MASTERING
MICROSOFT
OFFICE XP
PREMIUM EDITION

MASTERING™
MICROSOFT®
OFFICE XP
PREMIUM EDITION™

Gini Courter and Annette Marquis
with Karla Browning

SYBEX®

San Francisco • Paris • Düsseldorf • Soest • London

Associate Publisher: Cheryl Applewood
Contracts and Licensing Manager: Kristine
O'Callaghan
Developmental Editor: Bonnie Bills
Editors: Anamary Ehlen, Debby English, Linda
Recktenwald
Production Editor: Nathan Whiteside
Technical Editors: Maryann Brown, Charles Horn-
berger, Scott Warmbrand
Book Designers: Patrick Dintino, Catalin Dulfu, Franz
Baumhackl, Robin Kibby
Electronic Publishing Specialist: Adrian Woolhouse
Proofreaders: Nelson Kim, Laurie O'Connell, Nancy
Riddiough, Yariv Rabinovitch, Nanette Duffy, Dennis
Fitzgerald, Shannon Murphy, Juddith Hibbard, and
Ted Pushinsky
Indexer: Nancy Guenther
CD Coordinator: Christine Harris
CD Technician: Kevin Ly
Cover Designer: Design Site
Cover Illustrator/Photographer: Jack D. Myers

This book is dedicated to all the incredibly talented members of the International Association of Administrative Professionals (IAAP), whose Office questions always keep us on our toes.

To Karla's family—Matt, Carol, Kirby, and Megan—who took up the slack so she could write.

And to Charlotte who keeps the dream alive.

ACKNOWLEDGMENTS

It can be a bit of a gamble to undertake a large project, knowing the end result depends on the work of so many others. Having worked for six years now with the wonderful people at Sybex, we no longer see it that way. We continue to be impressed with the skill and dedication of our Sybex team and we are exceedingly fortunate to work with the certainty that they will make sure our final product is no less than great.

Special thanks to Bonnie Bills, our developmental editor, who pushed us to put our wonderful "personalities" back into the book and provided much welcomed assistance with the subsequent structural changes.

Production editor Nathan Whiteside did an outstanding job of keeping the project on track and smoothing the bumps over graphics issues so we could focus on writing. Anamary Ehlen went above and beyond by helping with chapter restructuring and offered significant improvements to make the text even more readable. Thanks to you both and for the additional assistance of Debbie English and Linda Recktenwald for making the author review stage a relatively painless one. We'd also like to thank Maryann Brown, Charles Hornberger, and Scott Warmbrand, our tech editors, who reviewed the book for accuracy and made sure we were presenting it like it is.

Kim Keener, the world's greatest administrative assistant, stepped in at the last minute to edit dozens of graphics and keep the book on schedule. Kim, once again, you've saved our collective skins!

For helping to make the CD-ROM something worth including, we want to thank Dan Mummert. He tracked down software, secured permissions, and made sure we had everything we needed. Christine Harris and Kevin Ly helped put it all in a convenient format and made sure it all works. You've been a big help!

We also can't say enough about our compositor: Adrian Woolhouse. We write words—he makes them attractive and gets the pages out to the printer on time. We appreciate the incredible job and all the hard work of our entire production team.

Karla Browning would like to extend special thanks to Dave and Deb for being there when she couldn't. It's such a great comfort to know someone else is handling things and handling them well.

And finally, we want to thank you, our readers. You are the ones who plow through the pages, try things out, scratch your heads in frustration, and say "Wow" at a moment of discovery. You send us feedback and suggestions. We would not be here without you, and we appreciate your faithfulness and, especially, your diligence.

CONTENTS AT A GLANCE

CONTENTS

8   Simplifying with Styles, Outlines, and Templates   231

9   Creating Merge Documents in Word   257

10   Creating and Distributing Word Forms   301

34 Managing Your Time and Tasks

INTRODUCTION

Microsoft Office XP is the most feature-packed version of Office to be released to date. Office XP has everything you need to produce any kind of print or online document you can conceive. Beyond the traditional word-processing, spreadsheet, and database tools, Office XP includes a massive array of Web creation and collaboration tools, data analysis and reporting tools, and graphic design features that give everyone the ability to create any type of publication and manage any type of data imaginable.

OFFICE XP EDITIONS

If you have applications that your friends or colleagues don't, or if you seem to be missing out, it could be that you have a different edition of Office XP. Microsoft is offering several editions of its Office suite to address the different needs of individuals, small business owners, and large corporations. The Office applications are bundled together as follows:

Edition	Applications
Standard	Word, Excel, Outlook, and PowerPoint
Small Business*	Word, Excel, Outlook, and Publisher
Professional	Word, Excel, PowerPoint, Outlook, and Access
Professional with Publisher*	Word, Excel, PowerPoint, Outlook, Access, and Publisher
Professional, Special Edition	Word, Excel, PowerPoint, Outlook, Publisher, Access, FrontPage, and SharePoint Team Services
Developers	Word, Excel, PowerPoint, Outlook, Publisher, Access, FrontPage, SharePoint Team Services, and Visual Basic for Applications (VBA) 6.0 development system and other programming support

*If you buy Office XP bundled with a new machine, you'll be able to choose between Office XP Small Business and Office XP Professional with Publisher.

All of the editions include Microsoft Internet Explorer and a number of smaller applications, such as Microsoft Clip Organizer, Microsoft Draw, Microsoft Photo Editor, and Microsoft Graph. Additions to the Office XP lineup include Microsoft Office Document Imaging and Microsoft Office Document Scanning. These new tools make it possible to treat scanned documents just as any other Office documents. First you scan the document using any installed scanner and Microsoft Office Document Scanning. Then you use Microsoft Office Document Imaging to view scanned documents on the screen, rearrange multipage documents, select and manipulate recognized text, and send documents to others in e-mail. You can even use Microsoft Office Document Imaging to search image files to find specific text.

The Microsoft Office Small Business Tools—including the Microsoft Business Planner, Microsoft Direct Mail Manager, Microsoft Small Business Customer Manager, and Microsoft Small Business Financial Manager—provide small business owners with business advice and practical tools to help set up, organize, and run a business. These tools are also included with all versions of the Microsoft Office suite except Standard.

WHO THIS BOOK IS FOR

Mastering Microsoft Office XP Premium Edition is specifically written to meet the needs of the advanced beginner and intermediate Office user. If all you need to do is write a letter now and then, send some e-mail, and create a budget for your business, this book is overkill. If you want to learn to develop custom applications using the Office XP suite with VBA and other programming tools, this book will not meet all your needs. We wrote this book for the intermediate Office user who wants to stretch their skills to help them do their jobs more efficiently, have more control over their data, and produce documents that rival the ones they used to send out to a commercial printer. We assume that you have some familiarity with the Office suite or similar applications. However, just to be sure, we review some the basic skills such as saving a file and moving and copying text with a particular emphasis on what's new in this version of Office. We then quickly move on to the features we have found to be the most important to the vast majority of Office users.

When we are not writing books, we are training users to put Office to work for them. We train teachers to apply Office in the classroom, administrative professionals to make their employers shine, customer service personnel to help track their interactions with customers, sales managers to take Office on the road with them, and department heads to help run their departments. What we have learned is that there are a million-and-one ways in which these different types of users need what Office

XP has to offer. We can't present all of them in the 1400 pages that make up this book. We have chosen to include the features and techniques that we have found to be the most valuable to the widest variety of people we train. We've included examples and strategies that are taken directly from our work with these good, solid, everyday Office users. To our trainees and, we imagine, to most of the readers of this book, Office XP is a tool to help you get your jobs done—it should not be the job itself. We've written this book to help you learn how to use this tool to make your job easier.

 NOTE Sybex publishes a Mastering book nearly the size of this one for each of the major Office XP applications. If you need an even more in-depth understanding of any of the applications, we suggest that you consult the Mastering book relative to that application. You can find the books at the Sybex Web site: www.sybex.com.

USING THIS BOOK

This book is designed to serve double duty as both a training manual and an on-the-spot reference. If you want to learn a specific application, you can start at the beginning of that section and work your way through to the end. We've presented the topics in a logical sequence based on our experience with training thousands of Office XP users. Each skill builds on the skills that precede it. Office XP now fully incorporates the use of speech and handwriting to input text and commands. We cover those features up front so you can put them to use in learning specific applications. Word is the tool that most users work with on a daily basis so we cover it next. We chose to introduce the office graphics tools that cross over applications—Microsoft Clip Organizer, Microsoft Draw, and Microsoft Graph—early on so you can make use of these tools as you learn Excel and PowerPoint, which follow. Next are sections on using the Office integration tools and Web tools in these applications. We then move on to Outlook and Access. If you are using the book as a training manual, you will find it helpful to focus on the applications in this order. The companion CD is chock-full of additional chapters, free software, shareware, and demo software. You'll find all you need to know about Microsoft Publisher, FrontPage, and SharePoint Team Services in the bonus chapters on the CD.

Throughout the chapters, you'll find sidebars, which are brief, boxed discussions that call your attention to related topics. In general, these sidebars provide additional information about a topic or more detailed explanations of issues presented in the text. "Mastering the Opportunities" sidebars describe techniques you can use to apply Office XP in your work setting. "Mastering Troubleshooting" sidebars show you how to avoid or recover from common mistakes or problems that users encounter.

You'll also find Tips, Notes, and Warnings scattered throughout the books to highlight additional useful information. We've introduced a special tip called an Expert Tip. These are tips that will save you time, make you more efficient, and take you to the next level in your skills. Expert Tips look like this one from Excel:

EXPERT TIP Suppose you've received a database with 10,000 records, many of them duplicate records. Don't eliminate the duplicates manually. Set up a criteria range without criteria (column headings only) and use the Unique Records Only option to extract a list without duplicates. This is far easier to do in Excel than in Access. Before you start creating the queries to eliminate duplicates in Access, consider exporting the table to Excel to eliminate the extra records.

NEW▶

To focus on features introduced or greatly improved in Office XP, look for the New symbol shown here.

The book is divided into eight parts, each of which covers specific skills related to an application or group of applications. In addition, we included a couple of useful appendices.

If you still want more, check out the CD for additional chapters and look for the CD icon throughout the book for references to the CD. Whenever we refer to files on the companion CD, even if you are reading chapters on the CD, you will see the CD icon in the left margin. This is print out that you'll find is label material, software, or other tools to expand your knowledge of the subject being discussed.

Here is a description of what each part of the book contains.

Part I: Harnessing the Power of Office XP

Chapters 1 and 2 are designed to get you started finding your way around Office XP. In Chapter 1, we've included a detailed review of all the cool new features in Office XP, such as the new Office XP task panes to open and create documents, use the Clipboard, search for clip art, and do other things more easily than ever before. We also introduce you to some changes to basic Office features such as personalized toolbars, the Open and Save dialog boxes, and Help, and to the dramatic improvements in crash-related document recovery. Chapter 1 also shows you the new Smart Tags components. These handy little icons appear whenever Office recognizes a pattern of information so you can take action on it. Smart Tags are available when you paste, when AutoCorrect makes changes to your text, and even when you type an address that you might want to add to your Outlook Contacts. Although still in their infancy, Smart Tags show a lot of potential. Chapter 2 is a must read if you're planning to use the new speech and handwriting tools with Office XP. Once you get these tools up and running, you can use them as your input method for the rest of the chapters.

Part II: Creating Quality Text Documents Using Word

Part II gives you a complete view of Word, from basic editing and formatting to advanced collaboration features. Chapters 3–5 teach you how to apply paragraph formatting, such as borders, bullets, and numbers, and to use language tools, such as the spelling and grammar checkers. You'll also learn to create newspaper-type columns and to display data in columns and rows using Word's powerful Tables features.

Once you've mastered the fundamentals, we introduce some of the "fun stuff" in Chapters 6 and 7. You'll learn how to create and insert graphics with the Office graphics tools, which cross over all applications. We chose to cover these tools early on, so our readers who are working their way through the book front to back can make use of them in Excel, PowerPoint, and other applications we cover later on.

Chapters 8–12 take you deeper into Word's powerful higher-level skills. You'll learn all about how to insert and position graphics and how to streamline your work with styles, outlines, and templates. Other powerful features you'll explore include mail merge, Word forms, working with large documents, and collaborating with others.

Part III: Crunching Data with Excel

Part III presents the major tools in the premier spreadsheet application, Excel 2002, from the point of view of the business Excel user. Excel has always been a strong application, and the enhancements and additions to Excel 2002 only make it better. In Chapters 13–21, you'll learn how to enter and format spreadsheets, create formulas, design and edit charts, and how to use Excel's powerful data management and analysis tools. If you've wondered about pivot tables, Goal Seek, and other advanced Excel tools, here's your chance to learn all about them in a way that actually makes sense!

Part IV: And Now, Presenting with PowerPoint!

Part IV takes you on a tour of PowerPoint. You'll learn how to create a presentation, how to add formatting and animation, and how to make a PowerPoint presentation. PowerPoint seems to be one of the easier applications to learn, but that doesn't mean it's short on features: there is plenty of power in PowerPoint, especially with the dynamic new animation schemes. You've never seen presentations look so good.

Chapters 22–25 take you through all of the features you'll need to become a Power-Point expert in no time.

Part V: Integration and Collaboration for Power Users

If Microsoft wanted users to use each of the tools in Office XP independently, they would not have packaged them as a single suite. The power of Office XP is that you can exchange data between applications, so you are always using the best tool for the task you want to accomplish. In Part V, Chapters 26 and 27, we'll show you how to exchange data between applications using object linking and embedding and how to use the import and export features of various applications. You'll learn how to collaborate with others on Office XP documents and share Office XP data.

Part VI: Making the Web Come Alive with Office XP

Office XP's Web tools are scattered throughout each of the applications. Although you may choose to use a dedicated Web-creation application such as Microsoft FrontPage, you may find that you can accomplish your objectives with the tools you already know. Word, Excel, and PowerPoint 2002's Web tools are nothing to sneeze at. In Chapter 28, we'll provide an overview of all the Web creation tools available in Office XP and help you decide which ones you want to use. In Chapters 29 and 30, we'll show you how to use the Web tools included in Word, Excel, and PowerPoint.

Part VII: Getting Organized with Outlook

There is no better way to keep your life organized and your communication in order than with Outlook 2002. In Part VII, Chapters 31–35, you'll learn how to keep contact information, manage your time and tasks, and track e-mail correspondence. If you have access to Microsoft Exchange Server, you'll also learn how to work with others across the Exchange Server network, sharing calendars and assigning tasks.

Part VIII: Creating and Using an Access Database

Access is a powerful program that anyone who understands their data can use to create useful database applications, even without programming skills. In Part VIII, Chapters 36–40, you'll have a chance to create a database from scratch after obtaining a basic background in database design and structure. You'll learn how to design tables, create forms for data entry, and write reports and queries to extract data from the database. When you've mastered these skills, you'll have a solid foundation on which to develop your own Access applications.

Appendix A: Customizing the Office Environment

Microsoft is a master of options. Each of us likes to do things a little bit differently than the person next to us. With a little background in how to customize the Office XP environment, you can make Office work just the way you like it. In Appendix A, we'll show you how to customize and set application options and to create your own toolbars.

Appendix B: Troubleshooting Office XP

Even the most experienced Office users, such as your authors, occasionally have something go wrong. If you know how to diagnose the problem and find a way around or through it, you can save yourself hours of needless headaches and grief. You'll find Mastering Troubleshooting sidebars throughout the chapters to help with the most common problems you might encounter. In Appendix B, we've tried to incorporate those things that typically go wrong and those infrequent things that can drive you up a wall. Written in a Q & A format, the appendix covers questions we've received from readers of *Mastering Office 2000* and our Office trainees. We suggest you review this chapter even before you have a problem so that you know where to look when problems do arise.

Bonus Chapters on the CD-ROM

Assuming that after you've devoured this book, you're still hungry for more, we've included three additional parts that include 10 bonus chapters on the companion CD. Part IX includes four chapters on Publisher 2002, a desktop publishing software designed for the rest of us. You can use Publisher 2002 to create newsletters, flyers, cards, reports, and a million-and-one other documents. In Chapters 41–44, we'll show you how.

Part X covers the exciting new Microsoft SharePoint *team sites*—team Web sites that contain document sharing, discussions, announcements, calendars, shared contacts, and a host of other features to keep your team in touch.

Part XI includes five chapters on Microsoft FrontPage 2002, the tool of choice for serious Web developers. If you plan to develop and manage a Web site, FrontPage is the tool you'll want to use. In Chapters 46–49, we'll show you how to create Web pages and link them together to make a Web site. In Chapter 50, we'll show you how to manage the site with FrontPage's Web site management tools.

Two additional appendices provide some critical reference material. Appendix C contains all the important commands you need to control Office applications with your speech. Print out the file to have the speech commands at your fingertips. If you have not yet installed Office XP, you'll want to read Appendix D to see all the installation options available to you. All in all, the CD is a great extension of the book itself, so don't forget to check it out—see the back of this book for a more complete list of what's on the CD.

CONVENTIONS USED IN THIS BOOK

Throughout this book, you will find references to the Standard and Formatting toolbars. The Standard and Formatting toolbars are the two toolbars most commonly displayed in previous versions of Office applications, such as the Word toolbars shown here.

Starting with Office 2000, Microsoft chose to personalize toolbars and menus. By default, you see one toolbar with the buttons you use most commonly. Menus are collapsed to display only the most recently used commands and, after a pause, uncollapsed to display those commands you haven't used recently. As you work with additional buttons and menu commands, Office adds them to the toolbars and menus, and removes less frequently used buttons and commands.

Buttons displayed on the personalized toolbar still "belong" to either the Standard or Formatting toolbar. In this book, you will see figures and graphics that display the single toolbar option and others that show the more traditional two-toolbar display. In either case, the text refers to the native location of the button, that is, the Standard or Formatting toolbar. To learn how you can turn off personalized toolbars and menus, refer to Appendix A.

We've also included a couple of typographic variations to help you distinguish certain kinds of text: **boldface type** shows any text you would type into Office dialog boxes or speak to give commands and `this font` shows any kind of programming instructions such as URLs, Excel formulas, HTML, or Visual Basic code.

WHERE TO GO FROM HERE

Even when you reach the end of this book, you have not reached the end of learning about Microsoft Office XP. If you'd like to learn more about a particular Office application, we recommend the individual Mastering books published by Sybex (www.sybex.com). *Mastering Access 2002 Premium Edition* (by Celeste Robinson and Alan Simpson), and our own *Mastering Microsoft Outlook 2002* and *Mastering Excel 2002*, for example, are each devoted to a single Office product. Each book will take you even further into a specific application than we can here.

If you were intrigued by topics in the CD chapters, we'd recommend *Mastering Microsoft FrontPage 2002 Premium Edition* (by Daniel A. Tauber, Brenda Kienan, and Molly E. Holzschlag) for more help with Web publishing.

Finally, don't forget to check the Microsoft Web site frequently: www.officeupdate .microsoft.com. Like all Microsoft products, Office XP will continually evolve. Look in the Office Update and Developers' areas of the Web site for patches, add-ins, graphics, and sample files, as well as the latest news about unique uses for Office XP programs.

WE'D LOVE TO HEAR FROM YOU!

We hope this book provides you with the skills you need to master Microsoft Office XP. We would love to hear what you think. We always enjoy hearing from our readers and are especially interested in hearing about your experiences and accomplishments with Office XP. You can contact us by writing or e-mailing to:

Gini Courter, Annette Marquis, and Karla Browning
c/o Sybex, Inc.
1151 Marina Village Parkway
Alameda, CA 94501
E-mail: authors@triadconsulting.com

Harnessing the Power of Office XP

LEARN TO:

- Explore the Office XP user interface

- Learn the new features of Office XP

- Manage files and format documents

- Get help when you need it

- Set up the Speech Recognition System

- Dictate and correct text

- Give voice commands

- Use handwriting recognition tools

CHAPTER 1

PRESENTING OFFICE XP: WHAT YOU NEED TO KNOW

FEATURING

- Exploring the user interface

- Using task panes

- Working with the Office Clipboard

- Working with toolbars

- Getting help

- Using new input methods

- Recovering documents

According to Microsoft, the XP name given to the newest versions of Office and Windows is short for "experience." A company press release says that these latest offerings are designed to "symbolize the rich and extended user experiences Windows and Office can offer by embracing Web services that span a broad range of devices." In short, Microsoft is suggesting that these products will take you to the next level of user experiences. We'll let you be the judge of that. What we will say is that Office XP offers a collection of new tools, enhanced favorites, and old standbys that make this version of Office worth a serious look.

For an experienced Microsoft Office user, exploring a new release of Office is like returning to your old hometown after many years away. It's distressing—perhaps even alarming—when you drive through town and everything looks different. But you eventually run across the friendly faces of some old friends and start feeling better. As time passes, some changes, like the new gourmet restaurant, become such a regular part of your life you wonder how you ever did without them.

When you initially "drive through" Office XP, you're going to find some old friends, but some of them, such as Word mail merge and PowerPoint animations, have had extensive plastic surgery. Microsoft's programmers have completely revamped the user interface, and at first blush it can be a bit disconcerting. Buttons look different, new windows, called task panes, open up unexpectedly, and Option buttons appear on the screen where you least expect them. They've also added a number of new features such as Smart Tags that provide a whole host of new options for auto-correcting, pasting, and working with data in your documents. And they've incorporated speech and handwriting recognition tools designed to let you throw away your keyboard—although we recommend you hang onto it a little while longer. As with any major Office revision, some of the changes are amazing and will make you wonder how you ever did it the old way. Others are mere irritants that you'll want to disable as soon as you can. We encourage you to give all the new features a try, but if you decide you really can't stand something, refer to this book because whenever possible, we tell you how to turn it off.

 NOTE Some of Office's more irritating features, such as the ever-cheerful Office Assistant, are turned off by default in Office XP. Your comments do make a difference in Redmond!

In this chapter, we'll focus on what you need to know as you start working in this new version. Most of the new features we discuss apply to more than one application, so we'll point out where to learn more about how the features impact specific applications.

Exploring the Office XP User Interface

NEW▶ The first thing you notice when you fire up one of the Office XP applications is the new *task pane* on the right side of the application window. The contents of the task pane support a range of features from opening documents to searching for clip art. Although sometimes intrusive and awkward to use, the task panes bring a lot of features to the forefront of the Office XP applications.

After you get over the surprise of the task panes, you might also notice the change in the look of Office XP toolbars. In this section, we'll discuss what's really changed behind the scenes with the functionality of toolbars and dialog boxes, such as Open and Save As. You'll also find information about the fundamental changes in the Online Help features in Office XP.

Task Panes Put Options at Your Fingertips

Task panes fire up and close automatically depending on your activity in the application. For example, the New Document task pane, shown in Figure 1.1, appears in place of the New dialog box whenever you start an application. If you close the New Document task pane, it reappears whenever you choose File ➢ New from the menu.

FIGURE 1.1

The New Document task pane lets you open existing documents and create new ones.

To activate the task pane manually, choose View ➢ Task Pane. You can then select the task pane you want to use from the menu at the top of the pane. The list of panes varies by application. Word's Task Pane menu appears in Figure 1.2.

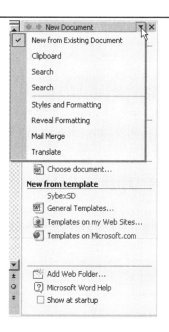

After you select a task pane from the list, you can go back to previous task panes by clicking the Back button to the left of the task pane name. Use the Forward button to return to the next pane in a series of previously opened panes. To close the task pane, click the Close button to the right of the task pane name.

You may find task panes to be intrusive and annoying when you first encounter them. If you're an experienced Office user, it will even take a while to get used to using them—old habits die hard. We recommend that you give them a chance, however. They are pretty good at getting out of your way when you are ready to work, and they add some functionality that never existed in Office before—for example, Word's Reveal Formatting task pane (see Chapter 8, "Simplifying with Styles, Outlines, and Templates") and the Translate task pane (see Chapter 4, "Putting Text and Language Tools to Work").

The New Document Task Pane

The New Document task pane is immediately visible when you launch Word, Excel, and PowerPoint. The task pane is divided into five sections:

Open A Document Lists the most recently saved documents and has a More Documents link that opens the Open dialog box

New Allows you to open a Blank Document or a Blank Web Page

New From Existing Document Makes it easy to base a document on a previously saved document without running the risk of overwriting the saved document

New From Template Lists recently used templates, General templates, templates saved to a Web Folder, and templates available from www.microsoft.com.

Miscellaneous Options Allow you to add a Web Folder, access Word Help, and disable the Show At Startup option that opens the New Document task pane when you launch the application

As soon as you select a document to open, the New Document task pane closes automatically to get out of your way while you work.

The Office Clipboard Task Pane

Microsoft introduced the Office Clipboard in Office 2000, and it quickly became one of the most exciting new features for users who create documents that cross Office applications. With the Office 2000 Clipboard, you could cut or copy more than one thing and paste the items individually or as a group. In Office XP, the Office Clipboard takes a giant leap forward in several significant ways:

- The number of items you can collect on the Clipboard has increased from 12 to 24.

- The Clipboard has been converted from a toolbar-based palette of icons to a task pane with larger previews of the individual items.

- The Clipboard is nearly as handy as the system clock or volume control. An icon appears in the Windows system tray from which you can control the Office Clipboard when it is not visible and which notifies you when something is being added to it.

The Office Clipboard task pane, shown in Figure 1.3, activates automatically when you cut or copy more than one item. You can open it manually in one of three ways:

- Select Clipboard from the open Task Pane menu shown earlier in Figure 1.2.

- Choose Edit ➢ Office Clipboard.

- Hold Ctrl and double-press (as in double-click) the C key.

When the Clipboard task pane is open, you can cut or copy items from your document and either paste them immediately or store them for later use. When you are ready to paste, you can choose to paste an individual item from the Clipboard task pane or click Paste All or Clear All to paste or delete all of the items on the Clipboard.

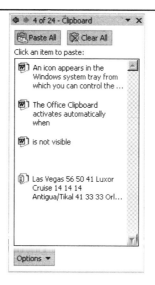

FIGURE 1.3

Use the Clipboard task pane to store up to 24 items you eventually want to paste into a document.

Setting Office Clipboard Options

The Office Clipboard has four options you can set to customize how the Clipboard task pane behaves. You can change the option settings by clicking the Options button at the bottom of the Clipboard task pane. These options are:

Show Office Clipboard Automatically With this option set, the Office Clipboard task pane appears automatically after you cut or copy a second item.

Collect Without Showing Office Clipboard This option, turned off by default, allows you to collect items with the task pane closed and out of your way.

Show Office Clipboard Icon On Taskbar This great option displays the Office Clipboard icon in the Windows system tray so you can cut and copy items from non-Office XP applications and store them on the Office Clipboard for pasting into an Office document.

Show Status Near Taskbar When Copying This option displays a screen tip above the Office Clipboard icon in the system tray to indicate that an item is being copied and how many items the Clipboard currently is holding.

The Office Clipboard is one of the most welcome enhancements to Office XP. It was a great feature when it was introduced in Office 2000 and it is even more power-ful now.

 TIP The Office Clipboard is not limited to use within Office. As long as the Clipboard is running in an Office application, you can cut and copy items from other applications, such as Internet Explorer or a graphics application, to the Office Clipboard for use in an Office document.

The Search Task Panes

NEW▶

If you've ever misplaced a document or needed to find every mention of a client's name in a group of documents, the new Basic Search and Advanced Search task panes are invaluable. These new task panes extend the search tools available in previous Office versions by searching for a specific text string in all of your documents. Although this feature has been available in Windows search tools, this is the first time you've been able to conduct your searching directly within an Office application. When you find the documents you are looking for, you can edit them in the application where they were created or copy a link to them to the Office Clipboard. Using this second choice, you can create a document directory that contains links to all the documents related to a specific topic. This is a great way to organize materials that are spread all over your drives and a key reason you may want to use Office Search instead of the traditional Windows search tools.

 NOTE To locate a text string within the open document, Find is still available in Office XP by choosing Edit ➢ Find or by clicking the Browse button on the vertical scroll bar and choosing Find.

To activate the Search pane, choose File ➢ Search, or if the task pane is open, select it from the Task Pane menu. In the Basic Search task pane, shown in Figure 1.4, you can enter text and have it search across your local computer and network drives and throughout Outlook to find what you need.

FIGURE 1.4

Use the Basic Search task pane to search through all of your files for the documents you need.

To enter a search, follow these steps:

1. Enter text in the Search Text box. Office looks through the body of documents, document properties, and keywords. Enter more words to narrow the search. Basic Search finds all word forms—for example, a search on *win* gives you *win*, winning, and winner.

2. Select the Locations you would like to search from the Search In drop-down list. You can search Everywhere or limit your search to any combination of My Computer, My Network Places, and Outlook's folders.

3. Select the type of results you would like from the Results Should Be drop-down list. You can choose different types of Microsoft Office files, Outlook items, and Web pages.

4. Click the Search button. The results are returned in the Search Results task pane, shown in Figure 1.5.

FIGURE 1.5

*The search results
appear in the Search
Results task pane.*

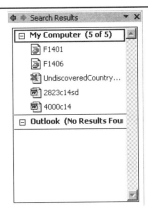

 NOTE When you use Office Search, you may find some surprising results. If you look closely at the results in Figure 1.5, you'll see that two of the files it returned are image files. Microsoft Office Document Imaging, a new product included with Microsoft Office XP, actually performs OCR (Optical Character Recognition) while it is generating TIFF image files. It then adds the text it recognizes to the Indexing Service, which Office also runs behind the scenes, so that even image text can be identified through a search. You can access Microsoft Office Document Imaging directly by opening the Microsoft Office Tools menu on your Programs menu.

When you want to start a new search or narrow the existing one, click the Modify button on the Search Results task pane to return to the Basic Search task pane.

Using Advanced Search

When you need to establish more exact conditions for a search, click the Advanced Search link on the Basic Search task pane. In the Advanced Search task pane, shown in Figure 1.6, you can choose from a long list of properties and set conditions for each one. For example, you can search for only documents that were modified after a certain date and contain a certain word.

FIGURE 1.6

Use the Advanced Search task pane to conduct a more precise search of your files.

To use the Advanced Search tool, follow these steps:

1. Select a property of the files that you want to locate from the Property drop-down list.

2. Select a condition that you want the property to meet from the Condition drop-down list.

3. Enter a value that you are looking for in the Value text box.

4. Click Add to save the search parameter.

5. Select And or Or to include another search parameter.

6. Repeat steps 1–5 until you have entered all the parameters for the search.

7. If you want to modify one of the search parameters, use the spin buttons to display the search parameter you want and then click the Remove button. Make any changes to the Property, Condition, or Value and click Add, or click Remove again to delete it.

8. Set Search In and Results Should Be search options.

9. Click Search.

Let's say, for example, you want to find all the documents created between two specific dates: 7/1/01 and 7/31/01. In the Property drop-down list, select Created On to search for the document creation date. In the Condition drop-down list, choose On or

After and enter **7/1/01** in the Value text box. Click Add to save the first condition. If you stop here, Office will return all the documents created on or after 7/1/01. To add the second condition, select And. Creation Date should still be selected in the Property text box. Select On or Before as the Condition and enter **7/31/01** in the Value text box. Click Add to add the second condition. When you've finished entering your search parameters, select where you want to search in the Search In list and what kind of documents you want to see in the Results Should Be list. When all of the parameters are set, click Search to begin the search for your documents.

 MASTERING THE OPPORTUNITIES

Setting Document Properties for Easy Searching

If you are wondering where document properties come from in the first place, you are not alone. You would not be the first person to ask, how does it know I created this document and why doesn't it use my full name? Some document properties, such as Creation Date and Modified Date, are created automatically by Office when you save an Office document. Other properties, such as Author, Title, Category, Keywords, and Description, can be set by you in the document's Properties dialog box. You can access this dialog box for any open document by choosing File ➤ Properties. The first tab of the five-tab dialog box, the General tab, displays the filename, location, file size, and critical dates such as Creation Date, Modified Date, and Accessed Date—that is, after the file has been saved the first time.

The second tab, Summary, is a place for you to enter critical information about the document—its title, subject, author, manager, company, categories, keywords, and comments (description). The Author field is filled in automatically from the data entered on the User Information tab of the Options dialog box. You can change it on the Summary tab or change it permanently in the application's Options dialog box (Tools ➤ Options). If you'd like to be able to see an outline of the headings in a Word document, be sure to select the Save Preview Picture check box; the summary appears on the Contents tab.

The third tab, Statistics, displays similar data to the General tab but goes into even more detail, such as the date it was last printed, how many revisions it has had, and the total editing time for the document (the actual time the document has been open by someone). You can also learn about the document size, from bytes to pages and everything in between.

Continued

MASTERING THE OPPORTUNITIES CONTINUED

The Contents tab displays the document's title—if the Save Picture Preview check box on the Summary tab is checked—and the headings of a Word document, the macro sheets of an Excel workbook, and the design template and slide titles of a PowerPoint presentation.

To enter even more data about a particular document, click the Custom tab. Follow these steps to set the Custom properties:

1. Select a property from the list or enter your own in the Name text box.

2. Select a data type: Text, Date, Number, or Yes or No.

3. Enter a value in the Value text box. The value must match the data type you set in step 2. If it doesn't match, Office changes the data type to Text.

   OR

   If you have bookmarks in Word, named ranges in Excel, or selected text in Power-Point, you can select the Link To Content check box to link the property to the specific contents. Use this option when you want to identify a named location in a document. After selecting the check box, select the named location from the Value drop-down list.

4. Click the Add button.

You can add as many custom properties as you want, but you can only enter one value per property. Most of the time, that makes sense—you can only have one Date Completed, for example. However, you may want to use some properties, such as Reference, more than once. If you need to enter additional values, create a new property, such as Reference1, Reference2, and so on.

Because the Property dialog box is available anywhere you can see a file—the Windows Explorer, My Network Places, Office Advanced Search, the Open dialog box, to name a few—entering properties can give you critical information about a document without even having to open it. To see the properties for a document, right-click a filename and choose Properties.

If you decide properties are essential to your business and want to be prompted to enter properties each time you save a document for the first time, choose Tools ➤ Options and on the Save tab, select Prompt For Document Properties.

Cataloging Your Image, Sound, and Motion Files with the Clip Organizer

NEW▶

The Microsoft Clip Organizer, formerly known as the ClipArt Gallery, has been totally revamped for Office XP. It's a much more powerful tool designed to keep track of all of your media files, not just those supplied by Microsoft. Although previous versions of the gallery had this potential, very few users actually took advantage of it. In Office XP, the first time you click the Insert Clip Art button on the Drawing toolbar or choose Insert ➢ Picture ➢ Clip Art, you have the option of cataloging image, sound, and motion files located on any of your local drives. Click the Options button on the message box that opens to select the folders you would like it to search to create the catalogs. It takes a few minutes to identify all your local folders and a few minutes more after you select the folders you want to actually create the catalog. However, it is worth the wait. After the cataloging is complete, you can use the Insert Clip Art task pane to search for your own images, as well as those in the Microsoft clip collection. For more about organizing your clips and using the Insert Clip Art task pane, see Chapter 6, "Beyond Text: Making the Most of Graphics."

 TIP To take full advantage of the Clip Organizer's search power, be sure to edit the keywords on the cataloged images. When the Insert Clip Art task pane opens, click Clips Organizer in the See Also section. The Clips Organizer shows your Collections List and displays thumbnails of images in the selected collection. Right-click any media file and choose Edit Keywords.

Additional Task Panes

Each application that uses task panes—Word, Excel, PowerPoint, and Publisher—has additional task panes that are specific to that application. The task panes provide easy access to a wealth of tools and are definitely worth exploring. To learn what task panes a particular application has available, choose View ➢ Task Pane and click the Task Pane drop-down list found on the task pane header next to the Close button. You'll find additional information about the task panes in the chapters of this book pertaining to individual applications.

Personalized Menus and Toolbars Respond to the Way You Work

In Microsoft Office 2000, Microsoft introduced the personalized menus and toolbars feature. Recognizing that most users only use a small percentage of menu and toolbar options, Microsoft redesigned them to bring the tools you use to the forefront. In personalized toolbars, the Standard and Formatting toolbars share one row and only the most frequently used tools appear on each portion of the toolbar. Personalized menus move frequently used menu items to the top of the list, and the menus themselves display only a portion of the available menu options.

This personalized menus and toolbars feature has been unequivocally either loved or hated by Office users. Microsoft heard their users' feedback and—for those in the latter category—made the feature a little easier to turn off. We consider this a blessing since we recommend that everyone turn it off before entering a single character in a document. After you have an application mastered, you might choose to make use of personalized menus and toolbars, but do not try it if you are learning an application. In our opinion, this is an invitation to indescribable aggravation.

Another less controversial change in Office XP is the new look of the toolbars and menus. When selected, toolbar buttons and menu options in Office XP turn blue with a darker blue border. Microsoft describes this as a streamlined, flatter look that is designed to take advantage of high-color displays and new Windows 2000 technologies. That may be the case, but the biggest advantage is you can look at another user's screen or a picture in a book and know at a glance which version of Office you are looking at. Beyond that, the change won't impact your use of the Office products.

Working with (or without) Personalized Menus and Toolbars

In Office XP, menu bars and toolbars adapt to the way you use the Office applications. Menus are collapsed, displaying only commonly used commands (see Figure 1.7) until you expand them to see the full list. To fully expand a collapsed menu, click the Expand arrow at the bottom of the menu, or simply hover over the menu for a moment.

FIGURE 1.7

Menus are initially collapsed, and can be expanded to show all of the available commands.

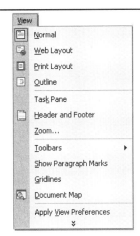

Personalized toolbars means that some buttons that were traditionally located on the Standard and Formatting toolbars are no longer displayed so that both toolbars can fit together on a single row. To display both these toolbars on separate rows or to access a button that is not visible, click the Toolbar Options button located at the right end of a toolbar to open the Toolbar Options menu:

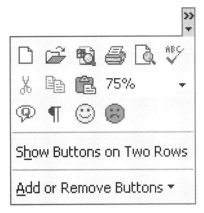

To see all of the buttons on the Standard and Formatting toolbars and display the Standard and Formatting toolbars on separate rows, choose Show Buttons On Two Rows. If you decide to keep the single row display and have need for a button that is not currently displayed, select it from the buttons on the Toolbar Options menu.

Here's where the personalization kicks in. Unless you have unused space on your toolbar, the new button replaces some other button you haven't used in a while, and hopefully don't want to use next. Approximately 20 buttons are visible on a single toolbar—depending, of course, on the width of the buttons you have selected, the size of your monitor, and your monitor's resolution. You'll find buttons that were displaced from one of the toolbars on the Toolbar Options menu the next time you need them. Theoretically, with increased use, most of the buttons you use regularly will be displayed on your toolbars.

 TIP You can change the width of one or another of the toolbars sharing one row and consequently display more buttons from that toolbar by pointing to the vertical hash marks immediately to the right of the Toolbar Options button on the Standard portion of the toolbar. The pointer changes to a four-headed arrow, and you can drag right or left to access more buttons.

If you find that the personalized menus take more than a little getting used to and you would like to restore your application to a more predictable (Office 97 style) interface, choose Customize from the Toolbar Options menu or right-click any toolbar and choose Customize. On the Options tab of the Customize dialog box, enable two check boxes: Show Standard And Formatting Toolbars On Two Rows and Always Show Full Menus.

 NOTE If you're new to an Office application, it makes sense to turn off the personalized toolbars and menus feature, both to avoid the endless frustration of searching for buttons and so you can see all of the standard application features. When you've settled into the application, you can make an informed decision about whether you want to enable personalized toolbars.

Adding Toolbar Buttons Is a Snap

If you're looking for a button that isn't visible on either the Standard or Formatting toolbar or the Toolbar Options menu, select Add Or Remove Buttons from the Toolbar Options menu, then select Standard or Formatting to display the list of all buttons for the respective toolbar. A button that is checked is currently displayed on either the toolbar or the Toolbar Options menu. Check any button to make it visible on the toolbar. For more information about customizing toolbars and menu bars, see Appendix A, "Customizing Office XP to Your Work Environment."

Open and Save As Dialog Boxes Make It Easier to Work with Files

NEW▶

Most of us prefer to avoid filing at all costs. However, keeping electronic documents organized requires all of us to become filing pros. Anything Microsoft can do to ease this burden is a step in the right direction. In Office XP, the Open and Save As dialog boxes have been subtly modified so that they're more flexible and functional. One of the most practical and easily overlooked changes is that you can now resize the dialog boxes. Just drag an edge to make the dialog box large enough to display all of the files in a folder—definitely worth the price of admission!

The Places bar, introduced in Office 2000, is the icon list on the left side of the Open and Save As dialog boxes. Although the concept was good, users complained that it wasn't customizable—the folders you needed to access most frequently still required the navigational skills of Magellan. A couple of third-party applications sprouted up to respond to these complaints, and now Office XP rises to the challenge with an easy-to-customize Places bar.

Another addition to the Save As dialog box makes it possible to reduce file size by compressing images used in the document. This may not mean much in a Word document with two or three images, but in a PowerPoint presentation, it can make a dramatic difference in the size of your presentation file.

Adding Folders You Frequent to the Places Bar

The Places bar in the Open and Save As dialog boxes (see Figure 1.8) comes with icons for History, My Documents, Desktop, Favorites, and Web Folders.

History is the list of the most recently modified or created Office documents, folders, and drives on your system. If you stored or opened an Office document, it's listed in History. The list is initially sorted in descending order based on modification date (see Figure 1.9), but you can also sort by name or type size by clicking the appropriate header on the list.

FIGURE 1.8

The Open dialog box features a customizable Places bar.

Places bar —

FIGURE 1.9

Choose History to open or save in a recently used folder or drive.

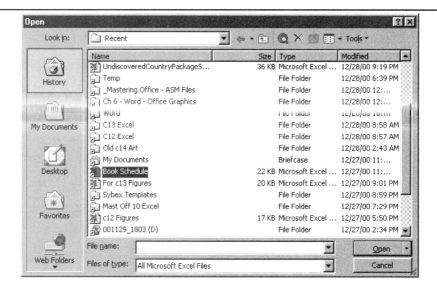

To clear the History list, choose History in the Places bar, and then select Tools ➢ Clear History from the dialog box menu.

My Documents opens the My Documents folder on your local drive. Desktop displays the files on your Desktop. Favorites opens your Favorites folder, and My Network Places displays your favorite shared folders on Web sites, including network drives, inside and outside of your network. These may be popular destinations in your search for the file you want to open, but chances are it takes you more than a few clicks to find the folders you frequent.

Customizing the Places Bar

NEW ▶

If you are tired of navigating through the same folder structure to find the folders you use most, stay tuned—you can customize the Places bar to include frequently used folders from your computer or network. To add a folder to the Places bar, you have to navigate to the folder one last time. When you find it, select the folder, then choose Tools ➤ Add To "My Places" from the Open or Save As dialog box menu. If you can't see where the icon was added, click the More Places arrow at the bottom of the Places bar.

———— More Places arrow

After you've added a folder to the Places bar, you can rearrange the icons on the Places bar. Select the icon you wish to move up or down, right-click, and choose Move Up or Move Down from the shortcut menu. If you add more than a folder or two, you probably also want to switch the display to smaller icons—right-click anywhere on the Places bar and choose Small Icons from the menu.

NOTE There's only one set of Open and Save As dialog boxes, shared by all the Office applications. Folders added to the Places bar in any application appear in all applications. When you clear the History list for one app, you're clearing it for all applications.

Compressing Pictures to Reduce File Size

Now that photographs and other high-quality images are becoming as common as stick figure clip art used to be, documents, through no fault of their own, are getting larger. The Save As dialog box has an additional feature to address this file size issue. In Office XP, you have the option to compress pictures while saving a document. This is a great option if you are concerned about file size and not as concerned about the quality of your images. Be forewarned though—compression may result in loss of image quality, especially if you are using high color photographs.

To access the Compress Pictures option, choose File ➤ Save As. In the Save As dialog box, open the Tools menu and choose Compress Pictures to open the Compress Pictures dialog box.

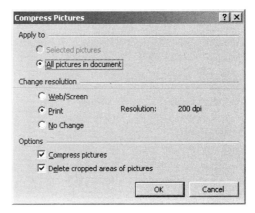

 NOTE   If you want to compress only some of the pictures in the document, select those pictures before opening the Save As dialog box.

If you have pictures selected, choose Selected Pictures. Choose the resolution you want for the pictures. If the document is for the Web or for screen viewing, such as a PowerPoint presentation, you can choose Web/Screen. This sets the resolution at 96dpi (dots per inch)—not great resolution but adequate for a lot of screen uses. If you are planning to print the document, 200dpi may be acceptable for you. If you plan to print to a high-resolution printer and want to maintain the resolution of the images in the document, choose No Change.

You are not done there, though. If you really want to maintain full image quality, you have to clear the Compress Pictures check box. If you keep the Compress Pictures check box selected, Office applies JPEG compression to high-color pictures, and a loss in image quality is the probable outcome.

The final option on this dialog box, Deleted Cropped Areas Of Pictures, may help reduce image size without a quality loss. When you crop a picture in an Office application, the cropped portion of the picture is hidden but is not actually deleted. If you are sure you don't need it, you can select this option to delete it from the image and reduce picture size as a result.

When you have the options set the way you want them, click OK and save the document. The Compress Pictures options are applied to the pictures in your document.

 WARNING After you have compressed a picture and have lost image quality, it cannot be restored. Be sure to save a copy of the image in its uncompressed form before setting the compression options.

Help Is Only a Click Away

Microsoft, like all the leading software companies, spends a great deal of effort designing help systems that will be useful for the people who use their software. This isn't altruism; good online help results in lower costs for help desk functions both at Microsoft and at the large corporations who purchase and support software. In Office 97, Microsoft introduced a social help interface: Clippit and other office assistants. In Office 2000, Clippit was redesigned as a free floating agent, removing it from the small window that kept it contained in Office 97 apps. In both versions, however, Clippit was considered annoying to many, cute to some, and downright frustrating to everyone at some time or another. Clippit or one of its cronies was the first thing you saw when you started an application, and sooner or later, most people wanted to know how to shut it off. Clippit became the Office feature we loved to hate.

With Office XP, Microsoft has taken a different approach to our social interactions. Clippit doesn't appear until its presence is requested (Help ➢ Show The Office Assistant). In place of the social, over-eager help agent, there's an incredibly passive Ask A Question box, sharing a row with the menu bar:

Type a question for help ▾

Type a question, and suggested avenues of inquiry are presented, ending with an offer to continue your search online at the Microsoft Web site:

The Ask A Question box maintains a history, so you can search again on questions asked previously. The history is cleared at the end of the application session.

Although some people require the social interaction only the Office Assistants can provide, we're excited to see a more reserved approach to asking for help and think many of you will be too.

New Ways to Let Office Know What You Really Want to Do

Office XP invites your interaction and gives you more options about how you want to handle actions that you take than any other version of Office. Microsoft has made an effort to make error messages more friendly and more specific and has added Smart Tag Options buttons that appear when you complete certain tasks. The Options buttons you will encounter most frequently are Paste Options, AutoCorrect Options, and Smart Tag Options.

More Powerful Paste Options

NEW▶

Cut/Copy and Paste features have been around since Windows was in its infancy, but never before have they been so flexible and so powerful. In Office XP, you can make choices about pasting that can save considerable time and effort. In Word, for example, you can choose whether you want to keep the original formatting of the text or change it to the formatting of its new location. Figure 1.10 shows an example of copying text from one Word document to another. When you paste text using any of the traditional paste methods (Paste button, Ctrl+V, Edit ➤ Paste), the Paste Options button appears next to the pasted text. If you click the button, you have options to keep the original (source) formatting, change to the formatting of the current document (destination), or insert plain text. If none of those options is sufficient, you can choose Apply Style Or Formatting and make your own choices.

FIGURE 1.10

Paste options let you decide how text is formatted when you paste it into a document.

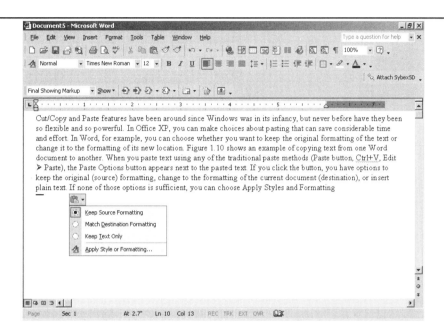

The paste options you have available depend on the type of pasting you are doing: Word to Excel, Word to Word, Excel to PowerPoint, and so forth. If you learn to use these options effectively, they will save you a lot of formatting hassles after the paste is completed. You can find out more about using paste options in the chapters pertaining to specific applications and also in Chapter 26, "Breaking the Application Barrier."

Reversing AutoCorrect

AutoCorrect, the feature that automatically corrects your mistakes and makes you think you are a better speller than your fourth grade teacher ever dreamed possible, has gotten smarter, kinder, and more reliable in Office XP. AutoCorrect has changed in two major ways:

• When you correct an automatic correction by retyping the original text, Auto-Correct won't attempt to correct you again.

- If you point to auto-corrected text, an AutoCorrect Options button appears that lets you reverse the current auto-correction, change the AutoCorrect list so that the auto-correction will be prevented in the future, and edit AutoCorrect Options.

The AutoCorrect Options button appears as a short blue line under the word when you point to a word that AutoCorrect has already corrected. If you click the blue line, the Options menu opens.

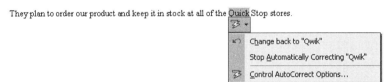

If you begin to correct a word that AutoCorrect has automatically capitalized or changed using one of its other standard rules, the Options menu gives you a choice to undo the change AutoCorrect made, to turn off the rule entirely, or to not apply the rule if these circumstances reoccur.

Data Smart Tags Make Everyday Tasks Easier

NEW ▶   How many times have you copied and pasted someone's name and address from a Word document to an Outlook contact? How many times have you typed someone's name in a report and remembered you needed to schedule a meeting with that person? Smart Tags identify key data items, such as addresses, places, dates, and times, in your documents so you can take some action related to them. Figure 1.11 shows a Smart Tag in action. In this example, a person's name is identified as a Smart Tag—the purple dotted line underneath the name is the indicator. When you point to the name, the Smart Tags Action button appears. Click the Action button to see the Smart Tags choices available to you.

FIGURE 1.11

Smart Tags identify key data elements such as names and addresses in your documents for action.

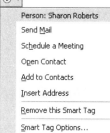

Smart Tags options are found in the AutoCorrect dialog box. The Smart Tags tab, shown in Figure 1.12, lists the Smart Tags currently available. Notice that Person Names is not turned on by default. If you type a lot of names in your documents, you probably want to keep this option off. If you are an average name-dropper, we recommend you add names to the active list to access the options shown in Figure 1.11.

FIGURE 1.12

You can set Smart Tag options in the AutoCorrect dialog box.

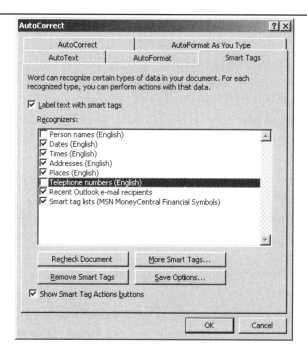

Smart Tags show a lot of promise. However, it may be a little while before Smart Tags are fully developed and show the level of consistency one would expect to see.

For example, place names, including cities and states, are often ignored by Smart Tags. On a positive note, Microsoft is offering a free software developer's kit (SDK) so businesses can develop their own Smart Tags to include specialized uses such as product lists, inventory items, and department lists. Microsoft also plans to develop other Smart Tags that can be downloaded from their Office Update site (`www.officeupdate .microsoft.com`). Expect third-party vendors to follow suit. If you'd like to know more about Smart Tags, see Chapter 4.

New and Improved Collaboration Tools

Microsoft is working to improve the functionality of Web pages you create in Office by providing tools that turn them from repositories of static data into living, breathing information animals. Office XP offers tools to make collaboration easier and provides data analysis and reporting tools that can be used on active data accessible on the Web. Office XP Web collaboration features include:

NEW▶

SharePoint team sites Team sites are comprehensive Web sites with all the tools you need to collaborate with a team, including discussions, document sharing, and a host of other useful components.

Presentation broadcast Viewing a PowerPoint presentation across the Web can be a communal affair with real-time chat and live information sharing about the presentation's content.

Online meetings Using Microsoft NetMeeting, users can activate a meeting across a network from any of the Office applications. Participants can use options for real-time collaboration on documents, including chat and whiteboard windows.

For teams that want to analyze live data across a network, Office XP offers three valuable tools:

Office Web Components Web Components let you work interactively with real-time data across an intranet using pivot tables, spreadsheets, and charts.

Web Query Wizard This wizard takes data from any site on the Web and brings it into Excel for your analysis. Data can be refreshed on request or can be set up to automatically refresh at specified intervals.

Data Access Pages Developing live Web databases is a practical possibility. If you've ever tried to create active server pages from your database, you know that it is no easy task—until now. Data Access Pages provide front-end forms in HTML format that are linked to data housed in Access. When users make changes on the forms from their browsers, the changes are immediately reflected in the database.

Working Together with a SharePoint Team Site

NEW ▶

One of the most interesting innovations in Office XP is the ability to create Share-Point *team sites*. Team sites replace Web Folders, which were locations on a Web server where you could access shared documents. Expanding greatly on the Web Folders concept, SharePoint team sites are complete Web sites with a number of features designed to let you share documents, have discussions, and communicate with your team. Team site features include:

- Document libraries where you can post documents you want to share
- Discussion boards to communicate with your team about important issues (or the scores of last night's basketball games)
- Web document discussions where your team can add comments and make revisions to documents
- Announcements to display the latest team news
- Team events to alert team members about upcoming events
- Surveys for team members to express their opinions about important issues
- Shared favorites where members can post links to useful Web sites
- Custom lists where you can create a list for anything

You can create a fully working team site, like the one shown in Figure 1.13, in no time at all.

NOTE To create a SharePoint team site, you must be able to access a server that is running SharePoint Team Services. SharePoint Team Services is only available in the Office XP Developer's Edition and for a short time in the Office XP Professional Special Edition. You can find information about installing and using SharePoint Team Services in Chapter 45, "Using SharePoint Team Services for Team Collaboration," on the companion CD.

PART

I

HARNESSING THE
POWER OF OFFICE XP

After you create a team site, you can subscribe to it so you get an e-mail notice any time something has changed. You can save documents to your team site directly from Office XP programs, making it easy to keep the site up-to-date. In addition, if you are not satisfied with the team site's design, you can customize it using FrontPage 2002.

Team sites have a ton of potential and are a welcome replacement to the less-than-reliable Web Folders of Office 2000. Take the time to create a site, and your team will thank you for it.

Moving beyond the Keyboard

NEW▶ Office XP incorporates two exciting new input methods: speech and handwriting. Speech recognition technology has seen major advances recently, due to software and especially hardware improvements. The Microsoft Speech Recognition System uses Lernout & Hauspie's speech recognition engine for dictation and application command and control. Microsoft clearly admits that the speech recognition tools are not designed to be totally hands free. You still need your mouse and keyboard to use the tools effectively. We still have a way to go before we are talking to our computers a la Star Trek, but if you've been intrigued by this new technology, it's definitely worth exploring. Office XP's foray into speech recognition is a valid effort and beats repetitive motion sprain or carpal tunnel syndrome any day—although you may find yourself getting hoarse if you are at it long enough.

NOTE Lernout & Hauspie (L&H), based in Belgium, is the premier company in speech recognition software. With their recent purchase of Dragon Systems, L&H have control of the two most effective speech recognition systems available today: L&H Voice Express and Dragon NaturallySpeaking.

Handwriting recognition is a whole new and interesting method of inputting electronically. Office XP's handwriting tools let you draw text with your mouse or on an external drawing pad that is immediately recognized and converted to text. Although this feature works with a mouse, handwriting tablets designed for this purpose give this feature a much more natural feel and are a lot more fun.

Chapter 2, "Inputting Text with Speech and Handwriting Recognition Tools," provides you with all of the information you need to make speech and handwriting as useful to you in the 21st century as the mouse and keyboard were in the last years of the previous century.

Minimizing the Impact of Crashes

Microsoft has gone all out in Office XP to protect your documents when the unexpected happens. In addition to the traditional AutoRecovery features, Office XP has a number of new options that save documents when an application crashes, recovers corrupt documents, and lets you choose which version of a recovered or saved document you want to use. If you have a pretty stable network and operating system environment, you may only run into these features on very rare occasions. Others who are less fortunate may get to know them intimately. Either way, it's helpful to know what to expect and what choices to make when your software or hardware crashes, and you are faced with those critical decisions about how to recover your work.

Saving When You Crash

NEW▶ The Document Recovery feature is new to Word, Excel, and PowerPoint. After a crash occurs, Office opens a message box, like the one shown in Figure 1.14, which gives you the option of recovering your open documents and restarting the application. Clear the check box if you just want to forget it and go home.

FIGURE 1.14

Office XP apologizes for your inconvenience while giving you the option of recovering your lost work.

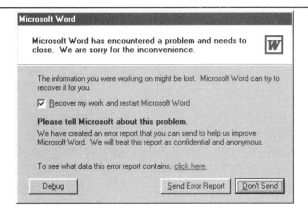

If you are willing to stick it out, you also have the option of sending an error report to Microsoft to help them develop fixes that will avoid similar crashes in the future. You can choose to click the Send Error Report or Don't Send button. If you choose to send an error report, Office dials or connects with Microsoft and sends the report. In the meantime, if you elected to recover your data, you see this message window.

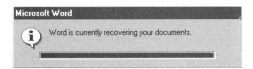

When the application restarts, you have the option of restoring this recovered version of the document (see "Recovering Documents with the Document Recovery task pane" later in this section).

Setting Timed Recovery Save Options

Timed Recovery Save is the traditional AutoRecovery feature. While Document Recovery will probably save a more current version of your document, Timed Recovery Save is still valuable when the power goes out and there is no time to save your work.

You can increase or decrease the frequency of AutoRecovery on the Save tab of the Options dialog box in Word, Excel, and PowerPoint or an e-mail message form in Outlook. The setting affects all four applications, so you can set it in any one of them.

Recovering Documents with the Document Recovery Task Pane

NEW▶

When your software or your system crashes and you restart an Office application, you are immediately presented with a Document Recovery task pane on the left side of the document window, like the one shown in Figure 1.15. It lists any documents that were open at the time of the crash and indicates whether it is the original document that was last saved by user, a recovered document that was last saved by AutoRecovery, or a recovered document that was last saved by Document Recovery. You'll also see the time that the document was saved so you can make comparisons to determine which one might be more current. If you're still not sure, click the arrow next to the document you think you want and choose Open.

FIGURE 1.15

The Document Recovery task pane shows you any version of the document that is available to recover.

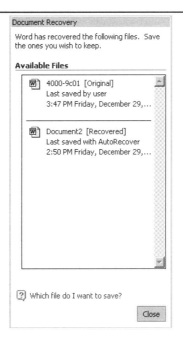

If you find the one you want to save, click the arrow next to the document again and choose Save. When you've recovered the documents you want, click Close on the task pane to get it out of your way.

Microsoft Office Application Recovery

Even when an application is nonresponsive, it's possible that you can recover your document in Word, Excel, and PowerPoint. If you can open the Windows Start menu and reach Programs, find the Microsoft Office Tools group and choose Microsoft Office Application Recovery. This tool will attempt to break into the nonresponding application and save the day, or at least your documents. It's worth a try.

Corrupt Document Recovery

If a Word or Excel document becomes corrupted, the application will attempt to repair it before reopening it. You may get this dialog box when you attempt to open it.

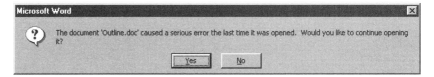

Click Yes to try to recover the document. You can also invoke this feature manually from the Open dialog box (see "Open and Save As Dialog Boxes Make It Easier to Work with Files" earlier in this chapter.)

Making Use of Office Safe Mode

If an Office application fails to start and you have to shut it down using the Task Manager (press Ctrl+Alt+Del), the next time you attempt to open the application Office gives you the option of starting the application in Safe Mode. By choosing this option, you can disable any add-ins or code that may be causing the problem.

Other Recovery Features

In addition to the myriad features for users, Office XP contains a number of new features to help system administrators, help desks, and Microsoft track persistent problems. These features, including Client Logging, Crash Reporting, Hang Reporting, Corporate Tracking, and Setup Failure Reporting, make the future stability of Office even more promising. If you'd like to know about the reliability features of Office XP, refer to www.officeupdate.microsoft.com.

INPUTTING TEXT WITH SPEECH AND HANDWRITING RECOGNITION TOOLS

FEATURING

- Setting up speech recognition

- Dictating text

- Correcting text

- Giving voice commands

- Tweaking the speech recognition system

- Using handwriting recognition tools

- Using soft keyboards

- Drawing on screen

- Correcting handwriting

n the dawning years of the twenty-first century, computers are not quite as advanced as Arthur C. Clarke dreamed in *2001: A Space Odyssey*. We can't yet interact with them as if they were human. Don't let that discourage you, however. With Office XP's new speech and handwriting recognition tools, you can issue verbal commands to your software and dictate documents to your own personal, electronic transcriptionist. The Speech Recognition System works in Word, Excel, PowerPoint, Outlook, Access, and even FrontPage. While it may still be a far cry from Clarke's vision of Hal, a computer with a little too much personality for most people's taste, these tools add an entirely new dimension to office productivity.

In this chapter, we'll show you how to set up the speech and handwriting recognition tools and how to use them most effectively. We'll point out their strengths and weaknesses and give you some tips for avoiding their pitfalls. We'll also let you know what hardware you'll need to make this new software worthwhile.

Preparing to Use Office XP's Speech Recognition Tools

NEW▶ Speech recognition has come a long way in the last five years. Certainly, software developments have played a part in its moving into the mainstream. But it's hardware advancements that have really tipped the scales. The availability of more memory, faster processors, better microphones, and larger hard drives are all players in the speech recognition equation. Before deciding whether you want to delve into this new technology, take a look at the following hardware and software requirements recommended by Microsoft:

- A high-quality, close-talk (headset) microphone with gain adjustment support (USB preferred)
- A 400MHz or faster computer
- 128MB or more of memory
- Windows 98 or later or Windows NT 4.0 or later
- Microsoft Internet Explorer 5 or later

 NOTE *Gain adjustment support* is a feature in microphones that amplifies your input for use by the speech recognition software.

Although not indicated by Microsoft, you also need a good-quality sound card—read the sidebar "Can a Different Microphone Help Me Improve Recognition Accuracy" for suggestions. Most sound cards are designed primarily for quality output. Only recently have sound cards been designed to handle input to complement speech and voice recognition software.

NOTE *Speech recognition* software is software that translates spoken words into typed text. *Voice recognition* hardware and software identifies individual voice patterns and is primarily designed for security purposes.

Be aware that the hardware requirements for processor speed and RAM are minimum requirements. Although we have used speech recognition on 128MB of RAM and a slower processor, it is less than ideal. In fact, you may even find it interfering with your ability to run other software without crashing. If you can afford to upgrade to 196MB of RAM, you'll find it makes a drastic difference.

MASTERING TROUBLESHOOTING

Why Won't Speech Run Right on My System?

Speech recognition has some special requirements depending on the operating system you are using and exactly what you want to do with it. If you would like to use speech to make Office as hands-free as possible, consider the following requirements:

- If you are running Windows 98 (not Microsoft Windows 98 Second Edition) and you want to dictate into dialog boxes, you should download the Microsoft Active Accessibility Redistribution Kit (RDK). Although we recommend upgrading to Windows 98 Second Edition if at all possible, you can download the RDK from Microsoft at www.microsoft.com/enable/msaa/download.htm#RDK.

- If you are running Windows NT 4.0, be sure you are using Internet Explorer 5.5.

- If you are using HTML format for your e-mail messages, and you are running Microsoft Windows 2000 with Microsoft Internet Explorer 5.5, you need Internet Explorer 5.5 Service Pack 1 (SP1).

After you've selected and installed the sound card and microphone, you're just two short steps away from speaking your text and commands:

1. Set up your microphone with the Microphone Wizard (less than 5 minutes).

2. Create speech files with the Voice Training Wizard (less than 20 minutes).

MASTERING TROUBLESHOOTING

Can a Different Microphone Help Me Improve Recognition Accuracy?

Before you even attempt to use the speech recognition tools, Microsoft recommends a minimum of a 400MHz processor and 128MB of RAM. As with any recommended minimum, you will not see optimal performance at this level. You need 192MB to 256MB to give you more stability and improve the software's accuracy. If you meet these requirements and are still having problems with accuracy, it could be your microphone.

At the time of this writing, Microsoft recommends only one microphone for use with its Speech tools, the Microsoft SideWinder Game Voice, which also lets you control games with voice commands. We have tried several other headset-style microphones with varying degrees of success. USB microphones with gain adjustment support are clearly the best choice. You can choose from desktop, headset, collar, and digital microphones. If you go with a headset or collar, choose one that fits you well and is comfortable so that the microphone stays positioned near your mouth at all times—off to the side of your mouth is usually best. Microphones with a swivel arm such as the Labtec Axis 501 make it easy to move it out of the way and return it to the same position when you are ready to dictate. If you choose a desktop model, be sure you keep it in the same place each time you dictate. Moving it around could affect accuracy, especially if the distance changes. Finding quality microphones for under $50 that are especially designed for speech recognition is becoming easier. The key is to not just settle for the microphone that came with your computer. Chances are it will not do the job for you. Invest a few dollars and you'll have a lot more fun with Speech.

Setting Up Your Microphone

Locate the microphone and headphone jacks on your computer and plug in your microphone. If you have a USB microphone, plug it into the USB port. You can run the Microphone Wizard from any Office application. Choose Tools ➢ Speech from the menu bar. The Language bar appears, floating somewhere over the application window:

NOTE Options on the Language bar may vary depending on the options you've installed and what is active at the current time. For more about Language bar options, see "Working with the Language Bar" later in this chapter.

If the microphone has not been previously set up, you are prompted to run the Microphone Wizard. The wizard adjusts the volume from your microphone so that it works well with the Office applications. Even if the microphone has been set up before, we recommend running it again to adjust its settings to your preferences. If you are not prompted for the Microphone Wizard, choose Tools ➢ Options from the Language bar to open the Speech Properties dialog box.

Click the Configure Microphone button in the Speech Properties dialog box to start the Microphone Wizard. Follow the instructions in the wizard to configure your microphone for optimal use with Microsoft Office XP.

 NOTE If you're using your headset microphone and laptop in a hotel room rather than your office, it's a good idea to invest a few minutes and run the wizard again to ensure the best recognition.

Training the Speech Recognition System

After the microphone is configured, you will use the microphone to train the Speech Recognition System. Train the system in the environment where you intend to use it: if you're going to use it in your office, train the system in your office with the normal level of office noise. The first time you set up your microphone, the voice training process starts automatically as soon as your microphone is configured. If you need to start it manually, choose Tools ➢ Training on the Language bar to create a user profile and begin training the system to recognize the way you pronounce words. You read the text that's displayed in the dialog box, and the Speech Recognition System highlights each word as it recognizes it, as shown in Figure 2.1. Your first training session will probably take around 20 minutes. You can pause at any point and continue later, but we don't recommend it. If you stop prior to the end of the session, you need to start at the beginning the next time you wish to train.

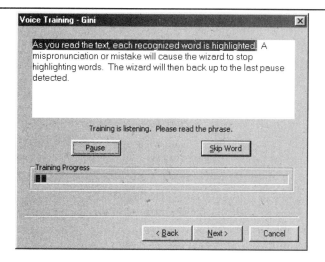

As you read the session text, each recognized word is highlighted by the Speech Recognition System.

When you've completed the introductory training session, your speech settings are saved in a speech profile. The system keeps a separate profile for each user. After you've worked with the Speech Recognition System in Office XP applications for a little while, we suggest going back for more training using other materials to increase recognition. Just choose Tools ➤ Training on the Language bar and choose one of the sessions from the list.

NOTE When you complete training, Office plays a short training video to help you get started. It's worth seeing just to hear how Microsoft suggests using the tools.

Using the Speech Recognition System

You can use the Speech Recognition System in Office XP in three ways:

- Dictate or correct text
- Issue voice commands to activate buttons, menu commands, and dialog boxes
- Play back printed text from a document

Dictating in Office XP

To use the dictation or voice command features of Office XP, open the Tools menu on any application and choose Speech. This activates the Language bar.

NOTE If you've never used speech recognition software before, we suggest you start dictating in the application where you feel most comfortable. For most people, that is Word.

Click the Microphone button on the Language bar to turn the microphone on. When the microphone is active, you can see additional options on the Language bar for Dictation and Voice Command. To the right of Voice Command is a yellow balloon that displays messages as you dictate. Some messages, such as Too Soft, let you know to speak up. When you are in Voice Command mode, this message box displays the last recognized command or what you could have said rather than using the mouse or keyboard.

To begin dictating text, make sure the Dictation button is blue. If it is not, click it and then begin speaking to enter text in your document. Speak each word clearly, and speak the names of the punctuation marks (comma, period, question mark). When you want a new paragraph, say **New Paragraph**. When you first begin, don't worry about making corrections. Just keep dictating and get comfortable with developing an appropriate speed and rhythm. If you are getting good recognition, keep going and worry about editing later. Don't forget to speak punctuation marks.

In addition to punctuation marks, you can also use the commands listed in Table 2.1 in Dictation mode.

TABLE 2.1   COMMANDS YOU CAN SAY IN DICTATION MODE

You Say	To
New Line	Start text on the next line.
New Paragraph	Start a new paragraph.
Mic Off	Turn the microphone off.
Tab	Press the Tab key once.
Shift Tab	Backspace a Tab.
Enter	Press the Enter key once.
Spelling Mode	Spell out the next word. You have to pause for a second after spelling out the word to switch back to normal Dictation mode.
Forcenum	Enter a number or symbol instead of spelling it out such as 2 instead of two. Pause for a second after using this command so it can revert to normal Dictation mode.

> **TIP** If you want to enter several numbers, dictate the numbers without the Forcenum command. Speech recognizes strings of numbers and enters them as numbers rather than text. It even formats phone numbers for you automatically.

You can dictate in any Office XP application. In Outlook, select the text box in an open form before you begin speaking. In Excel, cell navigation is part of dictation: precede the direction with the words **Go To**, **Go Up**, **Go Down**, **Go Left**, or **Go Right** and then indicate how many cells—**One Cell**, **Two Cells**, and so on.

When you are finished dictating or need to take a break, click the Microsoft button again to turn Speech off or click Voice Command and say **Microphone**.

Making Corrections and Enhancing Recognition

If the speech recognition system does not accurately recognize a word or string of words, select the words and click the Correction button to hear a recording of your dictation of the word or phrase. Choose the correct words from the list of suggestions, or select and respeak the words. Remember, you can always use the mouse and keyboard to make corrections if the words you want are not in the list.

If you would like to add words to the speech dictionary to aid in recognition, you can add them individually or you can use the Speech tools to review a document and identify any words it does not know. This second option is particularly valuable if you have a document that contains a lot of words that are unique to your business. To add words individually, follow these steps:

1. Click Tools on the Language bar.

2. Click Add/Delete Words to open the Add/Delete Words dialog box.

3. Select a word from the list or enter your own word.

4. Click Record Pronunciation and say the word correctly.

5. Repeat steps 3 and 4 until you have added all the words you want to add.

6. You may also want to delete a word that was automatically added to the list from your documents. Select the word and click Delete.

7. Click Cancel when you are finished adding and deleting words.

To review an entire document for words that are not in the speech dictionary, choose Tools ➤ Learn From Document. When the document has been reviewed, a Learn From Document dialog box appears with the list of words it identified. Select and delete words you don't want to add. Click Add All to add the rest of the words. If you'd like to add pronunciation, follow the steps listed above to access the Add/Delete Words dialog box.

Giving Voice Commands in Office XP

You can switch from dictating text that you want recognized to giving voice commands to operate the application by clicking the Voice Command button on the Language bar. You can use voice commands to move the insertion point within a document, to activate a toolbar button or a menu, and to input responses in a dialog box.

For example, suppose you want to designate specific page setup options for a document. You want your document to have landscape orientation with 1" left and right margins on 11"✕8.5" paper with a different first page header. Use your voice to make these setting changes:

1. Say **Voice Command** to switch to Voice Command mode.

2. Say **File** to open the File menu.

3. Say **Page Setup** to open the Page Setup dialog box.

4. Say **Margins** to select the Margins tab.

5. Say **Tab**, **Tab**, **Tab** to set the left margin—the insertion point should move into the Left Margin text box.

6. Say **Down Arrow**, **Down Arrow**, **Down Arrow** to reduce the left margin to 1.0".

7. Say **Tab** to move the insertion point to the Right Margin text box.

8. Say **Down Arrow**, **Down Arrow**, **Down Arrow** to reduce the margin to 1.0".

9. Say **Paper** to switch to the Paper tab.

10. Say **Paper Size** to open the Paper Size drop-down list.

11. Say **Legal** to select Legal from the drop-down list.

12. Say **Layout** to switch to the Layout tab.

13. Say **Different First Page** to select the Different First Page check box.

14. Say **OK** to accept the changes and close the dialog box.

When you are dictating or entering text, you can use voice commands to move the insertion point around your document. Table 2.2 shows voice commands that are available throughout Office XP.

TABLE 2.2   OFFICE XP VOICE NAVIGATION COMMANDS

You Say	Keyboard or Mouse Equivalent
Return **Enter**	Press Enter
Backspace **Delete**	Press Backspace
Space **Space Bar**	Press the spacebar
Escape **Cancel**	Press Esc
Right Click **Right Click Menu** **Show Right Click Menu** **Context Menu** **Show Context Menu**	Right-click a menu
Tab	Press Tab
Control Tab	Press Ctrl+Tab
Shift Tab	Press Shift+Tab
End **Go End**	Press End
Home **Go Home**	Press Home
Up **Go Up** **Up Arrow** **Arrow Up**	Press up arrow

Continued

TABLE 2.2 (continued) OFFICE XP VOICE NAVIGATION COMMANDS	
You Say	**Keyboard or Mouse Equivalent**
Down **Go Down** **Down Arrow** **Arrow Down**	Press down arrow
Left **Go Left** **Left Arrow** **Arrow Left**	Press left arrow
Right **Go Right** **Right Arrow** **Arrow Right**	Press right arrow
Previous Page **Next Page** **Page Down**	Press Page Down
Page Up	Press Page Up

 NOTE If you are having trouble using a particular voice command, minimize the application you are working in or switch to another application and then switch back to the application and try it again. Chances are it will work better after this little kick.

 For a list of the voice commands that are available in each specific application, refer to Appendix C, "Speech Recognition Commands in Office XP," on the companion CD. We've designed this appendix so that you can print it out and keep it handy as you become familiar with the speech commands.

 NOTE Some people think that speech and handwriting recognition tools are ways to avoid learning how to use applications. However, to use these tools effectively in Office, you must first know how to use the application you want to work in or you will not know how to use the voice commands. Speech and handwriting will help people who don't know how or are unable to type, but those users still have to learn how an application works before they can use it.

Tweaking the Speech Recognition System

Speech recognition is a trade-off between recognition and accuracy. Words are recognized in context; the more surrounding words the system has to examine, the more likely it is to determine which word you actually spoke. The more words the system examines, the longer it takes to display your dictated text on screen.

If the lag between dictation and display is too long, or if the percentage of incorrectly recognized words is too high, you can change the recognition/accuracy settings to improve recognition or speed. You can also adjust the Rejection Rate setting if the system frequently ignores menu commands in Voice Command mode.

To access the Speech Recognition System settings, choose Tools ➤ Options from the Language bar menu. In the Speech Properties dialog box (see Figure 2.2), select your profile, and then click the Settings button to open the Recognition Profile Settings dialog box, shown in Figure 2.3. Here you can adjust Pronunciation Sensitivity and the Accuracy vs. Recognition Response Time. If you set the sensitivity too high, you may find that it's trying to translate all of your *ums* and mumbles, so keep this setting toward the center. If you have a fast processor and lots of memory, increase the accuracy levels for the best recognition. To have the system automatically adjust and learn from your speech patterns as you are dictating, make sure the Background Adaptation check box is selected.

FIGURE 2.2

In the Speech Properties dialog box, you can create new profiles and augment your speech training.

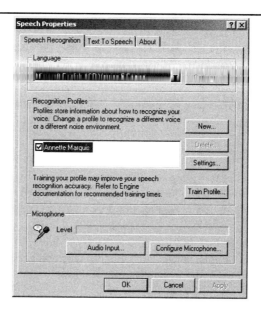

FIGURE 2.3

Use the settings in the Recognition Profile Settings dialog box to tweak the performance of the Speech Recognition System.

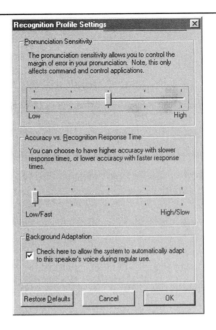

Creating a New Profile on Your Computer

Speech recognition files are specific to each person's voice and should not be shared. If another user wants to use speech on the same computer, they need to set up an additional speech profile. You may also find it useful to have a different profile at work and at home if the noise level is drastically different. To set up a user profile, choose Tools ➤ Options on the Language bar and click the New button on the Speech Recognition tab of the Speech Properties dialog box (see Figure 2.2). The Profile Wizard will guide you through the steps to create another user profile.

After you create a user profile, you can select the profile you want to use from the Speech Properties dialog box or from the Tools button on the Language bar. Choose Current User to verify the current user or select a different one.

Removing Speech Recognition Services

If you've given Speech a fair trial and you decide that it just isn't for you (or for your computer), you can remove the text service from Office XP without uninstalling the entire feature from your computer. To remove the service, right-click the Language bar and choose Settings to open the Text Services dialog box shown in Figure 2.4.

Select the speech service you have installed in the Installed Services list and click Remove (the speech service is the one with the microphone in front of it). After it is removed, it no longer loads with your software and as a result frees up any memory it was using. If you decide you want the speech service back, just reverse the process, clicking Add in the Installed Services list.

To uninstall the speech recognition service completely from your computer, use Add/Remove Programs in the Control Panel.

NOTE If you have text services installed for more than one language, select the language first from the Default Input Language drop-down list and then remove the speech text service.

FIGURE 2.4

Remove the text service from Office XP with the Text Services dialog box.

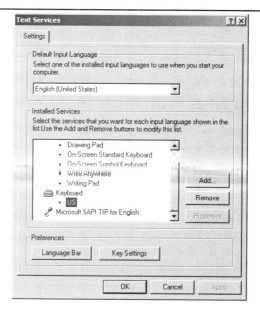

Working with the Language Bar

The Language bar is a completely new kind of Office toolbar. Rather than docking in the application window, the Language bar floats above it. You can move the Language bar around the application window by pointing to the left edge—the pointer becomes a four-header arrow so you can drag it where you want it.

To control the Language bar, right-click anywhere on it for a shortcut menu of options.

Minimize Positions the Language bar as an icon on the Windows system tray—just to the left of the clock. Click the icon and select Show The Language bar to activate it for use.

Transparency Makes the Language bar turn clear when not in use so as not to disrupt whatever is beneath it. Can be toggled on and off.

Text Labels Toggles between showing text and icons on the Language bar buttons.

Additional Icons In Taskbar Adds a microphone and handwriting icon to the Taskbar when the Language bar is minimized. You can activate Dictation or Handwriting mode by clicking the Taskbar button.

Settings Takes you to the Text Services dialog box.

Close The Language bar Shuts down the Language bar completely. To reactivate, choose Text Services in the Windows Control Panel and choose to show the Language bar from the Language Bar Preferences.

You can also control which buttons appear on the Language bar by clicking the Options button (the small downward-pointing arrow on the right end of the bar). Select the buttons you would like to have available on the Language bar from the list of Correction, Speech Tools, and Help.

MASTERING THE OPPORTUNITIES

Using Text To Speech with Excel

Text To Speech is a feature that reads back to you text you have entered into a document. Designed as one of Microsoft's new Accessibility features, Text To Speech is only available, at this point, in Excel. Microsoft is working hard to develop software that is accessible to people with disabilities, so we expect that this feature will be expanded in future releases.

Continued

MASTERING THE OPPORTUNITIES CONTINUED

Before using the Text To Speech feature, you first want to visit the Speech Engine settings in the Windows Control Panel, available by clicking the Speech icon. On the Text To Speech tab, you can choose whether you'd like to have Michael or Michelle reading to you. Be sure to have your headset on so you can preview both of the voices before making this momentous choice. You can also adjust the speed at which your choice speaks to you, so if you are from New York you can have it read faster and if you're from New Orleans you can slow it down. You are now ready to activate Text To Speech. To use the feature, start Excel and choose Tools ➢ Speech ➢ Show Text To Speech Toolbar.

To start reading from a particular position on the worksheet, click that cell and then click the Speak Cells button on the Text To Speech toolbar. By default, Michelle (or Michael) reads across the rows until she comes to the last cell of the worksheet and then returns to column A. Click the Stop Speaking button to stop the operation. To change directions and have her read down the column rather than across the row, click the By Columns button. If you'd like Michelle to speak entries as you enter them, click the Speak On Enter button. Just close the toolbar when you are finished with the Text To Speech tools.

Handwriting Recognition

NEW ▶ Handwriting recognition offers a wealth of opportunity for new types of computers. No longer tied to a keyboard, new computing devices will offer the same freedom that legal pads and steno books have given us for years. Already personal digital assistants (PDAs) and handheld computers such as Palms and Pocket PCs offer handwriting recognition as the primary input method. Tablet computers are beginning to show up in the catalogs of computer hardware resellers. Including handwriting recognition in Office XP brings us one step closer to throwing out our keyboards and giving users more natural and flexible computing options.

The Handwriting tools in Office XP, which are not part of the standard installation, include soft keyboards, on-screen drawing, and actual handwriting recognition. If you would like to use them, run the Office XP Setup program and add Handwriting in the Office Shared Features folder under Alternative User Input.

Using Soft Keyboards

As part of the set of Handwriting tools, Office XP offers two on-screen keyboards: Standard and Symbol. The Standard keyboard, shown in Figure 2.5, is a traditional QWERTY keyboard that floats on the screen.

The Symbol keyboard, shown in Figure 2.6, is a collection of language symbols for written languages other than English. The Standard keyboard option offers little advantage to the desktop or laptop user—it is designed primarily for the handheld computer market. The Symbol keyboard, however, used in conjunction with a traditional keyboard, can be an effective shortcut for users who have to type in languages that require keys not readily available on the QWERTY keyboard.

FIGURE 2.5

The Standard keyboard offers handheld computer users a familiar input method.

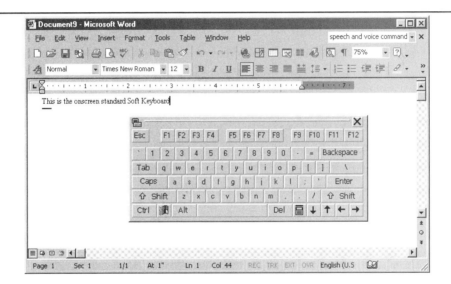

FIGURE 2.6

The Symbol keyboard gives ready access to characters that are not available on the QWERTY keyboard.

To activate either the Standard or Symbol soft keyboards, click the Handwriting button on the Language bar to select the keyboard you want you want to use.

If you would like to add the keyboard to the Language bar so you can easily turn it on and off, click the Options button at the right end of the Language bar (the small black arrow) and choose Microsoft Handwriting Item from the menu. With this option turned on, whatever handwriting item you select in the Handwriting menu appears on the toolbar.

Click the keys on the soft keyboard to enter text on the screen. When you want to turn the keyboard off, click the Close button on the keyboard (or the Handwriting button on the Language bar).

Drawing On Screen

The Drawing Pad is designed to make it easy to insert a quick drawing into a document. Although you have many more tools available to you using the Drawing toolbar, the Drawing Pad offers simplicity and flexibility for alternative computer devices. To activate the Drawing Pad, click Handwriting on the Language bar and choose Drawing Pad. This opens the Drawing Pad shown in Figure 2.7.

FIGURE 2.7

Use the Drawing Pad to create and insert simple drawings into a document.

NOTE If the Drawing Pad button doesn't appear on the Language bar, click the Language bar's Option button and select Microsoft Handwriting Item from the list of button choices.

To use the Drawing Pad, just point and draw. You don't have any pen or brush choices, but you can change the width and color of the lines you draw. Click the Options button in the title bar of the Drawing Pad to open the Draw Options dialog box, shown in Figure 2.8. You must return to the Draw Options dialog box every time you want to change pen color or width.

FIGURE 2.8

Change the pen color and width and also the toolbar layout of the Drawing Pad in the Draw Options dialog box.

 To clear the Drawing Pad window, click the Clear button on the Drawing Pad toolbar. To erase your last stroke, click the Remove Last Stroke button.

  When you are ready to insert your masterpiece into your document, click the Insert Drawing button. If you decide it needs a little more work in another application, click the Copy To Clipboard button.

Using Handwriting to Input Text

Handwriting recognition in Office XP is amazingly accurate even if all you have available to you is your trustworthy mouse. Obviously, handwriting tablets will become more common as more people experience the ease at which Office converts even the most illegible scrawl into typed text. Figure 2.9 shows how accurately Office XP converts handwriting.

To activate handwriting, choose Lined Paper from the Write menu on the Language bar and then click the Lined Paper button. This opens the Lined Paper Writing Pad shown in Figure 2.9.

You have the option of writing so that it is automatically converted into text. You can also leave it as handwriting if, for example, you want to sign a letter.

To use automatic handwriting recognition, click the Text button on the Writing Pad. If you print on the Lined Paper writing surface, your letters are immediately transcribed. If you write cursive style, your writing is automatically transcribed when you pause for more than a second or two.

To write using the mouse, hold the mouse button down to write; release it to move to the next word. It definitely takes a little work to get used to writing this way, but with a little practice, you'll do fine.

FIGURE 2.9

Office XP can accurately convert even this scrawl into typed text— it truly is amazing!

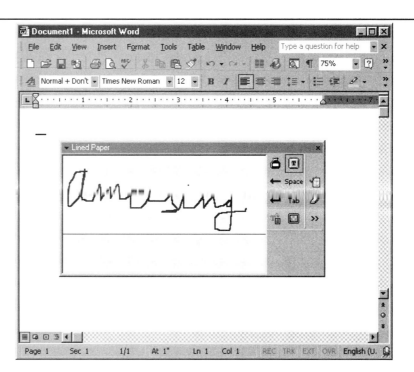

NOTE If you have access to a graphics tablet (as you might use with 3-D or Computer-Aided Drafting software), you will find handwriting a much more pleasant experience. You will also find new tablet-PCs and handwriting tablets available in your local or online computer store. If you have a laptop with a touchpad, you can purchase a pack of PDA styluses or a stylus pen and use the touchpad as your writing surface—depress the left touchpad button as you write. As far as tablets go, we've been impressed with the WACOM Graphire (www.wacom.com). The tablet comes with a cordless pen and mouse—you must use the mouse on the tablet—and a bunch of bundled software. Some of the software is unnecessary with the handwriting and drawing features in Office XP, but they still give you some cool toys to play with and a solid well-made tablet all for under $100.

 If you would prefer to transfer your handwriting without having it transcribed, click the Ink button on the Writing Pad. Be sure to write directly above the line on the Writing Pad to have your writing appear inline with the text. Use this option to add a real signature to an e-mail or letter.

The text you write appears in whatever size font you have selected. If you're working in a 10-point font, then the handwriting appears very small. If you would like to format the handwriting, select it just as you would any other text and change the text size, color, and alignment or even add bold, italics, and underline.

Correcting Your Handwriting

Whether you are using the Ink or Text tools to enter handwriting, you can correct mistakes that Office or you make in the text. To correct transcribed text, right-click any word and select the correct word from the list of choices just as you would if the word were misspelled.

You can also select the erroneous word and click the Correction button on the Writing Pad to see a list of word alternatives.

If you want to correct handwriting itself, right-click the word and choose Ink Object and then choose either Alternate List or Recognize. Either way, Office converts the handwriting into typed text. If you want to make a correction and keep the handwriting, the only option is to rewrite it.

Finding Help for Speech and Handwriting Recognition

Although you'll find some help files in each application, the general help files on speech and handwriting recognition are available on the Language bar. Click the yellow question mark Help button on the Language bar and choose Language bar Help. Choose Use Speech on the Contents tab to get help for speech and handwriting recognition.

You can also find extensive help on the Microsoft Office Update site at www.officeupdate.microsoft.com.

CREATING QUALITY TEXT DOCUMENTS USING WORD

LEARN TO:

- Enter text and apply formats

- Find and replace text and formats

- Lay out pages with columns and tables

- Create your own graphics and charts

- Define and apply styles

- Create merge documents

- Manage large documents

- Work collaboratively using versions and revision marks

Working with Text and Formats in Word

I n this world of lightning-speed technological advances, the written word still serves as one of the most essential forms of communication in our society. If you know how to produce high-quality written documents, you can make the right impression even before your recipient reads a single word. In this chapter, you'll learn the essentials of creating documents using Word 2002. You'll also learn how to produce good-looking printed documents by taking advantage of some enhanced printing options. Whether you are new to Microsoft Word or are stepping up to the latest version, knowing these fundamentals is guaranteed to enhance your personal or corporate image.

Although the Word application window is consistent with those of the other Office XP applications (introduced in Chapter 1, "Presenting Office XP: What You Need to Know"), there are a few differences you should know about. Figure 3.1 identifies features of the Word application window that differ from those in the other Office XP applications. The Word document window, contained within the application window, includes a ruler bar that you can use to set tabs and margins and to adjust columns. You'll find View buttons at the left end of the horizontal scroll bar and Browse buttons at the bottom of the vertical scroll bar. The Browse buttons help you review your documents page by page or by any other identifiable object.

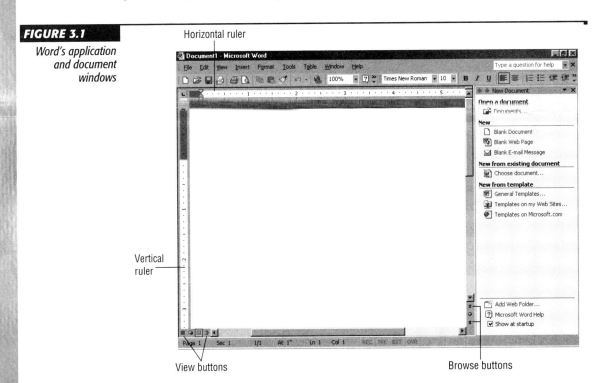

FIGURE 3.1

Word's application and document windows

Horizontal ruler

Vertical ruler

View buttons

Browse buttons

Getting a Different Perspective

You probably know how to use scroll bars to move around in a document. You'll be happy to know that Word 2002 has a number of other tools that make it easy to navigate documents of any length. Rather than using the arrows at the top and bottom of the vertical scroll bar, drag the scroll box to make a ScrollTip appear, showing the page number you are scrolling past. If the document has headings, the heading also appears in the tip.

To review specific features of a lengthy document, you may find that browsing is even quicker than using the scroll bars. On the bottom of the vertical scroll bar is a set of Browse buttons: Previous Page, Select Browse Object, and Next Page.

Click the Select Browse Object button to display a toolbar, shown in Figure 3.2, and then select the object type you'd like to browse.

PART

II

CREATING QUALITY TEXT
DOCUMENTS USING WORD

FIGURE 3.2

Browse Objects menu

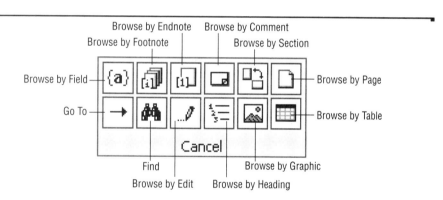

Objects are files or documents created in another application and inserted into a document: for example, pictures, line art, or an Excel worksheet placed in a Word document. In this menu, the term also includes other document landmarks you might want to browse: Fields, Endnotes, Footnotes, Sections, Comments, Pages, Edits, Graphics, Headings, and Tables. If you choose the Go To or Find button, a dialog box asks you where you want to go or what you want to find.

When you decide which object you want to browse, select the object's icon from the toolbar, then use the Previous and Next scrollbar buttons to move to the previous or next object of that type. If you choose to browse by any object type other than Page, the Previous and Next buttons turn blue to remind you that another choice is active. To return to "normal" browsing, open the Select Browse Object menu and choose Browse By Page.

Using Word Views

Word 2002 gives you several ways to view documents, depending on whether you are writing, outlining, preparing to print, or just reading a document. To the left of the horizontal scroll bar are the View buttons.

Normal View Best used for entering, editing, and formatting text. Headers, footers, graphics, and columns are not visible in this view.

Web Layout View Designed to be used when reading documents on the screen. There are no visible margins or page breaks in Web Layout view, making it easier to scroll through a document without interruption.

Print Layout View Allows you to work with your document exactly as it will look when it is printed.

TIP Word 2002 now lets you hide top and bottom margins as well as page breaks in Print Layout view. Just move the mouse to the top of any page. When you see the screen tip that says Hide White Space, give it a click. Margins disappear and page breaks are displayed as dark gray lines. To see this extra space again, place the mouse near a page break and click when you see the Show White Space icon and screen tip.

Outline View Useful when you are developing a document's structure and content and want to create a preliminary outline or review the outline as you are working.

In addition to the four standard views, the Document Map gives you the ultimate in navigational control. To use the Document Map, you must apply styles to your document's headings. (For more about applying heading styles, see Chapter 8, "Simplifying with Styles, Outlines, and Templates.") Each heading appears in the Document Map as a hyperlink, as shown in Figure 3.3. Click a heading to move immediately to that section of your document.

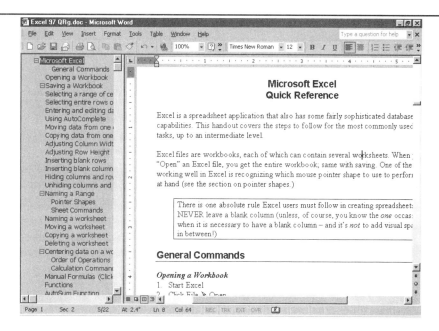

FIGURE 3.3

The Document Map provides an easy way to jump directly to the part of a document that interests you.

PART

II

CREATING QUALITY TEXT
DOCUMENTS USING WORD

This is a good time to open any Word document and spend a few moments examining any features described above that are unfamiliar. If you don't have a Word 2002 document, open any WordPerfect or Word document, and Word 2002 automatically converts it.

EXPERT TIP If you need to convert a number of documents, either from other formats into Word 2002 or from Word 2002 to other formats, use the Batch Conversion Wizard. Use My Computer or the Windows Explorer to move all the files (or copies of the files) to the same folder. In Word, choose File ➢ New. In the New dialog box, click the Other Documents tab, then double-click the Batch Conversion Wizard and follow the steps to select the files to convert. Word 2002, Word 2000, and Word 97 use the same file format. You can open these types of documents in any of these three versions of Word without the need to convert them first.

Entering Text

Word 2002 tries to make your life easier right from the first letter you type by watching what you're doing and figuring out how it can be most helpful. As you enter text,

Word takes several behind-the-scenes actions (see Figure 3.4). These actions include the following:

- If the Office Assistant is active, it evaluates what you are doing to see if it has any suggestions to offer. (See Chapter 1 for more about using the Office Assistant.)

- The AutoCorrect feature automatically corrects misspelled words that are in its dictionary, such as "teh" and "adn."

- The Spelling and Grammar feature reviews your text to determine if there are other possible misspellings or grammatical errors.

 TIP The accuracy of the Grammar feature is significantly improved when compared to Word 97 when it was first introduced. However, be careful about accepting its advice without verifying the accuracy of the suggestions. It still makes more than its fair share of errors. See Chapter 4, "Putting Text and Language Tools to Work for You," for more about the Grammar feature.

FIGURE 3.4

The Office Assistant with the Grammar feature in action

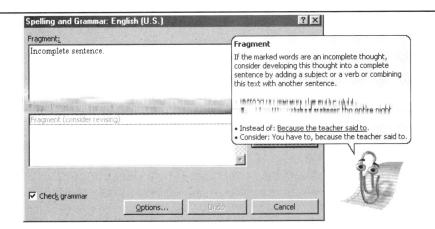

To enter text in Word, begin typing in the document window. Alternatively, you may use the dictation or handwriting tools available with Office XP. (See Chapter 2, "Inputting Text with Speech and Handwriting Recognition Tools," for more about these features.) Text you enter displays at the flashing insertion point (cursor). The insertion point moves over to accommodate the new text. You can also overtype existing text by pressing the Insert key on the keyboard. This puts you into Overtype mode; as you type new text, old text is deleted. Most users prefer Insert mode rather than Overtype mode. To return to Insert mode, just press the Insert key again.

In Normal view, Word displays a black horizontal line at the left margin.

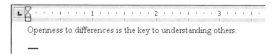

This represents the end of your document. In Normal or Outline view, you cannot move the insertion point or insert text or objects below the marker.

Moving the Insertion Point

Word provides several ways to move the insertion point using the keyboard. You can use the arrow keys to move the cursor up a line, down a line, and one character to the left or right, or use the special keys listed in Table 3.1.

TABLE 3.1   NAVIGATION KEYS

Key	Action
Home	The beginning of the current line
End	The end of the current line
Ctrl+Home	The beginning of the document
Ctrl+End	The end of the document
Page Up	Up one screen
Page Down	Down one screen
Ctrl+Left Arrow	One word to the left
Ctrl+Right Arrow	One word to the right

 TIP Ctrl+Page Up and Ctrl+Page Down move the insertion point to the previous or next Browse object. If Browse By Page is the object selected, Ctrl+Page Up/Page Down is the same as Page Up/Page Down.

Click-and-Type Lets You Type Anywhere You Want

In addition to providing more graphically realistic displays, Print Layout and Web Layout views offer one incredible advantage over Normal and Outline views. With support for a feature called Click-and-Type, in these views you are free to type anywhere on the screen without regard to where you last left the insertion point.

Move the I-beam around the screen and notice that the icon changes to an I-beam with an alignment indicator (left, center, or right). Wherever you *double*-click, Word automatically inserts the additional hard returns and tabs to place the insertion point there. Double-click in the center of the page to type centered text; double-click near the right margin for right alignment.

>
> **TIP** Click-and-Type is an optional feature that is turned on by default. The setting to turn it off/on is under Tools ≻ Options ≻ Edit. Simply check or uncheck the Enable Click-And-Type feature at the bottom of the dialog box.

Click-and-Type is especially useful when you want to use more than one alignment in the same line, as those shown here.

TRIAD Consulting, LLC   1 Triad Towers   Traverse City, MI 49684

Just double-click the appropriate side of the screen and start typing.

> **TIP** If you are interested in how Word manages this Click-and-Type trick, click the Show/Hide Paragraph Marks button (on the Standard toolbar) to see the hard returns and tabs that Word adds to your document.

Editing Quickly and Easily

You can spot a Word power user because they use the minimum number of steps to complete a task. They're not just proficient; they're efficient, particularly with skills that are used frequently in Word. Knowing several ways to select and replace text will let you streamline many of the other tasks you'll be doing with your documents.

Selecting Text

Although you can always drag to select text, Word offers you a number of other options. Any of these methods can be used, but some methods are easier to use in certain situations. For example, if you've ever tried to drag to select text over multiple pages, you have already experienced the wonders of an out-of-control accelerated mouse pointer. But if you choose another method, such as Shift-select (see Table 3.2 below), you can select text smoothly without getting any new gray hairs.

NEW▶

In Word 2002 you can (finally!) select multiple, noncontiguous sections of text (see Figure 3.5). Select the first section, then hold Ctrl while dragging additional sections of text. Any formatting or other feature you use applies to all the selected text.

TABLE 3.2   SELECTING TEXT WITH THE MOUSE

To Select	Do This
A word	Double-click anywhere in the word.
A sentence	Hold Ctrl and click anywhere in the sentence.
A paragraph	Triple-click anywhere in the paragraph.
Single line	Move the pointer into the left margin. When the pointer changes to a right-pointing arrow, point to the desired line and click.
Entire document	Choose Edit ➢ Select All from the menu, or hold Ctrl and click in the left margin or triple-click in the left margin.
Multiple lines	Move the pointer to the left margin. With the right-pointing arrow, point to the first desired line, and then hold down the mouse button and drag to select additional lines.
Multiple words, lines, or sentences	Move the I-beam into the first word, hold the mouse button, drag to the last word, and release.
Multiple words, lines, or sentences using Shift-select	Click in the first word, move the I-beam to the last word (with the Shift-select mouse button released), hold Shift, and click. Everything between the two clicks is selected.
Multiple, noncontiguous sections of text	Select the first bock of text you want, and then hold Ctrl and drag each additional block of text you want to select.

 TIP Special tip for keyboarders: You can hold Shift and use any of the navigation keys to select text. For example, hold Shift and press Home to select from the current word to the beginning of the line. Hold Shift and press the down arrow to select from the current insertion point position to the line below.

CREATING QUALITY TEXT
DOCUMENTS USING WORD

II

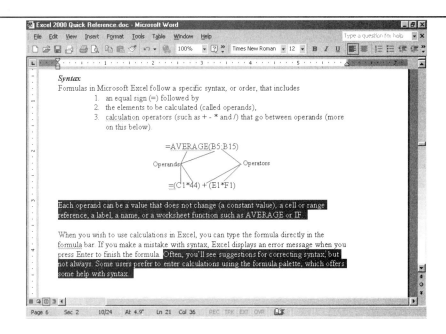

Correcting Mistakes

The easiest way to correct mistakes is to select the troublesome text (using any of the methods listed in Table 3.2) and just start typing. Pressing any key immediately deletes the selected text. To correct mistakes that you make while typing:

- Use the Backspace or Delete keys.
- Click the Undo button on the Standard toolbar.
- Press Ctrl+Backspace and Ctrl+Delete to delete whole words at a time.

Copying and Moving Text

NEW▶

The traditional method of moving and copying text is using the Cut, Copy, and Paste features on the toolbar and menu bar: select text, click Cut (or Copy), move the insertion point to a new location, and click Paste. Word 2002 offers enhanced paste options to give you more control over the formatting of pasted text.

The Paste Options icon is one version of Office XP's new Smart Tags feature. Smart Tags are a set of buttons shared by all Office XP applications. These buttons appear when you need them, giving you options for correcting mistakes or making formatting choices. Once you paste text into a document, the icon appears at the lower right of that text. Click it to see options for formatting the pasted text:

Keep Source Formatting Retains the text's original formatting

Match Destination Formatting Applies the formatting of the paragraph you have pasted into

Keep Text Only Pastes unformatted text

Apply Style or Formatting Opens the Styles And Formatting task pane, where you can choose another format that may differ from both the source and destination

---

NOTE If you're pasting items from a bulleted or numbered list, Word displays paste options that apply to lists. For more information about list options, see "Creating Lists, Numbers, and Symbols" later in this chapter.

If you wish to disable Paste Options, you can turn the feature off by clicking Tools ➤ Options ➤ Edit and disabling the Show Paste Options Buttons check box. If you're using it, however, you'll be interested in the new Smart Cut and Paste settings on the same tab in the Options dialog box.

NEW ▶

Enabling Smart Cut and Paste causes Word to behave consistently in applying the paste options you choose. It can also save you considerable clean-up time by deleting extra spaces and paragraphs that occur as a result of a paste action. Figure 3.6 shows Word 2002's new Smart Cut and Paste settings. Not sure exactly what an option does for you? Click the Question Mark in the title bar of the Settings dialog box, and then click the feature you want to know more about.

PART II

CREATING QUALITY TEXT
DOCUMENTS USING WORD

FIGURE 3.6

Save time and energy when you cut and paste by enabling Smart Cut and Paste settings.

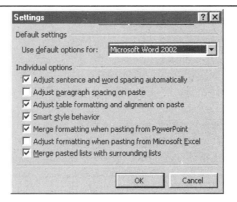

Using Drag-and-Drop

You'll find it more efficient to move or copy text short distances using a method called *drag-and-drop*. Drag-and-drop works best when you can see both the *source* (the location of original text) and the *destination* (the place that you want the moved or copied text to appear). Select the text you want to move or copy, hold down the right mouse button, and drag the insertion point to where you want to paste the text. Release the mouse button, and then select Move Here or Copy Here from the shortcut menu.

You can also use the left mouse button to drag-and-drop selected text, but Word won't open the shortcut menu. Instead, the selection is moved to the new location with no questions asked. If you want to copy text with the left mouse button, hold down the Ctrl key while dropping the text.

 TIP The shortcut menu with commands to move or copy appears when you drag-and-drop a selection or object in many Windows applications, including the Windows Explorer.

 If you want to use drag-and-drop in a large document, split the screen so you can see different pages of the document at the same time. To split a document, point to the small horizontal bar directly above the vertical scroll bar. When the mouse pointer changes to the Resize tool, drag down to create a separate window. You can also choose Window ➤ Split and position the divider where you would like it by clicking it into place. To return to a full window, drag the Resize tool back to the top of the document or choose Window ➤ Remove Split.

Working with Two or More Documents at Once

The beauty of being able to move and copy text is that once you've typed it, you shouldn't have to type it again—ever! It's very common to take words, paragraphs, even multiple pages from one document and use them in another. When you do this, both documents must be open, and you need to switch between the two to move the text around. To switch between several different open documents, you can click the Window menu and choose the one you want to activate, or you can click that document's button on the Taskbar.

 TIP By default, you should see Taskbar buttons for all open documents. If you don't, choose Tools ➤ Options ➤ View and make sure Windows In Taskbar is enabled.

If you want two documents on screen at once—to drag-and-drop text between them, for example—open the documents and choose Window ➤ Arrange All to see all open documents. When you want to work on just one of the documents again, click the Maximize button on the document's title bar.

Printing Your Documents

The dream of a paperless office may not be a long way from reality. In the meantime, however, we are still expected to generate hard copies of most documents we create. A few tricks can make all the difference in producing a printed document that reflects the professional appearance you want to convey.

Previewing Your Document

Previewing your document before printing gives you a chance to see how the pages break and whether there are any layout problems that will make the document look less than its best. Word 2002 offers you two ways to see how your document will look when it is printed:

- Print Layout view (View ➤ Print Layout) gives you the most WYSIWYG (what you see is what you get) picture of your printed document. In this view, you are able to enter text, insert graphics, and work in columns while seeing how your printed document will turn out.

- Print Preview allows you to view multiple pages of the document at once, zoom in and out of pages easily, adjust margins, and shrink the document by one page to prevent a small carryover from appearing on a page by itself.

 To open Print Preview, click the Print Preview button on the Standard toolbar or choose File ➤ Print Preview. Your screen should look like Figure 3.7.

PART

II

CREATING QUALITY TEXT
DOCUMENTS USING WORD

FIGURE 3.7

Use Print Preview to see how your document will appear on paper.

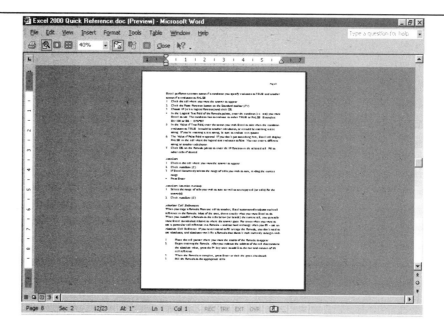

Table 3.3 shows the options available on the Print Preview toolbar.

TABLE 3.3   OPTIONS IN PRINT PREVIEW

Button	Button Name	Placeholder
	Print	Prints the document
	Magnifier	When pressed, click the document to zoom in or out. Click the button to inactivate it if you want to edit the document.
	One Page	Shows only one page of the document.
	Multiple Page	Shows up to six pages at one time.
50%	Zoom	Changes the magnification level.

Continued ▸

TABLE 3.3 (continued) OPTIONS IN PRINT PREVIEW

Button	Button Name	Placeholder
	View Ruler	Turns the vertical and horizontal rulers on and off.
	Shrink To Fit	Reduces the document by one page to prevent spillover.
	Full Screen	Turns full-screen mode on.
	Close Preview	Closes Print Preview.
	Context-Sensitive Help	Activates Help with the next button you click.
	More Buttons	Opens the More Buttons menu to customize the Print Preview toolbar.

Inserting Page Breaks

Word paginates documents automatically—when text exceeds the length of a page, Word moves to the next page by inserting a soft page break. After you've previewed your document, you might decide you want a page to break earlier: for example, at the end of a cover page or just before a new topic. To insert a hard page break that forces the page to break at the insertion point's current location, press Ctrl+Enter.

Changing Page Orientation and Paper Size

If you think that your document would look better in *landscape* orientation (11 × 8.5) than in *portrait* (8.5 × 11), you can change the orientation in Page Setup. Choose File ➢ Page Setup ➢ Margins or double-click the gray frame at the top of the ruler bar to open the dialog box shown in Figure 3.8.

FIGURE 3.8

Use the Margins tab of
the Page Setup dialog
box to change page
orientation as well as
margins.

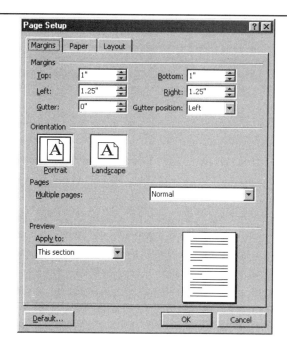

Change paper size for one or more pages by clicking the Paper tab in the Page
Setup dialog box (shown in Figure 3.9). You can change to another paper size entirely,
including a custom size for nonstandard forms like note cards or half-sheets. If you
choose a custom size, enter the dimensions for height and width. By default, Word
applies the change to the entire document. If you want to apply a different page size
to the balance of your document, position the insertion point at the beginning of the
page you want to change, go to Page Setup, change the page size, and choose This
Point Forward in the Apply To tool. Word automatically inserts a section break and
applies the new page size to the pages after the break (to learn more about section
breaks, see Chapter 5, "Designing Pages with Columns and Tables"). To apply the
change to a single page and not all the pages that follow it, move the insertion point
to the end of the last page that you want to have this formatting, select This Point
Forward, and change back to the original paper size.

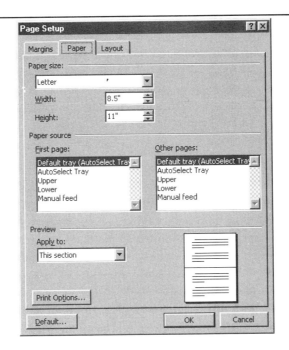

FIGURE 3.9

Choose a paper size and source on the Paper tab of the Page Setup dialog box.

The Paper Source feature is helpful when you're sending the document to a printer with multiple trays. You can choose to print Page 1 of your document from one tray and the rest of your pages from another tray. If your office keeps the corporate letterhead in the upper tray and plain white bond in the lower, you can print a multiple-page letter without leaving your desk—except to pick it up, of course!

Creating a Title Page for a Document

After you have the page orientation and paper size set, you may want to create a title page for your document. One easy way to do this is to enter the text you want on the title page and then center text vertically on the page between the top and bottom margins. To activate this feature, position the insertion point on the page you want to align. Choose File ➢ Page Setup and click the Layout tab. Under Vertical Alignment, you will find three options:

Top   This is the default setting; text lines up with the top margin.

Center   Text on the page is centered between the top and bottom margins.

Justify   Text is spread out so that lines are the same distance apart with the top line at the top margin and the bottom line at the bottom margin.

PART

II

CREATING QUALITY TEXT
DOCUMENTS USING WORD

Setting Margins

Word's default *margins* are 1.0 inch on the top and bottom and 1.25 inches on the left and right sides of the page. To change margins, use the Margins tab of the Page Setup dialog box, shown previously in Figure 3.8.

To change a document's margins, take these steps:

1. Position the insertion point where you want the margin changes to take effect.

2. Choose File ➤ Page Setup to open the Page Setup dialog box, and click the Margins tab.

3. Use the Top, Bottom, Left, and Right spin-boxes to set the amount of white space on the top, bottom, left, and right sides of the document.

4. Use the Gutter spin-box to add additional space to a document that will be bound. If the binding material takes up a half inch, adding a **0.5"** gutter will maintain equal white space on the portion of the document that extends past the binding. (You could, of course, set the left margin to **1.5"** instead.) The default gutter position is on the left of the page. For documents that will be top-bound, choose Top from the Gutter Position drop-down list.

5. Choose a setup option from the Multiple Pages drop-down list:

    Normal Prints the document as shown in Print Preview using only the front side of each piece of paper.

    Mirror Margins Helpful with back-to-back (duplex) printing. This option changes the preview to a two-page document and replaces the Left and Right margin controls with Inside and Outside margin controls. Setting the outside margin changes the two margins that will be back to back: the left margin of the left page, and the right margin of the right page in the preview. The inside margins are the right margin of the left page and the left margin of the right page. Pages that have a portrait orientation are divided in half horizontally. Landscape pages are divided vertically.

NEW▶

    Book Fold For booklet-type documents. Again, the Left and Right margin controls change to Outside and Inside. Word switches the document to Landscape orientation (if it's not already set up that way) and displays a Sheets Per Booklet drop-down list. You can make multiple booklets out of one document. If you wish the document to be printed as one booklet, choose All from the Sheets Per Booklet list. For multiple booklets, choose the number of pages you want to include in a *single* booklet. This setting ensures that the folded booklet will be correctly paginated.

6. Set the Apply To option to either Whole Document or This Point Forward. The default for the Apply To tool is Whole Document. This Point Forward applies margin settings from the insertion point to the end of a document.

7. Click OK to return to the document.

If you prefer, you can change margins using the vertical and horizontal rulers in Print Layout view. Point to the margin line on the ruler, and the pointer changes to a double-headed arrow.

When you hold down the mouse button, a dotted line extends through the document showing the location of the margin. Drag the dotted line in the desired direction to adjust the margin.

MASTERING THE OPPORTUNITIES

Printing a Booklet in Word

Producing a booklet using Word 2002 is much easier than it has ever been. (If you have the option, Microsoft Publisher is still a better tool for producing booklets. For more about using Publisher, see Part IX.) Word 2002 can produce 5.5″ × 8.5″ booklets where pages are automatically numbered and printed in the correct order. Some printers support booklet printing, making it even easier for you. But with even the oldest printer, you can use the 2 Pages Per Sheet option in Page Setup (click the Margins tab) to print two pages on a single 8.5″ × 11″ sheet and insert alternating page numbers on inside and outside margins (mirror margins) for booklet printing.

When creating a multipage booklet, start with a new blank document and set it up as a booklet. That way you have better control over the placement of text, graphics, and other elements. After you've chosen setup options, focus on the content. Finally, choose the correct print options and let Word do the rest.

Continued

MASTERING THE OPPORTUNITIES CONTINUED

To create a new booklet:

1. Choose File ➤ Page Setup.
2. Click the Margins tab and select Book Fold from the Multiple Pages list. (Word automatically changes the document to Landscape orientation.)
3. If you're making multiple booklets out of the document, choose the number of pages per booklet from the Sheets Per Booklet drop-down list. If the document will be one booklet, leave the default selection of All.
4. Set other Page Setup options as desired (Inside and Outside margins, for example).
5. Click OK to exit Page Setup.

Once you've entered the text and added graphics, headers, footers, a cover page, a back page, and any other elements you want, you must set printing options:

1. Choose File ➤ Print.
2. Set print options according to the kind of printer you have. For duplex printers, click Properties and enable duplex printing. Make sure you're printing in Landscape orientation as well. For other types of printers, enable the Manual Duplex check box in the Print dialog box. Word will print all of one side and then prompt you to turn the stack over to print the rest.
3. Choose a Page Range. In this case you want to choose All to print every page in the booklet. If you choose to print Current Page, Word prints the page you indicate plus other pages that belong on that sheet of paper. If you choose to print Selection, you'll get the selection with the default page layout instead of book fold.

Choosing Other Printers and Print Options

If you click the Print button on the Standard toolbar, Word uses the default print options—one copy of the document is sent to the Windows default printer. If you want to change the print settings, choose File ➤ Print to open the Print dialog box, shown in Figure 3.10.

PART

II

CREATING QUALITY TEXT
DOCUMENTS USING WORD

FIGURE 3.10

The Print dialog box lets you choose a printer, a range of pages to print, and other options.

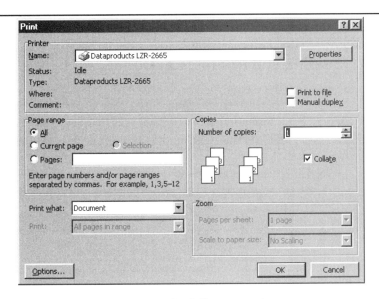

In the Print dialog box you can use the following options:

- Choose another printer.
- Click the Print To File option so that someone without Word can print the document (you must have the printer drivers installed for the printer that the document will be printed on and select that printer from the Printer Name drop-down list).
- Print only designated pages of a document, including current page, a range of pages, or selected text.
- Select whether you want to print even pages, odd pages, or both from the Print drop-down list.
- Increase the number of copies and have them collated (pages 1, 2, and 3 for each copy rather than all copies of page 1, then all copies of page 2, and so on).
- Print multiple pages per sheet and scale the document to fit a different paper size.
- Choose to print the document's properties (who created it, when it was created, how many words, characters, and so on.) or other lists such as AutoText entries.

- Elect to print a marked up document, or a list of markup changes. (See Chapter 12, "Working Collaboratively with Word," for more information about markup.)
- Print the Styles or AutoText entries used in the active document. (Chapter 8 has information on Styles, and Chapter 4 covers AutoText.)
- Print a list of shortcut keys (Key Assignments) for the active document.

Set the print options the way you want them and click Print to send the document to the printer.

Creating and Printing Envelopes and Labels

One of the time-saving features of Office XP is its ability to maintain address books that are shared between the applications. (See Chapter 31, "Understanding Outlook Basics," for information about Outlook address books.) Combine that with Word's Envelopes and Labels feature, and it has never been easier to prepare documents for mailing.

To print an envelope, take these steps:

1. If you are writing a letter, enter the name and address you want on the envelope as the inside address in the letter.

2. Choose Tools ➤ Letters And Mailings ➤ Envelopes And Labels and choose the Envelopes tab, shown in Figure 3.11.

3. The name and address you entered should appear in the Delivery Address box. If not, close the dialog box, copy the name and address, reopen the dialog box, and use Ctrl+V or Shift+Ins to paste it. If you have an Outlook address book, click the Address Book button and select a name from the list of contacts.

 NEW▶

4. If you use electronic postage software, click the E-Postage Properties button to set options such as the weight and class for the postage you'll be using.

5. Choose to enter or omit a return address. If you've used Envelopes and Labels before and chosen a default return address, it appears automatically.

6. Click the Options button to open the Envelope And Printing Options dialog box.

7. Click the Envelopes Options tab to set envelope options such as envelope size, delivery-point bar code, and fonts.

 NOTE Users with text in Asian languages will be pleased to know that Word 2002 now supports vertical text on envelopes. This feature is only available if Simplified Chinese, Traditional Chinese, Japanese, or Korean is enabled through Microsoft Office Language Settings.

8. Click the Printing Options tab to set printing options such as feed method and the printer tray that contains the envelope.

9. Click the Print button to send the envelope to the printer.

10. Click the Add To Document button to add an envelope page to your document. Figure 3.12 shows the document in Print Preview.

FIGURE 3.11

The Envelopes tab of the Envelopes And Labels dialog box

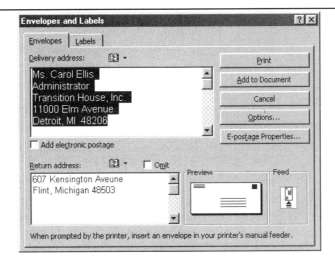

FIGURE 3.12

An envelope and letter in Print Preview

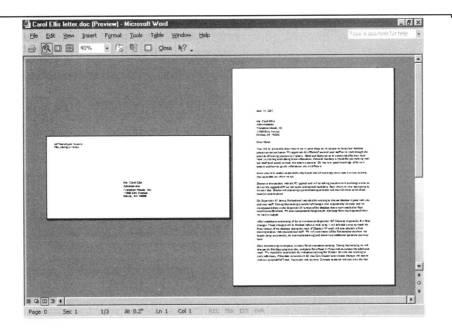

 TIP To have your return address appear as the default in the Envelopes And Labels dialog box, choose Tools ➢ Options ➢ User Information and enter your mailing address.

The Labels feature gives you the option to print one label or a full page of the same label. (See Chapter 9, "Creating Merge Documents in Word," for information about using Mail Merge to create individualized labels for different people.) To create and print labels, do the following:

1. Click the Labels tab of the Envelopes And Labels dialog box (Tools ➣ Letters And Mailings ➣ Envelopes And Labels), as shown in Figure 3.13.

2. Choose whether you would like a Full Page Of The Same Label or a Single Label. You can even specify which row and column to print on to use up those partial sheets of labels left over from other printing jobs.

3. If you want to print a full page of return address labels, click the Use Return Address check box.

4. Click the Options button to select a label style other than the default label—Avery Standard, 2160 Mini Address labels.

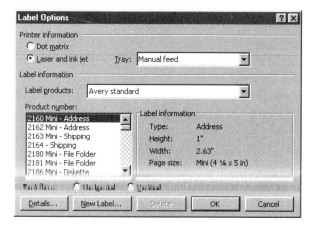

5. Choose the Label Product and Product Number you want to use from the lists provided. Click the Details button to see the actual measurements and layout of the labels you have selected or the New Label button to design a custom label size.

6. Click OK to close either page and OK again to return to the Envelopes And Labels dialog box.

NEW▶ 7. If you use electronic postage software, click the E-Postage Properties button to set options such as the weight and class for the postage you'll be using.

8. Click the Print button on the Envelopes And Labels dialog box to print the labels.

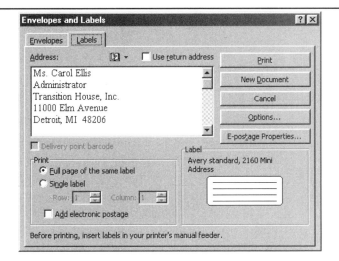

If you are creating return address labels or labels that you want to save, click the New Document button on the Labels tab to paste the labels into a new document. Save the document before sending the labels to the printer. The next time you want to print the same labels, open the saved label document and send it to the printer.

Making Fonts Work for You

All the fonts used by Windows programs are managed by Windows, so fonts available in one Office XP application are available in all the others. Unless you want to apply unique formatting like a double underline, you'll be able to make most of your font formatting changes by selecting text and using the buttons on the Formatting toolbar. The toolbar includes buttons and drop-down menus that let you choose a font, font size, effects (such as bold, italics, and underline), and font color. If you need font options that are not available on the toolbar, select text and then open the Font dialog box (see Figure 3.14) by choosing Format ➢ Font.

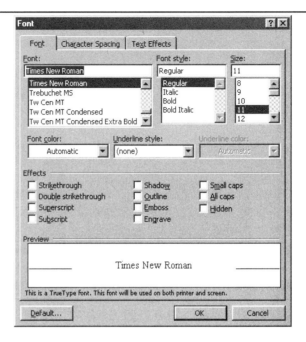

Word's Font dialog box has three page tabs: Font, Character Spacing, and Text Effects. On the Font tab, you can select font attributes and see how a font will look by noting the changes in the Preview box as you apply desired Font Style, Size, Underline Style, Font Color, and Effects. For example, Word 2002 provides 17 different underline options.

NEW▶ Once you've spent a fair amount of time formatting text to get it just right, you will probably want to use the same formatting in another section of the document. Word 2002's new Styles And Formatting task pane makes reapplying formats very easy. Select the unformatted text, and then follow these directions:

1. Turn the task pane on (if it's not already visible) by choosing View ➢ Task Pane.

2. Make sure the task pane is displaying Styles And Formatting (click the drop-down bar at the top of the task pane to select Styles And Formatting).

3. Choose the formatting you'd like from the list in the task pane.

NOTE Here we've described just *one* use of Styles And Formatting in the task pane. This powerful new feature is covered in depth in Chapter 8.

Ever wish you could quickly return text to its default settings? Word 2002 makes it easy. To remove formatting from selected text, choose Edit ➢ Clear ➢ Formats or choose Clear Formatting from the list in the task pane.

Applying Special Text Effects

There are 11 effects that you can apply from the Font dialog box. You can use Strikethrough and Double Strikethrough to show proposed deletions in a contract or bylaws. Use Superscript and Subscript to place special characters in formulas (H_2O or πr^2). Shadow, Outline, Emboss, and Engrave stylize the text so that it stands out, as shown in Figure 3.15.

FIGURE 3.15

Text effects in Word

This text is shadowed.
This text is outlined.
This text is embossed.
This text is engraved.

PART

II

CREATING QUALITY TEXT
DOCUMENTS USING WORD

Small Caps and All Caps are typically used in documents like letterheads or business cards. The Small Caps effect converts lowercase letters to smaller versions of the capital letters. To use Small Caps, enter all the text in lowercase or mixed case, select the text, and then apply the Small Caps effect.

Hidden text doesn't print and can be seen only when Show/Hide is enabled. This effect was much more commonly used when there weren't more effective ways—like Comments (see Chapter 12)—to include nonprinting, invisible document notes.

TIP If you are circulating a document and marking revised text for review, you don't need to apply Strikethrough manually. Instead, you can use Word 2002's newly enhanced Track Changes feature (see Chapter 12).

Changing Character Spacing

Use character spacing to adjust the distance between characters. For example, you can spread a title like *MEMORANDUM* across a page without having to space two or three times between characters.

MEMORANDUM

Character spacing is commonly used in advanced desktop publishing when you want to size and scale characters precisely.

Adding Animated Text Effects

Animated text effects are a cute text enhancement designed for documents that will be read on screen. There are six animation options that cause your text to blink, sparkle, or shimmer: Blinking Background, Las Vegas Lights, Marching Black Ants, Marching Red Ants, Shimmer, and Sparkle Text. To apply animation, select the text you want to animate, choose Format ➢ Font ➢ Text Effects, and select one of the six animation options. To turn it off, select the text again and select None from the list of options, or you can choose Edit ➢ Clear ➢ Formats to return text to its default settings. Keep in mind that the latter choice removes *all* font and paragraph settings.

 NOTE A word of advice: Apply animation sparingly, and don't apply it until you are finished editing document text. Overdone, it is pretty annoying, and animated documents use more computer resources, slowing down your system and making file sizes larger.

Highlighting Text for a Distinct Look

If you want to call someone's attention to a particular part of your text, you can *highlight* it so that it stands out for review. This is the computer equivalent of using a highlighter pen on the printout. If you have a color printer, the text will appear highlighted when printed. (Don't overlook the value of highlighting sections of text as a self-reminder.)

 Select the text you want to highlight and click the drop-down arrow next to the Highlight button. Click a color from the palette to apply it to the selected text. The button saves the last chosen pen color, so if you want to use the same color again, just select text and click the Highlight button directly. To turn highlighting off, select the highlighted text and choose None from the Highlight button drop-down list.

 If you prefer, you can choose a color to apply and highlight several sections of text. With no text selected, click the Highlight drop-down arrow and choose a highlight color. Drag the highlight pointer over the text you want to highlight. The highlight pointer remains active until you click the Highlight button again to turn it off.

Aligning and Formatting Paragraphs

In addition to formatting text or characters, skilled Word users know how to format lines and paragraphs of text. In this section, you'll learn how to use indents and tabs and to control how text flows on the page.

Aligning Text

Word provides four options, illustrated in Figure 3.16, for aligning paragraph text: Left, Center, Right, and Full (justify).

This paragraph is **left-aligned**. Left alignment is the most common alignment. It means that the text lines up with the left margin and leaves a ragged edge at the right margin. Left-aligned text is the easiest to read.

This paragraph is **centered**. Centering is generally used for headings and desktop publishing creations. Centered text is equally positioned between left and right margins.

This paragraph is **right-aligned**. Right alignment is used in headers and footers and other text you intend to be put off to the side. It means that text lines up with the right margin and leaves a ragged edge on the left. Right-aligned text is the hardest to read.

This text is **justified** or fully aligned. Justified text appears formal because text lines up evenly with the left and right margins. It is often used in documents with columns of text. Sometimes the paragraph looks unbalanced because too many spaces have to be inserted between words.

To align text, position the insertion point anywhere in the paragraph and click one of the alignment buttons on the Formatting toolbar.

Indenting Paragraphs

Word 2002 offers three ways to access paragraph-indenting features: the Formatting toolbar, the ruler, and the Paragraph dialog box.

You'll find the easiest method to change indents uses commands on the Formatting toolbar. Click anywhere in the paragraph you want to indent or select multiple paragraphs; then click the Decrease Indent button to reduce the left indent by a quarter inch. Click the Increase Indent button to extend the indent.

TIP New in Word 2002, you can drag-and-drop bulleted and numbered paragraphs to change their indent settings. Just place your mouse over the bullet or number and drag horizontally. The entire list goes with you.

Creating Indents Using the Ruler

The second method of indenting paragraphs—using the ruler—can take a little work to master, but it's a visual way to set left, right, hanging, and dual indents. You can use the ruler to set tabs as well as indents and set left and right margins in Page Layout view.

 TIP If you prefer to do most of your work without the ruler, hide the ruler by choosing View ➢ Ruler. To make the hidden ruler temporarily visible, point to the narrow gray line under the command bars (at the top of the document) and the ruler will reappear. When you move the pointer away from the ruler area, the ruler will slide back under the command bars.

There are four indent markers on the ruler, described here:

First-Line Indent Works the same as pressing Tab on the keyboard.

Hanging Indent "Hangs" the remaining lines in a paragraph to the right of the first line when this marker is positioned to the right of the first line indent marker. (Sometimes called an outdent.)

Left Indent Sets a paragraph off from the rest of the text by moving all lines in from the left margin.

Right Indent Moves text in from the right margin and is typically combined with a left indent to make a *dual indent*. Dual indents are used most commonly to set off block quotations.

To change the indents for existing text, select the paragraph or paragraphs you want to indent and drag the indent marker on the ruler to the desired location. Moving the first-line or the hanging indent marker indents or outdents the first line of each paragraph. Moving the left or right indent marker indents all lines of each paragraph.

Left Indent

If you forget which marker is which, point to any marker for a moment and view the screen tip. You can use the ruler to set indents before entering text. Position the insertion point where you plan to enter the new text before dragging the indent marker to the new location. The indents will apply to all newly entered text until you change the indent settings.

TIP If you select paragraphs that do not share the same indent settings, one or all of the indent markers on the ruler is dimmed. Click the dimmed marker(s) to make the indent settings the same for all the selected paragraphs.

Indenting Using the Paragraph Dialog Box

The third way to set indents is by using the Paragraph dialog box, shown in Figure 3.17. To access the dialog box, choose Format ➤ Paragraph or right-click and choose Paragraph from the shortcut menu.

FIGURE 3.17

*The Paragraph
dialog box*

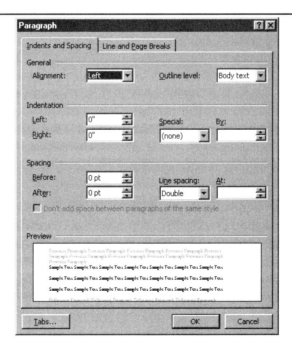

Follow these steps to indent using the Indents And Spacing tab of the Paragraph dialog box:

1. Select the text you want to indent and open the Paragraph dialog box (select Format ➤ Paragraph, or right-click and choose Paragraph).

2. Click the Indents And Spacing tab if it is not already selected.

3. Click the spin arrows next to the Left and Right text boxes or enter decimal numbers directly in the text boxes.

4. Click the Special drop-down arrow to select First-Line or Hanging indent. If you want the indent to be more or less than 0.5 inch, enter the special indent value in the By box.

5. Click OK to close the Paragraph dialog box and see your changes.

Setting Line Spacing Options

Word 2000 provides a number of options for adjusting *line spacing*, the vertical distance between lines of text. These options include the following:

Single   Provides enough room to comfortably display the largest character on a line

1.5 lines   Gives you one-and-a-half single lines

Double   Provides twice as much room as single spacing

At Least   Lets you enter a minimum line spacing for the selection

Exactly   Evenly spaces all lines regardless of the size of the fonts or graphics included in those lines

Multiple   Used to enter line spacing greater than triple

To change the line spacing for existing text, take the following steps:

1. Select the text whose line spacing you want to change.

2. Click the Line Spacing button on the Formatting toolbar to apply the last setting used. If you want something other than the last setting, click the drop-down arrow to see additional choices up to triple spacing.

3. For greater than triple spacing, or to use the At Least, Exactly, and Multiple options listed above, click the More choice on the drop-down list to open the Paragraph dialog box.

4. Click the Indents And Spacing tab if the page is not visible.

5. Click the Line Spacing drop-down list to select the desired line spacing.

6. If you are choosing At Least, Exactly, or Multiple, enter a number in the At box. For example, you can triple-space selected paragraphs by choosing Multiple and entering **3** in the At box.

7. Click OK to return to the document and review the changes.

To see all the formatting that is applied to a paragraph, choose Help ➤ What's This? and then click on the paragraph. The Reveal Formatting task pane appears, displaying paragraph and font formatting related to the paragraph. Click the Close button on the task pane to turn it off.

Using Tabs

Tab stops are markers. Pressing the Tab key moves the cursor from one tab stop to the next. One of the most common uses of a tab is to indent the first line of a paragraph.

 TIP Tabs can be used to create parallel columns, vertically aligning text within a document. However, Word's Tables feature—presented in Chapter 5—provides a much better option for creating parallel columns.

A new document includes tab stops at half-inch intervals. The default tab stops are dark gray tick marks that appear on the gray bar at the bottom of the ruler. The default settings can be changed by using the ruler or the Tabs dialog box. You'll need to choose both the alignment type and the location for each tab stop you want to use. There are five basic types of tab stops, shown in Figure 3.18:

Left This is the default type; text appears to the right of the tab stop.

Center Text is centered under the tab stop.

Right Text appears to the left of the tab stop.

Decimal This type is used for numeric entries. Text lines up with the decimal point.

Bar This type is used to create a vertical line between columns of tabbed data.

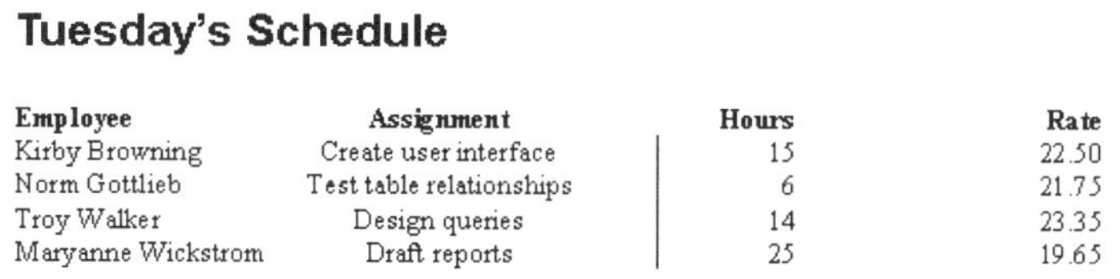

PART

II

CREATING QUALITY TEXT
DOCUMENTS USING WORD

FIGURE 3.18

The five types of tab stops are all used in this document.

Tuesday's Schedule

Employee	Assignment	Hours	Rate
Kirby Browning	Create user interface	15	22.50
Norm Gottlieb	Test table relationships	6	21.75
Troy Walker	Design queries	14	23.35
Maryanne Wickstrom	Draft reports	25	19.65

Setting Tab Stops Using the Ruler

Center Tab

At the left end of the ruler is a Tab Selection button that allows you to select the type of tab you want to set. By default, the button is set on Left Tab. Click the button to toggle through the different tab choices.

TIP You may notice two additional stops on the Tab Selection tool after the five tab choices. These are First-Line Indent and Hanging Indent. Use them to make it easier to select the indent markers on the ruler. When either tool is selected, you can click anywhere on the ruler (avoid the top gray bar) to move the corresponding indent marker to that position.

After you have chosen the type of tab you want to set, click the ruler at the position where you want the tab. The tab-stop marker appears, and all the default tabs to the left of the new tab stop are deleted. If you want to move the tab stop, drag the marker to a new location on the ruler.

If you want the tab stops to apply to existing text, be sure to select the text first—before clicking the ruler. Unless you select the entire document or the last paragraph in the document, the tab stops only apply to the selected paragraph(s). You can, however, set the tab stops for a blank document before you start entering text, and then the tab stops can be used throughout the document. To clear a tab stop, simply drag it off the ruler.

Setting Tab Stops and Leaders Using the Tabs Dialog Box

You can also create tab stops using the Tabs dialog box. Make sure the insertion point is located where you want the new tab stops to begin. (If the text you want to format is already entered, select it.) Access the Tabs dialog box, shown in Figure 3.19, by choosing Format ➤ Tabs from the menu.

FIGURE 3.19

The Tabs dialog box

In the Tab Stop Position text box, type the location for the tab stop you want to create. In the Alignment control, choose how you want text to align at the tab stop. The Leader control lets you select a *leader* to lead the reader's eye across the text. Leaders are used most commonly in documents such as agendas, price lists, and schedules. The leader (see Figure 3.20) precedes the tabbed text.

FIGURE 3.20

Text with tab stops and leaders

TELEPHONE LIST

CAROL FALLIS 810-555-2320
KIRBY BROWNING 517-444-7777
MATTHEW BRATCHER 810-732-4747
KIM HESTER 714-555-9000
MIKE FALLIS 302-678-1003

Click the Set button to add the new tab stop. Repeat these steps to set any other tab stops. Some users find the Tabs dialog box an easier way of changing tab stops than dragging arrows around the ruler. To change tab stops using the Tabs dialog box, follow these steps:

1. Select the tab stop from the list below the Tab Stop Position control.

2. Change the Alignment and Leader options.

3. Click Set to apply your changes.

To remove an existing tab stop, select it from the list and click the Clear button. Clicking Clear All removes all of the tab stops you added and reverts to the default tab settings. When you are finished setting tab stops, click OK to close the Tabs dialog box.

PART

II

CREATING QUALITY TEXT
DOCUMENTS USING WORD

To see where tabs have been typed in existing text, click the Show/Hide Paragraph Marks button on the Standard toolbar. You'll see a right-pointing arrow to indicate a tab.

˙Tuesday's·Schedule¶

¶

Employee	→	Assignment	→	Hours	→	Rate¶
Kirby·Browning	→	Create·user·interface	→	15	→	22.50¶
Norm·Gottlieb	→	Test·table·relationships	→	6	→	21.75¶
Troy·Walker	→	Design·queries	→	14	→	23.35¶
Maryanne·Wickstrom	→	Draft·reports	→	25	→	19.65¶

Creating Lists, Numbers, and Symbols

Word 2002 makes it easy to create bulleted and numbered lists. To apply numbers to existing text, select the paragraphs and click the Numbering button on the Formatting toolbar. Use the Bullets button to bullet existing paragraphs of text. You can also begin numbering or bulleting by clicking the Numbering or Bullets button before you type your first paragraph.

Word will also create numbered and bulleted lists for you. If you begin a list with a number, Word automatically numbers subsequently created paragraphs. Begin with an asterisk and Word bullets each additional paragraph you type. To see how Word's automatic numbering and bullets feature works, follow these steps:

1. Type the number **1** and a period, space once, and then enter the text for the item. For bullets, begin with an asterisk and a space.

2. Press Enter. Word automatically numbers the next item **2** and depresses the Numbering button on the Formatting toolbar, or it bullets the next item and depresses the Bullets button.

NEW|▶

3. Word also displays an icon (shown here) to the left of the first bulleted/numbered item. If you don't want to use Word's automatic bulleting/numbering feature, click the icon and choose Undo Automatic Numbering to undo automatic numbering this time or Stop Automatically Creating Numbered Lists to disable this feature entirely.

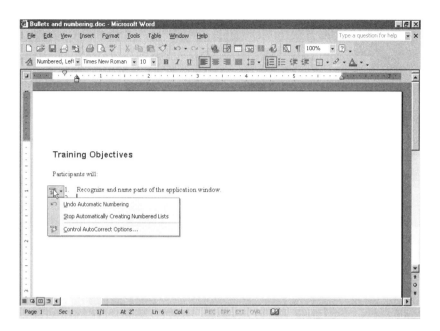

4. Assuming you haven't turned off automatic numbering, continue typing text and pressing Enter to create more numbered or bulleted paragraphs.

5. When you are finished creating the list, press Enter twice to turn automatic numbering or bullets off.

If you want to use letters rather than numbers in automatic numbering, type **A.** rather than **1.** to begin. Word numbers the second and succeeding paragraphs B, C, D, and so on. If you number your first paragraph **I.**, Word uses Roman numerals. Word now supports international alphabet numbering. That means you can letter paragraphs using the alphabet for any language installed on your system.

TIP If automatic numbering or bullets do not work when you follow the steps above, choose Tools ➢ AutoCorrect Options to open the AutoCorrect dialog box. On the AutoFormat As You Type tab, make sure that Automatic Bulleted Lists and Automatic Numbered Lists are checked.

Modifying the Bullet or Number Format

When you use the Bullets and Numbering features for the first time, Word supplies a standard round bullet and leaves a default amount of space between the bullet or number and the text that follows. You can choose a different bullet character, number format, or spacing before entering your list, or you can modify the format of an existing list. If the bulleted or numbered list has already been entered, select the paragraphs you want to change. To change formats, choose Format ➢ Bullets And Numbering from the menu bar to open the Bullets And Numbering dialog box, shown in Figure 3.21.

FIGURE 3.21

The Bullets And Numbering dialog box

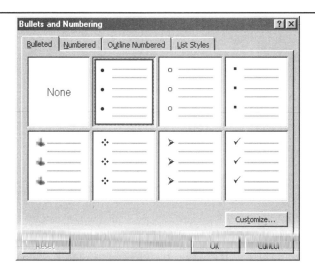

Click the tab for either Bulleted or Numbered. The dialog box displays eight styles for bulleted text and eight styles for numbered. You can simply select any of the styles shown.

If you really feel creative, click the Customize button to open the Customize Bulleted or Numbered List dialog box. (The Customize button is dimmed if None is selected.)

Here are the steps to apply a custom bullet format:

1. Select Format ➢ Bullets And Numbering.

2. Click the Bulleted tab and click Customize. (You must first select a bullet style if one is not already selected.)

3. From the Customize Bulleted List dialog box, select the bullet character you want to customize or click the Character button to select a bullet from one of

the installed font symbol sets. If you prefer, you can click the Picture button to open the Picture Bullet dialog box and select a graphic bullet.

4. To change the size or color of the bullet, click the Font button to open the Font dialog box. The Font button is only available if you've selected a Character bullet.

5. To change the distance of the bullet from the left margin, change the Bullet Position Indent At text box.

6. To change the distance from the bullet to the text, change the Text Position Indent At text box, or change the Tab Space After setting.

7. Click OK when you have finished customizing the bullet.

To apply a custom number format, follow these steps:

1. Select Format ➢ Bullets And Numbering.

2. Click the Numbered tab and click Customize (you must first select a number style if one is not already selected).

3. From the Customize Numbered List dialog box, enter a number format by choosing a number style and then adding any text before or after the field code.

WARNING Be careful not to delete the field code (the lightly shaded number that appears in the Number Format box). If you delete the code and retype a number, you'll get that number repeated for all paragraphs, rather than consecutive numbering.

4. Enter the starting number if it is other than 1.

5. Adjust the Number position and the Text position as desired.

6. Click OK to save your changes.

To remove numbers and bullets from text, select the bulleted or numbered list and click the Bullets or Numbering button on the toolbar to turn bullets or numbering off.

MASTERING TROUBLESHOOTING

Troubleshooting Bullets and Numbering

When you are creating a document with bullets and numbers, you may find that they are behaving differently than you expect. For example, you may find that the font is different for the number than for the text following the number or the bullet character is different than what you expect. Here are a few solutions to common problems that you may experience using bullets and numbers in your documents:

The font format of the bullet or number is different than the format of the text. This occurs when you turn on bullets and numbering before turning on text formatting. To make the bullet or number match, select the bulleted or numbered list, open the Bullets And Numbering dialog box, choose Customize, and click the Font button. Change the font formatting to match the text.

Numbers continue from the previous list rather than starting over at 1. When the two lists follow each other with no text between them, the numbering continues from the previous list. To choose whether to restart or whether to continue numbering, select the list, open the Bullets And Numbering dialog box, and click Restart Numbering or Continue Previous List. If you want to start numbering at a number other than 1, click Customize and enter the number in the Start At text box.

The bullet character used in a document does not appear the same when the document is opened on another computer. If the bullet you choose is from a font that is not installed on both computers, Word will substitute a bullet from another font. Either install the font on the second computer or change the bullet to one that comes from a font available on both computers.

Applying Multilevel Numbering

If multilevel numbering brings back memories of tediously outlining ninth-grade social studies papers, then you are in for a treat. With Word 2002, you can create multilevel bullets and numbering as easily as pressing a key.

To create a multilevel bulleted or numbered list, like the list shown in Figure 3.22, follow these steps:

1. Begin just as you would for a single-level list by entering the first item in the list.

2. Press Enter and then, to move in one level (demote), press Tab. Type the second-level text.

3. Press Enter again and continue entering second-level points.

4. To move in another level, press Tab again.

5. To return to a higher level (promote), press Shift+Tab.

6. When you have entered all the points, press Enter twice to turn off Automatic Bullets And Numbering.

1) Hiring Process
    a. Develop job description
        i. Get feedback from committee
        ii. Talk with Board
    b. Determine the number of hours required
    c. Make proposal to the board
    d. Develop recruitment plan
        i. Set up interview committee
        ii. Identify ad placements
        iii. Contact resources
    e. Implement recruitment plan
2) Supervision Process

 NOTE If you'll be creating a PowerPoint presentation with the same content as a Word document, start the Word document as a multilevel outline. Choose File ➤ Send To ➤ Microsoft PowerPoint to create a presentation with each first-level heading on a separate slide that includes lower-level headings as points and subpoints.

Customizing multilevel lists is similar to customizing single-level lists, except that you have to make decisions regarding bullet or number style and positioning for each level in the list. Open the Customize Outline Numbered List dialog box by selecting the list and choosing Format ➤ Bullets And Numbering, click the Outline Numbered tab (use this tab regardless of whether you are using bullets or numbers), and click the Customize button. Select a Level 1 Format, Style, and Start At number (if applicable) just as you would with a regular (non-multilevel) list. Simply repeat the process for each level in the outline.

NEW ▶ If you've spent some time customizing a multilevel list, you may want to save it as a *style* so that you can easily use it in other documents. Select the multilevel num-bered list, click Format ➤ Bullets And Numbering, and choose the List Styles tab, shown in Figure 3.23.

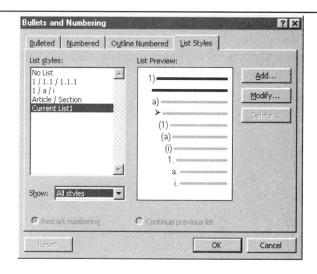

FIGURE 3.23

Word 2002's new List Styles feature lets you easily save custom list styles for use in other documents.

The List Preview shows formatting for Current List 1 (the list you selected before opening the dialog box). To Save this list formatting as a style:

1. Click the Modify button and enter a name for the List Style, overwriting the default of Current List 1. (The Add button allows you to keep Current List 1 and create another style based on it. If you just want to overwrite Current List 1, use Modify.)

2. Enable the Add To Template check box.

3. If you wish to make other modifications to the list formatting, use the controls in the dialog box.

4. Click OK. Click OK once more to close the Bullets And Numbering dialog box.

NOTE Styles are a very powerful feature for reusing formatting in a document or across documents. To learn more about them, see Chapter 8.

Inserting Special Characters

Many symbols used regularly in business documents aren't on the standard keyboard—the copyright sign (©), for example. Word 2002 makes many of these common symbols available to you with simple keystrokes and through the Insert ➤ Symbol option on the menu bar.

Choose Insert ➢ Symbol to open the Symbol character map, shown in Figure 3.24, and the Special Characters tab, shown in Figure 3.25.

FIGURE 3.24

The symbol character map

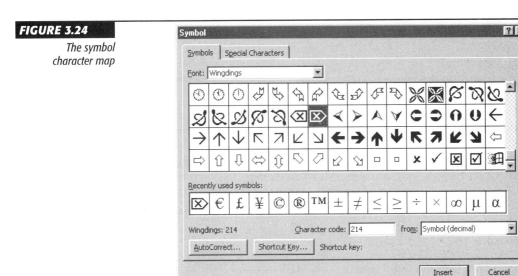

FIGURE 3.25

The Special Characters tab

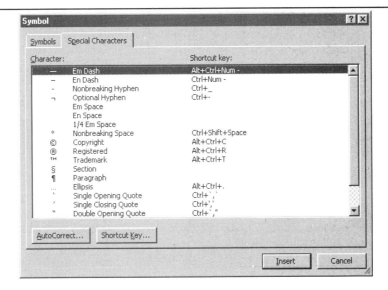

NEW ▶

The Symbol dialog box has been greatly improved in Office XP. Symbols are much larger (you can actually see them now!), and the dialog box is resizable to increase/decrease the number of symbols on screen at one time. Further, a Recently Used Symbol display allows you to quickly find and select a symbol if it's among the last 16 used.

EXPERT TIP As an alternative to browsing through rows and rows of symbols, you can type a three-digit number in the Character Code field to display the corresponding symbol. Although it is unlikely you'll memorize the character codes for all the symbols you use, inevitably someone will ask you, "Where did you find that symbol?" Rather than giving them lengthy instructions about where to find it on the symbol grid, just select it on your own machine and make note of its character code. Then instruct your colleague to open the Symbol dialog box, choose the font the symbol is in, and type its character code.

Once you find the symbol you want to use, choose it from the symbol font sets or special characters and then click the Insert button to insert the symbol into your document. If you need the symbol more than once, open the Symbol dialog box again and look for it under Recently Used Symbols.

Word also lets you streamline access to symbols that you need to use frequently. From either page of the Symbol dialog box, you can click a button to define a shortcut key for the selected character, and from the Special Characters page you can also define an AutoCorrect entry (the AutoCorrect tool is discussed in Chapter 4. Enter a character string that will automatically be replaced with the desired symbol—enter (p) for ¶, for example. Make sure it is a character string you don't use in other situations, or you will find it replaced with the symbol every time you type it.

 TIP To automatically insert en dashes (–) and em dashes (—) in your documents, make sure that the Hyphens (--) With Dash (–) check box is selected on the AutoFormat As You Type tab (Tools ➢ AutoCorrect ➢ AutoFormat As You Type). To insert an en dash, insert a space after a word, type one or two hyphens, and then follow the dashes with more text. For example, 1 - 2 becomes 1–2. To insert an em dash, enter two hyphens between two words without inserting any spaces. In this case, 1--2 becomes 1—2.

Updating Date and Time Automatically

Word 2002 includes 17 different formats you can use when inserting the current date and/or time, so the format you want is probably among them. Choose Insert ≻ Date And Time to open the Date And Time dialog box.

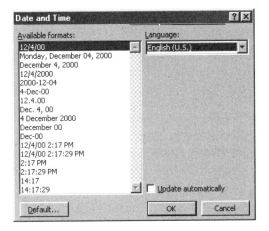

Select a format from the list. If you would like to automatically update the field to the current date and time every time you open the document, click the Update Automatically check box. This inserts the date and time as a field rather than as text. A Date And Time field is most useful when a document is in draft form and you want to know when it was last worked on, or when a memo or notice is regularly printed and mailed and should always have the current date. The Date And Time field is only updated when you print the document or right-click the field and choose Update Field. Go to Print Preview to see the changed date and time. When you return to the document, the date and time will be updated.

WARNING Don't click the Update Automatically check box on the Date And Time dialog box when the date on a document is important in maintaining a paper trail. If you want to have evidence that you typed your response to the IRS before their 30-day deadline, you'd better not use a date code. Otherwise the document will have today's date when you open it, not the date you actually created it!

To change the default date and time settings for new documents, select the format you prefer from the Data And Time dialog box and click Default. Word will ask you to confirm that you want to change the default format to the selected setting. Click Yes to confirm your choice.

CHAPTER 4

Putting Text and Language Tools to Work for You

FEATURING

- Creating and applying frequently used text
- Finding and replacing text and formats
- Checking spelling
- Improving grammar
- Using the Format Checker
- Finding the right word with the Thesaurus
- Using Word's translation tools
- Working with Smart Tags

Professional typists know that minimizing the number of keystrokes is the key to high-powered efficiency. For those of us who don't type at lightning speed, every keystroke we eliminate can result in noticeable time savings. Word 2002 has tools to help you streamline your work and check your text—including your grammar—efficiently. There's even a thesaurus to help you find that perfectly descriptive word or phrase.

Creating and Applying Frequently Used Text

In many businesses, it's not uncommon to use standard phrases and other "boiler-plate" text over and over again. Word has two features that let you easily insert frequently used text and graphics. The first feature, AutoCorrect, is common to most Office XP applications. In this section, you'll find in-depth information about using AutoCorrect. The second feature, AutoText, is unique to Word and allows you to store formatted text or graphics—even entire paragraphs—and then recall them with a couple of keystrokes.

Using AutoCorrect

AutoCorrect is the feature that changes "teh" into "the" and "adn" into "and" without a bat of the eye. AutoCorrect maintains a dictionary of commonly mistyped words, and when you mistype one, AutoCorrect fixes it automatically. AutoCorrect is also the feature discussed in Chapter 3, "Working with Text and Formats in Word," that changes the keystrokes **:)** into smiley faces ☺ and **(c)** into the copyright symbol ©.

NEW▶ Word 2002's auto-behavior is enhanced to cover instances where two adjacent words are misspelled only because the space between them is misplaced: *int othe* becomes *into the* automatically! Further, you'll find it helpful that AutoCorrect now interacts with Automatic Language Detection so that corrections are appropriate to the language you're typing in.

Because some of the AutoCorrect changes can be a bit disconcerting, you have the option of turning these features on and off as desired. Figure 4.1 shows the AutoCorrect dialog box; you can access it by choosing Tools ➢ AutoCorrect Options.

To add a word or phrase to the AutoCorrect dictionary, you can either select the text in the document or enter the words in the Replace and With text boxes in the AutoCorrect dialog box. If you select text in your document and open the AutoCorrect dialog box, the text appears in the With text box. You have the option of saving this AutoCorrect entry as plain or formatted text. Text that you enter directly in the Replace and With text boxes can only appear as plain text.

 NOTE AutoCorrect is case sensitive. If text appears in the Replace column in uppercase, it must be typed in uppercase for AutoCorrect to replace it.

PART

II

CREATING QUALITY TEXT
DOCUMENTS USING WORD

FIGURE 4.1

AutoCorrect options automatically correct common typing mistakes.

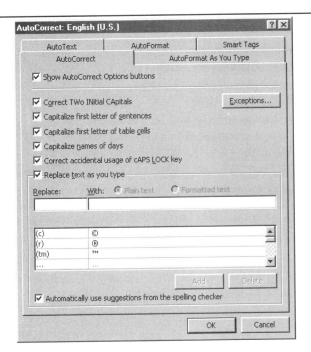

Although AutoCorrect is typically used to correct single words, you can use it to insert entire paragraphs or even longer segments of formatted text. If, for example, you routinely type highly technical words that are difficult to spell, you could enter the terms into AutoCorrect and let Word spell them for you. Just be careful to use a "Replace" word that you don't typically type. Every time you type this word, Word replaces the text with the AutoCorrect entry.

AutoCorrect is designed to prevent typing and spelling errors, but it is also valuable as a shortcut tool. You can enter words that you type regularly into your AutoCorrect list to save yourself time and keystrokes—long company names, for example, or legal or medical terminology. Just enter a code that you will recognize, such as **USA**, and

AutoCorrect expands it for you into *United States of America*. However, if you think you will ever want to use the abbreviation without expanding it, enter a slash (/) or some other character in front of the abbreviation (**/USA**) when you create the Auto-Correct entry. Then you can choose whether to have AutoCorrect supply the long form (by typing **/USA**) or use the abbreviation (by typing **USA** without the slash).

 When you click in or select text that has been inserted by AutoCorrect, a small blue rectangle appears below the first couple of letters in the text:

TRIAD Consulting, LLC

Place the mouse over the blue rectangle and you'll see the AutoCorrect icon. Click the icon to display a drop-down menu of choices related to the auto-corrected text:

Change Back To Undoes the AutoCorrect action this one time

Stop Automatically Correcting Removes the AutoCorrect entry from the dictionary

Control AutoCorrect Options Opens the AutoCorrect dialog box shown previously in Figure 4.1

 If you prefer, you can "un-auto-correct" by deleting the inserted text and manually retyping the original text. If you do, Word won't auto-correct that type of text again until you press Enter twice in the document.

TIP Another way to restore the actual characters in your document rather than the Auto-Correct symbol is to press the Backspace key (or click Undo) immediately following Word's AutoCorrect action. Word replaces the symbol with the original characters.

NOTE Word's new AutoCorrect options are just one example of Smart Tags. These new time-saving features all work similarly. Icons appear with options to undo automatic features, choose formatting, or insert information from other office programs. See "Making Smart Tags Work for You," later in this chapter.

Using AutoText and AutoComplete

AutoText is similar to AutoCorrect, with two significant differences:

- AutoCorrect works automatically; AutoText has to be invoked.

- An AutoText entry displays an AutoComplete tip that completes the text without having to type the entire entry.

To create an AutoText entry, follow these steps:

1. Select the text and/or graphics you want to store as AutoText. To include the text's format, such as font and font style, make sure you include the paragraph mark in the selection (click the Show/Hide button on the Standard toolbar to be sure).

2. Choose Insert ➤ AutoText ➤ New to create the entry (see Figure 4.2). You are prompted to give the entry a name—make it at least five characters and easy to remember.

3. Click OK to close the AutoText dialog box.

FIGURE 4.2

Create a new AutoText entry by entering a name in the Create AutoText dialog box.

Inserting an AutoText Entry

By default Word displays an AutoComplete tip as soon as you type the first four characters of the AutoText name. To accept the AutoComplete tip, press Enter. (Word 2002 even tells you to do so in the tip!) If you do not want to insert the AutoText entry, just keep typing. As soon as you type a letter that is inconsistent with the AutoText name, the tip disappears. If you're not seeing AutoComplete tips, make sure that option is enabled on the AutoText tab of the AutoCorrect dialog box (Insert ➤ AutoText ➤ AutoText or Tools ➤ AutoCorrect Options ➤ AutoText) as shown in Figure 4.3.

WARNING If the name you give to a new AutoText entry is something that's close to entries already in the AutoText list, you won't see an AutoComplete tip as you're typing. You have two choices: select and delete the entry from the AutoText list in the AutoCorrect dialog box, then re-create it under a different name or insert the AutoText manually by choosing Insert , AutoText , Normal and clicking the entry.

FIGURE 4.3

Turn on the Show AutoComplete Suggestions option on the AutoText tab of the AutoCorrect dialog box.

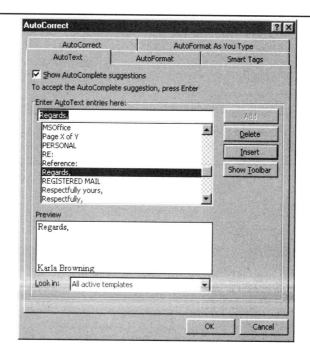

If you want to insert an AutoText entry manually—for example, when the name is less than four characters or when you have turned off the AutoComplete option—type the AutoText name and then press F3 or choose Insert ➢ AutoText and click the entry you want. (Usually entries you create are stored in the Normal category.) As Figure 4.4 shows, Word provides a number of canned AutoText entries that you can access from the Insert ➢ AutoText menu.

FIGURE 4.4

*The AutoText menu
offers categories for
standard entries you
can define.*

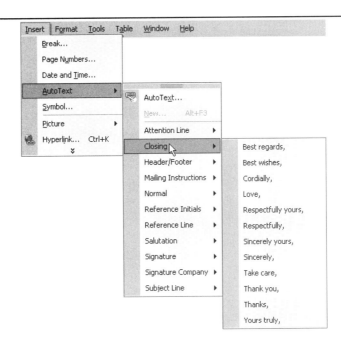

 TIP If you're inserting a lot of AutoText into a document, you can turn on the AutoText toolbar by choosing View , Toolbars , AutoText or choosing Insert , AutoText and dragging the narrow gray bar at the top of the menu to make it float. The toolbar's All Entries drop-down menu is the same as the menu bar's AutoText menu.

You can delete AutoText entries on the AutoText tab of the AutoCorrect dialog box (shown earlier in Figure 4.3; choose Insert ➢ AutoText ➢ AutoText) by selecting the entry you want to delete and clicking Delete.

MASTERING THE OPPORTUNITIES

Preparing Client Proposals and Other Documents with AutoText

A client proposal is often a collection of boilerplate paragraphs interspersed with paragraphs that respond to the specific needs of the client. Although a formal proposal might be best prepared using a template (see Chapter 8, "Simplifying with Styles, Outlines, and Templates," for more about creating and using templates), Word's AutoText feature allows you to add standard paragraphs, such as a privacy statement and general company description, to any document. Rather than searching for the last document you used them in each time you need them, you can use AutoText to call them up with only a few keystrokes.

To prepare the AutoText entries, open any document that contains the paragraphs you want to be able to reuse. Select the first paragraph you want and choose Insert ➢ AutoText ➢ New. If your company uses standard paragraph numbers in its proposals— for example, "I. Company Description"—you may want to call the AutoText entry by its number, such as **Para I**, **Para II**, and so on. If not, give the paragraph an easy-to-remember and descriptive name. When you click OK, Word saves the entry. Repeat this process for the other standard paragraphs.

When you have created all the AutoText entries you may need for a typical proposal, you are ready to go. Start writing, and whenever you need one of the standard paragraphs, AutoText inserts it for you. With a little forethought, you'll never have to go searching for text again.

Finding and Replacing Text

One of the fastest ways to make repetitive changes throughout a long document is to use Find and Replace. Find helps you locate a text string, and Replace substitutes new text for the existing string.

Follow these steps to use Find and Replace:

1. Click Select Browse Object and then click Find to open the Find And Replace dialog box, shown in Figure 4.5.

2. Enter the characters you want to search for in the Find What text box.

NEW▶

3. To have Word simultaneously select all occurrences of a text string in the document, enable the Highlight All Items Found In check box. If the string you want to locate is in the document's headers or footers, you must choose to search headers and footers from the drop-down list below the check box.

4. Click Find Next.

5. Close the Find dialog box and click the Next Find/Go To button at the bottom of the vertical scroll bar. Browse through each of the occurrences of the text string.

FIGURE 4.5

The Find And Replace dialog box

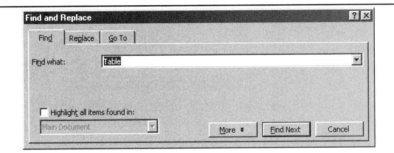

The More button in the Find And Replace dialog box provides you with additional searching options. You can have Word search the entire document (All), or for faster searching, just choose to search above (Up) or below (Down) the insertion point. You can also have it search for words that are in the same case as you entered (Match Case).

When Word searches, it will search for all occurrences of the text string—even if it does not form a whole word. For example, if you are searching for *will*, you will find *William*, *wills*, and *willful*, unless you click Find Whole Words Only. If you would like all forms of the word, turn on the Find All Word Forms check box and you'll get plurals, past tense, and so on. *Wildcards* are characters that stand for any character. If you enter **j*ing**, you will locate all words that start with *j* and end with *ing*. The text you enter in the Find What field can contain a wildcard so long as the wildcard is preceded and followed by at least one character. When you use a wildcard search, you must enable the Use Wildcards check box. The Sounds Like option gives you words that start with the same sound—entering **kind** will find *cannot*; **boy** will return *by*.

You can also look for text formatted a certain way by using the list that opens when you click Format. Click Special to find codes such as column breaks and paragraph marks; Figure 4.6 shows the complete list. For example, if you want to tighten up a document that contains two paragraph marks at the end of every paragraph resulting in a blank line between paragraphs, use Special to look for two paragraph marks and replace them with one.

FIGURE 4.6

You can find and replace any of these special characters or objects.

Paragraph Mark
Tab Character
Any Character
Any Digit
Any Letter
Caret Character
Column Break
Em Dash
En Dash
Endnote Mark
Field
Footnote Mark
Graphic
Manual Line Break
Manual Page Break
Nonbreaking Hyphen
Nonbreaking Space
Optional Hyphen
Section Break
White Space

Using Replace

To replace text, open the Find dialog box and click the Replace tab. Enter the text you want to find in the Find What text box and the text you want to replace it with in the Replace With text box. You can choose to replace one occurrence at a time by clicking Find Next and then Replace. Or, if you're very sure of what you are doing, choose Replace All to complete the replacements in one step. When Word is finished, it opens a dialog box that tells you how many replacements it made.

WARNING Be careful with Replace All. You might think you want to replace all occurrences of she with he, but do you really want to change ashen to ahen? Or shed to hed? Double-check your criteria by clicking the Find tab, enabling Highlight All Items Found, and clicking Find All. Peek behind the Find And Replace dialog box and see what Word has selected. When you're sure you've got the criteria right, return to the Replace tab and click Replace All.

If you must repeat a Find and/or Replace operation, click the drop-down list in the Find dialog box. You can select recently used items from the list rather than typing them again.

 TIP If you find that Replace caused some unexpected results, click Undo to return the document to its original state. Undo undoes all of the replacements in one easy step. Just to be on the safe side, however, it's a good idea to save before starting a major Replace operation.

Navigating through a Long Document with Go To

Find and Replace also gives you the option to Go To a specific type of text or object such as a page, footnote, or graphic. Click the Go To tab of the Find And Replace dialog box and select the type of item you would like to go to, then enter the corresponding name or the number of the item, as shown in Figure 4.7.

FIGURE 4.7

Use Go To to review similar objects or text throughout a document.

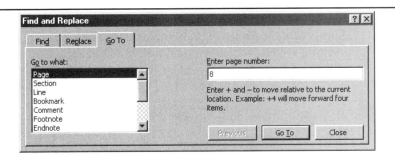

Go To is most useful in very long documents when you want to review all the occurrences of a specific type of text.

Checking It Twice with Spelling and Grammar

Spell-checking software has been around for a long time, but if you really want it to work for you, it helps to understand how the Spelling tool works and which custom options are available to you. Office comes with an extensive English dictionary and, if you install the Language Pack, dictionaries for other languages (see the "Mastering

Multilingual Editing" sidebar later in this section). When you run Spelling and Grammar or have the Check Spelling As You Type option turned on (Tools ➤ Options ➤ Spelling And Grammar), Office checks each word against these dictionaries. When it doesn't find a word, it flags it for you to verify. You have a number of ways of dealing with a word that isn't in the Office dictionary:

Ignore Once This option ignores the selected occurrence of the word.

Ignore All This option ignores all occurrences of the word in this document.

Add This option adds the word to the Custom dictionary so Office will recognize it in the future.

Change This option changes the word after choosing one of the suggested corrections or editing the word manually.

Change All This option changes all occurrences of the word in this document after choosing one of the suggested corrections or editing the word manually.

AutoCorrect This option corrects the word (after choosing or entering a correction) and adds it to the AutoCorrect dictionary.

Right-clicking a red underlined word gives you the option to select a word from a list of choices, ignore all occurrences, add the word to the dictionary, change the language, or choose from a list of AutoCorrect entries. To get the full set of options listed here, run Spelling and Grammar from the Standard toolbar; when Spelling finds a possibly misspelled word, you'll see the window shown in Figure 4.8.

FIGURE 4.0

Choose the correct spelling of a word from the list of choices offered by Office in the Spelling And Grammar dialog box.

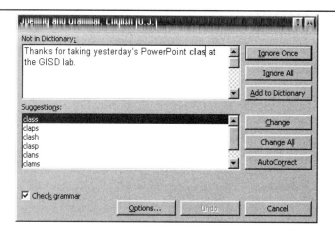

WARNING AutoCorrect and Spelling use two different dictionaries. When you add a word to the Spelling dictionary, it is not added to the AutoCorrect dictionary and vice versa.

Working with Custom Dictionaries

When you choose Add from the list of Spelling choices, the identified word is added to the default custom dictionary. The next time you type that word, Office recognizes it and ignores it. Have you ever accidentally added a word that was misspelled? Word 2002 makes it easier than ever to edit the custom dictionary and remove the word you added in error. Further, if you work in a field with lots of specialized terminology, you can save time and trouble by editing the dictionary directly. To access the dictionary and add new words or edit existing words, follow these steps:

NEW▶

1. Choose Tools ➢ Options and click the Spelling And Grammar tab.

2. Click Custom Dictionaries to open the Custom Dictionaries dialog box.

3. Select the dictionary you want to open and choose Modify. This opens a dialog box that contains a list of words already added to the dictionary. Chances are you'll see your company name or other information you entered when you installed Office XP.

4. To add a word, enter it in the Word field and click the Add button.

5. Remove words from the dictionary by selecting them from the list and clicking the Delete button. If misspelled words are in the dictionary, delete them, and then add them back in with the correct spelling.

6. Select another language from the Language drop-down list and add words in that language, if you wish.

7. When you have finished adding or editing words, click OK three times to close all dialog boxes.

All of the words you enter directly into the dictionary should pass a spelling check with flying colors.

PART

II

CREATING QUALITY TEXT
DOCUMENTS USING WORD

MASTERING THE OPPORTUNITIES

Making Custom Dictionaries Available across the Enterprise

If you work in a specialized business with its own nomenclature (that's just about every business today), making a custom dictionary available will save everyone in the organization time and energy. With Office XP, you can house the dictionary on the server and give every user access to it. Because processing happens locally, there is no need to distribute it to every user. See Appendix D, "Installing Office XP," on the companion CD for more information about installation options.

To create a custom dictionary, follow these steps:

1. Choose Tools ≻ Options and click the Spelling And Grammar tab.
2. Click Custom Dictionaries to open the Custom Dictionaries dialog box.
3. Click New to create a new custom dictionary.
4. Enter a name and file location for the dictionary. The default location is \\Windows\Application Data\Microsoft\Proof\ but you can choose any other location. Click Save.
5. The dictionary appears in the list of available dictionaries. Select the new dictionary and click Modify to open it.
6. Add words to the dictionary, clicking Add after each word. This might be an extensive task in companies with a great deal of specialized terminology. But remember, you only have to do it once!
7. Click OK to close all dialog boxes.

Additional computers on the network must be configured to use the custom dictionary. To do this, follow these steps on the other computers:

1. Choose Tools ≻ Options and click the Spelling And Grammar tab.
2. Click Custom Dictionaries to open the Custom Dictionaries dialog box.
3. Click Add and locate the custom dictionary file. Click OK to add the dictionary to the list of active dictionaries.

Office uses each of the active dictionaries when it checks spelling. You can deactivate a dictionary by clearing the check box in the Dictionaries dialog box. To remove a dictionary from the list of available dictionaries, select the dictionary from the list and choose Remove. Removing a dictionary does not delete it. You must actually delete the file directly to delete an entire dictionary.

Improving Your Grammar

NEW▶

Word 2002's Grammar Checker uses "natural language processing" to evaluate sentence structure and word usage to determine if you may be making grammatical errors. Although the feature is quite similar to earlier versions, the default settings for Word 2002 grammar checking have changed slightly. You can choose to have Word check grammar only to catch mistakes with capitalization, punctuation, subject-verb agreement, and common grammatical problems like sentence fragments and misplaced apostrophes. Or you can add style checking which also flags passive sentences, colloquialisms, wordiness, unclear phrasing, and more. By default, Style options are turned off. That means Word doesn't automatically check for passive sentences as it did in the past. To adjust grammar and style options, choose Tools ➢ Options ➢ Spelling And Grammar. Choose Grammar And Style from the Writing Style drop-down list or click the Settings button to turn on/off the individual grammar and style checking options shown in Figure 4.9.

FIGURE 4.9

Word 2002 offers over two dozen options for checking grammar and style.

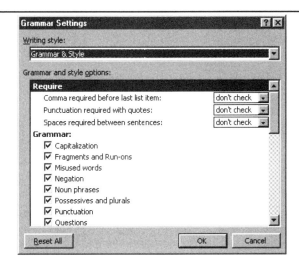

By default, Word checks grammar along with spelling when you click the Spelling And Grammar button on the Standard toolbar. If you have used other grammar checkers in the past, including those in previous versions of Word, you'll see some real differences here. Word 2002 not only identifies possible errors on the fly, but it will also make suggestions about how to rewrite the text to make it grammatically correct.

Checking Your Entire Document

When you are ready to check your total document, click the Spelling And Grammar button or choose Tools ➤ Spelling And Grammar. Word reviews the entire document and stops at any misspelled words or grammar questions. You can choose to accept or ignore the suggestions. If you would rather not be challenged every time Word encounters a sentence in passive voice (for example), click Ignore Rule in the Spelling And Grammar dialog box the first time Word identifies one. You'll be in the clear for the rest of the current document. Click Next Sentence to resume the process. If you would prefer not to check the grammar, clear the Check Grammar check box. In Figure 4.10, the Grammar Checker identifies a sentence written in passive voice and makes a suggestion about how the sentence could be reworded to give it more punch.

FIGURE 4.10

The Grammar Checker can suggest improvements when it identifies a problem.

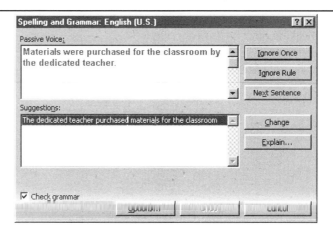

 NOTE When Word is checking spelling and grammar, watch the label on top of the text box in the Spelling And Grammar dialog box. It identifies the reason the text was flagged, such as Fragment, Use of I, Contraction, and so on, so you're not left trying to figure it out yourself.

 When you've finished checking the entire document, Word notifies you that the process is complete, and you're offered the option to check formatting.

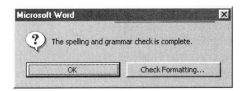

Click the Check Formatting button to have Word review the document for inconsistencies in fonts and styles while offering suggestions to correct the inconsistencies. (See Chapter 3, "Working with Text and Formats in Word," for more on Fonts and Chapter 8, "Simplifying with Styles, Outlines, and Templates," for more on Styles.)

Checking Grammar on the Fly

To have Word flag formatting inconsistencies with a wavy green line so that you can review them on the fly, choose Tools ➢ Options ➢ Edit and enable the Mark Formatting Inconsistencies check box. When you encounter a flagged word or phrase, right-click it. Grammar Checker gives you four options on the shortcut menu:

- Make one or more suggested corrections.
- Leave the text alone (Ignore).
- Open the Grammar dialog box.
- Get help about the sentence, available only if the Office Assistant is active.

If you choose About This Sentence, the Office Assistant provides additional information about the grammar rule at issue. Figure 4.11 shows the Office Assistant providing additional information about the passive sentence flagged earlier. You can also choose Grammar from the shortcut menu to open the Spelling And Grammar dialog box, another place where you can learn why the text was flagged. Click the Explain button in the lower-right corner of the dialog box to see the same information you'd see if you chose About This Sentence.

TIP If you would prefer to wait until you have finished entering and editing text to check the spelling and grammar, you can turn off the automatic Spelling and Grammar option. Choose Tools , Options , Spelling And Grammar and click the Check Spelling As You Type and the Check Grammar As You Type check boxes.

PART

II

CREATING QUALITY TEXT
DOCUMENTS USING WORD

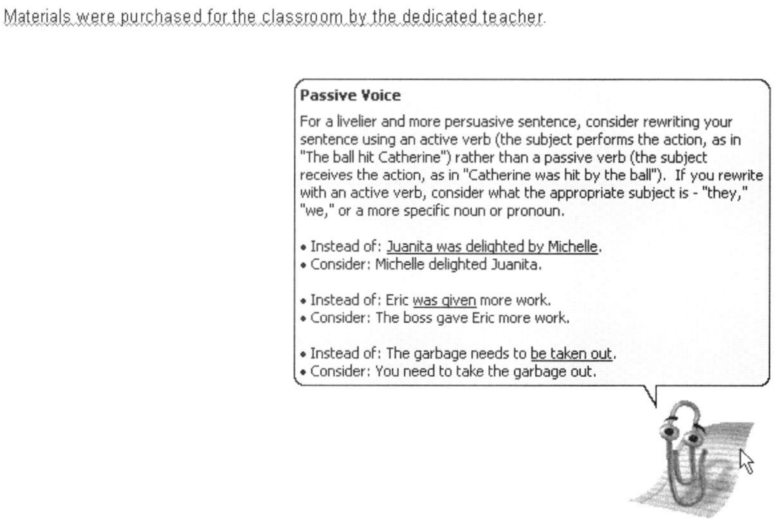

FIGURE 4.11

The Office Assistant provides information about a flagged sentence.

Materials were purchased for the classroom by the dedicated teacher.

Passive Voice

For a livelier and more persuasive sentence, consider rewriting your sentence using an active verb (the subject performs the action, as in "The ball hit Catherine") rather than a passive verb (the subject receives the action, as in "Catherine was hit by the ball"). If you rewrite with an active verb, consider what the appropriate subject is - "they," "we," or a more specific noun or pronoun.

• Instead of: Juanita was delighted by Michelle.
• Consider: Michelle delighted Juanita.

• Instead of: Eric was given more work.
• Consider: The boss gave Eric more work.

• Instead of: The garbage needs to be taken out.
• Consider: You need to take the garbage out.

  The status bar at the bottom of the application window includes an icon that shows you the status of Spelling and Grammar in your document. An X means that there are flagged words or phrases in the document. A check mark means that the document has been checked. If there are flagged words, you can double-click the icon to advance through them one by one, but it's generally easier to use the Spelling And Grammar button on the toolbar.

 WARNING Although Word 2002's Grammar Checker is a dramatic step forward in electronic proofreading, it regularly makes recommendations to fix text that is already correct or misses sentences that are obviously wrong. If you are uncertain, check another grammar reference.

MASTERING THE OPPORTUNITIES

Mastering Multilingual Editing

As more businesses find themselves interacting on a global scale, it is becoming essential to have people on your staff who can correspond in different languages. Office XP lets you edit text in approximately 60 different languages or language variations. (All languages may not be available in your copy of Office XP. Information about obtaining updates to the Language Pack is available on the Microsoft web site, `http://officeupdate.microsoft.com`.)

No, Office won't fully translate for you; you have to know enough of the language to create the text yourself (with *some* help from Word 2002's language translation feature). But Office will let you check the spelling and grammar, use AutoCorrect, and apply hyphenation and word-breaking rules. You can even read Help files and display menus and dialog boxes in some languages. To install and enable the multilingual features of Office XP, follow these steps:

1. Install the Language Pack (it is found on its own CD-ROM). The Language Pack works with the Windows Installer and makes it easy to install different languages as the need arises. Go to Add/Remove Programs in the Control Panel and choose Install. The Language Pack has its own setup files that are separate from the Office XP setup.

2. Choose Start ➢ Programs ➢ Microsoft Office Tools ➢ Microsoft Office Language Settings.

3. Select the languages that you want to use for menus and dialog boxes and for Help.

4. Click the Enabled Languages tab and select the languages you would like to be able to edit. You can choose to enable as many languages as you would like.

5. When you click OK or Apply, you are told that you must quit and restart all open Office applications. If you click Yes, Office will take care of this for you, prompting you to save if you have any unsaved documents. If you prefer not to restart, your settings won't take effect until the next time you launch an Office XP application.

After you have installed the languages you want, return to Word and start entering text in the new language. Word quickly figures out that you are working in another language and the appropriate spelling and grammar tools are invoked.

Continued

PART

II

CREATING QUALITY TEXT
DOCUMENTS USING WORD

MASTERING THE OPPORTUNITIES CONTINUED

If Office recognizes the language but you haven't installed the spelling and grammar dictionaries, it asks if you'd like to install them now. Once the appropriate dictionaries are installed, you can run Spelling and Grammar on a document with multiple languages, and Office automatically uses the correct language when it gets to that section.

When you enable some languages, you also get additional formatting options and language tools. For example, when you enable Japanese, you get a Format menu option called Asian Layout and a Tools ➢ Language menu option called Japanese Consistency Checker. Depending on the language, you also may find additional options available in the Options dialog box (Tools ➢ Options).

To set another language as the default language, choose Tools ➢ Language ➢ Set Language. In the Set Language dialog box, you can also indicate if you want to turn off Language AutoDetect and if you don't want to check spelling and grammar automatically.

Using the Thesaurus Command

The Thesaurus is there to help you find more descriptive, entertaining, or precise words to liven up your text. Rather than highlighting errors that you may have made, the Thesaurus offers help only when called upon.

To use the Thesaurus, take these steps:

1. Right-click a word (in any language you've installed!) and choose Synonyms to see a quick list of synonyms.

2. Click the word you want to use or choose Thesaurus from the shortcut menu to open the Thesaurus dialog box shown in Figure 4.12.

3. Click words in the Meanings column that best represent your context to see synonyms for them. Double-click to get a list of words that have the same or similar meaning.

4. Enter a new word to look up in the Replace With Synonym text box.

5. To review previously looked-up words, click the Previous button or select from the drop-down list under Looked Up.

6. When you find the word you want, select it and click Replace.

FIGURE 4.12

The Thesaurus dialog box

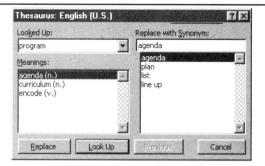

 NOTE   The Thesaurus command is not available on the shortcut menu if the word you want to look up is flagged for a spelling or grammar check. You must either take care of the spelling or grammar problem first or select the word and use the Thesaurus command from the menu under Tools ➢ Language ➢ Thesaurus.

Customizing the Spelling and Grammar Options

Word gives you a lot of freedom to determine how intrusive you would like Spelling and Grammar to be in checking your work. Click Tools ➢ Options and click the Spelling And Grammar tab to access a set of options as that shown in Figure 4.13 (notice that the options may reflect other languages for which you've enabled spell checking).

PART

II

CREATING QUALITY TEXT
DOCUMENTS USING WORD

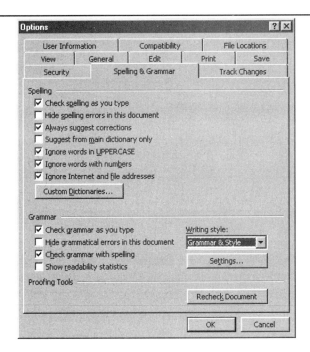

Use the Spelling and Grammar options to control what words get checked and how aggressively Word checks them. As you know, you can clear the Check Spelling As You Type and the Check Grammar As You Type check boxes to avoid getting distracted by the wavy red and green lines under all the purported misspelled words and grammatical errors. Alternatively, if you'd like Word to check your spelling and grammar in the background but not tell you about it, check the Hide Spelling Errors In This Document and Hide Grammatical Errors In This Document check boxes. (You can then go back and view the errors later.) To skip over words that may be just an annoyance, make sure that the Ignore Words in UPPERCASE, Ignore Words With Numbers, and Ignore Internet And File Addresses check boxes are checked.

 NOTE   Consider adding not-quite-words, such as Internet addresses that you use often, to a custom dictionary so that Spelling can check them and flag any typos for you.

As discussed previously under "Improving Your Grammar," Word includes options for writing styles or usage levels: Grammar Only and Grammar And Style. Each of these styles has unique grammar and style rules Word will check for in your documents.

Checking Your Document's Readability

Whenever you communicate in writing, the reading level of the audience can determine how much of your message they comprehend. Sadly, it isn't uncommon for adults to read at the fifth- or sixth-grade level; most daily newspapers in the U.S. are written for a middle school reading level. You can spend a lot of money crafting and printing elegant promotional materials for your new product, but if your potential customers can't understand them, you won't make a sale. Word protects you from speaking over or under the heads of your audience by providing you with a summary of your document's readability statistics. These statistics include word, character, paragraph, and sentence counts, average sentences per paragraph, words per sentence and characters per word, the percentage of passive sentences, the Flesch Reading Ease scale, and the Flesch-Kincaid Grade Level. Figure 4.14 shows the readability statistics for this chapter.

PART

II

CREATING QUALITY TEXT
DOCUMENTS USING WORD

FIGURE 4.14

Word provides a number of measures to help you establish the readability of your documents.

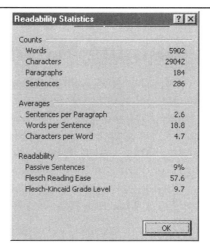

To review a document for readability, turn on the option in the Spelling And Grammar dialog box (Tools ➤ Options ➤ Spelling And Grammar). Click the Show Readability Statistics check box and click OK to save the changes. Word automatically calculates the readability statistics the next time it finishes running Spelling and Grammar. If you need word count more frequently, you can choose Tools ➤ Word Count to display the same stats without running Spelling and Grammar.

The grade level and reading ease scores are calculated using the same variables: sentence length and syllables in a word. The Flesch Reading Ease score is on a scale of 1 to 100, with 100 being the easiest to read. Reading ease is based on sentence length and the average syllables in each word. For documents other than legal or technical documents, shoot for a score in the range of 60 to 70. The Flesch-Kincaid Grade Level score is based on graded reading levels for schools in the United States. A score of 9, for example, means that a ninth grader can read and comprehend your document. For nonformal business documents, aim for a score of 7; few of your readers will feel you've "talked down" to them, and nearly all will understand the text.

If your document's reading ease score is lower or the grade level is higher than is acceptable for the intended audience, there are two remedies:

- Replace long multisyllabic words with shorter, more commonly used words.

- Break long sentences into several shorter sentences.

Use the thesaurus (Tools ➣ Language ➣ Thesaurus) to search for shorter words. The Spelling and Grammar feature can search for very long sentences. As you run Spelling and Grammar check, click the Options button to open the Spelling And Grammar dialog box. Click the Settings button and select the check boxes for the Wordiness and Sentence Length styles. Click OK twice to continue checking your document.

Keeping a Running Word Count

NEW▶

As we mentioned earlier, you can choose Tools ➣ Options ➣ Spelling And Grammar to enable the feature that shows readability statistics, including word count, for the current document. However, if you're likely to be counting and recounting frequently, it might be easier to turn on the Word Count toolbar shown in Figure 4.15. Choose View ➣ Toolbars ➣ Word Count or choose Tools ➣ Word Count and click Show Toolbar. Click the Recount button to update document stats on the spot. Use the drop-down list to select the count statistic you wish to view: words, characters with spaces, characters without spaces, lines, pages, or paragraphs. When you click Recount, all statistics update.

By default, Word bases its count on all text in the active document except footnotes and endnotes. You can, however, elect to include footnotes and endnotes, or you can count just a portion of the text. To include footnotes and endnotes in the count, choose Tools ➣ Word Count and enable that feature in the Word Count dialog box. To count a portion of the document, select the text you wish to count (remember, you can select noncontiguous blocks if you wish), and then click Recount.

FIGURE 4.15

The Word Count toolbar offers on-the-spot document statistics.

¡Que Bueno! Translating Text

NEW▶

In today's global business world, multilingual capabilities, once considered a luxury, are becoming a necessity. Any company with a Web site can receive communications from all over the world—in any language! With Word 2002, you can translate words into another language, insert the translated text into your document, and access more robust translation services via the Web. Figure 4.16 shows Word's translation tools in action.

NOTE You'll find that translating in Word works best if you attempt to convert only single words. For longer sentences and paragraphs, you'll probably need some type of translation service, which you can access those through the task pane.

FIGURE 4.16

Translate words and short phrases into another language using the Translate task pane.

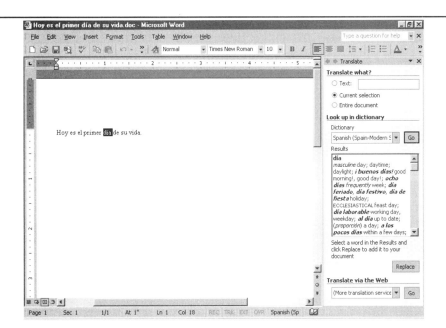

To use translation, do the following:

1. Choose the Translate feature from the task pane drop-down menu. If the task pane isn't already open, choose Tools ➢ Language ➢ Translate to open the task pane and activate translation.

TIP You can also open the task pane by right-clicking selected text and choosing Translate from the shortcut menu.

2. Choose an option from the Translate What section. If you choose Text, type the text you wish to translate in the text box. You can choose Current Selection even if you have no selected text; simply select it now.

3. Select the dictionary you wish to use for translation and click Go. If you haven't installed the appropriate dictionary, Word will prompt you to do so. The dictionary choice is disabled if you've chosen to translate the entire document because you must use a Web-based translation service for full sentences and other large amounts of text.

4. If you wish to use translation results in your document, select the word(s) in the Results box and click Replace. Text from Results appears in place of selected text in the document. If you had no text selected in the document, Word places selected Results at the insertion point.

5. To translate sentences and paragraphs, use the Translate Via The Web feature. Choose a previously used service from the drop-down list, or choose More Translation Services, and click Go. Word opens your default browser where you can quickly navigate to the translation options shown in Figure 4.17. It takes you a couple of clicks to get there but it is well worth the trip. Figure 4.18 shows the results of our very first attempt at translating a short sentence. Impressive!

FIGURE 4.17

Translate larger amounts of text using a Web translation service.

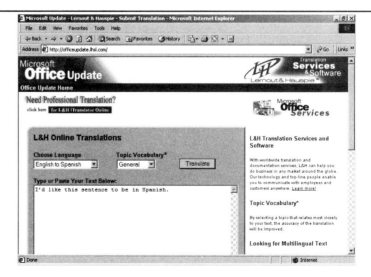

FIGURE 4.18

Translation results using Lernout & Hauspie's free Web translation service

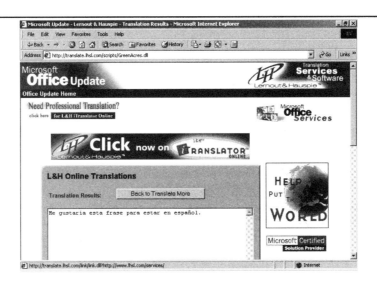

Making Smart Tags Work for You

NEW▶

It is easy to insert address information from Outlook into a Word document. But have you ever tried the reverse? Sure, you can copy and paste information into an Outlook contact form, but it's cumbersome to open another program and paste the information into multiple fields. This is one instance where Word's new Smart Tags can make data entry a breeze.

Smart Tags work like this: As you enter text, Word attempts to recognize and categorize the text you are typing. If you type a person's name, for example, Word recognizes it as a name and applies a Smart Tag *label*. This label provides options for actions you can take with names—for example, adding that person to your Outlook contact list.

By default, Smart Tags are only enabled for certain *recognizers* (types of text): person names, addresses, dates, times, and locations. You don't have to do anything special to see Smart Tags. Just enter recognizer text in any document, and you'll see a purple dotted line beneath the labeled text. Figure 4.18 shows a document with several Smart Tags.

PART

II

CREATING QUALITY TEXT
DOCUMENTS USING WORD

FIGURE 4.19

Word's new Smart
Tags let you perform
actions for which you
typically have to
launch another
program.

To use the options on any Smart Tag label, simply move the mouse over the purple dotted underline; a Smart Tag Actions button appears. Click the button to see a menu of actions you can perform and choose the one you want. Table 4.1 shows the more common Smart Tag labels and the options they offer.

TABLE 4.1   SMART TAG LABELS AND OPTIONS

Smart Tag Label	Typical Options
Person Names	Send Mail, Schedule A Meeting, Open Contact, Add To Contacts, Insert Address. This option is not on by default.
Dates	Schedule A Meeting, Show My Calendar.
Addresses	Add To Contacts, Display Map, Display Driving Directions.
Telephone Numbers	Add To Contacts. This option is not on by default.
Recent Outlook E-mail Addresses	Insert Display Name (appears as AutoText).

The recognizers listed in Table 4.1 represent a small sample of available Smart Tags. To have more choices, choose Tools ➢ AutoCorrect Options ➢ Smart Tags to open the Smart Tags tab of the AutoCorrect Options dialog box, shown in Figure 4.20. Choose More Smart Tags to visit the Web, where you'll find Smart Tags from a variety of sources. Some come from Microsoft; others are developed by third parties who may design Smart Tags and actions for specific products or services. For example, if you work in engineering, you might be able to click an "engineering specification" Smart

Tag in your document that allows you to see details about the spec or review the math behind it.

You can also use the Smart Tags tab of the AutoCorrect dialog box to adjust these options:

- Turn off Smart Tags by clearing the Label Text With Smart Tags check box.

- Turn off Smart Tag Actions buttons by clearing the Show Smart Tag Actions Buttons check box.

- Remove Smart Tags from a document by clicking the Remove Smart Tags button and then confirming the command when the message box appears.

- Save Smart Tags with your document by clicking the Save Options button and enabling the Embed Smart Tags check box.

- Review a document for Smart Tag recognizers by clicking the Recheck Document button.

FIGURE 4.20

Adjust Smart Tag options in the AutoCorrect dialog box.

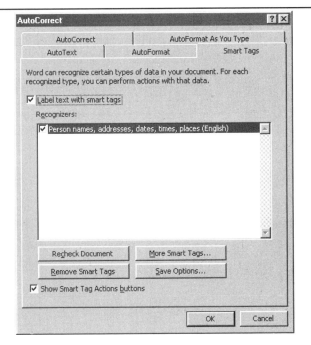

If you don't see Smart Tags in your document, check these options:

- Choose Tools ➢ Options ➢ View and make sure the Smart Tags feature is enabled in the Show list at the top of the dialog box. If it is disabled, you won't see the purple dotted underlines.

- Choose Tools ➢ AutoCorrect Options ➢ Smart Tags and make sure Label Text With Smart Tags is enabled.

 NOTE Smart Tags vary with the language in use and the grammar options you've enabled.

Using Smart Tags in E-Mail

If your e-mail recipients use Outlook 2002, they can view Smart Tags you send in e-mail messages. This can be very helpful for adding new contact information, calendar items, and so forth.

You don't have to do anything to make this work; the feature is on by default. To disable it, choose Tools ➢ Options ➢ General, and then click the E-mail Options button. On the General tab of the E-mail Options dialog box, clear the Save Smart Tags In E-mail check box.

If you don't want mail recipients following your download links via a Smart Tag, you must enable Personal Information Security, as it is off by default. Follow these steps:

1. Choose Tools ➢ Options ➢ Security.

2. Enable the Remove Personal Information From This File On Save check box.

CHAPTER 5

DESIGNING PAGES WITH COLUMNS AND TABLES

FEATURING

- Understanding sections
- Numbering pages
- Creating headers and footers
- Working with columns
- Entering and editing text in columns
- Revising column structure
- Creating and revising tables
- Formatting tables
- Changing table properties

Headers and footers that contain page numbers and other relevant information make a lengthy document easier to follow. Word can help you with everything from automatically numbering the pages to inserting different headers and footers on odd and even pages. You can also adjust hyphenation and other text flow options to make sure your final document looks its best.

If you are charged with writing your department's newsletter, you don't have to panic. Designing a newsletter with two or three columns on each page is a snap using Word's columns feature. If you are writing a financial report or creating a meeting agenda, tables make it easy to display data in columns and rows.

Understanding Sections

Word uses sections to organize documents for formatting purposes. A *section* is a contiguous portion of a document that has a specified number of columns and uses a common set of margins, page orientation, headers and footers, and sequence of page numbers. Word automatically inserts section breaks when you do the following:

- Format text as columns
- Change Page Setup options and indicate that you want the changes to apply from This Point Forward

You can manually insert a section break to apply a different page size or header and footer formatting within a document. For example, if you want a different header in each chapter in a document, put section breaks between the chapters before you create the headers.

To manually insert a section break:

1. Position the insertion point where you want the break to begin and choose Insert ➢ Break. The Break dialog box appears, as shown in Figure 5.1.

2. In the Section Break Types area, select one of the following options to specify where you want the new section to begin:

Next Page Inserts a section break and starts the new section at the beginning of the next page. You might use this type of break when you want to change page orientation.

Continuous Inserts a section break without inserting a page break. Any subsequent text you type directly follows the existing text. This break works well when you want to change the number of columns.

Even Page Inserts a section break and starts the new section at the beginning of the next even-numbered page in the document. If the section break is inserted on an even-numbered page, Word leaves the intervening page (an odd-numbered page) blank.

Odd Page   Inserts a section break and starts the new section at the beginning of the next odd-numbered page in the document. If the section break is inserted on an odd-numbered page, Word leaves the intervening page (an even-numbered page) blank.

3. Click OK to insert the section break.

FIGURE 5.1

The options in the Break dialog box allow you to specify what type of break to insert in a document.

Section break marks can be seen in both Normal and Outline views by default. You can also see section break marks in both Web Page and Print Layout views when you display nonprinting characters in your document. To do so, use either of the following procedures:

- Click the Show/Hide ¶ button on the Standard toolbar.
- Choose Tools ➤ Options ➤ View, check the Hidden Text check box in the Formatting Marks area, and then click OK.

Section break marks appear as double-dotted lines with the words *Section Break* and the type of break (*Continuous*, for example) in them, as shown below.

Section Break (Continuous)

To delete a section break, place the insertion point anywhere on the break, and press Delete.

Creating and Modifying Page Numbers

Whether or not you have inserted section breaks, you may want a simple way to automatically number the pages. Nothing could be more effortless than Word's Page Numbering feature. Follow these steps to use this feature:

1. Choose Insert ➤ Page Numbers to open the Page Numbers dialog box, shown in Figure 5.2.

2. In the Position drop-down list, select Bottom Of Page (Footer) or Top Of Page (Header) as the location for your page numbers.

3. In the Alignment drop-down list, select Left, Center, Right, Inside, or Outside to specify the location of the page number within the header or footer.

4. To prevent the page number from appearing on the first page of your document, click the Show Number On First Page check box to clear the check from it.

5. When the page numbers appear with both the position and alignment you want in the Preview area, click OK to have Word number the pages in your document.

FIGURE 5.2

Use the options in the Page Numbers dialog box to place sequential page numbers in your document.

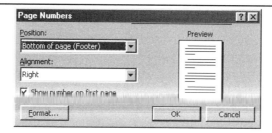

Page numbers appear on your screen in both Print Layout view and Print Preview, and they are automatically updated as you edit your document.

NOTE You can disable Word's automatic repagination feature in both Normal and Outline views by removing the check mark in the Background Repagination check box on the General tab in the Options dialog box. With automatic repagination disabled, Word won't display the page number for the current page in the status bar. In Web Layout view, Print Layout view, and Print Preview, you cannot disable background repagination.

MASTERING THE OPPORTUNITIES

Bound for Success: Printing on Both Sides of the Page

To create professional-looking business reports, contracts, proposals, or any document you want to bind along its left edge, you can combine the Inside and Outside page-number alignment options with mirror margins (on the Margins tab in the Page Setup dialog box) to print a document on both sides of the paper. Mirror margins automatically make the margins on facing pages "mirror" each other so that the inside margins (the right margin on the left page and the left margin on the right page) are equal to each other, and so are the outside margins (the left margin on the left page and the right margin on the right page). Usually, you will want the inside margins to be larger than the outside margins to allow space for binding the document. You can specify the amount of space to add to the inside margin by adjusting the value in the Gutter text box on the Margins tab.

If you select Inside as the page number alignment, the page numbers appear on the right side of the left page and on the left side of the right page. When you select Outside as the alignment, the page numbers appear on the left side of the left page and on the right side of the right page. Each selection you make appears in the Preview area of the Page Numbers dialog box.

PART

II

CREATING QUALITY TEXT
DOCUMENTS USING WORD

Changing the Page Number's Format

You can also change the format that is applied to the page numbers by applying a different numbering style and by having Word automatically insert the chapter number in front of the page number. For example, in a long document such as a proposal, it's common to number the pages of the table of contents using lowercase Roman numerals and the pages containing the text of the proposal using Arabic numerals.

To change the format of the page numbers in your document:

1. Choose Insert ➢ Page Numbers to display the Page Numbers dialog box.

2. Click the Format button to display the Page Number Format dialog box, shown in Figure 5.3.

3. Select the format for the page numbers in the Number Format drop-down list.

4. To have Word automatically place the chapter number in front of the page number, click the Include Chapter Number check box and then specify how you want the chapter number to appear using the following options:

- In the Chapter Starts With Style drop-down list, select the Heading style that you are using for each chapter in your document.

- In the Use Separator drop-down list, select the character you want to appear between the chapter number and the page number.

5. To specify the number at which you want to start numbering for the document, choose either of the following options in the Page Numbering area:

Continue From Previous Section Starts the page numbering in the current document section with the number next to the last number in the previous section. If this is the first section in the document, the number starts with 1.

Start At Allows you to specify the number you want for the first page of your document. Choose this option if you want to start the page numbering at a number other than 1.

6. Click OK in the Page Number Format dialog box and again in the Page Numbers dialog box to return to the document.

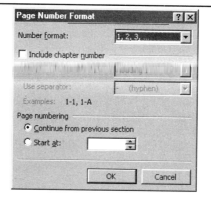

FIGURE 5.3

Display the Page Number Format dialog box to change the formatting applied to page numbers in your document.

If your document has more than one section, such as the proposal mentioned above, you can set up different page numbering for each section. To do this, position the insertion point on the first page of the document (in this case, the table of contents, which is the beginning of the first section of the proposal), choose Insert ➢ Page Numbers to add page numbering, and then click Format to set up the formatting for this section's numbering. Then move the insertion point to the first page of the *second* section (the proposal's chapters) and repeat the process. You will probably want to select the Start At option in the Page Numbering area of the Page Number Format dialog box to specify that the text of the proposal starts on page 1.

Repeat the process for any additional sections. If you want the page numbering to continue from the previous section, choose that option in the Page Number Format dialog box. If you want to remove page numbers, you need to edit the header or footer where the page number appears. See the following section to learn how to edit the headers and footers in your documents.

Creating Headers and Footers

Page numbers are certainly useful, but you may also want to include other information on each page. For example, the current date, your name, and the name of your company are additional pieces of information that often appear on each page of a document. For this type of information, use headers and/or footers. Headers are placed in the top margin and footers in the bottom margin on each page in the current section of the document.

To place a header or footer in your document, choose View ➤ Header And Footer. The existing document text is immediately dimmed and the Header section at the top of your document opens. A floating Header And Footer toolbar, like the one shown in Figure 5.4, also appears.

FIGURE 5.4

When you view your document's header or footer, the Header And Footer toolbar appears.

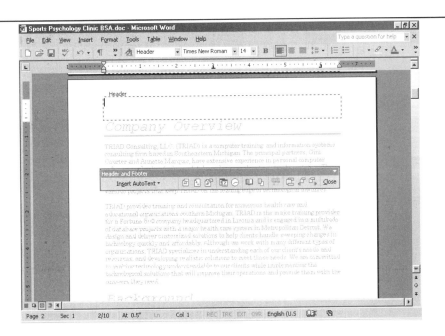

Enter the text you want to appear in the Header section. Use the Header And Footer toolbar buttons, shown in Figure 5.5, to help you edit the headers and footers.

FIGURE 5.5

Use the buttons on the Header And Footer toolbar to edit the document's header and footer.

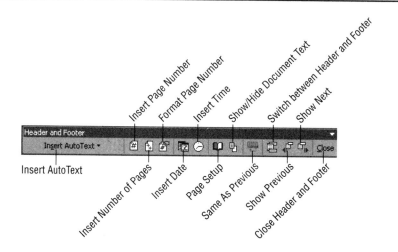

Whether you are creating headers, footers, or both, the process is the same:

1. Choose View ➤ Header And Footer to display the Header section in the active section of the document.

2. Enter text, insert graphics, and use the Header And Footer toolbar to insert AutoText, page numbers, and date and time codes.

3. To create a footer, click the Switch Between Header And Footer button on the Header And Footer toolbar to move the insertion point to the footer, and then add any necessary text or field codes.

4. To create different headers and footers in different sections, click Show Previous or Show Next to activate the footer in the previous or next section of the document, and then make any necessary changes to that footer. Click the Switch Between Header And Footer button on the Header And Footer toolbar to activate that section's header, and then edit it as necessary.

5. When you are finished editing your document's header(s) and footer(s), click Close to close the Header And Footer toolbar and return to your document.

Unless you change the header and footer in a section of a document with multiple sections, all of the headers and footers will be the same in every section.

Creating Alternate Headers and Footers

Word contains two options that allow you to further edit the position of your document's header and footer. You can choose not to display the header or footer on the first page, and you can display different headers and footers on odd and even pages. These features are particularly useful for long documents, which may contain a cover page and may be bound.

For example, you would not want the document's header and footer to appear on the title page of the sample proposal mentioned above. In addition, you might want one header and footer to appear on the left pages of the proposal and a different header and footer to appear on the right pages. To change the positions of your document's header and footer:

1. Click the Page Setup button on the Header And Footer toolbar to display the Layout tab of the Page Setup dialog box, shown in Figure 5.6.

2. Choose from the following options:

   • Select the Different Odd And Even check box to create different headers and footers for even- and odd-numbered pages.

   • Select the Different First Page check box to create a different header and footer for the first page.

3. Click OK in the Page Setup dialog box.

FIGURE 5.6

Display the Layout tab in the Page Setup dialog box if you want to create alternate headers and footers.

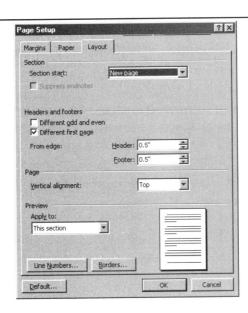

If you check the Different First Page box on the Layout page in the Page Setup dialog box, Word provides a new section titled First Page Header. Just leave the header and footer blank on the first page to suppress its display.

If you want to create different headers or footers for odd and even pages, check the appropriate box in the Page Setup dialog box. Word provides two new sections titled Odd Page Header on the odd-numbered pages and Even Page Header on the even-numbered pages. Enter the first header or footer, and then click the Show Next button on the Header And Footer toolbar to enter the opposite page header or footer.

TIP If part of your header or footer is "cut off" on the printed document, it may be situated outside of your printer's print area. To fix it, adjust the From Edge setting on the Layout tab of the Page Setup dialog box. The higher the number, the farther the header/footer is positioned from the edge of the page.

Taking Care of Loose Ends

Before you print the final version of a document, you should clean up dangling words, bad line and page breaks, and extra spaces that detract from the appearance of your document. There are three ways to clean up these loose ends:

- Are there spaces at the ends of lines because long words wrap to the beginning of the next line? If so, use hyphenation.

- Does the document have text strings that should be kept together but are broken over two lines? If so, use nonbreaking spaces.

- Are there paragraphs or lines of paragraphs that should be kept together but currently break across two pages? If so, use Line And Page Breaks options to specify how you want the text to flow within the document.

NOTE Make sure you have done all of your editing and formatting before attempting any of this final cleanup. When you add, delete, or reformat text, you have to clean up the document all over again.

Using Hyphenation

Word 2002 includes options for either automatically or manually hyphenating your documents. With hyphenation, you can prohibit Word from hyphenating words in caps. You can also indicate the size of the *hyphenation zone*, the distance from the right margin that Word scrutinizes for words to hyphenate. Increase the area if you want more words hyphenated; decrease it if you don't mind ragged edges.

 TIP Your document may contain blocks of text that you don't want Word to hyphenate. To prevent automatic hyphenation, select the text block, choose Format ➢ Paragraph ➢ Line And Page Breaks, and turn on the Don't Hyphenate option.

When you have Word automatically hyphenate your document, hyphens are added as you type in the document. If you would like more control over how Word hyphenates your documents, you can choose to manually hyphenate your document. When you do, Word reviews your document, locates candidates for hyphenation, and then recommends a location for the hyphen.

To hyphenate your document:

1. Choose Tools ➢ Language ➢ Hyphenation to display the Hyphenation dialog box shown in Figure 5.7.

FIGURE 5.7

Display the Hyphenation dialog box when you want to place hyphens in the current document.

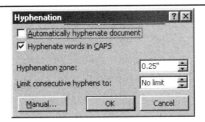

2. To allow hyphens to be placed in words that consist of all capital letters, leave the Hyphenate Words In CAPS box checked. Clear the check box to prevent Word from inserting a hyphen in words that appear in all capital letters.

3. If necessary, adjust the value in the Hyphenation Zone text box to specify the distance from the right margin in which Word will check for words to be hyphenated.

4. If necessary, adjust the value in the Limit Consecutive Hyphens To text box to specify the number of consecutive lines that can end in a hyphen.

5. To insert hyphens in your document, choose either of the following options:

- To have Word automatically insert hyphens in your document as you type, check the Automatically Hyphenate Document check box, and then click OK.

- Click the Manual button to display the Manual Hyphenation dialog box shown in Figure 5.8, click in a different location for the hyphen if necessary, and then choose Yes to insert the hyphen in the document. To prevent hyphenating the selected word, choose No. Word automatically displays the next word in the document for which hyphenation is recommended.

FIGURE 5.8

The Manual Hyphenation dialog box allows you to specify where you want the hyphen to appear in a recommended word.

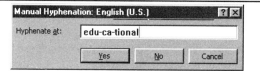

 NOTE Word's Manual Hyphenation feature is not installed in the typical Office installation. When you click the Manual button on the Hyphenation dialog box, you may be prompted to insert the Office CD and install the feature.

When Word makes a hyphenation recommendation, it is more concerned about spacing than about proper hyphenation. It frequently leaves two characters at the end of a line, or it recommends some other awkward place for the hyphenation. Use your own judgment, and if you're not sure, refer to a dictionary or hyphenation guide.

 TIP If you are creating a document, such as a newsletter, in which you want the right edge to be even rather than ragged, click the Justify button on the Formatting toolbar to apply that format to each paragraph.

TIP To prevent a word or phrase that already contains a hyphen (like a phone number) from breaking at the end of a line, insert a nonbreaking hyphen by holding down Ctrl+Shift when you type the hyphen. To enter an optional hyphen, a hyphen that breaks a word or a phrase at the designated place if it occurs at the end of a line, hold down Ctrl when you type the hyphen.

Nonbreaking Spaces

Occasionally, you might have a text string, such as an address, that should not be separated at the end of a line. You can protect this string by inserting *nonbreaking spaces* instead of regular spaces within the text string. These are similar to nonbreaking hyphens; text connected with nonbreaking spaces moves to the next line rather than breaking between lines. To insert a nonbreaking space, hold down Ctrl+Shift when you press the spacebar.

Handling Page Breaks

Word 2002 offers a number of other ways to keep text together so that your document looks professionally printed. One of these options, called Widow/Orphan control, is on by default. This feature prevents the first line of a paragraph from being left alone at the bottom of the page (an orphan) or the last line of a paragraph from appearing by itself at the top of a new page (a widow).

Using the Line And Page Break options, you can keep selected lines of text or entire paragraphs together. In addition, you can have Word insert a page break before a paragraph when you want the entire paragraph to be placed at the top of a page.

To specify how to break document text:

1. Select the text, then choose Format ➤ Paragraph ➤ Line And Page Breaks to display the Line And Page Breaks tab in the Paragraph dialog box, shown in Figure 5.9.

PART

II

CREATING QUALITY TEXT
DOCUMENTS USING WORD

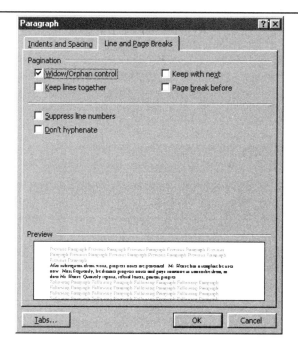

2. Choose any of the following options in the Pagination area:

- Clear the Widow/Orphan Control check box to prevent Word from automatically keeping text together at the bottom and top of pages.

- Check the Keep Lines Together box to prevent lines of the selected paragraph from being separated by a page break. The entire paragraph moves to the top of the next page.

- Check the Keep With Next box to keep the selected paragraph from being separated from the following paragraph by a page break (used, for example, to keep a heading with the first paragraph of text that follows).

- Check the Page Break Before box to insert a manual page break before the paragraph that contains the insertion point.

3. Click OK in the Paragraph dialog box.

 TIP You can also insert a manual page break before a specific paragraph by positioning the insertion point where you want to place the page break and then pressing Ctrl+Enter.

Working with Columns

Some information is most effectively presented in *newspaper columns*, in which text flows from the bottom of one column to the top of the next. All Word documents consist of at least one column. If you create newsletters, flyers, reports, announcements, or other publications that contain multiple text columns, you'll probably use Word's newspaper columns feature quite a bit.

Entering and Editing Text in Columns

Working with newspaper columns requires a little advance design work. You'll find that it is often easier to enter document text into a single column, and then convert the text into multiple columns. When you are ready to work with columns, switch to Print Layout view so you can actually see the columns as they will appear on the page. Then follow these steps:

1. Select the text you want to place in columns.

2. Perform either of the following actions to create columns of equal width:

   - Click the Columns button on the Standard toolbar to open the selection palette, and then drag to select the number of columns you want.

   - Choose Format ➤ Columns to display the Columns dialog box shown in Figure 5.10, adjust the value in the Number Of Columns text box, and then click OK.

PART

II

CREATING QUALITY TEXT
DOCUMENTS USING WORD

FIGURE 5.10

You can create columns using the options in the Columns dialog box.

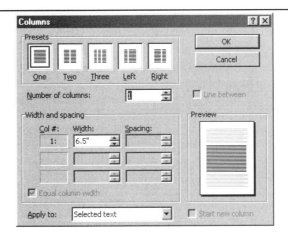

The selected text is rearranged into columns, and column markers are visible on the horizontal ruler.

NOTE Because of the space between the columns, a block of text poured into two or more columns takes up more room than it does in a single-column page. As a result, you may have to edit text to get it to fit on a prescribed number of pages.

Balancing Column Length

You can create *balanced* columns—that is, columns of equal length—for some documents. For example, a newsletter is a type of document that often contains multiple columns of the same length.

To create balanced columns, move the insertion point to the end of the text, choose Insert ➤ Break ➤ Continuous, and then click OK to insert a continuous section break.

 TIP If you want to begin a new page after the balanced columns, position the insertion point after the continuous page break and either press Ctrl+Enter or choose Insert ➤ Break ➤ Page Break and click OK to enter a manual page break.

Revising Column Structure

While you are creating a document with multiple newspaper columns, you may decide to change the appearance of your document by changing the number of columns in it.

To change the number of columns in a document with multiple columns, position the insertion point anywhere in the columns section and then either:

- Click the Columns button on the Standard toolbar, and then drag to select a new number of columns.

- Choose Format ➤ Columns, adjust the number in the Number Of Columns text box, and then click OK.

 TIP To revert to a single column, choose one column or switch to Normal or Outline view and delete the section markers.

When you create columns with the Columns button, Word makes all the columns the same width. If you want columns of differing widths, drag the Move Column marker on the horizontal ruler.

To change the amount of white space between the columns (the *gutter*), point to the right or left edge of the Move Column marker on the ruler and drag the desired distance.

Using the Columns Dialog Box

As you have already seen, you can use the options in the Columns dialog box, shown in Figure 5.10, to create multiple newspaper columns and to change the number of columns in your document. Several other options in the Columns dialog box allow you to further change the appearance of columns. For example, you can use the options to establish columns of a specific width or to lock column width so that they are equal.

To specify exactly how your columns should appear, choose Format ➤ Columns, choose any of the following options in the Columns dialog box, and then click OK:

- Specify the number and position of the columns in the Presets area. If you choose One, Two, or Three, the Equal Column Width check box is automatically selected, so when you change the width of one column, the width of each column is automatically changed. When you choose Left, the left column is narrower than the right column. When you choose Right, the left column is wider than the right column.

- Create up to nine columns by adjusting the value in the Number Of Columns text box.

- Specify the exact width and spacing between each column by adjusting the values for each column in the appropriate Width and Spacing text boxes.

- Click the Line Between check box to have Word insert vertical lines between each of the columns.

Keeping Text Together in Columns

All the tools that you use to keep page text together, including nonbreaking spaces, nonbreaking hyphens, and the Line And Page Breaks options, also work within columns. Word's Columns dialog box provides you with one more option for controlling where text breaks between columns:

1. Move the insertion point to the beginning of the text you want to reposition in the next column, and then choose Format ➤ Columns to open the Columns dialog box shown previously in Figure 5.10.

2. Change the Apply To control to This Point Forward.

3. Click the Start New Column check box.

4. Click OK to insert an End Of Section mark and move the text to the next column.

Creating Parallel Columns with Tables

Parallel columns, such as the names and numbers in a phone book, display corresponding text in columns. Although tabs can be used to present information in parallel columns, it is far easier to use Word's powerful Tables feature. With tables, every block of text can be easily formatted, edited, deleted, and moved around without affecting the remainder of the text. Tables are one of the most versatile tools in the Word toolkit.

The handiest ways to create tables in Word are:

- Click the Insert Table button on the Standard toolbar, and then drag to highlight the number of columns and rows you want in your table. As you drag, the number of rows and columns is displayed at the bottom of the button's menu. When the number of rows and columns is correct, release the mouse button to insert the table in your document.

- Click the Tables And Borders button on the Standard toolbar to display the Tables And Borders toolbar. The Draw Table button is selected by default, and the mouse pointer appears as a pencil. Drag the pencil to create a rectangle about the size of the table you want. When you release the mouse button, the outside border of the table appears in your document. Drag with the pencil again to draw in column and row borders.

NOTE Although you can use the Draw Table feature to create a table, it's generally easiest to create the table using the Insert Table button. Use the Draw Table button to insert additional columns and rows inside an existing table. See "Modifying Table Structure" later in this chapter.

If you want to specify exact measurements and formatting for the table when you create it, you can use a third method, which is in the Insert Table dialog box:

1. Choose Table ➢ Insert ➢ Table to display the Insert Table dialog box shown in Figure 5.11.

2. Adjust the value in the Number Of Columns text box to specify the number of columns in your table.

3. Adjust the value in the Number Of Rows text box to specify the number of rows in your table.

4. Choose one of the following options in the AutoFit Behavior area:

Fixed Column Width Allows you to specify the exact width of each column in the table by adjusting the value in the adjacent text box. Alternatively, choose Auto to have Word adjust the width of each column equally so the table spans from the left to the right margin.

AutoFit To Contents Automatically adjusts the width of each column in the table to fit the longest cell contents in that column.

AutoFit To Window Automatically adjusts the size of the table to fit the window of a Web browser or document, even if the size of the window changes.

5. To save the settings you specified in the Insert Table dialog box so that Word displays them each time the dialog box is displayed, click the Remember Dimensions For New Tables check box.

6. Click OK to insert the table in your document.

 NOTE See "Formatting Tables" later in this chapter to learn how to use Word's Table AutoFormat option, which is also available in the Insert Table dialog box.

FIGURE 5.11

With the options in the Insert Table dialog box, you can simultaneously create and specify the exact size of the new table.

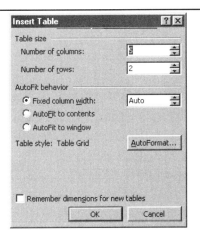

WARNING   When you delete a table, any data in the table is also deleted.

To delete a table, click any cell in the table and then choose Table ➤ Delete ➤ Table.

Positioning a Table

When you insert a table using the button on the Standard toolbar, or by using the Table menu, the table grid appears at the insertion point. However, you can easily move your table on the active page. To do so, position the mouse over the table until a four-headed arrow appears in a box at the upper-left corner of the table. Position the mouse pointer over the box and then drag the table. An outline of the table appears as you drag. When the outline is in the position you want, release the mouse button to drop the table in its new position on the page.

 Word now supports drag-and-drop copying of tables. Hold the Ctrl key while dragging the table to make a copy. Be sure to release the mouse button *before* letting go of the Ctrl key.

Nesting Tables

One of Word's newer features now allows you to insert a table in an existing table *cell*, the rectangle formed by the intersection of a column and row. To do so, click in the cell where you want to insert a table, and then use any of the methods above to insert the table.

Working with Text in a Table

Once you have created a table, you can enter text by clicking in any cell and then typing the characters you want in that cell. You can also use any of the following keys to activate a cell so you can enter text:

- Press the Tab key or the → key on the keyboard to move to the next cell to the right.
- Hold down Shift+Tab or press the ← key to move one cell to the left.
- Press the ↑ or ↓ key to move the insertion point to the cell above or below the current cell.

NOTE If you created your table by drawing it, click the Draw Table button on the Tables And Borders toolbar or close the toolbar to change the pointer from a pencil back to an I-beam. Then click in the cell and begin typing.

Since pressing the Tab key takes you to the next cell in a table, you might conclude that you can't use tabs within table cells to indent text you're typing. But you can! Just press Ctrl+Tab to indent text within a table cell.

To format text in a table, you must select it just as you would any other text. Table 5.1 shows how to select portions of a table.

TABLE 5.1   SELECTING IN TABLES

To Select	Action
A cell	Triple-click in the cell or click the cell selection pointer by placing the mouse near the left border of the cell.
A row	Move the mouse to the left margin outside of the table, point to the row, and click.
Multiple rows	Select the first row, hold down the mouse button, and drag down the desired number of rows.
A column	Move the mouse pointer above the column until it changes to a downward arrow and click, or hold down the Alt key and click in the column.
Multiple contiguous columns	Select the first column, hold down the mouse button, and drag through the desired number of columns; or use any method to select the first column and then hold down Shift and use any method to select the last column.
Multiple noncontiguous columns	Select the first column, hold Ctrl, and select additional columns.
Entire table	Choose Table ➢ Select ➢ Table, or click the table's Move icon above the top-left corner.

Formatting Text in Tables

Each table cell can be formatted separately. You can center text in the first column, left-align it in the second column, and right-align in the third column. You can apply boldface formatting to the *header row*, the row with the column names, and italicize other rows. Whatever you can do to a paragraph, you can do to the text within a cell.

Use the buttons on the Formatting toolbar or the commands on the Format menu to apply fonts, font effects, alignment, bullets and numbering, and indents and spacing to the text in a table.

You can also change the vertical alignment of the text in the active table cell. To do so, click the Align Position drop-down button on the Tables And Borders toolbar or right-click inside the table, highlight Cell Alignment, and then click one of the text alignment options that appear.

The alignment assigned to the active cell appears on the Align Position button on the toolbar.

TIP The Align Position button is one of several submenus that you can float as a free-standing menu. When you want to apply several different formats to a document, this saves the trouble of repeatedly opening the menu. To make the submenu float, click the Align Position drop-down arrow to open the menu. Point to the move handle (the gray bar at the top of the menu) and drag the menu into the document window.

Rotating Text in Tables

Occasionally, the best (or only) way to fit table text into the available space is to rotate the text so that it is no longer running in the traditional horizontal direction across the page. For example, you may need to rotate text if a table has many columns that require long headings. With Word's Change Text Direction feature, you can rotate text in a table so that it runs vertically, facing either right or left. To do so:

1. Select the cell or group of cells that contain the text you want to rotate.

2. Choose one of the following methods to change the text direction:

   • Click the Change Text Direction button on the Tables And Borders toolbar. The first click rotates the text so that it is facing right, the second click flips it to face left, and the third click returns it to horizontal.

- Right-click inside the table, and then choose Text Direction in the shortcut menu to display the Text Direction dialog box shown in Figure 5.12. Choose the rotation you want for the text in the Orientation area. The change appears in the Preview area. Click OK to define the direction of the text in the selected cell.

As the text rotates, so do some of the buttons on the Formatting toolbar. The alignment buttons and Numbering, Bullets, Decrease Indent, and Increase Indent buttons all rotate in the same direction as the text in the cell, as shown in Figure 5.13. The Columns button on the Standard toolbar also rotates. The Change Text Direction button on the Tables And Borders toolbar changes to display the rotation that will take place when you next click that button.

FIGURE 5.12

You can use the Text Direction dialog box to change the direction of the text in selected cells.

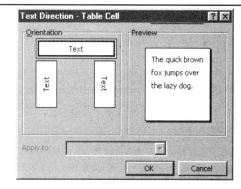

FIGURE 5.13

Some of the buttons on the Formatting toolbar change to reflect the rotation you've applied to the text in the active table cell.

When you rotate text, even the insertion point rotates, so editing can be a little disconcerting at first. The main thing to remember is that you have to drag the mouse vertically to select text. Once you've gotten the hang of that, you're all set.

Modifying Table Structure

One of the best reasons to use tables instead of tabs in your documents is that tables are easily modified. You can add or delete rows and columns, change column and row widths, and merge and split cells without upsetting the rest of the table text.

Further, you can set the table alignment and specify how you want document text to wrap around the table by changing the table's properties. In addition, tables can be indented a specified distance from the left margin of the page.

Adding and Deleting Rows, Columns, and Cells

You can easily adjust the number of rows in an existing table by either adding new rows or deleting existing rows. Use one of the following methods to place new rows exactly where you want them in a table:

- Select the row below where you want your new row to be and click the Insert Row button on the Standard toolbar. (It occupies the same physical space as the Insert Table button on the Standard toolbar. When you select a row the Insert Table button becomes the Insert Row button.)

- To add a row at the end of a table, simply move to the last cell in the table and press Tab. Word adds a new row with the same formatting as the current row.

- If you want to insert several rows in the middle of the table, select the number of rows you want to insert and choose Table ➢ Insert ➢ Rows Above or Table ➢ Insert ➢ Rows Below to have Word insert rows above or below the selection. Alternatively, click the Insert Table button drop-down list on the Tables And Borders toolbar and choose Insert Rows Above or Insert Rows Below.

- To insert rows above the selected rows, right-click the table and choose Insert Rows in the shortcut menu.

NOTE   As you select different parts of the table, the Insert Table button on the Standard toolbar changes. For example, if you select a column, the Insert Table button changes to the Insert Column button. The Insert Table button on the Tables And Borders toolbar behaves similarly, but not identically—rather than changing depending on what is selected, it displays the command most recently chosen from its drop-down menu.

To delete selected rows, either choose Table ➢ Delete ➢ Rows or right-click and choose Delete Rows from the shortcut menu.

WARNING When you delete a table row, all the data in that row is also deleted.

Inserting columns works in a similar way to inserting rows. New columns created in a table with fixed column width are the same width as the ones you select to create them, so you may have to adjust column widths if the table no longer fits into the width of the page.

Use one of the following methods to place new columns exactly where you want them in a table:

- Select the column to the right of where you want your new column to be and click the Insert Columns button on the Standard toolbar. (It occupies the same physical space as the Insert Table button.)

- To insert a column at the end of a table, click the Show/Hide ¶ button on the Standard toolbar, select the marks to the right of the last column, right-click the table, and then choose Insert Columns.

- Select the number of columns you want to insert and choose Table ➢ Insert ➢ Columns To The Left or Table ➢ Insert ➢ Columns To The Right to have Word insert columns to the left or right of the selection. Alternatively, click the Insert Table button drop-down list on the Tables And Borders toolbar and choose either Insert Columns To The Left or Insert Columns To The Right.

To delete selected columns, either choose Table ➢ Delete ➢ Columns or right-click the table and then choose Delete Columns.

 WARNING When you delete columns in a table, all the data in those columns is also deleted.

You can also insert new cells, rows, or columns into a table by following these steps:

1. Select the cells in the position in which you want to insert new cells.

2. Choose Table ➢ Insert ➢ Cells or click the Insert Table drop-down list button on the Tables And Borders toolbar and choose Insert Cells to display the Insert Cells dialog box shown in Figure 5.14.

3. Choose one of the following options to tell Word where you want the new cells to be placed in your table:

    Shift Cells Right Inserts the new cells in the position of the selected cells, and then moves the selected cells to the right

PART

II

CREATING QUALITY TEXT
DOCUMENTS USING WORD

Shift Cells Down Inserts the new cells in the position of the selected cells and then moves the selected cells, and every cell below the selected cells, down a number of rows equal to the number of inserted cells

Insert Entire Row Inserts new rows above the selected cells

Insert Entire Column Inserts new columns to the left of the selected cells

4. Click OK to insert the specified cells.

Display the Insert Cells dialog box when you want to insert cells in a specific location in a table.

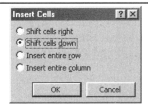

You can also delete selected cells, rows, and columns. To do so:

1. Select the cells you want to delete, and then choose Table ➢ Delete ➢ Cells or right-click inside the table and choose Delete Cells to display the Delete Cells dialog box.

2. Choose one of the following options:

Shift Cells Left Deletes the cells and their contents and shifts any cells that are to the right of the selection to the left to replace the cells that were deleted

Shift Cells Up Deletes the cells and their contents and shifts any cells below the selection up to replace the cells that were deleted

Delete Entire Row Deletes the row that contains the insertion point, including all the data in that row

Delete Entire Column Deletes the column that contains the insertion point, including all the data in that column

3. Click OK in the Delete Cells dialog box.

 WARNING When you delete selected cells, rows, and columns, all the data in the selection is also deleted.

TIP To quickly add columns or rows to a table, especially when you want them to span only a portion of the table (also referred to as splitting cells), click the Draw Table button and drag the Pencil pointer across or down the cells you want to cross.

Changing the Column and Cell Width and the Row Height

The easiest way to make adjustments to both columns and rows is to drag their borders. To do so, just move the mouse pointer to the border between the row or column until it changes to a double-headed arrow, and then drag that border in either direction. Column borders can be dragged left (to decrease the column width) or right (to increase the column width). Row borders can be dragged up (to decrease the row height) or down (to increase the row height).

 NOTE You can't adjust row borders by dragging when you're in Normal or Outline view.

Hold down the Alt key while you drag either border to display the measurement of the row or column in the ruler. Column sizes are displayed in the horizontal ruler above the columns; row sizes appear in the vertical ruler when you are in Print Layout view.

 NOTE To increase the width of a column while simultaneously decreasing the widths of each column to its right, hold down Ctrl while dragging the column's right border. Each column's width is changed proportionately.

There may be times when you want to make all the columns the same width or all rows the same height (for example, when creating a calendar). You can have Word do the work for you. Follow these steps to do so:

- Select the columns you want to be the same width and click the Distribute Columns Evenly button on the Tables And Borders toolbar or choose Table ➢ AutoFit ➢ Distribute Columns Evenly.
- Select the rows you want to be the same height and click the Distribute Rows Evenly button on the Tables And Borders toolbar or choose Table ➢ AutoFit ➢ Distribute Rows Evenly.

There are several other ways to quickly change the row height and column width of an entire table after you have entered your data in the table. You can select the table, or click in any cell in the table, and then perform one of the following actions:

- To change the row height and column width simultaneously to fit the contents of each cell, choose Table ➢ AutoFit ➢ AutoFit To Contents or click the drop-down list on the Insert Table button (Tables And Border toolbar) and then choose AutoFit To Contents. The height of each row is adjusted to fit the cell with the tallest contents. The width of each column is adjusted to fit the widest contents.

- To adjust the width of the table to fit the window in Web Layout view, choose Table ➢ AutoFit ➢ AutoFit To Window or click the drop-down list on the Insert Table button (Tables And Borders toolbar) and then choose AutoFit To Window.

You can also specify an exact row height, column width, cell width, and vertical alignment in selected cells by using Word's Table Properties dialog box (for more about the Table Properties dialog box, see "Changing Properties for the Entire Table" later in this chapter). In addition, you have some row options for tables that span more than one page.

To change the properties of selected rows:

1. Select the row or rows whose properties you want to change.

2. Choose Table ➢ Table Properties ➢ Row, or right-click the table and choose Table Properties ➢ Row, to display the Row tab in the Table Properties dialog box, shown in Figure 5.15.

3. To change the height of the selected rows, click the Specify Height check box to place a check in it, adjust the value in the text box to the height you want, and then select either At Least or Exactly in the Row Height Is drop-down list.

4. To specify how you want Word to display a table that spans multiple pages, choose either of the following options:

   Allow Row To Break Across Pages Permits a selected row that contains multiple lines of text to be continued on the next page. This may be harder to read but allows you to fit more text into the available space.

   Repeat As Header Row At The Top Of Each Page Duplicates the contents of the selected top row or rows of the table on subsequent pages of the table.

5. If necessary, click Previous Row or Next Row to select that row, and then apply any necessary properties to that row as indicated in steps 2 through 4.

6. Click OK to apply the row properties you selected.

FIGURE 5.15

Change the properties of the selected row(s) on the Row tab in the Table Properties dialog box.

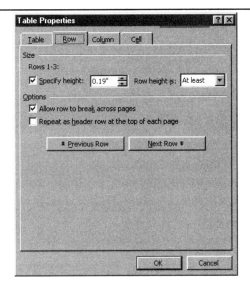

When you choose At Least in the Row Height Is drop-down list, you've specified that the rows will maintain a minimum height regardless of what is in them. Use Exactly when you want to designate a row height that doesn't change. This is useful when you are creating calendars, for example, where you want the row height to stay the same regardless of the contents.

TIP If you want to break a table across two pages, you can enter a page break in the table. Select the row you want to appear on the next page, and then press Ctrl+Enter to create a manual page break.

Use the options on the Column tab in the Table Properties dialog box to specify how the width of the selected column is determined, as shown in the following steps:

1. Select the column or columns whose widths you want to change.

2. Choose Table ➤ Table Properties ➤ Column, or right-click the table and choose Table Properties ➤ Column, to display the Column tab in the Table Properties dialog box, shown in Figure 5.16.

3. Choose from the following options in the Size area to adjust the width of the selected column:

   • Check the Preferred Width check box and then adjust the value in the related text box to the width you want for the column.

- In the Measure In drop-down list, choose Inches to specify an exact column width or Percent to have Word automatically adjust the column when other columns are resized.

4. Click either Previous Column or Next Column to select that column, and then choose the property options you want for that column.

5. When you have selected the options you want for each column, click OK in the Table Properties dialog box.

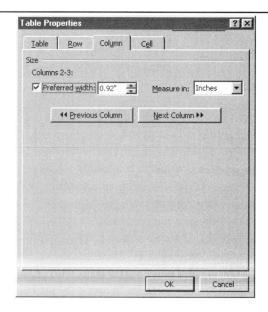

You can also choose specific properties for selected cells, such as the width of a cell, the cell's text alignment, and even the cell's margins. To do so, follow these steps:

1. Select the cell whose properties you want to change.

2. Choose Table ➢ Table Properties ➢ Cell, or right-click the table and choose Table Properties ➢ Cell, to display the Cell tab in the Table Properties dialog box, shown in Figure 5.17.

3. To change the width of the selected cell, use the following options in the Size area when appropriate:

- Check the Preferred Width check box and then adjust the value in the related text box to specify the width of the cell.

- In the Measure In drop-down list, choose Inches to define an exact cell width or Percent to define the width of the cell relative to the width of the table.

4. Choose Top, Center, or Bottom to specify the vertical alignment of the text in the cell.

5. For additional options, click the Options button to display the Cell Options dialog box. Choose any of the following options. Then click OK to return to the Table Properties dialog box.

   Same As The Whole Table Applies the same margins in each cell in the table. Or clear the check box and adjust the appropriate values in the Top, Bottom, Left, and Right text boxes to specify the corresponding margin for the selected cell.

   Wrap Text Automatically wraps text to the next line in the cell when the insertion point reaches the right margin of the cell.

   Fit Text Reduces the text so that it all appears on one line in the cell. The font size is not changed, only its appearance is.

6. Click OK in the Table Properties dialog box.

PART

II

CREATING QUALITY TEXT
DOCUMENTS USING WORD

FIGURE 5.17

Use the options on the Cell tab in the Table Properties dialog box to change the width or alignment assigned to the selected cell.

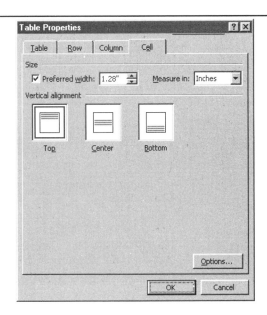

Merging and Splitting Cells

It doesn't take long when working with tables to discover that you don't always want the same number of cells in every row or column. You might want to put a title in a single cell that spans the top of the table or you might be creating a form and want fewer columns for the totals. When you want to make one cell from two or more cells, you *merge* the cells. When you want to separate a single cell into multiple cells, you *split* the cell.

Use any of the following methods to merge selected cells:

- Select the cells you want to merge and choose Table ➤ Merge Cells.

- Right-click the table and choose Merge Cells in the shortcut menu.

- Click the Merge Cells button on the Tables And Borders toolbar.

- If you prefer the visual approach, you can use the Eraser on the Tables And Borders toolbar to erase the border between cells you want to merge. Just click the Eraser button, and then click on the border you want to remove.

Follow these steps to split a selected cell:

1. Choose Table ➤ Split Cells, right-click the table, and choose Split Cells, or click the Split Cells button on the Tables And Borders toolbar to display the Split Cells dialog box shown in Figure 5.18.

2. Adjust the value in the Number Of Columns text box to specify the number of columns to split the cell into.

3. Adjust the value in the Number Of Rows text box to specify the number of rows to split the cell into.

4. Check the Merge Cells Before Split box if you want to merge more than one selected cell before you perform the split. This check box is not available if only one cell is selected.

5. Click OK to split the cells.

The Split Cells dialog box contains options that allow you to specify how you want to split selected cells.

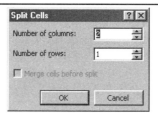

You can also click the Draw Table button on the Tables And Borders toolbar and then use the pencil to draw cell borders where you want to split cells.

The ability to define exactly how you want the cells, rows, and columns to appear in a table makes working in tables both useful and practical. You can, for example, create a table for use as an order form for your company, such as the one shown in Figure 5.19.

FIGURE 5.19

You can create a sample order form using Word's table and text formatting features.

ORDER FORM			
Item	Price	Quantity	Total
		Total	
		Sales Tax	
		Grand Total	

The Order Form table was created by inserting a table with four columns and ten rows, merging some cells, leaving the default borders, and changing the formatting applied to text in the cells. Then, the widths of the four columns were adjusted, and the alignment of the text entered in the cells was changed. You can use any combination of these procedures to create a table to your own specifications.

Formatting Tables

Before you print your table, you might want to put some finishing touches on it to give it that polished, professional look. Word offers both automatic and manual table-formatting options to add and remove borders, change border types, and add colors and shading. Word also lets you specify some properties for your tables.

Using AutoFormat

Word's Table AutoFormat feature provides you with a variety of formats that you can apply in one easy step. Table AutoFormat applies borders, shading, fonts, and colors based on the format selection you make. In addition, you can choose AutoFit to have Word resize the table to fit its contents. Most of the formats include special formatting for the header row, last row, and first and last columns since these often contain titles or summary information.

Follow these steps to have Word automatically format your table:

1. Click anywhere in your table and choose Table ➤ Table AutoFormat, or click the AutoFormat button on the Tables And Borders toolbar, to open the Table Auto-Format dialog box shown in Figure 5.20.

2. Select a Category of table styles to choose from.

3. Choose the name of the format to apply to the table in the Table Styles list box. A sample of the selected format appears in the Preview area.

4. If you wish to apply special formats to an area of your table, enable the Heading Rows, First Column, Last Row, and/or Last Column check boxes in the Apply Special Formats To area.

NEW

5. To adjust Borders, Shading, Font, Color, Fill and other table formats, click the Modify button to open the Modify Style dialog box. Make the formatting changes you want (be sure to apply the formatting to the appropriate portion of the table). Click OK when you're through.

NOTE Chapter 8, "Simplifying with Styles, Outlines, and Templates," has detailed information about creating, modifying, and saving styles.

---

6. When the table in the Preview area looks the way you want your table to appear, click OK in the Table AutoFormat dialog box.

FIGURE 5.20

Display the Table AutoFormat dialog box when you want Word to apply a saved set of formatting to your table.

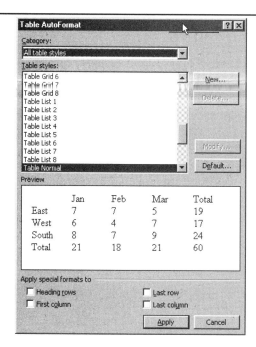

If you're not satisfied with the table's appearance, click the Undo button on the Standard toolbar, or open the Table AutoFormat dialog box again, and select a different format.

 NOTE It's always a good idea to save your document before applying any auto-formatting. It's better to be safe than sorry.

Adding Your Own Borders and Shading

You don't have to settle for Word's predesigned table AutoFormats. You can adjust the table AutoFormats manually or start from scratch, whichever you prefer. Either way, you'll want to display the Tables And Borders toolbar before you begin formatting your table, so you can use the buttons and drop-down list options on the toolbar to apply formatting to selected cells.

The Line Style, Line Weight, and Border Color buttons allow you to select the formatting you want to apply to the borders of selected cells. All three buttons are dynamic, which means that your most recent choice appears on the button. Border options include the following:

- Click the Line Style drop-down list arrow, and then select the style of the cell's border.

- Click the Line Weight drop-down list arrow, and then select the size of the cell's border.

- Click the Border Color button to display a color menu, and then select the color for the border.

TIP You can use the pencil pointer (Draw Table button) to draw over borders that you want to format. Make sure you draw over the entire length of the border, or the line style, weight, or color will not be applied.

Once you have selected the style, weight, and color for the border, you can then apply the border to selected cells. To do so:

1. Select the cells to which to apply the border you chose.

2. Click the Border drop-down list button on the Tables And Borders toolbar to open a menu containing 13 border choices.

3. Click the type of border you want to apply.

NOTE Inside Border can be applied only to two or more cells. Outside Border affects the border around a single cell or a group of cells; typically, you apply outside borders to the entire table.

You can also change the background color of selected cells. To apply a background color, follow these steps:

1. Click the cell that you want to apply a background color to, or select all the cells to be formatted with the same background color.

2. Click the Shading Color drop-down list button on the Tables And Borders toolbar, and then select the background color in the color palette that appears.

The Shading Color palette contains many different shading colors, including various shades of gray. One word of warning: If you plan to make photocopies of your printed table, be aware that some shades of gray do not copy or fax well.

Borders and shading are not limited to use in tables. You can apply the same skills you just learned to any paragraph of text. Just select one or more paragraphs and click the Borders button or choose Format ➢ Borders And Shading.

 TIP To gain complete control over the borders you want to apply, choose Format ➢ Borders And Shading to display the Borders And Shading dialog box. The options for table and cell borders appear on the Borders tab, and the options for shading cells appear on the Shading tab. On the Borders tab, select the line style, color, and width you want and then click the Preview window to turn desired borders on and off.

Centering Tables Horizontally

If you've adjusted the column widths or if you've moved a table, it may no longer be centered horizontally on the page. Word lets you center the table between the left and right margins so that it appears nicely positioned when you print your document.

To center the table horizontally on the page, follow these steps:

1. Use one of the following methods to select the entire table:

   • Choose Table ➢ Select ➢ Table.

   • Click the Move icon that appears at the top-left corner of the table when you move your mouse pointer over the table.

   • Hold Alt and double-click inside the table.

2. Click the Center button on the Formatting toolbar.

Changing Properties for the Entire Table

Word's Table Properties feature allows you to specify precisely the width and position of a table in your document. You can have regular document text wrap around a narrow table, and you can specify the distance between the table and the text.

To change the properties of a table:

1. Click in any cell in the table whose properties are to be changed.

2. Choose Table ➤ Table Properties ➤ Table to display the Table tab in the Table Properties dialog box, shown in Figure 5.21.

3. To specify an exact width for the table, check the Preferred Width check box in the Size area, and then do the following:

   • Adjust the value in the Preferred Width text box to specify the table's width.

   • In the Measure In drop-down list, choose either Inches, to have the value in the Preferred Width text box appear in inches, or Percent, to change the value to percent. If you choose Inches, the table width will be as wide as the value. If you choose Percent, the table width will be proportioned to the specified percentage in relation to the width of the page between the left and right margins.

4. Choose Left, Center, or Right in the Alignment area to specify the position of the table between the left and right margins.

PART

II

CREATING QUALITY TEXT
DOCUMENTS USING WORD

FIGURE 5.21

Display the Table tab in the Table Properties dialog box to change the size, alignment, or text-wrapping properties of the active table.

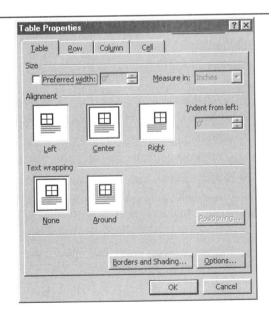

5. Adjust the value in the Indent From Left text box if you want to specify how far the table is to be indented from the left page margin.

6. Choose either of the following options in the Text Wrapping area to specify how you want the regular document text to wrap around the table:

None Places the table above the document text

Around Places the table in the document text

7. If you chose Around in step 6, click the Positioning button to display the Table Positioning dialog box shown in Figure 5.22, and then choose any of the following options:

- In the Horizontal area, the distance from the left edge of the page to the left edge of the table is displayed. Type a different measurement if you prefer, or select Left, Right, Center, Inside, or Outside to specify the horizontal position of the table. Then choose Margin, Page, or Column in the Relative To drop-down list to specify what the Position is related to.

- In the Vertical area, the table's current distance from the previous paragraph appears in the Position drop-down list. Type a different distance or choose Top, Bottom, Center, Inside, or Outside to specify the table's vertical position. Then choose Margin, Page, or Paragraph in the Relative To drop-down list.

- In the Distance From Surrounding Text area, adjust the values in the Top, Bottom, Left, and Right text boxes to specify the distance between the table's borders and surrounding document text.

- Check the Move With Text check box in the Options area so the table can move vertically in the document when you move the paragraphs surrounding it.

- Check the Allow Overlap check box in the Options area to allow the table to be partly covered with text or pictures when you are viewing it in a Web browser.

Click OK in the Table Positioning dialog box when you have finished selecting options.

8. Click the Borders And Shading button to bring up options (previously discussed) for applying borders and shading to the table.

9. Click the Options button to change default cell margins, to add cell *spacing* (blank space between cells), or to turn on the Automatically Resize To Contents feature for the entire table.

10. Click OK in the Table Properties dialog box.

FIGURE 5.22

When document text wraps around the active table, display the Table Positioning dialog box to specify the position of the table in the document text.

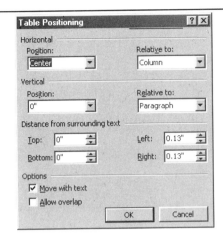

Adding Calculations to Tables

Although Word supports formulas and calculation in tables, we do not recommend using Word for calculation. Unlike Excel formulas, Word table formulas do not automatically recalculate, creating a huge risk of error if numbers in the table are changed.

If you need to use calculations in a table, we suggest you create the table in Excel and paste it into Word. If the data exists in Excel, open the workbook, select the range of cells, and copy them to the Clipboard. In Word, choose Edit ➢ Paste Special to open the Paste Special dialog box. Choose Microsoft Excel Worksheet Object from the list in the dialog box and click OK to embed the selected Excel range in the Word document. When you double-click the Excel object, the Word toolbars are replaced with Excel's toolbars and menus so that you have access to Excel's tools, including automatic recalculation, in Word.

 NOTE You can learn about options related to pasting between applications in Chapter 26, "Breaking the Application Barrier." You embed or link the table from Excel to Word. Either of these options is superior to adding a calculation directly to a table in Word.

Sorting It Out

Organize your data by sorting on any field: last name, zip code, department, or anything else you find useful. Rows can be sorted in *ascending order* (A to Z, or 0 to 9) or *descending order* (Z to A, or 9 to 0).

Click in the column you wish to sort on and click the Sort Ascending or Sort Descending button to rearrange the order of the rows.

NOTE Chapter 9, "Creating Merge Documents in Word," includes an in-depth section on sorting data in tables as well as data in regular paragraphs.

CHAPTER 6

BEYOND TEXT: MAKING THE MOST OF GRAPHICS

FEATURING

- Adding illustrations from Clip Organizer

- Managing your clip collection

- Using the Picture toolbar to enhance images

- Adding graphical lines and bullets

- Inserting other pictures from files

T he old saying "A picture is worth a thousand words" is true—pictures, or graphics, can really enhance your message. Pictures add visual interest to a document and often make it more inviting. In some documents, such as newsletters, graphics have come to be an expected ingredient. Graphics can illustrate a concept, serve as a corporate logo, or simply make your document look better. Graphics can consist of charts, line art, text, clip art, or photos. You can either use existing images stored in a file or create your own graphic objects.

In this chapter, you'll learn how to use Microsoft's Clip Organizer as a central catalog for all your media files, how to insert graphics from a variety of sources into Word documents, and how to make them appear where and how you want them to.

NOTE Throughout the book, we've interspersed information about how to work with graphics within individual applications in the chapters that relate to each application. So to learn what's different about working with images in Publisher, for example, be sure to check out Chapter 42, "Working with Graphic Objects in Publisher," on the companion CD.

Organizing Your Clips with Microsoft Clip Organizer

NEW▶ Microsoft Clip Organizer, shared by all of the Office applications, has been dramatically revised in this version of Office. It contains an even larger selection of clip art, including pictures, sounds, and motion clips. Although you can still browse the clips by category (referred to as *collections*), it is now much easier to search for the clips you want. In addition, it is even simpler to add clips from your own collection or download additional clips directly from Microsoft's online clip gallery, Microsoft Design Gallery Live. Finally, Clip Organizer is a great place to catalog and manage all of the graphics, sound files, and animated graphics files you have stored anywhere on your system.

In Office XP, the task pane offers options for searching or organizing clips. You can quickly access clips online, or look at tips for finding the perfect clip.

NOTE Not all of the clips visible in Clip Organizer are installed in a typical Office installation. When you insert a clip that is not installed, you may be prompted to insert the Office XP CD that contains the clip.

To access clip art, click the Insert Clip Art button on the Drawing toolbar, or choose Insert ➢ Picture ➢ Clip Art to display the task pane with clip art options as shown in Figure 6.1. The first time you do this you are prompted to catalog your media files. You'll have better luck searching for clips if you let Office do this, and it only takes a few minutes.

FIGURE 6.1

The Insert Clip Art task pane allows you to search for and insert clip art from a number of sources.

Searching for the Clip You Want

Microsoft assumes you are probably too busy to spend time going through hundreds of images to find the one you want. So rather than relying on luck to find the perfect graphic, the task pane gives you immediate access to Clip Organizer's built-in Search feature. Search saves time, frustration, and that inevitable feeling of hopelessness that comes from browsing through the vast clip collection. To search for a specific type of clip, follow these steps:

1. Enter a keyword or two in the Search Text box. (See Table 6.1 for tips on what to enter.)

2. Choose which collection(s) you wish to search by selecting from the Search In drop-down list.

3. Choose the type of file you're looking for—clip art, photographs, movies, or sound—in the Results Should Be list.

4. Click the Search button to display clips that meet your criteria. Figure 6.2 shows results of an Office Collections keyword search on **business, computer**.

TABLE 6.1 SEARCH TIPS	
Search For	**Results to Expect**
A particular word: **school**	Clips that are cataloged with *school* as a keyword
Multiple words separated by commas: **school, teacher**	Clips that have one or both of the keywords you typed
Words in quotes: **"school teacher"**	Clips that have *school teacher* as a keyword
Multiple words without quotes or commas: **school teacher**	Clips that have both keywords you typed
Filenames with wildcards: **sc*.jpg**	Media clips with filenames such as `school.jpg` and `scooter.jpg`

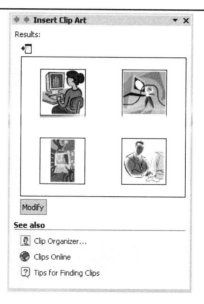

FIGURE 6.2

The task pane displays search results.

Scroll through the search results to find the clip(s) you want to use. To see nine clips at once instead of six, click the Expand icon at the top of the pane. If you wish to search again, click the Modify button to modify search criteria.

When you move the mouse over a clip, a drop-down indicator, called the Clip Options button, appears on its right border. Click it to see a shortcut menu with options for things you can do to that clip.

To insert a clip, click it. (You can also choose Insert from the shortcut menu if you've displayed it.) Once the clip is placed in your document, chances are you will want to adjust its size, position, and text-wrapping properties. See "Inserting Pictures into Documents," later in this chapter.

Finding Similar Clips

When you've found the perfect clip, you can instruct Clip Organizer to find additional clips that share a similar design style with the first one. Click the clip's drop-down menu and choose Find Similar Style. The results may have nothing in common with the content of the original clip, but you can use this feature when you want to incorporate a consistent look throughout your document.

Exploring Your Clip Collection

Using the new Microsoft Clip Organizer's Explorer interface, shown in Figure 6.3, you can now browse your stored clips and reorganize clips using the file management tools you already know, such as cut, copy, and paste and drag-and-drop.

FIGURE 6.3

Microsoft Clip Organizer's Explorer interface lets you preview your clips and use file management tools to organize them into collections.

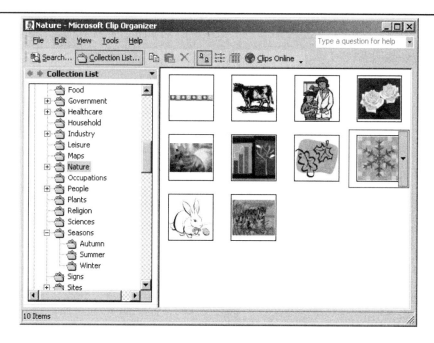

Rather than folders, Clip Organizer displays collections. You can create new collections and move and copy clips into existing collections. Clip Organizer automatically creates three collections in the My Collections folder. These are:

Favorites   Your most frequently used clips, such as your company's logo or other similar clips.

Unclassified Clips   Clips that you have not added to other collections. Included in this collection are clips that Clip Organizer identifies when it reviews your system to look for media clips.

Pictures   Photographs or other clips that you want to classify as Pictures.

In addition, Clip Organizer creates folders of Office Collections and Web Collections. Office Collections holds the media clips that come with Office. Click the Expand button (plus symbol) in front of Office Collections to see the list of included collections.

The Web Collections folder lets you access media clips from Microsoft's online clip gallery, Design Gallery Live. You must be connected to the Internet to access the clips in Web Collections. Expand the folder and then select a collection just like you did in the Office Collections folder. The only difference is that the clips that appear are from an ever-changing collection on the Web.

TIP Microsoft Clip Organizer is a freestanding application you can also launch directly from the Programs menu. Look for a folder called Microsoft Office Tools and launch it from there. You can organize your clips, import clips from other sources, search and browse the clips, and insert clips into applications that are not part of the Office suite.

Browsing the Collections

Some collections have subcollections that you can also access by clicking the Expand button in front of them. You know when a collection contains some clips because thumbnails of the clips appear in the right pane, as shown earlier in Figure 6.3.

 TIP If you'd prefer to see a list of the media files, choose View ➢ List. Choose View ➢ Details to see the Name, Size, Type, Caption, Keywords, Duration, and Date.

In Thumbnails view, you can distinguish sound files by the speaker icon and file name that appear in place of an image. Movie files, or animations, are designated by the yellow star in the bottom-right corner.

j0214098...

 NOTE Animated graphics are only animated when displayed in a Web browser or viewed in a PowerPoint slide show. They do not move when inserted into Word documents unless you preview the page in a browser. Refer to Chapter 29, "Creating Web Pages in Word and Excel," to learn more about using animated graphics.

Organizing the Clips You Find

After you find the perfect clips, you can save future searching time by adding them to the Favorites collection or to another collection of your choice. For either option, point to the clip and click the Clip Options button to open the shortcut menu. Choose Copy To Collection or, if it's a clip that is not part of the original Clip Organizer, choose Move To Collection. This opens the Copy To Collection dialog box shown in Figure 6.4. Choose Favorites or select another collection from the list. After you choose the collection you want, click OK to add the clip to that category and close the dialog box.

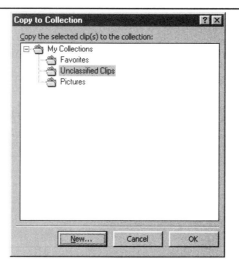

 TIP Press and hold Ctrl to select multiple clips you want to move or copy to a collection. To select contiguous clips, press and hold Shift to select the first and last clip you want to move or copy.

Creating a New Collection

If you would like to create a new collection, open the Copy To Collection dialog box (see previous section) and click the New button, or click any of the collections in the My Collections folder and choose File ➤ New Collection. This opens the New Collection dialog box. Enter the name of the new collection and select the folder you would like it to be a part of. When you click OK, the new collection appears in the list. In this example, we created a Logos collection in the Favorites folder.

PART

II

CREATING QUALITY TEXT
DOCUMENTS USING WORD

 NOTE You can't create a new collection in the Office Collections or Web Collections folders. You must select a folder in My Collections before attempting to create a new collection.

Assigning Keywords to Clips

To make it easier to find clips, clips can be assigned *keywords*, which are used by Clip Organizer's Search tool to locate the clips you are searching for. The media files that come with Office already have keywords assigned. Figure 6.5 shows a piece of clip art and the accompanying keywords that will help you find this clip.

FIGURE 6.5

A variety of keywords makes it easier to find the clips you are looking for.

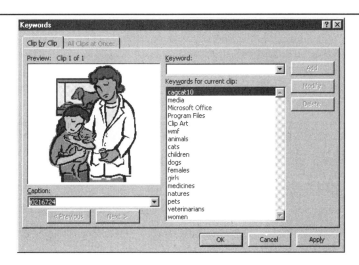

You can add additional keywords and delete existing keywords from any of the clips in My Collections. To add, delete, or modify keywords of individual clips, follow these steps:

1. Point to the clip you want to change.

2. Click the Clip Options button and chose Edit Keywords from the shortcut menu. This opens the Keyword dialog box, such as the one shown in Figure 6.5 above.

3. To edit the keywords of each clip individually, use the Clip By Clip tab.

4. To delete a keyword, select the keyword you want to delete and click the Delete button.

5. To add a keyword, click in the Keyword text box and enter the new keyword or, if it's a keyword you've added previously, select it from the drop-down list. Click the Add button.

6. To modify a keyword, select the keyword, make the editing changes you want to make and click the Modify button.

7. Click the Next button to edit the keywords of the next clip or click OK to apply the changes and close the dialog box.

To add, delete, or modify keywords of a group of clips, select the clips you want to edit: to select multiple clips, hold Ctrl and click each clip; to select multiple contiguous clips, click the first clip and hold Shift while you click the last clip. Then follow steps 2–7 above, selecting the All Clips At Once tab, shown in Figure 6.6, to make your edits.

EXPERT TIP   If you are editing clips in My Collections, you might also want to add a caption to the clip. The caption appears when you point to the thumbnail of the clip in Clip Organizer. If a clip does not have a caption, the list of keywords appears when you point to the thumbnail. To add a caption, right-click the thumbnail and choose Edit Keywords. Enter the caption in the Caption text box of the Clip By Clip tab and click OK. Also remember to edit keywords if you've added clips to Clip Organizer (see "Improving Your Clip Collection" later in this chapter) or have copied clips to a new collection for use in a specific project.

FIGURE 6.6

Use the All Clips At Once tab to add, delete, or modify keywords for multiple clips.

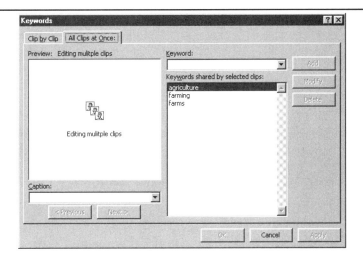

 NOTE You can add and delete keywords from a clip in the Office Collections and Web Collections folders only if you've previously copied the clip to My Collections.

 MASTERING THE OPPORTUNITIES

Organizing Clips According to Your Own Projects

One of the best ways to gain control of your clips is to create your own collections and keywords and organize the clips according to the projects you're working on. Let's say, for example, you produce a monthly newsletter for your department or organization. You can create a collection for the newsletter and copy all the design clips that designate special sections of the newsletter to this collection. To make it even easier, you can add custom keywords and captions to help you quickly find all the clips you need through a keyword search. While you are at it, you may also want to create collections to organize photographs of your company's products, your company logos, and photos of key employees to use as the needs arise. (See "Importing Clips into Clip Organizer" later in this chapter to add your own photos to Clip Organizer.) As you are preparing for the next issue, continue to organize the artwork as you go along. When you are ready to produce the newsletter, all the art you need is right at your fingertips.

Improving Your Clip Collection

The Clip Organizer is not at all limited by the clips that come with Microsoft Office. If you really want to make it useful, add all the photographs, clip art, sound files, and motion clips you have available to you, even if they come with their own cataloging software. Having access to all the clips you need in one place not only makes it more convenient but improves the overall quality of your work by offering you the greatest number of choices. You can add clips you already have in your collection, and you can download clips directly from Microsoft's Design Gallery Live as you need them.

Importing Clips into Clip Organizer

When you import clips into Clip Organizer, you have three options for how you handle the import process. To access any of these options, choose File ➢ Add Clips To Organizer. From here, you can choose:

Automatically Searches your hard drive for graphic, sound, and motion files and adds them to Clip Organizer for you. The clips are added to a collection called Unclassified Clips. Keep in mind that when you choose this option, Clip Organizer may even add clips used by applications and Web sites that you've accessed.

On My Own Adds clips you select to Clip Organizer. Click the Add To button on the Add Clips To Organizer dialog box to specify which collection to add the clips to.

From Scanner Or Camera Imports clips directly from an installed scanner or camera. If the scanner or camera you plan to use does not appear in the Device drop-down list, make sure the device is properly installed and working.

Removing Clips from Clip Organizer

In both the Automatically and On My Own options, Clip Organizer creates a shortcut to the clip files but does not change their file locations. If you delete a clip from Clip Organizer, the file is still available in its original location.

To delete a clip from Clip Organizer, select Delete From Clip Organizer from the Clip Options shortcut menu or click the Delete From Clip Organizer button on Clip Organizer toolbar. This option deletes the clip from all Clip Organizer collections it is in.

To delete a clip from a specific collection, choose Delete From [*Collection Name*] from the Clip Options shortcut menu.

Accessing Shared Clip Organizer Catalogs

If your company's system administrator has created shared Clip Organizer catalogs and made them available on the server, you can add them to your Clip Organizer by choose File ➢ Add Clips To Organizer ➢ On My Own and choosing Shared Catalogs

(*.mgc) from the Files Of Type drop-down list in the Pictures – Add Clips To Catalogs dialog box. Locate the shared catalog and click Add to include the catalog in your Clip Organizer.

 NOTE To access the clips in a shared catalog, you have to be logged on to the network and have access to the file location where they are stored.

Finding New Clips on Microsoft Design Gallery Live

 Microsoft has made sure that you have all the clips you need by posting a special Web site just for Clip Organizer users filled with over 100,000 graphic images and sounds, including clip art, photographs, sound clips, and motion files. The site is updated regularly and always has featured clips based on the season or upcoming holidays.

To access Microsoft Design Gallery Live, click the Clips Online button on the Clip Organizer toolbar or the link from the Insert Clip Art task pane.

In Design Gallery Live, you can browse by category or search for keywords. Searching is the best way to find what you are looking for quickly. To search, follow these steps:

1. Enter a search term in the Search For text box (see Figure 6.7). To get the best results, be descriptive but not too precise. For example, if you wanted clips of women basketball players, search for **basketball players**. **Basketball** would give you balls, nets, and players and **women basketball players** would return no clips.

2. Choose a category from the Search In drop-down list. If you are unsure, choose Everywhere.

3. Choose the type of results you want from the Results Should Be drop-down list: Anything, Clip Art, Photos, Sound, or Motion.

4. Choose the order you want the results to appear in from the Order By drop-down list: Newer, File Size, or Media Type.

PART

II

CREATING QUALITY TEXT
DOCUMENTS USING WORD

FIGURE 6.7

Microsoft Design Gallery Live is a great place to find clip art, photos, sounds, and motion clips.

When you get results, use the page controls in the top-left corner of the page to see additional pages of clips.

18KB

When you find the clips you want, you can download them one at a time or you can collect them all first and then download then all at once. To download them one at a time, click the drive icon with the downward-pointing red arrow at the base of the clip.

EXPERT TIP   If you access Design Gallery Live from a fast Internet connection, you may want to increase the number of clips that Design Gallery Live displays on a page. Click the Options link in the top navigation bar of Design Gallery Live and change the grid size by increasing the number of columns and rows and clicking Update. If you notice too much degradation in speed, go back to Options and choose Restore Defaults.

The clip is immediately downloaded and Clip Organizer opens, showing only the downloaded clip. Right-click the clip to add a caption, recategorize it, and edit the keyword list (the clip comes with keywords already assigned). Close Clip Organizer and reopen to see all the Clip Organizer clips.

NOTE   If Microsoft Clip Organizer is not running when you download the clip, you can find your new clips by clicking the Downloaded Clips category the next time you launch Clip Organizer.

To collect clips to download once you've selected them all, click the check box under the clip. If you want all the visible clips, click the Select All link. As you add clips to the download, you will notice the counter at the top of the page increase. When you are ready to download the files, click the Download *x* Clips link. When you are ready, click Download Now.

Download 2 Clips

EXPERT TIP The Microsoft Clip Organizer maintains a database of the clips, captions, collections, keywords, and other properties. Proper maintenance of this catalog, especially if you have added or deleted clips from the catalog, makes it run faster and with fewer problems. On a routine basis, you can compact the catalog and repair any corrupted data by choosing Tools ➢ Compact from the Clip Organizer menu.

Inserting Pictures into Documents

Finding the perfect clips is more than half the battle. Positioning them in your document so they enhance rather than detract from your message is the rest. Word makes it easy to work with pictures, but knowing a few tricks will give you full control of how your clips appear in your documents.

When you insert a picture into a document, the bottom of the picture is aligned with the text at the location of the insertion point. This default text-wrapping style, In Line With Text, is rather limiting—you can only move the clip as if you were moving a block of text, one character or one line of text at a time.

For more flexibility with how the clip integrates with the text and with how easily it is to move around the document, choose a different text-wrapping option by clicking the Text Wrapping button on the Picture toolbar. You can access these options from the Picture toolbar that opens automatically when you select a picture (for details about all of the tools on the Picture toolbar, see "Modifying Pictures with the Picture Toolbar" later in this chapter).

You can also access text-wrapping options if you right-click the clip and choose Format Picture, or click the Format Picture button on the Picture toolbar, and then click the Layout tab of the Format Picture dialog box, shown in Figure 6.8.

When you change the clip's layout to Square, Tight, Behind Text, or In Front Of Text, you can adjust the horizontal alignment of the clip using the Horizontal Alignment options on the Layout tab of the Format Picture dialog box. Choose Other if you want to reposition the picture by dragging it with your mouse. Click OK to save the new layout changes.

 NOTE Choosing any of the Alignment options does not restrict your ability to reposition a picture.

You can now reposition the picture by dragging it with the four-headed arrow pointer to a different location on the page while retaining the new text-wrapping style you set for the picture.

Resizing Clip Art

When you click a picture (or any object) to select it, eight handles appear around the outside: four at the corners and one on each side. When you point to any one of these handles, the pointer changes to a two-headed resize arrow. Drag any handle to resize the object in the desired direction. Drag one of the corner handles if you want to resize the object while maintaining the object's original proportions.

NOTE   As long as you resize a picture using a corner handle, Word 2002 automatically maintains the picture's original proportions. To turn this feature off, clear the Lock Aspect Ratio check box on the Size tab in the Format Picture dialog box (right-click the picture and choose Format Picture). You can still maintain proportions even with this option turned off by holding Shift while dragging a corner handle.

Gaining Control of Positioning and Wrapping

When you need more precise positioning of your graphics and want better control of how text wraps around the picture, click the Advanced button on the Layout tab of the Format Picture dialog box (right-click a picture and choose Format Picture).

Use the Picture Position tab, shown in Figure 6.9, to set the Horizontal and Vertical position relative to the Alignment (Left, Center, Right) or the Absolute Position. For Horizontal position, you can also choose Book Layout (position of left and right margins on opposite pages).

PART

II

CREATING QUALITY TEXT
DOCUMENTS USING WORD

FIGURE 6.9

The Picture Position tab of the Advanced Layout dialog box lets you control the exact positioning of a picture.

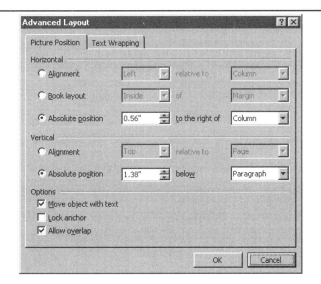

The Picture Position page also gives you these options:

Move Object With Text   Clear this check box to position the picture on the page so it does not move, even if the paragraph it is located in moves.

Lock Anchor Click this check box so you can move a picture while anchoring it to a particular paragraph so that it always stays in the same relative position to that paragraph.

Allow Overlap Click this check box to allow two pictures with the same text wrapping to overlap each other.

If you are not satisfied with how close the text is to the picture, click the Text Wrapping tab of the Advanced Layout dialog box, shown in Figure 6.10, to change the Distance From Text properties to increase or decrease the distance.

The Text Wrapping tab also provides options if you want the text to wrap only on one side of the picture or the other. To indicate this, choose Left Only, Right Only, or Largest Only. To wrap text on the left and right sides of the picture, select Both Sides.

For another option and even more precise control of how text wraps around the picture, choose Edit Wrap Points by clicking the Text Wrapping button on the Picture toolbar and selecting Edit Wrap Points. This adds numerous points in the picture, as you can see in Figure 6.11. Drag any one of the points to push the text away from that part of the picture.

FIGURE 6.10

Use the Text Wrapping tab in the Advanced Layout dialog box to change how text wraps around a picture.

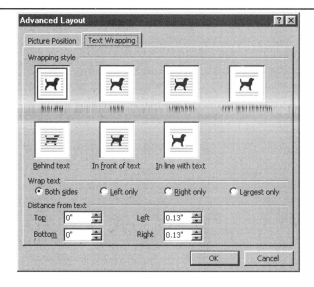

PART

II

CREATING QUALITY TEXT
DOCUMENTS USING WORD

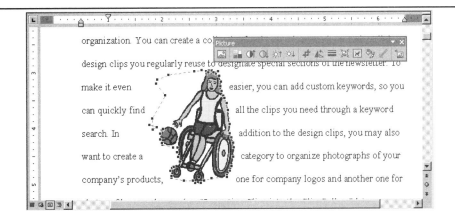

FIGURE 6.11

To change how closely text wraps around a picture, you can drag individual points to move the text further away.

 NOTE Many of the settings you learned about in this section in relation to pictures, such as the options on the Picture toolbar and the Format Picture dialog box, can be applied to any object you insert into a Word document regardless of the source application—Excel charts, Microsoft Draw objects, WordArt objects, and so on. If the Picture toolbar does not appear automatically when you select an object, right-click any visible toolbar and choose Picture to activate it. For more about inserting and working with other objects in Word documents and the other Office applications, refer to Chapter 7, "Getting Creative with the Office XP Graphics Tools."

Rotating Images

NEW▶ At the top of each picture you insert into a document is a green-filled circle above the center handle. This is the Free Rotate tool and it allows you to rotate the picture in any direction. When you point to the tool, the pointer changes to a circular arrow. When you click the arrow, the pointer changes to four circular arrows. Drag the pointer to rotate the image.

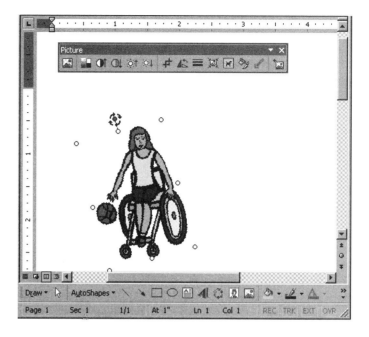

Modifying Pictures with the Picture Toolbar

Although Word does not have the features of photo-editing software such as Microsoft Photo Editor or a third-party photo-editing package such as Adobe Photo-Shop, you still have some basic editing options available to you within Word. When you want to change a picture by adjusting the contrast or brightness, setting the transparency, or cropping it, the Picture toolbar may just have the tools you need. Table 6.2 describes the buttons you can find on the Picture toolbar.

TABLE 6.2   THE PICTURE TOOLBAR BUTTONS

Button	Name	Use
	Insert Picture	Inserts a picture from a file.
	Color	Determines the appearance of the picture: Automatic (applies the most appropriate format, usually the defaults); Grayscale (converts each color to a shade of gray); Black & White (changes each color to black or white, converting the image to line art); or Watermark (changes the picture to a bright, low-contrast format that can be placed behind document text).
	More Contrast	Increases color intensity.
	Less Contrast	Decreases color intensity.
	More Brightness	Adds white to lighten the colors.
	Less Brightness	Adds black to darken the colors.
	Crop	Trims rectangular areas from the image.
	Rotate Left	Rotates the picture 90 degrees to the left with each click.
	Line Style	Formats the border that surrounds the picture.
	Compress Picture	Reduces the size of graphics by changing the resolution of the picture for Web/Screen and Print uses, compressing the picture by applying JPEG compression to high-color pictures (may result in a loss of quality), and deleting cropped areas of a picture.

Continued ▶

PART

II

CREATING QUALITY TEXT
DOCUMENTS USING WORD

TABLE 6.2 (continued)		THE PICTURE TOOLBAR BUTTONS

Button	Name	Use
	Text Wrapping	Determines the way document text wraps around the picture.
	Format Picture/Object	Displays the Picture tab in the Format Object dialog box so you can change the format to exact specifications.
	Set Transparent Color	Used like an eyedropper to make areas of JPEG pictures transparent. Used extensively in Web design.
	Reset Picture	Returns the picture to its original format.

 NOTE The Crop and Set Transparent Color buttons are used with areas of the picture. All other buttons affect the entire picture.

Inserting Pictures from Other Sources

In addition to using Clip Organizer as a source of art, you can insert pictures into your document from any file you can access. You can also format pictures inserted from a file by using the buttons on the Picture toolbar. To insert a picture that isn't in Clip Organizer, follow these steps:

1. Choose Insert ➢ Picture ➢ From File, or display the Picture toolbar and click the Insert Picture button to open the Insert Picture dialog box, shown in Figure 6.12.

2. Select the name of the file that contains the picture.

3. Click the Insert button to insert the selected picture into your document.

FIGURE 6.12

You can insert pictures into your documents from a variety of sources using the Insert Picture dialog box.

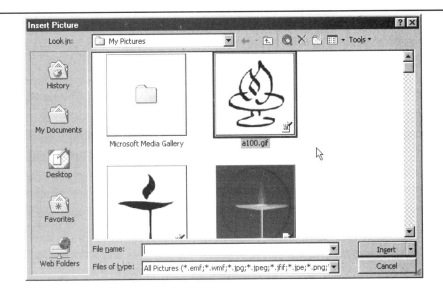

  MASTERING THE OPPORTUNITIES

Adding Graphical Lines, Bullets, and Page Borders

Adding clip art and photographs isn't the only way to add flair to a Word document. Word 2002 has features that allow you to insert graphical lines and bullets in place of the standard lines and bullet characters and to decorate your pages with graphical page borders. These finishing touches make your documents more interesting and more noticeable and after all, isn't that the point?

To insert a graphical line, follow these steps:

1. Position the insertion point where you want the line to appear.
2. Choose Format ➢ Borders And Shading.
3. Click the Horizontal Line button at the bottom of the Borders tab of the Borders And Shading dialog box. This launches the Horizontal Lines dialog box that searches your clip collections.
4. When you have selected a line, click OK to insert it into your document.

You can format the line by right-clicking it and choosing Format Horizontal Line.

Continued

MASTERING THE OPPORTUNITIES CONTINUED

To use graphical bullets in a bulleted list, follow these steps:

1. Select the list you want to bullet or position the insertion point where you want the first bullet to appear.
2. Choose Format ➤ Bullets And Numbering.
3. Select any bullet other than None and click Customize.
4. Click the Picture button to see the Picture bullet dialog box with all the picture bullets from your clip collections.
5. When you have selected a bullet, click OK to insert it into your document.

To add an artsy page border, choose Format ➤ Borders And Shading. Click the Page Borders tab and select a border from the Art drop-down list.

Inserting Scanned Graphics and Digital Photos

With today's digital cameras, scanners, and endless CDs filled with photos and clip art, it's pretty easy to capture just the right images for your documents. It may take a little legwork, but if it's out there, there is a way to turn it into a digital image. Office has built-in tools to accept images directly from scanners and digital cameras.

To import images from a digital camera, scanner, or other TWAIN device, first make sure the device is connected to your computer and the software for the device is installed through Windows. Then, follow these steps:

1. Set up the picture in the scanning device.
2. Choose Insert ➤ Picture ➤ From Scanner Or Camera.
3. Select the device you want use from the Device drop-down list.
4. Choose the resolution you want—Web Quality or Print Quality—depending on how you plan to use the picture.
5. Click Insert, or if you are using a scanner and want to change the image settings, choose Custom Insert. If the Insert button is unavailable because your scanner doesn't support automatic scanning, you must choose Custom Insert.

You can modify, reposition, and resize scanned images and digital photos just like any other images.

CHAPTER 7

GETTING CREATIVE WITH THE OFFICE XP GRAPHICS TOOLS

Graphics tools are available everywhere you look in Office XP. If you have even the smallest creative bone in your body, there is a tool for you. Here are just a few of the imaginative things you can do with the Office XP graphics tools that we'll cover in this chapter:

- Design graphical text
- Design flow charts
- Create conceptual diagrams
- Draw organizational charts
- Add watermarks to Word documents
- Apply graphical bullets and lines
- Create charts

You can add all of these graphic touches to your documents by using a few of Office XP's extra tools such as Microsoft Draw and Microsoft Graph. In this chapter, we'll show you how to make the most of these tools with a special emphasis on AutoShapes, WordArt, and the new Diagram Gallery. So hold on and watch for that creativity to seep out.

Using Microsoft Draw

If you want to design your own graphic objects, Microsoft Draw has a bundle of tools for you to use. You can unleash your creativity or just have fun drawing your own graphics using the drawing tools on Office XP's Drawing toolbar. Drawing is available in Word, Excel, and PowerPoint, and the drawing tools are available in the Access Toolbox. You use the same methods to create a drawing with the drawing tools, no matter which application you are using.

 NOTE You can also create a drawing in Word, Excel, or PowerPoint and paste it into an Access form or report or into another document.

The Drawing toolbar is displayed by default in PowerPoint. To display it in Word or Excel, use either of these methods:

- Click the Drawing button on the Standard toolbar.
- Right-click any toolbar or choose View ➤ Toolbars, and then select Drawing in the toolbar list.

When you display the Drawing toolbar, your Word document automatically changes to Print Layout view if it is not already in that view.

NOTE The Drawing toolbar includes two broad categories of menus and buttons. The first set, beginning with the AutoShapes drop-down list button and ending with the Insert Picture button, is used to create drawing objects. The remaining buttons on either side of this set are used to format existing objects.

Working with the Drawing Canvas

NEW▶

Although the Drawing toolbar is shared by Word, Excel, and PowerPoint, Word 2002 offers an additional, new tool to help you create quality drawings. With the *Drawing Canvas*, you can now create drawings in which multiple objects maintain their position in relation to each other. You can easily adjust the size of the Drawing Canvas to fit any size drawing you create. You can also format the Drawing Canvas itself by adding colors, lines, and fills, changing the size of the drawing area, and adjusting the layout in relation to text on the page. The biggest advantage you'll find using the Drawing Canvas is that you can easily copy and paste your drawing into other documents and other applications. Let's say you need a flow chart to appear in a Word document and a PowerPoint presentation. Create it once using the Drawing Canvas, and you can reuse it over and over again. To activate the Drawing Canvas and the Drawing Canvas toolbar, shown in Figure 7.1, just click any object tool on the Drawing toolbar.

PART

II

CREATING QUALITY TEXT
DOCUMENTS USING WORD

FIGURE 7.1

The Drawing Canvas adjusts to fit any size drawing and keeps drawing objects together.

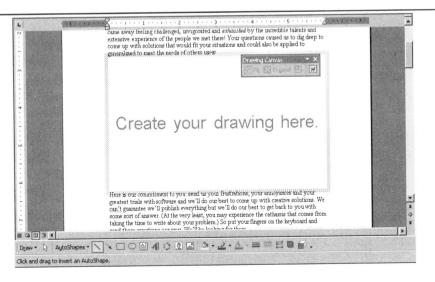

You can add any number of different objects, such as lines, ovals, rectangles, AutoShapes, and WordArt to the Drawing Canvas and then resize and reposition them in the *canvas*, or drawing area. When you move the Drawing Canvas, all of the objects contained within it move together as if they were a single object.

Circumventing the Drawing Canvas

If all you want is a simple line or other single object, using the Drawing Canvas may seem like overkill. To create an object without using the Drawing Canvas, click the object button you want on the Drawing toolbar. When the Drawing Canvas appears in your document, press the Esc key to dispose of it. You can then drag to create the object without the added overhead of the Drawing Canvas.

Resizing the Drawing Canvas

If you decide to use the Drawing Canvas, you have several options for resizing it to fit your drawing. The easiest method is to drag the handles in the corners or at the sides, as shown here:

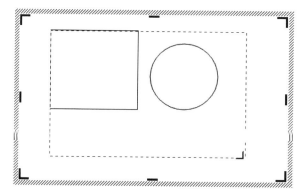

As soon as you add more than one object to the Drawing Canvas, you can click the Fit Drawing To Contents button on the Drawing Canvas toolbar to shrink the canvas to the exact size of the objects it contains—the edges of the canvas touch the edges of the objects. Click the Expand Drawing button if you want to create a larger drawing area. Each click expands the drawing in even increments.

The most precise method of adjusting the size of the Drawing Canvas is to right-click anywhere within its borders and choose Format Drawing Canvas. Click the Size tab and enter the desired height and width in the appropriate text boxes. You can also scale the drawing by entering percentage values in the Scale Height and Width text boxes.

Adding and Deleting Objects

To add an object such as an oval or rectangle to an existing Drawing Canvas, click anywhere in the Drawing Canvas to select it and then click the object button. If you skip this step, Word creates a new Drawing Canvas just for the new object.

To delete an object from the Drawing Canvas, click the object and press Delete.

Keeping Things in Proportion

If you drag the handles of the Drawing Canvas, you'll notice that the height and width of the object stay in proportion. You will also find that when you enter a height on the Size tab of the Format Drawing Canvas dialog box, the width also changes. The relationship between the height and width of an object is called the *aspect ratio*. The Lock Aspect Ratio property is turned on by default so you don't end up with drawings that become hopelessly out of proportion through wanton resizing. If you are feeling frisky and want to have more freedom over the height and width of the Drawing Canvas, clear the Lock Aspect Ratio check box in the Format Drawing dialog box before adjusting its size.

 TIP Office can convert existing Microsoft Draw Server OLE objects into built-in Drawing Canvases. Right-click the Draw object and choose Convert.

Inserting AutoShapes

Whether or not you plan to use the Drawing Canvas in Word, when you click the AutoShapes button in any application, a drop-down menu appears with a list of AutoShape categories. AutoShapes consist of lines; basic shapes such as triangles, cylinders, hearts, and braces; block arrows; flow-chart shapes; and many more. Choose the More AutoShapes option to see the complete list.

The easiest way to insert AutoShapes into your document is to display the AutoShapes toolbar, click the category that contains the shape you want, and then click the shape to select it. Use either of the following methods to display the AutoShapes toolbar:

- Click the AutoShapes button on the Drawing toolbar, point to the top of the toolbar, and drag it to make it float.
- Choose Insert ➤ Picture ➤ AutoShapes.

To insert an AutoShape in your document (other than a Curve, Freeform, or Scribble line, discussed below):

1. Click the AutoShapes drop-down list button on the Drawing toolbar, and then highlight a category to display its menu of AutoShapes. Alternatively, display the AutoShapes toolbar and click the button of the category you want to use.

2. Click an AutoShape, position the insertion point where you want to place the AutoShape, and then click in your document to insert it.

When you click to insert the selected AutoShape, it is created in its default size. If you want to create a custom size, position the insertion point in your document after selecting an AutoShape; notice that the mouse pointer appears as a crosshair. Drag diagonally (from the top left to the bottom right) to insert an AutoShape in a custom size. If you've already inserted the AutoShape, you can drag one of the AutoShape's corner *handles*, the small circles that surround a selected AutoShape, to increase or decrease its size proportionally.

 TIP If you intend to add a lot of AutoShapes in the same category, you can drag the title bar at the top of the menu and place the menu in the document as a floating toolbar. For example, when creating a flow chart, you can drag that menu's title bar so the AutoShapes on it are easily available while you work, as shown in Figure 7.2.

FIGURE 7.2

Drag the AutoShape category menu's title bar to create a floating toolbar, making it easier for you to quickly insert shapes in your document.

Callout AutoShapes are text boxes used for annotating other objects or elements. When you insert a callout in your document, the insertion point automatically appears inside the callout. To place text in any closed AutoShape except those created using the Lines category, right-click the AutoShape and choose Add Text in the shortcut menu. When you do, the insertion point appears in the object, and the Text Box toolbar appears. (See the explanation on using text boxes in the "Adding Line Art Objects" section later in this chapter.)

Curve, *Freeform*, and *Scribble* objects are AutoShape line objects that consist of multiple line segments you create individually. The line segments are extremely small in Curve and Scribble objects; in fact, they are so small that the lines appear to be curved. You can easily see the various line segments in a Freeform object. To create a Curve, Freeform, or Scribble AutoShape, follow these steps:

1. Click the AutoShapes drop-down list button and highlight Lines to display its menu of AutoShapes.

2. In the menu, click Curve, Freeform, or Scribble.

3. Position the mouse pointer where you want to begin the line, and then click to start it. Gradually move your mouse to a different location and click again to form the first segment of the line. Continue until the line appears as you want, and then double-click to form the end of the line.

If your object is a closed Freeform, double-click near the beginning of the line to close it. Alternatively, right-click the selected Freeform, and then choose Close Curve in the shortcut menu that appears.

Creating Flow Charts

Almost anyone involved in business today has been asked at one time or another to create a flow chart. Even if you don't know what all the different shapes mean, a basic flow chart is a great way to analyze the steps of a process. AutoShapes provides all the tools you need to create professional-looking flow charts with minimal effort.

To create a flow chart you need two objects: *shapes* and *lines* to connect the shapes. With AutoShapes, you can create the flow-chart shapes and then use Connectors to connect the shapes. After two shapes are connected, they retain their connection when moved. Figure 7.3 shows a simple flow chart using Connectors.

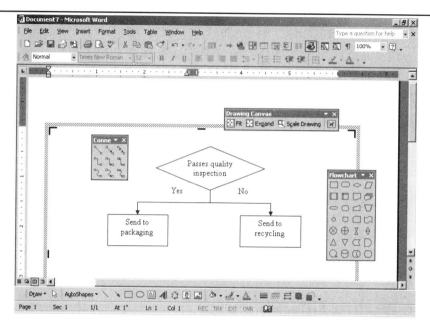

To create a flow chart, follow these steps:

1. Select the first FlowChart shape you want to use from the AutoShapes ➤ Flow-Chart menu. Click in your document or within a Drawing Canvas to create the shape.

2. Right-click and choose Add Text to place the shape in Edit mode so you can enter text into the shape. Resize as necessary.

3. Create a second flow-chart object and position it appropriately.

4. Select a Connector from the Connectors menu on the AutoShapes menu.

5. Move the pointer into the first flow-chart object. Blue handles appear on the sides of the object.

6. Click the handle you want to connect and drag toward the second object. When blue handles appear on the second object, drag the line to connect to the side you want.

7. Repeat steps 1–6 until you have completed your flow chart.

Adding Line Art Objects

Line art objects include AutoShapes, lines, arrows, rectangles, ovals, and text boxes. You can easily insert any of these objects in your document by using the appropriate tool on the Drawing toolbar. To draw a line or arrow, follow these steps:

1. Click the Line button or the Arrow button. (Press the Esc key if you do not want to use the Drawing Canvas in Word.)

2. Move the pointer, which now appears as a crosshair, to the position where you want the line to begin.

3. Hold down the left mouse button and drag to draw the line.

4. Release the button to create the line, and then click the Line or Arrow button to turn off that tool.

When you use the Arrow tool, an arrowhead appears at the end of the line where you released the mouse button.

TIP If you want a line or arrow that is absolutely horizontal or vertical in relation to the page, hold down the Shift key while dragging.

The Line and other object buttons work like the Format Painter button: When you have more than one object to draw, begin by double-clicking its button. The button stays pressed, allowing you to draw more objects, until you click any other drawing object's button. If you don't want to draw any more objects, just click the button that is depressed on the Drawing toolbar to change your mouse pointer back into an I-beam. To draw a rectangle or oval, follow these steps:

1. Click the Rectangle or Oval button.

2. Move the pointer, which now appears as a crosshair, to the top-left corner or edge of the object you want to draw.

3. Hold down the left mouse button and drag down and to the right to draw the object.

4. Release the button to create the rectangle or oval and turn off the Drawing tool.

TIP To create an exact circle or square, hold down Shift while dragging.

Because both the rectangle and oval are closed objects, you can add text in them just as you can in the closed AutoShapes. Right-click the object, and then choose Add Text in the shortcut menu to position the insertion point inside the object and display the Text Box toolbar.

 TIP If you need a series of identical objects, create one object and then paste as many copies of that object as necessary in the locations you want.

Creating and Applying Text Boxes

 Use the Text Box tool to create text that floats on a layer above standard document text. Draw the text box as you would a rectangle. When you release the mouse button, the text box is active—an insertion point appears in it, and a lined border appears around it. You can type the text you want in the active text box.

You can also create a text box around existing text. For example, if you are creating a newsletter, it may be easier to type the text and then change the way it is laid out. Text boxes are particularly useful in documents that contain graphics, because they allow you to move text to any position, including within the margins. To create a text box around existing text:

1. Select the text you want to place in a text box.

2. Click the Text Box button on the Drawing toolbar.

When you create a text box this way, the text box is selected—a shaded border with handles appears around the text box, but the insertion point is not in it. When the text box is selected, you can drag it to a different location on the page. You can also use the handles surrounding the selected text box to change its size. This is important, because text boxes do not automatically conform to the size of their contents—in other words, they don't grow as you add text or shrink when you delete text.

To activate a text box when you want to edit or format the text, just click inside the text box to place the insertion point in it. You can then select the text and apply formatting to it using the options and buttons on the Formatting toolbar and the commands on the Format menu.

To delete a text box, select it and press Delete. When you delete a text box, all the text in it is also deleted.

The Text Box toolbar appears when you draw a text box in your document, as shown in Figure 7.4.

FIGURE 7.4

Use the Text Box tool-
bar to create links
between text boxes.

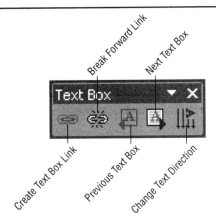

Use the buttons on the toolbar to perform the following actions:

- Activate or select a text box, click the Create Text Box Link button on the Text Box toolbar, and then click an empty text box to link the two text boxes in your document. Any text that does not fit in the first text box automatically flows into the next linked text box. For example, your company newsletter may contain a story that is continued on another page. If you place the beginning of the story in a text box, you can link it to the text box that contains the rest of the story.

- Create and store the text for linked text boxes in a separate file and make any formatting and editing changes there. Then copy the text into the first text box. Text that will not fit is automatically poured into the next linked text box.

- Activate the text box that contains the link (the one that was selected or active when you created the link), and then click the Break Forward Link button to break a link between two text boxes.

- Click the Previous Text Box button or the Next Text Box button to select the previous or next linked text box. This is helpful because you can see where each linked text box falls in line.

- Click the Change Text Direction button to rotate all the text in the active text box. The first time you click the button, the text turns to the right. When you click again, the text turns so that it is facing left. The third time you click the button, the text returns to its normal position. You can use rotated text in a text box to provide visual interest in a document.

PART

II

CREATING QUALITY TEXT
DOCUMENTS USING WORD

You can delete a linked text box without deleting its contents. The contents spill into the other text boxes that the deleted text box was linked to. You may need to resize those text boxes to accommodate the additional text.

Designing WordArt

WordArt is used to create a graphic object out of text. You can use WordArt to create text logos, emphasize titles, and add excitement to a document. For example, you can create a vibrantly colored title page for a proposal or report. To create WordArt:

1. Place the insertion point where you want the graphic and click the Insert Word-Art button on the Drawing toolbar to open the WordArt Gallery dialog box, shown in Figure 7.5. Alternatively, choose Insert ➢ Picture ➢ WordArt to open the WordArt Gallery dialog box.

FIGURE 7.5

You can choose a style for your text graphic in the WordArt Gallery dialog box.

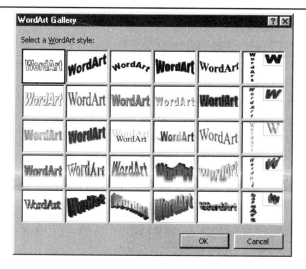

2. Click the style you want for your text graphic in the Select A WordArt Style area.
3. Click OK to display the Edit WordArt Text dialog box, shown in Figure 7.6.
4. Type the text in the Text area of the dialog box.
5. If necessary, apply the following formatting to the text in the Text area:
   - Select a different font in the Font drop-down list.
   - Select a different font size in the Size drop-down list.
   - Click the Bold and/or Italics button to apply that formatting.

6. Click OK to place the WordArt object in your document and open the floating WordArt toolbar.

PART

II

CREATING QUALITY TEXT
DOCUMENTS USING WORD

FIGURE 7.6

Type the text for your WordArt graphic in the Edit WordArt text box.

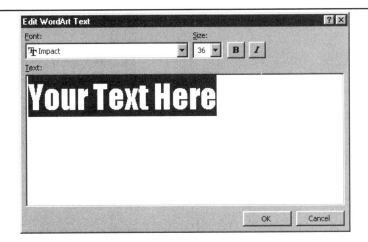

When the WordArt object is placed in your document, it is selected and the small, square sizing handles appear around it. The WordArt toolbar is only displayed when a WordArt object is selected in your document. You can use the buttons on the WordArt toolbar to edit and apply formatting to your WordArt object. The toolbar buttons are described in Table 7.1.

 NOTE To deselect an object, just click anywhere in the document. Deselected objects appear just as they will when the document is printed.

TABLE 7.1   WORDART TOOLBAR BUTTONS

Button	Name	Use
	Insert WordArt	Displays the WordArt Gallery dialog box to create a new WordArt object.
Edit Text..	Edit Text	Displays the Edit WordArt Text dialog box to edit text.

Continued ▶

TABLE 7.1 (continued)   WORDART TOOLBAR BUTTONS

Button	Name	Use
	WordArt Gallery	Opens the WordArt Gallery dialog box to change the WordArt style.
	Format WordArt	Opens the Format WordArt dialog box so you can format colors, size, position, and wrap properties.
	WordArt Shape	Opens a shape menu so you can select the basic shape into which the text will be poured.
	Text Wrapping	Displays a menu so you can select how text wraps around the WordArt object.
	WordArt Same Letter Heights	Makes all letters the same height, irrespective of case.
	WordArt Vertical Text	Changes the WordArt orientation from horizontal to vertical. Click again to reverse.
	WordArt Alignment	Opens an alignment menu with standard options and unique WordArt options.
	WordArt Character Spacing	Opens an adjustment menu so you can change space between characters.

Formatting Objects

Even though you can create some pretty cool shapes with the tools on the Drawing toolbar, they are pretty boring without a little formatting. After you create the objects you want, you can add color, lines, fills, and shadows and even make them 3-D. Most of the formatting tools you need are available on the Drawing toolbar. If you want even more options, right-click any object and choose Format [*Object Type*].

To select a single object, just click the object. To select multiple objects, either hold down Shift while clicking each object or click the Select Objects tool and drag a rectangle around the objects you want to select. Use the following tools to format a selected object:

Fill Color Displays a palette of colors. If you want an object without any color, choose No Fill. You can drag the Fill Color palette onto your screen as a floating menu, which is useful if you want to apply different fill colors to several objects. You can also choose More Fill Colors on the menu to create a custom color and Fill Effect to apply a gradient, texture, pattern, or a picture as the fill for an object.

Line Color Displays the Line Color palette. Choose a color to apply to the lines in and around the selected object. Like the Fill Color palette, the Line Color palette can be dragged onto your document so it becomes a floating menu. You can create a custom color for the line or apply a pattern to it for different effects.

Font Color Displays the Font Color palette. Choose a color for the text in a selected object such as a text box or callout. Drag the Font Color palette to make it a floating menu. You can use it to create custom colors to apply to the text in selected objects.

TIP Click the Fill Color, Line Color, or Font Color button to apply its current color to a selected object.

Line Style Displays a menu that contains various line styles. Click the style you want for the lines in and around a selected object. Alternatively, select More Lines from the menu to open the Format AutoShape dialog box and display the Colors And Lines tab. You can change the line style, color, and weight as well as many other attributes of the selected object.

NOTE The Format Text Box dialog box, which appears when you double-click the border of a text box, contains options similar to those of the Format AutoShape dialog box. Each dialog box allows you to change the fill color, line style, line weight, size, scale, and text wrapping style for a selected object. The Format Text Box dialog box also allows you to change the text box's internal margins and convert it to a frame. If the text box is a callout, you can also change the style of the callout.

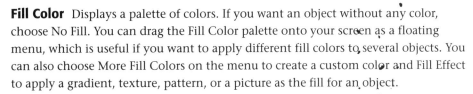

PART

II

CREATING QUALITY TEXT
DOCUMENTS USING WORD

Dash Style Displays a menu of dashed line styles. Click one of the styles to apply that style to all of the lines in the selected object. You can change the weight of the line by selecting it in the Line Style menu. To change the lines back to a solid line, select that style in the Dash Style menu.

Arrow Style Displays a menu of arrow styles. Select the style to apply to the ends of the selected line. You can choose an arrowhead or one of various other line termina-tors. If the combination of line endings you want isn't in the menu, choose More Arrows to display the Format AutoShape dialog box, set a beginning and ending style for the line, and then click OK. Arrow styles can be applied only to lines, arrows, and open AutoShapes.

The Draw menu, which appears when you click the Draw button on the Drawing toolbar, also contains some commands that allow you to change the appearance of a selected object. These commands include the following:

Text Wrapping Lets you select how you want the regular document text to appear in relation to the selected object.

Edit Points Changes the appearance of a Curve, Freeform, or Scribble AutoShape. When you use this command, each position in which you clicked your mouse while drawing the AutoShape appears with a small, black move handle. Drag the handle to change its position, thereby changing the appearance of the AutoShape.

Change AutoShape Replaces the current AutoShape with a different one. When you do, the AutoShapes menu appears. Choose the category that contains the AutoShape, and then choose the replacement. Any text in the AutoShape remains in the new shape.

NOTE You cannot use the Change AutoShape command to change the shape of a Line AutoShape. Instead, you must use the Edit Points command and drag the endpoints to dif-ferent positions. Alternatively, you can delete a Line AutoShape and insert an AutoShape in a different category.

Set AutoShape Defaults Inserts subsequent AutoShapes of the kind selected with the same formatting applied. Every new AutoShape of that type will appear in the same size, color, and so on, until you specify a different default.

Special Shadow and 3-D Effects

Shadow and 3-D effects are designed to give a selected drawing object more depth. You cannot apply both shadow and 3-D formatting to an object. If you apply a 3-D effect to a shadowed object, the shadow is removed. If you apply a shadow to an object that has 3-D formatting, the 3-D effect is removed. Any drawing object can have either a shadow or a 3-D effect applied to it.

Click the Shadow button to display a menu of various shadow styles, and then click the style you want for the selected object. To change the format of the shadow, click the Shadow button again, and then choose Shadow Settings to display the Shadow Settings toolbar. The toolbar buttons and their uses are described in Table 7.2.

TABLE 7.2   THE SHADOW SETTINGS TOOLBAR BUTTONS

Button	Name	Use
	Shadow On/Off	Displays or removes the object's shadow
	Nudge Shadow Up	Pushes the shadow up
	Nudge Shadow Down	Pushes the shadow down
	Nudge Shadow Left	Pushes the shadow to the left
	Nudge Shadow Right	Pushes the shadow to the right
	Shadow Color	Displays a palette so you can select the color for the shadow

PART

II

CREATING QUALITY TEXT DOCUMENTS USING WORD

To choose the 3-D effect to apply to a selected object, click the 3-D button on the Drawing toolbar, and then click the option you want in the menu that appears. To change the formatting applied to the 3-D effect, click the 3-D button again, and then choose 3-D Settings to display the 3-D Settings toolbar. Table 7.3 shows how to use the buttons on the toolbar to quickly change the format of the 3-D effect.

TABLE 7.3   THE 3-D SETTINGS TOOLBAR BUTTONS

Button	Name	Use
	3-D On/Off	Hides or displays the 3-D effect applied to the object
	Tilt Down	Tilts the 3-D effect toward the object
	Tilt Up	Tilts the 3-D effect away from the object
	Tilt Left	Rotates the 3-D effect to the left
	Tilt Right	Rotates the 3-D effect to the right
	Depth	Allows you to select or specify a different depth for the 3-D effect
	Direction	Allows you to select a direction the 3-D effect points to and to specify whether the direction is Perspective (extends all sides of the effect to a single point) or Parallel (extends all sides of the effect parallel to one another)
	Lighting	Adjusts the position and intensity of the "light" shining on the 3-D effect to present a different appearance
	Surface	Allows you to select the appearance of the composition of the 3-D effect
	3-D Color	Displays a palette so you can select the color for the 3-D effect

Arranging Objects

The Draw menu on the Drawing toolbar includes other options for manipulating objects. For example, you can change the position of a selected object on the page, display a grid to help you position an object precisely, and even group objects in order to move or edit them simultaneously.

Drawing objects are placed in separate layers on top of the text in a document, in the order in which they were created. To move objects from layer to layer:

1. Select the object you want to reposition.

2. Click the Draw button and choose Order to display the Order menu. If necessary, drag the menu by its title bar to display the Order toolbar.

3. Choose one of the following options to change the order of the selected drawing object:

   • Choose Bring To Front to place the selection above (on the top layer of) other graphic objects. Choose Send To Back to place the selection below (on the bottom layer of) other graphic objects.

   • Choose Bring Forward or Send Backward to move the selected object one layer at a time.

   • Choose Send Behind Text to place a selected object behind (below) the text layer of your document. Choose Bring In Front Of Text to place selected objects in front of the text layer.

PART

II

CREATING QUALITY TEXT
DOCUMENTS USING WORD

 TIP Use the Send Behind Text command to create a watermark for a single page. Place the watermark in a header or footer (View ➢ Header And Footer) to have it appear on every page of a document. The graphic does not have to be confined to the header or footer area.

If you're doing detailed work, consider turning on a grid of invisible horizontal and vertical lines to help you precisely align various objects in the drawing. The grid works by automatically pulling each object you draw into alignment with the nearest intersection of gridlines. You can display the gridlines and adjust the distance between them to help you as you draw. To turn on the grid:

1. Click the Draw button on the Drawing toolbar.

2. Choose Grid to display the Drawing Grid dialog box shown in Figure 7.7, choose the appropriate options (described below) to define the specifications for the grid, and then click OK. The options include the following:

Snap Objects To Grid Toggles the grid on and off.

Snap Objects To Other Objects Aligns drawing objects with both the horizontal and vertical edges of other drawing objects when selected.

Horizontal Spacing Specifies the distance between the horizontal gridlines.

Vertical Spacing Specifies the distance between the vertical gridlines.

Horizontal Origin and Vertical Origin Specifies the beginning point for the gridlines, relative to the edges of the page. Alternatively, check the Use Margins box to specify the margins as the beginning point for the gridlines.

Display Gridlines On Screen Toggles the gridlines display on and off. Check the Vertical Every box, and then adjust the value in the Vertical Every and Horizontal Every text boxes to a number greater than zero to display both sets of gridlines.

To save the gridline settings you specified so they become the default, click the Default button and choose Yes in the message box that appears asking if you want to change the default gridline settings. The default gridline settings are stored in the Normal template and are used until you change them again.

FIGURE 7.7

You can set options to display a grid to help you align objects within a drawing.

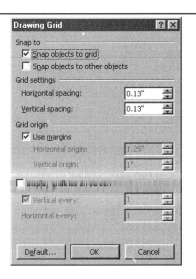

There are several other ways to adjust the positions of selected objects in a drawing. Click the Draw button on the Drawing toolbar and then choose from the following:

Nudge Pushes the selection incrementally Up, Down, Left, or Right

Align Or Distribute Sets alignment options relative to the page, the Drawing Canvas, or other objects

NOTE If one object is selected, click Relative To Page on the Align Or Distribute toolbar to make the alignment buttons available. Relative To Page aligns the selection in relation to the edge of the page. When multiple objects are selected, turn off Relative To Page if you want the objects aligned in relation to each other. Then choose one of the alignment options to specify the alignment you want use.

Rotate Or Flip Changes the orientation or direction of an object

Grouping and Ungrouping Objects

When your drawing is complete, you can group all the drawing objects so that they are treated as a single object. When you group objects, you can select all of the objects by selecting any one object in the group. Any formatting you apply is applied to every object in the group. For example, if you have selected a group of AutoShapes and you choose to apply a shadow, the shadow appears on each object in the group.

You can also use the Nudge, Align Or Distribute, and Rotate Or Flip commands to manipulate the position of the group, or you can simply drag the group to a new location on the page to move every object in the group. To combine several objects into a group:

1. Hold down Shift while you click each object to select it.

2. Click the Draw button on the Drawing toolbar and choose Group.

The handles on the multiple-selected objects are replaced with one set of handles that can be used to size or move the entire object.

If you want to move, resize, format, or delete an individual element in a group, you can ungroup the grouped object, thereby changing the group back into separate objects. Each object can then be edited independently of the group. To ungroup a grouped object:

1. Click the group to select it.

2. Click the Draw button on the Drawing toolbar and choose Ungroup. Alternatively, right-click the group and choose Grouping ➤ Ungroup.

 TIP Clip art images are often composed of a group of objects. To change the appearance of a clip art object, ungroup it and then edit individual objects as necessary. Office may tell you that it first needs to convert the object to a Microsoft Drawing object. Tell it OK, and you can then manipulate the object any way you want.

When you have finished editing, select one of the objects and regroup them so you can move or size the entire image. To regroup an ungrouped set of objects:

1. Select any object that was previously in the group.

2. Click the Draw button on the Drawing toolbar and choose Regroup. Alternatively, right-click the object and choose Grouping ➢ Regroup.

 NOTE   Although objects created in a Drawing Canvas move as if they are grouped, they are independent objects and cannot be resized together without grouping them first.

Constructing Diagrams and Organizational Charts

 Microsoft Org Chart has been available as an add-in application for many versions of Office. For the first time, however, you can create organizational charts as a built-in feature of Office. In addition, you can create other types of diagrams such as Cycle and Venn diagrams.

 To create a diagram, click the Insert Diagram Or Organizational Chart button on the Drawing toolbar. This opens the Diagram Gallery from which you can choose a diagram type. Table 7.4 shows the types of diagrams you can choose and how you can use them.

 TABLE 7.4   TYPES OF DIAGRAMS

Button	Name	Use
	Organizational Chart	Shows organizational relationships between people or departments
	Cycle Diagram	Represents a process that has a continuous cycle
	Radial Diagram	Shows relationships of multiple entities/concepts to a central point
	Pyramid Diagram	Illustrates entities or concepts that are based on a foundation

Continued ▌▶

Button	Name	Use
(Venn icon)	Venn Diagram	Demonstrates entities that overlap
(Target icon)	Target Diagram	Identifies steps toward a central goal

TABLE 7.4 (continued) TYPES OF DIAGRAMS

Creating an Organizational Chart

When you select the Organizational Chart from the Diagram Gallery, Offices creates an organizational chart object with four boxes: one manager and three subordinates, as shown in Figure 7.8. You can add additional boxes, delete boxes, and reposition boxes to fit your specific needs.

PART

II

CREATING QUALITY TEXT
DOCUMENTS USING WORD

FIGURE 7.8

An org chart object gives you a head start on creating your organizational chart.

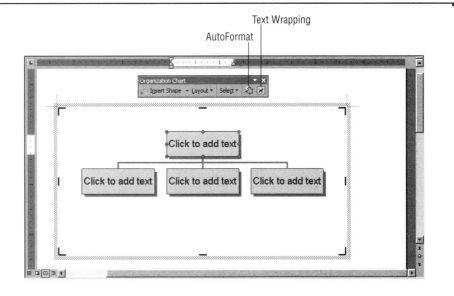

Click in any of the boxes to enter up to two lines of text. To add additional boxes, select the boxes to which the new box is related and choose Insert Shape from the Organizational Chart toolbar. If you click the down arrow to the right of the Insert

Shape button, you can choose to add a subordinate, co-worker, or assistant. To delete a box, click to select it and press Delete.

 NOTE If you work in company that has a nontraditional organizational structure—for example, shared leadership, a partnership, or another less hierarchical structure—you have to be creative to represent your structure with this tool. You cannot position an additional box at the top level. In this case, you might want to use the top level to represent your overall company, board, or maybe even your customers. Another option is to create your organizational chart using AutoShapes and Connectors (see "Inserting AutoShapes" and "Creating Flow Charts" earlier in the chapter).

Changing the Layout of the Org Chart

The Layout button on the Organizational Chart toolbar gives you options to change the layout of your chart from the standard horizontal configuration to one that is more vertical. To change the layout, select the manager shape at the top of the section you want to alter and then select Both Hanging, Left Hanging, and Right Hanging (and, no, we're not talking about chads on Florida's ballots) from the Layout drop-down menu.

You can also change the size of the org chart object by choosing Fit Organizational Chart To Contents, Expand Organizational Chart, or Scale Organizational Chart from the Layout menu. To have Office automatically rearrange and resize the org chart to fit the object frame, choose AutoLayout from the Layout menu.

Selecting Sections of the Org Chart

As charts become more complex, it becomes harder to select individual sections that you want to move or alter in some way. You can use the Select button on the Organizational Chart toolbar to do your selecting for you. Select the first box in a section you want to select and then choose from the following:

Level Selects all the boxes on the same level

Branch Selects all subordinates

All Assistants Selects the assistants in the branch you select

All Connecting Lines Selects the lines connecting with the box you select

Applying Styles from the Style Gallery

To make your org chart stand out, click the AutoFormat button on the Organizational Chart toolbar. This opens the Style Gallery shown in Figure 7.9. From here, you can choose a style for your chart that affects the box shape and style, colors, fills, and lines.

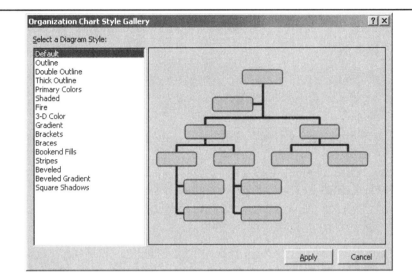

Wrapping Text

After you complete an organizational chart and want to position it within a report or larger document, you may become concerned with how the text wraps around the object. You can change the text wrapping by clicking the Text Wrapping button on the Organizational Chart toolbar.

Creating Conceptual Diagrams

The other five types of diagrams available from the Diagram Gallery when you click the Insert Diagram Or Organizational Chart button on the Drawing toolbar can be used interchangeably to represent a process or related concepts. Select the type of diagram that most closely resembles the message you want to communicate. See Table 7.4 earlier to review the types of diagrams and how they can be used.

The Diagram toolbar, shown in Figure 7.10, is similar to the Organizational Chart toolbar with only a couple of exceptions.

FIGURE 7.10

Use the Diagram tool-bar to add elements and format the diagram.

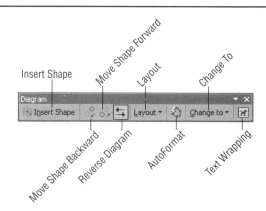

In addition to the Insert Shape, Layout, AutoFormat, and Text Wrapping buttons, you also have the ability to change the level or position of a particular shape using the Move Shape Backward, Move Shape Forward, and Reverse Diagram buttons. You can also use the Change To button to convert a diagram from one type to another—for example, if you created a Pyramid diagram but now feel a Venn diagram would better communicate your message.

Creating Charts with Microsoft Graph

Office XP has two charting tools: Excel and Microsoft Graph. If you don't know anything about creating charts and need to choose a tool to learn, choose Excel (refer to Chapter 15, "Creating Easy-to-Understand Charts"), the full-featured charting tool. Not an Excel user? Need a chart in the next 10 minutes? Then launch Microsoft Graph.

Use Graph to create charts for PowerPoint presentations, Word documents, and other uses. To launch Microsoft Graph, choose Insert ➢ Object from the application menu to open the Object dialog box. Choose Microsoft Graph Chart and click OK.

NOTE In PowerPoint, you can launch Graph by clicking the Insert Chart button on the Standard toolbar or choosing Insert ➢ Chart from PowerPoint's menu. If a slide already contains a chart placeholder or Graph chart, double-clicking the placeholder or chart launches Microsoft Graph for editing.

Graph contains two windows: a datasheet, which includes sample data, and a chart, as shown in Figure 7.11. Replace the labels (text) in the top row and left column with your labels and the values in the remaining cells with your numbers, and you have a basic bar chart. To delete a column or row you don't need, click its header and press Delete. Close the datasheet at any point to place the chart in your document.

PART

II

CREATING QUALITY TEXT
DOCUMENTS USING WORD

FIGURE 7.11

Enter text and values on Microsoft Graph's datasheet page to create a chart.

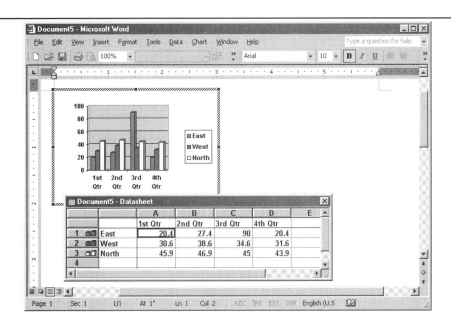

Resize and reposition the chart object as you would any other object. You must select the chart to resize it; a selected chart object has hollow handles. Double-click the chart to open the chart object so you can edit the individual objects inside it; when you can edit the chart, the object handles are solid, and you cannot move the chart object. To select the entire object again for moving or sizing, click outside of the chart to close it, then click once on the chart object.

Using Existing Data in a Chart

If you already have data, don't reenter it—you can import or copy data into Microsoft Graph. Graph can convert data from Excel, text files, SYLK files, Lotus 1-2-3, and CSV (comma-separated) files that can be exported from most spreadsheet and database programs.

To import data from an existing file, start Graph just as you would if you were creating a chart from scratch. Then choose Edit ➢ Import File on the Graph menu to open the Import File dialog box. After you select a file, the Import Data Options dialog box opens so you can select which part of the workbook or worksheet to use. Turn on Overwrite Existing Cells to replace the current data in the Graph datasheet. Turn this option off, and the imported data will be appended at the end of the current data in the datasheet.

Copying or Linking Existing Data

Use Copy-and-Paste or Paste Special to use existing data from Word or Excel to create a chart. Select and copy the data in its source application. In Graph, select the first cell where you want the data to appear. Choose the upper-left cell to overwrite the existing data, or select the left cell in an empty row to append the data. Paste the data, or choose Edit ➤ Paste Link from the Graph menu, to link the chart to the table or worksheet. (With linking, changes you make to the data in the source application will be automatically reflected in the Graph chart.)

If you often work in Excel, you probably create most of your charts there. However, you can choose to create charts from within Word or PowerPoint using Microsoft Graph and have access to most of Excel's formatting features as well.

Formatting a Chart

Graph is an OLE server, which means it creates objects you can use in other applications. While your chart is active or whenever you double-click a chart in a document, the toolbars and menus change from the primary application to Graph's. You have all the features you'll need to create a great-looking representation of your numerical data. Table 7.5 describes the buttons that are unique to the Graph toolbar.

TABLE 7.5   MICROSOFT GRAPH TOOLBAR BUTTONS

Button	Name	Use
	Format [*Object Name*]	Opens the Format [*Chart Object*] dialog box.
	Import File	Imports files for use in Graph.
	View Datasheet	Toggles the datasheet on and off.
	By Row	Displays data series by row. First row of the table provides x-axis labels.
	By Column	Displays data series by column. First column of the table provides y-axis labels.
	Data Table	Toggles between showing and hiding the data table with the chart.
	Chart Type	Allows you to change to another chart type such as 3-D Pie or Area.
	Category Axis Guidelines	Toggles to show or hide major vertical guidelines on chart.
	Value Axis Guidelines	Toggles to show or hide major horizontal guidelines on chart.
	Legend	Toggles to show or hide legend.

With the chart selected, right-click in the Chart Area and choose Chart Options to open the Chart Options dialog box.

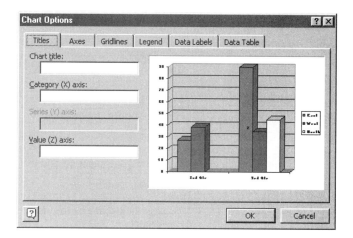

Use the dialog box options to add titles, display minor as well as major gridlines, show and position a legend, display data labels, and include the datasheet as part of the chart object.

Formatting a Chart

To format an individual chart object (for example, the columns, all the data in a row or column, the chart background, or the legend), select the object in the chart, or choose it from the Chart Objects drop-down list on the toolbar. Then double-click the selected object, right-click and choose Format [*Object Name*], or click the Format Object button on the toolbar to open the relevant dialog box. For example, the Format Data Series dialog box is shown in Figure 7.12.

NOTE When you select an entire data series for formatting and then double-click an item in the chart to open the formatting dialog box, the formatting is applied *only* to whichever point in the data series you double-clicked. If you want to apply formatting to the entire data series, select it using any of the methods described above, and then open the Format dialog box using the toolbar button, rather than double-clicking the chart object.

The following tabs give you several options to format individual chart objects:

Patterns Change borders and shading of the selected chart objects.

Shape Change the shape of bars in your graph when formatting a data series.

FIGURE 7.12

The Format Data
Series dialog box
appears when you've
selected a data series
for formatting. Format
dialog boxes for other
objects offer similar
options.

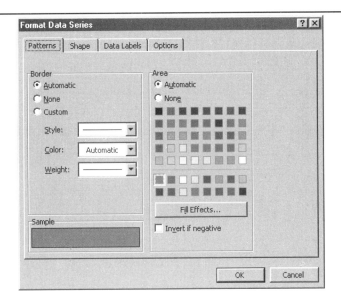

Data Labels Display values or percents on points in a series.

Options Increase the depth of the chart and the space between each category of columns.

When you've made all your choices, click OK.

Whether you choose to create your charts in Microsoft Excel or to use Microsoft Chart, you can create charts that convey exactly what you want to say in a way that many people can easily understand. The key to creating an effective chart is to make sure that you understand what it says—if you can understand it, you will be able to successfully convey your message to others.

SIMPLIFYING WITH STYLES, OUTLINES, AND TEMPLATES

FEATURING

- Creating an outline

- Promoting and demoting headings

- Viewing and printing selected levels

- Modifying an outline

- Getting to know styles

- Creating your own styles

- Redefining styles

- Using templates

- Creating your own templates

Success in the business world today is all about making efficient use of resources, avoiding repetition, and thinking ahead. Word 2002 has a number of features designed with these objectives in mind. Learning to use outlines, styles, and templates may take a bit of practice, but once they become part of your routine, you'll wonder how you lived without them.

Creating an Outline

Outlining lets you make use of Word's built-in heading styles to view the major topics covered in your document—without having to scroll through pages and pages of text. You can collapse and expand heading levels to see more or less of your document at one time, making it easier to ensure you've covered the essential subject matter. You can even print a collapsed outline of your completed document to use as a summary.

Word's Outline feature is particularly helpful for planning long documents such as annual reports, academic documents, and complex sales proposals. With outlining, you can type the points you want to include in a document and then arrange them in a logical sequence. If you decide to rearrange the document, you can move entire sections in one simple operation.

When you create an outline in Word 2002, you create the document's headings and subheadings in Outline view. After you finish the outline, it is often easier to switch to Normal or Print Layout view to enter the body text. You can switch back to Outline view anytime to focus on the document's organization.

To create the first-level headings in a new document, follow these steps:

1. Click the Outline View button to the left of the Horizontal scroll bar, or choose View ➤ Outline to change to Outline view. The Outlining toolbar appears, and the default style is set to Heading 1, as shown in Figure 8.1.

2. To begin the outline, type the text of your first heading and press Enter.

3. Repeat step 2 for each first-level heading you want to enter in your outline.

FIGURE 8.1

The Outlining toolbar appears when you change to Outline view.

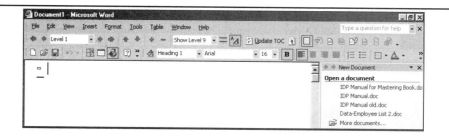

The Heading 1 style does not refer to only the first heading, but to the first *level* of headings, each of which is formatted with the same style (the default style for Heading 1 is Arial 16-point bold). You can have several first-level headings in your document. For example, when you are creating an outline for a document that contains chapters, each chapter can be a first-level heading, formatted in the Heading 1 style. You can choose to enter all your first-level headings and then go back and enter lower-level headings, or you can switch back and forth between levels.

To change an outline heading to a lower-level heading (or *demote* it), press Tab while the insertion point is anywhere in the paragraph. The second-level headings are formatted with the Heading 2 style (Arial 14-point bold italic). Figure 8.2 shows the nine outlining levels Word has available to use. If you want to change to a higher heading level (or *promote* the heading), press Shift+Tab.

FIGURE 8.2

Word contains nine built-in outline levels.

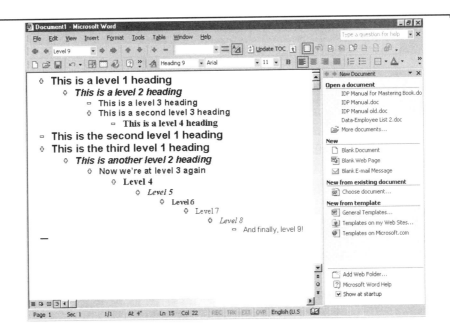

 NOTE An outline created in Word's Outline view is not a traditional multilevel, indented, numbered outline. Even though the levels appear indented in Outline view, all of the heading styles are actually left aligned. Switch to Normal or Print Layout view and see for yourself. To create an indented outline with multilevel numbering, go to Format ➢ Bullets And Numbering and choose the Outline Numbered tab.

Promoting and Demoting Headings

You have already seen that you can press the Tab key to demote or Shift+Tab to promote the paragraph that contains the insertion point while you are in Outline view. Word offers several other ways to promote and demote selected outline headings.

 NOTE The plus (+) outline symbol indicates that the heading contains at least one subheading. The minus (-) outline symbol indicates that the heading has no subheadings.

To promote or demote selected headings, do any of the following:

- Position the mouse pointer over the first outline symbol (plus or minus) beside the selection and drag to the left to promote or to the right to demote that heading and its subheadings.

- Click the Promote or Demote button on the Outlining toolbar.

- To demote headings to body text, click the Demote To Body Text button on the Outlining toolbar. Body text appears with a small square icon as its outline symbol.

- Click the Promote To Heading 1 button to change the selected level to a Heading 1 format.

Although it is not necessary to select an individual paragraph when you want to promote or demote, you will find it useful to select all of the paragraphs when you want to promote or demote multiple headings. Use one of the following methods to select the outline headings.

- To select a single outline heading without its subheadings, move the mouse pointer to the left of the *outline symbol* (the plus or minus symbol) and click.

- To select a single outline heading and its subheadings, click the plus symbol to the left of the main heading.

- To select multiple headings at the same level and any subheadings between them, move the mouse pointer to the left of the outline symbol and drag downward.

You can also hold Shift while clicking the outline symbol in front of each main heading.

MASTERING THE OPPORTUNITIES

Numbering Your Outline Headings

By default, Word's outline headings are not numbered. Instead, the headings rely on indentation and character formatting to show their correlation to each other. Technical publications, contracts, and other documents sometimes need section numbering, and Outline view provides a convenient way to do that accurately. You can also add bullets to headings for visual emphasis. Follow these steps:

1. In a new or existing document, click the Outline View button next to the horizontal scroll bar, or choose View ➤ Outline, to change the document to Outline view.

2. Choose Format ➤ Bullets And Numbering and click the Outline Numbered tab.

3. Choose one of the bulleted or numbered styles for the outline. A preview of each appears on the Outline Numbered tab. You can click the Customize button here to adjust the settings for each level of the numbered outline.

4. Alternatively, choose one of the styles on the List Styles tab of the Bullets And Numbering Dialog box. Then choose Modify to edit the style to suit your needs exactly. Click OK in the Modify Style dialog box to save the formatting changes to the selected style.

5. Click OK in the Bullets And Numbering dialog box to return to the document. A number or bullet in the first-level style you've chosen (for example, I. or 1.) appears automatically.

6. Enter your first heading and press Enter. Word supplies II. and you can enter your next heading.

7. To demote a level, press Tab. To promote a level, press Shift+Tab.

If you revise the outline (and document) by moving headings, Word renumbers them for you.

Viewing and Printing Selected Levels

Whether you have finished a fully developed report or created a simple outline, you may find it useful to focus on a portion of the outline. You can expand and collapse various sections of the outline so you can see and print as much or as little of the outline as you find useful.

To hide, or *collapse*, everything below a given level, choose from the Show Level drop-down list on the Outlining toolbar.

For example, if you choose Show Heading 3, only levels 1, 2, and 3 are displayed. All Headings 4 through 9 and body text are hidden.

There are two ways to tell when some outline headings are collapsed:

• The Show Level field on the Outlining toolbar tells you which levels are displayed.

• A wavy line appears below the lowest heading that is displayed, as shown in Figure 8.3.

FIGURE 8.3

When outline headings are hidden, a wavy line appears below the lowest heading that is displayed.

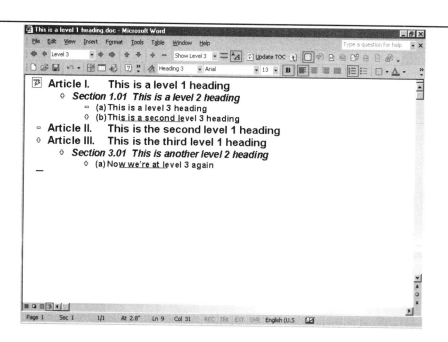

When you are ready to redisplay, or *expand*, all the outline headings, choose Show All Headings from the Show Level list on the Outlining toolbar.

If you want to focus on a particular point, you can collapse all the lower levels and then expand just the subheadings (and any accompanying body text) at the level you want to see. To do so:

1. Collapse the outline by choosing Show Heading 1 from the Show Level list.

2. Move the mouse pointer to the left margin and click to select the heading you want to expand.

3. Perform either of the following as appropriate:

- Click the Expand button to expand one level at a time, or double-click the plus symbol to the left of the heading to expand all levels in the section.
- Click the Collapse button to collapse one level at a time, or double-click the minus symbol to the left of the heading to collapse all levels in the section.

After you've created your outline, you can enter body text in one of the following ways:

- Type the body text as a heading in the outline, and then click the Demote To Body Text button on the Outlining toolbar, or position the insertion point in the outline, click the Demote To Body Text button, and then type.

- Switch to Normal or Print Layout view and enter body text under each heading. Just click to the right of the heading you want to write about, press Enter to begin a new paragraph, and type the text. If you decide you are not satisfied with the outline, you can switch back to Outline view at any time and rearrange it.

After you have entered body text in your outline, you can collapse or expand the outline using the same methods described above to collapse or expand outline headings. To display only the first line of each paragraph of body text in the outline, click the Show First Line Only button on the Outlining toolbar. The remainder of each paragraph is represented by an ellipsis (...) at the end of the line.

Finally, you can toggle the default Show Formatting feature off to display the outline without the formatting applied to the heading styles. This saves quite a bit of space. You still see the headings' indentation, and if you switch to Normal or Print Layout view, all the character and paragraph formatting are visible again. Click the Show Formatting button on the Outlining toolbar to turn this feature off (or back on).

Printing a Word Outline

One of the great things about Outline view is that you can print the entire outline or any portion of it without the corresponding text. Collapse or expand the outline so it shows just what you want to print, and then click the Print button on the Standard toolbar. Although Print Preview shows the entire outline, don't worry about it—only the expanded sections and headings will actually print.

NOTE   Heading styles are directly supported in Outline view. Even if you didn't originally create a document in Outline view, as long as you used heading styles, you can use the outlining features.

Modifying an Outline

Not only can you collapse and expand an outline, you can also select a section of the outline and move it to another location. This is a convenient way to restructure your document. To do so, use either of the following methods while you display the outline in Outline view:

- Click the plus icon in front of the section, or the square icon in front of a paragraph of body text, and drag it toward its new location. As you drag, the mouse pointer changes into a double-headed arrow, and a horizontal line appears, as shown in Figure 8.4. Drop the section when the line is in the correct location.

- Select the level, body text, or outline section to be relocated, and then click the Move Up or Move Down button on the Outlining toolbar. Click as many times as necessary to move the selection to the correct location.

FIGURE 8.4

To change the position of a section of the outline, drag it with the two-headed mouse pointer and drop it when the horizontal line is in the desired position.

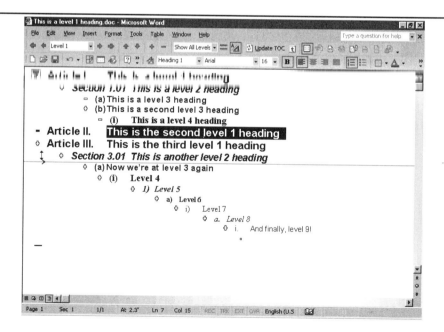

WARNING It's easy to rearrange your document in ways that you didn't anticipate. Save your document before any major restructuring.

Working with Styles

In the first part of this chapter, we showed you how to use heading styles to create a flexible outline for a document. Heading styles are just the tip of the iceberg when it comes to Word 2002's *Styles* feature. Styles can be applied to any kind of text and include fonts, sizes, font attributes, alignment, character spacing, paragraph spacing, bullets and numbering, borders, indenting, and just about any other formatting you can think of. Styles can save you countless hours of reformatting, because once you've applied styles to your text, a simple change in the style changes all the text formatted in that style.

Word has four main types of styles: table, list, character, and paragraph styles. Table and list styles are covered in more detail later in this chapter. *Character styles* define formatting that applies only to text characters, such as fonts and font styles; *paragraph styles* include character formatting but also define formatting that applies to the entire paragraph, such as indents and alignment. When you create a new document, Word makes styles available based on the template you select. In fact, every paragraph in a new document (created when you select Blank Document from the New dialog box or click the New Blank Document button) is created using the Normal paragraph style. Normal paragraph style consists of Times New Roman 10-point type, English language, single line spacing, left paragraph alignment, and widow/orphan control. In Word, you can apply a large number of predesigned styles or create and name your own special styles.

PART

II

CREATING QUALITY TEXT
DOCUMENTS USING WORD

 NOTE A new blank document is based on the Normal template (normal.dot). Word includes a number of other templates in addition to the Normal template. See "Using Templates" later in this chapter for more information about templates and how to use them.

Applying Styles

Body text ▾

When you open a new Word document, you'll find the default list of paragraph and character styles available for your use in the Style drop-down list at the far left of the

Formatting toolbar. To apply one of the default styles, click the drop-down arrow in the Style box and select the style you want to use. You can apply a style prior to entering text or apply it to selected text. If you select an entire paragraph and its paragraph mark, all of the formatting is applied to the paragraph. If you select only text, the character formatting in that style is applied to the selection.

NOTE   To be sure you've selected the hidden paragraph mark, select a single paragraph by triple-clicking or multiple paragraphs by moving the pointer to the left margin and dragging to select the paragraphs with the right-pointing arrow.

NEW▶   Now in Word 2002, styles can be applied from two locations: the Style drop-down list and the task pane. Just click the Styles And Formatting button to open the task pane and display a list of available formatting like the one shown in Figure 8.6.

Whether you're looking at the task pane or the Style drop-down list, each style type is formatted to show its characteristics. If modifications have been made after applying the style, you'll see those too. In the active document shown in Figure 8.5, the Formatting Of Selected Text box indicates the user applied Heading 1 style (Ariel 24-point type) and then centered the selected text.

FIGURE 8.5

The task pane displays the style of selected text and shows available formatting in the active document.

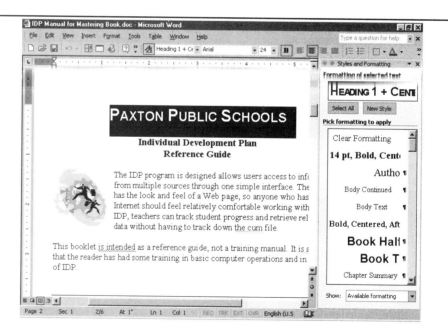

If the styles in the Style drop-down list do not display the characteristics of the style, the option has been turned off. To turn it on, right-click any toolbar and choose Customize. In the Options tab of the Customize dialog box, enable the List Font Names In Their Font check box, and then click Close.

NEW▶

MASTERING TROUBLESHOOTING

Diagnosing a Formatting Problem

When paragraph and character styles are applied to text and then formatting changes are made to some or all of the text, it can become difficult to know what formatting is applied. The task pane makes it easy to see the style of selected text. Turn on the task pane by clicking the Styles And Formatting button, and you'll see the style of the selected text at the top. But you may want more information than styles provide. To get details about the formatting of the style, use Word's Reveal Formatting feature. It lets you review all the paragraph and font formatting applied to any text. To activate Reveal Formatting, open the task pane (View ➢ Task Pane) and choose Reveal Formatting from the task pane selection list. If you prefer, you can choose What's This from the Help menu and then click any character in the document to open the task pane and see Font, Paragraph, and Section formatting.

Font formatting shows font type, style, and size and also language settings. Paragraph formatting shows alignment and indentation settings. Section formatting displays margin, layout, and paper settings.

Click other text in the document to see the formats applied there. You can also compare formatting in different areas of your document by following these steps:

1. Click in one area of your document to reveal its formatting
2. Enable the Compare To Another Selection check box in the task pane.
3. Click in another area of your document to reveal its formatting. Both formats are displayed at the top of the task pane, and formatting differences are displayed as shown here.

Continued

MASTERING TROUBLESHOOTING CONTINUED

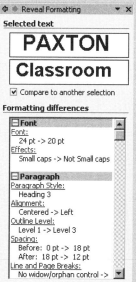

4. You can resolve unintended discrepancies in formatting by clicking the blue underlined text in the task pane to bring up the appropriate dialog box to make necessary changes.

5. Go back to the top of the task pane and click the arrow to the right of the second format. Word provides a drop-down list of actions you can take in your document.

Select All Text With Similar Formatting A handy way to find all instances of a particular type of formatting in a document. Once they're all selected, you can modify the formatting in one place; the changes apply to all the selections.

Apply Formatting Of Original Selection Applies the top format to the currently selected text.

Clear Formatting Removes formatting from the currently selected text.

To close Reveal Formatting, simply close the task pane, or choose to display another set of tools in the task pane.

Using Other Predefined Styles

By default, only the basic styles in your document, along with any new styles you create, appear in the Style drop-down list on the Formatting toolbar and in the task pane. You can control which styles appear in the Style lists for the current document by following these steps:

1. Display the Styles And Formatting task pane.

2. Select one of the following in the Show drop-down list:

Show: Formatting in use

Available Formatting Shows Word's basic built-in paragraph and character styles, any styles you apply or modify, any new styles you create, and a Clear Formatting option

Formatting In Use Displays the styles and other formatting used in the active document as well as a Clear Formatting option

Available Styles Displays all of Word's built-in styles, as well as any new styles you create

All Styles Displays all of Word styles plus any you create or modify

 NOTE When you change the list of displayed styles in the task pane, the Style drop-down list on the Formatting toolbar reflects your choice too.

If you find a style you'd like to use in your document, click it from the list in the task pane or from the Style drop-down list on the Formatting toolbar. The style is applied to any selected text or is activated for new text.

A Style All Your Own

After you start working with styles, it won't be long before you're dissatisfied with the basic selection of paragraph styles and want to create your own. There are several ways to do so.

To quickly create a new paragraph style based on an existing style, follow these steps:

1. Apply formatting to the paragraph until it appears the way you want.

2. Click in the Style drop-down list on the Formatting toolbar to highlight the name of the current style.

3. Type the name of your new style and press Enter.

PART

II

CREATING QUALITY TEXT
DOCUMENTS USING WORD

As an example, look at the newly created paragraph style in Figure 8.6. The characters appear in 26-point Comic Sans MS font. The paragraph is centered and has a shadow border. When you click in the Style drop-down list, type **Enthusiastic**, and press Enter, you've created a new style named Enthusiastic. The new style name appears in the Style drop-down list on the Formatting toolbar.

 NOTE To apply the new style to other text, use the same technique as with built-in styles: select the text and then select the style from the list.

The next new paragraph you type after the paragraph with the newly created style will have the same style applied to it. If you want to apply a different style to it, just select the name of the style in the Style drop-down list on the Formatting toolbar.

NEW▶ You can also create a new character or paragraph style in the task pane. To do so, follow these steps:

1. Click the Styles And Formatting button on the Formatting toolbar to open the task pane.

2. Click New Style to display the Style dialog box shown in Figure 8.7.

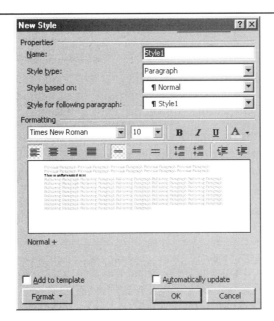

FIGURE 8.7

The New Style dialog box allows you to create new styles for use in the open document or to be saved with the active template.

PART

II

CREATING QUALITY TEXT
DOCUMENTS USING WORD

3. Create the new style by changing the following options in the Properties area:

Name Type a descriptive name for the new style.

Style Type Select either Paragraph, Character, Table, or List.

Style Based On Select the name of an existing style on which to base the new style. Many new paragraph styles are based on the Normal paragraph style, and many character styles are based on the character formatting contained in the Normal paragraph style.

Style For Following Paragraph If you'd like to revert to another style in the paragraph following the new style, select the name of the style. For example, if you apply the Heading 1 style, type a heading, and press Enter, Word automatically switches to the Normal style for the subsequent paragraph.

4. To choose the formatting for the paragraph, use the controls in the dialog box or, for more options, click the Format button (at the bottom) and then choose Font, Paragraph, Tabs, Border, Language, Frame, or Numbering to display the dialog box for that feature. Select any options you want in that dialog box to apply the new format. If you want to apply a style using a shortcut key combination, choose that option from the Format choices.

5. Repeat step 4 until the format you want appears in the Preview and Description areas of the New Style dialog box.

6. Choose either of the following options, if desired:

Add To Template   Stores the new style in the template on which the document is based—for example, Normal. If you do not check this box, the new style is stored only in the active document.

Automatically Update   Redefines the new style with formatting you apply manually to the paragraph in your document. Every paragraph in the document to which this style is applied will also be updated to contain the new formats.

7. Click OK in the New Style dialog box.

 WARNING   Word does not inform you when you make changes to a paragraph style for which you've chosen Automatically Update. Unless you are very confident about the changes you are making, it is safer to keep this option turned off. Because the formatting of every paragraph to which the style is applied will also be changed, the Automatically Update option may give you some unexpected results.

When you no longer need a style you created, you can delete it. When you do, Word automatically applies the Normal paragraph style to all paragraphs in the document to which the deleted style was applied. For example, if you've applied Word's Normal Indent style to a paragraph in a document and then delete the style from the document, Word automatically applies the Normal style to every paragraph that has the Normal Indent style.

 NOTE   You cannot delete any of Word's built-in styles from the Normal template. However, you can delete all but the Normal and Heading styles from the active document and modify styles that can't be deleted. If a style cannot be deleted, the Delete button in the Style dialog box is inactive when the style is selected. If you'd like to modify a built-in style to meet your needs, see the next section.

To delete a style from the current document:

1. Make sure the style is displayed in the task pane list.

2. Click the drop-down list next to the style you'd like to get rid of. Choose Delete.

3. In the message box that appears, choose Yes to confirm that you want to delete the style.

Changing Existing Styles

After you've created and applied a paragraph style, you may decide that you don't like the font or you need some extra spacing between paragraphs. It's in situations like this that styles really shine. You can modify a style, and it will automatically change all the text formatted in that style throughout the entire document.

To quickly change a style:

1. Make sure the style is displayed in the task pane list.

2. Click the drop-down list next to the style you'd like to get rid of. Choose Modify to open the Modify Style dialog box shown in Figure 8.8.

3. Make the desired changes in the following options:

   Name The name of the style is displayed in the Name text box. Type a different name if you want to create a new style.

   Based On Select the name of an existing style on which to base the new style.

   Style For Following Paragraph Select a style to be applied to paragraphs that follow those in the style you are redefining.

4. To choose the formatting for the paragraph, use the controls in the dialog box or, for more options, click the Format button (at the bottom) and then choose Font, Paragraph, Tabs, Border, Language, Frame, or Numbering to display the dialog box for that feature. Select any options you want in that dialog box to apply the new format. If you want to apply a style using a shortcut key combination, choose that option from the Format choices.

5. Repeat step 4 until the format you want appears in the Preview and Description areas of the New Style dialog box.

6. Choose either of the following options, if desired:

   Add To Template Stores the new style in the template on which the document is based—for example, Normal. If you do not check this box, the new style is stored only in the active document.

   Automatically Update Redefines the new style with formatting you apply manually to the paragraph in your document. Every paragraph in the document to which this style is applied will also be updated to contain the new formats.

7. Click OK to close the Modify Style dialog box and apply the new formatting to all text with that style.

PART

II

CREATING QUALITY TEXT
DOCUMENTS USING WORD

FIGURE 8.8

Display the Modify Style dialog box when you want to change the properties of an existing style.

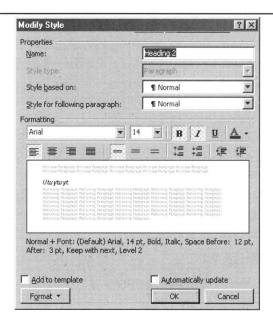

> NOTE   If you modify the Normal style, Word automatically changes other heading styles to match it.

Table and List Styles

NEW▶

When you spend a considerable amount of time developing a custom format for a table or for a bulleted or numbered list, you'll probably want to save it. Word 2002 lets you save table and list styles just as you would with paragraph and character styles. Follow the same basic steps as you would to modify any style. Modify and save list styles from the List Styles tab of the Bullets And Numbering dialog box (Format ➢ Bullets and Numbering). Modify and save table styles from the Table AutoFormat dialog box (Table ➢ Table AutoFormat).

Using Templates

Every document is based on a *template*, a collection of document formatting options, styles, and content that is available when you create a new document. By default, each new, blank document you create is based on the Normal template. You saw earlier in this chapter that when you create or modify a style you would like to have available every time you create a new document, you need only check the Add To Template check box in the New Style or Modify Style dialog box.

 NOTE   The Normal template also includes your AutoText entries, macros, toolbars, custom menu settings, and shortcut keys.

To help make your work easier, Word comes with templates for preformatted documents and template *wizards*, small programs that walk you through a series of steps to customize a preformatted document. Word includes additional templates and wizards for legal pleadings, letters and faxes, memos, publications, reports, and Web pages, as well as several other miscellaneous documents.

 To create a document based on the Normal.dot template, just click the New Blank Document button on Word's Standard toolbar. When you do, a new, blank document appears on your screen.

NEW ▶ Follow these steps to create a document based on a different template or wizard:

1. Choose File ➢ New to display the New Document task pane, shown in Figure 8.9.

2. Click General Templates in the New From Template list to open the Templates dialog box shown in Figure 8.10.

 NOTE   If you choose Templates On My Web Sites, you can browse templates on a Web server or connect to the Internet to browse templates. If you choose Templates On Microsoft.com, you can download templates from Microsoft.

3. Click the appropriate tab in the Templates dialog box to display the tab containing the template and wizard icons for that category.

4. Select the template or wizard icon you want to use to create a new document. (If you've used the Language Pack to install other language tools, you'll see templates in those languages.) A sample of the contents and formatting contained in the selected template appears in the Preview area.

5. Choose Document in the Create New area.

6. Click OK to open the new document.

NOTE   You may have noticed—in the task pane and in the Templates dialog box—the templates that create new Web pages and new e-mail messages. For information about creating Web pages in Word, see Chapter 29, "Creating Web Pages in Word and Excel." For information about creating and addressing e-mail messages, see Chapter 32, "Using Outlook As a Communications Tool."

FIGURE 8.9

The New Document options in the task pane offer various ways for starting a new document or opening existing files.

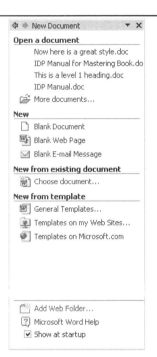

Word's built-in templates usually include placeholders where you can insert your text. They also generally include instructions to help you use the template. Wizards provide you with a series of steps where you enter information, choose settings, and click Finish when you're done. When the wizard or template results are displayed, you can enter additional text or make any other changes to the document. Then you must save it just as you save a document based on the Normal template.

PART

II

CREATING QUALITY TEXT
DOCUMENTS USING WORD

FIGURE 8.10

The Templates dialog box offers numerous choices for preformatted documents.

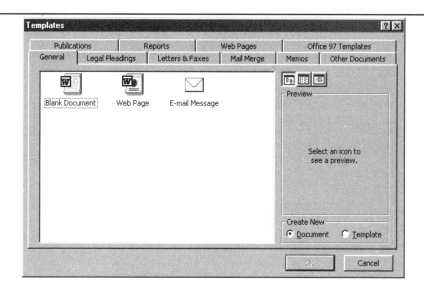

Creating Your Own Templates

Templates allow you to store the layout and formatting for an entire document, along with any necessary styles, AutoText entries, macros, and toolbars, so you don't have to spend time re-creating them the next time you create a similar document. You can either customize Word's templates for your own use or create new templates from scratch.

For example, you can open a document based on the Contemporary Letter template, fill in the information that is the same for all your business letters, such as your company name and return address, your name and job title, and even a logo or other graphic, and then save the document as a customized template. Using custom templates saves you the time and energy required to perform these same actions over and over again. When you want to write another letter, just open a document based on your customized template and fill in the body of the letter.

There are times when you may want to create a template completely from scratch. In that case, you can use the Normal template, which appears as the Blank Document template on the General tab in the New dialog box.

You can edit a template directly or open a document based on the template and then save the document to a template file. When you save a customized template, you must give it a name with the .dot file extension. You'll also need to specify where to store the template file. If you store it in the Templates folder, it appears on the General tab in the New dialog box. You can store it with similar templates by creating a folder with the same name as the sheet tab you want the template to appear on. Save the template to that folder and it appears on the corresponding sheet tab. Alternatively, you can create a new folder in the Templates folder in which to store the template file. When you do, a tab with the name of the new folder appears in the New dialog box.

 WARNING If you edit the template directly and then choose Save, you will overwrite the original template. Instead, choose Save As and assign the template file a different name. This is particularly important when you are basing your new template on the Normal.dot template.

Follow these steps to create a template:

1. Choose File ➤ New to display the New Document task pane shown previously in Figure 8.9.

2. Click General Templates to open the Templates dialog box shown previously in Figure 8.10.

3. To create a template from scratch, select the Blank Document icon on the General tab. To create a template based on any other template, click the tab of the category that contains the template, and then select its icon on the displayed tab.

4. Choose Template in the Create New area, and then click OK. If you choose Document, Word just opens a new document based on the selected template.

5. Enter any text and graphics that you want to appear every time you choose the template. Change formatting and add styles to the template that you want to have available.

6. Choose File ➤ Save As to display the Save As dialog box.

7. In the Save As Type drop-down list, choose Document Template (*.dot). The Templates folder, shown in Figure 8.11, is automatically selected as the storage location for the file in the Save In drop-down list.

8. Choose one of the following options to specify where to store the template file:

   • Leave Templates in the Save In drop-down list to have the new template appear on the General tab in the New dialog box.

   • To have the template appear on a tab other than General in the Templates dialog box, select the name of the folder in the Save As dialog box. If the folder you want does not appear, create a new folder with the exact same name as the tab that appears in the New dialog box. When you save the template to this folder, it appears in the corresponding tab of the New dialog box.

- Create a new folder in the Templates folder in which to store the file. Each subfolder in the Templates folder appears as a page tab in the Templates dialog box.

9. If desired, type a different name for the new template in the File Name text box.

10. Choose Save to save the new template file.

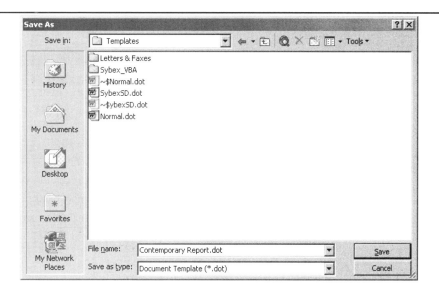

FIGURE 8.11

The Templates folder contains all the templates and template categories that appear in the New dialog box.

Managing Your Templates with Organizer

When you've created your own styles, AutoText entries, toolbars, or macros in a document or template, you can choose to apply them in other documents at any time. When you create a new document, it is based on the normal.dot template. If you wish to apply a different template, do the following:

1. Choose Tools ➢ Templates And Add-Ins to open the Templates And Add-ins dialog box shown in Figure 8.12.

2. Click the Attach button to open the Attach Template dialog box. Locate, select, and open the template you wish to attach.

3. The Attach Template dialog box closes, and the styles, AutoText entries, toolbars, and macros of that template are now available in the current document.

You can use Organizer to copy any styles, AutoText entries, toolbars, or macros in a document or template to another template. You can also rename a style or even delete a style from a template, including the Blank Document (Normal) template.

 WARNING Many documents use the styles stored in the Normal template. If you delete a style in the Normal template, it is deleted from existing documents based on the Normal template.

Take these steps to copy a style you've created in your current document into the Normal template:

1. Choose Tools ➢ Templates And Add-Ins to open the Templates And Add-ins dialog box shown previously in Figure 8.12.

2. Click the Organizer button to open the Organizer window shown in Figure 8.13.

3. On the left side of the Styles tab is a list box displaying the styles in the current document; on the right is a list of styles in the Normal template. Highlight the style (or styles) you want to save in the template and then click the Copy button. The new style appears in the list on the right.

4. Click Close when you have made all the necessary changes.

Use Organizer in a similar manner to copy, delete, or rename AutoText entries, custom toolbars, and macro projects to a different document or template.

TIP You can change the document or template that is named in either list box by choosing Close File below the appropriate list box and then choosing Open File to open a different document or template file. When you do, the styles, AutoText, toolbars, and macros in that file appear in the list box on the corresponding page.

PART

II

CREATING QUALITY TEXT
DOCUMENTS USING WORD

FIGURE 8.13

Use the Organizer to copy styles, AutoText entries, toolbars, and macros from one template to another.

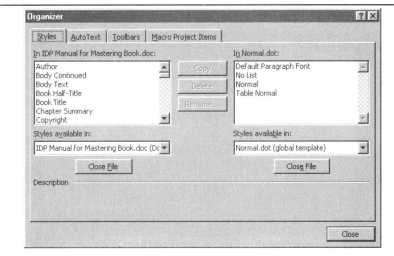

 MASTERING THE OPPORTUNITIES

Saving a Template to a Web Server

NEW Are some templates used frequently by your entire office staff? Now with Office XP and Windows 2000, you can store these commonly used templates on a Web server where users can access them with just a couple of clicks! Here's how:

1. Create or open the template you want to store on the Web server.
2. Click File ➢ Save As to open the Save As dialog box.
3. In the Save As Type list, choose Document Template.
4. Type a name for the template in the File Name box.
5. On the Places bar (at the left), choose My Network Places.

Continued

MASTERING THE OPPORTUNITIES CONTINUED

6. Navigate to the shortcut for the Web server to which you want to save your template. Double-click the server shortcut.

7. Click Save.

Now the template is stored in a place where many people can easily access it. When you're ready to use the template, follow these steps:

1. Click File ➢ New to open the New Document task pane. Click the Templates On My Web Sites link to open My Network Places.

2. Navigate to the Web server on which the template is stored.

3. Locate and select the template.

4. Click Create New and begin working on your new document.

5. Save the document and assign it a new filename so that you don't overwrite the original template.

CHAPTER 9

CREATING MERGE DOCUMENTS IN WORD

FEATURING

- **Understanding mail merge**

- **Creating a main document**

- **Choosing recipients**

- **Using existing data**

- **Creating a new data source**

- **Sorting and filtering the data source**

- **Creating directories and lists**

- **Creating envelopes and labels**

- **Merging documents**

I f Word was only a word processor, it would not enjoy near the popularity it currently does in the marketplace. Word's appeal comes in the strength of its additional features such as its powerful mail merge application. Mail merge allows you to combine data with form letters, labels, and reports to produce customized documents with a fraction of the effort of traditional word processing. And it's even easier in Word 2002!

With mail merge you can input data directly into Word or import data stored in an Excel spreadsheet, an Outlook address book, or an Access database. Word's mail merge feature is one way you can use the Office XP applications to put your data to work in a variety of useful ways.

Understanding Mail Merge

Whether you want to send a form letter to 5 people or 500, you can use Word to personalize each one and to create mailing labels or envelopes. You've heard about mail merge and you may have even used it, but you may never have realized that Word's mail merge feature is much more than a tool to create form letters and mailing labels. Don't let the term *mail merge* limit your thinking—you can use mail merge to create telephone directories, birthday lists, name tags, or any type of list or customized document you can imagine.

A mail merge requires two documents: a *data source* (also called a *recipient list*) in which the individual records are stored and a *main document* that refers to the fields in the data source. These two documents then come together to create the final *merge document, a document that uses the text and layout in the main document and the* data in each record of the data source.

NEW ▶   There are five types of main documents:

Letters   Letters, memos, or reports you want to personalize

E-mail messages   Electronic mail items sent through Outlook

Envelopes   Envelopes fed directly into your printer

Labels   Address labels or any other kind of label, such as name tags, videotape or disk labels, and file folder labels

Directories   Lists of data, such as phone lists, course catalogs, or membership directories

A data source consists of a number of individual *records*. A record contains all the information gathered about the item. For example, a record about a person may contain a name, address, telephone number, and date of birth. Each record is made up of a series of *fields*; a field is the smallest amount of data collected. A record about a person probably contains quite a few fields. The person's name might consist of four fields in the record—SocialTitle, FirstName, MiddleInitial, and LastName. The address might contain a separate field for the StreetAddress, City, State, and PostalCode. Any item you might need to work with individually should have its own field. The ability to store data such as your personal or business contacts, product catalog information, or purchasing records puts extra power in your hands. Using Word, you can access the data stored in any of the following:

- A data source file created using Word

- A file created with other Microsoft Office products such as an Excel database (list), Outlook contacts, or an Access database

- A database file created using any type of software and saved in a supported file format or as a delimited text file

 NOTE Word merge supports dBASE, FoxPro, and HTML data files, as well as any database you can query with Microsoft Query, including Oracle and SQL Server.

Creating or Specifying the Main Document

NEW▶

The Mail Merge Wizard helps you create a main document, create or select a data source, and then produce merged documents. You must create, or at least specify, which document is the main document before you create or select a data source. Your main document can be any document, including a new, blank document.

Follow these steps to create a main document:

1. Open an existing document or create a new document to serve as the main document. You can also create a new main document after you've started the Mail Merge Wizard.

2. Choose Tools ➢ Letters And Mailings ➢ Mail Merge Wizard to display Step 1 of the Mail Merge Wizard, shown in Figure 9.1. (If the task pane is already visible, you can choose Mail Merge from its selection menu.)

3. Choose a document type from the list that appears in Step 1. Then click Next: Starting Document at the bottom of the task pane to move to Step 2.

FIGURE 9.1

Display the Mail Merge Wizard in the task pane when you want to create either a main document or a new Word data source file.

4. Choose a start option:

Use The Current Document Allows you to work with the active document, whether it is a file you have already opened or a blank page you will edit later

Start From A Template Lets you select from the Template's dialog box, introduced in Chapter 8, "Simplifying with Styles, Outlines, and Templates"

Start From Existing Document Allows you to open a previously created Word file

5. After choosing a start option you may, at any time, modify the document by adding text or changing formatting.

6. Although Word doesn't prompt you to do so, if you've spent a fair amount of time on the main document, you should save now.

NOTE When you save a merge document, it's a good idea to indicate the type of document somewhere in the filename. We suggest that you begin main documents with the word *Main* and, when appropriate, the name of the data source it is linked to (*Main–Acknowledgment Letter to Customers*) so that you can identify your main documents easily.

Although this is by no means the end of the mail merge process, this is the biggest part of what you must do to create a main document. The rest involves adding merge codes for the data fields you want to use. Since you must select recipients before you add merge codes, we will discuss recipients next. To learn about merge codes, see "Adding Merge Fields to a Main Document," later in this chapter.

Selecting Recipients

The next step (Step 3 of 6) in the Mail Merge Wizard is to create or select a data source to use with your main document. Your data source can be used over and over again, with more than one main document. For example, if you want to send a form letter to your company's customers, you can use the same data source file for both the main form letter document and the main mailing labels document.

You are given three options for selecting recipients:

- Use an existing list if you've already created a data source in Word, Excel, Access, dBASE, or another ODBC-compliant program.

- Select from Outlook contacts if you're planning to send the document to people in your Outlook contacts list.

- Type a new list if you don't have an existing data file and you're not using Outlook contacts.

Using an Existing Data Source

If you already have data in an Excel worksheet, an Access database, an Outlook address book, or a dBASE, FoxPro, or delimited database, there is no need to re-create that data in Word. A data source file usually consists of a table with a *header row*, the first row in the table that contains the names of the fields for which you will enter data. Each field name is in a separate column in the row. The records, which contain the data, are entered in subsequent rows in the table. For example, each cell in the column that contains the LastName field will contain the last name of an individual.

NEW ▶ Follow these steps to use an existing data source:

1. In Step 3 of the Mail Merge Wizard, choose Use An Existing List.

 2. Click the Browse icon to open the Select Data Source dialog box. By default, the Look In field is set to the My Data Sources folder. Select another folder if appropriate; then select and open the file you'd like to use for this merge.

3. If you're using an Excel workbook or Access database, Word displays the Select Table dialog box (shown in Figure 9.2) so that you can select the sheet, named range, or table that contains the data you need for the merge. If you're using spreadsheet data, be sure to enable or disable First Row Of Data Contains Column Headers as appropriate. Then click OK to display the Mail Merge Recipients dialog box shown in Figure 9.3

4. In the Mail Merge Recipients dialog box, choose the records you want for the merge. Deselect the records you don't want by clearing the check boxes in front of them. You can also sort and filter records by using the column headers in this dialog box. (Sorting and filtering are discussed in greater depth later in this chapter.) Click OK when you're finished selecting recipients.

TIP If you plan to use most of the records, click Select All and clear the check marks from the ones you don't want. If you only plan to use a few of the recipients listed, click Deselect All, and then check the ones you want.

5. Once you've selected recipients, Word closes the dialog box and displays information about the selected recipients in the task pane. If you wish, you can select a different list or edit the existing recipient list. Select either option and repeat the steps above to modify the data source as needed.

This completes the recipient selection part of the mail merge process. Click Next: Write Your Letter to proceed to Step 4 where you insert merge codes and finalize the main document.

FIGURE 9.2

The Select Table dialog box allows users to choose a worksheet, named range, or table as a data source.

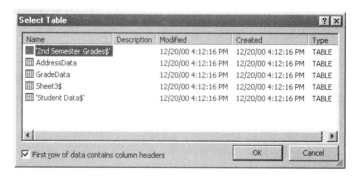

FIGURE 9.3

The Mail Merge Recipients dialog box is used for selecting records from a data source.

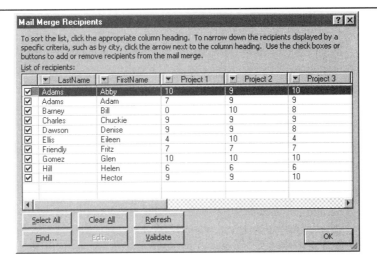

Using an Excel Worksheet As a Data Source

Excel worksheets are also tables, which, as you've seen, can be used to create a data source. An Excel data source is called a *list*. In Excel, each column is described with a label (the field name), and each row contains an individual record.

There are several things to keep in mind when you are using an Excel worksheet as your data source:

- The list cannot contain any blank rows or columns. Excel considers a blank row or column to indicate the end of the list.
- The column labels (field names) must be in the first row of the list. You can add special formatting to the column labels to differentiate them from the data entered in each record.
- Items in the list can be sorted by multiple fields in Word when you're selecting recipients, or in Excel when you're setting up the data.

If you typically use only *some* of the data in the worksheet as the data source, you may find it easier to name a range in Excel, rather than spend extra time selecting recipients in Word. In Excel, select the range of cells that contains the list items, including the column labels in the first row of the list, and then assign it a range name. Make sure you

Continued

CONTINUED

include the column labels as the first row in the named range, because Excel uses the data in the first row as the merge field names. Use one of the following methods to create a range name:

- Select the range of cells and then type the name you want for that range in the Name box at the left of the formula bar.
- Select the range of cells and then choose Insert ➢ Name ➢ Define to display the Define Name dialog box. Type the name in the Names In Workbook text box and then choose Add. Choose OK when you are finished entering range names.

Make sure you resave the file after you name the range. When you're ready to use the named range as a data source, simply follow the same steps you would in any merge. When Word displays the Select Table dialog box, the named range(s) appear in the list along with the sheet tab names. Select the one you want and click OK.

Creating a New Data Source in Word

If you haven't created a data source before you start the Mail Merge Wizard, Word provides the means to do so as part of the process. You can use the default address fields Word provides, or create your own fields.

NEW ▶ Word 2002 has made it possible to use just about any field name you can imagine. However, this newly available freedom in naming fields could have adverse effects if you share a data source with another user who isn't running Word 2002. It's still a good idea to follow these rules, which are absolutes in earlier versions of Word and in other data applications:

- Field names should be less than 40 characters long. Some programs won't recognize larger names, and shorter is better for easy reference.
- Each field name must be unique—no two fields in a data source can have the same name.
- Field names should not contain spaces and should begin with a letter rather than a number. You can use the underline (_) character to separate words, but it is easier to omit spaces and underlines and simply capitalize the first letter of each word in a name, such as StreetAddress or DateOfBirth.
- Stay away from using periods, commas, colons, semicolons, slashes, or backslashes in field names.

This is a good time to think about how you will use your data. If you use only one field, Name, for both first and last names, you can't open a letter with "Dear Joe." By separating names into FirstName and LastName fields, you have more options for how you can use the name in your main document. If you're feeling formal and might want to use "Dear Mr. Smith" as the salutation, you will want to include a Title or Honorific field for Mr., Mrs., Ms., and other social titles.

Addresses should be separated into StreetAddress or Address, City, State (or Province), and ZipCode or PostalCode. Later, you can choose to print labels that are sorted by ZipCode, or print envelopes and letters only for clients in Arkansas.

If you are creating several different data source files, it's helpful to use the same field names in each data source. For example, if you use "FirstName" in one data source, use this field name consistently—don't use "FNAME" or "First" in other source files. When you use the Mail Merge Wizard to create your data source, you can select many commonly used field names from a built-in list to help you keep your field names consistent. If you use the same field names, you'll often be able to use the same main documents with different data source files, rather than creating new main documents.

PART

II

CREATING QUALITY TEXT
DOCUMENTS USING WORD

NOTE When you create a data source as part of the mail merge process, an .mdb file is created, not a Word .doc file as in previous versions.

Creating a recipient list from scratch starts at Step 3 of the wizard. Choose Type A New List.

📋 Create...

Click the Create icon to open the New Address List dialog box shown in Figure 9.4. You'll see the list of commonly used address fields Word provides for you. If these fields are all you need, simply type the data you want in the appropriate field, and press Tab or Enter to move to another field. You don't have to enter data in every field, but if you're not going to use a field, consider deleting it as described below.

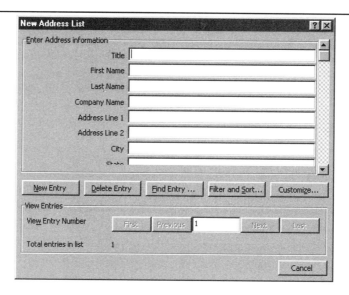

FIGURE 9.4

The New Address List dialog box provides fields to enter data for a new recipient list.

To add, delete, reorder, or rename fields, click the Customize button and Word displays the Customize Address List dialog box shown in Figure 9.5. You can do any of the following:

- Select a field you don't need and click the Delete button to remove it from the data source. Confirm the delete by clicking Yes in the message box, but be aware that if you've previously entered data in that field, you are deleting the data as well as the field.

Change the name of a field by selecting it and clicking the Rename button. Type a new name for the field in the Rename Field dialog box, overwriting its original name.

- Adjust the order of the fields by clicking the Move Up and Move Down buttons. This is particularly helpful if you are typing data from a written page and the fields are in a different order on the page than they are in the New Address List dialog box.

- Add another field by clicking the Add button and typing the name of the field you wish to add in the Add Field dialog box.

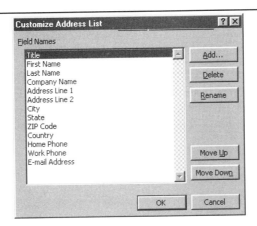

FIGURE 9.5

The Customize Address List dialog box allows you to add, delete, rename, and reorder fields in a recipient list.

When you've adjusted the fields to your satisfaction, click OK to close the Customize Address List dialog box and proceed with entering data in those fields.

It's easy to enter records in your new recipient list using the Data Form in the New Address List dialog box shown previously in Figure 9.4. Although it's possible to open the data source file (once it's saved) and enter the records directly in the data source's table, that is typically more difficult. The advantage to using the Data Form is that it displays only one record at a time. If you open the data source file, all the records are displayed, which can make it difficult to keep track of the field you're entering data for. And you have to know a bit about Access to work with the data directly.

Follow these steps to enter data in the new data source:

1. Type the information for the first field in the text box beside its name and then press Tab or Enter to move the insertion point to the next field's text box.

2. Repeat step 1 until you've entered data for each field in the first record. Then choose New Entry or press Enter to place the current data in the data source and to display the next empty record. Continue entering data.

3. Use the navigation buttons at the bottom of the New Address List dialog box to view the Next, Previous, First, and Last records. You can also type the number of a record and press Enter to display it. If you wish to remove a record, navigate to it and click the Delete Entry button.

NOTE There are options for sorting and filtering data as you create the data source. These features are discussed in the next few sections.

4. When you are finished entering data in the records, click Close to return to the main document. Word prompts you to save the data source.

 TIP When you save a data source file, it's a good idea to name the document so that it is easily identifiable as a data source file. You might want to begin all of your data source file names with *Data*; for example, *Data-Customers*.

Once you have saved the new data source, Word returns you to the main document. The task pane displays the filename and path of the data source you just created. If you wish to make changes to the data in the list, click Edit Recipient List to open the Mail Merge Recipients dialog box discussed earlier and shown previously in Figure 9.3. You also have the option to open another data source if you don't want to use the one you just created.

Editing Records

 Your data source records can be edited within the Mail Merge Recipients dialog box shown previously in Figure 9.3. You can enter new records, edit, delete, search, sort, filter, and validate records. Click Edit Recipient List in the task pane to open the Mail Merge Recipients dialog box.

To add a new record, select any record and click the Edit button. Word displays the data form that you saw previously in the New Address dialog box. Click the New Entry button to navigate to a blank form. Enter the data as you normally would. When you're finished, click Close to return to the Mail Merge Recipients dialog box. The new records appear with the others.

To delete a record, select it and click Edit. Make sure the record you want to delete is displayed in the data form, and then click the Delete Entry button. Click Close to return to Mail Merge Recipients.

To add, remove, reorder, or rename fields in the data source, click Edit to bring up the data form; then click Organize to open the Customize Address List dialog box, shown previously in Figure 9.5.

Sorting Records

By default, the Data Form and Mail Merge Recipients dialog box display records in the order you entered them. Therefore, Word merges them in the order you entered them unless you modify that order by sorting. You can organize your data source by sorting any field that you find useful. For example, you may want to see a list of the names of your customers in alphabetical order by their last names. Records can be sorted in *ascending order* (A to Z or 0 to 9) or in *descending order* (Z to A or 9 to 0).

To sort, open the Mail Merge Recipients dialog box at Step 3 of the Mail Merge Wizard. (Just click Edit Recipient List in the task pane.)

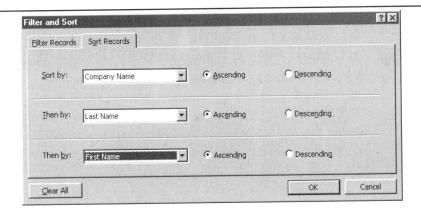

As you already know, Word displays recipients in table format with field names at the top of each column of data. Click any field name for an ascending sort on that field. Click the field name again for a descending sort.

There may be times when your data requires a *multilevel sort*—by last name and then first name, for example, or by company and then by last name. In any multi-level sort, there is, at the very least, a primary sort field and a secondary sort field. Word allows you a *tertiary* (third-level) sort field as well. For example, an elementary school's student list would typically be sorted by grade level (the primary field), last name (the secondary field), and then first name (the tertiary field.) This ensures that Sam Smith the second grader appears in the list before Judy Smith the fourth grader. And Judy appears in the list before Zack Smith, who is also in the fourth grade.

You can't perform multilevel sorts in the Mail Merge Recipients dialog box. Each sort works independently of the next. Instead, click the drop-down arrow on any field name to open a menu of choices. Select Advanced to open the Filter And Sort dialog box, and click the Sort Records tab to display the sorting options shown in Figure 9.6.

FIGURE 9.6

Word allows up to three levels of sorting in a data source.

Select the primary, secondary, and tertiary sort fields from the drop-down arrows, choose whether you want an ascending or descending sort on each field, and click OK. Figure 9.7 shows the Mail Merge Recipients dialog box after sorting by the fields shown in Figure 9.6.

FIGURE 9.7

The Mail Merge Recipients dialog box displays this data sorted by company and then by last and first names.

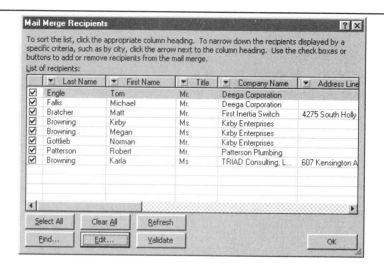

Filtering Records

Often, a data source contains more records than you want to use in a merge. As you know, you can deselect individual records by clearing the check box in front of the record in the Mail Merge Recipients dialog box. You can also *filter*, or separate, records based on criteria that you establish. Click the drop-down arrow on any field in the Mail Merge Recipients dialog box. You'll see a list of unique values for that field and two other typical filtering choices. Choose from the following options:

Unique Values Selects only those records that contain that value. Using the data in Figure 9.6, you might choose to send a sales promotion only to those customers at Kirby Enterprises.

Blanks Selects only those records with no data in the field. For example, you might want to send a memo to employees for whom you have no emergency contact.

Non Blanks Selects records that have data in a field. If you're mail-merging to an e-mail, you certainly want to filter the data for those records with e-mail addresses.

Advanced Establishes filter criteria through a query.

In the database world, a *query* is a tool used to select a group of records that meet specific criteria. To use a query to filter the records before you merge the main document and the data source, follow these steps:

1. In the Mail Merge Recipients dialog box, click the drop-down arrow on any field and choose Advanced. The Filter And Sort dialog box opens as shown in Figure 9.8. Make sure the Filter Records tab is selected.

2. In the Field drop-down list, select the field you want to use to select records.

3. Select one of the comparison operators in the Comparison drop-down list.

4. In the Compare To text box (at the far right of the dialog box), enter the text string you are looking for in the selected field.

5. Choose OK to filter the records with one criterion.

For example, if you wanted to merge records with a zip code of 48439, you would choose the ZipCode field from the Field drop-down list and Equal To from the Comparison drop-down list. Then you would type **48439** in the Compare To text box. Table 9.1 indicates the results from using other Comparison operators when you choose ZipCode as the field and enter a Compare To value of 48439.

FIGURE 9.8

The Filter Records tab of the Filter And Sort dialog box allows you to specify the criteria necessary to merge only the records you want.

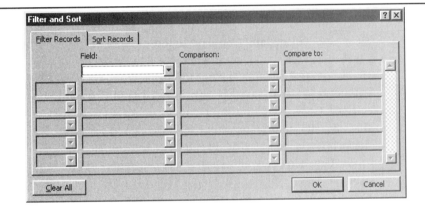

PART

II

CREATING QUALITY TEXT
DOCUMENTS USING WORD

TABLE 9.1   EFFECT OF COMPARISON OPERATORS

Comparison	Selects Records
Equal To (the default)	With the ZipCode value of 48439
Not Equal To	With any ZipCode value that is not 48439
Less Than	With ZipCodes in the range 00000–48438
Greater Than	With ZipCodes in the range 48440–99999
Less Than Or Equal	With ZipCodes 00000–48439
Greater Than Or Equal	With ZipCodes 48439–99999
Is Blank	Where there is no value in the ZipCode field
Is Not Blank	Where any ZipCode value is included

Continued

TABLE 9.1 (continued)	EFFECT OF COMPARISON OPERATORS
Contains	The string "48439" is somewhere in the field
Does Not Contain	The string "48439" is not in the field

Using And and Or

Once you enter a Compare To text string, the word And appears in the drop-down list to the left of the second row of the Filter Records tab in the Filter And Sort dialog box. You can enter multiple query criteria and select, for example, the records for people in California where the data source doesn't list a zip code. The single most confusing thing about writing queries is knowing when to use And and when to use Or.

Choosing And means both comparisons must be true for a match. If you enter the Field, Comparison, and Compare To information in the example given above, choosing And will select all records where the State is California *And* the ZipCode field in the data source is blank. Records for people from Arkansas, Oregon, or Massachusetts will not be selected. Records for people living in California with a zip code will not be selected. Choosing Or means a match will be found if either comparison is true. In this case, all Californians will be selected, as well as anyone from any other state who doesn't have a zip code listed in the data source.

Use Or when you want to select two different possible values for the same field. For example, when you want to send a mailing to all your customers in California and Nevada, you should select records where State is equal to California *Or* State is equal to Nevada. You wouldn't select And, because no single record includes both states.

There is one time you use And when making two comparisons in the same field: when you want to select records within a numeric range. For example, you might want to send an advertisement to all families with annual incomes between $25,000 and $40,000. In this example, you would select Income greater than $25,000 *And* Income less than $40,000. If you used Or, all records would be selected, as every level of income is either less than $40,000 or more than $25,000.

 TIP Here's a general rule for troubleshooting queries: If you expected some records to be selected but none were, you probably used And when you should have used Or. If you got a lot more records than you expected, you probably used Or when you should have used And.

Searching for Records

You may need to find a record in a data source that contains specified text in order to edit the record. To do so, follow these steps:

1. Click the Find button in the Mail Merge Recipients dialog box to open the Find Entry dialog box.

2. Type the text you want to find in the Find text box.

3. Select a Look In option. Search all fields or choose the field where the text is stored in the This Field drop-down list.

4. Click Find Next to have Word highlight the first record in the data source that contains that text in the field. Make any edits as necessary.

5. Click Find Next again have Word highlight the next record that contains the specified text and make any necessary edits.

6. Repeat step 5 as necessary. If Word finds no records that match your search criteria, it displays a message box saying so.

7. Click OK to return to the Mail Merge Recipients dialog box. Choose Close to return to the active document and Mail Merge Wizard.

Validating Recipient Data

NEW▶

Data validation has always been a powerful feature in spreadsheet programs. Excel's data validation tools are some of the best available. And now you've got that power in Word. When you're merging with a very large data source, it's impossible to hand-check every printed document for accuracy. Address validation can help eliminate certain errors ahead of time. For example, all zip codes should have at least 5 digits. If you're using zip+4, the entries in that field would have 10 digits (5 + 4 + 1 for the hyphen.) Data-validation tools can check to make sure that all entries in the zip code field are either 5 digits or 10 and notify you if that's not the case.

Address validation is available in the Mail Merge Recipients dialog box, but you must install third-party address validation software to use this feature. Address validation software, such as FirstLogic's PostalSoft (www.firstlogic.com), facilitates bulk mailing by verifying the accuracy of addresses and zip codes, resulting in faster and less expensive delivery. If you click the Validate button with no validation software installed, Word invites you to visit the Web for information about such programs.

Using Outlook As a Data Source

If you store names, addresses, and other recipient data in Outlook, mail merge is easier than ever! At Step 3 of the Mail Merge Wizard, choose Select From Outlook Contacts, and then click Choose Contacts Folder. Outlook prompts you to select a profile.

Choose the Outlook profile that contains the contact folder you wish to use. (More on Outlook profiles in Chapter 35, "Working behing the Scenes in Outlook.") Once you've chosen a profile, the Select Contact List Folder dialog box appears as shown in Figure 9.9.

Select the appropriate folder and click OK. The Mail Merge Recipients dialog box opens with Outlook contact data displayed. Proceed with selecting, sorting, and filtering as you normally would.

FIGURE 9.9

The Select Contact List Folder dialog box lets you choose an Outlook contacts folder as a mail merge data source.

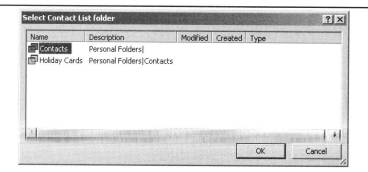

Using a Word Table As a Data Source

With the vast improvements to mail merge, you may find that you never have occasion to create a Word table for use as a data source. However, if you are a mail merge user from way back, chances are some of your existing data sources may be in Word table format. You can use the tools in the Mail Merge Recipients dialog box to manipulate the data in a Word table, just as you would with any data source. However, if you prefer to work with the table directly, you'll want to be familiar with the Database toolbar shown in Figure 9.10. Choose View ➢ Toolbars ➢ Database to display it.

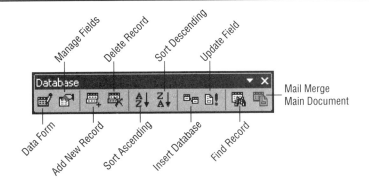

FIGURE 9.10

Word's Database tool-bar lets users work directly with records in a Word table.

 NOTE You can convert any existing Word table to a data source by deleting text that precedes the table in the document, deleting any blank rows in the table itself, and renaming column headers so that they follow field name conventions. Word recognizes a document that meets these requirements as a data source. To use other database options with a table other than a data source, choose View ➢ Toolbars and then select Database to display the Database toolbar.

You can add records to the data source by inserting another row and typing the data for the record. (See Chapter 5, "Designing Pages with Columns and Tables," for more information about working in Word tables.) If you prefer to enter or view records using the Data Form, click the Data Form button.

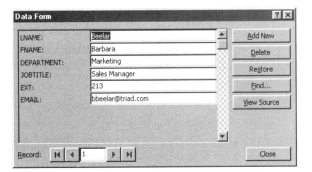

This Data Form is similar to the New Address List dialog box shown previously in Figure 9.4, with options for adding, deleting, and finding records. Edit as desired and click Close to return to the table. You should see your changes immediately.

To add, remove, or rename fields in your data source, click the Manage Fields button on the Database toolbar to open the Manage Fields dialog box.

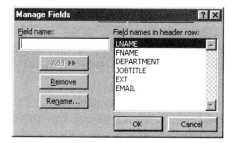

In the Manage Fields dialog box, you can perform any of the following, and then click OK when you're finished.

- To create a new field in the data source, type a name in the Field Name text box and click Add. The new field name appears at the end of the list in the Field Names In Header Row list box, and a new column is created beside the last column in the data source.

- To remove a field from the data source, highlight its name in the Field Names In Header Row list box and click Remove. Click Yes to confirm that you want to remove the field, along with the data stored in it.

 WARNING When you remove a field from the data source, the data in that field is also removed. Be certain that the data is not needed for any other purpose before removing a field.

- To rename a field, highlight its name in the Field Names In Header Row list box, click Rename to display the Rename Field dialog box, type a new name for the field in the New Field Name text box, and then click OK.

The Database toolbar has buttons for adding and deleting records. When you click the Add New Record button, Word inserts a new blank row at the bottom of the table. When you click Delete Record, be sure your insertion point is resting in the row you want to delete.

Sorting the Table

As you know, you can organize your data source by sorting any field that you find useful. The sort options in the Mail Merge Recipients dialog box were discussed previously in this chapter. If you want to directly sort the records in a Word table, you can use the sorting buttons on the Database toolbar. To sort the records in a data source, place the insertion point anywhere in the column you want to sort by, and then do the following:

- Click the Sort Ascending button to sort the records in the data source in ascending order according to the data in that field.

- Click the Sort Descending button on the Database toolbar to sort the records from highest to lowest, or Z-to-A order.

To sort the data source by more than one field—for example, to sort an alphabetized customer list by last name and then by first name—you'll need to use the Sort dialog box. Place the insertion point anywhere in the table you want to sort and choose Table ➢ Sort to display the Sort dialog box, similar to the one shown previously in Figure 9.6.

Follow the steps discussed earlier in this chapter with these two additions:

- In the My List Has area, choose Header Row to indicate that the data is in a table with field names in the first row.

- The Sort dialog box also has an Options button. In sorting a mail-merge data source, you probably won't need to use the Sort Options dialog box, but if you're taking advantage of Office XP's multiple-language features, you might want to select another language whose sorting rules you want to use in the Sorting Language drop-down list.

Click OK in the Sort dialog box to sort the data.

 WARNING It's a good idea to save your document before you sort and to always check your data immediately after a sort to make sure it sorted correctly. If it did not sort correctly, click Undo or close the document without saving and reopen your saved copy.

The Database toolbar also has a Find button. The tool works very similarly to the Find button in the Mail Merge Recipients dialog box.

If you were working on the data source during the process of a mail merge, click the Mail Merge Main Document button on the Database toolbar to return to the main document. You can switch back and forth between the main document and the data source using the buttons on the Taskbar.

PART

II

CREATING QUALITY TEXT
DOCUMENTS USING WORD

MASTERING THE OPPORTUNITIES

Sorting Any Table or List

The Sort dialog box is Word's tool for sorting any kind of table or list, not just mail-merge data sources. You can even sort a series of ordinary text paragraphs by first word. (You could use this technique to create an alphabetized glossary for a training manual, for example.) The procedure is generally the same as described in "Sorting the Table," particularly if you are sorting a table with a header row, but there are a few variations:

- If you're sorting anything other than a table, begin by selecting all the list items or paragraphs before choosing Table ➤ Sort.
- When you're sorting a table, the Sort By drop-down list shows you a list of field names or descriptive text in each cell in the header row of the table. You can indicate up to three sort levels when sorting data in a table or data source. You should also check whether or not your table has a header row.
- If you selected several columns in a document that has multiple columns of text, the Sort By drop-down list contains a list of the columns by number, such as Column 1, Column 2, and Column 3. You can sort by up to three columns, and you should make sure that No Header Row is selected for the list.
- If you've selected a bulleted list or several paragraphs of text, the Sort By list gives you only two options: Paragraphs and Field 1. Choose Paragraphs to sort by the first word in each paragraph, or Field 1 to sort by the first field or tabular column.

NEW❘▶ Word now sorts First Name and Last Name in the same column, even though you know better than to put them together!

 NOTE The Insert Database and Update Field buttons on the Database toolbar are discussed later in this chapter. See the sidebar "Inserting an External Database into a Word Document."

Adding Merge Fields to a Main Document

After you have created or identified the data source, you are ready to add *merge fields* and any additional information you need to the main document. There are two kinds of text in a main document. *Regular text* is text that will be the same in each version of the merged document, such as the body text in a form letter. *Variable text* is text that will be different in each merged document and is represented by a merge field. Merge fields have the same names as the field names in the data source. For example, the recipient's name and address is variable text in the main document.

You can edit the regular text in your main document as necessary, using the same methods as those you use to edit any other document. Insert a merge field where you want text from the data source to appear in your final, merged document.

Return to the Mail Merge Wizard, Step 3 if you're not already there. Click Next: Write Your Letter to proceed. The task pane displays several choices for adding regular and variable text.

Follow these steps to add merge fields and other information to your main document:

1. Click Address Block to display the options for addressing your letter, shown in Figure 9.11 Choose whether or not you want to include the recipient's name, and then select a name format from the list if applicable. Enable or disable the Insert Company Name check box. If you want to include the postal address, enable that choice and choose an option for including or excluding country and region data.

PART

II

CREATING QUALITY TEXT
DOCUMENTS USING WORD

FIGURE 9.11

The Insert Address Block dialog box lets you choose the fields to use in addressing letters to be merged.

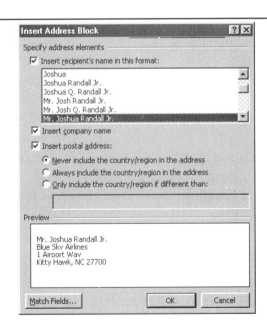

2. If the preview in the Insert Address Block dialog box doesn't show the address information you want, try clicking the Match Fields button to bring up the Match Fields dialog box.

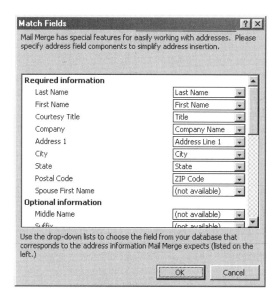

Use the drop-down lists on the right to select the name of the field in your data that corresponds with the address field Word displays on the left. For example, Word uses the term Postal Code, and many databases call this same field Zip Code. When you're done, click OK twice to close both dialog boxes. The address block field appears in the document with double arrows (<< >>) around the field name.

 WARNING Merge field codes must be entered using the options in the Mail Merge Wizard. You cannot simply type << before the field name and >> after it to make it a merge field.

 NOTE By default, merge fields appear with gray shading when the insertion point is anywhere in the field. To have them always appear with gray shading in your main document, choose Tools ➢ Options ➢ View. In the Show area, choose Always in the Field Shading drop-down list and click OK.

3. To have Word insert a greeting line for you, click Greeting Line in the task pane to open the Greeting Line dialog box shown in Figure 9.12. Select the components you want from the drop-down lists until the preview shows the data as you want it displayed in the main document. Select a backup greeting for instances where the data fields you need to create the greeting line are empty. If appropriate, use the Match Fields feature to adjust greeting fields. Click OK when you're finished.

 NOTE Word offers options for inserting postal bar codes and electronic postage. These features are discussed in "Creating Envelopes and Labels," later in this chapter.

FIGURE 9.12

Let Word insert a greeting line for you using fields available in the Greeting Line dialog box.

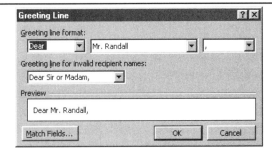

4. To insert other fields from your data, position the insertion point in the document at the position the field should appear and click More Items in the task pane. The Insert Merge Field dialog box opens as shown in Figure 9.13. Choose whether to display Word's Address Fields (the default) or the fields from your database. Select the field you want and click Insert. Click Close to return to the main document. Position the insertion point and repeat the process for each field you wish to place in your main document. It's a bit cumbersome, but you must close the Insert Merge Field dialog box each time you want to reposition the cursor.

FIGURE 9.13

The Insert Merge Field
dialog box allows
users to insert Word
address fields or any
field from the data
source.

5. Continue typing and inserting fields until you are finished with the main document. If you haven't already saved, now is a good time to do so. Figure 9.14 shows a main document ready to be merged.

6. Once you have saved the main document, you can attach a different data source to it. Just click Previous: Select Recipients in the task pane and follow the steps you normally would for selecting a data source. Only one data source can be attached at a time. Now you can see the advantage of using consistent field names in your data source files!

 NOTE A main document can be attached to only one data source at a time, but a data source can be attached simultaneously to multiple main documents.

7. When you have finished setting up and saving the main document, Word provides you with an opportunity to preview the merge results before completing the actual merge. Click Next: Preview Your Letters to proceed.

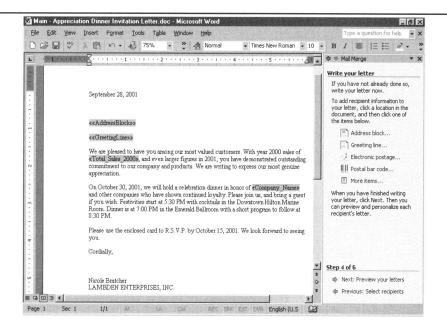

MASTERING THE OPPORTUNITIES

Using an If..Then..Else Field to Vary Text

From time to time when you're creating form letters, you may want to vary the text of the letter based on a field in the data source. For example, a teacher sending progress reports wants to add a sentence that reads, "Please contact me for a conference," but only for those students who have grades below C. The operations manager sending notice of a plant-wide meeting wants most employees to show up at 9:00 AM but requires employees in the Facilities department to come an hour early to set up.

An If..Then..Else field lets you vary the text of your main document based on the value in a data field. Here's what you do:

1. Proceed through Step 4 of the Mail Merge Wizard as you normally would.

2. At Step 4, as you are preparing the main document, position the insertion point where you want the If..Then..Else field to appear.

Continued

MASTERING THE OPPORTUNITIES CONTINUED

3. Click the Insert Word Field button on the Mail Merge toolbar. (Choose Tools ➢ Letters And Mailings ➢ Show Mail Merge Toolbar to display the Mail Merge toolbar if it isn't already visible. The buttons on this toolbar are fully discussed in "Using the Mail Merge Toolbar," later in this chapter.)

4. Choose If..Then..Else to open the Insert Word Field: IF dialog box.

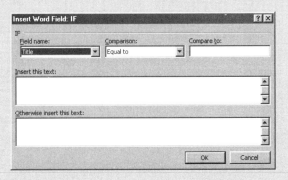

5. Use the Field drop-down list to choose the field on which you are basing the varied text.

6. Choose a comparison from the Comparison list. (See Table 9.1 earlier in the chapter for a description of comparisons).

7. Type a value in the Compare To field.

8. Click in the Insert This Text box and enter the text you want to appear in merged documents that meet the condition you specified.

9. Click in the Otherwise Insert This Text box and enter the text you want to appear in documents that do *not* meet the condition you specified.

10. Click OK to close the dialog box and insert the field.

11. Use the Preview step to review records, making sure the text varies according to the condition you specified.

12. If you have made an error (specified the wrong condition, for example), you must delete the Word field with the error and insert a new field with the correction.

In our plant-wide meeting notice example, the operations manager would choose Department in the Field Name list, choose Equal To in the Comparison list, and enter **Facilities** in the Compare To field. In the Insert This Text field, she might say, "Please arrive at 8:00 AM to set up the auditorium. The meeting starts at 9:00 AM." In the Otherwise Insert This Text box, she could add, "Please arrive promptly at 9:00 AM."

The field you use to specify a condition need not be part of the main document. In other words, you can use any field in the data source for the If..Then..Else field. It doesn't have to appear anywhere in the main document.

Previewing the Merged Document

When the main document and data source are merged, Word generates a separate document or listing (if you are setting up a catalog) for each record in the data source, based on the layout of the main document. Before you perform the merge, it is a good idea to see a sample of how the merged document will appear. Step 5 of the Mail Merge Wizard provides preview and editing options, as shown in Figure 9.15.

FIGURE 9.15

At Step 5 of the Mail Merge Wizard, users can preview their finished documents before actually performing the merge.

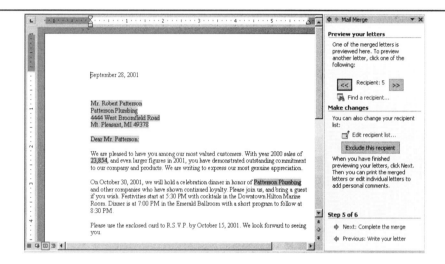

Step 5 automatically shows what the first record in the merge document will look like. To see the next record, click the double right arrow. The task pane shows which recipient number you're currently viewing. Click the double left arrow to see the previous record.

If necessary, you can make any additional edits to the main document while you're previewing the merged data. For example, if you did not place a colon or other punctuation after the greeting, you can insert it now. If you make any changes to the main document, be sure to save it again.

You can also make changes to the data source at this step. Exclude any recipient by displaying their merged record in the document window and then clicking the Exclude This Recipient button in the task pane. If you prefer, you can click Edit Recipient List to open the Mail Merge Recipients dialog box and make any of the changes discussed in this chapter. Changes to the data source are automatically saved.

PART

II

CREATING QUALITY TEXT
DOCUMENTS USING WORD

NOTE You can sort and filter any data source in the Mail Merge Recipients dialog box. However, you can only edit fields and field names for data sources in Word table format or those created with the Mail Merge Wizard. The Edit feature is disabled for other types of data.

If you are content with the setup of both the main document and data source, you're ready to complete the merge. Skip to "Merging Documents" to proceed, or read the following sections to learn about alternative types of main documents.

Creating Directories

A *directory* (also referred to as a *catalog*) is a main document used to create lists. Each record is listed directly under the previous record on the same page. Word 2002's Mail Merge tool is greatly improved, showing little of its former awkwardness. Just as with a letter merge, you can sort and filter records before performing the merge. In some cases this makes it easier to read the directory. (See the sidebar "Inserting an External Database into a Word Document" if you need to create something more ambitious.)

A directory merge follows the same basic process as any other merge with just a couple of differences:

- At Step 1, select Directory from the list of Document Types.

- At Step 4 when you set up a directory main document, you can either create a table to hold the merge field codes or use tabs to separate the codes. Using a table produces consistent results with the least amount of hassle (see Chapter 5 for more Information about creating tables). Place only text you want repeated with each record of the data source, but don't include other surrounding text. If, for example, you want a heading to appear above the records in the list, don't enter it now, or your merged document will include a heading, a record, another heading, another record, and so forth.

- The Preview step only allows you to see records one at a time. Although you don't get a complete view of the completed directory, you can still spot problems. This is a good time to make any adjustments to the table width or to the width of any column in the main document.

After you have merged the data source and main document (see "Merging Documents" later in this chapter), you can add titles, column headings, and any other information to the merged document before you print it, as shown in Figure 9.16. You probably won't want to save the results of merged catalogs, particularly if the underlying data changes frequently. However, if you had to add a lot of heading and title information after the merge, go ahead and save it for future reference.

FIGURE 9.16

Insert titles, column headings, and any other general information in a catalog after you have merged the main document and the data source.

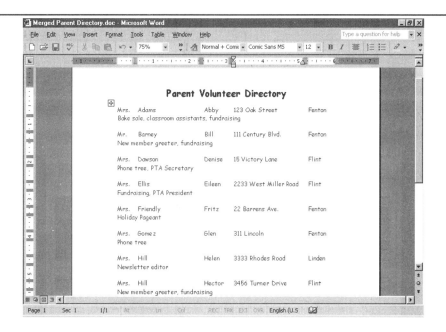

MASTERING THE OPPORTUNITIES

Inserting an External Database into a Word Document

As an alternative to using mail merge to create catalogs, Word lets you easily insert data from an external data source, such as an Excel or Access table, into a Word document. Using this feature, you can create a catalog where the data is linked directly to the data source; this way, you can update data without merging again. And unlike the Catalog Mail Merge feature, Insert Database allows you to insert data into a document that already contains text.

Follow these steps to insert an external database into a Word document:

1. Open a new, blank document, or open a document that contains the data source you want to replace.

2. Display the Database toolbar (View ➤ Toolbars ➤ Database).

Continued

PART

II

CREATING QUALITY TEXT
DOCUMENTS USING WORD

MASTERING THE OPPORTUNITIES CONTINUED

3. Click the Insert Database button on the Database toolbar to display the **Database** dialog box.

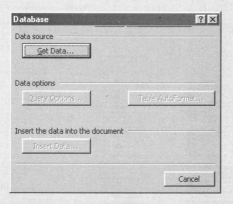

4. Choose Get Data to display the Open Data Source dialog box and then select the name of the folder that contains the database in the Look In list box.

5. Select the file extension of the database file in the Files Of Type drop-down list, highlight the name of the database file that contains the records you want to insert into Word, and then choose Open. (If you would like to connect to another type of ODBC-compliant database, click the New Source button to open the Database Connection Wizard.)

6. If the Select Table dialog box appears, specify the table, query, or worksheet that contains the data. You will only see this option if the data source you're using contains multiple tables.

7. To filter or sort the data or to select specific fields, click the Query Options button and enter the criteria. Click OK to return to the Insert Data dialog box.

8. You can choose an AutoFormat for the table by clicking the Table AutoFormat button and selecting the options you want in the dialog box. Click OK when you're finished here.

9. Choose Insert Data in the Database dialog box to display the Insert Data dialog box. Then choose any of the following options, and click OK:

Insert Records Choose All to insert all of the specified records, or choose From to insert a range of records, and then type the number of the first record in the adjoining text box and the number of the last record in the range in the To text box.

Continued

Creating Envelopes and Labels

Labels and envelopes are two other types of main documents. Specialty labels are available at office supply stores, allowing you to create labels for any use. Word can merge to various sizes of envelopes, including standard, business, note card, and other sizes. If your printer can print on envelopes and labels, you can create them in Word. (You must also know how to load the envelopes and labels. If you're not sure, consult your printer manual.)

Preparing Labels

Follow these steps to create labels:

1. Display the Mail Merge Wizard and then choose Labels in the Select Document Type options.

2. Click Next: Starting Document.

3. Choose a Starting Document option. If you began with a blank document, you can choose Change Document Layout to create a label from scratch or choose Start From Existing Document to use an existing label setup.

4. Click Label Options to set up the label you want to use. Select the manufacturer of your labels in the Label Products drop-down list. (If the manufacturer of the labels you have is not listed, look on the label box for the Avery equivalent. If there is one, choose Avery. If there isn't an Avery equivalent listed, get different labels, if at all possible. It's a lot of work to enter all the measurements manually, but you can do so by clicking the New Label button.) Select the product number (or Avery equivalent) that appears on your label package in the Product Number list box. (Chapter 3, "Working with Text and Formats in Word," has additional

information on setting up labels.) If you're using a printer that has multiple feed trays, select the one you wish to use from the Tray drop-down list at the top of the Label Options dialog box. The default for these types of printers is Manual Feed, so you may want to choose an automatic feed option if you are printing many pages.

5. Click Next: Select Recipients.

6. Attach a data source by browsing to open an existing list, choosing an Outlook folder, or creating a new address list.

7. Modify the recipient list, if desired, by clicking Edit Recipient List and then sorting or filtering, or selecting individual records. Click Next: Arrange Your Labels to proceed.

8. Set up the labels with the fields you want to use. Insert and format the fields on the first label. Then click Update All Labels to place those fields on every label.

 WARNING Don't delete the Next Record field Word automatically inserts on every label but the first. If you do, the first record is repeated on every label!

---

9. Click Next: Preview Your Labels to get an idea of how the final merged document will appear. Figure 9.17 shows name badges at the Preview stage.

10. Use the navigation buttons to browse through the labels in Preview mode. Just as with other main document types, you can also edit the recipient list at this point, if you wish.

11. Click Next: Complete The Merge when you are ready to proceed.

 TIP If you want to save the Label main document, include the word *Labels* (instead of *Main*) at the beginning of the filename.

FIGURE 9.17

Create name tags using labels as the main document type.

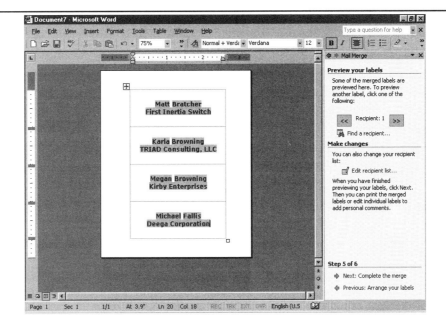

Preparing an Envelope

Creating an Envelope main document is similar to creating a Label main document. Follow these steps:

1. Display the Mail Merge Wizard and then choose Envelopes in the Select Document Type options.

2. Click Next: Starting Document.

3. Choose a Starting Document option. If you began with a blank document, you can choose Change Document Layout to create an envelope from scratch or choose Start From Existing Document to use an existing envelope setup.

4. Click Envelope Options and set up the envelope you want to use. Select an envelope size and font options as appropriate. Refer to Chapter 3 for more on the specifics of setting up an envelope. When you're finished, click OK and Word places the envelope in the document window.

5. Click Next: Select Recipients.

6. Attach a data source by browsing to open an existing list, choosing an Outlook folder, or creating a new address list.

7. Modify the recipient list, if desired, by clicking Edit Recipient List and then sorting or filtering, or selecting individual records. Click Next: Arrange Your Envelope to proceed.

8. Position the insertion point on the envelope and insert the fields you want to use. Word automatically includes the fields on every envelope in the merge.

9. Insert a postal bar code, if desired, to speed up the delivery process. Click Postal Bar Code to open the corresponding dialog box.

Use the drop-down lists to choose the database field that corresponds with the zip code and street address fields in Word. Click OK when you're finished; the bar code field appears on the envelope at the insertion point.

NOTE There is a text box on the label to help place recipient address fields. To see it, just click once in the area where you would expect to insert address fields. (If you don't see the text box right away, click again in another spot.) Once the text box is visible, the insertion point appears in the appropriate position and you can insert an Address Block field.

10. If you have electronic postage software installed, you can select that option in the task pane.

11. Click Next: Preview Your Envelopes to get an idea of how the final merged product will appear. Figure 9.18 shows an envelope in Preview mode, ready to be merged.

12. Use the navigation buttons to browse through the labels in preview mode. Just as with other main document types, you can also edit the recipient list at this point, if you wish.

13. If the envelope appears as you wish, save it to a file that begins with *Envelopes*.

14. Click Next: Complete The Merge when you are ready to proceed.

Preview envelopes to make sure the address fields are placed appropriately.

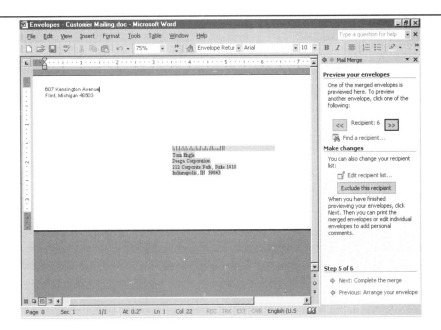

Envelopes appear with the return address specified as the mailing address on the User Information tab in the Options dialog box. An Envelope main document is easy to edit once you have set it up. To remove the return address from preprinted envelopes, just select it and press the Delete key.

TIP To change the return address on your envelope main document, choose Tools ➢ Options to open the Options dialog box. On the User Information tab, type a different name and address in the Mailing Address text box and click OK.

Using a Mail Merge Template for a Main Document

NEW▶

Word 2002 now includes templates designed specifically for mail merge. (For more about templates in general, see Chapter 8, "Simplifying with Styles, Outlines, and Templates.") You can choose from an assortment of letters, fax cover sheets, and directories. The templates come with commonly used merge fields already inserted, which save you steps, allowing more time for the really important things—like lunch!

Using a template is even easier than using a blank main document. Start the merge process as you normally would. At Step 1, choose either Letters or Directory as your document type. Click Next: Starting Document and then proceed as follows:

1. In the Select Starting Document area of the task pane, choose Start From A Template.

2. Click Select Template to open the Mail Merge tab of the Select Template dialog box.

3. Choose from the available templates here, or select another tab in the dialog box and choose one of those templates if you wish.

 NOTE There are three Merge Address List templates of varying styles—Contemporary, Elegant, and Professional. The Merge Address List templates produce directories.

4. Click OK to close the dialog box and open the template.

5. Proceed through the rest of the steps as you normally would. Depending on your data source, you may have to delete some of the fields included in the template, or replace them with correct fields from the data source before you complete the merge.

Using E-mail As Main Documents

If you are comfortable creating letters as a main document, you'll have no trouble with e-mail. The steps to create an e-mail main document are exactly the same. There are slight differences when you actually perform the merge, and those differences are discussed in the next section.

Merging Documents

Once you've created a main document and attached a data source, you are ready for the actual merge. This happens at Step 6 of the wizard. If you are still at Step 5, click Next: Complete The Merge to proceed.

The choices you see at Step 6 depend on which type of main document you are using. For each main document type you will be able to perform at least one of the following options.

Print Opens the Merge To Printer dialog box. Once again you're given the choice to merge all records, the current record, or a range of records.

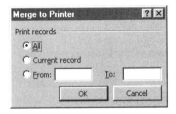

When you click OK, Word sends the results of the merge directly to the printer. Therefore it is prudent to send the current record or a small range just to make sure everything goes as expected. If you send the entire merge results and something is wrong, the error is multiplied by the total number of records you have in your data source. Choose All only if you have previewed your merge and everything is in perfect order (check that nobody has left purple and green paper in the printer!).

Edit Individual Letters (or Labels or Envelopes) Opens the Merge To New Document dialog box. (It looks just like the Merge To Printer dialog box.) Choose which records you wish to merge and click OK to have Word conduct the merge and create a new document with the results. Labels appear in columns, form letters and envelopes are separated by page breaks, and catalogs display each record. You can review the results of the merge (and even modify individual letters) before sending the merge document to the printer. Once the merge is printed, there is no reason to save the merge results. If you need to print it again at a later date, you'll want to do the merge again in case you've updated any of the records in the data source.

E-mail Opens a similar dialog box. With this option, however, you must select the database field that contains the recipients' e-mail address. If you're merging to e-mail, you may type a subject line and choose a mail format.

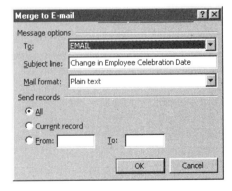

PART

II

CREATING QUALITY TEXT
DOCUMENTS USING WORD

Then you can select the records you wish to merge and click OK. Word fires up Outlook (or your default e-mail client). Send the e-mail as you normally would.

 NOTE Merging to e-mail works with any MAPI-compliant mail program, so you don't necessarily have to use Outlook. If you experience problems using a program other than Outlook, consult Microsoft's Knowledge Base for suggested fixes. In your browser's address bar, type **www.microsoft.com**. Using the link bar at the top of the page, place your mouse over Support, and then click the Knowledge Base link.

Using the Mail Merge Toolbar

NEW▶ Although the wizard nicely streamlines the mail merge process, users who are already familiar with the feature from way back may be wondering what happened to the Mail Merge toolbar. Not only is it still around, it's improved! Table 9.2 describes the buttons on the Mail Merge toolbar. At any step in the process, choose Tools ➤ Letters And Mailings ➤ Show Mail Merge Toolbar to display it.

TABLE 9.2   MAIL MERGE TOOLBAR BUTTONS

Button	Button Name	Function
	Main Document Setup	Opens a dialog box where you can choose a different type of main document (letters, envelopes, labels, e-mail, and so on).
	Open Data Source	Opens the Select Data Source dialog box so you can choose another data source for the merge.
	Mail Merge Recipients	Displays the Mail Merge Recipients dialog box so you can edit, sort, filter, and validate data.
	Insert Address Block	Opens the Insert Address Block dialog box to quickly insert address information in a main merge document.
	Insert Greeting Line	Displays the Greeting Line dialog box for inserting greeting line fields.

Continued ▶

TABLE 9.2 (continued)   MAIL MERGE TOOLBAR BUTTONS

Button	Button Name	Function
	Insert Merge Fields	Opens the Insert Merge Field dialog box for inserting any field from the data source in the main document.
Insert Word Field ▾	Insert Word Field	Offers a list of Word fields, such as If..Then..Else, for inclusion in the main document. For more on Word If..Then..Else fields see the "Using an If..Then..Else Field to Vary Text" sidebar earlier in this chapter.
	View Merged Data	Replaces the field names in the main document with data from the first record in the data source.
	Highlight Merge Fields	When field shading options are set to Never or When Selected, this button allows you to toggle field shading off and on.
	Match Fields	Opens the Match Fields dialog box for selecting the database fields that correspond with Word's typical address fields.
	Propagate Labels	Updates all labels with the merge fields inserted on the first label.
	Record Selectors	When View Merged Data is turned on, the record selectors allow you to display the first, next, previous, or last record. You can also type a number and press Enter to see a particular record.
	Find Entry	Opens the Find Entry dialog box with options to search for a text string in a particular field or in all fields.
	Check For Errors	Provides options for detecting and reporting omission errors before merging.
	Merge To New Document	Completes the merge and displays results in a new document.
	Merge To Printer	Completes the merge and sends results directly to the printer.
	Merge To E-Mail	Completes the merge and sends the resulting e-mail messages.

PART

II

CREATING QUALITY TEXT
DOCUMENTS USING WORD

MASTERING TROUBLESHOOTING

Troubleshooting Merge Problems

There are three basic reasons for merge problems:

- Document incompatibility
- Problems with the data source
- Problems with the main document

Document incompatibility means that either the data source or the main document isn't a valid Word mail merge file. A dialog box will appear, telling you that the main document has no merge codes or that the data source is invalid. Examine the file in question. If it is a data file, make sure it has field names, that there is no extra text at the beginning of the file, and that the data is in a table. If the problem is the main document, open it and check to make sure you have selected the correct data source file and that it has merge field codes. Even if both files seem to be okay, structural problems with individual records (like missing fields) can cause Word to stop in the middle of a merge.

You can have Word check the data source for omission errors before merging. With the main document active, click the Check For Errors button on the Mail Merge toolbar to open the Checking And Reporting Errors dialog box, shown below. Using this tool is much like checking spelling before printing.

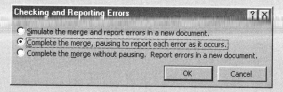

Choose one of the following options, and then choose OK:

- Have Word simulate a merge and report errors in a new document.
- Merge the two documents and report errors while the merge is taking place.
- Merge the two documents and report errors in a new document.

If you expect errors, simulation is best. If you don't think there will be errors (always our hope), go ahead and have Word merge, stopping along the way to report any errors it finds. When Word finds an error, a dialog box will open. Depending on the kind of error,

Continued ▯▶

MASTERING TROUBLESHOOTING CONTINUED

you may be allowed to fix the error and then continue merging. If you can't fix it, note the information provided and click OK to continue finding errors. When Error Checking is complete, close the merged document and fix the data source and/or main document files before merging the documents again.

Even if Word finds no errors and your documents merge, you may still find mistakes in your merged document. There is an easy way to decide if a mistake is in the main document or in the data source. If the mistake appears in every merged document, look for the problem in the main document. For example, if there is no space between the first and last names in your merged form letters, you need to put a space between the merge codes for FirstName and LastName in the main document. Spelling errors in every merged document should lead you to suspect that you forgot to check the spelling in the main document before merging.

If a mistake appears in some but not all merged documents, the problem is in the data source. If a merged first name is spelled incorrectly in one of the merged letters, it's misspelled in the data source. Close the merged file, open the data source file, correct the error, and then merge the documents again.

CHAPTER 10

CREATING AND DISTRIBUTING WORD FORMS

FEATURING

- Designing a form

- Creating a template for a form

- Using frames and text boxes

- Adding form fields

- Protecting and using forms

Let's say you've just been asked to create a vacation request form for the employees in your new start-up company. You could create the form in Word, print it, make copies, file them, and wait for someone to ask you for one. Each employee who wanted to request a vacation could request a form from you, fill it out, and hand carry or ask you to send it to their supervisor for a signature. The supervisor could then, if they remember, sign it and return the signed copy to you. You could copy it, return a copy to the employee, and file the other one. The result is endless paperwork, lost forms, and countless interoffice envelopes. By the time the form jumps through all its hoops, the vacation date has come and gone.

What we've just described is the office of the past—not today's twenty-first century office. In today's office, you can create an online form that you send via e-mail to the employee requesting it, or you can post it on your corporate intranet. After the employee completes and submits the form via e-mail or over the Web, the supervisor reviews it, marks it approved or declined, and returns a copy to you and the employee without ever touching a printed document. It's all over in a matter of minutes—no copies, no lost forms, no missed vacations—and it's a win-win situation for everybody.

Designing a Form

The most difficult part of creating an online form is designing it to meet your users' needs. Before you start creating your online form, sketch it on paper or use an existing printed form as a model. If you already have a paper-based form that people are familiar with, pull it out and use it as a model for the online form. A little pre-work will give your form a head start and will save you the time and frustration of trying to design the form while you're creating it.

You also need to decide if you want to create an online form that you will distribute via e-mail or post to a shared network folder or create an online form that you will post to your intranet. Although you can create both types of forms in Word, you cannot convert one type of form to another. It's essential that you choose the distribution method prior to creating the form. In this chapter, we'll show you how to create an online form you can send via e-mail. To learn how to create an online form on a Web page, see Chapter 29, "Creating Web Pages in Word and Excel."

Once you have determined a design and distribution method, you'll follow a several-step process to create the form. First you create a template so that the form can be used again and again without users overwriting it. Then you must create the layout for the form, often using a table to control the placement of information. After the layout is set, you can insert text, frames, fields, and other form elements. Now that you understand the process, let's discuss the specifics of each step.

Creating a Template for a Form

Because you'll want to use the online form over and over again, you need to create the form as a template. As soon as you open a new, blank template in which to create your form, go ahead and save it. That way, you can just click Save each time you make a change that you want to keep.

To have the template available when creating a new document, save the template in one of the existing template folders. If you create many online-form templates, create a new folder in the Templates folder in which to store them. When you do, an Online Forms tab appears in the New dialog box. This feature makes it easy for users to locate the templates when they want to create a form based on one of them.

To create a new template file, follow these steps:

1. Choose File ➢ New, select General Templates in the task pane, and then choose Blank Document in the Templates dialog box. Choose Template in the Create New area, and then click OK to close the dialog box.

2. Click the Save button on the Standard toolbar to display the Save As dialog box.

3. Choose the folder in the Templates folder in which you want to store the template. Alternatively, create a new folder in the Templates folder by clicking the Create New Folder button in the Save As dialog box.

4. Name the template and click Save—Word automatically adds the .dot extension to the file, designating it as a template.

NOTE If you forget to choose Template as the type of file to open in step 1 above, you can still save the document as a template file by selecting Document Template (*.dot) in the Save As Type drop-down list in the Save As dialog box.

Now that you have a new, blank template, you are ready to begin inserting the text and other objects that will be used repeatedly in the form. The easiest way to lay out the form is by using a table. Tables allow you to place text on different parts of the screen without worrying about user-entered text wrapping to a new line. Tables also make it easy for the user to enter text in the appropriate location. The user can press Tab to move from one cell to another.

Word comes with the Forms toolbar, a set of tools used to create online forms. The Forms toolbar includes buttons to insert form fields, to create tables and frames, to position questions and prompts on the page, to turn form-field shading on or off, and to protect the text and other objects on the form so that users can enter data only where you have placed form fields.

To display the Forms toolbar, right-click any toolbar and choose Forms. Click the Draw Table or Insert Table button on the Forms toolbar to create a table in the new template.

 NOTE See "Creating Parallel Columns with Tables" in Chapter 5 for additional information about creating and formatting tables.

Figure 10.1 shows an example of an online form that was created using a table. The borders have been turned off except for some of the bottom cell borders, which provide the lines for users' responses. As you can see, rows and columns aren't evenly distributed, and extra cells have been inserted to provide the appropriate spacing for items on the form.

FIGURE 10.1

Use tables to create online forms with rows and columns that are not evenly distributed.

After you enter descriptive labels and prompts in the table, you can split cells, merge cells, change borders, and adjust column and row widths as needed. Because the form is to be viewed online, don't forget to add colors, shading, and graphics to really make an impression.

Using Frames and Text Boxes

If you're not using a table to handle form layout, the Forms toolbar has an option for *frames* that allows you to place an item precisely at any position on a form. Frames are containers for text, graphics, comments, fields, and other Word elements. Since you move or resize a frame with a simple click and drag, it's often easier to manipulate text and objects if you place them inside frames. Furthermore, certain reference elements such as a table of contents, footnotes, endnotes, and comments must be in a frame. See Chapter 11, "Making Large Documents Easy to Use," and Chapter 12, "Working Collaboratively with Word," for additional information on using reference features.

Text boxes are similar to frames. They also serve as containers for text and objects, but you often have more formatting flexibility with text boxes than you do with frames. For example, you can use many of the drawing tools to enhance the appearance of a text box, but not a frame. So if you want to jazz up your form by showing its title in 3-D, use a text box, not a frame. See Chapter 7, "Getting Creative with the Office XP Graphics Tools," for more information about creating text boxes using Office XP's drawing tools.

Both frames and text boxes can be formatted by adding or removing visible borders, backgrounds, and even shadows. (Use Format ➢ Borders And Shading for frames; use this same command *or* drawing tools for text boxes.) In early versions of Word, you had to place graphic objects in frames to get text to wrap around them. In Word 2002, if you want text to wrap around a graphic, it is not necessary to use a frame. However, if you open an old Word document that uses frames, Word keeps them.

  **NOTE** Don't confuse the object frames discussed here with HTML frames, which are used to display multiple Web pages on a single screen. HTML frames are discussed in Chapter 47, "Enhancing a Web Page with Images," on the companion CD.

 To insert a frame, click the Insert Frame button and then drag to create a rectangle the approximate size of the text or object you want to place in the frame. By default, a frame appears with a black border in the size and location in which you created it. A newly created frame is active—the insertion point is placed inside it, and a shaded border appears around the outside of its regular border. You can immediately begin to type text in a frame.

Unlike text boxes, frames expand to accommodate their contents. For example, if you type text in a frame, it automatically grows so that all the text you type is inside the frame. Resize and move frames much the same as you would a text box: click the shaded border of an active frame to select it and then drag one of the black handles that appear around its borders. The mouse pointer changes to a two-headed resize arrow when you position it over a handle on the frame's border. To manually reposition a frame, select it, and when the mouse pointer changes into a four-headed move arrow, drag the frame to a new position.

To change the size or position of the frame to an exact specification and to change the way text wraps around the frame, follow these steps:

1. Right-click the frame and choose Format Frame, or select the frame and choose Format ➢ Frame, to display the Frame dialog box shown in Figure 10.2.

2. To change the way text wraps around the frame, choose one of the following options in the Text Wrapping area:

None This places text above and below the frame, but no text appears on either the right or left side of it.

Around The default, this places text above and below the frame and on both the right and left sides.

3. To change the size of the frame, specify any of the following options in the Size area:

Width Choose Exactly, and then adjust the value in the adjacent At text box to specify an exact width for the frame. Alternatively, choose Auto to allow the frame's width to conform to a size that holds its contents.

Height Choose At Least, and then adjust the value in the adjacent At text box to specify the minimum height for the frame. If you prefer, choose Exactly and adjust the value in the At text box to specify an exact height for the frame; or choose Auto to allow the frame's height to conform to the size that holds its contents.

4. To define the horizontal position of the frame, specify any of the following options in the Horizontal area:

Position Choose Left, Right, Center, Inside, or Outside to define the position of the frame in relation to the Page, Margin, or Column, which is selected in the Relative To drop-down list. If the frame is inside the margin of the page, you can type the distance from the edge of the page in the Position drop-down list.

Distance From Text Adjust this value to specify the amount of space between the edges of the frame and the text on the left and right side of the frame.

5. To define the vertical position of the frame, specify any of the following options in the Vertical area:

Position Choose Top, Bottom, Center, Inside, or Outside to define the position of the frame in relation to the Margin, Page, or Paragraph, which is selected in the Relative To drop-down list. Alternatively, type a measurement in the Position drop-down list to specify the position of the frame in relation to the margin, page, or paragraph.

Distance From Text Adjust this value to specify the amount of space between the edges of the frame and the text above and below it.

Move With Text Allows the frame to move its vertical position up or down on the page when the paragraph to which it is anchored moves.

Lock Anchor Locks the frame's anchor to the paragraph that currently contains it. For example, check the Lock Anchor box to lock the frame that contains a caption to the graphic the caption describes.

6. Click OK to apply the selected options to the frame.

FIGURE 10.2

The Frame dialog box contains options that allow you to specify the exact size and position of a selected frame.

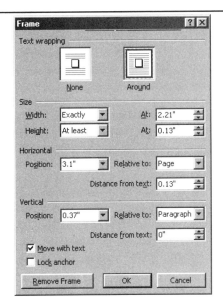

If you decide that you no longer want a frame in your form, you can delete it. Use either of the following methods:

- Select the frame and then choose Format ➤ Frame to display the Frame dialog box. Choose Remove Frame to remove the frame without removing its contents.

- Select the frame and then press Delete to remove both the frame and its contents.

You can use the options available in the Borders And Shading dialog box to change the appearance of the frame's borders and shading. To do so, follow these steps:

1. Right-click a frame and choose Borders And Shading to display the Borders And Shading dialog box.

2. Choose the border for the frame on the Borders tab and the shading or fill color for the inside of the frame on the Shading tab.

3. Click OK when you have applied the border and shading you want.

 TIP The tools on the Tables And Borders toolbar can also be used to apply some formatting to frames. For example, you can change the text direction in a selected frame using the Change Text Direction button on the Tables And Borders toolbar.

If it's text you want to position, Word 2002 text boxes, found on the Drawing toolbar, are also an option. With text boxes you can apply 3-D effects, shadows, fills, and background. In addition, you can both change the orientation of the text and flip and rotate the text boxes themselves. For more information about text boxes and other graphic tools, see Chapter 7.

Adding Form Fields

After your form is laid out, you must add *form fields,* or placeholders, that other people can use to submit their information. You can insert three types of form fields from the Forms toolbar:

Text form fields   Open fields of any length where users can enter text

Check box form fields   Check boxes that a user can check or clear to indicate yes or no answers

Drop-down form fields   Lists of choices from which users can choose a response

The form fields are controls just like those you find in dialog boxes. When your form is completed and you turn on protection, users will be able only to enter text, add or remove check marks, or select one of the choices in the fields. The rest of the document will be off-limits to them.

 NOTE A *control* is an object such as a text box or drop-down field that you can use to display or enter data or perform an action.

  To insert a form field, position the insertion point where you would like the field to appear, and then click the Text Form Field, Check Box Form Field, or Drop-Down Form Field button on the Forms toolbar.

It's helpful to have the Form Field Shading feature turned on while you are creating the form so that you can see where the fields are, especially text form fields. Form Field Shading is a toggle, which is turned on by default when you first display the Forms toolbar.

After you have entered a field in the form, you'll need to specify the options you want to apply to the field. To do so, either select the field and click the Form Field Options button on the Forms toolbar, right-click the field and choose Properties from the shortcut menu, or double-click the field to open its Form Field Options dialog box.

When you display the Text Form Field Options dialog box, shown in Figure 10.3, you can choose any of the following options for the selected field and then click OK:

Type Select Regular Text, Number, Date, Current Date, Current Time, or Calculation to specify what type of data the user can enter in the field. The field only accepts input of the correct type. For example, the user cannot enter text in a field that is specified as a date field.

Default Text If you want, type the choice that users would most commonly give. If you enter a default choice, then the user must type any different choice in the text box.

Maximum Length Adjust the value either to Unlimited or to a specified number of characters, which limits the length of user entries.

PART

II

CREATING QUALITY TEXT
DOCUMENTS USING WORD

FIGURE 10.3

The Text Form Field Options dialog box contains options to specify what type of text can be entered in the field.

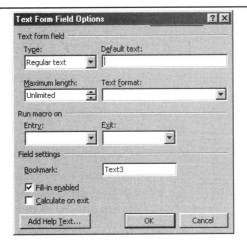

Text Format Choose Uppercase, Lowercase, First Capital, or Title Case to specify how the text will appear in the form field.

Run Macro On Select the name of the macro you want to run whenever the insertion point enters or leaves the field. This feature is optional.

NOTE See Chapter 18, "Automating Excel with Macros," for additional information on creating and using macros. Any macros you want to run when entering or exiting the form field must be stored in the form's template.

Field Settings Type the name of a bookmark in the Bookmark text box to have a macro reference the contents of this field. Check the Calculate On Exit check box to have Word update and calculate all the fields after any exit macros run. Check the Fill-In Enabled box to allow users to enter text in this field.

 NOTE See "Using Bookmarks" in Chapter 11 for information on creating and using bookmarks in your documents.

Add Help Text You can also add help text to the form field. See "Offering Help" later in this chapter.

When you display the Check Box Form Field Options dialog box, shown in Figure 10.4, you can choose any of the options for the selected field and then click OK. These two options are unique to check box form fields:

Check Box Size Choose Auto to make the check box the size of the text. Alternatively, choose Exactly and adjust the value in the adjacent text box to specify the exact size in points for the check box.

Default Value Choose either Not Checked or Checked as the default value for the field when the form is opened.

FIGURE 10.4

Choose the size and default value for a check box in the Check Box Form Field Options dialog box.

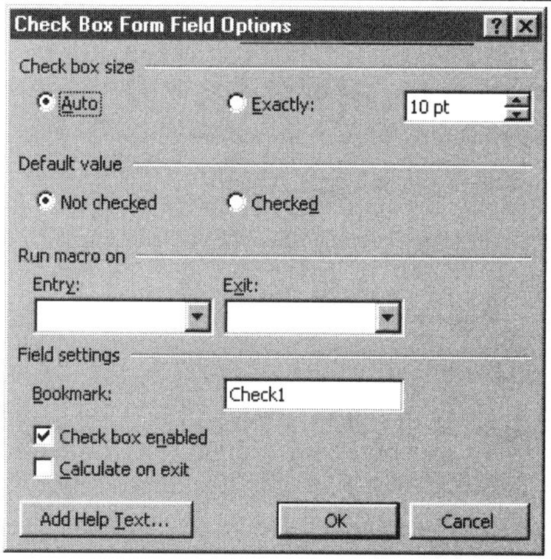

When you display the Drop-Down Form Field Options dialog box, shown in Figure 10.5, you can choose any of the options for the selected field and then click OK. These three options are unique to drop-down form fields:

Drop-Down Item Type an item here and choose Add to place it in the Items In Drop-Down List box.

Items In Drop-Down List Click either the ↑ or ↓ Move button to move the item highlighted in this box to a different position in the list. The items appear in the drop-down list on your form in the order in which they appear in the Items In Drop-Down List box.

Add/Remove To edit an item in the drop-down list, select it in the Items In Drop-Down List box and then click Remove to remove it from the list box and return it to the Drop-Down Item text box. Press Delete to delete the item, or edit the item and then choose Add to return it to the list.

PART

II

CREATING QUALITY TEXT
DOCUMENTS USING WORD

FIGURE 10.5

Enter the items for a drop-down list in the Drop-Down Form Field Options dialog box.

The first item in the list box appears on the form as the default. You may want to enter a blank item (press the spacebar several times before you choose Add) as the first choice. Alternatively, you can enter instructional text as the first item (for example, **Select your department**). However, if you provide one of these options, you cannot prevent users from selecting it as their choice. Another consideration is that the length of the text string for the first item determines the width of the drop-down list field on the form. Think carefully about this before deciding which way you want to go.

Offering Help

Creating a good form is half the battle. The other half is getting the users to complete it properly. You can make it easier for others to know how to complete the form by adding online help to each of the form fields. This simple enhancement could endear you forever to your users and, even more importantly, make sure you get back the data you are hoping to receive.

To add help text to the form field:

1. Open the form field's Options dialog box by right-clicking the form field and choosing Properties.

2. Click the Add Help Text button to display the Form Field Help Text dialog box shown in Figure 10.6.

3. On the Status Bar tab, choose one of the following options to specify what help text will appear on the status bar when the field is selected:

   None Provides no help text on the status bar for the form field.

   AutoText Entry Allows you to use a previously created AutoText entry as the help text that appears on the status bar. Select the AutoText entry in the adjacent drop-down list.

   Type Your Own Allows you to type up to 138 characters of help text in the text box.

4. On the Help Key (F1) tab, choose one of the following options to specify what help text will appear in a message box when the field is selected and the user presses F1.

   None Provides no help text for the form field when the F1 key is pressed.

   AutoText Entry Allows you to use a previously created AutoText entry as the help text that appears when you press F1. Select the AutoText entry in the adjacent drop-down list.

   Type Your Own Allows you to type up to 255 characters of help text in the text box.

5. Click OK in the Form Field Help Text dialog box.

 If you make changes to form fields—for example, if you click a check box after a form is protected—click the Reset Form Fields button to clear all entries.

PART

II

CREATING QUALITY TEXT
DOCUMENTS USING WORD

FIGURE 10.6

Add online help for a form field by choosing the location of the help text in the Form Field Help Text dialog box.

Protecting and Using the Form

Your form is almost ready to distribute. Make sure the form appears just as it will when the user opens a document based on your form's template. For example, you'll probably want to:

- Turn off form field shading because it presents a neater appearance. In addition, the form field shading doesn't accurately reflect the length of the form field, so it may be confusing to the users.

- Hide the gridlines if you used a table to create your form. When you do, only the descriptive labels and any cell borders you displayed appear on the form. This means that when you open a document based on the form template, the gridlines are hidden.

- Turn off the Forms toolbar.

After you're sure that everything is exactly the way you want it, click the Protect Form button to protect the form so the user can only enter data in the form fields. When you protect the form, the descriptive labels, formatting, and layout of the form cannot be changed. In addition, you will no longer have access to most toolbar and menu options.

NOTE In previous versions of Word, clicking the Protect Form button and choosing Tools ➢ Protect Document cleared any changes you made to form fields as you were testing the form, such as checking a check box or selecting an option button. In Word 2002, clicking the Protect Form button does not clear these changes. To clear them, you can choose Tools ➢ Protect Document or click the Reset Form Fields button on the Forms toolbar to clear them yourself.

The last step before distributing the form to users is to save the form template. Although many of the toolbar buttons and menu commands are no longer available, you can still save the template by clicking Save.

After protecting your form, it's always smart to test the form by filling it out to check that the *tab order,* the order in which the fields are activated when you press Tab, is correct. Depending on how you created the table and positioned the items in it, it may not tab logically through the fields. To correct this, you may have to insert blank cells or reposition items on the form. You may also find that you made a field's length too short or that you didn't include all the options in a drop-down list. Use the form as if you were a potential user; if possible, ask a colleague to test the form for you. It's amazing how easy it is to overlook something when you already know what data is expected in a field.

If you need to edit the form, be sure to open the form's template (not a document based on the template, but a copy of the form). You can then turn on the Forms toolbar and click the Protect Form button. You will again have free rein to do whatever you want to the form (within reason, of course!).

When users open a protected-form document, such as the one shown in Figure 10.7, they are only able to select a form field. Instruct the user to press Tab and Shift+Tab to move forward and backward through the fields. Users will have limited access to toolbar buttons and menu options. They can enter their information and then save or print the document so they have a copy of it. The form can also be e-mailed to a colleague using the File ➢ Send To ➢ Mail Recipient (As Attachment) command.

FIGURE 10.7

When you open a protected form, the first field is selected so the user can enter the appropriate information.

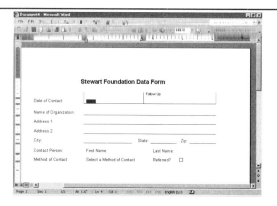

 NOTE See Chapter 33, "Tracking and Documenting Contacts with Outlook," to learn more about using Outlook to send your form as a file attached to an e-mail message.

CHAPTER 11

MAKING LARGE DOCUMENTS EASY TO USE

FEATURING

- Adding and revising footnotes and endnotes
- Deleting and converting notes
- Using bookmarks
- Creating cross-references
- Indexing for easy reference
- Easy navigation with hyperlinks
- Generating and modifying a table of contents
- Managing large documents
- Creating and printing master and subdocuments
- Converting existing documents

When you are responsible for creating documents that exceed the typical one- and two-page letters, you need more in your toolbox than the everyday Word tools. Word 2002 comes with a number of features to help you tackle lengthy documents, including footnotes, endnotes, tables of contents, indexes, hyperlinks, and cross-references, to name a few. Master documents take you a step further and help you organize multiple documents in a single volume while retaining their individual components. With a little forethought and some extra effort, you can make your documents easy to follow and help your readers find what they are looking for. Word 2002 takes the headache out of these additional touches, providing you with one more way for your work to stand out.

Adding Footnotes and Endnotes

NEW▶

When you want to give readers more information about your topic or a reference to the source of your information, Word gives you options for inserting both *footnotes*, which appear at the bottom of the page, and *endnotes*, which appear at the end of the document. Word automatically numbers the notes for you and calculates how much space footnotes will need at the bottom on the page. Now, in Word 2002, you can choose a number format for footnotes and endnotes, and apply different formats to individual sections, all from within one dialog box! Where was this feature when *we* were typing term papers?

 NOTE You can insert both footnotes and endnotes in the same document. For example, you may want to insert footnotes to add comments to the text of a page and endnotes to add source information, such as a bibliography, at the end of a report.

Each time you insert a footnote or endnote, Word automatically inserts a *note reference mark* (a character in the text of the document that tells the reader to look for additional information) in your document at the location where you inserted the note. The reference mark can be automatically numbered using Arabic numerals (1, 2, 3, and so on) or using the consecutive numbers or symbols you specify in a different format. You can also choose to insert a custom mark or symbol to use as the note reference mark in your document. Automatic numbering is, of course, the easiest because Word knows what the next reference mark number should be. If you choose a custom mark, you must select the symbol each time you insert a new note, even if you are using the same symbol for every note. This is much easier in Word 2002 since the Insert Symbol dialog box now displays recently used symbols.

To insert a footnote or an endnote, switch to Normal or Print Layout view and follow these steps:

1. Position the insertion point where you'd like the note reference mark to appear, and then choose Insert ➢ Reference ➢ Footnote to display the Footnote And Endnote dialog box shown in Figure 11.1.

PART

II

CREATING QUALITY TEXT
DOCUMENTS USING WORD

FIGURE 11.1

Display the Footnote And Endnote dialog box each time you insert a note reference mark in your document.

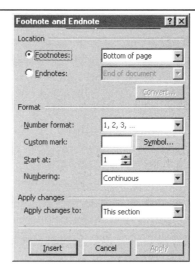

2. Select Footnote or Endnote in the Location area to specify what type of note you want to insert. Choose a placement option from the drop-down list to the right of the note type you specified.

   • Choose Bottom Of Page to place footnotes just above the bottom margin on the page that includes the note reference mark or Below Text to place the footnotes below the last line of text on a short page of text.

   • You can choose to display endnotes at the end of the document or at the end of each section.

3. Choose a Number Format from the drop-down list or, if you prefer, type the character you wish to use in the Custom Mark field or click Symbol to select a character from Word's symbol fonts.

4. If you're numbering footnotes/endnotes, enter a Start At number and then specify one of the following numbering options:

   Continuous Inserts consecutive numbers or symbols in the numbering format selected

Restart Each Section Restarts footnote numbering, using the Start At number you specified, at each section break

Restart Each Page Restarts numbering, using the Start At number you specified, at each page break

5. Choose an Apply To option.

6. Click OK to close the Footnote And Endnote dialog box.

When you insert a note in a document, Word inserts the note reference mark you specified and then:

- In Normal view, the Note pane opens. Type the text of your note beside the note reference mark. You can then press F6 to move the insertion point into the document window in the position where you inserted the note. In this way, both the Note pane and the document window appear on your screen at the same time. You can work in either pane by repositioning the insertion point either with the mouse or by pressing the F6 key. You can also click Close to hide the Note pane and return to your document. Insert another note or choose View ➢ Footnotes to redisplay the Note pane.

- In Print Layout view, the insertion point moves to the actual location where the note will appear in your document. Type the text of the note, and then press Shift+F5 or double-click the note's reference number to return to the location where you inserted the note reference mark in your document.

 TIP You can use Shift+F5 anytime to return the insertion point to the last three locations in the document where you edited text.

You can decide which view is easier to use when working with notes. In either view, when you want to review your note, all you have to do is point to the reference mark. The mouse pointer changes to an I-beam with a note attached to it, and a second later the note text appears. Just move the mouse pointer away, and the note disappears.

If you are not satisfied with the location of the notes, the note reference marks, and the way the notes are numbered, you can make some changes to it. For example, you can change the format of automatically numbered notes (Arabic numerals such as 1, 2, 3) to uppercase or lowercase letters, Roman numerals, or a list of symbols, which Word uses in a set pattern. You can also specify a position for the location of the notes in your document. Any changes you make to the way the notes appear are applied to all the footnotes or endnotes in the document.

To change the way footnotes and endnotes appear, use the following steps:

1. Select the note reference number you wish to change and choose Insert ➢ Reference ➢ Footnote to display the Footnote And Endnote dialog box shown previously in Figure 11.1.

2. Choose a different Number Format, Custom Mark, Start At number, or Numbering type.

3. If you wish to convert a footnote to an endnote, or the reverse, choose a different option in the Location area of the dialog box. You can convert this one instance, or you can change them all. If you wish to change them all, click Convert to open the Convert Notes dialog box. Select from the following options:

   Convert All Footnotes To Endnotes Changes all footnotes into endnotes

   Convert All Endnotes To Footnotes Changes all endnotes to footnotes

   Swap Footnotes And Endnotes Simultaneously changes all footnotes to endnotes and all endnotes to footnotes

4. Click OK in Convert Notes dialog box, and then click OK the Footnote And Endnote dialog box to both insert a note in the new format and change all existing notes to the new format.

Revising Footnotes and Endnotes

Now that you have footnotes and endnotes scattered throughout your text, you may need to edit one of the notes. There are several ways to activate a note so you can edit it:

- Double-click any reference mark in Normal view to open the Note pane at the bottom of the screen. All notes of the same type appear in the pane—just scroll to the one you want to edit, make your changes, and click Close.

- If you are looking for a specific note in Normal view, click the Select Browse Object button on the vertical scroll bar, choose Go To, select Footnote or Endnote, enter the reference mark number you are looking for, and choose Go To. The insertion point automatically moves to the note in the Note pane.

- Move the insertion point into the notes area in Print Layout view and select the text you want to edit. Type the new text to replace the selected text.

You cannot edit the note reference mark directly in the document. Instead, you must delete the note, choose Insert ➢ Reference ➢ Footnote so you can change the numbering or custom mark symbol, and/or then retype the text of the note.

PART

II

CREATING QUALITY TEXT
DOCUMENTS USING WORD

TIP If you are changing a note reference mark and know you have to retype the note text, why not select the text and copy it to the Clipboard first? Once you've modified the reference mark, you can just paste the text back into the Note pane.

Deleting Notes

When you want to delete a note entirely, click before or after the reference mark and press the Backspace or Delete key twice—the first time selects the reference mark, and the second time deletes both the mark and the note. Deleting the text inside the Note pane or at the bottom or end of the document does not delete the reference mark in the document.

Using Bookmarks

Bookmarks are named locations in a document. It's useful to be able to mark an item or a location that you want to return to later, especially when you are working with long documents. The bookmark could be a place where you need to insert some additional information before finishing the final draft, or a location in the document that contains information pertinent to the current topic. You can also create a bookmark to serve as the destination of a hyperlink in a document (see "Adding Hyperlinks to Make Navigation Easy" later in this chapter). Whatever the reason, by inserting bookmarks you can easily move to specific text or objects in a document without having to scroll.

Bookmark names can include both numbers and letters, but they must begin with a letter. Although you cannot include spaces in a bookmark name, you can include the underline character to use instead of a space in names that consist of multiple words.

To insert a bookmark, use the following steps:

1. Select the text, graphic, table, or other object you want to mark. Alternatively, position the insertion point in the location you want to mark.

2. Choose Insert ➤ Bookmark to display the Bookmark dialog box, shown in Figure 11.2.

3. Type a name in the Bookmark Name text box.

4. Choose Add to create the bookmark and return to your document.

By default, you cannot see bookmarks in your document. To display bookmarks, you can do the following:

1. Choose Tools ➢ Options and display the View tab in the Options dialog box.

2. Check the Bookmarks check box in the Show area.

3. Click OK in the Options dialog box.

Large, gray brackets ([ ]) surround text or graphics to which bookmarks were added. A gray I-beam appears in the location in which a bookmark was inserted where no item was selected. The brackets are nonprinting characters, so if you're working a lot with bookmarks, it's handy just to leave them turned on.

Use the options available in the Bookmark dialog box to delete existing bookmarks, to display hidden bookmarks, such as cross-references, or to move to a different document location that was marked. To manage your bookmarks, use the following steps:

1. Choose Insert ➢ Bookmark to display the Bookmark dialog box.

2. To edit or move to bookmarks in a document, use one of the following options:

• To delete a bookmark, highlight its name in the Bookmark Name list box and choose Delete.

• To change the order in which the bookmark names are displayed in the Bookmark Name list box, choose an option in the Sort By area. Choose Name to display the bookmark names alphabetically. Alternatively, choose Location to display the bookmark names in the order in which they are located in the document.

• To select the document location or item that is marked, highlight the name of the bookmark in the Bookmark Name list box and choose Go To.

PART

II

CREATING QUALITY TEXT
DOCUMENTS USING WORD

3. When you are finished making changes or have found the location you want, click Close to return to your document.

Another way to move to and select a bookmark in your document is to use Word's Go To feature:

1. Click the Select Browse Object button at the bottom of the vertical scroll bar.

2. Select Go To in the menu that appears to display the Find And Replace dialog box.

3. Choose Bookmarks in the Go To What list box and select the name of the bookmark in the Enter Bookmark Name drop-down list.

4. Click Close to return to your document.

When you close the Go To dialog box, you can use the Previous Find/Go To and Next Find/Go To browse buttons, located above and below the Select Browse Object button on the vertical scroll bar, to move to and select each of your bookmarks.

Creating Cross-References

Use *cross-references* to refer to text or objects elsewhere in a document. Cross-references are used to automatically keep references within a document up-to-date throughout editing. For example, you might direct a reader to see a paragraph in a different chapter: "See 'Employee Benefits' in Chapter 5 for more information." If the Employee Benefits section is later moved to Chapter 4, you can rest assured that the reader will still look in the right place, because the cross-reference will be updated when the Employee Benefits section is moved.

 NOTE To insert cross-references to more than one document, change the documents into subdocuments of a master document. See "Managing Large Documents" later in this chapter for additional information.

Cross-references can be linked to bookmarks, headings, numbered items, footnotes, endnotes, equations, figures, and tables—and you can choose how the reference will appear in the document. For example, if you want to refer to a heading, you can have the cross-reference indicate the actual text of the heading, the page number where the text is found, or just the word "above" or "below."

To insert a cross-reference in a document, use the following steps:

1. For a text cross-reference, type any optional text before the position in which you want to insert the cross-reference. For example, type **See page** and then press the spacebar to insert a space. For a hyperlinked cross-reference, position the insertion point where you want the hyperlink.

2. Choose Insert ➢ Reference ➢ Cross-Reference to display the Cross-Reference dialog box shown in Figure 11.3.

3. Select the type of item to which the reference will refer in the Reference Type drop-down list. A list of the items of that type in the document appears in the list box.

4. Select the item in the For Which Numbered Item list box to which the cross-reference will refer.

5. Choose what you want to include in the reference in the Insert Reference To drop-down list. This item will be inserted in the position of the insertion point in the document. For example, select Page Number to have the page number of the item selected in step 4 appear beside your optional text.

6. Choose Insert to insert the cross-reference.

7. Repeat the steps above to insert as many cross-references as necessary, and then click Close to return to your document.

PART

II

CREATING QUALITY TEXT
DOCUMENTS USING WORD

FIGURE 11.3

The Cross-Reference dialog box allows you to insert a reference to information in another location in the same document.

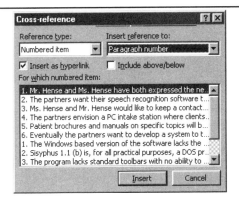

Cross-references are inserted as fields in the document. By default, the results of the field codes appear. If you want to see the actual field code, right-click the field and choose Toggle Field Codes. To display the results of the field code, right-click the field again and choose Toggle Field Codes.

NOTE   The Field Code commands do not appear on the shortcut menu if the field codes contain a grammatical error, such as no space between the field code and the period of the previous sentence. You must correct the grammatical error before Word will display the shortcut menu with the Field Code commands.

 MASTERING THE OPPORTUNITIES

Mastering Field Codes

Field codes are used in documents as placeholders for data that may change. Fields help you automatically enter some types of information. Some fields that are commonly used in documents include the Page field, which automatically updates the page numbers, and the Date field, which automatically inserts today's date (retrieved from Windows). In document-heavy businesses, the filename and path to a saved document are often displayed in a footer, making it easy to locate a file from a printed document. Speaking of printing, in businesses where a document undergoes several edits, it helps to use a field code to display the date each draft is printed. That way an attorney knows at a glance which version of the contract is more recent before he meets with the client to review it!

By default, the results of field codes appear in your documents rather than the field codes themselves. When field codes are displayed, they appear in curly brackets ({ }). To change the view so that the field codes, rather than the results, are displayed, follow these steps.

1. Choose Tools ≻ Options, and display the View tab in the Options dialog box.
2. Click the Field Codes check box to place a check mark in it.
3. Click OK in the Options dialog box.

Fields are inserted when you use specific commands, some of which are located on the Insert menu. For example, to insert page numbering (the Page field code), choose Insert ≻ Page Numbers, choose the position and alignment, and then click OK. If you want to manually insert field codes, do not type the curly brackets. Instead, press Ctrl+F9 to have Word insert the field-code brackets and then type the appropriate data between them.

Word's field codes can be found in the Field dialog box, which is displayed when you choose Insert ≻ Field.

If you make any changes to the document, you should manually update the results of the field codes. To do so, follow these steps:

1. Choose Edit ➤ Select All to select the entire document.

2. Press F9, or right-click the selection, and then choose Update Field in the shortcut menu.

TIP To have Word automatically update all the field codes in a document before you print it, choose Tools , Options, display the Print tab, check the Update Fields check box in the Printing Options area, and then click OK.

Hyperlinking Cross-References for On-Screen Viewing

If your document is intended for use online or on screen, leave the Insert As Hyperlink check box checked to create a more active kind of cross-reference. When a user points to a hyperlinked cross-reference, a screen tip appears telling the user they will go to a location in the current document if they hold Ctrl and click the hyperlink. Hold Ctrl (the mouse pointer changes to a hand) and click once to move to the location in the document to which the hyperlink cross-reference refers.

TIP If you prefer to follow hyperlinks with a single click as you do on the Web, disable the Ctrl+click feature by choosing Tools , Options , Edit and clearing the check box in front of Use Ctrl+click To Follow Hyperlink.

If you'll be moving back and forth in your document, you may find it helpful to turn on the Web toolbar. Right-click any toolbar and choose Web. Click the Back button on the Web toolbar to return to the point of origin, the hyperlink cross-reference. Click the Forward button to jump once again to the position to which the hyperlinked cross-reference refers.

Be careful not to delete an item that is referenced or the link will be broken. If the cross-reference is a hyperlink, Word will take your readers to another location that contains similar text. Users clicking the See Employee Benefits hyperlink could find themselves, for example, on the Termination of Employment page—probably not the message you want to convey.

Indexing for Easy Reference

You can make lengthy documents more user-friendly by creating an index of key words and phrases. Index entries can consist of individual words, phrases, or symbols that you select in your document; a topic that extends through several pages that you have named as a bookmark; or a topic that references another index entry.

Although marking index entries is a manual process, Word automates the creation of the index and will update it on request. Word automatically inserts the XE (Index Entry) field code for each marked entry. You can either mark the entries individually or have Word mark every instance of the same entry.

To mark the first index entry, follow these steps:

1. Select the text you want to include in the index and press Alt+Shift+X to display the Mark Index Entry dialog box shown in Figure 11.4.

2. The selected text appears in the Main Entry text box. If necessary, edit the text so it appears as you want it in the index.

3. To place subentries below the main index entry when the index is generated, type up to two additional entries, separated by a colon, in the Subentry text box. For example, when the main entry is Graphics, type **text box:Auto-Shape** to include both of those topics below the Graphics topic in the index.

4. Choose one of the following options in the Options area to specify what type of index entry you want the marked text to be:

   Cross-Reference Adds the cross-reference text you type to the index entry instead of the page number. When you select this option, type the name of another index entry after See in the corresponding text box. For example, if the main entry is Text Box, type **graphics** after See.

   Current Page Automatically adds the page number after the marked entry.

   Page Range Allows you to select a previously named bookmark, which defines text that spans multiple pages, in the adjacent drop-down list.

5. To add bold or italic formatting to the entry's page number, check the Bold or Italic check box in the Page Number Format area.

6. Choose one of the following to mark the index entry:

   Mark Labels only the selected text in your document as an index entry

   Mark All Labels every occurrence of the selected text in your document

---

 NOTE You can also display the Mark Index Entry dialog box by choosing Insert ➤ Reference ➤ Index And Tables and then clicking Mark Entry.

The Mark Index Entry dialog box stays open while you return to your document and select the next text you want to appear in the index. When you click back in the dialog box, the selected text appears in the Main Entry text box.

PART

II

CREATING QUALITY TEXT
DOCUMENTS USING WORD

FIGURE 11.4

Use the Mark Index Entry dialog box to create several different types of entries for an index in the current document.

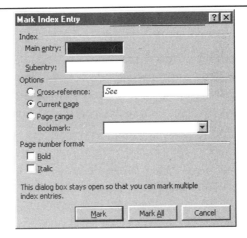

 NOTE A cross-reference index entry occurs only once in the index. As a result, you can choose Mark, but not Mark All, when marking cross-references.

 MASTERING THE OPPORTUNITIES

Marking Index Entries Using a Concordance File

A *concordance file* is a regular Word file that Word uses to automatically mark index entries in your document. A concordance file contains a two-column table. The exact text to be marked in the document is typed or pasted into the first column, and the text that is to appear in the index for that entry is typed in the second column. When you are ready, Word searches through the document for the text in the first column and marks it with an index entry field that includes the text in the second column.

Businesses with common terminology or technical jargon often use a concordance file to mark index entries. It saves the user from having to mark each entry individually

Continued

MASTERING THE OPPORTUNITIES CONTINUED

when the same terms are marked again and again over different documents. You can always use the concordance file as a starting point and add the terms that are specific to each document.

You must first set up the concordance file. To do so, follow these steps:

1. Open a new, blank document.
2. Create a two-column table.
3. Type (or paste) the text you want Word to mark for the index entry in the first column. The text must be entered exactly as it appears in the document.
4. Press Tab to move the insertion point to the next cell and type the index entry for the text that appears in the first column.
5. Repeat steps 3 and 4 for every index entry. To make sure Word marks all occurrences of the text you want, be sure to include all forms of the word in the concordance table. For instance, you should include *hibernate*, *hibernating*, and *hibernation* on the left column and type the word *bears* for all three in the right column.
6. Save the file.

Once you've created the concordance file, follow these steps to have Word mark the index entries in the document:

1. Choose Insert ➢ Reference ➢ Index And Tables to display the Index tab in the Index And Tables dialog box.
2. Choose AutoMark and select the name of the concordance file, and then choose Open. Word searches the document for the text in the left column of the concordance file and uses the text in the right column for the index entry.

When you are finished marking entries, get up from your chair and stretch for a minute. It's a tedious process but well worth it, because Word will use the marked index entries to automatically generate the index.

When you're ready to generate the index, follow these steps:

1. Press Ctrl+End to move the insertion point to the last page of your document, and then enter a heading for the index. Press Enter a couple of times to leave some space after the heading.
2. Choose Insert ➢ Reference ➢ Index And Tables to display the Index And Tables dialog box shown in Figure 11.5.

3. Choose any of the following options to specify how you'd like to format the index:

Type Select an option to specify how all subentries will appear below main entries. The Indented option places subentries below main entries; the Run-In option places subentries on the same line as main entries.

Columns Adjust the value to specify the number of columns that will appear in the index. Choose Auto to have the index appear with the same number of columns as the document.

Language Select the language for the index.

Right Align Page Numbers Check the check box to have Word place the entries' page numbers along the right margin of the page or column. Then select dots, dashes, underline, or none as the character that appears before the right-aligned page numbers.

Formats Select the styles to apply to the index. If you choose From Template, choose Modify to display the Style dialog box and then make any necessary changes to the selected index style.

4. When the sample index in the Print Preview area appears with the formatting you want for your index, click OK to generate the index in the position of the insertion point.

FIGURE 11.5

Display the Index tab in the Index And Tables dialog box when you are ready to generate the index.

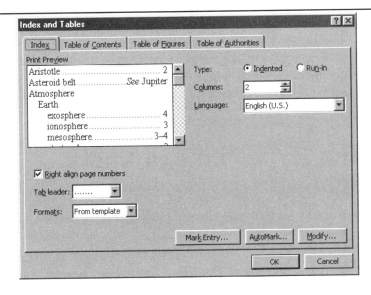

NOTE Apply a heading style to the index heading if you want to include it in your table of contents later. See "Generating a Table of Contents" later in this chapter to learn about creating a table of contents.

Word gathers the marked index entries and then uses them to create the index. A continuous section break mark is automatically inserted before and after the index. Go through each entry in the index to make sure it says what you want it to say and that the references are accurate. If you find any errors, you can fix them in the index, but any changes made to the index itself will be lost if you regenerate the index. Instead, make any necessary changes in the Index Entry (XE) fields inserted in the document and then regenerate the index.

 NOTE Just as with cross-references, you can't see Index entries unless the Show/Hide button on the Standard toolbar is turned on.

To regenerate the index after making changes, follow these steps:

1. Choose Insert ➢ Reference ➢ Index And Tables and then click OK to regenerate the index.

2. Word selects the existing index and displays a dialog box asking whether you want to replace it. Choose Yes.

If you edit the document after you generate the index, some of the page numbers in the index may no longer be correct. You can update the index without regenerating it because the entire index is a field. (The index that appears is the result of entering the Index field code at the insertion point.) To update the index, click anywhere in it and press F9. Any edits or formatting you've applied directly to the index are replaced when you update it.

Adding Hyperlinks to Make Navigation Easy

A *hyperlink*, a connection between two areas of a document or two different documents, is commonly used in Internet and intranet sites and other documents that are to be viewed online. By clicking a hyperlink, you can move to a different location in the same document, a different file, or even an address on the World Wide Web. For example, you can insert a hyperlink in a Word document that opens a PowerPoint presentation.

Hyperlinks are underlined and appear in a different font color. (If they don't stand out, no one knows to click them!) By default, hyperlinks appear in a blue font on your screen. Once you click the hyperlink, it changes to magenta.

 NOTE Type the e-mail or Web page address directly in a Word document to have Word automatically insert the address as a hyperlink. If the address does not appear as a hyperlink, check the Internet And Network Paths With Hyperlinks check box on the AutoFormat As You Type tab and AutoFormat tab in the AutoCorrect dialog box (Tools ➤ AutoCorrect Options).

There are several ways to create hyperlinks in your documents. The easiest way is to drag into your Word document selected text or graphics from a Word document or PowerPoint slide, an Excel spreadsheet range, or an Access database object. The document that contains the selection must have previously been saved.

When you drag the selection, Word automatically knows the location of the object you dragged. It is not necessary to create bookmarks in the destination document or to name ranges in the destination worksheet before you drag a selection.

To create a hyperlink by dragging selected text or a selected object, use the following steps:

1. Open the file that contains the text or other object and also open the Word document in which a hyperlink is to be inserted.

2. Display both files on your screen. If the two files are both Word files, use the Window ➤ Arrange All command to have the two open documents arranged horizontally on your screen. If the destination file is an Access, Excel, or PowerPoint file, open the file and display the location the hyperlink will jump to and then resize both applications' windows so you can see them on your screen.

3. Select the object the hyperlink will jump to in the destination file.

4. Hold down the right mouse button and drag the selection into the position you want for the hyperlink in your Word file.

5. Release the button and choose Create Hyperlink Here from the shortcut menu.

TIP You can also use the Clipboard to create a hyperlink. Copy the data or object to the Clipboard and position the insertion point where you want to create the hyperlink. Choose Edit ➢ Paste As Hyperlink to create the hyperlink in your Word document.

When you point to the hyperlink, the path to its destination file appears in a screen tip. If you position the insertion point within the hyperlink text, you can then edit it. Use the arrow keys to position the insertion point. If you use your mouse, selecting the hyperlink text can be a little tricky because you'll often jump to the destination file.

You can also insert a hyperlink to an e-mail or Web page address, specify descriptive text for the hyperlink in a screen tip, or browse for the exact path of a hyperlink's destination file using the options available in the Insert Hyperlink dialog box.

To use the Insert Hyperlink dialog box to insert a hyperlink, follow these steps:

1. Position the insertion point where you want to insert the hyperlink and choose Insert ➢ Hyperlink to display the Insert Hyperlink dialog box, like the one shown in Figure 11.6.

2. Specify the following options for the destination:

    • Click Existing File Or Web Page in the Link To area. Then type the path to the file or the address of the Web page in the Address text box. Alternatively, adjust the Look In control and select one of the files or Web pages that appears in the list box. The addresses in the list box change depending on which option (Recent Files, Browsed Pages, or Current Folder) is selected in the Link To bar.

 TIP If you choose a Web page, you can click the Target Frame button to select an exact location on the page or to open the page in a separate window.

    • Choose Place In This Document in the Link To area. Then select the name of a heading or a bookmark or one of the locations listed in the Select An Existing Place In The Document list box and click OK to insert the hyperlink and close the dialog box.

    • Choose Create New Document in the Link To area. Then type a filename for the document in the Name Of New Document field. Choose whether you wish to edit the new document now (Word will display the blank document immediately) or later (Word saves the blank document and inserts the hyperlink—you can open the blank document and edit it at any time).

- Choose E-mail Address in the Link To area. Type the address in the E-mail Address field (or select one from the list of recently used e-mail addresses). Type a subject line for the e-mail, if you wish.

3. To have descriptive text appear as the hyperlink in your document, type it in the Text To Display text box.

4. By default, the address in the Address box appears as the screen tip for the hyperlink. Choose ScreenTip to display the Set Hyperlink ScreenTip dialog box, type the descriptive text that will appear in the screen tip when you point to the hyperlink in the ScreenTip Text box, and then click OK.

5. Click OK to insert the hyperlink in your document.

FIGURE 11.6

Use the options in the Insert Hyperlink dialog box to insert a hyper-link to a file, a Web page, an e-mail address, a location in the current document, or to create a new document as the hyperlink's destination.

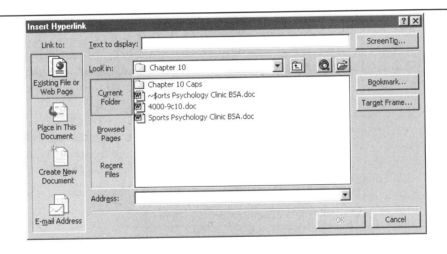

Generating a Table of Contents

Creating a table of contents (TOC) is similar to creating an index. However, instead of marking entries to generate the table of contents, you apply Word's built-in heading styles to the text that is to appear in the TOC. Word automatically selects the document's headings and lists them in the table of contents. If you did not apply heading styles when you created the document, you can go through the document and apply them before you create the table of contents.

In Word 2002 the document headings are entered as hyperlinks in the table of contents. You can point to one of the headings to move immediately to that position in the document. If the document is to be printed, display it in Print Layout view so the page numbers appear along with the headings. If the document is to be viewed online, display it in Web Layout view so that the headings are displayed as hyperlinks.

To create the table of contents, follow these steps:

1. Position the insertion point at the beginning of the document and choose Insert ➢ Reference ➢ Index And Tables to display the Index And Tables dialog box, previously shown in Figure 11.5.

2. Select the Table Of Contents tab in the Index And Tables dialog box, shown in Figure 11.7.

3. Choose any of the following options for your TOC:

   Show Page Numbers Check this box to have page numbers appear when the document is viewed in Print Layout view or when the document is printed.

   Right Align Page Numbers Check this box to have displayed or printed page numbers aligned along the right margin of the page. Adjust the Tab Leader control to select None, dots, dashes, or underline as the character to appear before the page number.

   Formats Select the formatting you want for the table of contents. If you choose From Template, choose Modify to display the Style dialog box and then make any necessary changes to the TOC headings.

   Show Levels Adjust the value in the text box to display the number of heading levels you want to appear in the table of contents.

4. Click OK to generate the table of contents.

When you generate the table of contents, a page break is inserted above the insertion point, and Word enters the TOC field code on the new page.

FIGURE 11.7

The Table Of Contents tab in the Index And Tables dialog box shows you samples of the table of contents in both Print Preview and Web Preview views.

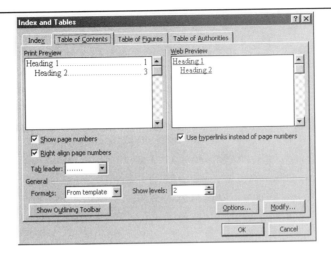

Using Other Options to Create a Table of Contents

You can also create a table of contents using a combination of outline levels, existing styles (other than heading styles) and TC (table of contents entry) fields. If you want to use other styles or outlining, simply assign each style a TOC level and/or outline level. To mark table of contents entries exactly as you want them to appear in the table of contents, insert TC field codes immediately before the text entry you want to include in the table of contents. Click Insert ➤ Field and choose TC to insert a TC field code. Follow these steps to use either option to create a table of contents:

1. Choose Insert ➤ Reference ➤ Index And Tables ➤ Table Of Contents and then click Options to display the Table Of Contents Options dialog box.

Continued

CONTINUED

2. Check the Styles check box to have Word build the table from available styles in your document and then assign each style the appropriate TOC level by typing the level in the adjacent TOC Level text box.

3. Check the Table Entry Fields check box if you inserted TC field codes in the document.

4. Enable the Outline Levels feature if you'd like to include text marked with outline levels in place of or in addition to styles in your TOC.

5. Click OK to return to the Index And Tables dialog box.

6. Choose the formatting for the table of contents from any of the available options.

7. Click OK to generate the table of contents.

Modifying a TOC

Although you can directly edit the text in the table of contents, any changes you make will be lost if you regenerate the table or update the TOC field code. In addition, you need to use the arrow keys to move to the text you want to edit because each table of contents entry is a hyperlink.

Generally, it's a good idea to update the entire table of contents instead of editing it. For example, if you edit the text of the document, the page numbers in the table of contents may be incorrect.

When you want to update the table, move the insertion point into it and press F9. Or, if the Outlining toolbar is turned on, click the Update TOC button on it. If the page numbers still don't seem to be correct, check the following:

• Index entry fields are formatted as hidden text. To hide them and other hidden text so they do not appear in the document (and increase its on-screen length), click the Show/Hide ¶ button on the Standard toolbar. Then update the table of contents.

• Remove any hidden section or page breaks from the document, and then update the table of contents.

If you decide that you want fewer (or additional) heading levels to appear in your TOC, choose Insert ➤ Reference ➤ Index And Tables ➤ Table Of Contents and adjust the number of heading levels. You can also change the tab leader by selecting a different one from the Tab Leader list. When you click OK, the TOC regenerates with the requested number of levels. In some documents, you may even want two TOCs—one with all heading levels and one with only the first-level headings.

Managing Large Documents

As a policy manual, personnel handbook, report, contract, or similar document gets longer, it uses more resources to open, save, or print. It takes forever to scroll down a couple of pages, and editing becomes a nightmare. With a little foresight, you can avoid this dilemma by starting with an outline and then dividing the entire document, called the *master document*, into various related documents, called *subdocuments*. You—and others in your work group—can then work with subdocuments as autonomous entities. However, at any point you can work with the entire master document so that you can have continuous page numbering, add headers and footers, create a table of contents, attach an index, and insert cross-references—all those things you cannot do with individual, unrelated documents.

What if you're already 10 chapters into a large document? Don't despair—those kind people at Microsoft were thinking of you when they created master documents. Word 2002 can combine separate documents into one master document and divide one long document into several subdocuments. So there's no excuse for working with a document that's out of control—the remedy is right at your fingertips.

Creating Master Documents and Subdocuments

To create a new master document from scratch, open a new document and display it in Outline view. To change to Outline view, choose View ➢ Outline or click the Outline View button next to the horizontal scroll bar.

The Master Document tools appear on the Outlining toolbar. Create an outline just as you normally would (see "Creating an Outline" in Chapter 8), using the same heading level for each section that you want subdivided into its own document.

When you have finished creating the outline, select the headings and text you want to split into subdocuments. Click the Create Subdocument button on the Outlining toolbar, and Word creates individual subdocuments using the highest-level heading text you selected as the subdocument name.

The master document displays each subdocument in a box with a small subdocument icon in the upper-left corner when displayed in Master Document view (the default). Click the Master Document View button on the Outlining toolbar to display the master document in Outline view. When you do, the subdocument icon and box no longer appear, and the display shows the section break marks that Word inserted before each selected heading when you created subdocuments.

When you save the master document, each subdocument is automatically saved in a separate file in the same folder as the master document, using the first part of the heading text as the filename. In addition, each subdocument automatically becomes a hyperlink in the master document. When the master document is open, you can simply click the hyperlink of a subdocument to open it for editing. In addition, you can open a subdocument when the master document is not open, using the same methods you would use to open any other file.

NOTE To open a subdocument before you save the master document, double-click its subdocument icon.

The primary purpose of creating a master document is to be able to work with discrete sections of the document. It makes sense, then, to collapse the master document so that just the document names are visible. Word automatically displays the master document with collapsed subdocuments when you open the master document file. If you want to see all the text in the entire document, click the Expand Subdocuments button on the Outlining toolbar. The button is a toggle switch—clicking the Collapse Subdocuments button on the Outlining toolbar will collapse the subdocuments again.

The subdocuments of a master document can be *locked*, which makes them read-only files. Read-only files can be viewed, but no changes can be saved to them. To lock a subdocument, click the Lock Document button on the Outlining toolbar. Click the Lock Document button again to unlock a locked subdocument.

NOTE In Master Document view, subdocuments are collapsed by default and always appear to be locked—the subdocument icons have padlocks, even if they are not. To see whether the subdocuments in a master document actually are locked, click the Expand Subdocuments button on the Outlining toolbar.

Word automatically locks an open subdocument. If someone opens a subdocument that is already open, it opens as a read-only document. In addition, subdocuments that are shared as read-only are locked, as are subdocuments stored on a read-only file share.

When the master document is expanded, you can work with it as if it were one document by switching to Normal or Print Layout view. You can apply page numbering; insert headers and footers, a table of contents, index, and cross-references; and adjust styles just as you would in a normal document. The styles in the master document's template are used for all the subdocuments when the document is printed. If you want to use different formatting for a subdocument, change the formatting in the master document section that contains the subdocument. The page numbers, borders, headers, margins, and number of newspaper columns can be changed in individual sections of a master document.

NOTE You can use a different template in a subdocument. To do so and then print the subdocument with different styles from those in the master document, open the subdocument in its own window and print it from there. You can also change the section's formatting by opening the subdocument in its own window and then making the changes.

Converting Existing Documents

For a document to be converted to a master document, you must apply Word's built-in heading styles to some of the text so you can work with it in Outline view. After you have applied heading styles, you can switch to Master Document view and follow the same steps you would to create a new master document.

If you have several documents that you want to combine into one master document, follow these steps:

1. Open a new, blank document or a document based on the template you want to use for the master document. Make sure you are in Outline view or you won't see the tools you need on the Outlining toolbar.

2. Position the insertion point where you want to insert an existing document and click the Insert Subdocument button on the Master Document toolbar to display the Open dialog box.

3. Select the name of the file to insert and click Open. The subdocument appears expanded by default.

4. Click the Collapse Subdocument button if you wish to collapse the subdocument. Word prompts you to save if it's a new master document.

5. Click a subdocument's icon to select it. Press the Shift key while you click to simultaneously select another subdocument.

Once you've selected files, you can can do the following:

- To merge two subdocuments, select both files and click the Merge Subdocuments button on the toolbar.

- To split one subdocument into two, place the insertion point where you want to split and click the Split One Subdocument button.

- To delete a subdocument, select it and press the Delete key.

- To convert a subdocument to master document text, select it and click the Remove Subdocument button.

Printing Master Documents

When all the text is entered in the subdocuments and all the formatting is applied to the master document along with a table of contents, index, and any other document items, you are ready to print the master document. Word allows you to print the entire master document or only specified details, depending on the heading levels and text displayed on your screen.

To print the entire master document, do the following:

1. Click the Expand Subdocuments button on the Outlining toolbar to expand the subdocuments.

2. Change the display to Normal or Print Layout view.

3. Print as you would any other document.

To print only some of the details of the master document, follow these steps:

1. Click the Expand Subdocuments button on the Outlining toolbar to expand the subdocuments.

2. Use the Show Heading buttons and the Expand and Collapse buttons on the Outlining toolbar to specify the amount of detail you want to print.

3. Print the document as you would any other document.

The printed master document is now ready to be bound, copied, or distributed as you sit back and wait for the accolades that will surely be showered upon you for your Herculean effort!

CHAPTER 12

WORKING COLLABORATIVELY WITH WORD

FEATURING

- Saving multiple versions of a document

- Tracking changes to a document

- Accepting or rejecting changes

- Inserting comments

- Highlighting changes

- Adding comments using document summary information

- Protecting documents

- Routing documents

- Comparing and merging documents

M any companies today use a team approach to completing word-processing projects. Your company's human resources or policy manual, for example, is probably the result of the efforts of many different people. The ability to work together on these complex documents saves time, money, energy, and paper. Word 2002 is designed to make working together easier and more productive. In this chapter, we'll cover Word's Reviewing tools and protecting and routing documents. In Chapters 28 and 29, you can find out about using Office XP's new Web features to work together on documents over the company intranet.

Saving Multiple Versions of a Document

Word's Reviewing tools, including versioning, tracking changes, comments, and the highlighter, allow you to keep your online documents intact while permitting others' input. In addition, Word allows you to protect a document so that the tracked changes and comments cannot be edited. You can easily access all of the Reviewing tools from the Reviewing toolbar. To display the toolbar, right-click any toolbar and then choose Reviewing.

When working with others, one of Word's most useful features is its capability to save multiple versions of a document. For example, if you are sending an online document to be reviewed by team members or supervisors, you can save the original version, and then save the version that includes the changes suggested by reviewers.

Prior to versioning, if you wanted to change and save a document and keep the original intact, you had to remember to save the revised document using a different filename. If you're like most people, there were those inevitable times when you saved without thinking and, with one click of the mouse, wiped out any vestige of the original document. Word's versioning feature allows you to save multiple versions of a document within the document itself and open a different version to edit.

 NOTE Word saves only the changes that were made to the document, not the entire document, when you save a version.

To save a version of the active document, follow these steps:
1. Choose File ➢ Versions to open the Versions In [*Document*] dialog box, shown in Figure 12.1. Previous versions (if any) appear in the list box with information about each saved version. (More on this below.)

2. Click Save Now to open the Save Version dialog box. The date, time, and name of the person creating this version are displayed at the top of the dialog box.

3. Type any comments you want to make about this version of the document in the Comments On Version text box.

4. Click OK. The Versions icon appears on the right side of the status bar to let users know that this document contains a version.

FIGURE 12.1

If you've saved previous versions of a document, they appear in the Versions In [Document] dialog box.

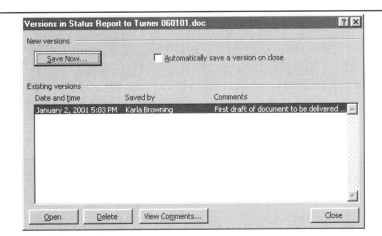

Word can automatically save a version of the document each time it is closed. This feature is useful if you need to keep track of who made changes to the document and when they were made. The most recently saved version of the document displays by default the next time you open the file.

Word also allows you to manage the versions in other ways. For example, you can see how many versions of the document have been saved, the date and time each was saved, and the name of the person who created each version. The most recent version appears highlighted at the top of the list.

Any existing version can be saved to a separate file. When the version is in a separate file, you can make sure that the reviewers are evaluating the most recent version (by circulating only that version), or you can compare it to another file to find changes that were made with Track Changes (discussed later in this chapter) turned off. You can also delete a saved version, which is useful when your file becomes large and seems to open and navigate more slowly.

PART

II

CREATING QUALITY TEXT
DOCUMENTS USING WORD

WARNING When you save a document as a Web page (see Chapter 28, "Exploring Office XP's Web Creation Tools"), any versions it contains are lost. Save the file as a regular document before you save it as a Web page, and use the document file to create any subsequent versions.

Use the following options to manage your versions and the size of the file:

1. Choose File ➤ Versions to display the Versions In [*Document*] dialog box, shown previously in Figure 12.1.

2. Check the Automatically Save A Version On Close check box to have Word save the document each time the file is closed.

3. Click Save Now to display the Save Version dialog box (shown in Figure 12.2), if you want to save the current version of the file. Alternatively, highlight the version you want to manage, and then use any of the following options:

   Open Opens the selected version in another window on your screen. (The document is also open and appears in its own window.)

   Delete Deletes the selected version when you no longer need it. After selecting this option, click Yes in the message box that appears to confirm the deletion.

   View Comments Displays a message box containing all of the comments that were entered by the reviewer when the selected version was saved.

4. If necessary, click Close to return to your document.

 NOTE When you delete a version of a document, you're only marking it for deletion. The version isn't deleted until you save the document.

Tracking Changes to a Document

Although saving each version of a document is helpful, it can still be difficult to identify where all the changes were made. To make that easier, Word can track each change to a document and allow you to accept or reject individual revisions or all revisions in one fell swoop. When Word's Track Changes feature is turned on, any changes to the document are indicated on your screen, and you can choose to print them when you print the document.

 NEW▶ To preserve document layout, Word now shows some of the changes inline and others in balloons in the margin of the document. With inline changes, newly inserted text appears both underlined and in a different color; deleted text appears with a strikethrough character through it and in a different color. In all cases, a vertical line in the outside margin indicates each line in the document where text has been changed.

NOTE   You must be in Print Layout or Web Layout view to see tracked changes in balloons.

To begin tracking changes, use one of the following methods to enable the feature:

- Click the Track Changes button on the Reviewing toolbar. The button is a toggle switch, so you can click it again to turn off the Track Changes feature.

TRK
- Double-click the dimmed TRK option on the status bar or right-click it and select Track Changes. This option is also a toggle switch, so you use the same method to turn off Track Changes when you are finished editing the document.

- Choose Tools ➢ Track Changes from the menu.

By default, each user's changes are visible. If a number of changes are made to the same section of a document, it gets pretty difficult to tell what text the document really includes. Each user's changes are visible by default. You can modify the tracking feature so that only formatting changes are visible, only insertions and deletions are visible, comments are not visible, or changes for a specific reviewer are visible and others are hidden. To do so, follow these steps:

NEW▶ 1. Click the Show drop-down list on the Reviewing toolbar.

2. Hide comments, insertions and deletions, and/or formatting by clicking the appropriate choice to remove the check mark.

3. To select a specific reviewer's changes, choose Show ➢ Reviewers and clear the check marks from the reviewers whose changes you do not wish to see.

As other people open the document, any changes they make appear in different colors (up to eight authors can work on one document before colors repeat). If you would prefer that all inserted text appear in one color and all deleted text in another, you can select a specific color for each. In addition, you can change the way Word indicates inserted and deleted text, changed formatting, or changed lines of text in the document.

Follow these steps to specify the formats and characters you want Word to use when tracking changes:

1. Click the Show drop-down list on the Reviewing toolbar and choose Options, or right-click the TRK icon on the status bar and then choose Options, or choose Tools ➢ Options to display the Track Changes tab, shown in Figure 12.2.

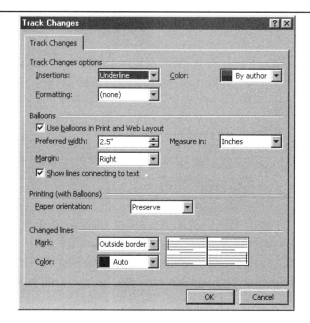

2. In the Track Changes Options area:

   • Choose an option from the Insertions drop-down list. Select (None), Color Only, Bold, Italic, Underline, or Double Underline as the format to apply to inserted text.

   • From the Formatting drop-down list, select (None), Color Only, Bold, Italic, Underline, or Double Underline as the format to apply to formatting changes.

3. Choose a Color Option for revisions:

   • Select the color in which all revisions appear or choose Auto to display all text changes in the default font color (usually black).

   • Choose the By Author option to have Word assign a different color to the first eight reviewers who insert text, delete text, or change the formatting applied to the document text.

4. In the Balloons area:

- Enable or disable the option to Use Balloons In Print And Web Layout.

- If you leave balloons enabled, use the spin control to select a Preferred Width and change the Measure In setting to reflect your preferred unit of measurement. Select whether to display the balloons in the right or left margin, and enable or disable the Show Lines Connecting To Text option depending, again, on your preference.

5. To set options for how Word prints with balloons, select a paper orientation from the drop-down list:

Preserve   Prints using the orientation specified in the Page Setup dialog box.

Auto   Lets Word print using the layout it deems best for the document.

Force Landscape   Prints the document in landscape orientation, leaving the most room for balloons

PART

II

 NOTE   These orientation options only apply if you choose Document Showing Markup in the Print dialog box. If you choose to print just the document, the regular page setup settings remain in effect.

6. In the Mark drop-down list, select (None), Left Border, Right Border, or Outside Border as the location for Word to insert a vertical line in the margin when any changes have been made to a line of text. Then choose a color for the line.

7. Click OK when you have finished adjusting Track Changes options.

To display information about a change, just point to the marked text to see a screen tip that indicates the type of change, who made it, and the time and date it was made.

 NOTE   If you wish to change the font in markup balloons, modify the Balloon Text style. For more information about creating and modifying styles, see Chapter 8, "Simplifying with Styles, Outlines, and Templates."

CREATING QUALITY TEXT
DOCUMENTS USING WORD

Choosing a Display for Review

When a document "makes the rounds," it is usually examined by people with different purposes in mind. For example, an author is usually interested in seeing changes in relation to how the original text was written. A proofreader needn't see changes at all. In fact, displaying multiple changes might interfere with accurate proofreading. Word 2002 allows you to display tracked changes from different points of view. Now it is even easier to review changes prior to accepting or rejecting them.

By default Word displays Final Showing Markup. Select from the Display For Review drop-down list on the Reviewing toolbar if you wish to see the document from another point of view. Choose from the following options:

Final   Shows how the document will look if you accept all changes.

Original   Shows how the document will look if you reject all changes.

Final Showing Markup   Displays deleted text in balloons and inserted text inline. Changes to formatting are visible. With this display, you can easily review suggested insertions because they are displayed inline.

Original Showing Markup   Leaves deletions inline and displays insertions and changes to formatting in balloons. Authors generally prefer this display for easy review of proposed changes.

Working with Changes in the Reviewing Pane

There may be times when you prefer to view a list of changes outside of the document text. Word 2002's new Reviewing pane allows you to do just that! Simply click the Reviewing Pane button on the Reviewing toolbar or click Show ➢ Preview Pane to display the pane below the horizontal scroll bar, as shown in Figure 12.3.

Four different sections in the Reviewing pane separate changes made to different parts of the document. Scroll the pane to see Main Document Changes And Comments, Text Box Changes, Footnote Changes, and Endnote Changes. If no changes have been made to a particular part, Word displays None.

You can adjust changes directly in the Reviewing pane if you wish. To do so, follow these steps:

1. Scroll to the change you wish to modify.

2. Click once in the pane to activate it, and then click again to place the insertion point.

3. Select, delete, insert, and format text as desired.

The Reviewing Pane button is a toggle. To hide the Reviewing pane, simply click the button again.

FIGURE 12.3

The Reviewing pane allows you to view and modify changes outside of the document text.

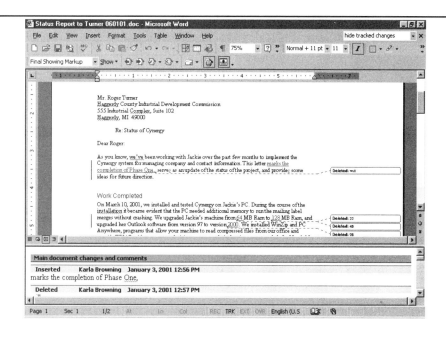

Accepting or Rejecting Changes

After a document has been edited by all reviewers, you can decide to accept or reject the changes. Here are your options on the Reviewing toolbar:

- To navigate through the document, click the Previous button to select the change preceding the position of the insertion point, or the Change button to select the change following the position of the insertion point.

NOTE If the Reviewing pane is turned on, the Change and Previous buttons automatically scroll the pane as needed.

- Click the Accept Change button to agree to the selected change, or the Reject Change button to remove the proposed change and return the document to its original text in this instance.
- To accept all changes to a document, click the drop-down arrow next to the Accept Changes button and choose Accept All Changes In Document.
- To reject all changes in a document, click the drop-down arrow next to the Reject Changes button and choose Reject All Changes In Document.

- If you've chosen not to display certain tracked changes—turned off formatting changes under the Show list, for example—you can choose Accept All Changes Shown or Reject All Changes Shown from the drop-down lists on the Accept and Reject buttons. Only changes you have chosen to display are affected.

TIP Click the Undo button on the Standard toolbar immediately after accepting or rejecting a change to return to the original edit.

Making Comments

When you're creating or editing a document with others, it's often valuable to be able to make comments that aren't part of the printed document but can be viewed on screen. Word 2002's Comments feature fits the bill. You can insert comments, view comments from one or all reviewers, and print the comments. Now in Word 2002, you can easily insert and play back voice comments.

When you insert a comment, Word places a comment indicator at the insertion point and displays the text of the comment in a balloon. If you are in Normal view, balloons are not visible, so the Reviewing pane opens instead.

To insert a comment, follow these steps:

1. Position the insertion point where you want to place the comment, and then either click the New Comment button on the Reviewing toolbar or choose Insert ➤ Comment.

2. Type the text of your comment in the Reviewing pane (for Normal view) or directly in the balloon (for Web Layout, Print Layout, and Outline views).

3. To insert another comment in Normal view, press F6 (which toggles between the document and Reviewing panes) or click in the document pane, and then repeat steps 1 and 2. To insert another comment in any other view, place the insertion point at the appropriate place in the document and repeat steps 1 and 2.

4. Toggle the Reviewing Pane button to hide the comments and other tracked changes in Normal view.

The steps for inserting a voice comment are slightly different, but no more difficult:

1. Place the insertion point at the appropriate location in the document.

2. Click the drop-down arrow next to the New Comment button.

3. Choose Voice Comment to open the Sound Object In Status Report dialog box.

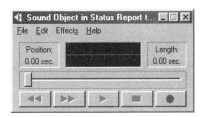

4. Click the Record button—it's the only one enabled—and then say your comment.

5. Click the Stop button when you're done commenting.

6. If you wish to rerecord your comment, click the Seek To Start button and repeat steps 4 and 5.

7. When you're finished, click the Close button to close the dialog box.

PART

II

CREATING QUALITY TEXT
DOCUMENTS USING WORD

WARNING If you're having trouble rerecording a comment, make note of its position and length as displayed in the dialog box. If you wish to rerecord a comment (rather than just add to it), make sure you speak over the entire position and length of the original sound.

Text comments are visible in balloons by default in Outline, Web, and Print Layout views. To make them visible in Normal view, or if you've disabled balloons in the Track Changes options, you must display the Reviewing pane. You can hide comments in Print Layout view by choosing Show ➤ Comments on the Reviewing toolbar to remove the check mark.

Voice comments are indicated by the sound icon at the point the voice comment was inserted (or in the appropriate position in the Reviewing pane). Double-click the sound icon to hear a voice comment.

NOTE If you can't hear comments on playback, you may need to adjust the volume of your speakers. If sound quality is still poor (or if you can't hear a thing), check your microphone setup. See Chapter 2, "Inputting Text with Speech and Handwriting Recognition Tools," for additional information about microphone configuration.

To see information about the comment's author, and the date and time commented, just position the mouse pointer over the comment balloon or sound icon for a moment—the information appears in a box above the text. If you're using the Reviewing pane, this information is automatically displayed with each comment, as shown in Figure 12.4.

 NOTE Word pulls the author's name from the User Information tab of the Options dialog box. If a generic or unrecognized name is being used for comment information, edit it there.

FIGURE 12.4

Text comments can be displayed in margin balloons and/or the Reviewing pane; voice comments appear as icons in the text.

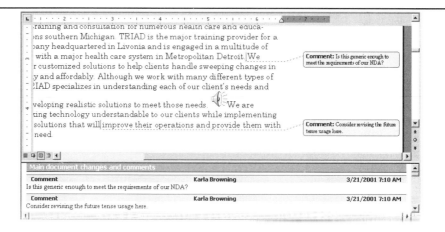

You have several choices for editing comments:

- Click directly in the balloon and edit the comment there.

- Click in the Reviewing pane and edit the comment's text as usual.

- To edit a voice comment, right-click the sound icon and choose Wave Sound Object ➤ Edit to display the Sound Object In Status Report dialog box. Click the Record button and say your new comment.

You can browse comments right along with other tracked changes using the Next and Previous buttons on the Reviewing toolbar. Once all comments are addressed, you can delete them from the document. You can delete them one at a time, by reviewer, or all at once.

To delete a single comment, do any one of the following:

- Click in the balloon you wish to delete and click the Reject Change/Delete Comment button on the Reviewing toolbar.

- Click in the balloon you wish to delete and click the drop-down arrow next to the New Comment button. Choose Delete Comment.
- Right-click the balloon you wish to delete and choose Delete Comment.
- Click the comment you wish to delete in the Reviewing pane and proceed with any of the above three actions.
- Select the sound icon of a voice comment and press Delete on the keyboard.

To delete comments by a particular reviewer:

1. Choose Show ➢ Reviewers on the Reviewing toolbar and clear the check boxes for the reviewers with comments you *don't* want to delete.

2. Click the drop-down arrow next to the Reject Change/Delete Comment button and choose Delete All Comments Shown.

To delete *all* comments in a document, click the drop-down arrow next to the Reject Change/Delete Comment button and choose Delete All Comments In Document.

Printing Tracked Changes and Comments

You can choose to print a document showing tracked changes and comments. Or you can print the list of changes without the document text. In either case, choose File ➢ Print to display the Print dialog box.

If you want to print the document showing comments and tracked changes, choose Document Showing Markup in the Print What drop-down list. Word adjusts the zoom level and page orientation as needed to display changes on the printed page.

To see a list of changes and comments, choose List Of Markup from the Print What drop-down list in the Print dialog box. The document changes and comments are printed consecutively along with the number of the page on which the comment is located.

Highlighting Text

Word 2002's highlighter is one of the easiest tools to use when you want to make sure that anyone reviewing an online document notices a particular section of text. Imagine using a highlighter pen, and you know almost everything you need to know to use this formatting feature.

To begin highlighting:

1. Click the Highlight button drop-down arrow and select one of the 15 colors in the palette. (Skip this step to accept the default highlight color, yellow.)

2. Click the Highlight button. The pointer changes into a highlighter pen with an I-beam attached.

3. Drag the pen over the text you want to highlight.

Because the highlighter includes an I-beam, you can highlight text as you select it. For example, double-click to highlight a word, and triple-click to highlight a paragraph.

When you are finished highlighting in your document, click the Highlight button again to turn off the highlighting feature. If you need to remove highlighting from text, select it and change the highlight color to None.

WARNING Some highlighting colors obscure the underlying text. Use a light color, such as yellow, if you intend to print a document with highlighting on a monochrome or dot matrix printer.

Adding Comments Using Document Summary Information

Every Windows file has a Properties sheet that contains information about the file—when it was created, who created it, when it was last modified, and so on. File properties help you to identify, locate, and organize your files. Word 2002 takes properties one step further by letting you enter detailed information about the document that others can view from the Open dialog box without actually opening the document.

NOTE Excel spreadsheet files, Access database files, and PowerPoint presentation files also have accessible Properties sheets.

There are three different types of file properties:

- *Automatic* properties are those that Word assigns values to. For example, the size of the file and the date it was created are both automatic properties.

- *Preset* properties are those for which you can enter specific text information—for example, the title, subject, comments, and keyword information.

NOTE When you use the AutoSummarize feature, a tool for generating executive summaries or abstracts of documents, Word automatically fills in the properties for keywords and comments. To disable this feature, choose Tools ➢ AutoSummarize, and then clear the Update Document Statistics check box.

- *Custom* properties are those you select from a built-in set of named properties, or those you create yourself. Custom properties can be linked to specific items in a file. For example, you can link a bookmark in a Word document to a custom property, and then search for all Word files that contain a property with that bookmark.

 TIP To automatically display the Document Name Properties dialog box when you save a file for the first time, choose Tools , Options , Save. Check the Prompt For Document Properties box and choose OK.

To display and add to the preset document properties:

1. Choose File ➢ Properties, and then, if necessary, click the Summary tab to display the options shown in Figure 12.5.

PART

II

CREATING QUALITY TEXT
DOCUMENTS USING WORD

FIGURE 12.5

Display or edit the properties of the active document on the Summary tab in the [Document Name] Properties dialog box.

Status Report to Turner 060101.doc Properties

General | Summary | Statistics | Contents | Custom

Title:

Subject:

Author: Karla Browning

Manager:

Company: TRIAD Consulting, LLC

Category:

Keywords:

Comments:

Hyperlink base:

Template: Normal.dot

☐ Save preview picture

OK   Cancel

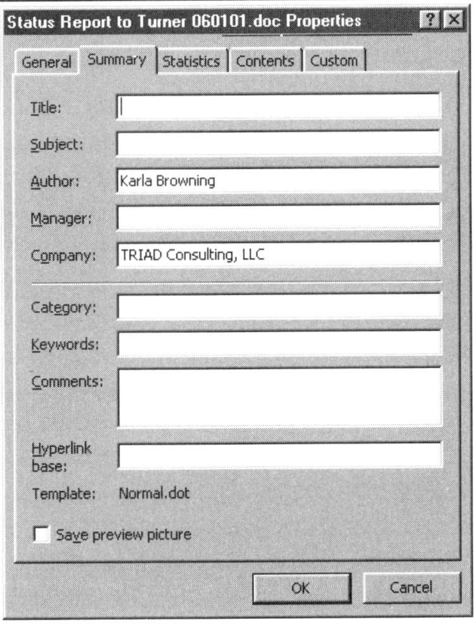

2. Enter any of the following information in the corresponding text box:

Title The Title text allows you to search for the file based on the text entered. The title can be different from the filename.

Subject Type a short description of the main topic of the document. The file's subject allows you to group it with files about the same subject, so you can search for all files regarding a particular topic.

Author Type the name of the document author. The user name for the computer on which it was created is entered automatically.

Manager This text is used to group files with the same project manager. Users can search for all the files that have the same manager when looking at a particular project.

Company This text box contains the name of the company that was entered when Office XP was installed on that computer. If you are doing work for a client, type the name of the company for which the document was created so users can search for all documents relating to that company.

Category If projects are grouped into classes or categories, type the class name. Users can access the information provided to search for all files in that category.

Keywords Type the keywords to use when searching for this file.

Comments Type any notes about the file so users can search for the file based on its comments.

Hyperlink Base Type the base address for all hyperlinks in the document. The address can be an Internet URL, such as `http://www.microsoft.com;` a path on your hard drive, such as `C:\My Documents\Personal;` or a path to a server, such as `\\Server\Shared\Newsletter Projects`. To use the hyperlink base address, you must type the name of the file, not browse for it, in the Type The File Or Web Page Name field in the Insert Hyperlinks dialog box.

3. Check the Save Preview Picture box to display a preview of the first page of the document (if it is a template) in the Templates dialog box.

4. Click OK in the [*Document Name*] Properties dialog box.

NOTE When you enable the Save Preview Picture check box, it increases the size of the file. For Word documents, you don't need a preview picture to preview the file in Word. Simply switch to Preview view in the Open dialog box to preview a Word document before you open it.

To view the properties of an unopened document:

1. Click the Open button on the Standard toolbar to display the Open dialog box, and then highlight the name of the file.

2. Choose Tools ➤ Properties to display the [*Document Name*] Properties dialog box, and then select the Summary tab, if necessary.

 NOTE You can click the Properties button in the Windows Explorer window to display the properties of the highlighted file. If you select the file in a folder viewed as a Web page, the Explorer will display the Author and Title properties and the preview (if you enabled the Preview property).

To preview the document:

1. Click the Open button on the Standard toolbar to display the Open dialog box, and then highlight the name of the file.

2. Click the Views drop-down list button to display its menu, and then choose Preview.

To search for all the files with a specified property, follow these steps:

1. Display the Open dialog box, and then choose Tools ➤ Search ➤ Advanced to display the Advanced tab of the Search dialog box.

2. Select the property that contains the information in the Property drop-down list.

 3. You must use Includes as your condition when searching for a property.

4. Type the text for that property in the Value text box.

5. Click Add to place the search criteria in the list box.

6. If you wish to use additional search criteria, select And or Or and repeat steps 2 through 5 until you've added all search criteria to the list box.

7. Select other search options as appropriate. Choose a Search In option and choose a Results Should Be option. Narrowing down the search by defining choices here can greatly reduce the amount of time it takes to display complete search results.

PART
II

CREATING QUALITY TEXT
DOCUMENTS USING WORD

8. Click Search to display the name of every file that meets the criteria you specified. Double-click a file to open it.

9. To clear search criteria and return to the Basic tab of the dialog box, click the Restore button.

 TIP You can search for files in the task pane using these same tools. Display the task pane (View ➢ Task Pane) and choose Search from the Task Pane drop-down list. Click Advanced Search at the bottom of the pane to search by document properties as described in the steps above.

Protecting Documents

Although you may not think there is much in your documents that anybody else would want, the gloomy truth is that your documents could become victims of corporate espionage or of unscrupulous colleagues out to pass your work off as their own. Add to that the risk that some well-meaning but misguided individual might revise one of your documents without your consent, and it's clear that it never hurts to be too careful when protecting your files and your work.

Word 2002 provides the following options to protect your documents:

• You can require a password to open the document.

• You can require a password to modify the document. Users without the password can open a read-only copy of the document. If they make changes to the document, they can't overwrite your original document. They must enter another filename or location.

• You can suggest, but not require, that users open the document as read-only.

• You can prevent changes from being made to a document you route for review, except for comments or tracked changes.

NEW▶

• You can add a digital signature to a document.

 WARNING Word gives you a stern warning that password-protected documents cannot be opened if you forget the password. Take this warning seriously. If you forget the password to open a document, Word will not let you open the document.

Passwords, which are case-sensitive, must be at least 1 character but no more than 15 characters in length, and can consist of letters, numbers, spaces, and symbols. A combination of uppercase and lowercase letters with numbers, spaces, and symbols is best—**bl%Ack ?9** is an example of a password that would be difficult to break. When you choose a password option, the password is not visible on the screen as you type it. Instead, Word asks you to reenter the password for verification.

To apply document protection when you save a document for the first time, follow these steps:

1. Click the Save button on the Standard toolbar to display the Save As dialog box.

2. Choose Tools ➢ Security Options to display the Security dialog box, shown in Figure 12.6.

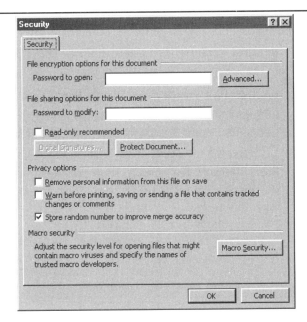

FIGURE 12.6

Display the Security options when you want to provide password protection or recommend read-only status to a document.

3. Choose any of the following options in the File Encryption Options For This Document area:

Password To Open Type a password to limit access to those who know the password.

Password To Modify Type a password to allow those who know the password to open the document and edit it. Users who don't know the password can open the file as a read-only document if they know the Password To Open or if you don't specify a Password To Open.

Read-Only Recommended Check this box to have Word ask the user whether or not to open the document as a read-only document. You do not need to specify a password when you recommend that a document be opened as read-only, but you can't prevent users from ignoring the recommendation.

NEW ▶

Advanced Choose a specific encryption type for your password to open in the Encryption Type dialog box. For example, if you wish to use a password longer than 15 characters, choose RC4. Click OK to close this dialog box.

4. Click OK in the Security dialog box. If you specified a password in step 3, the Confirm Password dialog box appears. You are prompted to confirm each password you entered.

5. Type the password again in the Confirm Password dialog box, and then click OK.

6. Enable or disable the Privacy options as follows:

Remove Personal Information From This File On Save Enable to hide information that appears with comments (the author's name, for example).

Warn Before Printing, Saving Or Sending A File That Contains Tracked Changes Or Comments Does just what it says, giving you the opportunity to remove these elements before you inadvertently share this information with others.

Store Random Number To Improve Merge Accuracy Disable this feature to remove the possibility of showing that two documents are related. You'll take a hit on accuracy when you merge documents, however. (See "Using Compare and Merge" later in this chapter.)

7. Click Save in the Save As dialog box.

 NOTE To password-protect a file you've already saved, choose Tools ➢ Options and click the Security tab. Alternatively, choose File ➢ Save As and follow steps 2 through 4 above.

To change or delete a password, open the document and reenter or delete the password on the Security tab.

Using a Digital Signature

NEW▶

In an age where a virus can send e-mail from you to everyone in your address book, document authentication is more important than ever. With Word 2002 you can *digitally sign* your important documents to confirm through electronic encryption that the information originates from you, it is valid, and it has not been modified since signed.

In order to digitally sign a document, you must have a digital certificate. There are several ways to do this, each with its own set of considerations.

Commercial Certification Authorities Companies such as VeriSign issue digital certificates upon approval of an application submitted by you or your company. This process can be time consuming, as information on the application must be fully verified by the certification authority before your digital certificate is issued. Furthermore, there is usually a cost associated with commercially issued digital certificates.

Information Technology Departments Some companies are equipped to issue their own digital signatures using tools such as Microsoft Certificate Server. Sometimes companies contract with an outside group qualified as a certification authority. Contact your network administrator or IT department to learn about the availability of certification services within your company.

Selfcert.exe Tools like this allow you to create your own digital certificate. Because the certificate isn't issued by a formal certification authority, however, it is considered unauthenticated and won't get past most security settings in Office XP.

Once you obtain and install your digital certificate, you can digitally sign files (and macros). To use a digital certificate, make sure you've finished all modifications to the file, and then follow these steps:

1. Choose Tools ➤ Options ➤ Security.

2. Click Digital Signatures to open the Digital Signature dialog box shown in Figure 12.7. Previous signers, if any, appear in the list box.

3. To add your own certification, click Add to open the Select Certificate dialog box. If you're working in Normal view, Word displays a prompt regarding hidden text and pictures. Click Yes to this prompt and Word switches you to Print Layout view. Then Word prompts you to save the document if it hasn't previously been saved.

4. Installed certificates appear in the Select Certificate dialog box. Click View Certificate to see details about the selected certificate. Then click the one you want to use and click OK three times to close all dialog boxes.

PART

II

CREATING QUALITY TEXT
DOCUMENTS USING WORD

FIGURE 12.7

Digitally sign important documents by attaching a digital certificate in the Digital Signature dialog box.

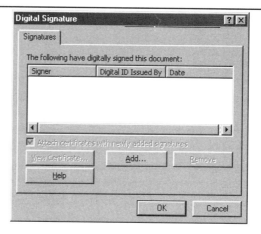

Protecting a Document before Review

If you're sending a document to several people for review, you probably want to make sure that none of the reviewers, either by accident or intention, hides their changes by turning off the Track Changes option, or by accepting or rejecting changes. You might want to make sure that the reviewers can insert comments, but not insert or delete any of the document's text. If the document is a form, you probably want to protect the form by ensuring that only the data in the form's fields can be entered, but that users cannot alter the structure or labels in the form.

 NOTE Word can warn you before sending files with tracked changes. That way you'll remember to turn document protection on. To enable the warning feature, choose Tools ➢ Options ➢ Security and check the box that says Warn Before Printing Saving Or Sending A File That Contains Tracked Changes Or Comments.

Follow these steps to protect your document against such revisions:

1. Open the document that is to be sent for review.

2. Check to see if the document contains more than one version. If it does, save the current version to a file with a different filename to prevent reviewers from seeing any previous versions of the document.

3. Choose Tools ➤ Protect Document or click the Protect Document button on the Security tab of the Options dialog box to display the Protect Document dialog box shown in Figure 12.8.

4. Choose one of the following options:

Tracked Changes Tracks all changes made by reviewers and prevents reviewers from either turning off the Track Changes feature, or from accepting or rejecting any changes. Reviewers can also insert comments in the document.

Comments Prevents reviewers from making any changes to the document text. They can insert comments, however.

Forms Prevents reviewers making any changes to a document except in form fields or unprotected document sections.

5. If you chose Forms in step 4, choose Section, enable the check box for each section in the document you want to protect, and then click OK. The sections are listed in the Protected Sections list box.

6. Type a password in the Password (Optional) text box, and then click OK to allow reviewers who know the password to turn off the Track Changes feature, accept or reject changes, edit regular document text, or edit the structure or labels in a form. Retype the password in the Confirm Password dialog box, and then click OK.

7. Save the document.

When a password is required, users must enter the password before they can unprotect the document.

PART

II

CREATING QUALITY TEXT DOCUMENTS USING WORD

WARNING If you don't require a password, anyone can unprotect a document by simply choosing Tools , Unprotect Document.

Routing Documents

Being connected to your colleagues—by a local or wide-area network, or through electronic mail—makes sharing and exchanging documents a snap. Word 2002 lets you dispatch a document in several ways.

Sending a Document for Review

 When you're satisfied with the first draft of the document and the protection you've applied, you are ready to send it to your reviewer(s). If you want to send the document to multiple reviewers all at once, or if you just want to send it to one person, consider using Word's new Send For Review feature. Word produces an e-mail message with the document attached. The automatically generated subject heading and message text indicate the document is for review. Further, Word turns on the Reviewing toolbar for your recipients. It's almost foolproof!

NOTE When you wish to send a document to a list of reviewers one at a time and in order, use the Routing feature discussed in the next section.

To send a document for review, choose File ➢ Send To ➢ Mail Recipient (For Review). Then follow these steps:

1. Address the message as you normally would.

2. Change the subject and message text if you wish.

3. Click Send.

 When the recipient opens the attachment, the Reviewing toolbar is already in place. Once the reviewer makes her changes, she can follow the same procedure to return the document to you. When you've decided to end the review cycle, click the End Review button (it's only visible when a document is sent using the above procedure) on the Reviewing toolbar. Confirm your decision in the message box and click OK. Word hides the Reviewing toolbar but leaves Tracked Changes on. You can quickly turn it off manually by double-clicking the TRK indicator in the status bar.

Using a Routing Slip

Word includes a routing slip feature, which specifies how to send an outbound document to reviewers. The routing slip can dispatch a document in either of the following ways:

- Use a routing slip to send a copy of the document simultaneously to all reviewers.

- Use a routing slip to send the same document to each reviewer, one at a time, in the order you specify so that subsequent reviewers can see the changes proposed by earlier reviewers. You can keep track of the location of the document when it is routed this way.

The routing slip can be saved with your document. A routed document is sent as an attachment to an e-mail message.

Routing requires a MAPI-compliant e-mail program, such as Outlook or Outlook Express or a VIM-compatible program such as Lotus cc:Mail.

To attach a routing slip to a document, follow these steps:

1. Choose File ➢ Send To ➢ Routing Recipient to display the Routing Slip dialog box shown in Figure 12.9.

2. Click the Address button to display your e-mail system's address book. Highlight the name of a reviewer, and then choose To to place the name in the Message Recipients list box. Choose the name of each reviewer in this way, and then click OK to return to the Routing Slip dialog box. Each name you selected appears in the To list box.

3. Type a subject for the e-mail message in the Subject text box. By default Word uses the word *Routing* followed by a colon and the title as entered in the document's properties (File ➢ Properties).

4. Type the e-mail message to send with the attached document in the Message Text box.

5. Choose one of the following options to specify how the document is to be routed to the reviewers:

    One After Another Sends the document to each reviewer in the order in which they are listed in the To list box at the top of the Routing Slip dialog box. Click the ↑ or ↓ Move button to change the order of the highlighted name.

    All At Once Simultaneously sends a copy of the document to each person listed in the To list box.

6. Check either of the following check boxes as necessary:

    Return When Done Automatically sends the routed document back to you when the last reviewer closes it.

Track Status Automatically sends you an e-mail message as the document is sent to the next reviewer in the list when the document is routed using the One After Another option.

7. Select (None), Tracked Changes, Comments, or Forms as the method of protection for the document in the Protect For drop-down list.

8. Click one of the following buttons to send the routing slip with the attached document:

OK Adds the routing slip to the document and closes the Routing Slip dialog box without sending the document. Choose this option when you want to edit the document before sending it.

Route Adds the routing slip to the document and sends it.

If you are routing the document to One After Another, you can choose to use the route settings previously established, or you can alter the routing slip before sending the document. To use existing settings, choose File ➤ Send To ➤ Next Routing Recipient to open the Send dialog box, and then choose either of the following options:

Route Document To *Reviewer Name* Sends the document to the next person on the list when you click OK.

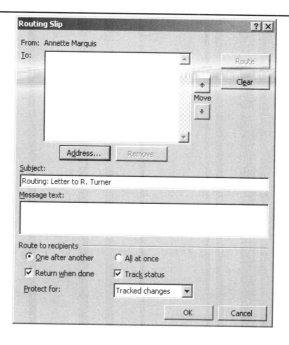

FIGURE 12.9

Use the options in the Routing Slip dialog box to send a document as an e-mail attachment to reviewers.

Send A Copy Of Document Without Using The Routing Slip Opens a new message in Outlook with the document already attached. Select the name of the reviewer in the address book, type any accompanying e-mail message in the text area, and then click Send to place the message in your Outbox. Click Send And Receive to actually send the message.

Alternatively, choose File ➢ Send To ➢ Other Routing Recipient to open the Routing Slip dialog box again so that you can change any of the route settings, or even add someone new. When you're done making changes, click Route to send the document right away or click Add Slip to close the dialog box and return to the document. If you've chosen Add Slip, you can route the document later by choosing File ➢ Send To ➢ Next Routing Recipient.

As each reviewer finishes reviewing a document that is sent One After Another, he or she must select File ➢ Send To ➢ Next Routing Recipient to send the document to the next reviewer in the list.

You can't remove a routing slip once it's added to a document. But you can make changes to it as we've described above, and you can choose not to use it. When you close a document with a routing slip, Word reminds you that the document is set up for routing:

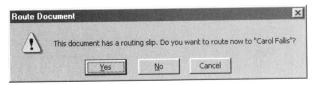

Click Yes to close the document and send it using existing route settings. Click No to close the document and ignore the routing slip. Click Cancel to return to the document.

Using Compare and Merge

So what happens if a novice user, thinking he is being extra careful, opens a routed file and uses the Save As command to give the document a new name? His changes are now on a different copy than those of the other reviewers. Fortunately, Word's Compare and Merge feature can get you through the inconvenience in a snap—before you even have time to enroll the novice user in a training class.

NOTE Compare and Merge should not be confused with the Mail Merge feature discussed in Chapter 9, "Creating Merge Documents in Word."

NEW When you compare and merge, Word shows differences between the documents as tracked changes. In Word 2002, that means you see balloon indicators in the margins. You can merge changes from multiple reviewers into a single document before you decide whether to accept or reject changes. To identify changes between two different documents and choose how to reconcile those changes, do the following:

1. Open one of the documents for comparison.

2. Choose Tools ➢ Compare And Merge Documents. The Compare And Merge Documents dialog box appears (it looks very much like the Open dialog box).

3. Locate and select the other file for comparison.

4. Enable or disable the Find Formatting and Legal Blackline check boxes as desired. The Legal Blackline option creates a new document that shows only the differences between the two documents without changing the original documents. Word creates the new document by assuming that all previously tracked changes in those documents are accepted.

5. Choose one of the following from the Merge drop-down list in the bottom-right corner of the dialog box:

Merge Displays all changes in the target document (the one you just located in the Merge And Compare dialog box).

Merge Into Current Displays all changes in the current document (the one you opened first).

Merge Into New Document Displays results in a new, third document that you can choose to save.

Compare The only choice available if you enabled Legal Blackline. When the documents you are comparing contain tracked changes, you must confirm that Word can accept those changes and proceed. Remember, the original documents remain unaltered. Word creates a third document that shows where the two differ once changes are accepted.

 NOTE If you've used the Versions command to maintain a history of changes and want to compare an earlier version, you must first save the earlier version under a different name.

Concurrent Editing

Now in Word 2002, multiple users can edit the same document at the same time. You don't get real time simultaneous editing—each user can't see what the other is changing. But two or more people can now open the file for modification, where previously only one could modify, and other users had to open a read-only copy. When the first user saves and closes his file, other users are given options to see that document and use Compare and Merge to update their own file with the first user's changes.

PART

II

CREATING QUALITY TEXT
DOCUMENTS USING WORD

PART III

CRUNCHING DATA WITH EXCEL

LEARN TO:

- Enter and format text and numbers

- Create charts

- Work with formulas and functions

- Manage data with Excel

- Analyze and report Excel data

- Import external data with Excel to work with other data sources

- Link workbooks and use 3-D cell references

- Use Excel's proofing tools

- Use Excel in a workgroup

CHAPTER 13

CREATING AND PRINTING EXCEL WORKSHEETS

FEATURING

- Entering data in Excel

- Working with numbers

- Using AutoFill features

- Formatting text

- Adding borders and colors

- Changing worksheet layout and other formatting

- Printing and previewing

I n this chapter, we'll create an Excel worksheet, and enter text, numbers, and formulas. As we create the worksheet, we'll format it so you can see the most efficient formatting methods. We assume that you're familiar with Word or another Office application. If you're completely new to Microsoft Office XP, you might want to review Chapters 1 and 2 before you return here to begin working in Excel. On the other hand, if you're already familiar with earlier versions of Excel, you'll probably want to skim through the introductory material here to pick up new tricks that will help you work more efficiently. Look for the NEW icon in the margin to find out about the latest improvements in Excel 2002.

Entering and Editing Cell Entries

Welcome to Excel 2002, the number cruncher! If you've used earlier versions of Excel, you'll find many new features that are welcome additions. If you're moving to Excel from another spreadsheet program, you're in for a real treat. Simply put, Excel 2002 is the best spreadsheet program ever designed—a powerful program with plenty of features to help you work more effectively.

The Excel Application Window

The Excel application window (see Figure 13.1) includes the standard title bar, menu bars, and toolbars. The *task pane* is displayed at the right side of the application window. Below the toolbars is a strip that contains the *name box* and the *formula bar*. The Excel status bar displays information about current selections, commands, or operations. The right end of the status bar displays NUM if the keyboard's Num Lock is on.

NEW▶   The Ask A Question button, used to get information from Excel Help, appears at the right end of the menu bar. The button's down arrow lists topics you've recently looked up.

Excel 2002 uses personalized menus and toolbars, so the Standard and Formatting toolbars appear side by side and the menus expand after a slight delay to show less frequently used options. Buttons you use less frequently move to the end (or off the end) of the toolbar to make room for more frequently used buttons.

FIGURE 13.1

The Excel 2002 application window

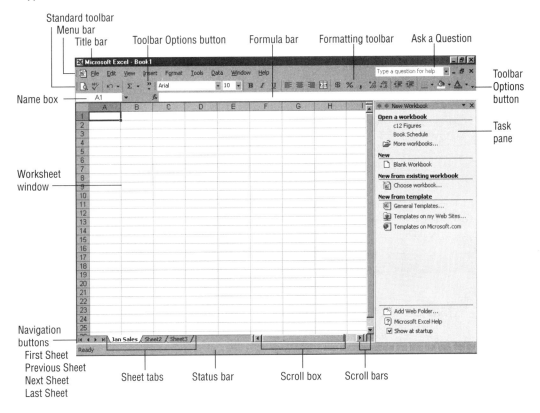

 NOTE To display the two default toolbars on separate rows, click the Toolbar Options button at the right end of either toolbar and choose Show Buttons On Two Rows. See Chapter 1, "Presenting Office XP: What You Need to Know," for information on customizing or disabling the personalized menu and toolbar features.

Workbooks and Worksheets

When you launch Excel, the Excel application window opens with a new Excel *workbook*. A workbook is a multipage Excel document. Each page in the workbook is called a *worksheet*, and the active worksheet is displayed in the document window. By default, a new workbook has three sheets. You can add or remove sheets from a workbook as needed.

 TIP If you typically need a different number of worksheets than the three offered by default, change the number of default sheets. Choose Tools , Options to open the Options dialog box. On the General tab change the Sheets In New Workbook setting to the desired number of worksheets.

At the left end of the horizontal scroll bar are *sheet tabs* and *navigation buttons*. Click a sheet tab to move to another worksheet or use the navigation buttons to scroll through the sheet tabs (see Figure 13.1).

 TIP To quickly move to any worksheet, right-click the navigation buttons and choose the sheet name from the shortcut menu.

Worksheet Components

Each worksheet is divided into columns, rows, and cells, separated by *gridlines*, as shown in the worksheet in Figure 13.2. *Columns* are vertical divisions. The first column is column A, and the letter A appears in the *column heading*. The horizontal *rows* are numbered. Each worksheet has 256 columns (A through IV) and 65,536 rows—plenty of room to enter all your data!

A *cell* is the intersection of a row and a column. Each cell has a unique *address* composed of the cell's column and row. For example, the cell in the upper-left corner of the worksheet (with the text *Worksheet Title* in Figure 13.2) is cell A1. Even though some of the text appears to run over into cell B1 in the next column, all of the text was entered in cell A1. The *active cell*, C2 in Figure 13.2, has a frame around it called the *cell pointer*, and the headings in the active cell's column (C) and row (2) are highlighted. When you enter data, it is always placed in the active cell.

 TIP Right-click any cell or selected cells to display a shortcut menu of frequently used commands. You can, for example, change the cell's format, or cut, copy, or paste its contents.

FIGURE 13.2

A worksheet consists of cells organized into rows and columns.

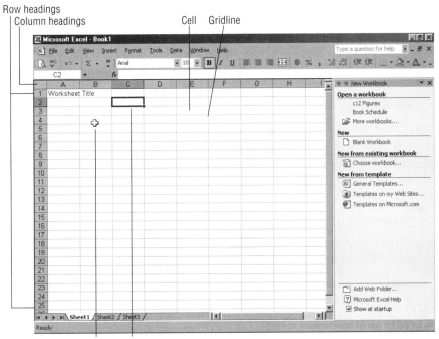

Row headings
Column headings
Cell   Gridline

Mouse pointer   Cell pointer

Moving the Cell Pointer

To activate a cell with the mouse, simply click in the cell. To move the pointer one cell to the left, right, up, or down, use the keyboard arrow keys. Use Ctrl and the arrow keys to move to the edge of the current *data region:* an area of the worksheet with data entered in cells, bounded by the edges of the worksheet and empty rows and columns. Frequently used keyboard commands are shown in Table 13.1.

PART

III

CRUNCHING DATA
WITH EXCEL

TABLE 13.1 KEYSTROKES TO MOVE THE CELL POINTER	
Key(s)	**Moves**
Home	To column A in the current row
Ctrl+Home	To cell A1
PgDn	Down one screen
PgUp	Up one screen
Alt+PgDn	Right one screen
Alt+PgUp	Left one screen
Ctrl+→	Right edge of current data region
Ctrl+←	Left edge of current data region
Ctrl+↑	Top of current data region
Ctrl+↓	Bottom of current data region
Ctrl+PgDn	Next worksheet
Ctrl+PgUp	Previous worksheet
Ctrl+Tab or Ctrl+F6	Next workbook or window
Ctrl+Shift+Tab or Ctrl+Shift+F6	Previous workbook or window

To quickly view other areas of the worksheet, use the scroll bars. Drag the scroll bar's scroll box to scroll more than a couple of rows or columns. Note that scrolling doesn't change the active cell—scrolling lets you view other parts of the worksheet, but the active cell is wherever you left the cell pointer. To scroll long distances, hold the Shift key while dragging the scroll box, and Excel will scroll farther for each movement of the mouse.

To use Excel efficiently, get comfortable moving the cell pointer using both the keyboard and the mouse. It's easier to use the keyboard when you are entering data (so your hands don't have to leave the keyboard) and the mouse when you need to scroll a long way or you already have your hand on the mouse for another task.

Entering Text and Numbers

Two types of data can be entered directly in cells in a worksheet:

Numbers Values you may want to use in calculations, including dates. Dates are often used in calculations to determine, for example, how many days to charge for an overdue video or how many months of interest you have earned on a deposit. *Formulas*, which are calculations, are a specific kind of number entry.

Text Any entry that isn't a number.

You can also insert other data into worksheets, including maps, graphics, hyperlinks, text copied from Word documents, and more, but the process differs from entering numbers or text directly in a cell.

To enter data in a cell, first activate the cell, and then begin typing the data. As soon as you begin entering characters from the keyboard, an insertion point appears in the cell, the text you are entering appears in the cell and the formula bar, and the formula bar buttons are activated.

If you make a mistake while entering data, click the Cancel Formula button (the red X) to discard the entry you were making and turn off the formula bar buttons. You can also cancel an entry by pressing the Esc key on the keyboard.

Clicking the Enter button (the green check mark) on the formula bar finishes the entry and turns off the formula bar buttons. Pressing the Enter key on the keyboard does the same thing but also moves the cell pointer down one cell. So if you are entering columns of data, the Enter key is more efficient than the Enter button. Moving to another cell always finishes an entry as if you clicked the Enter button before you moved the cell pointer.

NOTE Some Excel features are disabled while you are entering data in a cell, so you should always finish an entry by entering or canceling it before moving on to other tasks.

There is another way to finish an entry: simply move to another cell by clicking the cell or using the arrow keys. Before Excel switches the focus to the new cell, it finishes the entry in the current cell.

Saving Time with AutoComplete

Excel has an *AutoComplete* feature, which keeps track of text entered in a column and can complete other entries in the same column. For example, if you have already typed **Jones** in cell A1 and then enter the letters **Jo** in A2, Excel automatically fills in **nes** to make **Jones**. If **Jones** is the correct text, simply finish the entry by pressing Enter, moving to another cell, or clicking the Enter button. If the AutoComplete entry is not correct, just continue entering the correct text to overwrite the AutoComplete entry.

NOTE AutoComplete is turned on by default. To turn it on or off, select Tools ➢ Options and check or clear the Enable AutoComplete For Cell Values check box on the Edit tab.

AutoComplete resets each time you leave a blank cell in a column. AutoComplete may seem annoying at first, but it's worth getting used to, particularly when you're entering columns of data with a lot of repetition: repeated department names, cities, states, or other such information. If your data doesn't have many repeats, simply ignore AutoComplete and fully type each entry.

AutoComplete doesn't complete until you've entered unique text. If many of your entries begin with the same characters, try Pick From List. Right-click in the cell and choose Pick From List from the shortcut menu to select from a list of column entries.

EXPERT TIP If you type the same entry many times in Office applications, consider adding it to Office's AutoCorrect list (Tools ➤ AutoCorrect). In the AutoCorrect dialog box, type in a few unique characters signifying the word or number, and then type out the full entry. Excel (and the other applications) will automatically substitute the full entry when you enter the abbreviation. See Chapter 4, "Putting Text and Language Tools to Work for You," for more information about how to use AutoCorrect in Office.

Revising Text and Numbers

You can change an entry in a cell using two methods:

Type Over If you activate the cell and type a new entry, the old entry will be replaced. This is the easiest way to change a number (for example, *15* to *17*) or to replace text with a short word. If you find yourself accidentally typing over important data, hit the Esc key before changing cells or pressing Enter to restore the cell's original contents.

Edit Portion If the original entry is long and requires only minor adjustment, you might prefer to edit it. Click the cell and edit the entry in the formula bar, or double-click the cell or press F2 to open the cell for editing and edit directly in the cell. When you are finished, press Enter or click the Enter button to complete the entry.

 NOTE If double-clicking a cell doesn't open it for editing, the Edit Directly In Cell option may be turned off on the Edit tab of the Options dialog box. Choose Tools ➤ Options to view or change the current setting.

Deleting Cell Contents

To delete the contents of a cell completely, activate the cell and then either press the Delete key on the keyboard or right-click and choose Clear Contents from the short-cut menu. Don't choose Delete from the shortcut menu—that command is used to delete the row or column, not just the entry in the cell. If you've used other spread-sheet programs, you may be in the habit of deleting cell contents by pressing the spacebar to overwrite the contents. In Excel, cells with contents you can't see (like a space) have a way of messing things up later on, so you should get used to using the Delete key instead.

Selecting Multiple Cells

In Excel, at least one cell is always selected: the active cell. To select a *range* (a group of one or more cells), move to the center of the first cell in the range. The mouse pointer should be the large plus symbol used for selecting. Hold down the mouse button, and drag to the last cell you want to select before releasing the mouse button.

To select all the cells in a column or row, click the column heading or row heading. To select multiple columns or rows, select one heading and drag to select the others. When you point to row or column headers to select them, the mouse pointer changes to a row or column selection arrow.

To select the entire worksheet, click the Select All button, the gray rectangle at the upper-left corner of the worksheet above the row headings, or hold Ctrl and press A (for All).

If the cells, columns, or rows you want to select are *noncontiguous* (not next to each other), select one of the ranges you want to select, and then hold down the Ctrl key while selecting the others.

You'll want to look at the mouse pointer frequently while working in Excel. A mouse movement of 1/32 inch is the difference between selecting, moving, and copy-ing a cell, as shown in Table 13.2.

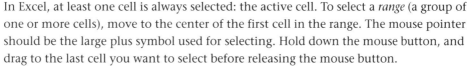

TABLE 13.2   EXCEL POINTER SHAPES

Pointer	Use
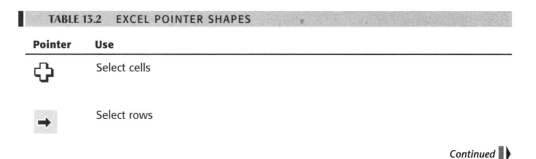	Select cells
	Select rows

Continued

PART

III

CRUNCHING DATA
WITH EXCEL

TABLE 13.2 (continued) EXCEL POINTER SHAPES	
Pointer	**Use**
↓	Select columns
↔	Adjust column width
↕	Adjust row height
✛	Move the contents of selected cells
+	Fill (copy) cell entries

Working with Numbers

You use a *formula* when you want to perform a calculation in Excel, so you'll appreciate some of the new formula features built into Excel 2002. Formulas are what make a spreadsheet a spreadsheet—the driving force behind the magic of Excel. You don't have to be a math major to use formulas, because Excel does the math correctly every time. Even if your checkbook never balances, you can use Excel's formulas and your data to calculate totals, averages, and other results accurately, quickly, and easily.

Excel uses standard computer operator symbols for mathematical and logical operators, as shown in Table 13.3.

TABLE 13.3 Mathematical and Logical Operators	
Operation	**Symbol**
Addition	+
Subtraction	−
Multiplication	*
Division	/

Continued ▶

TABLE 13.3 (continued) MATHEMATICAL AND LOGICAL OPERATORS	
Operation	**Symbol**
Exponentiation (to the power of)	^
Precedence (do this operation first)	enclose in ( )
Equal to	=
Not equal to	<> (this is typed as two symbols)
Greater than	>
Less than	<

Creating Formulas

There are a number of ways to create formulas, some more efficient than others. We'll begin with simple formulas that have one math operation. For example, the Second Hand News Payroll worksheet (see Figure 13.3) needs a formula to multiply Wilson's pay rate times the hours worked in order to calculate gross pay. There are two ways to create this formula: using point-and-click, or typing the formula using cell addresses.

FIGURE 13.3

The payroll worksheet needs formulas for Gross Pay.

	A	B	C	D
1	Second Hand News			
2				
3	Payroll for January 30			
4				
5	Name	Pay Rate	Hours	Gross Pay
6	Wilson	10	40	
7	Williams	9	41	
8	Ulmeyer	10.25	30	
9	Tier	9	16	
10	Stephens	9.75	44	

Point-and-Click Formulas

Point-and-click is the highly reliable method that Excel is known for. Each element of the formula appears in the formula bar as you type or select it. The following steps will get you started with this intuitive approach:

1. Activate the cell where you want the result to appear.

2. Type an equal sign (=).

3. Click the first cell you want to include in the formula.

4. Type an operator (+, -, *, /, ^).

5. Click the next cell in the formula.

6. Repeat steps 4 and 5 until the entire formula is entered.

7. Finish the entry by pressing Enter or clicking the Enter button on the formula bar. (Don't just click on another cell—Excel will include it in the formula!)

Cells that contain formulas display the formula results—the answer. To see the formula, select the cell and look at the formula bar.

Formulas are dynamic, so the results automatically change each time the numbers in the underlying cells are revised. In our worksheet, if Wilson's hours or pay rate change, Wilson's gross pay will also change because we created a formula based on the contents of two cells rather than typing in the values (**=10 * 40**) or an answer (**400**). Typed-in numbers don't change unless they are edited. This is the reason for a Very Important Excel Rule: *Never* do math "in your head" and type in the answer in a cell where you or other users would reasonably expect to have a formula automatically calculate the answer.

Traditional Typing Technique

The traditional spreadsheet approach is to type the formula using the cell addresses of each cell you want to include in the formula: **=b6*c6**. It's easier to type the wrong cell address than to click on the wrong cell, so typing the entire formula is a less desirable way to create a formula. If you need to reference widely disparate cells that are a challenge to move to and select, consider naming the cells (see the "Naming Ranges" section in Chapter 14) and then pasting the names rather than typing the addresses.

Using Natural Language Formulas

There is another technique for entering formulas, called *natural language formulas.* Support for natural language formulas was introduced in Excel 97 but didn't receive the rave reviews that Microsoft had anticipated. In Excel 2002, support for natural language formulas is available but is disabled by default. To turn on natural language formulas, choose Tools ➢ Options to open the Options dialog box. On the Calculation tab, enable the Accept Labels In Formulas check box.

Continued ▯▶

You'll notice in Figure 13.3 that Column B is labeled Pay Rate and Column C is labeled Hours. With Labels In Formulas enabled, you can use the column labels to enter your formula. Click in cell D6, type **=pay rate * hours**, complete the entry, and Excel will know exactly what you mean.

The natural language approach assumes that you know a couple of subtle things about worksheet design. You should always make sure that every row and column label is unique. There shouldn't be two columns or rows labeled Totals, or Excel will simply grab the nearest one, not necessarily the correct one. The entire label should fit into one cell. If the column label is Hours Worked, don't put Hours in one cell and Worked in the cell underneath. If you do, you can't refer to Hours Worked in a natural language formula (or anywhere else in Excel). For long labels, enter the label and then use the text-wrapping option discussed in "Aligning Text" later in this chapter.

Complex Formulas

Complex formulas involve more than one operation. For example, you might have separate columns for hours worked in the first week of the pay period and hours worked in the second. You'll want to add the hours together before multiplying by the pay rate: = Hours Week 1 + Hours Week 2 * pay rate. When you have more than one operation in a formula, you'll need to know about the *order of operations*, a short set of rules about how formulas are calculated:

1. Formulas are calculated from left to right.

2. Exponentiation ("to the power of") operations are always performed before any other operations. Multiplication and division are always done before any addition or subtraction. Excel will make two left-to-right passes through the formula in the preceding paragraph and do the multiplication (*hours week 2* multiplied by *pay rate*) on the first pass. Then it will come back through and add the hours worked in the first week to the gross pay for the second week. Calculating the gross pay this way would not make your employees happy.

3. To force Excel to add or subtract before it multiplies or divides, use parentheses. Any operation in parentheses is calculated first. If you want the hours for the two weeks added together first, just throw a set of parentheses ( ) around the addition part of the formula. Notice that you never need to include parentheses if you're only doing one operation, only when you need to tell Excel how to order two or

more operations. Parentheses are often added to a formula simply to make it more readable.

 TIP To add parentheses to an existing formula, select the cell containing the formula and click in the formula bar, or press F2 and edit in the cell.

Creating Totals

While the basic mathematical operators work well for formulas that contain a few cell addresses, it would be cumbersome to create a formula to add 100 cells if you had to use the point-and-click (or traditional typing) method. Excel includes functions to create totals, averages, and other operations commonly used in business, accounting, statistics, and other fields. We'll examine five common summarization functions here. Other common functions are covered in the chapters that follow.

In Excel 2002, the AutoSum button on the Standard toolbar has been enhanced to provide quick access to these summarization functions:

SUM Returns the total of all values in a range of cells

AVERAGE Returns the arithmetic mean for a range of cells

COUNT Returns the number of cells in a range that contain numbers

MAX Returns the highest value from a range of cells

MIN Returns the lowest value from a range of cells

Follow these steps to create a formula using the AutoSum button:

1. Select the cell where the result of the formula will appear, usually to the right or below the numbers you wish to sum.

2. Click the drop-down arrow on the AutoSum button.

3. Choose the type of summary formula you want to create.

4. Excel selects a nearby range of numbers to summarize. If the selection is not correct, select the numbers you wish to summarize.

5. Press Enter.

EXPERT TIP Excel has a one-step method for creating row and column totals using the *AutoSum* button on the Standard toolbar. Begin by selecting the cells that contain the numbers you want to total. Then choose a summarization method from the AutoSum button menu. Excel will add a formula to the empty cell (whether or not you selected it) and perform the calculation you selected. In order to get both row and column totals, you must select an extra column and row. Otherwise Excel only totals the rows in the cell beneath the range.

If you would like a blank row before the formula, simply select two extra cells below the range of cells to summarize. Excel always places the formula in the last empty cell selected. If you want to create totals or averages for multiple rows or columns and a grand total/grand average, select all the numbers before clicking AutoSum, as illustrated in Figure 13.4. In this example, Excel will create formulas in row 9 and column E for each selected row and column.

FIGURE 13.4

Using AutoSum to summarize rows and columns

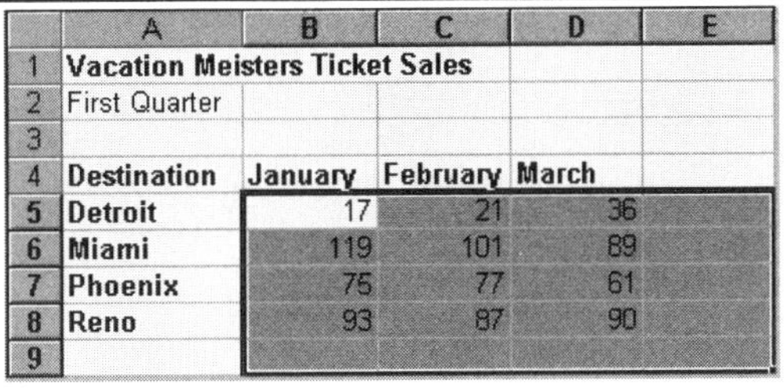

	A	B	C	D	E
1	Vacation Meisters Ticket Sales				
2	First Quarter				
3					
4	Destination	January	February	March	
5	Detroit	17	21	36	
6	Miami	119	101	89	
7	Phoenix	75	77	61	
8	Reno	93	87	90	
9					

Revising Formulas

There are two reasons you might want to revise a formula:

- You entered an incorrect formula.
- You've added new data and need to change the formula to reflect the new entries.

When you double-click a cell with a formula to open it for editing, Excel formats each cell address or range address in the formula a different color and places a border of the same color, called a Range Finder, around the cell or range. This makes it easy to see whether a formula refers to the correct cells. You can enter a new formula, overwriting the original formula. Or you can edit the existing formula.

Changing the Formula Reference

If you want to change the formula reference to refer to a different cell, you can use the keyboard or the Range Finder, as explained in the following steps.

PART

III

CRUNCHING DATA
WITH EXCEL

To use the keyboard:

1. Double-click the cell or press F2 to open the cell for editing.

2. Select the cell reference to change in the formula.

3. Click on or move to the cell you want to refer to.

4. Press Enter.

If the formula you're revising uses row labels instead of cell addresses, select the column or row label and type the correct label to replace the original entry.

To use the Range Finder:

1. Double-click the cell or press F2 to edit the cell.

2. Grab the border of the Range Finder and move it to the correct cell. (You're moving the Range Finder, so the mouse pointer should be an arrow.) If you need to include additional or fewer cells in a range, drag the square handle at the lower-right corner of the Range Finder to include the correct cells. Don't worry if the range needs extending left or up. The Range Finder's handle works if you drag it over itself from right to left or bottom to top.

3. When you are finished editing the formula, press Enter or click the Enter button.

If the cell reference you want to change is a range, the reference will include the first cell in the range, a colon, and the last cell in the range, like this: B10:B15. To revise this reference in a formula, select the entire reference, move into the worksheet, and drag to select the cells for the new formula, or move and then extend the Range Finder.

 NOTE Unions and intersections are two special types of ranges. A *union* is all the cells in two separate ranges. If you want, for example, to refer to cells C2 through C8 and those in C20 through C28, the ranges would be (C2:C8,C20:C28). By using a comma to separate the two ranges, you're indicating that you want all cells from both ranges. An *intersection* is just what it sounds like: a place where two ranges come together or overlap. For an intersection, use a blank space instead of a comma: The intersection (C2:C10 A10:J10) refers to just one cell, C10, where the two ranges overlap. Intersections are almost always used in natural language formulas.

Filling Formulas, Numbers, and Dates

In the Payroll example, the formula for each employee's gross pay is the same: `hours * pay rate`. If you've already created one working formula, all you need to do is *fill* it to the other cells. Filling is a form of copying.

Begin by activating the cell that has the formula you want to copy. There is a square box in the lower-right corner of the cell pointer called the *fill handle*. Move the mouse pointer toward the fill handle until the mouse pointer changes to the fill pointer shape.

Press the mouse button and drag the fill handle down to select the cells you want to copy the formula to. Release the mouse button, and the formula will be filled to the other cells. Now that you have read about the process, try it out by following these steps:

1. Select the cell that contains the formula you want to copy to other cells.

2. Drag the fill handle to select the cells where you want the formula copied.

3. Release the fill handle to fill the formula.

4. Optionally, click the AutoFill Options button and choose a fill option from the menu.

> **TIP** A common mistake that new Excel users make is selecting the wrong cell or cells in step 1. Select only the cells that contain the formula you want to copy.

When you fill by dragging a cell's fill handle, Excel copies the contents of the cell to the destination cells. If the content of the original cell includes a formula, Excel adjusts the formula relative to its new location. For example, if a formula is copied from row 5 to row 6, all row references are increased by 1. Fill a formula from column D to column E, and all column references are adjusted to reflect the change in position.

The fill feature provides a fast way to enter numeric data as well. When you fill a number (like the number 1), Excel fills the destination cells with the same number. If you want to increment the number, hold Ctrl while you fill to create a series: 1, 2, 3, and so on. If you're filling dates, you don't need to hold Ctrl to increment. Excel automatically increments when you fill dates by dragging the fill handle.

>
>
> **TIP** If you don't want to increment dates, you can use the Fill commands from the Edit menu. Select the cell you want to copy and the adjacent destination cells. Choose Edit ➤ Fill ➤ Down, Right, Up, or Left. Excel swiftly copies the source cell contents into all of the destination cells. The shortcut keystroke to fill down is Ctrl+D; Ctrl+R fills to the right.

Using the Auto Fill Options

NEW▶

When you release the mouse button at the end of a fill operation, Excel places an AutoFill Options button at the lower-right corner of the selected destination cells. Click the button to open the options menu, as shown in Figure 13.5.

FIGURE 13.5

Select a fill method from the AutoFill Options menu.

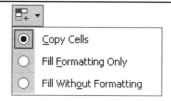

When you fill formulas, you have three choices:

Copy Cells Copies the original cell's formula and formatting to the destination cells. This is the default option.

Fill Formatting Only Copies the original cell's formatting—the same as using the Format Painter.

Fill Without Formatting Fills the formula, but the destination cells retain their original formatting.

The AutoFill Options button disappears when you choose an option or take other action in the worksheet.

Filling Series

Excel supports a wide variety of fill options. For example, by selecting one source cell and filling it, you can create:

- A linear (n=n+x) numeric series by incrementing the fill value by a specific *step value*. For example, if the source cell contains the number 10, you can have Excel add 5 to each successive cell to create the series 10, 15, 20, 25, and so on.
- A geometric (n=n*x) numeric series by multiplying the fill by a specific step value.
- A series of days, weekdays, months, or years.

If you initially select more than one cell, you can extend a linear or geometric series based either on the source cells or the trend in the source cells.

 TIP You can quickly fill a linear series by selecting two cells in the series and then dragging the fill handle. For example, if you select two cells with the values 5 and 10 and then drag the fill handle, Excel will fill with the values 15, 20, 25, and so on. Enter dates or numbers in two rows in a worksheet. Select both cells and double-click the fill handle to fill the balance of the empty cells in the column with sequential dates or numbers.

Here are the steps to access all the options for the AutoFill feature.

1. Select the source cell or cells and the adjacent destination cells.

2. Choose Edit ➤ Fill ➤ Series to display the Series dialog box, shown in Figure 13.6.

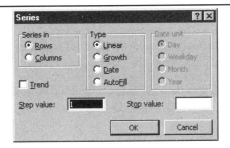

3. Select the series category in the Type area:

   Linear For series that increase by *adding* the same value to each successive cell.

   Growth For series that increase geometrically by *multiplying* by a value.

   Date Enabled only if the source cell contains a date. Select Date and select the date interval (Day, Weekday, Month, or Year) in the Date Unit area.

   AutoFill For formulas or other series types. Excel determines what series type to use based on the cells selected. This option is the same as filling by dragging the fill handle.

4. For Linear or Growth series types, check the Trend box or fill in a Step Value and/or Stop Value:

   Trend Check this box if you selected a range of cells with progressive values. Excel will determine what the trend is and fill the blank cells accordingly.

Step Value Enter the value you want Excel to use in incrementing the Linear or Growth series of values. Precede negative values with a minus symbol.

Stop Value Optionally enter the maximum value (or minimum if the Step Value is negative) allowed in the series.

5. Click OK to fill the cells.

6. Select a fill option from the AutoFill Options button menu.

 WARNING If you choose Growth and enable the Trend option, Excel calculates the trend and then adjusts the source cell values to smooth the trend, so the values you originally selected may also be changed.

 TIP To quickly fill or copy numbers, formulas, series, and even formats, select the source cells and then drag using the right mouse button. When you release the right mouse button, Excel will display the AutoFill shortcut menu. The menu will only include the options that are relevant to the data in the source cells.

Formatting Numbers

Excel lets you present numbers in a variety of formats. Formatting identifies numbers as currency or percentages and makes numbers easier to read by aligning decimal points. You format selected cells with three tools:

- The Formatting toolbar
- The Format Cells dialog box
- The shortcut menu

In even the simplest worksheets, you'll want to do some formatting to align numbers and their corresponding labels. The default format for text is left-aligned; numbers are right-aligned. The default format for numbers, General, doesn't display zeros that have no effect on the value of the number. For example, if you enter **10.50**, Excel doesn't display the extra or *trailing* zero because 10.5 has the same numeric value. Unless all your numbers have the same number of decimal places, you'll need to format the numbers to make them easier to compare.

Using the Formatting Toolbar

To format cells with the toolbar, select the cells and then click a button to apply one of the formats shown in Table 13.4. Click any cell to turn off the selection.

TABLE 13.4   NUMERIC FORMATTING FROM THE FORMATTING TOOLBAR

Button	Style	Effect
$	Currency	Displays and lines up dollar signs, comma separators, and decimal points: 75.3 as $75.30. Excel uses the currency symbol (for example, the $) selected in Regional Settings in the Windows Control Panel.
%	Percent	Displays number as a percentage: .45 as 45%.
,	Comma	Same as Currency, but without dollar signs: 12345.6 as 12,345.60.
.00	Increase Decimal	Displays one more place after the decimal: .45 as .450.
.00	Decrease Decimal	Displays one less place after the decimal: .450 as .45. If decreasing the number of digits eliminates a nonzero digit, the displayed number will be rounded. For example, if you format 9.75 with no digits following the decimal, Excel will display 10.

When you format a number, you change its appearance in the worksheet, not its value. For example, if you format the number 10.575 for two decimal places, the number will be displayed in the cell as 10.58. If you then multiply the cell by 10, the result is 105.75, not 105.80. To view the unformatted contents of a cell, click the cell and look at the formula bar. The number entered in the cell appears in the formula bar exactly as entered regardless of the format that has been applied to the cell.

 TIP If you're going to multiply formatted numbers (for example, in an order, payroll, or inventory system) use the ROUND function. For more information on functions, see Chapter 14, "Using References, Names, and Functions."

Using the Format Cells Dialog Box

The Format Cells dialog box has more numeric formulas that don't appear on the Formatting toolbar. With the cells you wish to format selected, open the dialog box in any of these three ways: choose Format ➢ Cells from the menu bar, press Ctrl+1, or right-click in the selection and choose Format Cells from the shortcut menu.

The Format Cells dialog box has separate pages for Number, Alignment, Font, Border, Patterns, and Protection. Figure 13.7 shows the Number tab, which includes a list of format categories (see Table 13.5) and controls for the number of decimal places, thousands separator, and treatment of negative numbers. Choose a category, and then fill in the other options.

FIGURE 13.7

The Format Cells dialog box has options that don't appear on the toolbars.

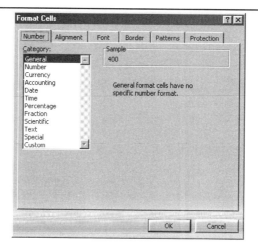

TABLE 13.5   NUMERIC FORMATTING IN THE FORMAT CELLS DIALOG BOX

Category	Description
General	The default format.
Number	Like General, but with set decimal places, a thousands separator, and formatting for negative numbers.
Currency	Numbers are preceded with a dollar sign immediately before the first digit. Zero values are displayed.
Accounting	Dollar signs and decimal points line up. Zero values are shown as dashes.
Percentage	The same as the Percent toolbar button.
Scientific	Numbers are displayed in scientific notation: for example, 1.01E+03.

NOTE If you point to the button on the Formatting toolbar with the dollar symbol, the screen tip indicates it is the Currency Style button. However, when you apply this button's format, Excel applies the Accounting format, with dashes for zeros and the dollar signs lined up. Microsoft has decided not to fix this discrepancy, which was introduced in a much earlier version of Excel, because it could confuse existing users.

The Format Cells dialog box includes six more specialized formatting categories:

Date Used for displaying dates in a variety of formats.

Time Includes options for mixed date and time displays, 24-hour clock times, and stopwatch results.

Fraction Includes formats based on either the number of digits to display in the divisor (1, 2, or 3) or the fractional unit (halves, quarters, tenths, and so on).

Special Converts numbers to text and includes formats for different types of numbers that aren't mathematical values: Zip Code, Zip Code + 4, Phone Number, and Social Security Number.

Text Changes a number to text without adding other formatting. This is useful for numeric labels that may include leading zeros, such as employee ID numbers. All the regular numeric formats strip off leading zeros. You must apply the Text format *before* entering the cell's contents: numbers entered and later formatted as Text will always be treated as numbers.

 WARNING Unlike the other formatting categories, Special and Text change the underlying value of the number. If you format a number with Special or Text, you will no longer be able to use the number in mathematical operations—unless you first reformat the cells with some other format.

 TIP If you only have a few numbers that need to be treated as text, you can enter them manually. Simply type an apostrophe (') before the number, and Excel will treat the number as text. Be aware, however, that you may have problems linking or importing these apostrophized numbers into other applications such as Access.

Custom Provides a list of custom formats for numbers, dates, and times that you can select from or add to.

NOTE For codes used to create custom formats, fire up the Office Assistant and ask for help on "custom formats."

Excel never displays part of a number. If a number can't be displayed as formatted, Excel displays an error ##### in the cell. Point to the right edge of the column heading and double-click to adjust the column width and display the cell contents.

Formatting Text

Even if you've never used Excel previously, you already have most of the skills you need to format text in Excel. Select the cells you want to format, and then choose a formatting option from the Formatting toolbar. Fonts, font weights (bold, italic, and underline), font size, and font colors work the same way in Excel as they do in Word and PowerPoint. In this section, we'll focus on text formatting unique to Excel.

Aligning Text

By default, Excel left-aligns text and right-aligns numbers. The default settings reflect common-sense rules about worksheet construction:

- Columns of text should be left-aligned because we're used to reading left-aligned text.

- Columns of numbers should be kept in the default (right) alignment and formatted so that the decimal points align and numbers can be visually compared easily—unless the numbers are actually text, such as item numbers, seat assignments, or Social Security numbers.

- Column labels should appear over the contents of the column. If the column is filled with numbers, the heading should be right-aligned or centered. Labels for text columns should be left-aligned or centered.

Use the buttons on the Formatting toolbar to override the defaults and align text and numbers at the left, center, or right within cells. Excel's fourth alignment, called Merge And Center, *merges* selected cells into one cell and centers the contents of the top-left selected cell across the new merged cell. Worksheet titles are often merged and centered.

To merge and center a title, select the cell containing the title and the cells in the same row for all the used columns in the worksheet, and then click the Merge And Center button. Excel only centers the text in the top-left cell of the selection, so if your worksheet's title is in more than one row, you'll need to merge and center each title row separately. If you make a mistake, select again and merge and center the correct cells.

There are more alignment options that don't appear on the Formatting toolbar. To see all the alignment options, select the cells you want to format and choose Format ➤ Format Cells, or right-click and choose Format Cells from the shortcut menu to open the Format Cells dialog box. The Alignment tab of the Format Cells dialog box is shown in Figure 13.8.

FIGURE 13.8

The Alignment tab of the Format Cells dialog box

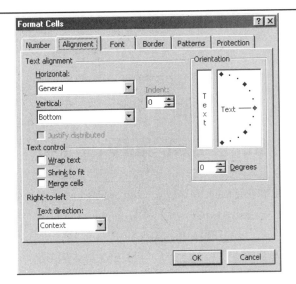

Rotating Text

Use the rotation tools on the Alignment tab of the Format Cells dialog box to orient text vertically or to rotate text to a specific orientation.

Consider rotating column labels when you have lengthy column headings for narrow columns containing relatively small values—for example, an attendance worksheet that uses dates to label columns, but contains only single characters such as *P* or *A* in the columns.

PART

III

CRUNCHING DATA WITH EXCEL

These steps will guide you through the process:

1. Select the cell containing the words to be rotated, and then select Format ➢ Cells and click the Alignment tab in the Format Cells dialog box. Choose one of the following options:

   • To orient text vertically (180°), click the pane with the vertical word *Text* in it.

   • To rotate text to another orientation, either use the Degrees spin box or drag the Text indicator in the rotation tool.

2. Click OK to apply the rotation.

Merge, Shrink to Fit, and Wrap Text

If you want a vertical title to cross several rows, use these steps:

1. Select the title and the cells you want to merge it across.

2. Select Format ➢ Cells from the menu or right-click the selection and choose Format Cells from the shortcut menu to open the Format Cells dialog box.

3. Enable the Merge Cells check box in the Text Control section of the Alignment tab.

4. Click OK to apply the changes.

Or use the Formatting toolbar to achieve the same result:

1. Select the title and the cells you wish to merge it across.

2. Click the Merge And Center button on the Formatting toolbar.

3. Optionally, click the Align Left or Align Right button to change the alignment in the merged cells.

Shrink To Fit reduces the size of the type within selected cells so the contents fit. Wrap Text wraps the contents of a cell if it would exceed the cell's boundaries. Both Shrink To Fit and Wrap Text use the current column width (see "Adjusting Column Width and Row Height" later in this chapter) to determine how much to shrink and where to wrap the selection. Follow these steps to apply shrink or wrap text control:

1. Adjust the column width.

2. Select the cell(s) you wish to format.

3. Choose Format ➤ Cells, or right-click in the selection and choose Format Cells from the shortcut menu.

4. On the Alignment tab of the Format Cells dialog box, enable either Shrink To Fit or Wrap Text.

5. Click OK.

If you narrow or widen a column after you shrink or wrap a label, you'll need to reshrink or rewrap the formatted cells.

EXPERT TIP   If you want the contents of a cell to wrap at a specific point regardless of the column width, force the text to wrap to the next line by pressing Alt+Enter when you enter the text. Alt+Enter inserts an invisible line break character and enables the Wrap Text check box, so if you edit the text to remove the line break, the text will wrap to the width of the column. There's a minor disadvantage to this method: the entry occupies more height in the formula bar, so you can't access the column headings when the cell is selected.

Applying Borders and Color

Borders and colors, when used effectively, make worksheets easier to understand. A *border* is a line drawn around a cell or group of cells. *Fill color* is used to highlight the background of part of a worksheet; *font color* is applied to text. Simply bordering or applying a fill color to totals or other summary cells provides visual cues that users appreciate.

If you don't have access to a color printer, you might still want to use color in frequently used worksheets that you work with on screen. Color distinguishes worksheets that would otherwise look similar—for example, the Sales department's budget could have a blue title, and Production's title could be burgundy.

The Border, Fill Color, and Font Color buttons are on the Formatting toolbar. All three buttons have drop-down arrows that open menus with related options. Select an item from the menu to apply it to the selected cells and make it the default item for the button.

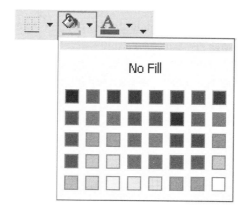

Borders can completely surround a group of cells, surround each cell individually, or underline or double-underline the selected range. (The double underline is often used to highlight grand totals in worksheets.) To apply a border, follow these steps:

1. Select the cells to be formatted.

2. Click the Border drop-down arrow and select a border to apply to the cells. That border becomes the default border for the Border button.

3. To apply the same border to other cells, select the cells and simply click the Border button.

The Fill Color and Font Color buttons are used the same way.

 TIP To change the border color for selected cells, choose Format , Cells to open the Format Cells dialog box. On the Border tab, select a color from the Color drop-down list.

 TIP If you have a lot of borders, colors, or font colors to apply, you can display any or all of the button menus as palettes that float on your worksheet. Open the menu and point to the dark gray bar at the top of the menu. Drag the menu into the worksheet and release the mouse button.

When you're finished with the menu, click its Close button. To add borders or color to non-contiguous ranges, select one range, and then hold the Ctrl key and select the other ranges you want to apply the format to before clicking the Border, Fill Color, or Font Color button.

Adjusting Worksheet Layout

As your workbook grows, you'll want to modify its layout so that it's easier to use both on screen and as a publication on paper or the Web. Excel's column and row structure make it easy to radically change the appearance of a worksheet in a few simple steps.

Adjusting Column Width and Row Height

By default, Excel columns are slightly more than eight characters wide. If the data in a worksheet is wider or much narrower than the column, you'll want to adjust the *column width* so it is wide enough to contain the data, but not so wide that data seems lost.

WARNING Some users simply leave blank columns rather than adjusting column widths: for example, skipping column B because the entries in column A are too wide for column A. Don't leave blank columns if you or anyone else may ever want to sort the rows in a worksheet. Blank columns and rows identify the limits of a database, so data on the other side of the blank column will not be sorted, mixing up the data. For more information on this, see "Sorting an Excel Database" in Chapter 16.

You can adjust column width either by dragging the column border or by double-clicking to AutoFit the column width to the existing data. You can also select several columns and either adjust them manually to a uniform width or AutoFit each one to its contents. Here are the general steps:

1. Select the column(s) you want to adjust.

2. Position the mouse pointer at the right edge of a selected column's headings. The pointer will change shape to a double-headed column adjustment pointer.

3. Double-click to have Excel adjust the widths of the selected columns to fit their contents. Or, to adjust the columns manually to the same width, drag the right border of a column's heading to make the column wider or narrower.

If you prefer using the menu to set column widths, follow these steps:

1. Select the column(s) you want to adjust.

2. Choose Format ➤ Column ➤ AutoWidth to set all column widths to fit the contents.

   OR

Choose Format ➢ Column ➢ Width to open the Column Width dialog box. Enter a value from 0 to 255 to indicate how many characters can be displayed in the column. Click OK.

 TIP If the default column width doesn't work for most of your worksheets, change the default. Choose Format , Column , Standard Width and type a new value in the Standard Width dialog box.

To copy a column width from one column to another, click a cell in the column with the desired width and copy it (select Edit ➢ Copy, right-click and choose Copy, or type Ctrl+C). Then select the destination column. Select Edit ➢ Paste Special or right-click and choose Paste Special from the shortcut menu to open the Paste Special dialog box. Click the Column Widths option button in the Paste area and then click OK.

Changing Row Height

You can adjust row height the same way you adjust column width. If you move the pointer to the lower edge of a row heading, the pointer will change to an adjustment tool. Double-click to adjust the row height to fit the font size; drag to manually increase or decrease size.

While it's easy to adjust row height, it can add to the amount of work you are required to do in the future. By default, Excel changes a row's height when you increase or decrease the font size used in the row. If you change the font size in a row you've previously adjusted, Excel will not adjust the row to fit—you'll need to adjust it manually. Choose Format ➢ Row ➢ AutoFit to return responsibility for the row's height to Excel.

Inserting and Deleting Rows and Columns

To insert a column between (for example) the current columns A and B, begin by selecting column B. Right-click and select Insert from the shortcut menu or choose Insert ➢ Columns from the menu bar to insert a column. To insert multiple columns, select more than one column before inserting. For example, you can insert three columns to the right of column A by first selecting B, C, and D. Insert rows in the same fashion.

Deleting rows and columns is much like inserting. Begin by selecting one or more rows or columns. When you delete a row or column, all information in the row or column is deleted, including cells in the column or row that are outside of the current display. To delete rows or columns, first select the rows or columns and then choose Edit ➢ Delete from the menu, or right-click in the selection and choose Delete from the shortcut menu.

 TIP Before deleting a presumably empty row or column, there's a quick way to check to make sure it's truly empty. Select any cell in a row, and then hold Ctrl and press the right arrow key. If the row is empty, you'll end up in column IV. Hold Ctrl and press the down arrow in an empty column, and the pointer will move to the cell in row 65536.

To quickly insert or delete a single row or column, select the row or column heading by right-clicking and selecting Insert or Delete from the shortcut menu. To clear the contents of a selected row but leave the emptied row in place, press the Delete key on your keyboard.

Inserting and Deleting Cells

Sometimes you'll need to add or delete cells in part of a worksheet without inserting or deleting entire rows or columns. Follow these steps to insert cells:

1. Select the range where new cells should be inserted, right-click, and choose Insert from the shortcut menu to open the Insert dialog box.

2. If you choose Shift Cells Down, the cells in the selection and all cells below them in the same columns are shifted. If you choose Shift Cells Right, cells in the same rows are moved to the right.

3. Click OK to apply the selected action.

To delete cells, select the range of cells you wish to delete, and then right-click and choose Delete from the shortcut menu. Choose to shift cells up or to the left and click OK. You can also use the Insert or Delete dialog boxes to insert or delete rows or columns.

PART

III

CRUNCHING DATA
WITH EXCEL

Moving and Copying Cell Contents

We assume that you're comfortable moving and copying in Word or other Windows applications. You'll notice a few differences when copying and moving cells and cell ranges in Excel:

- If you paste cells on top of existing data, the existing data will be overwritten. Before pasting, make sure that there are enough blank cells to accommodate the selection you want to paste. For example, if you want to move the contents of column E to the right of column A without overwriting column B, begin by inserting a blank column between A and B.

NEW▶
- *Cut-and-paste* and *copy-and-paste* now operate the same in Excel as in other Office applications. Thanks to the Office Clipboard, you can copy or cut a selection, perform other operations (such as inserting rows or columns), and paste later. Enhanced in Office XP, the Clipboard now saves the contents of up to 24 copy operations from any Office application (and many other Windows apps), so you can copy or cut several selections, and then begin pasting. The Clipboard toolbar opens automatically when you cut or copy more than one item without pasting. You can also choose Edit ➢ Office Clipboard to display the Clipboard.

- When you cut a cell in Excel, it is copied to the Clipboard but is not removed from the worksheet until you paste it in its new location by pressing Enter or clicking the Paste button.

- When you get ready to paste, just click the first cell, row, or column where you want pasted cells, rows, or columns to appear. If you select more than one cell to paste into, the selected range must be exactly the same size as the range you want to paste.

- When you copy a selection, you can paste it more than once. Use the Paste button to paste all but the last copy. Press Enter to place the final pasted copy.

Follow these steps for simple cut, copy, and paste operations:

1. If you're pasting into the middle of existing data, insert blank cells, rows, or columns for the data you want to move or copy.

2. Select the data you want to move or copy. To move, click the Cut button, choose Edit ➢ Cut, press Ctrl+X, or select Cut from the shortcut menu. To copy, click the Copy button, choose Edit ➢ Copy, press Ctrl+C, or select Copy from the shortcut menu.

3. Select the first cell, row, or column where you want to place the moved or copied data.

4. Press Enter to move or copy the data to its new location.

TIP Even if you plan to paste only once, there's a good reason to use Paste rather than simply pressing Enter. When you Paste, Excel displays a Paste Options button at the bottom of the pasted selection. Click the button to choose to copy Formatting Only, to retain column widths and formatting, or to match the pasted cells' format to the format of the surrounding cells.

Data Transfers between Worksheets

To move or copy data from one worksheet to another, cut or copy the selection and then click the sheet tab for the sheet that you want to paste into. Click in the appropriate cell and press Enter to paste.

Data Transfers between Workbooks

To move or copy a range of cells from one workbook to another, make sure both workbooks are open. Select and cut or copy the data, choose Window from the menu bar, and pick the destination workbook from the list of open workbooks. Click in the destination cell and press Enter.

To copy or move an entire worksheet to a new workbook or an open workbook, right-click the worksheet tab and choose Move or Copy from the shortcut menu.

TIP To paste items from the Office Clipboard, select Edit , Office Clipboard or hold Ctrl and press C twice. The Clipboard opens, showing the items currently held on the Clipboard. Select an item and then choose Paste from the item's options menu to paste it into the worksheet beginning at the active cell.

Using Drag-and-Drop

When you're moving or copying cells between worksheets or workbooks, it's easiest to rely on the Clipboard and the Cut, Copy, and Paste buttons on the Standard toolbar. When you can see both the cells to be moved or copied and the destination on screen without scrolling too far, however, the *drag-and-drop* method is quicker and more efficient:

1. Select the cells and move the mouse so that it points to any part of the cell pointer except the fill handle. The mouse pointer will change to a four-headed move arrow.

PART

III

CRUNCHING DATA
WITH EXCEL

2. Hold down the mouse button and drag the cells to their new location. To copy the cells, hold the Ctrl button while you release the mouse button.

NEW|▶ In Excel 2002, drag-and-drop has been greatly enhanced to support some features previously reserved for Paste Special operations. To access advanced features:

1. Select the cells to be moved or copied. Point to any part of the cell pointer except the fill handle.

2. Hold down the *right* mouse button and drag the cells to their new location.

3. Release the mouse button. A shortcut menu opens so you can select whether you want to move or copy the cells, copy formats only, copy values only, insert hyperlinks or links to the cells, shift the current cells and move, or shift the current cells and copy.

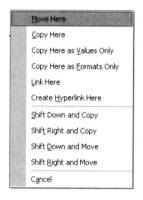

4. Choose the desired option from the menu.

Applying AutoFormats and Styles

Excel includes a number of canned worksheet designs, including formal business, list, and 3-D formats. These AutoFormats offer a quick way to apply a standard format to all or part of a worksheet. Before you use AutoFormat, select the cells to be formatted. This will usually include all the text and numbers in the worksheet, but you may wish to apply an AutoFormat to titles or data only. Follow these steps to AutoFormat a worksheet:

1. Select the range of cells you wish to format.

2. Choose Format ➢ AutoFormat from the menu to open the AutoFormat dialog box.

3. Click the Options button to expand the dialog box to display all the formatting elements you can apply.

4. Choose a format from the list of AutoFormats.

5. Deselect any formatting options you don't want to include.

6. Click OK to apply the selected format.

AutoFormats are composed of styles—specifications about one or more formatting options. If you have a format that you use often, you can create your own style. To create a style:

1. Select a range of cells that includes the format.

2. Choose Format ➢ Style from the menu to open the Style dialog box.

3. Enter a name for the style. Deselect any formatting elements you wish to exclude.

4. Click the Modify button and change any format options you wish in the Format Cells dialog box. Click OK to close the dialog box.

5. Click Add to add the style. Click OK to close the Style dialog box.

To apply a style, select the range you wish to format. Choose Format ➢ Style to open the Style dialog box. Select the style from the Style Name drop-down list and then click OK to apply the style to the selected cells.

To modify a style, open the Style dialog box, and choose the style in the Style Name drop-down list. Change any formatting options you wish and then click the Add button to update the style. Styles hang around forever unless you delete them. To delete a style, open the Style dialog box, select the style from the drop-down list, and click Delete.

 NOTE For more information on creating and using styles, see "Working with Styles" in Chapter 8.

Previewing and Printing

Print Preview, Page Setup, Page Break Preview, and Print are all interrelated. Print Preview, Print, and Page Setup function much as they do in the other Office XP applications. *Page Break Preview*, a view available only in Excel, displays the current page breaks and allows you to adjust them.

Adjusting Margins in Print Preview

Clicking the Margins button in Print Preview (choose File ➤ Print Preview) displays the current margin settings. Point to any of the margin lines, and the pointer will change to an adjustment tool, as shown in Figure 13.9. Press the mouse button to display the name and current setting for the margin on the Excel status bar. Drag a margin to adjust it.

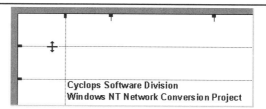

Cyclops Software Division
Windows NT Network Conversion Project

Excel's default margins are 0.75" on each side and 1" on the top and bottom, with a 0.5" header and footer margin. Headers and footers print in 0.5" of space between the header/footer margin and the regular margin. The top and bottom margins define the limits of the printed worksheet, and the header and footer margins define the areas where the header and footer will print. If you use headers and footers, the top and bottom margin values need to be greater than the header and footer margin values, or part of the worksheet may print on top of the header and footer.

Changing Page Setup

To change page setup, choose File ➤ Page Setup from the menu to open the Page Setup dialog box. (If you're already in Print Preview, click the Setup button; from Page Break Preview, right-click and choose Page Setup from the shortcut menu.) The Page Setup features are divided into four tabs: Page, Header/ Footer, Margins, and Sheet.

Page Settings

Use the Page options of the Page Setup dialog box, shown in Figure 13.10, to set page orientation, scaling, paper size, and print quality:

1. Open the Page Setup dialog box by choosing File ➤ Page Setup or by clicking the Setup button in the Print Preview window. Click the Page tab.

2. Adjust the following settings to suit your document:

   Orientation The direction of print in relation to the paper it is printed on. Portrait, the default setting, places the short edge of the paper at the top and bottom. If your worksheet is wider than it is long, consider using Landscape orientation.

Scaling Reduces or enlarges the print. If you simply need to make the print larger, use the Adjust To control and choose a size greater than 100%. The Fit To control instructs Excel to reduce a worksheet that exceeds a specific number of pages so it will fit.

Paper Size Lets you choose a paper size other than the default (for example, legal paper).

Print Quality Measured in dots per inch (dpi). Higher dpi means clearer print quality but slower printing.

First Page Number Used to start printing from a page number other than 1.

3. Click OK to apply the settings.

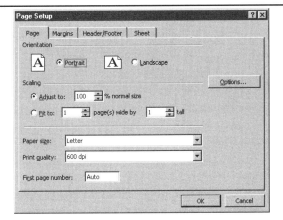

 NOTE   The Options button appears on every tab of the tab Setup dialog box. The button opens the Windows property sheet (or the manufacturer's property sheet) for the printer that's currently selected.

PART

III

CRUNCHING DATA WITH EXCEL

Headers and Footers

A header appears at the top of each page of a document. Footers are printed at the bottom of the page. The default setting is no header or footer. If you want a header or footer, choose or create it in the Header/Footer tab in the Page Setup dialog box, shown in Figure 13.11.

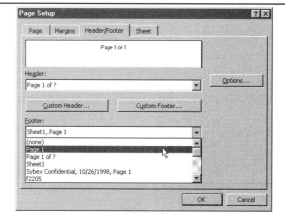

The current header and footer settings are displayed in the two preview panes. To choose a different predesigned header, click the Header drop-down list. Choose a footer the same way, using the Footer drop-down list. When you select a different header (or footer), the preview pane will reflect the change.

 TIP To create a new header or footer, click the Custom Header or Custom Footer button.

Setting Margins in the Page Setup Dialog Box

The preview in the Margins tab of the Page Setup dialog box (see Figure 13.12) displays the margins as dotted lines. You can change the margins here using the spin arrows for each margin.

FIGURE 13.12

Set margins, including space for headers and footers, in the Margins tab of the Page Setup dialog box.

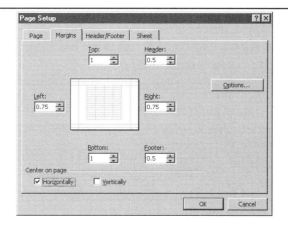

Use the Center On Page controls to center the printed worksheet horizontally between the side margins or vertically between the top and bottom margins. As you change settings on the Margins tab, the Preview will change to reflect the new margin settings.

Changing Sheet Settings

The Sheet settings (see Figure 13.13) relate to the features that will appear in the printed copy, including the print area, repeating rows and columns, and gridlines.

FIGURE 13.13

Use the Sheet settings to repeat rows or columns on each printed page.

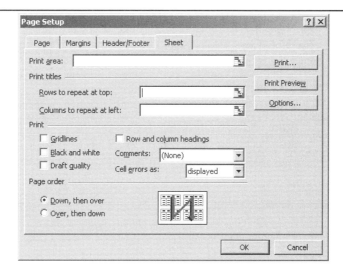

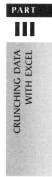

PART

III

CRUNCHING DATA
WITH EXCEL

If you find it difficult to select cells with the Page Setup dialog box in the way, click the Collapse Dialog button to minimize the dialog box while you select cells. This button is located on the Sheet tab in the Page Setup dialog box to the right of the Print Area, Rows To Repeat At Top, and Columns To Repeat At Left text boxes.

Click the Expand Dialog button to return to the Page Setup dialog box. This button is located to the right of the same text boxes mentioned above, when they appear as solo floating text boxes. Take these steps to change sheet settings:

1. Choose File ➢ Page Setup to open the Page Setup dialog box. Click the Sheet tab.

2. Specify ranges for a Print Area and rows and columns to be repeated as titles on each printed page by entering them from the keyboard or by using the mouse:

Print Area By default, Excel prints from the home cell A1 to the last occupied cell in a worksheet. To specify a different range, click the Collapse button in the Print Area text box to collapse the dialog box, select the area you want to print, and click the Expand button to expand the dialog box. If the Print Area includes noncontiguous cells, each contiguous range will print on a separate page.

Print Titles Repeats columns or rows on each page of the printout. Specify these rows or columns in the Rows To Repeat At Top and Columns To Repeat At Left text boxes. Excel requires a range for these entries (such as A:A to print column A on each page) even if you're only selecting a single row or column.

NOTE   The Print Area, Rows To Repeat, and Columns To Repeat controls are only enabled when you open the Page Setup dialog box from the menu (choose File ➢ Page Setup or View ➢ Header and Footer). If you go to Page Setup from Print Preview or the Print dialog box, you won't be able to change these three settings.

3. Enter option settings in the Print and Page Order sections:

Print Or Hide Gridlines Indicates whether gridlines will be printed, but does not affect their display in the worksheet. Turning off the print gridlines gives your worksheet a cleaner appearance and can make it easier to read.

TIP   To turn off screen gridlines, choose Tools , Options and clear the check mark in the Gridlines option on the View tab of the Options dialog box.

Draft Quality Prints the worksheet without gridlines or graphics.

Black And White If you used colors in the worksheet but won't be printing on a color printer, click this control to speed up the print process.

Row And Column Headings Prints the row numbers and column letters. This is a useful feature when you are editing or trying to locate an error in a worksheet.

Page Order Establishes the order in which multipage worksheets are printed.

Comments If the print area contains comments, you can choose to print them as they appear or on a separate page at the end of the print job. By default, comments are not displayed, so if you wish to print them as they appear, you'll also need to show them.

NEW▶   **Cell Errors As** Used to hide error messages (for example #NAME and ####) in the printed version of the worksheet.

4. Click OK.

Tips and Tricks for Printing

When you are ready to print your worksheet, here are some tips that will help you print exactly what you want to see.

- To see what will be printed with changing views, press Ctrl+Home to move to cell A1, then press Ctrl+Shift+End.

- If your printed copy includes extra pages that appear to have no content, you have a cell "out there" with something in it—a character, a space, or formatting such as a fill. To quickly move to the last occupied row and column in a worksheet, hold Ctrl and press the End button. To completely clear the contents of a seemingly blank cell, choose Edit ➢ Clear ➢ All.

- You've completely cleared all the cells you don't want to print and Excel still prints blank pages. What gives? Try this trick to force Excel to reexamine the boundaries of the worksheet. Choose File ➢ Save As (not Save) from the menu, and save the file using the same name (or another name—it works either way).

- The easiest way to set the Print Area is from the worksheet, not from Page Setup. Select the cells to be printed and choose File ➢ Print Area ➢ Set Print Area from the menu. When you want to print the entire worksheet again, choose File ➢ Print Area ➢ Clear Print Area.

Continued ▌▶

PART

III

CRUNCHING DATA
WITH EXCEL

CONTINUED

- You can set Page Setup options for multiple worksheets by selecting the worksheets before opening the Page Setup dialog box. Click the sheet tab of the first worksheet you want to print. Hold down Shift and click the last tab to select contiguous worksheets, or hold down Ctrl and click the tabs of each of the worksheets you want to print. Danger, Will Robinson: When worksheets are grouped, entries made on one worksheet are transferred to all the grouped worksheets. To ungroup the sheets, right-click any of the grouped sheets' tabs and choose Ungroup from the shortcut menu. Remember to ungroup the worksheets after you've changed the Page Setup to avoid accidentally overwriting data on grouped sheets. For more on worksheet grouping, see Chapter 19, "Using Excel to Present Information."

- The Page Order setting isn't as useless as it initially appears to be. If your print area is at least two pages wide and two pages long, the Page Order determines which page will be numbered Page 2—the page below Page 1, or the page to the right of the Page 1.

Setting Print Options

Excel offers flexible page breaks and print areas so you can manage the often-difficult task of printing unwieldy spreadsheets on standard-size paper. The Page Break Preview feature is a good tool for managing the printable areas of a spreadsheet, while the Print dialog box delivers complete control over which pages will print.

Page Break Preview

Page Break Preview is a view of the worksheet window that shows the print area, by page, and the page order. In Page Break Preview, areas that will be printed are white; cells that won't be printed are gray. Each printed page is numbered.

To view and adjust page breaks, follow these steps:

1. From the Print Preview window, click the Page Break Preview button, or choose View ➢ Page Break Preview from the worksheet window.

2. Using the mouse, drag the page break to print a larger or smaller number of rows or columns on the page.

3. Choose View ➢ Normal View to close Page Break Preview.

NEW▶ When you switch to Page Break Preview, you see how each page will print based on the current settings in the Print Setup dialog box. If you haven't change the Page Setup, the print job is shown as it will appear if printed at 100%. If you extend the page break for any page (making it wider or longer than the default setting), Excel will change the scaling on all pages, reducing the print type so the page still fits on the paper specified in Page Setup.

Inserting Manual Page Breaks

To add a manual page break, select the first column or row you want to appear in the page after the break. Right-click and choose Insert Page Break from the bottom section of the shortcut menu.

Removing Manual Page Breaks

To remove a manual page break, right-click in the row below a horizontal page break or in the column to the right of a vertical page break and choose Remove Page Break from the shortcut menu. To remove all manual page breaks, right-click any cell and choose Reset All Page Breaks from the shortcut menu. In Page Break Preview, you can also remove a page break by dragging it outside the print area. To return to Normal view, choose View ➢ Normal View from the menu.

Changing Print Settings

When you click the Print button on the Standard toolbar, Excel prints one copy of the selected worksheet(s) using the current settings from the Print and Print Setup dialog boxes. To adjust print settings, choose File ➢ Print to open the Print dialog box, shown in Figure 13.14.

Use the Print Range controls to print some, but not all, of the pages of a multiple-page print job. In Excel, you cannot specify noncontiguous pages as you can in Word, so if you want to print pages 1–4 and 6–8, you either have to print twice or choose the cells on those pages and specify them as your print area.

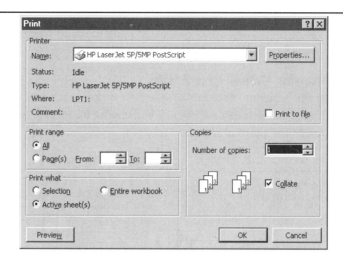

In the Print What control, specify which part of the worksheet or workbook you want to print. The Selection option provides another way to override the default print area: select the cells you want to print, and then print the selection. Choose Workbook to print every worksheet that has content in the active workbook. To print some but not all worksheets in a workbook, select the sheets before opening the Print dialog box. The Active Sheets option will be selected in the Print What control. If your page header or footer includes page numbers, the worksheets will be numbered consecutively in the order in which you selected them.

Checking Worksheet Spelling

Misspelled words automatically cast doubt on the accuracy of an entire worksheet. Excel includes two tools to help you correct spelling errors. *AutoCorrect* automatically fixes common typos and *Spelling* checks all the text in a worksheet to ensure that it is error-free. If you are not in the home cell when you begin the spelling check, Excel will check from the cell pointer to the end of the worksheet, and then ask if it should return to the top of the worksheet and finish checking. When Spelling is complete, Excel will notify you that it has finished checking the entire sheet.

Spelling is a shared feature of all the Office XP products, so words you add to the dictionary or to AutoCorrect are added to the common custom dictionary you use with Excel, Word, PowerPoint, and Access.

CHAPTER 14

Using References, Names, and Functions

FEATURING

- **Grouping worksheets to manage projects**

- **Creating and naming ranges**

- **Using labels as cell references**

- **Using functions and references**

- **Using absolute, relative, and mixed references**

- **Using worksheet functions**

- **Using financial functions**

- **Manipulating text with functions and formulas**

- **Using IF functions**

- **Manipulating dates with functions**

- **Linking workbooks**

Excel is designed to help you manage complex projects with finesse. You can name cells or ranges and use the names for both navigation and in place of cell addresses in formulas, making your worksheets easier to understand and update. Excel includes hundreds of functions that supply ready-made solutions for computing all types of typical and not-so-typical values. We'll review many of the frequently used functions in this chapter. By utilizing Excel's capability to add or remove worksheets, you can organize and use worksheets related to the same project in one workbook and create formulas that refer to multiple worksheets.

Working with Worksheets

If you've moved to Excel from another spreadsheet program, you may not have realized what a powerful organizational tool an Excel workbook is. Some spreadsheet programs save each worksheet independently as a separate file, requiring you to open five or six files when you work on a large project. With Excel, you can cluster worksheets for similar projects in a single workbook so you can see and work with the entire project at one time.

You can move through the various worksheets (Sheet1, Sheet2, and so on) associated with the project as easily as you flip through pages in this book. Simply click the worksheet's sheet tab. To change a worksheet's name to something more descriptive, double-click the sheet tab, type a new name of up to 32 characters, and press Enter:

$$\boxed{|◄|◄|►|►|}\ \mathbf{Sheet1}\ \diagup\ Sheet2\ \diagup\ Sheet3\ \diagup\ Sheet4\ \diagup$$

 NEW► You can change a sheet's tab color to make it easier to differentiate sheets by using, for example, specific colors for different departments or different quarters of the fiscal year. Right-click a sheet tab and choose Tab Color from the shortcut menu, or select the sheet and choose Format ➤ Sheet ➤ Tab Color from the menu to open the Format Tab Color dialog box. Select a color from the palette and click OK to apply the color to the tab.

TIP If you do not see any sheet tabs at the bottom of the application window, choose Tools ➤ Options and click the View tab. Check the Sheet Tabs check box in the Window Options area.

Selecting Worksheets

To select one worksheet, click its sheet tab. If you want to print more than one sheet or copy a couple of sheets into another workbook, you can select multiple worksheets. Hold the Ctrl key while clicking each sheet tab. To select consecutive worksheets, click the first tab, hold Shift, and click the last worksheet tab you want to select. To select all worksheets in a workbook, right-click any tab and choose Select All Sheets from the shortcut menu.

Using Grouped Worksheets

When more than one worksheet is selected, the worksheets are *grouped*. Data entered into one sheet is entered into all sheets in the group, making it easy to enter the same title in cell A1 of the three worksheets in the same workbook. It's not unusual to need a number of worksheets with common formatting and data entry. For example, if you work with quarterly budgets, you might want to create a workbook with worksheets that contain the same column headings, row headings, and formulas. With Excel, there are two ways to do this: by grouping the worksheets and then entering the data and formulas common to all four sheets, or by creating one worksheet and then copying it three times. Generally, it's easier to create and copy the worksheets, as you'll soon see.

Grouping is most useful when the worksheets already exist and you need to enter the same information in the same cell on each sheet. Rather than enter a number in cell B16 on all four sheets, group them and enter the value once.

TIP Now in Excel 2002, you can use fill to copy across several sheets. Enter the data on the first sheet. Select the range you wish to fill, and then select the sheets you wish to copy the data to. Choose Edit ➢ Fill ➢ Across Worksheets. In the dialog box, choose All, Formats, or Contents and then click OK.

Grouping is useful for more than data entry. You can format individual cells or ranges; set column widths and row heights; change print setup options including headers, footers, and print areas; and print grouped worksheets.

 WARNING Remember to ungroup worksheets immediately when you are finished entering, moving, or formatting common data. Otherwise, entries you make on one worksheet will be made on all worksheets, overwriting the existing entries on the other sheets in the group.

Ungrouping Worksheets

To ungroup worksheets, right-click any grouped worksheet and choose Ungroup Sheets from the shortcut menu, or click any worksheet in the workbook that is not included in the group.

 TIP To ungroup one or more sheets from the group while maintaining the rest of the group, hold Shift and click the tabs of the sheets to be ungrouped.

Copying and Moving Worksheets

You can copy or move worksheets within and between workbooks. To move worksheets within the same workbook, select the sheet tab(s), drag the tab to the new location (marked by a small triangle just above the tab), and drop it:

To copy a worksheet in the same workbook, hold the Ctrl key while dragging. The copy will have the same name as the original sheet, followed by the copy number:

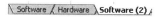

Moving or copying worksheets between workbooks is a bit more complicated.

1. Open the workbook you want to move or copy to. (You can switch between open workbooks by using the Excel's Window menu.)

2. Select the worksheet you want to copy, and then either choose Edit ➤ Move Or Copy Sheet from the menu bar, or right-click the sheet tab and choose Move Or Copy from the shortcut menu to open the Move Or Copy dialog box, shown in Figure 14.1.

3. In the To Book drop-down list, select the name of the open workbook where you want to move or copy the sheet, or choose New Book.

4. To copy the worksheet, select the Create A Copy option check box at the bottom of the dialog box before clicking OK.

You can use this dialog box to move and copy worksheets within the same workbook if you prefer the dialog box to the drag-and-drop method.

FIGURE 14.1

Use the Move Or Copy dialog box to move sheets within and between workbooks.

Inserting and Deleting Worksheets

To insert a new worksheet, right-click any sheet tab and choose Insert from the shortcut menu, or choose Insert ➢ Worksheet from the menu bar. If you want to insert the default blank worksheet, it's faster to use the menu bar. When you insert a sheet from the shortcut menu, the Insert dialog box (which is similar to the New dialog box) opens and prompts you to select the type of worksheet to add: a worksheet, chart, macro, dialog box, or another template. If you select an uninstalled template, you'll be prompted to insert your Microsoft Office XP CD so the template can be installed.

To delete one or more selected sheets, choose Edit ➢ Delete Sheet from the menu bar, or right-click the sheet(s) and choose Delete from the shortcut menu. You'll be prompted to confirm the deletion. Be careful here; you can't use Undo to restore an accidentally deleted sheet.

 TIP If you frequently find yourself adding sheets to workbooks, increase the default number of sheets in a new book. Select Tools ➢ Options from the menu bar, and change the Sheets In New Workbook setting on the General tab of the Options dialog box.

Naming Ranges

A *name* is an alias for a cell or range of cells. Names provide multiple benefits, which become more important as you create increasingly complex workbooks:

- Names can be used in formulas and are easier to remember than cell addresses.

- When a cell moves, the name moves with it.

- You can use a name in place of a cell or range address in a formula or function argument.

- Names identify the cell's contents: *PayRate*, *TotalSales*, and *Quantity* are more descriptive formula references than cell addresses.

- When you copy a formula that uses a name, the effect is the same as using an absolute cell reference.

The rules for using range names include the following:

- Names can be up to 255 characters long and can include letters, numbers, underscores, or periods.

- The name must begin with either a letter or the underscore character.

- You cannot use spaces, commas, exclamation points, or other special characters.

- Names cannot be valid cell addresses: *FY2001* cannot be used as a name, but *FYr2001* can be.

- Names are not case-sensitive: *INTEREST RATE* and *Interest Rate* are the same name.

- A name must be unique within a workbook; you can't use the same name on two different sheets.

The traditional practice is to exclude spaces, and to mix uppercase and lowercase letters, beginning each word within the name with an uppercase letter: *InterestRate*. If you include a space, Excel converts it to an underscore—*Interest Rate* is converted to *Interest_Rate*. This means that you have to remember to type the underscore when referring to the name.

Excel allows you to assign names that might be disallowed in many programs. For example, you can assign the names of program features like cell, column, and row to cells or cell ranges. You're also allowed to assign names that are the names of functions: SUM, COUNT, and so on. To avoid confusion, you probably shouldn't do this, even though Excel allows it.

There are three ways to name a range:

- Use the Name box in the formula bar.

- Use the Define Name dialog box.

- Create names from a row or column of labels.

Naming a Range Using the Name Box

Using the Name box at the left end of the formula bar is the easiest way to name ranges:

1. Select the range to be named; hold Ctrl if you need to select noncontiguous cells.

2. Click in the Name box.

3. Type a valid name for the range and press Enter.

You must press Enter to create the name; you can't simply click in another cell. Click the drop-down arrow in the Name box to open a list of the named ranges in your workbook.

Using the Define Name Dialog Box

The Define Name dialog box, shown in Figure 14.2, provides another way to name ranges, and it is the only place you can change or delete existing range names. The dialog box displays a list of the names already defined in the active workbook. Here are the steps for defining a range name using the dialog box:

1. Select the range of cells you want to name.

2. Choose Insert ➢ Name ➢ Define from the menu bar.

3. Type a name for the range in the Names In Workbook text box and click Add.

4. Click OK to close the dialog box.

FIGURE 14.2

In the Define Name dialog box, you can define, delete, or edit a range name.

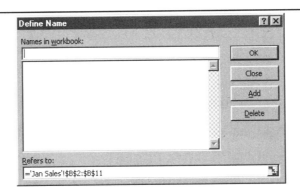

Changing a name or the range referred to by a name is equally easy. First, choose Insert ➢ Name ➢ Define to open the Define Name dialog box.

- To change the name used to refer to a range of cells, select the name from the list of named ranges. Select the name in the Names In Workbook text box, over-type the old name with the new name, and click Add.

- To change the cells referred to by a name, select the name from the list of names. Select the range in the Refers To text box. Select the correct range of cells in the worksheet (you can click the Collapse button in the Refers To text box to hide the dialog box), and then click Add.

To delete a name, select the name from the Names In Workbook list and click the Delete button.

Creating Names from a Row or Column

You can define a group of labels in a row or a column at one time using the Create Names dialog box, shown in Figure 14.3.

1. Select the range to be named. Include the cells you want to use as names as either the top or bottom row, or the first or last column selected.

2. Choose Insert ➤ Name ➤ Create from the menu bar to open the Create Names dialog box.

3. In the Create Names In area, select the row (Top or Bottom) and/or column (Left or Right) that contains the labels you want to use to name the selected range.

4. Click OK to apply the names and close the dialog box.

How Excel Creates Range Names from Labels

Excel edits text as needed to make valid names. Excel uses these standards to generate names from labels or other text:

- If the label for a column or row contains spaces, Excel will replace the space with an underscore: *Interest_Rate*.

- If the cell contents begin with a number, like *8-Mar* or *4 bags*, Excel will add an underscore to the beginning of the name: *_8-Mar* or *_4 _bags*.

- Excel will not create a name for a cell that contains *only* a number (like 1998, 78, or 1254.50). Excel will let you go through the motions, but it won't create the name.

Using Names As References

After you've defined a range, you can enter the range name anywhere a regular cell reference is valid. For example, you can enter the name of a range as an argument for a function: =SUM(Totals) to sum the cells in the range named Totals. Names also serve a valuable navigation function, particularly in large workbooks and worksheets. To move to and select a named range anywhere in the workbook, click the drop-down arrow in the Name box and select the name from the list.

Names created from column and row labels can be used to refer to specific cells at the intersection of the named row and column. In the Vacation Meisters Ticket Sales worksheet shown in Figure 14.4, the range A6:G6 is named *Detroit. Total* refers to E4:E14. The formula =Detroit Total will return the value (74) at the intersection of the two ranges: the intersection of row 6 and column E.

FIGURE 14.4

The formula in this worksheet uses row and column labels to return the value at the intersection of row 6 (Detroit) and column E (Total).

Range: Detroit

Range: Total

	A	B	C	D	E	F	G
1	Vacation Meisters Ticket Sales						
2	First Quarter						
3							
4	Destination	January	February	March	Total	Average	% TOTAL
5							
6	Detroit	17	21	36	74	25	9%
7	Miami	119	101	89	309	10	143%
8	Phoenix	75	77	61	213	71	288%
9	Reno	93	87	90	270	90	87%
10							
11	Total for Month	304	286	276	866		
12	Average for Month	76	72	69	217	=Detroit Total	
13	Minimun for Month	17	21	36	74		
14	Maximum for Month	119	101	90	309		
15							

PART

III

CRUNCHING DATA WITH EXCEL

Creating External and 3-D Range Names

You can use the Define Name dialog box to create names that refer to cells in any open workbook. For example, you may want to refer to a workbook that includes sales and expense totals for the third quarter. Rather than re-create, copy, or link to these figures in your annual sales workbook, you can create names (*Total3rdSales, Total3rdExpenses*) that refer to them. When you refer to a cell in another workbook, the reference is an *external reference*. You name external ranges as you would name ranges in the current workbook, then use the names as external references in formulas. To name a range in another workbook for use in the current workbook:

1. Open both workbooks.
2. Switch to the workbook where you want to create the name.
3. Open the Define Names dialog box (Insert ≻ Name ≻ Define).
4. Type a name for the reference in the Names In Workbook text box.
5. Click in the Refers To text box. Click the Collapse button.
6. Use the Window menu to switch to the workbook that contains the range you want to name.
7. Select the range you want to name.
8. Click the Expand button to expand the Define Names dialog box.
9. Click Add to create the range name.

External ranges don't appear on the Names drop-down list in the active workbook, but you can use them in formulas as you would internal named ranges. Type the range name, or choose Insert ≻ Name ≻ Paste to paste the named range into a formula.

There is a potential downside—if the other workbook is deleted, moved, or renamed, Excel won't be able to find the named range.

A *3-D name* refers to the same cell in more than one worksheet in a book. For example, in a budget workbook the total sales figure is always in cell D87 of each worksheet. You can create a 3-D name that refers to D87 across multiple worksheets. Follow these steps to define a 3-D range name:

1. Choose Insert ≻ Name ≻ Define from the menu bar.
2. In the Names In Workbook text box, type the range name.
3. Delete any reference in the Refers To text box, and type =.

Continued ▯▸

CONTINUED

4. Click the tab for the first worksheet you want to reference, hold Shift, and select the tab for the last worksheet to be referenced.

5. Select the cell or range to be named.

6. Click Add to add the name, and click OK to close the dialog box.

While 3-D range names have a limited navigation use, they're very useful in summary formulas for workbooks that contain a series of periodic worksheets.

Using Functions and References

Functions, such as the SUM, COUNT, AVERAGE, MIN, and MAX functions discussed in the previous chapter, are used to calculate results used in statistics, finance, engineering, math, and other fields. *Functions* are structured programs that calculate a specific result: a total, an average, the amount of a monthly loan payment, or the geometric mean of a group of numbers. Excel includes hundreds of functions. Most are included in the typical installation, but others, like the Engineering functions, must be installed separately. Each function has a specific order, or *syntax*, that must be used for the function to work properly.

Functions are formulas, so all functions begin with the equal sign (=). The equal symbol is followed by the *function name*, followed by one or more *arguments* separated by commas and enclosed in parentheses:

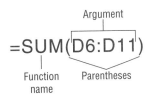

Excel's functions are grouped into the 10 categories listed in Table 14.1.

PART

III

CRUNCHING DATA WITH EXCEL

TABLE 14.1   EXCEL FUNCTIONS

Category	Examples
Financial	Calculates interest rates, loan payments, depreciation amounts, and so on; additional financial functions are included in the Excel Analysis Toolpak Add-in.
Date & Time	Returns the current hour, day of week or year, time, or date.
Math & Trig	Calculates absolute values, cosines, logarithms, and so on.
Statistical	Includes common functions used for totals, averages, and high and low numbers in a range; advanced functions for t-tests, Chi tests, deviation.
Lookup & Reference	Searches for and returns values from a range; creates hyperlinks to network or Internet documents.
Database	Calculates values in an Excel database table.
Text	Converts text to uppercase or lowercase, trims characters from the right or left end of a text string, concatenates text strings.
Logical	Evaluates an expression and returns a value of TRUE or FALSE, used to trigger other actions or formatting.
Information	Returns information from Excel or Windows about the current status of a cell, object, or the environment.
Engineering	Included with Office, but must be installed separately from the Analysis Toolpak.

You don't have to learn all the functions—but you should know the common functions thoroughly and know enough about other functions so that you can find them as you need them. The AutoSum functions (SUM, COUNT, AVERAGE, MIN, and MAX) are the only functions included on the Standard toolbar. You can access all the functions (including SUM) using the Insert Function button on the formula bar, or by selecting More Functions on the AutoSum button menu.

Entering Functions

While there are methods and shortcuts for entering functions in formulas, you'll always follow these general steps:

1. Decide which function to use.

2. Select the function.

3. Enter required and optional arguments for the function.

Before entering a function, click in the cell where you want the results to be displayed. Click the Insert Function (*f*x) button in the formula bar to open the Insert Function dialog box shown in Figure 14.5.

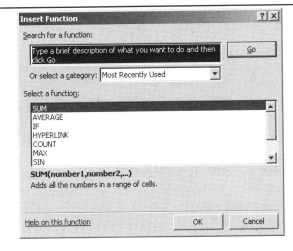

Selecting and Finding Functions

NEW▶

If you know the category of the function you need to use, select the function's category from the Category drop-down list. If you know the function's name, but not the category, choose All in the Category drop-down list. Choose the function in the Select A Function pane, and then click OK to begin entering arguments.

If you're not sure which function to use, enter some information about what you're attempting to do in the Search For A Function text box. Click Go to search for functions.

Click on the function name in the Select A Function pane to display the function's syntax and description below the pane. If you need help, click the Help On This Function hyperlink to display the Excel Help page on the selected function. When you've located the function you want to use, click the OK button.

Choosing a Function from the Formula Bar

If you've recently used the function you want to use, type = to start the formula. The Name box will change to a Function box, displaying the name of the last function that was entered from the list of functions. In Figure 14.6, IF was the last function used. Click the Function drop-down arrow to open the list of recently used functions.

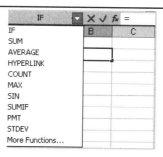

If the function you want is on the list, select it. If the function you want is not
listed in the Function box, choose More Functions at the bottom of the list to open
the Insert Function dialog box, shown previously in Figure 14.5.

Entering Function Arguments

NEW▶

When you select a function, Excel moves the function to the formula bar and opens
the Function Arguments dialog box. The dialog box displays a description of the function and one or more text boxes for the function's arguments, as shown in Figure 14.7.
For common functions that use a single range of cells as an argument, Excel will
"guess" which numbers you might want to use and place the range in the argument
text box. Required arguments are bold, like **Number 1** in Figure 14.7. These text boxes
must be filled in to successfully use the function.

In Figure 14.7, you can't select the cells for the argument because the Function
Arguments dialog box covers the cells. Click the Collapse Dialog button to shrink the
dialog box.

Confirm that the correct cells are selected, or use the mouse to select the correct cells, before expanding the palette with the Expand Dialog button. After you have selected all the required arguments, click OK to finish the entry and close the Function Arguments dialog box.

As with any formula, the results of the function are displayed in the active cell. The function itself is displayed in the formula bar when the cell is active.

These steps summarize how to use Excel functions:

1. Click in the cell where you want the result of the function to appear.

2. Type an = symbol. Choose a function from the recently used functions list. If the function does not appear on the list, open the Insert Function dialog box by choosing More Functions.

   OR

   Clicking the Insert Function button on the formula bar.

   OR

   Choosing More Functions from the AutoSum drop-down menu.

3. Choose a category from the drop-down list and a function from the Select A Function pane. Click OK to open the Function Arguments dialog box.

4. In the Function Arguments dialog box, select the text box for the first argument. Click the Collapse Dialog button if necessary, and then select the cells you want to include in the argument. Click the Expand Dialog button to return to the Function Arguments dialog box. Repeat this step for all required arguments and any optional arguments you need to use.

5. Click OK to complete the entry and close the dialog box.

Relative and Absolute Cell References

When you copy a formula from one cell to another, Excel automatically adjusts each cell reference in the formula. If, for example, the formula in cell J15 is =H15+I15 and you copy the formula to J16, it is automatically adjusted to =H16+I16. In this example, H15 and I15 are *relative cell references*—references made by simply clicking in the cell or typing a cell address when creating a formula. The relative change from one row (15) to another (16) is reflected in the formula when the formula copies: the rows in the cells are increased by one.

NOTE When copying cells in Excel, it doesn't matter if you copy and paste, drag-and-drop, or drag the fill handle. Excel treats formulas the same way, regardless of the copy method you employ.

Most of the time, this is exactly what you want Excel to do. When you copy a formula from one column to another, you want Excel to adjust the column references. A copy from one row to another should result in a change in the row numbers used in the formula. However, there are exceptions.

For example, in the Vacation Meisters worksheet originally shown in Figure 14.4, we would like to know the percentage of tickets sold for each destination city. We calculate a city's percentage by dividing the city's total into the grand total for all cities. In Figure 14.8, a formula was entered to divide the total Detroit tickets (74) into the grand total (866). The formula for Detroit is fine—but it's obviously wrong when copied to the other cities.

FIGURE 14.8

The formula in cell G6 was correct, but yielded wrong results when copied down the column.

	A	B	C	D	E	F	G	
1	Vacation Meisters Ticket Sales							
2	First Quarter							
3								
4	Destination	January	February	March	Total	Average	% TOTAL	
5								
6	Detroit	17	21	36	74	25	9%	── Correct result
7	Miami	119	101	89	309	10	143%	
8	Phoenix	75	77	61	213	71	288%	── Incorrect results
9	Reno	93	87	90	270	90	87%	
10								
11	Total for Month		100	116	966			
12	Average for Month	76	72	69	217			
13	Minimum for Month	17	21	36	74			
14	Maximum for Month	119	101	90	309			

So what happened? The formula in G6 was =E6/E11. When the formula was filled from G6 to G7, Excel changed each cell reference, just as it did when we filled the totals in column E. (In your worksheets, you can see which cells are referenced in a formula by double-clicking on the formula.)

The formula in G7 was changed to =E7/E12, and the change from E11 to E12 created the problem. Rather than dividing Miami's total into the total for all destinations, it divided it into the average in cell E12. The formulas for Phoenix and Reno have a similar problem.

When you fill this formula, you want E6 to change to E7 *relative* to the formula's new location, but you don't want E11 to change at all. The reference to E11 should be *absolute*—not changeable.

Absolute Cell References

You can instruct Excel not to change the reference to E11 by making it an *absolute cell reference*. Absolute cell references are preceded with dollar signs: $E$11. The dollar signs "lock in" the cell reference so Excel doesn't change it if you fill or copy the formula to another cell.

The dollar sign in front of the E instructs Excel not to change the column; the dollar sign in front of the 11 locks in the row. So as you fill the formula to the other cities, E6 will change to E7, E8, and E9, but E11 will always be E11.

You create the absolute cell reference in the original formula. If you never intend to fill or copy a formula, you don't need to use absolute references, and they won't fix a formula that doesn't work correctly to begin with. (The original formula for Detroit in G6 worked just fine.) If you are typing the formula, just precede the column and row addresses with a $. You can also create the absolute cell reference using the F4 key, as you will see in the steps below.

TIP Another way to handle this situation is by naming cell E11 (*QtrTotal* would be a good name) and using the name in the formula in G6. Names are always absolute, so when the formula is filled, the name will always refer to E11.

Follow these steps to create a formula that includes an absolute cell reference:

1. Place the cell pointer where you want the results of the formula to appear.

2. Begin entering the formula. After you click on the cell that should not change when the formula is copied, press the F4 key once to add $ to the row and column of the cell reference.

3. When the formula is complete, press Enter or click the green check mark.

When you fill the formula to the appropriate cells, the absolute cell reference will not change.

Mixed Cell References

You can also create a *mixed reference*, making part of a cell address absolute and part relative, by locking in either the column or the row. Use mixed references when you want to copy a formula down *and* across to have a reference change relatively in one direction but not in the other.

For example, E$5 will remain E$5 when copied down because the row reference is absolute, but it can change to F$5, G$5, and so on when copied across because the column reference is relative.

TIP The Absolute key (F4) is a four-way toggle. The first time you press it, it locks both the column and row: $E$11. Press it again, and only the row is locked: E$11. The third time you press the Absolute key, the column is locked: $E11. Press it a fourth time, and both row and column are relative: E11.

Using Excel's Financial Functions

Excel has more than 50 built-in financial functions, and you don't have to be an accountant to find ways to use many of them. You'll find functions for a variety of essential operations, including:

- Five ways to calculate depreciation on assets or inventory
- Tools to manage the profits you invest
- Functions that help you determine the cost of borrowing against your business line of credit

The financial functions use a variety of arguments, but these are the most common:

Fv The future value; what a loan or investment will be worth at a future time when all payments have been made

Nper The number of periods; the number of months, years, days, or other periods for an investment or loan

Pmt The payment; the amount you periodically receive from an investment or are paid on a loan

Pv The present value; the initial value of an investment or loan

Rate The interest rate on a loan; the discount or interest rate on an investment

The amounts of a periodic payment, present value, interest rate, and the total number of payments have a fixed relationship to each other. If you know any three of these, you can use one of the Excel financial functions to calculate the fourth:

NPER Calculates the number of periods

PMT Calculates the payment amount

PV Returns the present value for the amount loaned or invested

RATE Returns the interest rate

With these four functions, you can determine how much interest you paid on a loan or how much income you will receive from an annuity. The worksheet in Figure 14.9 uses the PMT function to calculate a monthly payment for various present values at an interest rate entered by the user.

When you work with the financial functions, you need to make sure that all the arguments in a function are based on the same period: a day, month, or year. For example, in Figure 14.9 the payments are monthly, but the number of periods and user-entered interest rate are based on years.

FIGURE 14.9

A worksheet for calculating loan payments uses the PMT function.

	A	B	C	D	E	F	G
1	LOAN PAYMENT CALCULATOR						
2							
3	Enter an interest rate here:		12%				
4							
5			AMOUNT BORROWED				
6	Loan Life (Yrs)	$ 5,000	$ 10,000	$ 15,000	$ 20,000	$ 25,000	
7							
8	1	$444.24	$888.49	$1,332.73	$1,776.98	$2,221.22	M
9	2	$235.37	$470.73	$706.10	$941.47	$1,176.84	O
10	3	$166.07	$332.14	$498.21	$664.29	$830.36	N
11	4	$131.67	$263.34	$395.01	$526.68	$658.35	T H
12	5	$111.22	$222.44	$333.67	$444.89	$556.11	L Y
13	6	$97.75	$195.50	$293.25	$391.00	$488.75	P
14	7	$88.26	$176.53	$264.79	$353.05	$441.32	A Y
15	8	$81.26	$162.53	$243.79	$325.06	$406.32	M
16	9	$75.92	$151.84	$227.76	$303.68	$379.61	E N
17	10	$71.74	$143.47	$215.21	$286.94	$358.68	T

In the PMT function arguments, then, Nper has to be multiplied by 12 and Rate divided by 12 so that all the arguments are based on a period of one month, as shown in Figure 14.10. *iRate* is a named range, referring to cell C3, where the user enters an interest rate.

The Function Arguments dialog box showing PMT arguments for the Loan Payment Calculator worksheet

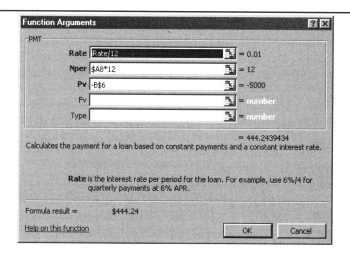

The Depreciation Functions

Businesses must select a depreciation method as assets are placed in service, and the method can't be changed later (unless you want to file additional paperwork). The worksheet in Figure 14.11 uses several of the depreciation functions to indicate methods a business could use to depreciate assets. (Row 17 has three #NUM errors, which we'll explain shortly.)

A worksheet for comparing different asset depreciation methods; Excel has a built-in function for each method.

	A	B	C	D	E
1	**6 YR ASSET DEPRECIATION MODEL**				
2					
3	Name of Asset	Printer			
4	Yrs of Useful Life	5			
5	Month Purchased	1			
6	Cost	$ 1,470			
7	Salvage Value	$ 50			
8					
9		ANNUAL APPRECIATION			
10					
11	Year	Declining Balance	Double Declining Balance	Straight Line	SYD (Sum of Yrs Digits)
12	1	$661.62	$588.00	$284.00	$473.33
13	2	$367.38	$352.80	$284.00	$378.67
14	3	$187.00	$211.68	$284.00	$284.00
15	4	$95.18	$127.01	$284.00	$189.33
16	5	$48.45	$76.20	$284.00	$94.67
17	6	#NUM!	#NUM!	$284.00	#NUM!

The depreciation functions use these arguments:

Life The years of useful life of the asset

Salvage How much the asset will be worth when it's past its useful life

Months The number of months the asset was in service the first year

To easily name a number of ranges, use the Define Name dialog box (Insert ➤ Name ➤ Define). Enter the range name in the Names In Workbook text box. Click the Collapse button in the Refers To text box, select the range, and click Add. When you've created the last range name, click OK to close the dialog box.

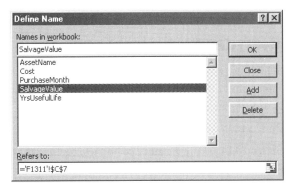

The arguments for the Declining Balance formula in cell B12 are shown in Figure 14.12.

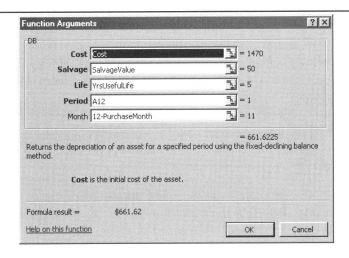

PART

III

CRUNCHING DATA
WITH EXCEL

FIGURE 14.12

*Arguments for the
Declining Balance
(DB) function*

Three of the four depreciation methods return an error for year 6 (row 17 of the worksheet in Figure 14.11). Note that each of the cells with an error has a triangle in the upper-left corner. In the final year, the depreciation can't be calculated using the same depreciation function. Instead, the depreciation is any remaining amount that has not been depreciated in former years. In cell B17, for example, an appropriate formula would be =Cost-SalvageValue-SUM(B12:B16).

If you click in a cell with an error, an error options button is displayed. From the button's menu you can get help diagnosing and solving the problem that created the error. See "Auditing Worksheets" in Chapter 17 for information on handling errors in Excel worksheets.

Using Everyday Statistical Functions

Excel includes a fistful of complex statistical functions. Everyday functions that you may not think of as statistical functions are also included in the list, including all the functions on the AutoSum button:

COUNT Returns the number of numbers in a range

COUNTA Returns the number of entries, including text entries, in a range

AVERAGE Sums the numbers in a range and divides the total by the number of numbers

MEDIAN Another kind of average, calculates the value in the middle of a range

MODE Returns the value that occurs most frequently

MAX Returns the largest value in a range

MIN Returns the smallest value in a range

COUNT is used to calculate the number of cells that have values, including dates, in the specified range. If you want to count the number of entries including text entries in a range, use the COUNTA function rather than COUNT.

> **TIP** Subtract COUNT from COUNTA for the same range to approximate the number of cells that are occupied with text rather than numbers.

AVERAGE returns a value called the arithmetic mean—the total of all the values in a range divided by the number of values in the range. When we talk about averages—bowling scores, test grades, speed on several typing tests—it's the arithmetic mean we're referring to. However, there are two other types of averages: MEDIAN and

MODE. MEDIAN tells you which value is the middle value in a range, and MODE tells you which value occurs most frequently.

You can routinely use MEDIAN to test the usefulness of an AVERAGE. In a perfect bell curve, mean (AVERAGE), MEDIAN, and MODE are the same value. If MEDIAN and AVERAGE values are close to each other, then there either aren't too many incredibly high or incredibly low values in the range, or they offset each other. If the MEDIAN is much lower than the AVERAGE, there are some very high values that "pull up" the AVERAGE. A higher than average MEDIAN means that there are a few very low values.

NOTE The AVERAGE function is SUM/COUNT on a range. The AVERAGEA function is SUM/COUNTA for a range, so each text value adds 1 to the divisor, but does not increase the SUM used as the dividend.

In Figure 14.13, we've used the SUM, COUNT, COUNTA, AVERAGE, AVERAGEA, MEDIAN, and MODE functions on the range of cells in D4:D18 to quickly report information about pledges for a company fundraiser:

SUM The total in cell D20

COUNTA The number of employees in G7

COUNT The number of pledges in G8

AVERAGE The average pledge in G9

AVERAGEA The per employee pledge in G10

MEDIAN and MODE For the results in G11 and G12

Nonpledges are recorded as None in the worksheet, so the AVERAGE function returns the average of those who pledged to the fundraising effort. If nonpledges had been recorded as zero, then the AVERAGE would include the nonpledges, dropping the average to the per employee figure in G10, as there would be no text entries.

NOTE The COUNTBLANK function returns the number of empty cells in a range.

FIGURE 14.13

The statistical functions can be used to quickly summarize results for reporting.

	A	B	C	D	E	F	G
1	2000-2001 Gold Seal Pledges						
2							
3	**Last Name**	**First Name**	**Department**	**Amount**			
4	Adams	Abby	Admin	$ 100			
5	Benth	Greg	Production	$ 100			
6	Brown	Howard	HR	$ 50			
7	Candy	Chuck	Production	None		**Employees**	15
8	Fitzgerald	Elizabeth	Production	$ 100		**Pledges**	11
9	Griffin	Nancy	Admin	$ 250		**Average**	$ 145
10	Hing	Ellen	Production	None		**Per employee**	$ 107
11	Issacs	Helen	Production	$ 100		**Median**	$ 100
12	Jaimison	Mason	Admin	None		**Mode**	$ 100
13	Kzatz	Randall	Technical	$ 300			
14	Lieberman	Dave	Production	$ 150			
15	Main	Bill	Technical	None			
16	Stevens	John	Production	$ 100			
17	Swinzer	John	Production	$ 150			
18	Talus	Charles	Admin	$ 200			
19							
20			**Total**	$ 1,600			

Rounding Numbers in Excel

Everyone thinks they know how to round a number, but if you ask three different people about rounding, you'll get three different answers. Excel has a rounding function for each of these three people and a few of their friends, too. Whether you want to round, round up, round down, or simply get rid of the noninteger portion of a number, there's a function to support your calculation. Excel's rounding functions are listed in Table 14.2.

TABLE 14.2   EXCEL'S ROUNDING FUNCTIONS

Function/Syntax	Description	Examples
ROUND(number, number of decimal places)	"True rounding" rounds away from zero to the number of decimal places you specify.	ROUND(2.75,1) = 2.8 ROUND(31.45,-1) = 30
ROUNDDOWN(number, number of decimal places)	Always rounds toward zero.	ROUNDDOWN(2.75,1) = 2.7 ROUNDDOWN(-3.95,1) = -3.9
ROUNDUP(number, number of decimal places)	Always rounds away from zero.	ROUNDUP(2.72,1) = 2.8 ROUNDUP(-3.95,1) = -4
CEILING(number, significant interval)	Rounds away from zero to the nearest significant interval.	CEILING(398,30) = 420 CEILING(3.72,.25) = 3.75

Continued ▶

TABLE 14.2 (continued) EXCEL'S ROUNDING FUNCTIONS		
Function/Syntax	**Description**	**Examples**
EVEN(number)	Rounds positive numbers up and negative numbers down to the nearest even number.	EVEN(45) = 46 EVEN(-45) = -46
FLOOR(number, significant interval)	Rounds toward zero to the nearest significant interval.	FLOOR(398,30) = 390 FLOOR(3.72,.25) = 3.5
INT(number)	Rounds down to the nearest integer.	INT(4.67) = 4 INT(-4.67) = -5
ODD(number)	Rounds positive numbers up and negative numbers down to the nearest odd number.	ODD(44) = 45 ODD(-44) = -45
TRUNC(number)	Truncates a number by discarding the noninteger portion of the number.	TRUNC(23.67) = 23 TRUNC(-45.6) = -45

Manipulating Text with Functions and Formulas

Many Excel users do little or no math with Excel. Instead, they use Excel's powerful text and date functions to massage data for use in other applications, such as SQL Server. Excel readily converts a wide variety of file formats, so it's the tool of choice for fixing imperfect data that you receive from customers or vendors. A chunk of text data is called a *text string* or *string*. Strings can include spaces, symbols, or numbers as well as characters.

Removing Extra Spaces with TRIM

Spaces at the end of a text string entry are called *trailing spaces*; those at the beginning are *leading spaces*. Trailing spaces can be accidentally added when a user hits the space-bar before moving to another column or field in any application. For a large number of extra spaces, however, you can't beat data created in a mainframe database. Some mainframe programs export fixed-length fields of data and fill unused field lengths with blank spaces. For example, if the City field in a database is 15 characters wide, a 10-character city name will be followed by five spaces. If the exported data needs to be used to create mailing labels, the spaces must be removed or a large gap will appear between the city name and the state name.

Extra spaces in data are inconvenient and difficult to remove manually. You can't see them, and even if you could, manually deleting spaces is tedious work. If you use a find and replace operation, you risk deleting spaces within a string that shouldn't be removed. If you replace all the spaces in the City column, you'll remove the space within a city (for example, the space between Los and Angeles) as well as the extra spaces (following Angeles). Removing extra spaces, while retaining the spaces within a string, is a task for the TRIM function.

The TRIM function strips only the leading or trailing spaces from a text string. If, for example, cell J5 contains the text string Los Angeles followed by four spaces, the formula =TRIM(J5) will return Los Angeles without the spaces.

Copying the Results of Text Functions

All of the text-handling tools are formulas. If you delete the cell that contains the original data, the cell containing the formula that relies on the deleted cell will return an error. To preserve the results of the formula so you can delete the original data, you'll use a variation on copy and paste.

Begin by selecting and copying the cells with the text formulas. Click in an empty area of the worksheet where you want to paste the results of the formula. You can press Enter to simply paste the selection, or you can use one of the following options to paste the values with or without their original formatting:

- Choose Edit ➢ Paste Special or right-click and choose Paste Special to open the Paste Special dialog box. Choose the Values option in the Paste section and click OK to paste the results of the formula beginning in the active cell.

- Right-click and choose Paste from the menu. After Excel pastes the selection, click the Paste Options button at the bottom-right corner of the selection. Open the Paste Options menu and choose Values Only or Values And Source Formatting to retain the formatting from the source range.

Parsing Data with LEFT, RIGHT, and MID

The LEFT and RIGHT functions return a specified number of characters from the beginning or end of a string. If, for example, you receive a mailing list with the city and two-character state abbreviation in one cell (see the sample in Figure 14.14), you can use RIGHT to list just the two-character abbreviation. We'll use the worksheet shown in Figure 14.14 throughout this section, so you may wish to create it in Excel to try the functions we'll be using.

FIGURE 14.14

This spreadsheet con-
tains useful data that
can be massaged with
text functions.

	A	B	C	D	E
1	Name	Address	City/State	MemberID	Phone
2	Olson, Diane	1414 Los Gatos Tr.	Los Angeles, CA	1997-DO1414	(213) 555-9867
3	Smith, Bettie	459 Linwood Ave.	Detroit, MI	2001-BS0459	(313) 555-1234
4	Sinkford, William	3901 Eastview St.	Cambridge, MA	1996-WS3901	(617) 555-2100
5	Madden, Patsy	2415 Williamston Dr.	Livonia, MI	1998-PM2415	(734) 555-7359

The syntax for the RIGHT function is *=RIGHT(string, number of characters)*. To return the two-character state abbreviation from cell C2, use this formula: =RIGHT(C2,2).

The RIGHT function is often combined with TRIM to make sure that the characters returned from the right end of the string aren't blank spaces. To strip spaces from the end of the combined city/state string in our example, first TRIM the string, then apply the RIGHT function: =RIGHT(TRIM(C2),2). Excel trims extra spaces from the text in C2, and then returns the rightmost two characters.

Working with Nested Formulas

The formula =RIGHT(TRIM(C2),2) contains a *nested function:* the results of the TRIM function are the first argument for the RIGHT function. You can easily enter nested functions using the Function Arguments dialog box and the Function list on the formula bar. Start with the RIGHT function. Click the Insert Function button on the formula bar and choose RIGHT from the list of Text functions (or enter the text string right in the Search For A Function text box and choose it from the list of Recommended functions provided). Click OK to open the Function Arguments dialog box. In the formula bar, the function name RIGHT is bold. In the Function Arguments dialog box, the cursor is in the text box for the first argument, Text:

Continued

CONTINUED

Open the drop-down list of functions at the left end of the formula bar and choose TRIM, or select More Functions to open the Insert Function dialog box and choose TRIM from the list of Text functions. When you close the Insert Function dialog box, the Function Arguments dialog box changes to display the arguments for the TRIM function, and the function TRIM is bold in the formula bar:

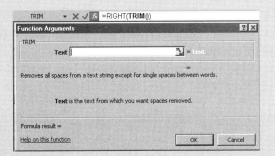

Click in the cell you want to TRIM to enter the argument for the TRIM function. Use the formula bar to switch the function displayed in the Function Arguments dialog box. To display the arguments for the RIGHT function, click the RIGHT function name in the formula bar. To display the argument for the TRIM function, click TRIM in the Function Arguments dialog box.

Excel supports up to seven levels of nesting in a formula.

To return the area code (the first three characters) from a 10-digit phone number in cell E2, use =LEFT(E2,3). If the phone number includes parentheses around the area code, you can use LEFT and specify five characters, but the result will include the parentheses. To return the area code without parentheses, use the MID function. The syntax for the MID function is =MID(*string, starting with, number of characters*). =MID(E2,2,3) will return the second, third, and fourth characters in the telephone number in cell E2.

Using UPPER and LOWER to Change Case

If you're a Word user, you may miss the familiar Change Case command that appears on Word's Format menu. Excel's equivalents are the UPPER and LOWER functions, which convert a string to all uppercase or all lowercase letters. Use UPPER to make a data set that contains uppercase and mixed case entries consistent. The only argument for the UPPER and LOWER functions is the text you want to convert. In our worksheet in Figure 14.14, =UPPER(C2) will return LOS ANGELES, CA.

NEW▶

Excel's equivalent of the Word Title Case option is the PROPER function. Like UPPER and LOWER, PROPER has only one argument: the cell that contains the text you wish to present in proper case. The first letter of each word will be capitalized, and all remaining characters will be in lowercase.

Finding a Character with SEARCH

The SEARCH function locates one string within another, so it can be used to find a single character in a string. The syntax for the function is =SEARCH(*string to find, string to search in, starting with character*); the result is the position of the string to find within the string to search. The final argument, *starting with character*, is optional. If you don't specify where Excel should start searching, it begins at the start of the string. For example, to find the comma character in the combined city/state string in cell C2 (see Figure 14.14), use =SEARCH(",",C2). Excel will return the value 12.

NOTE The SEARCH function is not case sensitive.

We'll combine SEARCH with LEFT to return the city from the string in Figure 14.14 that includes the city name, a comma, and the state abbreviation by substituting the SEARCH formula above for the second argument in the LEFT function that specifies how many characters to return: =LEFT(C2,SEARCH(",",C2)).

TIP To determine the length of a text entry, use the LEN function. LEN returns the length of a string, and has only one argument: the string or its cell address: =LEN(B2).

Putting Text Strings Together

Excel has one tool for assembling text strings: the CONCATENATE function. Concatenation is addition for text; each string is appended to the end of the prior string. The arguments for the function are each of the strings you want to add together, separated by commas: =CONCATENATE(*string1,string2,string3*...) The strings can be cells, or text entered in parentheses. To concatenate a first name in cell A10 with a last name in B10, use this formula: =CONCATENATE(A10," ",B10). The second argument, " ", puts a space between the two names.

PART

III

CRUNCHING DATA WITH EXCEL

If you're just concatenating a couple of fields, it's easier to use the symbol for con-catenation: the ampersand (&). Place the ampersand in your formula between strings. This formula has the same result as the CONCATENATE formula in the previous para-graph: =A10&" "&B10.

Converting Delimited Text to Columns

Excel has another spiffy tool for massaging data: the Convert Text To Columns Wizard. The wizard is used to separate a column of data that has a set delimiter—for example, a comma between a city and state or last and first names, or a hyphen between a cat-alog number and an item number—or is fixed-length data.

Before invoking the text to columns command, save your worksheet. Select the column you want to split, and then choose Data ➤ Text To Columns from the menu to open the Convert Text To Columns Wizard. In the first step of the wizard, choose Delimited to split a column of data separated by a delimiter and click Next. In the second step of the wizard, shown here, choose the delimiter used in the data, or select Other and type the delimiter in the text box:

The wizard will separate your data into columns based on the delimiter you select. If, for example, you select a comma as a delimiter, Excel will place this data into three

Continued

CONTINUED

columns, and remove the commas: AAA, ,CCC. The text AAA will appear in the first column, the second column will be blank, and CCC will be placed in the third column. If you enable the Treat Consecutive Delimiters As One check box, the two commas will be treated as one, and CCC will be placed in the second column.

When you've set your delimiters and the check box, click the Next button. In the third step of the wizard, select a format for each column of data and a destination for the columns of separated data.

If you don't specify a destination, the first column of data is placed in the original column, and the remaining columns are placed to the right of the original column. If the columns to the right of the original column aren't empty, you'll be prompted to overwrite them. Click OK to convert the text into separate columns of data.

If you're cautious, you can use the Treat Consecutive Delimiters As One option to strip out spaces. For example, if you have a column of last names followed by commas and first names, you can set both the comma and the space as delimiters and enable the Consecutive Delimiters check box as shown above. Excel will regard the comma and space following the last name as a single delimiter and discard them both, placing last names in the original column and first names in the next column. This assumes that the original column contains no last names or first names that include spaces.

Using IF Functions

Your computer's processor is capable of two different types of operations: arithmetic operations and logical operations. Adding, subtracting, multiplying, and dividing are arithmetic operations. Logical operators, such as greater than, less than, and not equal to, allow you to compare two or more values or text strings to filter or sort in Word, Access, and Excel. Excel's logical functions place that selection power inside a formula. Use logical functions (also broadly referred to as IF functions) any time you want to apply one formula or another, based on the contents of a cell, such as:

- Overtime pay if total hours are more than 40
- Shift premiums
- Commission calculation rates that vary based on the total sales volume
- Different vacation-day allocations based on seniority
- Two concatenation formulas for full names for people with and without middle initials or names

IF

The syntax of the IF function is =IF(*test, result if true, result if false*). In the payroll worksheet in Figure 14.15, we have a few employees who worked more than 40 hours; these employees should be paid time and a half for hours in excess of 40 hours. Without the IF function, we would need two different formulas: one for employees who worked overtime, and another for those who did not.

FIGURE 14.15

Use the IF function to select the proper Gross Pay formula for each employee based on the number of hours worked.

	SUM	▼ ✗ ✓ *fx*	=IF(C5<=40,C5*D5,40*D5+(C5-40)*D5*1.5)					
	A	B	C	D	E	F	G	H
1	Gold Seal Production							
2	Payroll: Week Ending April 26							
3								
4	Last	First	Hours	Rate	Gross Pay			
5	Benth	Greg	40	15.25	=IF(C5<=40,C5*D5,40*D5+(C5-40)*D5*1.5)			
6	Candy	Chuck	48	15.00	IF(logical_test, [value_if_true], **[value_if_false]**)			
7	Fitzgerald	Elizabeth	44	15.00	690.00			
8	Hing	Ellen	24	15.25	366.00			
9	Issacs	Helen	40	14.75	590.00			
10	Lieberman	Dave	40	14.75	590.00			
11	Stevens	John	36	15.00	540.00			
12	Swinzer	John	40	16.00	640.00			

For employees who worked 40 hours or less, the formula in the Gross Pay column is simply their hours multiplied by their rate: if Greg Benth works 40 hours or less, his gross pay would be =C5*D5. For employees who worked 40 hours or more, the formula needs to reflect overtime. The first 40 hours are paid at the regular rate; hours over 40 are paid at the rate multiplied by 1.5. When Greg works more than 40 hours, the formula will be: =40*D5+(C5-40)*D5*1.5.

Now, we'll place these two formulas, and a test to determine whether an employee's hours are less than 40, in an IF statement. Here's the IF statement created in E5 to calculate Greg's gross pay: =IF(C5>40,40*D5+(C5-40)*D5*1.5,C5*D5). This formula works for all employees' Gross Pay. Excel checks the hours, and then applies the first formula if the hours are over 40 or the second formula if they are not.

TIP You can quickly fill Greg's formula to the other employees by selecting Greg's formula, pointing to the fill handle, and double-clicking.

There are always two ways to write an IF statement. Rather than testing to see if an employee worked over 40 hours, we could test to see if the hours were less than or equal to 40, then swap the two formulas within the IF function: =IF(C5<=40,D5*C5, 40*D5+(C5-40)*D5*1.5).

Nesting IF Functions

If you need to test for more than one condition or apply more than two different calculations in a formula, nest one IF function inside another. For example, Figure 14.16 includes cell ranges normally stored in three different worksheets: a monthly sales report and a table of commission formulas that are applied based on geography. Our IF statement needs to only test for two regions: North and South. All other regions (the East and West regions) receive the same commission.

There are two regions to test for before applying a commission.

	A	B	C	D	E
1	Commission Worksheet				
2					
3	Number	Name	Region	Sales	Commission
4	AJ45	Allison	North	151,985	
5	AL13	Barb	West	180,637	
6	AJ47	Don	North	212,637	
7	AJ91	Barry	East	129,874	
8	AJ57	Myha	South	172,658	
9	AL21	Jamal	East	176,692	
10	AL22	Betty	South	247,958	
11	AL23	Scott	West	309,987	

The formula for cell E4, shown in the formula bar in Figure 14.17, applies a 5% commission in the North region, 5.5% in the South region, and the 6% commission to all other regions (East and West): =IF(C4="North",D4*5%,IF(C4="South",D4*5.5%, D4*6%)). Note that the formula ends with two close parentheses, one to close each IF function.

Nest IF functions to test for more than one condition to determine which formula should be applied.

	A	B
1	Format	Displays
2	Short Date	1/1/01
3	Four digit year	1-Jan-2001
4	Medium Date	1-Jan-01
5	Long Date	January 1, 2001

The key to creating nested logical functions is to understand how they work, so it's worth analyzing how Excel processes this nested function:

1. If the region in column C is North, the result of the first test is true, so Excel immediately moves to the second argument of the IF function and calculates the 5% commission. The rest of the formula is ignored.

2. If the region is not North, the result of the first test is false. Excel immediately moves to the third argument in the IF function and begins executing the test to see if the region is South.

3. If the region is South, Excel executes the second argument of the second IF function and applies the 5.5% commission calculation. The rest of the formula is ignored.

4. If the region is not South, then Excel executes the third argument of the second IF function and applies the 6% commission.

 NOTE You can nest up to seven IF functions in one formula.

As soon as any IF function conditions are met, Excel processes the second argument (the *result if true* argument) of that function and ignores any functions nested within the IF statement. The next example illustrates the most efficient way to build nested IF functions to apply up to four different commissions based on a numeric value—sales volume—rather than region:

Sales Over	Percent
-	5.0%
200,000	5.5%
250,000	6.0%
300,000	6.5%

When you create an IF based on ranges of values, start at one end of the range or the other, and work through the range sequentially. These two functions would produce identical results:

```
=IF(D4>300000,6.5%*D4,IF(D4>250000,6%*D4,IF(D4>200000,5.5%*D4,5%*D4)))
=IF(D5<=200000,5%*D5,IF(D5<=250000,5.5%*D5,IF(D5<=300000,6%*D5,6.5%*D5))))
```

In the second IF function in the second formula, you don't have to test to see if D5 is less than or equal to 250,000 *and* greater than 200,000. If the value of cell D5 is less than 200,000, Excel won't get to the second IF function. See the "Working with Nested Formulas" sidebar earlier in this chapter for the easiest way to create complex nested functions.

MASTERING TROUBLESHOOTING

Trapping Errors with IF Statements

One of the most common errors in Excel, the Division By Zero error, occurs when you divide a number by 0. This often happens when you create a worksheet with formulas in advance of entering data. If cell B27 is empty and cell B30 contains the formula =B10/B27, the error message #DIV/0 appears in cell B30. The user opening the workbook to enter data is greeted with an error message.

If you wrap the formula =B10/B27 in an IF statement that tests if B27 has a value greater than zero, you can omit the error message: =IF(B27>0,B10/B27,0).

To see if a cell is totally blank, use the ISBLANK function. ISBLANK returns one of two values, TRUE or FALSE, so it works well as the first argument in an IF function: =IF(ISBLANK(B27),0,B10/B27).

Using Specialized IF Functions

The specialized IF functions are statistical functions with a logical basis. Use SUMIF and COUNTIF to total or count values in range based on the value in that range or a corresponding range. Divide SUMIF by COUNTIF to calculate the average as if Excel included an AVERAGEIF function. To demonstrate how these incredibly useful functions work, we'll expand the commission worksheet as shown in Figure 14.18.

FIGURE 14.18

SUMIF and COUNTIF summarize data based on a criterion.

	A	B	C	D	E
1	**Commission Worksheet**				
2					
3	**Number**	**Name**	**Region**	**Sales**	**Commission**
4	AJ45	Allison	North	151,985	7,599.25
5	AL13	Barb	West	180,637	9,031.85
6	AJ47	Don	North	212,637	11,695.04
7	AJ91	Barry	East	129,874	6,493.70
8	AJ57	Myha	South	172,658	8,632.90
9	AL21	Jamal	East	176,692	8,834.60
10	AL22	Betty	South	247,958	13,637.69
11	AL23	Scott	West	309,987	20,149.16
12					
13					
14		**North**	**South**	**East**	**West**
15	Total Sales	364,622	420,616	306,566	490,624
16	Total Commission	19,294	22,271	15,328	29,181
17	Total Salespeople	2	2	2	2
18	Average Sales	182,311	210,308	153,283	245,312

PART

III

CRUNCHING DATA WITH EXCEL

The SUMIF Function

The syntax for the SUMIF function is =SUMIF(*criteria range, criteria, range to sum*). The two ranges can be the same if, for example, you're totaling the occurrences of a specific entry in a cell. The third argument, *range to sum*, is optional. If the *criteria range* and the *range to sum* are the same, you only have to specify the *criteria range* and *criteria*. In cell B15 of the commission worksheet, we'd like to total the sales in column D, but only for the salespeople in the North region. SUMIF will evaluate each record and only include it in the total sales if the person is from the North region.

The COUNTIF Function

The syntax for the COUNTIF function is =COUNTIF(*criteria range, criteria, range to count*). The COUNTIF function works like COUNTA, rather than COUNT, so you can count the number of cells in a range that match a text string.

MASTERING THE OPPORTUNITIES

Using Named Ranges As Function References

The SUMIF and COUNTIF functions use ranges as arguments: the range of cells you want to apply a condition to, and the range of cells you want to total or count if the condition is true. Naming both cell ranges saves time when we create the formulas. If we don't name the ranges, we'll need to make our references absolute so Excel won't change the column references when we copy the formulas from North to the other three regions. Naming the ranges has the added benefit of making the formulas more understandable.

To name the three ranges in Figure 14.18, we selected the C3:E11, and then chose Insert ➤ Name ➤ Create. In the Create Names dialog box, we enabled only the Top Row check box and clicked OK.

In this workbook, names really pay off for two reasons: the workbook uses functions that refer to absolute ranges, and since we'll want to copy the functions, we need Excel to treat them as absolutes. When you need to supply a criteria range or database range in a function, consider naming the range before creating the formulas.

After naming the three ranges, we created four formulas in column B (North); and filled the formulas to columns C (South), D (East), and E (West):

14		North	South	East	West
15	Total Sales	364,622			
16	Total Commission	19,294			
17	Total Salespeople	2			
18	Average Sales	182,311			
19					

The four formulas in column B (North) are:

- Total Sales in B15: =SUMIF(Region,B14,Sales)
- Total Commission in B16: =SUMIF(Region,B14,Commission)
- Total Salespeople in B17: =COUNTIF(Region,B14)
- Average Sales in B18: =B15/B17

The absolute references to Region, Sales, and Commission are not altered by the fill operation. The reference to the criteria in B14 changes from North in column B to South, East, and West as the formulas are filled across the columns.

 NOTE The commission worksheet contains a database. In rows 3 through 11, each row is a data record with information about one salesperson. For more information about working in an Excel database, including sorting, filtering, creating subtotals, and using COUNT and SUM with multiple conditions, see Chapter 16, "Managing Information with Excel."

Manipulating Dates with Functions

Excel includes a number of formats for dates and times, but ideally, the date or time is stored as a value rather than text. In Figure 14.19, the date 1/1/2001 is displayed in a number of formats, but the values entered in column B are all the same: 1/1/01. Date and Time formats are applied on the Number tab of the Format Cells dialog box.

PART

III

CRUNCHING DATA
WITH EXCEL

FIGURE 14.19

The format doesn't change the underlying value of the dates in column B.

	A	B
1	Format	Displays
2	Short Date	1/1/01
3	Four digit year	1-Jan-2001
4	Medium Date	1-Jan-01
5	Long Date	January 1, 2001

The fact that dates and times are numbers means you can complete mathematical operations on cells that contain dates or times. The following are examples of the calculations you can complete in Excel:

- Subtract today's date from a book's due date to see if it is overdue
- Add days to a project's beginning date to calculate the date when the project should be completed
- Determine how many days fall between two dates
- Sort dates in chronological order
- Subtract the start time for a task from the ending time to determine how long it took to complete the task

Excel includes time/date conversion and mathematical functions. The conversion functions convert or extract date and time data and include tools to handle dates and times stored as text. The mathematical functions are used for addition and subtraction.

NOTE When you enter dates, Excel generally recognizes them as dates. If, for example, you enter 1/1/2001, 1-1-2001, or January 1, 2001, Excel will recognize it as a date. Dates imported from another application may not fare as well; imported dates are often stored as text entries. Use the date and time conversion functions to convert text dates to number dates.

Entering and Storing Dates and Times In Excel 2002

If you enter a date with a two-digit year (1/1/01), Excel applies the following rule to determine which century to place the date in:

- For year values 00-29, Excel assumes the date is in the 21st century: 1/1/2000 through 12/31/2029.
- For year values 30-99, Excel assumes the date is in the 20th century: 1/1/1930 through 12/31/1999.

If your workbook includes dates prior to 1/1/1930 or after 12/31/2029, enter all four digits of the year so that Excel won't need to interpret the date. If you want to force Excel to display four-digit years, change the Short Date Style setting on the Regional Settings tab of the Windows Control Panel (Start ➤ Settings ➤ Control Panel).

Continued

CONTINUED

Excel stores all dates as numbers called *serial values*. You may have seen a date's serial value if you changed the format on a date to a nondate number format. If you haven't changed Excel's default calculation settings, the serial value of 1/1/2001 is 36892. (The serial values are often incorrectly called Julian dates.) If you subtract 1/1/2001 from 1/2/2001, Excel actually subtracts 36892 from 36893 to determine that there is one day between the two dates.

To ensure compliance with worksheets created on a Macintosh computer, Excel supports two date systems. In the default 1900 system used in Windows applications, January 1, 1900 has the serial value 1. In the 1904 system, used by the Macintosh operating system, 1/1/1904 is assigned serial value 1. Both systems have values for dates up to December 31, 9999. There will be a Y10K problem in Excel worksheets, but none of us will be here to worry about it.

To switch to the 1904 system, choose Tools ➤ Options to open the Options dialog box. On the Calculation tab, enable the 1904 Date System check box. (If you open a worksheet created with Excel for the Mac, Excel will automatically enable the 1904 Date System check box.) Note, however, that this will not change the serial values Excel has assigned to dates you've already entered in workbooks.

Excel stores times as decimal fractions, based on a 24-hour clock. Midnight (0:00:00) is 0; noon (12:00:00) is 0.5; and one second before midnight (23:59:59) is 0.99999999. Format the decimal fractions using the Time formats in the Format Cells dialog box.

Table 14.3 lists commonly used date and time conversion functions. Following the table, we'll provide some examples of how the functions are used in business settings.

TABLE 14.3 COMMON DATE AND TIME CONVERSION FUNCTIONS

Function	Description	Syntax
DATE	Creates a serial value (which you can format using any of the date formats) from three numbers: the year, month, and day	=DATE(*year, month, day*)
TIME	Creates a decimal number time from three numbers: hour, minute, and second	=TIME(*hour, minute, second*)
NOW	Returns the serial value for the current date and decimal fraction for the current time from your computer's system clock	=NOW()

Continued ▐▶

TABLE 14.3 (continued)   COMMON DATE AND TIME CONVERSION FUNCTIONS

Function	Description	Syntax
TODAY	Returns the serial value for the current date from the computer's system clock	=TODAY()
DAY	Returns the day number (1 to 31) from a text string, date, or serial value	=DAY(*date*)
MONTH	Returns the month value (1 to 12) from a text string, date, or serial value	=MONTH(*date*)
YEAR	Returns the year value (1 to 9999) from a text string, date, or serial value	=YEAR(*date*)
HOUR	Converts a text string or decimal fraction to an hour	=HOUR(*string or fraction*)
MINUTE	Converts a text string or decimal fraction to a minute	=MINUTE(*string or fraction*)
WORKDAY	Returns the first workday (nonweekend day) based on a starting date, a number of days, and optionally, a list of holiday dates	=WORKDAY(*start date, days, list of holidays*)
NETWORKDAYS	Returns the number of days, excluding weekends and optionally holidays, between a start date and an end date	=NETWORKDAYS(*start date, end date, list of holidays*)

Use the DATE and TIME functions to construct dates and times when the arguments (*year, month, day, hour, minute,* or *second*) are supplied by a cell entry or another formula. For example, in the customer detail worksheet in Figure 14.20, a user enters the four-digit year in cell B4.

FIGURE 14.20

Use the DATE function to construct a date from cell contents or formulas.

	A	B	C	D	E	F	G
1	Customer Sales Detail						
2	**Reel World Solar**						
3							
4	Year						
5							
6							
7	Number	Sale Date	Name	Region	Order	Commission	
8	AJ45	3/1/99	Allison	North	36,100	1,805.00	
9	AJ45	5/17/00	Allison	North	37,900	1,895.00	
10	AJ45	4/19/01	Allison	North	25,000	1,250.00	
11	AJ45	11/12/99	Allison	North	51,985	2,599.25	
12	AJ47	4/1/99	Don	North	41,560	2,078.00	
13	AJ47	7/5/00	Don	North	66,895	3,344.75	
14	AJ47	6/4/99	Don	North	74,374	3,718.70	
15	AJ47	6/3/00	Don	North	29,808	1,490.40	
16							
17				Total Sales for			
18							

The formula =DATE(B4,1,1) returns the beginning date in that year; =DATE(B4,12,31) returns the last day in the year. Nest these formulas in a couple of IF functions to place an X to mark the rows that contain sales for the year entered by the user, as shown in column G of Figure 14.21:

```
=IF(ISBLANK($B$4),"",IF(B8>=DATE($B$4,1,1),IF(B8<=DATE($B$4,12,31),"X",
"",""))
```

Making an X in a cell is pretty useless if that's the only result. Use the X in the cell as the criteria to apply a conditional format to the data as shown in Figure 14.21, and it becomes more useful. (See "Applying Conditional Formatting" in Chapter 16 for other slick formatting options.)

Use the SUMIF function to evaluate the values (X or no X) in column G and total the cells in the range named OrderTotal in column E that fall within the year entered in B4: =SUMIF(G8:G15,"X",OrderTotal). Cell E17 has a formula that concatenates a string and the year entered by the user: ="Total Sales for"&" "&B4 to accurately label the total created with SUMIF.

 TIP If you find the Xs in column G annoying, they're easy to hide: Simply change the font color to the same color as the fill used for conditional formatting. If there's an X, it blends in. If there isn't an X, it doesn't matter. Or, remove the conditional formatting from the cells in column G and change the font color in column G to white.

FIGURE 14.21

Use the date functions to mark or summarize based on a date.

	A	B	C	D	E	F	G
1	Customer Sales Detail						
2	**Reel World Solar**						
3							
4	Year	2000					
5							
6							
7	Number	Sale Date	Name	Region	Order	Commission	
8	AJ45	3/1/99	Allison	North	36,100	1,805.00	
9	AJ45	5/17/00	Allison	North	37,900	1,895.00	X
10	AJ45	4/19/01	Allison	North	25,000	1,250.00	
11	AJ45	11/12/99	Allison	North	51,985	2,599.25	
12	AJ47	4/1/99	Don	North	41,560	2,078.00	
13	AJ47	7/5/00	Don	North	66,895	3,344.75	X
14	AJ47	6/4/99	Don	North	74,374	3,718.70	
15	AJ47	6/3/00	Don	North	29,808	1,490.40	X
16							
17			Total Sales for 2000		134,603		

The NOW and TODAY functions have no arguments. Both consult the computer's system clock. TODAY returns the current date; NOW returns the current date and time. The NOW function can be nested in the TIME function to calculate the current time. The YEAR function returns the year from a date, serial value, or text string date.

 TIP To convert the year (or any other date) to text, wrap it in a TEXT function: =TEXT(YEAR(*date*)).

When you sort a list of birth dates or hire dates, the dates are sorted in chronological order. If you have every employee's birth date or hire date in an Excel workbook, you can use the MONTH and DAY functions to create a birthday list or anniversary list that you can sort by month and day, rather than by date. Figure 14.22 shows a list of birth dates, months, and days sorted by month, then date. In cell E2, the formula is simply =MONTH(D2). The day formula in cell F2 is =DAY(D2). For information on sorting in Excel, see "Sorting an Excel Database" in Chapter 16.

FIGURE 14.22

Use the MONTH and DAY functions to extract birth months and days from a list of birth dates.

	A	B	C	D	E	F	G
1	Last Name	First Name	Department	Birthdate	Birthmonth	Birthday	BirthText
2	Benth	Greg	Production	1/19/57	1	19	19-Jan
3	Kzatz	Randall	Technical	2/12/66	2	12	12-Feb
4	Talus	Charles	Admin	2/28/46	2	28	28-Feb
5	Candy	Chuck	Production	3/8/79	3	8	8-Mar
6	Swinzer	John	Production	3/22/72	3	22	22-Mar
7	Adams	Abby	Admin	4/12/69	4	12	12-Apr
8	Brown	Howard	HR	5/5/55	5	5	5-May
9	Main	Bill	Technical	5/29/70	5	29	29-May
10	Fitzgerald	Elizabeth	Production	7/7/52	7	7	7-Jul
11	Griffin	Nancy	Admin	8/13/72	8	13	13-Aug
12	Stevens	John	Production	8/15/80	8	15	15-Aug
13	Issacs	Helen	Production	9/24/46	9	24	24-Sep
14	Lieberman	Dave	Production	10/8/63	10	8	8-Oct
15	Jaimison	Mason	Admin	11/11/65	11	11	11-Nov
16	Hing	Ellen	Production	12/5/77	12	5	5-Dec

Converting Text Strings to Dates

When you import dates from another application, they may be imported as text strings, just as if you'd typed an apostrophe in front of a date entered in Excel, or applied the text format before typing the date in the cell. You can easily tell that a date is text rather than a value by widening the column that the date appears in. Dates are numbers, so they should be right-aligned in the cell. Text entries are left-aligned.

The DATEVALUE function converts a text string date to a serial value; the syntax of the function is DATEVALUE(*text string date*). There's only one catch: DATEVALUE only works for dates in the 20th century. Use DATEVALUE when dates prior to 12/31/1999 from another application are imported as strings to convert them to serial values. There is no corresponding function for dates beginning in 2000, or prior to 1900. Instead, you need to use a nested formula to create a serial value.

If cell B30 contains the text string 1/12/2003, the following formula, using the DAY, MONTH, YEAR, and DATE functions, will convert the string to serial value:
`=DATE(YEAR(B30),MONTH(B30),DAY(B30))`.

Functions That Exclude Weekends

A life without weekends sounds incredibly unattractive, so Excel has two functions that take weekends into consideration. WORKDAY and NETWORKDAYS automatically exclude weekends when calculating results, and both can be beefed up to also exclude holidays.

NOTE If these functions don't appear on the list of Date functions, you may need to install the Analysis Toolpak. Choose Tools ➢ Add-Ins to see if the Toolpak is installed. If it's not, browse to find `Analys32.x11` (generally in the `Microsoft Office\Office\Library\Analysis` folder) or use Windows Find (Start ➢ Find or Start ➢ Search to locate it). If `Analys32.x11` is not installed, run Office Setup to install the Analysis Toolpak. After installation, choose Tools ➢ Add-Ins in Excel and click the Analysis Toolpak check box.

The WORKDAY function takes a start date, adds a number of days, and produces the next workday. If you add, for example, one day to a Friday, the WORKDAY function will return the date for the following Monday. The worksheet shown in Figure 14.23 is a chart of due dates for three-day rentals. The due dates skip weekends: =WORKDAY(A4,3) takes the date in cell A3 and adds three workdays. If you have a list of holiday dates, name the range *Holidays* and enter the range as the third argument for the function to have Excel treat dates on the list as nonworking days: =WORKDAY (A4,3,Holidays).

The NETWORKDAYS function returns the number of workdays between a starting date and an ending date, excluding Saturdays, Sundays, and holidays from a range of dates you specify.

FIGURE 14.23

The WORKDAY function skips weekends.

	A	B	C	D
1	THREE DAY RENTAL PICKUP AND DUE DATES			
2				
3	PICKUP DATE:	DUE BACK ON:		
4	April 2, 2001	April 5, 2001		
5	April 3, 2001	April 6, 2001		
6	April 4, 2001	April 9, 2001		
7	April 5, 2001	April 10, 2001		
8	April 6, 2001	April 11, 2001		
9	April 9, 2001	April 12, 2001		
10	April 10, 2001	April 13, 2001		
11	April 11, 2001	April 16, 2001		
12	April 12, 2001	April 17, 2001		
13	April 13, 2001	April 18, 2001		
14	April 16, 2001	April 19, 2001		
15	April 17, 2001	April 20, 2001		
16	April 18, 2001	April 23, 2001		
17	April 19, 2001	April 24, 2001		
18	April 20, 2001	April 25, 2001		
19	April 23, 2001	April 26, 2001		
20	April 24, 2001	April 27, 2001		

MASTERING THE OPPORTUNITIES

Exporting a List of Holidays from Outlook

Both WORKDAY and NETWORKDAYS have an optional argument: a list of holiday dates that can also be excluded. You need to provide the list. If your organization has a holiday list in an Office document, simply copy and paste the list in Excel, and include the list's range as the third argument in the function. If your organization simply uses standard holidays, you can create an Outlook Calendar view that includes holidays and their dates, formatted so that Excel will readily recognize them as dates. (You can type the dates in Excel, but Outlook contains holidays for the next six years, so you can save time by using the Outlook dates.) Using the Clipboard, you can copy these dates from the Outlook Calendar into Excel for greater precision in the WORKDAY and NETWORKDAYS functions.

The Outlook view you'll create uses the Categories field to determine which dates are holidays. If you have special organizational holidays (Founder's Day, the annual staff picnic and softball game, the spring retreat) when the business is closed, add them to your Outlook Calendar and include them in the Holiday category before copying the holidays to paste in Excel.

This is a multi-step process, but if you save the view you create in Outlook, it will be a simple copy and paste operation in future years. Of course, you won't need to do it for a while unless additional holidays are added to your company's calendar as Outlook exports six years of holidays. Follow these steps to export the list of holidays from your Outlook calendar.

1. In the Outlook Calendar, open the Define Views dialog box (View ➤ Current View ➤ Define Views).
2. Select the Events view and click the Copy button in the dialog box to create a copy.
3. In the Copy View dialog box, enter a unique name for the View and click OK.
4. In the View Summary dialog box, click the Filter button.
5. In the Filter dialog box, click the Advanced tab.
6. In the Define More Criteria section of the Advanced tab, click the Field button to expand the Field menu.
7. Choose All Appointment Fields, then Categories from the menu.
8. Verify that Outlook placed "contains" in the Conditions text box.

Continued ▌▶

MASTERING THE OPPORTUNITIES CONTINUED

9. In the Value text box, type **Holiday**:

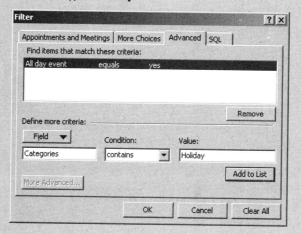

10. Click the Add To List button to add the Criteria to the list.

11. Click OK to close the Filter dialog box.

12. In the View Summary dialog box, click the Fields button to open the Show Fields dialog box. The completed view only requires two fields: Subject and Start. Use the Add and Remove buttons to create the two-field list in the Show These Fields In This Order pane. Click OK to close the Show Fields dialog box.

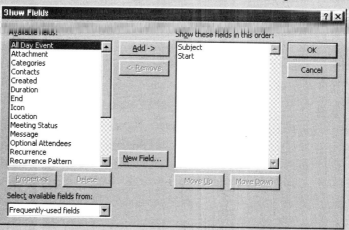

Continued

13. Click OK to close the View Summary dialog box, and Apply View to apply the view and close the Define Views dialog box.

14. Right-click the Start column button in Outlook's Information Viewer and choose Format Column from the shortcut menu. Choose a short date format for the Start column and click OK.

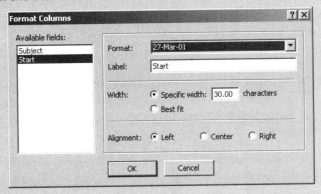

15. Click the Start button to sort the Start dates in ascending order.

16. Choose Edit ≻ Select All to select all the appointments, then copy them to the Clipboard.

17. Paste the selection into an Excel workbook:

	A	B
1	**Subject**	**Start**
2	Independence Day	7/4/00
3	Labor Day	9/4/00
4	Columbus Day	10/12/00
5	Thanksgiving Day	11/22/00
6	Christmas Eve	12/24/00
7	Christmas Day	12/25/00
8	New Year's Eve	12/31/00
9	New Year's Day	1/1/01
10	Martin Luther King Day	1/15/01
11	Lincoln's Birthday	2/12/01

18. Select and delete rows that aren't required (past dates and holidays that are working days for your organization such as Groundhog Day). If, for example, your organization works on President's Day, sort by Subject, select and delete all President's Day rows, and then resort by Start.

19. Name the range of dates imported from the Start field.

PART

III

CRUNCHING DATA WITH EXCEL

Linking Workbooks

A *link* is a reference to a cell or range in another workbook. Links are commonly used to avoid double-entering workbook information. For example, say you work in a company where departments are responsible for their own budgets. As the time to finalize the coming year's budget approaches, each manager is working furiously on his or her budget. The vice president for finance has a master budget that summarizes the department budgets.

It's not practical to put all the department worksheets and the master budget in one large workbook, because many people would need to use the workbook at the same time. Instead, if the managers link the workbooks together, they won't have to fight with each other or with the vice president over whose turn it is to work with the budget. (Experience indicates that the vice president almost always wins.)

The vice president's workbook will include links to cells in the departmental budget workbooks. As the department managers change their numbers, the changes can be automatically reflected in the vice president's master budget workbook so the managers and the VP are all working with the most current data. Each link establishes a relationship between two workbooks. The vice president's workbook is called the *dependent workbook*, because each value there depends on a value in another workbook, which is called the *source workbook*.

There are two ways to create a link: by using an open workbook as a source or by referring to a workbook's disk or network location. The first method is much easier to use. It's the same as creating any other reference in a formula, but you need to switch to the source workbook before selecting the cell to reference in the formula.

Before creating the formula that includes a link, open the source workbook. Then, in the dependent workbook, begin entering the formula with an equal sign (=). At the point in the formula where you want to include a cell reference from the source workbook, choose Window on the menu bar and select the source workbook. Click on the cell that you want to reference, and it will be included. Notice that the cell reference includes the workbook and worksheet names as well as the cell address:

Cell address

='[Book Schedule.xls]Proposed'!$B$3

Workbook name   Sheet name

You may prefer to arrange the source and dependent workbooks so that you can see the "result" cell and the cell to be referenced at the same time. With both workbooks open, choose Window ➢ Arrange to open the Arrange Windows dialog box.

Choose how you want the open workbooks arranged, and then use each workbook window's sizing tool to further size and arrange the windows.

 TIP You can arrange copies of a single workbook so you can work in different parts of the workbook in separate windows. Choose Window ➢ New Window and then open the Arrange Windows dialog box and arrange the windows.

If the workbook is not open, you must provide all the information that Excel needs to find the source workbook, including the full path. For example, if you want to refer to cell D4 in the Sales sheet of the Proposed Dept. Budget workbook, stored in the Sales Management folder on the C drive, the reference would be: `'C:\Sales Management\ [Proposed Dept. Budget.xls]Sales'!D4`. There are many places to make a mistake when typing an entry like this. Try to create links with open source workbooks whenever possible.

Linking with Paste Link

If you simply want to include a cell from another workbook (as opposed to using it in a formula), create a link by copying and paste-linking.

Open both workbooks; then select and copy the cell(s) from the source workbook. Activate the destination workbook, and choose Edit ➢ Paste Special from the menu bar or right-click and choose Paste Special from the shortcut menu to open the Paste Special dialog box. Click the Paste Link button.

 Or, right-click and choose Paste from the shortcut menu. After Excel pastes the selection, click the Paste Options drop-down list and choose Link Cells.

Updating Links

When you open the dependent workbook and the source workbook is not open, Excel will ask if you want to update the links. If both workbooks are open, changes in the source workbook are automatically updated in the dependent workbook.

If the source workbook can be opened by other users, however, they could be making changes to that workbook while you are working with the dependent workbook. In this case, the links will not be updated automatically; you have to instruct Excel to update the links.

With the dependent workbook open, choose Edit ➢ Links to open the Edit Links dialog box. From the Source list, choose the source workbook that you want to update. Click the Update Values button to update the dependent workbook with information from the latest saved version of the source workbook.

Creating 3-D Cell References

In Excel, you can reference ranges that occur in the same cell or group of cells on two or more worksheets. For example, Figure 14.24 shows the July, August, and September worksheets for reporting different types of media sold at various locations; all three worksheets have exactly the same layout. The Third Quarter worksheet summarizes the figures from the three monthly worksheets. Because all the worksheets have exactly the same layout, you can total all worksheets at one time with a 3-D cell reference.

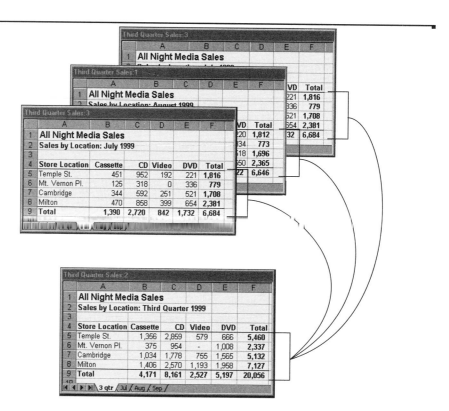

FIGURE 14.24

Three monthly worksheets combined into a summary quarterly worksheet by using 3-D cell references

First make sure that the worksheets you want to reference are next to each other. Then simply create the formula as you normally would, using AutoSum.

To insert a 3-D argument, hold Shift and select the worksheets that include the cells you want to insert in the argument. (The sheet with the formula will also appear to be included; just ignore it.) Then select the cell(s) that you want to include and finish creating the formula:

 =SUM(Jan:Mar!B5)

Formulas with 3-D references can be filled and copied like other formulas.

TIP If you plan to create and use many 3-D cell references, or 3-D references that span workbooks as well as worksheets, you should consider using 3-D range names. See the sidebar "Creating External and 3-D Range Names" earlier in this chapter.

CREATING EASY-TO-UNDERSTAND CHARTS

ore than one in four adults can't easily calculate how much change they should get when they give the fast food cashier $5.00 for a $2.37 meal purchase. The proliferation of PCs and calculators has lessened the perceived importance of math skills, so the numerically challenged aren't spending their days sitting in basic math classes. These folks are your co-workers, customers, and supervisors. They serve on committees and boards that approve or reject projects and expenditures dear to your heart and your organization's bottom line. Excel's charting feature is a tool that helps bridge the gap between the figures in spreadsheets and the people who need to understand them, making numbers accessible to people who can't or don't work well with numbers.

And even folks who like numbers appreciate a well-built chart. Charts make it easier to compare and understand numerical values and highlight information that can be lost in a long list of numbers. Every chart tells a story. Stories can be simple ("See how our sales have increased") or complex ("This is how our overhead costs relate to the price of our product"). A well-designed chart provides context and focus so the story you want to tell is easily understood.

Charts are constructed with *data points,* which are the individual numbers in a worksheet, bundled into *data series,* which are the groups of related data points within a column or row. For example, Figure 15.1 shows the Undiscovered Country Travel Destination Package Sales worksheet we'll use to create charts in the first portion of this chapter. Each of the numbers in the worksheet is a data point. There are many possible sets of data series in this worksheet: one set includes five data series—one for each destination's row. Another set includes a data series for each month's column. Each column or row of numbers is a series.

<table>
<tr><td>FIGURE 15.1</td><td colspan="5"></td></tr>
</table>

FIGURE 15.1

Each number in this worksheet is a data point, and each row or column is a potential data series.

	A	B	C	D	E
1	Undiscovered Country Travel				
2	Destination Package Sales				
3					
4	Destination	April	May	June	Q2 Total
5	Las Vegas	56	50	41	147
6	Luxor Cruise	14	14	14	42
7	Antigua/Tikal	41	33	33	107
8	Orlando Express	34	48	45	127
9	Daytona	87	34	19	140

A Quick Overview of Chart Types

Excel supports a broad selection of chart types. Your data and the story you want to illustrate determine the type of chart you will plot the data on. In this chapter, we'll focus on the chart types used most frequently for business charts in North America.

Pie Charts

Use *pie charts* to show the relationships between pieces of an entity. The implication is that the pie includes *all* of something. In the simple pie chart shown in Figure 15.2, the pie shows all the tickets sold in the second quarter. The pie chart type isn't appropriate for illustrating *some* of anything, so if there's not an obvious "all" in the data you're charting, don't use a pie.

FIGURE 15.2

A pie chart from the Destination Package Sales worksheet

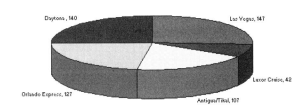

Destination Packages - 2nd Quarter

A pie chart can only include one data series. If you select more than one data series, Excel uses the first series and ignores all others. No error message appears, so you won't necessarily know that the chart doesn't show the data you intended to include, unless you examine the chart carefully.

Pie charts almost always show relationships at a fixed point in time—the end of the year, or a specific month, day, or week. It is possible to create a pie chart with more than one time frame; however, this kind of information would be better represented in a series chart.

When you create a pie chart, you don't need to create worksheet formulas to calculate percentages. Excel totals the data points in the series and then divides the value of each data point into the series total to determine how large each data point's pie slice should be. Don't include a total from the worksheet as a data point; this doubles the total Excel calculates, resulting in a pie chart with one large slice that represents exactly 50 percent of the pie.

Series Charts

In a *series chart*, you can chart more than one data series. Series charts let you compare the data points in the series, such as April vs. June, or Las Vegas compared to Orlando. Series charts are open-ended; there is no requirement that the data shown is all the data for a month or year. There are several types of series charts, so you can often

PART

III

CRUNCHING DATA
WITH EXCEL

improve the usefulness of a series chart simply by changing the chart type. The charts shown in Figures 15.3, 15.4, and 15.5 were created using the same data series.

Line, Ribbon, and Area Charts

The series chart in Figure 15.3 is a *line chart* showing the relationship between ticket sales and each destination during the first quarter. The chart includes a data table that lists the values illustrated by the chart. Each data series is a destination. Line charts are available in a 2-D version as shown or in a 3-D version called a *ribbon chart*. An *area chart* is a line chart with the area below the line filled. Line, ribbon, and area charts are typically used to show one or more variables (such as sales, income, or price) changing over time with time on the x-axis.

FIGURE 15.3

Line charts are typically used to illustrate changes over time.

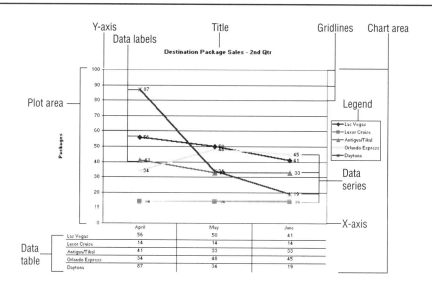

Column and Bar Charts

In Figure 15.4, the data is presented as a *bar chart*. The bars are bulkier, thus giving added substance to the chart. In the line chart (Figure 15.3), what the user notices is the trend up or down in each line and the gaps between the lines. The bar chart makes all ticket sales seem more substantial, but it also makes the difference between destinations even more clear. Changing the chart type shifts the focus to the difference between destinations rather than the trend for each destination.

Line and area charts share a common layout. The horizontal line is the *x-axis*, and the vertical line is the *y-axis* (the same x- and y-axes you may have learned about in algebra class). In a bar chart, however, the chart is turned 90 degrees so the x-axis is on the left side.

With a little help from Excel, you can combine columns with line or area charts and embellish line or column charts with 3-D effects. You can move beyond the column/bar spectrum and use tubes, pyramids, cones, or cylinders to represent data or transform regular bars into floating 3-D bars.

FIGURE 15.4

The bar chart focuses the user on the difference between destinations.

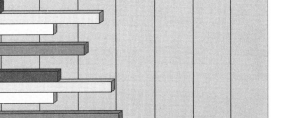

When you need to show totals and the data points that make up the total, the natural choice is a *stacked bar chart* or *a stacked column chart*. A stacked 3-D column chart is shown in Figure 15.5. Stacking adds another dimension to the chart, since it allows the user to compare sales between as well as within time periods—like providing a column chart and a pie chart for each time period.

PART

III

CRUNCHING DATA WITH EXCEL

FIGURE 15.5

The stacked column chart provides total and detail information.

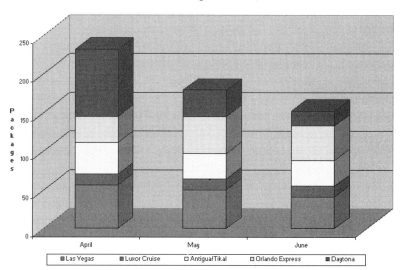

In a 2-D chart, the x-axis is the *category* axis and the y-axis is the *value* axis. In a 3-D chart, the y-axis becomes the *series* axis, and values are plotted on the third axis, the *z-axis*, which provides the "third dimension" of depth in the chart. Don't worry about memorizing which axis is which in each chart type; there are ways to know which is which when you're creating or editing the chart.

Excel includes other chart types suitable for presenting scientific, statistical, and financial data. *Scatter charts* are used to present experimental results. *Surface* and *contour charts* are good for presenting 3-D and 2-D changes in data. *Radar charts* show data values in relation to a single metric. *Stock charts* present values for between three and five series of data, including open, high, low, close, and volume trading information.

Creating a Chart

The easiest way to create a chart is by using the Chart Wizard. In most circumstances it's also best to use the wizard because it provides easy access to all the chart options you might need. Here's an overview of the steps for creating an Excel chart with the Chart Wizard:

1. Select the ranges you want to include in the chart.

2. Click the Chart Wizard button on the Standard toolbar.

3. In the first wizard step, select a chart type and subtype, then click Next.

4. In the second step, verify that you have selected the correct range and choose to have the series represented by rows or by columns. Click Next.

5. In the third step, set options for the chart, including titles, data labels, and legend placement. Click Next.

6. In the fourth step, select a location for the chart. Click Finish.

Selecting Data for the Chart

First, select the data that you want to include in the chart. With the exception of the chart's title, everything that appears in the chart should be selected from somewhere in the worksheet. Column and row labels provide text for the axes and legend. Make sure that the ranges you select are symmetrical: If you select four labels in rows 9–12 of column A, select data points from the other columns in rows 9–12. If you select labels in columns A–D of row 5, then the data series you select should also be in columns A–D. Figure 15.6 shows the data selected to create the charts originally shown in Figures 15.3 through 15.5.

FIGURE 15.6

Select all the data required for the chart-data points and text that will serve as labels.

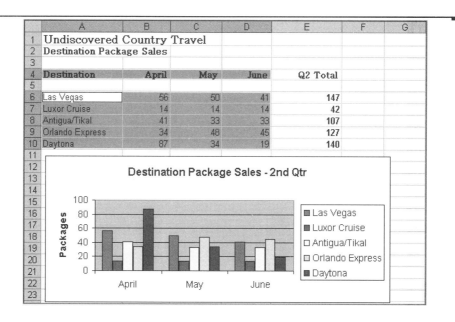

TIP The selection in Figure 15.6 doesn't include the empty cells in row 5. If you include blank rows or extra empty columns in your selection, you'll have empty spaces in your chart. Remember that you can hold the Ctrl key to select noncontiguous ranges of data. If you select some cells you don't want to include, press the Esc key and start selecting again.

Using the Chart Wizard

 With the text and numbers selected, click the Chart Wizard button on the Standard toolbar. The Chart Wizard and the Office Assistant both open. You can close the Assistant, if you want to. The Chart Wizard includes a button that will reopen the Assistant if you need help.

In the first step of the Chart Wizard, choose a chart type in the Chart Type list box (see Figure 15.7). If the type of chart you want isn't listed, check out the chart types on the Custom Types tab.

FIGURE 15.7

Choose a chart type and subtype in the first step of the Wizard.

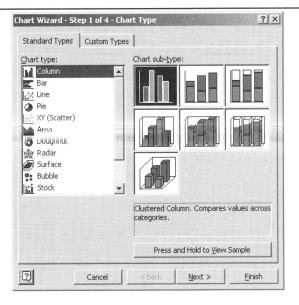

 For information about a chart type, select the type, click the Chart Wizard's Office Assistant button, and choose Help With This Feature. The Assistant will offer to provide a sample of the selected chart. Microsoft Excel Help will then slowly display, showing detailed explanations of all the charts and their respective elements.

The wizard creates a preview so you can check the chart's general appearance using your data. After choosing a chart type in the left pane on the Standard Types tab, choose a subtype in the right pane. To see a rough sample of the type and subtype using your data, use the Press And Hold To View Sample button in the Chart Wizard. When you've selected a type and a subtype, click Next to continue.

In the second step, shown in Figure 15.8, check the Data Range tab to make sure the range you selected is correct. If it isn't, use the Collapse Dialog button and select the proper range before continuing. Choose Rows or Columns in the Series In option group, and the preview will change to reflect the range and series arrangement you specify. Figure 15.9 shows the preview by Rows (months on the x-axis) and Columns (destinations on the x-axis).

FIGURE 15.8

In the second step of the wizard, check the selected data range.

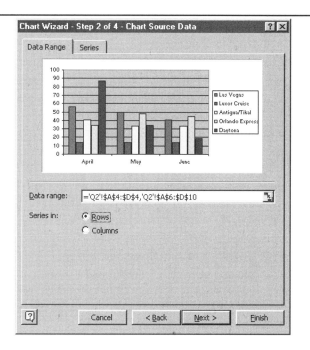

PART

III

CRUNCHING DATA
WITH EXCEL

FIGURE 15.9

Indicate whether the chart's series are in rows or columns.

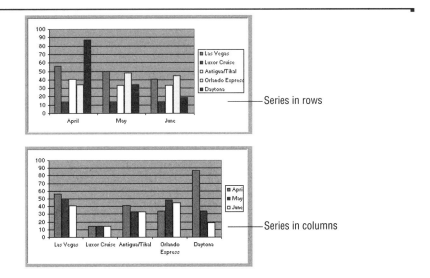

Series in rows

Series in columns

Select the Series tab (shown in Figure 15.10) to verify selected ranges and values for the series used in the chart. Select any of the items listed in the Series list box to see which cells or cell ranges in the spreadsheet correspond to the selected series and category labels. Use the Collapse Dialog button next to the series' Name or Values text boxes, or the Category (X) Axis Labels text box to change the ranges used for these chart elements.

To remove a series, select the series in the list and click the Remove button. To add a series, click the Add button. Specify a cell reference for the label and a range for the series data.

TIP You don't need to use data from your worksheet as the series names. In Figure 15.10, each series' name comes from column A, the name of the destination. To make the names more descriptive, select the cell reference in the Name box and type the new entry: for example, Luxor (Egypt). Repeat this for each series.

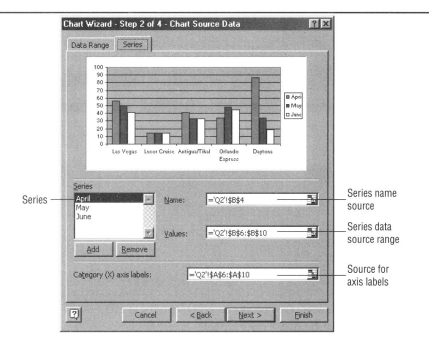

FIGURE 15.10

Verify the series data, name, and axis labels on the Series tab.

In the third step, use the tabs (shown in Figure 15.11) to set options for various aspects of the chart:

Titles Enter titles for the chart and axes.

Axes Display or hide axes.

Gridlines Display gridlines and display or hide the third dimension of a 3-D chart.

Legend Display and place a legend.

Data Labels Display text or values as data labels.

Data Table Show the selected range from the worksheet below the chart.

As you change options, the chart preview reflects your changes. When you've finished setting options, click Next to continue.

PART

III

CRUNCHING DATA
WITH EXCEL

FIGURE 15.11

Set the chart's titles, labels, and display options.

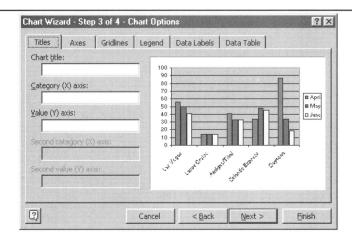

NOTE Every chart needs a title. The title provides information that is not already included in the graphical portion of the chart. The chart's picture, legend, and title taken together should answer any questions about the timing, location, or contents of the chart.

In the last step of the Chart Wizard, you can choose to place the chart on the current worksheet or on a new, blank sheet in the same workbook. If the chart is placed on its own sheet, it will print as a full-size, single-page chart whenever it is printed. If you add it to the current worksheet as an object, it will print as part of the worksheet, but can also be printed separately.

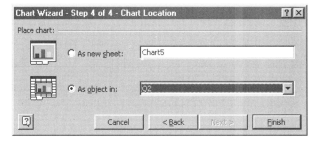

Enter a new sheet name (or choose As Object In and select the worksheet in which to place the chart) and click Finish to create and place the chart. The Office Assistant will open and offer further help with charts. The Excel Chart toolbar will open in the workbook window. You can move a chart object to its own worksheet or make a chart an object in another worksheet (like a picture that you can reposition and resize). Select the chart or chart object, right-click, and choose Location from the shortcut menu to open the Chart Location dialog box.

Editing and Formatting Charts

After you create and save your chart, use Excel's editing and formatting tools to modify it or improve its appearance. If you placed the chart as an object, you'll probably need to move and resize the chart to place it correctly in an existing report or worksheet. Moving and resizing are only the beginning. You can add, delete, and reorder data series, display error bars and data labels, or change the fill, font, and spacing of various chart elements.

Moving, Sizing, and Printing Chart Objects

If you place the chart as an object in the current worksheet, you'll inevitably need to resize and move it so it will print well with the existing data. The chart object floats on a layer above the worksheet, so it may cover part of the worksheet data or fall across a page break. Fortunately, moving a chart (or any other object) in Excel is a snap!

 NOTE The Office applications handle all objects in roughly the same way as a chart object, so if you've worked with WordArt or clip art in Word or PowerPoint, you know how to move and resize chart objects. You'll find detailed information about working with objects in Chapter 26, "Breaking the Application Barrier."

When the Chart Wizard closes, the chart displays square *handles* on the corners and sides to show it is selected. If the chart isn't selected, click once on the chart to select it. To deselect the chart and return to the worksheet, click anywhere in the worksheet except on the chart object. When the chart is selected you can move it by pointing to the chart (anywhere inside the chart frame except the plot area) and holding the mouse button down. When the pointer changes to a four-headed arrow, drag the chart to its new location. To change the chart's size, move the mouse pointer to one of the chart's handles. Hold the mouse button and drag the handle to stretch or shrink the chart. Handles on the sides of the chart change the size in one direction (width or height). To increase width and height in proportion, use a corner handle.

> EXPERT TIP Turn on Page Break Preview when sizing and moving charts to make sure they remain within the boundaries of a page. The View menu doesn't include the Page Break Preview command when a chart is selected, so click anywhere in the worksheet to deselect the chart, choose View ➢ Page Break Preview, and select the chart.

Printing Charts As Objects or Worksheets

If you placed your chart as an object in the current worksheet, you can still print it separately. If the chart is selected when you print, the chart will print by itself on a full page. If the worksheet is selected, the worksheet prints, including the chart object.

- To print a worksheet, including a chart object, activate any worksheet cell before printing.
- To print a chart object as a full-page chart, select the chart before printing.

Adding a Data Series

You can modify Excel charts quickly and easily. If you have an existing series chart, you can select and drag excluded series to add them to chart. Here are the steps for adding a data series to a chart:

1. In the worksheet, select the data series to be added.

2. Drag the series and drop it in the chart.

If you prefer a more structured approach, or wish to change the label for the series, use the Chart Wizard. Select the chart object or chart worksheet and click the Chart Wizard button. Click Next to move to the second step of the Chart Wizard and add or adjust series on the Series tab. This is also a fine place to delete a data series.

Deleting a Data Series

A chart is a collection of graphic objects. The chart object contains a data series object, which contains data point objects. To access the objects, first select the chart. Then click a series to select the entire series. The series will have handles.

 TIP To select a data point, first select the chart, then the series, then the data point.

When an object is selected, you can delete or format the object. Use these steps to delete a data series from a chart:

1. In the chart, select the data series or any data point in the series.

2. Press the Delete key on the keyboard.

 NOTE Press the Delete key when the chart is selected to delete the entire chart object.

Formatting Charts

The *chart area* (see Figure 15.12) is a rectangular area within the chart window bounded by the chart border that contains all of the parts and pieces of the chart including the title, legend, and the border surrounding the chart object. Changing the size of the chart object changes the size of the chart area.

FIGURE 15.12

The chart area is the entire chart. The plot area is the graphical area of the chart.

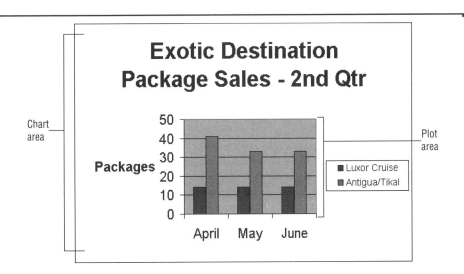

The *plot area* (see Figure 15.12) is bounded by the axes and contains the columns, lines, wedges, or other objects used to represent the data points. Objects that form the boundaries of the plot area have fixed location areas and cannot be moved or individually sized. For example, the x-axis labels must be located near the x-axis.

PART

III

CRUNCHING DATA
WITH EXCEL

Resizing and Deleting Objects in a Chart

You can, however, resize all the objects in the plot area by increasing or decreasing the plot area itself. (There's an exception to this rule; see "Exploding Pies" later in this chapter.) Objects outside the plot area and axes can be sized or moved to other locations in the chart area. The title and legend can be placed above, below, or in the plot area.

Any object in a chart can be selected and then formatted or deleted, with the exception of individual data points. Data points can be formatted, but only data *series* can be added or deleted. To select a data point, first select the data series, and then click the data point once.

Formatting the Chart with the Chart Toolbar

Common formatting options are available on the Chart toolbar (View ➢ Toolbars ➢ Chart). The first button is used to select one of the objects in the chart; the other buttons format the entire chart or selected text. See Table 15.1 for descriptions of the buttons on the Chart toolbar.

TABLE 15.1 CHART TOOLBAR BUTTONS

Button	Button Name	Function
Chart Area ▾	Chart Objects	Selects the object chosen from the list.
	Format Object	Opens the Format dialog box for the selected object.
	Chart Type	The drop-down arrow opens a menu of chart types; clicking the button applies the type indicated on the button face.
	Legend	Displays or hides the legend.
	Data Table	Displays or hides the data table.
	By Rows	Uses the selected worksheet rows as a data series.
	By Columns	Uses the selected worksheet columns as a data series.

Continued ▶

Button	Button Name	Function
TABLE 15.1 (continued) CHART TOOLBAR BUTTONS		
	Angle Clockwise	Angles selected text downward.
	Angle Counterclockwise	Angles selected text upward.

Formatting Individual Objects

The difference between a "good" chart and an outstanding chart is often found in a number of small, almost insignificant changes. The chart shown in Figure 15.12 is the chart as it appears right out of the Wizard. Figure 15.13 shows the same chart after we've invested three minutes to format a few of the chart objects.

FIGURE 15.13

The chart shown in Figure 15.12 with formatting changes.

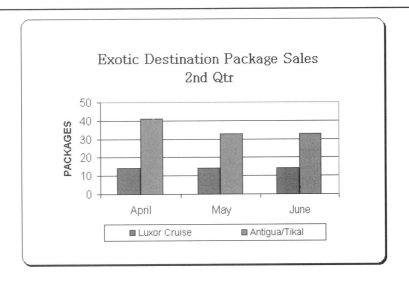

We made the following formatting changes:

- Plot area pattern set to None
- Plot area increased
- Corners on chart area rounded
- Legend positioned at bottom

PART

III

CRUNCHING DATA WITH EXCEL

- Legend text box resized
- Y-axis label retyped in caps and rotated
- Axis labels' font size decreased
- Title font size decreased and edited to break across lines
- Title font changed to match worksheet font

To format chart objects such as a data series, select the object from the Chart Objects drop-down menu on the Chart toolbar. Double-click any selected object or click the Format Objects button to open the formatting dialog box for the object. For example, double-clicking any column in a data series opens the Format Data Series dialog box, shown in Figure 15.14.

FIGURE 15.14

Double-click any object to open its formatting dialog box.

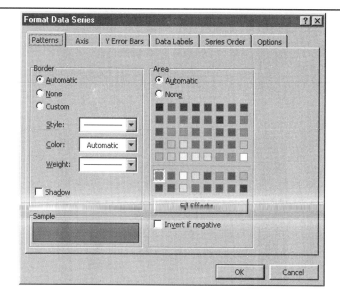

There are five or six tabs in this dialog box; depending on the chart type, the dialog box may include tabs for Shape, Axis, or Y Error Bars. Each tab contains a group of settings for the selected data series that include:

Patterns Applies a selected color and pattern for each series.

Axis Adds a second vertical axis at the right end of the plot area scaled to the selected series. The chart must contain two or more series.

Y Error Bars Adds a graphic display of sampling errors when the data in the chart is a statistical sample being applied to a larger population.

Data Labels Adds a descriptive label or the numeric value for each data point in the series.

Series Order Reorders the series in a chart; especially useful with 3-D charts, where the selected range is charted in reverse order.

Options Settings for the bar or column overlap, gap, and color variation.

For more information on a specific control within a formatting dialog box, click the Help button and then click the control.

Similar options are available when you double-click a selected data point, the plot area, chart area, or other chart object. To change font and alignment settings for axis labels (such as the April, May, and June x-axis labels in Figure 15.13), select the axis and open the Axis dialog box.

EXPERT TIP To quickly format an object, select it, right-click, and select Format from the shortcut menu. If the entire chart is selected, Chart Options appears on the menu. If you want to change the type of chart from a pie to a bar chart, for example, you can also choose Chart Type from the shortcut menu.

Inserting and Formatting Titles

If you didn't give the chart a title while creating it, you can add one at any time. Select the chart, right-click, and open the Chart Options dialog box from the shortcut menu. In the Titles tab of the dialog box, you can edit or format existing titles (including placeholders) in a selected chart without having to use the Chart Options from the shortcut menu. To change the text in a title, click once to select the title, and then edit the selected text.

To wrap a title into multiple lines, place the insertion point where you want the second line to begin, hold the Ctrl key, and press Enter.

Double-click a title (or select the title, right-click, and choose Format Title from the shortcut menu) to open the Format Title dialog box. Use the controls in the Pattern, Font, and Alignment tabs to format the title as you would format other text.

 TIP To change all the fonts used in a chart, double-click in the chart area and change fonts in the Format Chart Area dialog box. If you don't like the results, click Undo to revert to the original style.

PART

III

CRUNCHING DATA WITH EXCEL

Exploding Pies

If you want to emphasize specific data points in a pie chart, you can *explode* the pie chart by moving one or more pieces of the pie farther from the center. In Figure 15.15, the Antigua/Tikal slice has been exploded. Although you can select an exploded pie in the Chart Wizard, the wizard explodes either all slices of the pie or the first slice, depending on which explosion sample you choose. It's easier to create an unexploded pie of the type you want, and then edit the chart to explode selected slices.

FIGURE 15.15

Explode a pie slice to emphasize a particular data point.

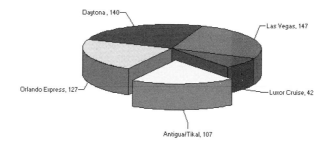

Destination Packages - 2nd Quarter

If you want to explode all the slices in a chart, select the chart and then select the pie in the plot area. Drag any slice away from the center to explode all the pie slices. To explode a single slice, select the chart and then click the pie to select the data series. With the series selected, click to select the slice you want to explode. Drag the slice away from the center.

When you explode all slices in a pie, each slice gets smaller as you increase the space between the slices. If you explode slices individually, the other slices remain centered in the plot area, and the slices don't get smaller.

MASTERING THE OPPORTUNITIES

Changing 3-D Views

You can change the perspective for 3-D charts using the 3-D View tool in the Chart menu. With this tool, you can tilt and rotate 3-D series charts and pie charts to emphasize specific data series or individual data points. For example, here's the pie from Figure 15.15 rotated and tilted so that the exploded slice is at the bottom right in the foreground where it is more noticeable. The slice also stands out better, because its lighter color is next to the darker color of the adjacent slice.

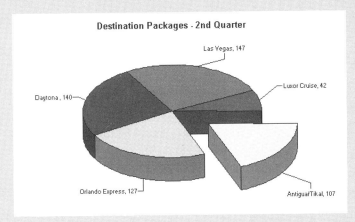

A 3-D chart looks three-dimensional because objects in the "foreground" are larger than objects in the "background." Some purists reject 3-D charts because the resizing of objects to create the 3-D appearance distorts the actual values represented by the objects: the slice at the bottom of a 3-D pie chart is larger than it would be if it appeared at the top of the pie. Many users willingly accept the distortion created by 3-D charts because they "like the look" or they use the distortion to exaggerate a point.

For more complex charts, optimizing the view is essential if you want to convey the data's message to viewers. Important chart objects can be obscured by other chart objects that appear closer. The larger foreground objects dominate the chart's visual impact, possibly drawing attention away from smaller elements that could be important points in a presentation or report. When a 3-D column chart includes multiple series, you'll often need to change the 3-D view or rearrange the series so that all the data is visible. Use these steps to change a chart's 3-D view:

1. Select the chart and choose Chart ➢ 3-D View to open the 3-D View dialog box.

Continued

MASTERING THE OPPORTUNITIES CONTINUED

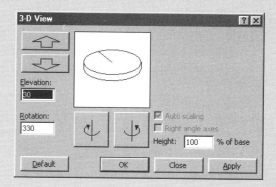

2. Click the Elevation arrows on the left to change the *elevation,* or degree of tilt of the chart. The wire-frame preview changes to show the effects of your setting, as does the number in the Elevation box.

3. Use the Perspective arrows to change the ratio of the front of the chart to the back; increasing the *perspective* increases the depth of the chart. (3-D pie and bar charts don't have Perspective controls.)

4. Click the clockwise or counterclockwise rotation buttons to change the chart's horizontal orientation. The Rotation settings and the preview will change to reflect your choices.

5. Type in a different percentage in the Height text box to collapse or expand the chart's height (the z-axis) relative to its width (the x-axis). A higher percentage will make the chart taller or wider while a lower percentage will make it shorter or smaller.

6. Click OK to apply changes and close the dialog box.

To return the chart to the original settings, click the Default button and check the Auto Scaling box.

There's also an alternate way to change the 3-D perspective, elevation, and rotation on 3-D series charts: choose Corners from the Chart Objects menu on the Chart toolbar and use the handles to tilt or rotate the chart.

CHAPTER 16

MANAGING INFORMATION WITH EXCEL

FEATURING

- **Understanding Excel databases**

- **Sorting a database**

- **Using filters**

- **Using subtotals to summarize data**

- **Extracting a subset from a database**

- **Using a Data Form for data entry, editing, and searching**

- **Using Excel's Dfunctions**

- **Applying conditional formatting**

- **Creating array formulas using the Conditional Sum Wizard**

n this chapter, you'll use Excel's database capabilities to create and manage lists. The capabilities cover the entire range, from basic sorting and filtering to extracting data based on criteria, removing duplicate records from a database, and applying database and array formulas to worksheet ranges.

One of the first questions many Office users ask (and many others fail to ask) is how Excel's database features compare to the features found in Access. You want to know when Excel's database features will be sufficient, and how to decide which of the two database tools to use. This chapter will help you evaluate that issue in terms of your own needs.

Basic Database Concepts

In its simplest form, a *database* is a list with a specific structure, defined by its *fields:* the categories of information it contains. A telephone directory, for example, is a database with fields that include last name, first name, middle initial, address, and telephone number. Database software allows you to do two distinct things: organize, or *sort*, the data in a specific order (for example, alphabetized by last name); and *filter*, or query, the data to find specific information (for example, all the entries for a specific city). If software doesn't allow you to sort and filter, it's not database software.

An individual listing in the phone book is a *record* in the database, containing a single set of the fields: one phone user's last name, first name, middle initial, address, and telephone number. Each field must have a unique *field name:* LastName, last name, LASTNAME, and LastNameforListing are all possible field names for a field containing last names. In Excel, fields are columns, and each record is an individual row.

The Traverse Tree Sales worksheet (shown in Figure 16.1) is an Excel database. Each field is a separate column. Column labels (*Month, County, Type, Quantity, Bundles,* and *Cost*) are field names. Each individual row is a record.

Creating a database is as simple as creating any other worksheet, but there are additional rules for worksheets that you intend to use as databases:

- *Blank rows and blank columns* signal the end of a database. Don't leave a blank row between column headings and data records. DO leave a blank row after all records and before totals, averages, or other summary rows. Don't leave blank columns within a database, and make sure there are no blank columns hiding between the columns of a database that you inherit.

- *Field names* at the tops of columns must be unique within a database. Be consistent: label every column.

FIGURE 16.1

An Excel database is a
section of a worksheet
defined by empty rows
and columns.

	A	B	C	D	E	F
1	TRAVERSE TREE SALES					
2	County Cooperative Tree Orders					
3						
4	Month ▾	County ▾	Type ▾	Quanti ▾	Bundle ▾	Cost ▾
5	Jan-01	Genesee	White Pine	37000	74	44,326
6	Jan-01	Genesee	Blue Spruce	12500	25	17,475
7	Jan-01	Oakland	Blue Spruce	22500	45	31,455
8	Jan-01	Oakland	White Pine	15500	31	18,569
9	Jan-01	Oakland	Concolor Fir	13500	27	16,173
10	Feb-01	Genesee	Frazier Fir	6500	13	7,787
11	Feb-01	Lake	Blue Spruce	42500	85	59,415
12	Feb-01	Lake	White Pine	32000	64	38,336
13	Feb-01	Oakland	Scotch Pine	11000	22	13,178
14	Mar-01	Kalkaska	Blue Spruce	13500	27	18,873
15	Mar-01	Kalkaska	Concolor Fir	10000	20	11,980
16	Mar-01	Lake	Frazier Fir	14500	29	17,371
17	Mar-01	Lake	Concolor Fir	12000	24	14,376
18	Apr-01	Kalkaska	Frazier Fir	7500	15	8,985
19	Apr-01	Lake	Blue Spruce	31000	62	43,338
20	Apr-01	Lake	White Pine	26500	53	31,747
21						
22	Click here for web information on spring planting.					

Any worksheet you've already created can be used as a database, but you might
have to delete or add rows, delete columns, or edit column labels to meet these
requirements.

Choosing a Database Application: Excel or Access

There's a myth that all databases must be created in Access. Don't believe it. Excel 2002
is, in many ways, the database tool of choice. You can create simple databases more
quickly in Excel than in Access. Excel has a huge user base, so there are more people
with Excel skills than Access skills. A database created in Excel can be easily sorted
and filtered by beginning Excel users. Put that same database in Access, and you've
increased the difficulty level for both of these tasks. Excel's data manipulation tools
and data functions are almost as powerful as those in Access, and the statistical functions in Excel are unmatched in Access. Excel and Access use the same engine, the Jet
Engine, to perform database functions, so databases created in Excel sort and filter as
fast or faster than the same databases in Access.

NOTE In the last three releases of Office, Microsoft has been evolving Access to make it a
superior front-end form and report tool for SQL Server databases. These changes make
Access a slower desktop database.

Excel is an outstanding database tool. There are, however, four factors that will force you to use Access or another database rather than Excel: complexity, size, integrity, and security.

Database Complexity

The type of database you can create in Excel is known as *flat file*: a single worksheet or *table*. A more elaborate database structure consists of many such database tables, related by common fields. Traverse Tree Sales could create a more complex database with one table for customers, another for suppliers, and a third, like that shown in Figure 16.1, for orders. When you need to create more than one table and relate the tables, you've generally outgrown Excel. To relate data from more than one table, you need a *relational database* so you can pull together information from different tables to answer complex questions. Microsoft Access and Microsoft SQL Server are both relational databases.

Database Size

Excel databases are limited to the number of rows in a worksheet: you can store only 65,535 records in a worksheet. With Access, the only record limitation is the amount of space on your hard drive. If you're creating a database with lots of fields—for example, to store and analyze the results of a multipage survey—you'll notice another limitation: Excel can handle only 256 fields. While a single Access table has the same limitation, Access' relational ability means you can separate fields into two or more tables without compromising your ability to analyze data across the tables.

Data Integrity

Data in an Excel worksheet is always at risk. Users can accidentally delete information, overwrite or change formulas, insert or delete columns, or fail to save changes before closing the workbook. You can protect areas of a worksheet, but you can't make an Excel workbook foolproof. With Excel, the integrity of the data is determined by the knowledge and sense of adventure of the least skilled user.

With Access, data integrity is foremost. Access saves every record automatically so users don't have to remember to save. Users work with data in forms and reports, effectively isolating the data from the user. You can create forms that restrict access to fields, or provide view-only access to critical data. If your mission-critical database will be used by inexperienced or low-level users, Access has all the tools you need to protect data integrity.

Data Security

Excel 2002 has vastly improved worksheet protection, but for desktop database security, it's hard to beat Access. Access meets or exceeds industry standards for data security. You can grant users or groups of users permissions to view existing data, add new data, or edit data. You can effectively deny access to sensitive data while allowing users to view other fields as appropriate. If you need to limit users' exposure to data, you need Access 2002.

Even if your analysis of the data's complexity, size, integrity, and security results in a decision to use Access rather than Excel, you'll want to know how to use Excel's database features. Excel's list management features are powerful tools for manipulating tables and smaller sets of records from larger databases. Some tasks are easily done in Excel but difficult to do in Access. You can save an Access table in the Excel format, manipulate the data, and return it to Access.

> **NOTE** The boundary between Access and Excel is intentionally fuzzy. As Access is improved to work incredibly well with SQL Server, tools like the Access Links add-in bridge the gap between Excel and Access, allowing you to export directly to Access from Excel, or to create Access forms for use with Excel databases.

Entering Data in an Excel Database

Excel worksheets usually include more numbers than text; databases are the exception. Two text features, AutoComplete and Pick From List, are of little use in a budget, but very useful in a database.

AutoComplete, discussed in Chapter 13, "Creating and Printing Excel Worksheets," examines the other cells in the column and fills in the remaining text. For example, if the database field is state names and you begin entering **Cal**, AutoComplete will fill in **ifornia** if *California* appears elsewhere in the column. Press Enter to accept the AutoComplete entry, or keep typing to enter a different value.

The Pick From List feature displays the values used in the column (the same value list that AutoComplete uses) so you can choose from the list. Right-click in a cell and choose Pick From List from the shortcut menu to open the list of text entries from the column. Select an entry from the list.

Pick From List is most useful when you have less than 20 entries that begin with the same characters: for example, a list of account numbers formatted as text or similar location names (U of M - Ann Arbor, U of M - Dearborn, U of M - Flint, and so on).

AutoComplete won't kick in until the characters you've already entered are unique: in this example, that's at least 10 characters. It's more efficient to right-click, select Pick From List, and choose the correct entry.

Extending Formats and Formulas

With the Extend List Formats And Formulas option enabled, Excel 2002 automatically formats new database records (added at the bottom of the database) to match the other records and copies formulas from the previous row. In the database in Figure 16.1, for example, a date entered in cell A21 will be formatted with the mmm-yy format, and the formulas in columns E and F will be extended to cells E21 and F21 after data is entered in columns A through D. This option is enabled by default. If it has been turned off, follow these steps to turn it back on:

1. Choose Tools ➤ Options to open the Options dialog box.

2. On the Edit tab, enable the Extend List Formats And Formulas check box.

Sorting an Excel Database

To sort the data in a database, first select any cell in the database; then choose Data ➤ Sort from the menu to have Excel select the records in the database and open the Sort dialog box, shown in Figure 16.2.

Order the rows in a database with the Sort dialog box.

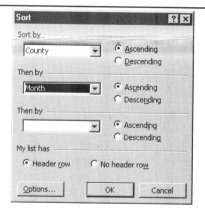

Excel will select all cells above, below, to the right, and to the left of the cell you selected until it encounters a blank column and row. Excel will examine the top row of the database and either assign it as a record by including it in the selection, or deselect it, assuming it is a row of column headings. The last section of the Sort dialog box lets you correct an incorrect selection by specifying whether you have a header row.

NOTE If you didn't select a cell within the database before choosing Data ➢ Sort, Excel will notify you that there was no list to select. Close the message box, select a cell in the database, and choose Data ➢ Sort again.

In a telephone book, records are sorted initially by last name. This is called a *primary sort*. If you know that some records may have the same entry in the primary sort field (two Smiths), specify a *secondary sort* on another field, like the first name. And if you might have two David Smiths, you can use the middle initial for a *tertiary sort*. Note that the secondary and tertiary sorts occur only in case of an identical value at a higher level of sorting.

You can sort up to three levels using the Sort dialog box. Records can be sorted in *ascending order* (A–Z or 1–100) or *descending order* (Z–A or 100–1). In the Sort By box, enter or select the field name you want to sort by. Choose a sort order. If some of the records may have the same value in the Sort By field, use the first Then By text box to select the field you want to sort by when there is a tie in the primary sort field. For databases with many similar records (like a long customer list), you might want to add a tertiary sort, using the second Then By box. When you have made all the sort selections, click OK to sort the database according to your specifications.

Using the Toolbar Sort Buttons

  You can also sort a database (or any worksheet range bounded by blank columns and rows) using the sort buttons on the Standard toolbar. Select a single cell within the column you want to sort by. Click the Ascending Sort or Descending Sort button to sort the database.

This is an easy way to sort, but it has one major drawback: Excel doesn't allow you to verify that the correct cells have been selected as the database. We recommend sorting the database once using the Data ➢ Sort dialog box to ensure that you and Excel agree on what should be included in the database. After the first sort, use the toolbar buttons.

WARNING If some columns of data are not selected, the selected columns will be sorted but the unselected columns will not be, ruining the integrity of the data by mixing up the records. (This is why you never include empty columns in a database.) Always check to be sure that all columns were included before sorting. Click Undo immediately if some columns were omitted in a sort.

When you know how Excel sorts, you can use the sort buttons to do secondary and tertiary sorts. When Excel sorts the records in a database, it only rearranges records when necessary. If a list is already sorted by city, sorting it by state will create a list sorted first by state, and then by city within each state, because the existing city sort will only be rearranged to put the states in order.

 TIP If you need to sort by more than three fields, use the toolbar buttons. Sort the least important field first and work backward through the sort fields to the primary sort field.

Filtering a Database

There are many times you'll want to work with a database *subset:* a group of records in the database. For example, you might want to print all sales records for one salesperson, all the orders from one client, or all the customers who haven't made a purchase this year. A *filter* is used to select records that meet specific criteria and temporarily hide all the other records.

Applying an AutoFilter

To have Excel set up an AutoFilter, select any cell in the database and choose Data ➤ Filter ➤ AutoFilter. Excel reads every record in the database and creates a filter criteria list for each field. Click the drop-down arrow that appears next to each field name (see Figure 16.3) to access the field's criteria list.

(see Figure 16.3)

FIGURE 16.3

Click the drop-down arrow next to the column heading to choose AutoFilter criteria.

	A	B	C	D	E	F
1	TRAVERSE TREE SALES					
2	County Cooperative Tree Orders					
3						
4	Month	County	Type	Quanti	Bundle	Cost
5	Jan-01	Genesee	(All)	37000	74	44,326
6	Jan-01	Genesee	(Top 10...)	12500	25	17,475
7	Jan-01	Oakland	(Custom...)	22500	45	31,455
8	Jan-01	Oakland	Blue Spruce Concolor Fir	15500	31	18,569
9	Jan-01	Oakland	Frazier Fir	13500	27	16,173
10	Feb-01	Genesee	Scotch Pine White Pine	6500	13	7,787
11	Feb-01	Lake	Blue Spruce	42500	85	59,415
12	Feb-01	Lake	White Pine	32000	64	38,336
13	Feb-01	Oakland	Scotch Pine	11000	22	13,178
14	Mar-01	Kalkaska	Blue Spruce	13500	27	18,873
15	Mar-01	Kalkaska	Concolor Fir	10000	20	11,980
16	Mar-01	Lake	Frazier Fir	14500	29	17,371
17	Mar-01	Lake	Concolor Fir	12000	24	14,376
18	Apr-01	Kalkaska	Frazier Fir	7500	15	8,985
19	Apr-01	Lake	Blue Spruce	31000	62	43,338
20	Apr-01	Lake	White Pine	26500	53	31,747

- The default criteria setting in each field is All, which means that the contents of the field are not being used to filter the records.

- Top 10 is used in numeric fields to display the top or bottom 10, 5, or any other number or percentage of values.

- Custom prompts you to create a custom filter (see "Creating a Custom Filter," below) for choices that don't appear on the list.

When you apply a filter, all the records not included in the subset are hidden, as shown in Figure 16.4, where the records are being filtered based on Type. The number of records found and the total number of records in the database are displayed in the status bar. Each record retains its original row number; the row numbers of filtered records appear in blue. The drop-down arrow for the filtered field turns blue to show that it is being used to filter the database.

FIGURE 16.4

Records displayed as filter results keep their original row numbers.

	A	B	C	D	E	F
1	TRAVERSE TREE SALES					
2	County Cooperative Tree Orders					
3						
4	Month ▾	County ▾	Type ▾	Quanti ▾	Bundle ▾	Cost ▾
10	Feb-01	Genesee	Frazier Fir	6500	13	7,787
16	Mar-01	Lake	Frazier Fir	14500	29	17,371
18	Apr-01	Kalkaska	Frazier Fir	7500	15	8,985
21						
22	Click here for web information on spring planting.					

To open the AutoFilter list in a column, either click the filter arrow or select the column heading with the AutoFilter arrow and press Alt+↓. Table 16.1 lists other keyboard shortcuts you can use with Excel's AutoFilter lists.

TABLE 16.1   AUTOFILTER KEYBOARD SHORTCUTS

Key	Action
↓	Move down one list item.
↑	Move up one list item.
Alt+↑	Close the list.
Home	Move to the start of the list (All).
End	Move to the last item in the list.
Enter	Apply the selected item.

PART

III

CRUNCHING DATA
WITH EXCEL

Filter on more than one field to select, for example, all the Scotch Pine sales in Oakland County. Set the criteria using each field's drop-down list. Only records that meet all the criteria you selected will be included in the filtered subset.

To display the entire database, change the filter criteria for all filtered fields back to All, or simply choose Data ➤ Filter ➤ Show All. You'll know at a glance that all filters are set to All because the drop-down arrows and the row headings will all be black again.

Using the Top 10 Filter

Top 10 filters display records based on their value. You can only use Top 10 filters with numeric fields. When you choose Top 10 as your filter criterion, the Top 10 AutoFilter dialog box opens:

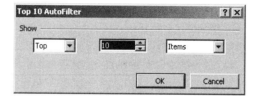

In the first drop-down list, choose Top or Bottom, depending on whether you want to see the highest or lowest values in the database. In the spin-box control, enter a number larger than 0. In the last control, choose Items or Percents. For example, to see the top 10 percent of the scores in a column of test scores, choose Top, enter **10**, and then choose Percents. The Top 10 filter only works with values: numbers, dates, and times

NOTE If you use a handful of filters frequently, consider saving filtered versions of the database as views. For information on views, see Chapter 17, "Solving Business Problems with the Analysis Tools."

Creating a Custom Filter

When you filter using the drop-down criteria, you are looking for records that exactly equal specific criteria. Custom filters give you access to other ways to set criteria:

- All records with fields that are *not* equal to a criterion
- Records that are greater than or less than a criterion
- Records that meet one condition *Or* another

To create a custom filter, choose Custom from the drop-down criteria list to open the Custom AutoFilter dialog box, shown in Figure 16.5.

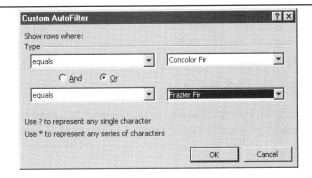

Click the filter operation drop-down list to choose an operator. The list includes common logical operators like Equals and Is Greater Than Or Equal To, as well as complex operators to filter for records that do or do not begin with, end with, or contain a *string* (one or more characters) you specify. The values drop-down list on the right is populated with the record entries in the field from the field criteria list. To find all records that are *not* in Lake County, for example, choose Does Not Equal as the operator, and select Lake from the drop-down list. You can also enter text in the criteria controls. Notice in the dialog box that you can use the wildcard characters * and ? to broaden the search string.

To find all orders for Oakland and Ottawa counties, you could

- Use the wildcard character and search for equals O*
- Use the Begins With type and search for begins with O

The And and Or options are used when you want to filter by more than one criterion in a column. And is used to establish the upper and lower ends of a range and is almost always used with numerical entries: Quantity is greater than 100 And Quantity is less than 201 leaves only the quantities between 101 and 200.

Or is used to filter by two different criteria: Lake County *Or* Oakland County. If you use And when you mean Or, you'll often get a *null set:* no records. (There are no records in Lake County *And* Oakland County—it's one or the other.) If you use Or when you mean And, you'll get all the records. (Every record is either less than 201 *Or* greater than 100.)

If you print the database while it is filtered, only the filtered records will print, so you can quickly generate reports based on any portion of the information in the Excel

database. The filter criteria drop-down arrows don't print, so there's no need to turn the AutoFilter off until you are done working with a database.

Filtering appears as if it would be useful when you need to chart parts of the data in the database. You could filter the records you want to chart, then select and chart the information as you would normally. This is true. Bear in mind, however, that when the filter criteria change, the chart will change.

To turn the AutoFilter off, choose Data ➤ Filter ➤ AutoFilter.

 NOTE If you need to create charts for specific filtered data sets or subtotals, see the sections "Creating a Subset" and "Creating Subtotals" later in this chapter.

Creating a Subset

There are times when you will want to work with or distribute a subset of the database. For example, we have a database with 5,000 records—but only 700 of them pertain to our current project. It would be easier to work with a smaller database that includes only the 700 records we need. We can quickly create a subset of the 700 records using copy and paste:

1. Filter the active database to display the records you wish to copy.
2. Select the filtered database, including the column labels and any other titles you wish to copy.
3. Click the Copy button or choose Edit ➤ Copy.
4. Select the first cell where you want the new database to appear.
5. Press Enter to paste the database.

Remember that this filtered data is not linked to the original database, so changes in the original aren't reflected in the subset. Don't invest time updating and maintaining this as a separate database. If you need to work with a subset that remains up to date, use Microsoft Query (see Chapter 19, "Using Excel to Present Information") to link directly to the Excel database.

Using Advanced Filters to Extract a Subset

Complex filters quickly outgrow the Custom dialog box. If you need to create subsets like these, filtered by more than two criteria in a field, or with a combination of And and Or statements, you need the Advanced Filter:

- Quantities over 10,000 for Lake and Genesee counties and quantities over 15,000 for Kalkaska county
- All fir trees for Oakland and Lake counties, and Concolor Fir only for all other counties

You create subsets with complex criteria by *extracting* the subset's records from the database using Excel's Advanced Filter. The Advanced Filter is more complex, but incredibly powerful: you establish a *criteria range* that includes the column labels from your database and one or more criteria that you enter directly below the labels. Excel filters the database through the criteria range to create the subset.

 NOTE The Advanced Filter feature isn't just for extracting data; you can filter a list in place just as you do with AutoFilter.

The criteria range is the heart of advanced filtering. If the criteria range is incorrect, the extracted data will be wrong—so take your time with this. The column headings must be precisely the same as they are in the database, so begin by copying the column headings to another location in your workbook (a separate worksheet that you name *Criteria* is good).

Then, type the criteria you want to establish. For example, if you want to extract records where the Quantity is over 10,000, enter **>10000** in the cell just below the Quantity column label. If you have more than one criterion in a single column (for example, County = Genessee *Or* County = Oakland), use one cell for each criterion:

	A	B	C	D	E	F
1	Month	County	Type	Quantity	Bundles	Cost
2		Genesee				
3		Oakland				

There are two ways to filter for two criteria in separate columns, based on whether you want to use And or Or. Enter criteria on the same row for an And condition:

	A	B	C	D	E	F
1	Month	County	Type	Quantity	Bundles	Cost
2		Genesee				>25000
3						

Or place criteria on separate rows for an Or condition:

	A	B	C	D	E	F
1	Month	County	Type	Quantity	Bundles	Cost
2		Genesee				
3			Blue Spruce			

PART

III

CRUNCHING DATA WITH EXCEL

In this example, criteria are established to find quantities over 20,000 in Oakland County *Or* over 10,000 in Lake County:

	A	B	C	D	E	F
1	Month	County	Type	Quantity	Bundles	Cost
2		Oakland		>20000		
3		Lake		>10000		

You can't create this last criterion with an AutoFilter. You would need to create two sets of filters, one for each county.

TIP You'll need to refer to the criteria range in the Advanced Filter dialog box, so you might want to name it (Insert ➤ Name ➤ Define).

After the criteria range is set, click anywhere in the database and open the Advanced Filter dialog box (Data ➤ Filter ➤ Advanced Filter) shown in Figure 16.6.

FIGURE 16.6

Select the database, criteria range, and location for the extracted data in the Advanced Filter dialog box

Excel will automatically select your entire database for the List Range text box. Use the Criteria Range text box to identify your criteria range, including the column labels.

Choose whether you want to filter the records in their current location (as Auto-Filter does) or extract the records by copying them to another location. If you choose another location, the Copy To text box will be enabled so that you can select the first cell of the range where the filtered records should be copied. As with any copy operation, just select one cell—if you select a range, it must match exactly the range required by the extracted data. Be sure that there is room in the destination area for the incoming data.

You can enter a cell in any open workbook in the Copy To text box, so you can put the filtered subset of your database in a different workbook or a different worksheet than the original database.

If you want to eliminate duplicate records from the filtered list, turn on the Unique Records Only check box. Finally, click OK and Excel will filter in place or extract data as you have indicated.

EXPERT TIP Suppose you've received a database with 10,000 records, many of them duplicate records. Don't eliminate the duplicates manually. Set up a criteria range without criteria (column headings only) and use the Unique Records Only option to extract a list without duplicates. This is far easier to do in Excel than in Access. Before you start creating the queries to eliminate duplicates in Access, consider exporting the table to Excel to eliminate the extra records.

When you use advanced filtering to filter in place, the filtered subset will have blue row numbers, just as it does with AutoFilter. To turn the filter off, choose Data ➢ Filter ➢ Show All.

Creating Subtotals

You can create subtotals based on any field in the database. A *subtotal* is not necessarily a sum: it can be an average, count, minimum, maximum, or other statistical calculation based on a group of records.

Before subtotaling, you must sort the database on the field you wish to subtotal on. For example, if you want to subtotal each month's orders, first sort the database by month. Follow these steps to create subtotals:

1. Sort the database by the field you wish to subtotal on.
2. Choose Data ➢ Subtotals to open the Subtotal dialog box, shown in Figure 16.7.
3. Choose the field you sorted by from the At Each Change In text box.
4. Select a type of subtotal from the Use Function drop-down list.
5. In the Add Subtotal To control, select each field you want to subtotal. You can subtotal more than one field at a time, but you have to use the same function: average three fields, sum three fields, and so on.

FIGURE 16.7

FIGURE 16.7

Create summary totals and averages in the Subtotal dialog box

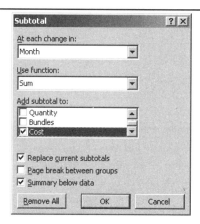

6. If necessary, change the following settings:

Enable Replace Current Subtotals Replaces a former subtotaled set with new subtotals. If you want both sets of subtotals to appear (for example, sums and averages), deselect this check box.

Page Break Between Groups Places each subtotaled set of records on a separate page.

Summary Below Data Places a summary (grand total, grand average) row at the bottom of the database.

7. When you have entered the information for subtotals, click OK to generate subtotals, as shown in Figure 16.8.

When you apply subtotals, Excel automatically applies an outline and displays the outline symbols as shown in Figure 16.8. Use the outline symbols to display the level of detail you wish to see or print.

NOTE If the outline symbols do not appear, choose Tools ➢ Options and enable the Outline Symbols check box on the View tab of the Options dialog box.

FIGURE 16.8

The Traverse Tree Sales worksheet with subtotals

Row Level Details

	A	B	C	D	E	F
1	**TRAVERSE TREE SALES**					
2	County Cooperative Tree Orders					
3						
4	**Month**	**County**	**Type**	**Quantity**	**Bundles**	**Cost**
5	Jan-01	Genesee	White Pine	37000	74	44,326
6	Jan-01	Genesee	Blue Spruce	12500	25	17,475
7	Jan-01	Oakland	Blue Spruce	22500	45	31,455
8	Jan-01	Oakland	White Pine	15500	31	18,569
9	Jan-01	Oakland	Concolor Fir	13500	27	16,173
10	**Jan-01 Total**			101000		127,998
11	Feb-01	Genesee	Frazier Fir	6500	13	7,787
12	Feb-01	Lake	Blue Spruce	42500	85	59,415
13	Feb-01	Lake	White Pine	32000	64	38,336
14	Feb-01	Oakland	Scotch Pine	11000	22	13,178
15	**Feb-01 Total**			92000		118,716
16	Mar-01	Kalkaska	Blue Spruce	13500	27	18,873
17	Mar-01	Kalkaska	Concolor Fir	10000	20	11,980
18	Mar-01	Lake	Frazier Fir	14500	29	17,371
19	Mar-01	Lake	Concolor Fir	12000	24	14,376
20	**Mar-01 Total**			50000		62,600
21	Apr-01	Kalkaska	Frazier Fir	7500	15	8,985
22	Apr-01	Lake	Blue Spruce	31000	62	43,338
23	Apr-01	Lake	White Pine	26500	53	31,747
24	**Apr-01 Total**			65000		84,070
25	**Grand Total**			308000		393,384

Hide Details

To display a specific level of the outline, click the appropriate Row Level Detail symbol.

Click the Show Detail and Hide Detail symbols to display or hide details for a subtotal. The outline symbols do not print, but if you've added a couple of layers of subtotals, you may wish to turn off the outline symbols to regain the space they occupy at the left edge of the Excel window. To remove the outline symbols but retain the subtotals, choose Data ➢ Group and Outline ➢ Clear Outline. To remove subtotals from a worksheet, open the Subtotal dialog box again (see Figure 16.7) and click the Remove All button.

PART

III

CRUNCHING DATA
WITH EXCEL

Copying Subtotals

When you copy a *filtered* database, Excel only copies the rows that are visible. If you copy *subtotals*, even with the detail collapsed, Excel copies (and pastes) the hidden rows. There's an easy way to copy subtotals, but you could spend the better part of a workday trying to find it.

1. Begin by collapsing the subtotals so that only the data you wish to copy is visible. Select the data you wish to copy.

2. Choose Edit ➢ Go To to open the Go To dialog box.

3. Click the Special button to open the Go To Special dialog box.

4. Enable the Visible Cells Only option and click OK.

5. Click the Copy button.

6. Move to the first cell where you want to paste the copied selection and click Paste.

Importing Data from Other Applications

Excel works with a wide range of file types, so Excel users often need to import data stored in files created with other programs. It's easy to import data files from other Microsoft Office applications, but getting the stuff from non-Office programs can be more challenging. Fortunately, Excel readily opens files saved as plain text, and most programs can save files in this format. Formatting doesn't import well. Be prepared to reformat columns, reapply fonts, and apply other formatting changes that are lost during an import operation.

 TIP Excel 2002 supports HTML and XML as native formats, so markup language files open as readily as Excel workbooks, and Excel workbooks can be saved as HTML and XML documents. See Chapter 20 for more information on working with HTML and XML documents in Excel 2002.

Here are the steps to open a non-native file (a file created in another application) in Excel:

1. Select File ➢ Open. In the Files Of Type list box, leave the default of All Types or select the relevant source file type (for example, XML, Text, or an earlier version of Excel). Locate and select the file and click Open.

2. If your file opens, begin working with it. If it does not open, or looks very garbled in Excel, open it in the original application and save the file as an Excel file, or save it as a text file and use the steps in the next section to get it into Excel.

In some instances, an attempt to open a file results in a "file not valid" error message. There are two possible reasons for this message: Excel doesn't support the file type, or the type is supported but the converter is not installed. Excel supports a number of file formats, including Lotus 1-2-3 and Quattro Pro. The Lotus 1-2-3 converter is installed by default; the Quattro Pro converter is only installed in a custom installation.

NOTE For information on installing text and graphic converters for Office XP, see Appendix D.

If the file type you wish to open isn't supported by Excel, return to the original application, save the file as a delimited text file, and reopen it in Excel with the Text Import Wizard, described in the next section.

EXPERT TIP Most files can be imported if you have access to the file's native application or an application that can convert the document. If you're familiar with the file formats that each of your applications supports, you'll often be able to find an application to use as a translation tool to move from one format to another. For example, Excel imports WordPerfect tables poorly. However, with the appropriate converters installed, Word opens WordPerfect documents and appropriately displays WordPerfect tables. And you can copy/paste data directly from Word to Excel. To move data from WordPerfect to Excel, then, either save the WordPerfect document as a Word document, or open the WordPerfect document directly in Word and save it as a Word document. Copy the table, and paste it in the Excel worksheet.

Parsing Imported Data with the Text Import Wizard

When Excel can't open an imported file directly, you can use the Text Import Wizard to open the file and parse it into an Excel spreadsheet. When you *parse* a file, Excel examines it, converts text items to appropriate data types, and places the data in rows and columns. In order to be parsed successfully, a text file must already resemble a spreadsheet or table, with each paragraph corresponding to a record or row, and with a consistent character, usually a comma or tab, used to mark the column breaks.

Here's how to open a text file, parse its contents, and import it using the Text Import Wizard:

1. Select File ➢ Open and select Text Files in the Files Of Type list box.

2. Locate and select the file. Click Open. The first step of the Text Import Wizard appears, as shown in Figure 16.9.

In the first step of the wizard, indicate whether the file is delimited or fixed length.

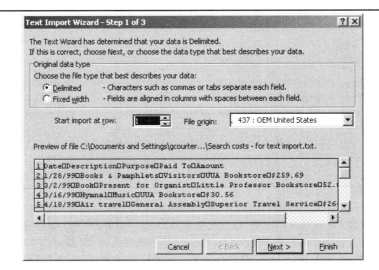

3. The wizard attempts to determine what type of text file it is opening. Set or verify the data type option:

Delimited Text files where data fields are separated by commas, tabs, or another consistent symbol or character

Fixed Width Nondelimited files in which each field is a specific length; space between fields is padded with zeros or spaces

4. Use the Start Import At Row spin-box control to skip titles or blank rows at the beginning of the file. The row you select should contain column headings if the file contains them or the first row of data.

5. If you are importing a Mac or DOS file rather than a file created in a Windows application, select the appropriate operating system from the File Origin drop-down list. Click Next to move to the second step of the wizard.

6. Excel adds the column boundaries (see Figure 16.10). If the columns aren't correct, change the symbol used as the delimiter. When you have selected the correct delimiter, each column will contain data from one field. Click Next.

FIGURE 16.10

Check the column boundaries in the second step of the wizard.

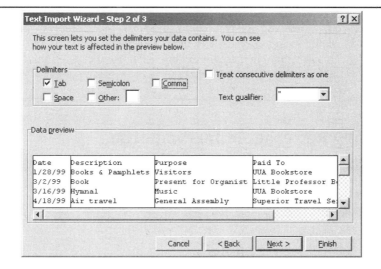

 TIP This is your only chance to correctly separate the data into fields. If you've tried each of the delimiters and the columns are still incorrect, your file may have fixed-width fields, or consecutive delimiters. Click Back to return to the first step to set the Fixed Width option. Enable the Treat Consecutive Delimiters As One check box in the second step to have Excel disregard consecutive delimiters.

7. In the final step in the Text Import Wizard, choose the format for each of the newly defined columns. Select a column and choose the format. (Double-check the formats for date columns, which Excel often assumes are Text.) Select the Do Not Import option to skip the selected field. The default format setting is General. The format used in the column appears in the header. If you want all of the columns to have the same format, but something other than General, hold Shift and click on each column until all are selected. Choose a format from the options in the Column Data Format area.

TIP Eurodata alert: click the Advanced button to choose separators if you're importing data that uses decimal and thousands separators other than the period and comma.

8. Click Finish when the formats have been set.

PART

III

CRUNCHING DATA
WITH EXCEL

TIP You can use Excel's internal parsing tool to separate a column of data into two columns (for example, a column of full names into first and last names). First insert a blank column to the right of the existing column. Then select the column of data and choose Data ➢ Text To Columns.

Using Refreshable Text Importing

If you will be updating the original text file containing the data you plan to import, you can establish a link to this source file so that every time it is changed, those modifications will appear in the Excel file, too. This process, known as *refreshable text importing*, uses the Text Import Wizard, too, but accesses it through a different menu command.

To implement refreshable text, use these steps:

1. Select the first cell where you will place the imported data.

2. Choose Data ➢ Get External Data ➢ Import Text File from the menu.

3. Select the file and click Import to launch the Text Import Wizard.

 NOTE Refresh the data by selecting Data ➢ Refresh Data, selecting the appropriate text file in the Import Text File dialog box, and clicking Import. If you only want to import a portion of the text file as refreshable text, construct a query using the Microsoft Query tool, discussed in Chapter 20.

Using Data Forms

Data Forms provide an easy way to enter or search for data. Because Data Forms have a portrait orientation, they're particularly helpful when the columns in your database exceed the width of the screen. Using the form allows you to see all the database fields at once without scrolling horizontally.

To create a Data Form, select any cell in a database and choose Data ➢ Form. The first record in the database will be displayed in the Data Form (see Figure 16.11). In the form, use the vertical scroll bar or the up and down arrow keys to browse the records. Use the Tab key to move between fields in the form; pressing Enter moves to the next record.

If you're an experienced Excel user, Data Forms may not look all that interesting. For the power user, Data Forms become more useful when you consider other users entering data in your workbooks. Data Forms offer a nearly bulletproof way to let a less-accomplished user enter data. The contents of *calculated fields* (see the Bundles and Cost fields in Figure 16.11) are displayed without a text box, so users can't accidentally overwrite formulas. (The formulas still work: if you change a value that a calculated field is based on, Excel will recalculate the field.) If your users are overwriting formulas in critical worksheets or getting lost scrolling across the screen, show them how to open the Data Form, give them a five-minute orientation to working with the form (see the section below), and turn them loose.

FIGURE 16.11

A Data Form for the Traverse Tree Sales database

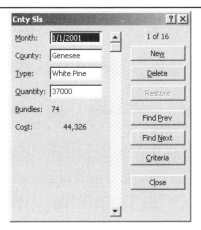

Adding and Deleting Records in a Data Form

Click the New button or scroll to the last record of the database to open a New Record form. Enter each field in the appropriate text box control. When you have entered information for the last field, press Enter or click the New button again to continue entering new records. Press the ↑ (up arrow) key or click the scroll bar to close the New dialog box.

To delete the record currently displayed in the Data Form, click the Delete button. A dialog box will appear, warning that the record will be permanently deleted. Pay attention to the warning—clicking Undo will not bring the record back. Click OK to delete the record's row from the database.

PART

III

CRUNCHING DATA WITH EXCEL

NOTE Excel's AutoComplete and Pick From List features don't work with the Data Form, so you have to type each entry fully.

Searching for Records

You can use the Data Form to search for individual records that meet specific criteria. This is like filtering, but you view the records one at a time. This is a good way to locate specific records that you need to delete.

The following steps outline how to search for records with a Data Form:

1. Open the Data Form if it is not already open.

2. Click the Criteria button to open the Criteria form, which looks amazingly like the Data Form.

3. Enter the search criteria for one or more fields in the text box controls. Excel joins two criteria with And, so it will only find records that meet both criteria. You can't search for records that meet either criteria (Or). For advanced searching, use a filter. If you want to erase the search criteria, click the Criteria button again. Click the Clear button to delete the criteria, and then click the Form button to return to the form.

4. Click Find Next to find the first record that meets the criteria. Use Find Next and Find Prev to view the records that meet the search criteria.

5. Click the scroll bar to view all records in the database.

Using Dfunctions to Summarize a Database

Excel 2002 includes functions designed specifically for databases. The database functions, or *Dfunctions*, are similar to the Advanced Filter command: they apply a criteria range to a database. The generic syntax for the Dfunctions is:

=FUNCTIONNAME(*database range*, *column to search*, *criteria range*)

The Dfunctions are very useful when the criteria that serves as the basis of a summary changes. In the database we've used thus far in this chapter, we can use types of trees, county names, quantities, or ranges of quantities as criteria. The results of the Dfunction formulas will change based on the criteria we use.

Most of the Dfunctions mirror Excel's regular set of summary functions. Use DSUM, DCOUNT, DAVERAGE, DMIN, and DMAX as you would use the nondatabase versions of the same functions.

TIP DGET returns a unique value (if there is a single record that meets a criteria) from a database.

Construct a criteria range by copying and pasting the column headings in another area of your workbook. The database and the criteria range are used in every Dfunction, so it makes sense to name both ranges. In Figure 16.12, we've inserted rows and added a criteria range (A4:F5, named Criteria) directly below the worksheet titles and above the database in A7:F23 (which we named TreeData). Three formulas and corresponding labels were added to the right of the database:

```
Total Quantity: =DSUM(TreesData,"Quantity",Criteria)
Total Orders: =DCOUNT(TreesData,"Quantity",Criteria)
Average Order: =DAVERAGE(TreesData,"Quantity",Criteria)
```

FIGURE 16.12

The Dfunctions summarize data in a column based on values—or lack of values—in a criteria range.

	A	B	C	D	E	F	G	H	I
1	TRAVERSE TREE SALES								
2	County Cooperative Tree Orders								
3									
4	Month	County	Type	Quantity	Bundles	Cost			
5									
6									
7	Month	County	Type	Quanti	Bundle	Cost			
8	Jan-01	Genesee	White Pine	37000	74	44,326			
9	Jan-01	Genesee	Blue Spruce	12500	25	17,475		Total Quantity	308,000
10	Jan-01	Oakland	Blue Spruce	22500	45	31,455		Total Orders	16
11	Jan-01	Oakland	White Pine	15500	31	18,569		Average Order	19,250
12	Jan-01	Oakland	Concolor Fir	13500	27	16,173			
13	Feb-01	Genesee	Frazier Fir	6500	13	7,787			
14	Feb-01	Lake	Blue Spruce	42500	85	59,415			
15	Feb-01	Lake	White Pine	32000	64	38,336			
16	Feb-01	Oakland	Scotch Pine	11000	22	13,178			
17	Mar-01	Kalkaska	Blue Spruce	13500	27	18,873			
18	Mar-01	Kalkaska	Concolor Fir	10000	20	11,980			
19	Mar-01	Lake	Frazier Fir	14500	29	17,371			
20	Mar-01	Lake	Concolor Fir	12000	24	14,376			
21	Apr-01	Kalkaska	Frazier Fir	7500	15	8,985			
22	Apr-01	Lake	Blue Spruce	31000	62	43,338			
23	Apr-01	Lake	White Pine	26500	53	31,747			

When there are no criteria in the Criteria range, the Dfunctions sum, count, and average all the records in the database. In Figure 16.13, we've specified criteria in the criteria range; the three formulas using the Dfunctions summarize the data based on the criteria.

FIGURE 16.13

FIGURE 16.13

Add criteria to the range to conditionally sum, count, and average.

	A	B	C	D	E	F
1	TRAVERSE TREE SALES					
2	County Cooperative Tree Orders					
3						
4	Month	County	Type	Quantity	Bundles	Cost
5		Lake	White Pine			

Total Quantity	58,500
Total Orders	2
Average Order	29,250

Adding Dfunctions to a worksheet makes it a useful tool for ad hoc reporting. For information on the other Dfunctions—DVAR, DVARP, DSTDEV, DSTEVP, and DPRODUCT—search Excel Help for database functions.

Applying Conditional Formatting

With *conditional formatting*, you can apply formats to selected cells based on a *condition*. Conditional formatting is not a database feature, but some of the most striking examples of conditional formatting are those used in databases. You can apply font attributes, borders, or patterns to cells based on whether the condition is true or false. Conditional formatting is one of Excel's more amazing features. You used to apply all formats manually, selecting each cell and applying the formats. Of course, if the values changed, you had to do it all over again. In Figure 16.14, all of the Quantity values greater than or equal to 25,000 are bold with a border.

FIGURE 16.14

Use conditional formatting to highlight values in a database.

Month	County	Type	Quantity	Bundles	Cost
Jan-01	Genesee	White Pine	**37,000**	74	44,326
Jan-01	Genesee	Blue Spruce	12,500	25	17,475
Jan-01	Oakland	Blue Spruce	22,500	45	31,455
Jan-01	Oakland	White Pine	15,500	31	18,569
Jan-01	Oakland	Concolor Fir	13,500	27	16,173
Feb-01	Genesee	Frazier Fir	6,500	13	7,787
Feb-01	Lake	Blue Spruce	**42,500**	85	59,415
Feb-01	Lake	White Pine	**32,000**	64	38,336
Feb-01	Oakland	Scotch Pine	11,000	22	13,178
Mar-01	Kalkaska	Blue Spruce	13,500	27	18,873
Mar-01	Kalkaska	Concolor Fir	10,000	20	11,980
Mar-01	Lake	Frazier Fir	14,500	29	17,371
Mar-01	Lake	Concolor Fir	12,000	24	14,376
Apr-01	Kalkaska	Frazier Fir	7,500	15	8,985
Apr-01	Lake	Blue Spruce	**31,000**	62	43,338
Apr-01	Lake	White Pine	**26,500**	53	31,747

To apply conditional formatting to a selection, follow the steps below, which are explained in detail in the next section:

1. Select the cells you want to format.

2. Choose Format ➤ Conditional Formatting from the menu to open the Conditional Formatting dialog box.

3. Choose Cell Value Is or Formula Is.

4. Select a conditional operator.

5. In the Condition text box enter a value, cell reference, or formula.

6. Click the Format button. Set up a format for this condition and click OK.

7. If you have additional conditions or formats, click the Add button and repeat steps 3–6 for each condition.

8. Click OK to close the dialog box and apply conditional formatting.

Setting the First Condition

From the first drop-down list, choose Cell Value Is to base the formatting on the value in the cell or Formula Is to base the formatting on a formula that returns a value of True or False. Don't let this confuse you; it doesn't matter whether the cell contains a typed-in value or a formula. If you want the format to be applied based on the number or text that appears in a cell, use Cell Value Is. If you wish to format an entire row based on the value in one cell in the row, use Formula Is.

In the second drop-down list, choose one of the conditional operators: Between, Not Between, Equal To, Not Equal To, Greater Than, Less Than, Greater Than Or Equal To, or Less Than Or Equal To. In the text box, either type a constant (like **300** or **Oakland**), select a cell in the worksheet, or enter a formula (more on this in a few pages).

Click the Format button to open an abbreviated version of the Format Cells dialog box. Some of the formats are disabled (like font type and size), so you know you can't use them for conditional formatting. You can, however, pile on borders, shading, and different colors to make cells jump off the page.

Choose the format options you want to apply when the condition is True, and then click OK to return to the Conditional Formatting dialog box. Click OK to close the dialog box, and the formats will be applied to the appropriate cells.

Setting Additional Conditions

What if you want more than one conditional format? For example, you might want to show sales increases in blue and decreases in red. In this case, you need two conditions. Create the first condition in the Conditional Formatting dialog box, and then click the Add button to add another condition.

You can create up to three conditional formats for a range of cells. The formats are applied in the order in which they appear in the dialog box, so sequence is everything. In Figure 16.15, we've added two more conditional formats for the Quantity column. The results, however, will be the same as in Figure 16.14.

Condition1 formats any cell with a value greater than or equal to 25,000, then proceeds to the next cell in the range. If a value meets Condition1, Excel never tests Conditions 2 and 3. And if a value fails the first condition, it won't meet the second or third conditions. To apply these three formats successfully, we need to reverse their order, checking first for the condition of >=35000 then for >=30000 and finally for values >= 25000.

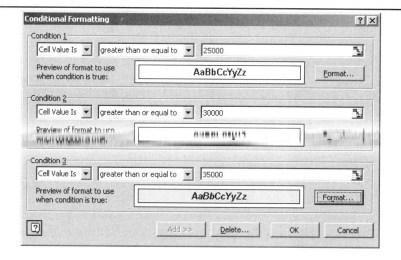

FIGURE 16.15

These conditional formats are in the wrong order; only the first format will ever be applied.

Deleting Conditional Formatting

To delete a conditional format, select the formatted range and choose Format ➤ Conditional Formatting. Click the Delete button at the bottom of the Conditional Formatting dialog box to open the Delete Conditional Format dialog box.

Check the formats you want to delete, and then click OK.

Using Cell References in Conditions

You can compare the value in a cell to the value in another cell in the worksheet. For example, you might select a cell that shows an average and apply a conditional format to all the numbers that are above that average. In this example, each cell you conditionally format will refer to the cell that contains the average, so you'll use an absolute cell reference. Simply click on the cell with the average to place the absolute reference in the condition text box.

EXPERT TIP   You don't have to apply conditional formatting to all the cells in a range at once. Create one or more conditional formats for a single cell and tweak them until they're exactly what you want; then select the entire range you want to format, including the formatted cell. Choose Format ➤ Conditional Formatting, and the dialog box will open, displaying the format you created. Just click OK, and the format will be adjusted and applied to the other selected cells.

Using Formulas As Conditions

Now add one more flourish, very useful in databases: you can compare a cell to a formula. For example, in Figure 16.13, we used a county in a criteria range to summarize data using the Dfunctions. By highlighting the rows that are being summarized, users can easily see the records that underlie the summaries, as shown in Figure 16.16. It's slick and interactive; when the user enters a county name in the criteria range, the totals change and the records for that county are highlighted.

FIGURE 16.16

Use formulas as conditions to format all the cells in a row based on the value in one cell.

	A	B	C	D	E	F	G	H	I
1	TRAVERSE TREE SALES								
2	County Cooperative Tree Orders								
3									
4		County							
5		Lake							
6									
7	Month	County	Type	Quantity	Bundles	Cost			
8	Jan-01	Genesee	Blue Spruce	12,500	25	17,475			
9	Jan-01	Oakland	Blue Spruce	22,500	45	31,455		Total Quantity	158,500
10	Feb-01	Lake	Blue Spruce	42,500	85	59,415		Total Orders	6
11	Mar-01	Kalkaska	Blue Spruce	13,500	27	18,873		Total Cost	$ 204,583
12	Apr-01	Lake	Blue Spruce	31,000	62	43,338			
13	Jan-01	Oakland	Concolor Fir	13,500	27	16,173		Average Order	26,417
14	Mar-01	Kalkaska	Concolor Fir	10,000	20	11,980			
15	Mar-01	Lake	Concolor Fir	12,000	24	14,376			
16	Feb-01	Genesee	Frazier Fir	6,500	13	7,787			
17	Mar-01	Lake	Frazier Fir	14,500	29	17,371			
18	Apr-01	Kalkaska	Frazier Fir	7,500	15	8,985			
19	Feb-01	Oakland	Scotch Pine	11,000	22	13,178			
20	Jan-01	Genesee	White Pine	37,000	74	44,326			
21	Jan-01	Oakland	White Pine	15,500	31	18,569			
22	Feb-01	Lake	White Pine	32,000	64	38,336			
23	Apr-01	Lake	White Pine	26,500	53	31,747			

PART

III

CRUNCHING DATA WITH EXCEL

Here are the steps we followed to modify the worksheet and add formula-based conditional formatting. We're taking a slightly longer approach than necessary for clarity.

1. Establish and format a two-cell range, named Criteria, in cells B4:B5.

2. Select the first record in the database (A8:F8).

3. Choose Format ➢ Conditional Formatting.

4. Select the Formula Is format type.

5. Enter the formula for this row: **=$B8=$B$5**, as shown in Figure 16.17.

FIGURE 16.17

Enter a formula for the selected row.

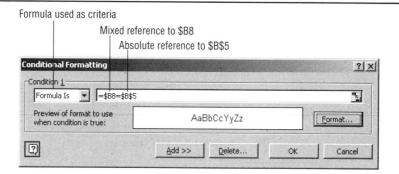

Formula used as criteria

Mixed reference to $B8

Absolute reference to $B$5

The conditional format formula must start with an = symbol and return a value of True or False When you create a conditional format, Excel automatically makes all references absolute references. We edited the first cell reference (using F4) to make the reference to B8 a mixed reference: $B8. If we make this a relative reference, only the cells in column A will be formatted; if it's absolute, we can't copy it to the other rows in the database.

6. Click the Format button and select a format. Click OK to close the Format dialog box.

7. Click OK to apply the conditional format to the first row.

8. Select the first record.

9. Click the Format Painter button and apply the format to the other records in the database.

OR

Click Copy. Select the remaining records. Choose Edit ➢ Paste Special to open the Paste Special dialog box. Choose Formats and click OK.

OR

Click Copy. Select the remaining records and click Paste. Open the Paste Options menu and select Formatting Only:

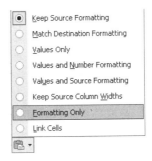

Take the time to sort out the absolute and mixed cell references in the conditional formula: the payoff is worth it. This combination of conditional formatting and Excel's Dfunctions creates a ruggedly useful worksheet.

 TIP When you're comfortable with the cell references, select the entire database in step 2 and continue to create the cell references in the Conditional Formatting formula as if it was going to be copied from the first row to the remainder of the database. You'll be finished at step 7.

Using the Conditional Sum Wizard

The Conditional Sum Wizard is an Excel add-in that creates *array formulas*: nested formulas that combine logical and statistical functions to summarize information from a database. Array formulas embed the criteria in the formula rather than store it separately as a criteria range. You'll use the Dfunctions for flexible criteria. Array formulas are best used when there are multiple criteria that don't change. In our example, we'll use the Conditional Sum Wizard to total the cost for each county.

While you can build array formulas using the Function Arguments dialog box, if you're building an array formula that's based on a condition, the Conditional Sum Wizard is much quicker. The Conditional Sum Wizard is not installed by default. Choose Tools ➢ Add-Ins to open the Add-Ins dialog box and install the Conditional Sum Wizard. (If you installed from CD, you'll be prompted to insert it.)

To use the wizard, select any cell in the database and choose Tools ➤ Conditional Sum. In the first step of the wizard, shown in Figure 16.18, make sure the database is selected.

FIGURE 16.18

Verify that the database is selected.

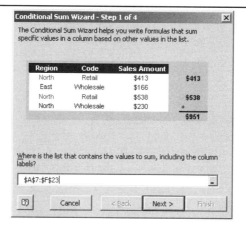

In the second step of the wizard, shown in Figure 16.19, select the column to be totaled based on the condition. Build a condition by selecting a column to search, an operator (Is), and a value. Click Add Condition to add the condition to the formula. Our goal is to total sales for each county, so we created a condition for a single county name.

FIGURE 16.19

Select a column, logical operator, and value to build a condition.

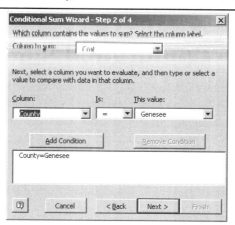

You can add other conditions. The conditions are treated as And rather than Or conditions, so we can't, for example, choose County = Genesee and County = Lake. We could, however, choose County = Genesee and Bundles > 10.

There are two types of array formulas: those that return a single value, and those that return an array of values. The Conditional Sum Wizard creates a single formula, but your answer to the question in Step 3 of the wizard shown in Figure 16.20 determines whether the formula can be easily copied to create an array of values.

FIGURE 16.20

Choose to create a formula that can be easily copied.

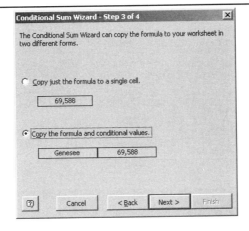

If, for example, we choose the first option (Copy Just The Formula To A Single Cell), then Excel will embed the value string (Genesee) in the formula:

{=SUM(IF($B$8:$B$23="**Genesee**",$E$8:$E$23,0))}

If we choose the second option (Copy The Formula And Conditional Values), the wizard will copy the string Genesee to a cell that we specify and include a relative reference to the cell in the formula so we can easily copy it:

{=SUM(IF($B$8:$B$23=**A25**,$E$8:$E$23,0))}

If you chose to copy just the formula, in the final step of the wizard you'll be prompted for a location for the formula. If you chose to copy the formula and values, you'll be prompted twice: once for the value and again for the conditional formula. Figure 16.21 shows our worksheet after the placing the formula and conditional value. The formula is expanded.

PART

III

CRUNCHING DATA WITH EXCEL

FIGURE 16.21

The worksheet with the conditional value and formula in place.

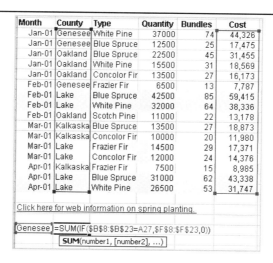

Month	County	Type	Quantity	Bundles	Cost
Jan-01	Genesee	White Pine	37000	74	44,326
Jan-01	Genesee	Blue Spruce	12500	25	17,475
Jan-01	Oakland	Blue Spruce	22500	45	31,455
Jan-01	Oakland	White Pine	15500	31	18,569
Jan-01	Oakland	Concolor Fir	13500	27	16,173
Feb-01	Genesee	Frazier Fir	6500	13	7,787
Feb-01	Lake	Blue Spruce	42500	85	59,415
Feb-01	Lake	White Pine	32000	64	38,336
Feb-01	Oakland	Scotch Pine	11000	22	13,178
Mar-01	Kalkaska	Blue Spruce	13500	27	18,873
Mar-01	Kalkaska	Concolor Fir	10000	20	11,980
Mar-01	Lake	Frazier Fir	14500	29	17,371
Mar-01	Lake	Concolor Fir	12000	24	14,376
Apr-01	Kalkaska	Frazier Fir	7500	15	8,985
Apr-01	Lake	Blue Spruce	31000	62	43,338
Apr-01	Lake	White Pine	26500	53	31,747

Click here for web information on spring planting.

Genesee =SUM(IF($B$8:$B$23=A27,$F$8:$F$23,0))

SUM(number1, [number2], …)

To copy the formula, first copy or enter the other conditional values below the value used in the formula, and then fill the formula to the adjacent cells:

Genesee	69,588
Lake	204,583
Kalkaska	39,838
Oakland	79,375

TIP Array formulas are enclosed in braces { }. When you edit an array formula, the braces are removed. Press Ctrl+Shift+Enter when you are finished editing to denote that you are entering an array formula, and Excel will replace the braces.

CHAPTER 17

SOLVING BUSINESS PROBLEMS WITH THE ANALYSIS TOOLS

FEATURING

- **Using Goal Seek**

- **Using Solver**

- **Creating scenarios**

- **Adjusting views**

- **Using data validation**

I n this chapter, we'll examine Excel's analysis tools. You already know how to use many of these business analysis tools: Excel's functions and formulas. For more advanced work, Excel includes specialized forecasting tools often referred to as What If tools, used in What If analysis. (Using What If tools is sometimes called *wiffing*, short for *What-If*ing.) You'll learn about features that separate casual users from Excel experts, proficiencies that make other users wonder, "How did they *do* that?"

Excel worksheet errors pose another kind of business problem. Whether the errors are formula errors or data entry errors, the result can be incorrect decisions based on faulty data. It's no coincidence, then, that we're ending the chapter on forecasting with a section on error diagnosis and avoidance. If you're going to base your business decisions on Excel information, it's a good idea to make sure the underlying data is correct.

Forecasting and Modeling

Business forecasts—predictions of business factors like product demand, production costs, income, and expenses—are the weather report for a business unit's future. Like a weather forecast, a business forecast may be inaccurate. However, there is one important difference between a weather forecast and a business forecast: while we can't change the weather, managers can monitor the progress of a business and make decisions to move actual performance closer to the forecast.

Business forecasts try to simulate future behavior of variables like gross profit based on information gathered from a variety of sources. A forecast may be based on:

- Historical information: last year's sales, weighted averages of past performance, experience from similar business units

- Judgments or educated guesses by people in a position to help predict future performance: managers, clients, sales staff

- Information about the external environment: prices charged by competitors, the local employment level, regulatory changes, or the current interest rate

The more good sources of information you consider, the more accurate your forecast will be. There are different ways to construct forecasts. In Excel, forecasting always involves creating a model: one or more worksheets with formulas to show how different variables interrelate.

Making Assumptions

Forecasting is always based on assumptions. Each model has specific, built-in assumptions, but there are general assumptions common to most models. One general assumption is that the future will be much like the present: the world's financial markets won't fall apart during the life of an equipment lease, so you will need to make a lease payment this month and every month in the future until the end of the lease. You also assume that a forecast will not be perfect. There will always be some neglected piece of information that affects the forecast because a model is a simulation of reality, not reality itself.

Another assumption is that the distant future is more difficult to predict than the near future. (That's why it is difficult to get 50-year mortgages.) No one could have accurately predicted the last four years of stock market prices, the market penetration of PCs over the past decade, or the success mapping the human genome. As the time involved in a forecast increases, the accuracy of the forecast decreases, even if the model was essentially accurate in the short term when it was constructed.

Building an Accurate Model

There are several steps involved in building a model and using it to forecast performance:

1. Determine what you need to forecast with the model: Gross sales? Best price? Optimal number of staff?

2. Make explicit assumptions.

3. Define and collect information for the model.

4. Create the model in Excel.

5. Use the model to forecast the future value of variables.

6. Compare real performance to the model and adjust the model (or change actual performance) as necessary.

The amount of effort spent on each step should be based on the importance of the information you intend to obtain from the model. You don't want to spend hours researching a decision to save two dollars. But you need to spend sufficient time when you are creating a model to support decision making that involves hundreds of thousands of dollars.

NOTE Excel's analysis tools require something to analyze. You'll use your own data to create a model that works for your organization. The worksheets that we created, shown in Figures 17.1, 17.2, and 17.8, are included in the WellBilt.xls worksheet on the companion CD.

Scenario: WellBilt Corporation

We'll use a fictitious company, the WellBilt Corporation, to work with Excel's analysis tools. The WellBilt Manufacturing Corporation makes a variety of PC accessories. WellBilt's CD Division makes organizers for compact discs.

1. **What We Need to Determine:** WellBilt needs to decide how many organizers the CD Division should make each month. We've been put in charge of collecting and modeling the information needed to decide how the CD Division can maximize gross profit for the next 12 months.

2. **Assumptions:** WellBilt assumes that they will be able to sell CD Organizers to large computer stores as they have in the past. More assumptions will be added as information is collected.

3. **Required Information:** We need to collect information on the income generated by organizer sales and the expenses involved in manufacturing the CD Organizers. Some of the expenses are *fixed expenses*: expenses that are the same amount no matter how many CD Organizers are manufactured. Other expenses (like labor and materials) are *variable expenses*.

The Accounting Department predicts that the CD Division's fixed monthly expenses are not expected to change ($80,000 for building mortgage, maintenance, and salaries) in the next year. There are several pieces of variable cost information: hourly employees make $6.00; overtime hours are paid at time and a half. During a month, the current workforce can build 48,000 organizers without working overtime. Each CD Organizer takes an hour to make and uses $1.25 in raw materials.

The Marketing Department uses an Excel worksheet to determine sales at various prices for the CD Organizer. They have determined that the formula `Price=$20-(Quantity/5000)` expresses the price needed to sell a particular quantity. In other words, customers will spend no more than $20 for a WellBilt CD Organizer. At a price of $19, WellBilt can sell only 5,000 units. For each additional 5,000 units sold, WellBilt must drop the price $1. This month, WellBilt manufactured and sold 45,000 units.

Creating the Wellbilt Business Model

We have enough information to create an Excel model of the basic factors that influence production and pricing for CD Organizers. We also have some new assumptions:

that the information from Accounting and Marketing is accurate, and that their information will be valid for next year.

EXPERT TIP Use extensive commenting in worksheets used for forecasting. Every number or formula you enter has some basis, but it's not always easy to reconstruct the source in six months or a year. If, for example, you enter information obtained from a Web site, right-click in the cell and choose Insert Comment from the shortcut menu. Enter the URL for the Web site and the date and summarize the information (which can be removed from the Web page at any time).

The Accounting department information contains an If statement: if production is less than or equal to 48,000 units, then the cost of labor is $6 per hour. Hours in excess of 48,000 cost $9 per hour. Since this month's sales were 45,000, let's begin by modeling production of sales of 45,000 units. The worksheet, with formulas displayed at the right, is shown in Figure 17.1.

FIGURE 17.1

The basic model for current production

	A	B
1	WellBuilt Manufacturing	
2	CD Organizer Production	
3		
4	Income	
5	Units Produced	45,000
6	Unit Price	11.00
7	Total Income	495,000
8		
9	Expense	
10	Fixed Expense	80,000
11	Labor Expense	270,000
12	Material Expense	56,250
13	Total Expense	406,250
14		
15	Gross Profit	88,750

B
45000
=20-(B5/5000)
=B5*B6
80000
=IF(B5<48000,B5*6,(48000*6)+(B5-48000)*9)
=1.25*B5
=SUM(B10:B12)
=B7-B13

Now we can expand the model to include three levels of production—40,000, 45,000, and 50,000—by adding column headings, entering units produced in row 5, and copying the formulas and fixed expenses to the other two columns. Figure 17.2 shows all three levels of production.

FIGURE 17.2

The CD Division
model includes cost
figures at three levels
of production.

	A	B	C	D
1	WellBuilt Manufacturing			
2	CD Organizer Production			
3				
4	Income	High	Medium	Low
5	Units Produced	50,000	45,000	40,000
6	Unit Price	10.00	11.00	12.00
7	Total Income	500,000	495,000	480,000
8				
9	Expense			
10	Fixed Expense	80,000	80,000	80,000
11	Labor Expense	306,000	270,000	240,000
12	Material Expense	62,500	56,250	50,000
13	Total Expense	448,500	406,250	370,000
14				
15	Gross Profit	51,500	88,750	110,000

Now we're ready to check the accuracy of the model. Is the gross profit for the current month close to $88,750? If it is not, we know that information is missing from the model; if the difference between the model and reality is significant, we'll want to track down the factors that account for the difference and include them in our model. If current gross profit is close to the $88,750 forecast, we can be more confident about the model's ability to predict gross profit at other levels of production.

If we needed to recommend one of the three production levels at this point, we would recommend production of 40,000 CD Organizers (column D in Figure 17.2). We make more money making fewer organizers. Our goal, however, was to find the level of production that maximizes gross profit.

We could continue adding columns and copying formulas until we arrived at an optimum. Fortunately, there's a better way. We'll use Excel's Goal Seek and Solver features to determine values outside the current model. Use Goal Seek analysis when you want to find a specific solution by changing one variable. Excel's Solver, a linear programming tool, supports multivariate analysis and is the tool designed for most real-world problems where more than one variable can change.

Using Goal Seek

Goal Seek is used to calculate backward—to determine the values necessary to reach a specific goal. If you have a worksheet model, you can use Goal Seek to get a specific answer. For example, one of the WellBilt managers wants to know how many units must be manufactured and sold to result in gross profits of exactly $100,000 per month. You know the goal, and Goal Seek will help you find the answer.

Goal Seek changes an underlying value (the Units Produced in row 5) until the value in the goal cell (Gross Profit) is equal to the goal ($100,000). Excel will begin by trying an upper and lower value for the Units Produced. If the goal falls between the initial values, Goal Seek then narrows the value in small increments until the Gross Profit value is within 0.01 of the goal. If the goal value is outside the initial range, Goal Seek will try larger values. Each attempt to meet the goal is an *iteration*. The default settings (Tools ➤ Options ➤ Calculation) instruct Excel to try 100 iterations before giving up.

Here are the steps to use Goal Seek:

1. Open the workbook that has the figures you want to calculate from.

2. Choose Tools ➤ Goal Seek from the menu to open the Goal Seek dialog box, shown in Figure 17.3.

3. Enter references or values in all three controls of the Goal Seek dialog box:

    Set Cell The cell that will contain the goal result. There must be a formula in this cell.

    To Value The target value.

    By Changing Cell The cell that contains the value that will be incrementally changed to try to reach the goal in the Set Cell. This cell must contain a value.

4. Click OK to start Goal Seek.

5. To accept the solution, click OK in the Goal Seek Status dialog box to enter the Goal Seek solution. To reject the solution, click Cancel.

FIGURE 17.3

Select a cell to contain your goal, a target value, and a variable cell in the Goal Seek dialog box.

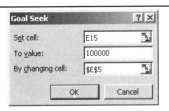

When you choose to keep the Goal Seek solution, the solution overwrites the existing values with the solution values. To retain the data from the existing model, begin by copying any one of the columns to use with Goal Seek (see Figure 17.4).

FIGURE 17.4

When a solution is found, the solution value is entered in the worksheet.

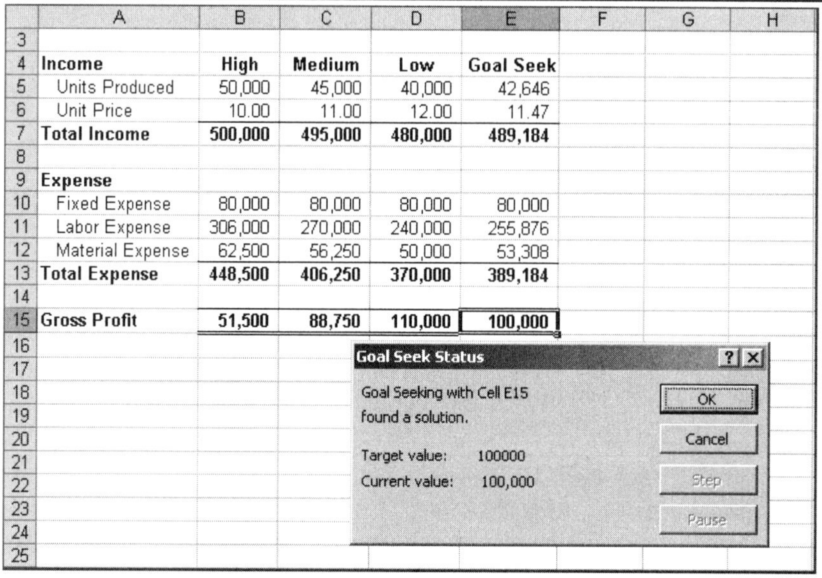

	A	B	C	D	E	F	G	H
3								
4	Income	High	Medium	Low	Goal Seek			
5	Units Produced	50,000	45,000	40,000	42,646			
6	Unit Price	10.00	11.00	12.00	11.47			
7	Total Income	500,000	495,000	480,000	489,184			
8								
9	Expense							
10	Fixed Expense	80,000	80,000	80,000	80,000			
11	Labor Expense	306,000	270,000	240,000	255,876			
12	Material Expense	62,500	56,250	50,000	53,308			
13	Total Expense	448,500	406,250	370,000	389,184			
14								
15	Gross Profit	51,500	88,750	110,000	100,000			
16								
17								
18								
19								
20								
21								
22								
23								
24								
25								

Goal Seek Status

Goal Seeking with Cell E15 found a solution.

Target value: 100000
Current value: 100,000

OK   Cancel   Step   Pause

The dialog box indicates both the goal value and Goal Seek's progress in matching the value. In this case, the match is exact. Goal Seek was able to find a value for Units Produced that resulted in a Gross Profit of exactly $100,000. Clicking the OK button replaces the figures in the Set Cell and Changing Cell with the Goal Seek results. Clicking Cancel leaves the original figures in the two cells.

Some problems don't have a solution. Figure 17.5 shows the Goal Seek message box when a solution cannot be found. The target value entered for Gross Profit was 250,000. Goal Seek has already tried 100 numbers. The last number tested—a very large, negative number—is displayed as the Current Value; the other numbers in column E are so large that they can't be displayed in the current column width. Goal Seek has already tried both positive and negative numbers as large as the Current Value shown in the dialog box. It's unlikely that additional iterations would result in a solution.

Even when Goal Seek can't find a solution, however, you know more than you knew before. Given the values for price, fixed expenses, and variable expenses, Well-Bilt cannot make $250,000 a month from the CD Division no matter how many CD Organizers they manufacture (or fail to manufacture).

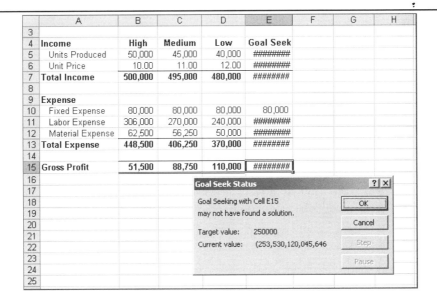

FIGURE 17.5

Goal Seek displays a message when a solution cannot be found.

Using Solver

Solver is used to find an *optimal* solution: the largest or smallest value rather than a specific value goal (like 100,000). Optimization has many business applications. Solver can be used to find the least expensive solution to a problem, or a solution that maximizes income. Solver can also be used, like Goal Seek, to find a specific value. Use Solver rather than Goal Seek when you need to change values in multiple cells or apply constraints.

Our original assignment was to maximize gross profit. This is a job for Solver. As with Goal Seek, a Solver solution overwrites existing data; you must copy the model to another column if you want to retain the solution.

   1. Choose Tools ➢ Solver to open the Solver Parameters dialog box, shown in Figure 17.6.

NOTE If you don't see Solver on the Tools menu, click Tools ➢ Add-Ins and choose Solver Add-In in the Add-Ins dialog box. Excel may prompt you for the CD to install this feature.

PART

III

CRUNCHING DATA WITH EXCEL

2. Enter references or values in the following controls:

Set Target Cell Solver's Target Cell is the same as Goal Seek's Set Cell: the cell that the final result should appear in. If this is the active cell when you fire up Solver, it's automatically entered.

Equal To Set the Max, Min, or Value Of option to solve for the largest or smallest possible number, or a set value.

By Changing Cells As with Goal Seek, the By Changing Cells is the cell that Solver is to change to find the solution indicated. After you select a Target Cell, click the Guess button to have Solver examine the formula in the Target Cell and find all of its predecessor cells that contain values. Delete any guessed cells that Solver should not change as part of the solution.

3. After you have made choices for these three controls, click the Solve button.

FIGURE 17.6

Use Solver to find the optimal solution to a problem.

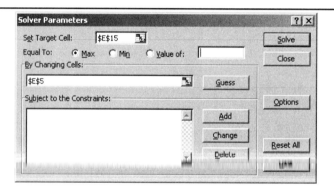

Like Goal Seek, Solver will try 100 iterations before reporting that it cannot find a solution. A successful solution is shown in Figure 17.7. Choose to Keep Solver Solution or Restore Original Values. (Saving scenarios is discussed in "Using Scenarios," later in this chapter.) If you choose Keep Solver Solution, the original values will be overwritten. You cannot undo this change.

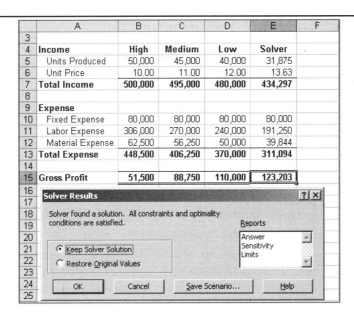

FIGURE 17.7

Keep or discard the Solver solution.

 NOTE We have the answer to our question: given the current fixed costs, variable costs, and pricing structure, WellBilt can maximize gross profit by producing 31,875 CD Organizers.

Using Solver with Multiple Variables

Goal Seek is limited to changing one variable, but Solver can work with multiple variables at the same time. Solver also lets you specify *constraints*—limits for individual variables—to guide the optimization process. Our current What If scenario has only one changing variable—Units Produced—and no constraints except those already included in the model's formulas. Many business problems are more complex: the optimal solution is not Choice A or Choice B, but a mix of the two. This type of business problem requires a type of analysis called *linear programming*—finding the best intersection between two or more courses of action.

What Should WellBilt Build?

Thanks to our model, the CD Division is now maximizing gross profit. A work team in the CD Division suggests that the division expand its product line. Each of the

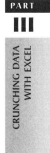

PART

III

CRUNCHING DATA WITH EXCEL

division's four machines can make DVD Organizers as well as CD Organizers. DVD Organizers sell for a higher price, but they also take longer to produce. Based on our earlier Solver solution in Figure 17.7, each CD Organizer results in $3.87 gross profit for the division ($123,203/31,875). Marketing predicts that DVD Organizers can be priced to gross $5.16 per unit.

We need to determine whether the CD Division will increase profit if they dedicate part of their machine time to DVD Organizers. WellBilt could simply try a new product mix for a couple of months, but we can easily model the mix of products that will maximize profits. There are some specific constraints:

- It takes 3 pounds of material to make a CD Organizer. It takes 3.1 pounds to make a DVD Organizer.

- The division can obtain 400 pounds of material daily. Currently the material is used to make 124 CD Organizers.

- Forty-five minutes of machine time is required to make a CD Organizer. DVD Organizers take one hour of machine time. In a 24-hour day, a machine can turn out 32 CD Organizers, or 24 DVD Organizers. WellBilt has four machines.

Determining Wellbilt's Optimum Production

We'll begin by creating a model that includes the relevant information for CD and DVD Organizer production to help determine the best production mix. This model doesn't need a lot of formulas. A model with formulas displayed is shown in Figure 17.8. Row 5 models the current production mix per machine: 33 CD Organizers produced per machine in each 24 hour period, which gross $3.87 each. The current mix for all four machines is 131 total.

The number of hours in a day places a constraint on the optimal solution. The Hours constraint is the number of hours spent producing CD Organizers (CD Qty * CD Hours) plus the hours used to created DVD Organizers (DVD Qty * DVD Hours). There are only 24 hours in a day, and only four machines, so this number will need to be less than or equal to 96. The Solver Parameters dialog box allows you to specify constraints like this.

The available pounds of material provide the other constraint. There are only 400 pounds to be divided between the two products. The Material constraint (CD Qty * CD Material + DVD Qty * LD Material) cannot exceed 400.

There are two additional constraints: we can manufacture no fewer than zero DVD Organizers or CD Organizers. If you don't specify these constraints, Solver often returns a solution that includes manufacturing a negative number of a product.

After you've constructed your model, including constraints, open the Solver Parameters dialog box (Tools ➢ Solver), shown in Figure 17.9.

FIGURE 17.8

The DVD Proposal worksheet models the materials and time required for current production.

	A	B	C	D	E	F
4	Current	Qty	Machine Hours	Material	Gross/ Unit	Total Gross
5	CD Org per machine	31	24	100	3.87	=E5*B5
6	CD Org four machines	=B5*4	=C5*4	=D5*4	3.87	=E6*B6
7						
8	**Proposed**					
9	CD Organizer	1	0.75	3	3.87	=E9*B9
10	DVD Organizer	1	1	3.1	5.16	=E10*B10
11						
12						Total =F9+F10
13	**Constraints**					
14	Hours	=B9*C9+B10*C10				
15	Material	=B9*D9+B10*D10				

Must be <= 96 hours

Must be <= 400 pounds

Maximize this value

FIGURE 17.9

Set constraints to reflect real resource limitations that affect your model.

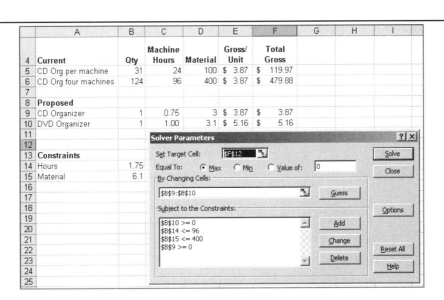

Follow these steps to set multiple constraints:

1. In the Solver Parameters dialog box, set the Target Cell, Equal To option, and By Changing Cells range.

2. To add a constraint, click the Add button to open the Add Constraint dialog box.

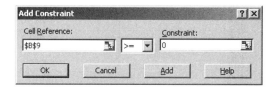

3. Select the cell that contains the formula to be constrained and an operator, and enter a value for the constraint. Click Add to add the constraint and create another constraint, or click OK to add the constraint and close the dialog box.

4. Click Solve to have Solver calculate a solution, as shown in Figure 17.10.

5. To keep the results, select Keep Solver Solution in the Solver Results dialog box and click OK.

FIGURE 17.10

Keep the original values or accept Solver's solution.

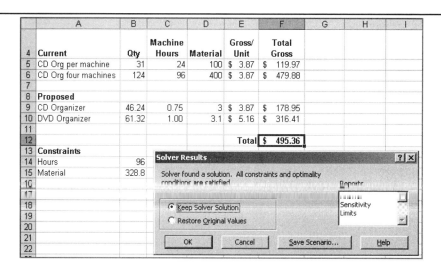

Producing 46.24 CD Organizers and 61.32 DVD Organizers each day uses only 329 pounds of material and every available hour of machine time: the optimal solution. The increased efficiency also results in greater profits: $496.36 per day, an increase of $15.48 per day, over $4,000 per year.

Saving Solver Models

NEW▶

In Excel 2002, you can save and rerun Solver models. Create the model first: in the Solver Parameters dialog box (Tools ➤ Solver), set up the Solver parameters, including the constraints. Then click the Options button to open the Solver Options dialog box.

Click the Save Model button to open the Save Model dialog box, shown here:

A vertical range of cells beginning with the target cell is suggested. You don't need to save the model in the suggested range, but you need to select either a single cell or the same number of cells as the suggested range. Click OK to save the model.

To reuse a model, open the Solver Parameters dialog box, click the Options button, and click Load Model. In the Load Model dialog box, select the entire range of cells saved as the model.

Although we've used an example from manufacturing, Excel 2002's analysis tools are used in many types of businesses. Hospitals use Solver to determine optimal staffing. Banks use Goal Seek to calculate necessary reserves at changing interest levels. Fast food chains use Solver to minimize the amount of time customers stand in line waiting to order a burger by increasing staffing during peak hours. Whenever you are trying to meet a goal, increase efficiency, or maximize profit, Excel's What If tools provide information to support a decision-making process.

Using Scenarios

Wouldn't it be nice if you could save models that reflect different scenarios: best case, worst case, current, and most likely? Excel has just the tool for this type of What If analysis! Create and save different groups of values using Excel's Scenarios feature, and then view the results of different scenarios with just a couple clicks.

Let's take a look at WellBilt's gross profits in a worst-case scenario. We know from using Solver that while they maintain a single manufacturing line (CD Organizers), WellBilt can maximize their gross profits by producing 31,875 CD Organizers at a per unit price of $13.63 (see Figure 17.7). Now let's create a scenario that projects gross profits if WellBilt can only use one of its four machines. It's easiest to begin by clicking in the cell that contains the variable you are changing. Since we're experimenting with Units Produced, we'll select E5. Follow these steps to create a scenario:

1. Choose Tools ➤ Scenarios to open the Scenario Manager.

2. Click the Add button to open the Add Scenario dialog box shown in Figure 17.11.

PART

III

CRUNCHING DATA WITH EXCEL

FIGURE 17.11

Create a variety of What If scenarios with the Add Scenario dialog box

3. Type a name for the scenario (like Single Machine Production) in the Scenario Name field.

4. Enter the address of the cell or cells you wish to change in the Change Cells field. Enter additional details about the scenario in the Comment field. If you're sharing the workbook with other users, you may choose to protect the scenario by preventing changes or hiding it.

5. Click OK to open the Scenario Values dialog box and enter the value for this scenario.

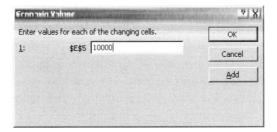

6. Click OK to return to the Scenario Manager. Click Add to continue creating scenarios. Close the Scenario Manager when you're finished.

To display a scenario, open the Scenario Manager (Tools ➤ Scenarios) and choose a scenario from the list. Click the Show button to display the scenario results in your worksheet.

Goal Seek and Solver both support scenarios. To save the results of an analysis operation as a scenario, click the Save Scenario button in the Solver or Goal Seek Results dialog box.

Creating Views

A *view* is a specification for the appearance of an Excel workbook. The default view is the appearance of a workbook when it was last saved. If you close a workbook with the third sheet activated, it opens with the third sheet activated. A view always includes:

- The size and position of the Excel application window and child windows, including split windows
- The hidden/unhidden status of worksheets and columns
- The active sheet and active cells when a view is created
- Column widths
- Display settings including the zoom ratio

Optionally, a view can also include:

- Print settings, including print area
- Hidden/unhidden settings for columns and rows
- Filter settings

Saving custom views enables you to quickly switch between different view settings: for example, a managerial view that displays cost columns and a customer view that hides detailed costs.

To create a custom view, first set the print and display options and hide any rows, worksheets, or columns that you wish to hide. Activate the sheet and cells that should be activated when the view is initially enabled. Then follow these steps:

1. Choose View ➤ Custom Views to open the Custom Views dialog box.

2. Click the Add button to open the Add View dialog box.

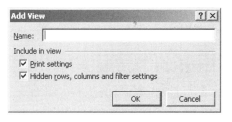

3. Enter a name for the view.

4. Disable the check boxes if you wish to omit the current print settings and hidden rows/columns and filter settings from the view.

5. Click OK to create the view and add it to the Custom Views dialog box.

To apply a view, choose View ➢ Custom Views. Select the view in the Custom Views dialog box and click Show.

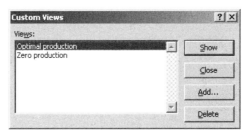

 NOTE If you'd like to know more about Solver, Goal Seek, Scenarios, and Views, we recommend *Mastering Excel 2002*, published by Sybex and written by yours truly.

Auditing Worksheets

Excel makes numbers look believable—even when results are so incorrect that no one should believe them. Part of analyzing a worksheet is checking the completed worksheet for errors, before you or other people rely on the results for decision making.

You can make two kinds of errors when creating a worksheet. One is a *data entry error*: typing the wrong number, misspelling a word or name, or forgetting to type both parentheses in a pair. Excel will let you know when you miss a parenthesis, but there is no software tool that can check to be sure you enter all your numbers correctly. You can ensure that a number is in an acceptable range (see "Minimizing Data Entry Errors" later in this section), but your experience and knowledge of historic values is the best guide.

Resolving Logical Errors

The other kind of error is a *logical error*: adding rather than subtracting, or multiplying the wrong numbers. Some logical errors violate Excel's rules about how formulas are constructed and result in an error message in the cell or an interruption from the Office Assistant. Those errors are the easy ones to catch and correct. But errors that don't violate Excel's internal logic are the really nasty ones, because nothing jumps out and says, "This is wrong!" If you are familiar with the data, you can check the logic yourself to make sure the results make sense. If you are not conversant with the data, find someone who is and review the worksheet with them.

Working with Error Codes

Excel has eight error codes that pop up in cells to let you know that a formula requires your attention. The first is the ###### error, which may be telling you that the data is too wide for the column. This is easy to fix (hardly an error, but you get the idea). The codes, listed in Table 17.1, give you information about what caused the error.

TABLE 17.1   EXCEL ERROR CODES

Error Code/ Error Name	Cause
#####	1. Data is too wide for the cell, *or* 2. You subtracted one date from another, and the result is a negative number. Double-check your formula.
#DIV/0 Division by Zero	The number or cell reference you divided by is either zero or blank. If you see this in cells you just filled, you needed an absolute cell reference in the original formula.
#N/A Not Available	1. You omitted a required argument in a function, *or* 2. The cell that contains the argument is blank or doesn't have the kind of entry the function requires.
#NAME	1. You misspelled the name of a range or function, *or* 2. You referred to a name that doesn't exist, *or* 3. You used text in a formula or format without putting it in quotes, *or* 4. You left out the colon in a range (B3:D7).
#NULL	You referred to an intersection that doesn't exist by using a space between two ranges in an argument.
#NUM	1. You used text or a blank cell in an argument that requires a number, *or* 2. You entered a formula that creates a number too large or too small for Excel to handle.
#REF Invalid Reference	You deleted some cells that this formula requires, so the formula can't find the cell that it refers to. You may have deleted some cells by pasting other cells over them.
#VALUE	You entered text when a formula requires a number or a Boolean value (True or False).

When a cell contains an error (other than the error that occurs when data is too wide for the column), select the cell to display the Error Options button. Click the button, and then open the Error Options menu to get more information about the error and how to correct it.

Resolving Circular Cell References

Circular cell references result in immediate messages from Excel. A *circular cell reference* occurs when a formula refers to the cell that it is in. For example, when the formula =SUM(J15:J20) is entered in cell J20, Excel tries to add J20 to itself over and over again. Excel will iterate 100 times; then it will give up and show an error message letting you know you have a circular cell reference:

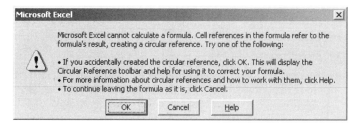

Click OK, and Help opens with information about circular references. (Help only opens the first time you create a circular reference in a session.) Excel displays a blue dot next to the formula that created the circular reference and displays Circular: and the reference for the offending cell in the status bar. If Help opened, clicking the cell with the circular reference opens the Circular Reference toolbar (or you can turn it on from the View menu.)

The drop-down list in the toolbar displays the current circular reference; clicking the drop-down list shows all the circular references in all open workbooks. The first two buttons on the toolbar are used to trace dependents and precedents.

Dependents are cells with formulas that rely on the cell in the drop-down list; *precedents* are the cells that are referred to in this cell's formula. Click the Trace Dependents button to see cells that depend on the active cell. Click the Trace Precedents button, and Excel will show you the precedent cells:

The precedent arrow shows that all the cells in the row, including the last cell, are included in the formula in the last cell.

Click the Remove All Arrows button, and Excel will turn the arrows off. Then move to the circular reference cell and fix the formula so that it does not include a reference to itself.

TIP If there's a circular cell reference anywhere in an open workbook, CIRCULAR appears on the status bar. Use the drop-down list in the Circular Reference toolbar to find the reference.

In the example we've used so far, the circular reference was easy to find, because the formula referred directly to the cell it was stored in. Indirect circular references are harder to find. Just continue clicking the Trace Precedents button, and you'll eventually find a formula that refers to the cell where the circular reference was reported.

Minimizing Data Entry Errors

The best source for data is the person who knows whether or not the data is correct. If you type your business address or hourly rate incorrectly, you're likely to notice it. Courter's Rule of Data Entry (related to Murphy's Law) is that the person entering data is often the person farthest removed from the reality the data represents. In some institutions, data entry personnel haven't a clue about the data that they enter, as they have no first-hand experience about the data. But even when knowledgeable people enter data, mistakes occur. When you're in a hurry, you don't have time to check every number.

Data validation allows you to build business rules into each cell so that grossly incorrect entries produce error messages. Business rules are the policies and procedures, formal and informal, that govern how a business operates. Examples of business rules include: no refunds after 30 days; no one ever works more than 80 hours in a week; and all employees must be at least 16 years of age. Here are the steps (detailed below) to create a validation rule:

1. Select the cells you want to validate. Hold Ctrl to select noncontiguous cells.

2. Choose Data ➢ Validation to open the Data Validation dialog box.

3. To set a validation rule, on the Settings tab set validation criteria for entries allowed, data, and minimum and/or maximum, as shown in Figure 17.12. Clear the Ignore Blank check box to require an entry in the cell.

PART

III

CRUNCHING DATA WITH EXCEL

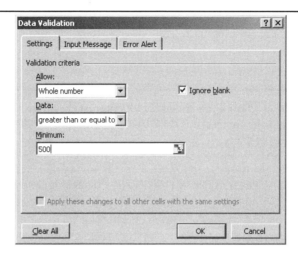

4. To provide information when a user clicks on the cell, enter a message and optional title on the Input Message tab. Make sure the Show Input Message When Cell Is Selected check box is checked.

NOTE People who use the same worksheet regularly get annoyed by input messages. To provide less intrusive help, create a separate validation entry for the column or row heading that only includes an input message.

5. If you want to display a user message when invalid data is entered, choose a Style and enter an Error Message and optional title on the Error Alert tab. Choose a style—Stop, Warning, or Information—based on the severity of the error. To display the message, check the Show Error Alert After Invalid Data Is Entered check box.

6. Click OK.

7. Test the input message, validation, and error message by entering invalid data in one of the cells you selected.

TIP Input Messages can be great additions to worksheets and templates you build for other people to use, even if you don't want to validate data. On the Settings tab, leave the default Any Value setting, and then enter your message on the Input Message tab.

You don't have to include an error message as part of data validation. You might prefer to let users enter data and then have Excel show you or another user all the data that isn't valid. If a person is entering data that they are familiar with, provide an error message so they can immediately correct invalid data. If the person entering data isn't in a position to correct it, skip the error message and handle the validation afterward.

To remove Data Validation or Input Messages, select the cells, open the dialog box, and click the Clear All button to clear all three tabs of the dialog box.

Using the Formula Auditing Toolbar to Check Validation

The Formula Auditing toolbar includes the tracing tools from the Circular Reference toolbar, a Trace Error button to check the precedents for error codes, and buttons to circle or clear circles from entries that violate validation rules. The Formula Auditing toolbar is one-stop shopping for error checking in your worksheet. Turn on the toolbar by choosing Tools ➤ Formula Auditing ➤ Show Formula Auditing Toolbar from the menu.

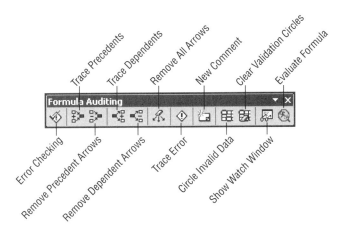

If you don't assign an error alert to your validation rules, there's no visible indication when a user enters invalid data. To view invalid entries, click the Circle Invalid Data button on the Formula Auditing toolbar. Each invalid entry will be circled in red. Click the Clear Validation Circles button to remove the circles.

 NOTE For more information on auditing, search for Audit in Excel 2002 Help.

CHAPTER 18

AUTOMATING EXCEL WITH MACROS

FEATURING

- Recording a macro using the Macro Recorder

- Running macros

- Examining and editing Visual Basic code

- Understanding Visual Basic

- Using Visual Basic in Excel

Excel 2002 is more than just a spreadsheet or data analysis tool. This chapter looks at the most powerful Excel tool of all—its *programmability*. With macros and VBA, you can create your own software telling Excel exactly how you want it to work. You'll use Visual Basic (VB) to program in the Office XP applications. There are two ways to create VB programs. The simplest method is to record *macros*—VB programs that run within Excel. Or, if you're already familiar with Visual Basic, you can create Excel macros by opening the Visual Basic interface and typing code. You'll learn about Visual Basic and Visual Basic for Applications later in this chapter, but you don't have to know how to program in any version of VB to create macros in Excel 2002.

 NOTE While Excel's Macro features are included in a typical installation, the Office XP Administration Kit allows installers to omit Visual Basic and all the VB tools when they install Office XP. If the Macro menu items do not appear or are disabled, talk to your network administrator.

Creating Macros in Excel

In Excel, as in Word and PowerPoint, you can use the Macro Recorder to create macros. You turn on the recorder, complete the steps you want to repeat, and save the macro. The next time you need to complete the steps, you run the macro. Before recording a macro, you should practice the steps you want to record, because once you begin recording, *all* your actions are recorded, mistakes included.

Take note of the conditions your macro will operate under and set up those conditions. Will you always use the macro in a specific workbook? If so, open the workbook. Will the macro always be used to change or format a selected range? Then have a range selected before you begin recording the macro, just as you will when you run the macro later.

When you have practiced the steps and set up the same conditions the macro will run under, select Tools ➢ Macro ➢ Record New Macro to open the Record Macro dialog box, which is shown in Figure 18.1.

FIGURE 18.1

*The Record Macro
dialog box in Excel*

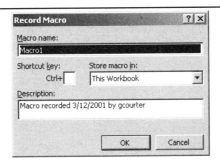

The suggested name is Macro1. (Microsoft didn't waste a lot of imagination here.) Visual Basic names, including macro names, can be up to 255 characters long, and they can contain numbers, letters, and underscores but not spaces or other punctuation, and they must begin with a letter. You can enter uppercase and lowercase letters in a name. Visual Basic will preserve your capitalization style, but it is not case sensitive: it won't recognize FixMyName and fixmyname as different names. Enter a more descriptive name for the macro.

NOTE If your organization uses a naming convention, you'll probably prefix the macro name with mcr for macro or bas for Visual Basic code. Some companies only use the bas prefix, whether or not you create the macro with a macro recorder. Check the standards for your organization if you're not sure.

Enter a new description. If other users will have access to the macro, include your name and contact information (extension or e-mail address).

Storing a Macro

In the Store Macro In drop-down list, select the document you want the macro stored in. In Excel, a macro's storage location determines how you'll be able to access and run it later:

- If you select the current workbook (or another workbook), the macro will only be available in that workbook. If you want to use the same macro somewhere else, you'll have to copy or re-create it. Macros that are stored in a workbook, including a template, are called *local macros*.

- Storing an Excel macro in the Personal Macro Workbook creates a *global macro*, which is available to all workbooks created in Excel.

CRUNCHING DATA WITH EXCEL

All global macros are loaded each time you launch Excel, consuming valuable resources. And macro names you use globally can't be reused in individual workbooks. Unless a macro is going to be widely used, it's best to store it locally.

In Excel, you can assign a shortcut keystroke combination to macros. While you can assign macros to shortcut keys, you should use extreme caution when making assignments. Most of the Ctrl combinations and many of the Ctrl+Shift combinations are already in use. It's safer to assign frequently used macros to a command bar or a button. You don't have to make this decision when you record the macro; you can add a macro to a command bar at any time, as you'll see later in this chapter.

 MASTERING THE OPPORTUNITIES

Macro Storage and the User Interface

The decisions about where to store macros and where to place buttons or menu items that let users run the macros are related. Users should *always* be able to find the commands for available macros. And they should *only* be able to see commands if the macros are available. Clicking a button for a macro that Excel can't find will result in an error message.

For example, let's say you're creating macros to automate an Excel workbook that will be distributed to your clients at a variety of locations. In this case, you should store the macros locally in the workbook you'll distribute. The buttons that users click to run the macros should be displayed in the distributed workbook and should not be visible if your client switches from your workbook to another open workbook. To achieve this, you can create a custom toolbar that will be turned on when the workbook opens and off when it closes, or add freestanding command buttons that run the macro. Either way, the buttons should be available always and only when the macros are available. For information on adding worksheet command buttons, enter the term command button in Excel 2002 Help.

You may also create macros that everyone in your department uses in a variety of documents. For example, you may create a macro that adds a custom footer to an Excel workbook. The footer will include the date, time, filename, and the text © *All rights reserved* with the year and your company and department name. This is a good candidate for a global macro. Store the macro in the Personal Macro Workbook and place a button or menu command that runs the macro on the Excel 2002 menu bar or Standard toolbar.

For information on customizing or creating Office XP toolbars, see Appendix A.

After you've set the recording options in the Record Macro dialog box, click the OK button to begin macro recording. The message *Recording* is displayed at the left end of the status bar and the Stop Recording toolbar opens. The Macro Recorder records the actions you take, but not the delay between actions, so there's no rush. If you want the macro to enter text, enter the text now. Type carefully—if you make a mistake, then reverse it later, the mistake and correction will be included when you replay the macro unless you edit the macro (see "Working in the Visual Basic IDE" later in this chapter). To include menu commands in the macro, just make menu selections as you normally would.

 TIP When you format text in a macro, choose the formatting options from a Format dialog box rather than clicking toolbar buttons to select font style and alignment. If you use the toggle buttons, the results when you run the macro are unpredictable: if selected cells are already italicized, clicking the Italics button turns italics off.

 When you are finished entering all the steps in the macro, click the Stop Recording button on the Stop Recording toolbar. The toolbar will close automatically. You don't need to do anything special to save the macro now. Local macros are saved when you save the workbook. Excel saves global macros when you end your Excel session.

Absolute and Relative Cell References in Macros

In Excel macros, all cell references are absolute by default. If you click in a cell during macro recording, the macro will select that cell each time you play it back. This is not always useful. For example, you might want a macro to format selected cells and move to the cell below the selection. When you record the macro, the cell below the selection is J22. But each time you play the macro, you don't want Excel to select J22; you want to select the cell below the cells you just formatted.

 To use relative cell references, click the Use Relative References button on the Stop Recording toolbar. The macro will record references relative to the current cell until you click the button again to turn relative references off. Then you can record other actions using absolute references.

Running Macros from the Macro Dialog Box

To run a macro, choose Tools ➤ Macro ➤ Macros to open the Macro dialog box, shown in Figure 18.2. Select the macro from the list and click the Run button. The macro will execute. You can't enter text or choose menu options while the macro is executing. When the macro is done playing, Excel will return control to you. It's a good idea to save any open workbooks before you run a new macro. If you've made a mistake during recording, the playback results may not be what you expected.

 NOTE If there is an error, you can record the macro again using the same name, or delete the macro in the Macro dialog box. You may also have to click Undo a few times to back out of any problems the macro created.

FIGURE 18.2

Run macros directly from Excel's Macro dialog box.

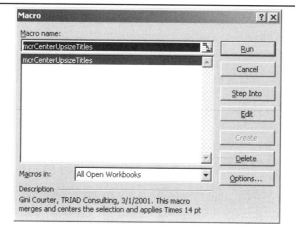

 MASTERING TROUBLESHOOTING

Terminating an Infinitely Looping Macro

You can accidentally create a macro that won't be able to run to completion because it gets caught in a loop. If, for example, you write a macro that subtracts 1 from the value in cell B10 until B10 >=20, it will run forever, continually subtracting, if the initial value in B10 is already less than 20. It's easier to create this kind of error in the Visual Basic Editor, but it's also possible to record an infinitely looping macro with the Macro Recorder.

Continued ▐▶

Deleting Macros

There are two ways to delete a macro: by overwriting or by deleting. If you need to improve the way a recorded macro executes, record the macro again, using the same name. You are prompted to overwrite the existing macro with the new one. If you no longer need a macro, choose Tools ➢ Macro, select the macro from the macro list, and click the Delete button.

The global macro workbook, PERSONAL.XLS, is open, but hidden, when Excel is running. You can't delete macros from hidden workbooks using the Macro dialog box. To delete a macro from the global workbook, choose Window ➢ Unhide to open the Unhide dialog box.

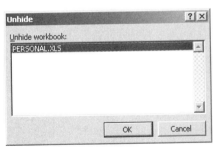

Unhide the workbook and then open the Macro dialog box to delete the macro. If you're feeling adventurous or are VB-experienced, you might prefer to select the macro in the Macro dialog box and click Edit to open the Visual Basic Editor. Select all the lines of code in the macro and delete them to delete the macro.

NOTE If the Unhide command is disabled, there are no global macros, so PERSONAL.XLS does not load with Excel 2002.

Opening a File That Contains Macros

If you can add code to an Excel 2002 workbook, so can the people who write viruses. Viruses are self-replicating programs. When you open a workbook that contains a virus, the virus copies its code into the default Excel template, effectively becoming a global virus. From that point forward, every workbook you save using the template will be infected, which means that every file you give to someone else on a disk or via the Internet will also contain the virus.

Office XP does not include virus detection software; you're responsible for installing antivirus software on your computer. Your computer is at risk unless you never receive files from another computer via disk, CD, network, or Internet connection. (Why would you even own a PC?) However, Excel scans workbooks to see if they contain macros. Based on your security settings, Excel 2002 disables the macros, notifies you that the workbook has macros, or does nothing. To view or change your macro security settings, choose Tools ➤ Macro ➤ Security to open the Security dialog box.

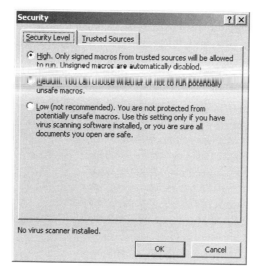

If you run a lot of macros in Excel, choose Medium security. You can decide whether you want to open the workbook with macros enabled, or disable them.

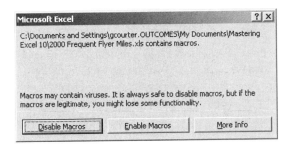

Clicking the More Information button doesn't give you more information about the macros in the workbook; it opens the Excel help topic on macros and security.

Disabling the macros gives you an opportunity to look at them in the Visual Basic Editor without endangering your computer. If you decide the macros are legitimate, just close the Visual Basic Editor and reopen the workbook. If you know that the workbook contains macros that you or a co-worker put there, choose Enable. If, on the other hand, you received the workbook unsolicited in an e-mail message from a friend who just loves to pass along the latest hot item from the Net, you should consider disabling the macros or not opening the file.

A macro's code includes the macro's description. Note that this is yet another good reason to always note your name and contact information when creating a macro: it gives other users less reason to delete the macro and a way to reach you if they're still not sure.

Understanding the Visual Basic Family and Office XP

Visual Basic (VB) is a friendlier and vastly more powerful version of the easy-to-learn BASIC programming language that was included with every version of DOS. VB isn't just an Office XP language; you can use VB to create programs without Office. VB is an interpreted rather than a compiled language, which makes it easier to learn. When you run Visual Basic code, the code is interpreted line by line, so you can receive instant feedback on code errors. This makes *debugging*—finding and fixing your errors—far easier. Visual Basic code can also be compiled, which makes it run faster. You can create code in the interpreter and then compile the debugged VB code.

Continued

PART

III

CRUNCHING DATA
WITH EXCEL

CONTINUED

Visual Basic is an event-driven language, which means that it responds to user *events* like clicking on a button or switching between worksheets. You write a VB program and attach it to an event. For example, if you write code that should run when the user clicks a particular button, you'll attach it to the button's Click event. The current version of Visual Basic is VB 6, but we've been working with beta 1 of Visual Basic.NET, the next generation of VB, for a few months. The final version will be released sometime in 2001.

Visual Basic for Applications (*VBA*) is a streamlined subset of Visual Basic that works within a *host application* like Excel 2002. VBA's focus is extending the capabilities of the host application, so it doesn't include the tools needed to create applications outside of a host. Instead, it includes huge libraries describing all the objects you can program in each application; VBA is included with Office XP and includes libraries for Excel, Word, and the other Office XP applications. If you have Microsoft Project 2000 or Visio on your computer, you also have their VB libraries. The commands used in VB and VBA are identical. Some programmers, however, suggest that VBA is harder to use because it's not enough to just know the Visual Basic language. You also have to be a power user in every Office application you want to use as a basis of a custom application. If you're not a great Excel 2002 user, you'll probably never create a stunning VBA application based on Excel 2002.

Another subset of Visual Basic is called *VBScript*, a more simplified programming language for use on the Internet. VBScript was designed to compete with Netscape's JavaScript. VBScript is generally used in two places: HTML pages (Web pages) and Outlook forms. Unlike VBA, VBScript does not support all of the Visual Basic syntax. There are things you can do in VB that you cannot do in a script, including using financial and statistical functions and certain input/output operations. (You can also use VBA to automate Outlook 2002, so you have the best of both worlds.) VB and VBA code are interchangeable, but both types of code require fairly extensive rework for use in VBScript.

Working in the Visual Basic IDE

Excel 2002 macros are created in Visual Basic and directly accessible in the Visual Basic Editor. To examine or edit a macro, choose Tools ➢ Macro ➢ Macros to open the Macro dialog box, select the macro you want to examine, and click the Edit button to open the Visual Basic Integrated Development Environment (IDE), also referred to as the VB Editor (see Figure 18.3). To go directly to the VB Editor from Excel, choose Tools ➤ Macro ➤ Visual Basic Editor.

FIGURE 18.3

The Visual Basic IDE includes a Code window, the Project Explorer, and a Properties window.

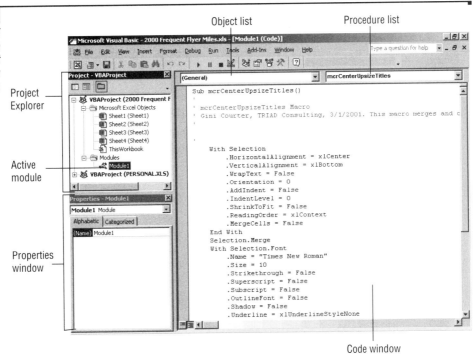

Object list

Procedure list

Project Explorer

Active module

Properties window

Code window

In Figure 18.3, the Project Explorer and Properties window are open to the left of the Code window. The Project Explorer shows all the open VBA projects. Every document can have one VBA project associated with it; the project is stored with the document. The project in Figure 18.3 has two types of project components: *application objects* (worksheets and a workbook) and a *module*. A module is a container for VB code. Each macro you create with the Macro Recorder is placed in a new module. Projects can include other types of objects, including forms for user interaction and references to templates or other documents.

PART

III

CRUNCHING DATA
WITH EXCEL

 TIP If you have lots of macros, the Project Explorer will quickly fill up with modules. Cut and paste to move the macros to one module window, or use two or three modules to organize your macros by functionality, and then delete the empty modules. To delete a module, right-click it in the Project Explorer and choose Remove Module *N* from the short-cut menu.

The Properties window displays the properties for the object selected in the Project Explorer; it will be familiar if you've designed tables, forms, or reports in Microsoft Access.

The Code window displays code from the active component in the Project Explorer. Double-click a module or select the module and click the View Code button in the Project Explorer to display the module's code in the Code window. If there are a number of macros in a module, select the macro name from the Procedure list at the top of the Code window.

Code lines that begin with an apostrophe (') are *remarks* that explain the code. In the Visual Basic Editor, remarks are color-coded green. The code itself is displayed in the default text color, black.

The code below is a simple Excel macro that selects and previews the first chart in the workbook, Chart 1. We created the macro by recording two actions with the Macro Recorder: selecting the chart, and clicking the Print Preview button on the Standard toolbar. The Macro Recorder generated this Visual Basic code:

```
Sub basPrintChartOnly()
'
' basPrintChartOnly Macro
' Macro recorded 3/1/2001 by Gini Courter
'

    ActiveSheet.ChartObjects("Chart 1").Activate
    ActiveWindow.SelectedSheets.PrintPreview
End Sub
```

You need to be slightly familiar with the VB Editor if you want to edit macros created with the Macro Recorder, or if you want to create macros that can't be recorded. The Macro Recorder is limited to elements that are visible in the interface. There are other objects that are best manipulated, or can only be set, with code (more on this in a moment).

Independent blocks of VB code are called *procedures*. There are three kinds of procedures in VBA: functions, subroutines, and property procedures. You already know what a *function* is from your work with Excel: functions are code that returns a value as the result of one or more calculations, comparisons, or other operations. A *subroutine* is code like our macro that performs an action, but doesn't return a value. The code begins with the word Sub (for *subroutine*) and ends with End Sub. Following Sub is the macro name we entered in the Record Macro dialog box and a set of parentheses. In a function, the parentheses show the names of the argument variables that are used or generated by the function. Most macros don't have input or output variables, so the parentheses are empty. The user name, the date recorded, and other remarks are from the Description box in the Record Macro dialog box.

Two lines of code follow. The first line activates Chart 1 on the active sheet:

```
ActiveSheet.ChartObjects("Chart 1").Activate
```

`ActiveSheet.ChartObjects("Chart 1")` identifies the object; `Activate` is a *method* of the object. Methods are actions for objects. Activate is a method common to many objects, because almost any Excel object—from a cell to a toolbar button—can be activated.

The second line sends the selected sheets to Print Preview. Because the chart is selected, the preview only includes the chart—that's how Excel always behaves when you print or preview with a chart selected. The object is `ActiveWindow.SelectedSheets`, and `PrintPreview` is the method being used:

```
ActiveWindow.SelectedSheets.PrintPreview
```

When the VB interpreter hits the End Sub line, it's finished running the macro. It returns *focus* (control) to the host application, Excel, which is displaying Chart 1 in the Print Preview window. The user can choose to print the chart or close the Preview window.

You don't need to know much about programming to do some simple editing here. For example, you can have the macro print Chart 2 simply by changing the name of the chart object. You can copy this macro two or three times and create macros to print different chart objects in the active worksheet. (Each macro must have a different name, so be sure to change the macro name following the word Sub in the first line of the macro.) When you finish editing, close the Visual Basic window to save your changes and return to Excel.

The formatting macro created earlier in this chapter (and shown in the VB Editor in Figure 18.3) created a lot of extra code. We changed two settings on the Font page and one setting on the Alignment page of the Format Cells dialog box, but Excel recorded the settings for every option on both pages:

```
Sub mcrCenterUpsizeTitles()
'
' mcrCenterUpsizeTitles Macro
' Gini Courter, TRIAD Consulting, 3/1/2001. This macro merges and centers
the selection and applies Times 14 pt
'
    With Selection
        .HorizontalAlignment = xlCenter
        .VerticalAlignment = xlBottom
        .WrapText = False
        .Orientation = 0
```

```
        .AddIndent = False
        .IndentLevel = 0
        .ShrinkToFit = False
        .ReadingOrder = xlContext
        .MergeCells = False
    End With
    Selection.Merge
    With Selection.Font
        .Name = "Times New Roman"
        .Size = 10
        .Strikethrough = False
        .Superscript = False
        .Subscript = False
        .OutlineFont = False
        .Shadow = False
        .Underline = xlUnderlineStyleNone
        .ColorIndex = xlAutomatic
    End With
    With Selection.Font
        .Name = "Times New Roman"
        .Size = 14
        .Strikethrough = False
        .Superscript = False
        .Subscript = False
        .OutlineFont = False
        .Shadow = False
        .Underline = xlUnderlineStyleNone
        .ColorIndex = xlAutomatic
    End With
    Selection.Font.Bold = True
End Sub
```

You can edit this macro to delete the settings that you don't want the macro to change—options like underline, color, strikethrough, or outline font—by deleting the entire line that includes the name of the setting. When you're finished editing, choose File ➢ Close And Return To Microsoft Excel to close the VB Editor.

Creating a Procedure in the VB IDE

The basPrintChartOnly and mcrCenterUpsizeTitles macros are *general procedures.* The code isn't tied to any particular button or control and only runs on demand. General procedures are very useful. You can assign these macros to a toolbar button, a command button, the macro menu, a menu bar, or all of the above. We'll create another general procedure using the VB Editor; we need to create this procedure in the Editor because there's no way to record the actions we want the macro to perform.

From Excel 2002, open the VB Editor. Then insert a new module (Insert ➤ Module), or open an existing module. Choose Insert ➤ Procedure from the menu to open the Add Procedure dialog box.

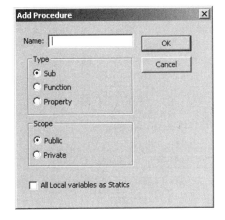

Enter a name for the procedure—**basTitleHeader**—in the Name text box. Choose the Type of procedure you're creating: a subroutine (Sub). The Scope is a procedure's range: Private procedures can only be called by other procedures in the same module; Public procedures can be called by any procedure in the same application. Select Private for this subroutine. Click OK to add the first and last lines of the procedure (called a *stub* or *snippet*—no relation to Clippit) to the Code window.

When you create a macro with the Macro Recorder, you're prompted for a description. When you create a macro in the VB Editor, you need to remember to write a note that includes your name, the date, and a brief description of the macro. Type an apostrophe, hit the spacebar, and then enter at least your name and today's date. Feel free to add more descriptive information if you wish. Press Enter to move to the next line, type an apostrophe, and press Enter again to leave a blank line between your remarks and the code.

PART

III

CRUNCHING DATA WITH EXCEL

Our procedure will use the contents of the first two cells in the active sheet to create a header. The contents of cell A1 will be placed in the left header, and the contents of A2 in the right header. Here's the completed code:

```
Sub basTitleHeader()
lheadtxt = Range("A1").Value
rheadtxt = Range("A2").Value
ActiveSheet.PageSetup.LeftHeader = lheadtxt
ActiveSheet.PageSetup.RightHeader = rheadtxt
End Sub
```

This macro can be easily edited to refer to different cells or place the contents in the footer (LeftFooter, CenterFooter, or RightFooter) rather than the header.

Getting Help with VBA and Excel 2002 Objects

When you enter code, you refer to objects in Excel like headers and ranges. For a list of objects, use the VBA libraries, which are just a click away in the Object Browser. Click the Object Browser button (or choose View ➢ Object Browser) to open the browser.

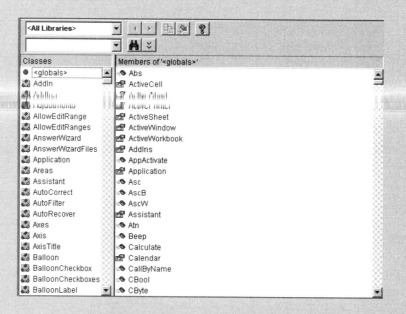

Continued

CONTINUED

The Excel library should already be selected, but you can choose other libraries from the Project/Library drop-down list. To search for an object, enter part of the object's name in the Search Text box and click the Search button. When you choose an object in the Classes pane, you'll see a list of properties and methods for the object in the right (Members) pane of the browser. If you want more information about the selected object, click the Help button in the Object Browser.

For a more global view of application objects, browse the object model, the map of all the objects in an application. The model shows each object and how it relates hierarchically to other objects in the application. To access the object model for an application, open the application, launch Help, and search for the word *object*.

One final macro uses the contents of a cell, but uses it as a filename rather than contents for a footer or header. It includes an error trap to display a message box if A1 is blank or the contents of A1 can't be used as a filename.

```
'basTitleSave macro
Public Sub basTitleSave()
On Error GoTo ErrTrap
BookName = Range("A1").Value
ActiveWorkbook.SaveAs (BookName)
ErrTrap: MsgBox ("Cell A1 does not contain a valid file name. The file has
not been saved.")
End Sub
```

Many VB programmers got their start with Office macros. If you've followed along with the examples in the text, you've created two simple but useful (and endlessly modifiable) macros in the Visual Basic Editor. Install the VB Help files from the Office XP CD and have at it.

Mastering Visual Basic and VBA

If you want to learn more about Visual Basic, don't overlook the Visual Basic Help files included with Office XP. They're a vast improvement over the relatively skimpy development help provided with some earlier versions of Office.

Continued ▐▶

PART

III

CRUNCHING DATA WITH EXCEL

CONTINUED

For free technical help, visit the Visual Basic Technical Resources site at `http://msdn.microsoft.com/vbasic/technical/default.asp`. Then move to the Visual Basic Web Directory at `http://www.vb-web-directory.com` for a list that includes non-Microsoft resources, as well.

Mastering Visual Basic 6 by Evangelos Petroutsos (Sybex, 1999) is an excellent, well-indexed VB reference that every VB and VBA programmer should have at hand.

Sybex also publishes very useful guides to VBA application development for individual Office components. Visit `www.sybex.com` and check out the Developer's Handbook series for Excel, Word, and Access.

We also recommend the *Microsoft Office and Visual Basic for Applications Developer* magazine by Informant Communications group. Visit the Web site at `http://www.msofficepro.com/`.

CHAPTER 19

USING EXCEL TO PRESENT INFORMATION

FEATURING

- Outlining a worksheet

- Creating pivot tables

- Modifying pivot tables

- Adding calculated fields and items

- Creating PivotCharts

- Getting by without DataMap

T his is the second of three chapters that focus on using Excel to analyze and present information. In Chapter 17, we examined Excel's analysis or What If tools, Goal Seek and Solver. This chapter focuses on presenting Excel information in easily understood chunks, using outlines for formula-based data such as budgets and pivot tables and PivotCharts for summary reports of database data. In Chapter 20, we'll focus on bringing all of Excel's power to bear on data from other applications.

Grouping and Outlining

Applying an *outline* adds outline symbols that let you quickly display or hide rows and columns of detail in a worksheet. Figure 19.1 shows a worksheet with an Auto Outline applied. Using the outline symbols on the outline bars above and at the left edge of the worksheet, the user can quickly shift from displaying all the worksheet detail, as shown in Figure 19.1, to the detail for Print Expenses and subtotals for other expense areas as shown in Figure 19.2.

FIGURE 19.1

Outlining adds symbol buttons at each level of the worksheet. Use the symbol buttons to hide or display levels of detail.

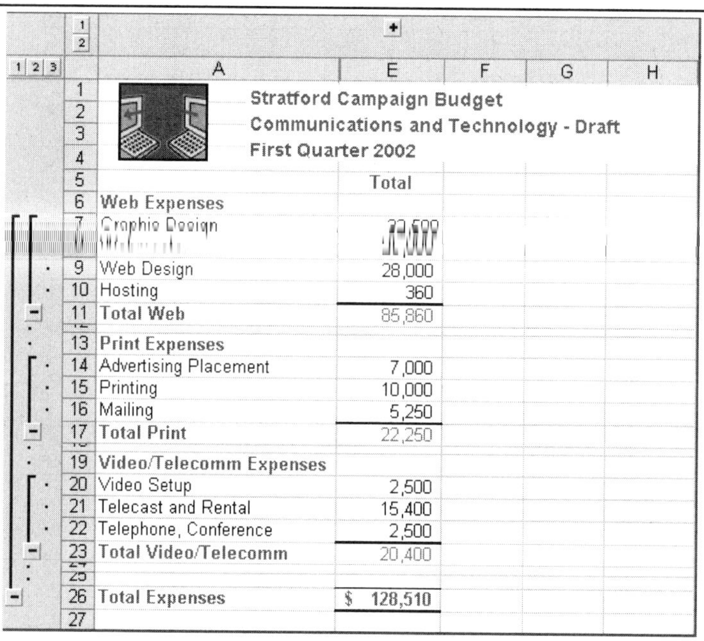

	A	E	F	G	H
1		Stratford Campaign Budget			
2		Communications and Technology - Draft			
3		First Quarter 2002			
4					
5		Total			
6	Web Expenses				
7	Graphic Design	22,500			
9	Web Design	28,000			
10	Hosting	360			
11	Total Web	85,860			
13	Print Expenses				
14	Advertising Placement	7,000			
15	Printing	10,000			
16	Mailing	5,250			
17	Total Print	22,250			
19	Video/Telecomm Expenses				
20	Video Setup	2,500			
21	Telecast and Rental	15,400			
22	Telephone, Conference	2,500			
23	Total Video/Telecomm	20,400			
26	Total Expenses	$ 128,510			
27					

FIGURE 19.2

The worksheet shown in Figure 19.1, with the line item details hidden

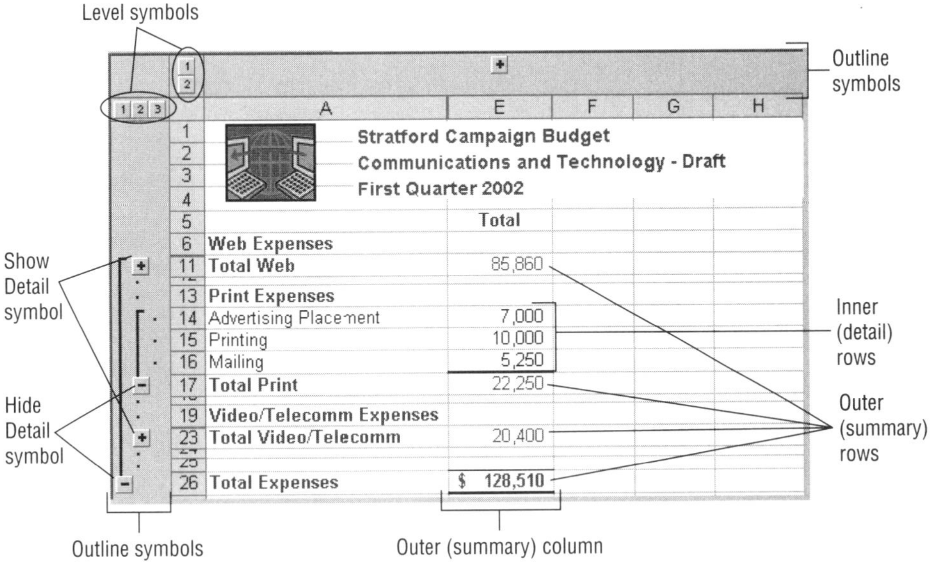

An outline can have up to eight detail levels; the higher (or outer) levels of detail summarize the lower (inner) levels. There are three ways to create an outline:

- Add subtotals to a database (Data ➤ Subtotals), and Excel 2002 automatically outlines the database.

- Auto Outline a worksheet that includes formulas that create a hierarchy (formulas that add or use summary functions such as SUM).

- Create the outline manually using Excel's Group And Outline tools (see the next section). Use this method when your worksheet structure won't support an Auto Outline, or when you want to omit some outline levels.

To outline, select a range to outline, or click anywhere in the worksheet to outline the worksheet, and then choose Data ➤ Group And Outline ➤ Auto Outline. When you apply an Auto Outline, Excel analyzes the formulas in the worksheet and adds outline symbols outside the column and row indicators. To display a hidden level of detail, click the level symbol at the top left of the outline bar. For example, click the level 2 symbols to show the first level of detail for all levels, as shown in Figure 19.3. To display the detail for a specific outer level (in Figure 19.2, the detail rows for Print Expenses), click the Show Detail symbol for that outer level.

If the outline symbols don't appear, they may be turned off. Choose Tools ➤ Options and click the View tab. Enable the Outline Symbols check box, and then close the Options dialog box.

PART

III

CRUNCHING DATA WITH EXCEL

FIGURE 19.3

Use the level symbols to display or hide levels of detail.

	A	B	C	D	E
1		Stratford Campaign Budget			
2		Communications and Technology - Draft			
3		First Quarter 2002			
4					
5		January	February	March	Total
6	Web Expenses				
11	Total Web	39,620	27,120	19,120	85,860
13	Print Expenses				
17	Total Print	7,750	4,250	10,250	22,250
19	Video/Telecomm Expenses				
23	Total Video/Telecomm	500	1,000	18,900	20,400
25					
26	Total Expenses	$ 47,870	$ 32,370	$ 48,270	$ 128,510

The outline symbols do not print, so you can leave the outline on. If you prefer to turn it off and regain some space on the screen, choose Data ➢ Group And Outline ➢ Auto Outline again.

EXPERT TIP   In Figure 19.2, the worksheet titles at the top of the worksheet are displayed even though the underlying columns B, C, and D are hidden. The titles are in a text box created with the Drawing toolbar. The text box was formatted, the border line removed, and the object positioning (a Properties setting) changed to Don't Move Or Size With Cells so the text box size won't change when the detail columns are hidden. Right-click any worksheet object and choose Format Object to set the object's properties.

Reviewing Worksheet Structure for Outlining

You can't outline all worksheets. As with sorting and filtering databases, there are some structural requirements for outlining worksheets. Excel can't Auto Outline worksheets that violate these rules, so noncompliant worksheets are candidates for manual outlining. Manual outlining takes more time; before you manually outline a worksheet, review these rules and, if necessary, make a few structural changes to your worksheet. You can also change Excel's Group And Outline settings and then apply an Auto Outline.

Arranging Columns and Rows for Outlining

Summary columns need to have a specific orientation relative to detail columns. For example, if three specific columns of detail—B, C, and D—are followed by a summary column E, then the summary columns must *all* follow (be on the right of) the detail columns. If column A is a summary of columns B, C, and D, then *all* summary columns must precede the detail columns. Either summary first or detail first is acceptable; a mix of the two is not. If the relationship of summary columns to detail columns is not consistent, rearrange the columns in your worksheet.

NEW▶

Excel's default setting is that summary columns follow detail columns; if the summary column is to the left of the detail, you must change the Group And Outline Direction setting (Data ➢ Group And Outline ➢ Settings). The same rule applies to summary rows. You can, however, have summary columns on the left and summary rows below detail rows, and vice versa.

For both rows and columns, the pattern applies to all levels. If, for example, you have detail rows followed by a subtotal row, the grand total row must follow all the subtotals: level 3 detail precedes level 2 subtotals; level 2 subtotals precede level 1 totals.

Changing Excel's Group and Outline Settings

If your summary rows or columns are above or to the left of the detail rows and columns, choose Data ➢ Group And Outline ➢ Settings to open the Settings dialog box shown below. Change one or both Direction settings to describe the data in your worksheet. To apply an Auto Outline with the new Direction settings, click Create. To manually create an outline using these settings, click OK.

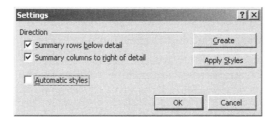

Manually Outlining a Worksheet

When you manually outline a worksheet, you determine which sections are outlined. Follow these steps to manually outline a worksheet:

1. Select the first section of rows or columns that contain detail data. Begin with the lowest level of data you wish to group. Do not select the summary row or column for this section of detail.

2. Choose Data ➢ Group And Outline ➢ Group to group the detail section.

3. Continue selecting detail sections and repeating steps 1 and 2 for all sections of the lowest detail level.

4. Select a section of rows or columns that contain the next level of detail, including the summaries omitted in step 1 above.

5. Choose Data ➤ Group And Outline ➤ Group to group the section.

6. Repeat steps 4 and 5 until the worksheet is completely grouped.

Manually outlined ranges must follow the same structural rules as worksheets that are Auto Outlined.

To turn off an outline, choose Data ➤ Group And Outline ➤ Clear Outline.

Ungrouping Data

An Auto Outline might be almost exactly the outline you'd create manually, but include extra groups. To ungroup a level, select the detail rows or columns (not the summary row or column that contains a formula). Choose Data ➤ Group And Outline ➤ Ungroup to remove the group. If this is the only group in its level, the outline level button will also be removed.

Creating Pivot Tables and PivotCharts

PivotTable Reports, Excel's equivalent of the Access cross-tab query feature, is a powerful data summarization tool. A *pivot table* summarizes the columns of information in a database in relationship to each other. The graphical equivalent of a pivot table, a *PivotChart* displays different views of data, depending on what you choose to put in it. The Traverse Tree Sales example we used in earlier Excel chapters (see Figure 19.4) is a small database, but it would still take several subtotal operations, requiring time and effort, to answer the following questions:

• How many trees of each type were delivered each month?

• How many Blue Spruce were delivered in March? In April?

• What was the total expenditure by tree type for each county?

You could sort the list and then add subtotals to answer any one of these questions. Then, to answer any other question, you would have to sort and subtotal again. A single pivot table, shown in Figure 19.5, will allow you to answer all of these questions, and more.

FIGURE 19.4

Use PivotTable Reports and PivotCharts to summarize data from databases like the Traverse Tree Sales database.

	A	B	C	D	E	F
1	**TRAVERSE TREE SALES**					
2	**County Cooperative Tree Orders**					
3						
4	**Month**	**County**	**Type**	**Quantity**	**Bundles**	**Cost**
5	Jan-01	Genesee	White Pine	37000	74	44,326
6	Jan-01	Genesee	Blue Spruce	12500	25	17,475
7	Jan-01	Oakland	Blue Spruce	22500	45	31,455
8	Jan-01	Oakland	White Pine	15500	31	18,569
9	Jan-01	Oakland	Concolor Fir	13500	27	16,173
10	Feb-01	Genesee	Frazier Fir	6500	13	7,787
11	Feb-01	Lake	Blue Spruce	42500	85	59,415
12	Feb-01	Lake	White Pine	32000	64	38,336
13	Feb-01	Oakland	Scotch Pine	11000	22	13,178
14	Mar-01	Kalkaska	Blue Spruce	13500	27	18,873
15	Mar-01	Kalkaska	Concolor Fir	10000	20	11,980
16	Mar-01	Lake	Frazier Fir	14500	29	17,371
17	Mar-01	Lake	Concolor Fir	12000	24	14,376
18	Apr-01	Kalkaska	Frazier Fir	7500	15	8,985
19	Apr-01	Lake	Blue Spruce	31000	62	43,338
20	Apr-01	Lake	White Pine	26500	53	31,747
21						
22	Click here for web information on spring planting.					

FIGURE 19.5

This PivotTable Report of the Traverse Tree Sales database summarizes deliveries by County, Type, and Month.

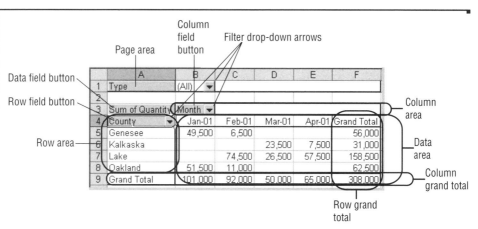

Creating a Pivot Table with the Wizard

Select any cell in a database and choose Data ➤ PivotTable And PivotChart Report to launch the PivotTable And PivotChart Wizard, shown in Figure 19.6.

Step 1: Identifying the Data Source and the Type of Report

In Step 1 of the wizard, select the type of data you want to work with: data in a single Excel database, data from an external source like Microsoft Access, data that you want to consolidate from several worksheets or sources, or an existing pivot table. Basing a pivot table on an existing pivot table results in a leaner file. Specify whether you want a PivotTable Report or a PivotChart.

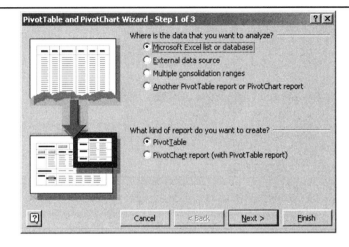

Step 2: Verifying the Data Range

In Step 2, verify the range of the database. If there is no range selected, or if the range is incorrect, select the correct range before clicking the Next button.

Step 3: Layout and Destination

In the third step (see Figure 19.7), specify the destination, layout, and options. The default destination is a new worksheet. To place the pivot table in an existing worksheet, click Existing Worksheet. Identify a cell address for the upper-left corner of the pivot table.

At this point, you can click Finish and lay out the pivot table in the worksheet. If you prefer to use a more structured tool to create the table layout (as you were forced to do in Excel 97), click the Layout button to display the PivotTable And PivotChart Wizard Layout dialog box, shown in Figure 19.8. We discuss layout options next.

FIGURE 19.7

*Step 3 of the
PivotTable And
PivotChart Wizard—
selecting a destination*

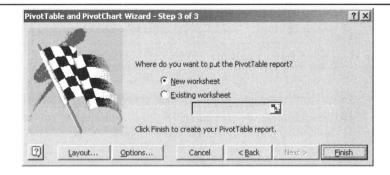

FIGURE 19.8

*Designing a table's
Layout*

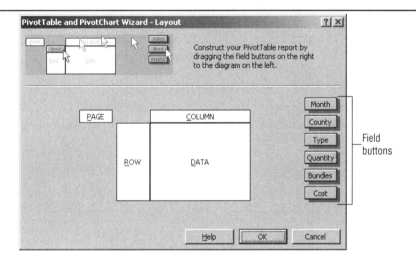

Each of the four pivot table areas—Page, Column, Row, and Data—has a corresponding layout area in the Layout dialog box. At the right side of the dialog box is a group of *field buttons*, one for each field name in the database. Design the pivot table layout by dragging the field buttons into one of the four sections of the layout area. Click OK to close the Layout dialog box and return to the PivotTable And PivotChart Wizard. Click Finish to create the pivot table.

Pivot Table Layout

When you complete the wizard, Excel displays the pivot table, the PivotTable toolbar, and the PivotTable Field List, as shown in Figure 19.9.

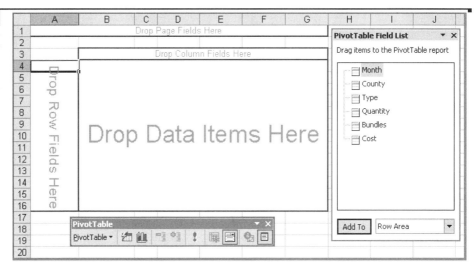

FIGURE 19.9

Design the pivot table by dragging fields from the Field List to the Data, Row, Column, and Page areas of the report.

You create a table by placing fields in each of the areas. Use the Field List controls or drag-and-drop to place fields. In the Field List, select a field and choose an Add To location in the drop-down list; then either click the Add To button or double-click a field to move it there.

TIP   Drag the Field List to the left or right edge of the window to dock it as a task pane.

Most users simply drag an item from the Field List and drop it in one of the four areas. As we show in the margins here, the mouse pointer changes to reflect the area you are pointing at. In Excel 2002, field buttons appeared on the PivotTable toolbar. Field names were often truncated to fit the buttons, so this is a major improvement.

  Place fields you want to compare in the Row and Column areas, indicated by the changing mouse pointer. For example, you might want to compare sales regions by month, or types of trees sold by county. The Row and Column areas are somewhat interchangeable; however, your pivot table is easier to use if it isn't too wide. When the table is created, Excel will examine the fields you've chosen. Each unique entry becomes a row or column heading—an *item*—in the pivot table. If one of the fields has fewer entries than the other, it's a better candidate for the Column area.

> **NOTE** If you click the Layout button in the third step of the wizard, each area has a corresponding layout area in the Layout dialog box. At the right side of the dialog box is a group of *field buttons*, one for each field name in the database. Design the pivot table layout by dragging the field buttons into one of the four sections of the layout area.

While you can filter items in the Row area and Column area, the Page area is used specifically to filter the pivot table. If you need to create separate reports for values in one or more columns, drag their field buttons to the Page area.

Information in the Data area is summarized (SUM, AVERAGE, COUNT), so numeric fields are generally placed there. If you place a text field in the Data area, you can only COUNT the number of entries for each column and row.

As you drop a field button into the Data area, Excel indicates the default summary type for the data. SUM is the default for values; COUNT is the default for columns that contain text entries, dates, or times.

> **EXPERT TIP** If a column of numbers includes text entries, you're limited to COUNT, even if most entries are numeric—a good reason *not* to use text values like None or NA to indicate the absence of a value. Use Replace (Edit ➤ Replace) to replace text entries like NA with blanks; simply leave the Replace With text box blank. Blanks are also easier to filter. To quickly locate all the blank entries in a column, turn on an AutoFilter (Data ➤ AutoFilter) and choose Blanks from the list of values on the column's filter list.

Changing the Summary and Format for Data Fields

To change the type of summary, click the Field Settings button on the PivotTable toolbar or double-click on the field button in the Data area to open the PivotTable Field dialog box. Choose the type of summary you want to use from the scroll list.

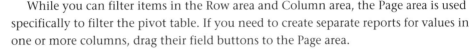

The default number format in a pivot table is General. Click the Number button in the PivotTable Field dialog box to change formats, or use the menu and toolbar to format the completed pivot table.

 NOTE Click the Options button to extend the PivotTable Field dialog box and perform custom calculations (see "Using Custom Calculations in Pivot Tables," later in this chapter).

While you're in the PivotTable Field dialog box, you can enter a new name for the field that's less verbose than *Sum of Quantity* or *Count of Quantity*. You cannot give the pivot table field the same name as the underlying database field (Quantity in our example), but you can name it *Quantity_*. The underscore is almost invisible on the field button.

 TIP You can rename fields in your pivot table without opening the PivotTable Field dialog box. Click the field button, overtype the name in the formula bar, and press Enter.

Setting Pivot Table Options

Pivot tables are constructed objects. Unlike a regular worksheet, pivot table rows and columns are created and populated based on settings. The PivotTable Options dialog box is anything but optional; you'll save lots of time if you know what you can change in this dialog box.

Right-click anywhere in the pivot table and choose Table Options, or click the Pivot-Table menu on the PivotTable toolbar and choose Table Options to open the PivotTable Options dialog box, shown in Figure 19.10. If you're going to create several pivot tables in a worksheet, name them. If you don't name a pivot table, Excel will give it the default name: PivotTable1 for the first, PivotTable2 for the second, and so on.

Figure 19.10 shows the default settings for Format Options and Data Options. Two frequently changed options are the grand totals and the empty cells options. If you don't want grand totals in your pivot table, this is the place to turn them off. Enable the For Empty Cells, Show check box to suppress the automatic display of zeros for empty pivot table cells.

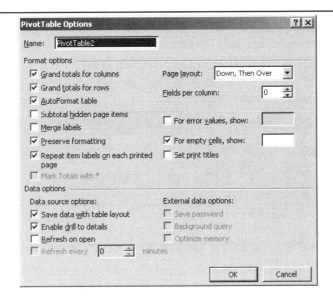

PART

III

CRUNCHING DATA
WITH EXCEL

FIGURE 19.10

Name the pivot table and set options for totals in the PivotTable Options dialog box.

 NOTE You can set options in the PivotTable Wizard. In the final step of the wizard, click the Options button to open the PivotTable Options dialog box.

Creating Pivot Tables from External Data Sources

In applications other than Excel, pivot tables are often called cross-tab reports. If you've worked with cross-tab reports in Microsoft Access or a reporting tool like Crystal Reports, you already appreciate the ease of use of Excel's PivotTable Report feature. Both Crystal Reports and Access are great software, but neither compares to Excel for ad hoc cross-tabular reporting, particularly if you want to quickly change the report layout. The good news is that you can use Excel to create pivot tables for external data from other data sources, including:

- Access databases
- SQL Server databases
- Oracle databases
- Lotus 1-2-3 worksheets
- Any ODBC database that you have a driver for

There are two ways to retrieve external data for a pivot table: by opening an Office Data Connection (.odc file) or by using Microsoft Query.

Using an Office Data Connection

To use an Office Data Connection in Excel, open the data source by choosing Data ➤ Import External Data ➤ Import Data from the menu. Select the data connection, import the data, and then start the PivotTable Report Wizard.

NOTE For information on creating Office Data Connections, see "Importing Data" in Chapter 20.

Using Microsoft Query in a PivotTable Report

If you want to use an existing query or any data source other than the current workbook or an Office Data Connection, use Microsoft Query. Microsoft Query is not installed during the typical Office XP installation, so have your Office XP CD on hand when you start the PivotTable And PivotChart Wizard:

1. Select Data ➤ PivotTable And PivotChart Report and choose External Data Source in the first of the three wizard steps.

2. In the second step of the wizard, click the Get Data button.

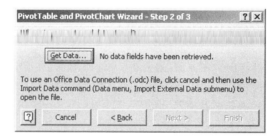

If Microsoft Query is not installed on your system, you will be prompted to install it from the Office XP CD.

3. After Microsoft Query is installed, the Microsoft Query Choose Data Source dialog box appears. If you're unfamiliar with Query, refer to Chapter 20 for instructions on using query to pull data into Excel from other applications.

Filtering Items

To filter data displayed in the pivot table, click the filter drop-down arrow on the field button for the field you wish to filter to open a list of items in the field.

Select the items you want to display and click OK to close the list and filter the pivot table.

 TIP Do you want to include this filtered table in a report you're creating in Word? Select and copy the filtered pivot table. Open the Word document and place your insertion point where you want to place the pivot table. Click Paste to embed the pivot table in the Word document. Click anywhere in the pivot table to turn on the Excel toolbars so you can format the table.

Changing Pivot Table Layout

When you're analyzing a database, you'll often want to summarize it in a number of ways. What you learn from one pivot table raises questions that only another pivot table can easily answer. Rather than create a new pivot table, you can change the layout of an existing pivot table by dragging a field button to another area. Excel 2002 automatically updates the pivot table.

You can place more than one field in each area to create a richer analysis. In Figure 19.11, for example, the Row area contains both the County and Month fields, and the Data area includes summaries for Cost and Quantity. The County field has been filtered to display only Lake and Kalkaska counties. Conditional formatting has been added to the table so the user can visually separate the two fields in the Data area.

NOTE See Chapter 16 for information on conditional formatting.

FIGURE 19.11

The pivot table areas can include multiple fields.

	A	B	C	D	E	F	G	H
3				Type ▼				
4	County ▼	Month ▼	Data ▼	Blue Spruce	Concolor Fir	Frazier Fir	White Pine	Grand Total
5	Kalkaska	Mar-01	Trees	13,500	10,000			23,500
6			Total Cost	18,873	11,980			30,853
7		Apr-01	Trees			7,500		7,500
8			Total Cost			8,985		8,985
9	Kalkaska Trees			13,500	10,000	7,500		31,000
10	Kalkaska Total Cost			18,873	11,980	8,985		39,838
11	Lake	Feb-01	Trees	42,500			32,000	74,500
12			Total Cost	59,415			38,336	97,751
13		Mar-01	Trees		12,000	14,500		26,500
14			Total Cost		14,376	17,371		31,747
15		Apr-01	Trees	31,000			26,500	57,500
16			Total Cost	43,338			31,747	75,085
17	Lake Trees			73,500	12,000	14,500	58,500	158,500
18	Lake Total Cost			$102,753	$14,376	$17,371	$70,083	$204,583
19	Total Trees			87,000	22,000	22,000	58,500	189,500
20	Total Total Cost			$121,626	$26,356	$26,356	$70,083	$244,421

To remove a field from the pivot table, drag the field button out of the pivot table area. A large *X* appears on the button. Release the mouse button to drop and delete the field. To add a field to the pivot table, drag a button from the Field List. Add, delete, or rearrange the field buttons, and then click the Finish button to return to the pivot table.

TIP The PivotTable toolbar and Field List are only displayed when you select one or more cells in a pivot table. If the toolbar does not appear, right-click any toolbar and select PivotTable from the list. If neither the toolbar nor Field List appears, click in the pivot table and choose Data ➢ PivotTable And PivotChart Report to open the last step of the wizard. Click OK to close the wizard and display the pivot table tools.

Applying a Format

There are 22 different AutoFormats designed specifically for pivot tables. The first 10 AutoFormats are indented formats designed to resemble traditional printed database reports that were, in turn, based on outlines used in text documents. These PivotTable

Reports look very little like pivot tables and a lot like reports you'd spend a fair amount of time creating and formatting in Access or another reporting application. The indented levels allow users to read section values down a column and clearly demarcate the breaks between values, as shown in this section of a PivotTable Report:

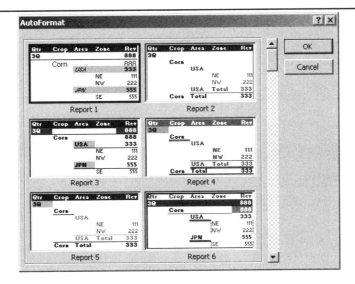

Quantity	Type			
County ▼	Month ▼	Blue Spruce	Concolor Fir	Frazier Fir	Grand Total
Kalkaska	Mar-01	13,500	10,000		23,500
	Apr-01			7,500	7,500
Kalkaska Total		13,500	10,000	7,500	31,000
Lake	Feb-01	42,500			42,500
	Mar-01		12,000	14,500	26,500
	Apr-01	31,000			31,000
Lake Total		73,500	12,000	14,500	100,000
Grand Total		87,000	22,000	22,000	131,000

To apply an AutoFormat, right-click the pivot table and choose Format Report from the shortcut menu or click the Format Report button on the PivotTable toolbar to open the AutoFormat dialog box, shown in Figure 19.12.

FIGURE 19.12

Select an indented report format or traditional pivot table format for your table.

Keeping the Pivot Table Updated

A pivot table is dynamically linked to the database used to create the table. If you edit values within the database, simply choose Data ➤ Refresh Data or click the Refresh Data button, and Excel will update the pivot table to reflect the database changes.

However, if you add rows or columns to the database, you *cannot* simply refresh the data. You must return to the PivotTable And PivotChart Wizard and identify the new range of records that should be included in the table. If you don't, the pivot table values won't include the added data.

To update the range being used in the pivot table, choose Data ➤ PivotTable And PivotTable Chart Report from the menu or click the PivotTable menu in the toolbar and choose Wizard. Move to the second step of the wizard and reselect the database. Click the Finish button to close the wizard and return to the updated pivot table.

Using Custom Calculations in Pivot Tables

Excel 2002 supports two types of custom calculations in pivot tables: you can change the summarization function and basis for a data field, or you can add a calculated field or item to a pivot table. In the pivot table, double-click the field button for the field to open the PivotTable Field dialog box, or select the field and then click the Field Settings button on the PivotTable toolbar. Click the Options button to expand the dialog box; then choose one of the functions listed in Table 19.1 from the Show Data As drop-down list.

Many of the functions use a Base field and a Base item. Base fields and Base items are like filters in that the Base field is a column in your database, and the Base item is a value from that field.

TABLE 19.1 FREQUENTLY USED ADVANCED PIVOT TABLE FUNCTIONS

Function	Result/Use
Difference From	Shows the data in the Data area as the difference from the value you specify for the Base field and item. Used to compare sales in dollars or units to a specific sales figure.
% Of	Displays the data in the Data area as a percentage of the value you specify for the Base item. Used to show a percentage comparison between sales or revenues and a target figure, where sales that hit the target would be 100%.

Continued

TABLE 19.1 (continued)	FREQUENTLY USED ADVANCED PIVOT TABLE FUNCTIONS
Function	**Result/Use**
% Difference From	Shows the difference between the data in the Data area and the value you specify as the Base item, as a percentage of the base data. Used to show how much sales exceeded or fell short of a target; sales that hit the target would be 0%.
Running Total In	Displays the data in the data area as a running total. Used to show cumulative progress (by month, week, or other time period) toward a goal.
% Of Total	Displays each data item as a percentage of the grand total of all the data in the pivot table. Used to show each entry's contribution to the grand total as a percentage.

The Pivot Table Report includes data from the database. You can perform calculations on the data by inserting a calculated field in the Data area or a calculated item in the Column or Row area. For example, we could add a field to our pivot table to calculate the cost of the tree deliveries summarized in the pivot table. Calculated fields perform calculations on the totals in the pivot table, not on the values in the individual records.

Inserting a Calculated Field

To insert a calculated field:

1. Select any cell in the pivot table.

2. Open the PivotTable menu on the PivotTable toolbar.

3. Choose Formulas ➢ Calculated Field to open the Insert Calculated Field dialog box.

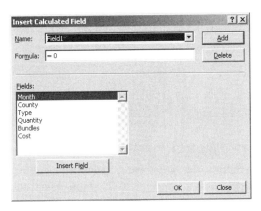

PART

III

CRUNCHING DATA WITH EXCEL

4. Type a name for the field in the Name text box.

5. Enter a formula for the calculated field in the Formula box. Use the Fields list and Insert Field button to use a field in the formula.

6. Click Add to create the field.

7. Click OK to close the dialog box and return to the pivot table.

The calculated field is added to the pivot table.

 TIP To change the order of the data fields in the table, right-click the field you wish to move, choose Order from the shortcut menu, and select from the menu choices.

Inserting a Calculated Item

Calculated item formulas are calculated for each record in the database, then summarized in the pivot table. You add a calculation to all items in a field, but you can modify the calculation for individual items. To insert a calculated item:

1. Select the field or any item in the field that you want to create a calculation for.

2. Choose PivotTable ➤ Formulas ➤ Calculated Item from the PivotTable toolbar to open the Insert Calculated Item dialog box.

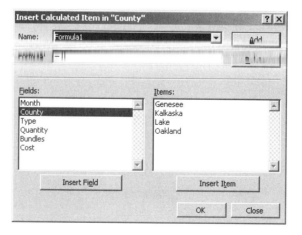

3. Type a name for the calculated item in the Name text box.

4. Enter a formula for the calculated item in the Formula text box. Use the Fields and Items lists and Insert Field and Insert Item buttons to add fields or items to the formula.

5. Click Add to add the formula.

6. Click OK to close the dialog box and return to the pivot table.

Modifying a Calculated Item for Specific Items

You modify formulas for calculated items in the formula bar. Select the cell that you wish to change (hold Ctrl and click to select additional cells). Edit the formula on the formula bar and press Enter.

Drilling Down in a Pivot Table

Even though the cells in the Data area of a pivot table contain summary information, you can *drill down* through a pivot table to view all the detail that underlies an individual summary figure. Double-click any nonzero value in the Data area, and Excel opens a new worksheet to display the records that were used to create that cell of the summary. Figure 19.13 shows a pivot table and the results of drilling down in the White Pine sales in Lake County.

Double-click on any data cell to drill down to the data.

Total Cost	Type					
County	Blue Spruce	Concolor Fir	Frazier Fir	Scotch Pine	White Pine	Grand Total
Genesee	$17,475		$7,787		$44,326	$69,588
Kalkaska	$18,873	$11,980	$8,985			$39,838
Lake	$102,753	$14,376	$17,371		$70,083	$204,583
Oakland	$31,455	$16,173		$13,178	$18,569	$79,375
Grand Total	$170,556	$42,529	$34,143	$13,178	$132,978	$393,384

Month	County	Type	Quantity	Bundles	Cost
4/1/2001	Lake	White Pine	26500	53	31747
2/1/2001	Lake	White Pine	32000	64	38336

If you can't drill down in a worksheet, the option may be disabled in the Table Options dialog box. Right-click the pivot table and choose Options to open the dialog box.

Creating Separate Pivot Tables

Rather than printing the pivot tables of different departments or counties on different pages, you might want to create a series of pivot tables—one for each department or county. You can do this quite simply. First, make sure that the field you want to create individual tables for (such as County) is in the Page area of the table. Then take the following steps:

1. Arrange the layout so that the field that you want to use to separate the tables is in the Page area.

2. On the PivotTable toolbar, choose PivotTable ➢ Show Pages.

3. Choose the field you want to create separate pivot tables for and click OK.

Excel inserts new worksheets and creates a pivot table for each item in the selected field.

Creating PivotCharts

PivotCharts help users understand data in a way that conventional database reports cannot. You can base a PivotChart on an existing pivot table or a database. If you create a PivotChart based on a database, Excel creates an *associated pivot table* before creating the chart, so if you need to create a table and a chart, save a step by creating the chart. The default PivotChart type is a simple column chart, but you can switch to any of the chart types that are suitable for summary data.

You can rearrange the data fields in the chart, but the chart will start out with the pivot table's row fields assigned to the category axis (the horizontal, or x-axis) in the chart. Similarly, the column fields in the table become the series (the vertical, or y-axis) fields in the chart. PivotCharts also have optional page fields. Refer to the earlier section, "Creating a Pivot Table with the Wizard" to decide what to drag onto the Category, Series, and Data areas of the chart.

Here are the steps for creating a PivotChart:

1. Click anywhere in the database and select Data ➢ PivotTable And PivotChart Report.

2. In the first step of the wizard, select PivotChart (With PivotTable) and click Next.

3. In the second wizard step, verify that the correct data range is selected and click Next.

 NOTE If you have already created a pivot table with the selected data range, Excel prompts you to create a chart based on the existing pivot table. Doing so saves memory and disk space, so if you have an existing pivot table that won't be deleted, base new tables or charts on it. If more than one pivot table exists for the data, Excel will prompt you to pick the one you want to use.

4. In the third step in the wizard, choose a location for the associated pivot table. You can change the layout and other options here, as described in "Creating a Pivot Table with the Wizard." Click Finish.

Both PivotChart and PivotTable Report objects can be copied and pasted into documents in other applications. If you want to use your PivotChart in a PowerPoint presentation, create it in Excel as an object rather than on a new worksheet. Then select and copy the object, switch to PowerPoint, click the slide, and paste or paste link (Edit ➤ Paste Special).

If you based your chart on an existing pivot table, or visited the Layout dialog box in the wizard, your chart will have columns, labels, and a legend, as shown in Figure 19.14. If you did not set the layout in the wizard, you'll see a blank PivotChart and the PivotTable toolbar with fields from the database. Drag fields from the toolbar onto the labeled chart areas to create the chart.

FIGURE 19.14

The PivotChart has many of the same options as the pivot table, including filter drop-down lists.

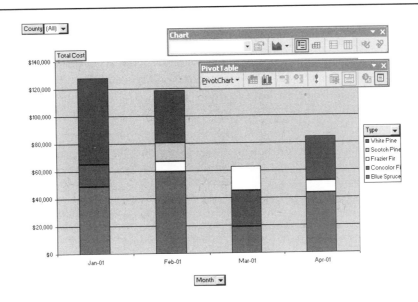

The chart fields have many of the same properties as pivot table fields. Use the filter drop-down lists to filter chart items, select a button to rename the field, or double-click a data button to change the summarization method. Use the Chart toolbar and menu to modify the chart elements as you would any Excel chart.

To use calculated fields in a PivotChart, add the fields to the associated pivot table. The field buttons will be available on the PivotTable toolbar in the associated PivotChart.

NOTE Office XP includes Office Web Components for publishing dynamic pivot tables and charts in Web pages. See Chapter 29 for information on Web publishing in Excel.

Mapping Geographic Data in Excel

NEW▶ Unlike recent versions of Excel, Excel 2002 does not include Microsoft Map. Microsoft Map has been replaced with MapPoint, which is not included with Office XP. The difference between Microsoft Map and MapPoint is like the difference between Microsoft Works and Microsoft Office XP: when you need a business-quality mapping application, you've already outgrown Microsoft Map. MapPoint is now in its fourth version, MapPoint 2002, and includes plenty of high-end features like Web maps with hyperlinks as well as tens of thousands of dollars of demographic data for the U.S. and Canada. For more information on MapPoint, visit the Microsoft Office Web site: http://www.microsoft.com/office.

CHAPTER 20

IMPORTING AND EXPORTING DATA IN EXCEL

FEATURING

- Exporting Excel data to Access 2002

- Importing data

- Connecting to ODBC data sources

- Using Microsoft Query to query data sources

- Creating Web queries

- Using OLAP cubes

I n this chapter, we travel beyond the limits of Excel to work with Access and other databases. Excel is the most powerful data conversion tool on most users' PCs: if you can't open a data file in other applications, don't give up until you've taken a shot at it with Excel. Excel opens a wide variety of files in their native formats, includes converters for other file formats, and has an import wizard to help you identify and map imported data. Add Microsoft Query to the mix, and you can work in Excel with live data from other sources including databases created in Access, Oracle, dBASE, and FoxPro, as well as text databases with delimited or fixed length records. Add an ODBC connection, and Excel's reach extends to the vast majority of business databases. If you're a corporate data creator or user, you'll quickly appreciate Excel's dominance as a data analysis and presentation tool for a wide range of external data.

Working with Access and Excel

Access 2002 and Excel 2002 have a special relationship: they use the same data engine and are designed to work together. From Access, you can easily move or copy Access data to Excel, import Excel data, or link to an Excel worksheet or range.

From Excel, you can copy Excel data into Access or convert an Excel worksheet to an Access database. Access data is only a step away from Excel; as you'll see later in this chapter, you can query Access databases with Microsoft Query and work with the data in Excel, where you have access to pivot tables and charts and analysis and presentation tools.

 TIP For an improved interface for data entry, load the AccessLinks add-in. With AccessLinks, you can create Access forms and use them in Excel or use Access reports to provide a consistent look for your Excel databases. Download AccessLinks from the Microsoft site.

Copying Data from Excel to Access

To copy data from Excel to Access, the columns must be in the same order as the fields in the Access table. You can rearrange the columns in Excel, or open the table that you want to paste records into in Access Table Design view and rearrange the columns. (Don't do the latter unless you're experienced with Access.) Data in the columns must meet the requirements set in the Access table design: if an Access field requires a date, the Excel data must be a date (or blank). If an Access field is required, each row in the Excel database must have an appropriate entry in the column.

1. In Excel, select the data to be copied. Do not select the column headings.

2. Copy the data to the Clipboard.

3. In Access, open the table where you want to paste the data.

4. On the Access menu, choose Edit ➢ Paste Append to paste the data.

Importing Data

NEW▶

It's even easier to work with external data in Excel 2002. You can easily link to data from most data sources using the Select Data Source dialog box shown in Figure 20.1.

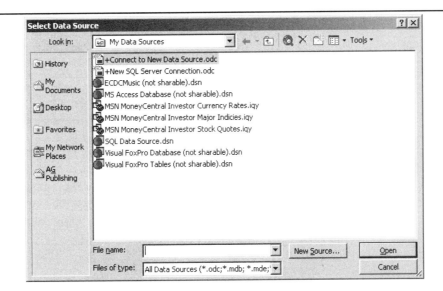

FIGURE 20.1

Import data from a wide range of sources in Excel 2002.

While Microsoft named this feature Importing in Excel 2002, the result isn't an import in the traditional sense of data that's copied and converted. The result is a refreshable link to an external data source from files like these:

- OLEDB data sources
- ODBC data sources
- Exchange Server folders
- Web queries

PART

III

CRUNCHING DATA WITH EXCEL

- HTML and XML files
- SQL databases
- Access databases

When you copy data and manipulate it in Excel 2002, the data is frozen in time: if you're working with data you copied yesterday, the data set doesn't include changes made today. Importing uses a connection to the data, so that you can always retrieve the most current data.

Using an Existing Data Source

Choose Data ➢ Import External Data ➢ Import Data from the menu to open the Select Data Source dialog box. Select a data source to import the data into Excel and choose a location for the imported data.

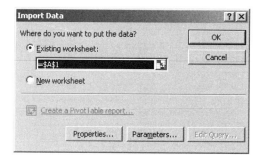

You may be prompted to provide more information. For example, if you select the Microsoft Network MoneyCentral Investor Stock Quotes Web query, you'll be prompted to supply a parameter list of stock ticker symbols separated by commas.

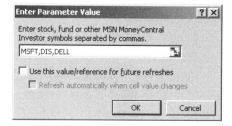

After you've entered symbols, Excel imports the data from the data source, as shown in Figure 20.2. This is a Web query that retrieves data from the Internet, so you must have an Internet connection to import data.

FIGURE 20.2

*Imported stock
information from
MoneyCentral*

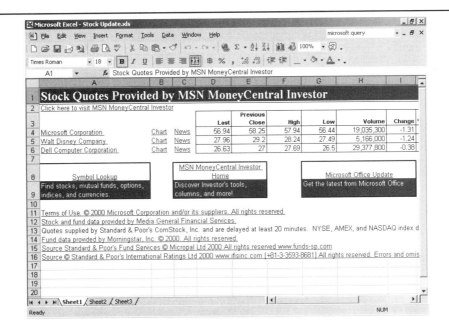

Creating a New Data Source

Creating a new data source is straightforward, but not easy. For data sources other than ODBC data sources, you are prompted to type the names of servers and file locations rather than selecting them from drop-down lists. If you're not familiar with data sources in your organization, read the next section and then invest a few minutes with your network administrator to get the information you'll need.

Choose Data ➢ Import External Data ➢ Import Data from the menu to open the Select Data Source dialog box. Click the New Source button or double-click +Connect To New Data Source to launch the Data Connection Wizard. In the first step of the wizard, select the type of data source you need to create:

- SQL Server
- SQL Server OLAP (Online Analytical Processing) Services

PART

III

CRUNCHING DATA
WITH EXCEL

- ODBC DSN (for databases and spreadsheets)
- Oracle
- Other/Advanced (Outlook and other sources)

The next steps depend on the type of data source you selected in the first step. If, for example, you choose Other/Advanced, in Step 2 of the wizard, you select a specific data type, as shown in Figure 20.3, and connection information.

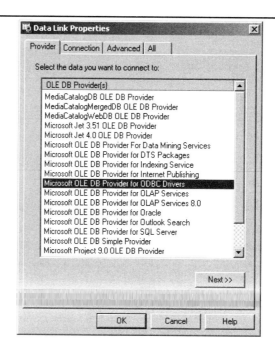

FIGURE 20.3

Choose an Other/Advanced data type in the Data Connection Wizard.

If you chose ODBC DSN, you select an ODBC data source type in the second step. Then you select the data source: the file of the type you selected that contains the data you want to import. Follow the steps to complete the wizard. In the last step of the Wizard, shown in Figure 20.4, enter a name for the data connection. The default save location for user-defined data sources is the My Data Sources folder in My Documents, but you can select another location. If you wish, enter a description and keywords that can be searched with Office Search.

FIGURE 20.4

Enter a name, location, and description for the new data source.

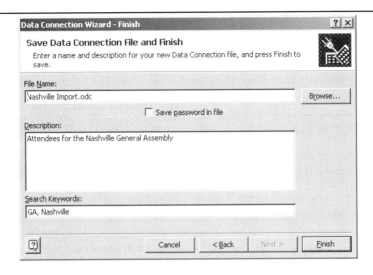

Click Finish to close the Data Connection Wizard and return to the Select Data Source dialog box. Choose the data source and click Open to open the data source. In the Import Data dialog box, specify a worksheet location for the imported data. All the records from the data source are imported when you click OK.

Click the Create A PivotTable Report link in the Import Data dialog box to immediately move to the last step of the PivotTable Wizard.

NOTE See Chapter 19, "Using Excel to Present Information," for information on creating PivotTable Reports and PivotCharts.

PART

III

CRUNCHING DATA
WITH EXCEL

Retrieving External Data with Microsoft Query

The Import External Data feature will meet most, but not all, of your data needs. If you need to preprocess data, use Microsoft Query. You can use Query, an add-in included with Office XP, to perform the following tasks:

- Sort or filter rows or columns of data before importing.
- Create parameter queries.
- Join multiple tables.

You launch Query from Excel by choosing Data ➤ Import External Data ➤ New Database Query. If you select an external data source in the PivotTable Report Wizard, Microsoft Query is launched automatically.

While you can use Query with other applications, there are several good reasons to work with Query data in Excel, including the number of users who are already familiar with the application's tools. If you offer to create a Microsoft Query for a colleague, they'll probably express some degree of gratitude. When you offer to help them access the data they need in Excel, you'll generate some real excitement.

Before you can use Query to import data, you must install Query and make sure the ODBC driver or OLAP data source driver that you need is installed on your computer. In the Typical installation, Microsoft Query is set to Install On Demand. If your first use of Query results in an error message, simply bypass Install On Demand. Start the Office XP CD; Microsoft Query is on the list of Office Tools in the Microsoft Office XP Setup dialog box.

 TIP You can launch Query without Excel; you'll find the `msqry32.exe` program in the folder where the other Office XP applications are installed.

Understanding Data Sources

Improved software and hardware for microcomputer access to mainframe data have radically changed the role of PCs in business, and Office XP continues the trend toward greater desktop access to hard-core corporate data with support for ODBC (Open Database Connectivity) as well as OLEDB. ODBC is an open standard for database access. ODBC was not developed by Microsoft, but it is often thought of as a Microsoft standard because Windows was the first operating system to support ODBC.

Access and SQL Server are both *ODBC-compliant*, as are many other database programs. Widespread use of the ODBC standard means that you can query data from a variety of sources on your PC, whether or not the data was created on a PC. For example, you may want to create an Excel PivotChart to present information stored in an Oracle database. To do this, you will use a combination of software:

- Microsoft Query to create a query
- Excel 2002 to open the query
- The ODBC Driver Manager, which is part of Windows
- A specific ODBC driver designed to allow Query to "talk to" the Oracle database
- The Oracle database

The combination of a database and the ODBC driver to connect to it is called a *data source*. Office XP includes ODBC drivers for the following programs:

- Microsoft SQL Server
- Microsoft SQL Server OLAP Services 7.0 and later
- Microsoft Access 2000 and 2002
- dBASE
- Microsoft FoxPro
- Microsoft Excel
- Oracle
- Paradox
- Text databases

ODBC-compliant databases usually ship with their own ODBC drivers, and there are third-party drivers available. If you want to use Office XP to analyze information in a database that's not listed above, first check with the database manufacturer to find out how to get a 32-bit ODBC driver; often, you'll find that it was included with the software. You can also check the Microsoft Web site for ODBC drivers that were not included with Office XP. The driver will have a setup program to assist with installation.

PART

III

CRUNCHING DATA
WITH EXCEL

ODBC Drivers

Before you can set up a data source, you must have the appropriate driver. There are two types of ODBC drivers: 16-bit and 32-bit. If you're using Office XP, you can use the 32-bit drivers. Use of the 16-bit drivers depends on your operating system. Windows NT Workstation supports both 16- and 32-bit drivers; only 32-bit drivers are supported under Windows 95/98 or Windows 2000. If you're running Windows 95/98 and working with vendors to acquire an ODBC driver, make sure you specify a 32-bit driver.

The newest ODBC drivers have their own installation programs. Older drivers, which required setup through the Control Panel, are no longer supported in the version of ODBC that ships with Office XP.

If you're new to ODBC, don't let the abbreviations and driver discussion intimidate you. The bottom line is this: the majority of databases that you'll encounter support ODBC. If a database supports ODBC, you can connect to the data and then use the familiar and powerful tools in Excel to manipulate the data. The steps are:

1. Fire up Microsoft Query.
2. Create a data source or select a source that you or someone else created.
3. Use Query to select data from the data source.
4. Return the Query data to your Excel workbook.

Selecting an External Data Source in Microsoft Query

From an Excel worksheet, choose Data ➢ Import External Data ➢ New Database Query to launch Microsoft Query. Query will display the Choose Data Source dialog box, shown in Figure 20.5. The Databases tab of the dialog box shows a mixture of existing data sources and ODBC drivers you can use to create data sources. The Queries tab has a list of queries you've previously created and saved. You'll find out about OLAP Cubes (the third tab of this dialog box) later in this chapter.

 TIP There are default folders that Query searches for data sources and queries. To add other folders, click the Options button in the Choose Data Source dialog box.

FIGURE 20.5

*Select a data source
for the query.*

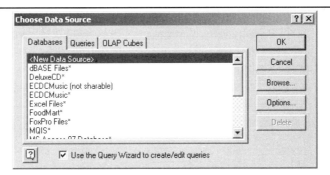

Microsoft Query isn't the only program that creates ODBC data sources, so if you've created data sources to use with programs like Seagate Crystal Reports, Cognos PowerPlay, or Cognos Impromptu, they'll be listed on the Databases tab. If you've already created a data source for the database you want to query, simply select it from the list and click OK.

Setting Up a New Data Source

To create a new data source, choose New Data Source at the top of the list on the Databases tab and click OK to open the Create New Data Source dialog box, shown below. In the first text box, enter an easy-to-remember name for your data source; you can use the name of the database. In the second text box, choose the appropriate driver from the list of ODBC drivers, and then click the Connect button to launch the ODBC driver.

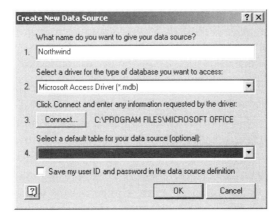

PART

III

CRUNCHING DATA
WITH EXCEL

Setting Up Your Database

The ODBC Manager will display the Setup dialog box for the driver you selected. The dialog box you see will request specific information to complete the ODBC connection depending on the database type you chose.

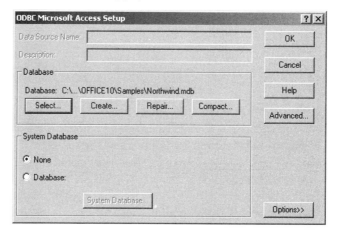

Click the Select button to choose an existing database in the Select Database dialog box. (You can click the New button to create a database, but we advise you to spend some time designing it first!) If the database is secured, use the second section of the dialog box to choose the system database that validates your login, and then click the Advanced button and enter your login name and password in the Set Advanced Options dialog box. If there is no security set for the database, leave the default System Database setting of None. (Consult your database administrator or your help guide information about these choices.) Click OK to close the Select Database dialog box and return to the Create Data Source dialog box.

Selecting a Default Table and Login

If you're going to create a number of queries based on the same table in the data source, you may want to set the table as the default table in the Create Data Source dialog box. If a default table is selected, it's the only table displayed in the Query Wizard, which can really speed up creating queries in a large database with many tables.

The check box at the bottom of the Create Data Source dialog box allows you to save your user ID and password as part of the data source so you won't have to re-enter them each time you connect to the data source.

Click OK to create the data source. You'll return to the Select Data Source dialog box, where you can choose the data source. Query includes a wizard that you'll use to create simple select queries as you would in Access. For more complex queries, you'll use the Microsoft Query window. The Query Wizard is enabled by default. To turn it off, clear the check box at the bottom of the dialog box before you click OK to close the Select Data Source dialog box and open Microsoft Query.

MASTERING THE OPPORTUNITIES

Limiting Access to Data Sources

When you set up your data source, you can restrict access to it so that you're the only user, or so that only people who have access to your computer can use the data source. Access restrictions depend on the type of data source you create: User DSN (data source name), System DSN, or File DSN. User data sources are specific to the current user and are available only on the machine where they're created. Create a User data source when you're the only person who needs to use the data source. System DSNs are local to the machine but are not user-specific, so they can be shared with other people who use your computer. File DSNs are available to all users whose computers have the ODBC driver used to create the data source, so you can share them with other people in your department or workgroup. Some ODBC drivers only let you set up one or two of the types of data sources. For maximum control when creating data sources, use the ODBC Data Sources (32-bit) application in the Windows Control Panel.

Creating Queries with the Query Wizard

The Query Wizard opens with a list of the *views* (database queries), tables, and columns (fields) in your data source. In Figure 20.6, the open data source is the Northwind sample database that is included with Office XP. The left pane works like the Windows Explorer. Tables and views have an expand symbol; click the symbol to display the table's fields.

The right pane displays the columns included in your query. Select a view, table, or individual column, and use the pick buttons to move the selection to the right pane. If you need a reminder about the contents of a column, select the column in the left pane, and then click the Preview Now button in the dialog box to display data from the column as shown in Figure 20.6.

Preview Now

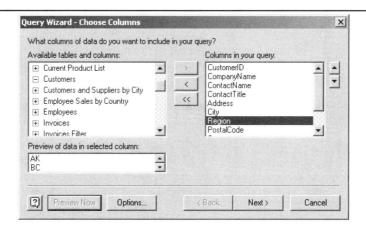

You can select data from more than one table or view. When you have finished selecting columns, click the Next button. If you selected columns from more than one table, the Query Wizard will check to see if there are existing relationships between all the tables before proceeding. If any table from which you included columns is not related to the other tables you selected, you'll be dumped out of the Query Wizard and into Query so you can indicate the appropriate relationships. (If this happens, see the later section, "Defining Relationships in Query.")

In the next step of the Query Wizard, use the drop-down lists and text boxes to specify filter criteria if you want to restrict the results based on values in specific columns. Use the And operator between criteria when all conditions must be met; use Or when any of the conditions should place a record in the query result set. For example, use Or to see Customers in Canada and Mexico, as shown in Figure 20.7. After the filters have been set, click Next.

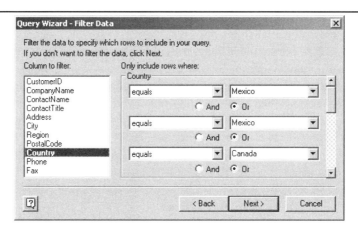

NOTE   If you aren't going to filter, sort, or join tables in a query, you should just use Excel's Import Data feature. It's easier and faster.

You can set up to three sort columns; then click Next. In the final step of the Query Wizard, you can save the query as an IQY file (which you can open directly from Excel next time) by clicking the Save Query button. Then choose one of three ways to work with your data. You can return the data to Excel, work with it in Query, or create an OLAP cube. If you choose to return the data to Excel, you can use all the Excel tools you're familiar with to work with the data. After choosing an option, click OK to close the Wizard and work with your result set. If you choose the first option, an Excel dialog box will open so you can specify the placement of the results.

Editing a Query

To edit a query, choose Data ➢ Import External Data ➢ Edit Query from the menu to open the Query Wizard. The filter page is a bit tricky. Columns that are already used in a filter are bold, but the filter isn't displayed automatically. To see the current filter, click the bold column name in the left pane. Change filtering or sorting criteria and click Finish to return to Microsoft Excel.

Defining Relationships in Query

Sometimes Query makes you clean up relationships simply because you didn't choose fields from enough tables. In Figure 20.8, we selected fields from only two tables — Employees and Categories—because we wanted to determine the total value of each employee's sales in each category. The problem is, there isn't a related field that appears in both the Employees and Categories tables, and Query lets us know about it.

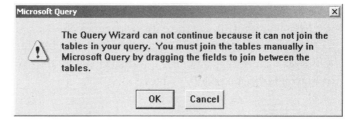

The path from Employees to Categories requires five tables. Employees take Orders, which have Details about Products, and Products fall into Categories. We need related fields from the Orders, Order Details, and Products tables to create the query, so if we click OK, the Query Wizard closes and we're left in the Microsoft Query Window, shown in Figure 20.8.

NOTE In a well-built database, the fast way to find a relationship between tables is to see if the primary key of either table appears as a foreign key in the other table. For more information about keys, both primary and foreign, see "Determining Fields" and "Understanding Table Relationships" in Chapter 37.

FIGURE 20.8

The Query window shows tables and their relationships.

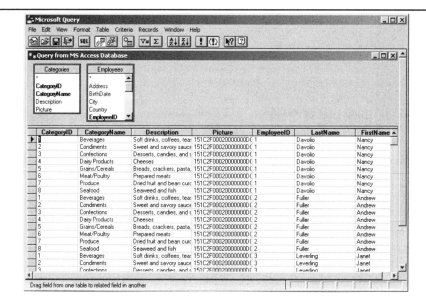

The Query window shows tables and their relationships.

Don't assume anything just because there's data in the Query Window grid. The data is the result of a cross join or full outer join, which returns every record in one table for each and every record in the other table: data in abundance, but generally not what you want. To get the data we need, we must relate the tables.

 To add another table to the grid, click the Add Tables button to open the Add Tables dialog box, select a table, and then click Add to add the table. Click Close when you're finished adding tables.

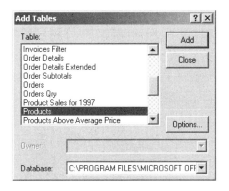

When the tables you selected are all related, you'll be able to rearrange the tables using drag-and-drop and follow the join lines from the first table to the last, as shown in Figure 20.9.

FIGURE 20.9

Join lines connect related tables in a query.

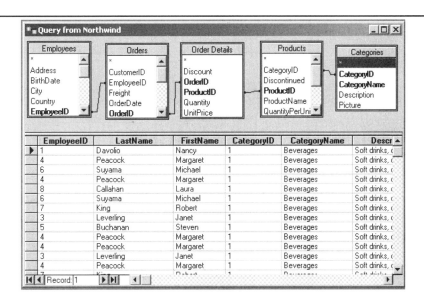

How does Query do this? It joins fields with the same name, which means that the joins it creates may not be correct, particularly if the person who designed the database wasn't consistent when naming fields. To delete a join, select it and press Delete on your keyboard. To create a new join, drag the field from one table and drop it on the field that represents the same data in the other table.

To edit a join, select it and double-click to open the Joins dialog box shown in Figure 20.10. Choose the join that best describes the data you would like to see in your query results.

Edit the default join to return all the records from one table and related records from other tables.

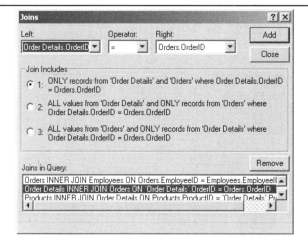

When you've finished adding tables and editing joins, choose File ➤ Return Data To Microsoft Excel to work with your imported data.

Retrieving Data with a Web Query

With Excel 2002's Web Query feature, you can retrieve data from any accessible table on an intranet or the Internet. To retrieve Web data, make sure you're appropriately connected to the Internet or a network intranet and choose Data ➤ Import External Data ➤ New Web Query. The New Web Query dialog box opens, displaying the home page from your browser, as shown in Figure 20.11.

To navigate, enter a URL or select a page from the Address drop-down list. The list comes from your browser history. If you need to create many Web queries, you can save time by clearing the browser history and then visiting each of the pages in your browser before creating Web queries. When you open the Address drop-down list, it will only include the pages that you have visited since you cleared the history.

Each importable table is marked with a yellow arrow icon. HTML supports nested tables, so many pages have lots of tables (see Figure 20.11). Point to an icon to highlight the corresponding data in the table. Click the icon to select the table; the icon changes to a green check mark. Select the tables you wish to import.

FIGURE 20.11

Choose a table to import in the browser window.

To save the query in your list of data sources, click the Save Query button at the top of the dialog box. Click the Import button to return the data to Excel.

Setting Web Query Options

Click the Options button to open the Web Query Options dialog box, shown in Figure 20.12, and set the options described in Table 20.1.

FIGURE 20.12

Change formatting and redirection settings in the Web Query Options dialog box.

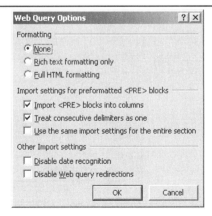

TABLE 20.1   WEB QUERY OPTIONS

Option/Setting	Description
Formatting: None	The default.
Formatting: Rich Text	Excel-like formatting, but without hyperlinks or merged cells.
Formatting: Full HTML	Full formatting, including merged cells and hyperlinks.
Import <PRE> Blocks Into Columns	Enable to use the delimiters in preformatted sections to determine how to parse the data into columns. Disable to place each row of preformatted data in a separate worksheet cell.
Treat Consecutive Delimiters As One	Disable to treat delimiters as you would in a text data file; enable to ignore consecutive delimiters.
Use The Same Import Settings For The Entire Section	Enable to apply the Treat Consecutive Delimiters setting to all preformatted blocks on the page; disable to specify treatment for individual blocks.
Disable Date Recognition	Turn on to ensure that numbers similar to dates (part numbers, for example) are not converted to dates in Excel.
Disable Web Query Redirection	Enable to prevent redirection of the query if the data source moves.

Working with Query Results in Excel

In Excel, you can use the query result set as you would any native Excel data. You can, for example, add formulas, create totals or averages, and chart the information. The real charm of both Import and Query, however, is their ability to refresh data from the data source on demand. When you open a query using Data ➢ Import External Data, the External Data toolbar also opens.

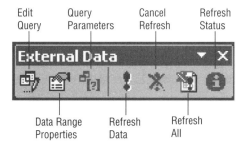

NOTE If the External Data toolbar does not open, right-click any toolbar and choose External Data to display the toolbar. The toolbar does not open if you open a query with the File ➢ Open command.

To view the latest data from a data source, click the Refresh Data button, and Query will rerun your query. The Refresh All button reruns all queries in the current workbook. If your queries are complex and take a long time to run, or if you have a number of queries, you'll appreciate being able to cancel a refresh or get refresh information at the click of a button.

If you want to change the query design, click the Edit Query button to launch Microsoft Query and reopen the Query Wizard so you can add or delete tables and columns, or change filters or sort order.

NOTE If you rearrange the columns or change the sort order or filter criteria in Excel, Query uses the new layout when it refreshes the data. The following section has information on retaining or discarding layout changes.

 MASTERING THE OPPORTUNITIES

Creating Parameter Queries

You can create a parameter query in Query as you would in Access. If you've been working with Web queries, leave the page where the Web query data is located before following the steps below; otherwise, you'll end up in the Web Query dialog box rather than Microsoft Query. In the final step of the Query Wizard, choose View Data Or Edit Query In Microsoft Query, and the Query window will open. If the Criteria grid is not displayed, choose View ➢ Criteria to display it. In the Criteria Field drop-down list, select the field for which you want to set a parameter. For example, to create a parameter query where users determine the state abbreviation (for example MI, NV, CA) used in the query, set the appropriate state field as the Criteria Field.

Continued

MASTERING THE OPPORTUNITIES CONTINUED

In the Criteria row just below the field, enter the user prompt in brackets: **[Enter a two-letter state abbreviation:]**. Query will immediately create the message box with the user prompt. You can simply cancel the message box or enter a value to see how your criteria work. Enter additional Or criteria in the remaining rows. To create And criteria, set a Criteria Field and criteria in the next column.

To return to Excel when you're finished, choose File ➤ Return Data To Microsoft Excel from the Query menu.

Creating a parameter query is particularly helpful when users need to change criteria frequently. In Excel, click the Query Parameters button on the External Data toolbar.

This opens the Parameters dialog box, where you can change the source for a parameter to a cell in the workbook (or a fixed value). This way, you can let users enter a value in (for example) cell A3, click the Refresh Data button, and see the query results for the new value they entered.

Setting Excel Data Range Properties

One of the disadvantages of working with Query data in Excel is that users can forget to refresh the data and copy formulas in adjacent columns when more records are returned in the query results. Automated refresh settings are just one of the properties you can set for the range of data returned by Query.

 Begin by clicking the Data Range Properties button on the External Data toolbar to open the External Data Range Properties dialog box shown in Figure 20.13. These properties don't affect the query that you saved (or didn't save) in Microsoft Query. They determine how the query behaves in Excel:

Name The Excel name for the data range.

Save Query Definition Saves the definition as part of the Excel worksheet so that it can be refreshed later without choosing Tools ➤ Get External Data and retrieving the saved query. Enabled by default.

Save Password Saves the password you entered to open the query data source. Enabled by default.

Enable Background Refresh Allows you to work on other tasks in Excel while data is being refreshed. If you disable this check box, you must wait for Query to refresh the data before continuing.

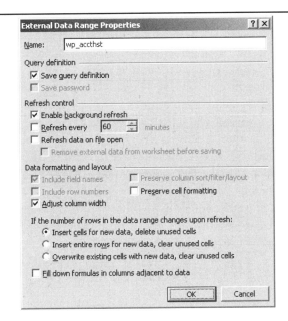

FIGURE 20.13

Use the External Data Range Properties dialog box to set refresh information for the query data.

Refresh Every *X* Minutes Ensures that the data range is refreshed at the interval you specify. Be careful with this, particularly when a query result set can grow or is accessed over a network with high peak volumes. You can become incredibly unpopular with colleagues who use this workbook if you refresh every 30 minutes and it takes 15 minutes for Query to refresh the data range.

Refresh Data On File Open Launches Query and refreshes the data each time the workbook is opened rather than waiting for *X* minutes to refresh. This is a good option when data changes less frequently than users open the workbook. Many corporate data stores are refreshed once a day or once a week during off-peak hours, so a refresh when the file opens is probably adequate. With Refresh Data On File Open selected, you can choose to Remove External Data From Worksheet Before Saving. When the file is saved and closed, the external data is dumped, which saves drive space. The next time the workbook is opened, the query is run again and the data refreshed.

There are two distinct types of Data Formatting And Layout options. The first two options on the left pertain to the external data source; the options in the right column relate to Excel. You can Include Field Names or omit them if you want to create different column labels and Include Row Numbers from the external data source.

When data is refreshed, Excel will automatically Adjust Column Width to fit the data unless you turn this third option off. Preserve Column/Sort/Filter/Layout and

Preserve Cell Formatting are both enabled by default. With the default settings, if you rearrange columns in Excel and then apply a format to a column of query results, both the new arrangement and the format will be retained when the data is refreshed.

The last time you ran your query, it returned 10 rows of data; if it returns 13 rows next time, how should Excel deal with the extra rows? Use the option buttons to choose the method you want Excel to use (insert cells and delete unused cells, insert entire rows and clear unused cells or cell replacement, row replacement, or both) when the number of rows changes on refresh. If you have other worksheet columns with formulas that rely on the external data range, enable the Fill Down Formulas In Columns Adjacent To Data check box to have Excel copy the formulas down to extra rows or remove formulas from rows that no longer have external data.

When you've adjusted the properties to meet the needs of the workbook's users, click OK to save the properties and close the dialog box.

3-D Pivot Analysis with OLAP

OLAP (Online Analytical Processing) is a natural extension of traditional Excel pivot tables. Pivot tables analyze data in two dimensions. For example, you can create a pivot table to analyze your company's sales by area, by date, or by product. If you create a pivot table to summarize dates by quarter and sales by region, you can drill down and view sales for a month or a particular day, or you can look at sales for the states within a region. Until Excel 2000, the pivot table toolkit had a serious limitation: you couldn't adequately analyze three or more dimensions (sales by region *and* date *and* product) simultaneously. OLAP is a three-dimensional data analysis tool for analyzing the multidimensional data that abounds in corporate databases.

 TIP OLAP uses PivotTable Reports, Microsoft Query, and ODBC. Refer to Chapter 19 for information on pivot tables; refer to the ODBC and Microsoft Query sections earlier in this chapter for help with these topics.

Understanding OLAP Cubes

An *OLAP cube* is a special type of query with data organized in the categories you use for analysis so you can quickly generate new analyses or reports based on the data. You create OLAP cubes from any ODBC data source with Microsoft Query, or you can attach to an existing data cube created by one of your co-workers or an OLAP provider. If cubes are well designed, you won't need an abundance of them. One cube containing data on, for example, sales, can replace a plethora of queries and pivot tables created about specific aspects of sales information.

An OLAP cube is organized in *dimensions*, and a given dimension may have two or more *levels* of information, ranging from the more inclusive and general to the more specific and detailed. In a PivotTable or PivotChart Report, a dimension is placed in a Row, Column, or Page area. For example, a cube of data about sales might have these dimensions and corresponding levels:

Sales dates Years, quarters, months or weeks, days

Geography Country, state/province, city

Products Product category, product

The lowest level of this cube, called a *measure*, would be the detail about sales: the quantity of each product sold. The measures are placed in the data area of a pivot report. People who use your cube will analyze data by expanding and collapsing dimensions and swapping dimensions to see the changes in the measures.

 TIP *Dimensions* are the Row, Column, and Page areas in a traditional pivot table. *Measures* are the fields used in the Data area.

If you serve as an information technology person in your company or department (formally or informally), you'll quickly realize that OLAP is a powerful feature. You can create cubes to help your users analyze data, even if they know nothing about joins or queries, rather than spending your time creating specific reports. If you're an end user, you'll appreciate the power to robustly analyze and report on your data without asking for assistance.

Opening an Existing OLAP Cube

There are three ways to access an existing OLAP cube. If the cube was already used in an Excel PivotTable or PivotChart, just open the Excel workbook. The workbook includes the information required to launch Microsoft Query and connect to the OLAP data source.

Using an Existing OLAP Query

If the OLAP cube was saved in Microsoft Query but not in Excel, choose Data ➢ Import External Data ➢ Import Data and set the Files Of Type to OLAP

Queries/Cubes. Select the OLAP query. Excel will run the query and prompt you to choose a location for a pivot table.

Selecting an Existing OLAP Data Source

If there is no query based on the OLAP cube but a data source using the cube exists, select the data source as you would for any query based on an external data source. Open Excel and choose PivotTable Chart/PivotTable Report from the Data menu. In the first step of the wizard, choose External Data Source. In the second step, click Get Data to open the Choose Data Source dialog box. Select the OLAP Cubes tab and select an OLAP data source; then click OK to connect to the data source and return to the PivotTable Wizard.

Creating a New OLAP Data Source

If you need to create a new data source using a cube or OLAP server, begin by choosing the External Data Source option in the PivotTable And PivotChart Wizard. In Step 2 of the wizard, click Get Data to open the Choose Data Source dialog box. On the OLAP Cubes tab, choose New Data Source and click OK to open the Create New Data Source dialog box.

Enter a name for the data source. Select Microsoft OLE DB Provider For OLAP Services 8.0, which is included with Office XP, as the provider. Click the Connect button to open the MultiDimensional Connection dialog box, shown in Figure 20.14.

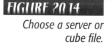

FIGURE 20.14

Choose a server or cube file.

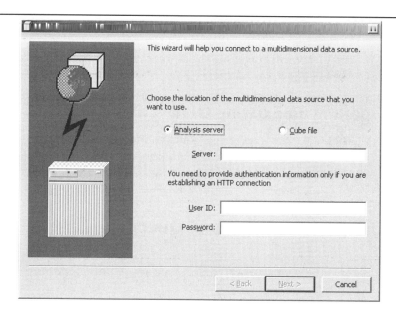

If you're connecting to an analysis server, enter the OLAP server resource name provided by your system administrator or database administrator in the text box. To connect to a cube, choose the OLAP Cube option, and then enter the cube filename or browse and select it. If you don't have a cube or an analysis server, see the next section, "Creating a New OLAP Cube."

Click Finish to connect to your server or cube and return to the Create New Data Source dialog box. Click OK to create the data source and add it to the list in the Choose Data Source dialog box. Click OK to return to the PivotTable Wizard.

EXPERT TIP OLAP data is delivered to a desktop in two ways: from a relational database using Microsoft Query and ODBC, or from an OLAP database. With an OLAP database, summary calculations are performed on the analysis server and then sent over the network to Excel. Server-based queries run much more quickly than those based on relational databases that require Excel to receive all the detail data and then perform summary calculations on your workstation. Analysis servers allow users to analyze data sets that have too many records for Excel to manage. On the other hand, OLAP cubes created with relational databases give you a way to look at complex data even if your company doesn't have an OLAP server. You can create the cube to filter the records returned from a database, allowing Excel to handle a larger number of records (without running out of system resources) than it would be able to if all fields were being retrieved by Excel.

Creating a New OLAP Cube

If you can connect to an ODBC data source, you can create OLAP cubes by setting up a data source, creating a query based on the data source, and saving the query as an OLAP query.

Setting Up a Data Source

From Excel, choose Data ➢ Import External Data ➢ New Database Query. If necessary, create and then select a Database data source as discussed earlier in this chapter. In the illustrations that follow, we're creating a cube using the Northwind database included with Office XP, the same database we used with Microsoft Query earlier in this chapter.

Creating a Query

In the Query Wizard, choose the tables and fields that you need for your cube. Choose carefully: you can't edit a cube, so if you omit a field, you have to create a new cube. Select tables and fields that represent the levels, dimensions, and measures you'll want to analyze in the cube.

Saving a Query As an OLAP Query

In the last step of the Query Wizard, select Create An OLAP Cube From This Query. If you think you may want to create a similar cube later with slightly different fields, click the Save Query button. Click Finish to launch the OLAP Cube Wizard.

EXPERT TIP You'll select measures that you want to summarize when you create the cube. If you want to summarize a field twice, you need to add it to the query twice. For example, if you want to count *and* total the values in a field, you'll have to place the field in your query twice. You can't select a field more than once in the Query Wizard, but you can in Query itself. In the last step of the Query Wizard, choose View Data And Edit Query In Microsoft Query to return to Query, where you can drag additional fields into the query grid. After you've examined the query results, choose File ➢ Create OLAP Cube from the Query menu bar to launch the OLAP Query Wizard.

The OLAP Cube Wizard opens with an explanatory page. Click Next to move to the first step of the wizard, shown in Figure 20.15. In this step, decide which of the fields you want to use as measures *(data fields)*. The fields you select here will end up in the Data area of your PivotTable Report in Excel. The OLAP Cube Wizard examines your data, checks the fields that may be measures, and assigns a summarization method: COUNT for text and primary key fields, and SUM for other numeric fields. Uncheck fields to show that is not a data field when you're finished selecting. The fields that you don't check can be used in the next step as dimensions/levels. Of the fields selected by the wizard in Figure 20.15, we'll keep two: OrderID and Quantity.

To change the summarization method for a field, click in the Summarize By column and select the function (Sum, Count, Min, Max) you want to use. Edit the Data Field Name to change the display name for a field. For example, in Figure 20.15 you might choose to change the name Count of Order ID to Number of Orders or even simply Orders. You can also change field display names later in Excel; shortening the names creates easier-to-use field names in the task pane. Click Next to move to the second step, selecting dimensions and levels.

The wizard does not select dimensions for you; instead, you begin with a blank screen. In your PivotTable Report, dimensions will be placed in the Row, Column, and Page areas. Select the highest level in any dimension in the left pane, and drag-and-drop it on Drop Fields Here To Create A Dimension in the right pane to create a dimension, as shown in Figure 20.16. Add more dimensions the same way.

FIGURE 20.15

Select fields to be summarized in the OLAP Cube Wizard.

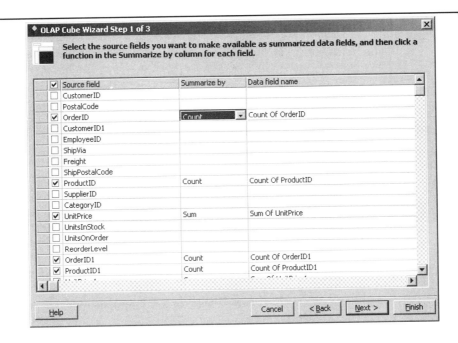

FIGURE 20.16

Select dimensions in the second step of the wizard.

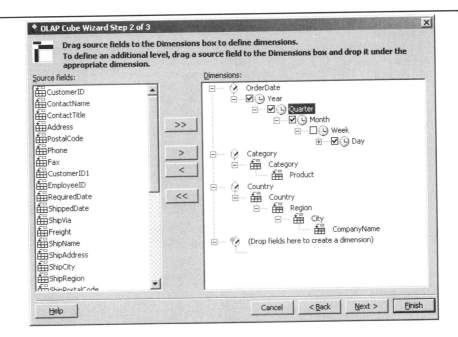

Date fields create their own levels—years, quarters, months, weeks, and days—that you can choose to include or omit. (You can't select both months and weeks to include, because weeks cross months.) For other dimensions, you'll need to create your own levels. For example, to create a Product level within the Categories dimension, drop the Product field directly on Category to create another level within Category (see Figure 20.16). Similarly, drop Region on Country and City on Region to create a geographical dimension.

 TIP To edit a level or dimension name, right-click and choose Rename from the shortcut menu. You can also remove, cut, and paste dimensions. When you remove a field or dimension, it moves to the bottom of the list in the left pane. You cannot copy a dimension.

The third step of the wizard, shown in Figure 20.17, offers three ways to save your OLAP cube. The correct choice depends on several factors: the system resources available to the people who use the cube, the amount of data the cube will contain, and how frequently users change pivot reports. If a cube will see heavy-duty use, you may want to create three identical cubes, saved three different ways, and test the response of each to determine which choice is best.

FIGURE 20.17

Choose a save method for the cube.

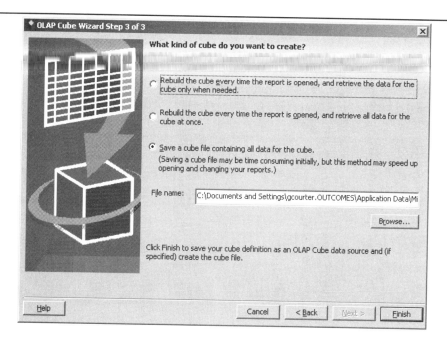

The first option stores the information required to generate the cube in your OLAP Query (and PivotTable Report in Excel). When you open the query, the cube is created and populated with the data for the fields currently used in the pivot table. Additional data is retrieved on demand. The limited initial data means that this is a good choice when users frequently *look* at the PivotTable Report based on this cube but don't *change* the report very often.

The second option stores the cube information the same way, but when the cube is opened in Query or Excel, all the data that might be required by the pivot table is downloaded at once. This is a better choice when users often change the layout of the pivot table, but it will, of course, take longer to load initially and it requires more memory than the first option.

The third option creates a separate cube file (with a .cub extension) that includes all the data for the cube. If you've got disk space and memory in quantity and need to rearrange your pivot tables a lot, this is a great choice. It takes longer to save this file the first time, but it will open more quickly than the first or second options because Query doesn't have to re-create the cube.

 TIP Use the third option to create an offline cube so you can work with the cube even when you can't connect to the database it was created from. Refresh the data when you reconnect.

Select an option and click Finish. Immediately, Query opens a Save As dialog box to prompt you to save a *cube definition* (.oqy) file. This file is separate from the cube file or cube creation instructions you selected in the wizard. You can't edit the cube directly, but you can create new cubes from the cube definition file. Open the cube definition file in Query and launch the OLAP Cube Wizard again to create a new cube. The .oqy file is added to the Queries tab of the Choose Data Source dialog box, so you can use it as you would any other query in Excel. Save the .oqy file, and Query will begin creating the OLAP cube. You are asked whether you want to return the cube to Excel and begin analyzing your data. When you choose Yes, Excel prompts you for a location for the data table.

Working with a Cube in Excel

 In Excel, the OLAP cube dimensions and measures appear on the PivotTable task pane. It's worth noticing a field's icon; if the field is a summarized field, the icon has numbers. Dimensions have a lined icon. You can't place dimensions in the Data area, or measures in the Page, Row, or Column areas of the table. Each dimension's field button includes all the levels you chose or added for the dimension, so dragging the OrderDate dimension into the PivotTable Column area, as shown in Figure 20.18, or the PivotChart x-axis brings along the years, quarters, and so on.

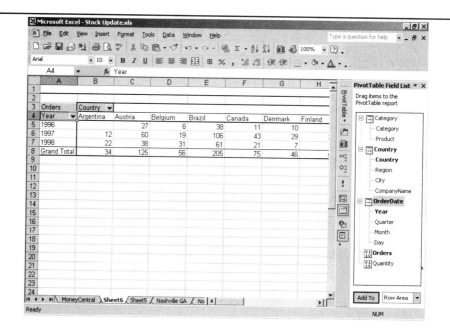

FIGURE 20.18

Drag dimensions into the Page, Column, and Row areas and measures into the data area.

Digging into Dimensions

Dimensions are what separate a cube from a traditional pivot table. There are three ways to display more data in a dimension: drilling down a dimension, using the Show Detail and Hide Detail buttons on the PivotTable toolbar, or selecting from a tree view of the dimension. Drill down by double-clicking the level in which you want to see more detail. In Figure 20.19, for example, you could double-click 1996 to see the four quarters; double-clicking one of the quarters would expand the months or weeks.

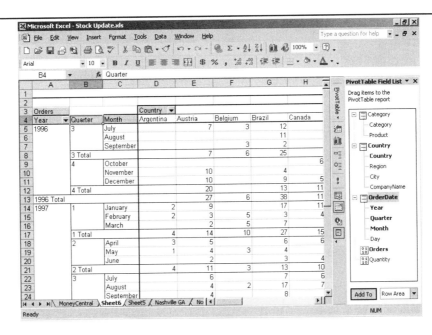

FIGURE 20.19

Double-click a dimension to see more detail.

Instead of double-clicking each entry to expand an entire dimension, use the Show Detail and Hide Detail buttons. Select the row or column button and click the Show Detail button to expand every entry one level. Click again to expand the detail by two levels. You can show or hide a selected item as well as an entire row or column.

To expand, collapse, or filter a dimension, click the drop-down arrow on the dimension button to open a tree view of the dimension.

Use the plus and minus icons to expand and collapse the display, and use the check boxes to show or hide levels and items in a level. Click once on a checked box to add a double check mark, which displays the data in that level and the next level of detail.

Save your Excel workbook to save the information required to connect to the query and cube. The next time you need to work with this cube, you can simply open the workbook and Excel will connect to the cube file.

CHAPTER 21

Using Excel's Workgroup Tools

FEATURING

- Working with existing templates

- Creating templates

- Inserting comments in cells

- Using lookup functions

- E-mailing and routing workbooks

- Sharing workbooks

- Tracking changes

- Resolving conflicts

- Merging workbooks

Excel supplies powerful assistance for maintaining spreadsheet consistency throughout your workgroup, department, or organization. We'll start with templates, which allow you to provide a uniform look for your worksheets. Macro-powered templates are an easy way to have other users enter data consistently so it can be analyzed with ease. When you share or circulate nontemplate Excel files among reviewers, Excel's revision features will help you keep track of changes and comments.

Using and Creating Templates

Templates are workbooks that are used to create other workbooks. Templates let you quickly construct workbooks that are identical in format, giving your work a standardized look. Excel includes some templates; you can create others for your personal use or for users in your workplace unfamiliar with Excel or your organization's standards for workbook formatting.

Templates are a big time-saver when you need to periodically create workbooks with identical or similar features—much faster than copying an existing workbook and deleting the information you don't want to keep. With a template, you determine the look and feel of data. If, for example, you have a number of clients that send you data, you can send them a template with data validation to ensure that the data is entered in the proper columns with appropriate formatting.

An Excel template can include text, numbers, formatting, formulas, and all the other features you already use. When you open a template, Excel opens a copy and the original template is not altered. This protects the original template from accidental changes—yet another reason to save workbooks created for other users as templates.

There are several ways to distribute a template. You can set a template as the default template so it will be used for every new workbook. You can keep a template for your own use, or store the template in a shared folder on a network or intranet so others can use it.

Working with Existing Templates

Excel includes predesigned templates that you can use or modify. To open a template, choose File ➢ New from the menu to display the New Workbook task pane. (The New button on the Standard toolbar opens an empty Excel workbook based on the default template.)

Click the General Templates link to open the New dialog box. The General templates are on the Spreadsheet Solutions tab. Select any template icon to preview the template. To open a template, double-click the icon or select it and click OK. If the template is not installed, Excel will install it. You may be prompted for the Office XP CD.

Click Templates On My Web Sites to locate templates stored on a local intranet or Internet site. To locate more templates, click Templates On Microsoft.com. Predictably, most templates on Microsoft.com are Word templates, but there's an adequate selection of Excel templates for Finance and Accounting and Business Forms. To preview a template, click the template link and agree to the license agreement. To download the template, click the Edit In Excel link on the preview page and save the template.

Entering Data

The Sales Invoice template, shown in Figure 21.1, is a typical Excel template. The cells with standard text and formulas are protected; you can't select, for example, the Total cells in column M.

FIGURE 21.1

The Sales Invoice template is a typical Excel template

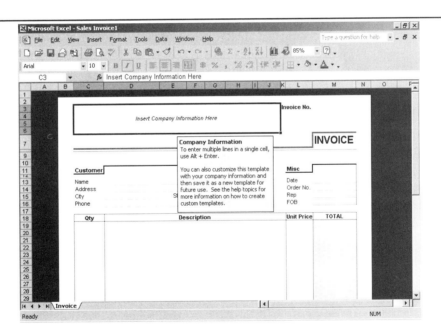

Select a cell with an italicized placeholder—*Insert Company Information Here*—to view a screen tip. Some templates include comments; cells with a red triangular comment indicator include comments. To view a comment, move the mouse over the cell.

Creating Templates for Personal Use

You can create a template for workbooks that you use frequently. For example, you might use Excel to complete a weekly payroll and put all the payroll worksheets for one month into a separate workbook.

Rather than constructing a new workbook each month, you can create a monthly payroll template. At the beginning of each month you can create a new workbook from the template. Your template will differ from a regular workbook in four specific ways:

- You'll save the file as a template (.xlt file extension) rather than a regular workbook (.xls).

- It will contain only the text, formulas, and formatting that remain the same each month.

- The template will include visual formatting clues and comments to assist users.

- It will be saved in the Office Templates folder or a shared folder for others to use.

You can create a template from scratch or base it on an existing workbook. If you're using an existing workbook, first make sure that all the formulas work, and that numbers and text are formatted appropriately. Remove the text and numbers that will be entered each time the template is used. Don't remove formulas—although the results of the formula change, the formulas themselves remain the same.

 NOTE If you're creating a template from scratch, you still need to enter (and then remove) values to test the template's formulas before saving the template.

When saving a template, be sure to follow these steps:

1. Click the Save button or choose File ➢ Save As.

2. In the Save As Type control, choose Template from the drop-down list. The Save In control will change to the default Templates folder.

3. Enter a name for the template in the File Name text box.

4. Click the Save button.

Creating Templates for Other Users

Presumably you know where you should and shouldn't enter data in a workbook you use regularly. You're familiar with the data to be entered. If you create a template for a frequently used workbook, you don't need to build in a lot of assistance.

When you create a template for other users, you can't assume that they know how to use it. Even if the folks using the template initially are experienced users, those who succeed them may know little or nothing about your organization, Excel, or your template. If you don't invest the time required to create a solid template, you'll get to be the trainer and help desk for your template when new employees use it. The following features make a template easier to use:

- Borders and shading let users know where they should—and shouldn't—enter text or other information.

- Cells that shouldn't be altered are protected (see "Protecting Workbooks, Worksheets, and Ranges" later in this chapter).

- Comments (choose Insert Comment from the shortcut menu) provide assistance where users might have questions about data entry.

- Data validation (see Chapter 17, "Solving Business Problems with the Analysis Tools") provides input messages and error messages to guide data entry.

- Any extra worksheets are removed from the workbook.

When you're finished creating the template, choose File ➤ Save As, and save the workbook as type Template. You can create a folder within the Templates folder to hold your personal templates. Other than the General tab, tabs in the New Workbook dialog box represent folders in the Templates folder. The template will be included on the General tab (or tab representing the folder you created) of the New dialog box. Save the template in a shared folder to make it accessible for other users.

 WARNING Don't save templates in Exchange Server folders. When a user opens a template from a public folder, they open the original template.

Editing a Template

To modify a template, open the template from the Templates folder with File ➤ Open rather than File ➤ New. When you are finished editing, save and close the template. You're not limited to templates you created; you can modify the canned Microsoft templates as well. See "Protecting Worksheets and Ranges" later in this chapter for information on unlocking the standard templates.

 NOTE　It's good practice to save your version of a standard template with a new name.

As you gain experience with Excel, you can add other features to templates, like command buttons and custom toolbars. Use Excel's Help feature to find more information on template design and modification. Refer to Chapter 18, "Automating Excel with Macros," for information on recording simple macros which you can attach to buttons or menu options.

EXPERT TIP　The File menu includes a list of recently opened files. After you create a template, the list will include the template you just created. If you or another user opens the template from the File menu, the template—not a copy of the template—will open. To clear the recently used file list from the menu, first save and close the template; then choose Tools ➢ Options to open the Options dialog box. On the General tab, turn off the Recently Used Files check box and click OK to close the Options dialog box and clear the list. Reopen the Options dialog box and enable the check box, and Excel will resume displaying recently used files with the next files you save.

Using Lookup Functions

Excel's lookup functions can be used in any workbook, but they are particularly useful in templates. Lookups retrieve information from an Excel database based on a user entry. For example, a user can enter a customer number, and Excel will return the customer's name, mailing address, last order date, or other information from a database. Returning the data from a list ensures consistency in the guise of user convenience.

In the template shown in Figure 21.2, a user enters a salesperson's ID in B3; the salesperson's name and region are returned to cells B5 and D5. When a customer's ID is entered in column B, the customer name and discount are retrieved from another database.

The Commission Calculation worksheet uses VLOOKUP functions to return salesperson and customer information.

Calculation worksheet

Lookups to SalesStaff database

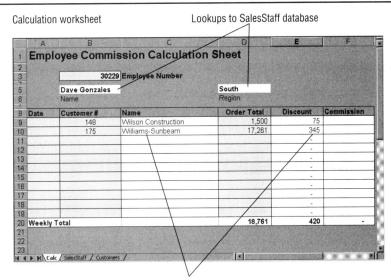

Employee Commission Calculation Sheet

| | 30229 | Employee Number | | | |

| Dave Gonzales | | | | South | |
| Name | | | | Region | |

Date	Customer #	Name	Order Total	Discount	Commission
	148	Wilson Construction	1,500	75	
	175	Williams-Sunbeam	17,261	345	
				-	
				-	
				-	
				-	
				-	
				-	
				-	
				-	
				-	
Weekly Total			18,761	420	-

Lookups to Customers database

SalesStaff database

EmplNum	LastName	FirstName	Region	Years
11983	Kershner	Irwin	East	3
20923	Billings	Bart	North	5
20957	Adams	Alicia	East	3
22764	Barker	Chuck	North	5
30229	Gonzales	Dave	South	3
41984	Wilson	Jeremy	West	7
45832	Brackett	Art	South	4
55672	Vu	Myha	East	1
56566	Lorenzo	Elmo	South	4

Customers database

Customer Number	Company Name	Address	City	State	ZipCode	Discount
141	Lassiter Manufacturing	950 Pierce Lane	Boise	ID	83703	2%
148	Wilson Construction	3611 E. Perkins	Sandusky	OH	44870	5%
151	Johnson Controls	3000 Plaza Blanc	Santa Fe	NM	87505	2%
153	Delta Construction	2600 Pali Hwy	Honolulu	HI	96817	0%
161	Fellowes Corp.	Pittman Avenue	Camp Hill	AL	36850	3%
172	Newell Office Group	1300 Lincoln	Newton	MA	02165	2%
175	Williams-Sunbeam	2501 Adams Ave.	Ogden	UT	84401	2%
178	Borgman Controls	14021 Borgman	Pine River	MN	56474	0%

There are three lookup functions: LOOKUP, HLOOKUP, and VLOOKUP. The generic LOOKUP function is the least used. The VLOOKUP and HLOOKUP functions have 90 degrees of difference. HLOOKUP searches horizontally through the first row of a database to find a matching value, and VLOOKUP searches vertically. The organization of a database—with each record occupying a row rather than a column—makes the VLOOKUP, which searches in the first column of a database, the most frequently used lookup function. The syntax for the VLOOKUP function is:

```
=VLOOKUP(lookupvalue, tablearray, indexnumber, rangelookup)
```

Lookup value The cell that contains the value you want Excel to locate in the first column of the database.

Table array The database range.

Index number The number of the column that contains the value Excel should return; the first column is column 1.

Range lookup An optional argument and a Boolean value (TRUE or FALSE) that indicates whether the table array is sorted on the first column. If FALSE, then Excel will only return a value when it finds an exact match for the lookup value in the table array. If TRUE or not specified, Excel will return the last value that is greater than or equal to the lookup value.

 TIP Set the range lookup to FALSE if you're searching in a primary key field (such as a customer number or part number), even if the list is sorted.

The table arrays (databases) shown in Figure 21.2 are stored on other sheets of the workbook in named ranges: SalesStaff and Customers. The simple VLOOKUP function used in D5 is shown in Figure 21.3: =VLOOKUP(B3,SalesStaff,4,FALSE). The formula uses the lookup value in B3 (the salesperson's number) to search the SalesStaff database. When Excel finds an exact match for the value in B3 in the first column, it returns the value in column 4, the region, to cell D5. The lookup is nested in an IF statement that uses an ISBLANK function to ensure that Excel displays a blank rather than an #N/A error when cell B5 is empty. The complete formula is:

```
=IF(ISBLANK(B3),"",VLOOKUP(B3,SalesStaff,4,FALSE))
```

The full name displayed in B5 uses two lookup functions and concatenates the first name from the third column of the database with the last name from the second column to display the full name:

```
=IF(ISBLANK(B3),"",VLOOKUP(B3,SalesStaff,3,FALSE)&" "&VLOOKUP(B3,SalesStaff,
2,FALSE))
```

The VLOOKUP formulas in columns C and E refer to the Customers table. This formula returns the customer name from the second column of the range:

```
=IF(ISBLANK(B9),"",VLOOKUP(B9,Customers,2,FALSE))
```

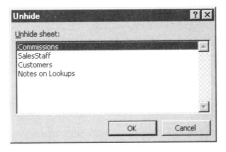

FIGURE 21.3

The formula for the Region returns a value from the fourth column of the SalesStaff range.

In the formulas thus far, we've displayed an empty string ("") when the lookup value was empty. We can't do this in the formulas in column E. The formulas in column E multiply the customer's discount from the database by the sales figure in column D. Multiplying by a string results in an error, so we'll place a zero in the cell if the lookup value in column B is empty:

```
=IF(ISBLANK(B9),0,VLOOKUP(B9,Customers,7,FALSE))*D9
```

Hiding Worksheets

In our template, the sheets that contain the SalesStaff and Customers worksheets are normally hidden (Format ➤ Sheet ➤ Hide) from the user. To unhide hidden sheets in a workbook, choose Format ➤ Sheet ➤ Unhide to open the Unhide dialog box, shown below. Select the sheet you wish to display and click OK to display the worksheet.

PART

III

CRUNCHING DATA WITH EXCEL

Protecting Workbooks, Worksheets, and Ranges

If it's this easy to display the hidden sheets in our template, we'll only be hiding them from novices. Templates need to be further protected to prevent users from unhiding the hidden sheets. You can protect workbooks, worksheets, and ranges in Excel 2002.

Protecting Workbooks

To protect a workbook, choose Tools ➢ Protection ➢ Protect Workbook from the menu.

To protect the structure of a workbook so that worksheets can't be hidden, unhidden, renamed, moved, inserted, or deleted, enable the Structure check box. To lock in the size and position of the workbook's windows when the workbook is opened, enable the Windows check box.

To prevent other users from turning off the protection, type a password and click OK. You'll be prompted to type the password again. Workbook passwords are case sensitive.

 WARNING If you lose the password, you won't be able to remove the workbook protection without resorting to utilities that break passwords. Many companies don't allow their employees to install this type of software for obvious reasons.

Protecting Worksheets and Ranges

Each cell in a workbook has a locked property which is enabled by default. The property is enforced when you protect the cell's worksheet. Before protecting a worksheet, you can unlock selected cells in one of two ways:

• Disable the cells' Locked property to unlock the cells for all users.

- Use the new Allow Users To Edit Ranges feature to provide specific users with permission to edit the cells.

With either option, the remaining worksheet cells are locked only when you protect the worksheet.

 NOTE The standard Excel templates are protected and must be unprotected before you can unlock cells.

Unlocking Ranges

To unlock cells, select the cells and choose Format ➤ Format Cells or right-click and choose Format Cells from the shortcut menu to open the Format Cells dialog box. On the Protection tab, turn off the Locked check box.

Allowing Users to Edit Ranges

 In prior versions of Excel, you could set two levels of password-based permission: read only, or read/write permission. If a user could edit some cells, they could edit all cells. The new range-editing feature provides two new types of security: user-based and range-based. Permission can be granted based on either passwords or network authentication, and different permissions can be granted for specific ranges of cells. For example, in our workbook, we might let one user edit customer address information and another user edit only customer discount data.

 NOTE This feature is dependent on the operating system, and it only works with Windows 2000.

To grant permission to edit ranges before protecting a worksheet, choose Tools ➤ Protection ➤ Allow Users To Edit Ranges to open the Allow Users To Edit Ranges dialog box.

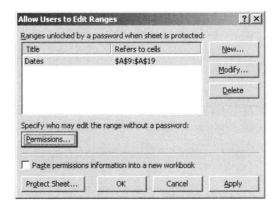

Click the New button to add a range. In the New Range dialog box (shown below), enter a name for the range. Specify the range in the Refers To Cells text box. Hold Ctrl to select noncontiguous ranges. If the workbook will be used by users who aren't on your network (including remote users), enter a password for this range. Users will be required to enter the password to edit cells.

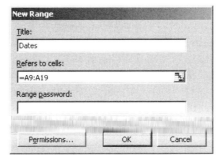

If all users with edit permission will be logged on to your network, click the Permissions button to open the Permissions dialog box. Click the Add button to select users or groups from your network and allow or deny editing rights without a password. Click OK until you return to the Allow Users To Edit Ranges dialog box. Click Add to specify permissions for another range.

When you are finished setting password or network-authenticated permissions for users, click the Protect Sheet button to open the Protect Sheet dialog box. Enter a password (which you'll need to know if you ever want to change permissions for the worksheet) and verify the worksheet features you wish to protect. Click OK to protect the worksheet.

To unprotect a worksheet, choose Tools ➤ Protection ➤ Unprotect Worksheet. You'll be prompted for the password you entered in the Protect Sheet dialog box. After unprotecting the sheet, you can modify or delete the settings for the sheet and ranges.

Working with Workgroups

Excel's sharing and tracking features make it easy for you to collaborate with others by sharing the same workbook file among multiple users. Excel's workgroup features range from simple tools for distributing files for comments—e-mailing and routing—to powerful features that allow you to distribute copies of workbooks and merge changes from the copies into a single file. Excel minimizes the potential for problems by giving you control over how the changes made by all of the users are merged into a single, error-free file.

E-mailing Workbooks

There are two ways to e-mail Excel worksheets to another user. You can send an entire workbook as an attachment, or send a copy of the active sheet as HTML in the body of an e-mail message. Send the entire workbook when the recipient has Excel and you want them to be able to manipulate the data in Excel. When you send a copy of the active sheet, the recipient can view the information but cannot alter it. They do not, however, need Excel to view the worksheet; they only need Outlook or a Web browser.

 NOTE To e-mail a worksheet as HTML, you need Outlook. To e-mail a message as an attachment, you need Outlook, Outlook Express, or another MAPI- or VIM-compatible messaging system.

To e-mail the entire workbook, choose File ➤ Send To ➤ Mail Recipient (As Attachment). To e-mail the active sheet as HTML, choose File ➤ Send To ➤ Mail Recipient. The Office Assistant will prompt you to send the entire workbook as an attachment, or the active sheet as an e-mail message.

Routing Workbooks

Routing lets recipients view a workbook in a particular order. For example, you may want to have one of your co-workers review a workbook before you send it to your administrative assistant so that your assistant can see the changes or comments that your co-worker made. You can also use routing to send a workbook to a distribution list. You can track the status of the routed workbook as it moves from one recipient to the next. After all recipients have reviewed the workbook, it automatically returns to you. To route a workbook:

1. Open the workbook.

2. Choose File ➢ Send To ➢ Routing Recipient to open the Routing Slip dialog box.

3. Click the Address button to open the Select Recipients dialog box and add recipients as you would in Outlook. You will be prompted to allow access to the Outlook address book.

4. Select the recipients in the order that you want them to receive the workbook.

 TIP If you choose a distribution list as the recipient, all the members of the list are treated as a single recipient and will receive the workbook at the same time. To route the workbook to members of a distribution list in order, select the individual members, rather than the name of the list.

5. Click Route to route the workbook.

OR

Click Add Slip to prepare the workbook for routing at a later time. When you're ready to route the workbook, open it and choose File ➤ Send To ➤ Next Routing recipient.

Posting Workbooks

You can post an Excel workbook directly to a Microsoft Exchange folder. The workbook will appear in the list of items in the folder in Outlook and the Exchange Web client, and users with access to the folder will have the same permissions for the workbook as they do for other items in the folder. To further protect a workbook, assign passwords (or set permissions to edit ranges) to the workbook before posting it; users will be prompted for their passwords when they open the posted workbook. To post a workbook to an Exchange folder:

1. Choose File ➤ Send To ➤ Exchange Folder to open the Send To Exchange Folder dialog box.

2. Select the folder you want to post a copy of the workbook in.

3. Click OK.

 TIP If you post a shared workbook, sharing will be turned off.

Sharing Workbooks and Tracking Changes

Sharing allows more than one user to access a workbook at the same time. Tracking stores information about workbook changes by user. Sharing and tracking are intertwined. You can only track changes in a shared workbook; tracked changes are kept for a duration set in the Share Workbook dialog box.

Sharing Workbooks

If you want others to be able to use a workbook while you have it open, you need to share the workbook and ensure that it is stored on a shared drive that other users can access. Choose Tools ➤ Share Workbook from the menu to open the Share Workbook dialog box.

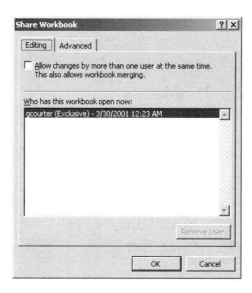

By default, the current user has exclusive rights to a workbook. On the Editing tab, enable the Allow Changes check box to make the file accessible to other users. Then move to the Advanced tab to set options for tracking changes and resolving conflicts explained in the next sections.

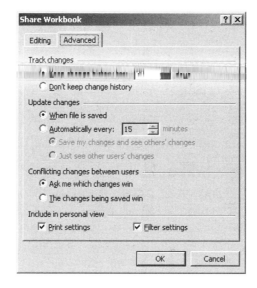

If you choose to track changes in a *change history*, select the number of days the change history should be kept.

TIP You can only track changes in shared workbooks. To use the tracking feature on workbooks that only you use, password-protect the shared workbook and don't give anyone the password.

Whether you track changes or not, you need to set when changes are updated. The default is to update changes only when the file is saved. This means that each time you (or another user) save, Excel will save your changes and update your workbook with changes made by other users. You can choose to have your workbook updated Automatically every set number of minutes; if you then choose the Save My Changes option, your changes will be saved when the update occurs. If you update changes Automatically, other users still won't see your changes until you save—unless they also choose to see saved changes Automatically rather than waiting until they save.

When two or more users make different changes in the same cell, it causes a conflict. Set the Conflicting Changes option to indicate how conflicts should be resolved. Excel can prompt you to resolve conflicts or automatically accept the saved changes.

The Personal view contains your print and filter settings for the workbook. These settings do not affect other users' view of the workbook. Use the check boxes to include or exclude these settings when the workbook is saved.

When you close the dialog box, Excel will prompt you to save the workbook. If you return to the Shared Workbook dialog box, you'll notice that you no longer have the workbook open exclusively, as other Excel users can now open it.

Tracking and Updating Changes

When you track changes in a workbook, Excel notes each change in each workbook cell. Display the changes by choosing Tools ➢ Track Changes ➢ Highlight Changes and enabling Track Changes While Editing.

When tracking is enabled, a changed cell has a cell indicator in the upper-left corner, color-coded by user. Hover over the cell, and Excel displays a screen tip to show you the changes that have been made.

> **gcourter, 3/30/2001 12:36 AM:**
> Changed cell D25 from '2/1/2001' to '1/31/2001'.

Working in a Shared Workbook

When Highlight Changes is enabled, each change made is noted in a comment, and changed cells are flagged with a cell indicator in the upper-left corner. Excel assigns a different triangle color to each user who modifies the workbook, so you can visually inspect the workbook to find all the changes made by one user. When you save the workbook, you accept the changes, so the triangle and comment disappear.

Some Excel features aren't available in shared workbooks. For example, while a workbook is shared, you can't do any of the following:

- Delete worksheets

- Add or apply conditional formatting and data validation

- Insert or delete ranges of cells (you can still insert and delete individual cells, rows, and columns), charts, hyperlinks, or other objects (including those created with Draw)

- Group or outline data

However, you can use the features before you share a workbook, or you can temporarily unshare the workbook, make changes, and then turn sharing on again. See Excel's Online Help for the complete list of limitations of shared workbooks.

 WARNING If you unshare a workbook, it cannot be merged with other copies of the shared workbook. For more information, see "Merging Workbook Changes" later in this chapter.

Resolving Conflicts

If changes you are saving conflict with changes saved by another user, you'll be prompted to resolve the conflict (unless you changed the Conflicting Changes setting in the Advanced tab of the Share Workbook dialog box). In the Resolve Conflict dialog box, you can review each change individually and accept your change or others' changes, or accept/reject changes in bulk.

Viewing the Change History

You can examine all the changes that have been saved in a workbook since you turned on the change history. Choose Tools ➢ Track Changes ➢ Highlight Changes to open the Highlight Changes dialog box.

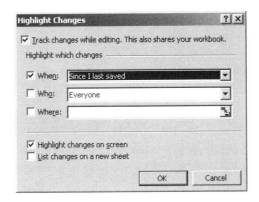

In the dialog box, select the time period for the changes you want to review, and specify the users whose changes you want to see. If you only want to see changes for a particular range or sheet, select the range you want to view. You can view the changes on screen or on a separate worksheet in the workbook.

When you view the change history on a separate worksheet, you can filter the changes to find changes made by different users or on specific dates. When you remove a workbook from shared use, the change history is turned off and reset. If you want to keep the changes, select the information on the History worksheet and copy it to another worksheet before unsharing the workbook.

Accepting or Rejecting Changes

You can review a workbook and accept or reject changes in bulk or individually as you do in Microsoft Word. To begin reviewing, choose Tools ➢ Track Changes ➢ Accept Or Reject Changes to open the Select Changes To Accept Or Reject dialog box.

Specify the time period, users, and cell range you wish to review. If you don't specify a range, you'll review the entire workbook. Click OK to open the Accept Or Reject Changes dialog box.

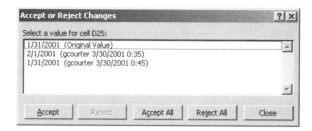

To accept or reject all changes, click the Accept All or Reject All button. To accept or reject a specific change, select the change and then click the Accept or Reject button. Click Close when you are finished reviewing changes.

Merging Workbook Changes

If you anticipate many conflicting changes in a shared workbook, or if you want users to be able to make changes independently and then review all changes at once, make and distribute copies of the shared workbook. To create the copies, use Save As and give each copy of the workbook a different name. Then you can merge the copies when users are done with their changes. You can only merge workbooks that have the same change history, so it's important that none of the users turns off sharing while using the workbook (see the sidebar "Protecting Workbooks for Merging"). The history must be complete when you merge the workbooks.

If, for example, you set the number of days for the history at 30 days and users keep the workbooks for 32 days, you won't be able to merge the workbooks. Before you make copies of the shared workbook, make sure you set the history to allow enough time for changes and merging. If you're uncertain, set the history to 1000 days or an equally ridiculous length of time.

Follow these steps to merge shared workbooks:

1. Open your copy of the shared workbook that you want to merge changes into.

2. Choose Tools ➢ Compare And Merge Workbooks. If you haven't saved your copy of the workbook, you'll be prompted to do so.

3. In the Select Files To Merge Into Current Workbook dialog box, choose the copy (or copies) of the shared workbook containing the changes you wish to merge. Click OK.

Protecting Workbooks for Merging

To prevent users from turning off sharing or changing the change history, password-protect the workbook before sharing and distributing it. The process for protecting shared workbooks is changed in Excel 2002:

1. Choose Tools ➢ Share Workbook to open the Share Workbook dialog box.
2. Select the Editing tab and make sure the Allow Changes By More Than One User At The Same Time check box is enabled.
3. On the Advanced tab, select Keep Change History For, and enter a number of days that vastly exceeds the number of days the workbooks will be shared. If you're not sure, enter 1000. Set any other options you wish on the Advanced tab.
4. On the Editing tab, turn the Allow Changes check box back off so the workbook is not shared. Click OK.
5. Choose Tools ➢ Protection ➢ Protect And Share Workbook.
6. Enable the Sharing With Track Changes check box.
7. Type a password in the Password text box.
8. Reenter the password when prompted.
9. Save the workbook.

AND NOW, PRESENTING WITH POWERPOINT!

LEARN TO:

- **Create a basic presentation**

- **Format text and slides**

- **Add objects, transitions, and slide animation**

- **Use PowerPoint in a workgroup**

- **Prepare notes, handouts, and overhead transparencies**

- **Automate and narrate your presentation**

CHAPTER 22

CREATING A PRESENTATION

FEATURING

- Using the AutoContent Wizard

- Switching between PowerPoint views

- Entering and editing text

- Using design templates or blank presentations

- Applying slide layouts

- Importing slides from existing presentations

- Importing an outline from Word

Voices in the room fall to a hush as you make your way to the podium. Several speakers have been before the board already, not one of them with an idea as good as the one you are about to present. You know what they say—it's all in the delivery. This is where you make it or break it. Gathering your notes and your wits, you take a deep breath and begin...

It wasn't so long ago that it was common to watch presenters fumble with black-and-white overheads, using a piece of cardboard to help the audience track the progress of the presentation. Now it's fairly typical to see PowerPoint presentations in sales meetings, planning sessions, college lectures, and even elementary classrooms. If you're using PowerPoint 2002, you've got a huge edge. New animation features make it easy to create a presentation that truly stands out. When you make your next presentation—whether it's to demonstrate a product, outline a project, or sell an idea—PowerPoint 2002 offers a way to take the focus off you and put it where it belongs—on what you have to say!

Use PowerPoint to create electronic slide shows that can enliven even the most apathetic crowd. If you don't want to give your presentation electronically, you can create vivid, full-color overhead transparencies and valuable audience handouts that will supplement the most polished presentations. You can create presentations that run automatically, like those displayed in kiosks at trade shows. With PowerPoint 2002's enhanced Web features, you can create Web-ready presentations for display on the Internet that are natural tools to explain multistep processes. Whether you are creating slides for a departmental presentation or displaying information on the company Web site, PowerPoint allows you to quickly grab the attention of your audience and deliver your message in a most memorable way!

Steps to a Quality Presentation

Every PowerPoint presentation consists of a series of *slides*, text or objects displayed on a graphic background, as shown in Figure 22.1. You create your presentation by adding text and objects (like a chart, image, sound file, or video clip) to slides.

FIGURE 22.1

A PowerPoint slide

For every presentation you create in PowerPoint, you'll go through these steps:

1. Plan the presentation and gather materials you'll want to include.

2. Create the presentation by creating slides, entering and editing text, and arranging slides.

3. Apply a presentation design. Modify the design if necessary.

4. Format individual slides if you wish.

5. Add objects to the presentation.

6. Apply and modify transitions, animation effects, and links for electronic presentations.

7. Create audience materials and speaker notes.

8. Rehearse and add slide timings.

9. Present the presentation.

You don't have to work through all the steps sequentially. With PowerPoint, you can create and modify a few slides, adding objects, animation, and speaker notes, and then insert more slides. If you find the slides distracting, you can create your presentation's content as an outline and then work on the aesthetics.

Creating a Presentation Using the AutoContent Wizard

NEW▶ When you launch PowerPoint, the task pane automatically displays New Presentation options, as shown in Figure 22.2.

When you launch PowerPoint, options for starting a presentation appear in the task pane.

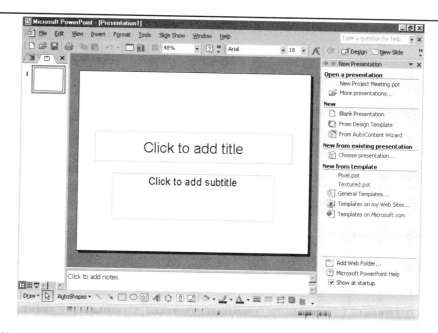

You can open an existing presentation or create a new presentation using one of the three listed options. We'll create our first presentation using the AutoContent Wizard and discuss the other creation methods, Design Template and Blank Presentation, later in this chapter.

NOTE To have PowerPoint start each session with the task pane hidden, choose Tools ➢ Options, select the View tab, and disable the Startup Task Pane check box. If this is your first experience with task panes, we recommend leaving it on for a while. It seemed like a nuisance to us at first, but we soon incorporated it completely into our work styles.

The AutoContent Wizard is helpful for beginning users of PowerPoint because it generates an outline and applies a considerable amount of slide formatting automatically.

It's also a good tool for a more advanced user whose presentation matches one of the AutoContent templates or who wants some help structuring a presentation. As its name implies, it is designed to suggest content.

The AutoContent Wizard works like any of the other wizards in Office. You move through a series of steps that help you design your presentation. In each step, click Next to advance or Back to return to a previous step.

1. If you have just launched PowerPoint, choose AutoContent Wizard from the task pane and click OK to start the wizard. (If the task pane isn't visible, turn it on by clicking View ➢ Task Pane. If necessary, click the task pane drop-down arrow and choose New From Existing Presentation to display options for beginning a presentation.) The first step explains the wizard. Click Next.

2. In the second step, choose the PowerPoint presentation type that most closely matches your topic. You can scroll through all the presentation types or narrow your choices by selecting a category from the button list. Click Next.

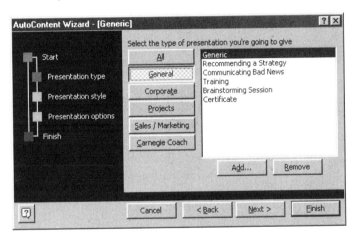

3. Select a style for your presentation. Will this presentation be displayed on the Internet? Will you be using black-and-white overheads? The choice you make now does not prohibit you from switching to another style later, but it limits the options PowerPoint displays in the wizard. Click Next.

NOTE If you are creating an online presentation, refer to Chapter 30, "Creating Online Presentations with PowerPoint," for more on PowerPoint's dynamic Web-publishing features.

4. In the fourth step of the wizard, enter the title that should appear on the first slide. If you would like to include additional information on every slide, such as a company, project, or department name or the current date, activate those features here. Click Next.

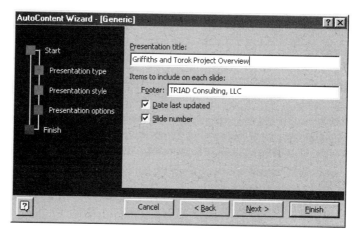

5. Click Finish to create the presentation.

Viewing Slides

One of the keys to working comfortably and efficiently in PowerPoint is understanding views. The term *view* refers to how you look at and work on your presentation. PowerPoint 2002 offers several different views, three of which are accessible from the View menu and view buttons: Normal view, Slide Sorter view, and Slide Show view. The other views, Master view and Notes Page view, have special features that we will discuss at length in Chapters 23 and 25. While you'll quickly choose one view as your favorite, you'll probably work in all of the views while you're building your presentation.

Normal View

When you click Finish, the AutoContent Wizard closes and the presentation is displayed in Normal view, as shown in Figure 22.3. The outline (with text suggested by the AutoContent Wizard) is displayed on the left; your first slide is shown on the right. The smaller pane at the bottom of the window allows you to add speaker notes for this slide.

Normal view is a *tri-pane view* that allows you to see three different aspects of your presentation within one window. The sections of the tri-pane window are resizable so you can choose the element(s) of the presentation you wish to focus on.

> **TIP** The Drawing toolbar is on by default. Hide it by choosing View ➤ Toolbars from the menu (or by right-clicking any toolbar) if you need a little extra room for the document window.

FIGURE 22.3

Figure 22.3: Normal view includes a large Slide pane, an Outline pane, and a smaller pane for notes.

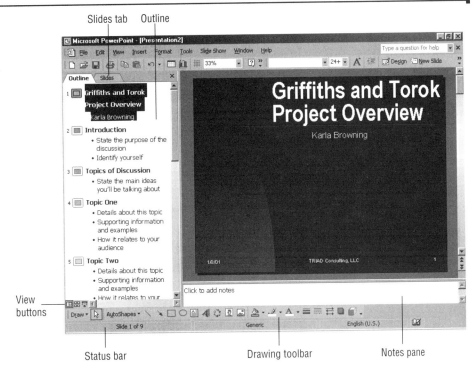

Slides tab   Outline

View buttons

Status bar   Drawing toolbar   Notes pane

NEW▶

The Outline pane in Normal view has two tabs: Outline and Slides. When the AutoContent Wizard finishes, the Outline tab, which shows the text on each slide, is displayed by default. For those of us who are visually oriented, it helps to display the slides themselves rather than the text of the slides. To see slide miniatures in the left-side pane, as shown in Figure 22.4, click the Slides tab.

When you're viewing slide miniatures in the left-side pane, the tabs at the top of the pane show icons rather than words. Click the Outline View icon to show slide text in the left pane.

TIP If you accidentally close the left-side pane that displays the outline and slide minia-tures, you can bring it back by clicking View ➢ Normal (Restore Panes).

FIGURE 22.4

FIGURE 22.4

Normal view lets the user display slide miniatures in the left-side pane.

 Three view buttons appear at the left end of the horizontal scroll bar; in Figure 22.3, the Normal View button is selected. The status bar displays the number of the active slide, the AutoContent presentation type, and the language used on the current slide.

You can change to Slide Sorter view or Slide Show view by clicking the appropriate view button at the bottom-left of the PowerPoint window or by choosing the view name from the View menu.

 Slide Sorter view allows you to see many slides at once. The number of slides shown depends on the zoom setting, your monitor size, and screen resolution. Power-Point defaults to 66 percent zoom, which allows you to see approximately 12 slides with display resolution settings of 800 × 600 pixels. If you wish to see more or fewer slides, you can adjust the zoom higher or lower or seize this opportunity to request a larger monitor from the appropriate person in your organization.

Click the Slide Show (From Current Slide) button to see how a slide will look in full-screen mode when you display your presentation. Click the mouse or press Enter to move from one slide to the next; if a slide has multiple lines of text, you might have to click once for each line. After the last slide, PowerPoint returns to the previous view. Press Esc if you want to end the slide show before the last slide.

When you switch from one view to another, the current slide remains current, regardless of view. For example, if you are on the fifth slide in Normal view and switch to Slide Sorter view, the fifth slide is selected. Clicking the Slide Show (From Current Slide) button begins the Slide Show with the fifth slide.

NOTE Slide Sorter view is discussed in more depth later in this chapter. For more information about Slide Show view, see Chapter 25, "Taking Your Show on the Road."

With the outline displayed in Normal view, presentation text is in the left pane of the tri-pane window. The selected slide is shown to the right of the outline. Below the slide is an area for notes if you choose to use them. Notes are hidden from the audience in an electronic presentation and are displayed in online or NetMeeting presentations only if you choose to display them. Unless you're adding notes to a Web presentation, think of the notes as somewhat private—the perfect place to put a reminder to distribute a handout or tell a specific joke, or the full text that you intend to present while the slide is displayed.

For efficiency's sake, you may wish to resize the panes in Normal view so that the one you're working in is larger. Simply point to any of the pane dividers, and your mouse pointer changes to the Resize tool. Drag to move the pane divider.

TIP If you don't see the Notes pane, point to the window divider directly above the Drawing toolbar. Click and drag upward to open the Notes pane.

There are several different ways to move between slides in Normal view. You can click anywhere in the outline to move to that slide. Or if slide miniatures are displayed in the left pane, simply click the one you want to view. You can also use the vertical scroll bar to move forward and backward through your slides, or use the PgUp and PgDn keys to browse slides. As you drag the vertical scroll bar, the slide number and slide title are displayed in a screen tip. If you wish to advance to the next slide or go back to the previous slide, you can use the double up- and double down-arrow buttons located at the bottom of the vertical scroll bar.

Which View Should You Use?

As you work in PowerPoint, you will discover that adjusting the view makes it easier to carry out certain types of formatting and editing. Similarly, you will find that certain types of editing are possible *only* in a specific view.

- In Normal view, you can enlarge the Outline pane to focus on text rather than objects or entire slides. You can't work with objects directly in the outline, but the text-only interface helps you focus on content rather than format.
- In Normal view, you can instead choose to make the outline smaller and enlarge the Slide pane to focus on the appearance of text and objects on each slide. Use this view when you want to position objects on a slide in relation to text.
- In Slide Sorter view, the focus is on entire slides, their order, and how they appear during the presentation.
- Slide Show view gives you a better idea of how your presentation will look when you eventually show it.

In general, choose Normal view to edit or insert text on slides, to insert objects, and for animation (see Chapter 24, "Objects, Transitions, and Animation"). Normal view lets you edit text either on the outline or on the slide, and the entire slide is displayed large enough to easily place objects and apply animation. Choose Slide Sorter view to change the order of slides or to apply slide transitions (see Chapter 24 for more information on transitions). Slide Show view is best used to preview your presentation before showing it or for full-screen preview of overheads.

Working on the Outline in Normal View

In the early stages of your presentation's development, you'll probably want to work in Normal view, which provides you with the most editing flexibility and allows you to see the text from multiple slides at one time: a bird's eye view of your presentation. As you know, you can resize the Outline pane to make it easier to work with text, yet you can still see in the right-side pane how the text you've entered fits on the slide. The Standard and Formatting toolbars are available for editing functions. You work with text as you would in Word.

NOTE When you begin your first presentation after installing PowerPoint, the toolbars are displayed on one row. Click the drop-down arrow at the end of the toolbar to see more buttons, or choose Show Buttons On Two Rows to see all buttons on both toolbars at once.

Entering and Editing Text

Replace the suggested contents in the slides created by the AutoContent Wizard before making substantial formatting changes. To edit, simply select the line of text you want to change by clicking the bullet or slide icon in front of that line. Overtype with new text. In a PowerPoint outline, there are five text levels below the slide title. Text entered at any level other than the title level is a point or a subpoint. Each level in the outline has a unique bullet.

Slide Title

- Level 1
  ◆Level 2
    ★Level 3
      • Level 4
        −Level 5

 TIP If you want to remove bullets from a level on all slides, don't format each slide. Choose View ➢ Master ➢ Slide Master and remove the bullets on the Slide Master. Click any view button to close the Slide Master. For more on the Slide Master, see Chapter 23, "Formatting and Designing a Presentation."

Working in a PowerPoint outline is similar to using Outline view in Word. As you type in the outline, press Enter at the end of a line to move to a new line. The new line is on the same level as the previous line. If you are at the end of a bulleted point when you press Enter, the next line starts with a bullet at the same level as the previous one. If you position the insertion point at the end of a slide's title and press Enter, PowerPoint inserts a new slide.

The Outlining toolbar is not visible by default in PowerPoint 2002. You must turn it on by clicking View ➤ Toolbars ➤ Outlining. If you haven't previously moved the Outlining toolbar, it displays vertically to the left of the outline.

After pressing Enter to start a new line, press the Tab key or click Demote to demote the text to a lower level. If you press Tab or click Demote again, you'll be at the next lower level.

To promote text to a higher level, either press Shift+Tab or click Promote. When you press Enter, you get a new line at the same level. To switch levels, you have to promote or demote.

In PowerPoint 2002 outlines, font size appears the same at each level. However, if you glance at the slide, you'll notice that PowerPoint automatically adjusts font size depending on the number of items contained on a slide, the available space in the text box, and the level at which the text is placed. This means that the text size for any given level can vary from slide to slide.

> **TIP** You can disable the feature that automatically adjusts font size by choosing Tools ➤ AutoCorrect ➤ AutoFormat As You Type. In the Apply As You Type settings, disable the Autofit Body Text To Placeholder check box. Note the similar option for title text. Disable it if you wish.

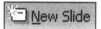

You can also add new slides to follow the slide where the insertion point is resting. Just click the New Slide button on the Formatting toolbar. The task pane opens with a list of layout options displayed. When you press the Enter key (notice that the insertion point is automatically positioned for a new slide title). You may select a different slide layout if you don't want to use the default. For more information, see "Selecting Slide Layouts" later in this chapter.

> **NOTE** If your insertion point is resting immediately in front of the title text when you insert a new slide, the new slide appears above, rather than below, the active slide.

Selecting Text, Lines, and Slides

Many of the methods used to select text in Word and Excel work here as well. Double-click a word to select it. To select a block of text, click at the beginning and Shift+click at the end. To select an entire point, click the bullet or icon in front of the text or triple-click anywhere within a point.

If you select a first-level point that has second-level points underneath it, the second-level points are also selected. Click and drag to select only the main point. Similarly, selecting the title using any method other than dragging selects the entire slide.

You can expand and collapse sections of the outline by using the Expand and Collapse buttons on the Outlining toolbar or by right-clicking a slide title and choosing Collapse or Expand from the shortcut menu. To collapse or expand multiple slides, select them and then right-click anywhere in the selection. Choose Expand or Collapse from the shortcut menu. You can also use the Expand All and Collapse All buttons to expand or collapse the entire outline.

Checking Spelling

PowerPoint includes the same spelling features as Word. AutoSpell automatically underlines misspelled words that you enter. Right-click an underlined word to see suggested correct spellings. Click the Spelling button on the Standard toolbar to check the spelling for an entire presentation. (For more information on spelling, see Chapter 4, "Putting Text and Language Tools to Work for You.")

EXPERT TIP   PowerPoint does not include a grammar check or a thesaurus. If you need to use these tools in a presentation, choose File ➢ Send To ➢ Microsoft Word. Choose the Outline Only option, and PowerPoint quickly saves your presentation as a Word document. In Word, choose Tools ➢ Spelling And Grammar to check both spelling and grammar. While you're at it, use Word's thesaurus to handle redundancies in the text. Make the necessary changes and send the Word document back to PowerPoint (File ➢ Send To ➢ Microsoft PowerPoint). This creates a new presentation, so if your grammar skills need a lot of support, check grammar before you invest time adding objects or applying designs, transitions, and animation to your presentation. When you're back in PowerPoint, you can still copy/paste text into Word if you want to quickly check grammar, or use the thesaurus, for newly added text.

Using Find and Replace

Use PowerPoint's Find feature to locate a text string in your presentation. You can replace existing text strings with new text by using Find and Replace. Choose Edit ➢ Find from the menu bar to open the Find dialog box. The feature works much the same as it does in Word (see "Finding and Replacing Text" in Chapter 4 for a refresher). Keep in mind a couple of things when you're using PowerPoint 2002's Find feature:

- If you use Find in Normal view, clicking Find Next moves to and selects the next text string that matches the Find What string.

- In Slide Sorter view, there isn't a Find Next button; instead, the button is Find All. Clicking Find All selects all the slides that contain the string.

Inserting, Deleting, and Moving Points and Slides

As you mouse over a bullet or slide icon in the outline, the pointer shape changes to a four-headed arrow, the tool for moving text and objects. To move a point (and all the subpoints beneath it), drag the bullet preceding that point. If you click a slide's icon, the entire slide—the title and any body text—is selected. Drag a slide icon to move the entire slide.

As you drag the selection toward its new location, a two-headed arrow replaces the four-headed arrow, and a horizontal line appears in the outline, as shown in Figure 22.5. If you drag-and-drop the horizontal line, the selected point(s) or slide move to the new location.

FIGURE 22.5

Moving a point using drag-and-drop

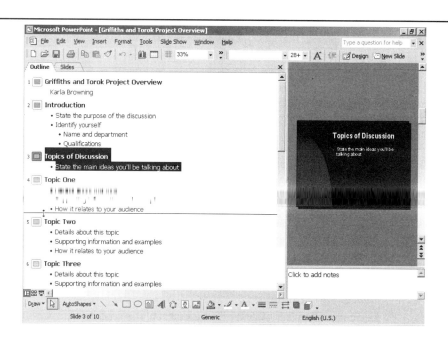

When you use drag-and-drop to rearrange slides or points, be sure to move the mouse vertically. Horizontal dragging causes the selected text to change levels. If you drag a bulleted point horizontally to the right, a vertical line appears in the outline. Drag-and-drop the horizontal line to the right to demote the text or to the left to promote the text.

> **TIP** You can also move entire slides in Normal view by switching to the Slides tab in the Outline pane and dragging a slide miniature to its new location.

If you prefer, you can use any of the traditional cut-and-paste and copy-and-paste methods to move and copy sections of an outline.

NEW▶

PowerPoint supports Smart Cut and Paste, which removes extra spaces when you delete text and inserts extra spaces when you paste from the Clipboard.

When there are options for formatting pasted text, PowerPoint 2002 displays the Paste Options button with the same choices you saw in Word 2002. Disable Paste Options by clicking Tools ➢ Options ➢ Edit and clearing the Show Paste Options check box. For more information about Paste Options in Word, see Chapter 3, "Working with Text and Formats in Word."

Delete slides, points, or subpoints as you would in a Word document: select the text and press the Delete key.

Working on the Slide in Normal View

If you only focus on the outline, it's easy to put too much on one slide, causing some lines of text to run off the bottom of the slide. Luckily you can catch this mistake in the Slide pane and quickly make necessary adjustments. But the Slide pane isn't just for viewing slides. You can insert, edit, move, and delete text directly on the slide. In fact, you may find it easier than working on the outline. While you can only work with one slide at a time, this view gives you a better feel for how the slide will actually look when complete.

Most slides include two text boxes, one for the title and one for the body text. When you click in the title or body, a frame appears around the text box, as shown in the previous slide. You can point to the frame and drag the text box to another location on the slide.

To add text to a slide, place your insertion point at the desired location in the text box. Promote or demote points and subpoints just as you would in Outline view, selecting the text first and either using the Promote or Demote buttons on the Outlining toolbar, or pressing Tab or Shift+Tab. To format the text in the box, select the text by clicking or dragging as you would in the outline; then change formats using the Formatting toolbar or Format menu.

Using the Slide Sorter

In Slide Sorter view, shown in Figure 22.6, you work with entire slides. You can't rearrange the text on a slide, but you can move or copy entire slides.

FIGURE 22.6

You can rearrange slides in Slide Sorter view.

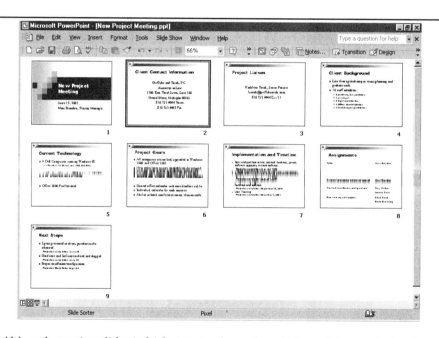

Although moving slides is fairly easy in the outline, it doesn't let you judge the overall visual impact of the presentation as you can when arranging slides in Slide Sorter view. For an overall balanced presentation, drag-and-drop allows you to distribute slides with graphic objects quickly and evenly among those that are text-only. (You may want to return to the outline to confirm that the text flows logically from slide to slide.)

TIP Double-click any slide in Slide Sorter view to display it in Normal view.

To drag-and-drop slides, switch to Slide Sorter view and follow these steps:

1. Click a slide once to select it. Use Shift+click to select multiple contiguous slides or use Ctrl+click to select multiple noncontiguous slides. A selected slide has a dark border around it, like slide 2 in Figure 22.6.

2. To move a selected slide, drag the slide toward its new location. A gray vertical line will appear. Drag-and-drop to move the line and the selected slide to the new location.

3. To copy a slide, hold Ctrl while dragging; release Ctrl after dropping the slide in place.

4. To delete slides in the Slide Sorter, select the slide(s) and then press Delete.

 TIP In Slide Sorter view, you can't always read the text on a slide. To display the title in a readable format, hold Alt and click the slide. When you release the mouse button, the slide miniature returns to normal.

Adding Notes

 PowerPoint lets you add notes to slides in any view. Look for the pane that says "Click to add notes," as shown previously in Figures 22.2 and 22.3. Click anywhere in the Notes pane and begin typing. Slide Sorter view does not have a Notes pane. Instead, select the slide for which you wish to record notes, and click the Notes button on the Slide Sorter toolbar.

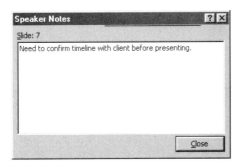

The Notes button opens a dialog box so you can enter notes about slides in a presentation. You can use this feature for speaker notes to be used during a presentation, but you can also use notes to keep track of other information about particular slides as you're creating a presentation. For example, there may be data that needs to be verified or alternative information you've considered adding to the slide.

 NOTE Remember that your audience at a live slide show never sees the text you have entered in the Notes pane unless you intentionally print your notes and hand them out.

To add notes from Slide Show view, right-click the slide and choose Speaker Notes from the shortcut menu. Again, you'll see the Speaker Notes dialog box. Any text you enter is displayed in the Notes pane in Normal view. To display the notes in Slide Show view, right-click on the slide and choose Speaker Notes to reopen the dialog box.

If you want to include graphics in your notes, you have to insert them in Notes Page view, not Normal view. Choose View ➢ Notes Page to access this view, shown in Figure 22.7. The default zoom setting in Notes Page view is usually too small to see anything. So the first thing you must do is increase the zoom setting; 75 percent seems to work fine. Then

1. Click the Notes area to enter text.

2. Format the text if you wish.

3. Insert graphics in the notes just as you would in a Word document. For more information about inserting graphics, see Chapter 6, "Beyond Text: Making the Most of Graphics."

FIGURE 22.7

You can enter notes with graphics in Notes Page view.

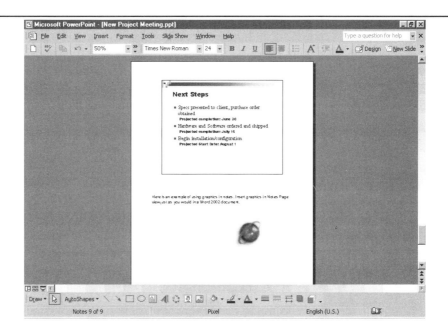

Other Ways to Create Presentations

The benefit of the AutoContent Wizard is that it helps you to develop your content. It is also helpful to beginning users, because the design templates used by the wizard include formats, transitions, and, in some templates, animation. All you need to do is enter text and you have a usable presentation.

If, however, you have already planned your content, you don't need to use the wizard. There are other ways you can create a presentation:

- Use a design template, which gives you a "look" without burdening you with text to alter or delete.

- Borrow the design from an existing presentation, which is useful if the presentations in your department (or for a project) should share a common design.

- Start from scratch with a blank presentation, enter your text first, and then apply a design.

- Import and modify an existing Word outline.

You can always apply another design to an existing presentation.

Using Blank Presentations or Design Templates

NEW▶

If you like to start with a blank slate, choose Blank Presentation from the task pane when you launch PowerPoint, or choose File ➢ New from the menu to open the New Presentation task pane. Choose Blank Presentation to have PowerPoint display a new blank slide with *Slide Layout* options in the task pane. Figure 22.8 shows a blank presentation window. Slide layouts determine the way objects are arranged on your slides; they are discussed more fully in the next section of this chapter.

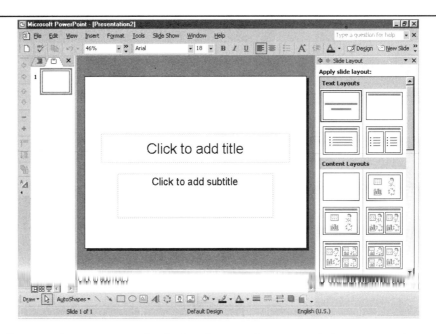

FIGURE 22.8

When you start with a blank presentation, PowerPoint 2002 displays Slide Layout options in the task pane.

Alternatively, you can use the design elements from any existing presentation or template to start a new presentation. To create a presentation using a design saved as a template, choose From Design Template in the task pane that opens when you launch PowerPoint. If PowerPoint is already running, choose File ➢ New to open the task pane.

When you choose From Design Template, the task pane shows Slide Design options. Templates are displayed in three categories: Used In This Presentation, Recently Used, and Available For Use. When you point to a template, a drop-down arrow appears to its right and a screen tip shows the template's filename. By default, templates are displayed as thumbnails. To enlarge them, click the drop-down arrow on any thumbnail and choose Show Large Preview. Remember, too, that you can resize the task pane to view more templates at once, as shown in Figure 22.9. Scroll through the templates until you find one you like.

FIGURE 22.9

Show large previews and resize the task pane to more easily view design templates.

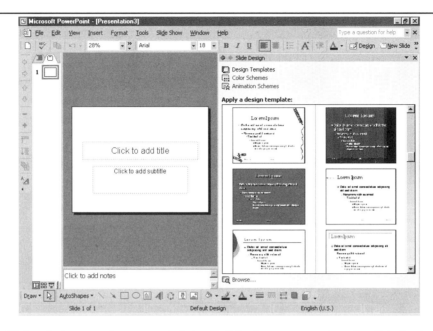

Click a design template to apply it to all slides in a presentation. Or click the drop-down arrow and choose Apply To All Slides.

NEW▶

You can apply a different template anytime the urge grabs you. And, in PowerPoint 2002, you can use more than one design template in a presentation. This assumes, of course, that the presentation contains more than one slide! To apply more than one design, follow these steps:

1. Display the presentation in Normal view, and choose the Slides tab of the Outline pane.

2. Display the Slide Design options in the task pane. (Click the drop-down arrow at the top of the pane and choose Slide Design - Design Templates.)

3. Select the slides you want to use with the first template. Hold Ctrl to select multiple noncontiguous slides.

4. Click the drop-down arrow on the design template you want to use for the selected slides.

5. Choose Apply To Selected Slides from the drop-down menu.

6. Repeat steps 3 through 5 to apply additional templates.

You can change the design template of a presentation at any time by choosing For-mat ➤ Slide Design from the menu or by selecting Slide Design - Design Templates from the task pane drop-down list.

For you die-hard previous-version users, feel free to browse through the templates in the old Apply Design Template dialog box. Simply click the Browse icon at the bot-tom of the task pane to open it.

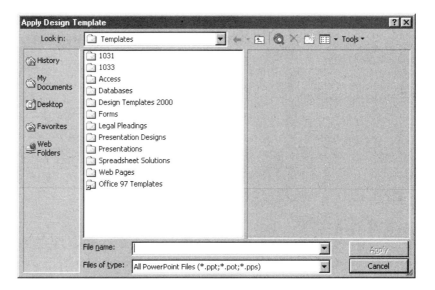

The dialog box opens to the Templates folder, so you won't see design choices right away. Choose a folder from the Look In control:

Design Templates 2000 Contains the templates from the most recent previous ver-sion of PowerPoint. Choose this folder to find designs such as Angles, High Voltage, and Whirlpool.

Presentation Designs Includes the new 2002 templates and a few holdovers from 2000. You'll find over a dozen striking new designs, including Eclipse, Fireworks, Net-work, Orbit, and Pixel. Try Crayons for a fun and informal look.

Presentations Holds designs with placeholder text from the AutoContent Wizard presentation types. Choose Company Meeting, Financial Overview, or Marketing Plan to get started. Save yourself some steps by using one of the online templates if you're planning to display the presentation on the Web.

To apply a design from an existing presentation rather than a template, change the Files Of Type drop-down list to All PowerPoint Presentations, and then locate and select the presentation with the design you want to use.

Selecting Slide Layouts

NEW▶

If you begin a presentation with a design template or chose to create a blank presentation, the presentation is empty. When you choose the design template option, PowerPoint displays design templates in the task pane. With blank presentations, PowerPoint opens the task pane displaying slide layouts, as shown previously in Figure 22.8. Slide layouts allow you to arrange objects in different ways on slides. Layouts contain placeholders for text, tables, charts, and other graphics you might wish to include in a presentation. (The Slide Layout task pane also opens when you click the New Slide button on the Formatting toolbar, as mentioned earlier in this chapter.)

 TIP If you don't want to see the task pane each time you insert a new slide, disable the Show When Inserting New Slides check box beneath the slide layout thumbnails.

Notice that when you display slide layouts in the task pane, there is a scroll bar; there are other layouts you might want to look at, including a blank slide with no placeholders. Point to any layout to see a screen tip describing its placeholders. No choice that you make here is carved in stone: you can always change a slide's layout. The task pane displays slide layouts in four categories:

Text Layouts Choose one of these if all you need is a title and some form of bulleted list. You can also select title only.

Content Layouts These layouts are for slides that include organization charts and other types of illustrative diagrams as well as tables, charts, video clips, pictures, and clip art. Choose the content layout that best meets your needs for relative size and number of objects to be included.

Text And Content Layouts Choose one of these to create a slide with bulleted text and one or more of the objects listed in the previous paragraph.

Other Layouts These include placeholders for specific object types. For example, you can choose bulleted text with a media clip, or title and table.

As you begin a new presentation, PowerPoint assigns a layout based on where you are in the presentation. The first slide is given the Title Slide layout. Subsequent slides use the Text layout. You can quickly and easily override these automatic choices when necessary.

Let's assume you are content with the Title Slide layout for the first slide. Your next task is adding text to the slide. Click the Title text box on the slide and enter your presentation's title. Click the Subtitle text box and enter any additional information you want to appear on the title slide. (If you prefer, you can enter all of the text for this slide on the Outline portion of the Normal view window.)

To add slides, follow these steps:

1. Click the New Slide button on the Formatting toolbar or choose Insert ➤ New Slide from the menu.

2. If the selected layout meets your needs, begin typing on the slide or click the appropriate object icon to insert the object you wish to use. (More on inserting objects in Chapter 24.)

3. If you wish to apply another slide layout, scroll the task pane and click the layout you wish to use. The layout is immediately applied to the slide, and you can continue by clicking the appropriate placeholder.

4. Depending on the slide layout you choose, there may be several text boxes for body text and other frames for objects. In all cases, when you have finished entering text in a text box, click outside of the text box to turn off the selection.

 WARNING If you add text to a slide using the Text Tool button on the Drawing toolbar, the text will not appear in your outline. The Text Tool button creates a text box object, not slide text.

Continue adding slides one by one to build your presentation. To change the layout of an existing slide, display it in Normal view and choose a different slide layout from the task pane.

 TIP To quickly insert a slide with the layout you want, click the drop-down arrow on the layout and choose Insert New Slide.

 NOTE If you later insert objects that weren't included in the original layout, PowerPoint's AutoLayout feature adjusts existing contents to accommodate the new insertion. Learn more about AutoLayout in Chapter 24.

Applying a Layout to Multiple Slides

It is not uncommon to create a presentation by inserting all slides with slide titles at once. Content is added later as you work on individual slides. If this is your work style, you will probably make layout decisions after the slides are created.

In PowerPoint 2002 you can apply layouts to multiple slides at once. Here's how:

1. Display the presentation in Normal view, and choose the Slides tab of the Outline pane.

2. Display the Slide Layout options in the task pane. (Click View ➢ Task Pane, and then click the drop-down arrow at the top of the pane and choose Slide Layout.)

3. Select the slides you want. Hold Ctrl to select multiple noncontiguous slides.

4. Click the drop-down arrow on the layout you want to use for the selected slides.

5. Choose Apply Layout or Apply To Selected Slides from the drop-down menu. (In this instance, both commands do the same thing.)

> **TIP** If you've changed the location or size or placeholders, or if you've changed fonts on a slide and wish to return to the slide's original layout and font settings, select the slide and click the drop-down arrow on the layout you're using. Choose Reapply Layout.

Table Slides

When you need to display information in parallel columns, as shown in Figure 22.10, select a Table Slide layout. The enhanced tables features in PowerPoint 2002 incorporate most of the powerful table tools from Word.

You can quickly and easily create tables. Customize the table by specifying the number of columns and rows, and by inserting and deleting text, applying borders, applying shading, changing fonts and alignment, resizing columns and rows, and modifying your table in dozens of ways.

1. Display slide layouts in the task pane.

2. Insert a new slide with a table placeholder.

3. Activate the Title text box and enter a slide title.

4. Double-click the icon to start a new table. The Insert Table dialog box opens.

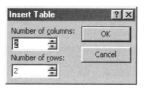

5. Use the spin boxes to indicate the number of columns and rows for your table, or select and overtype the default numbers.

6. Click OK. PowerPoint displays the empty grid.

7. If you wish, turn on the floating Tables And Borders toolbar (View ➢ Toolbars ➢ Tables And Borders).

8. The default tool on the Tables And Borders toolbar is the pencil, which is used to draw new rows or columns and to split cells. You can drag the pencil vertically, horizontally, or diagonally.

9. Click the pencil tool to "put it away." Your mouse pointer becomes an I-beam for selecting cells and typing text.

10. Use the other options on the Tables And Borders toolbar to apply formatting changes to borders, shading, and alignment.

FIGURE 22.10

Use a table slide when you need to display text in parallel columns.

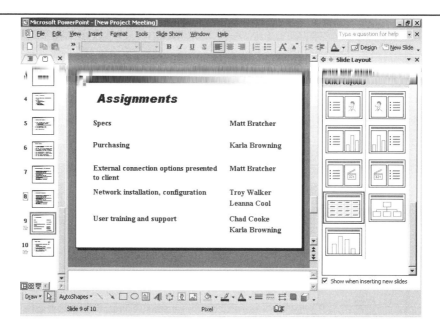

NOTE For a detailed description of table features, see Chapter 5, "Designing Pages with Columns and Tables."

Multi-Object Slides

The slide layouts in the task pane allow you to vary the arrangement of objects on your slides, including placeholders for tables, charts, graphics, text frames, and other objects. As we have previously discussed, some layouts include multiple placeholders with text placement beside, below, or above objects.

Although placeholders aren't necessary—charts, clip art, media clips, and other objects can be placed on any slide—the placeholders provide shortcuts to the objects you include most often. They save time by minimizing resizing, since objects are placed in a presized frame. In addition, when you need multiple objects on a slide, using a layout with placeholders ensures plenty of space for each object. It creates a balanced look and reserves enough space between objects that the slide does not look crowded. The result is more professional-looking slides.

Figure 22.11 shows a newly inserted slide with placeholders for two small objects and one large object. Within each placeholder are multiple icons representing commonly used objects available for insertion in that frame.

FIGURE 22.11

Choose one of the content layouts to easily insert multiple objects on a slide.

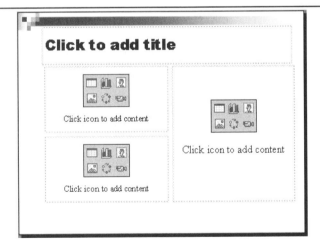

 To insert an object into one of the placeholders, simply click its icon. PowerPoint launches the appropriate application or dialog box to create and insert the object you need. At this point the assumption is that you know what to do with the tool you've launched. All object tools are covered in this book. Tables are discussed in the previous section of this chapter and in Chapter 5. Diagrams and charts are covered in Chapter 7. For more information about inserting clip art or sound and video objects, see Chapters 6 and 24.

 MASTERING THE OPPORTUNITIES

Creating an Organizational Chart

You can create professional-looking organizational charts right on your slides. In the task pane, choose one of the content layouts or choose the slide layout that includes an organizational chart and title (in the Other Layouts category). Click in the Title text box—if you're using one—and type a title for the slide.

The first couple of steps for getting started depend on which slide layout you're using. If you chose the Title And diagram Or Organization Chart, you must double-click the Organization Chart icon. If you chose one of the content layouts, you must click the Insert Organization Chart Of Diagram button. Both of these actions open the Diagram Gallery.

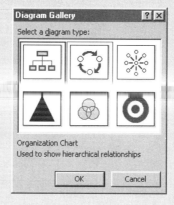

Choose the Organization Chart icon to launch the Organization Chart tools. You are automatically given four boxes—one manager and three subordinates—and the Organization Chart toolbar is displayed. Delete boxes you don't want by clicking them and pressing Delete.

Continued

MASTERING THE OPPORTUNITIES CONTINUED

Before you add a box, decide which level is appropriate for the person whose name will appear in the box. Select the box to which you wish to add another box, and then click Insert Shape on the toolbar. Choose a level to insert: manager, subordinate, assistant, etc. A new box appears with instructional text to select and overtype.

Choose a particular level or all levels for editing by clicking Select from the Organization Chart toolbar. Change the color, shadow, and border options on selected boxes by using the tools on the Drawing toolbar. Options for different chart styles and text formatting are also available. For additional information about formatting organization charts, see Chapter 7, "Getting Creative with the Office XP Graphics Tools."

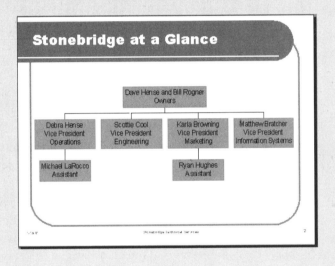

Using Slides from Existing Presentations

Applying a design from an existing presentation (Format ➤ Slide Design) uses a presentation's background, fonts, and formatting without any of the content. To borrow content, use the Slide Finder to take entire slides from an existing presentation and place them in the active presentation. To open the Slide Finder from any view, choose Insert ➤ Slides From Files. Click the Browse button and select the presentation that contains the slides you want to add to your presentation. If necessary click the Display button to add thumbnails of the slides to the Slide Finder, as shown in Figure 22.12.

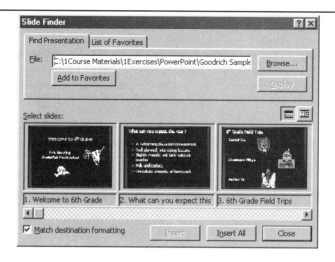

The slides appear with each slide's number and title below the slide. Use the horizontal scroll bar to move through the slides in order. To work more quickly, click the Show Titles button in the Slide Finder dialog box to display a list of slide titles with a single preview pane.

Click the Show Slides button to return to the thumbnails if you wish. Select the slide or slides you want (hold Shift or Ctrl to select multiple slides). Then do *one* of the following:

- Click Insert, and the selected slides appear in your presentation following the slide that was selected when you opened the Slide Finder. The text and any objects (like a picture or chart) on the slide are imported. The slide's design is *not* imported into the current presentation. Instead, each slide is reformatted upon being imported so that it matches the design of the presentation you are currently working on.

NEW▶
- Clear the Match Destination Formatting check box and then click Insert. Imported slides are positioned following the slide that was selected when you opened the Slide Finder. Imported slides retain their original formatting.

The Slide Finder remains open so you can browse to select another presentation and continue inserting slides. If you wish to use all slides in a presentation, open it and click Insert All.

EXPERT TIP   If you frequently use slides from a particular presentation, open it in the Slide Finder and click Add To Favorites. Confirm your decision to do so in the message box that appears. The next time you wish to insert slides from that presentation, you don't have to browse to select it. Just choose the List Of Favorites tab in the Slide Finder.

Creating a Presentation from a Word Outline

You can import a Word outline (see Chapter 8, "Simplifying with Styles, Outlines, and Templates") to create a PowerPoint presentation. The outline is inserted into the active presentation, so if you have just started, you can use the outline as the entire presentation. You may also use an outline as additional content in a partially completed presentation. If you choose to insert an outline into an existing presentation, each first-level heading becomes a new slide. To do this, follow these steps:

1. In any view, select the slide you want the inserted outline to follow.

2. Choose Insert ➢ Slides From Outline.

3. Change the Look In field so it points to the folder containing the Word outline.

4. Select the Word file you want to insert. In some cases, PowerPoint may prompt you to install the necessary converters. Do so and continue.

5. Click Insert.

 TIP   When you insert a Word outline, the complete document appears as part of your presentation. If you only want part of the outline, delete the extra slides after importing. If you have a rather lengthy outline from which you only need a few slides, consider copying those sections to a new Word document and importing from there.

If you're already working in Word, you can create a presentation from the active document by choosing File ➢ Send To ➢ Microsoft PowerPoint from the Word menu.

CHAPTER 23

FORMATTING AND DESIGNING A PRESENTATION

FEATURING

- Changing the color scheme

- Modifying the Slide Master

- Customizing the background

- Formatting and checking text

Now that PowerPoint has become so common in sales departments, marketing groups, classrooms, boardrooms, and offices throughout the world, there's a new focus in presentation design. Increasingly, users are looking for ways to make their presentations stand out. Different is better.

Although PowerPoint offers many eye-catching design templates to choose from, it won't be long before you feel the need to modify a template to better suit the content of a presentation. It's easy to choose one of PowerPoint's design templates to establish the primary background for your presentation and then change the background or colors to meet your specific needs—for example, using colors from your client's logo or your alma mater.

No matter how well you've done with the design, it's the presentation content that makes the difference between professional and amateur, selling and not selling, a high grade or a low one. Fortunately, PowerPoint offers several tools for checking text style and formatting—yet another way to make sure you look good at the podium!

Changing the Color Scheme

Consider the environment for your presentation when changing colors or backgrounds. For overheads, the lighter the background the better. Dark backgrounds work well for electronic or online presentations, but if you need to show a presentation with room lights on, choose a light background and dark text.

Color Schemes

When you're ready to make changes, open the task pane and choose Slide Design - Color Schemes to display color scheme options, as shown in Figure 23.1. If the task pane is already displaying design options, just click Color Schemes to bring up in the same place. For most templates, PowerPoint displays several standard schemes with the ability to edit them, creating your own custom color schemes. With only a few exceptions, like the Whirlpool template, the standard color schemes include the current color scheme, at least one alternate scheme, and one black-and-white choice. The number of standard schemes you see depends on the design template. The color schemes with the white background are designed for overheads, but they can be used for kiosk or Web presentations.

NEW ▶

A scheme can be applied to selected slides or to all of the slides in the presentation. To apply a new color scheme to all slides in a presentation, just click the thumbnail of the color scheme you like. With PowerPoint 2002, color scheme changes are made in real time so you can see modifications immediately and undo any you don't like.

To change only selected slides in the presentation, do the following:

1. Display the presentation in Normal view with slide miniatures showing in the left pane.

2. Select the slides to be modified.

3. Click the drop-down arrow on the color scheme you want to use. Choose Apply To Selected Slides.

FIGURE 23.1

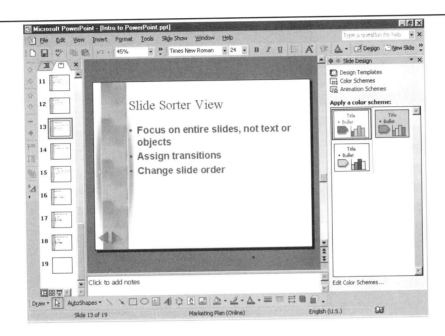

FIGURE 23.1

Change design template colors using the color scheme options in the task pane.

NOTE You can't change the color scheme in a blank presentation because there's no scheme to change.

If none of the standard schemes trips your trigger, create your own scheme. Select the scheme that's closest to the scheme you want and click Edit Color Schemes at the bottom of the task pane. This opens the Edit Color Scheme dialog box to the Custom tab, as shown in Figure 23.2. Select the element color you want to change and click the Change Color button to open the Colors dialog box. Choose a color from the array of colors presented, or if you want to mix your own, select the Custom tab to open the Color Picker.

If you wish, you can save the color scheme of the current design for future use by clicking the Add As Standard Scheme button on the Custom tab (see Figure 23.2). Added schemes are displayed on the Standard tab of the Edit Color Scheme dialog box.

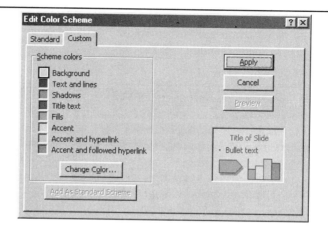

Modifying the Slide Master

Every design includes one or more *Slide Masters* that identify the position of the text and graphic objects, the style of the fonts, the footer elements, and the background for all slides. Most designs include a separate Title Master as well. Templates from earlier versions of PowerPoint usually have only one master.

NEW▶ To display master slides for a presentation, choose View ➢ Master ➢ Slide Master, or hold Shift and click the Normal View button. The master slide is displayed along with the Slide Master View toolbar. In PowerPoint 2002 you can see all Slide and Title Masters for a presentation in the pane at the left (see Figure 23.3). Note the gray lines connecting Title and Slide Master pairs. Point to any master and you'll see a tip with the name of the master design and the slides that are based on it.

NOTE Now that you can apply multiple design templates to presentations in Power-Point 2002, you may find yourself managing several master slides. For each design you use, there are generally two masters. For a long presentation with three different templates, you're looking at potentially six masters!

Every slide in a presentation is based on a Slide Master or Title Master. Changes that you make to the master are reflected in each slide that is based on the master. For example, if you want a graphic object (a company logo, perhaps) to appear on every slide, place it on the master rather than inserting it on each slide. To change the title font for all slides or the vertical graphic shown on the left side of the slide in Figure 23.3, change it on the master by following these steps:

1. To open the Slide Master, choose View ➤ Master ➤ Slide Master.

2. On the master, select any text box to modify its format. Use the buttons on the Formatting toolbar to format text or choose Format ➤ Font to change text color, size, or style.

3. To change bullet characters, select the level of bullet you wish to change and choose Format ➤ Bullets And Numbering from the menu. In Office 2002, the Bullets And Numbering feature is nearly identical in Word and PowerPoint. This feature is covered in depth in Chapter 3, "Working with Text and Formats in Word."

FIGURE 23.3

Changes to the Slide Master are reflected on all slides based on the master.

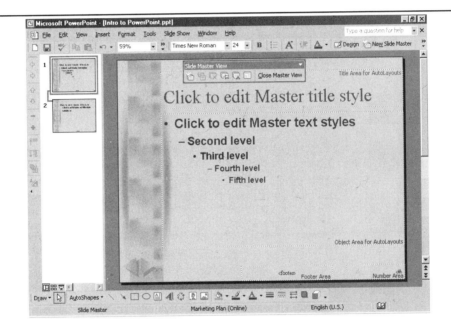

While you're working with the Slide Master, you can select and move or delete placeholders, including graphic objects and text boxes. Insert logos or other graphics you want to appear on every slide by choosing Insert ➤ Picture from the menu.

NEW▶

Microsoft has enhanced the Slide Master View toolbar for PowerPoint 2002. Not only can you close the master and return to your slides, there are also options for inserting, deleting, renaming, and preserving Slide and Title Masters. Table 23.1 describes the function of each button on the Slide Master View toolbar.

NOTE When you insert a new master, the design appears in the Used In This Presentation category of the Slide Design task pane. You can easily apply the design to any new slides when you are working in Normal view.

TABLE 23.1   THE SLIDE MASTER VIEW TOOLBAR

Button	Button Name	Function
	Insert New Slide Master	Adds a blank Slide Master to the presentation. You can insert and arrange placeholders, graphics, fonts, bullets, color schemes, and other slide elements to create your own master from scratch.
	Insert New Title Master	Adds a blank Title Master to the presentation. Only enabled if you add a regular Slide Master first and apply a design to it. Modify design elements on the new Title Master to create your own Title Master from scratch.
	Delete Master	Removes the selected master from the presentation. Reformats slides based on that master to match one of the remaining masters.
	Preserve Master	Prevents PowerPoint from automatically deleting a master when no slides are based on that master or when you apply a new design to slides that were originally based on that master.
	Rename Master	Opens the Rename Master dialog box, where you can type a new name for the selected master. Renaming one master in a Slide–Title Master pair also renames the other.
	Master Layout	Opens the Master Layout dialog box, where you can enable or disable certain elements (date, footer, slide number) on the selected master.
Close Master View	Close Master View	Returns you to Normal view after you finish changes to the master.

 TIP If you want to save slight modifications to a master while retaining the original, PowerPoint now lets you copy any slide, including a master. Choose Insert ➢ Duplicate Master Slide, modify the copy, and then rename the copy if you wish. In Normal view you can choose Insert ➢ Duplicate Slide to copy the selected slide.

Adding Slide Footers

When you use the AutoContent Wizard to create a presentation, one of the steps in the wizard prompts you to include the system date, slide number, and other text in a slide footer. These elements are placed in the Slide Master. You can add, delete, or modify the footer. Simply open the Slide Master and click the text box you wish to edit. If you added text, dates, and/or slide numbering in the AutoContent Wizard, their text boxes show generic text in the Slide Master. Select one of the footer text boxes and type any new information to overwrite the choices made in the AutoContent Wizard.

For users who prefer to edit inside a dialog box, choose View ➢ Header And Footer from the menu in Normal view or Slide Master view. The Header And Footer dialog box (shown in Figure 23.4) allows you to edit, add, or delete footer text on slides. Turn on the items you want to display, activate Don't Show On Title Slide, if desired, and click either Apply to place a footer on the current slide only or Apply To All to change the Slide Master. (If you opened the dialog box from the Slide Master, you can only choose Apply To All.)

FIGURE 23.4

Edit headers and footers on the Slide Master or in the Header And Footer dialog box.

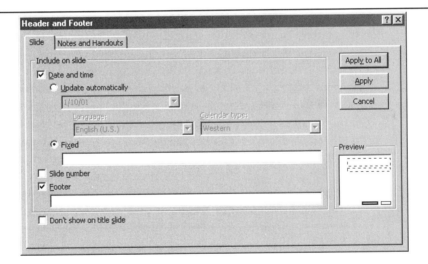

Customizing the Background

When you choose to apply a design template, the template includes, among other things, the color scheme and background color. Often, the background is more than just a solid color. It may have a shaded effect, a pattern, or a texture. A picture or graphic object may be part of the background. All these characteristics—shading, patterns, textures, and objects—form the background of the slide. Text and objects that you place on the slide are positioned on top of the background.

To change the background, choose Format ➤ Background, or in Normal view right-click the background and choose Background from the shortcut menu to open the Background dialog box.

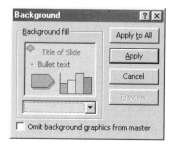

As with the color scheme, you can apply changes to selected slides or to the Slide Master. If the background graphic elements interfere with an object you've placed on a slide, remove the background graphics by enabling the Omit Background Graphics From Master check box and clicking Apply. The master background graphics won't be applied to the selected slide, but all other slides will retain background graphics. Figure 23.5 shows a slide with and without background objects. You may see slight differences in other slide elements—such as the title in Figure 23.5—by omitting background objects, but the slide retains the general presentation design. And now the chart, table, or image you've placed on the slide has less competition. If your presentation is chock-full of charts and graphics, omit the background graphics for all slides by enabling the check box and clicking Apply To All.

   NOTE   When you select Omit Background Graphics, you also omit the footer.

FIGURE 23.5

The top slide contains background objects. The bottom slide has its background objects omitted from the master.

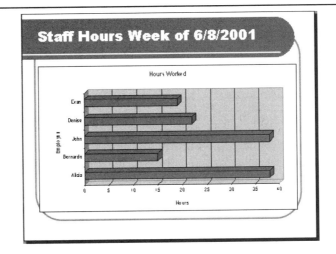

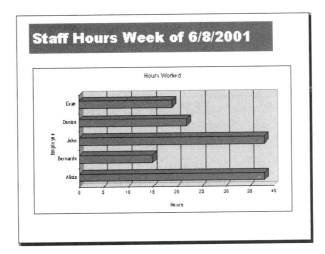

To change the background, click the drop-down arrow in the Background Fill area of the Background dialog box to open a drop-down list of the color scheme options.

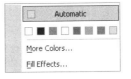

Choosing Automatic fills the background with the default fill color. Select one of the color-scheme colors or choose More Colors (which opens the Color Picker) to select a solid background color. For a walk on the wilder side, choose Fill Effects to open the Fill Effects dialog box.

 TIP You can apply the same Fill Effects options in Excel to fill chart elements and in any object you draw using the Drawing toolbar throughout Office XP.

In this dialog box, you can select a background from four different types of fills, as demonstrated by the four tabs: Gradient, Texture, Pattern, or Picture. The Gradient tab of the Fill Effects dialog box is shown in Figure 23.6.

Gradient A variegated color mix. The preset gradient schemes use two or more colors to create effects such as Early Sunset, Moss, and Parchment.

Texture A photolike fill ranging from wood and mineral textures to a fossil fish.

Pattern A repeated pattern such as diagonal lines or vertical stripes.

Picture An image in one of the many graphic formats PowerPoint supports.

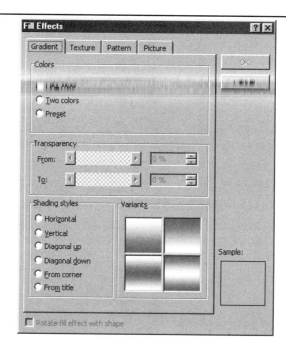

FIGURE 23.6

Select a gradient fill from the Gradient tab of the Fill Effects dialog box

To change the gradient or texture of a slide background, follow these steps:

1. Choose Format ➢ Background from Normal or Slide Sorter view, or right-click a slide (outside of any text boxes or objects) and choose Background from the shortcut menu.

2. Open the fill drop-down list and choose Fill Effects.

3. Select the Gradient tab of the Fill Effects dialog box. Select one of the gradient options: One Color, Two Colors, or Preset.

4. If you have chosen the two-color option, select the two colors you wish to use to create a custom gradient.

5. Select a shading style to determine the direction of the gradient (Horizontal, Diagonal Up, From Title, etc.)

6. Click OK, preview the gradient, and click Apply or Apply To All.

Or you can follow these steps to choose a different fill effect:

3. Select the Texture tab of the Fill Effects dialog box.

4. Select a texture from the previews.

5. Preview the new texture and click Apply or Apply To All.

 TIP To quickly apply the background from one slide to the entire presentation, select the slide, open the Fill Effects dialog box (Format ➢ Background ➢ Fill Effects), and click Apply To All.

To change the pattern for a slide background, do the following:

1. Choose Format ➢ Background from Normal or Slide Sorter view or right-click a slide (outside of any text boxes or objects). Choose Background from the shortcut menu.

2. Open the fill drop-down list and choose Fill Effects.

3. Select the Pattern tab of the Fill Effects dialog box (see Figure 23.7). Select contrasting foreground and background colors. The foreground color forms the pattern on top of the background color.

4. Click one of the pattern styles displayed in the dialog box and click OK.

5. Preview the new pattern and then click Apply or Apply To All.

FIGURE 23.7

The Pattern tab of the Fill Effects dialog box

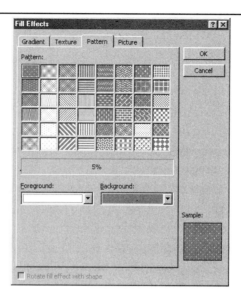

On the Picture tab, you use the Browse button to select a picture to apply to a background. PowerPoint supports many different graphic formats, from Windows metafiles to JPEGs.

Pictures used as backgrounds can be stunning. Landscapes and group photos are particularly effective. You don't need to worry about sizing the image—it fills the entire slide. You should, however, change the font on the slide to a contrasting color so text will be legible. Figure 23.8 shows a slide that uses the Horseshoe Falls (Niagara Falls, Canada). This was one of many geographically specific background photos in a presentation for an audience that included decision makers from the U.S. and Canada.

To use a picture as a slide background, do the following:

1. Choose Format ➢ Background from Normal or Slide Sorter view or right-click a slide (outside of any text boxes or objects). Choose Background from the shortcut menu.

2. Open the fill drop-down list and choose Fill Effects.

3. Select the Picture tab of the Fill Effects dialog box.

4. Click the Select Picture button to open the Select Picture dialog box.

5. Locate the picture you wish to use. Click OK.

6. Preview the new pattern and click Apply or Apply To All.

FIGURE 23.8

The right picture can make an excellent background image.

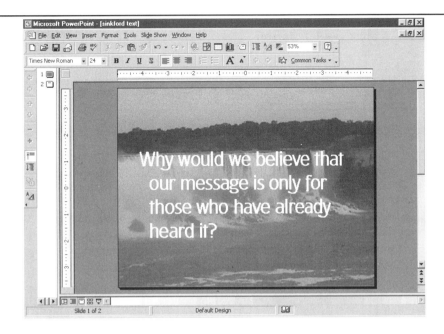

 TIP An easy way to build immediate rapport with your audience is to include pictures that are meaningful to them. When you use an image of a customer's building as the background to a presentation, it's a powerful way to say, "We visited your manufacturing facility." When you're collecting information for a proposal, use a digital camera to take photos of client sites for use in project and sales presentations (however, don't include images of people unless you have obtained their written permission). If you don't have a digital camera with good resolution, you can take 35mm photos and scan them on a high-resolution scanner.

Formatting and Checking Text

When you format text on individual slides, the formatting takes precedence over formatting from the Slide Master. Even if you apply a new design to the master, formatting applied to individual slides won't change, so you should make sure you are pleased with the overall design before formatting individual slides. You can apply standard Office text enhancements to text in your PowerPoint slides. Select the text to be formatted and then change font typeface, size, and attributes using the Formatting toolbar or the Format menu.

TIP PowerPoint designers spend a considerable amount of time putting together templates with colors, fonts, and other attributes that provide a coordinated look. If you sometimes arrive at work wearing a striped shirt and plaid pants and still want to experiment with your own designs in PowerPoint, ask a colleague to review the presentation after you make formatting changes.

Formatting is displayed by default in both Normal and Slide Sorter views. However, you can decide whether or not to display formatting. The Show Formatting button on the Outlining toolbar toggles between displaying and hiding text formatting. In Slide Sorter view, the Show Formatting button toggles between displaying the slide thumbnail and slide titles.

Two buttons that do not appear in Word or Excel are the Increase Font and Decrease Font buttons. Each click changes the font size in standard increments that increase as font size increases. Fonts 10 points and smaller change in 1-point increments; larger fonts change in greater increments.

Add a shadow to selected text by clicking the Shadow button; change the color of the text by clicking the Font Color button on both the Formatting and Drawing toolbars. When you click the arrow next to the Font Color button, the colors from the current scheme are displayed.

NOTE Select View ➤ Toolbars to turn the Drawing toolbar on or off. You can also right-click any toolbar and turn the toolbar off and on from the shortcut menu.

A Word about Fonts

Fonts fall into five categories: serif, sans serif, script, decorative, or symbol.

Continued ▯▶

CONTINUED

Serif fonts, like Times New Roman, are easily recognizable from the serifs attached to the ends and tips of letters. For example, the uppercase "N" shown below has feet, and the lowercase "t" has a curvy bottom. Serif fonts are best for body text in paragraphs because the serifs provide cues for the reader.

Sans serif fonts, like Arial, do not have fancy ends and tips on letters. These plain-vanilla fonts work well for headings.

Script fonts, such as Lucida Handwriting or Brush Script, are designed to look like cursive handwriting. Avoid script fonts at the office, since they project a more personal, rather than corporate, style.

Decorative fonts, like Old English or Desdemona, add impact to documents like flyers and banners. You'll see decorative fonts used on formal documents like wedding invitations. If you are the person in charge of creating and posting flyers for the annual company picnic, consider using a decorative font to draw people's attention to the posted document.

Symbol fonts are for inserting special characters like the copyright symbol, ©, or for choosing bullet characters. You have probably seen the trademark symbol, ™, used in business publications and the Greek letter Sigma, Σ. Other symbols work well for bullet characters.

This is Times New Roman, a Serif font

This is Arial, a Sans Serif font

This is Brush Script MT, a Script font

THIS IS DESDEMONA, A DECORATIVE FONT

Wingdings is a symbol font. Here are some Wingdings: ♿✗□♏◆✉

Aligning Text

Text can be left-aligned, centered, right-aligned, or justified. Align Left, Center, and Align Right are options on the Formatting toolbar. To justify text, choose Format ➤ Alignment ➤ Justify from the menu bar. The paragraph containing the insertion point is now justified. If you wish to justify multiple paragraphs, select them before choosing the menu commands.

Replacing Fonts

Use the Replace Font dialog box to substitute one font for another globally in a presentation. You might choose to replace fonts to change the look of a presentation, but there is sometimes a more pressing reason. If you open a presentation on a computer that doesn't have the presentation's fonts installed, another font is automatically substituted—unless the fonts were embedded in the presentation. (See Chapter 25, "Taking Your Show on the Road," for pointers on saving presentations for use on another computer.) This substitute font may not be good looking and occasionally it isn't even readable. Rather than changing various levels of the master, you can have PowerPoint change each occurrence of the missing font by following these steps:

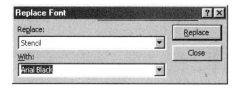

1. In Normal view, select the text box that includes the font you want to replace.

2. Choose Format ➤ Replace Fonts to open the Replace Font dialog box.

3. Select a replacement font.

4. Click Replace.

To replace fonts for *all* text boxes on *all* slides, switch to Slide Sorter view, select all slides (Ctrl+A is the fastest way), and follow steps 2 through 4.

Adjusting Line Spacing

In PowerPoint, you can add or subtract space between lines and before or after paragraphs, much as you add leading in desktop publishing. However, rather than entering extra blank lines between points or subpoints, you can use the Line Spacing dialog box to adjust the spacing between lines.

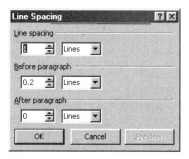

In Normal view, select the text you want to space. (This process works whether the text you select is on the outline or on the slide.) Choose Format ➢ Line Spacing to open the Line Spacing dialog box. Then set the lines or points (1 point = 1/72 inch) to be added as Line Spacing (between each line, even within a point or subpoint), Before Paragraph, or After Paragraph, and click OK.

Adjusting Tabs and Indents

The distance your insertion point moves when you press the Tab key is preset at one-half inch. You can see the default tab stops on the ruler in Normal view. Choose View ➢ Ruler to turn your ruler on, if necessary. To change the default tab settings for your presentation, do the following:

1. Switch to Normal view and display the ruler (View ➢ Ruler).

2. Select the text you want to change the tabs for.

3. On the ruler, drag the first default tab stop to its new position. All other tab stops will adjust so that the distance between each tab stop is the same.

If you click in a text box with multiple levels of main points and subpoints, you will see indent markers appear on the ruler, as shown in Figure 23.9. Each level of points has its own set of three indent markers. If you only have first-level bullets, you will only see three markers. If you have first- and second-level bullets, you will see six, and so on. You can use these indent markers to move text and bullets to the left or right, or you can indent just the text, moving it farther from the bullet that precedes it.

FIGURE 23.9

You can use indent markers on the ruler to move bulleted points or indent text.

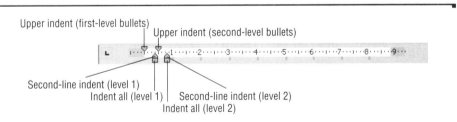

The upper marker sets the indent for the first line of the paragraph. Adjust the marker instead of pressing Tab if you want to give the appearance of a tabbed first line. Just drag the upper indent marker to the right; the other lines in that paragraph (and all paragraphs at that bullet level) will wrap to the left margin of the text box.

When you drag the triangular part of the lower indent marker, it adjusts all lines in the paragraph below the first line. If the first and subsequent lines of the paragraph are at the same setting (alignment), dragging this marker moves the entire paragraph in relation to the bullet. (The rectangular portion of the marker also moves when you drag the triangular portion.)

Drag the rectangular part of the lower marker to move the entire paragraph while maintaining the relationship between the first-line indent and the rest of the lines.

Take these steps to change indent settings for the current slide:

1. In Normal view, select the text you want to set indents for.

2. If the ruler isn't displayed, turn it on (View ➢ Ruler).

3. Drag the upper indent marker to change the indent for the first line of a paragraph.

4. Drag the lower indent marker to set the indent for other lines in a paragraph.

5. To change the indent for an entire paragraph, drag the rectangular box beneath the lower indent marker to move both upper and lower markers while maintaining the relationship between the upper and lower indent.

6. To change the distance from a hanging paragraph to the bullet that precedes it, drag the triangular portion of the bottom indent marker.

 PowerPoint 2002 has buttons for increasing and decreasing the indent setting on selected text. Click the Increase Indent button to move text to the right one level at a time. Click Decrease Indent to move text left one level at a time. If you think this sounds just like promoting and demoting, you're correct! The buttons do essentially the same thing.

Using the Style Checker

 PowerPoint 2000 can automatically check your presentation for consistency and style. When there are problems with punctuation or visual clarity, they are marked with a lightbulb. You can fix or ignore these inconsistencies, and there are options for changing the style elements PowerPoint checks. Automatic style checking is off by default. Turn it on by clicking Tools ➢ Options ➢ Spelling And Style and then enabling the Check Style control.

> **NOTE** The Office Assistant must be displayed to check styles.

1. Open the presentation you want to check for style and consistency.

2. Activate the Office Assistant, if it isn't already showing, by choosing Help ➢ Show The Office Assistant.

3. Locate slides that are flagged for errors.

4. Click the lightbulb to see a list of options.

5. Click the option you want to apply.

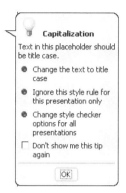

To change the elements that PowerPoint checks for, choose Change Style Checker Options For All Presentations in the list of options. If your presentation doesn't have any inconsistencies, choose Tools ➤ Options to open the Options dialog box. On the Spelling And Style tab of the dialog box, click Style Options to open the Style Options dialog box.

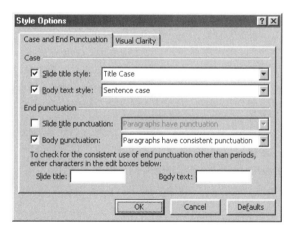

In the Case And End Punctuation tab of the dialog box, enable or disable case and end punctuation options so that your presentation is consistent. It is a good idea to check for consistent end punctuation on paragraphs. When you choose to use end punctuation, PowerPoint checks for periods by default. If you're using question marks or other end punctuation, type the punctuation symbols in the edit boxes so the style checker can look for it.

Click the Visual Clarity tab of the dialog box to enable or disable font and legibility checking. Use the spin boxes to set options for the number of fonts per presentation, font sizes, number of bullets, and number of lines of text.

If you wish to return to the original style options without readjusting manually, simply click the Defaults button in the Style Options dialog box.

CHAPTER 24

OBJECTS, TRANSITIONS, AND ANIMATION

FEATURING

- Adding objects

- Creating graphical bullets

- Modifying and adding transitions

- Adding animation

- Creating and animating charts

- Hiding slides

- Adding links to other slides

- Adding comments and CD audio

- Recording narration

A fter your presentation's content is under control, it's time to think about ways to add visual impact that supports and extends your message. Objects add interest that text cannot; well-chosen graphics provide another way for the audience to understand your message. Why not include your company logo on the introductory slide? Consider displaying those month-end sales figures in a Word table. Emphasize a particularly important point with a graphical bullet. At the end of the chapter, we'll tie the presentation together with audio, adding CD tracks and sound files, and recording narration. This is your opportunity to add the design elements that make a good presentation a great presentation.

Adding Objects

PowerPoint treats each item placed on a slide as an object. Even the text typed in the outline is placed in a text box. Most slides have at least two text boxes—one for the title and one for the bulleted text—and each text box is an object. We covered the title box and text box objects in Chapters 22 and 23. In this chapter, we'll focus on other, catchier objects that support content. The PowerPoint Online Help uses the term *text boxes* to refer to title boxes and text boxes (or simply text boxes) and uses the term *objects* to refer to objects other than the title box and text box. We'll use the same convention in this chapter. To add objects to slides, switch to Normal view.

 I I I" II ꟹ‖‖ ꜱᵇⱼₑₐₜ ꜱₖₐᵤᵢₐ ₐₚₚₑₐᵣ ꝋₙ ᵥₑᵥₑᵣᵧ ꝋ‖‖‖ (‖‖‖‖ ⸱ ꝙ‖‖‖ꝗ‖ ‖ꝙ‖ ꝇ꜐ꝗ‖ ꝛ‖ ⸱ ꝛ‖‖‖‖‖ ꝇ꜐‖ ꝛꝗ‖‖‖‖‖‖ꝓ add it to the Slide Master (see Chapter 23, "Formatting and Designing a Presentation").

Using Slide Layouts with Object Placeholders

The easy way to insert an object is to begin with a slide layout that includes the object, whether the object is text, clip art, a table, a chart, a sound or video clip, or any other object. To insert a new slide and display layout options, choose Insert ➢ New Slide from the menu. If you just want to see layouts without inserting a new slide, choose Slide Layout from the drop-down list at the top of the task pane. Figure 24.1 shows several examples of slide layouts that include text and objects.

FIGURE 24.1

Choose a layout that includes an object in the Slide Layout task pane

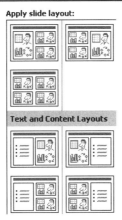

Apply slide layout:

Text and Content Layouts

Select a slide layout that includes the object you want to use. There are layouts with placeholders for charts, tables, organizational charts, media clips, and clip art, as well as generic objects. After selecting a layout, double-click the object's placeholder in the slide, and PowerPoint launches the appropriate application to either insert or create the indicated object.

 NOTE See Chapter 23 for more information on slide layouts.

Inserting Objects

NEW ▶

You can insert objects on any slide without changing the layout. In the absence of the placeholder that the layout provides, you must manually resize and position inserted objects. The PowerPoint grid takes the guesswork out of sizing and aligning. And now you can turn it on with a click of a button. Show/Hide Grid is available on the Standard toolbar. As you drag an object near a guide, the object "sticks" to the guide so you can easily align objects on the guide. This Snap To Grid feature is on by default. To adjust specifics of how the grid works, choose View ➢ Grid And Guides (or press Ctrl+G) to open the Grid And Guides dialog box.

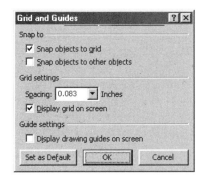

Clear the Snap Objects To Grid check box if you don't want objects to stick to the grid as you drag. Enable Snap Objects To Other Objects if you want to automatically line up objects that are positioned on the same gridline. Use the Grid Settings area of the dialog box to adjust spacing between gridlines or to toggle the grid off (as if you had clicked the Standard toolbar button). Enable the check box to Display Drawing Guides On Screen if you want to display two nonprinting lines that divide each slide into four equal quadrants. Design and graphics professionals often use layout guides for placing objects in ways that create a balanced look.

Inserting Clip Art

To insert a clip on any slide, choose Insert ➤ Picture ➤ Clip Art to open the task pane and search Microsoft Clip Organizer, as fully described in Chapter 6, "Beyond Text: Making the Most of Graphics."

NOTE If this is your first contact with clip art, you are prompted to categorize clips in Clip Organizer. It's a good idea to go through this process as soon as you get a chance. That way, existing picture files on your computer are available when you search for art in Clip Organizer. Chapter 6 can help you here as well.

Once your search results are returned, click the clip you want to use and it appears on the slide. Move and resize the clip as necessary.

If the clip art you are inserting needs to be exactly positioned relative to the slide's text or other objects, start with a slide layout that includes a clip art placeholder. Just choose Slide Layouts from the drop-down menu in the task pane and choose the layout that best suits your needs. As you may recall, the task pane displays slide layouts in four categories: Text, Content, Text And Content, and Other. Some placeholders (those listed under the Other Layouts category) launch clip art with a double-click, while some layouts (the Text And Content layouts) allow you to single-click. This may be a bit confusing, but you can always follow the rule for beginners: try a single click; if it doesn't work, try a double click! The appropriate click action opens the Select Picture dialog box, shown in Figure 24.2.

When you find the clip you want to use, click it and then click OK. The dialog box closes and the picture you selected is displayed on the slide, sized to the frame of the placeholder.

FIGURE 24.2

The Select Picture dialog box offers hundreds of clip art images you can add to presentations.

NEW▶

If you insert an object without a placeholder on a slide that's already "full," Power-Point automatically adjusts the slide layout to accommodate the new object. Often, you get results you don't want when this AutoLayout feature kicks in. Click the Automatic Layout Options icon to see a list of choices related to the slide layout.

Choose Undo Automatic Layout to return the slide to its preinsertion appearance. The inserted object stays on the slide, but you'll have to move and resize it to not obscure other slide objects. Choose Stop Automatic Layout Of Inserted Objects if you never want PowerPoint to adjust the slide layout when you insert additional objects. Or you can choose Control AutoCorrect Options to open a dialog box and disable automatic features you don't need.

NOTE AutoCorrect is a common feature in Office 2002 applications and is covered in detail in Chapter 4, "Putting Text and Language Tools to Work for You."

Aligning and Rotating Art

To quickly align or space objects, including clips, hold Shift and select the objects. On the Drawing toolbar, choose Draw ➤ Align Or Distribute and then choose an alignment or distribution option from the menu. If you're just "eyeballing" it—dragging objects to an approximate position—why not turn on the grid? Now that there's a Show/Hide Grid button on the Standard toolbar, it's only a click away. Object alignment is further discussed in Chapter 6.

 PowerPoint 2002 allows you to rotate any picture. As you previous-version users know, this feature was often disabled for certain file types. To rotate a graphic, place your mouse over the green handle and drag left or right.

Recoloring a Clip Art Object

The Picture toolbar opens automatically when you select a clip art object in Power-Point. If you or another user previously turned it off, click View ➤ Toolbars ➤ Picture to display it again.

 General use of the Picture toolbar is discussed in Chapter 7, "Getting Creative with the Office XP Graphics Tools." But one toolbar button is available only in PowerPoint: the Recolor Picture button. Clicking the button opens the Recolor Picture dialog box, shown in Figure 24.3.

FIGURE 24.3

Swap clip art colors in the Recolor Picture dialog box.

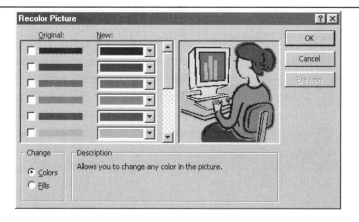

In the Change area, choose either Colors, which changes the colors of lines as well as fills, or Fills, which doesn't affect lines. To change a color, check the box in front of the color you want to change, and then select a new color from the corresponding New drop-down list. The sample changes as you assign new colors for the clip.

TIP If you need to recolor a clip art image in any other Office application, copy the image and paste it in a PowerPoint slide. Recolor the image in PowerPoint and then use the Clipboard to return it to the other Office application.

Inserting Media Clips from Clip Organizer

PowerPoint includes sounds and animated GIFs you can play during your slide shows. Some sounds, like the typewriter or laser sound, are accessed from animation effects (more on this later in the chapter). Other sounds and motion clips are in Microsoft Clip Organizer. Just as with clip art, you may find it easiest to insert clips by choosing a slide layout that includes a media clip placeholder. Simply click the Insert Clip Art icon to open a dialog box with available clips.

To insert a sound or video file on any slide, follow these steps:

1. In Normal view, display the slide you want to add a media clip to.

2. Choose Insert ➢ Movies And Sounds ➢ Movie From Clip Organizer or Sound From Media Gallery.

3. In the Insert Clip Art task pane, select the sound or motion clip (animated GIF) you want to add. Click the drop-down arrow and choose Preview/Properties to preview the selected sound or motion clip.

NOTE If you're inserting a media clip from a placeholder, the task pane doesn't open. Instead, you must use the Media Clip dialog box to search for and select the clip you want.

4. Click Insert from the drop-down menu or simply click the thumbnail icon to insert the object and place a sound icon or video object on the slide. When you insert a sound file, PowerPoint prompts you to choose to play the clip automatically or on mouse click.

5. To play a sound or video that doesn't play automatically, double-click the icon or object in Slide Show view.

 NOTE You need speakers (or headphones) and a sound card to play music and sounds. To view the current settings for sound on your computer, open the Control Panel and check the Sounds And Multimedia settings.

To insert a sound or video that isn't in Clip Organizer, choose the From File menu choice (Insert ➤ Movies And Sounds ➤ Movie From File, for instance). Locate, select, and open the file. Animated GIFs don't play in views other than Slide Show view. Click the Slide Show view button to preview the animated GIF on your slide. Many of the commands on the Picture toolbar are disabled for animated GIFs.

 NOTE You can add your own narration or CD audio to a presentation. See "Orchestrating the Soundtrack" at the end of this chapter.

Inserting Other Sound and Video Files

Microsoft provides a fine selection of sound clips, and you can download more sound and video clips from Clip Organizer online. But you're not limited to the Microsoft clips. You can download royalty-free sounds and video from a number of Web sites, grab a camera or microphone, and hit the field to interview customers. Or you can use the Windows Sound Recorder or Media Player to capture sound and video from your PC. To insert a sound or video file stored on your computer or network, follow these steps:

1. Choose Insert ➤ Movies And Sounds ➤ Sound From File or Movie From File.

2. Locate the file you wish to insert.

3. Click OK to insert the file.

If you need video for a presentation and don't have a video capture card or a digital video camera, don't despair. Most computer graphics companies and many full-service camera shops can create video files from your videotape or 8mm tape.

TIP The optimal screen display size for a video depends on your screen resolution. To have PowerPoint estimate the best video size, right-click the video object and choose Format Picture to open the Format Picture dialog box. On the Size tab, enable the Best Scale For Slide Show check box, and then choose the resolution for the monitor or projector you'll use for playback from the drop-down list. When you click OK, PowerPoint resizes the object.

PowerPoint supports a number of sound and video formats, but the Windows Media Player supports even more. If PowerPoint doesn't support the type of multimedia file you want to play in your presentation, insert the object as a Media Player object instead of a PowerPoint movie or sound file. To do so, follow these steps:

1. Choose Insert ➢ Object from the menu to open the Insert Object dialog box.

2. Choose Media Clip from the list of objects.

3. Click Insert.

4. Right-click the object and choose Media Clip ➢ Edit from the shortcut menu to open the Media Player toolbar in PowerPoint.

5. Choose Insert Clip from the menu. Select the type of clip you want to insert.

6. In the Open dialog box, select the clip and click Open.

7. Click in the background of the slide to end the editing session.

Right-click the Media Player object and choose Format Object from the shortcut menu to change the object's appearance on the slide. For more information about the Media Player, choose Help while you're editing a clip to open Windows Media Player Help.

TIP To hide the media clip icon from your audience, drag it off the slide in Normal view. In this case, you'll probably want to use custom animation (covered later in this chapter) to have the media clip play automatically when the slide is displayed.

Inserting Tables from Word

If you've already created a table in Word that you want to use in a presentation, you can copy it in Word and paste it onto a slide. A table larger than three columns by four rows will be too large to show up clearly on a slide, so keep it simple. If you want to create a Word table in the current presentation, choose Insert ➢ Table, or choose a Table AutoLayout from the task pane and double-click the Table icon on the slide. You are prompted to enter the number of columns and rows you want to include.

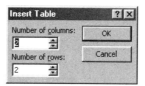

After you select the appropriate number of rows and columns and click OK, you can work with the table just as you would in Word. You may even want to use tools on the Tables And Borders toolbar. (Right-click any toolbar and choose Tables And Borders if it doesn't appear automatically.) For a thorough review of Word's table features, see Chapter 5, "Designing Pages with Columns and Tables."

Resize the table using the handles, or reposition the table by dragging it to a new location. If you need to edit the table, double-click the table object, or choose Toolbars ➢ Tables And Borders to turn the toolbar back on.

Customizing Bullets

You're probably used to choosing bullet characters in PowerPoint and Word from the myriad font sets installed with Windows and Office. If you thought Wingdings and Monotype Sorts were cool, fasten your seatbelt. In PowerPoint 2002, you can create a custom bullet from any picture file, giving you endless possibilities for emphasizing points on slides. We're particularly fond of the bullets we created from pictures of our cat's head, but it makes sense to use a custom Clippit bullet to illustrate a list of ways to get help in PowerPoint.

> Shift+F1
> Click the Office
>   Assistant button
> Choose Help >
>   Show the Office
>   Assistant

PART

IV

AND NOW, PRESENTING
WITH POWERPOINT!

Before you change bullet characters, decide whether you want to make the change on all slides or on just the selected slide. If you wish to make the change for all slides, be sure you are working from the Slide Master (View ➤ Master ➤ Slide Master). Then do the following:

1. Select the text that will use the new bullet. If you are working on the Slide Master, click in the appropriate level.

2. Choose Format ➤ Bullets And Numbering. The Bullets And Numbering dialog box opens, as shown in Figure 24.4.

FIGURE 24.4

Use the Bullets And Numbering dialog box to customize bullet characters.

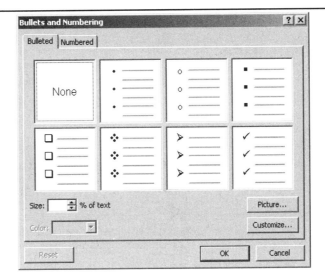

3. Select one of the seven bullet types displayed here and click OK.

   a. Alternatively, you can click Customize to open the Symbol dialog box, shown in Figure 24.5. Click the Font drop-down list to switch character sets. Select the character you wish to use and click OK.

   b. A third alternative is to click Picture to open the Picture Bullet dialog box, shown in Figure 24.6. Choose one of the displayed bullets, or to choose a picture from a file click the Import button, select the file you wish to use, and click Import.

FIGURE 24.5

Previewing a bullet character in the Symbol dialog box

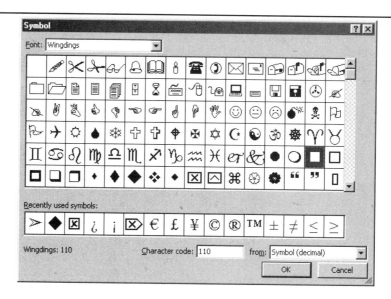

FIGURE 24.6

In the Picture Bullet dialog box, choose a picture from Clip Organizer to use as a bullet character, or import your own.

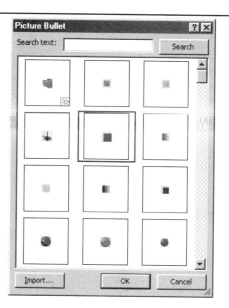

When you wish to use the picture bullet, look for it among others in Clip Organizer. To adjust the size of a custom bullet, use the Size spin box in the Bullets And Numbering dialog box.

TIP To create bullets of screen features (like our Clippit bullets), use a screen capture utility.

Modifying and Adding Transitions

An electronic presentation, or slide show, is a presentation displayed on a computer screen or projected with an LCD projector. Since slides are "changed" by the computer rather than by hand, you can add computerized special effects to a slide show that aren't possible when you use regular overheads for a presentation (unless you're an incredibly talented presenter who moonlights as a magician). A *transition* is a special effect added to the slide's initial appearance on-screen. The slide can appear from the right, dissolve in gradually, or fade through the background of the previous slide.

Individual slides can include *animation*—different steps used to construct the slide, one placeholder at a time. For example, the slide can first appear with a title only, and bulleted points can be added one by one. In earlier versions of PowerPoint, animation was called *slide builds*.

 NOTE Some of the design templates also include animated features—for example, one of the background objects may streak into place. You can modify this animation on the Slide Master.

If you started your presentation with the AutoContent Wizard or specific templates, your slides may already have transitions and/or animation assigned. Think of these as default settings; modify these transitions or add transitions in Slide Sorter view using the tools on the Slide Sorter toolbar, shown here.

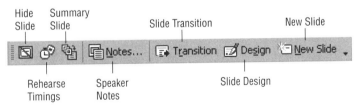

If a presentation doesn't have transitions, each slide simply appears in place of the previous slide—very plain-vanilla. Many of the PowerPoint 2002 design templates include transitions so there is more pizzazz.

PowerPoint 2002 offers the ability to apply and preview transitions without ever leaving Normal view. We suggest displaying thumbnails (rather than the outline) for ease of selecting multiple slides. PowerPoint does so by default when you open the Slide Transition task pane. To change or add transitions in Normal view,

1. Display the task pane (View ➣ Task Pane).

2. Click the task pane selection list and choose Slide Transition. The task pane displays current transition settings, as shown in Figure 24.7.

3. Select the slide(s) and then choose an effect from the Apply To Selected Slides list box.

TIP To select a slide, click it. To select multiple noncontiguous slides, click the first slide, hold down Ctrl, and click the other slide(s) you want to select. To select all slides, press Ctrl+A.

FIGURE 24.7

The Slide Transition task pane is available in both Normal and Slide Sorter views.

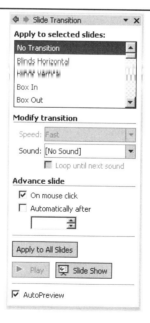

Many of the transitions listed differ only in direction—for example, Cover Up, Cover Down, and Cover Up-Left. PowerPoint 2002 has several new transition effects as well. Check out Newsflash, Comb, Shape, and Wedge & Wheel. Anytime you select a transition from the list, PowerPoint provides a preview of the transition using the selected slide. (Look fast—it doesn't take long.) To see the transition again, click Play at the bottom of the task pane. If you don't like seeing the automatic preview each time you make a transition selection, disable the AutoPreview check box at the bottom of the task pane. You can still click Play to see a preview when *you* decide it's appropriate.

If you prefer to add transitions from Slide Sorter view, click the Slide Transition button on the Slide Sorter toolbar to display the Slide Transition task pane. Choose the effect you wish to use from the list box in the task pane.

In Slide Sorter view, an *animation icon* below the lower-left corner of a slide indicates the slide has an assigned transition or animation. You can't tell from looking at the icon whether it has transitions, animations, or both. Click the icon to see a preview in the slide miniature.

 TIP To quickly return to Normal view from Slide Sorter view, double-click a slide.

Setting Transition Speed and Sound

Each transition has a default speed. You can change the speed for transitions, choose a different transition, or add sound effects to accompany a transition in the Slide Transition task pane, shown previously in Figure 24.7.

Select the slide(s) you want to adjust. Choose a new transition effect (if you wish) and then choose one of the Speed options from the drop-down list in the Modify Transition area of the task pane. If you assign a transition sound from the Sound drop-down list, you can choose to have the sound loop until another sound begins playing. The last choice on the drop-down list, Other Sounds, opens a dialog box so that you can select a sound file. PowerPoint uses wave sounds (WAV extension). You'll find some wave files in the Media folder in the Windows folder, but you can purchase CDs of wave files at many computer stores and download free sound bytes from the Internet (see the sidebar titled "Using Sound Files from the Internet").

The Advance Slide settings are used to enter timings for automatic slide advances. For now, leave the default On Mouse Click setting to require human intervention to change slides (see "Setting Slide Timings" in Chapter 25).

Any settings you choose are applied immediately to selected slides. If you wish, you can choose Apply To All Slides to apply the transition settings to every slide in the presentation. Effects, including sound, can be previewed by clicking the Play button in the task pane.

MASTERING THE OPPORTUNITIES

Using Sound Files from the Internet

If you work in a company or industry that frequently uses PowerPoint presentations, you may hear those canned sound bytes so many times they become irritating. If everyone in the room makes the drive-by sound along with the transition, it's time to try out some different sounds.

Use any Internet search engine to locate sites with the text string "WAV files." Select a site and browse the files until you find just the right sound. Right-click the file and choose either the Download or the Save As option. Select a Save location and click OK. Often, you come across sites where all you have to do is click a link to automatically download a sound file. In any case, once the sound file is saved to a folder you can access, assign it by choosing Other Sound from the drop-down list in the Slide Transition task pane.

Naturally, you will have to use discretion in selecting sound bytes for a professional presentation. Although *you* might want to communicate decisions about downsizing using the Tragic Soap Opera Organ from Joe's Original Wave Files (www.sky.net/~jdeshon/joewav.html), your boss may not find it amusing.

Some companies have strict policies regarding Internet usage and downloading files. Be sure you are working within your company's policies when using Internet sounds.

Adding Animation

NEW▶ Transition effects are used *between* slides; animation effects occur *within* a slide. Each title, bulleted point, or object on a slide can be added to the slide separately. Animating points focuses the viewer on the individual point you're discussing during the presentation. PowerPoint 2002 has new preset *animation schemes* that include separate effects for the slide title and bulleted paragraphs. You can apply a scheme to multiple slides with just a few clicks. You can apply preset animation schemes from Slide Sorter or Normal view. Display the task pane and then do the following:

 Animation Schemes

1. If the task pane is in Slide Design mode, click the Animation Schemes icon to display preset schemes. If not, click the task pane selection menu and choose Slide Design - Animation Schemes.

2. Select the slide(s) you want to animate.

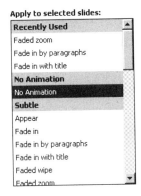

3. Choose a scheme from the scroll list in the task pane. Schemes are categorized as Recently Used, No Animation, Subtle, Moderate, and Exciting.

 WARNING It's possible (and very easy) for your presentation to come across as a bit *too* exciting. Keep transitions simple and occasionally throw in something different. If you use too many effects, you could wind up obscuring your message rather than enhancing it.

---

4. Schemes are applied to selected slides in real time. You'll see a preview as soon as you choose a scheme from the list. (If you don't see the preview, enable the AutoPreview check box at the bottom of the task pane.) Click Apply To All Slides if you wish to use the selected animation scheme on all slides.

 If you apply an animation scheme in Slide Sorter view, you'll immediately see the animation icon below the left corner of the slide. (It may have already been there if you previously applied a transition to that slide.) Click the icon, or click a slide and click Play to view animation.

 WARNING Preset animation schemes override existing transitions. If you don't want to lose the transitions you've applied, you must use custom animation (discussed in the next section).

When you animate some but not all elements on a slide, Slide Show view opens the slide displaying those objects and graphics that are *not* animated. Click (or press Enter on the keyboard) to animate the first slide element. Click again for each additional object.

Adding Custom Animation

Sound and motion can be combined in unique ways to generate a memorable electronic presentation. Use the custom animation tools to determine the order in which information is presented, to bring focus to important points, and to spice up tedious content.

NEW▶ Custom animation has been totally revamped for PowerPoint 2002. Not only are there over a dozen more effects from which to choose, you also have much better control over how you apply those effects. Now there are options for applying entrance, emphasis, path, and exit effects. That means you can animate an object to bounce in and then bounce out. You can even apply simultaneous animation so that multiple slide elements appear at once.

Switch to Normal view to apply custom animation; this feature is disabled in Slide Sorter view. Essentially you must follow two steps: select a slide object and then apply the custom effects you want for that object. Repeat those two main steps for each object on the slide that you wish to animate. It's helpful to animate items in the order you want them added to the slide during the slide show. However, as you'll see below, you can change the animation order with just a few clicks. Let's take a closer look at the steps you'll follow to apply custom animation:

1. In Normal view, navigate to the slide you want to animate.

2. Display the task pane and choose Custom Animation from the task pane selection menu (see Figure 24.8).

3. As the helper text indicates, you must select an object on the slide (the slide title, for example) and click the Add Effect button in the task pane.

FIGURE 24.8

PowerPoint displays helper text to assist with custom animation on nonanimated slides.

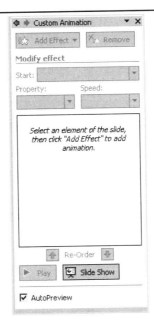

4. Then you must decide *how* and *when* you want to animate the selected object. Choose from these options:

Entrance To see an effect when the object enters the slide in Slide Show view. Objects animated with entrance effects do *not* appear on the slide when it transitions from the previous slide.

Emphasis To use an effect to draw attention to a particular slide element. Objects with emphasis animations appear on the slide when it transitions from the previous slide.

Exit To apply an effect as the object leaves the slide. As with emphasis effects, objects appear with the slide transition.

Motion Path To create a set of specific directions for the object to follow when it animates (more on this in the next section). Objects may or may not appear on the slide when it transitions—it depends on where you place the object in Normal view. If you position the object *off* the slide, it follows the motion path *onto* the slide (unless you goof and choose a path that doesn't move the object toward the slide!).

5. Once you've determined the how and when, you must select an effect. The choices available depend on which of the four animation types you chose in

step 4. For example, when you click Add Effect and choose Entrance for the selected slide title, you're presented with a list of most frequently/recently used effects. Choose one of these or click More Effects to see additional choices in a dialog box.

The dialog box choices are categorized as Basic, Subtle, Moderate, and Exciting. Some may be disabled. For example, the Faded Swivel choice shown here is unavailable because it is an exit animation. If the Preview Effect check box is enabled, you can click an effect to get an idea of what it does (you may have to drag the dialog box out of the way to see the preview on the slide). When you find the effect you want to use, click it and then click OK.

TIP Many effects—Wipe, Fly, Checkerboard, and Cover, to name a few—have an adjustable direction component. Choose the effect as you normally would and then, if you wish, select something other than the default from the Direction drop-down list in the task pane.

6. Repeat the procedure for each element you wish to animate. PowerPoint displays the *animation sequence*—the order in which animations occur—in the task pane (shown here) and places a nonprinting animation tag next to animated slide elements (see Figure 24.9). Each tag corresponds to the numbered item in the task pane.

Anytime you wish to preview the effects applied to a slide, just click Play at the bottom of the task pane. In preview mode, effects display automatically even if objects are set up to animate on mouse click. To get a feel for how the slide will behave during the actual presentation, click the Slide Show (From Current Slide) button.

To adjust the animation sequence, click the animated object in the task pane list, and then use the Re-Order buttons (below the list) to adjust its placement in the list. PowerPoint automatically adjusts the tags on the slide to reflect the new animation order.

NEW▶

But wait, there's more! What if you decide to use more than one animation on an object? For example, bulleted points with entrance effects can include an exit effect as well. To apply a second animation to an already-animated object, select it and follow steps 3 through 5. PowerPoint may display more than one tag on slide objects with multiple animations, or you may see the tag number followed by an ellipsis (…). The slide displayed in Figure 24.10 (later in this chapter) contains objects with multiple animations.

EXPERT TIP When you give a slide show, you want the audience to remember your presentation's *content*—not just the flashy effects. In general, you should develop an overall animation "theme," apply it consistently, and vary from the theme to highlight key points. Use one or two similar transitions throughout the presentation. For example, alternating left and right or top and down transitions of the same type provides variety without irritating your audience. (Avoid alternating rapid left/right transitions if you're keynoting after a big meal unless you have a supply of those small bags that the airlines use.) When a presentation has transitions, slides without transitions stand out, so No Transition effectively becomes another type of transition. Sound can be attention grabbing, but new sound on every slide is too much.

EXPERT TIP The same tips apply to animation. Choose a small group of animation effects. Text that flies in from the right feels normal because the side we read first enters first, so the majority of body text should enter the screen from the right rather than the left, particularly if your audience may include low-level readers. To add emphasis, then, have text enter from the left, top, or bottom, but make sure to leave the text on the screen for a longer period of time; it takes longer to begin reading text that enters from the left.

Applying Path Animation

NEW▶

We've frequently heard questions like these from longtime PowerPoint users:

- Can I make the racecar drive up the side of the slide and then across the top?
- Can I make a butterfly clip art "flit" across the screen?
- Can my drawn arrow make a figure eight and then come to rest in the upper-right corner of the slide?

We used to have to answer, "Yes, with difficulty." But now it's simple! PowerPoint 2002's path animation makes it easy for objects to follow virtually any path. You're sure to find just the right choice from several dozen built-in path selections. And if you don't, you can create your own by drawing a custom path. Path animation might seem a bit tricky at first, but here's what you need to know to be successful with it.

- Objects using path animation have a starting and ending point.
- The object's placement on the slide determines its starting point.
- The path animation you select determines the object's ending point. You can reverse the animation path, which also swaps starting and ending points.
- Paths can be locked or unlocked. Locked means the animation path is tied to that location on the slide, even if you move the object. When you choose unlocked, the path moves automatically anytime you move the object.

To apply a path animation, follow these steps:

1. Select the object you wish to animate.
2. Click Add Effect ➤ Motion Paths to open a menu of choices. Choose one of the menu options, or choose More Motion Paths to open the Add Motion Path dialog box.

PART

IV

AND NOW, PRESENTING
WITH POWERPOINT!

Additional motion paths are displayed in categories: Basic, Lines & Curves, and Special. Click a path to see its effect (make sure Preview Effect is enabled and move the dialog box out of the way if necessary). When you find the one you want to use, click it and click OK.

3. If you don't see an effect that suits your needs, you can choose Add Effect ➤ Motion Paths ➤ Draw Custom Path to create your own. See the sidebar titled "Perfecting Path Animation" for tips on creating custom paths.

4. Once you've applied a path animation, the path is displayed on the slide as a dotted line (see Figure 24.9). The starting point is indicated by a green arrow, and the ending point is indicated by a red arrow.

 TIP Drag the red and green arrows to adjust starting and ending points.

FIGURE 24.9

Slide objects show nonprinting numbered tags to indicate the order in which they are animated.

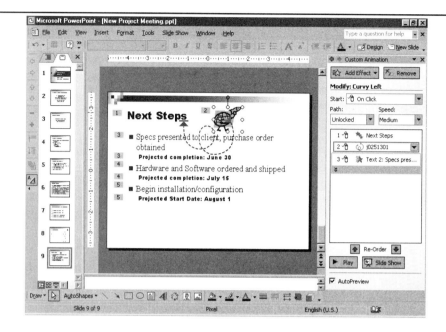

Adjusting Path Animation

At times you will want to make minor modifications to the animation path: make the curve a little wider or make the bounce a little lower. PowerPoint allows you to edit the path at certain points. Just select the object with the path animation you want to tweak, and then click the Path drop-down list in the task pane. Choose Edit Points to display handles on the animation path. Drag the handles—one at a time—to adjust the path.

To tie an animation path to a location on the slide and not the object you're animating, choose Locked from the Path drop-down list. If you later move the object, the path stays put. To have the path move with the object, choose Unlocked.

You can also reverse the direction the object travels along the animation path. Select the object and choose Reverse Path Direction from the Path drop-down list. Essentially, you are swapping the object's starting and ending points when you reverse the path.

MASTERING THE OPPORTUNITIES

Perfecting Path Animation

So you've grown tired of using the canned path animations (even though there are over 60 of them!). No problem; PowerPoint 2002 lets you draw your own custom path. The secret to having success with this feature is selecting the correct drawing tool and knowing the click sequence that produces the desired results with that tool. Select the slide object you wish to animate. Click Add Effect ➣ Motion Path ➣ Draw Custom Path and then use one of these tools:

- Choose the **Line** tool if you want to draw a straight path. Once the tool is selected, drag from the object to the ending point. Release the mouse, and the animation path immediately appears on the slide.

- Click the **Curve** tool to make a wavy path. Click once at the starting point, move the mouse to where you want the first curve, and click. Repeat until you have all the curves you need. Double-click to end the curve and display the path on the slide.

- Select the **Freeform** tool if you want to create a path that includes both straight and curvy line segments. Use clicks to create straight-line segments; drag when you want to draw wavy lines or other shapes. Double-click to finish.

- Use the **Scribble** tool to create virtually any path. One caution here: you'll have difficulty drawing straight lines. If you're going for that erratic look, Scribble will do it. Select the tool and drag from the object to the ending point. Release the mouse button to end the path.

Changing Speed, Timing, and Other Custom Animation Settings

So far we've discussed how to apply animation effects and how to adjust the animation sequence. But there's much more to it than that. For example, you can adjust the speed at which an object animates, apply sounds to accompany animation effects, change text color after animation, and create simultaneous animations. Further, you can determine whether each animation occurs with a click of the mouse or automatically based on timing. With all these choices, you can spend hours on animation alone!

To adjust the speed of an animation effect, select the object (by clicking it on the slide or in the animation sequence, or by clicking its animation tag on the slide). Then choose a different animation rate from the Speed drop-down list in the task pane.

> **TIP** To get an idea of the exact timing of an animation, display the Advanced Timeline. Just click the drop-down arrow next to the object in the task pane animation list, and choose Show Advanced Timeline.

NEW▶ Animations that are adjacent in sequence can be set up to occur simultaneously. When you want animations to happen at the same time, make sure they are next to each other in the animation list. Use the Re-Order arrows to position them if necessary. Then

1. Select the one that appears *farthest down* the list.

2. Click the Start drop-down list at the top of the Custom Animation task pane.

3. Choose With Previous.

Items that animate simultaneously are assigned the same numbered tag on the slide. And you can still apply more than one animation to items that animate at the same time. Figure 24.10 shows a slide with simultaneous animation and multiple animations for two of its objects.

The animation sequence for the slide in Figure 24.10 goes like this. After the slide transition, the objects tagged 0 do their thing: the text "Welcome to 6th Grade" dissolves in at the same time the bus graphic follows its path animation. The sequence continues as the numbered tags indicate. Next come "Mr. Vallier," then "Goodrich Middle School," and finally the oval graphic at the top of the slide. Then come the exit animations: all the text leaves the slide, but the graphic objects remain in position since no exit animations have been applied to these graphics

> **NOTE** It's fairly easily to understand an animation *sequence* from the tags on the slide. However, to see what specific effect has been applied to an object, you must click its tag. The effect appears at the top of the task pane below the Change icon. And remember, you can always click Play to get the full visual effect.

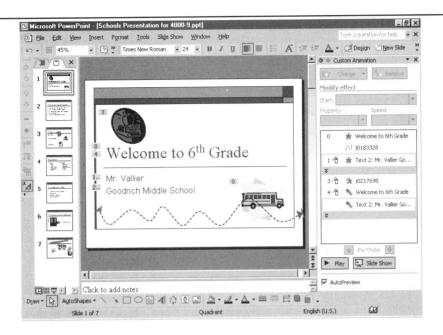

FIGURE 24.10

Objects with simultaneous animations are tagged with the same number.

Working with Text Frames

Although graphics can add information with pizzazz to an otherwise dull presentation, it's slide text that usually conveys your message in the most straightforward way. Therefore, it pays to spend a few minutes making sure slide text is introduced and emphasized in ways that make it easy to understand and remember. One way to do this is with an emphasis effect (discussed previously). However, if an audience member glances away during the critical moment, they may miss the emphasis and lose track of which bulleted point you are addressing. Using an after-animation dim color can help the audience keep up. (Just make sure you don't dim to a color that makes the text unreadable, or your note takers may become annoyed.) Or you might choose to repeat the emphasis until you click for the next bulleted point. Fortunately, there are several ways to fine-tune animation.

NEW ▶

Previous PowerPoint versions required that you apply the same effect to all paragraphs in a text frame. Now you can choose a different effect for each bulleted point. This feature gives you much more control and increases the likelihood of overkill at the same time! Seriously, though, there are ways to use varying effects without stupefying your audience. Here are some quick ideas:

- Wipe in the first several points and bounce in the last. (Or combine any two effects in this way.)

- Alternate two effects: one paragraph dissolves in, the next flies in.
- Use the same effect on each point, but vary the direction: stretch across, from bottom, from left, from right.
- Choose a different effect and direction for each point, but use the same effect sequence for every slide: wipe right, then ascend, curve up, and checkerboard across on every slide. We wouldn't recommend this for slides with more than four bulleted points, and that might be pushing it, depending on any other effects included in the presentation.

Consistency is the key. Choose one or two settings to alter between slides; don't change everything under the sun! Once the audience sees a consistent pattern (the earlier the better), they'll quickly know what to expect and focus more on content.

The task pane displays animated text frames collapsed by default.

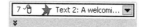

When you select the collapsed item and apply animation, the effect settings are the same for each paragraph in the text box—a quick and easy way to animate if you want to use the same effect within a frame. To access individual paragraphs within the text frame, click the double down arrows to display them. Click the double up arrows to collapse the detail at any time.

 TIP You can also select a specific paragraph by clicking its numbered slide tag. The list in the task pane expands automatically.

Adjusting Effect Options

Each animated object listed in the task pane contains a menu of choices related to the animation. Now that you know the difference between selecting a text box and selecting a specific item within a text box, we can proceed with modifying default animation settings. Select any text object you've previously animated, or animate one now if you are starting from scratch. Click the drop-down arrow next to the animated item in the task pane to display a menu of choices for that item.

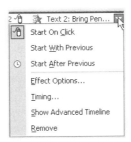

Choose Effect Options to open a dialog box with options for that animation. Figure 24.11 shows effect options for a text box with a Strips animation. Proceed as follows:

1. Select a different direction if you don't like the current choice. The Direction list varies according to the type of effect you've chosen. These same choices are available in the task pane, but you can change them here too.

2. Choose a sound to accompany the animation if you wish. Click the sound icon to adjust the volume of the sound. Keep in mind that depending on which object you selected in the task pane, you may be applying a sound to every bulleted point in the frame—overkill in most situations. (See the sidebar titled "Mastering Animation for Multiple Text Levels.")

3. Select an After Animation color to change the color of animated text as the next animation occurs. You can use this in multiple-point slides with rather dramatic effect; for example, you can have each point animate as white text and then change to gray when the next point enters, drawing the viewer's attention immediately to the new point and away from the previous point. If you're creating a presentation for an audience that includes members with lower reading levels—and that includes most audiences—make sure you dim points after animation. It's a simple way to make sure you don't leave slow readers in the dust.

WARNING Over 30 percent of the adult population learns best when taking notes. It's not that they don't trust your handouts; the physical act of writing triggers learning. If you don't want to really irritate a third of your audience, select an After Animation color that doesn't get lost in the background. Gray works well with many backgrounds (unless, of course, the background color of your template is gray).

4. The Animate Text list determines how text is introduced: all at once, by word, or by letter. If you introduce by word or letter, you must select a delay percentage.

WARNING Be careful here. It's exciting to see an occasional slide title fly in by letter, but you'll lose your audience at the second bulleted point if you animate text-heavy slides by word or letter.

5. When you have finished adjusting effect options, click OK to apply them. PowerPoint provides an immediate preview.

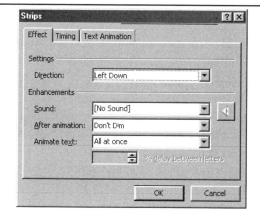

Effect options are available for any slide object. You can't introduce graphics by letter, of course, but you can choose a sound and a dim color for most. In addition, path animations offer the following options:

Smooth Start Causes the animation to gradually build speed rather than starting abruptly.

Smooth End Slows the animation as it reaches its ending point.

Auto-Reverse Plays the animation twice: once forward, once in reverse. Requires double the time.

Modifying Animation Timing

You can introduce a slide object automatically or as a *triggered* effect, which means it animates on mouse click. You needn't make the same choice for all slides, but if you're varying triggers on or between slides, you should practice the presentation until you've memorized where to click and where automatic advances occur.

To adjust timing, select an animation from the task pane list and click the drop-down arrow to display its menu. Then

1. Choose Timing to open the Timing tab of the effect dialog box shown here.

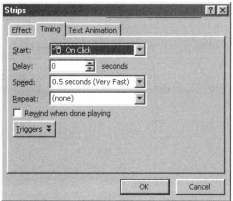

2. Choose a Start option. If you wish to automate the animation so that it proceeds without mouse clicks, choose After Previous. (The With Previous choice creates simultaneous animation, as previously discussed.)

3. If you wish to apply a time delay between the Start action and the animation, set the number of seconds in the Delay spin box.

NOTE The number of seconds that you enter is related to your processor speed and available memory. Five seconds lasts longer on a slower computer than on a faster computer with tons of available memory.

---

4. Use the Speed control to adjust how fast the animation occurs. For entrance, exit, and path animations, the speed setting determines how fast it takes the object to go from start to end position. With emphasis effects, the timing control establishes how long the animation lasts. These same timing choices are available from the Speed drop-down list in the Custom Animation task pane.

5. If you want to see an animation more than once, you can repeat it. Choose an option from the Repeat list to see an animation multiple times, until the next click, or until the next slide is displayed.

TIP You can use the repeat feature in conjunction with some of the emphasis effects. This is helpful in keeping the audience focused on the bulleted point you're currently addressing. As always, consider the annoyance factor and make sure the effect you're using doesn't obscure the message.

6. If you want an object to return to its original position after animation, enable the Rewind When Done Playing check box. This is particularly helpful with path animations. It causes the object to move from starting to ending point, pause for a moment, and then return to its original placement (which could even be off the slide).

7. Adjust triggers if needed. Choose Animate As Part Of A Click Sequence to play the animation in the order it appears in the task pane sequence, regardless of *where* you click during the slide show. Choose Start Effect On Click Of and select an object if you want to specify an exact click location to trigger the animation.

8. When you're finished, click OK. PowerPoint provides a preview that plays even triggered events automatically. To preview the show using actual triggers, click the Slide Show button in the task pane.

MASTERING THE OPPORTUNITIES

Mastering Animation for Multiple Text Levels

As you learned in Chapter 22, slide text can be arranged in outline levels. The slide title represents the highest level, and five additional levels are available for bulleted points.

PowerPoint lets you choose whether to introduce text by specific levels or all at once. Slides with multiple bullet levels could be overwhelming to listeners if introduced all at once (and you may not want them thinking ahead to subpoint 3 while you're addressing main point 2). If you have second- and third-level bullets and choose to introduce text by the first level, the second- and third-level bullets appear with the first-level bullet they fall under.

You animate points to draw the audience's attention to the point. If the second- and third-level points are simply supporting information or subpoints you want to dispense with quickly, animate by first level. If, on the other hand, you need the audience to

Continued

MASTERING THE OPPORTUNITIES CONTINUED

understand the subpoints or you intend to discuss each in some detail, animate at the second or third level. Here's how:

1. Select the text object you want to adjust. Remember, you can select *all* bulleted points in a text box, or you can choose to tweak them separately.

2. Click the down arrow next to the selected object in the task pane. Choose Effect Options ➤ Text Animation to display group settings.

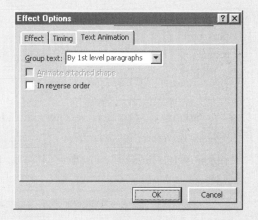

3. Select a Group Text setting. If you select By 3rd Level Paragraphs, paragraphs on levels 1, 2, and 3 enter with separate mouse clicks. To introduce subpoints together with the main point they fall under, group by the level of the main point (usually level 1).

4. If the text you're animating is part of a drawn shape, the Animate Attached Shape check box is available. Check it to animate the object along with the text. Disable it to animate text only.

5. Choose In Reverse Order to bring the last bulleted point in first, and so on.

6. Click OK when you're through. PowerPoint closes the dialog box and provides a preview of the animation.

Using Charts in Presentations

In Office 2002, there are two programs that create charts: Excel and Microsoft Graph. If you already have a chart in Excel, you can easily copy it and embed it in or link it to your slide. In early versions of Office, PowerPoint created the largest (possibly the only) user group for Microsoft Graph, because PowerPoint didn't support animation for objects created in Excel. Excel charts can be animated in PowerPoint 2000 and, of course, PowerPoint 2002.

 NOTE While Graph is a decent charting tool, it's only useful for simple charts. Excel is the best tool for creating and formatting charts. For information on charting in Excel, refer to Chapter 15; see Chapter 7 for instructions on using Microsoft Graph.

To place an existing Excel chart in a PowerPoint slide,

1. Open Excel.

2. Select the chart you want to use. The handles on the chart object border indicate that the entire chart is selected.

3. Copy the chart to the Clipboard.

4. In PowerPoint's Normal view, select the slide you want to place the chart on.

5. To *embed* the chart, click Paste or choose Edit ➢ Paste from the menu.

6. Alternatively, to *link* the chart, choose Edit ➢ Paste Special to open the Paste Special dialog box.

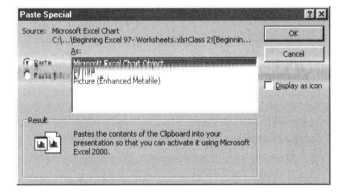

   a. Select the Paste Link option on the left. (To display an icon that you can click to display the chart, enable the Display As Icon check box.)

   b. Click OK to paste the linked chart.

If the workbook that the chart was copied from contains macros, you'll be notified and prompted to proceed or cancel.

> **TIP** When you link rather than embed a chart (or any other object), there are obvious trade-offs. Your chart contains current data, but if someone moves or renames the file containing the chart, or if you e-mail the presentation to someone who doesn't have access to the file, the slide cannot display charted data. Using a dial-up connection to access a linked chart in a real-time presentation is dicey, but when it doesn't work well, you'll have ample time to explain the variability of dial-up connections as your chart elements haltingly lurch their way across the screen.

 To insert a Microsoft Graph chart, click the Insert Chart button on the Standard toolbar or double-click a slide that has a chart placeholder.

Animating Charts

Charts illustrate numeric data; animation breathes life into the illustration. During your slide show, you can introduce an entire chart all at once or have chart elements appear by category, by data series, or as individual data points. Adding the data separately lets you apply emphasis where needed, and it allows your audience to digest one piece of information before you deliver another. You must animate the entire chart first, even if you are planning to animate individual elements. Navigate to the slide with the chart you wish to animate, select the chart, and choose Slide Show ➢ Custom Animation to open the Custom Animation task pane.

1. Click Add Effect and choose an entrance, exit, emphasis, or path animation. If you're planning to animate individual chart elements, be careful here. All the animation effects are available when chart elements are introduced all at once (see step 3). Only certain effects allow you to animate by element. For example, you can't have chart elements spiral in by category, but you can have them strip down.

> **NOTE** Many, but not all, of the directional effects work with individual chart elements: Blinds, Strips, Wipe, Stretch, Checkerboard, and Expand all work. Surprisingly, Fly does not. Experiment until you find one you like. Chances are, you'll use it again and again in your presentations.

2. Display effect options for the chart you just animated. (Click the drop-down arrow next to the object in the task pane and choose Effect Options.) Choose the Chart Animation tab of the dialog box. Chart Animation is available only if the selected object is a chart.

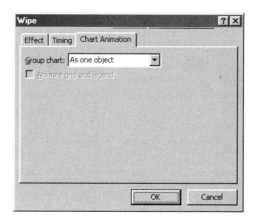

3. In the Group Chart drop-down list, select how you want the chart elements to appear.

All At Once Brings the chart in like a picture; the entire object appears.

By Series Causes all bars from a data series (all the bars, columns, or line segments that are the same color) to appear at once. For example, you might have all four quarters of the West Coast data appear, then the East Coast, etc.

By Category Brings in each x-axis cluster separately (all first quarter, then all second quarter, and so on).

By Element In A Series and By Element In A Category Work essentially the same as By Series and By Category, respectively, except that only one bar appears at a time rather than several bars at once. Choose By Series or By Category to set the order to animate the individual data points.

4. Turn on Animate Grid And Legend if you want to apply effects to those chart elements as well.

5. Use the Effect tab of the dialog box to assign a sound and an After Animation option if you wish. Adjust timings on the Timing tab just as you would with any object.

6. Click OK when you're finished. PowerPoint provides an immediate preview as long as the AutoPreview check box is enabled in the task pane.

NOTE As you add effects to a live presentation, you should increase your practice time. For a perfectly polished presentation, practice until you have memorized which slides animate automatically and which advance on mouse click. If it's difficult to memorize during practice, your presentation is probably overanimated.

Animating Video and Sound

Multimedia settings work just like text animation settings. Select a sound or video object and open the Timing tab of the effect options (shown earlier in the "Modifying Animation Timing" section of this chapter). If you choose to start After Previous, you don't have to click the object to play it. You can hide the object until it plays by assigning an entrance effect. To have the video loop, choose a Repeat setting other than None. Rewind a video clip automatically by enabling the Rewind When Done Playing check box. If you wish, assign a sound to play as the video plays. (Use the Effect tab for this.)

Hiding Slides

Many presentations contain "emergency slides" that are displayed only if certain questions or topics arise during the presentation. Creating and then hiding a slide gives you some leeway: anticipate the questions that will be asked during your presentation (and when they'll be asked), and create slides to allow you to answer the questions with authority. If a question isn't asked, you don't have to show the slide. If, on the other hand, a member of the audience asks how you plan to raise $10 million, you can whip out the hidden slide. The questioner doesn't need to know that the slide was shown only in response to their question.

 In Slide Sorter view, select the slide you want to hide, and then click the Hide Slide button on the Slide Sorter toolbar. A null symbol appears over the slide's number. To display the hidden slide during the presentation, if you have access to the computer's keyboard, type **H** while displaying the slide preceding the hidden slide.

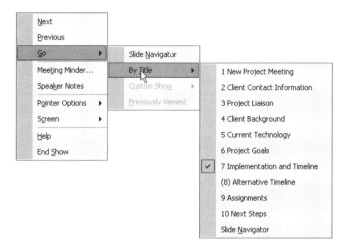

If you are using a mouse or a remote pointing device, you can right-click the slide before the hidden slide, choose Go ➢ By Title, and select the title of the hidden slide from the shortcut menu. However, the shortcut menu is very intrusive. Further, anyone in the audience who uses PowerPoint will know that the slide titles displayed in parentheses on the shortcut are hidden slides. That sort of defeats the purpose of hiding them. If you won't have access to a keyboard during a slide show, hyperlinks provide a slicker way to show hidden slides.

Adding Links to Other Slides

PowerPoint supports hyperlinks to other slides, other presentations, and URLs. Following a hyperlink moves the user from the current slide to another slide, another presentation, or a site on the Internet.

To create a hyperlink, switch to Normal view and select the text that will be used as a hyperlink. Normally, this text tells the user where they're going to end up: Click Here To Exit The Presentation, for example, or Click To View More Options. You don't want to use Click Here For Hidden Slide, so select some existing text that forms a logical jump-off point. With the text selected, right-click and choose Action Settings from the shortcut menu, or choose Slide Show ➢ Action Settings from the menu bar, to open the dialog box shown in Figure 24.12.

FIGURE 24.12

Create hyperlinks in the Action Settings dialog box.

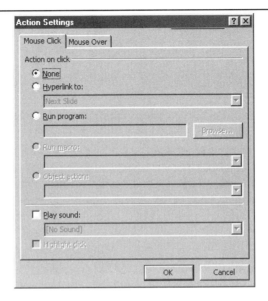

You can activate a hyperlink in two ways: by clicking it or by moving the mouse over it. Both pages of this dialog box are identical—choose a page based on which mouse action you want to trigger the hyperlink. Click the Hyperlink To option and select the slide you want to link to.

Choosing Next Slide shows the next slide, even if it's hidden. To choose a specific slide, choose Slide from the Hyperlink To drop-down list to open the Hyperlink To Slide dialog box.

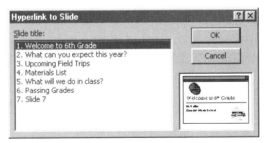

Choose a slide from the Slide Title list box, and then click OK. Click OK in the Action Settings dialog box to create the hyperlink. (The Use Relative Path For Link option is used with Internet URLs and files; for a link to another slide, it doesn't matter whether or not this option is enabled.)

When text is turned into a hypertext link, its formatting is changed. The text is underlined, and a contrasting font color applied. You won't be able to change the color or remove the underlining on the slide. If you want to camouflage hyperlinks, change their color to match surrounding text by using the Custom tab of the Edit Color Scheme dialog box.

WARNING   Don't change the hyperlink color scheme to match surrounding text if you are creating a kiosk presentation for users to click through themselves. They won't know it's a hyperlink if it doesn't stand out. (And if you're presenting a slide show created a few months ago, it's possible to forget the hyperlink without a visual cue.)

If you prefer, you can apply hyperlinks directly by selecting text and clicking Insert ➢ Hyperlink or clicking the Insert Hyperlink button on the Standard toolbar. Specific steps for creating hyperlinks this way are discussed in Chapter 11, "Making Large Documents Easy to Use."

Orchestrating the Soundtrack

In addition to (or instead of) the WAV files that you attach to transitions or include with animation, there are two other audio elements worth considering: CD tracks and narration. Assuming your computer has a CD drive, it's easy to use one or more sequential tracks from a CD as a soundtrack for your presentation. Add a microphone, and you can create narration for the entire presentation or add spoken comments to specific slides.

WARNING   If you won't be present when viewers use your presentation (in a kiosk or on a Web site), you won't know when viewers have special needs. If critical content is only included in the narration, note that hearing-impaired and deaf viewers—as well as Web users whose computers don't have sound cards—won't have access to the content. In a Web presentation (see Chapter 30, "Creating Online Presentations with PowerPoint"), you can display notes. For a kiosk presentation, make sure narrated content is handled redundantly in slide text.

Adding CD Tracks

While you don't need to have the CD you want to use in the CD drive to insert a track, you must close any other applications (such as the Deluxe CD player) that take exclusive control of your CD drive so that PowerPoint can access the CD drive. To insert a CD track, switch to Normal view and do the following:

1. Choose Insert ➤ Movies And Sounds ➤ Play CD Audio Track to open the Movie And Sound Options dialog box.

2. Select the starting and ending track(s) and times.

3. Enable the Loop Until Stopped check box if you want the song to play continuously until you stop the show.

4. Click OK.

5. Indicate whether the sound should play automatically or as soon as you click the icon.

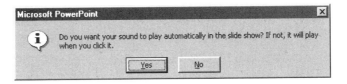

 6. In Normal or Slide Show view, double-click the CD icon to hear the audio track.

Who Owns the Music?

PowerPoint makes it easy to add a CD track or two to your presentation. So why don't more of the presentations you see include a bit of Bette, a few Cranberries, or a slice of Shania?

Broadly speaking, there are two kinds of music: copyrighted music and music in the public domain. Music copyrights can always be renewed. If you use copyrighted music in a public performance, you need to compensate the songwriter, so if you plug in your MIDI keyboard and record "Happy Birthday (to You)" for a public presentation, you owe a fee to the descendants of the two women who wrote it a century ago. On the other hand, "The Confutatus" from Mozart's *Requiem* is in the public domain, although it may be less suitable for a presentation at your boss' birthday bash.

Not all recordings of Mozart's music are in the public domain. If you intend to use a track directly from a commercial CD in a presentation for a conference, there are other permissions to obtain from the music publisher (companies like Sony, Warner Music, PolyGram, and BMG). Obtaining permission from these media megacompanies is a long process and often ends with a "No." They expect royalties as well as assurances that you'll use their music in an acceptable context.

Most public performances of music in the U.S. are licensed through one of three organizations: ASCAP, BMI, or SESAC. All three are member organizations for songwriters and music publishers. Three is the key here because it generally takes about three months to obtain permission to use a piece of music. (This shows signs of improvement; BMI recently partnered with LicenseMusic.com to create a Web-based process for locating and using music written by BMI members.) You'll need to know both the name of the song and the name of the songwriter to determine which of the three organizations to contact for permission to use the music. For more information on using music that is not in the public domain, visit one of these Web sites:

- http://www.ascap.com/ascap.html
- http://www.bmi.com/
- http://sesac.com

So, where can you quickly obtain music for your presentation? The Web, of course. Fire up any Internet search engine and search for **royalty free music** to find dozens of sites where you can download or purchase sound files and CDs.

Recording Audio Comments

Plug in your microphone, lower the ambient noise level in the room (in a home office this means to mute the TV, make the dog stop barking, and give each of the kids a Popsicle), and follow these steps to add a verbal comment to a slide:

1. Display the slide in Normal view.

2. Choose Insert ➤ Movies And Sound ➤ Record Sound to open the Record Sound dialog box.

3. Enter a name for the sound file.

4. Click the Record button (the reddish dot).

5. Talk.

6. When you are finished, click Stop (the blue rectangle).

7. Click OK to save the file.

 The sound icon appears on the slide. Right-click the icon and choose Custom Animation to animate your recorded comment. In the Custom Animation task pane, recorded sound files are listed as Media. To delete a voice comment from a slide, select the icon and then press Delete.

 TIP If you haven't recorded sound recently, it's a good idea to check your microphone level before recording. Choose Slide Show ➤ Record Narration and click the Set Microphone Level button.

Recording Narration

Narration—spoken audio that elaborates the content of the slides in a presentation—is used in kiosks, Web presentations, and instructional presentations, but it has other uses. Make an audio recording of your presentation, attach it as narration, and you have an easy answer to the question: "What did I miss?"

Narration overrides all other sounds in a presentation, so if you add narration to a presentation that has CD audio, animation sounds, or audio comments, only the narration plays. To mix narration and other sounds, record sound files for individual slides.

To record narration for your presentation, select slide 1 and choose Slide Show ➢ Record Narration from the menu to open the Record Narration dialog box, shown in Figure 24.13. PowerPoint checks the current drive for space for a sound file and displays the results as disk space and recording time.

FIGURE 24.13

The Record Narration dialog box indicates storage available for your sound file.

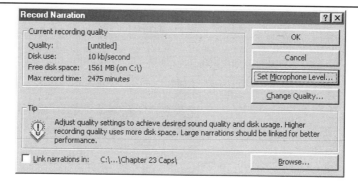

The narration's storage requirements depend on two factors: recording quality and time. Higher quality requires more storage space. If there isn't enough room (enough minutes) on the selected drive for the narration, you have two options:

• Click the Browse button and select another location.

• Lower the sound quality.

To change the sound quality, click the Change Quality button to open the Sound Selection dialog box.

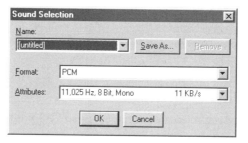

Choose a quality setting from the Name drop-down list. CD Quality is the best, Telephone the worst. To further tweak the quality, select a group of attributes from the Attributes drop-down list. If you choose attributes, you can save the selection by clicking the Save As button. This is a good idea if you'll be adding narration to more than one presentation for the same audience. Click OK to close the Sound Selection dialog box.

> **TIP** If your presentation file is large or the narration is going to be long or high quality, enable the Link Narrations dialog box to store each slide's narration as a separate file linked to the presentation.

Click the Set Microphone Level button in the Record Narration dialog box to make sure that your microphone is plugged in and delivers adequate sound for your presentation.

Click OK to start recording the narration. Move through the presentation, speaking your narration and advancing slides. At the end of the presentation, PowerPoint displays this message box.

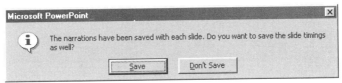

Choose Save to save the slide timings—the length of time between each click of the mouse—with the narration. To save the narration only, choose Don't Save.

A sound icon appears in the bottom-right corner of every slide to indicate that the slide includes narration. Delete a slide's narration by deleting the icon.

> **TIP** When you insert an audio comment with the Record Sound dialog box, the Sound icon is placed in the center of the slide. You can move the icon anywhere on the slide. We'd suggest not moving it to the lower-left corner (or lower-right, depending on the template) because the menu icon resides there.

To record (or rerecord) narration for part of a presentation, select the slide that you want to begin recording on. Choose Slide Show ➤ Record Narration. When you arrive at the slide that immediately follows the last slide you want to record narration for, press Esc to stop recording.

The narration begins automatically when the slide show starts. To view the presentation without its narration, choose Slide Show ➢ Set Up Show from the menu to open the Set Up Show dialog box. Enable the Show Without Narration check box and click OK; then choose View ➢ Slide Show, or click the Slide Show button, to start the slide show.

CHAPTER 25

TAKING YOUR SHOW ON THE ROAD

FEATURING

- Getting feedback from your workgroup

- Incorporating feedback

- Collaborating online

- Preparing notes and handouts

- Printing your materials

- Setting slide timings

- Saving custom shows for different audiences

- Setting up the slide show

O nce you have created, polished, and practiced your presentation, it's time to think about delivery. How will your audience see the presentation—in an auditorium, in a small conference room, over the company intranet? What are the differences between presenting on the road and presenting down the hallway? You must address setup issues thoroughly so that technical problems don't prevent you from showing a presentation you've worked for hours creating. It's equally important to head off glitches that might occur during your presentation—hyperlinks that no longer work, linked files that aren't available, or animations that don't play as expected. No matter how convincingly you recover, technical problems detract from your message. Fortunately, there are steps you can take to ensure that your presentation runs smoothly.

Getting Feedback on Your Presentation from Your Workgroup

Most of us wouldn't deliver new sales materials to a client without first having a colleague proofread them. Nor should you give a presentation that hasn't been scrutinized by someone else whose opinion you trust. The spelling checker catches most mistakes, but it can't do anything about a misspelled company name you've told it to ignore. And there's nothing quite like the feeling you get when you and a few hundred of your closest friends notice a spelling or grammatical error projected in five-foot-high letters in an auditorium.

Nearly all presentations can benefit from others' input. Have a colleague check your presentation for spelling and grammar errors the other tools can't catch. Get a second opinion about the appropriateness of your transitions and animations. Have someone outside your field of expertise check the presentation for jargon and general clarity.

The people who proof your presentation don't have to be in the next office. They could be anywhere in the world! Attach your PowerPoint presentation to an e-mail message so others' comments can be added, or use online collaboration, where you actually build your presentation with the help of a person or team at another location. Either way, you're getting suggestions from a second or third person as you're polishing your presentation.

Handling Security Issues

If the presentation you're sending for review contains sensitive material, it's your responsibility to ensure that only intended reviewers gain access to the file. E-mailing a document affords only a minimum level of security. While we can presume that reviewers must log on to retrieve e-mail, we can't know whether they leave their machine logged on while they are away from it. Bad practice, we know. Unfortunately, it's not all that uncommon.

Depending on how you're planning to distribute the file for review, you can use some or all of the following options for protecting a sensitive document:

- If you're saving the file to a network location, your network administrator can set up a shared folder. Ask the administrator to set permissions so that only you and your reviewers can open the folder where the presentation file is stored.

- Any file can be password protected in PowerPoint 2002. Choose Tools ➢ Options ➢ Security and enter a password to open and/or a password to modify. Use a password to open for files that you don't want unauthorized users to even browse. Enter a password to modify if you're concerned about unauthorized editing of the document, but you don't mind users opening it read-only.

- Use a digital signature to authenticate that a distributed document really comes from you. Your reviewers can in turn digitally sign their changed copies so you know for sure they did the actual editing. Choose Tools ➢ Options ➢ Security and click the Digital Signatures button to add a digital signature.

NOTE Security features are discussed more fully in Chapter 12, "Working Collaboratively with Word."

Incorporating Feedback

PowerPoint lets reviewers annotate slides with comments. The comments can be hidden, so you can keep the comments with the presentation as you're working on it. Figure 25.1 shows a slide with a comment added in the default comment location.

To add a comment, switch to Normal view and choose Insert ➢ Comment from the menu bar. The Reviewing toolbar and a yellow comment text box open. Your name appears at the top of the comment. Begin typing, and the comment appears in the text box. Comments are not visible in Slide Show view.

FIGURE 25.1

A slide with a reviewer's comment

NEW▶

Slide comments in PowerPoint 2002 are indicated by *markers*, small boxes with the reviewer's initials and a comment number. Point to a marker to see the text of a comment. Click a marker to display the comment until your next click.

You can place more than one comment on a slide. To insert another comment, click the Insert Comment button on the Reviewing toolbar. Click the Markup button to display or hide all comments in the presentation. Hidden comments are hidden in all views. Use the comment's handles to move or resize the comment as you would any other text box. Modify the text of a comment by clicking the Edit Comment button on the Reviewing toolbar.

You can delete each comment as you address it. Simply click at the edge of the comment to activate the frame and press Delete, or click the Delete Comment button on the Reviewing toolbar. If you want to keep the comments (perhaps for future enhancements to the presentation), you can either hide them or move them out of the display area if they are interfering with your work. Drag comment markers into the gray background area of Normal view.

Sending a Presentation for Review

NEW▶

Use any MAPI-compliant e-mail program to send a PowerPoint file to reviewers. If e-mail hasn't made it to your corner of the office yet, save the file in a shared network location. No network? Then use sneakernet. (Put the document on a floppy disk and walk it over to a colleague for review!)

To e-mail a presentation using Outlook, click File ➤ Send To ➤ Mail Recipient For Review. Outlook automatically creates a review request message—flagged for follow-up—with the presentation attached. You should send the file this way if you want to take advantage of PowerPoint's automatic change tracking.

WARNING You must also attach the files for any linked objects, or recipients won't be able to see them when they open the presentation.

You can still send a presentation for review, and take advantage of automatic change tracking, even if you're not using Outlook. To do so:

1. Click File ➢ Save As and choose Presentation For Review in the Save As Type drop-down list. Name the file and select a location as you normally would; then click Save. (If you're using floppy disks or a shared network folder to distribute the presentation to reviewers, make enough copies for all reviewers, and that's it—until the reviewed copies come back to you, that is!)

2. Attach the file to an e-mail message using the procedures established by your e-mail programs. Don't forget to attach linked files as well.

3. Send the e-mail.

 TIP Use the Office 2002 Routing feature to solicit feedback from multiple recipients in a specific order or all at once. See "Routing Documents" in Chapter 12 for additional information on routing.

NEW▶ If you're not using routing to distribute a presentation to multiple reviewers, you will wind up with presentation changes in separate files. Fortunately, PowerPoint 2002's Compare And Merge feature automatically handles this issue. Now you can enjoy the same flexibility you have in Word by incorporating modifications from several reviewers' files into one presentation. Then you can browse to apply or reject those changes all in one place.

Reviewing a Presentation

Recipients of a presentation for review need only double-click to open the file, make their changes, and return the file to you. Depending on how they received the file, recipients should do one of the following:

- Outlook recipients using PowerPoint 97 or 2000: When you finish making modifications in PowerPoint, click File ➢ Send To ➢ Mail Recipient As Attachment. Address and send the e-mail as usual.

- Outlook recipients using PowerPoint 2002: Click File ➢ Send To ➢ Original Sender. Or click the Reply With Changes button on the Reviewing toolbar to send the presentation back to its originator with any changes you have made. See the next section for information about tracking changes in PowerPoint.

• Recipients of e-mail in a program other than Outlook and those who have reviewed the file from a shared network folder: Make your changes and click Save. E-mail users should return the file to the original sender as an attachment. Shared folder users should notify the original author when you have finished your review.

• Reviewers using a floppy disk: Make modifications in PowerPoint and click Save. Close PowerPoint and walk (or mail) the disk back to the original author.

 NOTE Only the original author sees a reviewer's changes. And reviewers needn't worry about overwriting the original presentation file. PowerPoint presents reviewers' modifications for approval. The original author still has the ability to reject any or all modifications.

Tracking Changes in a PowerPoint Presentation

NEW▶ PowerPoint 2002 now offers the same robust reviewing features as Word, although there is a slightly different process for working with them. When you send a presentation for review, PowerPoint tracks changes in content, color schemes, animation settings, transitions, layout, formatting of text and objects, and much more.

When you receive a file with a reviewer's changes, do one of the following to display those changes in your original presentation:

• If you used Outlook to send the presentation for review, open the message and double-click the attachment. Click Yes when Outlook displays a message box prompting you to merge changes.

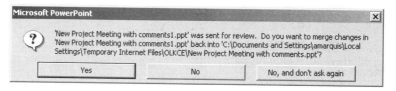

• If you used any other means for distributing the presentation to reviewers, open the original presentation and then click Tools ➢ Compare And Merge Presentations to display a dialog box where you must locate and select the reviewer's file. Click Merge.

PowerPoint 2002 displays markers next to the slide objects that have been changed. Point to a marker to see the reviewer's name and a description of the change. Use the Previous Item and Next Item buttons to browse markers in a presentation.

For each marker you see, decide whether to keep or discard the reviewer's changes. Click the Apply button on the Reviewing toolbar to keep the selected change, or click Unapply to reject it. The drop-down lists on these buttons offer options for applying/unapplying all changes to a particular slide or all changes in the active presentation. After you have chosen apply or unapply, you may wish to delete a change marker. To do so, click it and press Delete on the keyboard.

WARNING Be sure to address the change marker by clicking apply or unapply before deleting it.

Click the Reviewers button if you wish to review changes by one or more particular reviewers. Disable the check boxes next to the reviewers whose changes you don't want to see.

The Revisions Pane button toggles the Revisions pane on and off. If you prefer to see changes and comments in a list, as shown in Figure 25.2, turn it on. You can select reviewers, browse changes, and apply and reject changes in the Revisions pane.

Click a list item to see details about its changes.

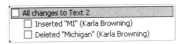

Enable a check box to apply a change. Clear a check box to unapply it. Apply all changes to an object by enabling All Changes To [*object name*]. If you prefer to see miniatures of slides with changes, select the Gallery tab in the Revisions pane.

TIP When you're finished looking at changes for a particular reviewer, switch to the Gallery tab of the Revisions pane, locate a miniature slide with changes from that reviewer, and then click the down arrow on that slide and choose Done With This Reviewer.

FIGURE 25.2

The Revisions Pane shows tracked changes in list format color-coded by reviewer.

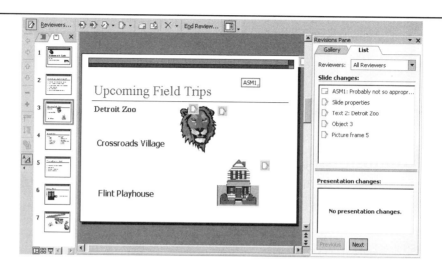

Ending a Review Cycle

As soon as you combine a reviewed presentation with your original, an End Review button appears on the Reviewing toolbar. Click it when you are finished reviewing file modifications.

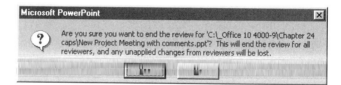

Confirm the end-review command in the message box, keeping in mind the following:

- You can no longer combine reviewed presentations with the original.
- Any unapplied changes remain unapplied, and you can't view them again.

WARNING If you have applied (or unapplied) all reviewer modifications, deleted all change markers, and saved your presentation, PowerPoint ends the review automatically.

Collaborating Online

PART

IV

AND NOW, PRESENTING WITH POWERPOINT!

You can get online, real-time feedback without leaving your desk using PowerPoint's online collaboration features. Many organizations implementing Office 2002 find that the tools for online collaboration are the software suite's most valuable new features. To access online collaboration, choose Tools ➤ Online Collaboration ➤ Web Discussions. For information on using online collaboration, see Chapter 27, "Collaborating in Office XP."

MASTERING THE OPPORTUNITIES

Developing a Presentation As a Team

If you are creating a presentation jointly with one or more people in your workgroup, you should save the presentation in a shared network folder or on a team site (see Chapter 45, "Using a SharePoint Team Site for Team Collaboration," on the companion CD). That way, each collaborator can access and edit the same file rather than having multiple unfinished drafts floating around on your network.

Start by working together to develop an outline, including slide topics and supporting graphics. Decide on a template (customized, if you wish) that all authors should use. Decide whether each person should animate their own slides or one person should add transitions and animation once all slides have been created. If each team member is responsible for transitions and animations, agree on the types of transitions and the level of animation you'll use.

After these basic decisions have been made, delegate parts of the outline to each team member for preparation of slides. Team members can work independently during the slide preparation stage, saving their work as they go along. When all slides are complete, you may wish to pull everyone together for a "polishing" meeting so each person has input in the final draft. If more than one team member will speak during the actual presentation, hold at least one rehearsal to ensure that the material flows smoothly between presenters.

If you don't have a network for sharing files, or a team site to work from, you can still collaborate on a presentation. Have each participant complete their slides in a separate presentation. Transfer them to one PC via floppy or Zip disk, and use the Slide Finder (see Chapter 22, "Creating a Presentation") or PowerPoint's Compare And Merge feature to incorporate all of the slides into one presentation.

Preparing Handouts and Notes

Handouts are pictures of the slides or the outline from a presentation that you give to participants. You can arrange handouts so they have two, three, four, six, or nine slides to a page, or you may choose to create a handout from your outline.

The Handout Master

You use the Handout Master to view and select the handout layouts. Choose View ➢ Master ➢ Handout Master to open the master, shown in Figure 25.3. The Handout Master toolbar opens automatically.

 TIP Settings for the masters, including the Slide Master and the Handout Master, are saved as separate workspaces within PowerPoint. If you close, for example, the Handout Master toolbar before switching out of the Handout Master, the next time you open the Handout Master the toolbar will not be displayed. Right-click any command bar or choose View ➢ Toolbars to display toolbars that were turned off in an earlier session.

The unlabeled placeholders (rectangles with dotted-line borders) show where slides are positioned in the layout selected in the Handout Master View toolbar. Click the appropriate button on the Handout Master View toolbar to select the number of slides you'd like to display on each page of the handout. PowerPoint 2002 now lets you choose one slide per page in addition to the other choices that were available in previous versions.

The Handout Master contains placeholders for the footer, header, date, and page number. By default, the footer area displays the title of your presentation (not to be confused with the presentation's filename). If you have chosen to number slides or display the date and time in the presentation, the Handout Master also includes these fields.

FIGURE 25.3

The Handout Master is a tool for preparing handouts from your slides.

To display or delete placeholders for date/time and page number, or to format or automatically update the date/time field, open the Header And Footer dialog box (View ➤ Header And Footer). Switch to the Notes And Handouts tab, shown in Figure 25.4. The header, footer, page, and date information you enter in the dialog box replaces the appropriate placeholders in the Handout Master when you print handouts.

FIGURE 25.4

Change settings to display date and/or time, page numbers, and fixed text in the Header And Footer dialog box.

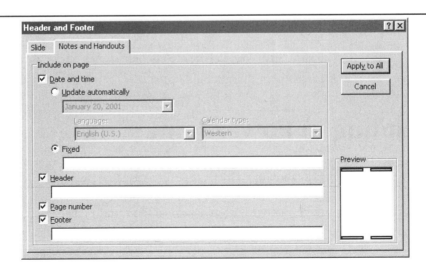

If you delete a placeholder and later change your mind about the deletion, Power-Point offers a quick and easy way to bring it back. Just click the Handout Master Layout button to display the Handout Master Layout dialog box.

Enable the check box next to any placeholder you wish to restore. If the place-holder already exists on the master, it is "grayed out" in the dialog box.

NOTE Click in any of the labeled placeholders to add text to the placeholder. It's easiest to edit the master if you change the Zoom setting to **75%** or **100%** so you can see the text.

Insert art or other graphics (a company logo, for example) just as you would on a slide. (Choose Insert ➤ Picture ➤ Clip Art or Insert ➤ Picture ➤ From File.) Format the background of your handouts by choosing Format ➤ Handout Background from the menu. To modify the slide color scheme for handouts, do the following:

1. Display the color scheme options in the task pane. (Choose View ➤ Task Pane, and then choose Slide Design ➤ Color Scheme from the task pane selection menu.)

2. Click the arrow next to the color scheme you want to use.

3. Choose Apply To Handout Master.

Printing in PowerPoint

When you click the Print button on the Standard toolbar, PowerPoint prints the entire presentation in the default setting—usually the Slide pane from Normal view. If the slides have a background, this can take some time, even on a laser printer. More important, it's rarely what you intended to print. In PowerPoint, it's always best to choose File ➤ Print to open the Print dialog box (shown in Figure 25.5) so you can select whether to print slides, handouts, notes, or an outline.

TIP You can replace the standard Print button with a button that opens the Print dialog box. Right-click any toolbar and choose Customize. With the Customize dialog box open, drag the Print button off the toolbar and drop it in the application window. On the Commands tab of the dialog box, choose the File category. In the Commands pane, select the Print... button and drag it onto the Standard toolbar. Close the Customize dialog box.

FIGURE 25.5

*Change print settings
for your presentation
in the Print dialog box.*

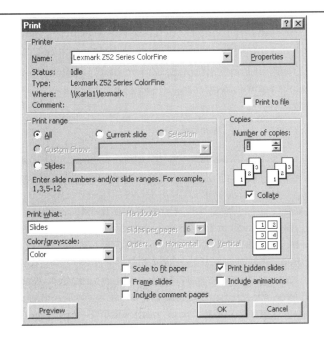

The default print setting is All Slides. To print some, but not all, slides, enter their numbers in the Slides text box. Choose what you want to print (slides, handouts, notes, or an outline) from the Print What drop-down list. If you are printing a color presentation on a noncolor printer, choose Pure Black And White from the Color/Grayscale list. This helps speed up the printing process. Choose Grayscale from this list to print black-and-white on a color printer.

NOTE Choose Tools ➢ Options and select the Print tab of the Options dialog box to change the default print settings for the current presentation and the default settings for printing graphics for all presentations.

If you're printing handouts with multiple slides per page, you must choose either a vertical or a horizontal printing order. Click the Frame Slides check box to print a simple box around each slide; this is a good idea if the slides themselves don't include a border. If there are hidden slides in your presentation, the default is to print them. You can disable that option by clearing its check box.

You can also choose how many slides per handout page to print in the Print dialog box. If you previously used the Handout Master to choose the number of slides per page, you can override that choice here.

Now you can preview what you're about to print! Just click the Print Preview button on the Standard toolbar (or choose File ➤ Print Preview) to display the presentation with current print settings. Figure 25.6 shows an outline in Print Preview.

The Print Preview toolbar, shown here, provides several options for changing print settings without reopening the Print dialog box.

You can use the scroll bar to browse the document preview, but there are also buttons on the toolbar for viewing previous and next pages. Change what you're printing by choosing from the Print What drop-down list. The Options button has settings for framing slides, printing comments, setting color options, adjusting print order, and more. About the only thing you can't do there is choose a different printer. You can even change from portrait to landscape orientation by clicking the appropriate button on the toolbar. This is particularly helpful if you're experimenting with different handout layouts.

NOTE You can't change the orientation if Print What is set to Slides. See the sidebar titled "Printing Report Covers from PowerPoint Slides" for information about printing slides using a different orientation.

When you're finished adjusting settings, click Close to leave the preview and return to work on your presentation, or click the Print button to open the Print dialog box (shown previously in Figure 25.5) and proceed with printing.

FIGURE 25.6

PowerPoint 2002 offers Print Preview with an Options button for changing print settings.

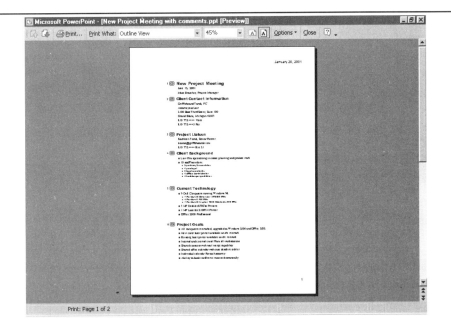

MASTERING THE OPPORTUNITIES

Printing Report Covers from PowerPoint Slides

If you're handing out a packet of materials, you can print the title slide of your presentation for use as a cover. In Normal view, navigate to your title slide.

If you are using a dark background for your presentation, it is a good idea to format the title slide temporarily with a light background; select the title slide and choose Insert ➢ Duplicate Slide to create a copy that you can reformat. Choose Format ➢ Slide Color Scheme and select a standard scheme that displays a light-colored or white background. If you have access to only a black-and-white printer, or if you'll be making copies of the cover on a black-and-white copier, choose the black-and-white scheme and click Apply.

Select File ➢ Page Setup from the menu to open the Page Setup dialog box shown here. Change the orientation from landscape to portrait and click OK.

Continued

MASTERING THE OPPORTUNITIES CONTINUED

Print as many copies of the report cover as you need by choosing File ➢ Print from the menu. Be sure to select Current Slide in the Print dialog box and use the spin box to select the number of report covers you need.

When you are finished printing, you must return the slides to their original landscape orientation. Delete the duplicate slide with the light background or choose Slide Show ➢ Hide Slide to retain it.

Creating Handouts in Word

You can use the power of Office automation to create handouts and reports for a Power-Point presentation in Word. The Send To Word feature transfers the text or slides from the current presentation to a Word document, which you can then edit (adding titles and additional text), format, and print to use as handouts. This tool uses a lot of system resources, so begin by closing other applications. Choose File ➢ Send To ➢ Microsoft Word to open the Send To Microsoft Word dialog box, shown in Figure 25.7.

Select how you want the presentation to appear: in one of the four handout-style layouts or as an outline. Choose whether you want to paste a copy from your presentation or link the Word document to the presentation. If you choose Paste Link, changes to the presentation will be updated in the Word document; however, you'll lose some of the editing flexibility in Word.

After selecting layout and paste options, click OK. PowerPoint launches Word and exports your outline or slides. Edit and print the document as you would a Word document. If you send slides (instead of an outline), this may take a few minutes because each slide is exported as a graphic object.

FIGURE 25.7

PowerPoint provides
options for creating
handouts in Word.

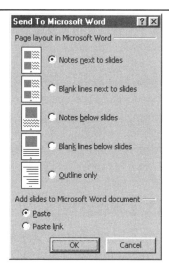

 TIP If you're only transferring an outline, click the Black And White View button on the Standard toolbar before opening the Send To Microsoft Word dialog box for easier formatting in Word.

Preparing 35mm Slides and Overhead Transparencies

If you have a desktop slide printer, you can print your presentation as 35mm slides for use in a traditional slide projector. Even if you don't, you can still convert the PowerPoint slides to 35mm. Genigraphics and other service bureaus can take your presentation (or selected slides from it) and convert it to 35mm. Save your presentation as you normally would and send it to a service bureau via e-mail or on disk. You can also visit http://www.genigraphics.com to learn how to upload your presentation.

 WARNING Some service bureaus may require that you save the presentation as a postscript file. Check with them first to be sure.

To print black-and-white or color transparencies for an overhead projector, simply insert transparency film in your printer, and then print the slides (without animations) using the Print dialog box.

TIP Transparencies look best with clear (white) backgrounds, black text, and occasional splashes of color. Avoid dark backgrounds or graphic-heavy templates more appropriate for on-screen presentations.

Setting Slide Timings

After you have finalized your slides, including transitions and animation (see Chapter 24, "Objects, Transitions, and Animation"), you are ready to rehearse your slides in preparation for the actual presentation. Rehearsal is vital—you'd rather discover problems in private than have them projected to a large audience.

Automated vs. Manual Advance

There are two ways to advance an electronic presentation. If the presentation is designed to run on its own—for example, in a booth at a trade show—you'll want to advance slides automatically. If your finished presentation will be used to illustrate a verbal presentation or will be posted on an intranet, you'll probably prefer to advance slides manually. If slides should advance automatically, only a bit more work is required to set the timings for each animation and transition.

If you are using manual advance, then your presentation is essentially completed. Rehearse the presentation a few times, making sure that you know how many times to click on each slide to display all the objects.

TIP You can always manually advance slides in a presentation, even if it includes slide timings. Choose Slide Show ➢ Set Up Show from the menu and choose an Advance option: Manually or With Timings.

Setting Automatic Timings

There are two ways to set slide timings: through rehearsal or manually in the Slide Transition task pane. (You can only enter animation timings by rehearsal.) It's easiest to create timings through rehearsal and then alter individual advances manually. Before setting timings, run through the entire slide show two or three times. Try not to advance slides and animations too quickly for your audience, because they will be seeing the slides for the first time. Make sure that your audience will have time to read the title, read each point, and see how a graphic illustrates the points. It helps to read the contents of each slide out loud, slowly, while rehearsing and setting the timings. When you're ready to record timings, switch to Slide Sorter view and follow these steps:

1. Click the Rehearse Timings button on the Slide Sorter toolbar or choose Slide Show ➢ Rehearse Timings. The first slide appears, and the Rehearsal toolbar opens.

2. The toolbar has two timers. The timer on the right shows the total time for the presentation. The left timer is the elapsed time for the current slide. Click anywhere on the slide for your next animation or your next slide. The timers automatically record the number of seconds that pass between transitions and animations.

3. The Rehearsal toolbar has three buttons: Next, Pause, and Repeat. Click the Next button (or anywhere on the slide) to move to the next slide or animation.

4. If you are interrupted in the middle of rehearsal, click the Pause button, and then click Pause again to resume.

5. If you make a mistake while rehearsing a slide, click Repeat to set new timings for the *current* slide. If you don't catch a mistake before a slide has been advanced, you can either finish rehearsing and then edit the slide time manually or close the toolbar and begin again.

6. When you complete the entire rehearsal for a presentation, or if you press Esc to end the rehearsal, you are prompted to save the timings.

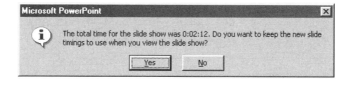

Choose Yes to save the timings as rehearsed. Choose No to discard the timings. In Slide Sorter view, the total time for each slide appears below the slide.

Editing Slide Timings

To edit an individual transition time, select the slide and click the Slide Transition button on the Slide Sorter toolbar. The rehearsed time, which you can edit, is displayed in the Advance Slide area of the task pane.

To re-rehearse timings for one or more slides:

1. Choose Slide Show ➢ Set Up Show from the menu to open the Set Up Show dialog box, shown in Figure 25.8.

2. In the Show Slides section, set the From and To controls to the range of slides you wish to change animation timings for.

3. Click OK to close the dialog box.

4. Choose Slide Show ➢ Rehearse Timings, or click the Rehearse Timings button on the Slide Sorter toolbar, to rehearse new timings for the selected slides. Save timings when prompted.

5. Choose Slide Show ➢ Set Up Show and set the Show Slides option to All.

FIGURE 25.8

The Set Up Show dialog box lets you choose the slides for which you wish to re-rehearse timings.

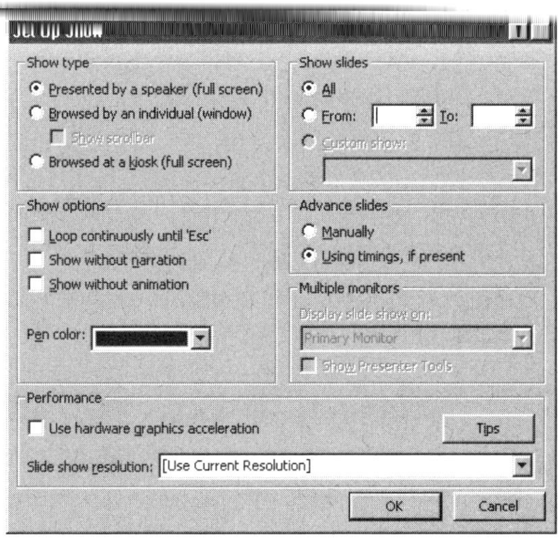

Customizing Shows for Different Audiences

Sometimes you need to create multiple versions of the same slide show to present to different audiences. For instance, you might have an East Coast and a West Coast version of the same sales presentation. Both versions use identical slides 1–12, but slides 13–25 are different, depending on where the client is located. You don't have to save each version as a separate file. In PowerPoint 2002, you can create a presentation within a presentation using the Custom Shows feature. To begin customizing, choose Slide Show ➢ Custom Shows from the menu to open the Custom Shows dialog box.

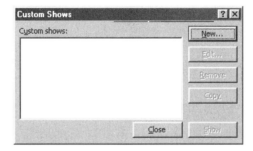

Click New to open the Define Custom Show dialog box.

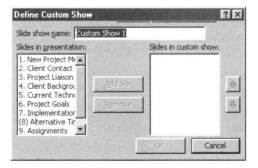

Name your show, overwriting the default name Custom Show 1. Select the slides you wish to include in this version of the show and click Add to move them to the Slides In Custom Show list. Use the Remove button to remove selected slides from the list.

Use the Move Up and Move Down arrows to change the slide order. Click OK to save the custom show and return to the Custom Shows dialog box. Define another custom show using the New button, or click the Edit button to edit a selected show. To remove the selected custom show, click the Remove button.

During a presentation, you can right-click, choose Go ➤ Custom Show on the shortcut menu, and select the custom show you want to display. The shortcut menu, however, is rather intrusive. You may prefer to set up the presentation so it displays the custom version when you start the slide show (see the upcoming section, "Setting Up the Slide Show").

 TIP You can switch to a custom show during a presentation by creating a hyperlink to that show. Choose Slide Show ➤ Action Settings or Insert ➤ Hyperlink from the menu. For more information, see "Adding Links to Other Slides" in Chapter 24.

Recording Narration

Sometimes voice narration is appropriate for a presentation. Perhaps a key team member can't attend but wants to view the slides at another time, or the presentation will be viewed on your organization's intranet. Shows designed to run at a kiosk in a dedicated area (rather than in a noisy display hallway) are also good candidates for narration. You can record narration before you run the slide show, or you can record it during the presentation and include comments from meeting participants for archival purposes. When recording narration, you need a computer with a sound card and a microphone. To show a presentation with narration, the computer needs only a sound card.

Voice narration is not always appropriate. Noisy convention halls make it difficult to hear and understand narration at a kiosk, and the narration really annoys the folks in adjacent display areas. Also, participants in a meeting might be hearing-impaired, which makes voice narration unsuitable. It's likely, too, that your Web presentation will sometimes be viewed on computers without sound cards. You can opt to show your presentation without previously recorded narration in the Set Up Show dialog box under the Slide Show menu.

When you record narration, you're creating sound files *and* a new set of slide timings. During recording you can right-click and pause if necessary. Right-click and choose Resume to begin recording where you left off. When you have finished recording, PowerPoint saves the narration with each slide and asks whether you want to save the new timings as well. This is a good idea; the new timings coincide with the narration, while previously recorded timings may not.

 NOTE Specific steps for recording voice narration are covered in depth in Chapter 24.

Setting Up the Slide Show

You've designed a good presentation, had it reviewed by a colleague, and practiced moving through the slides. Now you're ready to specify the settings that you'll use to deliver the show. Before you present the slide show, choose Slide Show ➢ Set Up Show, or hold Shift and click the Slide Show button, to open the Set Up Show dialog box, shown previously in Figure 25.8.

In the Show Type area, select a presentation method and then choose whether or not to use narration, animation, and looping in the Show Options area. In the Advance Slides area, choose Manually or Using Timings, If Present. To show the presentation continuously, choose Using Timings, If Present and click the Loop Continuously Until 'Esc' check box. In the Show Slides area, you can choose to show the entire presentation, certain slide numbers, or a custom presentation.

During the presentation, you can use the mouse pointer to draw on the slides to emphasize a point (see "Drawing on Slides" later in this chapter); select a pen color that contrasts with both the background and the text colors used in the slides.

Viewing on Two Screens

If you're running Microsoft Windows 98, Windows 2000, or Windows NT version 5, you can get the benefits of online broadcasting even if you're doing a live presentation to a group. PowerPoint's View On Two Screens option allows you to set up a show with one computer (say, your laptop) as the presenter and the other (a computer with a large monitor) as the audience. You get to see slides and notes while the audience sees only the slides.

 First, your computer must have dual-monitor software installed (Windows 98 or better). Second, connect the two computers using a direct-connect serial cable. Then, on the primary computer (the laptop, in this instance), choose Slide Show ➢ Set Up Show to open the Set Up Show dialog box (refer to Figure 25.8, shown earlier). Open the Display Slide Show On drop-down list and select the monitor you wish to use to show the presentation. The other monitor displays your presentation in Normal view. Enable the Show Presenter Tools check box to see a navigation panel on one screen, shown in Figure 25.9, making the presentation easier to navigate during the show.

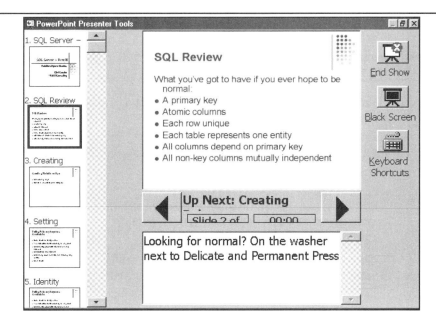

FIGURE 25.9

Presenter Tools provide an easy means to navigate the slide show when you're using multiple monitors.

Adjusting Performance

NEW▷ PowerPoint 2002 offers performance settings to help achieve smooth-running presentations when your processor speed may not be up to it. Choose Slide Show ➢ Set Up Show to display the Set Up Show dialog box, shown previously in Figure 25.8. If your video card supports it, enable the check box Use Hardware Graphics Acceleration to improve animation speed. Choose a resolution from the Slide Show Resolution list:

Use Current Resolution Does just as it says. The slide show runs at the screen resolution of the computer it's on. If the presentation isn't displaying properly, make sure the projector resolution matches the computer's resolution (see the sidebar titled "Improving Slide Show Performance" for more on this).

640 X 480 Causes the projector to use a lower screen resolution, but animations may run more smoothly (as opposed to being "choppy"). This setting uses less of the computer's resources to display the slide show, so text and graphics may not display as sharply; nevertheless, choose 640 X 480 if your presentation is running too slowly.

800 X 600 Displays text and graphics in better resolution, but if your animations lurch haltingly across the screen, use the lower-resolution setting, or enable graphics acceleration and try again.

When you've finished adjusting show settings, click OK to close the Set Up Show dialog box and save the slide show settings with the presentation.

MASTERING TROUBLESHOOTING

Improving Slide Show Performance

Technical problems are the last thing you need during a big presentation. Plan to spend at least an hour setting up and testing your equipment before the audience enters the room. In a perfect world, you should test everything a day before the presentation and again just before show time. Ah… would that it were a perfect world!

Projector Resolution Is Fuzzy

Ideally, the resolution on the computer should match the resolution of the projector. Adjust computer resolution in the Display Properties dialog box (Start ➤ Settings ➤ Control Panel ➤ Display ➤ Settings) or use the Set Up Show dialog box to choose a different resolution for the show (Slide Show ➤ Set Up Show). With some laptops, you may have to disable the display to get ideal resolution from the projector.

Nothing Appears on the Projection Screen

If there's no light or sound from the projector, check the simple things: Is it plugged in? Is the power strip turned on? Is the projector turned on? Is the bulb good? Is the lens cap off? If you've got power and light but still no image from the computer, check the following: Is the laptop toggled so that the video port is active? Are cables plugged in correctly and securely? Have you tried turning both machines off and back on? (Turn the projector on first, then the computer.)

Continued ▌▶

PART

IV

AND NOW, PRESENTING WITH POWERPOINT!

MASTERING TROUBLESHOOTING CONTINUED

Presentation Runs Too Slowly; Animations Are Choppy

Enable graphics acceleration and/or choose a lower resolution in the Set Up Show dialog box. You can also set color depth to 16-bit to get the best performance. (Use the Settings tab of the Display Properties dialog box; use the Control Panel to get there.) You might also consider compressing pictures in the presentation (see "Compressing Pictures to Reduce File Size" in Chapter 1).

Presentation Still Runs Too Slowly

Resize animated pictures so that they are smaller. Use less "exciting" transitions and animations. Fading, spinning, spiraling, and scaling are resource hogs. Use Fly, Wipe, Dissolve, and other basic effects instead. Use fewer simultaneous animations, and reduce the number of by-word and by-letter animations.

Displaying the Slide Show

Navigate to slide 1 and click the Slide Show (From Current Slide) button, or choose Slide Show ➤ View Show, to start the presentation. To advance to the next slide or animation, click anywhere on the slide background, or if you're using a keyboard, press Enter, Page Down, down arrow, or N.

A menu button appears in the lower-left or lower-right corner of the slide (depending on the template used in the presentation). Click the button to open the shortcut menu.

The shortcut menu provides additional options for navigating through your presentation. From the menu, you can move to the previous or next slide. To move to a specific slide, choose Go ➢ By Title and choose the slide you want to display, or choose Go ➢ Slide Navigator to open the Slide Navigator. Select a slide to move to, and click OK.

Ending on a Black Slide

When you click past the final slide in a slide show, you return to the PowerPoint window: a lot like Toto opening the curtain on the Wizard of Oz. To end on a blank slide and maintain the mystery, choose Tools ➢ Options to open the Options dialog box. Select the View tab and then click End With Black Slide.

TIP You can switch to a black (or white) screen at any point in a presentation—to distribute handouts or samples, answer a question unrelated to the current slide, or display a blank screen during a break. Press the B key on the keyboard for a black screen, the W key for a white screen. Press any key to continue with the presentation.

Saving a PowerPoint Show

A PowerPoint Show is a stripped-down PowerPoint file that includes only the presentation, fonts, and embedded OLE servers required to run the presentation, much like a shortcut to a show. PowerPoint Show files use the extension PPS rather than PPT, which is used for presentations. As a PPS file, the show can be shown but not edited, so this is an easy way to create a read-only version of a presentation before distributing it to others. Colleagues who receive the presentation attached to an e-mail message need only double-click the file icon to go directly to the slide show. Save the show on your desktop, and you're always just one click away from a slide show.

To save a finished presentation as a show, choose File ➢ Save As to open the Save As dialog box. In the Files Of Type drop-down list, choose PowerPoint Show. To run a PowerPoint show file, double-click the file's icon.

EXPERT TIP To run any presentation without displaying the PowerPoint interface, select the presentation's icon (on the Desktop, in My Computer, wherever). Right-click and choose Show from the shortcut menu.

Online Presentations

With Microsoft Windows Media Services and Online Presentation Broadcasting, you can show a presentation over a TCP/IP network or the Internet. Members of the audience view the presentation on their computers. You can schedule the meeting in advance either by phoning participants or by using Microsoft Outlook to schedule the meeting (see "Planning a Meeting with Others" in Chapter 34). During the presentation, you can take complete control while audience members watch (see Chapter 30), or you can use online collaboration (see Chapter 27), allowing participants to make changes to the presentation.

Drawing on Slides

During the slide show, you can underline or circle an object or text to make a point, check off points that have been discussed, or use lines to connect related points on-screen. Press Ctrl+P, or choose Pen from the shortcut menu, and the mouse pointer becomes a pen. Drag the pointer to draw on the current slide. Right-click and choose Arrow, or press Ctrl+A, to turn the pen off. The drawing isn't saved, so no "damage" is done to the slide.

 TIP If members of the audience (or you) want a hard copy of a slide that's been illustrated with the pen, hold Alt and press Print Screen to copy the slide and drawing to the Clipboard. After the presentation, paste the image from the Clipboard into a Word document. To capture up to a dozen illustrated slides during a presentation, open the Office Clipboard before starting the presentation. Screen shots captured with Alt+Print Screen are copied to the Office Clipboard if it is already open.

You can change the color of the pen tool before you begin a presentation by choosing Slide Show ➢ Set Up Show from the menu. Select a color from the drop-down list. Although it's somewhat intrusive, you can also change pen colors during your presentation. In Slide Show view, right-click and choose Pointer Options ➢ Pen Color from the shortcut menu.

Generating Meeting Notes

During a live or online presentation, you can enter minutes or action items in the Meeting Minder. Right-click in Slide Show view and choose Meeting Minder. Select the Meeting Minutes tab to enter meeting minutes.

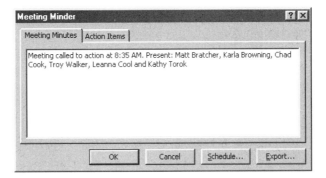

Type the text of the minutes and click OK to close the dialog box. At any time during the slide show, you can open the Meeting Minder and add to the minutes. You won't see minutes from previous slides until you export them. Select the Action Items tab to create and assign follow-up tasks.

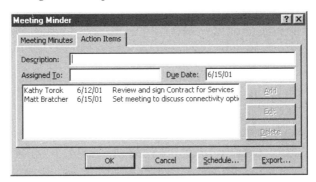

In the Action Items tab, enter the "to do" list generated during the meeting, including due dates and the person responsible for the item. If the date or responsible person changes or if the item is eliminated in later discussion, select the item from the list and edit or delete it. Click Schedule to launch Microsoft Outlook and enter this item on your Calendar or To Do list.

When the presentation is finished, click the Export button to export the minutes to Word and the action items to Word and/or Outlook.

Saving a Presentation for Use on Another Computer

Office XP includes a PowerPoint Viewer, which is used to display a presentation on a computer that doesn't include PowerPoint. To bundle your presentation and the viewer in one easy, compressed package, choose File ➤ Pack And Go to launch the Pack And Go Wizard. As you proceed through the wizard, you'll be asked to select a presentation, a destination drive, linking-and-embedding options, and whether the file should include the PowerPoint Viewer. The first time you use the viewer, you must download it from the Microsoft Web site, and the wizard prompts you to do so.

If your presentation includes linked objects or fonts that you may not be able to access on the computer used to display the presentation, choose to include linked files and to embed fonts.

 WARNING When you embed fonts and include linked files, even compressed files can become very large, requiring five, 10, or even more standard floppy disks. Packing time for these large files is considerable. You probably should use a Zip disk or other high-capacity medium to transport the presentation file between computers. If your e-mail system supports transmission of large amounts of data, consider sending the presentation as an attachment.

When it's time to unpack the presentation, take the following steps:

1. If you used portable media, insert the disk created by Pack And Go and then open Windows Explorer.

2. In Windows Explorer, select the drive and/or folder where the disk is located and then double-click the Pngsetup.exe file.

NEW▶

3. Enter a destination for the unpacked presentation and viewer. Now you can browse to select a folder location, and the unpack utility recognizes folder names with more than eight characters.

4. To start the slide show, double-click the PowerPoint Viewer (Ppview32.exe) and then click the presentation. If you did not include the viewer, you can start the slide show immediately after you unpack it. Pack And Go Setup prompts you with this option. If you choose not to immediately view the presentation, you can launch PowerPoint at any time and open the unpacked file.

 WARNING If you go directly to the show from the Pack And Go Wizard, a copy of your presentation is created in C:\Windows\Temp. Delete this temp file after the show, particularly if you're using someone else's computer.

EXPERT INTEGRATION AND COLLABORATION

LEARN TO:

- Convert, link, and embed data from one application to another

- Import and export data

- Create Office documents from Outlook

- Work together on written documents

- Send and receive instant messages

- Hold virtual meetings over the Web

CHAPTER 26

BREAKING THE APPLICATION BARRIER

FEATURING

- Converting files to Office formats

- Linking and embedding objects

- Working with embedded objects

- Creating new objects

- Using application-specific tools to share data

U sing only one of the Office XP applications at a time is like trying to build a house by doing all the hammering first. To build a house, you must constantly switch between your hammer, screwdriver, level, tape measure, saw, and drill. Office XP is no different from your toolbox. By switching between the Office XP tools, you maximize their effectiveness and save yourself a lot of work in the process. If you find yourself retyping or re-creating data or objects that already exist in another Office XP application, you're working way too hard. This chapter features a variety of methods to copy information from one application into another document by embedding, linking, or converting the existing data. We'll also explore the application-specific tools that allow you to access data and documents from another application.

Converting, Linking, and Embedding

Object Linking and Embedding, or *OLE* (pronounced o-lay), is a Windows protocol that allows applications to communicate with each other to create or update *objects:* data that can be embedded or linked in another application. Word documents, Excel worksheets and charts, Access tables, and PowerPoint slides are all examples of objects you can insert (embed or link) in other Office XP documents. For example, if you need to use an Excel chart in a Publisher or Word document or a PowerPoint presentation, don't re-create it—reuse it. You can also insert graphics, sounds, video, and virtually anything else you can select and copy to the Clipboard.

OLE requires two applications to complete its mission:

- An *OLE server* is a source application that can create an OLE object. For example, Excel is an OLE server because it can create a chart object.

- An *OLE client* is a destination application that can accept OLE objects. Power-Point is an OLE client because it can accept an Excel chart object.

When you use OLE, you have three choices for how you access the external data: you can convert it, link it, or embed it. Each technique has advantages and disadvantages and depends largely on what you need to accomplish. Table 26.1 compares the three options.

TABLE 26.1   CONVERTING, LINKING, AND EMBEDDING OBJECTS

Option	Result	Tools Available from OLE Server	Original File Location	Best Use
Converting	Pastes object into destination document in a format supported by the destination application; e.g., an Excel worksheet becomes a Word table.	None	Irrelevant; converted object is a copy.	When the source application will be unavailable or when you want to use the destination application's tools to format the object.
Linking	Maintains active link to OLE server. Changes can only be made in the source application and are reflected in the linked object.	All source application tools are available; double-clicking object launches OLE server.	Source file must be maintained in original location, or the link is broken.	When the linked object should always reflect the most current data, or to minimize the size of the destination document.
Embedding	Object is copied to destination document and retains attributes from OLE server application.	All source application tools are available; double-clicking object makes OLE server application tools available within client application.	Irrelevant; object is a copy.	When you want to be able to make changes to the object and either you won't have access to the original file or you want to capture data at a specific point in time.

PART

V

EXPERT INTEGRATION
AND COLLABORATION

Now we'll discuss each option in detail and give you examples of how to use them.

Converting Data

When you *convert* a selection, it is translated from its *native format* (the format used by the application it was created in) to a format that can be used directly by the application in which you place the selection. Converting creates a copy, much like a snapshot. After the selection is converted, you use the tools in the destination application to work with it. You can change the converted data without affecting the original.

The easiest way to convert (and embed or link) data in an Office application is to copy and paste. Open the *source application* that contains the text, picture, or other object you want to place in the *destination application*. Select the object and copy it to the Clipboard. In Figure 26.1, we've selected and copied data in an Excel workbook that we'll use in the examples that follow. After you copy the data you want, you can close the source application if you wish; in some cases, you are asked if you want to retain the contents of the Clipboard. Choose Yes to keep the data on the Clipboard so you can paste it.

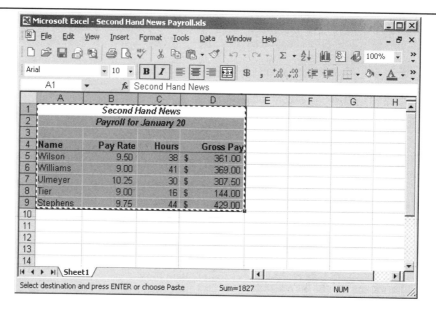

Open the destination document and place the insertion point where you want to paste the selection. To convert the data, simply paste it into the document. In Figure 26.2, the data from Excel has been pasted into Word, which converted the Excel data into a Word table.

You can use all the tools you normally use in Word tables to manipulate the converted table. None of the changes you make to the table, such as adding or deleting rows and columns, affect the original data in Excel.

FIGURE 26.2

Simply pasting the Excel data into Word converts it to a table.

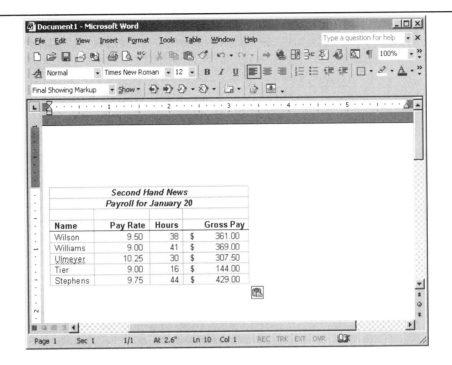

Choosing Paste Options

NEW▶

Office XP's new Smart Tags make converting objects even more flexible because you can choose to reformat the converted object based on the formatting of the destination document. As soon as you paste an object, the Paste Options button appears in the bottom-right corner of the object. Click the down arrow to open the Paste Options menu.

- ◉ Keep Source Formatting
- ○ Match Destination Table Style
- ○ Keep Text Only
- ○ Keep Source Formatting and Link to Excel
- ○ Match Destination Table Style and Link to Excel
- Apply Style or Formatting...

The first option, Keep Source Formatting, retains the formatting of the original object—in this example, the Excel worksheet. Match Destination Table Style changes the formatting to the default formatting of the document. If you choose this option when converting an Excel spreadsheet to a Word table, the table changes to HTML format. Keep Text Only removes all formatting and displays only text. We will cover the other paste options later in this chapter.

 NOTE If you are pasting an object that is not a table, such as text, the second option on the Paste Options menu is Match Destination Formatting rather than Match Destination Table Style.

Other Conversion Options

Converting the Excel data to a Word table is only one of several conversion options available to you. You can also paste it as a picture and use Word's drawing tools to position the graphic. To see further conversion choices, choose Edit ➤ Paste Special to open the Paste Special dialog box, shown in Figure 26.3.

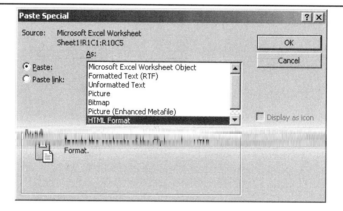

The source for the object (the name and range of worksheet cells) is displayed at the top of the dialog box. The list in the As box allows you to select how the information should be pasted. The choices include the following:

Microsoft Excel Worksheet Object Creates an object that can be linked or embedded (see the next section).

Formatted Text (RTF) Converts the worksheet to a Word table.

Unformatted Text Converts the selection to Word tabular columns.

Picture and Bitmap Convert the worksheet selection into a graphic that you can work with in Word using all the Word graphic tools. The Picture option creates a higher-quality graphic than Bitmap. You can place the graphic in a separate drawing layer by enabling the Float Over Text option.

Picture (Enhanced Metafile) Converts the selection into a Windows Metafile graphic.

HTML Format Converts the table to an HTML table. HTML is the default in Office XP.

Unformatted Unicode Text Converts the entries in the cells to unformatted Unicode text columns.

 NOTE Unicode is an international standard for encoding characters that includes all the characters in the world's major languages.

Of the choices listed, all but the first, Microsoft Excel Worksheet Object, convert the object into some other type of object. Choose a format and click OK to convert the selection and paste it into your document.

Embedding and Linking

When you *embed* an object, a copy of the object that retains its native format is placed in the destination document. The Excel object is still "in" Excel, but it appears in the Word document. If you change the object pasted in Word, the original selection in Excel remains unchanged.

With a *link,* a relationship is established between the selection in the native application and the pasted entry in the destination document. When you open the Word document, Word reloads the Excel selection directly from the worksheet. When you begin to edit the object, Word launches Excel, and you make your changes there. This ensures that the original data and the linked copy are synchronized; changes to the original data are reflected in the linked object. Linking has two advantages: it saves disk space and, more important, it is *dynamic.* If the source for the object changes, the change is reflected in all linked objects.

Embedding an Object

To embed or link, you use the Paste Special dialog box. First, select and copy the object. In the destination application, choose Edit ➤ Paste Special to open the Paste Special dialog box, shown earlier in Figure 26.3. From the As list, choose the description that includes the word "object" (for example, Microsoft Excel Worksheet Object) and click OK. Figure 26.4 shows the Excel object embedded in the Word document. You can tell it's an object because it has handles when selected. If you double-click the object to edit it, the native application (Excel) toolbars appear right in the Word application window, as shown in Figure 26.4.

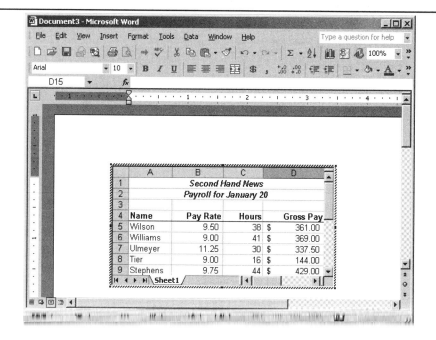

Use embedding when you want to be able to work with the object in the destination document using the source document's tools. Let's say, for example, you want to include an Excel spreadsheet in a PowerPoint presentation. If you simply copy and paste it, you can still edit the worksheet data, but you lose the formulas in the spreadsheet. Any changes you make to the numbers are not reflected in the totals or other formulas. However, if you insert the worksheet as a Microsoft Excel object, it looks the same, but now you can make changes to the data and be confident that the formulas will recalculate. If you want to insert the object into your presentation and still be able to edit it in Excel, this next Paste Special option is for you.

Creating a Link

To link the selection rather than embed it, enable the Paste Link check box in the Paste Special dialog box (see Figure 26.3). You can link any of the converted or embedded file types listed. For example, if you copy an Excel worksheet range and choose Paste Link to link it into a Word file with the Microsoft Excel Worksheet Object option, you create a dynamic link to the range in the original worksheet. Any changes you make to the worksheet are reflected in the Word document.

If you would like to create a hyperlink to another document, choose Edit ➢ Paste As Hyperlink. The text in the pasted object is underlined and colored blue to indicate it is a hyperlink. When you click the hyperlink, you are taken to the document in the native application. This is useful when you are creating a document that will be viewed online. Obviously, it is not much help in a printed document.

NEW▶

If you are pasting an Excel worksheet into Word, you can also create a link by pasting the object normally and then choosing one of these options from the Paste Options Smart Tag menu: Keep Source Formatting And Link To Excel, or Match Destination Table Style And Link To Excel. With this type of link, the object converts to a Word table, but the data maintains its link to Excel. Changes you make to the Excel worksheet are shared with the table, but double-clicking the table does not open Excel. You can distinguish this type of link because when you click the table, the data appears shaded, as it does in Figure 26.5.

PART

V

EXPERT INTEGRATION
AND COLLABORATION

FIGURE 26.5

You can use Office XP's Paste Options to create a link that converts the table to a Word table and still maintains an Excel worksheet, as this shading indicates.

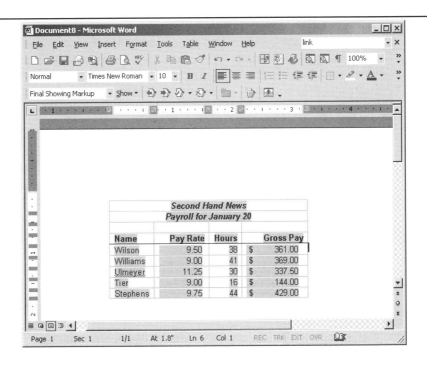

Working with Embedded and Linked Objects

To select a linked or embedded object, click it. Use the object's handles to size it, or press Delete to delete it. The real magic of OLE occurs when you double-click the object. After you double-click, wait a moment. If the object is embedded, the toolbars from the object's native application appear in the destination application. With a linked object, double-click and you are transported to the source document to edit the object.

 TIP Sometimes when you double-click an object, you see a message that the source application cannot be opened (especially if the source application is already open). If the source application is installed on your computer, click OK to close the message box, and double-click again.

Automatic and Manual Updating

When you create a link with Paste Special, *automatic link updating* is enabled. The object is updated each time the destination document is opened and each time the source document changes. You can choose to update links manually rather than automatically, giving you control over when a file is updated. This is particularly helpful when the source document is on a server and you don't want to wait for network traffic to clear. To change to *manual link updating*, select the linked object and choose Edit ➤ Links to open the Links dialog box. As the Update Method, choose Manual. When you are ready to update links in the destination document, open the Links dialog box again and click the Update Now button, or right-click a selected object and choose Update Link from the shortcut menu.

 WARNING If you use manual linking, don't forget to update before printing a report. You should adopt a consistent method for updating so you don't pass off last month's information as the latest data.

Inserting and Linking Entire Files

If you want to embed or link an entire file instead of a selection, it is often easier to *insert* the object or file into the destination document than to use copy and paste. In

Word and Publisher, you can insert text files directly from the Insert menu. In other applications, you can insert files by creating objects.

Inserting and Converting Text Files in Word and Publisher

If you're like many users, you use Word to pull together reports that include data from a variety of applications. Word is designed to let you convert files on the fly using the Insert command. To convert a file to a Word document or Publisher text, choose Insert ➢ File in Word or Insert ➢ Text File in Publisher; both open the Insert File dialog box. Choose the file you would like to insert—in Word, you may have to select a different file type from the File As Type drop-down list; Publisher already displays All File Types as the default. When the document is inserted, it is automatically converted to the correct format.

In Word you can also choose to insert a file and maintain a link to the original document. Let's say you use some standard text in several different types of reports that describe your organization. If you insert that text as a linked file, you can make changes to it in one place and have the changes appear in every document you use it in. To create a linked file, click the down arrow on the Insert button in the Insert File dialog box, and choose Insert As Link.

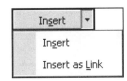

When you create a link to a file using this method, you must update the link manually. You cannot choose to have the link update automatically. If you make changes to the source document, right-click the linked document—the text should appear shaded—and choose Update Field, or choose Links from the Edit menu and click Update Now.

If you want to insert only part of a selected Excel workbook or Word document, click the Range button on the Insert File dialog box and enter a range of cells or a bookmark name before clicking the Insert button.

Embedding and Linking Other Types of Files

If you want to insert something other than a text file in Word or Publisher or want to insert any type of file in another Office XP application, you can create an OLE object from an existing file. Choose Insert ➢ Object ➢ Create From File to open the Create From File tab of the Object dialog box, shown in Figure 26.6.

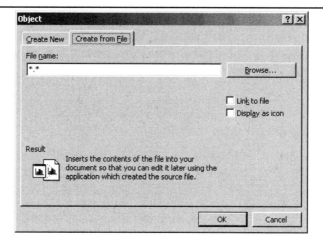

FIGURE 26.6

Use the Create From File tab of the Object dialog box to embed or link an entire file.

Select and open the file you want to embed or link, and choose Link To File if you want to maintain a link between the source and destination documents. Choose Display As Icon to insert the object as an icon. Click OK to insert the object in the destination document. Some files are inserted as icons whether or not you choose Display As Icon. A multimedia file, for example, appears as an icon in a Word document. Double-click the icon to play the file.

NOTE To insert or import sound or video files, you must have Windows Media Player installed on your system. Media Player comes with Windows and can be found on the Programs menu (Start ▸ Programs ▸ Accessories ▸ Multimedia ▸ Media Player). You can download the latest version of Windows Media Player, along with the Windows Media Player Bonus Pack with all kinds of cool add-ins, from www.microsoft.com\windows\windowsmedia.

MASTERING TROUBLESHOOTING

When Linked Files Are Renamed or Moved

Office XP can generally locate a linked file that has been renamed as long as it is still located in the same folder on the same drive. When you move a linked file, Office may

Continued ▌▶

MASTERING TROUBLESHOOTING CONTINUED

or may not be able to find the file in its new location. If you move the source file to another folder on the same drive and typically within the same folder branch, a new link is established and everything should work as expected.

However, if a linked file is moved to another logical drive or to a different folder branch, Office will no longer be able to find the file. Office XP displays the following error message.

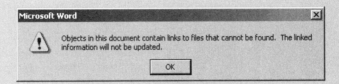

Moving the linked file back to its original location should repair the broken link. If you move a linked file successfully while the destination file is open, close the destination file, reopen it, and test the link again to make sure Office still knows where to find the linked file.

To repair a broken link, select the object and choose Edit ➢ Links. Click the Change Source button and locate the file you want to relink.

Creating New Objects

You can use the Object dialog box to create a completely new object. For example, you may want to include an Excel chart in a Word document. You don't have to open Excel and create the chart; you can create an Excel object directly in Word.

 TIP Because new objects exist only in the destination document, they cannot be linked, only embedded.

You probably have other applications on your computer, such as Microsoft Word-Art and Microsoft Graph, that also create objects. Choosing Insert ➢ Object from the menu bar opens the Object dialog box. The scroll list on the Create New tab, shown in Figure 26.7, displays the objects that can be created using applications installed on your computer.

FIGURE 26.7

Insert objects using the
Object dialog box.

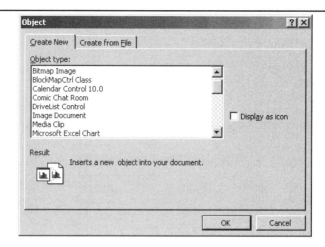

Select from the Object Type list, and click OK to launch the application tools you can use to create the object. Create the object, and then click outside the object to deactivate it.

The Object Type list on the Create New tab of the Object dialog box is amended as new applications are installed, but applications may remain on the list even if they have been removed from the computer. If you select an application that has been removed, the destination application provides an error message, warning you that it cannot find the application needed to create the object.

Using Application-Specific Tools to Exchange Data

In addition to using OLE, several of the Office applications have features that allow you to directly access data from other Office applications or to send data to another Office application. In Chapter 9, "Creating Merge Documents in Word," we discussed Word's Mail Merge feature and described how you can connect to data that resides in Access, Excel, and Outlook. That was just one example of some of the ways that you can exchange Office data. Here are a few more, broken down by application.

Excel

Excel has a number of tools that make it one of the best data conversion tools available. Excel opens a wide variety of files in their native formats, includes converters for other file formats, and has an import wizard to help you identify and map imported data. Using Microsoft Query, you can work in Excel with live data from other sources, including databases created in Access, Oracle, dBASE, and FoxPro, as well as text databases with delimited or fixed-length records. If you need data to move from one application to another, never give up until you've tried taking it through Excel. Chapter 20, "Importing and Exporting Data in Excel," covers Excel's importing and exporting tools in great detail.

Access

Access has tools to import items from other applications and to export data from Access for reporting and analysis. In Chapter 37, "Creating the Database Structure," you'll find information about how to import data from Excel and Outlook to use in Access databases. If you want to use Access data in a report you are creating in Word, or if you want to use Excel data analysis and calculation tools to analyze Access data, you can use the Access OfficeLinks feature to send the data where you want it. To use OfficeLinks, follow these steps:

1. Create a report in Access that contains the data you want to use.

2. Click the down arrow on the OfficeLinks button and choose Publish It With MS Word or Analyze It With MS Excel.

If you choose Word, Access launches Word, creates a rich text format file, and displays the data in columns separated by tabs. If you choose Excel, it launches Excel and creates an Excel workbook that contains the data from the report. In both cases, Office saves the newly created file to your default folder location.

PowerPoint

If you create an outline in Word before you begin writing that big report, you can make the outline serve double duty. By using PowerPoint's Insert Slides From Outline feature, you can create a PowerPoint presentation that exactly matches your Word outline. To use this feature, you must have a Word outline that uses heading styles (see Chapter 8, "Simplifying with Styles, Outlines, and Templates," for more about Word outlines and heading styles); every Heading 1 becomes a new PowerPoint slide. Choose Insert Slides From Outline from the PowerPoint Insert menu and—voila!—you have an instant PowerPoint presentation. Of course, you'll need to tweak the text and add design and formatting, but your content is all there for you to work with.

Outlook

Outlook was born to share data and to integrate with other applications. You can import and export data using Outlook's Import And Export Wizard, available on the File menu and described in Chapter 35, "Working behind the Scenes in Outlook." In addition to importing and exporting data, you can create a Word document, an Excel workbook, or a PowerPoint presentation from within Outlook; you can access the Outlook Address Book from Word; and you can save Outlook items to document folders on your local computer or network location. And this is only the beginning. If you need to move data into or out of Outlook for any purpose, there is probably a way to do it.

Creating a New Office Document from Outlook

If you want to e-mail a new Word, Excel, or PowerPoint document to someone, you don't need to leave Outlook to do it. You can create a new Office document directly from the New menu in Outlook. To create a new Office document, choose File ➤ New ➤ Office Document and then select Microsoft Excel Worksheet, Microsoft Word Document, or Microsoft PowerPoint Presentation from the New Office Document dialog box that opens. Click OK to launch the application. After you create and save the document, you can choose File ➤ Send To to e-mail the document or post it to a Microsoft Exchange folder.

Using Outlook Address Books in Word

You probably already know that you can access your Outlook address books when you are using Word's Mail Merge and Envelopes And Labels features (if you didn't, refer to Chapter 9). However, did you know that you can add an Address Book icon to your toolbar and access addresses anytime you want them? Follow these steps to put addresses at your fingertips:

1. From Word, choose View ➤ Toolbars ➤ Customize, or right-click any toolbar and choose Customize.

2. From the Commands tab, choose the Insert category and then scroll down the Commands list to find Address Book.

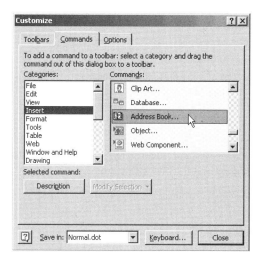

3. Drag the icon to the Standard toolbar or any other toolbar of your choice.

4. Click Close.

5. Click the Insert Address button to open the Select Name dialog box.

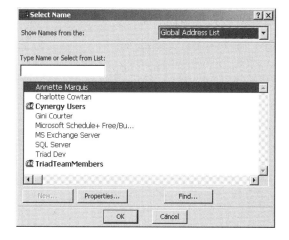

6. Choose the desired address book from the Show Names From The drop-down list.

7. Locate the address you want to insert. If you choose an Outlook Contacts folder you can choose which address you want: Mailing, Home, or Other.

8. Click OK to insert the address.

Once you have inserted an address, the name stays on the Insert Address button drop-down list for easy access.

PART

V

EXPERT INTEGRATION
AND COLLABORATION

Saving Outlook Items to Document Folders

If you are working in an environment where you are constantly receiving messages that your mailbox is too full, you may be interested to know that you can save your Outlook items to another folder location outside of Outlook and still access the items as if they never left.

Setting Up Shortcuts to Your Server Folders

To easily move your Outlook mail to the server, you should first set up shortcuts to your server folders. You can then drag-and-drop messages to the folder shortcuts.

1. Make the Outlook bar visible by choosing View ➢ Outlook Bar, and make the folder list visible by choosing View ➢ Folder List.

2. Click the Other Shortcuts button at the bottom of the Outlook bar.

3. Click the My Computer icon and locate the folder to which you want to create a shortcut. If it's on the network, click Network Neighborhood and locate your folder on the server.

4. To create new folders to store your mail, select the folder where you would like to place the new folder. Choose File New ➢ Folder and enter the new folder's name.

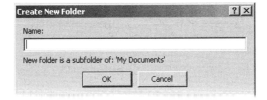

5. Drag the folder that you want to use to store messages to the Outlook bar and drop it there. Outlook creates a shortcut to the folder. Drag any additional folders you want to create shortcuts to.

6. To return to your mailbox, click Outlook Shortcuts and then click the Inbox icon.

 NOTE If you can't open network folders in Other Shortcuts, you may need to request permission from your network administrator or help desk.

Moving Messages to Your Folders

Once you have created folder shortcuts on the Outlook bar, you're ready to move messages to the folders.

1. Make the Outlook bar visible by choosing View ➢ Outlook Bar, and make the folder list visible by choosing View ➢ Folder List.

2. Make the messages you want to move visible in the right pane of the Outlook window.

3. Click the Other Shortcuts button at the bottom of the Outlook bar.

4. Select the messages you want to move. You can select multiple messages by holding Ctrl while clicking the messages you want, or to select consecutive messages, click the first one and hold Shift before clicking the last one.

5. Point to any one of the selected messages, and right-drag (drag with the right mouse button) and drop the messages on the server folder icon (you can also hold Shift and left-drag if you prefer).

Opening Messages from Your Server Folders

Even when your messages are stored in folders outside of Outlook, you can still open them as Outlook items.

1. Make the Outlook bar visible by choosing View ➢ Outlook Bar, and make the folder list visible by choosing View ➢ Folder List.

2. Click the Other Shortcuts button at the bottom of the Outlook bar.

3. Click the folder shortcut on the Outlook bar that contains the message you want to access.

4. Double-click the message in the right pane to open it as an Outlook item.

 NOTE You can reply to and forward stored messages just like any other Outlook messages.

Exchanging Other Types of Office XP Data

As you can see from the examples in this chapter, Office XP is made to move data, and the Office XP applications are made to work together to make this happen. If you are looking for a way to move data around and you're unsure of what method to use, check the File, Insert, and Tools menus of both the source and the destination applications. Typically, this is where you can find the importing, exporting, inserting, and converting tools to accomplish your objective. And in your search for the right tool, remember this Office XP adage: if you entered it once, you should never, ever have to enter it again.

CHAPTER 27

COLLABORATING IN OFFICE XP

FEATURING

- Working together on written documents

- Scheduling meetings with others

- Delegating and sharing tasks

- Communicating with others over the Web

- Sending and receiving instant messages

- Holding a virtual meeting with NetMeeting

- Sharing contact data with a team

People used to think that computers would offer us lives of leisure. Only our index finger would suffer any strain as it pushed buttons all day to take care of our every need. For most of us, reality has set in, and all we can count on it is that pushing buttons all day causes repetitived motion strain and faster computers result in a faster-paced work environment. We're being pushed from every direction to think faster, accomplish more, and always keep at least five steps ahead of the competition. Companies all over the globe are discovering that the best way to accomplish these aims is to encourage teamwork. Collaboration is a way to maximize the talents of each person, avoid rework, and use resources efficiently.

Microsoft designed Office XP to provide an infrastructure to support collaboration. They also designed the tools to make teamwork possible. Some of these tools are so extensive that we have dedicated entire chapters to them in this book. In this chapter, we provide an overview of all the primary workgroup tools, refer you to the chapters where you can find more detail about these tools, and introduce you to some new ways you can use Office XP to collaborate with your co-workers to get the job done.

Writing, Revising, and Working Together on Documents

Before the Web was even a dream in Tim Berners-Lee's mind, people have been collaborating on written documents. Not too long ago that meant printing multiple double-spaced copies and distributing them to team members for their revisions and comments. Someone then had the arduous task of consolidating all those handwritten corrections into a single coherent document. When word processing software such as Word and WordPerfect first introduced revision tracking in documents, it was viewed as a miraculous achievement. Revision tracking is now a staple in many industries (the publishing industry is a prime example), and other enhancements—such as saving multiple versions, routing, and master documents—have taken collaboration on written documents to a whole new dimension.

 NOTE Tim Berners-Lee, while serving as a software consultant for CERN Laboratory in Switzerland, is the inventor of the World Wide Web and the Hypertext Markup Language (HTML) that makes it possible.

Saving Multiple Versions of a Word Document

Although saving multiple versions is limited to use in Word, it's an idea whose time has come. The Versions feature, described in detail in Chapter 12, "Working Collaboratively with Word," lets you create a document and save a version of it in which you can record who saved it, the time and date it was saved, and any comments about the version. You or someone else can then open the document, make changes to it, and resave it as a different version. A version is not the same as a copy—only one copy of the document file exists. Within that file, Word tracks and displays different versions upon request.

Adding Your Comments

Versions may be limited to Word, but comments are everywhere. You can enter comments in Word documents (Insert ➤ Comment), in Excel worksheets (Insert ➤ Comment), and in PowerPoint presentations through the Notes pane. Comments are an effective way of communicating with team members about something in a document, reminding you of work left to be finished and documenting the purpose of a document.

You can also add comments to any document on its Properties sheet, shown in Figure 27.1, which you can access from the File menu of any application.

FIGURE 27.1

You can add comments to the Properties sheet of any document.

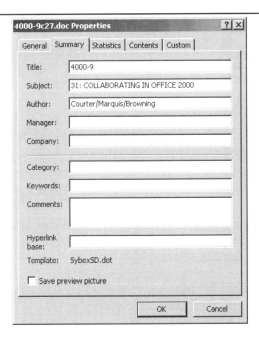

NOTE You can find out more about comments in Word in Chapter 12 and in Excel in Chapter 21. The Notes pane in PowerPoint is discussed in Chapter 22.

Tracking Changes

The most powerful text-based collaboration tool is the Track Changes feature in Word and Excel. With this feature, which has been completed revised in Office XP, you can make revisions to your heart's content and then in a single motion accept them or reject them all. You can also review each one and choose whether to accept or reject the change. When you distribute a document in which you've turned on Track Changes, you are able to maintain a record of every insertion, deletion, and move, including who made the change and when it was made.

Figure 27.2 shows a document that has been revised with revision tracking turned on. Inserted text is underlined, and deleted text is crossed out. Revision tracking also assigns each author a different color so it's evident at first glance that revisions were made by different people. Pointing to any revision shows a screen tip with the reviser's identity, the date and time of the revision, and what was done.

FIGURE 27.2

With revision tracking active, you can immediately see what text was inserted and by pointing to the text, find out the identity of the reviser.

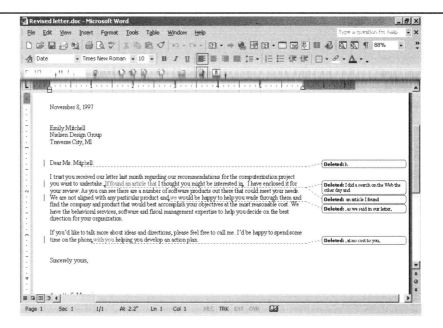

Revision tracking has a number of options and a dedicated toolbar for reviewing revisions (the Reviewing toolbar). To find out more about revision tracking in Word, refer to Chapter 12, and in Excel, Chapter 21.

Sharing Workbooks

To track changes in Excel, you must also share the workbook. When you share a workbook, more than one person can have the workbook open at the same time. Any changes that one person makes are shared with anyone else who has the workbook open as soon as the workbook is saved. Sharing a workbook is also covered in more depth in Chapter 21.

 TIP Sharing a workbook is an effective strategy when you want to work with someone else across a network. While you're discussing changes over the phone, you can immediately see each other's changes simply by saving the file.

Using Master Documents to Share the Load

In Chapter 11, "Making Large Documents Easy to Use," we showed you how to more easily manage large Word documents by converting them to a master document and subdocuments. You can also use a master document to work collaboratively on a large project. A master document serves as a container for other linked documents. The linked subdocuments can be opened independently of the master document or opened within the master document for page numbering and ease in printing. Changes made to the independent subdocument or to the subdocument as part of the master document are immediately reflected.

Subdocuments make it easier to divide up the work and still have a cohesive, unified document when you are finished. Subdocuments are no different from any other Word document, so you can still use revision tracking and all the other Word collaboration features with them. And because subdocuments can be assigned different passwords (Tools ➢ Options ➢ Save), you can restrict who has access to change or even view particular sections of a document. That's pretty hard to do in a single document!

Master documents may be intimidating the first time you work with them, but with just a little work, you'll consider them a nice addition to your collaboration tool chest.

Routing Documents

Routing is an incredibly useful tool to a team because you can distribute documents to a group of people all at once or successively. When you route a document successively, each reviewer has the benefit of seeing the changes made by previous reviewers. If you have a chain of command or some sort of logical review sequence, routing allows you to make sure the document moves along, and it can identify any holdups along the way.

Routing is not limited to documents needing revision. You can attach a routing slip, like the one shown in Figure 27.3, to Word documents, Excel workbooks, and PowerPoint presentations as a way of sharing information, delivering policies and procedures, highlighting financial accomplishments, or even distributing online forms.

FIGURE 27.3

You can attach a routing slip like this one to documents, workbooks, and presentations.

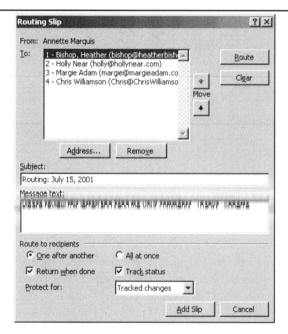

 NOTE For more about routing, refer to Chapters 12 and 21.

Scheduling Meetings and Managing Tasks

Collaborating on written documents is important, but sometimes you just have to get together and talk about it. Outlook has built-in tools to help you schedule meetings and share tasks with each other.

Scheduling Meetings

Finding a time when everybody can get together for a meeting can be the hardest part of holding a meeting. Outlook's Calendar can put an end to the countless hours spent scouring schedules for that one free hour you all have in common. As long as each person you want to meet with keeps their calendar updated in Outlook, you can use the Plan A Meeting feature of the Calendar, shown in Figure 27.4, to find an available time slot, send out invitations to the meeting, and track responses automatically. This capability is based on accessing each person's Free/Busy information shared through Microsoft Exchange Server or, new in Office XP, over the Internet.

PART

V

EXPERT INTEGRATION
AND COLLABORATION

FIGURE 27.4

Planning a meeting has never been easier or quicker than with Outlook's Plan A Meeting feature.

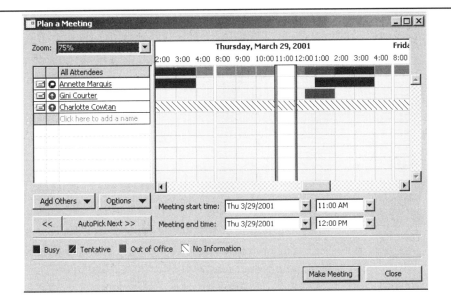

 NOTE You can learn all about planning meetings in Chapter 34, "Managing Your Time and Tasks."

Viewing Multiple Schedules at Once

NEW▶ If you need to see the contents of other people's calendars and they give you permission to do so, Outlook has a couple of built-in ways to access individual calendars. Using folder permissions and establishing delegates, both discussed in Chapter 35, "Working behind the Scenes in Outlook," are effective ways to share your calendar with someone else. In many businesses, however, meetings are scheduled with the same groups of people over and over again. If this is true in your business, a nifty addition to Outlook 2002 called Group Schedules could save you from having to select the same names every time you want to schedule a meeting. With this tool, you can create and save a group schedule that you can open whenever you need to see what everyone is up to.

To set up a group schedule, follow these steps:

1. Switch to Outlook's Calendar and click the Schedules button on the Standard toolbar.

2. Click the New button in the Group Schedules dialog box to create a new group schedule.

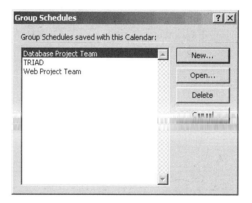

3. Enter a name for the new group schedule and click OK.

4. Select the names of the people you want to include in the group on the Group Schedules time grid. You can do this by clicking in the Group Members column and entering the names. Or to add names from the address book, click the Add Others button and choose Add From Address Book.

5. After you've added the names, click the Save And Close button.

Outlook closes the Group Schedules dialog box along with the time grid. To view the group schedule you created, click the Schedules button. Select the group you created and click Open. To see details about anyone's schedule, point to the time slot, and a screen tip appears with the rest of the appointment information (see Figure 27.5).

 NOTE To see the details of someone's schedule, you must have at least Reviewers permissions to that person's calendar. If you have questions about how to set up permissions, see Chapter 35 for the complete story.

PART

V

EXPERT INTEGRATION
AND COLLABORATION

FIGURE 27.5

Point to any time slot to see the details of someone's calendar.

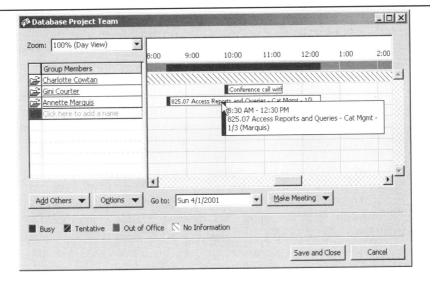

You can use the Group Schedules tool to schedule an appointment with the members of the group. Select any time on the time grid—drag to create a longer appointment—and open the Make Meeting menu to select from the available options.

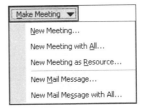

If you'd rather see only working hours in the time grid or you don't care about seeing appointment details, click the Options button on the Group Schedules time grid and toggle either option on or off.

 NOTE For Microsoft Outlook 2000, Microsoft made an Outlook add-in available on its Web site called Multiple-Calendar Viewer. This was a valuable utility for viewing up to five people's calendars at one time side by side on your screen. The biggest advantage of Multiple-Calendar Viewer over Group Schedules was that you could view everyone's schedules and then schedule an appointment on just one of the calendars—exactly what the doctor ordered for physicians, dentists, therapists, attorneys, or any office where you want to schedule a client with the first available professional. At the time of publication of this book, we have no word on whether this add-in will be upgraded for Outlook 2002. If you are interested, check for it at www.officeupdate.microsoft.com.

Delegating and Sharing Tasks

Whether or not you're in a supervisory or other leadership position, Outlook's Tasks feature, shown in Figure 27.6, makes it possible to share tasks with others and automatically track progress on completion of these tasks. If you have a stake in whether or not a task is completed, you can request that Outlook send you a message every time the task is updated. When you open this message, Outlook updates the copy of the task in your task list. If you do not have a monitoring stake in the task's completion, you can still send a task to someone else and leave no trace of the task on your list. Either way, the new task owner has the information they need to remind them of the task before them. You can find more about assigning tasks to others in Chapter 34.

PART

V

EXPERT INTEGRATION
AND COLLABORATION

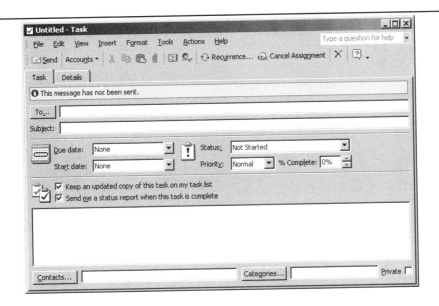

FIGURE 27.6

The task-tracking features provide automatic updates every time the task owner changes the task status, due date, or percent complete.

MASTERING THE OPPORTUNITIES

Assigning Tasks in a Team

A practical application of the using the Tasks feature on a team is to designate a "task-taker" at each team meeting. This person's responsibility is to maintain the list of things people agreed to do during the meeting and to record the date each task is due. At the end of the meeting, the task-taker returns to their workstation and records the tasks in Outlook, being careful to assign them to the appropriate individual. Because the task-taker is not responsible in any way for completing the tasks, they turn off the task-tracking features. As a result, shortly after returning from the meeting, all the meeting participants have the things they agreed to do recorded for them in their task lists. It makes it a lot harder to forget that they agreed to something and also verifies that everyone left the meeting with the same understanding of the next steps.

Outlook's Tasks feature can also be used to monitor tasks assigned to team members through Microsoft Project. Microsoft Project's TeamAssign feature can directly access Outlook Tasks. When a project team member updates a TeamAssign task, Outlook can update the Project file with information about the task's status, including Actual Work (time spent on the task recorded on a timeline). For more information about using tasks in formal project management, we recommend *Mastering Project 2000*, brought to you by your authors and Sybex, ISBN 0-7821-2656-1.

Communicating with Others across the Web

If you and your associates can't get together for a face-to-face meeting, you still have several options for getting together virtually. You can send and receive instant messages using MSN Messenger, hold virtual meetings using Microsoft NetMeeting, broadcast PowerPoint presentations to a group over the Web, and conduct document-centered Web discussions with Microsoft SharePoint Team Services. Each of these methods provides options for collaboration and input impossible to obtain before the Web existed.

NOTE For information about how to broadcast PowerPoint presentations to a group, see Chapter 30, and for more about Web discussions using Microsoft SharePoint Team Services, see Chapter 45 on the companion CD.

Holding Virtual Conversations

If you haven't yet held a virtual conversation, you may soon find yourself behind the eight ball. Virtual conversations—including instant messaging, live chat, online meetings, and audio and video conferencing—are gaining in popularity in both personal and business interactions. Microsoft Outlook 2002 includes support for instant messaging using the MSN Messenger Service and Microsoft Exchange Instant Messaging service. You can also use Outlook to schedule and log in to online meetings using Microsoft NetMeeting or Microsoft Exchange Conferencing and online presentations using Windows Media Services.

Joining the IM Revolution

Instant messaging, or IM, is becoming a popular way to communicate with business associates, colleagues, friends, and family. MSN Messenger Service, shown in Figure 27.7, is included with Internet Explorer 5. To make sure you have the latest version of MSN Messenger Service, go to http://messenger.msn.com. Instant messaging is enabled by default in Outlook 2002, so instant messaging is activated whenever you log in to Outlook and have a live network or Internet connection.

FIGURE 27.7

MSN Messenger Service is a great tool to use when you want instant communication and no long-distance charges.

To install MSN Messenger, choose Tools ➢ Options from the Outlook menu and select the Other tab. Check to see that the Enable Instant Messaging In Microsoft Outlook check box is enabled, and then click the Options button. You are prompted to open the MSN Messenger download Web page. Click Yes and then connect to the Internet if you are not already connected.

This takes you to the Microsoft Office Update site, where you need to select your country and then click Download Now. To use MSN Messenger Service, you must have a Microsoft Passport or a Hotmail account. A Passport is a central user name and password that gives you access to any participating Passport Web sites. A Hotmail account is a free Web-based e-mail account. If you do not have a Passport, click Get A Passport. If you already have a Hotmail account, you can use this information to get your Passport. If you don't, you can get both at one time. Complete the profile information to obtain a Passport. After you have a Passport, you can download MSN Messenger. Choose the option to Run This Program From Its Current Location, and click OK to begin setup.

After MSN Messenger is installed, an icon appears in the Windows system tray. This icon indicates that you are signed in. A red X on it indicates that you are not signed in. Before you can start communicating with anyone, however, you must add them to your list and invite them to start using the service. They, of course, must also be running MSN Messenger. If they are not, they are invited to download it and get set up.

When you invite someone to be active on your list, they have the option to make themselves visible to you or not. You can contact them only if they agree to participate with you, so it's a pretty closed club. You don't have to worry that anyone under the sun could be sending you instant messages. If you don't want to hear from them, just say no. You can even block a sender if later on you decide the romance is over. Just right-click their name in the MSN Messenger window and choose Block.

When you are interested in communicating with someone, you are instantly notified that they are online. You can choose to converse with them then or wait until you have something important to say. When they send you a message, a message window activates, like the one in Figure 27.8. To respond to their message, enter your text in the box at the bottom of the screen and click Send.

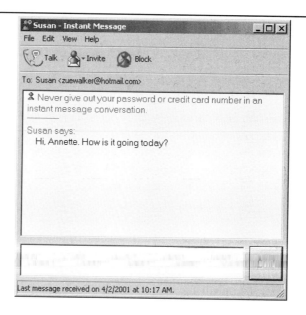

When you are finished talking, just say goodbye and don't send any more messages. The person remains active and available as long you both are online. If you don't want to be bothered by anyone, right-click the MSN Messenger Service icon in the Windows system tray and choose My Status from the shortcut menu. From there you can choose from a list that indicates you are not available.

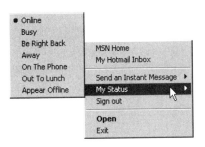

In addition to sending instant messages, you can use MSN Messenger to send e-mail to a contact's Hotmail account, send a text or alphanumeric message to a pager, make a telephone call, and send an invitation to start a Microsoft NetMeeting.

Holding a Virtual Meeting

Virtual meetings allow a group of geographically separated people to work together on documents over the Web. While MSN Messenger lets you hold a conversation with a group of people, Microsoft NetMeeting adds full meeting functionality to the online experience. With NetMeeting, participants have the power to simultaneously examine a document and make changes to it through each person's workstation, share a whiteboard, take control of another computer, use audio and video, and transfer files to each other.

 NOTE Microsoft NetMeeting is not included with Office XP. You can install it from the Windows 2000 CD or download the latest version from www.microsoft.com/windows/netmeeting.

You can access NetMeeting from MSN Messenger (Tools ➤ Send An Invitation ➤ To Start NetMeeting). You can also use Outlook's Calendar to schedule a NetMeeting—just click the This Is An Online Meeting check box in an open Appointment form.

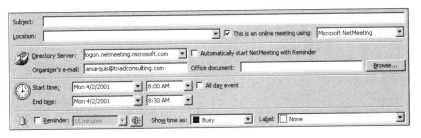

PART

V

EXPERT INTEGRATION AND COLLABORATION

You can then enter information about the Directory Server you want to use, the organizer's e-mail address, and the path to an Office document you want to share during the meeting. When the meeting time comes, Outlook automatically starts NetMeeting and signs you in to the meeting. Figure 27.9 shows the NetMeeting window when a meeting is in progress.

FIGURE 27.9

From the NetMeeting window, you can click one of the buttons at the bottom to share an application, chat, use the whiteboard, or transfer files.

If you would like to hold a NetMeeting with just a couple of people, you can use your standard Internet connection. However, if you plan to have a large group meeting, you should have access to a conferencing server, such as Microsoft Exchange Conferencing Server, to manage the conference for you. For more about Microsoft Exchange Conferencing, visit www.microsoft.com/catalog and choose Exchange 2000 Conferencing Server from the Alphabetical List Of Products drop-down list.

NOTE Microsoft used to maintain a group of conferencing servers for public use. Because of the amount of unseemly traffic they were receiving, they have discontinued access to these servers. If you would like access to a public NetMeeting server, you can still find one at http://communities.msn.com/TheNetMeetingZone.

For more information about NetMeeting, visit www.microsoft.com/windows/netmeeting.

Managing Team Contact Data in Outlook and Exchange

One of the biggest challenges facing many businesses today is how to keep teams in communication with each other about their clients or customers. It is not uncommon for several people from a company to have contact with the same person from a client's company. It can be difficult to look as if you have your act together when a client receives two calls from different people at your company about the same issue. With Outlook 2002, running on a Microsoft Exchange Server, your worries are over. You can set up a contact-based information system that includes contact information, e-mail messages, journal entries, and tasks all linked to individual contacts and shared by all members of your team. Before anyone contacts a client, they can review previous activities and communication and know exactly what's happening between your company and the client.

Setting up the folder system to support this contact management system requires a little work on the part of an administrator and a little more on the part of the participants. In this section, we'll outline the steps for setting up the folder system and putting it into action. Follow each of these steps carefully and sequentially to make sure that everything works the way it should.

Setting Up the Folder System

The person designated as the contact management administrator needs to be given administrative rights to create public folders on the Exchange Server or needs to work with the Exchange Server administrator to create the folders and assign user permissions.

Creating a Set of Public Folders

To create a set of public folders, follow these steps:

1. Expand Public Folders in your mailbox and select All Public Folders; then choose File ➢ New Folder to create the first folder in the system. This is a Contacts folder.

2. Create Email, Journal, and Tasks subfolders under the Contacts folder.

The folder structure should look something like this.

Assigning User Permissions

To assign user permissions to each of the new folders, follow these steps:

1. Right-click the Contacts folder and choose Properties.

2. Select the Permissions tab.

3. Click Add to add the users.

4. By default all users are given Author permissions, as shown in Figure 27.10. If you want to change this, select an appropriate role for each user or design a custom role (for more about roles, refer to "Setting Permissions for Others" in Chapter 35).

5. Click OK to assign the permissions.

6. Repeat steps 1 through 5 for each of the subfolders you created.

FIGURE 27.10

Author permissions give users the right to create and read items in the folder, but they can edit and delete only those items that they create.

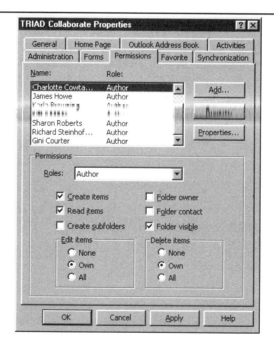

Defining Folder Groups for Activities Tracking

The contact management system relies on the Activities tab of the contact form. On the Activities tab, you can view all Outlook items that are linked to the contact. By default, when the Contacts folder is a public folder, Outlook does not identify the folders to be searched for linked activities. You must define the folders you want Outlook to examine. You can do this by following these steps:

1. Right-click the Contacts folder and choose Properties.

2. Select the Activities tab.

3. Click New to identify the first folder you want to search.

4. Name the folder group—we recommend giving it the same name as the folder you plan to select. Figure 27.11 shows the View Titles And Folders dialog box.

5. Click the first subfolder and click OK.

6. Repeat steps 3 through 5 for each of the subfolders you created.

7. Select the default folder you'd like to appear on the contact form Activities tab drop-down list.

8. Click OK to save the Activities properties. The Activities tab should look like the one in Figure 27.12 (with the folder names you've entered).

PART

V

EXPERT INTEGRATION
AND COLLABORATION

FIGURE 27.11

Enter the name of the folder group, and select a folder to add to the group.

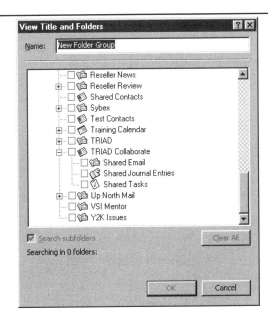

NOTE In public folders, you must individually select each folder and place it in its own folder group—you can only create folder groups that contain multiple folders in personal mailboxes.

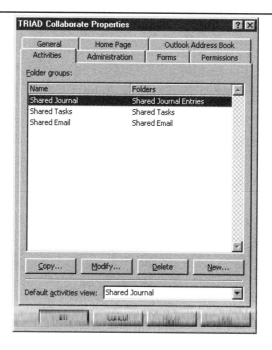

Customizing the Activities View

When a team member opens a contact form and selects the Activities tab, it's helpful if they find useful data in the Activities list. You can predefine what fields appear in each of the subfolders so no one has to go searching for critical data. To set up the Activities views, follow these steps:

1. Create a sample contact in the new Contacts folder (entering a name is sufficient) and select the Activities tab.

2. Right-click in the information viewer and select Show Fields to open the Show Fields dialog box.

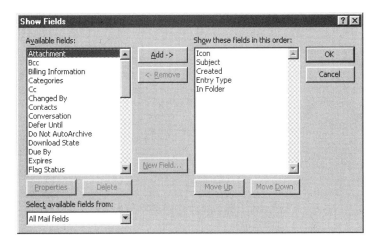

3. Select the fields you want to display and click Add (you may have to switch the Select Available Fields From drop-down list to correspond to the type of folder you are modifying—e.g., choose All Journal Fields to modify the Journal folder's view).

4. When you have finished selecting fields, click OK.

5. You can also choose Group By, Sort, and Other Settings from the shortcut menu to modify other characteristics of the view, or choose Customize Current View to open the View Summary dialog box, shown in Figure 27.13.

6. Select another folder from the Show drop-down list and repeat steps 2 through 5 until you have created the view for each folder.

PART

V

EXPERT INTEGRATION
AND COLLABORATION

7. Close the contact form when all views have been created.

FIGURE 27.13

You can use the View Summary dialog box to create the desired view.

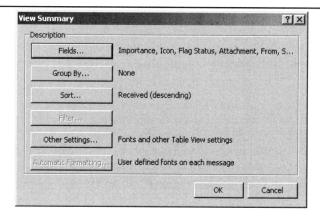

NOTE For more about creating custom Outlook views, refer to "Creating Custom Views" in Chapter 35.

Sending a Folder Link to Team Members

To notify the team members that the folder is ready for their use, select the Contacts
folder and choose File ➢ Folder ➢ Send Link To Folder, or right-click the folder and
choose Send Link To Folder. Address the e-mail message to each member of the team
(or if you've created a personal distribution list, enter the list name—see Chapter 32).

Putting the Folder System to Use

When the team members receive the link to the Contacts folder, they are ready to go,
with only a few minor adjustments.

Adding Folders to Favorites

Assuming that these folders are going to be used often, team members probably want
to add them to the Favorites folder. To do this, follow these steps:

1. Select the Contacts folder and choose File ➢ Folder ➢ Add To Favorites.

2. In the Add To Favorites dialog box, enter a Favorites folder name if you want to
change it from the original name.

3. Click the Options button to expand the dialog box.

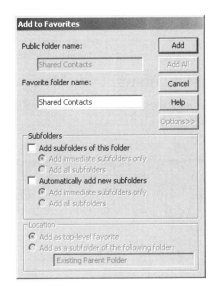

4. Select the Add Subfolders Of This Folder and Automatically Add New Subfolders check boxes. Leave Add Immediate Subfolders Only selected for both options.

5. Click Add to add the folders and subfolders to Favorites.

NOTE The options described in step 4, Automatically Add New Subfolders and Add Immediate Subfolders Only, are not required, so if you have reason to make other choices, you can do so without affecting the operation of these folders.

Setting Up the Contacts Folder As an Outlook Address Book

Team members must set up the Contacts folder as an Outlook address book to be able to access the e-mail and fax addresses stored with the contacts. To set this property, follow these steps:

1. Right-click the Contacts folder and choose Properties.

2. Select the Outlook Address Book tab.

3. Check the Show This Folder As An Email Address Book check box.

4. Enter a different name for the address book, if desired.

5. Click OK to save the property setting.

NOTE Changing the Outlook Address Book property also enables the QuickFind toolbar to search through this folder to find a contact.

Creating New Items

When a team member wants to create a new journal entry, e-mail, or task related to a contact, the first step is to open the contact. From the Actions menu, choose the desired action.

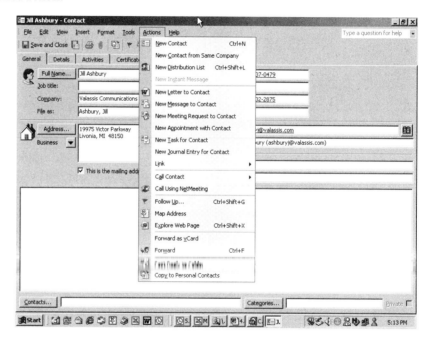

The most critical difference between creating a typical Outlook item and creating an Outlook item stored in a public folder is that you must choose File ➤ Move To Folder rather than choosing the Save or Save And Close commands. The Save and Save And Close commands store the item in the default mailbox folders rather than in a public folder. The Move To Folder command opens the Move Item To dialog box, from which you can choose the appropriate public folder.

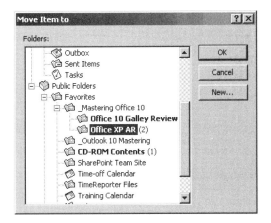

Sending E-mail Directly to a Folder

You can also e-mail items directly to folders in Outlook 2002. This means that you can forward or Bcc (Blind Carbon Copy) incoming and outgoing messages so that they are also stored in the appropriate folders. To e-mail directly to a folder, you must first add the folder to an address book. Then you can include the folder name just as you would any other message recipient.

Adding an E-mail Folder to an Address Book

To add an e-mail folder to an address book so it can receive mail sent directly to the folder, follow these steps:

1. Right-click the folder and choose Properties.

2. On the Administration or Summary tab, click the Personal Address Book button.

3. Click OK to close the Properties dialog box.

 NOTE A Personal Address Book is not available by default in Outlook 2002. Outlook adds the e-mail folder to the Contacts folder instead.

Viewing Associated Activities

When a team member wants to view activities associated with a contact, all they have to do is open the contact and select the Activities tab. When they select the type of activity they'd like to view (Journal, Email, or Tasks), Outlook immediately begins searching for and displaying those items, as shown in Figure 27.14. Double-click any entry to open the item.

Select the Activities tab to see the items linked to the open contact.

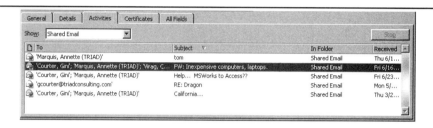

Now that the system is up and running, you are able to track communications and stay up-to-date on everything happening with a contact. Outlook provides the structure to make working as a team easier than ever!

MAKING THE WEB COME ALIVE WITH OFFICE XP

LEARN TO:

- Explore Office XP's Web design tools

- Publish and manage Web pages

- Create Web pages in Word

- Put an Excel spreadsheet online

- Publish PowerPoint presentations on the Web

CHAPTER 28

Exploring Office XP's Web Creation Tools

FEATURING

- Choosing between the Office Web design tools

- Setting Web publishing options

- Saving documents as Web pages

- Publishing Web pages

- Managing published Web pages

M icrosoft Office XP was designed with the Web in mind. In fact, the vast majority of enhancements to Office overall are related to the Web. Creating a Web page is the easy part; making it attractive, responsive, and interactive takes some knowledge and an array of special tools. Microsoft has worked to simplify the many tools they include in the Office suite. Although it has some limits, Office XP has sufficient power to make quality Web development a realistic possibility for Office users. In this chapter, we'll help you differentiate the Web-related tools contained in Office XP so you can pick the tools that work best for your situation. We'll also review the general Web publishing options and how you save, publish, and manage a published Web page.

Filling Your Web Design Toolbox

Every one of the Office XP applications offers something for the Web. With some applications, such as Word, Publisher, and FrontPage, you can create fully functioning Web sites. Other applications, such as Excel and Access, offer tools to create individual Web pages and special objects that you can include in existing pages. Access, through the use of Data Access Pages, makes database data available to your Web visitors. In PowerPoint, you can create presentations for the Web and even broadcast presentations to a select audience. Although Outlook doesn't include any Web design tools, you can use Outlook as a browser, display home pages for folders, access contacts' Web pages, and store URLs on the Outlook bar.

Table 28.1 examines each Office XP application and identifies the strengths and limitations of its Web tools.

TABLE 28.1   OFFICE XP WEB TOOLS

Application	Web Tools	Strengths	Limitations
Access	Make live database data available to the Web with Data Access Pages.	Data Access Pages can be used for interactive reporting, data entry, and data analysis. Pages are reasonably easy to design once you decide what you want users to do. You can open any HTML page in Access as a Data Access Page.	Users must have Internet Explorer 5 and a Microsoft Office XP license, so Data Access Pages are not for general distribution on the Web. They also have limited flexibility from a Web design perspective.

Continued ▶

TABLE 28.1 (continued)   OFFICE XP WEB TOOLS

Application	Web Tools	Strengths	Limitations
Excel	Publish static or interactive spreadsheets and pivot tables.	Can save and publish workbooks or individual pages; includes Excel tools with the worksheet object for direct data manipulation.	Need to open the page in a Web editing program such as FrontPage to add additional content to the page.
FrontPage	Create and manage small- and large-scale Web sites; has most of the tools you need for Web page creation and Web site management; provides Web page templates and wizards.	Web page editing and formatting tools are as consistent with Word as HTML allows; reports and views help manage Web sites; Explorer-type interface offers easy file management.	Creates a lot of extraneous HTML code; shared borders and navigation bars are great when they work but can be difficult to master; FrontPage 2002 server extensions must be installed on server to take full advantage of tools.
Outlook	Add Web links to contacts; open Web pages directly in Outlook; assign home pages to folders; add URLs to the Outlook bar.	Integrates the Web with other contact and folder management activities.	Cannot create Web content; must edit folder home pages in FrontPage.
PowerPoint	Publish presentations and create online broadcasts; can also create hyperlinks to Web pages in typical presentations.	Easy way to present summary information to users; few new skills needed to learn to design and publish presentation. The full-screen slides look great.	Presentations run as Web pages; cannot add additional content to the pages.
Publisher	Create Web pages and entire Web sites.	Built-in wizards and templates make Web design easy and fun.	A limited set of automated components and no Web site management tools.
Word	Create Web pages and Web sites in HTML; includes themes, frames, and form creation tools.	Little new to learn; great for intranet content providers who have to update and maintain a limited number of pages.	Can't view or edit HTML code; no Web site management tools.

PART

VI

MAKING THE WEB COME
ALIVE WITH OFFICE XP

Introducing the Best Web Tools

Given all the Web tools at your fingertips, here is a summary of what we think works best for the common Web-related tasks:

- If you are planning to create and maintain a full-service Web site with multiple pages, hyperlinks, user forms, graphics, and maybe even a little sound and video, we recommend that you start in FrontPage and use that as your primary Web design tool.

- If you have other users who are creating and updating simple Web pages that you want to incorporate into a larger Web, you may want to encourage them to use Word or Publisher rather than taking the time to teach them FrontPage. They will be eternally thankful!

- Use Excel, Access, and PowerPoint to add interactive content where appropriate.

- Take advantage of Outlook's Web tools, particularly adding hyperlinks to contacts' Web sites and viewing SharePoint team sites through Outlook (see Chapter 45, "Using a SharePoint Team Site for Team Collaboration," on the companion CD).

In the rest of this chapter, we'll take you through some of the common Web publishing options you will find through Office XP. Although these are a bit technical, it helps to know what's available before you start creating and publishing Web pages.

Setting Web Publishing Options

In each Office XP application when you can create HTML Web pages—Word, Excel, PowerPoint, and to a lesser degree Access and Publisher—you can change the default settings for HTML publishing in the Web Options dialog box. The available options differ slightly, depending on the application you are using. However, several of the options are available in most applications; we'll review those for you here.

NOTE Because FrontPage is dedicated to Web publishing, all of its options are related to Web publishing.

To access the Web options, choose Tools ➢ Options. Click the Web Options button on the General tab to open the Web Options dialog box, like the one shown in Figure 28.1 for Excel. Use the pages of this dialog box to set specific options for creating Web pages in Office XP.

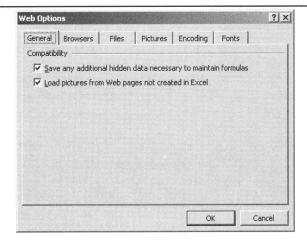

FIGURE 28.1

Set options for your Web page in the Web Options dialog box.

 NOTE Check the Web Options dialog box in each Office application to see the options that are specific to that application.

General Options

The General options vary the most depending on the application. In Excel, for example, you can set options for font formatting and the inclusion of hidden data and indicate whether pictures should be displayed when you open an HTML page in Excel. While in Access, you can only adjust the color of hyperlinks.

 TIP To find out about a specific option on the General tab or any other tab of the Web Options dialog box, click the What's This button in the title bar and choose the option you want to know about.

Browser Options

If you are creating Web pages for use on your company's intranet, you probably have a pretty good idea which browser most people have access to. If you select that browser as the target browser on the Browsers tab shown in Figure 28.2, you can make sure everyone will have access to the cool stuff you add to your Web site. The options listed at the bottom of the page turn on and off depending on which target browser you choose. Supported features are selected, and unsupported features are unselected.

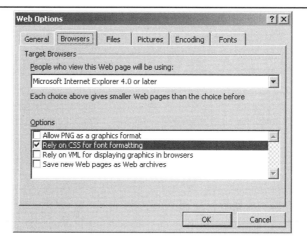

Use the Browsers tab to set options related to browsers, such as how graphics are handled.

Use these options to set how you want to display graphics. Advanced browsers like IE 5 support Vector Markup Language (VML) and Portable Network Graphics (PNG). Displaying graphics in VML and allowing PNG as an output format result in smaller Web graphics, which download and save much more quickly. If you've ever waited while your low-speed modem slowly downloaded a dozen graphics, you know that ⬚⬚⬚ ⬚⬚⬚ ⬚⬚⬚ ⬚⬚⬚⬚⬚ ⬚⬚⬚⬚ ⬚⬚⬚⬚ ⬚⬚⬚⬚ ⬚⬚⬚⬚ ⬚⬚⬚⬚ ⬚⬚⬚⬚ ⬚⬚⬚⬚ ⬚⬚⬚⬚ ⬚⬚⬚⬚⬚ ⬚⬚⬚ ⬚⬚⬚⬚ ⬚⬚⬚⬚⬚, ⬚⬚⬚⬚ with older browsers like IE 4 won't see any graphics at all—and IE 4 isn't all that old.

NOTE Internet Explorer 5.0 or later supports saving new Web pages as Web archives. Use this option to save snapshots of Web pages in single MIME-encoded files using the .mht or .mhtml file format.

File Options

The settings on the Files tab determine how the application saves files when you publish your document. These file options are available in many of the Office XP applications.

Organize Supporting Files In A Folder Enabled by default; this option creates a separate folder for supporting files such as graphics when the document is saved. The folder's name is the document's name with _files appended. For example, the folder of supporting files for My Presentation is named My Presentation_files. This option helps keeps your files organized and looking more like a Web site. If you clear the check box, be sure you can keep track of all of the files associated with the pages you create.

Use Long File Names Whenever Possible Disable this option if you're saving your presentation on a network file server (rather than a Web server) and Windows 3.1 or non-Windows users on your network need to open your presentations.

Update Links On Save This option automatically checks to make sure the links to supporting files such as graphics, background textures, and bullets are updated when the Web page is saved.

Check If Office Is The Default Editor For Web Pages Created in Office Clear this option only if you want to use a non-Office application as your default Web page editor. Otherwise, Office will ask you every time you try to save a Web page in Office if you want to make an Office application the default editor for the page. If you are setting Word options, you can specifically set Word as the default editor for the page.

In Excel, use the Files tab options to set a location from which you want to download Office Web Components from your corporate intranet. When you designate a file location, Office Web Components are loaded and installed automatically when you open an Excel workbook that uses them. This download location must be set up by your system administrator.

Picture Options

On the Pictures tab, shown in Figure 28.3, you can set the size of a target monitor and the number of pixels to improve layout and resolution. 800 × 600 is still the most common resolution used today, but the proliferation of laptops and high-resolution monitors make this difficult to predict. 800 × 600 is probably still a safe bet for most Web development.

FIGURE 28.3

Use the Pictures tab
options to set the size
of the target monitor.

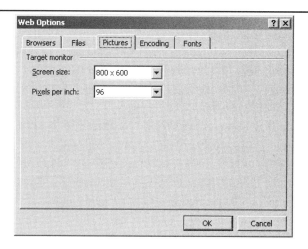

Encoding and Font Options

On the Encoding tab, you can choose the language code you want to save with the Web page. If you are using another language from the Office Language Pack to create the Web page, be sure to save the corresponding encoding with the Web page.

The Fonts tab, shown in Figure 28.4, sets the appropriate character set—Arabic, Cyrillic, English/Western European, and so forth—to use with your Web page. This is also where you set the default font and font size on the Web page. If a user opens the Web page and they have the default font on their system, that's the font the page will use. If they don't have the default font, Windows substitutes another font. It's a good idea to choose a common font that you can be confident most users will have available to them if you want your pages to display correctly.

FIGURE 28.4

On the Fonts tab, you can choose the character set and the default Proportional Font and Fixed-Width Font to use on your pages.

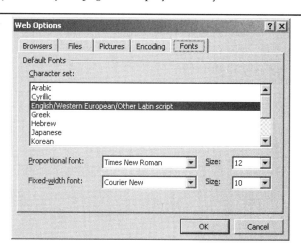

MASTERING THE OPPORTUNITIES

Assigning a Hyperlink Base for a Document

If you are creating Web pages for a corporate intranet (or a Web site where all linked pages reside on the same domain), you can establish a hyperlink base for a document that provides a consistent path to where linked documents are located. This makes it easy to link to documents because you don't have to enter the entire path. It also means that if you change the location of the linked documents, all you have to do is change the hyperlink base and all the links in the document will still be viable. To set a hyperlink base for a document:

1. Open the document's Properties sheet (File ➤ Properties) and click the Summary tab.
2. In the Hyperlink Base box, type the path you want to use for all the hyperlinks you create in this document.

If you want to override the hyperlink base and identify a fixed location for a particular link, just enter the full path to the link in the Insert Hyperlink dialog box.

Saving Documents As Web Pages

In some of the Office XP applications (except Access and Outlook), you can save documents as Web pages using the Save As Web Page option on the File menu. The Save As Web Page dialog box from Word is shown in Figure 28.5.

Click Change Title to open a dialog box where you can enter a title to appear in the browser's title bar when the page is displayed. (The filename is the default title.) In Word, you simply click Save to save an HTML version of the document. With PowerPoint and Excel, you can set other options, and with Publisher, you can create more than just Web pages—you can create an entire Web site.

NOTE Chapters 29 and 30 provide application-specific information on Web publishing in Word, Excel, and PowerPoint. Chapter 40 covers Web publishing with Access.

PART

VI

MAKING THE WEB COME
ALIVE WITH OFFICE XP

When you save as a Web page, you have the option of saving a page title that is different from the filename.

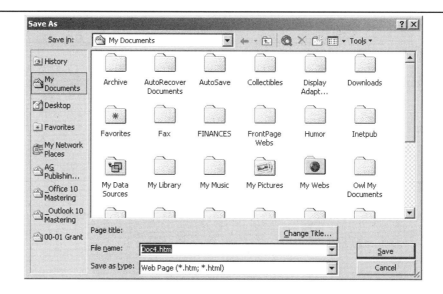

When you create an HTML document, you have several options for where you save it. You can save an HTML document to any of the following:

- Private folder where you can work with it just like any other Office document
- Shared folder where other users can open it in its original application
- Web folder where other users can open it in a browser
- Web server where it can become part of an intranet or Internet Web site

In order to save some of these shared folders on a Web server, you need appropriate permissions. Check with your server administrator if you want to save a document to one of these shared locations.

TIP Before you save a document as a Web page, create a folder in which to save the page and any related Web pages. This organizes the Web files and makes the supporting subfolders easy to find.

If you move or copy a Web page to another location, you must also move or copy the supporting folder in order to maintain all links to the Web page.

Saving a Web Archive

NEW▶ If you want to send a snapshot of a Web page you created in Office XP to someone and don't want to send all the accompanying supporting files, you can save the page as a Web archive. This file format applies MIME encoding, used to encode e-mail attachments, to the page so it can be saved as a single document. It is only supported by Internet Explorer 5.0 or higher, so make sure your recipient has the latest version of IE and that they have Outlook Express 5.0 or higher installed.

To save a Web page as a Web archive, choose File ➤ Save As Web Page and then select Web Archive (*.mht, *.mhtml) from the Files Of Type drop-down list.

You can open Web archives directly in Internet Explorer or in the Office application you used to create it.

Saving vs. Publishing

There are two ways to save Web documents in Excel and PowerPoint:

- Saving as a Web page
- Publishing a Web page

 NOTE Office XP Help uses the terms *save* and *publish* interchangeably, but there are differences between them that are worth knowing about.

Saving a document as a Web page saves the document in HTML format and makes the page viewable in a browser. You may want to save a document first as an Office document and then save it again as a Web page. When you want to make changes to the Web page, open the Office document, make the changes there, and resave it as a Web page. This reduces the formatting losses you may experience if you open an HTML document in an Office application.

The option to publish a Web page is available in Excel, PowerPoint, and Publisher. *Publishing* a Web page automatically makes a copy of the page, requiring you to enter a different name or path for the file. It also provides you with options that are not available by simply saving. For example, publishing a PowerPoint presentation allows you to set such additional options as which slides are displayed and whether Speaker's Notes are available. Figure 28.6 shows the Publish As Web Page dialog box that opens when you click the Publish button on the Save As dialog box in PowerPoint.

Excel allows you to publish individual worksheets, but you have to save a workbook as a Web page before you can access the entire book in a browser. So why would you want to publish? Publishing allows you to select a range of cells or append a worksheet or a range of cells to an existing Web page. If you'd like to find out more about publishing Excel pages, refer to Chapter 29.

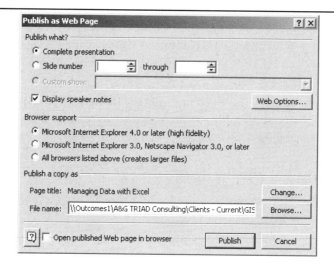

FIGURE 28.6

Publishing a PowerPoint presentation as a Web page allows you to select additional options that aren't available by saving.

Managing Published Web Pages

Managing Web pages you create in Office applications can be a bit tricky unless you also have Microsoft FrontPage 2002. FrontPage includes a number of Web site management tools that give you control over your published Web site. After you publish a Web page to a Web server, you cannot edit the page unless you have FrontPage available to open the page. That doesn't mean that all is lost, however. To make changes to a published Web page without FrontPage, open the copy of the Web page or original source document, make the changes you want to make, and republish the page to the same location. This overwrites the existing page with the modified version.

A major part of managing a Web page is verifying that the hyperlinks work; FrontPage includes a tool to verify hyperlinks. When you don't have FrontPage, the best way to do this is to access the page just as any other user would and check the hyperlinks in your browser. If the links work there, they are fine. If they don't, correct the hyperlinks in your copy and republish the page to the Web server.

For more information about FrontPage's Web site management tools, refer to Chapter 50, "Managing a Web Site with FrontPage," on the companion CD.

CHAPTER 29

Creating Web Pages in Word and Excel

FEATURING

- Creating Web pages using the Web Page Wizard

- Adding content to a Web page

- Creating hyperlinks

- Adding background sounds and movies

- Adding scrolling text

- Creating Web-based forms

- Working with frames

- Making a Web available for others to view

- Saving an Excel spreadsheet as a Web page

- Using the Office Web Components in an Excel Web page

Your supervisor has just asked you to create a series of Web pages for your corporate intranet. If you haven't created Web pages but have heard the lunchroom rumors about HTML, this new assignment can be pretty intimidating. Fear no more: Office XP will put your anxiety to rest. All you need to do is add a few new skills to your extensive bag of Word and Excel tricks, and you'll be producing dazzling pages in no time.

Word 2002 provides three ways to create Web pages:

- Using the Web Page Wizard
- Applying a Web template
- Converting an existing Word document

The Web Page Wizard creates not only Web pages but also full *Webs:* collections of pages with links between them. If the project you are undertaking involves multiple documents, the Web Page Wizard is generally the best choice, because it creates links for you and gives your pages a consistent look and feel. If you are providing content to your corporate intranet and you've been given a template to use, you may want to apply the template directly or convert an existing document without going through the wizard. However, after you use the wizard, you'll find it's a great tool whatever your goal.

Using Excel's Web tools, you can publish static and interactive spreadsheets, charts, and pivot tables. Interactive Web pages let users add formulas, sort and filter data, analyze data, and edit charts. In this chapter, we'll review Word's Web tools and show you how to add Excel components to make your pages even more valuable.

 NOTE What's the difference between a Web and a Web site? A Web becomes a Web site once it's published and assigned a URL that others can access.

Creating Web Pages Using the Web Page Wizard

The Web Page Wizard can create single pages or Webs that can be published as complete Web sites or appended to existing sites. If you want to create more than one page, it's a good idea to draw up the layout of your Web before you start the wizard (see Chapter 28 for more about designing a Web). You'll want to know the names of as many pages as possible so the wizard can create the links between them. If you have existing documents you want to include in the Web, be sure to know their names and where to locate them.

When you are ready to create your Web pages, choose File ➢ New from the Word menu. Select General Templates from the New Documents task pane. Select the Web Pages tab in the New dialog box and select Web Page Wizard. Click OK to start the wizard and Next to move on to the first step.

NOTE The Web Page Wizard may not be already installed. If you try to open the wizard, you may be prompted to install it on demand, so make sure you have access to the CD or network drive that Office was installed from.

The Title And Location page, shown in Figure 29.1, determines the official title of your Web. Although it can be changed later, it's important to give your Web a descriptive title, because the various Web search engines use the site's title when users search for a site on the Internet. A good title could mean the difference between someone finding your site or not.

By default, the wizard creates a new folder for your Web, so if you change the location, be sure you change it to an empty folder. The wizard creates additional subfolders for storing graphics and other supporting files, but the main pages are stored in the folder you specify. If you don't designate a unique folder, your Web files get mixed in with unrelated documents, making it difficult to manage the Web effectively. Enter the title and location and click Next.

FIGURE 29.1

Enter a descriptive title and folder location for your Web.

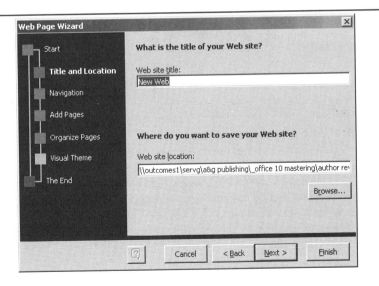

PART

VI

MAKING THE WEB COME
ALIVE WITH OFFICE XP

Using Frames for Navigation

The Web Page Wizard offers three choices for the layout of your pages, as shown in Figure 29.2:

Vertical Frame Runs down the left side of the page and contains links to the other pages in the Web.

Horizontal Frame Positioned across the top of the page and contains links to the other pages in the Web.

Separate Page Opens each page in a full window and does not use frames. Forward and Back buttons and appropriate links are added to the pages.

Choose the Navigation option you prefer and click Next.

FIGURE 29.2

The Web Page Wizard automatically creates navigation links between pages.

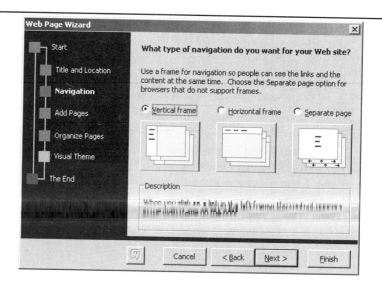

 NOTE Not all browsers support frames, and text readers (used by people with vision impairments) don't work well with frames. Many Web developers who use frames also offer visitors a no-frame alternative on the site's Welcome page, but if you can only choose one layout, choose the Separate Page option for the widest range of accessibility. For more information about making your Web sites accessible to people with disabilities, visit www.cast.org/bobby.

Differentiating Text Frames from Web Frames

You may already be familiar with text frames for positioning text on a page. *Text frames* are used extensively in PowerPoint and Publisher, and they can be used in Word and Excel to position a block of text outside of the normal paragraphs or cells. *Web frames* may contain text, but their primary purpose is to organize content on a Web page. Web frames typically appear on the top or left of a page and include navigational links that remain visible even when the visitor moves to a different page of your Web. See "Working with Frames" later in this chapter for more information.

Adding Pages

A Web created by the Web Page Wizard comes with three pages: a Personal Web Page and two blank pages. The Personal Web Page is a template that includes sections for work information, favorite links, contact information, current projects, biographical information, and personal interests. If you are not creating a personal Web with yourself as the focus, you can delete this page by selecting it and clicking Remove Page. The first blank page moves into position as the new home page for your Web.

 NOTE The home page is typically the first page visitors see when they visit a Web site, but a Welcome page that gives visitors options such as no frames or no graphics may precede it.

If you want to add additional pages to your Web, now is the best time to do so. As shown in Figure 29.3, you can add a new blank page, add a page based on a template, or insert an existing document into the Web. To add a blank page, click the Add New Blank Page button, and the new page appears at the bottom of the list (you will be given the option to rename pages in the next step of the wizard).

FIGURE 29.3

Add a new blank page, a template page, or an existing file to your Web using the Add Pages step of the Web Page Wizard.

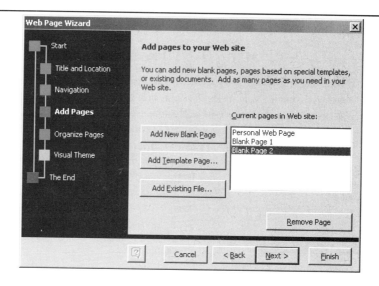

Selecting a Template for Your Page

Word includes seven Web page templates. Some of these templates include specific page layouts, such as the Left-Aligned Column and Right-Aligned Column templates. Others provide a structure for Web content, such as the Frequently Asked Questions and Table Of Contents templates. To review each of the templates, in the Add Pages step of the wizard, click the Add Template Page button. This opens the dialog box and preview window shown in Figure 29.4. Click any of the templates in the Web Page Template area to display a full page view of the template. When you have chosen the template you want to include in your Web, click OK. If you'd like to add another template page, click Add Template Page again and repeat the process.

NOTE   The Web page templates are also available outside of the wizard by choosing File ➢ New, selecting General Templates from the New Document task pane, and clicking the Web Pages tab.

FIGURE 29.4

A selected template is displayed as a full page behind the Web Page Templates dialog box so you can see what elements it contains.

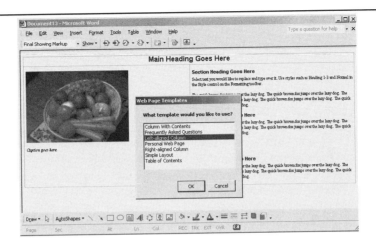

Adding Existing Documents

If you would like to convert any existing documents and add them to your Web, go to the Add Pages step and click the Add Existing File button. Locate and double-click the file you would like to include. The wizard saves a copy of the file as HTML and includes it in the Web folder. Repeat the process to add additional documents.

WARNING If you try to add an HTML page created in FrontPage 2002 or a page created in Excel or Access that uses the Office Web Components, it opens in its native application instead of being added in the wizard.

When you have finished adding pages, click Next to move on to the Organize Pages step of the wizard.

MASTERING TROUBLESHOOTING

When Multiple Word Pages Become One Web Page

When you insert a file in the wizard, it is added as a single page, even if it's a multipage document. If you have a document that you want to present as several individual pages,

Continued ▯▶

PART

VI

MAKING THE WEB COME
ALIVE WITH OFFICE XP

MASTERING TROUBLESHOOTING CONTINUED

use copy-and-paste to create and save a separate Word document for each page before launching the wizard, and then insert each document.

If you need to convert a number of existing Word documents to the HTML format, you can use the Batch Conversion Wizard. Create a new folder, and then move or copy all the Word documents to the folder. Choose File ➢ New. Select General Templates from the New Document task pane and click the Other Documents tab. Double-click the Batch Conversion Wizard. (If the wizard isn't listed in the New dialog box, you need to install it from the Office XP CD or your network installation point.) The Batch Conversion Wizard can also be used to recover corrupt documents and to convert files to and from the Word format from applications such as Pocket Word, Inkwriter, WordPerfect, Works, Windows Write, and Excel.

Organizing the Links

Now that you have the pages in your Web, you can rename them and change their relative order, as shown in Figure 29.5. This order determines the order of the links. Use the Move Up and Move Down buttons to rearrange the pages and the Rename button to change a page's name. Click Next to move on to the next step.

FIGURE 29.5

Putting the Web pages in order and giving them useful names will make the Web more organized.

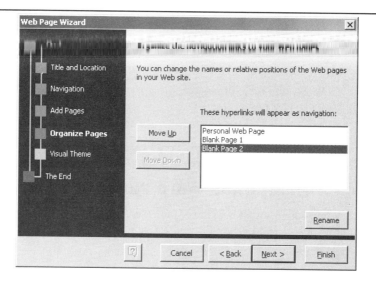

Applying Themes

Themes were first introduced in FrontPage 98 and are now included in several Office XP applications. A theme is a collection of colors, fonts, graphics, backgrounds, bullet characters, and styles that fit together. Office includes over 65 themes that can be applied to print publications, online documents, and Web pages. To select a theme, click the Browse Themes button in the Visual Theme step of the Web Page Wizard.

The Theme dialog box, shown in Figure 29.6, displays a preview of each theme listed on the left. Options for Active Graphics (typically appearing as animated bullets and horizontal lines) and Background Image are on by default. If you would also like to use Vivid Colors, click the check box. You can see the results of turning these options on or off in the preview window on the right, although you won't see active graphics actually move.

Once you decide on a theme (you can also choose No Theme from the top of the list), click OK. If you decide to use a theme, make sure Add A Visual Theme is selected in the Visual Theme step of the wizard.

Click Next to move to the last step of the wizard and click Finish. The wizard creates your Web pages, adds the links you specified, and saves the pages to the folder you chose.

FIGURE 29.6

You can apply Web themes to Web and print documents to create a consistent look and feel for all your publications.

PART

VI

MAKING THE WEB COME
ALIVE WITH OFFICE XP

Exploring Your Web

After the Web Page Wizard finishes its job, it opens the home page in Word. If you used frames in your Web site, the Frames toolbar opens (see more about frames in "Working with Frames" later in this chapter), but you have to open the Web toolbar manually if you want it available. The home page contains navigation links to other pages in the Web, either in frames—as shown in Figure 29.7—or at the top of the page if you choose the Separate Page option.

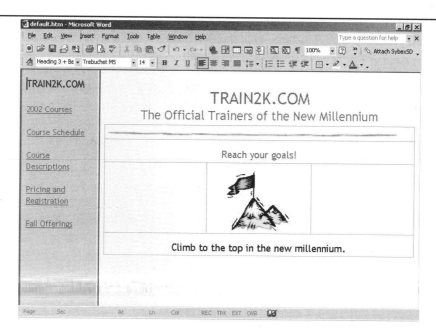

To view the other pages of the Web, point to any of the navigation links. The pointer changes to a hand and provides a screen tip about the file location of the hyperlink. Click the hyperlink to open the page. When the page opens, the Web toolbar, shown in Figure 29.8, also opens.

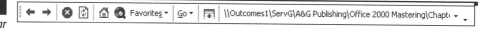

The Web toolbar is the standard Internet Explorer browser toolbar. Click the Back button to return to the home page.

> **EXPERT TIP**   To see the files the Web Page Wizard creates, open the folder in My Computer or Windows Explorer. You may notice a number of subfolders and files that you aren't familiar with. `Default.htm` —or `index.htm` if you are saving the Web on hard disk as opposed to a Web server—is the filename the wizard automatically assigns to the first or home page of the Web. The wizard creates a subfolder for each page and uses it to house graphics and other objects related to the page. For example, when you insert a graphic on a page and save the page, Word automatically saves the graphic to the page's corresponding subfolder. Graphics and other objects are not saved as part of a Web page but rather are saved separately and linked to the page. This is standard Web design protocol and helps keep the myriad of individual files streamlined and organized.

Adding Content to a Web Page

Editing Web pages in Word is not much different than editing other Word documents. You have access to all of Word's formatting and editing tools, including fonts, paragraph formatting, bullets, tables, and borders and shading. Web pages also include features that are not typically used in print documents: hyperlinks, frames, form controls, active graphics such as scrolling text boxes, and other special multimedia features. These tools are described in this section. If you learn to use these tools effectively, you'll be able to design Web pages that are dynamic, attractive, and effective.

Saving and Reopening a Web

If you create a Web using the Web Page Wizard, the wizard automatically saves the Web pages and associated files. After you make changes to any of the pages, click Save or choose File ➢ Save to resave the files just as you would any other document.

When you reopen a Web, you can choose to open individual pages for editing or the entire Web. The frame at the left or top of your Web pages is actually a separate page, so it will not open when you open individual pages. To make changes to the frames page, open the file `TOC Frame.htm`. To open the home page with the frame giving you access to the entire Web, open the file called `default.htm` or `index.htm`.

Creating Hyperlinks

Hyperlinks are what make the World Wide Web what it is. When Tim Berners-Lee, CERN researcher, developed HTML, his primary interest was in being able to access related documents easily—without regard to computer platform or operating system— by connecting the documents through a series of links. Hyperlinks allow readers to pursue their areas of interest without having to wade through tons of material searching for specific topics, and hyperlinks take readers down paths they might never have traveled without the ease of clicking a mouse. Adding hyperlinks to your documents moves information down off the shelf, dusts it off, and makes it a living, breathing instrument that people can really use.

Creating a hyperlink in an existing Web page is easy. Just follow these steps:

1. Enter or select some descriptive text in the page to define the link; for example, you could either type **Click here to view new courses** or select existing text that says *New Courses*.

2. Select the text, right-click within it, and choose Hyperlink to open the Insert Hyperlink dialog box, as shown in Figure 29.9.

3. Type a file or Web page name, or click the Existing File Or Web Page buttons to browse for the file. Click the Place In This Document button to create a link to another location in the same document, or click the E-mail Address button to create a link to an e-mail message form.

4. If you want to change the hyperlink text, enter new text in the Text To Display box.

5. Add a screen tip to the hyperlink by clicking the ScreenTip button and entering the text you want to appear in a screen tip.

6. Click OK to create the link.

For more about creating hyperlinks and bookmarks in Word documents, refer to Chapter 11, "Making Large Documents Easy to Use."

FIGURE 29.9

Create hyperlinks to other documents, Web pages, e-mail addresses, and other places in the same document by using the Insert Hyperlink dialog box.

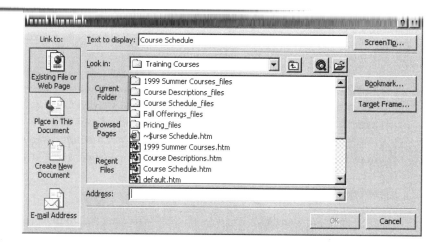

NOTE Word automatically creates a hyperlink when you type an address it recognizes as an Internet or file path address. If, for example, you type www.train2k.com, Word creates a hyperlink to that address. To turn hyperlink automatic formatting on or off, choose Tools ➤ AutoCorrect. Click AutoFormat As You Type and check or clear the Internet And Network Paths With Hyperlinks check box.

MASTERING TROUBLESHOOTING

Troubleshooting Hyperlinks

A hyperlink's effectiveness depends on its being able to locate the file or Internet address to which it is linked. If the file has moved or been renamed, or the address no longer exists, clicking the hyperlink returns an error message. It's important to regularly verify hyperlinks you've included in your site. If a link does not work, check the following:

1. Do you currently have access to the Internet or intranet site the link is calling? If not, check the link again when access has been restored.

2. Has the site or file moved? If so, right-click the link and choose Edit ➤ Hyperlink. Update the location of the linked file.

3. Does the file still exist? If not, right-click the link and choose Edit ➤ Hyperlink. Click Remove Link.

If the link still does not work after you have followed these steps, make sure the address is spelled correctly and there are no syntax errors in the address (for example, a comma instead of a dot).

If Edit Hyperlink does not appear on the shortcut menu when you right-click, it could be because the text contains a spelling or grammar error. Word displays the Spelling shortcut menu until the error is corrected.

Inserting Graphics

Visitors to a Web site expect to see more than just text. Fast-loading graphics add impact to your Web pages. The trick is to use small, attention-grabbing graphics on main pages and give visitors the option to view larger, more elaborate graphics by clicking to another page.

Inserting a graphic into a Web page is no different than placing one in a Word document. The Insert Clip Art task pane opens when you select Pictures ➤ Clip from the Insert menu; from the task pane you can choose art or any other clip art or photos you want to use (for more about inserting graphics in Word, see Chapters 6 and 7).

Web browsers don't support all the graphics features available in Word. To ensure that your Web pages look as good when viewed by a browser as they do in Word, features that are unsupported have been disabled. Only some of the wrapping styles available in Word documents, for example, are available for use in Web pages. As a result, you may find that once you've inserted a graphic, you have difficulty positioning it where you want it. To change how text wraps around the picture so you can more easily place the graphic where you want it, right-click the graphic and choose Format Picture or choose Format ➤ Picture from the menu. Select the Layout tab and change the Wrapping Style, as shown in Figure 29.10.

FIGURE 29.10

By changing the Wrapping Style, you can more easily position graphics.

You can also access the wrapping styles from the Picture toolbar that opens when you select a picture. Click the Text Wrapping button and choose a wrapping style from the menu that opens.

Inserting Alternative Text

A number of other options are available in the Format Picture dialog box. Because not all browsers can display graphics and some people just don't have the patience to wait for your beautiful graphics to appear on a Web page, it's possible to insert alternative text that describes the graphic. When the Web page opens, the alternative text appears while the page is loading, allowing visitors to click when they find the text they want without waiting for the graphic. To specify alternative text, select the Web tab of the Format Picture dialog box.

MASTERING TROUBLESHOOTING

Making Graphics Stay Where You Want Them

If you are having trouble positioning graphics on a Web page, you might want to try a Web designer's trick. Insert a table into the page. Three columns are usually sufficient, but add more columns if you want to line up a series of graphics. Then, position the graphic inside a cell of the table and change the table properties so the table expands to fill the size of the screen. To do so, follow these steps:

1. Click inside the table and choose Table ➤ Table Properties.

2. Select the Table tab and change Preferred Width to 100% Measure In Percent. (Although this step is not necessary, it makes it easier if you aren't sure about precise placement and sizing.) Click OK.

3. Now place the graphic inside the cell of the table that corresponds to the position you would like for the graphic. Click the Center button on the Formatting toolbar to center the graphic in the cell.

Before publishing the Web page, you can change the table's borders to No Borders. To do this, select the table, choose Format ➤ Borders And Shading, click the Borders tab, and click None. Your table won't be visible on the page, but the graphics will stay where you put them.

Using the Web Tools Toolbar

Word comes equipped with a Web Tools toolbar, shown in Figure 29.11, to help you add sounds and video, create forms, and add scrolling text. To turn on the Web Tools toolbar, choose View ➤ Toolbar and click Web Tools (be careful not to choose Web or you'll get the browser toolbar).

FIGURE 29.11

The Web Tools toolbar can help you add sounds, video, forms, and scrolling text.

Adding Background Sounds and Movies

Even though we don't seem to mind being constantly barraged by sounds from radio and television, most of us have not yet developed a fondness for sounds from the Web. Only occasionally will you happen upon a Web site that opens with background music drawing you in—or turning you away, as the case may be. However, if you'd like to add background sounds to your site despite all the evidence to the contrary, Word makes it easy for you to do.

To add a sound file to a page, follow these steps:

1. Check to see that you are in Web Layout view (View ➤ Web Layout).

2. Turn on the Web Tools toolbar by choosing View ➤ Toolbars ➤ Web Tools.

3. Click the Design Mode button on the Web Tools toolbar.

4. Move the insertion point to any obvious place on the page—it doesn't matter where you insert it as long as the icon remains visible.

III You can move into Design mode from any view, not just Web Layout view, but if you're working on a Web page, it's best to begin in Web Layout view so you know what your finished product will look like.

5. Click the Sound button on the Web Tools toolbar.

6. Enter the name of a WAV file or click Browse and locate the file.

7. Click the Loop down arrow to choose the number of times you want the sound to play, either 1–5 or Infinite.

8. Click OK.

9. Click the Design Mode button to return to your previous view. The sound file should begin playing immediately and will play whenever you open the page, as many times as you instructed it to.

NOTE Your browser (along with add-ins like RealPlayer—www.realplayer.com—and the Microsoft Windows Media Player) determines the types of sound files you can play. MIDI and WAV files are common, but MP3 (MPEG audio) files are becoming the most common. After you insert the file, test it in your browser and in browsers that your site's visitors would commonly use.

 To add a movie file, click the Movie button on the Web Tools toolbar (remember to click the Design Mode button and position the insertion point first). Enter the settings in the Movie Clip dialog box, as shown in Figure 29.12. It's a good idea to include an alternative image to display in browsers that do not support movie clips, or you can put the clip on a page so that users can choose whether or not to download it. However, even if a browser does support movie clips, the image will be small and difficult to see on most systems. If possible, test the display on several machines with different browsers to see how the movie file looks before making it a permanent part of your Web page.

FIGURE 29.12

To display a movie clip on a Web page, enter the settings for the clip you want to play and an alternative graphic for those browsers that do not support clips.

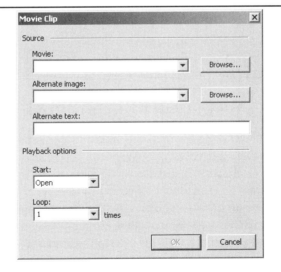

 To remove a sound or movie clip, switch to Design mode. Locate the Sound or Movie icon, like the ones shown here. Select the icon you want to delete and choose Edit ➢ Clear.

PART

VI

MAKING THE WEB COME
ALIVE WITH OFFICE XP

NOTE Movie clips consume a lot of bandwidth, so be cautious about using movie clips if most of your visitors use a dial-up connection to reach your site.

Adding Scrolling Text

Scrolling text is a way to grab your visitors' attention with a special announcement or notice. If you've used the Windows Scrolling Marquee screen saver, you're already familiar with the concept. To add scrolling text, follow these steps:

1. Click the Design Mode button on the Web Tools toolbar.

2. Position the insertion point where you want the scrolling text to appear.

3. Click the Scrolling Text button on the Web Tools toolbar.

4. Enter the text in the text box.

5. Set the options for Behavior, Direction, Background Color, Loop, and Speed.

6. Click OK to insert the scrolling text box.

7. Click the Design Mode button to exit Design mode; the text box doesn't scroll in Design mode.

You can resize or move the scrolling text box in Design mode as you would any text box in Word. To delete a scrolling text box, switch to Design mode, click the box to select it, and choose Edit ➣ Clear.

Viewing a Word Web Page in a Browser

If you are working on a Web site in Word, the easiest way to take a look at your work in a browser is to click File ➣ Web Page Preview. You'll want to do this on a regular basis to make sure the page looks the same in the browser as it does in Word. You don't want any surprises after you've finished your work on the Web. Use the navigation links on the page you preview to see other pages in the Web.

If you have your browser open and the Web you want to view is not open in Word, follow these steps to view the Web in the browser:

1. Start the browser.

2. Click File ➣ Open and locate the home page (default.htm or index.htm) for the Web site you want to view. Click OK.

3. Use navigation links to move from the home page of the Web site to the page you are working on.

Creating Web-Based Forms

To make the Web truly interactive, information has to go in both directions. Web users need the ability to send information to the site owners, and Web owners need to know who their visitors are and what they are looking for. Web forms provide a way for visitors to respond to surveys, register with a site, voice their opinions about issues, search your site, or submit feedback.

You can add a form to any Web page. When you add a form control from the Web Tools toolbar, Word automatically adds Top Of Form and Bottom Of Form boundaries to the form, as shown here:

Top of Form

Bottom of Form

Word comes equipped with 11 built-in controls for you to use on forms. Here's a quick look at each one.

 Check Boxes Use check boxes when users are allowed to select more than one option within a group. For example, you could have your check box say something like, "Send me more information about:" and then list various choices for the user to select from.

 Option Buttons Option buttons indicate that a user can select only one item from a group of options, such as indicating that they would like to receive information Daily, Weekly, or Monthly.

 Drop-Down Boxes Drop-down boxes give users a list of specific options from which they can choose one. For example, from a drop-down list of cities, you can pick yours to see its weather report.

 List Boxes List boxes are similar to drop-down boxes in that they give users a list of options to choose from. However, instead of clicking an arrow to open a list, users use scroll buttons to scroll through the list. List boxes allow users to select multiple choices by using Shift or Ctrl while clicking.

 Text Boxes Text boxes are fields where users can enter text, such as a name, address, or other specific information.

 Text Areas Text areas are open text boxes with scroll bars where users can write a paragraph or more to give feedback, describe a problem, or provide other information.

 Submit Button A Submit button is an essential element on a form, because a user must click the Submit button so that the data they entered is sent to the Web server for processing.

Submit With Image The Submit With Image control lets you substitute an image for the standard Submit button. Make sure users know they have to click this button to submit their data—and that clicking the button submits the data. For example, don't use the same image for a Next Page button and a Submit button.

 Reset Button Reset is a command button form control that clears the data in the current form so the user can start over.

 Hidden Hidden is a form field, invisible to the user, that passes data to the Web server. For example, a hidden control could pass information about the user's operating system or Web browser.

 Password In a Password control, typed text is replaced with asterisks so users can type passwords confidentially.

Laying Out a Form

Tables are a big help in laying out a form so that it looks organized. Create the table so it has twice the number of columns you would want to display in a single row. For example, in Figure 29.13, the third row contains three fields, so the table contains six columns. After you have inserted all the field names and form controls, save the page and open it in Internet Explorer or another browser to see how it looks.

Using a table to lay out form fields helps to align them in organized columns.

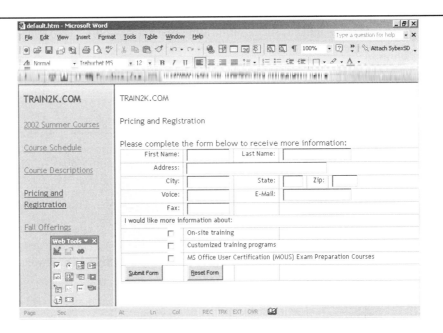

NOTE Because of the way different browsers display form fields, it is impossible to make every field line up perfectly with the fields above it unless you use tables.

Setting Form Field Properties

All form controls have properties that determine how they behave. Some form controls require that you set the properties before the control can be used. For example, you must enter the values that you want to appear in a drop-down list so the user has options to choose from. To set or edit a control's properties, double-click the control to open the Properties dialog box like the one in Figure 29.14.

If you haven't worked with control properties before, these dialog boxes can be a bit intimidating. Once you understand what you are looking at, you can choose which of the property settings to change and which to just leave alone. Each of the Properties dialog boxes has two tabs: Alphabetic and Categorized. They both contain the same properties in different order. The Alphabetic tab displays the properties in, you guessed it, alphabetical order. The Categorized tab groups the properties into various types: Appearance, Data, Miscellaneous, and so on.

FIGURE 29.14

Set or edit form field properties in Alphabetic tab of the Properties dialog box or view the same properties in collapsible and expandable groups on the Categorized tab.

PART

VI

MAKING THE WEB COME ALIVE WITH OFFICE XP

To make changes, double-click any of the properties to enter Edit mode. One change you should always make is to rename the control from the default name to a name that describes the field—for example, change *HTMLText1* to *FirstName*. Control names cannot contain spaces, but they can contain numbers and both uppercase and lowercase letters.

Entering Values for Drop-down Lists and List Boxes

To enter options for a drop-down list or a list box, type the first value in the Display-Values property. Enter a semicolon and no space before entering the next value. Figure 29.15 shows you the values in the control properties and the end result in a drop-down list. As you can see, the values you type each appear on a separate line in the list. To test the drop-down list box, exit Design mode and click the down arrow on the form control.

FIGURE 29.15

Enter values for a drop-down list in the DisplayValues property. When you view the page, the values you entered appear on separate lines in the drop-down list.

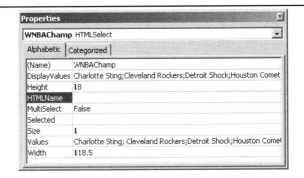

Make your choice for the 2002 WNBA Championship Team:

For more information about form control properties, refer to the Word Help topic "Form Controls You Can Use on a Web Page."

Adding Submit and Reset Buttons

After a user fills out your fabulous form, it would be nice if the data actually went somewhere. Every Web form needs Submit and Reset buttons to complete the form's functionality. The Submit button must be tied to some action so that the data knows where to go. The Reset buttons clears the form when the user makes mistakes and wants to start over. To insert Submit and Reset buttons, move to the end of the form—stay above the Bottom Of Form marker—and click the Submit or Reset buttons on the Web Tools toolbar.

To make the Submit button really work, you may need the help of your Web server administrator. Data can be stored in a comma-delimited text file, an Access table, or other database format. But before it can do that, it has to have a script, referred to as a *CGI script* or *form handler*, to tell it what to do with the data it collects. If you don't know how to write this script and you don't have a Web server administrator to help you, consider taking your form into FrontPage. FrontPage makes it easy to create these scripts by just answering a few questions in a dialog box. Refer to Chapter 49, "Enhancing the Interactivity of Your Web," on the companion CD for help in activating a form using FrontPage.

Working with Frames

A *frame* is a structure that displays a Web page on every other page of the Web site. The page that displays the frames is called a *frames page*. Although the Web Page Wizard is the easiest way to create a simple navigational frame, Word offers you the option of adding and deleting frames manually.

TIP There's a Frames toolbar that you can use to add, delete, and set the properties of frames. Right-click on any toolbar and choose Frames to display the toolbar.

To add a frame, choose Format ➢ Frames to open the Frames menu. If you want to add only a table of contents to the existing document, choose Table Of Contents In Frame. This option creates a table of contents for the displayed document based on heading styles used in the document. Figure 29.16 shows an example of a table of contents frame for this chapter. A link is created for each heading formatted using a heading style (for more about using heading styles, see Chapter 8, "Simplifying with Styles, Outlines, and Templates").

FIGURE 29.16

The Table Of Contents In Frame option creates a table of contents for the displayed document based on the heading styles.

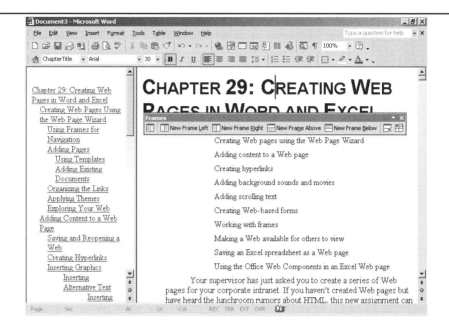

To create a page that you can use with frames, choose Format ➢ Frames ➢ New Frames Page to create the frames page. Choose Format ➢ Frames again to choose the position of the frame you would like to add. You can choose from several options about where to place the frame on the page. New Frame Above creates a header frame, and New Frame Below creates a footer frame. If you plan to add horizontal and vertical frames, add header and footer frames first so they extend the width of the page. Resize frames by dragging the frame border in the direction you want. After adding a horizontal frame, click in the main body of the page before clicking New Frames Left to add a vertical frame. Otherwise, you divide the header into two sections. Click in each frame to add content.

Saving a Frames Page

If you save the frames page before adding any content, Word saves all three frames as a single document. Unlike other Web pages, however, Word doesn't give this document a Title in the Save As dialog box. As soon as you add content to a frame, Word also saves the frame as an individual document. Because you are going to end up with several documents for each frames page you create, it's a good idea to create a folder to save in before saving a frames page. This keeps the main frames page and all the individual frames together in one easy to find place. Give the main frames page a name that reminds you it's a frames page. If it is the home page of the Web you are creating, however, save it as default.htm.

If you add graphics or other objects to a frame, Word creates subfolders to house them in. The subfolder has the name of the page followed by an underscore and the word files. For example, let's say you insert a graphic on a frame that you saved as Training Overview. Word creates a folder called Training Overview_files to store the graphic. It also creates an XML document in the folder called filelist.xml that keeps a list of all the images in the document. Each frame gets its own subfolder to hold image files. The example in Figure 29.17 shows the results of creating a frames page with three frames and inserting text and graphics on each page. In saving the main page as TRAIN2K Registration, Word also saved each frame as an individual document and created folders in which to store the images from each frame.

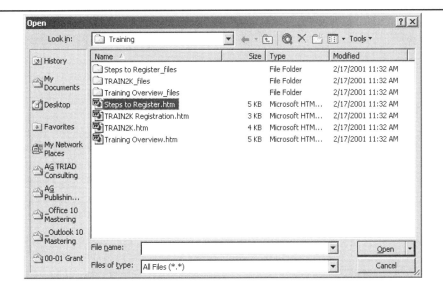

FIGURE 29.17

Word saves each frame individually and creates folders in which it saves image files.

Renaming Frames Pages

After Word creates folders in which to store images related to a frames page, the process of renaming a frame document is a little more complicated than renaming a normal document. To maintain the association between the document and the folder, you must first open the document you want to rename and resave it using File ➢ Save As to give it the new name. Word creates a new folder to store the image files. You must then choose File ➢ Open and delete the original document and associated *_files folder. It's an awkward process but it works. The key thing is to remember to discard the old document and folder so it doesn't confuse you down the road.

Setting Frame Properties

Right-click any frame, or select the frame and click the Frame Properties button on the Frames toolbar, to open the Frame Properties dialog box, shown in Figure 29.18. The initial page should be set to the frame that is open. However, you can change the page that opens in a frames page by selecting a different initial page from the drop-down list or clicking Browse to search for one. Give the frame a name by selecting or entering one in the Name box. Adjust the size of the frame by adjusting the size controls. By default, frames are set to a relative size. You can change the relative size to a specific pixel size or a percentage of the screen display by changing the Measure In option.

FIGURE 29.18

Use the Frame Properties dialog box to adjust the size of frames, borders, and other frame settings.

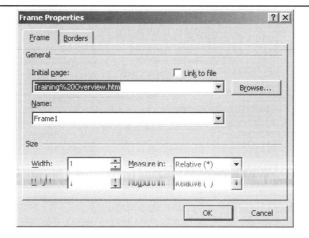

On the Borders tab of the Frame Properties dialog box, set whether you want to display frame borders and, if you do, what size and color you want them to be. You can determine if users will be able to adjust the frame size or not by clearing or checking the Frame Is Resizable In Browser check box. Turn scroll bars on or off using the Show Scrollbars In Browsers setting.

WARNING If you move a frames page to a different folder or drive location, you must copy all of the related frames documents to the same location.

Removing a Frame from a Frames Page

If you decide you want to remove a frame from a frames page, click in the frame and choose Format ➢ Frames ➢ Delete Frame or click the Delete Frame button on the Frames toolbar. You may want to save the frame under a different name before you delete it in case you decide you want to use it at a later time. To save the frame under a different name, right-click in the frame and choose Save Current Frame As.

EXPERT TIP Although Word 2002 provides some exciting Web page design options, creating a complex Web site requires some knowledge of HTML and other Web programming tools. While you are creating Web pages in Word, Word is writing the HTML and XML code behind the scenes. You can view this code and even edit it directly by choosing View ➢ HTML Source. This opens the Microsoft Development Environment design window where you can edit HTML and active server page (ASP) files. If you are not a programmer, this is a good place to take a look at what it takes to produce the content you are creating and see HTML in actual application. If you are a programmer, you can edit the HTML file and add Microsoft Visual Basic, JScript, and VBScript to your files.

Making a Web Available for Others to View

When you have your Web looking just the way you want, it's time to put it out there for others to use. In today's environment, you may be publishing a Web to your company's intranet, an extranet, or the World Wide Web. If you are developing for your company's intranet, contact the Web administrator to see how to proceed from here. It may be as simple as saving the files to a shared network folder.

If you want your Web pages to be available for the whole world to see, you need to publish the site to a Web server that others can access. The Web server may be within your company or run by a Web-hosting company. The cost of having a Web site hosted by an external company has come down dramatically, so unless you have a burning desire to run your own server, the smartest choice is to let a specialist do it. A good Web-hosting company is sure to have fast equipment, T1 lines for fast connections, and multiple phone lines to handle the heavy traffic that will be generated by your site. The company you choose can give you instructions on how to publish the Web to their server.

TIP If you need to find a company to host your Web, HostSearch.com (www.host-search.com) can help. HostSearch.com maintains an unbiased directory of Web hosting companies and lets you search for a host using a number of criteria including cost, space, and features. You can read reviews by actual users and compare up to five plans that meet your criteria.

Creating Web Pages with Excel

Excel 2002 is well-equipped to work with the Web. Not only can you save Excel worksheets as Web pages, you can open HTML files directly from Excel and drag-and-drop HTML tables from your browser directly into Excel worksheets. When you save or publish Excel 2002 worksheets as Web pages, the pages you create are either interactive or noninteractive. Noninteractive pages are simply static pages that users can look at to examine data, like those you could publish in prior versions of Excel. With the interactive opportunities made available by using the Office Web Components, users can work with the data via the browser using some of the same tools they would in Excel 2002.

 NOTE *Saving* and *publishing* Web pages in Office XP are not the same things. In Excel, for example, saving always creates noninteractive pages. See Chapter 28 for more information about Web publishing in Office.

Excel 2002 includes three Office Web Components, and each one supports specific kinds of interactivity. The components are:

- The Spreadsheet component inserts a spreadsheet where users can add formulas, sort and filter data, and format the worksheet.

- The Charting component is linked to data in the Spreadsheet component so that the chart can display changes when the data in the spreadsheet changes.

- The PivotTable component lets users analyze database information using most of the sorting, filtering, grouping, and subtotaling features of PivotTable Reports.

Understanding Office Web Components

The Office Web Components are based on *COM*, the *Component Object Model*. With these components, you don't need to learn Java to create the slick interactive interface your users are asking for. The COM standard defines groups of functions called *interfaces*. Interfaces like the Office Web Components are grouped into component categories, which are in turn supported by applications like Excel, Access, and Internet Explorer 4 and 5. COM objects used in Office XP are only interactive if the user's browser supports COM. If a user has an older browser, they'll still see the spreadsheet, chart, or pivot table, but they will not be able to manipulate it in their browser.

To create either an interactive or noninteractive Web page, open the spreadsheet you want to save to the Web. Then choose File ➢ Save As Web Page from the menu to open the Save As dialog box.

You'll notice a couple of differences between this and the typical Save As dialog box. You can choose to save the entire worksheet or just the selected sheet. To create interactive pages that Web site visitors will be able to work with, enable the Add Interactivity check box to add Office Web Components to your page. You can save an entire workbook as a Web page, complete with sheet tabs; however, the page cannot be interactive. To save an entire workbook, simply click Save to create the Web page and close the dialog box.

 NOTE To have Chart functionality, you must first create a chart in the worksheet and select it before opening the Save As dialog box.

Publishing the Active Sheet

If you want to publish the active sheet in the open workbook to a Web server, click Publish to open the Publish As Web Page dialog box, as shown in Figure 29.19.

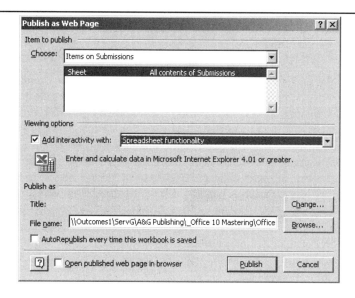

Choose what part of the workbook you want to publish. You can choose to publish the entire workbook without interactivity, you can choose a range of cells, or you can choose any of the sheets in the workbook.

If you have enabled interactivity, choose the component you wish to use from the drop-down list by selecting the kind of functionality you want users to have: spreadsheet or PivotTable.

NEW▶ In the Publish As section of the Publish As Web Page dialog box, click the Change ████████ ██ ████ ████ ██ ████████ █ ████ ████ █ ████ ███████ ██ ████ ████ ████ ██████ ████ want to publish to. In Excel 2002, you can select the AutoRepublish Every Time This Workbook Is Saved check box to take the hassle out of remembering to republish the worksheet every time you make a change.

If you want to immediately view your work in the Web browser, select the View In Web Browser button before you click Publish. When you are ready to publish, click the Publish button. Excel creates the Web page, including any interactivity you have specified. Figure 29.20 shows a Web page that includes the Spreadsheet component.

FIGURE 29.20

An interactive Excel
Web page that
includes the
Spreadsheet
component

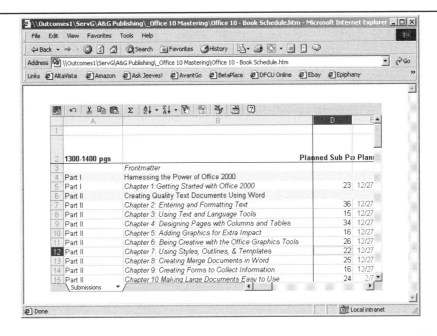

  Most of the toolbar buttons on a published Excel worksheet are familiar Excel buttons. There are two additions: the Export To Excel button and the Commands And Options button. The Export To Excel button re-creates the Excel worksheet at a user-specified location. The Commands And Options button opens additional user tools, as shown in Figure 29.21. Use this dialog box to change the format of a worksheet, work with formulas in the sheet, find worksheet data, and change worksheet and workbook options.

FIGURE 29.21

Users can change
the properties of
selected cells.

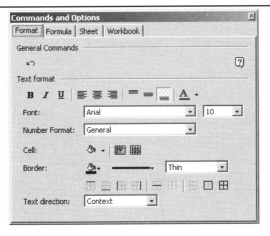

PART

VI

MAKING THE WEB COME
ALIVE WITH OFFICE XP

In Figure 29.22, we've published the same data using the PivotTable component. The COM object works like the Excel PivotTable Report with areas for row data, column data, and page data (filter data). See Chapter 19, "Using Excel to Present Information," for more information on PivotTable Reports.

FIGURE 29.22

The PivotTable component lets users interactively analyze data.

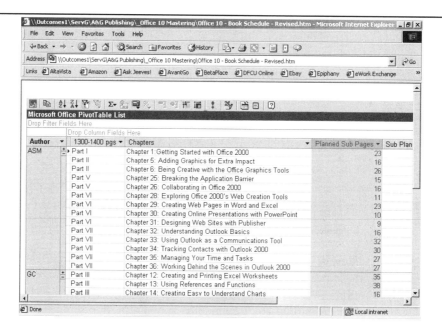

The Chart component displays both the chart and the underlying data (see Figure 29.23). Users manipulate the data to change the chart, just as they would in Excel. They can't change the chart type or other chart features, so make sure you create a chart that's useful before saving it as an interactive page (for more about creating Excel charts, see Chapter 15, "Creating Easy-to-Understand Charts").

FIGURE 29.23

The Chart component reflects changes in the underlying data.

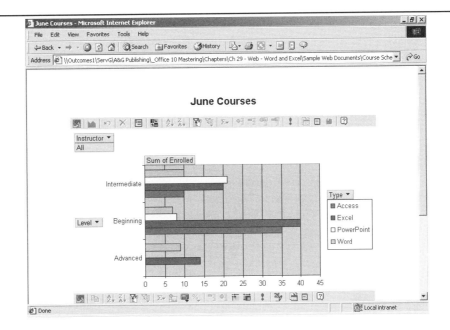

Appending to an Existing Web Page

If you already have a published spreadsheet and you'd like to add another Web component such as a chart or a pivot table to it, you can append the data to the existing page. To place a second component on a single Web page, choose File ➢ Save As Web Page and then click Publish to open the Publish As Web Page dialog box. Enter the existing HTML file in the File Name text box. When you click Publish, Excel prompts you to replace or add to the page. Choose Add To File to display more than one component on the page.

CHAPTER 30

CREATING ONLINE PRESENTATIONS WITH POWERPOINT

FEATURING

- Saving Web presentations

- Publishing Web presentations

- Setting PowerPoint Web options

- Setting up and broadcasting presentations

I f you have a presentation to give and your audience is spread out across the continent or across the globe, save the expense of bringing them all together. With PowerPoint 2002, you can deliver real-time presentations on the Internet or an intranet for an audience of one or one thousand, and you can save or publish presentations for individuals to use online at their convenience. In this chapter, we'll show you how to take your presentations to the Web and even broadcast them live with audio and video.

Preparing Presentations for the Web

PowerPoint 2002 gives you two methods for making presentations available for browsing on the Internet or your company's intranet: saving and publishing. When you save a presentation, other PowerPoint 2002 users connected to your network can access the HTML document, which allows them to edit the presentation. A published presentation, however, is like a published Web site: other users can view it and follow its links, but they cannot edit it. You'll probably want to save a presentation to a network file server while you and any colleagues are working on it; then, once it's ready to "go live," you can publish it to a Web server.

Before saving or publishing your presentation, it's a good idea to preview (File ➤ Web Page Preview) the way the presentation will look in your default browser. Then choose File ➤ Save As Web Page from the menu bar to open the Save As dialog box.

Saving a Presentation As a Web Page

The page title for the presentation is displayed near the bottom of the Save As dialog box. The title appears in the title bar of the user's browser; the default title is the presentation's title (from the title slide). To change the page title, click the Change Title button and enter a new title in the Set Page Title dialog box.

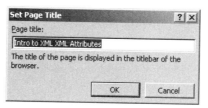

Click OK to return to the Save As dialog box. Click the Save button to save the presentation and close the dialog box.

Publishing a Web Presentation

With PowerPoint 2002, you can publish an entire presentation, selected slides, or even a single PowerPoint slide. The first page of a PowerPoint publication, displayed in Internet Explorer 5, is shown in Figure 30.1.

FIGURE 30.1

The published presentation includes navigation controls browser users expect to see.

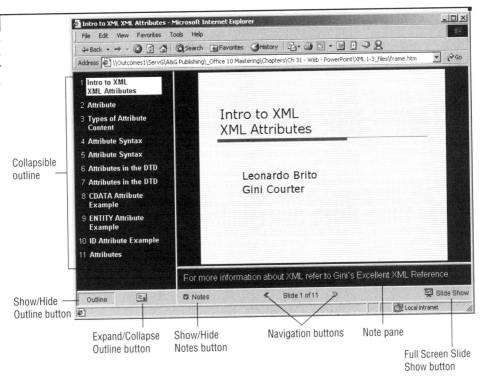

Collapsible outline

Show/Hide Outline button

Expand/Collapse Outline button

Show/Hide Notes button

Navigation buttons

Note pane

Full Screen Slide Show button

To publish your presentation, first choose File ➢ Save As Web Page; then click the Publish button in the Save As dialog box to open the Publish As Web Page dialog box, shown in Figure 30.2.

PART

VI

MAKING THE WEB COME
ALIVE WITH OFFICE XP

FIGURE 30.2

Set options for your Web presentation in the Publish As Web Page dialog box.

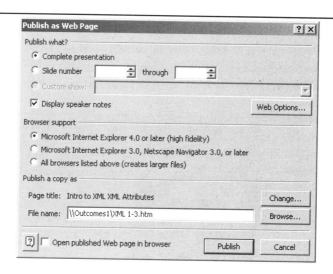

In the Publish What section, choose to publish the entire presentation, a range of slides, or a custom show you created using the Slide Show ➤ Custom Shows command. Enable the Display Speaker Notes check box if your presentation includes speaker's notes that you want users to see in a separate Note pane.

Setting Web Publishing Options

Click the Web Options button on the Publish As Web Page dialog box to open the Web Options dialog box. Use the four tabs of this dialog box to set options for publishing the current presentation. The General options available only in PowerPoint are detailed here; see Chapter 28, "Exploring Office XP's Web Creation Tools," for information about Web options used in all the Office applications.

TIP You can also access Web Options from the General tab of Options dialog box. From the main PowerPoint window, choose Tools ➤ Options, select the General tab, and click the Web Options button.

Add Slide Navigation Controls Your presentation will include an Outline pane with a collapsible outline (see Figure 30.1) in the color scheme you select, a Note pane, and navigation buttons below the presentation. Turn this option off if you're publishing a single slide.

NOTE In order to display Outline and Note panes in your published presentation, these panes must be turned on in the presentation before you publish. Also, you must have entered Notes on at least one slide prior to publishing.

Show Slide Animation While Browsing Your slide show will display animations within slides. If animations are manually advanced, the user will click the navigation buttons to switch slides and click the slides to move through the animations. There are no instructions to tell the user to do this, so we suggest you set automatic timings for all animations if you enable this check box.

Resize Graphics To Fit Browser Window This option is enabled by default. When you publish your presentation, this option automatically resizes graphics so they'll display best in the Screen Size setting specified in the Picture options.

When you've finished setting Web options, click OK to close the Web Options dialog box and return to the Publish As Web Page dialog box.

Selecting Browsers to Support

Choose the browsers you wish to support based on the intended distribution of your presentation. If you're publishing a presentation for your company's intranet, all you have to do is select your company's browser standard. For wider distribution (as with the Internet), there are additional issues to consider:

- Pages that link to your presentation serve as gatekeepers. If users need Internet Explorer 4 or higher to effectively view your home page, you may as well choose IE 4 support for your presentation that's accessed via the home page.

- The newer the browser, the more bells and whistles it supports. For example, IE 4 supports multimedia, including PowerPoint sound effects and movies. However, choosing the latest and most powerful browsers means that users may have to download a newer version of a browser to view your presentation. Even if you put a link to the browser's download page on your Web site, some users won't take the time to do this; they'll just browse elsewhere.

- The best browser format for WebTV is not necessarily the newest. With the number of WebTV users increasing, you may wish to choose the IE/Netscape 3 standard to maintain a broader user base.

- Choosing to support all browsers is the egalitarian approach and guarantees the widest possible access to your publication. However, it results in larger files, which means that everyone who wants to view your presentation will need more time to download it.

In the Publish A Copy As section of the Publish As Web Page dialog box, change (or leave the default) page title. Click the Browse button to select a destination for the presentation. If you wish to preview the presentation as soon as it is published, enable the check box at the bottom of the Publish As Web Page dialog box. Click Publish to publish a copy of the active PowerPoint presentation. If you change the presentation, you'll need to publish it again if you want the published copy to reflect your changes.

MASTERING TROUBLESHOOTING

Troubleshooting Web Presentations

After you publish a presentation, you may notice that the slide show (in PowerPoint) and the same presentation viewed as pages in your browser behave differently. Functionality that comes from PowerPoint isn't available in your browser. For example, when you right-click during a Web presentation, the presentation shortcut menu does not appear. This makes sense—your browser probably doesn't have a PowerPoint shortcut menu the rest of the time, either!

There are a number of PowerPoint features that don't work on a Web page, regardless of the browser support you select when you publish your presentation. Features that do not have Web support include:

- Embossed and shadow effects for fonts
- OLE multimedia objects
- Multislide sound effects (moving to another slide stops sound)
- Dimming effect on previous points on a slide
- Text animated by letter or by word rather than by paragraph
- Chart effects
- Spiral, stretch, swivel, and zoom effects

The browser you're using (or the browser you chose to support when you published) also affects the published product. Internet Explorer 3, for example, doesn't support sound and video playback.

Broadcasting Presentations

Rather than publishing a presentation and waiting for users to access it, you can schedule a Web broadcast over the Internet or an intranet and have everybody view it at the same time. Presentation Broadcasting is often used in place of a face-to-face meeting or conference call when you have participants at.remote locations, reducing the time and expense of traveling. Unlike a published presentation that users browse at their leisure, a broadcast occurs in real time, so you schedule the broadcast and invite participants in advance using Outlook (or another e-mail program). However, you can also record the broadcast and save it so that participants who could not attend or wish to review the presentation can do so.

Broadcasts come in two sizes: 1 to 10 participants and 11 or more participants. (This assumes that participants need their own Internet connections. If two people are sitting in front of the same monitor, count them as one participant.) You can use Internet Explorer 4 or 5 to broadcast to up to 10 people. For 11 participants or more, you'll need access to Windows Media Services, so talk to your Web administrator. Windows Media Services, which is available for free download from Microsoft and runs on Windows 2000 Server, is also required if you include live video, regardless of audience size.

There are three steps required to get ready for the actual broadcast:

- Selecting the broadcast options
- Selecting a shared folder and server
- Scheduling the broadcast

EXPERT TIP   Presentation Broadcasting uses Office automation to create appointments and invitations to the presentation in Outlook 2002. You can create and broadcast presentations regardless of your e-mail client, but if you intend to broadcast on a regular basis, you'll want to use Outlook and speak to your network or Web administrator about installing Windows Media Services or purchasing Windows Media Services from a third-party vendor. For more information about third-party vendors, choose the Advanced tab on the Broadcast Settings dialog box (Slide Show ➤ Online Broadcast ➤ Settings) and choose Use A Third Party Windows Media Service Provider. A browser window should open with links to third-party providers—check your Windows Taskbar for Internet Explorer if it doesn't appear on top of PowerPoint. As a way to attract customers, this service is being offered free for an undisclosed period of time. Ongoing rates are yet to be announced at the time of this writing so you might want to take advantage of it while it's still free.

Setting Up Your Broadcast

NEW▶

With the presentation you wish to broadcast open and active, choose Slide Show ➤ Online Broadcast ➤ Settings to open the Broadcast Settings dialog box, shown in Figure 30.3.

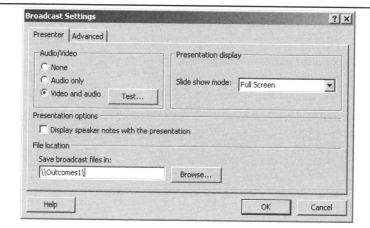

 NOTE   Online Broadcast is an install-on-demand feature in the standard Office installation. The first time you use this feature, you may be prompted to install it.

Selecting Broadcast Options

If you are broadcasting to 10 or more people using Windows Media Services, you can broadcast both audio and video (the default option in the Audio/Video settings in the Broadcast Settings dialog box). If you are not using Windows Media Services, you can choose Audio Only or None for no audio/video. As long as you have a microphone attached to your computer, you can broadcast audio. Click the Test button to run a test to make sure everything is running properly.

If you have annotated your presentation and want this material to be available to you, click the Display Speaker Notes With The Presentation check box on the Presenter tab of the Broadcast Settings dialog box. You can choose to display the presentation on your monitor as Full Screen or Resizable Screen in the Slide Show Mode drop-down list. Full Screen means you can't be shopping on eBay while your presentation is going on, but this is purely a matter of personal preference.

MASTERING TROUBLESHOOTING

Troubleshooting Audio/Video Set-Up

If, when you run the Audio/Video test in the Broadcast Settings dialog box, you get a Windows Media Encoding Error that says it cannot find the correct audio or video compression codec, you probably do not have the latest version of Windows Media Player installed on your system. A *codec*, which is short for compressor/decompressor, compresses the size of audio, video, and image files so that they don't use as much storage space or as much bandwidth when streamed across the Internet. PowerPoint 2002 expects to find the Windows Media Codec that comes with Windows Media Player 7.0 or later. You can find Windows Media Player 7.0 and the cool add-ons included with Windows Media Player Bonus pack on the CD that accompanies this book or for free download from www.microsoft.com/windows/windowsmedia.

NOTE You can schedule and broadcast a presentation on different computers. However, it's easiest to schedule the broadcast on the computer of the person who's hosting the presentation so PowerPoint will pick up their default description information.

PowerPoint saves the presentation before you broadcast, and you can indicate the file location where you want to save it in the Save Broadcast Files In text box at the bottom of the Presenter tab.

EXPERT TIP For the shared folder and the location where you save a recording of the broadcast, you must enter a server and folder with the file URL, \\server\\shared-folder; don't use network path syntax such as c:\My Documents\Broadcasts. Ideally, the shared folder's URL and the PowerPoint presentation's filename should not contain spaces; if they do, you'll have to double-check how the URL appears whenever it is referenced because the spaces will be represented by the characters %20. If the shared folder you want to use is on your computer or a mapped drive, click the Browse button and locate the folder to have the correct syntax automatically entered in the dialog box.

Setting Advanced Options

On the Advanced tab of the Broadcast Settings dialog box, shown in Figure 30.4, you can identify a remote Windows Media encoding machine and the URL for an audience chat room to accompany the presentation. In the Windows Media Server section, you need to indicate if you are using Windows Media Server or not. If you are not, then you have to limit the presentation participants to 10 or less. If you are using Windows Media Services locally, enter the name of the server on the network. If you would like to access a third-party Window Media Services provider, choose the last option.

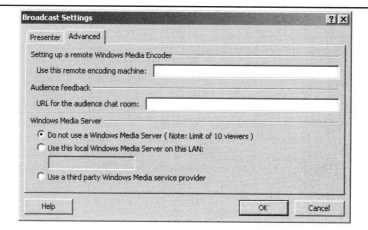

FIGURE 30.4

Use the Advanced tab of the Broadcast Settings dialog box to set up the servers you are going to use for the presentation.

NOTE In order to hold a chat, you must have access to a chat server and chat software such as Microsoft Chat or access to an online chat server such as MSN Chat (http://webchat.msn.com/).

When you are finished setting up the presentation, click OK. You are ready to schedule the broadcast.

Scheduling the Broadcast

After you set all the broadcast options, you can choose to start the broadcast immediately or schedule the broadcast to start at a later time. To start the broadcast immediately, choose Slide Show ➤ Broadcast ➤ Start Live Broadcast Now.

When you choose this option, Outlook opens. All you see, however, is the Outlook icon flashing on the Taskbar. Click the icon to see an Outlook alert that a program is trying to access e-mail addresses stored in Outlook. This is a security warning to prevent a virus from using your e-mail addresses to spread itself. Click the Allow Access For check box and indicate the number of minutes you would like to authorize—1 is generally sufficient.

The message box closes and is replaced by a PowerPoint dialog box that lists any presentations that you have set up for online broadcast and asks which one you want to broadcast. Select the presentation you want and click the Broadcast button to open the Live Presentation Broadcast dialog box, shown in Figure 30.5. Information you enter here appears on the Lobby page of the presentation.

FIGURE 30.5

Enter information about the presentation that will appear on the presentation's Lobby page.

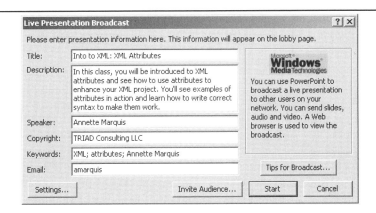

Click the Invite Audience button on the Live Presentation Broadcast dialog box to open an Outlook e-mail message form. Address the form to all of the people you want to invite and enter any more information about the presentation in the message box of the form. Send the message to invite the participants. Because you are starting the presentation right away, this assumes that you've already notified the participants in some other way, or you might find yourself presenting to an empty auditorium.

PART

VI

MAKING THE WEB COME
ALIVE WITH OFFICE XP

Preparing the Presentation for Broadcast

Click the Start button on the Live Presentation Broadcast dialog box to begin the presentation. Don't get nervous quite yet, though, you still have some steps to follow to prepare the presentation, such as setting up the microphone, doing a camera check, writing an audience message, and previewing the Lobby page. PowerPoint displays the Broadcast Presentation dialog box and shows you the status of the presentation as it prepares it for broadcast.

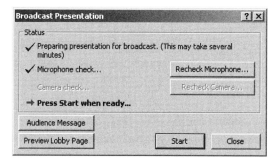

PowerPoint guides you through the microphone and camera check—just follow the instructions on the screen. To write an audience message that appears at the top of the Lobby page, click the Audience Message button. Although you can enter several lines of text, keep it brief. The message appears in a one-line, scrollable text box at the top of the Lobby page (see Figure 30.6). Click Preview Lobby Page to see what your participants will view as they wait for the presentation to begin.

NOTE If you are broadcasting the presentation immediately without scheduling a broadcast time, the Lobby page is simpler and does not contain the date and time information.

Click the PowerPoint icon on the Taskbar to reactivate PowerPoint. When you are satisfied with the settings, you can take a deep breath and click Start again for the real thing. The first slide of the presentation appears either in full screen or in a resizable window, depending on the choice you made in the original setup (see "Selecting Broadcast Options" earlier in this chapter).

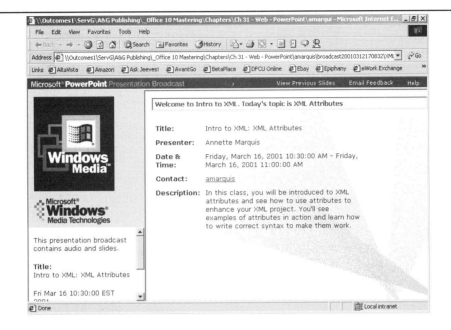

FIGURE 30.6

When participants access a broadcast, they enter through the Lobby.

Scheduling a Presentation for Broadcast Later

Rather than broadcasting a presentation immediately, you'll probably schedule most presentations for broadcast at a later time. Much of the setup for the broadcast is the same, but you must follow a few additional steps.

When you choose Slide Show ➤ Broadcast ➤ Schedule A Broadcast For Later or Reschedule A Live Broadcast, PowerPoint opens the Live Presentation Broadcast dialog box, shown earlier in Figure 30.5. However, instead of Invite Audience and a Start button, you have either a Schedule or Reschedule button. When you click the button, PowerPoint opens an Outlook appointment form so you can set a time and date for the meeting and invite participants, as shown in Figure 30.7.

FIGURE 30.7

*In an Outlook appoint-
ment form, you can
invite participants, set
the time and date of
the broadcast, and
add additional presen-
tation information.*

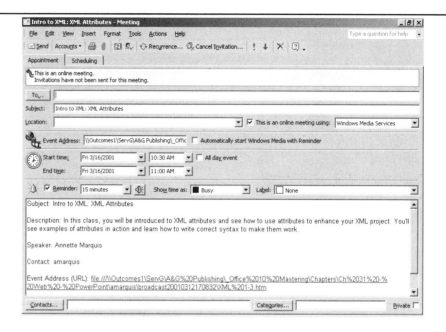

TIP If you're the person presenting the broadcast, you might want to set a reminder at least 15 minutes in advance and have Outlook automatically launch Windows Media when the reminder occurs.

After you send the appointment, PowerPoint creates and sends e-mail invitations to the attendees. If you don't use Outlook as your e-mail client, you need to enter the broadcast date and time in the message; PowerPoint automatically includes a hyperlink to the broadcast location that the participants can click to join the broadcast. PowerPoint then saves the broadcast version of the presentation. This can take several minutes for a lengthy presentation, but PowerPoint lets you know when the presentation is ready.

You'll receive e-mail responses from participants who use Outlook to let you know whether or not they will be attending the broadcast. After you read an e-mail response, the list of attendees on the Show Attendee Availability tab of the Outlook appointment item is automatically updated. The presentation appointment appears on your Outlook calendar. If you need to change broadcast times or cancel the broadcast, right-click the appointment and use the shortcut menu in Outlook, or open the

PowerPoint presentation and choose Slide Show ➢ Online Broadcast ➢ Reschedule A Live Broadcast.

 NOTE It's a good idea to rehearse your presentation between the time you send the invitations and the scheduled broadcast time. Chapter 25, "Taking Your Show on the Road," shows how to use PowerPoint's rehearsal tools.

Broadcasting the Presentation

A few minutes before the time of the actual broadcast, you can start preparing to make sure everything is set and ready to go. Open the presentation in PowerPoint and choose Slide Show ➢ Online Broadcast ➢ Start Live Broadcast Now to open the Live Presentation Broadcast dialog box, shown earlier in Figure 30.5.

Click the Start button and follow the instructions in "Preparing the Presentation for Broadcast" earlier in this chapter. The only difference you see here is that the timer is ticking down the minutes and seconds to the broadcast time. When the time reaches zero, click Start to start the broadcast.

The Lobby page is replaced with the first slide in your presentation. If you are using a microphone, begin speaking to welcome your audience and begin the presentation. Advance slides and animated objects just as you would in a live electronic presentation. When you click the last slide, the broadcast ends by displaying a black slide, and participants are returned to the Lobby page. If you recorded the presentation, participants can click the Replay Presentation button in their browser to view the presentation again.

 NOTE Depending on Internet or intranet access speeds, there could be a significant lag between the time you click and before slides change or animations appear. Monitor your browser window; it reflects what your participants are actually seeing. Participants can't easily remind you to slow down or speak more clearly, so take your time as you move through the presentation.

Participating in a Broadcast

You must have IE 4 or 5 to participate in a PowerPoint broadcast. To participate, you need an e-mail invitation. If you are using Outlook and you clicked the Automatically Start Windows Media With Reminder check box and set a reminder on the appointment form that invited you to the presentation, you are all set. When it's time for the presentation, Windows Media and your browser will start and launch the Lobby page for the broadcast. Adjust your audio volume so that the sound is clear. To view the entire presentation at your own pace, click the View Previous Slides link in your browser. In many presentations, you are allowed to e-mail questions or responses from your browser during the presentation. Some presentations also let you use Microsoft Chat to have a dialog with other participants.

GETTING ORGANIZED WITH OUTLOOK

LEARN TO:

- Find your way around the Outlook interface

- Organize your data with Outlook folders

- Manage your e-mail and contacts

- Take care of your to-do list with Tasks

- Schedule appointments, meetings, and events with Calendar

- Share your Outlook data

- Customize the Outlook environment

- Use Outlook when you are away from the Office

CHAPTER 31

Understanding Outlook Basics

O<!-- -->utlook can help you organize the mountains of information that can easily inundate your work life. The first few times you open Outlook, it's valuable to spend some time browsing. There is much to see and do here—as long as you know where to look and how to make Outlook work for you. Outlook contains six distinct tools (called *folders*) rolled into one: Contacts, Inbox (e-mail), Tasks, Calendar, Journal, and Notes. You can use all six or only one, depending on your individual needs and circumstances. The best part is that once you've learned how to use one folder effectively, you know most of what you need to use all of the folders. So start with the folder you know you want to use. Once you are comfortable with one of the folders, it will be much easier to move into the next, and the next. Before long you'll throw away your paper-based planner and start wondering how you ever lived without Outlook.

 TIP When you launch Outlook 2002, be careful not to select Outlook Express, a more limited e-mail and newsgroup application that is included with Internet Explorer.

Outlook Uses and Outlook Users

Outlook 2002 is a flexible tool that can be used in any business environment. You can use Outlook effectively on a stand-alone computer with or without a modem, or as part of a large corporate network with hundreds of computers and multiple sites around the globe. Regardless of your environment, you'll find tools that you can use to organize your information.

Outlook 2002 is referred to as a *desktop information manager (DIM)*, but it's that and more. You can use Outlook 2002 to organize all the information on your desktop, including a significant amount of information that you've probably kept only in paper form as well as information that you may never have organized at all.

With Outlook 2002, you can:

- Record the names, addresses, and other information related to personal and business contacts.

- Keep your to-do list and organize it by priority, by due date, or in other ways.

- Manage your appointments and track birthdays, holidays, and special events.

- Send electronic mail through the Internet or your corporate network.

- Keep notes about telephone conversations and meetings and, if desired, relate them to individual contacts.

- Schedule a meeting with other people in your workgroup or even across the Internet.
- Organize all of your personal information and files through one central interface.

And this is just the beginning. There is only one way to truly appreciate the power of Outlook 2002—you have to start using it. Once you do, you'll experience an increase in personal productivity and know that you'll be able to control and manage the information that crosses your desk. This application may even improve your outlook!

Outlook As a Personal Information Manager

Outlook 2002 includes six folders:

Contacts Replaces your manual address book or Windows address book. In Contacts, you keep personal and business contact information, names, addresses, e-mail addresses, and other information related to individuals. You can send contacts through Internet e-mail to other Outlook or personal information software users. You can also communicate with these contacts through e-mail, letters, phone calls, instant message, and NetMeeting, all initiated from within Outlook.

Tasks Your online to-do list. You can list your tasks, assign due dates, prioritize items, and even include shortcuts to Microsoft Office documents that are related to the task. You can also delegate tasks through e-mail to other people who are running Outlook.

Calendar Records your appointments, meetings, and other date-specific information, such as birthdays, holidays, vacations, and anniversaries in a date book. To make sure you still have time to get your work done, you can easily assign times in your calendar to work on items in your Task list.

Inbox Your source for sending and receiving electronic mail from home, the office, or on the road. If you have Internet access, you can use Outlook Express to participate in Usenet (NNTP) newsgroups and create private discussion groups.

Journal Lets you record what you've done. It can be used as a personal diary, a record of conversations and interactions with a client or customer, a time tracker to analyze how you spend your time, and a place to organize documents and communications related to a specific individual or project.

Notes An electronic notepad to replace all those little pieces of paper scattered all over your desk and stuck to the side of your monitor.

Outlook in a Corporate Setting

To experience all the incredible functionality of Outlook 2002, you must be running Outlook as a Microsoft Exchange Server client. You don't have to work in a large corporation to use Exchange Server. Many small companies are seeing the benefits of running Exchange Server, which is included in Microsoft Small Business Server and Microsoft BackOffice. Exchange Server an ideal system for companies organized around a virtual office. An Exchange Server enables your staff to dial in to the server from their homes or hotel rooms and have access to e-mail, to documents stored in public folders, and to shared calendars.

Whether you're in a corporation of thousands or one of five people working from home offices, Microsoft Exchange Server adds this functionality to Outlook 2002:

Calendar Lets you see when other users are free or busy; open other user's calendars with appropriate permissions; work with Microsoft Schedule+ for group scheduling; and delegate access to schedule appointments on your calendar.

Inbox Stores e-mail on the server in private or shared public folders rather than on your hard drive; uses server-based rules to filter your mail; supports voting, message flags, and message recall; allows deferred delivery of e-mail; sends and receives receipts when mail has been delivered or read; gives access to the Exchange Server Global Address List; allows users to access mail remotely; and uses client/server message replication.

Workgroup Functionality Creates private discussion groups (available also to Internet users) and works with collaboration, workflow, and project tracking applications such as Microsoft Project 2000, Microsoft Team Manager, and Microsoft Office XP products.

Outlook was clearly designed with the workgroup in mind. Its primary objective is to make collaboration in a workgroup setting efficient, friendly, and productive.

When Outlook is installed on a desktop, it creates a default *user profile,* a group of settings that define how you receive e-mail, where your personal information is stored, and what information services, such as Microsoft Exchange Server, are available. User profiles can be set up as roaming profiles, which means that you could log on to any computer in an office environment and have access to your personal information.

Exploring the Application Window

The Outlook application window, shown in Figure 31.1, has many familiar elements. The application window title bar identifies the application name and the active folder. On the far right side of the title bar are standard Minimize, Maximize/Restore, and Close buttons that control the application window. Underneath the title bar are two command bars: the menu bar and the Standard toolbar.

FIGURE 31.1

In the Outlook application window, you can use the Outlook bar to move among Outlook folders, such as Contacts, and the Information Viewer to see your data.

Menu bar   Standard toolbar   Ask a Question box

Folder banner

Outlook bar

Status bar

Information Viewer

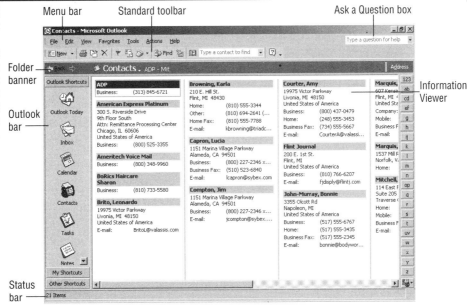

The vertical bar on the left side of the application window is called the Outlook bar. The icons let you navigate between the Outlook folders and easily access other folders. Outlook data is displayed in the *Information Viewer*: the large window to the right of the Outlook bar. Use the scroll bars on the Information Viewer to see data that does not appear in the display. The status bar displays messages and information—for example, the number of items in an active folder.

NOTE Every record in Outlook—a contact, a task, an appointment, an e-mail message, a journal entry, or a note—is referred to as an *items*. Items are stored in folders designated by the types of items they contain. You can create new folders and then move and copy Outlook items between folders to organize your data. See Chapter 35, "Working behind the Scenes in Outlook," to find out how to organize items in folders.

Toolbars

The toolbar menu options and buttons change depending upon which folder is active. For example, if the Contacts folder is active, open the Actions menu to create a new contact, send a message to a contact, call a contact, and so on. If you are in Calendar, the options on the Actions menu relate to creating new appointments, new events, and new recurring appointments. If you have difficulty finding a menu option that you know you saw somewhere before, switch to the folder in which you would most likely use that option, and you'll probably find it on one of the menus.

For more options in all folders, turn on the Advanced toolbar by choosing View ➢ Toolbars and clicking Advanced. This toolbar includes a number of truly useful buttons, some of which appeared on the Standard toolbar in Outlook 98. We recommend turning this toolbar on and leaving it on to save time searching for frequently used commands on the menu.

The first button on the Standard toolbar is the New button. This button is the easiest way to create any new item—a new task, a new contact, or a new appointment, for example. Just remember that what it creates depends on the currently active folder. When you point to the New button, a screen tip tells you what item the button is currently set to create. Regardless of which folder you are in, you can choose to create any new item by clicking the New button's down arrow. This opens the New menu, shown in Figure 31.2, listing all the items you can create in Outlook.

FIGURE 31.2

Click the New button's down arrow to create a new item of any type, no matter which folder you are working in.

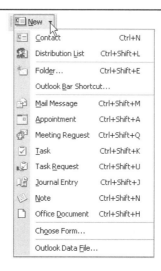

Prior to Office 2000, the toolbars in Outlook weren't fully customizable. In Appendix A, "Customizing Office XP to Your Work Environment," you'll find information on creating and customizing toolbars in Outlook and the other Office applications.

The Outlook Bar

The Outlook bar (see Figure 31.1) provides easy access to the Outlook folders and to other folders on your computer and network. The bar is divided into groups with *group buttons* such as Outlook Shortcuts, My Shortcuts, and Other Shortcuts. Click any of the icons in the Outlook Shortcuts group to activate that folder. Use the scroll bar button on the bottom of the group to see other icons in the group. Click one of the group buttons at the bottom or top of the Outlook bar to display the shortcuts in the group.

To change the size of the icons on the Outlook bar so that more can be displayed, right-click anywhere on the background of the bar and choose Small Icons from the shortcut menu.

If you decide that the Outlook bar takes up too much room on your screen, choose Hide Outlook Bar from the shortcut menu or click Outlook Bar on the View menu to turn the Outlook bar off. Click View ➢ Outlook Bar to make it visible again. If you like the Outlook bar, but prefer a leaner model, drag the vertical divider at the right edge of the Outlook bar to the left to narrow the Outlook bar.

The Folder List

The Folder List displays the folders in the current application—usually Outlook, but if you choose My Computer in the Other Shortcuts group, the Folder List looks a lot like the left pane of the Windows Explorer. To display the Folder List, choose View ➢ Folder List from the menu, click the Folder List button on the Advanced toolbar, or click the folder name in the *folder banner* to temporarily open the Folder List. The folder banner is the dark gray bar that contains the folder name (see Figure 31.1).

If you activate the folder list from the folder banner, click the pushpin button at the top-right corner of the Folder List to leave the Folder List open.

The Information Viewer

The Information Viewer is where it all happens—where Outlook displays all of your data. The Information Viewer displays multiple items or records at once. This is where you see all of your unread e-mail, a catalog of your contacts, or a list of your tasks. The best part about the Information Viewer is that it displays your data the way you want to see it. You can sort your data, group it together, and find records that meet specific criteria. Outlook 2002's default settings start with Outlook Today displayed in the Information Viewer.

Outlook Today

When you start Outlook for the first time, you may start in Outlook Today. Outlook Today's Web page interface, shown in Figure 31.3, provides you with the day-at-a-glance view of your world by listing your appointments, e-mail that has yet to be handled, and tasks that are due to be completed. In an ideal world, you would spend your day completing these responsibilities and then start fresh tomorrow with a brand-new list. Recognizing that few of us live in that ideal world, Outlook Today displays appointments for the next five days by default and includes tasks that are overdue as well as those that are due today. However, if you'd rather focus only on today or see more than five days of appointments, you can change some of the settings that control Outlook Today.

FIGURE 31.3

Outlook Today provides a summary of your days' activities.

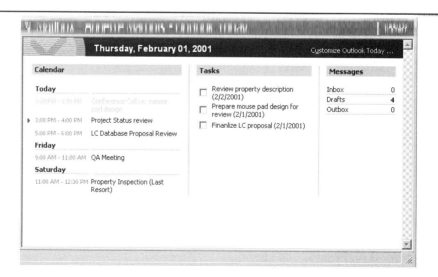

NOTE If Outlook Today does not appear automatically when you launch Outlook, you can display it by clicking the Outlook Today icon on the Outlook bar.

To change Outlook Today's options, click the Customize Outlook Today button in the upper-right corner of the Outlook Today window.

The Customize form, shown in Figure 31.4, opens so you can change the following:

Startup If you like Outlook Today's view of your world, enable the check box to have Outlook Today appear when you launch Outlook.

Messages Choose to display messages from your Inbox, Drafts, or Outbox folder.

Calendar Select the number of days (between 1 and 7) of calendar to display.

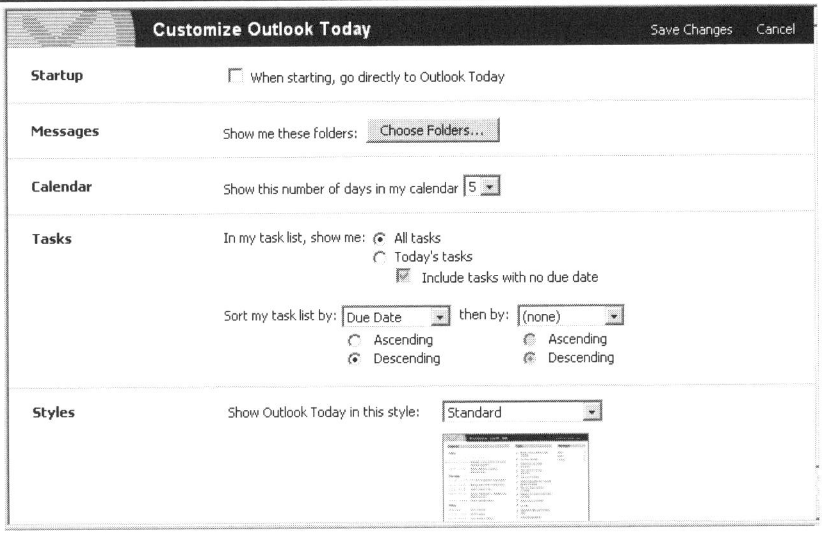

FIGURE 31.4

In the Outlook Today Customize page, you can change what data is displayed and the style in which you see it.

Customize Outlook Today — Save Changes Cancel

Startup ☐ When starting, go directly to Outlook Today

Messages Show me these folders: [Choose Folders...]

Calendar Show this number of days in my calendar [5 ▼]

Tasks In my task list, show me: ⦿ All tasks
○ Today's tasks
☑ Include tasks with no due date

Sort my task list by: [Due Date ▼] then by: [(none) ▼]
○ Ascending   ○ Ascending
⦿ Descending   ⦿ Descending

Styles Show Outlook Today in this style: [Standard ▼]

Tasks Select All Tasks, which shows complete and incomplete tasks, or Today's Tasks, which shows only those incomplete tasks that are due today. You can also indicate how you'd like the tasks sorted.

Styles Choose an Outlook Today theme.

When you have finished setting preferences, click Save Changes to return to Outlook Today.

Working in the Outlook Folders

Each Outlook folder has unique features. Some operations and features, however, are common to all six folders. In this section, we will explore the common features of the Outlook folders.

There are two ways to work with Outlook data: in the Information Viewer or on Outlook forms. You can enter data directly in the Information Viewer or double-click a record to open that item in a form. The Information Viewer displays a set of columns from multiple Outlook items. A form displays an individual Outlook item, which includes all the information about a particular contact, the entire contents of an e-mail message, or the details of a scheduled appointment. The Information Viewer lets you look at your data as a group—all the people from the same company or all of your unread e-mail—while forms let you focus on one record and see all its data.

Viewing Data in the Information Viewer

One of Outlook's greatest strengths is its capability to display multiple records based on different groups of settings. A *view* is a specific set of fields, sort order, grouping, filters, and formats presented in one of the five types of Outlook views: Card, Table, Timeline, Day/Week/Month, and Icon.

Each of the Outlook folders has a default view, but you can switch to other views or create your own view in every folder. In the default views, folder items are initially sorted alphabetically or chronologically. In some views, data is also grouped according to entries in a field. For example, to see all your contacts within each organiza-tion, you could group by company, and then optionally sort the contacts within each company by last name. Grouped views usually are indicated with the word "by" in their name.

Changing Views

Outlook 2002 makes it easy to display the data you need to work with. You can:

- Switch to a predefined view
- Rearrange an existing view
- Create your own view from scratch

To switch to another view, choose View ➢ Current View and select from the list of available views. Figure 31.5 shows the views available in Tasks.

 TIP If you turn on the Advanced toolbar (View ➢ Toolbars ➢ Advanced), you can select Views from the Current View drop-down list.

FIGURE 31.5

Each view type has a number of predefined groupings and views available such as these for Tasks.

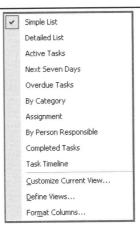

If you would like to maximize the power of organizing your data with views, learn more about views and how to create custom views in Chapter 35.

Rearranging Table Columns

Table views are the easiest to change—even easier than rearranging columns in an Excel worksheet. To rearrange the order of the columns in a table view, select a column heading in the header row, hold your mouse button down, and drag the column heading to its new location. When two red arrows appear where you want the column to be, release the mouse button.

Removing a Field in Table View

To delete a column, drag the column button off the header row and drop it when you see a large black X.

Sorting Items in Table View

To sort the data in a different order, click the heading of the column on which you want to sort. An upward or downward arrow appears in the heading.

An up arrow indicates that the data is sorted on that column in ascending (A to Z) order; a down arrow indicates descending (Z to A or, more commonly, 99 to 1) order. Click the heading again to change the sort direction.

Entering Data in the Information Viewer

In table views, you can enter data directly in items in the Information Viewer. For example, to add a contact in the By Company view, click at the top of the list where it says *Click here to add a new contact*. Type the contact information in the text boxes and press Enter to add the contact to Outlook's Contacts folder. Even if you can't enter data, most views allow you to edit data directly in the Information Viewer. To edit an item, click once in the field you want to edit. If an insertion point appears, you can edit the data. If it does not, you must edit the data in the item's form.

Using Forms to Enter Data

Creating a new record in any of the folders is as simple as clicking the New button on the Standard toolbar. Either switch to the folder you want to use before clicking the New button or click the button's drop-down list to select the desired item. The default form for a folder contains commonly used fields in that folder. To open the form for an existing record, double-click the item in the Information Viewer or right-click the item and choose Open.

Navigating a Form

When you open a form, such as the Contact form shown in Figure 31.6, the focus is on the first field in the form. Use Tab and Shift+Tab to move forward and backward between the fields, or click in any field to activate it. If a form has multiple tabs, like the Contact form's General, Details, Activities, Certificates, and All Fields tabs, select the page tabs at the top of the form to move between the tabs. Each form has its own toolbars that include general and folder-specific commands.

FIGURE 31.6

The Contact form is a multitab form with its own toolbar.

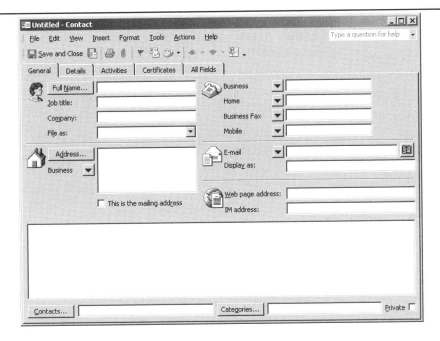

To move from record to record without closing the form and double-clicking the next item in the Information Viewer, click the Previous Item or Next Item button; this moves you directly to the next record. Outlook prompts you to save any changes that you made to the current record before moving on.

TIP If you'd rather use the keyboard to move between items, hold Ctrl and press the comma key to move to the previous item; pressing Ctrl+period opens the next item.

The drop-down arrows on each of these buttons let you move quickly to the first and last records in the folder. Click the arrow attached to the Previous Item button and choose First Item In Folder; click the arrow on the Next Item button and choose Last Item In Folder.

Entering Text and Numbers

Enter and select text in a form as you would in Word:

- Select text by dragging over it with the mouse pointer.
- Double-click to select a word and triple-click to select a line of text.

- Select all the text in a field by choosing Edit ➢ Select All.
- Select the Edit menu to access Cut, Copy, and Paste options or use the shortcut keys: Ctrl+X to cut, Ctrl+C to copy, and Ctrl+V to paste.
- Choose Edit ➢ Undo or click the Undo button (if it appears on the toolbar) to undo an action.
- Use Spelling to spell-check your document (Tools ➢ Spelling).

When you cut or copy two selections without pasting in between, the Office Clipboard task pane, the only task pane available in Outlook, opens automatically. You cannot open the Clipboard task pane manually as you can in the other Office applications. For more about the task pane, see Chapter 1, "Presenting Office XP: What You Need to Know."

 NOTE The default e-mail format in Outlook 2002 is HTML using Microsoft Word. As a result, all of the editing and formatting features available in Word are at your disposal when you are creating e-mail.

Using AutoDate

AutoDate lets you enter dates as text (in English, Spanish, or another language for which you've installed the Office Language Packs) and converts them into numeric dates. For example, suppose you know you want to schedule a meeting for three weeks from today but you aren't sure of the date. Rather than scrolling through the calendar to find the date, just type "3 weeks from today" into the field and AutoDate will convert the text to the actual date. It can also convert holidays, but only those with fixed dates such as Christmas and Cinco de Mayo. Outlook cannot convert movable holidays such as Hanukkah or Easter, even if you add the appropriate year.

 NOTE For information on adding holidays to your Outlook Calendar, see "Adding Holidays to Your Calendar" in Chapter 34, "Managing Your Time and Tasks."

Saving Data in a Form

 After you have finished entering data in a form, click the Save And Close button on the Standard toolbar or click the Windows Close button and choose Yes to save the item when prompted.

If you need to pause when entering data in a form, it's a good idea to choose File ➢ Save to make sure you don't lose your work. You won't be prompted for a filename because items are saved within the Outlook file.

If you want to use text from an item in some other Windows application, such as a Word document, use File ➢ Save As to save the item as an RTF (rich text Format) file on your hard drive or network location.

NOTE Outlook supports several file types in addition to RTF. You can choose to save an item as a text file (.txt), an Outlook template (.oft), or a message format (.msg). Contacts can also be saved as vCard files (.vcf) and Calendar items in vCalendar format (.vcs).

Printing in Outlook

Outlook printing is essentially a what-you-see-is-what-you-get feature, which means that whatever is on your screen is pretty close to what prints. If you want to print a list of contacts, display that list in the Information Viewer. If you want to print the contents of an individual e-mail message, open the message before you print.

Clicking the Print button on the Standard toolbar will print whatever is in the Information Viewer.

Special Printing Options

Outlook has a number of advanced page setup features that allow you to print pages that will fit right into your favorite paper-based planner, such as Day-Timer, Day-Runner, or Franklin. You can also print attractive schedules and directories from the choices available, such as the directory shown in Figure 31.7.

FIGURE 31.7

*A Contacts directory
using special printing
options*

To access these options, change the view in the Information Viewer to one that most closely matches what you want to print. For example, if you want to print a list of tasks, switch to one of the Task list views (View ➢ Current View). The directory in Figure 31.7 came from Address Card view in Contacts.

When you have your view set up, choose File ➢ Page Setup to choose your printing preferences. Then choose the style of layout you want from that menu. The menu choices presented depend on the folder and the current view. If the choice you want is not available, switch to a different type of view.

In the Page Setup dialog box, shown in Figure 31.8, the first choice you have is to choose the style of layout that you want. The options presented here depend on the type of items you are printing. Two styles are available in all folders:

Table Data is presented in a traditional format of columns and rows, as seen in Figure 31.9.

Memo This is the default style when printing the contents of a form.

After you choose a style, choose other page setup options such as formatting options, paper type and size, margins, page orientation, and headers and footers.

FIGURE 31.8

*The Paper tab of the
Page Setup dialog box
for Tasks*

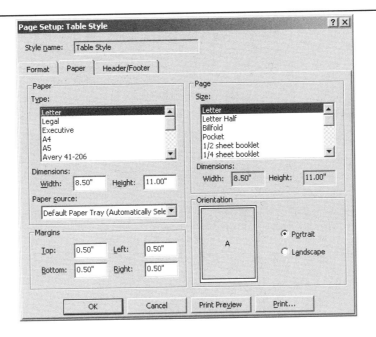

FIGURE 31.9

*Tasks printed using
the Table print style*

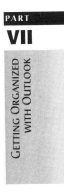

Outstanding Tasks
1/14/2001 7:53 PM

☐	!	✆	Categories	Subject	Due Date
☑			Valassis	Create Web Page outline for Publisher at Valassis	Mon 1/15/2001
☑			Clients	FW: Electronic Office Suite	Wed 1/10/2001
☑				Send Emily a book	Wed 1/10/2001
☑			Admin	Pay TRIAD bills	Tue 1/9/2001
☑	!		Training	Contact VCI managers to arrange requested computer training	Mon 1/8/2001
☑	!		Training	Write descriptions for Toronto IAAP Convention	Mon 1/8/2001
☑	!		Training	Respond to Information Requested for HP	Mon 1/8/2001
☑			Personal	Pay personal bills	Tue 1/2/2001
☑			Personal	Call Dave Gates re VL	Sat 12/16/2000
☑			Personal	Review checking account balances	Tue 12/12/2000
☑			UU	Send newsletter to Annie	Mon 12/4/2000
☑			UU	Revise Epiphany's database	Fri 12/1/2000
☑			Marketing	Create ad for OfficePRO	Thu 11/30/2000
☑			Mott Foundation	Print database documetor with TOC	Mon 11/27/2000
☑		✆	Valassis	Create a new intermediate excel exercise	Tue 11/7/2000
☑			UU	Send out marketing stuff to Board	Tue 10/24/2000
☑			UU	Call Livinsgton County Press for ad rates	Mon 10/16/2000
☑			UU	Call Oakland Press about ad rates	Mon 10/16/2000
☑			UU	Call Tri-County Times about ad rates - 3 weeks	Mon 10/16/2000
☑			Admin	Schedule Crystal Reports class with IKON	Tue 10/3/2000
☑			Marketing	Finish TRIAD School Marketing brochure	Tue 10/3/2000
☑		✆	UU	Send out: All Are Worthy Initiative Media Release	Mon 10/2/2000
☑		✆	Perry Database	Creater Hedaers for IDP	Mon 9/18/2000

NOTE The Calendar has several unique styles such as Daily, Weekly, Monthly, and Tri-fold styles. To find out more about printing calendars, see Chapter 34.

Using Print Preview

Previewing your document before you print it not only saves time but saves paper. You can get to Print Preview directly from the File menu or from any of the Page Setup dialog boxes. It's helpful to preview the document while you are making Page Setup choices so you can see the results of your selections.

When you are satisfied with the document's setup, click the Print button from Print Preview, or return to Page Setup and print from there.

CHAPTER 32

USING OUTLOOK AS A COMMUNICATIONS TOOL

FEATURING

- Creating and addressing e-mail messages

- Using address books

- Designing and using custom signatures

- Attaching items and files to messages

- Setting message handling options

- Using e-mail as a voting tool

- Receiving and replying to mail

- Creating rules to handle mail automatically

O f all of tools in the Outlook toolbox, the e-mail tools are, by far, the most commonly used. Many users send e-mail day in and day out and never even explore what else Outlook has to offer. In many ways, e-mail forms Outlook's central nervous system—messages are sent and received from all the other Outlook folders. Outlook's e-mail folders—Inbox, Outbox, Drafts, and Sent Items—process and store all these different kinds of messages, including meeting requests and cancellations, task assignments, status reports, voting messages, forwards, replies, delivery receipts, and everyday standard messages.

In Outlook 2002, even your everyday standard messages don't have to look ordinary. Outlook 2002 has a number of enhancements, such as default HTML mail, that make the days of boring, plain-text e-mail message obsolete. You can format messages with fonts, colors, graphics, stationery, signatures, and imported Office objects to make them look anything but ordinary.

In this chapter, we'll explore how to set up Outlook e-mail and how to use it to its fullest potential. We'll review the use of Word as the default HTML e-mail editor, sending and receiving attachments, message handling options, voting, and processing mail automatically with rules, colors, and junk mail filters.

Understanding Outlook E-mail Accounts

NEW▶

In Outlook 2002, you can connect to any number of POP3, IMAP, and HTTP Internet accounts; Microsoft Exchange Server networks; and other third-party networks to send and receive mail. You can also access directory services, such as those housed on LDAP servers and other address book sources. Depending on how your e-mail account are configured and whether or not you are currently logged in to a mail server, you may send and receive your mail automatically or you may have to wait until you dial your Internet Service Provider (ISP) or your Microsoft Exchange Server network. Outlook's new e-mail options let you decide whether you want your Internet mail to sit in your Outbox until you are ready to send it or you want Outlook to process it immediately as soon as you hit the Send button.

 NOTE To find out how to set up new mail accounts, refer to Chapter 35, "Working behind the Scenes in Outlook."

NOTE If you have used previous versions of Outlook, you may be wondering where e-mail configurations such as Internet Only and Corporate/Workgroup have gone. In Outlook 2002, all accounts are united into one configuration where you can set up Internet-only and corporate/workgroup mail services.

Outlook's E-mail Folders

Outlook uses four primary and one secondary folder to handle e-mail messages. When you receive a message, it's delivered to the *Inbox* folder.

If you click Save while you are creating a message (or choose Save Changes when you close a message form), a copy of the message is retained in the *Drafts* folder. When you instruct Outlook to send the message, the message is moved to the *Outbox*. If you use a dial-up connection, the message remains in the Outbox until you actually connect to your ISP and send the message (or until Outlook connects at an established time interval). If you have a continuous connection to the Internet (a cable or satellite modem, for example) or send and receive messages over your organization's network, the message has a very short stay in the Outbox.

After a message is sent from the Outbox, it is placed in the *Sent Items* folder or other folder specified in Outlook (see Chapter 35 to find out how to change the default settings for sent items).

Items deleted from any Outlook folder are placed in the *Deleted Items* folder, Outlook's equivalent of the Recycle Bin.

 TIP You can move quickly to the Inbox or the Outbox from any Outlook module. Hold Ctrl+Shift and press I for the Inbox or O for the Outbox.

Creating and Addressing E-Mail

 To create a message, choose File ➢ New ➢ Mail Message from the menu, or open the drop-down menu on the New Item button and choose Mail Message to open a message form, shown in Figure 32.1. Composing and sending a simple message is a three-step process: address the message form, type the message in the large open text box, and send the message.

FIGURE 32.1

Open a message form to create an e-mail message.

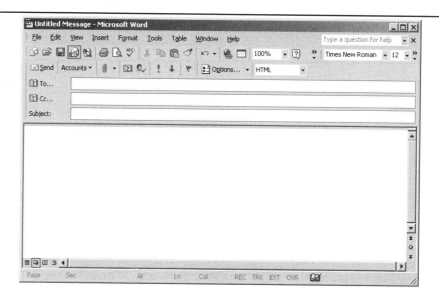

The message header includes text boxes for From, To, Cc, Bcc, and Subject. By default, the Bcc and From text boxes are not displayed. To display other text boxes, click the arrow on the Options button and select the text box you wish to display.

 NOTE You use the From text box if you have been given permission by another user to send mail from them. To find out how to set permissions for others, see Chapter 35.

Entering E-mail Addresses

There are three ways to enter e-mail addresses: from your address books, by typing the address manually, or by searching for the person's e-mail address with a directory service. Enter the recipient's name or e-mail addresses in the To text box, or click the To button to open the Select Names dialog box, shown in Figure 32.2. When you open the Select Names dialog box, Outlook displays the Global Address List if you are connected to a Microsoft Exchange Server or an Outlook Address Book if you are using an Internet e-mail account. Only address book entries that include either an e-mail address or a fax number are displayed.

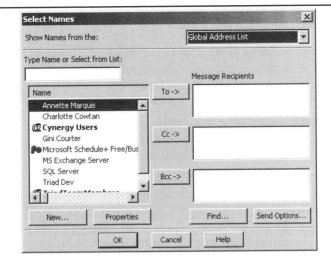

FIGURE 32.2

*Select message
recipients using the To,
Cc, and Bcc buttons in
the Select Names
dialog box.*

 NOTE To change the order of how the address books appear, see "Determining the Order of Address Books" later in this chapter.

NEW▶

In Outlook 2002, the names in the address list do not show the type of e-mail address next to the person's name (as you might be used to from Outlook 2000). To see if a particular listing is an e-mail address or fax number, use the horizontal scroll bar to view additional data about the address. The fields that are available depend on the type of address book you are accessing. In the Global Address List, you can scroll to see Business Phone, Office, Title, Company, Alias, and E-mail Type. In Outlook Address Books, such as Contacts folders, you can see E-mail Address, Display Name, and E-mail Type. These fields can help you verify that you have the right person and identify which e-mail/fax address you want to use. Unfortunately, the Select Names dialog box cannot be resized, so you are forced to follow the rows across without being able to see all the data at once (to access the Address Book dialog box where all the data is available, see "Accessing Address Books outside of a Mail Message" later in this section.

About Address Books

An address book is a list that, minimally, contains names, e-mail addresses, or fax numbers. You may have only one address book or you may have several of them, depending on the e-mail accounts you have set up in your Outlook profile. The most common address books are:

Global Address List An address book for members of your organization stored on a server, such as a Microsoft Exchange Server; sometimes called a *post office address list*. This address book can contain additional books that contain global distribution lists, conference rooms, contacts, users, and public folders.

Outlook Address Book A category of address books that includes Outlook's Contacts folder and potentially any other Contacts folder in your folder set. These address books only include contacts that have an e-mail address or fax number listed.

 NOTE If you have installed other mail services or use an Internet Directory Service (LDAP), you may also have additional address books.

Selecting an Address Book and an Address

If you have more than one address book, begin by choosing an address book from the drop-down list in the Select Names dialog box.

When the address book opens, either scroll to the person's name or begin entering the name in the Type Name text box until you find it. With the contact's name selected in the left pane, you can double-click to place it in the To box or click the To, Cc, or Bcc button to add the name to the list of recipients. Another option is to right-click the name and select To, Cc, or Bcc from the shortcut menu. To select a contiguous list of names, hold Shift while you select them or hold Ctrl to select noncontiguous names before clicking the To, Cc, or Bcc buttons. After you've added all the recipients, click OK to close the Select Names dialog box and return to the message form.

EXPERT TIP To and Cc recipients are listed in the header of the message, while recipients of blind courtesy copies are not. Therefore, recipients of the original message and courtesy copies won't know that the message was also sent to the Bcc recipients, while Bcc recipients won't know what other blind courtesy copies were sent. If you are responsible for sending out an e-mail newsletter or the same message to several competitors, you might consider putting everyone's name in the Bcc box. That way, no one will see who else received the correspondence and you aren't giving away other people's e-mail addresses without their permission.

Entering Addresses Manually

If you'd rather type than select, you can type an entire e-mail address in the To, Cc, and Bcc text boxes, or type enough of the contact's name for Outlook to find the recipient. When you enter text in one of these text boxes, Outlook automatically checks the text against the names in the address books. If Outlook finds the name in an address book, it substitutes the display name for the e-mail address. For example, gcourter@triadconsulting.com is replaced with *Gini Courter*. When you enter a full e-mail address, Outlook checks the address to verify that it has the proper form: two text strings separated by an @ symbol. If you are on an Exchange Server or other mail server, it may also verify that the address has a mailbox on the server. When Outlook finds an Internet address in the correct format or a mail server address in the Global Address List, it verifies it by underlining it in the message header.

WARNING Outlook is not able to verify that an Internet e-mail address is correct. It can only tell you that it's in the correct e-mail format (user name followed by @ symbol followed by top-level domain name).

If the text you enter is not a valid e-mail address or it is not in the address book, Outlook marks it with the wavy red underline used in Word to mark spelling errors. Right-click the name and select the correct recipient from the shortcut menu.

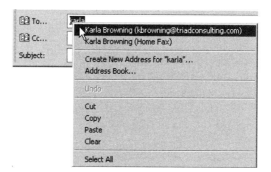

If the name does not appear on the shortcut menu, choose Address Book to open the Select Names dialog box or choose Create New Address For [*Name*] to create a new Contact item for the person (see Chapter 33, "Tracking and Documenting Contacts with Outlook," for more about entering contacts).

Determining the Order of Address Books

You can determine the order in which Outlook accesses your address books to locate a name. The order of address books determines which address list or Contacts folder Outlook searches first for an address.

To view or change the order, choose Tools ➢ Address Book from Outlook's Standard toolbar (outside of a mail message) and then choose Tools ➢ Options from the Address Book dialog box's menu. In the Addressing dialog box shown in Figure 32.3, select the address book you would like to show first when you open the Select Names or Address Book dialog boxes from the Show This Address List First drop down list Select the folder in which you would like to keep your personal addresses from the Keep Personal Addresses In drop-down list. Finally, use the up and down arrows to the right of the open text box to change the order of the address lists in which Outlook checks names before sending mail.

If an address book is not appearing in the list of address books shown here, click the Add button to add it to the list. When you have finished setting the order, click OK and then click the Close button on the Address Book dialog box.

TIP If a new Contact folder is not appearing in your list of available address books, you must go to the properties of the Contact folder (select the folder in the folder list, right-click, and choose Properties) and select the Show This Folder As An E-mail Address Book check box on the Outlook Address Book tab.

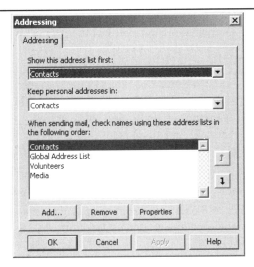

In the Addressing dialog box, you can change the order in which address lists appear, where your personal addresses are kept, and the order of address lists Outlook uses to process mail.

Resolving Ambiguous Names

If you don't clarify ambiguous recipients before clicking the Send button on a message, Outlook opens a dialog box so that you can select a name. For example, let's say you type **Jim** in the To text box. There are several Jims in your address book, so Outlook underlines the name. To choose the correct Jim, you can right-click the name and select the Jim you want from the shortcut menu. If you don't specify which Jim you want before you click the Send button, Outlook prompts you with a list of possible Jims.

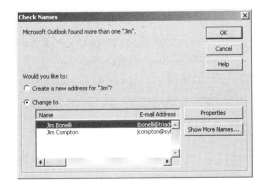

Select the Jim you want and click OK to address the message. The next time you enter **Jim** as a recipient name, Outlook automatically selects the name you chose from the menu or dialog box this time. To select a different Jim, continue typing the correct name or click the To button to select from the address book.

Automatically Suggesting Names

NEW▷

When you start typing an address in the message header, Outlook 2002 examines your address books and automatically suggests the e-mail address of the person it thinks you are typing. If you find this irritating, you can turn this option off. Choose Tools ➢ Options, click E-mail Options, click Advanced E-mail Options, and clear the Suggest Names While Completing The To, Cc And Bcc Fields check box.

> **NOTE** Just to put your mind at rest, Outlook doesn't really "think." Even though the new millennium is officially upon us, Hal, from *2001: A Space Odyssey* fame, is still on the drawing board.

Accessing Address Books outside of a Mail Message

To access your address books without opening an e-mail message, click the Address Book button on Outlook's standard toolbar. This version of the address book, shown in Figure 32.4, is resizable, and you can easily display all the available fields by dragging its bottom-right corner. You can also drag the column markers next to the column names to change column width.

FIGURE 32.4

If you access the address book from outside an e-mail message, you can resize the dialog box and change column width to display all the data.

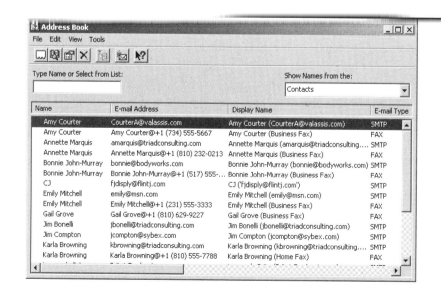

When you've found the e-mail address you want to use, select it and click the New Message button to open an e-mail message form.

Using Directory Services

A *directory service* is an address book maintained in an LDAP directory. *LDAP* (Lightweight Directory Access Protocol), developed at the University of Michigan, is an emerging Internet/intranet standard, used in many networking programs, that defines a common format for electronic directories. The directory could be on a local network server running Microsoft Exchange or on a public directory service you access via the Internet, such as Four11 or Bigfoot. The best time to use a directory service is when you know a person's name but don't have their e-mail address.

Public directory services may be available through your Internet Service Provider or they may have been created or enabled by your network administrator.

If clicking the Find button doesn't open a Find People dialog box, you don't have direct access to directory services. However, if you have an Internet connection, click Start ➤ Find ➤ People. Internet Explorer takes you to a search engine that allows you to search for individual e-mail addresses.

Creating a Contact from an E-mail Address

You can quickly create a contact from any verified e-mail address in the To, From, Cc, or Bcc text boxes. Right-click the underlined address and choose Add To Contacts from the shortcut menu. Outlook opens a blank Contact form with the e-mail address in both the Name and E-Mail text boxes. Correct the name, enter any additional information you wish, and then click Save And Close to close the form and return to your e-mail message. You can also add a contact on the fly from e-mail you receive by right-clicking the sender's or another recipient's e-mail address and choosing Add To Contacts from the shortcut menu.

NOTE   See Chapter 33 for information on creating contacts.

Creating and Using Distribution Lists (Groups)

When you work with a team or are a member of a committee or task force, you'll often address e-mail to the same group of people—the other members of your team. *Distribution lists* streamline this process. With a distribution list, you create a named list in your Contacts folder and then add all the members of your team or committee to the group. When you address your next e-mail message, you can send it to the distribution list (and all its members) rather than adding each of the members as individual recipients.

To create a new distribution lists in your Contacts folder, follow these steps:

1. Choose Tools ➢ Address Book to open the Address Book dialog box, and click the New Entry button to open the New Entry dialog box.

2. Choose Personal Distribution List. You can store personal distribution lists in any Contacts folder—you may want to create a subfolder in your main Contacts folder to store distribution lists (see Chapter 35 for more about creating folders).

3. Choose where you would like to store this list and click OK to open the Untitled - Distribution List dialog box, shown in Figure 32.5.

4. Enter a name for the list in the Name text box.

5. Click the Select Members button to open the Select Members dialog box.

6. Choose the address book that contains the first member you wish to add. Double-click an address to add the address to the distribution list. Continue selecting additional members.

7. When you've selected all the members of the distribution list, click OK to close the Select Members dialog box.

8. Click Save And Close to close the Distribution List dialog box.

FIGURE 32.5

In the Untitled - Distribution List dialog box, enter a name for the list and select the members you want to include in the list.

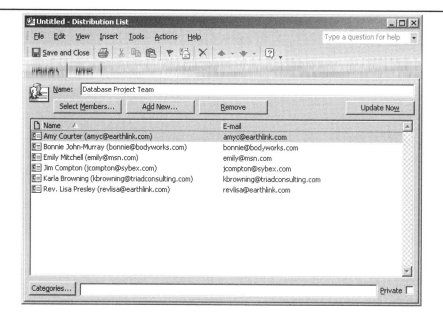

NOTE If you click the Add New button on the Distribution List dialog box, you can enter a display name and e-mail address and check whether you want to add this person to Contacts. If you do not add the information to Contacts, this person's address is accessible only in the distribution list.

 Figure 32.6 shows the new distribution list in the Contacts address book. Personal distribution lists are intermingled with contacts—look for the special group icon to tell them apart.

FIGURE 32.6

You can distinguish personal distribution lists in the Contacts address book by the special icon.

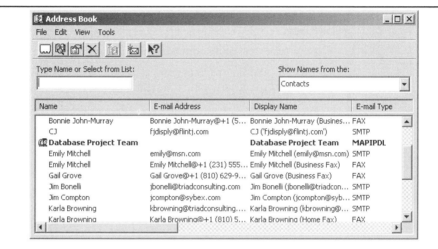

 NOTE If you're one of a group of users who needs the same distribution list, you can send the distribution list via e-mail as an attached item. See "Inserting Files and Items into Messages" later in this chapter. You might also talk with your Microsoft Exchange administrator about creating global distribution lists, which are stored in the Global Address List.

Addressing Mail to a Group or Distribution List

To send mail to all members of a group or distribution list, type the group name in the To, Cc, or Bcc text box on the message form, or click one of the three buttons to open the Select Names dialog box. Group names are bold in the Select Names dialog box and address books, and they are preceded by the group icon. Select the group name and click the To, Cc, or Bcc button to add the group's members as message recipients. To check the membership of a group, right-click the group name in the message's address boxes or in the Select Names dialog box and choose Properties to open the group's Properties dialog box.

Adding or Removing a Name from a Group or Distribution List

The membership of a team or committee can change as members leave the team and new members are added. Follow these steps to add and remove names from a group or distribution list:

1. Choose Tools ➢ Address Book from the menu and select the address book that contains the distribution list.

2. Double-click the name of the list you want to change or right-click a distribution list name and choose Properties to open the Distribution List Properties dialog box.

3. Click the Select Members button to add new group members.

4. To remove a member from a group, select the name you want to delete and click the Remove button in the Distribution List Properties dialog box.

5. When you've finished adding and removing members, click OK to close the Distribution List Properties dialog box.

Deleting a Distribution List

When a team's work is complete or a committee is disbanded, you probably won't need the distribution list anymore. To remove a distribution list, open the address book (Tools ➢ Address Book) and select the group you want to remove.

Right-click the name of the distribution list and choose Delete from the shortcut menu. When you delete a distribution list, any addresses that exist outside the list are also deleted.

 NOTE You can also delete the distribution list from the Contacts folder in which it resides.

Formatting Messages

NEW▶ In Outlook 2002, Microsoft Word is the default e-mail editor. If you stick with Word, you have Word's tools at your disposal. You actually compose your e-mail message in a Word document, as you can see in Figure 32.7.

FIGURE 32.7

Using Word as your e-mail editor makes all of Word's tools available for your use.

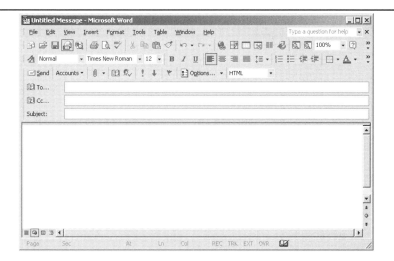

If you have a computer with not quite enough memory to support Word as the e-mail editor and you become uncomfortable with the speed hit you are taking, you can decide to use Outlook's built-in text editor. To switch to Outlook's text editor, choose Tools ➢ Options from Outlook's main window and click the Mail Format tab. Clear the Use Microsoft Word To Edit E-mail Messages check box. As you can see in Figure 32.8, you have a much more limited set of tools at your disposal when you make this choice.

FIGURE 32.8

Using Outlook's e-mail editor gives you a more limited set of formatting tools.

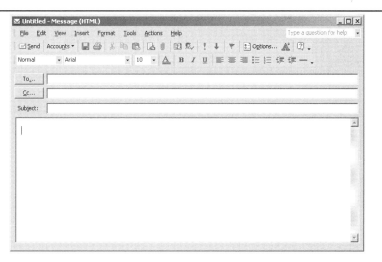

TIP If you like using Word to edit e-mail messages, you might like using it to read messages. On the Mail Format tab of the Options dialog box, you can also choose to use Word to read messages that you receive in rich-text format by selecting the Use Microsoft Word To Read Rich-Text Messages option.

In addition to selecting an e-mail editor, you may also choose from one of three e-mail formats: HTML, Rich Text, and Plain Text. For information about changing these options, see, "Setting a Message Format" later in this chapter. To learn what these format have to offer, continue with the next section.

Choosing a Message Format

NEW▶ Outlook 2002 supports three e-mail message formats:

- HTML is the default format in Outlook 2002. Your message is created in *Hypertext Markup Language* (HTML), the language used to develop pages on the World Wide Web. The HTML format supports an incredibly wide range of formatting, including backgrounds, horizontal lines, numbered and bulleted lists, and any other formatting you expect to see on a Web page. Most e-mail systems support HTML.

- With *Microsoft Outlook rich text* you can format fonts, align paragraphs, and use bulleted lists in your message. Outlook rich-text format (RTF) is only understood by Microsoft Exchange Client versions 5.0 and 4.0 and all Outlook versions.

- *Plain text* is created using a plain-text font, Courier New, and you can't apply any formatting to the message. Plain text is understood by all e-mail systems.

HTML is the default in Outlook 2002 because it is supported by a large number of e-mail systems. If the recipient's e-mail client only supports plain text, an HTML message appears as plain, unformatted text. With the availability of HTML, RTF messages are, for the most part, a thing of the past.

NOTE Outlook still uses RTF for special Outlook/Exchange Server messages such as meeting and task requests.

It's important to remember that while you can compose a message in any of these three formats, the appearance of the message depends on the formats supported by the recipient's e-mail software. Before you spend a long time formatting a message, you might want to check if the person receiving it will be able to see the formatting.

 NOTE When you reply to a message, Outlook automatically uses the original message's format for the reply.

What format to choose and exactly what tools are available for you to use depends on which of the two e-mail editors you are using to compose your message. Table 32.1 shows what tools to expect with each text editor in each available format.

TABLE 32.1   OUTLOOK EDITORS AND FORMATS

Text Editor	Message Format	Available Tools
Microsoft Word	HTML	Text formatting, numbering, bullets, alignment, horizontal lines, borders and shading, backgrounds, HTML styles, clip art, pictures, drawings, WordArt, hyperlinks, linked objects, links themes, columns, and tables. You also have access to AutoCorrect, AutoText, Spelling and Grammar, and other language tools. Almost anything you can create in Word, you can create in this format.
Outlook	HTML	Text formatting, numbering, bullets, alignment, horizontal lines, backgrounds, Spelling, hyperlinks, and HTML styles.
Microsoft Word	Rich text	Same as Microsoft Word HTML.
Outlook	Rich text	Text formatting, numbering, bullets, and alignment. Only supported by Exchange and Outlook clients.
Microsoft Word	Plain text	No formatting tools available—understood by all e-mail systems.
Outlook	Plain text	No formatting tools available—understood by all e-mail systems.

Setting a Message Format

You can set a message format for all messages, and you can choose a different format for a particular message. To set the default message format, follow these steps:

1. Choose Tools ➢ Options from the Outlook menu to open the Options dialog box.

2. Select the Mail Format tab, shown in Figure 32.9.

3. Choose the format you want to use from the Compose In This Message Format drop-down list.

4. To set specific options related to Internet mail, click the Internet Format button to open the dialog box shown in Figure 32.10.

5. Clear the check box under HTML options if you would rather include hyperlinks in your messages rather than actual image files.

6. Choose your preferred format when you send Outlook rich-text messages to Internet recipients from the Outlook Rich-Text Formats drop-down list. Unless all Internet recipients are running Outlook, chances are they will not be able to see rich-text formatting. Converting to HTML format is probably the best choice.

7. If you plan to use plain text, set your line wrapping preference and check the check box under Plain Text Options.

8. Click OK to close the Internet Format dialog box and OK again to close the Options dialog box.

 TIP   For an excellent article that explains encoding and decoding of messages and messages attachments in pretty understandable terms, see "Decoding Internet Attachments - A Tutorial" at `http://pages.prodigy.net/michael_santovec/decode.htm`.

FIGURE 32.9

Choose an e-mail editor and set message format options in the Options dialog box.

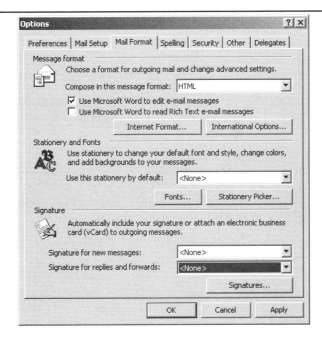

FIGURE 32.10

When sending mail across the Internet, you can set additional options about how messages are handled.

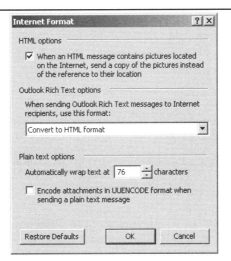

Setting a Format for an Individual Message

Even if your default format is HTML, you can choose to send an individual message using rich text or plain text. If you are using Word as your e-mail editor, choose a format from the Message Format button in an open e-mail message form.

When you use Outlook's text editor, you cannot change directly from HTML to rich text or from rich text to HTML—you must switch to plain text first. Formatting you've already applied is lost when you make this switch, so it's best to pick a format and stick with it until you finish composing a message. To change the format from HTML to plain text, click the Format menu in an open e-mail message form and choose Plain Text.

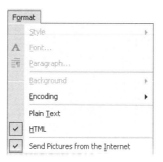

Click Yes to this warning message.

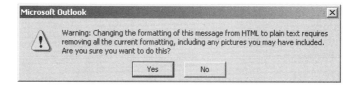

To change from plain text to rich text, click the Format menu again and choose Rich Text—all three format choices are available on the menu when you are using plain text.

Choosing Stationery

If you use an HTML editor, you can personalize your e-mail messages by choosing HTML stationery, a scheme that includes a font and a background color or picture. To select stationery, select HTML as your e-mail editor on the Mail Format tab in the Options dialog box (Tools ➢ Options from Outlook's main menu). Then choose a stationery pattern from the Use This Stationery By Default drop-down list.

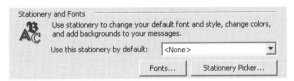

To see what the various stationery patterns look like, click the Stationery Picker button on the Mail Format tab of the dialog box to open the dialog box shown in Figure 32.11. Each stationery choice includes fonts and a background picture or color. Click OK when you've made your selection.

FIGURE 32.11

Select stationery from a list of choices in the Stationery Picker dialog box.

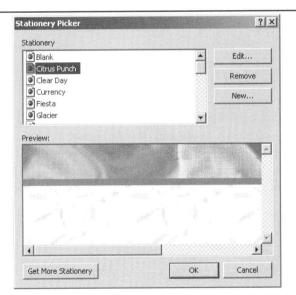

NOTE   Can't find a stationery type to meet your needs? Just click the Get More Stationery button, and Outlook launches your browser so you can visit the Microsoft Web site, where you can download more stationery patterns for free.

Editing Stationery

If you'd like to edit a stationery choice's default font, background, and colors, click the Edit button on the Stationery Picker dialog box. This opens the dialog box shown in Figure 32.12.

Edit stationery to your liking in the Edit Stationery dialog box.

Click the Change Font button to change the default font used in the stationery. Choose a picture to use as the background or click Browse to apply any picture as the background. If you'd prefer a color, select Color and click the color drop-down list to choose from a palette of background colors or select Do Not Include A Background In This Stationery. Click OK when you are finished editing your stationery selection.

TIP If you'd like to create your own stationery from scratch, click the New button on the Stationery Picker dialog box, give your stationery a name, and then make choices for font and background just as if you were editing an existing selection.

Selecting Fonts

Because most stationery includes fonts, if you select stationery, fonts are set based on this choice. If you would like to use your own fonts, click the Fonts button on the

Mail Format tab of the Options dialog box to open the Fonts dialog box, shown in Figure 32.13.

FIGURE 32.13

You can specify fonts to use in specific types of messages.

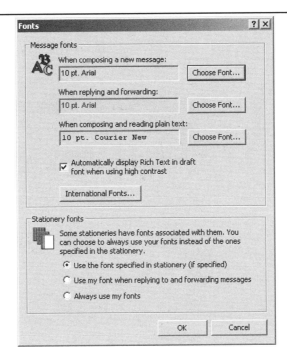

If you are not using stationery or if you would like to override the stationery fonts, you can specify a font to use when composing a new message, replying and forwarding, and when composing and reading plain text. To override the stationery fonts, be sure to choose Use My Font When Replying To Or Forwarding Messages or Always Use My Fonts in the Stationery Fonts section of the dialog box. When you have finished selecting font options, click OK and click OK again to save your stationery choices.

 WARNING Do not choose an obscure font that no one has. For the font to display correctly, the recipient who opens your mail must have the same font on their system.

Selecting Stationery and Fonts from a Word E-mail Message

You can also choose stationery and fonts from a new or reply Word e-mail message form. Click the arrow on the Options button and choose Stationery to open the Personal Stationery tab of the E-mail Options dialog box shown in Figure 32.14.

FIGURE 32.14

The E-mail Options dialog box is another place you can set stationery and font options.

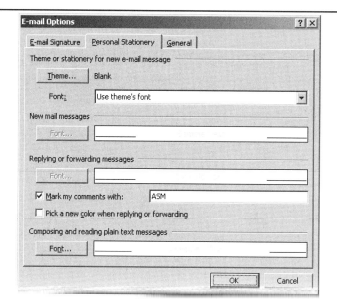

Click the Theme button to open a list of all of the themes available in Word. The themes specifically designed as stationery are designated by the word *stationery* in parentheses after the theme name. You can also assign fonts here, but you cannot edit a stationery choice. To change fonts, choose an option other than Use Theme's Font from the Font drop-down list. You must go through the Mail Format tab of Outlook's main Options dialog box to edit a stationery choice.

WARNING If you apply stationery and font choices through the E-mail Options dialog box within Word, any changes you make do not affect the open message. These changes are applied only when you open a new mail message.

Setting Other Stationery Options

You can also set options related to replies and forwards and plain-text messages on the Personal Stationery tab of the E-mail Options dialog box:

Mark My Comments With When you reply to or forward a message, you can mark your comments with your name, initials, or other text. Enable the check box and enter text into the adjoining text box. When you enter text in the body of the original message, your comments stand out based on your choice here.

Pick A New Color When Replying Or Forwarding Enable this check box to have your comments appear in a different color from the original message. You don't have any choice over the color; Outlook picks it for you.

Composing And Reading Plain-Text Messages If you don't like reading plain-text messages any more than you like sending them, you can click the Font button and change the font from the default Courier New to something a little easier on the eyes. The recipient will still see their own default font, however.

Setting General HTML Options

If you plan to use HTML as your message format, you'll want to review the General HTML options on the General tab of the E-mail Options dialog box. Click the arrow next to the Options button on an open e-mail message form and choose E-mail Signature or Stationery to access the options shown in Figure 32.15.

 NOTE One might logically assume you could choose Options from the Options menu to get to General HTML options, but this choice takes you to Message Options specifically related to the open message form.

On the General tab of the E-mail Options dialog box, you can choose how your messages are streamlined and packaged for mailing. You can set the following options:

Filter HTML Before Sending With this option selected, Outlook removes any formatting codes placed there by Word that are not needed by HTML. This option reduces the size of the message by stripping out these codes. However, some advanced formatting that is specific to Word may also be stripped out.

Rely On CSS For Font Formatting Cascading Style Sheets (CSS) eliminate the need to include font formatting in the message. Instead the message relies on the CSS that accompanies the message. If you clear this check box, the message may be larger, but it will display the same regardless of whether the e-mail program that reads it supports CSS.

NEW▶ **Save Smart Tags In E-Mail** New in Office XP, Smart Tags identify consistent elements—such as names and addresses—that it finds in documents so they can be used in different ways. E-mail programs that don't support Smart Tags will not display them, so it doesn't hurt to leave this checked.

When you are finished setting Personal Stationery and General options, click OK to save your changes. You have to close the open e-mail and create a new one to see the changes you made.

FIGURE 32.15

Set HTML General options to control how your messages are packaged for mailing.

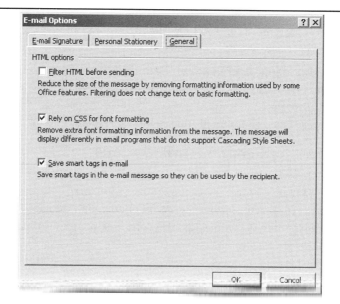

Designing Custom Signatures

A *custom signature* is text you add to the end of a message to provide any information you want all of the recipients of your e-mail to know, such as your contact data, confidentiality information, or advertisements for your products.

With Outlook 2002, you can create multiple custom signatures and select the signature you want to use with each message you send. This lets you create a formal signature for business messages and a friendlier signature for messages to friends and family.

To create a custom signature, follow these steps:

1. Choose Tools ➢ Options from the Outlook menu to open the Options dialog box.

2. On the Mail Format tab, click the Signatures button to open the Create Signature dialog box.

3. Click New and enter a name for the signature.

4. You can choose to start with a blank signature or base this new signature on any existing signatures or on an existing file. Make a choice of how you want to create the new signature and click Next to open the Edit Signature dialog box shown in Figure 32.16.

FIGURE 32.16

*Design a custom sig-
nature in the Edit
Signature dialog box.*

5. In the Signature Text box, enter or edit the text you want to include in your signature.

6. Click the Font and Paragraph buttons to select font, alignment, and bullets.

7. Click the Clear button if you want to start over.

8. If you want to apply additional HTML formatting, including hyperlinks and images, click the Advanced Edit button to launch an HTML editor, such a Front-Page, if it is available. (You can also insert hyperlinks and images if you create or edit the signature in the E-mail Options dialog box, discussed below.)

9. The vCard Options allow you to include your contact information as a "virtual business card" in the signature. If the recipient uses Outlook or contact management software that supports the vCard standard, they can drag or copy the attached vCard to add you to their list of contacts. Select a vCard from the list of available options or click the New vCard From Contact button to create a vCard.

10. When you've finished entering and formatting the text for your custom signature, click Finish to return to the Create Signature dialog box and OK to return to the Options dialog box.

The signature you just created is automatically set as the default, appearing in the text area of every new message. You can choose another default signature (or None) from the drop-down list. You can also choose a different default signature for replies and forwards.

 TIP Before creating a new signature, create a contact (see Chapter 33) that includes your business information and excludes private information (for example, your home phone number) that you wouldn't routinely provide to customers or vendors. You can then select this contact to send as a vCard with your messages in the Edit Signature dialog box.

Creating a Custom Signature inside a Word E-mail Message

When you create e-mail signatures from the E-mail Options dialog box within a Word e-mail message, you have a few additional options available, such as inserting hyperlinks and objects. To create signatures using these tools, follow these steps:

1. Open the E-mail Options dialog box from within a Word e-mail message form by clicking the drop-down arrow on the Options button and choosing E-mail Signature.

2. Enter a name for the signature.

3. Click in the open text box under Create Your E-mail Signature and enter the text you want to include.

4. Select the text to apply different fonts, font styles, alignments, and font colors.

5. Click the Insert Picture button to insert an image file.

6. Click the Insert Hyperlink button to include a hyperlink to a Web site, a document, or another e-mail message in your signature.

7. When you have finished creating your signature, click Add to add it to the list of available signatures.

8. If Word prompts you, say Yes if you would like to make this signature the default e-mail signature on new messages or select it from the Signature For New Messages and Signature For Replies And Forwards drop-down lists. Choose the most commonly used signature for the default.

9. To create additional signatures, click New and repeat steps 2–8.

Selecting a Custom Signature

Regardless of how you create it, if you use Microsoft Word as your e-mail editor, you must choose a default signature to have access to any of your signatures. You can always delete or edit a signature in an individual message. However, if you don't make one signature the default, you can't access any of them. When a signature has been inserted into a message, you can choose a different signature by right-clicking the signature in the e-mail message and making another choice from the menu that opens.

If you are using Outlook's text editor instead of Word, choose Insert ➢ Signature and select a signature from the menu; if the custom signature you want to use isn't displayed on the menu, choose More to open the Signature dialog box. Select a signature and then click OK to add the signature to the message.

Inserting Files and Items into Messages

You can insert a file or an Outlook item into an e-mail message to send it with the message. It doesn't matter which e-mail editor or message format you use; you can attach items and files to messages in any format. You can insert a copy of the file or item, the text of the file or item, or a hyperlink to the file.

Inserting a Copy of a File

To insert a file into a message, follow these steps:

1. Choose Insert ➢ File from the menu inside an open message form.

2. Click the Insert File button on the message toolbar to open the Insert File dialog box.

3. Locate the file as you would any document you want to open.

4. When you find the file, click the Insert button. The Insert File dialog box closes, and Outlook inserts an icon representing the file in a new text box labeled Attach in the message header.

NOTE A *file* refers exclusively to a document or object created outside of Outlook, such as a Word document, a graphic, or an Excel workbook. Something created within Outlook, such as an e-mail message or a task, is referred to as an *item*. See "Inserting Outlook Items into an E-mail Message" later in this chapter.

The file you inserted retains its original formatting and is included in its entirety in the message. Use this method for inserting a file when you want the recipient to work with a copy of the file in its original format. As a copy, changes your colleague makes are not reflected in the original file. To be able to open an attachment, the recipient must have an application on their system that can read the file's format. For example, to view an Excel workbook, the recipient must have Excel or an application that opens Excel files.

 WARNING By default, Outlook 2002 blocks attachment files (such as .bat, .exe, .vbs, and .js) that contain viruses. If you insert one of these file types, you are prompted whether or not you really want to send a potentially unsafe attachment. If you say Yes, Outlook will allow you to send the attachment. See "Grappling with Outlook's Security Features," later in this chapter, for more about Outlook's e-mail security features.

EXPERT TIP Here's a nifty file attachment shortcut. Click the Other Shortcuts group bar on the Outlook bar. Click My Computer or My Documents and locate the file you want to send as an attachment. Click the Outlook Shortcuts group bar to display the Inbox. Drag the file you want to attach from the Information Viewer and drop it on the Inbox in the Outlook bar. Outlook creates a new e-mail message with the file attached.

Inserting the Text of a File

If the recipient does not have an application to open the attached file, you can insert the contents of a text-based file as text. For example, rather than attaching a Word document, you can insert the Word document as text. As long as the recipient's e-mail system supports HTML messages, the document retains all of its formatting. You cannot, however, insert a graphic as text. To insert a file as text, follow these steps:

1. Choose Insert ➢ File from the menu on an open message form.

2. Click the Insert File button on the message toolbar to open the Insert File dialog box.

3. Locate the file as you would any document you want to open.

4. When you find the file, click the drop-down arrow on the Insert button to open the Insert menu. Choose Insert As Text. The Insert File dialog box closes, and Outlook inserts the text of the document in the body of the e-mail message.

Inserting a Hyperlink to a File

NEW▶

If the person (or people) you want to send a file to has access to a shared network drive or Web server, you can insert a file shortcut as a hyperlink, rather than attaching a copy of the document. This not only saves server and mailbox space, it allows you to work on the same file rather than having multiple copies floating around. To make this work, you must first move the file to a shared location and verify that the recipient has appropriate access to the file location. Then you can insert a hyperlink into an e-mail message so that the recipient can locate the correct file. To insert a hyperlink using Word as your e-mail editor, follow these steps:

1. In an open e-mail message form, click the Insert Hyperlink button or choose Insert ➤ Hyperlink from the menu to open the Insert Hyperlink dialog box, shown in Figure 32.17.

Use the Insert Hyperlink dialog box to insert hyperlinks in your e-mail signatures and messages.

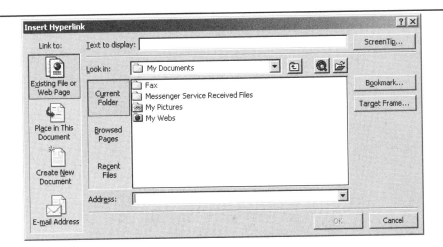

2. Decide if you want to create a link to a Web page, a document on a shared drive, or an e-mail address:

- To create a Web link, click the Browse The Web button to launch your browser so you can navigate to the site you want. When you get there, click the mail message in the Windows Taskbar to bring it forward. Outlook fills in the Text To Display and the Address for you. Edit the Text To Display text box as desired and click OK to create the hyperlink.

- To create a link to a document on a shared network drive, navigate to the folder that contains the document and select it from the list. Outlook fills in the Text To Display and the Address for you. Edit the Text To Display text box as desired and click OK to create the hyperlink.

- To create a link to an e-mail address so the recipient can send an e-mail to this address (generally this would be to an address other than yours), click the E-mail Address button on the Places bar. Enter the E-mail Address you want to use, a Subject if you want the message to contain a specific subject, and the Text To Display in the signature. Click OK to add the e-mail address link to the signature.

3. Close the Insert Hyperlink dialog box to return to the mail message and insert the link. Figure 32.18 shows an e-mail message that includes hyperlinks.

TIP If you know the Web address, you can type it into the e-mail message and select it before clicking the Insert Hyperlink button. Outlook automatically converts the text to a hyperlink. However, you cannot use this option to insert a link to an e-mail address or file location.

FIGURE 32.18

This e-mail message includes hyperlinks to a shared network file location, a Web site, and an e-mail address.

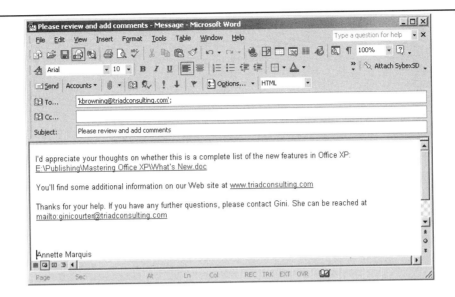

Inserting a Hyperlink Using the Outlook Editor

To insert a hyperlink into a message using Outlook as the editor, you must know the URL (Universal Resource Locator) and type it into the Hyperlink dialog box, shown here.

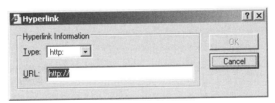

Follow these steps to enter a hyperlink:

1. Choose Insert ➤ Hyperlink.

2. Select the type of hyperlink you want to create: file, ftp, gopher, http, https, mailto, news, telnet, or wais.

3. Type the address in the URL text box.

4. Click OK to create the link.

Inserting Outlook Items into an E-mail Message

Because your mail recipients do not have access to your Outlook folders, you can only insert an Outlook item, such as a contact, in an e-mail message as an attachment or as text. To insert an item as an attachment, follow these steps:

1. Create a new e-mail message.

2. Click the drop-down arrow on the Insert button and choose Item In A Word Message or choose Insert ➤ Item from the menu in an Outlook message.

3. Select the folder that contains the item you want to insert in the Look In text box.

4. Select the item from the Items list. You can click any of the column headers to sort by that column; click it again to sort in reverse order. If you are inserting a contact, you can click the first contact in the list and start typing the contact's name to locate the contact you want.

5. If you want to insert more than one item of the same type, hold Ctrl until you have selected all the items.

6. If you are using Outlook as your editor, you can choose to insert the item as text rather than as an attachment. Select Text Only from the Insert As options.

7. Click OK to insert the items.

 TIP If you use Word as your e-mail editor, you cannot insert an Outlook item as text in Outlook 2002. You can, however, get around this obstacle so you can send the contents of Outlook items to people who do not run Outlook. And you can do it without changing your default editor. Before creating a new message, choose Actions ➤ New Mail Message Using ➤ Microsoft Outlook (HTML). Follow the steps above to insert the item as text. The next message you create, you'll be back to using Word.

Sending Your Message

You've selected an e-mail editor, addressed your message, added and formatted text, and inserted attachments and custom signatures; now you're ready to send your message to the recipients. But first, take a moment and examine Outlook's message-handling options to make sure your message is delivered and received with the same care you took while creating it.

Setting Message Options

Unlike the message format options for stationery and signatures, message options are set for the current message only, not for all new messages. Also, the options are the same regardless of which text editor you are using.

Click the Options button in the message form's toolbar to open the Message Options dialog box, shown in Figure 32.19. Table 32.2 explains each of the message-handling options.

FIGURE 32.19

Message options are set for a specific message.

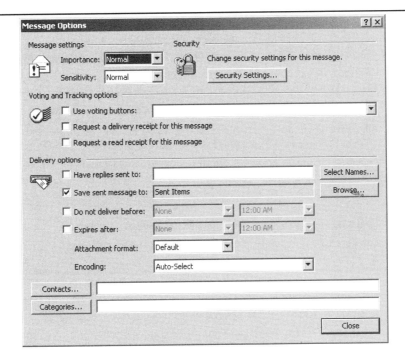

TABLE 32.2 MESSAGE-HANDLING OPTIONS	
Option	**Description**
Importance	Alerts the recipient about the importance of the message. Choose from Normal, Low, or High.
Sensitivity	Alerts the recipient about how sensitive the message is. Choose from Normal, Personal, Private, or Confidential.

Continued ▶

TABLE 32.2 (continued) MESSAGE-HANDLING OPTIONS	
Option	**Description**
Security Settings	A new feature of Outlook 2002 that lets you encrypt messages and attachments and designate a digital signature to secure the message.
Use Voting Buttons	Enables use of e-mail as a voting tool (see "Using E-mail As a Voting Tool" below).
Tracking Options	Notifies you when the message has been received and/or read; dependent on the capability and settings of the recipient's mail service.
Have Replies Sent To	Allows you to designate an individual to collect replies to the message.
Save Sent Message To	Indicates which folder you want the sent message stored in; Sent Items is the default.
Do Not Deliver Before	Keeps the message from being delivered before the specified date.
Expires After	Marks the message as unavailable after the specified date.
Attachment Format	Allows you to select among the three major attachment formats: MIME, UUencode, or BINHEX.
Encoding	If you have International Options set on the Mail Format tab of the Options dialog box to designate an encoding option rather than Auto-Select, you can choose a particular encoder here. Otherwise, Auto-Select is the only choice.
Contacts	Relates this message to a contact.
Category	Assigns a category to this message.

Using Read and Delivery Receipts

Delivery receipts are fairly reliable; most e-mail servers accurately reflect that a message has been received by the server. If, however, the recipient's e-mail address is valid but the server can't communicate with the recipient's e-mail client, the message may never be delivered by the recipient's server and you'll still get a receipt confirming delivery. Read receipts are less reliable. Some e-mail servers can't send read receipts, and others send read receipts along with the delivery receipts. Microsoft Exchange Server handles read and delivery receipts very well; if your message leaves the Exchange environment, read receipts in particular are less reliable.

TIP Some e-mail servers will send delivery receipts for messages sent in plain text or HTML, but not in rich-text format. To increase the chances of reliable delivery receipts, change to HTML.

Using E-mail As a Voting Tool

Gathering opinions, reaching agreement, and settling on a course of action are all part of working as a team. Outlook has a built-in tool to help generate and then gather responses from groups of e-mail recipients. It then even tabulates the results for you, showing you a log of everyone's votes. To activate voting, select the Options tab of an open e-mail message and then click the Use Voting Buttons check box.

You can add your own text to the voting buttons that appear, and you can add additional buttons—put a semicolon between the options or you'll get one big button. If you want to have someone else collect the results, enter their address in the Have Replies Sent To text box. When you've set up the options, click Send to distribute the ballots to the voting list.

 NOTE You will not see the voting buttons on your outgoing message. They only appear on the recipients' messages.

Recipients respond by clicking one of the voting buttons below the menu bar, as shown in Figure 32.20. Their responses are sent to the Inbox like any other message. When you open the message, you can see the current vote and you can click the Information bar to open a tracking form where you can view the results, as seen in Figure 32.21. The tracking form is also available in the sent message—open the message you sent in the Sent Items folder and select the Tracking tab.

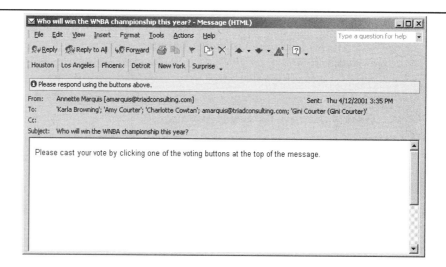

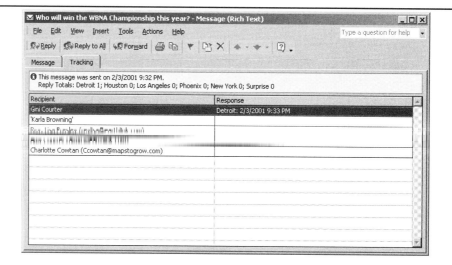

 NOTE Outlook 2002 automatically creates messages with voting buttons in rich-text format, regardless of the default format you have set.

Sending Mail Messages

You're ready to send your message to its recipients. Click the Send button on the message toolbar. You may be wondering how long the message will hang around in the Outbox. The answer: it depends.

NEW▶

In most Microsoft Exchange Server or other third-party server networks, mail leaves your Inbox and goes directly to the mail server for processing. However, in Outlook 2002, you can choose to hold all of your mail in the Outbox until you choose to send it. If you have ever clicked the Send button and then said to yourself, "I really shouldn't have done that," then this feature is for you. To set this option, choose Tools ➢ Options, select the Mail Setup tab, and clear the Send Immediately When Connected check box. With this option turned off, outgoing mail stays in your Outlook Outbox until you tell it to leave.

To move the message out of the Outbox and to the Internet or local mail server, do one of the following:

- Choose Tools ➢ Send/Receive and choose Send All from the Outlook menu to send, but not receive, messages to all of your e-mail accounts.

 NOTE In order to send and receive e-mail, you must first set up your e-mail accounts. If you would like to know how to do this, see Chapter 35.

- Click the Send/Receive button on the Standard toolbar or choose Tools ➢ Send/Receive and choose Send And Receive ➢ All to send and receive messages to and from all of your e-mail accounts.
- Choose Tools ➢ Send/Receive and select a specific account to send and receive messages to and from only one e-mail account.

 MASTERING THE OPPORTUNITIES

Sending Web Pages with Outlook and Internet Explorer

You can attach Web pages, including all the hyperlinks, in an Outlook e-mail message directly from Internet Explorer. Before you jump in, you need to check a couple of settings

Continued ▯▶

MASTERING THE OPPORTUNITIES CONTINUED

in Outlook 2002 and in Internet Explorer. In Outlook, you must be using HTML format (Tools ➢ Options ➢ Message Format and select HTML from the Compose In This Message Format drop-down list). To configure Internet Explorer, choose Tools ➢ Internet Options. Select the Programs tab and make sure Microsoft Outlook is listed as the e-mail program.

You're now ready to use Outlook e-mail from Internet Explorer. Browse to find the page you want to send. Make sure you're using the live page, not a cached page, by clicking the Refresh button. (If you send a cached page, it appears as an attachment rather than as a Web page in the message body.) After the page refreshes, choose File ➢ Send ➢ Page By E-Mail. If Outlook isn't running, IE launches it. In a few seconds, you see a mail message that includes the Web page.

Creating and Using Send/Receive Groups

NEW ▶   If you have more than one e-mail account, you can create Send/Receive Groups designating different send/receive options for each group. A group can contain one e-mail account or several. You decide what makes sense for your situation. Send/Receive Groups are particularly valuable when you are working offline because you can control how often you send and receive mail, the size of attachments you download, and whether you download headers of full messages. See "Working Away from the Office with Offline Folders" in Chapter 35 to learn how to create Send/Receive Groups that you can use offline.

Reviewing Mail Messages

When you are using another application and Outlook is running in the background, an envelope icon appears in the Windows system tray to notify you that you have received a message. Double-click the icon to activate Outlook and review your messages. In the Inbox Information Viewer, unread messages are boldface, so they are easy to spot.

Select a message, and the beginning of the message appears in the Preview pane below the messages. If the Preview pane is not open, choose View ➢ Preview Pane from the Outlook menu to display it. The previews usually let you see enough of a message to gauge its urgency. You can change the size of the Preview pane by adjusting the bar at the top of the pane up or down with the mouse pointer. You cannot preview messages that have been encrypted for security by the sender.

WARNING Viewing a message in the Preview pane can trigger some e-mail viruses, just as they would be if you opened the message that contains the attached virus. For increased security, turn off the Preview pane (View ➢ Preview Pane turns the pane display on or off).

The first four columns of the default Inbox view show the message's Importance, Message Icon, Flag Status, and Attachment information. If the sender set the importance of the message, it is displayed in the first column; high importance is marked with a red exclamation point, low importance with a blue arrow. Table 32.3 below shows the major icons used in the Inbox.

TABLE 32.3   INBOX MESSAGE ICONS

Icon	Message
❗	High Importance
↓	Low Importance
✉	Unread
✉	Digitally signed message
✉	Read
✉	Forwarded
✉	Replied to
⚑	Flagged for follow-up

Continued ▌▶

PART

VII

GETTING ORGANIZED WITH OUTLOOK

TABLE 32.3 (continued) INBOX MESSAGE ICONS	
Icon	**Message**
▽	Flagged; follow-up completed
📎	Includes an attachment
🗗	Meeting Request
🗐	Task Request
🖼	Digitally signed with an attached certificate

Opening Mail Messages

To open a message, double-click the closed envelope icon in front of the message—the same symbol that announced the message's arrival in the system tray. Outlook opens the message in a separate window. An information bar above the message header indicates if the message was flagged or had importance or sensitivity settings other than Normal. In Figure 32.22, the message header indicates that this message has high importance.

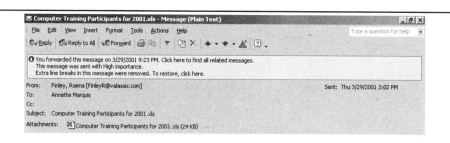

FIGURE 32.22

The message header contains important information about the message.

 TIP To open multiple messages, each in its own window, hold Ctrl and click to select each message in the list; then right-click and choose Open Selected Items.

To close a message, click the Close button in the message's title bar, choose File ➤ Close from the message's menu, or press Alt+F4. When you close a message, it remains in the Inbox, but is no longer bold.

EXPERT TIP   The To, From, and Subject fields in a received message have a gray background, which indicates that they can't be edited. In the case of the Subject field, this isn't true. You can change the subject of a message, including keywords in the subject to make it easier to find later. For example, a message with the subject "RE: Inquiry" that contains a quote you requested might be better titled "Design Quote." To change the subject, select the subject text and start typing. When you close the message, you'll be prompted to save changes.

 ### MASTERING THE OPPORTUNITIES

Mastering Message Security

When you need to send or receive secure data over the Internet, a digitally signed message can give you confidence that the message has not been altered. To send or receive a digitally signed message, you must receive a digital ID or certificate from a certified security authority, such as VeriSign, Inc. Your Microsoft Exchange Server administrator may also be able to issue a digital ID. You can use your digital ID to verify your signature and to encrypt your message so only the intended recipient (who must also have a valid digital ID) can read it.

A secured message has a Certificate button just above the message box.

To view the signature or encryption used with the message, click the Certificate button to open the Digital Signature dialog box. Outlook validates certificates by ensuring that:

- The contents of the message didn't change after the message was signed.
- The certificate is not revoked or expired.
- The e-mail address on the certificate matches the address on the message.
- The check mark in front of each item indicates that it is valid.

Continued

MASTERING THE OPPORTUNITIES CONTINUED

By default, Outlook notifies you before you open a message with an invalid certificate. You can check the Digital Signature dialog box to find the item that is not valid; it will be marked with a red *X* rather than a check mark.

If the certificate has expired, you can e-mail a message to the sender and let them know. Otherwise, it may be that the certificate is not from a certifying organization that Outlook already recognizes. If you know the certificate is acceptable, click the Edit Trust button in the Certificate or Digital Signature dialog box and choose Explicitly Trust This Certificate to accept this certificate in the future.

To find out more about digital signatures, visit www.thawte.com/, www.verisign.com, or www.globalsign.net.

Opening Messages with Attachments

NEW▶ Outlook 2002 displays attachments in the message header, as shown in Figure 32.22 in the previous section. To open the attachment, double-click the icon.

The first time you double-click an attachment created using certain applications, an Opening Mail Attachment dialog box warns you that this type of file may include a virus. This is just a standard precaution and does not indicate that there is anything unusual about this particular file. Choose whether you want to open the file or save it to disk, and click OK. If the file isn't from a trusted source and you'd rather not open it, click Cancel.

With some file types, you can disable the Always Ask Before Opening This Type Of File check box, and Outlook will quit prompting you about the particular file type.

After you select Open and click OK, Windows searches for the application needed to open the attachment, launches the application, and opens the file. If you don't have the required application, or if the file extension isn't properly registered in the Windows Registry, you're notified that the file can't be opened and told what action you could take to open the file.

Grappling with Outlook's Security Features

NEW▶ If you receive a lot of attachments, one of the first things you may notice is that Microsoft has significantly beefed up Outlook's security and warnings in Office XP. When you open an attachment with one of the file types that provide excellent containers for viruses, you don't have the option to open it. As a matter of fact, you can never open it—access to it is completely blocked. This should have an impact on the spread of many e-mail viruses, but it also creates havoc when you must have access to a certain file. The file types that Outlook blocks completely include some commonly used files such as Internet shortcuts, executables, and Microsoft Access databases. Table 32.4 shows you the file attachment extensions that Outlook blocks from access.

TABLE 32.4   BLOCKED FILE EXTENSIONS—LEVEL ONE FILE TYPES

File extension	File type
ade; adp; mda; mdb; mde; mdz	Microsoft Access files
bas; vbs; vbe; vb; vb	Microsoft Visual Basic and Visual Basic script files
bat; com; pif	Batch files and Microsoft MS-DOS programs
chm; hta; ins; isp	HTML and Internet files
cmd; msp; msi	Microsoft Windows NT Command Script and Windows Installer files
crt	Security certificates
exe	Programs
js; jse	JScript files
lnk; url	Shortcuts
msc; mst; pcd	Microsoft Common Console Documents
cpl; hlp; inf; reg; scr; shs	Miscellaneous files
sct; wsc; wsf; wsh	Windows Script files

If you receive an e-mail message with one of these attachments, you still see the paper clip to indicate that the message has an attachment. When you open the message, however, the attachment is not there. In its place, you see the following message in the Information area of the message.

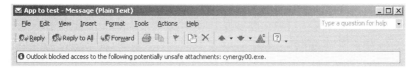

The only thing you can do about it is ask the sender to send it to you in a different format. For example, you could ask them to zip an Access database or copy a URL for a Web site into the message text instead of sending the link as an attachment.

NOTE If you are unfamiliar with zipping files, we suggest you install Winzip from the companion CD. It's shareware, so you can install the full version and then pay for it after you've tried it. It's well worth the investment.

Preventing File Blocking

If you regularly receive e-mail messages of a certain type and you want to be able to continue to do so, you (or if you are on a Microsoft Exchange Server, your server administrator) can prevent Outlook from blocking particular file types. Before you do this though, make sure you have excellent, up-to-date virus protection software. Use big-name software such as Norton or McAfee that stays on top of all the latest viruses and provides you with updates on a regular basis either for free or by subscription. When you are confident that your e-mail protection is working properly and you plan to keep it working properly, then, and only then, consider softening these security restrictions.

If you are on a Microsoft Exchange Server network, the Exchange Server administrator can customize the security settings by installing a special Outlook custom form in a public folder and then configuring the security options for both individual users and groups of users. You can get information on Outlook 2002 e-mail security and links to the downloadable files on the Office Update Web site—www.officeupdate.microsoft.com.

If you are not on an Exchange Server network, you can control your own settings but you have to be willing to edit the Windows Registry to do it. If you are not that daring, you can install Ken Slovak's Outlook Security add-in, found on the companion CD, which will edit the Registry for you. If you'd like to do it yourself, follow these steps to safely edit the Registry:

1. Click Start ➢ Run.

2. Type **regedit** in the Open text box and click OK.

3. Before you make any changes to the Registry, it's always a good idea to back it up first. To do that, choose Registry ➢ Export Registry Files. Identify the file location where you'd like to save the backup and give it a name such as **Before Security Changes**. Click Save to save the Registry file.

4. Click the folders to open this key: HKEY_CURRENT_USER\Software\Microsoft\Office\10.0\Outlook\Security.

5. Open the Edit menu and choose New ➢ String Value.

6. Enter **Level1Remove** as the name of the string value.

7. Right-click the new string value and choose Modify.

8. Enter the file extensions separated by semicolons that you do not want Outlook to block. For example if you would like to receive url and mdb files, enter **url;mdb**.

9. Click OK to save the new string value and then close the Registry.

10. Close Outlook and reboot before testing the new settings. You can send yourself a file with one of the newly unblocked extensions to test the changes.

If you decide at a later time to remove the new string value, you can reopen the Registry and delete it.

EXPERT TIP Microsoft suggests that the safest way to share potentially dangerous files is to post them to a shared network location or Web server. If you don't have access to a Web server of your own, you may want to check out some of the free Web services that allow you to upload and download files. Some provide as much as 200MB of free storage space and offer a good option for safe file exchange. Whalemail at www.whalemail.com provides 75MB and even allows you to send pickup notifications to the people you want to receive the file. Other similar services include www.visto.com and www.bigvault.com.

MASTERING TROUBLESHOOTING

Troubleshooting Attachments and Encoded Messages

Attachments

If you receive a file created with an application that you do not have on your computer, you may be able to associate the file with another application. For example, you don't have Adobe Illustrator but know that CorelDRAW will open Illustrator files. You can associate files with the Illustrator extension to CorelDRAW using Windows Explorer (View ➢ Folder Options ➢ File Types).

If you are uncertain whether you have a suitable application, look at the icon used to display the attachment. When the familiar Windows icon is displayed, there is no application associated with the file on your computer.

Continued ▯▶

MASTERING TROUBLESHOOTING CONTINUED

If you're not sure which program an attachment was created in, ask the sender before you follow the dialog box instructions. If the file can't be opened directly in any application, associating the file won't solve the problem. You may need to contact the sender and request that the file be converted to a format you can open.

Encoded Messages

Messages sent over the Internet are often encoded to preserve formatting and maintain the integrity of attachments. As discussed earlier, the most common encoding schemes are UUencode, the Unix-to-Unix encoding format, and MIME, the Multipurpose Internet Mail Extensions format.

Outlook automatically decodes messages encoded in both of these formats. The only way you will know that the message was encoded is by looking at the text at the beginning of the message. If you receive a message encoded with a scheme other than UUencode or MIME, the text of the message will appear to be garbled.

The sender may have chosen to encode the message. You can let them know that it isn't working, and that they can encode messages in MIME or UUencode and Outlook will decode them for you.

Often, however, the sender's mail program automatically encoded the message, so the sender doesn't know that the message was encoded. They may be able to change a mail format or delivery option and switch to UUencode or MIME, but they may not have the option. If you regularly receive encoded mail from users with other formats (like Mac users who use BINHEX), consider a separate decoding program. You can find out more about decoding e-mail attachments in an excellent article by Michael Santovec at http://pages.prodigy.net/michael_santovec/.

Replying to Mail

After you read a message, you can reply to the sender or to everyone who received the message, including those who received courtesy copies of the message. Select or open the message you want to reply to; then click the Reply button to address a reply only to the sender.

You can also select the Reply To All button to send a reply to the sender and all the other recipients of the message you received. Outlook opens a message form and enters the recipients' addresses in the To text box. You can add other recipients using the To, Cc, and Bcc buttons on the message form. Keep in mind that when you reply to a message, Outlook uses the same format as the original message to ensure that the recipient can read the reply. If the Bcc text box is not visible, click the Options button drop-down list and select Bcc.

NOTE   Reply To All does not reply to individuals who received a blind courtesy copy (Bcc) of the original message.

Forwarding Messages

Forwarding sends the entire message and any text you add to another recipient. To forward an open message, click the Forward button or choose Actions ➤ Forward from the message menu. If the message is not open, right-click the message in the Information Viewer and choose Forward from the shortcut menu.

Formatting Options for Forwarded Messages

To indicate how the original text and text you add should appear in the forwarded message, follow these steps:

1. Choose Tools ➤ Options on the Outlook menu to open the Options dialog box.

2. On the Preferences tab, click the E-mail Options button to open the E-mail Options dialog box.

3. Choose a format from the When Forwarding A Message drop-down list:
   - Attach Original Message
   - Include Original Message Text (the default)
   - Include And Indent Original Message Text
   - Prefix Each Line Of The Original Message

4. To add comments to replies and forwarded messages, enable the Mark My Comments With check box and enter your name, initials, or other text in the text box.

5. Click OK to close the E-mail Options dialog box.

6. Click OK to close the Options dialog box.

Flagging Messages for Further Action

You can't always reply to, forward, or even fully read and review a message when you receive it. Flagging messages ensures a message doesn't get lost and helps you stay organized. When you flag a message, you note the type of action that's required. You can even set a reminder so you don't forget to follow up on the message.

 NOTE   You can flag messages that you're sending or forwarding as well as those you receive. Flagging is a quick way to let the recipient know that they need to act on a message by a particular date.

 To flag an open message, choose Actions ➢ Follow Up from the message menu, or click the Follow Up button on the message toolbar. If the message is not open, right-click it in the Information Viewer and choose Follow Up from the shortcut menu. Choose a flag description from the list of choices or enter your own description in the Flag To text box, shown in Figure 32.23.

FIGURE 32.23

In the Flag For Follow Up dialog box, you can set the type of flag and the date and time you want the flag to notify you.

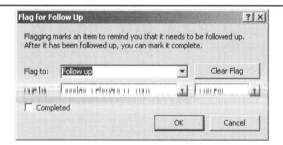

Choose a date to be reminded about the message using the Due By calendar control. If you want, edit the reminder time. When you're finished entering flag information, click OK to close the dialog box.

When you've completed follow-up with the message, you can either clear the flag or mark the action complete. You can sort by the Flag Status column in table views, so if you want to be able to sort or group messages that you've flagged as complete, change the flag status to complete. To clear the flag, open the Flag For Follow Up dialog box, click the Clear Flag button, and click OK. To mark a flag as complete, open the Flag For Follow Up dialog box and enable the Completed check box; then click OK to close the dialog box.

TIP You can right-click on a flag in any table view and choose Flag Complete or Clear Flag from the shortcut menu.

Organizing E-mail Messages

One of the most persistent challenges facing the networked business is presented by the proliferation of electronic mail. Learn how to organize your mail and you'll be more efficient and maintain your sanity in the process.

 Outlook makes it easy to organize and manage your Inbox, and all the tools you need are in one place—the Ways To Organize Inbox pane. Click the Organize button on the toolbar to open the pane at the top of the Inbox, shown in Figure 32.24. Using the pane, you can create folders for message management, create rules to color-code your message, change Inbox views, or open the Rules Wizard and automate management of the messages you receive.

FIGURE 32.24

With the Ways To Organize Inbox pane, all your message management tools are right at your fingertips.

The Ways To Organize Inbox pane has four tabs: Using Folders, Using Colors, Using Views, and Junk E-Mail. (Information about views, and more details about folders, can be found in Chapter 35.)

Using Folders

You can use the Using Folders tab of the Ways To Organize Inbox pane, shown in Figure 32.24, to move selected messages out of your Inbox and into a different folder. Hold Ctrl and select the messages you want to move. Then select a folder from the Move Message drop-down list; if the folder you want is not there (or not created yet), choose Other Folder at the bottom of the list. This opens the Select Folder dialog box where you can browse mailbox and public folders or create a new folder.

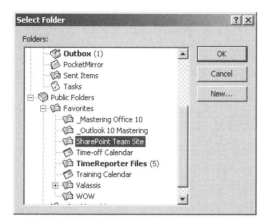

Creating Rules to Automatically Move Messages

Rules take the headache out of managing your Inbox by letting Outlook handle much of your mail automatically. In the Using Folders tab, shown in Figure 32.24, you create rules by example. If you want all messages from Karla Browning to be automatically placed in a specific mail folder, select a message from Karla in the Inbox or any other mail folder. Then choose From or Sent To in the Create A Rule drop-down list to indicate which type of messages should be moved. If you don't have a message from your recipient in any of your mail folders, enter the person's name in the text box. Use the Into drop-down list to select the folder where you want the messages to/from this person moved; then click the Create button to create the new rule. You'll know it worked because it will say Done next to the Create button.

The rule is applied to all new messages you send or receive.

NOTE You can create even more complex rules to handle mail messages. To find out about using the Rules Wizard to create rules, refer to Chapter 35.

Using Colors to Organize Messages

Message information (sender, subject, and so on) is displayed in the Windows text color by default; this is the color you get when you choose the Automatic color in any Windows application. The Using Colors tab, shown in Figure 32.25, lets you apply any of 16 colors to message descriptions based on who sent the message, to whom it was sent, and whether you are the only recipient.

FIGURE 32.25

Automatically apply colors to easily distinguish messages from each other.

To set the color based on the sender or recipient:

1. Choose a message from the sender or addressed to the recipient in the list view.

2. In the Color Messages drop-down lists, choose From or Sent To and a color you wish to apply.

3. Click the Apply Color button to create the color rule.

4. To distinguish messages sent only to you from those sent to multiple recipients, choose a color in the Show Messages Sent Only To Me drop-down list, and click the Turn On button to apply this rule.

 TIP Coloring all messages sent only to you lets you quickly locate messages that most likely require your attention.

You can create a new Automatic Formatting rule by following these steps:

1. Open the Ways To Organize Inbox pane by clicking the Organize button on the Standard toolbar.

2. Click the Using Colors tab in the Ways To Organize Inbox pane.

3. Click the Automatic Formatting button at the top right of the Ways To Organize Inbox pane.

4. Click the Add button in the Automatic Formatting dialog box, shown in Figure 32.26, to create a rule that Outlook temporarily names *Untitled*.

5. Type a descriptive name for the rule.

6. Click the Font button and choose a font.

7. Click the Condition button to open the Filter dialog box. In the three tabs of the dialog box, set the filter conditions.

8. Click OK to create the condition.

You can set automatic formatting options based on a variety of conditions.

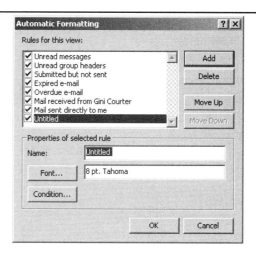

 NOTE To learn more about setting filter conditions, refer to "Creating Custom Views" in Chapter 35.

Selecting Views

Views determine how your data is displayed in the Information Viewer. The Inbox presently uses table view (columns and rows) to display Inbox items. However, the sort order, how the data is grouped, which fields are visible, and how it is filtered can be changed by choosing a different view. You can select predefined and custom views from the Using Views tab of the Ways To Organize Inbox pane, shown in Figure 32.27.

Views determine what data is displayed in the Information Viewer.

You can change the fields, sort order, grouping, filters, settings, and formatting of the current view by clicking the Customize Current View button in the top right of the Using Views tab. You can learn more about creating custom views in Chapter 35.

Using Junk Mail and Adult Content Rules

Businesses have used direct mailing (via snail mail) to market to individuals and companies for years. What marketing companies call direct mailing, others call "junk mail." Junk mail delivered to your electronic mailbox—also known as *spam*—can be just as annoying as its paper-based cousin. With Outlook 2002, you can automatically color or even move junk mail messages (right to your Deleted Items folder if you prefer) so you don't waste your time with them.

Although you may or may not consider them junk mail, adult content messages can also be automatically formatted for easy identification or moved to a separate folder to read at a later time.

To format junk e-mail or adult content messages, click the Junk E-Mail tab in the Ways To Organize Inbox pane, shown in Figure 32.28. Choose a color for each type of message (you can apply the same color to both), and then click the Turn On buttons. If you'd prefer the messages were deleted or placed in a specific folder, choose Move from the drop-down list and then select the folder to which you would like the messages moved.

FIGURE 32.28

Automatically format or move your junk and adult content e-mail using Outlook rules.

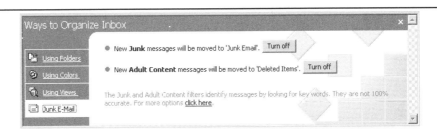

MASTERING THE OPPORTUNITIES

Filtering Junk Mail and Adult Content Mail

Outlook 2002 recognizes junk mail and adult content mail by filtering message content. Outlook filters messages, searching for phrases commonly used in direct marketing messages and adult content messages. For junk mail, phrases include: "cards accepted," "extra income," "money-back guarantee," and "100% satisfied." With adult content mail, Outlook searches for phrases like "over 18," "adults only," "adult web," and "xxx" in the Subject line.

It's worth knowing how Outlook and other programs with content filters determine which messages may be junk mail or have adult content. If you include phrases like "We're brainstorming ways to generate extra income" or "There must be over 18 ways to complete this analysis" in a piece of regular business correspondence, don't be surprised if your recipient never reads the message. To see all the phrases Outlook uses to filter mail, open the file `filters.txt` in the folder where Outlook was installed.

CHAPTER 33

TRACKING AND DOCUMENTING CONTACTS WITH OUTLOOK

FEATURING

- Creating contacts

- Entering address information

- Entering telephone numbers

- Entering e-mail, Web, and IM addresses

- Associating contacts and categories

- Entering additional contact details

- Viewing Activities

- Saving and deleting contacts

- Viewing contacts

- Communicating with your contacts

- Using Journal and Notes

As the old adage goes, "It's not what you know but who you know that counts." Outlook's Contacts folder is the place to record all of that critical data about who you know. You can record names and addresses, telephone numbers, e-mail addresses, Web page addresses, and a score of other information pertinent to the people with whom you communicate. And it doesn't stop there. After you enter a contact, you can send them a letter, write them an e-mail, schedule meetings and appointments with them, record tasks and journal entries related to them, even find a map to their house. In this chapter, you'll learn all about entering contact data and how you can use Outlook to communicate with your contacts.

Creating a Contact

In Outlook, a *contact* is an individual or organization you need to maintain data about. The information can be basic, such as a name and phone number, or be more detailed to include anniversary and birthday information, nicknames, and digital IDs. If you've been tracking contacts manually in a day planner or address book, you'll have some work ahead of you before Contacts can be fully functional. If you have addresses in any electronic format, an Excel worksheet, contact manager software such as ACT or ECCO, an e-mail program like Eudora or Outlook Express, or a database like Microsoft Access, you don't have to spend time reentering the data. Outlook can import data from a variety of sources. See Chapter 35, "Working behind the Scenes in Outlook," for information about how to import your data.

While Outlook is robust enough to manage your business and professional contacts, don't forget to take time to add personal contacts like friends and family members so all your important names, e-mail addresses, phone numbers, and addresses are in one place.

To enter contact data, you can open a blank Contact form in several ways:

Contacts

- If you're going to be entering a number of contacts, click the Contacts icon in the Outlook shortcut bar to open the Contacts folder. This makes it easier to create subsequent contacts and see the contacts that you've created.

- Choose File ➢ New ➢ Contact from the menu.

- Click the New Contact button on the toolbar.

- If you're working in another folder (for example, Calendar), choose File ➢ New ➢ Contact from the menu—you'll just need to look a bit farther down the menu selections to find Contact. The same list is attached to the toolbar; click the New Item button's drop-down arrow and select Contact from the menu.

- If your hands are already on the keyboard, there's no need to grab the mouse: press Ctrl+Shift and the letter C.

The Contact form is a multipage form, with tabs labeled General, Details, Activities, Certificates, and All Fields. The form opens with the General tab displayed, as shown in Figure 33.1. (To move to another tab, simply select a different tab.) In the text boxes on the General tab, you can enter the kinds of information you usually store in an address or telephone book.

FIGURE 33.1

Use Outlook Contact forms to collect and manage information about business and personal contacts.

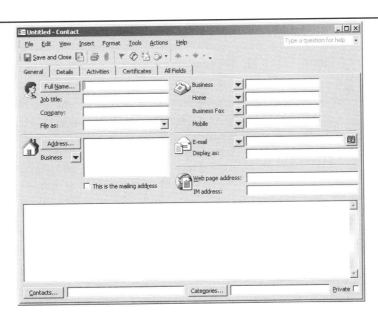

Entering Names, Job Titles, and Companies

To enter a contact's name, begin by entering the contact's name in the first text box on the General tab of the Contact form, next to the Full Name button. If you just want to enter the contact's first and last names, that's fine, but you can also include their title, middle name (or initial), and suffix. For example, **Mary Smith**, **Dr. Mary Smith**, or **Smith, III, Mr. Richard M.** are all acceptable ways of entering names.

When you've finished typing the contact's name, press Enter or Tab to move to the next field. Outlook parses (separates) the name into parts for storing it. If Outlook can't determine how to separate the parts of the name, or if the name you entered is incomplete (perhaps you entered only a first name in the Full Name field), the Check Full Name dialog box, shown in Figure 33.2, opens so you can verify that Outlook is storing the name correctly.

FIGURE 33.2

The Check Full Name dialog box appears when Outlook can't verify how a name should be stored.

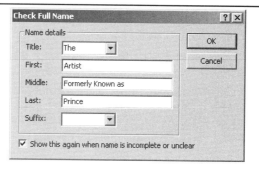

 If you are not sure how Outlook might parse a name, you can edit these fields manually by clicking the Full Name button to open the Check Full Names dialog box.

 TIP To instruct Outlook not to check incomplete or unclear names, clear the Show This Again When Name Is Incomplete Or Unclear check box in the Check Full Name dialog box before clicking OK. To turn checking back on, open a Contact form, click the Full Name button to open the dialog box, turn the option back on, and then click OK.

On the General tab of the Contact form, enter the contact's complete job title in the Job Title text box. If you don't know the contact's job title, simply leave the field blank. Enter the name of the contact's company in the Company field. In the File As field, either select an entry from the drop-down list or type a new entry to indicate how the contact should be filed.

If you choose to file contacts with the first name first, you can still sort them by last name, so it's really a matter of personal preference. If you'll usually look up the company rather than the individual, it's a good idea to file contacts by company name. For example, ABC Graphics assigned Jim as the sales representative to your account, but it might be more useful to file the contact as *ABC Graphics (Jim)* than as just *Jim*—particularly if you have trouble remembering Jim's name.

You aren't limited to the choices on the File As drop-down list. Select the text in the File As text box, and then enter the File As text you'd like to use. This allows you to enter formal names for contacts, but store them in a way that makes them easy to retrieve; you can enter **Ms. Emily Mitchell** as the contact name, but file your friend as *Emily* so you can find her quickly.

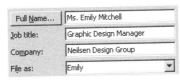

Entering Contact Telephone Numbers

This is truly the age of connectivity. While three mail addresses are sufficient for nearly everyone you know, it isn't unusual to have five, six, or more telephone numbers to contact one person: home phones, work phones, home and work fax numbers, mobile phones, ISDN numbers, and pager numbers. With Outlook, you can enter up to 19 different telephone numbers for a contact and display four numbers "at a glance" on the Contact form, as shown in Figure 33.3.

FIGURE 33.3

The Contact form displays four of the nineteen phone numbers you can enter for a contact.

When you create a new contact, the four default phone number descriptions Outlook displays are Business, Home, Business Fax, and Mobile. To enter a telephone number for one of those four descriptions, click in or tab to the appropriate text box on the General tab of the Contact form and type in the telephone number. You don't need to enter parentheses around the area code or add hyphens or spaces—just enter the digits in the telephone number, as shown here.

When you move out of the text box, Outlook automatically formats the digits, adding parentheses, spaces, and hyphens. If you enter a seven-digit telephone number, Outlook assumes the phone number is local and adds your area code to the number.

 WARNING If you include letters in your telephone numbers (like 1-800-CALLME), you won't be able to use Outlook's automated dialing program to call this contact.

To enter another telephone number, click the drop-down arrow for any of the four text boxes to open the menu of telephone number types.

Those telephone number types that have check marks are those you've already entered for this contact. Choose the type of phone number you want to enter from the menu; then enter the number in the text box.

Because Outlook only displays four numbers at a time, the numbers that are displayed in the four text boxes may not be the numbers you use most frequently. That's not a problem—just open the menu next to each text box and, from the menu, select the types you want to display.

Entering Country Codes for International Calls

To see the details of a phone number and set the country code for an international number, double-click the phone number to open the Check Phone Number dialog box.

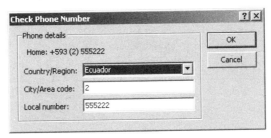

Select the country from the Country/Region drop-down list, and Outlook automatically inserts the country code into the number. Click OK to display the country code in the phone number text box.

Entering Contact Addresses

Outlook allows you to store three addresses—Business, Home, and Other—for your contact and designate one of the three as the address you want to use as the contact's primary address. To choose the type of address you want to enter, click the drop-down arrow in the address section, and select the address type from the list. The address type is displayed to the left of the arrow.

Click in the Address text box on the General tab of the Contact form and type the address as you would write it on an envelope. Type the street address on the first or first and second lines, pressing Enter to move down a line. Type the city, state or province, country, and zip code or postal code on the last line. If you don't enter a country, Outlook uses the Windows default country.

 NOTE The Windows default country is set in the Windows Control Panel under Regional Settings (Windows 98) or Regional Options (Windows 2000).

When you press Tab to move to the next field, Outlook checks the address just as it did the contact name. If the address is unclear or incomplete, the Check Address dialog box opens, as shown in Figure 33.4. Make sure the information for each field is correct, and then click OK to close the dialog box.

FIGURE 33.4

The Check Address dialog box opens to allow you to verify an incomplete or unclear address.

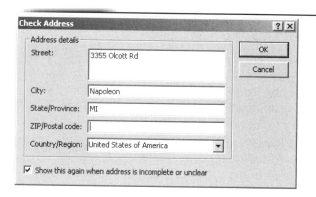

In Outlook, the primary address for a contact is called the *mailing address*. The mailing address is the address displayed in most views and is the address used when you merge a Word main document with your Outlook contacts. By default, the first address you enter for a contact is set as the mailing address. To change the address used as the mailing address, make sure the address you want to use (Home, Business, or Other) is displayed in the Address text box; then click the This Is The Mailing Address check box to make the displayed address the mailing address.

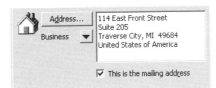

Entering E-mail Addresses

You can enter up to three e-mail addresses for a contact. The e-mail addresses, on the General tab of the Contact form, are labeled E-mail, E-mail 2, and E-mail 3, rather than "Business" and "Home" like mail addresses and telephone numbers. In many cases, the top-level domain of the e-mail address can help you distinguish which address is for business and which is for home use.

To enter an e-mail address, enter the entire address, including the user name and the domain name. When you move out of the e-mail address text box, Outlook analyzes the address you entered to ensure that it resembles a valid e-mail address. Outlook does *not* check to make sure that the address is the correct e-mail address for this contact or that the address exists. Outlook just looks for a user name, the @ symbol, and a domain name. If all the parts aren't there, Outlook opens the Check Names dialog box. If you cancel the dialog box, Outlook lets you keep the incomplete e-mail address even though it is not usable. Be sure to correct the address before continuing.

Understanding E-mail Addresses

Internet e-mail addresses have three parts: a user name, followed by the "at" symbol (@), and a domain name. The domain name includes the *host name* and may include a *subdomain name*.

Each e-mail account has its own *user name*. In Windows NT, user names include the owner's name, such as bjones, jonesb, or billjones. Many companies and e-mail providers also add a number to the user names, so they look like bjones1, or they include the person's middle initial so that Bill Jones and Barbara Jones don't have to fight over who gets to be the "real" bjones.

Continued ▐▶

PART

VII

GETTING ORGANIZED
WITH OUTLOOK

CONTINUED

The user name and domain name are separated with the @ symbol. The *domain name* begins with the host name. The *host name* is the name of the server that handles the e-mail account. For example, in the address `bjones@wompus.berkeley.edu`, the host name is `wompus`. (On one of the wompus server's hard drives, there's space for Bill Jones to keep his e-mail; the space is called his *mailbox.*) The *subdomain* is `berkeley`— the name or an abbreviated name of the organization that owns the server. The last part of the domain name, following the last period, is the top-level *domain*, which describes the type of organization. Prior to 2001, seven domains were available for use in the United States, with some of these being available internationally. These are:

com Commercial: for-profit organizations

edu Educational: schools, colleges, and universities

gov Governmental: federal, state, and local governmental units

mil Military: armed services

net Network: network access providers

org Organization: nonprofit businesses

int International organization

In 2000, the Internet Corporation for Assigned Names and Numbers (ICANN) approved seven additional top-level domains. The new domains are:

biz Designed for business use only—not available to individuals

info For use internationally for any information site

name For individual use such as adam.name and mary.c.adam.name

pro Restricted to attorneys, physicians, and accountants

museum Restricted to accredited museums worldwide

coop Restricted to business cooperatives such as credit unions and rural electric cooperatives

aero Restricted for use by the airline industry

In addition to these 14 domains, each country has its own two-letter domain such as `uk` for the United Kingdom, `ca` for Canada, `jp` for Japan. A large number of educational organizations use `us` (United States) as their domain rather than `edu`; the domain name `oak.goodrich.k12.mi.us` describes a host at Oaktree Elementary in Goodrich Public Schools, a K–12 district in Michigan. Some countries have offered their domains for sale to the general public. The people of Tuvala, for example, have formed an exclusive partnership with the dotTV Corporation and are offering dot-tv domain names for general use.

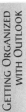

Some addresses used within mail systems aren't compatible with Internet mail. For example, many CompuServe addresses contain commas: 72557,1546. This is a valid e-mail address for a CompuServe member if you are also a CompuServe member and use CompuServe Mail to send your e-mail. However, it's not a valid *Internet* e-mail address. The only punctuation used in Internet addresses are periods and the @ symbol. If you want to send e-mail to this CompuServe address from Outlook or any other Internet mail system, the address must be modified for use on the Internet. For CompuServe addresses that consist of numbers, change the comma to a period and add the CompuServe domain name: 72557.1546@compuserve.com. For other addresses, talk with the person whose address you are entering and ask them for their POP3 or SMTP address.

NOTE   For the last few years, CompuServe users have had the option of adopting a user name at the cs.com domain.

Viewing Display Names

When you enter an e-mail address, Outlook automatically creates a display name and inserts it into the Display As text box.

This is the name that appears on an e-mail message form addressed to this person. If you want to change the display name, just type anything you'd like to see in the Display As text box.

Entering an E-mail Address from the Global Address List

If you are working on a Microsoft Exchange Server, your network administrator has already set up a Global Address List that includes everyone who has a mailbox on the network. In some organizations, complete contact data such as address and company information is entered when the mailbox is created. However, it is more typical to create the mailbox with nothing more than the person's name and e-mail address. In these cases, you may want to create a contact for people within your company about whom you need additional information.

If you are entering contact information for someone who is in your company's Global Address List or some other address book, you can click the Address Book button next to the e-mail text box on the General tab of the Contact form to open the

Select Name dialog box, shown in Figure 33.5. Select the address you want from the list and click OK. This automatically enters the person's internal e-mail address in the text box.

FIGURE 33.5

If the contact is already in the Global Address List, select their name from the list to enter their internal e-mail address.

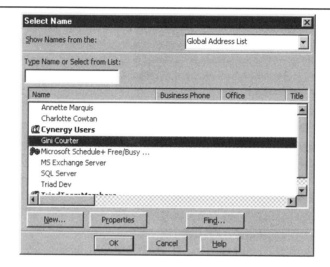

 TIP If you want to see what data is already included in the Microsoft Exchange Server mailbox, select the name from the Select Name dialog box and click Properties to open the Properties dialog box.

Choosing a Format for the Message

NEW|▶

The default format for messages created in Outlook 2002 is HTML created with Microsoft Word. If you are certain that this person's mail system does not support HTML messages (most up-to-date mail programs do), you can choose either plain text or rich text as an alternate format.

All versions of Outlook support a file format called *rich-text format* (*RTF*). With RTF, you can format an e-mail message as you would a Word document, using boldface, italicized text, and different fonts and font colors to provide emphasis in the message. If you're using Outlook on a server at work, your colleagues running Outlook on the network will be able to open RTF messages and see your text in all its formatted glory.

NOTE If your contact's e-mail service doesn't support RTF, the formatting of the message can make it harder to decipher the actual text of the message because it inserts funny codes. At best, the formatting doesn't appear, and you've spent time formatting for no good reason. For more about selecting e-mail formats and formatting Outlook HTML messages in Word, see to Chapter 32, "Using Outlook As a Communications Tool."

To change the message format, right-click an e-mail address on the General tab of a Contact form and choose Properties. This opens the E-mail Properties dialog box.

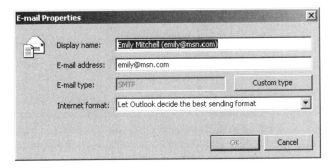

The default Internet Format is Let Outlook Decide The Best Sending Format. If you are uncomfortable letting software make decisions for you, you can choose plain text or Outlook rich-text format from the drop-down list.

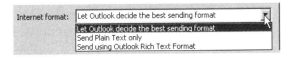

If you make a different selection, click OK to save the change or Cancel to close the dialog box without making a change.

 NOTE If you change the Internet format in the E-mail Properties dialog box and click OK, Outlook changes the E-Mail address to match the Display As address.

To access the advanced e-mail format options, right-click an e-mail address and choose Send Options. This opens the Send Options For This Recipient Properties dialog box, shown in Figure 33.6.

FIGURE 33.6

Use the Send Options For This Recipient Properties dialog box to set e-mail message formats for MIME and Plain Text/UUencode.

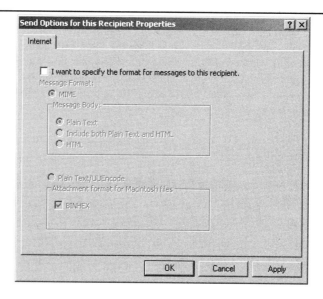

To specify the type of encoding to be applied to messages you send to this e-mail address, click the I Want To Specify The Format For Messages To This Recipient check box. You can choose either MIME or UUencode.

If you choose MIME, you can select Plain Text, Include Both Plain Text And HTML, or HTML. If you choose Plain Text/UUencode and you plan to send Macintosh files, you can choose to use the encoding standard BINHEX for the attachments.

Click OK to apply the options you selected.

NOTE   See Chapter 32 for a discussion of these encoding standards and how they affect e-mail messages and attachments.

Entering Web Information

To assign an Internet URL to a contact, enter the address in the Web Page Address text box in the Contact form. When you enter a World Wide Web URL in the Web Page Address text box, you don't need to enter the protocol, in other words, http. Enter the resource name (for example, `www.disney.com`), and when you leave the text box, Outlook automatically adds `http://` to the beginning of the URL. However, if you're entering an address for another type of protocol, such as gopher, telnet, or ftp, you must enter the entire URL, including the protocol and the resource. If you don't, Outlook still adds `http://` to the beginning of the URL, and it will be incorrect.

 NOTE If the URL you are pointing to includes standardized elements, Outlook can handle things other than WWW links. For example, `ftp.uunet.com` becomes `ftp://uunet.com` and `gopher.ucla.edu` becomes `gopher://gopher.ucla.edu`. However, if an ftp site begins with a WWW prefix (this is how most ISPs allow access to personal Web space), then it is still interpreted as a Web address.

To visit the user's Web site, simply point to the URL and the mouse pointer changes to the familiar browser-link hand shape. Click the link to launch your default browser and load the Web page.

Entering an Instant Messaging Address

The popularity of sending instant messages to others across the Internet has grown so dramatically that Microsoft incorporated the feature into Microsoft Exchange 2000 for use within a corporate setting. With Instant Messaging, you can have a conversation with someone without ever picking up the telephone or waiting for an e-mail response. Because these addresses sometimes vary from their typical e-mail address, you can enter a person's instant messaging or IM address in the IM Address text box below the Web Address text box on the General tab of the Contact form.

If you are not on an Exchange Server or if you want to exchange messages with someone who is not on your network, you can still activate Instant Messaging as long as you have an Internet connection. Connect to the Internet and then choose Options from the Outlook Tools menu (not from within a Contact form) and click the Other tab. Select the Enable Instant Messaging In Outlook check box and click the Options button to run the MSN Messenger Service setup. This will guide you through creating a free MSN Messenger account.

 NOTE Unfortunately, instant messaging protocols have fallen victim to the "Net wars" and remain proprietary. The consequence of this is that it's not possible at the time we are writing this book for a Microsoft Network member, for example, to exchange instant messages with someone who subscribes to America Online. We're hopeful that AOL will agree to change this situation, so tell your friends who subscribe to AOL to keep putting on the pressure.

Entering Contact Comments

The large text box at the bottom of the General tab of the Contact form is an open area for comments about the contact: anything from quick phrases to eloquent paragraphs. For example, if the contact is your sales representative, you might put your account number in the comments text box. Or you might note hobbies and favorite ice cream flavors. If your company hands out T-shirts, it's a perfect location for shirt sizes.

 TIP An excellent use of the comments box is to record directions to a contact's home or business. The next time you have to visit there, just click the Print button and you have their critical phone numbers, address, and directions on one piece of paper. If you sync Outlook with a PDA, the comments also sync (as long as they are not too long), and you have everything you need in one place.

Associating Contacts with Other Contacts

Often, contacts become contacts because someone you already know introduces you. If you would like to associate one contact with another to track referrals, organize families, or just record who introduced you, you can enter a contact in the Contacts text box. Click the Contact button at the bottom of the General tab of the Contacts form to open the Select Contacts dialog box shown in Figure 33.7.

FIGURE 33.7

You can associate a contact with one or more other contacts to demonstrate relationships between them.

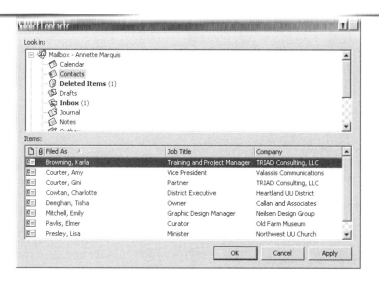

Select one or more contacts from the list. Hold Ctrl while clicking to select more than one associated contact. After you click OK, Outlook displays the associated contacts with links to their Contact data. Double-click a name to open its corresponding Outlook form.

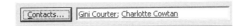

Assigning Categories

Categories are a way to organize Outlook items based on groupings you set. Outlook comes with a predefined set of categories you can use, or to make the most of categories, you can create your own. To assign categories to a contact, click the Categories button at the bottom of the General tab of the Contact form. This opens the Categories dialog box in Figure 33.8.

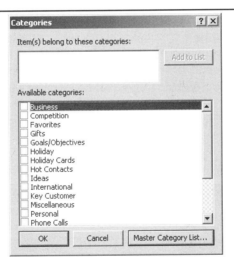

Click to select any of the categories listed. You can assign several categories to a single contact. Be aware, however, that some PDAs only accept a single category assignment. Click OK to assign the categories.

Making a Contact Private

If you're using Outlook on a network, you can give others permission to access your Contacts folder. However, you may have some contacts—your therapist or fortune teller, for example—that you prefer to keep private. In the bottom-right corner of the General tab of the Contact form, there's a check box marked Private. By enabling the Private setting, you prevent other users from seeing this contact, even if they have access to your Contacts folder.

 NOTE For more about sharing Contact folders, see Chapter 35, "Working behind the Scenes in Outlook."

Adding Details

On the Details tab of the Contact form, shown in Figure 33.9, you can record less-frequently used information about your contacts. Remember that you can sort and filter your contacts on these fields, so try to use standard entries. If, for example, you want to be able to find all the vice presidents in your Contacts folder, make sure you enter **Vice President** the same way for each contact.

FIGURE 33.9

Use the Details tab to record other information about your contact.

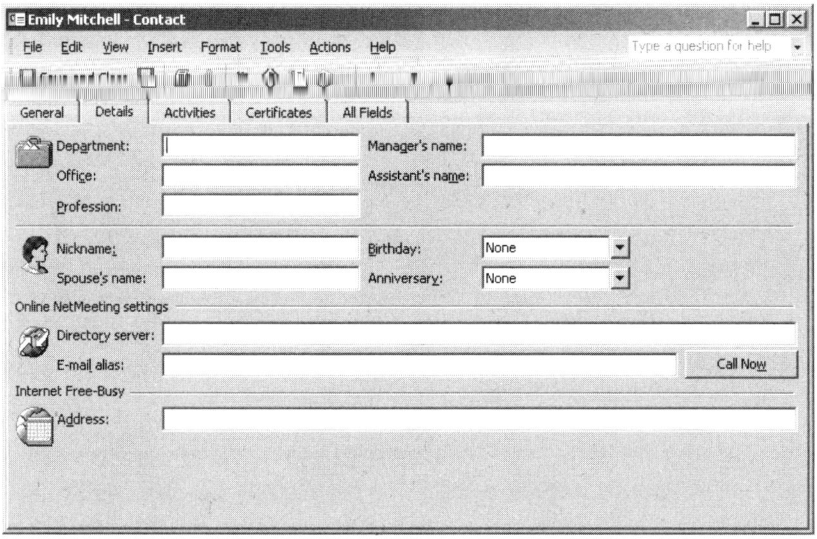

The Birthday and Anniversary fields have drop-down arrows that open a calendar. You can type dates directly in these fields, or you can select a date from the calendar. Click the arrow and the calendar opens, displaying the current month.

To choose the current date, click the Today button on the bottom of the calendar. To enter a different date in the current month, just click the date. Click the arrows in the calendar's header to scroll to the prior month or the next month. This is fairly tedious if you're entering a contact's birthday (unless she was born yesterday!). To scroll more rapidly, point to the name of the month in the header and hold down your mouse button to open a list of calendar pages. Continue to hold down the mouse button and move the mouse above or below the list of months to scroll through the years. Notice the position of the mouse pointer.

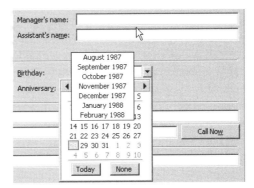

Without releasing the mouse button, select the month you want from the list. You can finally release the mouse button to select the actual date.

Entering NetMeeting Addresses

Microsoft NetMeeting is Internet-based collaboration software included with Outlook and Microsoft Exchange Server. With NetMeeting, you can work with one or more contacts "face to face" over the Internet, using video and audio as you would in a video conference call.

NOTE Some additional hardware is required to support NetMeeting's high-end video and audio functions.

You can use NetMeeting to send files directly to a meeting attendee, have open chat sessions for brainstorming ideas about projects, diagram ideas on a Net whiteboard, and work with other attendees in real time in shared applications.

NetMeetings are held on an Internet Locator Server (ILS); each meeting participant must log on to the server, which maintains a list of users so that other participants can find out who is available for a meeting. On the Details tab, you can enter two NetMeeting settings. Enter the ILS used for meetings with the contact in the Directory Server text box and the contact's E-mail Alias (usually their e-mail address), as shown in Figure 33.10.

FIGURE 33.10

Enter the ILS and alias the contact uses for NetMeetings in the Details tab.

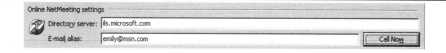

Accessing Your Contact's Schedule on the Internet

Free/Busy refers to the times that a user is available (for meetings, including Net-Meetings) or unavailable, according to their Outlook calendar. With Outlook, you can publish your free/busy times in two different ways: in Exchange Server on your local area network or over the Internet using the iCalendar standard. With Exchange Server, the only people who can see your free/busy times are colleagues who can log on to your network. By publishing your free/busy times on an Internet server, you make the schedule of free time available to people outside your network.

Before users can access your free/busy schedule, you need to tell them where the file that contains the schedule is located. The file can be stored on a server, ftp site, or Web page. If your contact has given you the URL for their free/busy schedule, enter it in the Internet Free/Busy text box on the Details tab of the Contact form.

 NOTE For more information on Internet Free/Busy, see Chapter 34, "Managing Your Time and Tasks".

Tracking Activities

The Activities tab of the Contact form, shown in Figure 33.11, displays a table of both automatic and manual entries related to the contact. The default view of the Activities tab shows the icon to designate the type of entry, the subject of the item, and the Outlook folder in which it resides.

PART

VII

GETTING ORGANIZED
WITH OUTLOOK

FIGURE 33.11

On the Activities tab of the Contact form, you can see all the entries related to the contact.

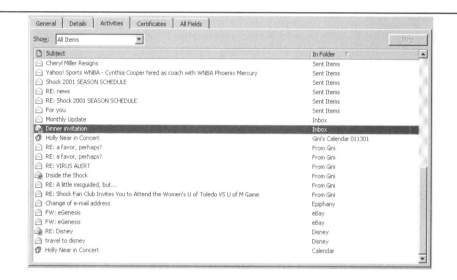

Previewing and Viewing Activities

If you want to see more detail about each of the entries, right-click anywhere in the Activities window (except on an entry) and select the AutoPreview option.

The first three lines of the note in each message entry are displayed, as shown in Figure 33.12. It's easy to know if the preview shows all the text in the note, including signatures, because the end of the note is marked <end>. If the note is longer than the preview and ends in the middle of a word, the preview ends with ellipses (…). To turn AutoPreview off, right-click and select AutoPreview again.

To see the entire entry, double-click the entry to open it.

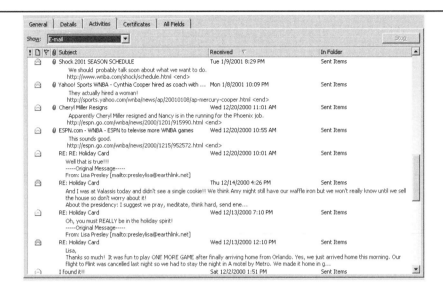

AutoPreview displays the first few lines of any message item.

Sorting and Grouping Activities

As with any Outlook view, you can click the heading of a column to sort the entries by the value in the column. For example, to arrange the entries by subject, click the Subject column heading.

To group items by a field, even if the field is not currently displayed, right-click in any open area of the Activities list (you may have to scroll down to the bottom) and choose Group By from the shortcut menu. Choose to group the data by a field that has repetitive entries such as the In Folder field. Figure 33.13 shows data grouped by In Folder. Click the plus symbol in front of a group to expand the items in that group and click the minus symbol to collapse it again.

To remove grouping, right-click and choose Group By again from the shortcut menu. Click Clear All and OK to remove all grouping.

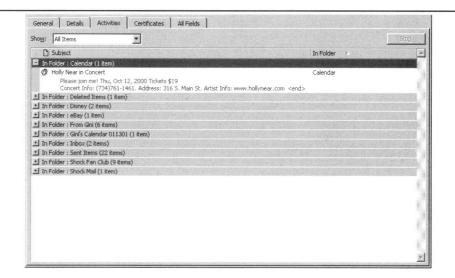

FIGURE 33.13

Grouping organizes your data so you can find just what you are looking for.

Viewing Certificate Information

A *certificate*, or *Digital ID*, is used to verify the identity of the person who sent an e-mail message. Digital IDs have two parts: a *private key*, stored on the owner's computer, and a *public key* that others use to send messages to the owner and verify the authenticity of messages from the owner. The Certificates tab of the Contact form shows Digital IDs that you've added for this contact. You can view the properties of the ID and choose which ID should be used as the default for sending encrypted messages to this contact.

Viewing All Fields

In the Contact form's All Fields tab, you can display groups of fields in a table format. The default display on this tab is User Defined Fields. Unless you or someone else has customized your Outlook forms and added fields, there won't be any fields displayed—but don't assume that this page is totally useless. Choose Personal Fields, for example, from the Select From drop-down list to have access to fields, shown in Figure 33.14, that are not displayed on any of the Contact form tabs, such as Children, Gender, and Hobbies. You can enter data directly into these fields and store them with the rest of the contact data.

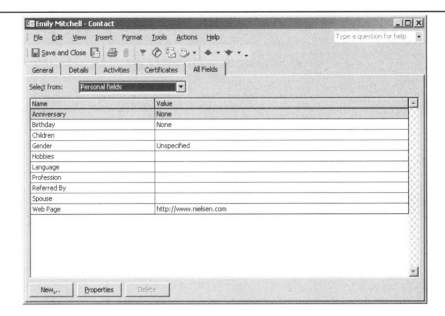

Saving a Contact

When you've finished entering information in the Contact form, click the Save And Close button, or choose File ➢ Save And Close to save this contact's information and close the form.

If you're going to be entering another contact immediately, it's faster to click the Save And New button, or choose File ➢ Save And New to save the current contact and open a blank form.

Adding a New Contact from the Same Company

Once you begin entering contacts, you'll often have several contacts from the same organization. The contacts have the same business address and the same or similar e-mail addresses and business telephone numbers. Outlook lets you create a contact based on an existing contact, so you don't have to enter the business information again. When you've finished entering the first contact, choose Actions ➢ New Contact From Same Company from the Outlook menu. (If the contact is closed, select the contact first in the Information Viewer.) The first contact is saved, and the business information for the contact is held over in the Contact form. Add the new contact's personal information and edit the business information as required.

Deleting a Contact

To delete a contact, select the contact or open the Contact form. Then choose Edit ➢ Delete from the menu, right-click and choose Delete from the shortcut menu, or press Ctrl+D. You are not prompted to confirm the deletion. However, if you immediately notice that you've deleted a contact erroneously, you can choose Undo Delete from the Edit menu to restore the contact.

Finding Contact Information When You Need It

When you need to find a contact in a hurry, don't worry about opening the Contacts folder and scrolling through a long list of entries. From any folder, click in the Find A Contact text box on the Standard toolbar and enter the contact you need to open.

You don't even have to type their full name. Enter a first or last name and Outlook shows you a list of possible hits.

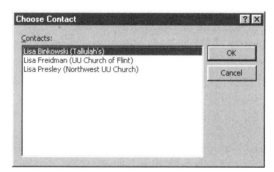

Select the contact you want to see, and Outlook opens the appropriate Contact form.

Using Predefined Views

The Contacts folder has seven predefined views: Address Cards, Detailed Address Cards, Phone List, By Category, By Company, By Location, and By Follow-up Flag. To switch to another view, choose View ➢ Current View on the menu, and select the view you want to apply.

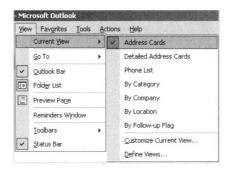

The Address Cards view, shown in Figure 33.15, is the default view in Contacts. It displays basic information about the contact: File As name, mailing address, e-mail address, and telephone numbers. Detailed Address Cards view displays additional data, including full name, job title, company name, and categories. Card views have a handy feature: an index on the right side that lets you quickly go to Contacts by the File By name. Clicking the *S*, for example, takes you to contacts whose File By name begins with the letter *S*. Many users choose either Address Cards or Detailed Address Cards as their default view for Contacts.

FIGURE 33.15

Address Cards view works just like an electronic version of a Rolodex.

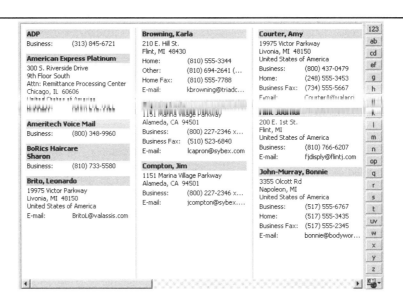

To learn all about applying and creating even more views for Contacts and printing directories of your contacts, refer to Chapter 35, "Working behind the Scenes in Outlook."

Locating a Contact

The easiest way to search through a long list of contacts is to enter a first or last name in the Find A Contact text box on the Standard toolbar. If Outlook only finds one name that matches your entry, it opens the Contact form for that person. If it finds more than one possible match, Outlook displays a list of possibilities that you can then choose from.

When you don't remember the contact's first or last name, you can search for other information about the contact by clicking the Find button on the Standard toolbar to open the Search pane at the top of the list.

If you're looking for a contact, enter all or part of their name, company name, or address in the Look For text box. By default, Outlook searches all text in each contact, including comments. To limit your search to just key fields and speed up your search, click the Options button at the far right end of the Search pane and unselect Search All Text In The Message.

Click the Find Now button to find all the contacts based on the text you entered in the Look For text box. When you find the contact you're looking for, just double-click it to open the Contact form.

Using Advanced Find

If you can't find the contact you're looking for in the Search pane, or if you're looking for text in specific fields or based on criteria other than text, consider using Advanced Find. Click Advanced Find on the Options menu to open the Advanced Find dialog box.

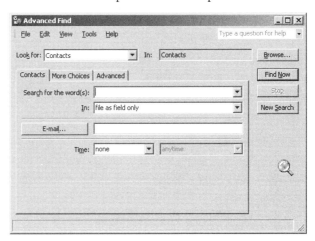

In the Advanced Find dialog box, you can select the type of item—Contacts, Tasks, and so on—and click the Browse button to select the folder you'd like to search. If you are searching Contacts, you can enter the name or other text you want to search for in the Search For The Words text box on the Contacts tab. Open the In drop-down list and select the category of field you want to search, such as Names fields, Address fields, and so on. Choose Frequently Used Text Fields for the broadest search. Using the Time options, you can search for contacts that were created or modified within a particular time frame. For example, you can find contacts you created today or modified in the last week.

Flip to the More Choices tab, and you can find contacts by categories. On the Advanced tab of the Advanced Find dialog box, shown in Figure 33.16, you can enter multiple, specific search criteria based on the values in fields. To enter a search criterion, click the Field button to open a menu of Outlook field types. Choose a type (for example, All Contact Fields), and then select the field from the menu.

From the Condition text box, choose the appropriate operator. The operators in the list depend on the type of data that will be in the field you selected. For example, with text fields, you'll choose between Contains, Is, Doesn't Contain, Is Empty, and Is Not Empty. In the Value text box, enter the value you want to find (or not find). You don't have to enter a Value for Is Empty and Is Not Empty fields. When you're finished building the search criterion, click the Add To List button to add it to the Find Items list.

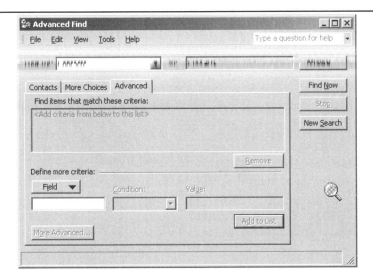

FIGURE 33.16

Use the Advanced tab to find contacts based on one or more specific fields.

When you've entered all the advanced criteria you need to conduct your search, click Find Now to find the contacts that match all the criteria you entered. You can enter search criteria on more than one tab and find, for example, contacts created in the last seven days in the Business category.

New Search

If you're finished with one search and want to search for other contacts, click the New Search button to clear the criteria you entered from all three tabs of the dialog box.

When you're finished with Advanced Find, choose File ➢ Close or click the Close button on the dialog box title bar to close Advanced Find and return to Contacts. To close the Search pane, click the Close button at the top of the pane or click the Find button again on the Standard toolbar.

Printing Contacts

If you've ever been asked to create an employee directory for your organization, you know the potential pitfalls. Someone (probably you) has to enter data, choose a layout for the directory, format all the data, and add headings. By the time you send the directory to your printer, you've invested a lot of time in design issues. Outlook includes a number of printing options that will help you quickly and easily create directories, phone lists, and other print resources that formerly took hours or days to create.

When you choose File ➢ Page Setup from the Outlook menu, you are presented with a list of styles to choose from. The available styles depend on the current view; so before you print, select the view that most closely resembles the printed output you want. For a simple employee telephone list, switch to Phone List view and choose the table view from the Page Setup menu. For complete names and addresses, choose a Card view. Table 33.1 identifies the Contact views and their corresponding print styles.

TABLE 33.1   PAGE SETUP STYLES

Style	Type of View	Default Printed Output
Table	Table	A list of contacts in columns and rows. Only available when you are in a table view such as Phone List view.
Card	Card	A two-column listing of names and contact information.
Small Booklet	Card	A multiple-section listing of names and contact information prepared for two-sided printing.
Medium Booklet	Card	A two-column listing of names and contact information prepared for two-sided printing.
Memo	Table	Data for the selected contact(s), with your name at the top of each entry.
Phone Directory	Table	A two-column listing of names and phone numbers, with a heading for each letter of the alphabet (very slick).

The Page Setup dialog box, shown in Figure 33.17, has three tabs: Format, Paper, and Header/Footer. In the Format tab, choose the format options you would like to apply to the style:

Sections To have each letter of the alphabet begin on a new page, choose Start On A New Page. For continuous presentation, choose Immediately Follow Each Other.

Number Of Columns As you increase the number of columns, Outlook decreases the font size.

Blank Forms At End This option allows space for users to add new entries in the correct section in the printed directory.

Contact Index On Side This check box will generate an index, like the index used in Address Card view, with the section's letters highlighted.

Headings For Each letter This feature gives you a highlighted letter at the beginning of each alphabetic section.

Fonts These lists offer you choices of fonts for the letter headings and body.

Shading This check box enables or disables gray shading in the letter tabs, letter headings, and contact names.

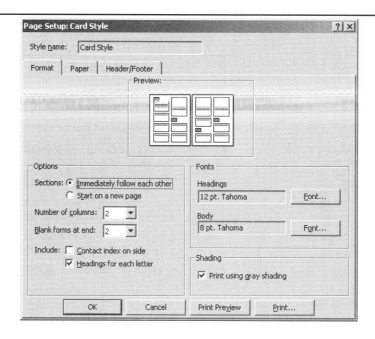

FIGURE 33.17

Use the Page Setup dialog box to design your printed Contacts directory.

After you make a change, you can click the Print Preview button to see how the change affects your printed output. Click anywhere in the preview to zoom in on the detail; click again to zoom out. To close Print Preview and return to the Page Setup dialog box, choose Page Setup. If you click Close, you close both Print Preview *and* Page Setup.

On the Paper tab of the Page Setup dialog box, choose the settings that describe the dimensions of the paper you're going to use.

On the Header/Footer tab, you can create a header and footer that contain text and document information. Headers and footers appear on each page of the finished product. If you're creating a 1/4-page booklet, a header will appear four times on the printed sheet, so it will be at the top of each page after it is folded.

The header and footer each have a left-aligned, a centered, and a right-aligned section. To include text in the header or footer, just click in the section and begin typing. Use the five buttons on the toolbar below the header and footer sections to include the page number, total number of pages, date printed, time printed, and user name in the header or footer.

When you've finished setting print options, click the Print button to open the Print dialog box. Select a printer from the Name list, the range of pages to print, and the number of copies. Click the OK button to send the job to the printer.

 TIP If you want to print a booklet with two-sided pages and you have a one-sided printer, choose Odd in the Number Of Pages drop-down list and print all the odd-numbered pages first. Turn the sheets over and reinsert them into the printer. Choose Even to print the rest of the pages. Outlook orders the pages so they can be folded into a booklet when they're all printed.

The printing process is the same in all the Outlook modules. Begin by selecting a view that supports the output you want. Preview the output in Print Preview. Change views, if necessary, and then adjust the Page Setup options to further define the final output. Finally, send the job to the printer, and think about how easy this was.

Dialing a Contact

Newer multimedia computers support a full range of *telephony* accessories, including headsets and built-in or monitor-mounted microphones. You don't need a lot of fancy hardware to use Outlook's telephony features. As long as you have a telephone connected to the line your modem uses, you can place telephone calls from Outlook. You don't need a fast modem to make telephone calls—your voice is simply routed from one port in the modem to the other. Outlook's telephone dialing program is called *AutoDialer*. You must be in the Contacts folder to use AutoDialer.

You can begin by selecting the contact you want to call. Then click the AutoDialer drop-down arrow to open the menu of all the telephone numbers for the contact. Choose a number from the list, and the New Call dialog box opens.

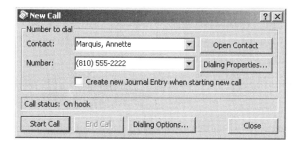

The contact's name appears in the Contact text box, and the phone number you select is in the Number text box. You can click the arrow in the Number box to see other numbers.

If you know your contact's telephone number, or have it in your telephone's speed dial listing, you could have dialed the number by now. AutoDialer is popular because of the check box that appears under the number. One simple click and Outlook opens a Journal entry for the contact while you place the call.

Click the Start Call button to have Outlook dial the number. If the Create New Journal Entry check box is enabled, a new Journal Entry form opens automatically. The New Call dialog box is still open (and remains open during the call). The Call Status reads *Connected*, and the End Call button is enabled.

When you've completed your call, click the End Call button to close the connection (you may have to move the Journal Entry form out of the way to see the New Call dialog box). Outlook automatically pauses the timer in the Journal item, and it enters the total time for the call in the Duration control. If you'd like to make some notes about the call, enter them in the open Notes area in the Journal item. You should also change the subject to describe the contents of the telephone call and assign a category if you wish. When you've finished entering information in the Journal form, click the Save And Close button to close the Journal entry.

Creating a Letter to a Contact

To write a letter to a contact (the traditional, snail-mail variety), select the contact and choose Actions ➤ New Letter To Contact. This starts the Microsoft Word Letter Wizard. Information available in the Contact form is filled in for you. When you complete the additional information in the Letter Wizard, Outlook passes control over to Word so you can write your letter. Complete the letter as you would any Word document. Close or minimize Word to return to Outlook.

Mail Merging Contacts with Word Documents

If you want to create labels, letters or envelopes, or a catalog of Outlook names and addresses, you can go to Word and use Outlook Contacts as a data source. For even more up-front options, you can access mail merge from within Outlook.

To access the mail merge features in Outlook, switch to Contacts, then follow these steps to initiate a mail merge:

1. Create a Contacts view, including the fields you want to merge and any filters you want to apply to the data (View ➤ Current View ➤ Customize Current View).

2. If you don't want to merge all of the visible contacts, select the contacts you want using Ctrl+Click.

3. Choose Tools ➤ Mail Merge to open the new Outlook Mail Merge Contacts dialog box, shown in Figure 33.18. Only selected contacts will be preselected.

4. Check whether you want to merge all the records or the selected records.

5. Check if you want to merge all contact fields or only the fields in the view you selected—with over a hundred contact fields, it is generally better to choose the fields you want, as described in step 1, to make the list more usable.

6. Identify if you want to create a new Word main document or if you have an existing Word document you want to use as the main document.

7. To save a copy of the contacts you include in the merge, check Permanent File and enter a filename.

8. Choose the document type—letters, labels, envelopes, or catalog—and indicate whether you want to merge to a new document, a printer, an e-mail, or a fax.

9. Click OK to launch Word and open the main document. You can now add merge fields and finish the merge in Word.

NOTE Word's mail merge features have been completely revamped in Office XP, so you'll want to take a look at Chapter 9, "Creating Merge Documents in Word," where they are discussed in detail.

FIGURE 33.18

Initiate Word's mail merge features from within Outlook.

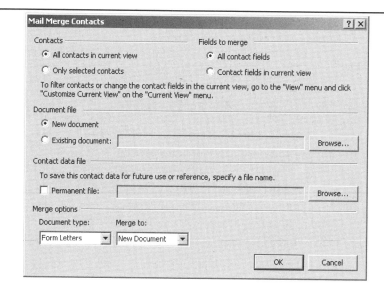

Documenting Your Communications in the Journal

Unfortunately, Outlook's Journal is probably the least understood and least used feature in all of Outlook. For those who use it, it is an invaluable record of the work you have done. It adds impressive content to performance appraisals, makes you look good when no one can remember what was said on a conference call, and provides documentation when you need backup in touchy situations. The Journal is the place in Outlook where you can keep a running history of your daily activities. You can use the Journal to make notes, record your impressions, organize e-mail communications, and track how long you spent working on a document.

Manually Recording an Event in the Journal

To access the Journal, click the Journal icon on the Outlook bar. The Journal opens in its default Timeline view, showing how you've spent your time and what events have occurred on a particular day. Figure 33.19 shows three phone calls that occurred over a three-day period.

PART

VII

GETTING ORGANIZED
WITH OUTLOOK

FIGURE 33.19

*The Journal's
Timeline view*

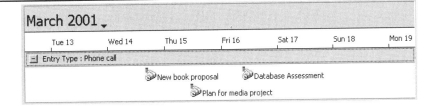

To expand an Entry Type group so you can see all of the entries it contains, click the Expand button (with the plus symbol) on the Entry Type group heading. To collapse a group that is already expanded, click the Collapse button (the minus symbol).

NOTE The first time you click the Journal icon on the Outlook bar, you may be surprised to find that there are already entries in the Journal. This is because the Journal is working behind the scenes, automatically recording work that you're doing in other Office applications. For a better understanding of these entries, and to learn how to change the automatic settings, see "Automatically Recording Journal Events" later in this chapter.

Only one type of Journal entry is visible in Figure 33.19, phone calls. In all, there are approximately 20 types of Journal entries that you can make. To create a new Journal entry, click the New button on the Standard toolbar and choose Journal Entry from the list. The Journal Entry form shown in Figure 33.20 opens. The default entry type is Phone Call. Just click the down arrow in the Entry Type field to see the other choices, such as Conversation and Microsoft Excel.

FIGURE 33.20

A Journal Entry form

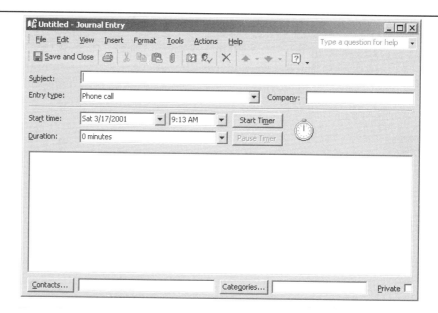

Creating a Journal entry is quite simple:

1. Enter a Subject for the Journal entry and choose the Entry Type from the drop-down list.

2. To associate a Journal entry with an existing contact, click the Address Book button and choose a contact from the Select Names dialog box.

3. Enter a Company name, if desired.

4. Enter a date and time in the Start Time field or, if you're making a phone call, click the Start Timer button to have Journal automatically time your conversation.

5. Record the length of the communication from the Duration drop-down list or type in an entry of your own. If you clicked the Start Timer button, click the Pause Timer button when you've finished your phone call to have Outlook automatically record the call's duration.

6. Type your notes about the communication in the open text box area.

7. Assign the Journal entry to a category by clicking the Categories button.

8. To exclude anyone who has access to your Outlook folders from reading this entry, click the Private check box.

9. Click the Save And Close button to record your Journal entry.

Automatically Recording Journal Events

Working behind the scenes, Outlook can help you keep track of your communications and monitor how much time you spend on your projects. Any action associated with a contact—such as sending or receiving e-mail, a meeting response, or a task request—can automatically appear in the Journal. Additionally, Outlook can record what other Office documents you work on and for how long.

To set up Outlook to automatically record items:

1. Choose Tools ➢ Options from the menu and click Journal Options to open the Journal Options dialog box, shown in Figure 33.21.

2. Select the items you would like to automatically record from the list of choices, including e-mail messages, meeting requests, and so on.

3. Mark the contacts for which you want to record items automatically.

4. Select the types of files you would like to record automatically from the list, which includes all of the Office applications and other compatible programs.

5. Choose whether you want double-clicking a Journal entry to open the entry itself (the default) or the item it refers to.

6. Click OK to save your choices in the Journal Options dialog box and click OK again to close the Options dialog box.

FIGURE 33.21

The Journal Options dialog box

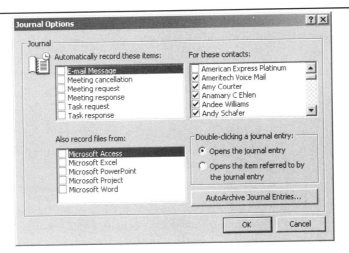

NOTE In earlier versions of Outlook, the Journal was the only way to track e-mail communication with a contact. Outlook 2000 replaced the Journal tab in a Contact form with Activities, which automatically searches through your Outlook mailbox for Outlook items related to a contact each time you open the tab. See "Tracking Activities" earlier in this chapter for more about how Activities works.

Unless you've chosen to open the referenced item directly, when you double-click a Journal entry, the Journal form opens containing an icon for the referenced item.

 NOTE When you set the Journal to automatically record documents that you work on in any of the Office applications, Outlook records the author of the document as the contact it associates with the Journal entry, using the Author field on the Summary tab of the document's properties. (To display the Summary tab, open the document in the application, choose File ➢ Properties, and click the Summary tab.)

Inserting Items and Files into Journal Entries

You can insert documents and Outlook items (or hyperlinks to them; see the sidebar, "Which Insert File Option Should I Choose?") directly into Journal entries. For example, if you had a phone conversation about a proposal you were writing for a client, you could insert a hyperlink to the Word document directly into the Journal entry. In the future when you wanted to review what you talked about, you could directly reference the proposal. Follow these steps to insert an item or file into a Journal entry:

1. Open the Journal entry and click in the Notes area of the Journal form.

2. Choose Insert ➢ File to insert a document or a link to a document created outside of Outlook or choose Insert ➢ Item to insert an Outlook item. The Insert File or Insert Item dialog box opens.

3. Locate the file or item you want to insert and select it.

4. Click the drop-down arrow on the Insert button to choose whether you want to Insert As Text, Insert As Attachment, or Insert As Hyperlink.

5. Click OK to insert the file. In the Notes area of the Journal entry, you'll see either the contents of the file, an icon representing a copy of the document or item, or a hyperlink to the document or item.

6. Double-click the icon or link to open the document.

MASTERING THE OPPORTUNITIES

Which Insert File Option Should I Choose?

There are significant differences between inserting a file as text, an attachment, or a hyperlink; you should make a careful choice each time you insert a file into an Outlook item.

Insert As Attachment The default choice is Insert, which is the same as Insert As Attachment. Be aware that when you insert an attachment, you are making a copy of the original document. When you double-click the icon in the Outlook item to open the document, you are opening and perhaps modifying the copy. The original document remains unchanged. Use this option if you want to send a file to someone who can open an Office attachment to an e-mail message.

Insert As Text This option is useful if you plan to send an item to someone who does not have Outlook or if you want to print the Journal entry and see the contents of the item. The actual text of the item or file is included in the Journal entry. To use this option for Office documents, you must first save the document as a text document.

Insert As Hyperlink This option creates a link to the document on your local or network drive. Use this option if you are inserting the document for your own reference and do not plan to e-mail the item to anyone outside your network. When you click the link to open this document, you are modifying the original document in its original location.

Your network administrator may have policies about version control and storage capacity. You may need to maintain a "paper trail" by keeping each stage of modification as a separate document, or you may need to minimize duplication of storage by keeping only a single copy of each document. Find out what the policy or practice is in your organization before making a decision of which insert option to choose.

Making Notes

Even after you are using Outlook to its fullest, you will still run across those odd pieces of information that have nowhere to go or that you want to keep at your fingertips: your flight information, the type of battery your cell phone uses, or information about your car insurance. They aren't related to a contact and they aren't an event, so what do you do with them? Outlook includes an easy way to organize all those notes that don't belong anywhere else. Choose Note from the New Item button (or hold Ctrl+Shift and press N) to open a Note window. Enter your text in the Note window that opens.

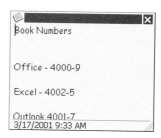

 TIP When you are entering a note, enter a title for the note and then press Enter before entering the contents of the note. Otherwise, the entire text of the note will be visible in the Notes Information Viewer.

Each note is automatically time- and date-stamped. Closing the window automatically saves the note. To view a note, click the Note icon on the Outlook bar to go to the Note window. Double-click a note to open it. Click the Note icon to access options for deleting, saving, and printing notes.

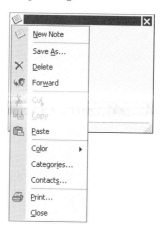

If a note gains importance and needs to become a task, a Journal entry, or an e-mail message, just drag the Note icon onto the appropriate icon on the Outlook bar or into the appropriate folder in the folder list.

Using Notes outside Outlook

You can take a note with you to any application or even park it on the Windows Desktop so it's ready and waiting for you. To copy a note to the Windows Desktop, restore the Outlook window (click the Restore button on the Outlook title bar) and drag the note to the Desktop. To move a note, right-drag the note onto the Desktop and choose Move Here from the shortcut menu. Outlook does not have to be open for you to edit the note, make additions to it, or delete the contents.

MASTERING THE OPPORTUNITIES

Making Notes Mobile

If you carry a 3Com Palm or other handheld computing device, chances are it synchronizes with Outlook's Notes module. It may have a different name for the folder; the Palm, for example, calls it MemoPad—look at your handheld device to see if there is a similar folder. Once you discover it, it opens a world of possibilities for having information at your fingertips. For example, copy your travel itinerary into an Outlook note and you never have to worry about finding your travel agent's printout again. This is especially valuable in the age of electronic tickets where you don't even have a ticket to refer to. If there is a document you want to take with you, copy and paste Word documents or Excel spreadsheets directly into a note. It's a good idea to check your handheld's documentation to see if there is a maximum file size, and you'll want to double-check the document on your handheld after you synchronize to make sure it made it there safely. Once you get in the habit of using notes, you'll find them an invaluable tool for the mobile professional.

CHAPTER 34

MANAGING YOUR TIME AND TASKS

FEATURING

- Creating tasks

- Setting up recurring tasks

- Assigning a task to someone else

- Completing a task

- Viewing and navigating the Calendar

- Scheduling appointments

- Configuring the Calendar

- Printing the Calendar

- Using the Calendar in a workgroup

f you're already a list keeper, you'll find that Outlook takes the To Do list to a new dimension by adding the ability to track progress, assign tasks to other people (our personal favorite), set reminders for tasks, schedule time to complete tasks, and evaluate the progress you are making. Even if making lists is not your favorite pastime, it's hard to ignore the power of Outlook's Tasks module. When you combine tasks with the flexibility and organization of Outlook's Calendar, it won't be long before you're keeping up with the most organized person you know.

Creating a Task

To create a task, you simply type the name of the task and its due date. You can also enter more detailed information about the task, taking full advantage of the power that Outlook has to offer.

To enter a task, click the Tasks icon on the Outlook bar. The default view in Tasks is the Simple List view, shown in Figure 34.1. The Simple List view has four columns:

Icon An icon that changes if a task is assigned to someone else or was assigned by someone else

Complete A check box indicating whether the task has been completed

Subject A descriptive name for the task

Due Date The date on which you expect or need to complete the task

You can enter a task directly into the Information Viewer by clicking in the Click Here To Add A New Task text box. The row turns blue, and the box that is active for editing is white. Type a subject in the Subject field. It's helpful if you make the subject descriptive but not too long—less than 30 characters is best so you can read it all in the column.

NOTE You must be in Simple List or Detailed List view to have the Click Here To Add A New Task text box. If you prefer to use another view, then create a new task by choosing Task from the New button.

FIGURE 34.1

*The Simple List view
of Tasks*

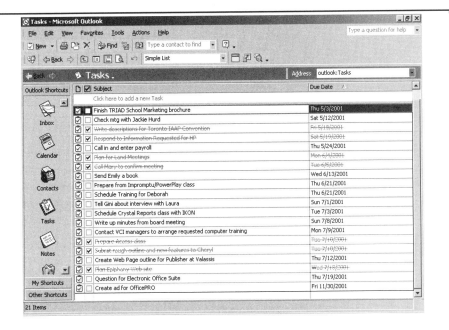

After you type a subject, press Tab to move to the Due Date field (Shift+Tab moves you back to Subject); the text box turns white.

Because Outlook recognizes natural-language dates using its AutoDate feature, you have multiple options for entering dates in this field. Just about anything you type into the field that remotely resembles a date is converted into a standard date format (Wed 8/18/01). You could type **8-18-01**; **aug 18**; **three weeks from now**; **a week from today**; **tomorrow**; **one month from next wed**. All are legitimate dates in Outlook (of course, they wouldn't all return the same date). Go ahead and try it—it's fun to see what AutoDate's limits are.

Click anywhere in the Task list to move the task into the list. Where the task appears in the list depends on how the list is currently sorted. Enter additional tasks the same way.

Entering Details about a Task

To take advantage of the powerful features built into Outlook, you need to add more information about the task than just the subject and due date. The most direct way to do this is to enter the data in a Task form. You can open the form for any existing task by double-clicking the task in the Information Viewer. To open a blank Task form, click the New button on the Standard toolbar (if Tasks is the active module in the

Information Viewer); or click the down arrow to the right of the New button to open the New menu, and choose Task from the list.

The Task form, shown in Figure 34.2, is composed of two tabs: Task and Details. The Task tab focuses on a description of the task (see "Completing a Task" later in this chapter for more information about the Details tab). Enter the subject in the Subject text box, and press Tab to move to the Due Date field. Click the down arrow to choose a date from the calendar, or enter a date in the text box. If the task is not scheduled to start right away, enter a Start Date to indicate when it should be started.

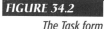

FIGURE 34.2

The Task form

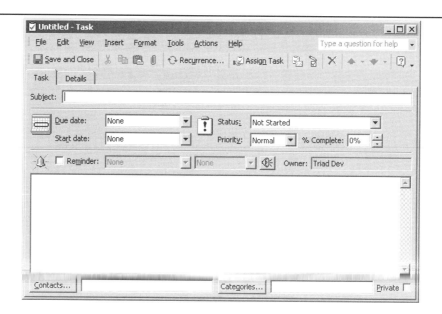

Setting Reminders

If you've entered a due date, Outlook automatically activates the Reminder check box. However, you don't have to enter a due date to use this feature. Click the Reminder check box to activate a reminder that will be displayed at a specified date and time.

The Time drop-down list has a choice for every half hour around the clock, so be careful to select the correct AM or PM time. There's nothing like setting a reminder for

12 hours after something was supposed to be completed! You can also type an entry in this box if you need a reminder at the quarter hour.

Reminders come with a sound by default. You have the option of disabling the sound or changing the sound file it plays. Click the speaker icon to access the Reminder Sound options.

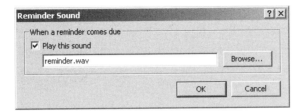

Clear the Play This Sound check box if you'd prefer your reminders appeared on your screen silently. If you would like to hear a sound but would prefer a different sound file, click the Browse button to locate the file you would like to use. Double-click the filename, and it appears in the Play This Sound text box.

TIP If you change the sound file within a task, it is only in effect for that specific reminder. To change the default sound file for all Reminders, go to Sounds in the Windows Control Panel and change the sound assigned to Microsoft Office Reminders. Sound files, or wave files, are designated by a .wav extension. If you would like to record your own reminder message or sound that plays when it is time to do a task, you can do so using the Windows Sound Recorder.

When the reminder time arrives, a reminder window appears in whatever application you're using at the time. However, in order to see the reminders you've set, Outlook must be running—in the background if necessary. If it's not, you won't see the reminder(s) until the next time you launch Outlook. See "Managing Reminders" later in this chapter to learn about options for handling reminders when they appear.

Updating Task Status

When you enter a task, Outlook assumes you haven't started working on the task yet. To help you manage your tasks and assess the status of certain projects, you have four other Status options in addition to Not Started available to you. Click the Status down arrow on the Task tab of the Task form to open the list of choices.

In Progress If a task is in progress, you might also want to indicate the percentage that is complete in the % Complete text box. Use the spin box to change the percentage, or type the actual percentage directly in the box.

Completed In addition to marking a task complete, you might also want to complete some additional fields on the Details tab. See "Completing a Task" later in this chapter.

Waiting On Someone Else It's helpful to set a reminder to yourself to call this person if you don't hear from them in a reasonable amount of time.

Deferred You may want to change the start and end dates so this task doesn't show up on your list of active tasks.

Setting Priorities

By setting a priority level for a task, you can be sure that your most important tasks receive most of your attention. The default priority is set at Normal. You have additional options of High and Low. High priority items are designated by a red exclamation point in the Information Viewer, and Low priority items are designated by a blue downward-pointing arrow.

Owning a Task

The Task Owner is the person who creates the task, or the person to whom the task is currently assigned. When you create a task, you are the owner by default. To give up ownership, however, all you have to do is assign the task to someone else. As soon as that person accepts the task, they officially become the new owner. To learn how to assign tasks to someone else, see "Delegating Tasks" later in this chapter.

Assigning Categories to Manage a Project

Categories are user-defined values that help to organize your data throughout Outlook. Chapter 35, "Working behind the Scenes in Outlook," provides a thorough discussion of how to create new categories and delete undesired categories. You have the same list of categories available to you as you have in Contacts or any of the other Outlook modules.

Categories can pull related tasks together, making it possible to view the tasks connected with a particular project. Just click the Categories button and assign each task to the same category from the Categories dialog box. When you return to the Information Viewer, you can sort by category, group all the tasks in the same category together, or even filter out just those tasks related to a single category (see Chapter 35 for more about creating custom views). Figure 34.3 is an example of a Task list grouped by category.

FIGURE 34.3

Task list grouped by category

Categories : Admin (2 items)					
☑	Call in and enter payroll	Not Started	Thu 5/24/2001	0%	Admin
☑	Schedule Crystal Reports class with IKON	Not Started	Tue 7/3/2001	0%	Admin
Categories : Marketing (5 items)					
☑	Finish TRIAD School Marketing brochure	In Progress	Thu 5/3/2001	0%	Marketing
☑ ↓	Send Emily a book	Not Started	Wed 6/13/2001	0%	Marketing
☑ !	Tell Gini about interview with Laura	Not Started	Sun 7/1/2001	0%	Marketing
☑	Question for Electronic Office Suite	Not Started	Thu 7/19/2001	0%	Marketing
☑	Create ad for OfficePRO	Not Started	Fri 11/30/2001	0%	Marketing
Categories : Perry Database (1 item)					
☑ !	Check mtg with Jackie Hurd	Not Started	Sat 5/12/2001	0%	Perry Database
Categories : Sybex (1 item)					
☑	Plan next book project	Not Started	Wed 2/28/2001	0%	Sybex
Categories : Training (2 items)					
☑	Schedule Training for Deborah	Not Started	Thu 6/21/2001	0%	Training
☑ !	Contact VCI managers to arrange requested c...	Not Started	Mon 7/9/2001	0%	Training
Categories : UU (1 item)					
☑ ↓	Write up minutes from board meeting	Not Started	Sun 7/8/2001	0%	UU
Categories : Valassis (3 items)					
☑ ! 0	Call Valassis Managers about custom training	Not Started	Mon 1/22/2001	0%	Valassis
☑	Prepare from Impromptu/PowerPlay class	Not Started	Thu 6/21/2001	0%	Valassis

> **TIP** To assign several tasks to the same category, click the Organize button on the Standard toolbar. Select all the tasks you want to assign to the same category (hold Ctrl while you click each task) and then select the Category from the Add Tasks Selected Below To drop-down list. If the category you want doesn't exist, create it first by entering its name in the Create A New Category Called text box.

Making a Task Private

If your Outlook folders are shared on a network, there may be times when you don't want others to see information about a task. Click the Private check box on the right-hand corner of the Task form to keep this task from being visible to others to whom you have given permission to access your Tasks folder.

> **NOTE** For more about privacy and security, see Chapter 35.

Setting Up Recurring Tasks

A *recurring task* is a task that you must complete on a regular basis—such as a monthly report, a weekly agenda, a quarterly tax submission. Anything that you have to do periodically qualifies. In Outlook you can enter the task once, and then set a pattern for it to recur on your Task list. Outlook doesn't care if you've completed this month's report; when the time comes for next month's, it adds another copy of the task with a new due date to your list.

To set up a recurring task, enter the task as you would any other task that needs completion. When you have the data entered for the first occurrence of the task, click the Recurrence button on the Standard toolbar within the Task form. This opens the Task Recurrence dialog box, shown in Figure 34.4.

FIGURE 34.4

Task Recurrence dialog box

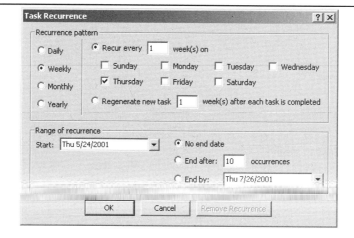

Here you can set the Recurrence Pattern and the Range Of Recurrence. To set the Recurrence Pattern, indicate whether the task needs to be accomplished Daily, Weekly, Monthly, or Yearly. If the task needs to be completed every three days, choose Daily; every two months, choose Monthly; and so on. Each of the four options gives you different choices for defining the actual pattern. Rather than choosing a specific date pattern, as an alternative, you can indicate how many days/weeks/months/years you want Outlook to wait after a task is marked as complete before it generates a new task.

Daily Choose between Every *N* Days or Every Weekday.

Weekly Indicate how often the task should occur: every week (1), every other week (2), every third week (3), and so on. This is the best option if the task needs to be completed every six weeks or every eight weeks (because some months have more than four weeks). Then mark on which day of the week the task needs to be accomplished.

Monthly Choose between specifying which date of each *N* month(s) or indicating the first, second, third, fourth, or last day of every *N* month(s); for example, the last Friday of every month or the third Thursday of every second month. You could also indicate the first weekday or the last weekend day of the month.

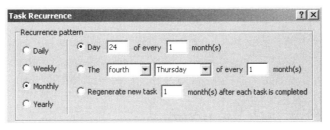

Yearly Indicate a specific date in a specific month (every May 5), or mark the first, second, third, fourth, or last day of a specific month (the first Friday in May).

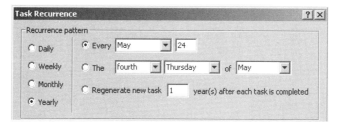

Sometimes you have to be creative to figure out how often a task really occurs. For example, if a task occurs two times a year on February 28 and August 31, do you use Monthly or Yearly? Because these dates are six months apart, you could use Monthly and indicate the last day of every six months (as long as the Start date was set to one of the two dates).

However, if this task is not so evenly spaced—May 31 and August 31 for example—you probably will have to enter two tasks: one for the May date every year, and one for the August date every year.

Defining the Range of Recurrence

The Range Of Recurrence refers to when the first task in the series is due and how long the task will continue (see Figure 34.4, shown previously).

You have your choice of:

No End Date The task continues into infinity (or until you tell it to stop).

End After *N* Occurrences You only need to complete the task a specific number of times, and then you are finished with it.

End By You only have to do this task until a certain date, and then you are free.

Once you have set the Range Of Recurrence, click OK to return to the Task form. Click Save And Close to save the task and return to the Information Viewer.

Editing Task Recurrence

To make changes to the recurrence pattern or range that you set, open the task and click the Recurrence Pattern button. Make your changes and then click Save And Close again. You may also edit the Subject of the task, but any changes you make affect only future occurrences of the task.

If you want to skip the next occurrence of a task but not interfere with the recurrence pattern, open the task and choose Skip Occurrence from the Actions menu. The due date automatically changes to the next date the task is due.

Remove Recurrence

To delete the recurrence pattern without deleting the task, open the task, click the Recurrence button, and click the Remove Recurrence button on the bottom of the Task Recurrence dialog box. Close the Task Recurrence dialog box and Save And Close the task. The task still appears on your list, but it is now there for one time only.

Delegating Tasks

If you work as a member of a team, or if you have people reporting to you, there are times when you may want to create a task for someone else to do. As long as the other person is running Outlook and you both have access to e-mail, you can assign tasks to each other.

Assign Task

To assign a task to someone else, create the task as you normally would, add task Recurrence, if appropriate, and click the Assign Task button on the Standard toolbar of the Task form. This opens a message form with the task included, as shown in Figure 34.5.

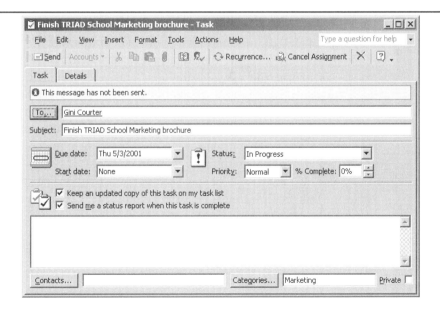

FIGURE 34.5

Assigning a task to someone else

Enter the person's e-mail address, or click the To button and choose the name from your address lists (see Chapter 32, "Using Outlook As a Communications Tool," for more information about addressing e-mail messages). You have two options related to this assignment.

Keep An Updated Copy Of This Task On My Task List Even though you have assigned the task to someone else, you may still want to know how the task is going. Every time the new owner of the Task revises the task in any way, a message is sent to you indicating that the task was updated. As soon as you open the message, the task is automatically revised in your Task list. When you close the task, the message is removed from your Inbox. This option is not available if the task is recurring.

Send Me A Status Report When This Task Is Complete When the new owner marks the task as complete, you receive an automatic status report message informing you that the task is complete. This status report message remains in your Inbox until you move it or dispose of it. Although you can assign a task to anyone who runs Outlook, if the person is not on your network, you will not receive automatic updates when that person makes revisions to the task.

If you would like to send a message along with the task assignment, enter the text in the message box. Click Send to transfer the message to your Outbox.

Assigning a Task to More than One Person

Create Unassigned Copy

It's possible to assign the same task to more than one person, but if you do, you cannot keep an updated copy of the task in your Task list. To assign the task to an additional person, open the task, click the Details tab, and click the Create Unassigned Copy button.

You are warned that you will become the owner again (the person you originally assigned the task to took over ownership of the task when they accepted it) and will no longer receive updates (unless you want to write them to yourself). Click OK to create the copy and assign the task.

If you really need to receive updates from more than one person about the task, create the task multiple times and assign it individually to each person. Include the person's name in the Subject so you can differentiate the multiple tasks.

Receiving a Task Assignment

When someone sends you a task, you receive an e-mail message with the words "Task Request" in the Subject. When you open the task, you can choose to accept the task or decline the task by clicking the appropriate button on the message form.

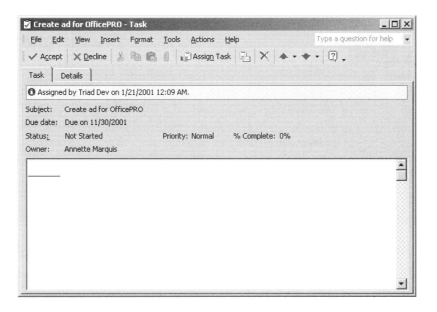

If you click Accept, the task is automatically added to your Task list, and you become the owner of the task. If you click Decline, the person who sent you the task retains ownership. Either way, the person who originated the task is sent a message indicating your response. When you click Send, you are given the option of editing the response before sending it, or sending it without editing. If you want to explain why you're declining your boss's request, click Edit The Response Before Sending and enter your explanation in the message.

Even after you accept a task, you can change your mind and decline the task. Just open the task and choose Decline Task from the Actions menu.

Passing the Task Along

If you receive a task from someone, it's possible for you to accept the task assignment and then turn around and assign the task to someone else (commonly referred to as passing the buck). When you accept the task, you become the owner of the task, and changes and updates you make are returned to the task's originator. When you reassign a task to someone else, that person becomes the owner and future updates are returned to you *and* the originator of the task. To reassign a task:

1. Open the e-mail message that contains the original task request, and click the Accept button to accept the task (if you have not already done so). This sends a Task Update to the originator indicating that you have accepted the task. You are now the owner of the task.

2. Open the task in your Task list and click the Assign button. Make sure the Keep An Updated Copy Of The Task On My Task List and the Send Me A Status Report When The Task Is Complete options are both checked so you won't lose track of the task.

3. Enter the e-mail address of the person you want to assign the task to, and click Send to send the Task Request to them. They are now the temporary owner of the task. When they accept the task, they become the task's owner.

4. When you receive a task update from the new owner, the originator also gets a message from you.

By following this process, you keep the task's originator informed, and you have someone else doing the work—not bad work, if you can get it!

Sending Status Reports

Even though Outlook does a great job of keeping a task's originator informed about the status of a task, you may need to incorporate more detail into a report than Outlook generates automatically. If you want to send a manual status report, click Actions ➢ Send Status Report from the Standard toolbar of the open task. Type in (or copy and paste) your status report. Click Send to send an update to the task's originator.

Creating Tasks from Other Outlook Items

Outlook's power comes from the incredible ease with which all of the components work together to make your life easier. How many times have you received an e-mail message asking you to do something? Unless you print the message and put it in the stack of papers on your desk and hope you run across it before it needs to get done, you may find yourself forgetting it was even asked of you. Outlook changes all that. The next time you receive an e-mail message asking you to do something, all you have to do is drag the message onto the Task icon on the Outlook bar.

Outlook automatically opens a Task form for you with the information already in it, including the actual contents of the e-mail message.

All you have to do is add Due Dates, assign the task to a category, and add any other details you want—and your reminder is all set. (You will, however, have to actually do the task yourself.)

You can use this trick to create Outlook tasks with any other Outlook item, such as a Journal entry, a Calendar item, or a Note.

Completing a Task

When you've finally completed a task, there is nothing more satisfying than checking it off your list. Outlook wouldn't want you to miss out on this pleasure, so it has incorporated a check box into the Simple List view. To mark a task complete, just click the check box in the Status column.

A completed task is crossed off the list. If the view you are using does not include completed items, such as Active Tasks view, the item is actually removed from the list altogether. To complete a task in Active Tasks view, change the Status to Completed or change the % Complete to 100%. Of course, you can always see it by switching to a view such as Simple List view, which shows all tasks. If you mistakenly check off a task as complete, just switch to Simple List view and clear the check box.

If you are interested in tracking more information about a completed task, you may want to open the task and click the Details tab of the Tasks form. It has several fields, shown in Figure 34.6, that are designed to be filled in when the task is completed.

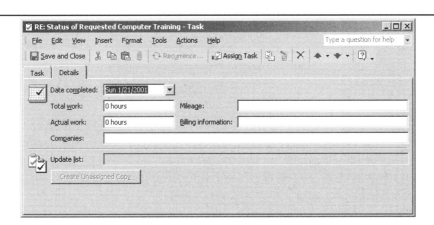

FIGURE 34.6

You can track additional information about a completed task on the Details tab of the Task form.

On this tab, you can record the date the task was completed, the planned number of hours (Outlook will translate to days), the actual number of hours, and other billing information you may want to track, such as the number of miles traveled on the job. If you have to submit an expense or billing statement at the end of the month, this is a great way to track the information you need.

Scheduling Your Time in Calendar

Calendar

When you first enter the Calendar by clicking the Calendar icon on the Outlook bar or choosing View ➢ Go To ➢ Calendar from the menu, Outlook displays Day/Week/Month view, seen in Figure 34.7.

FIGURE 34.7

The Calendar's Day/Week/Month view

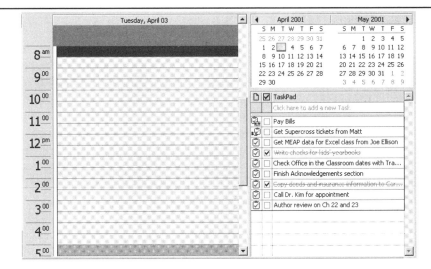

This view is actually a combination of a daily calendar, a monthly calendar, called the Date Navigator, and a list of tasks on the TaskPad. Within this view, you can easily switch from Day view to Work Week view, Week view, or Month view using buttons on the Standard toolbar.

The first button, Day, is the default view. The next button, Work Week, displays a work week of five days. If your work week is made up of different days, you can customize the week, using the Calendar options. (See "Configuring the Calendar" later in this chapter.) The Week button shows all seven days of the week in the typical week-at-a-glance format. The Month button displays a month at a time, alternating gray and white backgrounds to differentiate the months. Personal preference dictates which view you use most frequently. Choose the view that gives you the best sense of where you have to be and what you have to do.

Using the Date Navigator

The Date Navigator not only shows you the monthly calendar but also lets you select days to view in the calendar itself.

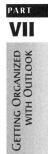

Click any date in the Date Navigator and that date becomes visible in the Information Viewer. Click the left and right arrows next to the month headings to select a different month. To select an entire week, move your pointer to the left side of the Date Navigator. The pointer changes position and points toward the Date Navigator. Click your mouse to select the week. To select multiple weeks, hold your mouse button down and drag, as shown here.

It's also easy to compare nonconsecutive days. Click one day and hold the Ctrl key down on the keyboard before selecting the next day.

To move quickly to a different month, click on the month name and select another month from the list. If the month you want is not immediately visible among the months displayed, pretend there is a scroll bar and drag outside the list.

Moving the mouse pointer farther away from the list increases the speed of the scroll. To slow down the scroll rate, move the mouse pointer closer to the list. To move to a previous month, position the mouse pointer above the list.

Any time you want to move quickly back to the current date, click the Today button on the Standard toolbar.

EXPERT TIP If you prefer to display only one month in the Date Navigator, move your mouse pointer to the left side of the Navigator. The pointer changes to a resize arrow; drag the border of the Date Navigator to the right until only one month is visible. To display more months, drag the border of the Date Navigator down or to the left.

Scheduling Appointments

Scheduling an appointment is as easy as clicking in the appointment slot in the Day view and entering the information. Once you have finished the entry, point to the lower border of the appointment slot and, with the two-headed arrow pointer, drag to identify the end time of the appointment. Drop the blue line just above the desired end time as shown in Figure 34.8.

FIGURE 34.8

Dragging to identify the appointment's end time

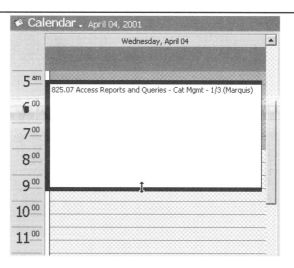

To change the start time of the appointment, drag the blue line above the appointment slot. If you want to maintain the length of the appointment but alter the start and end times, point to the blue line on the left side of the appointment and, with the four-headed arrow, drag the entire appointment to a new time. Once you begin dragging, the four-headed arrow changes shape to a pointer with a move box.

To change the appointment to a different day, drag the appointment with the four-headed arrow to the new date in the Date Navigator.

 NOTE To change the date of an appointment by dragging to a new date, the new date must be displayed in the Date Navigator. If the desired month is not visible, you must change the date by opening the Appointment form.

Entering an Appointment in the Appointment Form

When you want to enter more details about an appointment, double-click the appointment in the Information Viewer to open the Appointment form shown in Figure 34.9. In addition to the Subject and Start and End times, the Appointment form allows you to enter a location, to set a reminder, color code, and to enter other notes about the appointment.

FIGURE 34.9

The Calendar's Appointment form

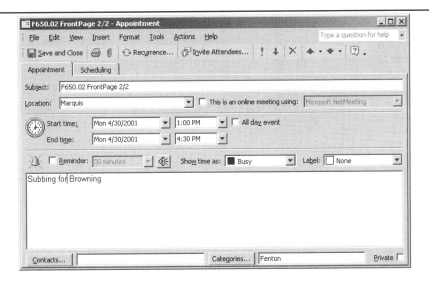

Click the This Is An Online Meeting check box if the meeting will occur over the Internet (for more information about online meetings, see Chapter 27, "Collaborating in Office XP").

To set the start and end times in an Appointment form, click the down arrow to the right of the Start Time and End Time fields. The first arrow opens a calendar from which you can select the date for the appointment. Use the left and right arrows next to the month name to select from a different month.

The arrow to the right of the second field opens a list of times. Be careful to select the correct AM or PM time, or you may be expecting to have lunch some day at midnight.

Managing Reminders

One of the biggest advantages of using an electronic calendar is that it can automatically remind you when it's time to go to your appointments. The default reminder is set for 15 minutes prior to a scheduled appointment, but you can select any time from 0 minutes to up to two days from the drop-down list, or you can type any reminder time in the text box. To turn off the reminder, click the check box to the left of the Reminder field.

At the scheduled time, the reminder appears as a small dialog box in whatever application is running at the time (as long as Outlook is running in the background). Outlook 2002 now uses a single window for all reminders, whether they're for appointments, events, or tasks. Figure 34.10 shows a reminder window with one active task and one appointment.

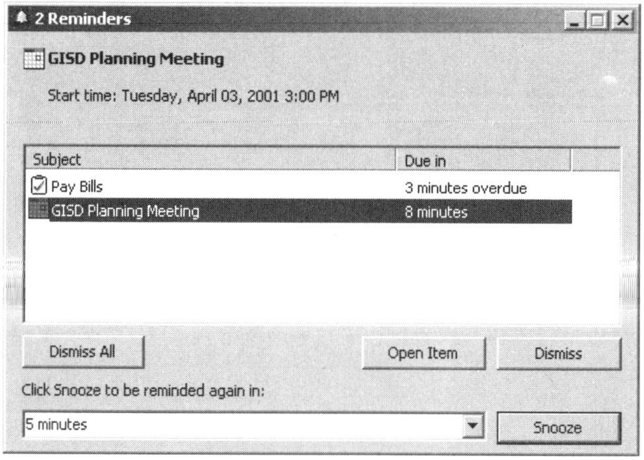

FIGURE 34.10

Outlook 2002 lets you handle reminders more efficiently by allowing you to deal with them all at once.

2 Reminders

GISD Planning Meeting

Start time: Tuesday, April 03, 2001 3:00 PM

Subject	Due in
☑ Pay Bills	3 minutes overdue
GISD Planning Meeting	8 minutes

Dismiss All   Open Item   Dismiss

Click Snooze to be reminded again in:

5 minutes   Snooze

When Outlook displays the Reminder window, choose one of the following options:

- Click Dismiss to dismiss the selected reminder, in which case Outlook assumes you are on your way to the appointment (or have tackled the task) and won't bother you again.

- Click Dismiss All to dismiss all displayed reminders. Outlook won't remind you about these items again.

- Select an item and click Snooze to be reminded again in a designated amount of time. To use this option, choose the desired time interval from the Click Snooze To Be Reminded Again In drop-down list and then click the Snooze button.

 TIP You can hold Ctrl or Shift to select multiple items for snoozing.

- Select one or more items and click the Open Item button to open the Appointment or Task form so you can review it and make changes if you wish.

When the Reminder dialog box opens, clicking anywhere outside the dialog box moves it to the Windows Taskbar. You can then open it at any time to respond to the reminder.

By default, an appointment reminder is accompanied by the Windows "ding." You can change the sound, as described in the "Setting Reminders" earlier in the Tasks section of this chapter. When you have set the Sound Reminder options, click OK to return to the Appointment form.

Scheduling Recurring Appointments

You probably have appointments that occur on a regular basis—for example, a weekly staff meeting, a daily project review meeting, or a monthly district sales meeting. With Outlook's Calendar, you can set up a meeting once and make it automatically recur in your calendar. Recurring appointments can be set up in the same way as recurring tasks described earlier in this chapter. The only difference is that you have to enter a Start and End time and Duration as shown in Figure 34.11.

FIGURE 34.11

Enter a Start and End time and Duration to set up a recurring appointment.

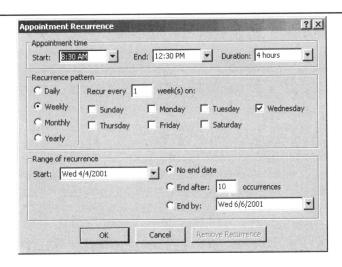

Scheduling Events

An event is an appointment that has no start or end time, such as a holiday, anniversary, or any other day that you want to note. To schedule an event, open an Appointment form, enter the subject and date information, and then click the All Day Event check box. This removes the Start Time and End Time fields from the Appointment form. You can set a reminder for an event and set a Recurrence Pattern just as you would for any other appointment.

Outlook assumes that an event does not occupy your time and therefore shows your time as Free. You may want to change this, however. For example, if the event you are entering is your vacation, you could set the Show Time As field to Out Of The Office.

Because there are no times associated with an event, events are displayed differently than regular appointments in the Information Viewer. In the Day view, an event appears at the top of the day's schedule. In the Week and Month views, events are displayed in bordered boxes, such as those shown in Figure 34.12.

FIGURE 34.12

In Month view, you can easily distinguish events by the borders around them.

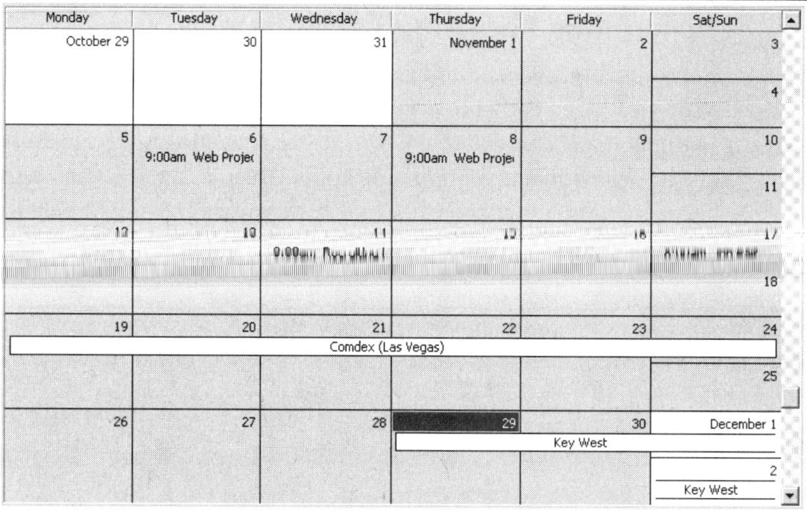

Scheduling a Multiple-Day Event

Multiple-day events are scheduled activities that have no set start and end times and span across several days. To enter such an event, open the Appointment form and set the start and end dates to coincide with the actual dates of the event.

MASTERING THE OPPORTUNITIES

Scheduling Time to Complete a Task

To help you manage your time more effectively, Outlook displays the TaskPad as part of the default Calendar view. This allows you to schedule time to work on individual tasks.

To schedule time to work on a task, display the day and select the time in the Information Viewer. Drag the task from the TaskPad to the designated time. Outlook creates an appointment based on the task and opens an Appointment form with the contents of the task already included in it. Set the other options just as you would for any other appointment.

When you complete the task, mark it complete on your Task list just as you would any other task. You'll be surprised at how much easier it is to check off items on your Task list when you schedule time in your daily calendar to complete them.

Color Coding Your Calendar

NEW▶

If you typically display your calendar in Day/Week/Month view, you'll love Outlook 2002's new color-coding feature for appointments and events. You can choose from 10 colors, and each color comes with a label such as Business, Important, Needs Preparation, Phone Call, and more. Naturally, you can edit these labels to fit your own business and personal needs. We found it handy to assign a color to each of our trainers. Now we can see who's doing a particular class at a glance.

There are two ways to color-code calendar items: manually or automatically, using rules. Before you decide which method to use, keep in mind that:

- Manual coloring always takes precedence over coloring applied by rules. So if you've applied manual coloring to a calendar item, you cannot format it with automatic coloring.
- If you've given another person access to your calendar through a public folder or other means, only manually assigned colors are visible. Automatic coloring is only visible to the person who applied it.
- You must be in Day/Week/Month view to see any coloring.

Before you apply calendar coloring, you should modify the list of labels so they reflect your own business practices. To do so, click the Calendar Coloring button on the Standard toolbar and choose Edit Labels. The Edit Calendar Labels dialog box opens as shown in Figure 34.13. Simply select the text of the label you wish to change and overtype it with your own text. Click OK when you're finished editing labels.

FIGURE 34.13

Modify the default color labels to make the most of Outlook 2002's new calendar coloring feature.

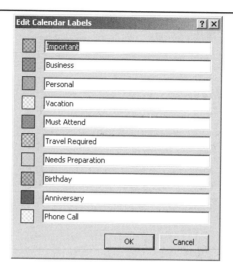

To assign a color manually, do any of the following:

- Select an appointment or event in the Day, Week, or Month area of the Information Viewer. Click the Calendar Coloring button on the Standard toolbar and choose one of the colors from the list.

- Right-click a calendar item and choose Label; then click the color you'd like to use.

- Double-click a calendar item to open the Appointment form. Click the Label drop-down list and choose a color from there.

To assign a color automatically, follow these steps:

1. Right-click a calendar item and click Automatic Formatting, or click the Calendar Coloring button on the Standard toolbar and choose Automatic Formatting. In either case, the Automatic Formatting dialog box opens.

2. Click Add to create a rule, and then type a name for the rule in the Name field.

3. Click the Condition button to establish criteria for the rule.

 NOTE See Chapter 35 for more information about creating rules and setting conditions.

4. Select a label from the Label drop-down list and click OK to apply the rule.

Remove calendar coloring by selecting the appointment and changing the color label to None. This works even if the coloring you have applied is the result of a rule. To delete all coloring associated with a rule, delete the rule. Right-click an appointment and choose Automatic Formatting from the shortcut menu. Select the rule and click the Delete button inside the Automatic Formatting dialog box.

Configuring the Calendar

Because people work very different schedules these days, Outlook has included a number of options that let you define the days you work, the hours that you want to display in your calendar, and on which day your work week starts. To change the Calendar options, choose Tools ➢ Options on the menu. Click the Calendar Options button to open the dialog box shown in Figure 34.14.

FIGURE 34.14

Calendar Options let you customize Calendar to fit your needs.

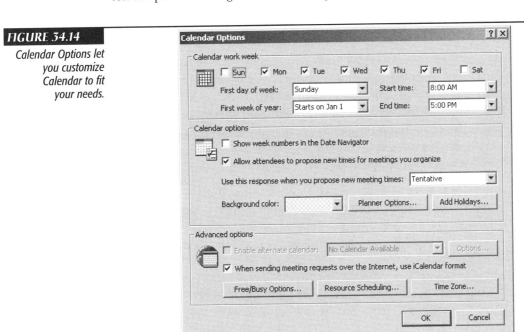

Set the Calendar options as follows:

Calendar Work Week Options

- Check the boxes for the days of the week to designate the days that make up your work week. Set the start and end times of your typical day using the Start Time and End Time fields.

- To keep your calendar in line with your staff schedules, you may want to indicate that your calendar starts on the first four-day week or first full week of the year rather than January 1. Make this selection from the First Week Of Year drop-down list.

Calendar Options

- Enable the Show Week Numbers In The Date Navigator check box if you need to know what week (1–52) you are in for planning purposes.

NEW▶

- If you want others to have the flexibility of suggesting alternative times for meetings you organize, enable that check box. (For more on the meeting planner, see "Using the Calendar in a Workgroup," later in this chapter.)

- Choose a default response for times when you propose alternative meeting times. Click the drop-down arrow next to Use This Response When You Propose New Meeting Times and choose from the list.

- Click the Background Color drop-down arrow to designate a different color for your calendar's background in Day and Work Week views.

NEW▶

- In Outlook 2002, you can display lunar calendar information and make appointments based on that calendar. If you've installed any of the languages that support a lunar calendar (Arabic, Chinese, Hebrew, Japanese, or Korean), you can turn on the Enable Alternate Calendar feature and choose the calendar you'd like to use.

NEW▶

- Click the Planner Options button to choose certain behaviors for the Meeting Planner (discussed later in this chapter).

- Click the Add Holidays button to add a variety of religious and national holidays to your calendar (see the next section).

Advanced Options

- Selecting When Send Meeting Requests Over The Internet, Use iCalendar Format converts appointment items into a format that can be used by people who don't run Outlook.

- Click the Free/Busy Options button to control how far in advance your free/busy information is available for others on your Exchange Server and how frequently it updates information with the server. If you want to share your free/busy information with others over the Internet, you can enter the URL where your information is available. See "Checking Others' Schedules First" later in this chapter for more about free/busy information.

- Click the Resource Scheduling button to set options for scheduling resources such as meeting rooms, AV equipment, and the like.
- Click the Time Zone button to adjust the time zone you are in and set a second time zone to view simultaneously—an invaluable option if you schedule meetings in one time zone that you plan to attend in another.

Adding Holidays to Your Calendar

You can add national and religious holidays to your calendar, including Christian, Jewish, and Islamic holidays. Choose Tools ➢ Options and on the Preferences tab, click the Calendar Options button. In the Calendar Options dialog box, click the Add Holidays button.

While it only takes a few clicks to add all the Yemeni holidays to your calendar, if you decide you really don't care about holidays in Yemen, it takes a little more effort to remove them from the calendar. You can delete them one by one for each of the three years of holidays Outlook adds, or you can delete all the holidays as a group and then add back in the ones you want. To quickly delete all the holidays in your calendar, choose View ➢ Current View ➢ By Category. All the holidays are in the Holiday category. Select the Holiday group heading and press Delete.

EXPERT TIP Outlook only imports holidays into the main calendar folder, so attempting to add holidays to a calendar subfolder or public folder only results in duplicate holidays being added to your main calendar. To have holidays appear in calendar subfolders, move or copy them to the subfolder after first adding them to the main folder. To do this, switch to By Categories view in the main calendar folder. Right-drag the holiday group to the subfolder and choose either Move or Copy from the shortcut menu that appears.

Printing the Calendar

Before you can print your calendar, you need to decide what style you want to use. By default, the view that is visible on your screen is the view that prints. For example, if you are in Day view, you'll print all your appointments for that day.

If you are more particular about your calendar's layout, choose File ➢ Page Setup to have a world of options available to you. Before a dialog box even opens, you are presented with a list of choices.

Choose the primary layout that you want for your calendar. The Page Setup options you see depend on the style you choose. Figure 34.15 shows the Format options for the Weekly Style.

FIGURE 34.15

*Page Setup options
for the Weekly Style*

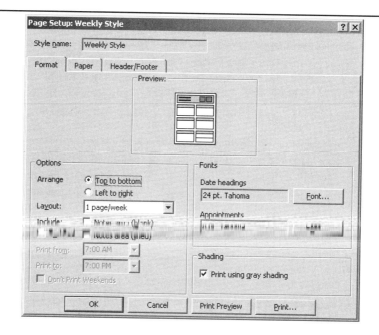

The first tab of the Page Setup dialog box gives you Format options. Here you can enable various check boxes to indicate what sections you would like to appear on the calendar page. You can even include an area for those handwritten notes. At any point in the Page Setup process, you can click the Print Preview button to see how your printed document will appear. If you are satisfied, click the Print button—if it needs more work, click Page Setup and you're brought right back here.

The Paper tab of the Page Setup dialog box is especially critical if you don't plan to print your calendar on standard 8.5" × 11" paper. You can set the paper type, size, dimensions, orientation, and margins, and you can identify what tray of the printer the paper is in.

> **TIP** If you are using a planner from the big three—Day-Timer, Day-Runner, or Franklin—take special note of the Page Size list. Your planner is probably listed, so you'll be able to select an exact match.

Headers and Footers

The Header/Footer tab of the Page Setup dialog box closely resembles Excel's dialog box for defining headers and footers (see Chapter 13, "Creating and Printing Excel Worksheets"). If you're familiar with Excel—or headers and footers in any application, for that matter—this will be a snap.

A *header* appears on the top of every page of your document—in this case, the calendar. A *footer* appears on the bottom of every page. Typically, you'll find the title and subtitle in the header. By default, Outlook includes the User Name (that's generally you), the Page Number, and the Date Printed in the footer. However, you can put any information anywhere you want it.

The header and footer sections are each divided into three subsections: left, center, and right. Click in any of the six text boxes to enter text in that section. Outlook provides you with placeholders for five variable fields that you can insert in either the header or the footer.

Page Number Inserts the actual page number of the document

Total Pages Can be combined with the page number placeholder to create expressions like "Page 1 of 4" (Page [*Page #*] of [*Total Pages*])

Date Printed Displays the date the calendar was printed, regardless of the date period shown in the calendar

Time Printed Displays the actual time the calendar was printed

User Name Displays the name of the user currently logged in to Outlook

To insert a placeholder, click in the section of the header or footer where you want the placeholder to appear, and then click the placeholder button.

TIP If you're printing a calendar in booklet form, you may want to reverse the header and footer on opposite pages. For example, if the date printed appears on the right side on odd pages, it would appear on the left on even pages. This gives your document a more professionally printed appearance.

When you have finished setting up the Page Setup options, click the Print button to print your calendar.

Creating Your Own Calendar Style

To save time and use a consistent format for your calendar from week to week, you can define a Page Setup style to use every time you print your calendar. Follow the steps below to define your own print style that will appear in the Page Setup menu list:

1. Choose File ➤ Page Setup ➤ Define Print Styles.

2. Choose to edit an existing style or to create a new style by copying an existing style.

3. If you choose to copy an existing style, enter a name for the new style in the Style Name text box at the top of the Page Setup dialog box.

4. Create your custom style using the Page Setup options.

5. Click OK to save your changes.

6. Select your newly created style from the Page Setup menu.

To delete a custom style, choose File ➤ Page Setup ➤ Define Print Styles, select the style you want to delete, and click Delete.

 TIP If you are editing an existing style, the original style will no longer be available. However, you can reset the original style by choosing Define Print Styles from the Page Setup menu, selecting the style, and clicking the Reset button.

Using the Calendar in a Workgroup

If you've ever worked in an office that holds lots of meetings, then you know first-hand the inordinate amount of time that is spent scheduling and rescheduling meetings. Some office studies have found that nearly 30 percent of secretarial time is spent scheduling meetings for managers and administrators. Group scheduling tools are one of the fastest-growing software markets today. Companies all over the globe are recognizing the need to simplify the process of scheduling meetings. Outlook is ready to address this challenge, as the Calendar module offers extensive tools for workgroup scheduling.

Planning a Meeting with Others

Outlook 2002 offers several ways to invite others to attend a meeting. The simplest way is to click the drop-down arrow on the New button and choose Meeting Request from the list of choices. This opens the Meeting e-mail message form, shown in Figure 34.16.

FIGURE 34.16

A meeting request message form

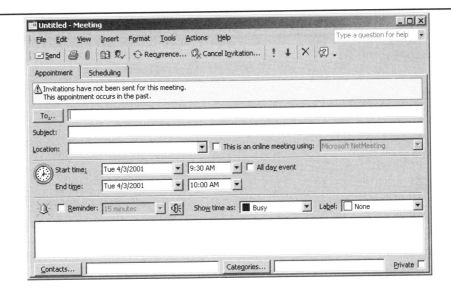

You'll see some differences between the Meeting form and the standard e-mail message form. First, notice the message informing you that invitations for this meeting have not yet been sent. Of course, you already knew that, but you can always find the status of an invitation here even after you send it. Second, in addition to the To and Subject fields, there is a Location field for you to identify where the meeting will take place. The other fields on the Meeting form are similar to a typical Appointment form.

To create a meeting request, follow these steps:

1. Click the down arrow on the New button and choose Meeting Request.

2. Click the To button to open the Select Attendees And Resources dialog box. (You'll probably recognize it as the familiar Select Names dialog box you've used many times in addressing e-mail.)

3. Double-click the names of those people whose attendance at the meeting is required.

4. If a person's attendance is optional, click their name and click the Optional button.

5. If your Microsoft Exchange administrator set up meeting rooms and other resources with their own mailboxes, select the resource you want to assign to the meeting and click the Resources button.

6. If someone you want to invite to a meeting is not in your address book, click the New button, select New Contact as the entry type, and click OK. Enter information about the contact in the Properties dialog box. Click Save And Close to add this person to your address book.

7. Click OK to close the Select Attendees And Resources dialog box and return to the Meeting form.

8. Enter the Subject and Location, and click the check box if this is an online meeting.

9. Fill in the Start Time, End Time, Reminder, and Show Time As fields just as you would for any other appointment.

10. If the meeting is going to be regularly scheduled, you can click the Recurrence button and set up the Recurrence pattern (see "Scheduling Recurring Appointments" earlier in the chapter).

11. Click the Send button to send out the meeting requests.

 NOTE Outlook automatically creates meeting and task requests in rich-text format, regardless of the default format you have set.

Responding to a Meeting Request

NEW▶

Each person you invite to the meeting receives an e-mail message labeled *Meeting Request*. When they open the message, they see the information about the meeting. Once they've decided whether they can attend, they can click one of the Accept, Decline, or Tentative buttons at the top of the Meeting form. And now, in Outlook 2002, there's another option: Propose New Meeting Time. Users who choose this last option can even see free/busy information of other invitees on their Exchange Server.

After an attendee clicks one of these four response buttons, Outlook generates an e-mail message back to you, the meeting request originator, indicating whether this person can attend or, if the attendee clicked Propose New Meeting Time, an alternate meeting time and/or date. If the person accepted the meeting request, it's automatically placed on their calendar. In addition, all of the responses are automatically tabulated, so there is no need to keep a manual count. It really couldn't be easier. To see a list of attendees and their responses to date, all you have to do is open the appointment in your calendar and click the Tracking tab, shown in Figure 34.17.

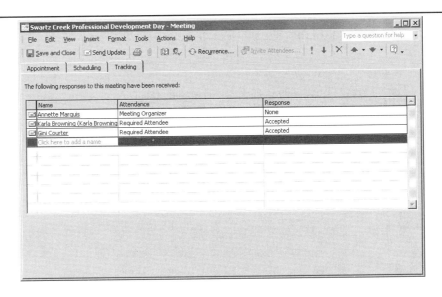

If, after seeing who has accepted your invitation, you decide to invite other people to this meeting, click the Invite Others button on the Scheduling tab. You'll then be able to generate new e-mail meeting requests.

That's all there is it is to it. Never again will you have to make 25 phone calls to get four people to attend a meeting. Now you'll actually have time to get some real work done.

Checking Others' Schedules First

Even the steps outlined above for requesting a meeting could backfire if you find that the majority of the people you need at your meeting can't attend at the time you requested. It might be easier to check individual schedules first and schedule the meeting at a time when all of your key people can attend. A lot of people get nervous when you talk about making their schedules available for others to see. Outlook has found the best of both worlds. It allows you to look at the individual's *free/busy* information; you can see when an individual is free, busy, out of the office, or tentatively scheduled. You cannot, however, see what they are doing or how they are spending their time (unless they have given you permission to do so). This seems to relieve most people's anxiety about Big Brother looking over their shoulder and still allows for the greatest success in scheduling meetings with the first request.

NEW▶

To check to see when someone is available to meet, open a Meeting form and select the Scheduling tab. The Scheduling tab, shown in Figure 34.18, lists all attendees in the left column. When you first open this page, Outlook automatically goes out to the network to gather the most current free/busy information. The grid on the right side of the page shows each individual's free/busy status.

NOTE When you click the Scheduling tab, Outlook immediately searches the network for your meeting invitees. If these folks aren't on your network, Outlook invites you to join the new (and free!) Microsoft Office Internet Free/Busy Service. You can click Join to sign up yourself, but you must ask your meeting invitees to do the same or you still won't be able to see their free/busy information.

FIGURE 34.18

The Scheduling tab of the Meeting form shows free/busy information.

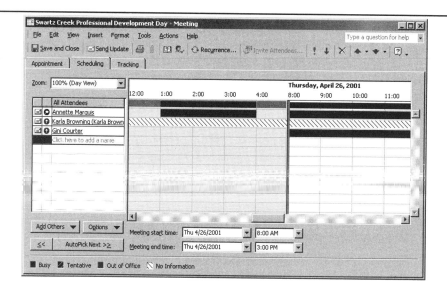

An individual's free time is not marked in the grid. If they are out of the office, a maroon bar extends across the time that they will be gone. If they are busy, you see a blue bar, and if they are tentatively scheduled, you see a slashed blue bar.

NEW▶

Point to any horizontal bar to see a screen tip with details of any appointment you have permission to view. If you find these screen tips annoying, turn them off by choosing Tools ➤ Options ➤ Calendar Options. Click the Planner Options button and disable the Show Popup Calendar Details check box.

The white vertical bar represents the duration of the meeting. The green border on the left indicates the start time, and the brown border represents the end time of the meeting.

The key to working with the Scheduling grid is to start by manually setting your preferred meeting time in the Meeting Start Time and Meeting End Time text boxes. Even if the desired attendees are not available at this time, this sets a beginning date and the duration of the meeting. Click the AutoPick Next button to locate the first time when all attendees are available. Notice that the Meeting Start Time and Meeting End Time text boxes change to correspond to the time indicated by the grid. If the first time that everyone is available is not agreeable to you, continue clicking AutoPick Next until you find a good time.

If, at any point, you decide to invite others to the meeting, click the Add Others button on the Scheduling tab. Click the Options button to access the following four options:

Show Only Working Hours Shows only work hours in the calendar

Choose Show Calendar Details Displays the details of free/busy time, but only if the selected attendees have given you permission to do so

TIP If you'd like this option on by default, minimize this scheduling window and choose Tools ➢ Options ➢ Calendar Options. Click the Planner Options button and enable the Show Calendar Details In The Grid check box.

AutoPick Determines whose schedules must be free for AutoPick to select an available time slot.

Update Free/Busy Forces Outlook to update the free/busy information on the server

As soon as you find an agreeable time for everyone you want to invite, return to the Appointment tab (if you wish) to verify that the start and end times have been adjusted accordingly. Then send the attendees' e-mail message. Now you can be pretty confident that the attendees will accept the meeting request.

EXPERT TIP Typically, Outlook only updates free/busy information from the Exchange Server every 15 minutes (that's the default Calendar option setting). If you are concerned that one of your invitees might be scheduling something at the same time, click the Option button on the Scheduling tab of the Appointment form and choose Update Free/Busy information. This gives you the most current data available.

Canceling a Meeting

Suppose you need to cancel a meeting that you arranged. Don't despair, you still don't have to make a slew of phone calls. Open the meeting in your calendar and click the Cancel Invitations button on the Meeting form toolbar. This generates e-mail messages to all attendees indicating that the meeting has been canceled. You are even given an opportunity to explain why you are canceling the meeting. You can then follow it up with another invitation to the meeting at the new date and time. What used to take hours is now handled in just a few minutes. Everybody's notified, everyone's calendar is updated, and no one had to be interrupted from their work to make it happen.

NOTE At last! Now Outlook gives you the ability to combine schedules for multiple people (and/or resources) into one window. This is clearly one of the most exciting new features in Outlook 2002. Suppose you regularly need to see schedules for all people in a particular department; or perhaps you need to periodically view availability of the conference rooms in your building. Group Scheduling makes it possible. For more about creating group schedules, see Chapter 27, "Collaborating in Office XP."

CHAPTER 35

WORKING BEHIND THE SCENES IN OUTLOOK

FEATURING

- Managing data and files in Outlook

- Creating and using rules to manage mail

- Moving and copying items

- Importing and exporting Outlook data

- Archiving and backing up your Outlook data

- Customizing Outlook to work the way you do

- Using Outlook on a Microsoft Exchange Server

Nowhere does Outlook do a better job of living up to its reputation as a desktop information manager than in its folder and file management features. You'll never have to launch Explorer or My Computer again. All of your file management needs can be accommodated from within Outlook. And when you want to exchange data with others over the Internet or a network, Outlook is ready to serve. Collaboration has never been easier. In this chapter, we'll introduce you to Outlook's powerful data management features, how to create custom views, what Outlook options are worth changing, and how to manage permissions when you want to share Outlook data. We'll also show you how to take all of your Outlook data on the road with you and synchronize it when you return home.

Managing Data and Files in Outlook

Whether you've realized it or not, each of the Outlook modules is organized as a folder, with all of the properties of other folders on your hard drive or network. Anything you already know about file management in Windows Explorer applies to working with folders and items in Outlook. You can move files, copy them, rename them, create subfolders under them, and view them in different ways. The easiest way to grasp the Outlook folder structure is to choose Folder List from the View menu. This opens a third pane in the Outlook window that clearly shows the folders and subfolders that make up the Outlook modules (see Figure 35.1). Click any folder to see its contents.

FIGURE 35.1

The Folder List view of Outlook

To create a new folder to organize Outlook items, follow these steps:

1. Choose File ➢ New ➢ Folder to open the Create New Folder dialog box shown in Figure 35.2.

2. Enter a name for the new folder.

3. Select the type of Outlook item you plan to keep in the folder.

4. Choose where you'd like to place the folder.

5. Click OK.

FIGURE 35.2

*In the Create New
Folder dialog box,
create an Outlook
subfolder to organize
your items.*

 MASTERING TROUBLESHOOTING

Why Can't I Access My New Contacts Folder from the Address Book When I Want to Send E-mail?

If you create a Contacts folder, you have to make it available as an Outlook address book in order to access the e-mail addresses from the Select Name dialog box when you are creating messages. Follow these steps to make a folder available as an Outlook address book:

1. Right-click the new Contacts subfolder and choose Properties from the shortcut menu.

2. Choose the Outlook Address Book tab of the Properties dialog box (discussed further in "Properties and Other Options" later in this chapter).

Continued ▶

3. Click the Show This Folder As An Email Address Book check box.

4. Enter a different name for the address book, if desired. This is the name that will appear in the Select Names dialog box and other dialog boxes that display the list of address books. Changing the name does not change the folder name—only the name of the address book created from the folder.

5. Click OK to save the changes and close the Properties dialog box.

Moving and Copying Items into Outlook Folders

To move existing Outlook items into a subfolder, open the folder that contains the items and drag the items to the new folder in the Folder List. To copy the items, hold down the Shift key while you drag. To select several noncontiguous items to move or copy, hold down the Ctrl key before selecting. To select contiguous items, select the first item and hold down the Shift key before selecting the last item in the list.

Deleting Items and Folders

To delete an item or a folder, select what you want to delete and click the Delete button from the Outlook menu. Deleted items and folders go into the Deleted Items folder, visible in the Folder List. The Deleted Items folder is similar to the Recycle Bin in that items you delete go there before being lost forever. There are some important differences, however, between the Recycle Bin and the Deleted Items folder.

First of all, files remain in the Recycle Bin until you empty it or restore the files to their original location. By contrast, items can be removed from the Deleted Items folder in four ways:

- By emptying the folder. To do this, right-click the folder and choose Empty Deleted Items Folder.

- Automatically upon exiting Outlook. To set this option, choose Tools ➣ Options and click the Other tab. Click the Empty The Deleted Items Folder Upon Exiting check box.

- By archiving the folder. Archiving cleans out items that are older than the time period you specify. See "Archiving Items" later in this chapter.

- By moving the items to another folder.

The Recycle Bin and the Deleted Items folder also differ in that files erroneously deleted from the Recycle Bin may be recoverable using file-recovery software, such as

Norton Utilities or the Windows Undelete utility. Because Outlook items are stored in folders known as MAPI data stores, or containers—essentially, records in a database—rather than independent files, items deleted from the Deleted Items folder cannot be recovered.

Sharing Outlook Data with Another Outlook Item

Once you start working with multiple Outlook modules, you can be even more efficient by tying existing items together. For example, to create a task related to a scheduled meeting, drag the appointment into the Task folder. Outlook opens a new Task form and inserts all the text from the appointment into the task. If you receive an e-mail about an appointment or want to schedule time to complete a task, drag the Outlook item into the new activity to make sure you have the information when you need it.

MASTERING THE OPPORTUNITIES

Maintaining Information Away from the Office

If you carry a personal digital assistant (PDA), such as a 3Com Palm computing device, and do not synchronize your e-mail, you can still carry the contents of e-mail messages with you on the road. Just drag the message into the Notes folder. All of the contents will be placed in a note, and the next time you synchronize, it will be transferred to your PDA. Copying and pasting the contents of a Word or Excel document into a note is another way to have the information you need without carrying a backbreaking briefcase everywhere you go. You'll learn more about synchronizing later in this chapter.

Archiving Items

The more you use Outlook, the more Outlook items you create. Pretty soon, your collection of Outlook items can become pretty unmanageable. Organizing Outlook items into subfolders is one way to keep things under control, but that won't solve the performance problems you may begin to experience when your folders become unwieldy. Deleting unneeded items can be helpful in maintaining manageable folders, but more than likely the day will come when you'll need something you deleted and have no way to retrieve it. So what's the answer? Archiving old Outlook e-mail, appointments, tasks, and Journal entries keeps Outlook fit and trim and still gives you access to your old data if you need it.

NEW▶ Outlook's archiving feature requires a few setup steps the first time you use it. However, archiving has been simplified in Office XP because you can now set Default Archive Settings that apply to all folders except where you've customized the settings. If you change the global settings, the changes apply to all folders that use the default settings. To set up archiving, follow these steps:

1. Go to Tools ➢ Options ➢ Other and click the AutoArchive button. Check to see that the global options shown in Figure 35.3 are set, and close the AutoArchive and Options dialog boxes.

2. To change the properties on an individual folder, right-click each folder (and subfolder) you want to archive and choose Properties. Choose the AutoArchive tab and set the individual folder AutoArchive settings.

3. To initiate the first archiving, choose File ➢ Archive to open the Archive dialog box.

4. From the Archive dialog box shown in Figure 35.4, choose to archive the selected folder and its subfolders only or to archive all folders according to their AutoArchive settings. If you do not choose to archive all folders according their AutoArchive settings, designate how old the items that you archive should be.

5. Click OK to begin archiving.

While Outlook is archiving in the background, you'll see a message in the status bar, and Archive Folders temporarily appears above Personal Folders in your file list.

FIGURE 35.3

You can set the AutoArchive options to archive old Outlook items automatically.

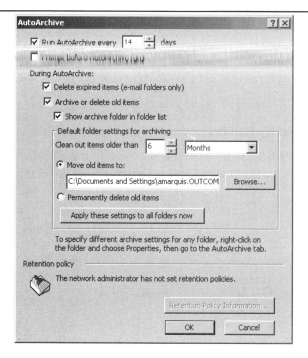

FIGURE 35.4

When you initiate archiving manually, you can choose to archive just one folder or all folders according to the AutoArchive settings.

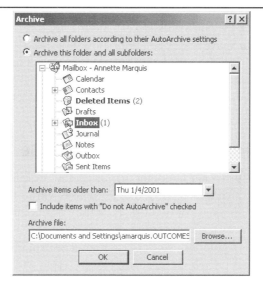

From this point on, AutoArchiving will commence the first time you launch Outlook after the interval you set in the AutoArchive options.

EXPERT TIP   If you would rather be prompted each time before AutoArchiving begins, be sure that the Prompt Before AutoArchive Runs option under Tools ➢ Options ➢ Other ➢ AutoArchive is selected.

Retrieving Archived Items

When you need an archived item, all you need to know is where you stored the archive folders. Choose File ➢ Open and select Personal Folders File. Find the file named archive.pst.

TIP   If you don't remember where you filed archive.pst, try the default file location for your operating system:
Windows 2000—C:\Documents and Settings*yourusername*\Local Settings\ Application Data\Microsoft\Outlook\Archive.pst
Windows NT—C:\winnt\profiles*yourusername*\Local Settings\Application Data\Microsoft\Outlook\Archive.pst
Windows 98—C:\Windows\Local Settings\Application Data\Microsoft\ Outlook\Archive.pst
If it's not in this location, use Windows' Search (Start ➢ Search) to track it down.

When you locate the file, click OK and Outlook displays Archive Folders in the file list. Click the plus symbol to expand the list, locate the item you need and drag it into your active folder, and then print it or commit it to memory. When you have found the information you need, you can drag it into your active mailbox folders, print it, or just read and close it. To close the Archive folders when you are finished with them, right-click Archive Folders in the Folder List and choose Close "Archive Folders."

Managing Windows Files and Folders

Outlook is not just a tool for managing and organizing Outlook items; you can conduct all of your file management activities within Outlook. To access files and folders on your computer or network, click the Other Shortcuts button on the Outlook bar. Click the My Computer, My Documents, and Favorites icons to see all of the files you would expect to see using My Computer or Explorer in Windows. If you turn on the Folder List (View ➢ Folder List), you get a split window just like you would find in Explorer, with folders in the left pane and folder contents in the right pane. Move, copy, rename, and create folders and delete files using the same methods as you would in Windows.

The key advantages to managing files and folders in Outlook are that you can customize the way you see your files and you can print your file list. You may choose to group files by file type or view a folder in Timeline view to see what files were created or modified during a specific period (for more about Outlook views, see "Creating Custom Views" later in this chapter). When you need a hard copy of your file list, set up the view the way you want it and click the Print button on the toolbar. Try doing that in Explorer!

Using Rules to Manage Mail

As you are struggling to keep up with the daily avalanche of e-mail, wouldn't it be nice to have a personal assistant who sorts and processes e-mail for you? Well, look no further! In Chapter 32, "Using Outlook As a Communications Tool," we introduced you to the Junk Mail and Adult Content Mail filters. Those are just a couple of the ways you can have Outlook manage your mail for you. Outlook's Rules Wizard can handle all the day-to-day management of your e-mail by sorting mail into folders, forwarding and copying certain mail, deleting junk, and even responding to some mail automatically. To access the Rules Wizard, choose Tools ➢ Rules Wizard from the Inbox. Figure 35.5 shows the Rules Wizard with a number of defined rules.

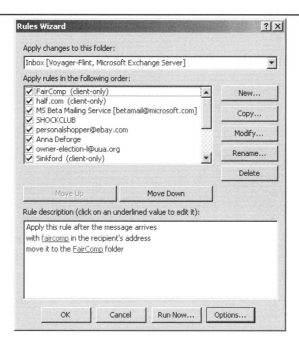

FIGURE 35.5

The Rules Wizard can help you get a handle on your mountain of e-mail.

To create a rule to handle your mail, follow these steps:

1. Open the Inbox and choose Tools ➤ Rules Wizard.

2. Click New and choose to create a rule from one of the templates shown in Figure 35.6 or choose Start From A Blank Rule. We recommend that you use a template until you are comfortable creating rules.

3. Click an underlined value in the Rule Description to edit the rule. For example, if you are using the Move New Messages From Someone template, then click People Or Distribution List and select the address of the person or distribution list that originates the mail. Then click Move It To The Specified Folder and select the folder you want the mail to move to. You can also create a new folder by clicking the New button on the Rules Wizard dialog box that opens.

4. After you specify the Rule Description, click Next.

5. Select any conditions, shown in Figure 35.7, you want checked before the rule is applied. For example, if you only want the mail from this sender moved to the folder you specified if it is addressed only to you, click the Sent Only To Me check box. You can apply several conditions to each rule you create. In this example, From People Or Distribution List is already selected based on the template you chose in Step 2. If an additional value is required based on your

choices, the value is underlined in the Rule Description section at the bottom. After you set the conditions and additional descriptions, click Next.

6. Choose what you want to do with the message. In the example we are using, Move It To The Specified Folder is already selected. You can also choose to have it forwarded to someone else, to notify you with a specific message, or a number of other actions. Remember to identify any values in the Rule Description box if the action you choose requires more detail. Click Next.

7. Identify any exceptions to the rule. For example, perhaps you don't want the message moved to the specified folder if it is marked with High Importance. To designate this, select the Except If It Is Marked As Importance exception. After you set any exceptions, click Next.

8. Enter a name for the rule and indicate whether you would like to run the rule immediately on messages in the Inbox. This is a great way to test the rule to see that it does what you want it to. Click Finish to return to the first Rules Wizard screen.

9. Repeat steps 2–8 to create additional rules.

10. You can change the order in which rules are processed so that a message that might be affected by more than one rule is handled on a priority basis. Click the Move Up and Move Down buttons to rearrange rules.

11. If you'd like to turn a rule off without deleting it, clear the check box in front of it. You can then reselect it when you want the rule to run again.

FIGURE 35.6

Choose one of the predesigned rule templates to create your rule.

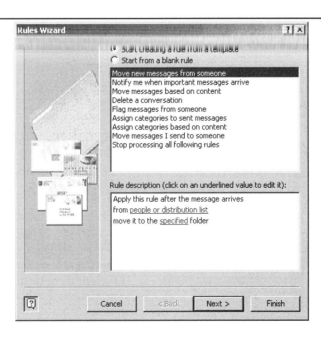

FIGURE 35.7

By applying conditions to the rules you create, you can be specific about when you want the rule to apply.

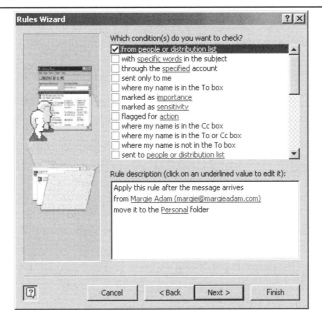

NEW▶   In Outlook 2002, you can now import and export rules. You can import rules that your coworkers have created on other computers and also export rules you've created to other computers, such as a laptop you are taking on the road. Click the Options button on the Rules Wizard dialog box and then choose Import Rules or Export Rules. The Rules Wizard files are saved as RWZ files.

Importing and Exporting Outlook Data

If you already have data in some other contact management or database system, or if you have a need to use Outlook data in some other system, Outlook's Import And Export Wizard can help you get that data where it belongs. Most of the time, this will be contact data—names, addresses, and phone numbers—but you can also import calendar information, tasks, and e-mail messages. Outlook's Import And Export Wizard recognizes data from a wide variety of other applications and can export data in a number of useable formats. In this section, we'll first examine importing from other applications and then look at export options.

Importing Outlook Items

The Import And Export Wizard walks you through the steps to import data from these contact managers:

- ACT! 2.0 and 3.0
- ECCO 2.0, 3.0, and 4.0
- Lotus Organizer 1.0, 1.1, 2.1, and 97
- Microsoft Outlook personal folders
- Schedule+ 1.0 and 7.0
- Sidekick for Windows 2.0

It will also convert data from these file formats:

- dBASE database files
- Microsoft Access
- Microsoft FoxPro
- Schedule Plus Interchange
- Microsoft Excel

If the file format you have isn't on either list, don't despair. Outlook also imports files in standard DOS and Windows formats:

- Comma-separated values (DOS and Windows)
- Tab-separated values (DOS and Windows)

 TIP If you want to import the external data into a separate folder before mixing it with your existing Outlook data, create a new folder prior to starting the Import And Export Wizard.

To import files from any of these formats, begin by choosing File ➢ Import And Export to open the Import And Export Wizard, shown in Figure 35.8. Follow these steps to import data:

1. In the first step of the wizard, choose Import From Another Program Or File, then click the Next button.

2. In the second step of the wizard, select the format for the information you want to import, then click Next.

FIGURE 35.8

Use the Import And Export Wizard to import contacts from another file format.

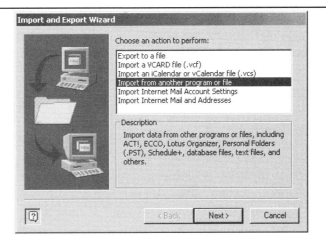

WARNING If you did not originally install the Import/Export file converters for Outlook, you are prompted to do so after the second step of the wizard. To continue, you must have access to the Office XP installation files either on a CD-ROM or through a network installation point. This process installs only the particular converter you need based on your choice in the wizard. If you want to install all of the converters, run the Office installation program to add new features.

3. In the third step of the wizard, select the file you want to import. Either enter the path and filename, or click the Browse button and select the file in the Open dialog box.

4. Before you click Next, you need to choose one of three options for dealing with duplicates—data you've entered in Outlook 2002 that also exist in the file you're importing. Unless you are importing an Outlook personal folder, you can't select records to import. The Duplicate options are designed to deal with these three possible scenarios:

   • If you haven't entered any data in Outlook, or if all the information in the imported file is more accurate than the Outlook information, choose Replace Duplicates With Items Imported.

   • If you've already entered some data into Outlook and kept it up-to-date, you may have correct information in both Outlook and the imported file. For example, if you're importing contact information, Outlook may have Jane Smith's new e-mail address at work, but her home phone number is only in the file you want to import. In this case, choose Allow Duplicates To Be Created. All the contacts in the import file are added to the existing contacts in Outlook. You'll have to check the information in both of Jane Smith's Contact forms, copy either the e-mail address or the home phone number to one of the two forms, and delete the other form.

- If the information in Outlook is the most recent information for each contact, choose Do Not Import Duplicate Items. If a contact already exists in Outlook, it won't be imported from the other file. Only data that are missing in Outlook will be added.

5. In the next step of the Import And Export Wizard, select the destination folder for the external data.

6. The next step of the wizard differs depending on the type of data you are importing. If the data live in a database, such as Access, you can choose in which data table the data you want reside. When you select the data table, the Map Custom Fields button becomes active.

7. You know where the imported data are going; now you can find out where each field belongs in Outlook. Click the Map Custom Fields button to open the Map Custom Fields dialog box, shown in Figure 35.9. The left pane of the dialog box shows the field names and a sample record from the data file being imported. The right pane of the dialog box shows fields in Outlook and the name of the imported field that will be used to fill the Outlook field. For example, the Last Name field from the Excel database will be used to fill the Name field in Outlook. Click the plus sign in front of the Name field, and it expands to show the components of the field. If you're not familiar with the data shown in the sample record, use the Previous or Next button to move to another record in the import file. To map a field, drag the field name from the left pane and place it next to the correct Outlook field in the right pane. After you've made sure all the fields are mapped correctly, click OK to close the Map Custom Fields dialog box.

8. Now click Finish to import the data from the import file and create new Outlook items.

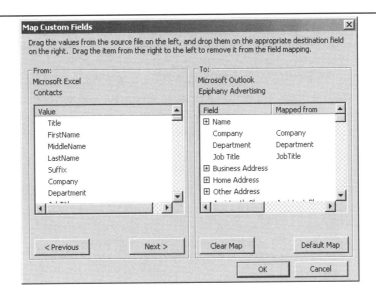

FIGURE 35.9

Use the Map Custom Fields dialog box to assign imported fields to Outlook contact fields.

While Outlook converts the data, a message box appears to show you Outlook's progress. You can't cancel the import, but don't worry, it doesn't take long. You can import hundreds of records in two or three minutes. When Outlook is finished importing records, the dialog box disappears. Your data is now available for you to use in Outlook.

MASTERING TROUBLESHOOTING

What If Outlook Doesn't Support My File Format?

In actual practice, you can import contacts from nearly any application. If, for example, you keep your contacts in a Lotus 1-2-3 spreadsheet, you can open the spreadsheet in Excel and save it as an Excel worksheet. Are your contacts in a table in Word? Copy and paste the table into Excel. We've converted files from a no-name 64K organizer using the Comma Delimited format, and we've combined contacts with fields in two separate Access databases by linking the tables from one database into the other, then creating a query to display the fields we wanted to put into Outlook. To import another group of contacts from Quattro 97, we had to save the file in Quattro as a previous version, then open and convert in Excel. The moral of the story? If Outlook doesn't support the format of the file you're importing, find a way to convert the file to a supported format.

MASTERING TROUBLESHOOTING

What If My Fields Don't Match Outlook's Fields?

When Outlook maps the import file, it looks for field names that are similar to those used in Outlook: Name, Address, Department, and so on. If you can change the field names in the import file, you won't need to spend as much time mapping custom fields.

Combined fields don't import well. For example, if the import file lists first and last name in a single field and middle initial in a second field, you'll need to separate the first and last names into two fields in the import table before you can import the data. Parsing (separating) data like this is most easily accomplished in Excel using the Text To Columns feature.

If most of the fields are mapped incorrectly, it's easier to begin mapping from scratch. Click the Clear Map button in the Map Custom Fields dialog box to start with a fresh map in the right pane.

You can use the four extra fields for imported data that doesn't have a corresponding Outlook field. User 1, User 2, User 3, and User 4 appear at the bottom of the list in the right pane of the Map Custom Fields dialog box.

If you have fields you don't want to import, you can either remove them from the import file before importing or remove them from the map. To remove a field from the map, drag the Mapped From value in the right pane and drop it anywhere in the left pane. Only mapped fields are imported.

If you make a mistake mapping fields and want to start over again, click the Default Map button in the dialog box to return to the map that was displayed when you opened the Map Custom Fields dialog box.

Exporting Outlook Data

It won't take long before you rely on Outlook as your primary data source for all kinds of information. If you have to create a report about your activities, conduct an analysis of your time, or use a list of contacts in a spreadsheet you're creating, it makes sense to export the data out of Outlook rather than re-creating it in another application. The Import And Export Wizard works as easily copying data from Outlook as it does bringing it in from other sources.

To export data, follow these steps:

1. Choose File ➢ Import And Export.

2. Select the type of file you want to create, including comma- and tab-separated values, dBASE, Access, Excel, and FoxPro databases, or a Personal Folder file. Click Next.

3. Choose the folder you want to export. You can export only one parent or sub-folder at a time (unless you are exporting a Personal Folder file; see "Backing Up Outlook Data" in the next section). Click Next.

4. Enter the name of the file that is created by the exported data. Click Browse to open a dialog box to help you locate the folder, and enter a filename. Click OK to close the dialog box, and click Next to move to the next step of the wizard.

5. Click Map Custom Fields to make sure that the data is mapped correctly (refer to "Importing Outlook Items" earlier in this chapter for more about mapping). If the incorrect fields appear in the To column, click Default Map to replicate all the fields in the From column.

6. Click OK to close the Map Custom Fields dialog box, and click Finish to export the file.

 TIP To create database tables or spreadsheets that contain only some of the fields in the folder you are exporting, open the Map Custom Fields dialog box and click Clear Map. Drag over the fields you want to move from the From column to the To column. When you export the data only, the fields you select will appear in the table that gets created in the database or spreadsheet file.

Backing Up Outlook Data

Growing to depend on Outlook as your personal information manager can be deadly if you don't regularly back up your Outlook folders. A hard-disk problem or a network snafu could wipe out all of your information. Backup is not as automatic as archiving, but it's just about as easy and is a critical task if your mailbox is not on a network. The trick is remembering to do backups—why not create a recurring Outlook task that reminds you to back up regularly?

To back up your folders, follow these steps:

1. Choose File ➤ Import And Export to launch the Import And Export Wizard.

2. Select Export To A File and click Next.

3. Choose Personal Folder File from the list of file types and click Next.

4. Select Personal Folders from the list of Outlook folders and click Include Sub-folders. You can also choose to back up a particular folder from your personal

folders or Microsoft Exchange mailbox (you can choose only one folder and its subfolders) and to filter the items based on criteria. Click Next when you've specified what you want to back up.

5. Choose a location and a filename for the backup. The default location depends on which version of Windows you have. Choose one of these options: Replace Duplicates With Items Exported, Allow Duplicates To Be Created, or Do Not Export Duplicate Items.

6. Click Finish to start the backup.

If you have a lot of e-mail and other items, expect the backup to take more than a few minutes. It's better to let the backup run without interference, so you probably want to set it up to run at the end of the day or as you are going to lunch.

 NOTE If you use Outlook on a Microsoft Exchange Server, your data is housed in your Exchange Server mailbox, which should be backed up by your server administrator. You may also have a set of personal folders to provide local storage for Outlook items—a handy place to keep items if there's a limit on the maximum size of your Exchange mailbox. If you are unsure about whether you can use personal folders, check with your Exchange Server Administrator to see what the policies are in your organization.

Customizing the Outlook Environment

There are many ways to customize Outlook to make it do things according to your working style. In fact, there are so many options scattered throughout Outlook that it is difficult to keep track of them all. Options or settings are found in three primary locations:

- On the Tools menu under Options
- On the Tools menu under E-mail Accounts
- On the Properties sheet of a folder

Additional options are sprinkled around Outlook. For example, options related to toolbars are found on the Customize Toolbars dialog box (View ➤ Toolbars ➤ Customize), and options related to the Outlook Today home page are found by clicking the Customize Outlook Today button on the top of the page. Although Microsoft has made an attempt at streamlining, don't expect to find every option you need in one place—you probably won't. When you already know the option you are looking for but aren't sure where to find it, your best bet is to ask the Office Assistant. It does a pretty good job of pointing you in the right direction.

NOTE Outlook's toolbars and menu bars are consistent with those in other Office XP applications. For information about customizing toolbars and menu bars, refer to Appendix A, "Customizing the Office Environment."

Setting Options in the Options Dialog Box

The majority of Outlook options are set in the Options dialog box (Tools ➤ Options), but navigating through the dialog box can give the most knowledgeable user a headache. The focus of this overview section is to let you know what options are available and where to find them.

Preferences

The first page of options in the Options dialog box, shown in Figure 35.10, is the Preferences page for each of the Outlook modules: E-mail, Calendar, Tasks, Contacts, Journal, and Notes.

FIGURE 35.10

The Options dialog box is filled with options you can set to make Outlook work the way you want it to.

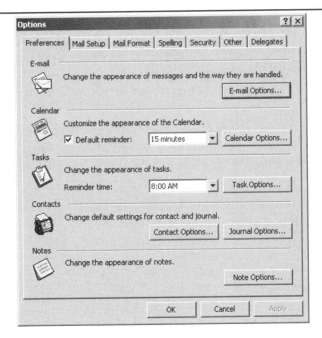

E-mail Options

In the E-mail area you'll find Message Handling options, including Advanced E-mail options related to saving messages, what happens when a message arrives, and default sensitivity and importance options. You'll also find options for tracking whether a message has been delivered and read, as well as options for replies and forwarded messages. Changing these options changes the default settings for all new messages. E-mail Options are covered in more detail in Chapter 32, "Using Outlook As a Communications Tool."

Calendar Options

In the Calendar area you'll find these options:

Calendar Work Week Options include settings for the days you want to appear in your calendar and start and end times for each day.

Calendar Options include displaying week numbers, setting color, and choosing if you want to give people the option to propose alternate times for meetings you organize.

> **Planner** Options control how you view calendars in the Meeting Planner time grid.
>
> **Add Holidays** Inserts religious and national holidays into your calendar (see "Adding Holidays to Your Calendar" in Chapter 34 before choosing this option).

Advanced Options are related to posting your free/busy information, scheduling meeting rooms, and setting time zones.

> **Free/Busy** Options let you determine how far in advance your calendar information should be available for others to use to schedule meetings and if you want that information posted to the Web.
>
> **Resource Scheduling** Is used when you are responsible for maintaining schedules for rooms and other resources for meetings.
>
> **Time Zone** Lets you designate the current time zone and set up a second time zone to show in your calendar.

Task Options

In the Task area you'll find these options:

Color Options change the colors to distinguish overdue tasks and completed tasks.

Assigned Task Options control whether tasks you assign are kept on your Task list and whether Outlook sends status reports when you complete an assigned task.

Reminder Time Changes the default time when you are reminded to complete a task.

NOTE To find more options related to tasks, see the discussion of the Other page later in this chapter.

Contact Options

In this area, the Name and Filing options determine how Full Name and File As names are displayed. You can also have Outlook check for Duplicate Contacts by leaving the Check For Duplicate Contacts check box selected.

Journal Options

The Journal's Automatically Record options let you set what type of items you would like to automatically record for specific contacts. You can also set Outlook to automatically record files you work on in other Office and Office family applications.

Note Options

The Appearance options give you choices of default note color, size, and font.

Mail Setup Options

NEW ▶

The second tab in the Options dialog box is Mail Setup:

E-mail Accounts Identifies the accounts where you can send and receive your e-mail and what address books you have access to. See "Adding E-mail Accounts to Your Profile" later in this chapter.

Send/Receive Gives you the option to indicate whether you want to send e-mail immediately when connected and also create and use Send/Receive Groups. See Chapter 32 for more about Send/Receive Groups.

Data Files Changes where you store e-mail and other Outlook folders. Use this option to create a set of Personal Folder files.

Dial-up Settings Controls how Outlook connects to and interacts with your dial-up connections.

Mail Format

Options under the Mail Format tab include message format settings, stationery and fonts, and signature. These options are covered in more detail in Chapter 32.

Message Format Options let you choose which format you want to use for your messages: HTML, plain text, or Microsoft Outlook Rich Text. Plain text is the most generic and can be read by all of your e-mail recipients. You can also choose to edit your e-mail message using Word—this option requires additional memory resources and may slow your system, but the interface is greatly improved in this version of Outlook.

Stationery And Fonts Options allow you to change the default fonts and stationery used for writing and replying to messages. Stationery options are available only if you choose HTML as your message format. Make sure the person you are sending to can read HTML messages.

Signature Sets up an automatic signature that is included in all of your outgoing correspondence. Click Signature Picker to create a new signature.

Spelling

The Spelling tab offers settings related to automatic spell-checking and spelling and international dictionaries. When the Always Check Spelling Before Sending option is checked, you can be sure that every e-mail message is correct before sending it out.

Security

E-mail and Web security is a major concern for businesses interacting over the Internet. Companies without adequate security controls in place are opening the door to corporate spying, sabotage, and other nasty stuff. Outlook 2002 has a number of features built in that help you secure your correspondence by validating who sent the e-mail and encrypting the contents so unauthorized people cannot view them.

On the Security page of the Options dialog box you can secure and encrypt your e-mail, avoid downloading harmful content from the Web, and designate a digital ID for use in electronic transactions.

 NOTE A digital ID is a unique code that can be assigned to companies or individuals (for a fee) by trusted third parties, such as VeriSign, Inc., based on information supplied. The purpose is to guarantee that parties in transactions are indeed who they claim to be.

Other

The Other page of the Options dialog box contains an assortment of options that have no obvious relationship to each other. If you're looking for a setting and you can't find it, you might just find it here.

General Options include a setting to empty the Deleted Items folder on exiting, a check box to make Outlook the default program for e-mail, Contacts, and Calendar, and an Advanced Options button.

Advanced Options include general settings such as which folder you want to start in when Outlook opens, whether you want a warning before permanently deleting items, turning on auto-selection, and providing feedback with sounds. You will also find additional options here related to Tasks, Notes, and Calendar to go with those on the Preferences page. If you are customizing Outlook and designing custom forms, come here to manage custom forms, install add-ins, and add COM components.

 NOTE For an extensive coverage of customizing Outlook and designing custom Outlook applications using VB, see our book, *Mastering Outlook 2002,* also from Sybex.

Preview Pane Settings control what happens when you read mail in Outlook's Preview pane.

Instant Messaging Is a check box to enable or disable Instant Messaging in Outlook. See Chapter 27, "Collaborating in Office XP," for more about communicating with MSN Messenger Service.

Delegates

Delegates are people you designate to be able to send mail on your behalf. To give other users access to your mail without being able to send mail for you, right-click the mail folder you want them to be able to open and change their permissions to that folder.

Setting Up Outlook Profiles and E-mail Accounts

Much of Outlook's work behind the scenes is dictated by the settings in your user profile. A *profile* is a file that contains information about your Outlook configuration. The profile, stored on your local computer, links you to particular e-mail accounts, directories, address books, and folders that may be stored locally, on a local area network, or on the Internet.

If you work for a company that has a local area network, your network administrator probably already created your Outlook profile on your computer. If you share a computer with others or use your computer for business and personal use, you can create additional profiles to distinguish one from another. In this section, you'll learn more about profiles and you'll see how to create profiles and add e-mail accounts.

Working with Outlook Profiles

Before creating an Outlook profile, you need to gather information about the e-mail accounts, directories, and folders that you want to include in your profile. Although you can always modify a profile later, the more you can set up at the onset, the faster you'll have access to the data you need.

 NOTE An Outlook profile is not the same as a Windows NT/2000 user account. A Windows NT/2000 user account manages network security and access to network folders. An Outlook profile manages access to a mailbox and public folders. However, when you're adding a new Outlook profile, you can keep it simple by giving it the same name as the Windows user account.

The first time you start Outlook 2002, the Outlook Startup Wizard guides you through the steps of adding your primary e-mail account to your profile. If you don't have all the information you need or you want to use Outlook without access to e-mail, you can tell it in the second step of the wizard that you do not want to configure an e-mail account.

 NOTE The Startup Wizard lets you add only one e-mail account, but you can add more after Outlook starts.

If you are ready to set up your primary e-mail account, you can add it in the third step of the wizard (see "Adding E-mail Accounts to Your Profile" later in this chapter for information about how to set up each account type). Using Outlook 2002, you can connect to e-mail accounts available through any of the following servers:

- Microsoft Exchange Server to access your mailbox, read and reply to mail, access public folders, and share documents
- POP3 (Post Office Protocol) server to download e-mail from an Internet Service Provider
- IMAP (Internet Message Access Protocol) server to download e-mail and synchronize your mailbox folders
- HTTP (Hypertext Transfer Protocol) server such as Hotmail to download e-mail and synchronize your mailbox folders
- Other workgroup and third-party mail accounts

When you finish the wizard, Outlook starts up and displays your Microsoft Exchange Server mailbox or, if you do not have access to a Microsoft Exchange Server, a set of Personal Folder files it creates on your hard drive. A Personal Folder file is the local *information store* for the profile, where Outlook keeps contacts, tasks, appointments, and other items associated with this profile. Personal Folder files have a `.pst` file extension.

When you use the Outlook Startup Wizard, Outlook creates a default profile named *Outlook*. This is the profile that Outlook uses each time you start Outlook unless you create an additional one.

NEW **NOTE** If you have used previous versions of Microsoft Outlook, you may be wondering what happened to the Internet Only and Corporate/Workgroup installations of Outlook. These differentiations have been eliminated in Outlook 2002. You can set up any POP3, IMAP, or HTTP account individually or combine one or more of these Internet mail accounts with Microsoft Exchange or other workgroup or third-party mail server.

Modifying the Default Profile

If more than one person works on the same computer, you should each have your own Outlook profile. Profiles help keep your personal computer personal by saving each user's mail and address book settings separately.

Even as an individual user, you might find a need for more than one profile. For example, you might have one profile on your notebook computer that you use when you're in your office, connected to a mail server that delivers both internal and Internet mail. To keep your business and personal lives separate, you might create a second profile that connects to dial-up e-mail service for your personal use.

You can designate a default profile that Outlook uses every time it starts, or you can ask Outlook to prompt you to select a profile when you launch Outlook. To create a new profile or modify an existing one, you need to access the Mail Setup dialog box, shown in Figure 35.11, from Windows Control Panel.

FIGURE 35.11

The Mail Setup dialog box gives you the choice to set up e-mail accounts, change settings for data files, or show profiles.

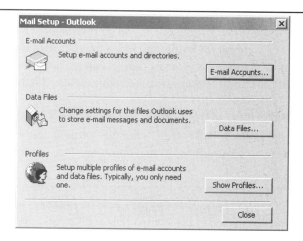

Mail

Choose Start ≻ Settings ≻ Control Panel on the Windows Taskbar to open Control Panel. Then double-click the Mail icon to open the Mail Setup dialog box. You can choose to add e-mail accounts to the default profile, modify where your data is stored, and set up multiple profiles.

Adding E-mail Accounts to Your Profile

The steps to set up the various types of e-mail accounts are slightly different. To set up a Microsoft Exchange account, you need the name of the Exchange Server and the user name (mailbox name). To set up a POP3, IMAP, or HTTP account, you need additional information such as the e-mail address, logon information, incoming and outgoing mail server names, and connection information. To set up other mail server accounts, you need information about how to connect to the mail server's post office.

Adding a Microsoft Exchange Server Account

To add an Exchange Server e-mail account for the default profile, follow these steps:

1. Open the Mail Setup dialog box (Start ≻ Settings ≻ Control Panel ≻ Mail) and click the E-mail Accounts button.

2. Choose Add A New E-mail Account and click Next.

3. Select Microsoft Exchange Server from the list and click Next.

4. Enter the name of the Exchange Server and the user name in the text boxes shown in Figure 35.12.

5. Click the Check Name button to verify that the Microsoft Exchange Server name exists and that it recognizes the user name. If the names are recognized,

they are underlined. If they are not recognized, a Microsoft Exchange Server dialog box opens. The name must be resolved before you are allowed to continue.

6. Check the Use Web Protocol To Connect check box on the Exchange Server Settings page if you are running Microsoft Exchange 2000 and plan to connect to the mailbox over the Web.

7. Click the More Settings button to review the default Exchange Server settings on the Microsoft Exchange Server Properties sheet, shown in Figure 35.13. The General tab of this Properties sheet controls the connection state at startup. The Advanced tab allows you to open additional mailboxes (your supervisor's, for example), encrypt information, and set up Logon Network Security and Offline Folders. The Connection tab is where you indicate how you want to connect to the Exchange Server when you are offline. The Remote Mail tab manages remote mail connections.

8. Make any desired changes to the Microsoft Exchange Server properties and click OK to save the changes.

9. Click Next and click Finish to finish setting up the Microsoft Exchange Server account.

FIGURE 35.12

Enter Microsoft Exchange Server settings to connect to an Exchange Server mailbox.

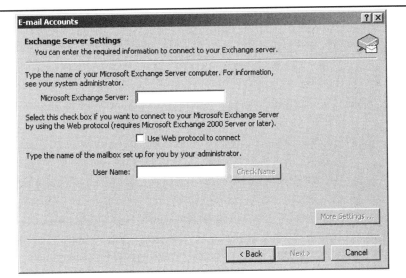

FIGURE 35.13

Modify the default
Exchange Server
settings in the
Microsoft Exchange
Server Properties
sheet.

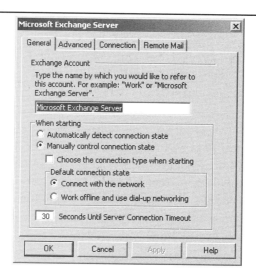

If you want to add additional e-mail accounts or modify your profile in any other way, you can initiate additional changes from the Mail Setup dialog box that appears when you finish the Microsoft Exchange Server setup.

Adding an Internet Mail Account

If you want to add an Internet mail account, such as a POP3, IMAP, or HTTP account, follow these steps:

1. Click the E-mail Accounts button on the Mail Setup dialog box (Start ➤ Settings ➤ Control Panel ➤ Mail).

2. Choose Add A New E-mail Account and click Next.

3. Select the type of account you want to create—POP3, IMAP, or HTTP—and click Next to open the E-mail Accounts page, shown in Figure 35.14. Regardless of the type of Internet mail account, you need to enter the same type of information.

4. Enter your name and e-mail address in the User Information text boxes.

 NOTE If the e-mail address you use is an alias, you can enter the alias here rather than the e-mail address given to you by the Internet Service Provider.

5. Enter the user name and password you need to log on to the Internet Service Provider (ISP) in the Logon Information text boxes.

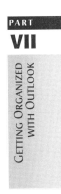

FIGURE 35.14

Enter Internet e-mail settings for your POP3, IMAP, or HTTP mail account in this dialog box.

E-mail Accounts   ? X

Internet E-mail Settings (POP3)
Each of these settings are required to get your e-mail account working.

User Information

Your Name:

E-mail Address:

Logon Information

User Name:

Password:

☑ Remember password

☐ Log on using Secure Password Authentication (SPA)

Server Information

Incoming mail server (POP3):

Outgoing mail server (SMTP):

Test Settings

After filling out the information on this screen, we recommend you test your account by clicking the button below. (Requires network connection)

Test Account Settings ...

More Settings ...

< Back   Next >   Cancel

6. Enter the names of the incoming and outgoing mail servers in the Server Information text boxes. Contact your ISP if you do not know this information—it is usually posted on the ISP's Web site.

7. Click the More Settings button to modify additional settings related to your Internet mail connection.

8. Enter additional settings in the Internet E-mail Settings dialog box, shown in Figure 35.15, regarding the account, including the name and other user information you would like to use, outgoing server information, connection information, and other advanced server-related information. If you are connecting using a phone line, be sure to click the Connection tab to designate the Dial-Up Networking connection you want to use.

9. Click OK to save changes you made to the Internet E-mail Settings page.

10. Click the Test Account Settings button on the E-mail Accounts page to have Outlook establish a network connection, find the outgoing mail server, find the incoming mail server, log on to the incoming mail server, and send a test message. If the test is successful, Outlook congratulates you and you can close the Test Account Settings dialog box. If the test is not successful, the Errors tab displays the source of the problem and recommends a course of action.

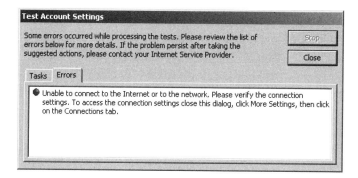

When you have corrected any errors and the test is successful, click Next and Finish to finish setting up an Internet mail account.

FIGURE 35.15

Modify account settings in the Internet E-mail Settings dialog box.

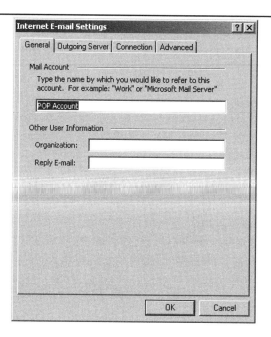

You can choose to add an additional Internet mail account or add another workgroup or third-party mail account. If your company uses a third-party mail server that has an Outlook connector, you can set it up so you can receive mail through Outlook.

Adding Directories and Address Books to a Profile

An address book is a directory of names with their e-mail addresses or fax numbers. An Internet Directory Service (LDAP or Lightweight Directory Access Protocol server) houses corporate and other directories on a server on the Internet.

If you have access to an LDAP server, follow these steps to add an Internet Directory Service to your Outlook profile:

1. Click the E-mail Accounts button on the Mail Setup dialog box (Start ➢ Settings ➢ Control Panel ➢ Mail).

2. Choose Add A New Directory Or Address Book and click Next.

3. Select Internet Directory Service (LDAP) and click Next.

4. Enter the Server Information and, if required, Logon Information in the text boxes.

5. Click More Settings to modify the Connection and Search options as necessary. Click OK to return to the Internet Directory Service (LDAP) Settings dialog box.

6. Click OK and click Finish to save the new service as part of your profile.

Adding Address Books

When you enter contacts into Outlook, Outlook adds data to an address book, called an Outlook Address Book, created from the Contacts folder. If you add new Contacts folders, you can designate them to be made available as Outlook Address Books if you want them to be. You can also create a Personal Address Book to track your most commonly used e-mail addresses.

To add a new address book, follow these steps:

1. Click the E-mail Accounts button on the Mail Setup dialog box (Start ➢ Settings ➢ Control Panel ➢ Mail).

2. Choose Add A New Directory Or Address Book and click Next.

3. Select Additional Address Books and click Next.

4. Select the type of address book you want to add from the list of choices: Outlook Address Book or Personal Address Book.

5. To add an Outlook Address Book, click Outlook Address Book, and Outlook immediately adds the address book and returns you to the Mail Setup dialog box. You can add only one Outlook Address Book.

6. To add a Personal Address Book, click Personal Address Book and set up the properties, including a name and location for the address book. You can add only one Personal Address Book.

7. Click OK to save the address book and return to the Mail Setup dialog box.

The Outlook and Personal Address Book account types can be added only once to a profile. You can create additional Contacts folders and add them to the Outlook Address Book service by setting the Outlook Address Book properties for the folder (right-click the folder, choose Properties, and choose the Outlook Address Book tab).

Properties and Other Options

Every Windows folder has properties, or attributes, related to it: how large it is, when it was created, and how many subfolders it has, for example. All of the Outlook modules and any subfolders you create also have properties that can affect the functioning of the folder. To access a folder's properties, like those shown in Figure 35.16, right-click the folder in the Folder List or on the Outlook bar and choose Properties.

FIGURE 35.16

Every folder has properties that define it.

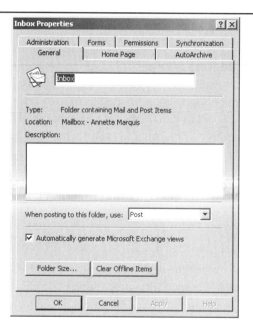

Use folder properties in Outlook to change the AutoArchive settings (discussed earlier in the chapter) for a folder, designate a home page to open when you open this folder (like the Outlook Today page), or assign a customized form to a folder. Every Outlook module has some settings that are unique to that folder type, and not all settings apply to all folders. Additional options may also be available if you are on a Microsoft Exchange Server network, so you'll want to explore the Properties dialog box of each folder in Outlook to see what options are available to you.

TIP If you are unsure of an option's purpose, find out more information about it by clicking the Question Mark button on the Property box's Title bar. If you are still unsure, keep the default setting.

Customizing the Outlook Bar

The Outlook bar is a navigational feature introduced in the original version of Outlook that has since become a standard tool available in a variety of other applications. FrontPage 2002, for example, uses a similar bar to navigate between views. The Outlook bar has a lot of flexibility that some users love and others choose to ignore. It's up to you to decide what role the Outlook bar will play for you.

The Outlook bar offers groups of shortcuts. The default groups—Outlook Shortcuts, My Shortcuts, and Other Shortcuts—can be renamed or deleted completely if you choose. You can also add additional groups for your own shortcuts. To rename or delete a group, click to open the group and right-click the Outlook bar (to add a new group, just right-click). Choose Add New Group, Rename Group, or Delete Group from the list of options.

To add a shortcut to the Outlook bar, drag the folder from the Folder List to the Outlook bar. Drop the folder when the black horizontal line appears where you want the folder to appear:

In addition to folder shortcuts, you can also create Outlook bar shortcuts to documents. If, for example, you're working extensively on a group of Word and Excel documents, you can add them to the Outlook bar and open the documents from within Outlook, just as you would add shortcuts to the Desktop so that you could open these documents by double-clicking the Desktop shortcuts. To add a document shortcut to the Outlook bar, follow these steps:

1. Click the Other Shortcuts button on the Outlook bar and click the My Computer shortcut.

2. Locate the document you want to create a shortcut to.

3. Drag the document from the table in the Information Viewer and drop it on the Outlook bar to create the shortcut.

4. Click the document's shortcut in the Outlook bar to launch the appropriate application and open the file.

Creating Custom Views

As you've seen while working in the various Outlook modules, views define how you see your Outlook data. There are five types of views available in Outlook:

Table view The default view in Tasks, this shows data in columns and rows.

Timeline view Used in Journal to see when activities occurred, this displays data across a timeline.

Card view This displays Contact data in an address-card format.

Day/Week/Month view Used with Calendar, this shows a Date Navigator and Day, Work Week, Week, and Month buttons to display data.

Icon view The default view in Notes, this displays a small or large icon for each Outlook item.

Views improve efficiency by making the data you need visible when you need it. Switching between views gives you a different perspective on your data and helps you capitalize on the powerful grouping features. Views also provide you with a valuable reporting tool. By creating custom views that are sorted, grouped, and filtered to extract the data you need, you can create time logs, calendars, project reports, schedules, company directories, correspondence logs, and a whole host of other management reports. When you use views effectively, raw data is translated into priceless information.

If you would like to create a new view, you have three options:

• Modify an existing view.

- Copy an existing view and modify the copy, leaving the original unchanged.
- Create a new view from scratch.

To modify an existing view, follow these steps:

1. Switch to the view you want to modify.

2. Choose View ➢ Current View ➢ Customize Current View to open the dialog box shown in Figure 35.17.

3. Click the Fields button to add or remove fields from the view.

4. Change the grouping of the data by clicking the Group By button.

5. Click the Sort button to set the fields you want to sort by.

6. Define criteria for records to display by clicking the Filter button.

7. Change display settings and fonts under the Other Settings button.

8. Click the Automatic Formatting button to apply special formatting rules to items, such as applying bold to unread items in the Inbox.

9. Click OK to apply the customized view.

FIGURE 35.17

Customize existing views by changing fields, grouping, sorting, filters, fonts, and formatting.

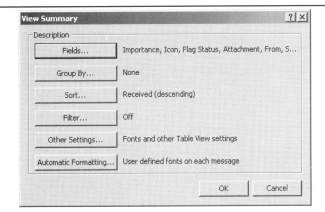

Making a copy of an existing view or creating a new view from scratch is essentially the same as modifying an existing view, but there are a couple of extra steps involved. To copy an existing view or create a new view, follow these steps:

1. Switch to the module for which you want the new view.

2. Choose View ➢ Current View ➢ Define Views to open the dialog box shown in Figure 35.18.

3. To copy an existing view for modification, select the view from the list, click Copy, and enter a name for the new view.

To create an entirely new view, click New, enter a name for the view, and select the type of view.

With either option, if you are on an Exchange Server network, indicate whether you want this view visible to everyone in this folder, visible only to you in this folder, or available in all Contacts folders.

4. Click OK and follow steps 3–8 in the procedure outlined earlier for modifying an existing view.

5. Click Apply View to make the new view the current view for this folder, or click OK to add the view to the list of available views but not apply it.

 TIP If you modify one of the default views and later decide to return it to its original state, choose View ➢ Define Views, select the view, and click Reset.

To delete a custom view, switch to the module that contains the view you want to delete. Choose View ➢ Current View ➢ Define Views, select the view you want to delete, and click the Delete button.

In the Define Views dialog box you can create a new view, make a copy of an existing view, or modify an existing view.

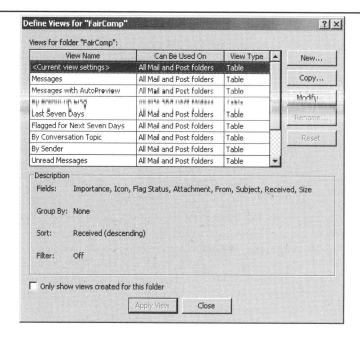

MASTERING THE OPPORTUNITIES

Creating and Using Categories

Categories are one of the most powerful features available in Outlook 2002 for organizing and viewing your data. Categories let you decide what individual Outlook items have in common. Although Outlook comes with a predefined list of categories, we recommend that you dump it and create your own list that has meaning to you. The same Categories list crosses over all Outlook items, so you can create categories that tie data together across Outlook folders. Let's say you are in charge of planning a large conference for your organization. By creating a category for the conference, you can assign the category to contacts, tasks, calendar items, and even e-mail related to the conference. You can then use Outlook's Advanced Find (Tools ➢ Advanced Find) to search for all the items in your mailbox related to the conference. You can also use By Category views in the individual Outlook folders to see all the tasks related to the conference, all the appointments, and so on. By using Categories in this way, you can turn Outlook into a simple project management tool to organize all your project-related data.

To access Categories, open any new Outlook item and click the Categories button at the bottom of the item form—if you open a Mail item, choose Tools ➢ Options to find the Categories button. This opens the Categories dialog box.

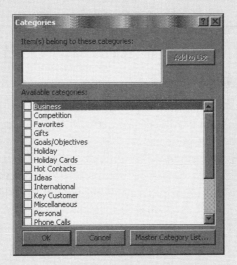

Continued ▐▶

MASTERING THE OPPORTUNITIES CONTINUED

Click the Master Category List button at the bottom of the dialog box. To clean out all or most of the items in the list, select the first item and scroll to the bottom of the list. Hold Shift and select the last item in the list. If you would prefer to keep some of the categories in the list, hold down Ctrl and deselect the ones you want to keep. When you are ready, click the Delete button.

To add a new category to the list, type it in the New Category box and click Add. Click OK to close the Master Category List. If you want to assign any of your new categories to the open item, click the check box in front of the category. You can assign more than one category to an item, but we suggest that you limit it to no more than two or three. For one thing, some PDAs can handle only one category at a time, and, in addition, By Category views repeat the item for each category it's assigned to.

If you would like to assign several Outlook items to the same category, click the Organize button on the Outlook's Standard toolbar in Calendar, Tasks, Contacts, or Journal. Click Using Categories to add selected contacts to a category and also create new categories. To assign categories to e-mail, you must open the message and choose Tools ➤ Options. To assign categories to Notes, open the note, click the Note icon, and choose Categories from the menu.

Outlook 2002 and Microsoft Exchange Server

Microsoft Exchange Server is server software that maintains and manages user mailboxes and public folders on a network server. Outlook is client software that maintains and manages personal folders on workstations and communicates with Exchange Server mailboxes and public folders. Although you can use Outlook without an Exchange Server or a network, with appropriate permissions from your network administrator, Exchange Server lets you create public folders containing calendar items, tasks, messages, or contacts and then share those folders with other users. Exchange Server also lets you take full advantage of assigning tasks and scheduling meetings in Outlook's Tasks and Calendar folders.

Creating Shared Outlook Items

You can access the public folders on your system by turning on the Folder List (View ➢ Folder List), clicking the Expand (plus) button in front of Public Folders, and then clicking the Expand button in front of All Public Folders.

If you have permission from your Exchange Server administrator, you can create pubic folders yourself. You can create a public folder by right-clicking All Public Folders and choosing New Folder. Name the folder in the Create New Folder dialog box and select which type of Outlook items it will contain. Verify that All Public Folders is selected and click OK to create the folder. You can find the new folder in the list of All Public Folders.

EXPERT TIP   You can also create a public folder by copying or moving an existing folder from your mailbox. Just right-drag the folder to All Public Folders and choose Copy (or Move) from the shortcut menu that opens. For example, you can copy your Contacts folder as a public Contacts folder and then delete the contacts that don't need to be shared. The default folders in your mailbox cannot be moved, only copied.

Establishing Favorites

The Favorites folder, located under Public Folders, is a folder to house those public folders that you access often. You can drag any public folder to which you have permissions to the Favorites folder. Outlook maintains a shortcut to the folder in the Favorites folder, providing you quick and easy access to those folders you need.

   NOTE   Only folders available in the Favorites folder can be made available for offline use—see "Working Away from the Office with Offline Folders" later in this chapter.

Setting Permissions for Others

Whether you want to give someone access to a public folder or you would like a coworker to have access to one or more of the folders in your personal mailbox, the process is the same. You select the folder, select a user, and assign them a role. *Roles* are bundled groups of folder permissions. The roles for folders, from most to least restrictive, are the following:

None   No access to the contents of a folder.

Contributor   Allowed to create new items.

Reviewer   Allowed to read existing items.

Author   Allowed to create new items, edit or delete items they have created, and read existing items.

Publishing Author   Same as Author but includes access to subfolders.

Editor   Same as Author but can edit or delete all items.

Publishing Editor   Same as Editor but includes access to subfolders.

Owner   All permissions, including the right to change folder permissions.

To add or remove permissions, follow these steps:

1. Select the folder for which you want to set permissions.

2. Choose File ➢ Folder ➢ Properties For *Folder Name* or right-click the folder and choose Properties to open the Properties dialog box shown in Figure 35.19.

3. Choose the Permissions tab.

4. Click the Add button to open the Add Users dialog box.

5. Select the person whom you want to allow access to your folder, and click OK.

6. Select the person's name in the upper pane.

7. Choose the appropriate role in the Roles drop-down list.

8. Click OK.

NOTE   If you give someone access to one of your personal folders, they can open your folder from their mailbox by choosing File ➢ Open ➢ Other User's Folder and selecting your user name and the folder they want to open. Use Delegate permissions, discussed earlier in this chapter, if you would rather that others respond to your e-mail on behalf of you rather than as you.

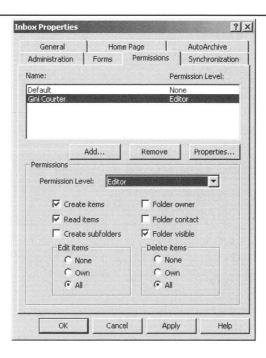

FIGURE 35.19
Set permissions for other users in the folder's Properties dialog box.

Working Away from the Office

Outlook has two methods for handling work while you're out of the office: *Remote Mail* and *offline folders*. With Remote Mail, you can download and read the messages that have been delivered in your absence, but you can't send messages (unless you have an Internet Service Provider and an Internet mail service configured in Outlook). Offline folders, a second set of folders kept on your remote computer, allow you to send *and* receive mail, tasks, and other items by dialing in to your organization's Microsoft Exchange Server. To use Remote Mail and offline folders, you must have your home or laptop computer configured to use Dial-Up Networking (DUN) or have some other network connection, such as a virtual private network (VPN). To use offline folders, you must have dial-up or network access to your Microsoft Exchange Server. See your system administrator for remote permissions and information on configuring remote access.

Managing Remote Mail

NEW▶

Remote Mail allows you to download selected messages to a remote computer after retrieving message headers from your e-mail accounts. This allows you to minimize connection time and pick up only the mail you need while you are away from the office. We recommend using Remote Mail when you are connecting to an Internet Service Provider to retrieve your mail. Before you can use Remote Mail, you must do the following:

1. On the Tools menu, point to Send/Receive Settings and then click Define Send/Receive Groups.

2. Select a group in the list and click Edit (see Chapter 32 for information about setting up Send/Receive Groups).

3. Select the Inbox check box. Follow the instructions on the screen for creating an offline folder file (.ost). If no instructions appear, the offline folder is already available on your computer.

4. If you set up a new offline folder file, click OK when prompted to synchronize the selected folders to the new offline folder file.

Downloading and Marking Headers

To download message headers when you are offline, choose Tools ➢ Send/Receive ➢ Work With Headers ➢ Download Headers From and select the e-mail account you want to use.

Browse through the headers and mark headers for messages you'd like to see by right-clicking the headers you want and choosing Mark To Download Message or Mark To Download Message Copy. You can click the Delete button to delete messages; however, when you delete messages remotely, they're actually deleted, not just moved to the Deleted Items folder, so use this feature cautiously.

Retrieving Messages You're Marked for Download

After you've marked all message headers, choose Tools ➢ Send/Receive ➢ Work With Headers, choose Process Marked Headers From, and choose the e-mail account you want to use. It's a good idea to make sure you've set up Remote Mail correctly and practiced using it before you grab your laptop and leave for the Caribbean.

Working Away from the Office with Offline Folders

Offline folders allow you to access your Microsoft Exchange Server account, use a folder remotely, work with all the items in the folder, and then synchronize (update) both the offline folder and the folder on your office server so the two are identical. Before you can work offline, you must set up an Offline Folder File:

1. Install and configure Dial-Up Networking or establish another network connection to your Exchange Server network.

2. Establish an Offline File Folder on your remote computer. Choose Tools ➢ E-mail Accounts and click View Or Change Existing E-mail Accounts. Then click Next.

3. Choose Microsoft Exchange Server in the list and click Change.

4. Click the More Settings button to open the Microsoft Exchange Server dialog box shown in Figure 35.20.

5. Select the Advanced tab and click Offline Folder File Settings.

6. Enter the name and path of the file you would like to use as the Offline Folder File. Offline.ost is the default.

7. Click OK. If the folder is not already created, you are prompted to create it. Click Yes.

8. Select the General tab of the Microsoft Exchange Server dialog box shown in Figure 35.20.

9. Choose between the When Starting options: Automatically Detect Connection State means that Outlook will determine whether you are online or offline when you start Outlook. Manually Control Connection State means that you can choose to always connect with the network or choose whether you are working offline or online each time Outlook starts. You can also choose to always work offline and use Dial-Up Networking. Choose this option if you are away from the office more than you are in so Outlook won't have to look for the network each time it starts.

10. Close the Microsoft Exchange Server dialog box and close the E-mail Accounts dialog box.

FIGURE 35.20

In the Microsoft Exchange Server dialog box you can create and configure offline folders.

NOTE You might also choose to create offline folders on your office computer so that you can continue to work when the network connection is lost. On a network computer, you don't need to set up Dial-Up Networking.

Designating Folders for Offline Use

 Before you synchronize for the first time, you need to tell Outlook which folders you want to synchronize for offline use. Follow these steps to designate which folders to synchronize:

1. Choose Tools ➤ Send/Receive Groups.

2. Select the group you want to use or click New to create a new group. Because these settings are different than other groups you may want to use, we recommend creating a new group called **Offline**.

3. Click Edit to edit the Send/Receive Settings dialog box shown in Figure 35.21.

4. Choose Microsoft Exchange Server from the Accounts list and select the Include Account In This Send/Receive Group check box.

5. Select each of the folders you want to synchronize, including any public folder Favorites. As you select a folder, click the Filter Selected Folder button if you'd like to apply a filter to the folder that applies to every Send/Receive Group this folder is in.

6. Select or clear the actions you'd like to apply to this group—see Figure 35.21.

7. Click the Limit Message Size button if you want to download messages only under a certain size.

8. Click OK when you've finished with the group settings to return to the Send/Receive Groups dialog box.

9. In the Send/Receive Groups dialog box, select Include This Group In Send/Receive under When Outlook Is Offline.

FIGURE 35.21

Select the folders and settings you want to include in the Offline Folder File synchronization.

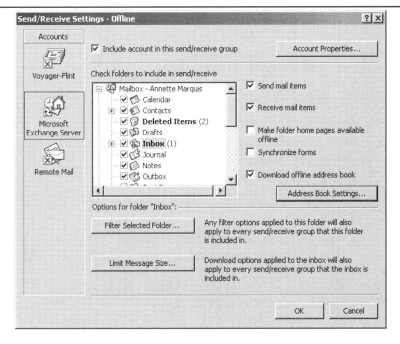

Synchronizing Offline Folders

NEW▶

Synchronizing your folders compares the contents of the offline and regular folders and adjusts items in both so that they are identical. For example, synchronization moves messages you've received at work to an offline folder and sends messages from your offline Outbox folder. If you delete a Contact item in your Offline folder, synchronizing deletes the item in your regular folder. Outlook 2002 uses Send/Receive Groups to synchronize with the offline folder file.

To synchronize all of your designated offline folders, choose Tools ➢ Send/Receive ➢ Send And Receive All. If you want to synchronize only a single folder, choose Tools ➢ Send/Receive ➢ This Folder.

Watch the right corner of the status bar for an indication of the progress of the synchronization. When the synchronization is complete, the status bar is clear.

You must synchronize before you disconnect the computer from the network and then once again when you return. You can also dial in to the Exchange Server while you are away and synchronize remotely.

CREATING AND USING AN ACCESS DATABASE

LEARN TO:

- **Plan a database**

- **Create a database structure**

- **Create and use forms**

- **Create reports and queries**

- **Creat Web pages**

CHAPTER 36

PLANNING A DATABASE

FEATURING

- Creating a database with the Database Wizard

- Understanding database objects

- Using the Database window

- Designing your own database

- Determining your database needs and purposes

- Planning the database structure

- Determining fields for your tables

- Understanding table relationships

For most computer users, databases represent a quantum leap in data management capability beyond other business software, where the most powerful and sophisticated features often require programming. That's also true of Access to some extent, but you can handle many of your company's data needs without writing a line of code in Access 2002.

The five Access chapters (this chapter through Chapter 40) cover the basics—everything you need to create a functional Access database. These Access chapters do not assume any familiarity with Access, but we do assume that you're a knowledgeable Windows computer user with some experience with Excel. And before you can design an effective database, you need an understanding of database design concepts.

Simple databases, sometimes called flat-file databases, allow you to work with only one list or table of information at a time (Microsoft Excel is an example of a flat-file database). Programs like Access, which is a relational database, let you separate your data into different tables and store each item of data (such as a customer address) only once. Then you relate the tables to each other so you can connect data such as a customer address and several customer orders. In a relational database, data storage can be more flexible, and data does not have to be duplicated.

You can create a great relational database with Access 2002, but there's nothing in Access to prevent you from creating a bad one. By "bad," we don't simply mean unattractive or even downright ugly; a database is bad when users can't perform simple tasks, or when even the designer can't retrieve data in meaningful ways. We've seen dozens of bad databases created by bright, dedicated people. They intended to create useful databases; they spent hours of time, often their personal time, building a database. When the database was completed, it fell far short of their expectations not because they needed to understand Visual Basic or high-end design concepts, but because they didn't understand the basics: design concepts that are often omitted from Access training courses.

This chapter includes many of the "data basics" you need to confidently create solid databases, but an in-depth discussion of database design is beyond the scope of this book. We heartily endorse *Database Design for Mere Mortals,* by Michael Hernandez (Addison-Wesley, 1997). This book offers a comprehensive look at principles of relational database design—including theory and practice—independent from any platform or product. You'll find the text well written and virtually free of technical industry lingo. If this is your first database—and it's more than just a walk through the wizard—read the book. Knowing the principles of design will save you hours of frustration with a finished product that doesn't meet your data needs.

In the first part of the chapter, we'll create a database using the Database Wizard. The wizard creates databases that perform as described, so you don't need to know anything about design to use the wizard. The wizard is limited, however, to a few databases that are commonly used in business. If there isn't a wizard for the database you want to create, of if you want to extend the functionality of the database created with the wizard, you'll need to know about database design—the concepts that aren't directly addressed in Access but are critical to creating a functional database. If you've taken a database design or systems analysis course, you may already be familiar with normalization, Entity-Relationship modeling, primary and foreign keys, and referential integrity. If some of these concepts are unfamiliar, spend some time in this chapter before you start creating your database. And if *none* of these concepts are familiar, pick up the Hernandez book and plan to spend a couple of weeks boning up on the basics of relational database design before constructing a mission-critical database

MASTERING THE OPPORTUNITIES

Do You Need the Complexity of a Relational Database?

Does your data need a relational database? If your data is simple and can be kept in a single table with no duplication (like a list of business contacts), it's easier to keep it in a flat-file database like Microsoft Excel. If your data requires lots of calculation and manipulation, those tasks are easier to perform in Excel. When you need to relate two types of data to each other (students and classes, sales managers and client accounts), you need to move to Access.

Whether you keep your data in Access or Excel, you can easily transfer it between the two programs. If your contacts are already in an Excel workbook, you can *import* the Excel file into Access as a table in a database. If you need data that's kept in another department and changes regularly, such as shipping charges, you can *link* to that table from your database and always have current data. And if you want to perform lots of calculations on data that's in an Access table, you can *analyze* it (by exporting a copy) in an Excel workbook.

PART

VIII

CREATING AND USING
AN ACCESS DATABASE

Creating a Database with the Database Wizard

With Access 2002, there are a number of ways to create a database:

- Use one of the Database Wizards included with Access 2002 if you're creating a database commonly used in business—for example, inventory control, event management, or contact management

- Convert an Excel workbook into an Access database
- Create a database entirely from scratch in Access
- Import or link to data in other data sources
- Use Access Project to create a database linked to a new or existing SQL Server database

We'll start by creating a database with the Database Wizard. You can use any of the Database Wizards to whip up a fully functional database that includes sample data. Several wizards are installed with Access 2002; each wizard asks a few questions about your preferences and then uses your answers to create a new database. We'll use the Contact Management database to illustrate using the wizard. The Contact Management database is a useful sample and parallels the Contacts folder in Outlook 2002.

Follow these steps to get started:

1. Choose Start ➢ Programs ➢ Microsoft Access. Access starts, and the task pane appears on the right side of a blank Access window. If the task pane does not appear, choose File ➢ New to display it.

2. The task pane lists the most recently used database files at the top, with options for creating new databases, projects, and data access pages. Click the General Templates option in the New From Template area to open the Templates dialog box.

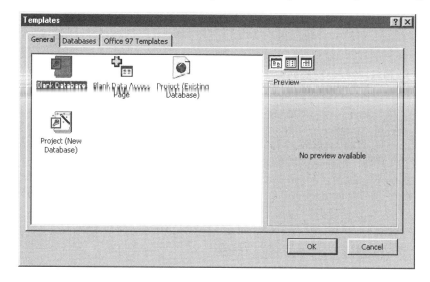

To create a database using the Database Wizard, follow these steps:

1. In the Templates dialog box, on the Databases tab, double-click the icon for the database you want to create—Contact Management, for example.

2. You're asked what to name the new database file and where to save it. In the File New Database dialog box (shown here), type a filename in the File Name box. In the Save In box, navigate to the folder where you want to save the database. Then click Create.

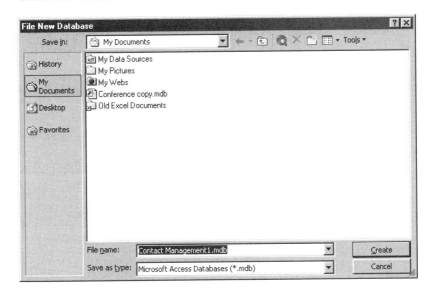

3. The Database Wizard starts with a window describing the database you're creating. Click Next.

 TIP To create the database immediately by using all of the wizard's default choices, click Finish in any Database Wizard dialog box.

4. In the second step of the wizard (shown in Figure 36.1), select the specific fields you want to include in each table. Select a table in the list on the left; in the list on the right, mark or clear fields to include in that table. Most of the fields listed are required; italicized fields are optional. Click Next when you've added optional fields and removed unneeded fields from each of the tables.

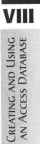

FIGURE 36.1

Select fields for your database in the second step of the Database Wizard.

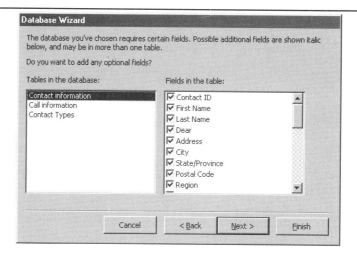

5. In the third step, select a style for database screen displays (such as forms), and click Next. (Click a style name to preview the style.)

TIP The default style, Standard, is the best choice. Standard uses no additional system resources because it uses the Windows system colors. The Standard style includes text boxes and controls that are used in other dialog boxes, so your users won't have to spend a lot of time determining where they can type or edit. And because Standard uses the system settings, your database behaves as all "real" Windows applications behave—screen colors reflect the user's choice of system colors.

6. In the fourth step of the wizard, select a style for printed database reports, and click Next. (Click a style name to preview it.)

TIP The style choice Compact doesn't look nearly as nice in print as it looks in the preview; users often complain that the headings are hard to read.

7. In the fifth step, type a title for your database or accept the wizard's suggestion. Enable the check box to place a graphic, such as a corporate logo, on database reports. Click the Picture button to browse, locate, and select the graphic file you wish to use. Click Next.

8. In the final step, make sure the check box labeled Yes, Start The Database is enabled, and click Finish.

The wizard creates the database; progress meters appear as different parts of the database are created. When the database is complete, Access displays the Main Switchboard, as shown in Figure 36.2. The Main Switchboard simplifies user interaction with the database.

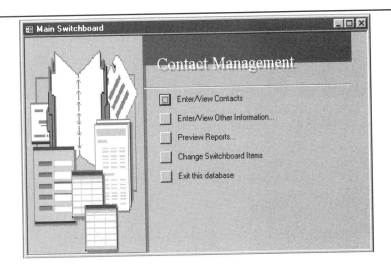

PART

VIII

CREATING AND USING
AN ACCESS DATABASE

If you close or minimize the Main Switchboard, you'll see the Database window; it may be minimized at the bottom of the Access application window.

TIP If you want a database to look at but don't want to create one at this time, open the Northwind Sample Database that's provided with Access 2002. Many of the illustrations in these chapters show the Northwind database. Just choose Help ➢ Sample Databases ➢ Northwind Sample Database. If it's not installed, Access prompts you to install it.

MASTERING THE OPPORTUNITIES

What Can a Wizard Do?

Why devote the extra time and energy to design and create a database with functionality that exists with only a few clicks? You may find that one of the Access wizards creates a database that does everything you need. At the very least, you may be able to use one of the wizards to create a database that serves as a starting point for a larger design. Here is a synopsis of what each wizard can do for you.

Asset Tracking Stores information about assets, their depreciation and maintenance histories, plus employees and vendors of your organization. Use it for tracking equipment purchased and maintained by your company. Answer questions like these: When was the last time we had a maintenance call on the fourth-floor copy machine? Is projector number 5 available for use?

Contact Management Is similar to the Contacts folder in Outlook 2002. Maintain information about the people you know and the dealings you have with them. Need to refresh your memory about your last phone call with a client? Curious about how many clients you've called this week? If you record the calls, the database can print a report for you.

Event Management Stores information about—you guessed it—events! Preserve information about events, the people who register and attend them, employees who work at the events, and sales associated with an event. Ever wonder how many of your seminars were attended by a particular person? The Event Management database can tell you.

Expenses Tracks employees and the details of their business expenses. You can create your own categories for expenses (lodging, vehicular, meals, etc.) and print reports on expenses by category or by employee. Maintain expense balances for employees by keeping track of their advances, checks issued, and amounts owed. The database includes an expense report form.

Inventory Control Maintains data about products you purchase and sell, orders and suppliers for those products, and your own employees. Keep track of the number and type of products you have on hand, set a reorder level for each product, and maintain an inventory log. Print reports on product transactions, cost comparisons, and purchases from various suppliers.

Ledger Works well for tracking deposits, withdrawals, and transfers among many different accounts. Accounts can be categorized (you pick the categories) and reported on individually or as a group. If your company uses accounting software (even small-business software like QuickBooks Pro), you probably don't need this database.

Continued

MASTERING THE OPPORTUNITIES CONTINUED

Order Entry Is the other side of the Inventory Control database. Use it to maintain details about products you sell, the customers who buy them, and the specifics of customer orders, shipping, and payment. Answer questions like these: What has Customer A ordered in the last six months? When did we invoice that last shipment to Customer B? What are my outstanding receivables for the month of June? Which of my employees had the most sales in July?

Resource Scheduling Lets you keep track of resource schedules (a resource could be a person, a piece of equipment, a conference room, etc.) and availability. Maintain a usage log for each resource and track customers' contact with a resource.

Service Call Management Provides a means for creating customer work orders and tracking them to completion. Maintain a service call history for each customer, including invoice and payment amounts. Access even figures your sales tax! Print reports for sales by month, work order status, and sales by employee.

Time and Billing Tracks projects, employee work hours, client billing, and payment. It's the service call management database for the company that bills by the hour. Find out which employee is billing the most time each month, review hours billed to a particular project, and print client invoices right from the database.

Understanding Access Database Objects

A database is a file used to store all the data pertaining to a specific enterprise, business, or project. Data for a single business might include product details, product categories, customer information, customers' orders, employee details, and shipping company details. All of this data is kept in a single Access file, the database, and is easily interrelated so you can find answers to questions such as these: How many orders were placed from customers in Arizona in November? Which employee handled the most orders in the first half of 2001? Access databases include seven types of objects: tables, queries, forms, reports, pages, macros, and Visual Basic modules.

Tables Are the building blocks of databases. Tables contain data: one table for each set of data in the database. For example, the Northwind database includes tables for Categories, Customers, Employees, and other sets of data.

Queries Are used to retrieve data from one or more tables; instructions to sort or filter the results—the data returned by the query—are saved with the query. Forms and reports are often based on queries rather than tables, so a user can enter data in more than one table (customers and orders, for example) or report on more than one table (customers and the orders they placed last month).

Forms Are input objects used to enter (or display) information from tables.

Reports Are the output from a database. They are usually printed.

Pages Are Web pages that can be used for input or output.

Macros Are instructions for manipulating data or other objects. Access does not have a Macro Recorder; you create macros using the Macro Builder.

Modules Contain Visual Basic code that serves the same purpose as macros.

Database structure is provided by tables designed to store data easily, accurately, and without redundancy. Tables are composed of fields, or categories of information, and records, or individual line-item entries, as shown in the Products table in Figure 36.3.

FIGURE 36.3

A table contains records, each of which is made up of a consistent set of fields.

Product ID	Product Name	Supplier	Category	
1	Chai	Exotic Liquids	Beverages	1C
2	Chang	Exotic Liquids	Beverages	24
3	Aniseed Syrup	Exotic Liquids	Condiments	12
4	Chef Anton's Cajun Seasoning	New Orleans Cajun Delights	Condiments	4E
5	Chef Anton's Gumbo Mix	New Orleans Cajun Delights	Condiments	3E
6	Grandma's Boysenberry Spread	Grandma Kelly's Homestead	Condiments	12
7	Uncle Bob's Organic Dried Pears	Grandma Kelly's Homestead	Produce	12
8	Northwoods Cranberry Sauce	Grandma Kelly's Homestead	Condiments	12
9	Mishi Kobe Niku	Tokyo Traders	Meat/Poultry	1E
10	Ikura	Tokyo Traders		
11	Queso Cabrales	Cooperativa de Quesos 'Las Cabras'	Dairy Products	1
12	Queso Manchego La Pastora	Cooperativa de Quesos 'Las Cabras'	Dairy Products	1C
13	Konbu	Mayumi's	Seafood	2
14	Tofu	Mayumi's	Produce	4C
15	Genen Shouyu	Mayumi's	Condiments	24
16	Pavlova	Pavlova, Ltd.	Confections	32
17	Alice Mutton	Pavlova, Ltd.	Meat/Poultry	2C
18	Carnarvon Tigers	Pavlova, Ltd.	Seafood	1E
19	Teatime Chocolate Biscuits	Specialty Biscuits, Ltd.	Confections	1C
20	Sir Rodney's Marmalade	Specialty Biscuits, Ltd.	Confections	3C

Record: 1 of 77

All the other database objects rely on the fields and properties of the tables. If you make significant changes to tables after creating forms and reports, you'll need to modify the forms and reports to reflect the changes. For maximum efficiency, make sure your tables are well designed before creating queries, forms, reports, or pages based on the tables.

MASTERING THE OPPORTUNITIES

About Access Project Files: Access Grows Up

One common complaint about prior versions of Access was that while Access functioned well with a modest amount of data, it was too small to handle large volumes of data. Starting with Access 2000 and continuing with Access 2002, that limitation has disappeared. You can create a database called an Access *project*, which contains only forms, reports, macros, and modules; this part of a database is often called a *front* end. You then link the project file to a SQL Server database, often called a *back-end data store*. For an in-depth look at projects in Access, check out *Mastering Access 2002 Premium Edition*, by Alan Simpson and Celeste Robinson (Sybex, 2001).

Using the Database Window

The Northwind database (Help ➤ Sample Databases ➤ Northwind Sample Database) opens with the splash screen form; all the Microsoft Office applications include a splash screen with copyright information. The Database window appears behind the splash screen. Click OK to close the splash screen form and activate the Database window, shown in Figure 36.4. The Database window is open whenever a database is open. The window can be hidden, but closing it closes the database.

NOTE Access 2002 allows users to open and modify Access 2000 databases without changing the native file format. The title bar of the Database window may indicate that the database is in Access 2000 format, if it was originally created in Access 2000 or earlier.

The object types are listed in the window's Objects bar. To see objects of a specific type, such as forms, click the type name in the Objects bar. Access displays all objects of that type in the Objects list to the right of the Objects bar.

VIII

CREATING AND USING
AN ACCESS DATABASE

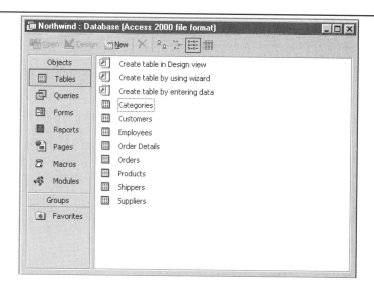

Click an object to select it, or type the first few letters of the object's name. Double-click an object to open it.

 TIP You can change this behavior so that objects in the Database window open with a single click. Choose Tools ➢ Options to open the Options dialog box. On the View tab, choose Single-Click Open.

Groups are an organizational tool introduced in Access 2000. A group can include shortcuts to objects of different types, so you can create groups and place shortcuts to related objects together. For example, you can create a Customers group that contains the Customers table, queries based on the table, and forms used to enter Customer data. When you need to make changes to the table, you can easily identify the other objects that might be affected. Create a group by right-clicking in the area under the Groups bar (see Figure 36.4) and choosing New Group from the shortcut menu. After you've named and created the group, drag objects from the other pages of the Database window to add shortcuts to the objects to the group. You can place shortcuts to an object in as many groups as you want.

NOTE If this is your first time freely exploring Access 2002, spend some time with the Northwind database to see what a database can do. In the Objects bar, choose Forms, double-click on the Main Switchboard to open it, and then check out the various functions of the Northwind database.

Designing Your Own Database

Before you begin constructing your database, you need to spend some time designing it. A poor design virtually ensures that you'll spend extra time reworking the database. Database developers often spend as much time designing a database as they do constructing it in Access. To design a database, you should follow these steps:

1. Determine the need or purpose of the database and what sort of output you'll generate—this helps you determine what data you need to be able to input.

2. Decide what tables the database should include.

3. Specify the fields that each table should include, and determine which fields in each table contain unique values.

4. Decide how the tables are related to each other, and then review and finalize the design.

5. Construct and relate the tables, and enter sample data for testing the database.

6. Create forms, reports, and queries to accomplish your data tasks.

 NOTE The rest of this chapter is an overview of the design process. Details and procedures for creating database objects—tables, queries, forms, and reports—can be found in Chapters 37 through 40.

Determining the Need or Purpose

Every database begins with a problem or need that creating a systematic data tracking system can solve. You might, for example, need to keep track of certain data about customers. Think about why you need the database: what will it allow you to do better than you do now? Send mailings to existing customers? Track orders? Study current

PART
VIII

CREATING AND USING
AN ACCESS DATABASE

customer trends to help identify potential new customers? You'll be able to answer all of these questions if you create the appropriate tables, queries, and reports.

If all of this data pertains to the same business, and one person is responsible for updating the data, it should all be kept in the same database; don't create a different database for each different purpose. A situation in which you'd want to create separate databases within the same business might be in a large company where several different departments are responsible for updating different aspects of company data. In that case, each department might have its own database, and your database designed for one department would link to tables in other departments' databases.

The list of functions to be included in a database is called the database scope. When you know what the completed database should be able to do, open a Word document and create a scope statement that describes the functions of the database as well as the things that it will *not* do. For example, the Northwind database includes information about employees, but it is not a payroll or human resources system. Northwind includes information about customer orders and it prints invoices. It does not, however, print customer statements or overdue-account notices.

A scope statement is critical if you're creating a database that others will also use, and you need to get agreement from your supervisor or colleagues on the functionality of the database. When your database can perform the functions listed in the scope statement, it's done—at least for now—and you can celebrate success. As you work on the database, your colleagues will have suggestions for improvement, some of which will be difficult to add. If you try to include them, you're an active participant in *scope creep*. If, however, you've gotten agreement (in writing is nice) on a scope statement, you can easily defer suggestions that are outside the scope so you can focus on completing the database on a relatively timely basis. When you try to incorporate too many additional features, you run the risk of finishing your database late or not at all; in many organizations, that would make your first database your last database. You're better off completing the database as designed and adding more features in a second or third iteration.

Deciding What Should Be Included

An *entity* is one unit or thing; in a relational database, each entity is in a separate table, and the *fields* in the table describe attributes of the entity. For example, customers are an entity with name, address, and other fields. The orders customers place from Northwind are another entity. The fields in the Customers table pertain to customers, and the fields in the Orders table are about orders.

Fields appear in only one table. In Northwind, it would be redundant to keep the customer's company name, contact name, and address in the Orders table. If a customer moved, the user would need to update the customer address in several places. Keeping customer data in a Customers table and order data in an Orders table is more efficient. When the customer moves, the user only has to change the address once in the Customers table, and it will always be current.

Entity-Relationship (E-R) modeling is a tool for describing and figuring out the tables and fields in your database. It's a great tool to use with Access because the Access Relationships window (see Figure 36.5) looks like an E-R model. You can create a model in any Office application using the Drawing toolbar, or simply use a piece of paper and a pencil or pen. Above each rectangle write the name of the entity: Customers, Orders, Employees, and so on. Draw a rectangle for each entity in your database. When you're well into the process and you've actually created the tables in Access, you can display your own E-R model by choosing Tools ➢ Relationships.

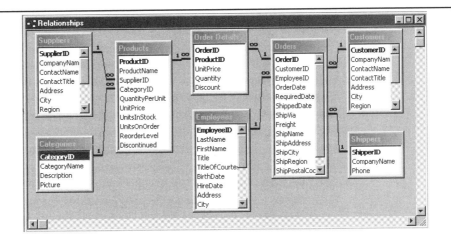

FIGURE 36.5

The Access Relationships window shows the entities (tables) and relationships in the database.

Determining Fields

Once you've established the tables you'll be creating, determine what information about each entity should be included. List all fields for the entity underneath the entity name in the rectangle. There are no free-floating fields in a database: every data field must be part of a specific table. Every field should be *atomic*: that means you store data in its smallest logical components. Street address, city, state, and zip code should be stored separately, rather than in one big field, so that you can create reports for all the customers in one state or zip code.

Within an entity, a field should appear only once. If, for example, we wanted to track a customer's credit card information, as many e-commerce sites and catalog companies do, we wouldn't include the credit card number and expiration date in the Customer entity unless we stored data on only one credit card. If we need to retain information on more than one credit card per customer, credit cards need to be a separate Credit Cards entity. If one customer can have many credit cards, we need two tables. To determine whether you need two tables, then, think about whether the entity you're examining (Customers) can have more than one of the fields you're adding (Credit Cards). If the answer is yes, create another entity.

Identifying Unique Fields

In a relational database, tables are connected to each other through unique fields: fields with values that occur only once in a table. Social Security numbers, for example, uniquely identify one person. A field or a combination of fields that uniquely identifies each record in a table is called a *primary key*. Other common primary key fields are the item number in a catalog, an employee ID, and a UPC for retail products. In some tables, it takes more than one field to create a primary key: a customer number and a date, or an order number and a shipment number.

When you save a table for the first time, you can let Access create a primary key for you; in that case, Access adds a field called ID that contains consecutive, nonrepeating numbers. Access assigns the numbers automatically, so each record in the table has a unique numeric identifier, but unlike an employee ID or a UPC, the numbers themselves have no meaning outside the database. Whenever possible, you should identify a primary key within the data rather than having Access create an ID field.

In your E-R model, put the primary key field at the top of each entity rectangle. Underline, bold, or star the name of the field to show that it's the primary key

 TIP Our database team often uses big sheets of plain white newsprint and large sticky notes—one for each entity—to model the database. When we get to the next section, we can move the entities around on the newsprint while we examine the relationships.

Understanding Table Relationships

A relationship links two tables by linking a common field that appears in both tables. For example, a record in an Orders table includes a Customer ID Number field from a Customers table. The customer's name isn't stored in the Orders table—just the Customer ID Number. The relationship between the Customer ID Number fields in the two tables tells the database that the orders with a particular Customer ID Number belong to the record with the same value in the Customers table. Including a Customer ID Number in the Orders table clearly identifies which customer placed the order, so you can find a customer's name and address for any given order.

A table's primary key is the field or fields used to uniquely identify each record in the table. When you include the key field in another table and use it to relate the two tables, the field in the related table is called a *foreign key*. You can then create a relationship between the foreign key and the primary key fields, which relates the two tables. In the Orders table shown in Figure 36.6, the Order ID field is a primary key. The Order ID field is also included in the Order Details table, where it is a foreign key. To relate the two tables, the developer connected the primary key from the table on the "one" side of a relationship (the primary table) to the foreign key in the "many" table (the related table).

FIGURE 36.6

*Two related tables:
Orders and
Order Details*

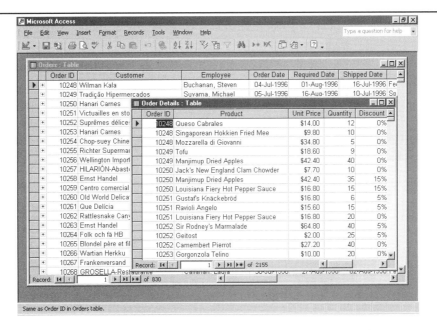

There are three types of relationships: one-to-one, one-to-many, and many-to-many. For each, there is a single correct way to model the data and create the tables so that Access will correctly interpret the relationship.

One-to-One   When two tables are related in a one-to-one relationship, each record in Table A has no more than one record in Table B. You don't see these relationships very often in databases; usually, the developer combines this information into one table. However, a single entity may be separated into two tables because there are too many fields to place in one Access table (more than 256 fields). Or only some of the records in a table may use additional fields, so these fields are placed in a separate table to avoid a lot of empty fields in the first table. For example, if some of your employees are high school interns, the Human Resources database may include a separate School Information table rather than having empty School Name, School Address, and Counselor fields in the Employees table. When two tables have a one-to-one relationship in Access, both tables have the same primary key.

One-to-Many In the more common one-to-many relationship, one record in Table A can be related to many records in Table B: for each Customer ID Number in the Customers table, there can be many records in the Orders table. But the reverse is not true: each order has only one customer.

Many-to-Many A many-to-many relationship means that a record in Table A can be related to many records in Table B, and a record in Table B can be simultaneously related to many records in Table A. For example, a student enrolled in multiple classes can have many teachers, and a teacher can have many students. Relational databases don't allow you to directly create many-to-many relationships. However, there are ways to get around this by creating linking tables.

When two tables have a many-to-many relationship, create a linking table. The linking table's fields are the fields that serve as the primary keys from both of the tables. Select all the fields in the linking table as the primary key of the linking table.

 NOTE There is a fourth way two tables are related: not at all. In Northwind, there is no direct relationship between Employees and Customers. Customers place an order with whatever employee answers the telephone at Northwind.

Work your way through the tables (the entities in your model) to determine how they're related. For each pair of tables, ask the three questions in Table 36.1. The last row indicates the relationship described by the answers.

TABLE 36.1   DETERMINING TABLE RELATIONSHIPS

Question	Answers				
1. Is there a relationship between records in Tables A and B?	Yes	Yes	Yes	Yes	No
2. Can a record in Table A be related to more than one record in Table B?	Yes	Yes	No	No	No
3. Can a record in Table B be related to more than one record in Table A?	Yes	No	Yes	No	No
Relationship	**Many-to-Many**: create a table with primary keys from A and B	**One-to-Many**: include primary key from A in B	**One-to-Many**: include primary key from B in A	**One-to-One**: include primary key from A in B	**No Relationship**: do not include fields from A in B, or B in A

In your database, the one-to-many relationship between two tables allows you to select a single record in one table and see all the related records in a different table. Access displays the related records in a subdatasheet. For example, in Figure 36.7, the Customers table is related to the Orders table. Clicking the plus symbol next to the Customer ID opens a subdatasheet that shows all the orders (in the Orders table) that the customer placed. The plus symbol becomes a minus symbol when the subdatasheet is opened. Click the minus symbol to close the subdatasheet. Subdatasheets are created automatically when you create the relationship between two tables in Access 2002.

 NOTE You can learn more about subdatasheets in "Adding Subdatasheets to Look Up Related Records" in Chapter 37.

A relationship also allows you to create multi-table queries that pull related data out of two or more tables, and reports that summarize data drawn from two or more tables.

NOTE   To learn more about relationships, see "Creating Relationships" in Chapter 37.

FIGURE 36.7

Access creates subdatasheets for related records in another table.

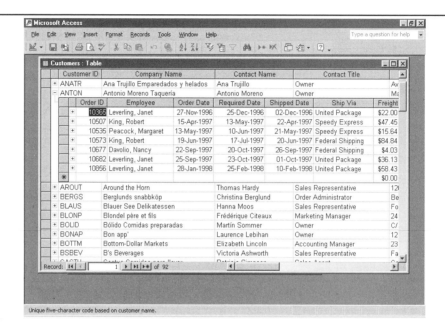

With the primary and foreign key fields in place, you're ready to relate the tables. There are two ways to create relationships in Access 2002: you can create a lookup field in the many table of a one-to-many relationship, or create the relationship directly in the Relationships window (see Figure 36.5). In Chapter 37, find out about lookup fields in "Creating Lookup Fields" and about creating relationships in "Creating Relationships."

In your Entity-Relationship model, draw lines between the related fields in tables. If two tables have a one-to-many relationship, draw a line from the primary key in the "one" table to the foreign key field in the related table. Write 1 and M near the ends of the lines to indicate the one and many ends of the relationship.

Reviewing the Design and the Table Relationships

After you've planned the tables and relationships, and before you begin constructing tables and typing data, you need to reexamine the structure of the database: tables, fields, and relationships. Make sure that:

- All fields are atomic; that is, fields should represent the smallest reasonable piece of data (FirstName and LastName rather than Name).
- Each table describes only one entity.
- Each table has a primary key.
- The only fields that appear in more than one table are primary or foreign keys.
- Related tables include primary and foreign keys, as indicated in the previous section.

When you're convinced that the design is well conceived, proceed to Chapter 37, where you'll begin creating tables and setting relationships.

 TIP   This is the best time to have an experienced database designer review your model. Make arrangements to consult with someone in your organization's IT or IS department. Take your E-R model and scope statement to the review.

CREATING THE DATABASE STRUCTURE

FEATURING

- Creating a new, blank database

- Creating and modifying tables

- Selecting a primary key

- Creating lookup fields

- Importing from Excel, Outlook, and other applications

- Linking to external data

- Modifying field properties

- Relating tables

- Setting referential integrity in relationships

- Entering data in a table

- Using subdatasheets for "drill-down" analysis

I n Chapter 36, "Planning a Database," we created a database using the Database Wizard. If there isn't a wizard for the database that you need to create, or if you want to modify the fields and tables created with a wizard, you need to work in Design view—the focus of this chapter. We'll start by creating and modifying database tables, and importing and linking to existing external data. For imported or created tables, we'll set field properties that ease data entry, ensure that only valid data is entered, and require users to provide entries in important fields. After the tables are created, we'll establish relationships between them and create referential integrity constraints to enforce the rules of those relationships. Finally, we'll enter, edit, sort, and filter data in table Datasheet view.

Creating a New Database

When you create a database from scratch, you have complete control over the database objects, their properties, and the relationships between tables. When you start Access, the task pane opens. To create a database without assistance from the Database Wizard, choose Blank Database and click OK.

After you click OK, you're prompted to enter a filename and a location for the database in the File New Database dialog box. A new database must be saved before you begin creating tables. After you've entered a filename, click Create to create and open a new database.

If the task pane isn't open, choose File ➢ New to open the task pane and create a new database.

Getting Data for the Database

There are three ways to add data to your new database:

- Enter it (using a keyboard or other device).
- Import it from an existing data source; the imported data is a copy.
- Link to an existing data source; when the data in the source changes, the changes are reflected in Access.

Some of the data you'll include in your database doesn't exist yet or only exists in a paper-based system. This data needs to be entered. You'll create tables to hold the data, specifying the fields to include in each table, and enter data in the tables you created. Other data already exists in an electronic form in an Excel workbook, Access or another database, or a text file. You can import or link to this data. If you choose to import, you can create tables for this data and then import the data into the tables. It's often easier, however, to import the data into an Access table first and then modify the table design. When you link to an external data source, you don't design or modify tables in Access. You use the fields and tables in the external data source. To work with external data, see "Importing vs. Linking" later in this chapter.

Creating Tables

To create a new table in a database, display the database tables by clicking the Tables icon in the Objects bar of the Database window. Three table-creation methods are listed:

- Create Table In Design View
- Create Table By Using Wizard
- Create Table By Entering Data

If you're creating a table with fields commonly used in business, begin with the Table Wizard, which includes all the tables and fields used in the General Templates. Fields chosen from the wizard include useful extras. For example, if you choose a phone number field from the Table Wizard, the field is already formatted with the parentheses and hyphens used to format a telephone number. After you're finished with the wizard, you can open the table in Design view and add fields or modify the fields you chose from the wizard.

For tables that only include fields specific to your organization, start in Design view. In Design view, you enter field names and specify all the properties of each field.

In early versions of Access, the last choice, Create Table By Entering Data, was named Create Table In Datasheet View. Don't let the name change fool you: this feature hasn't been improved. Creating tables in Datasheet view is very limiting; you can change the names of fields, add lookup columns, enter data, and that's about it. Access assigns attributes to the fields, sometimes incorrectly. We'd encourage you to simply ignore this third choice—Datasheet view is not a good place to create a table.

PART

VIII

CREATING AND USING
AN ACCESS DATABASE

 MASTERING THE OPPORTUNITIES

Naming Objects

Although Access allows you to name objects any way you want, we suggest that you follow the Leszynski/Reddick (L/R) naming convention so that your databases can be easily understood by other people who work with Access, including you. There are lists

Continued

MASTERING THE OPPORTUNITIES CONTINUED

of objects in Access that include all objects, and some that include both tables and reports. By using a standard naming convention, you'll be able to know at a glance the type of object you're selecting.

Stan Leszynski and Greg Reddick are a couple of well-known database developers who came up with this logical naming convention in the early 1990s to provide a common language for Access developers so they could coordinate their efforts more easily. In the L/R convention, an object name begins with a tag that identifies the kind of object it is: tbl (table), frm (form), rpt (report), qry (query), mcr (macro), or bas (VB code in a module). There are no spaces or punctuation in object names, and the first letter of each word in the name is capitalized. (While Access allows spaces in object names, many other databases do not. Omitting spaces makes it easier to transfer data to other programs.) For example, a table of customer orders might be named tblOrders; a query showing customer order information might be called qryCustOrders. We'll introduce other tags for specialized objects and controls in succeeding chapters.

The Access wizards don't use these naming conventions, but you can add tags to new object names yourself. Right-click an object in the Database window and choose Rename from the shortcut menu.

Creating a Table in Design View

In the Tables tab of the Database window, double click Create Table In Design View to open table Design view. Design view for an existing table is shown in Figure 37.1; you may want to use it as an example to follow as you create your first table from scratch. In the upper pane of the table Design view there are empty rows; use one row for each field in the table, giving each field a name, data type, and optional description. Before saving the table, you should assign one or more fields as the primary key.

FIGURE 37.1

Enter field names, types, and descriptions in the table Design view.

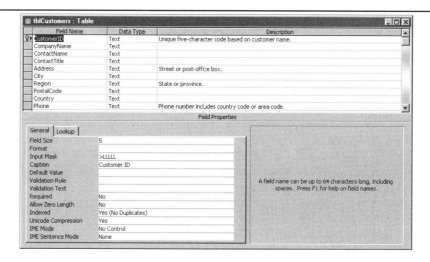

To create a table in Design view, follow these steps. The remainder of this section explains each step in detail.

1. Type the field name for the first field. Enter the field(s) that will be used as the primary key first so you can easily find the primary key when you open a table in Design view. Press Tab to move to the Data Type column, or click in the column.

2. Select a data type from the drop-down list. You can select a data type by typing its first letter; for example, if you know you want a Number data type, type **n** and press Enter or Tab to move to the Description area.

3. Enter a description for the field or leave it blank.

4. Press Enter or Tab to drop to the next blank row and enter the information for the next field. Continue until you have entered all fields.

5. When you have entered all the field names and data types, select the field(s) to designate as a primary key by clicking or dragging the row indicators. (Use Ctrl+click to select noncontiguous fields.) Click the Primary Key button on the toolbar to designate all the selected fields as primary key fields. If you want only a single key field, you can right-click and choose Primary Key from the shortcut menu.

6. Click the Save button on the toolbar or choose File ➤ Save to save the table. Enter a unique table name (beginning with the tbl tag) when prompted.

PART

VIII

CREATING AND USING
AN ACCESS DATABASE

7. To begin entering records, click the View button on the toolbar (see "Entering Data in a Table" later in this chapter); if you're not ready to enter data, close the table to return to the Database window.

Field Names

Field names should be descriptive and as unambiguous as possible. As with the names of tables, queries, and other objects, the convention is initial caps, no spaces. If your database includes customers, employees, and vendor contacts, naming a field First-Name won't be enough to distinguish the customer's first name from an employee's or vendor rep's first name. Use CustomerFirstName or CustFName to avoid ambiguity. The field name is internal—as you'll see later in this chapter, you can specify a different name (a Caption) that users will see—so the name only needs to be useful for you and future developers working on the database tables.

MASTERING TROUBLESHOOTING

Migrating Data When You've Used Names with Spaces

Access has always allowed spaces in object names, but spaces are discouraged because they present a problem if the table is exported to or linked to from another database. If you're going to convert your Access 2002 database to Microsoft SQL Server only, spaces are no longer a problem because SQL uses a unique identifier that Access assigns to each field name. If SQL Server is the only database you'll need to relate or migrate your Access database to, the decision to use spaces in your field names is up to you and your IS or IT department. If you want our opinion, we encourage you to stick with the L/R naming convention (described earlier in this chapter), which does not allow spaces in field names.

If you need to change names to remove the spaces (for example, to migrate Access data to a database that does not accept spaces in object names), Access 2002's Name AutoCorrect feature will change the names for you throughout the database. When you change the field name in one place, the name is changed wherever it occurs in the database objects. The field name is not, however, changed in Visual Basic code in the database.

Name AutoCorrect is turned on by default; you can turn it on or off by choosing Tools ➤ Options, selecting the General tab, and marking or clearing the check boxes under Name AutoCorrect.

Data Types

The *data type* constrains the kind of data that can be entered in the field. If, for example, you select the Number or Currency data type for a field, users won't be able to enter any character other than a digit, minus symbol, plus symbol, decimal point, or dollar sign (assuming your computer is configured to use U.S. currency symbols). Choose Yes/No, and user choices are even further constrained. Choose the data type that reflects the type of data you want users to be able to enter in the field. There are 10 items on the Data Type drop-down list.

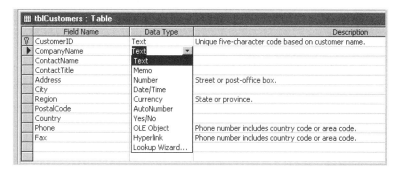

Text Words or numbers that won't be used in calculations (such as phone numbers and Social Security numbers). The maximum length for a Text field is 255 characters. Text is the default data type because it is used most frequently.

Memo An open field that is used for comments. Although you get many more characters than you do with a Text field (65,536), you can't easily sort or filter on a Memo field, so use this field type sparingly, if ever.

Number Numbers that are negative or positive values; unlike Excel, Access does not treat dates as numbers.

Date/Time Dates, times, and combinations of the two.

Currency Numbers in dollars or in dollars and cents.

AutoNumber A numeric field automatically entered by Access; it is used for a primary key field when none of the fields (or combination of fields) in a table is unique.

Yes/No A logical field that can have only one of two opposite values. Data in this field can be displayed six different ways: Yes or No, On or Off, True or False.

OLE Object An object, such as a photograph, a bar code image, or a document that was created in another application.

Hyperlink URL and e-mail addresses.

PART

VIII

CREATING AND USING
AN ACCESS DATABASE

Lookup Wizard Not really a data type, this is used to create a lookup field, which lets the database user select a value from a list, enhancing data accuracy by preventing typos (see the section "Creating Lookup Fields"). Fields created with the Lookup Wizard have one of the data types listed here; when you use the Lookup Wizard to get values from another table, Access creates a relationship between the two tables.

Unlike many other databases, Access databases can store not only text-based data but also objects. Set a field's data type to OLE Object (Object Linking and Embedding object) to store graphics, pictures (including pictures of bar codes), sounds, Excel spreadsheets, PowerPoint presentations or slides, or Word documents. For example, a Products table could include pictures of products or the logo for the products' manufacturer or supplier. A database to track your music collection could include an OLE field for samples from tracks on each CD.

NOTE In addition to choosing a data type, you must also set specific properties for each field in your table. Field properties are discussed later in this chapter.

Descriptions

There are two uses for the field's description. While you're creating a database, this is the best place to keep notes related to specific fields. For example, you may need to verify the data type for a field or do some research to determine the values to use on a drop down list created with the Lookup Wizard.

When the database is completed and you're ready to use the interface built, the field descriptions provide a passive help system. When a user moves to a field in a table or form, the text in the description appears in the status bar. If you've used the descriptions for your own notes, you can either turn off the status bar display or return to Design view to clean up the descriptions.

TIP Objects also have descriptions. These descriptions don't appear on the status bar but are useful for internal documentation. When a table is modified, you can note the changes in the description. To view the property sheet for an object, right-click the object (table, query, and so on) in the Database window and choose Properties from the shortcut menu.

Primary Key

The primary key is the field (or set of fields) that contains unique values within the table: Social Security numbers (if obtainable) for people, product numbers for products, ISBNs for books, FEINs for companies. If a single field can't serve as a primary key, try combining two fields. For example, in the Order Details table shown in the Relationships window in Figure 37.2, neither the OrderID nor the ProductID could be a primary key, since either could occur several times in the Order Details table. However, because each order lists each ordered product just once, every order-product combination is unique. If no combination of fields is suitably unique, you may need to include an AutoNumber field for a primary key. Values in AutoNumber fields are, by definition, unique.

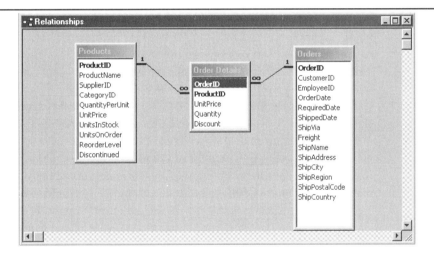

FIGURE 37.2

The Order Details table has a two-field primary key.

PART

VIII

CREATING AND USING
AN ACCESS DATABASE

 WARNING Access lets you create a table without a primary key. Do *not* do this. In a relational database like Access, every table *must* have a primary key for multi-table queries, reports, and forms to work properly.

Creating Lookup Fields

A lookup field gets its entries from either a table or a fixed list of values. Lookups represent the "one" side of a one-to-many relationship. To enter data in a lookup field, the user chooses a value from a list (as shown in Figure 37.3) rather than typing the entry. They can click on a list entry, use the arrow keys on the keyboard, or type the first letter or two of the list entry.

FIGURE 37.3

*Looking up an entry in
a lookup field*

Order ID	Product	Unit Price	Quantity	Discount
10248	Queso Cabrales	$14.00	12	0%
10248	Queso Cabrales	$9.80	10	0%
10248	Queso Manchego La Pastora	$34.80	5	0%
10249	Raclette Courdavault	$18.60	9	0%
10249	Ravioli Angelo	$42.40	40	0%
10250	Rhönbräu Klosterbier	$7.70	10	0%
10250	Röd Kaviar	$42.40	35	15%
10250	Røgede sild	$16.80	15	15%
10251	Rössle Sauerkraut	$16.80	6	5%
10251	Ravioli Angelo	$15.60	15	5%

Lookup fields speed data entry and ensure data accuracy because the user can't inadvertently misspell an entry chosen from a list. But lookup fields aren't just convenient features for users. The enforced accuracy of lookups really pays off when you create reports that sort or group on the values in a field. It's easy, for example, to present all the orders from North Dakota as a group if every user enters North Dakota the same way—**ND** or **North Dakota** or even **N. Dakota**—in each record. If the table includes several different renditions of North Dakota, you'll need to tell Access that ND and North Dakota (and every other state abbreviation and name combination) are equivalent.

Lookup fields are created with a Lookup Wizard. To create a lookup field, decide whether you want to present a list of values from another table or from a fixed list. A fixed list is good if the possible values are few and seldom change, because you don't need to create another table to hold the entries. For example, if you need to enter a credit card type (such as Visa, MasterCard, American Express, or Discover) on an Orders form, your database works faster if you create a fixed list of these names for the lookup field. If, however, your organization decides to start accepting Diner's Club cards, you'll have to correct the list in the table.

If you want to look up product names for an Orders form, a table lookup is a better idea because the list will change whenever you add products. When you look up items in a table, the user always sees the current list of items. The table must exist before you can create a lookup field using the table. It does not need to have records; however, it is easier to size the text boxes used to display table information if the table contains sample records.

TIP Lookup table names begin with the tag t1kp.

To create a lookup based on another table, in Design view follow these steps:

1. If you're creating a new field, enter the field name. Choose Lookup Wizard as the data type.

2. In the first step of the Lookup Wizard (see Figure 37.4), choose whether the data in the lookup will come from a typed-in list or an existing table. Click Next.

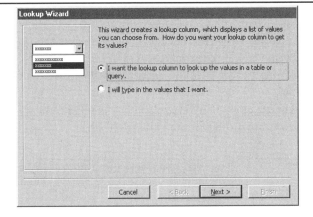

Looking Up Entries from a List

If you choose a typed-in list, in the next step of the wizard you choose a number of columns for the list and type in each item, as shown in Figure 37.5. Press Tab at the end of each item to create the next entry. Then adjust the width of the column so that it is slightly wider than the longest entry, and click Next.

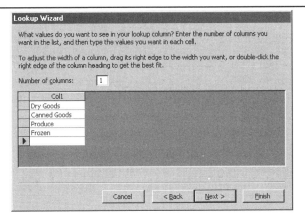

In the last step of the wizard, enter a label for the lookup column; the label will become the new field name when you click Finish. If you want, you can edit the field name in the table.

Looking Up Entries in a Table

If you choose to look up values in a table, you'll be prompted to select a table (or query) in the next step of the Lookup Wizard.

Select a table and choose the columns that you want to include in your lookup. In Figure 37.6, adding the CategoryName field will allow a user to select the category name from a list. The CategoryID field, the primary key, will be included automatically and is the value that is stored in the table where you're creating the lookup. If you choose more than one field, all the fields will be visible when the user opens the lookup list.

Double-click each field to add it to the list. When you have selected all the fields you wish to display in the lookup, click Next.

FIGURE 37.6

Choosing fields from a table for a lookup

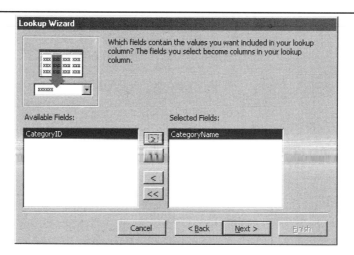

In the next step of the wizard, set the width of each column by dragging the right border of the column label. Unless the primary key field has meaning for your users, leave the Hide Key Column check box enabled. Click Next.

In the last step of the Lookup Wizard, enter a label for the lookup, which will become the new name for the field. Click Finish. You'll be prompted to save the table so that Access can create the relationship between the table you're working on and the table that provides the values for the new lookup field.

Verifying Lookup Relationships

To review the relationship that Access created, close the table and then open the Relationships window: choose Tools ➢ Relationships from the menu, or click the Relationships button on the toolbar. A number of relationships may already be defined, depending on how many lookups you've created in your database.

Click the Show All Relationships button to make sure all the relationships are displayed. The relationship between a Products table and a Categories table is shown in Figure 37.7. The CategoryID is the primary/foreign key field that relates the two tables.

FIGURE 37.7

Relationships are created automatically by the Lookup Wizard.

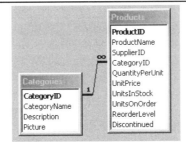

Populating the Lookup Table

After your fields are set up, you can enter data in the table. To open a table in Datasheet view from the Database window, select the table and click Open.

If the table is still open in Design view, click the View button on the left end of the toolbar to switch to the table's Datasheet view. If you've made design changes and haven't saved the table yet, you'll be prompted to do so before you switch views. Choose Yes; if you choose No, you remain in Design view. If you haven't already specified a name for the table, the Table Name dialog box appears. Enter a name for the table in the Table Name dialog box (beginning with **tbl** if you're using the L/R naming convention). If you forget to assign a primary key, a warning appears. Click Cancel, assign a primary key, and save again.

TIP When you change to a different view, the toolbars change to correspond to the view you are in, so don't be surprised if a toolbar looks different when you switch from Design to Datasheet view.

Creating a Table Using the Table Wizard

The Table Wizard is a fast way to create a table. When you select a field in the wizard, you're also selecting the field's data type and properties. The wizard includes sample tables and fields; browsing the lists may prompt you to include fields you hadn't included in your design. To create a table using the Table Wizard, double-click Create Table By Using Wizard on the Tables tab of the Database window.

1. In the first step of the wizard (shown in Figure 37.8), click a category option, Business or Personal, and select a table from the Sample Tables list.

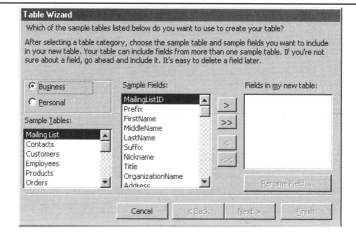

2. To include a field from the Sample Fields list, double-click the field name or use the arrow buttons to move the field to the list of Fields In My New Table.

3. To rename a field, select the field in the Fields In My New Table list. Click the Rename Field button to open the Rename Field dialog box. Enter a name for the field, and click OK.

4. Continue selecting tables and fields for your table. When you've selected all the fields you want to include in this table, click Next.

5. In the second step of the wizard, type a name for your table and select a primary key option.

   a. If you let Access set the primary key, it adds an AutoNumber field to the table. Do this if there is no field or combination of fields that can serve as a primary key, or if you intend to add more fields, including a primary key field, in Design view after finishing with the wizard. Click Next.

b. Choose No, I'll Set The Primary Key if the fields you selected include a primary key. Click Next to advance to the next step of the wizard. Select the key field from the list of fields in your table and choose the data type for that field using the option buttons. Click Next.

 TIP If your table needs a multifield primary key, choose the first option, and Access will add an AutoNumber field. When you're finished with the wizard, open the table in Design view, delete the AutoNumber field, and set the primary key.

6. If there are other tables in your database, the next step of the wizard (see Figure 37.9) prompts you to create relationships to the existing tables. You can create relationships now in the wizard or create them later in the Relationships window. If this is the first table in your database, you won't be asked about relationships, and you can skip ahead to step 7.

FIGURE 37.9

*Create relationships
between the new table
and existing tables.*

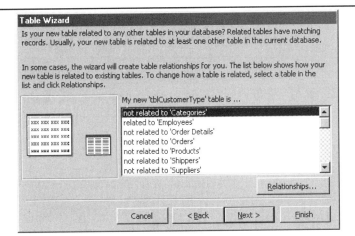

Access lists each table in the database and uses the field names and primary key/foreign key rules discussed in Chapter 36 to determine if the tables may be related. Access doesn't "know" anything about how your tables should be related; it simply compares field names for primary key fields and makes guesses about how they *might* be related. Access creates all the relationships in the list at the conclusion of the Table Wizard. This has all the potential of a bad night at the singles' bar: if you're not attentive, you'll end up with useless or potentially harmful relationships you really don't want to have.

To change a relationship, select the relationship description in the wizard and click the Relationships button to open the Relationships dialog box.

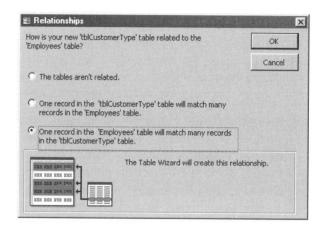

Select the option that describes the relationship between the selected table and the table you're creating, and click OK. Work your way through the list of tables, removing relationships that shouldn't be created and adding relationships if you wish. When you're finished with this step, click Next.

7. In the last step of the wizard, you have three choices. You can select Modify The Table Design to open the finished table in Design view (so you can further tweak the design); you can select Enter Data Directly Into The Table (so you can start entering data in Datasheet view); or you can let Access automatically create and display a form that will allow you to enter data into the table. Select the option you want, and click Finish.

Working with External Data

In Access 2002, you can add copies of tables from other applications to your database or connect directly to tables that exist in a separate database, including spreadsheet files. Access 2002 can import (copy) or link (connect to) data from prior versions of Access, third-party databases like dBASE and Paradox, spreadsheets like Excel and Lotus 1-2-3, and HTML tables from the Internet or an intranet. You can even link to an Outlook Address Book, and programmers will appreciate that the Import command now lets you choose XML (eXtensible Markup Language) documents. The capability to work with data from a variety of sources makes Access a powerful tool in today's workplace, where data can originate in a variety of applications. Before you retype data that already exists, it's worth your time to see whether you can import it directly into Access or transfer it to a program that Access can use.

Access 2002 can turn almost any data file into an Access database table. If you choose File ➤ Open to open an existing data file, the Open dialog box shows multiple data file types (Excel spreadsheets, other database types, text files) in the folder. Opening a file created in an application like Excel starts the Link Spreadsheet Wizard, which guides you through setting up a new database based on the data file. The new database contains a single table, linked to the original file, so you can use the data in Access without duplicating data. Creating an entire database for a single linked table isn't always the most efficient way to work with data, however, so read through the following sections on importing and linking tables into existing databases to determine which method is appropriate.

Importing vs. Linking

Importing data creates a copy of the data in a table in your database. Because a copy is created, the original data isn't affected, and further changes in the original data are not reflected in Access. With *linked* data, you are working with original data; when the source file changes, the changes are reflected in Access, and changes you make in Access are reflected in the source file.

Before you can bring external data into your Access database via importing or linking, you need to decide which method you want to use. For example, let's say that you're creating a new database, and a colleague in another department offers you an Excel spreadsheet that lists all the cities, states, and zip codes for your region. Should you import or link? If you know that the spreadsheet isn't routinely updated, you should import it. Cities, states, and zip codes rarely change, so updating isn't an issue with this data. When you import data, you can change field properties and rearrange or delete fields if you need to, so importing is more flexible from your point of view.

Contrast this with an Excel spreadsheet maintained by the Purchasing Department that lists current products in the inventory. New products are constantly added, and products are removed. You don't want salespeople who use your database to sell products you no longer carry, or fail to sell products that are in stock. You should link to this spreadsheet so your users always have access to current data.

Importing Data

To import external data, choose File ➤ Get External Data ➤ Import to open the Import dialog box. Select the type of file you want to import from the Files Of Type drop-down list. Locate and select the file, and click Import. See the following sections for details on importing from different types of applications.

TIP Not all import file filters are included in a typical Office XP installation. If the file type you want is not listed in the Files Of Type drop-down list, install additional import filters from your Office XP CD-ROM.

Importing Data from Spreadsheets and Other Databases

You can easily import data from Excel or Lotus 1-2-3. (Other spreadsheet filters are available with a custom Office installation.) To do so, follow these steps:

1. Choose File ➢ Get External Data ➢ Import to open the Import dialog box.

2. Select the file you wish to import. Click the Import button. (If you can't see Excel or Lotus files, change the Files Of Type drop-down list at the bottom of the Import dialog box.)

3. If you're importing from an Excel workbook with more than one named range or worksheet, you are prompted to select a worksheet or range (see Figure 37.10). Select the range or worksheet you want to import, and click Next.

FIGURE 37.10

Select a worksheet or range in the Import Spreadsheet Wizard.

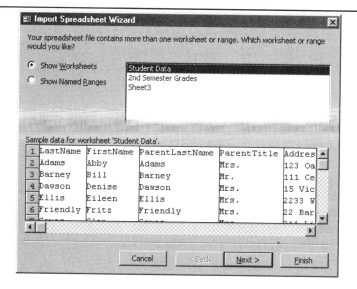

4. In the next step of the wizard (the first step you see if there is only one data source in the file you selected), indicate whether the spreadsheet's first row is data or column labels. Click Next.

TIP If some of the column headings aren't valid Access field names, Access notifies you that it will convert the names (using names like Field1, Field2, etc.). If you're importing this data into a new table, you can change these names in Design view after importing the data. If you intend to import the data directly into an existing table, however, this is a problem. Cancel the wizard, make sure the column headings in the spreadsheet match the field names in the existing table, and start again.

5. In the next step, choose whether you want Access to create a new table with this data or place it in an existing table. If you choose an existing table, the column labels in the spreadsheet and the field names in the table must be identical. Click Next.

6. If you've chosen to import the data into a new table, the next step of the wizard, shown in Figure 37.11, allows you to indicate whether the data in each column is indexed (more on this property later in the chapter); you can omit any columns of data you don't want by enabling the Do Not Import Field (Skip) check box. Click Next.

FIGURE 37.11

*Selecting the columns
you wish to import*

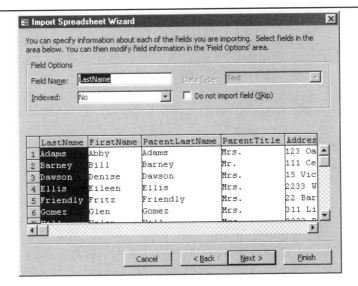

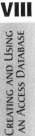

7. In the next step, choose whether to have Access add an AutoNumber primary key (not always the best idea), select an existing column as the primary key, or indicate that there is no primary key field.

TIP If the primary key includes more than one field, choose No Primary Key Field, and set the primary key in table Design view after you've imported the data.

8. In the last step of the wizard, name the table and click Finish. Access will import the data.

After the table is imported, you may want to make some changes in Design view. For example, if a Social Security number column was imported as numbers, you'd want to change the data type to Text and add an input mask to speed up data entry. Numbers that won't be calculated, such as zip codes and part numbers, should be changed if necessary to the Text data type to retain leading or trailing zeros. Data types and field properties (like input masks) are discussed at length later in this chapter.

When you import from a database other than Access, the Import Database Wizard opens, and the steps are similar to the steps in the Import Spreadsheet Wizard.

 MASTERING TROUBLESHOOTING

Handling Data Import Glitches

Access can successfully import or link only to valid databases. Most database applications can only be used to create valid databases; spreadsheet, text, HTML, and XML files may not be valid databases.

When you try to import invalid data, Access reports zero records imported at the end of the Import Wizard. Open the file in its native application and make whatever corrections are necessary to make it a valid database; then resave the file and try again.

If, for example, you try to import 50 rows of data from Excel, and Access reports that zero rows were imported, the Excel spreadsheet is probably not a valid Excel database. Open the Excel workbook, select any cell in the database range, and choose Data ➢ Sort. Excel will select the database range or display a message box indicating that no list is found—that the active cell is not part of a database. For more information on Excel database requirements, see Chapter 16, "Managing Information with Excel."

If some, but not all, rows and columns are selected, check for blank rows or columns within the database. If there is no list, look for advanced formatting in the range. An Excel database can't have merged cells; and multiline cells (created by pressing Alt+Enter when entering data) aren't accurately imported. When you've corrected the Excel database, save the workbook and try importing again.

You can also use Excel's tools to check text and markup databases. Launch Excel and open the HTML, XML, or text document to see how it performs with Excel's data tools.

Importing from Access

If you import from another Access database, you aren't limited to importing just data. You can import forms, reports, macros, and even relationships. When you choose an Access database in the Import dialog box, the Import Objects dialog box opens. Click the Options button to extend the dialog box to show other available options, as shown in Figure 37.12.

Select the tabs in the dialog box to display the type of object you want to import. On each object tab, click Select All to import all the objects, or select specific objects to import. You can import tables with all their data, or import table structures only. When you've selected all the objects you want to import, click OK to import the objects into the current database.

FIGURE 37.12

You can import more than data from another Access database.

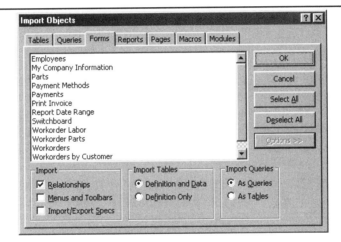

Importing from Outlook or Exchange

NEW▶

You can import items from any of the MAPI folders or address books in Outlook, and import or link to an Exchange address book. Follow these steps to import your Contacts folder from Outlook or Exchange:

1. Choose File ➢ Get External Data ➢ Import.

2. In the Files Of Type drop-down list, choose Outlook or Exchange to open the Import Exchange/Outlook Wizard, shown in Figure 37.13.

3. Locate and select your Contacts folder. Click Next.

4. Select whether you wish to import the contacts into a new table or an existing table. If you select an existing table, the field names must match the field names in Outlook. Click Next.

5. If you're importing the data into an existing table, you're done. Simply click Finish and wait while Access imports the data.

6. If you chose to import the data into a new table, verify the data type for each field. Enable the Do Not Import check box to skip the selected field. Click Next.

FIGURE 37.13

Use the Import Exchange/Outlook Wizard to import Outlook items.

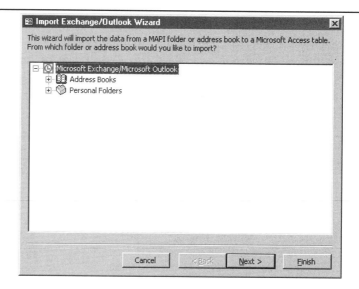

7. Next, choose whether to have Access add an AutoNumber primary key (still not the best idea), select an existing column as the primary key, or indicate that there is no primary key field. You can assign a primary key later in Design view if you want. Click Next.

8. In the final step enter a name for the new table. Click Finish to import the data.

Relax and grab a beverage—this operation can take a few minutes. Access notifies you when the import is complete.

NOTE You can't use this method to import user-created or custom fields. The import includes only the standard fields from the folder. If you need to import Outlook custom fields, you'll need a bit of Visual Basic code. On the Microsoft site, search for Knowledge Base article Q208232 for information on importing user-defined fields from Outlook 2000/2002 into Access.

Linking to a Spreadsheet or Database

If the data you want to include from another source gets updated periodically, you should link to the data rather than importing it. Examples of *dynamic data* include lists of customers or products, price schedules, current course offerings, etc. Linking to a table or worksheet is even less complex than importing. You can't change the structure of the linked table or worksheet, so you don't get an opportunity to skip columns.

Follow these steps to link to an external data source:

1. Choose File ➢ Get External Data ➢ Link Tables.

2. Select the type of data source you want to link to in the Files Of Type drop-down list, select the file you want to link to, and click Link to open the Link Wizard.

3. If you're linking to a spreadsheet or other non-Access file, select the worksheet, named range, or table you want to link to, and click Link. If you're linking to a table or set of tables in another Access database, select the table name(s) and click OK.

   If you're linking to another Access table, the table is linked and you're finished. If you're linking to a non-Access file, continue with step 4.

4. In the wizard, indicate whether the first row contains data or column labels, and click Next.

5. Enter the name you will use to refer to the external table or worksheet, and click Finish.

You can tell which tables in a database are links to other tables. Linked Access tables have a link arrow in front of the Access table icon; other linked file types have their own icons with the link arrow. In Figure 37.14, the tblShippingCompanies table is a linked Excel worksheet.

If you decide later that you don't want to maintain the link, select and delete the link in the Table tab of the Database window. The link is deleted, but the original data source is not affected.

FIGURE 37.14

Linked external files retain the icon from their native application.

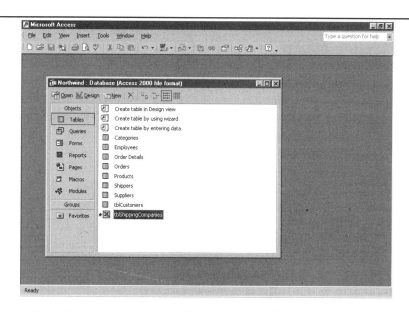

Setting Field Properties

Whether you import a table or create it with the Database Wizard, the Table Wizard, in Design view, or (ugh!) by entering data, you can modify the table and fields in Design view. Every field has properties that control how the field's contents are displayed, stored, controlled, or validated. Some properties are common to all fields, and some properties are only relevant to particular data types. In table Design view, the selected field's properties are displayed in the property sheet at the bottom of the window. For example, Figure 37.15 shows the properties for the EmployeeID field in the Northwind Orders table.

FIGURE 37.15

The two-tabbed property sheet at the bottom of the Design view window displays the properties for the selected field.

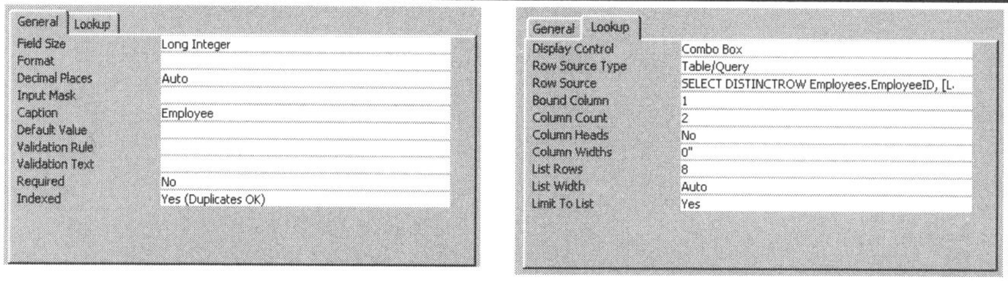

There are two property pages: one for general properties of the field and the other for lookup properties. Lookup properties are set when you use the Lookup Wizard, but you can tweak the properties after creating the lookup. Some properties have drop-down lists; the lists only appear when you click in the property text box.

General Properties

The following general properties are available for most field types. Some of the properties are not available for fields with the OLE Object or AutoNumber data type.

Field Size Property

For Text fields, the Field Size property is the maximum number of characters allowed in the field. For example, you might set the size for a State field to 2. A user isn't allowed to enter more characters than this field setting, so make sure you leave ample room for long names and addresses. For Number fields, the Field Size property limits the minimum and maximum value that can be entered as well as the type of value that is stored. The Integer field size, for example, can store whole numbers from –32,768 to 32,767. The Byte field size stores whole numbers from 0 to 255. Double is used for large numbers with fractional (decimal) portions. For help with the Field Size property, press Shift+F1 and click in the Field Size property text box.

PART

VIII

CREATING AND USING
AN ACCESS DATABASE

 TIP Access 2002's default numeric field size is Long Integer. If you want to store decimal numbers, you must choose another field size. You can change this default on the Tables/Queries page of the Options dialog box (Tools ➤ Options).

Format Property

The Format property indicates how the field's contents are displayed; choices are based on the field's data type. Set the data type first; then for Currency, Date/Time, Number, AutoNumber, and Yes/No fields, choose a built-in format setting from the drop-down list, or enter a custom format. Formats can also be specified for Text and Memo fields, although no drop-down lists of built-in formats are available.

Decimal Places Property

Number and Currency fields have one additional general property, Decimal Places, which specifies the number of digits displayed and stored after the decimal. The default is Auto. To force a specific number of decimal places for values stored in a field, you must set three properties: change the Field Size property to something other than Integer, Long Integer, or Byte; change the Format property to something other than General Number; and set the Decimal Places property.

Input Mask Property

When a user enters data in a Phone field, the punctuation (parentheses and hyphen) normally found in a telephone number can serve as a guide so that the user doesn't have to decide whether they need to type it. Formats for data entry that include placeholders and punctuation are called *input masks*. Input masks work only with Text and Date fields.

To set an input mask, open the table in Design view and follow these steps:

1. Save the table.

2. Select the field, and click the Input Mask text box in the property sheet.

3. Click the Build button that appears at the right end of the Input Mask text box to start the Input Mask Wizard. If the feature isn't installed, Access prompts you to install it.

4. In the first step of the wizard, select the type of input mask you want to create, and click Next to display options for changing the input mask.

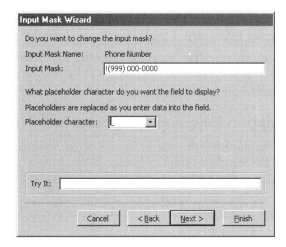

5. If you want, you can edit the input mask (for example, a telephone number might be punctuated as 000-000-0000 or 000.000.0000). If you alter the punctuation, take care not to delete the "!" at the beginning.

6. Select the placeholder you want to appear where the user should enter text, and click Next.

7. In the last step, click an option to indicate whether you want the data stored with or without the input mask. Storing the data with the input mask in place makes the database file a bit larger but preserves the special formatting so it appears in reports. Click Next.

8. Click Finish to save the input mask.

Caption Property

A *caption* is a label used for the field in Datasheet view and on forms and reports; feel free to use spaces and symbols here rather than in field names. If the Caption property is blank, the field name is used to label the field.

WARNING Don't overlook the importance of captioning fields. You probably don't want the labels on your data entry forms and printed reports to be *CompanyName, CompanyAddress,* etc. If you caption those fields now, you'll save an enormous amount of formatting time later.

PART

VIII

CREATING AND USING
AN ACCESS DATABASE

Default Value Property

Use the Default Value property to specify a value for new entries; the user can over-write the default value. Enter the most frequently entered value for the field. For example, if the majority of addresses in a table are from Georgia, enter **GA** as the Default Value property in the State field.

Validation Rule and Validation Text Properties

Validation means screening data to eliminate incorrect entries. Entering a value in a field's Default Value property is a passive way to validate data; if the user doesn't enter anything in the field, at least the default value is there. For more active validation, create a validation rule that all data entries must meet, and validation text to let the user know what constitutes a valid entry. In Access 2002, you can set validation for fields and records in tables and for controls in forms.

Field validation is set in a field's Validation Rule property. When the user tabs or clicks out of the field during data entry, Access checks to make sure the data entered matches the rule. If not, the validation text is displayed.

Record validation is set in the property sheet for the table. When the user moves to a new record during data entry, Access checks to make sure the entire record is valid. Record validation is used to compare one field to another to check, for example, that an employee's hire date occurred before the termination date.

Many field properties are *inheritable*. That means that the validation rule set in a table passes through to any form control based on the table. So, normally you won't use control validation, which is set in a form control's property sheet and which functions in the form but not in the underlying table. It's better to set validation once in the table than four times in four forms.

 NOTE Sometimes, however, you can only perform validation in a form. For example, you can create a form that displays information from an external linked table (see "Importing vs. Linking" earlier in this chapter). The linked table isn't part of your database, so you can't set validation at the table level. You can, however, validate entries in the form. In form Design view, right-click on the form control used to enter data for the field you want to validate. Choose Properties from the shortcut menu to open the control's property sheet. Click on the Data tab and set the Validation Rule and Validation Text properties.

To enter a validation rule for a field, open the table in Design view. Select the field in the upper pane, and click in the Validation Rule property text box in the lower pane. If the rule is simple (for example, minimum pay rate is $10), enter it using logical operators such as **>=10**. The validation rule can be a range, a minimum, or a maximum, as shown in the examples in Table 37.1. In the Validation Text property, enter an error message of up to 255 characters that Access will display when invalid data is entered. This is the message box for the Validation Text property from the first example in Table 37.1.

TABLE 37.1   DATA VALIDATION EXAMPLES

Example Field	Validation Rule	Requires User to Enter	Sample Validation Text
HourlyPayRate	>=10	A pay rate greater than or equal to 10	Pay rate must be at least $10/hour.
AccountCredit	<>0 Or Is Null	A positive or negative number, or no entry	Zero is not a valid entry. Enter a positive or negative number, or leave the field blank.
CheckDate	>=#1/1/01# And <#1/1/02#	A date in the year 2001	Enter a date in the year 2001.
VendorCode	Like "Z??????"	A seven-character vendor code beginning with the letter Z	This is not a valid vendor code. Enter the vendor code, including the initial Z.
Birthdate	<=Now()	A date prior to today	Enter a date prior to today's date.

 TIP If you need more space to type validation text, right-click in the Validation Text property and choose Zoom to open the Zoom window. When you finish entering text, click OK to close the Zoom window.

PART

VIII

CREATING AND USING
AN ACCESS DATABASE

NEW▶

To validate records, right-click anywhere in the Design view window and choose Properties from the shortcut menu to open the Table Properties window, shown in Figure 37.16. Now, in Access 2002, you can open the property sheet for the table and press Shift+F7 to switch the focus back to Design view.

FIGURE 37.16

Use the Table Properties window to define validation rules for records.

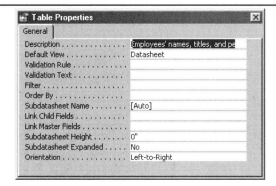

Create table-level validation rules and validation text just as you would for a field: enter the rule and text next to their respective property labels. Validation rules for records are often more complex than field rules, so you may need to use the Expression Builder, shown in Figure 37.17, to create complex field and record validation rules. To open the Expression Builder, click the Build button at the right end of the Validation Rule text box. With the Builder, you can access common functions and, for record validation, field names from the current table.

FIGURE 37.17

Use the Expression Builder to create complex validation rules.

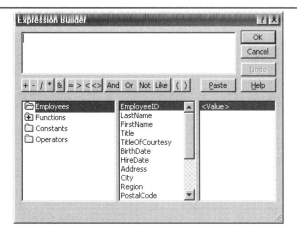

When you add validation rules for fields to a table that already has records, you are asked whether you want Access to apply the rules to the existing data when you save the table. If you choose to apply the rules to existing data, Access scans the existing data and tells you whether there are entries that violate the new rule. Access won't change the existing entries or tell you which ones they are; it just tells you whether any violate the rule. You have to filter or sort the table and locate the existing errors yourself. See the sections "Sorting Records" and "Filtering Records" near the end of this chapter.

Required and Indexed Properties

When a field's Required property is set to Yes, a user must enter data in the field before saving the record. A value of No means that data entry in the field is optional. These properties are important for primary key fields, but they can be set for any field in which you need to control data accuracy and completeness. For example, in an Employee table, you might require entries for first and last names. Don't set a field's property to Required if the data to enter in the field isn't always available to the person creating the record. For example, you may want to add a customer to the table before the billing department has established their credit limit. In this case, you can't require an entry in the CreditLimit field.

Indexing a field speeds up sorting, searching, and filtering on that field; however, too many indexes slow down record editing and entry. The primary key for a table is always indexed. You should index fields like LastName and State that will be frequently used for sorting reports or forms, or for looking up records. There are three possible values for a field's Indexed property: No, Yes (No Duplicates), and Yes (Duplicates OK). Choosing either Yes value creates an index for the field. Yes (No Duplicates) means that the value entered in the field must be unique.

For a single-field primary key, Access sets the Required property to Yes and the Indexed property to Yes (No Duplicates). With a multiple-field primary key, all fields are required, but duplicates are allowed within each field.

Allow Zero Length Property

The Allow Zero Length property, available only for Text fields, is a Yes/No setting that determines whether a text string with no length ("") is a valid entry.

TIP The default setting for Allow Zero Length is No. This works well for most Access databases. Users can't type a zero-length string, so allowing them isn't an issue. So where do you find zero-length strings? In legacy databases on mainframes or minicomputers. If you're planning to import legacy data into a table or think it might even be an option, change the Allow Zero Length setting to Yes for nonrequired fields in the table. It's easier to do this up front than to try to debug the incredibly unhelpful error messages you'll get later when Access refuses to import external data.

Lookup Properties

The Lookup tab (shown earlier in Figure 37.15) includes two types of properties: the Display Control property and properties that are only used in lookup fields.

Display Control Property

For Yes/No fields in your database, you should examine one property on the Lookup properties tab. A Yes/No field can be displayed as a text box (where users type Yes or No), a combo box (a drop-down list), or a check box. For most Yes/No fields, choose Check Box from the Display Control drop-down list.

Properties Used in Lookup Fields

The items in a list created with the Lookup Wizard appear in the order in which they're listed in the table. You can sort the items in a different order by modifying the query behind the lookup. To access the query in table Design view, select the field and open the Lookup property sheet. Click the Row Source property, and then click the Build button to open the query. For help with modifying queries, see Chapter 39, "Creating Reports and Queries."

For lookup fields, check the last property, Limit To List. Set this to Yes if users must choose from the list; set it to No to allow users to enter values that don't appear on the list.

 NOTE For complete information on any of the field properties, hold Shift and press F1, and then click in the text box for the field to display the Access 2002 help topic for the property.

Relating the Tables

Working with table relationships begins in the Relationships window. Use the window to view relationships created during table design with the Lookup Wizard and to create any other required relationships. You then edit each relationship to set referential integrity if the data requires it, and set cascading updates and cascading deletes so Access knows how to handle data changes that affect referential integrity.

Creating Relationships

When you create lookup fields with the Lookup Wizard, Access creates the required relationships. However, some of the relationships in a database may not be used for lookups. Refer to your Entity-Relationship model (see Chapter 36), and you'll probably find relationships between tables that don't involve lookups. You'll need to establish these relationships in the Relationships window.

Before you can relate two tables, the primary key field in the primary table must be included as a foreign key (or, in the case of a one-to-one relationship, as a primary key in the related table. The foreign key field in the related table must have the same data type and size as the primary key in the primary table—with one exception. If the primary key uses an AutoNumber data type, the foreign key field must use the Number data type and the Long Integer field size: the data type and field size of the entries created by AutoNumber fields.

To create a relationship, follow these steps:

1. Activate the Database window by clicking the Database Window button in the Access toolbar.

2. Click the Relationships button on the toolbar or choose Tools ➢ Relationships from the menu to open the Relationships window.

3. Make sure both the primary and related tables are displayed in the Relationships window. If they are not, right-click in the Relationships window and click Show Tables or click the Show Tables button on the toolbar to open the Show Tables dialog box. Select the table you want to add and click the Add button. Click Close to close the dialog box. Or if you have only a few tables in your database, right-click in the Relationships window and choose Show All from the shortcut menu.

4. Select the primary key field in the primary table and drag-and-drop it onto the matching field in the related table. The Edit Relationships dialog box, shown in Figure 37.18, opens.

FIGURE 37.18

Verify that the fields and relationships described in the Edit Relationships dialog box are accurate.

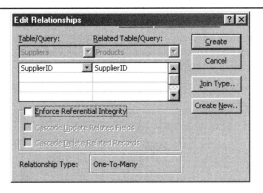

5. In the Edit Relationships dialog box, there are two items to check: that the related field names are correct and that the relationship type is correct. If the field names are incorrect, select the correct field names from the drop-down lists in the dialog box. If the relationship type is Indeterminate, click Cancel. If both of these items are OK, click Create to create the relationship and close the dialog box. A *join line* is drawn between the related fields in the Relationships window.

If Relationship Type is Indeterminate, Access doesn't know how to create the relationship because there's an ambiguity in the field properties for the fields you're attempting to relate. To fix this problem, you need to look in only three places: the Indexed and Required properties and the data types for the two fields. Right-click on one of the tables and choose Table Design from the shortcut menu to open the table in Design view. Both fields should have the same data type (with the exception for AutoNumber fields noted earlier). For a one-to-many relationship, the primary key field's index property should be Yes (No Duplicates), and the Required property should be Yes. In the related table, the foreign key's Index property should be Yes (Duplicates OK). Correct any discrepancies, and then save and close the table to return to the Relationships window and try again.

TIP If you prefer a visual tool for database construction, you can do most of your work in the Relationships window. Create each table with the bare minimum: one field with a data type. Then open the Relationships window and show all the tables. To continue designing a table, right-click the table and choose Table Design.

Setting Referential Integrity

Referential integrity ensures that records in a related table have related values in the primary table. Referential integrity prevents users from accidentally deleting or changing records in a primary table when records in a related table depend on them. This ensures there are no *orphaned* records in the related table, such as orders without customers or salaries without employees. By default, the relationships you create in Access 2002 are not subject to referential integrity rules. In most databases, you'll need to change this setting for some relationships.

 NOTE When referential integrity is applied, the join line in the Relationships window has a "1" symbol and an "infinity" symbol. The symbols indicate a one-to-many relationship between the tables with referential integrity enforced.

PART
VIII

CREATING AND USING
AN ACCESS DATABASE

For example, suppose a database includes two tables: Departments, with DepartmentID as the primary key, and Employees, which includes DepartmentID as a foreign key to show which department an employee is assigned to. When referential integrity is enforced in the relationship between these two tables, three restrictions are applied:

1. Entries in the related table require a matching entry in the primary table. Access doesn't allow users to use a DepartmentID value in the Employees table that doesn't already exist in the Departments table, so they can't make up departments.

2. The entries in the primary table are protected against deletion. Foreign key values (DepartmentIDs) that have been used in the related table protect their matching records in the primary table, so a user can't delete a department in the Departments table that's currently used in the Employees table.

3. The entries in the primary table are protected against updates. A user can't update the DepartmentID value OPS to Opers in the Departments table, because OPS is already referenced in the Employees table.

When users try to enter, delete, or update data that violates the referential integrity rules, Access displays a warning dialog box and ignores the change. Enforcing referential integrity ensures that the data entered from a lookup exists in the primary table. It also means that the primary tables in your database must be kept current. If users can't enter a department that doesn't exist in the database, new departments must be added to the database as soon as they become operational.

To change referential integrity in a relationship, open the Relationships window. Right-click the join line and click Edit Relationship. In the Edit Relationships dialog box (refer to Figure 37.18), enable the Enforce Referential Integrity check box to set it; clear the check box to turn off referential integrity. Click OK to close the dialog box.

Cascading Updates and Deletes

You can override the second and third restrictions outlined in the previous section and still maintain referential integrity by enabling Cascade Update Related Fields and Cascade Delete Related Records.

When you enable Cascade Update Related Fields, changing the value of a primary key in the primary table automatically updates that value in the foreign key of the related table's matching records. With Cascade Update enabled, you *can* change OPS to Opers. The change is automatically reflected in any Employees record that included OPS. In this example, Cascade Update may be useful.

When you enable Cascade Delete Related Records, deleting a record in the primary table deletes any related records in the related table. Deleting the Operations record from the Departments table deletes the record for any employee of the Operations department in the Employees table. Amazingly, you can change your organizational structure and downsize, all with one simple press of the Delete key! In this example, Cascade Delete is probably not useful.

Cascade operations work in only one direction, from primary to related records; changes to related records never travel backward to the primary record. Cascading updates and deletes make your database more efficient by ensuring that related records always match their primary records.

Choosing When to Use Referential Integrity

You need to decide whether to use referential integrity, cascading updates, and cascading deletes on a relationship-by-relationship basis. To make this decision, ask four questions about each relationship:

1. Do you want to limit the values in the related table to values that are already included in the primary table? For example, do you want to make sure that the only department IDs entered in the Employees table are those listed in the Departments table? If you do, enable referential integrity. If, however, users should be allowed to enter departments that aren't already in the Departments table, don't enable referential integrity.

NOTE If you want users to be able to enter departments that aren't in the Departments table and the DepartmentID field in the Employees table is used as a lookup, you also need to set the field's Limit To List lookup property to No.

2. Is the primary key an AutoNumber field? If so, there's no reason to enable Cascade Update Related Fields, because users can't change the values in AutoNumber fields.

3. Do you want users to be able to change the existing values in the primary key? If the department ID for the OPS department changes to MGMT, do you want to automatically update the ID for employees who work in OPS to MGMT? It depends on the purpose of the table. If you need to keep a record to document that an OPS department once existed and had employees assigned to it, don't allow the user to change the primary key value; leave Cascade Update Related Fields disabled. However, if you want to be able to immediately update all the OPS references, allow cascading updates.

4. Do you want to allow users to delete records from the primary table and all related records in the related table? If the OPS department is merged into another department, should deleting OPS from the Departments table also delete all the OPS department employee records? (Probably not!) If not, don't enable Cascade Delete.

A negative answer to the fourth question often takes you back to the first question. You have to choose between accurate supporting data, now and in the future, and the amount of dead data (from closed departments or customers who haven't ordered for years) you're willing to tolerate in lookup tables.

 TIP You can't set referential integrity if existing table data already violates the rules. For example, if you have entered employees in a department that isn't in the Departments table, you'll get an error. Add the department to the Departments table and try again. The error won't tell you where the problem occurred, just that there is one. If many records exist in both tables, a specialized query wizard can pinpoint the problem records. In the Database window choose Insert ➢ Query and then select Find Unmatched Query Wizard in the New Query dialog box.

To set or change the Cascade settings, open the Relationships window. Right-click the join line and click Edit Relationship. In the Edit Relationships dialog box, mark or clear the Cascade check boxes, and click OK.

PART

VIII

CREATING AND USING
AN ACCESS DATABASE

Entering Data in a Table

Before entering data in a table, you should have

- Created the table's fields and set data types, including lookups to lists or related tables

- Set field properties

- Defined the table's other relationships in the Relationships window

If you've completed these steps, it's time to *populate* the tables in the database by entering data. Datasheet view (see Figure 37.19) looks much like a spreadsheet, and skills that you've learned with Excel or other spreadsheets will serve you well here. To open Datasheet view, select the table in the Database window and click Open.

NEW▶ Access 2002 has two new shortcut key combinations to help you work between Design and Datasheet views. In Design view, Ctrl+> (or Ctrl+.—period) takes you to Datasheet view. In Datasheet view, Ctrl+< (or Ctrl+,—comma) takes you to Design view. Make sure you use the correct toggle. If you're already in Datasheet view and use Ctrl+>, Access thinks you want to make a pivot table and displays the windows you need for this feature (which we'll discuss in Chapter 40, "Creating Web Pages with Access.") To get back on track, you must close the extra windows, and reopen the table from the Database window.

FIGURE 37.19

The Customers table in Datasheet view

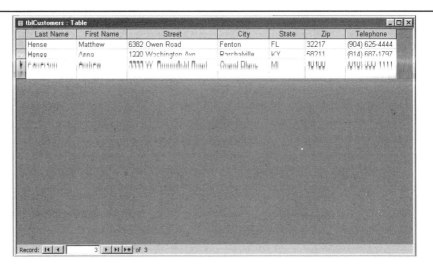

Click in the first field and begin typing the entry; then press Tab to move to the next field. Continue entering field information and pressing Tab until you reach the end of the record; then press Tab again to start another record. Click in any field you want to enter data in; press Shift+Tab to move one field to the left. Press the arrow keys to move one cell at a time in the arrow direction. Press Crtl+Z to undo an entry immediately after you type it.

> **TIP** Press Ctrl+' (apostrophe) to copy the entry in the cell above, or Ctrl+; (semicolon) to insert today's date.

The table columns are set at the default width, so some of the data, like addresses, won't fully display in the column. Maximizing the window displays more of the data, and you can adjust the widths of individual columns. Move the mouse to the right edge of the *field indicator*—the gray bar that is called a column heading in Excel. The mouse pointer changes to a column adjustment tool: a two-headed arrow. Drag to manually adjust the column, or double-click to resize the column to fit the existing data as you would in Excel.

Rearrange columns by dragging the field indicator to a new location. This only affects the layout in Datasheet view; the table design is unchanged. When you close the table, you are prompted to save the layout changes made when you adjusted or moved the columns.

Move around in the datasheet using the arrow keys on the keyboard, and pan the width of the table with the horizontal scroll bar at the bottom of the screen. The vertical scroll bar at the right screen edge moves up and down through the datasheet. (Scroll bars only appear when there is data that cannot be viewed within the current window.) The navigation buttons at the bottom of the screen are used to move to the first, previous, next, last, or new record.

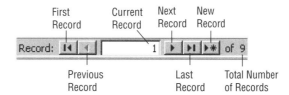

Entering Objects and Hyperlinks in Database Records

Fields with the OLE Object data type are used to store objects such as pictures or sound files. You can store hyperlinks to other files or Web sites in fields with a Hyperlink data type.

Adding Objects to Records

To enter an OLE object in a record, you can't just type in the object's filename—you have to insert the file. In Datasheet view, right-click in the OLE field in the record and choose Insert Object to open the Insert Object dialog box. You can create a new object to place in the field by choosing Create New, but if the object already exists on a local or network hard drive, choose Create From File, as shown in Figure 37.20.

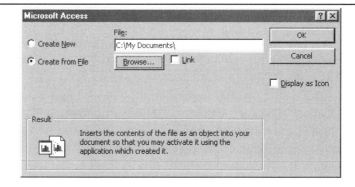

Click the Browse button and locate the OLE object file. If you want the object in the database to be updated when the file changes, enable the Link check box. If you prefer a copy of the object in the database, leave the Link box disabled, and the object will be *embedded* in the database (which also means it won't be updated if the file changes). Click OK to insert the OLE object file in the record.

The object, as it will be in a text description of the object's icon (such as a Word document, a MIDI sequence, or a bitmap) appears in the field. If only text is displayed, double-click the entry to open the object in its native format. For example, a Word document opens in Word; a video clip opens Windows Media Player and begins to play.

Adding Hyperlinks to Records

To enter a hyperlink in a record, open the table in Datasheet view. Type the URL for the hyperlink. The hyperlink turns blue and the text is underlined.

For more support while entering hyperlinks, right-click in the field and choose Hyperlink ➢ Edit Hyperlink to open the Insert Hyperlink dialog box. In the dialog box, you can insert a hyperlink to

- An existing Web page
- A new Web page
- An object in the current dialog box

* An e-mail address (mailto) that will launch the user's default e-mail client

You can enter display text (other than the hyperlink text) and a screen tip that appears when a user hovers over the hyperlink.

When you click the hyperlink, a browser launches and goes to the page or launches the appropriate application to handle the hyperlink. You cannot edit the link by clicking it, because that triggers the hyperlink. To edit or delete the hyperlink, right-click the hyperlink entry; then choose Hyperlink on the shortcut menu and select the command you want. If the hyperlink was misspelled or the address changes, click Edit Hyperlink, and then change the URL text in the Address box in the resulting dialog box. To change the entry in the table to something more meaningful than the URL (for example, *Course Catalog* instead of www.triadconsulting.com/ Course_Catalog_Wel.htm), change the entry in the Text To Display box. To delete the hyperlink, click Remove Hyperlink.

Editing Data

To edit data, move the mouse over the field you want to edit. The mouse pointer changes to an I-beam, and when you click in the field, an insertion point appears. Double-click to select a single word. To select and overtype the entire field, move the mouse to the left edge of the field. The pointer changes to a selection tool. Click once to select the field; begin typing to overwrite old data with new.

Deleting Records

To delete a record, click the *record selector* (also called a *row indicator,* the gray box that is called a row heading in Excel) to select the entire record, and press the Delete key or click the Delete Record toolbar button. Drag the record selector or press Shift+click to select consecutive records. Or right-click the record selector and choose Delete Record from the shortcut menu. Deleting records can't be undone, so a message box appears, prompting you to confirm the deletion. Access does not have a Recycle Bin.

When you finish entering or modifying table data, close the table. If you changed the table layout by adjusting column widths or rearranging columns, you are prompted to save the changes. You are not prompted to save the data you entered; each record is saved as soon as you move the insertion point to a different record.

 NOTE The record you're editing has a small pencil icon in its record selector, indicating that the data in that record isn't saved. When you move to or click in a different record, the pencil icon disappears, indicating that the record has been saved.

Sorting Records

Records can be sorted in ascending (A–Z) or descending (Z–A) order. They can be sorted by any field or by more than one field. For example, you can sort records by last name and then by first name, or by zip code and then by last name within each zip code.

To sort a table in Datasheet view, click anywhere in the column you want to sort by, and then click the Ascending Sort or Descending Sort button. To remove the sort order and return records to their original order, choose Records ➤ Remove Filter/Sort.

When you close a table that has been sorted, Access prompts you to save the changes. Choose Yes if you want to save the sort order so that when you open the table again, the records are displayed using the same sort order.

Multilevel Sorting

A *multilevel sort* sorts the records on the first field you specify and then sorts records with the same value using another specified field. For example, you can sort all the customers by state and then by zip code within each state. To apply a multilevel sort, choose Records ➤ Filter ➤ Advanced Filter/Sort to open the Advanced Filter/Sort window, shown in Figure 37.21.

FIGURE 37.21

Use the Advanced Filter/Sort window for multilevel sorts.

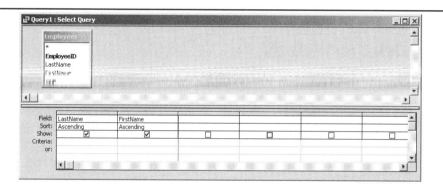

1. In the field list in the upper pane, double-click the field name for the first field you want to sort by (in our example with the Employees table, the LastName field). The field name appears in the first column of the grid. Then double-click the next field you want to sort by (in this example, FirstName).

2. In the Sort row, select a sort order (in this case, Ascending) from the drop-down list for each field.

3. Click the Apply Filter button on the toolbar (even though it's a sort) to close the window and apply the sort order. To remove the sort, choose Records ➤ Remove Filter/Sort.

NOTE In Excel, you can complete a multilevel sort by sorting the columns in reverse order. Access uses a different sorting method, so this doesn't work in Access.

Filtering Records

Applying a *filter* to an Access table temporarily hides records that don't meet criteria that you specify. You can create a filter based on text or a value you have selected, use a blank form to type in the values you want to see, or enter complex filtering and sorting criteria in a window similar to the Access query window.

Filter by Selection/Filter Excluding Selection

The easiest way to apply a filter in Access is with Filter By Selection. Click in the field that contains the value you want to use as a filter and then click the Filter By Selection button. For example, to find all the customers in Mexico, click in any record with Mexico in the Country field and then click the Filter By Selection button.

Only the records for Mexico are visible; all others are hidden. Navigation buttons at the bottom of the table show the number of filtered records.

To remove the filter, click the Remove Filter button. If you want to reapply the filter, click the same button again, which has now become an Apply Filter button.

If you want the filter to match only part of a field, select the part of the data you want to see. For example, if you want to see all the companies in area code 317, select the string "317" in the Telephone field. You can apply filters to filtered data to narrow the search even further.

If you would like to see all the records except those with a certain value—for example, all the customers that aren't in Mexico—locate a record with the value you want to exclude, right-click to open the shortcut menu, and choose Filter Excluding Selection.

Filter by Form

The Filter By Form method works the same way as filtering by selection, except that you set up your criteria on a blank form or datasheet.

Click the Filter By Form button to open the Filter By Form window, a one-row datasheet with field indicators at the top of the columns. Click in a field to open a drop-down list containing all the existing values in that field. Select the value to use as a filter, and click the Apply Filter button. Using this method, you can apply multiple filters to display records that meet all the criteria you select. It's called an AND filter because it filters for records that each meet criterion A, and criterion B, and criterion C, and so on.

You aren't limited to the values in the drop-down lists; you can use *comparison operators* (also called *logical operators*) such as less than (<), more than (>), and greater than or equal to (=>) in your criteria. For example, you can filter a Products table for records that show less than 10 Units In Stock and more than 10 Units On Order, as shown in Figure 37.22.

FIGURE 37.22

Use logical operators to create filter expressions.

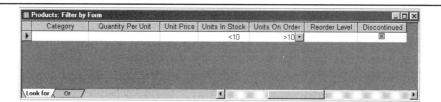

To see records that meet any of the specified criteria, but not necessarily all of them (an OR filter), click the Or tab at the bottom of the form before selecting the additional criterion. For example, you might want to see all customers in "CA" or "AZ." After you set criteria on the Look For and Or sheets, click the Apply Filter button.

Adding Subdatasheets to Look Up Related Records

Subdatasheets allow you to quickly view records in a related table, as shown in Figure 37.23. Subdatasheets leverage the one-to-many relationships in your database by allowing you to open the "one" table and display the related records in the "many" table. Essentially, you are "drilling down" to more detailed information available in the related table, a type of analysis similar to that provided by pivot tables in Excel.

When you open a table with related records in another table, the first column of the datasheet has *expand indicator icons* (small plus symbols). To display a sub-datasheet, click the expand icon next to the record you want to see details for. To hide the subdatasheet, click the *collapse icon* that precedes the record.

FIGURE 37.23

Looking up related records with a subdatasheet

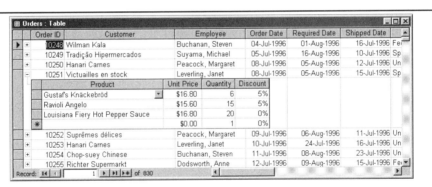

Subdatasheets are created automatically when you create a lookup field (which creates a one-to-many relationship), but you can insert them yourself if no lookup fields connect the two tables. To insert a subdatasheet

1. Open the primary table (on the "one" side of the relationship).

2. Choose Insert ➤ Subdatasheet to open the Insert Subdatasheet dialog box, shown in Figure 37.24.

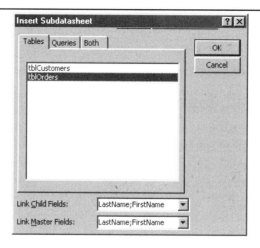

FIGURE 37.24

*The Insert
Subdatasheet
dialog box*

3. Select the related table (on the "many" side of the relationship).

4. Open the list in the Link Child Fields box and select the foreign key field in the related table.

5. Open the list in the Link Master Fields box and select the name of the primary key field in the primary table.

6. Click OK. If a relationship between the two tables doesn't exist, Access asks if you want to create one. Click Yes.

To remove a subdatasheet, choose Format ➢ Subdatasheet ➢ Remove.

 TIP Access does not display the foreign key in the subdatasheet. To display the foreign key, click in the subdatasheet and choose Format ➢ Unhide Columns from the menu.

CREATING AND USING FORMS

I n Chapter 37, "Creating the Database Structure," we created tables and entered data directly into the tables in Datasheet view. A datasheet in a table is similar to an Excel worksheet but not quite as easy to use. The user can't freeze columns to easily see which row they're working in, so it's easy to edit the wrong data or delete the wrong record. Tables are data containers; they're not the ideal place for users to enter or edit data. And in a relational database, users often need to enter data in more than one table: a new customer and the order they want to place; a new vendor and the products they supply.

Forms allow users to enter or view data without needing to know how the database tables are designed or related. A form doesn't need to include all of a table's fields, so the form may omit fields where users can't enter data, such as AutoNumber fields. A database's *user interface* is the collection of forms used to interact with the data.

A form can include data from multiple tables, providing one-stop data entry. You can design the form so that it looks just like a physical document that serves as the source document—a membership application, a customer data form, or another document used to collect data—to make it easier for users to enter data correctly. As with tables, there is more than one way to create a form. Access provides three form-creation methods: AutoForms, the Form Wizard, and form Design view.

 NOTE We'll continue to use the Northwind database for illustrations in this chapter so you can play along. Northwind.mdb is on the Office XP CD. See the note at the beginning of Chapter 36, "Planning a Database," for information on installing and locating the Northwind database.

Selecting a Form Layout

Most data entry forms are based on one of three layouts: datasheet, tabular, or columnar. Figure 38.1 shows a simple datasheet form for the Northwind Customers table. The datasheet form layout looks just like the table's Datasheet view, right down to the navigation buttons. Users can rearrange the columns and rows as they would in the table's Datasheet view.

FIGURE 38.1

A datasheet form resembles the table's Datasheet view.

Customers1

Custo	Company Name	Contact Name	Contact Title	Address
ALFKI	Alfreds Futterkiste	Maria Anders	Sales Representative	Obere Str. 57
ANATI	Ana Trujillo Emparedados y helad	Ana Trujillo	Owner	Avda. de la Constitución 222
ANTO	Antonio Moreno Taquería	Antonio Moreno	Owner	Mataderos 2312
AROU	Around the Horn	Thomas Hardy	Sales Representative	120 Hanover Sq.
BERG	Berglunds snabbköp	Christina Berglund	Order Administrator	Berguvsvägen 8
BLAU	Blauer See Delikatessen	Hanna Moos	Sales Representative	Forsterstr. 57
BLON	Blondel père et fils	Frédérique Citeaux	Marketing Manager	24, place Kléber
BOLIC	Bólido Comidas preparadas	Martín Sommer	Owner	C/ Araquil, 67
BONA	Bon app'	Laurence Lebihan	Owner	12, rue des Bouchers
BOTTI	Bottom-Dollar Markets	Elizabeth Lincoln	Accounting Manager	23 Tsawassen Blvd.
BSBE	B's Beverages	Victoria Ashworth	Sales Representative	Fauntleroy Circus
CACTI	Cactus Comidas para llevar	Patricio Simpson	Sales Agent	Cerrito 333
CENTI	Centro comercial Moctezuma	Francisco Chang	Marketing Manager	Sierras de Granada 9993
CHOP	Chop-suey Chinese	Yang Wang	Owner	Hauptstr. 29
COMN	Comércio Mineiro	Pedro Afonso	Sales Associate	Av. dos Lusíadas, 23
CONS	Consolidated Holdings	Elizabeth Brown	Sales Representative	Berkeley Gardens

Record: 1 of 91

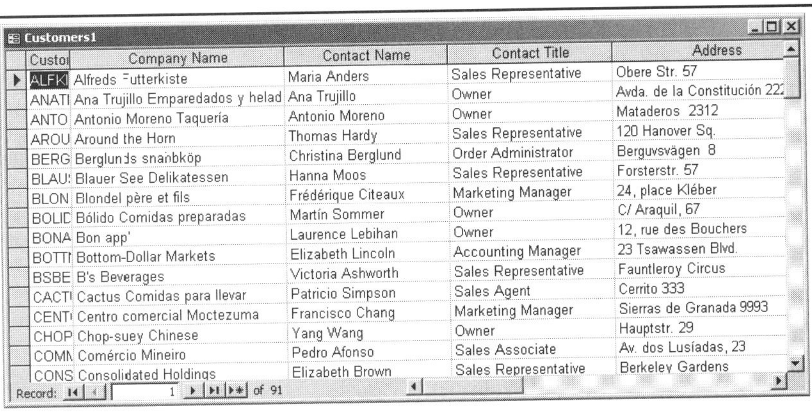

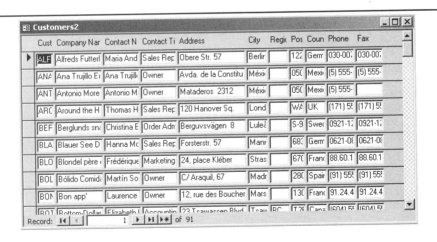

A tabular form for the Customers table is shown in Figure 38.2. Like the datasheet form, the tabular form presents multiple records. However, the form itself looks a bit more polished, and movement within the form is limited. While it's true that you can use combinations of keystrokes to move freely within the form and from record to record, the most typically used single keystrokes (Tab and Enter) only allow you to move from field to field within each record and from the last field in one record to the first field in the next record; furthermore, you can't navigate between records using the arrow keys on the keyboard.

FIGURE 38.2

A tabular form is a more polished version of the datasheet form.

Customers2

Cust	Company Nar	Contact N	Contact Ti	Address	City	Regi	Pos	Coun	Phone	Fax
ALF	Alfreds Futterl	Maria And	Sales Rep	Obere Str. 57	Berlir		122	Germ	030-007	030-007
ANA	Ana Trujillo E	Ana Trujill	Owner	Avda. de la Constitu	Méxi		050	Mexi	(5) 555-	(5) 555-
ANT	Antonio More	Antonio M	Owner	Mataderos 2312	Méxi		050	Mexi	(5) 555-	
ARC	Around the H	Thomas H	Sales Rep	120 Hanover Sq.	Lond		WA	UK	(171) 55	(171) 55
BEF	Berglunds sna	Christina E	Order Adr	Berguvsvägen 8	Luleå		S-9	Swec	0921-12	0921-12
BLA	Blauer See D	Hanna Mc	Sales Rep	Forsterstr. 57	Manr		683	Germ	0621-08	0621-08
BLO	Blondel père	Frédérique	Marketing	24, place Kléber	Stras		670	Franc	88.60.1	88.60.1
BOL	Bólido Comida	Martín So	Owner	C/ Araquil, 67	Madr		280	Spair	(91) 555	(91) 555
BON	Bon app'	Laurence	Owner	12, rue des Boucher	Mars		130	Franc	91.24.4	91.24.4
BOT	Bottom-Dollar	Elizabeth I	Accountin	23 Tsawassen Blvd.	Tsaw	BC	T2F	Cana	(604) 55	(604) 55

Record: 1 of 91

A columnar form, like the form shown in Figure 38.3, displays one record at a time. If the primary purpose of a form is data entry or editing one record at a time, a columnar form is best. Click the navigation buttons to move between records or enter a new record.

FIGURE 38.3

Columnar forms display one record at a time.

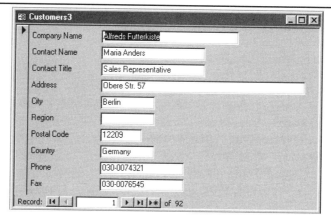

Both the tabular and datasheet forms display multiple records. A common use for a datasheet or tabular form is as a subform: a form within another form. For example, the Northwind Orders form is a columnar form that includes a datasheet subform, as shown in Figure 38.4. A form and subform are used to display data from a primary table and a related table.

FIGURE 38.4

This form displays data from two tables. The columnar form displays customer data; the datasheet subform displays customers' orders from the related table.

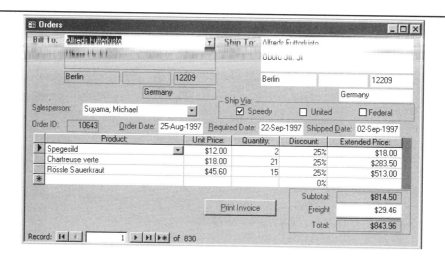

Creating AutoForms

AutoForms are quick and frill-free forms created with a few clicks on the Access tool-bars. AutoForms are based on a single table or query. You select the table or query and choose a layout, and Access creates the form. To create an AutoForm, choose Insert ➤ Form from the menu; or click the Forms button in the Objects bar of the Database window and then click the New button on the Database window toolbar to open the New Form dialog box shown here.

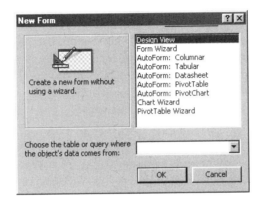

We'll stick with the basic form options for now; select the one you want (Tabular, Columnar, or Datasheet) from the AutoForm layouts. In the drop-down list, select the table you want to base the form on. Click OK to create and display the form. When you close the form, you are prompted to save it. The L/R prefix for forms is frm.

There's an even faster way to create an AutoForm. Begin by selecting the table on the Tables tab of the Database window. Open the drop-down menu on the New Object button on the Database toolbar. Choose AutoForm to create a columnar Auto-Form; or choose Form to open the New Form dialog box, where you can choose different types of AutoForms.

AutoForms are a good choice when you need a quick form that includes all the information from a single table. You might create an AutoForm to populate lookup tables in your database. But AutoForms are built for speed, not for comfort: Auto-Forms are labeled with field names rather than captions; fields are placed on the form in table order, including fields that have no value to the user.

If you don't want to display all the fields from a table, or if you need data from multiple tables, use the Form Wizard or Design view to create your form. See these other sections in this chapter: "Creating Forms for Multiple Tables" to learn about the Form Wizard, and "Modifying Form Design" to learn about Design view. First, however, we'll look at some basic form operations so you know how users interact with forms—critical knowledge when you're designing or modifying forms.

Entering and Editing in Forms

In a datasheet form, users enter and edit information exactly as they would in the table's Datasheet view. To select and edit a field, move the mouse pointer to the left edge of the field and click.

Tabular and columnar forms display each data field in a *text box control*: an editable area on a form that is bound to a field in a table. In tabular and columnar forms, drag to select all the text in a field before entering the correct data. To move to the next record in a form, tab out of the last text box control for the current record, or simply press Ctrl+Page Down. In all forms, you can use the navigation buttons to move between existing records and use the Delete Record button on the toolbar to delete the current record or selected records.

 NOTE A *control* is any element of an interface that a user can interact with or a developer can place, delete, move, or size: a text box, a button, a label, and so on. You'll see the term often in this chapter and the next because controls are the building blocks for forms and reports.

NEW Nothing messes up data like users' spelling errors. There are some steps you can take to minimize the potential for typographical errors (drop-down lists, for example) However, we can't overstress the importance having your users spell check their data. And now there's a Spelling tab in the Options dialog box (Tools ➢ Options), so you can set language options and create custom dictionary names just as you have always been able to do in other Office applications.

Printing Forms

Forms print as displayed on the screen. But don't click that Print button yet! When you click the Print toolbar button, Access prints every record in the active record set—in this case, that's your entire database. If the form is a columnar form, each record prints on a separate page; this can amount to a lot of dead trees. Reports, discussed in Chapter 39, "Creating Reports and Queries," are the Access object designed for printed output, so they provide many more options for printing single or multiple records.

To print the current record or selected records, displayed in a table's Datasheet view or in a tabular form, use the mouse to select the records you want to print. Choose

File ➤ Print from the menu bar to open the Print dialog box, choose Selected
Record(s) under Print Range, and click OK.

MASTERING THE OPPORTUNITIES

Printing Forms for Manual Use

One use for printed forms is as a blank form that you can distribute to others so they can
fill it out and return it for data entry. To print a blank form, open the form and display a
new record (choose Records ➤ Data Entry from the menu or click the New Record button on the navigation bar). If you print a totally blank record, the text boxes do not
appear. Type a space or period in one field so that the record is not blank, and choose
File ➤ Print Preview to preview and print the form. (If the underlying table has other data
entry requirements, you'll have to meet those before you can print the record.)

Searching, Sorting, and Filtering in Forms

You can search for, sort, and filter data in forms just as easily as in a table, and the
techniques are quite similar.

Searching for Records

Access provides an easy way to find individual records; it even allows you to look for a
partial name if you are unsure about how the name is spelled. Find and the related
Replace operation locate or replace *strings*, a group of consecutive characters.

To use the Find tool in Access, open any form and click in the field that contains
the data you're searching for. Click the Find button on the toolbar to open the Find
And Replace dialog box.

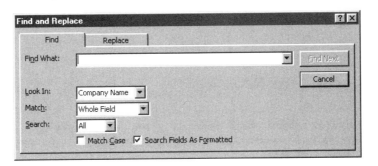

Type the search string you are looking for and click Find Next. Access searches through the records in the form and finds the first occurrence of the text you entered in the field you specified, as shown in Figure 38.5. (You might need to move the dialog box out of the way to see the search results.) If the search string occurs more than once, you can click Find Next again to find the next occurrence.

Use the Find feature to search for a value or a string.

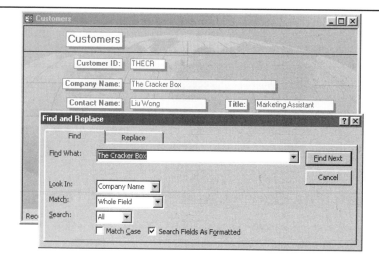

Access provides a number of useful options for advanced searching. Let's say, for example, that you only remember that a person's name starts with *Has*. You can change the search parameters in a number of ways. You can look for all records where the value in the ContactName field starts with *Has* by choosing Start Of Field in the Match box. If all you know about the name is that it has a *ch* near the end, you can choose to match Any Part Of Field. You can instruct Access to search all the fields in the form by selecting the form name in the Look In box, or just select the field name to search the current field.

To further refine your searches, you can specify that you want to match the case of the text string, and you can search up or down from your current position in the record set instead of searching the whole set. Searching up or down is an issue if the current set contains many thousands of records and searching in one direction would save time.

Replacing Data

To replace a text string with another string, select the Replace tab in the Find And Replace dialog box. The Replace settings are identical to the Find settings, except that you also enter a replacement string in the Replace With box.

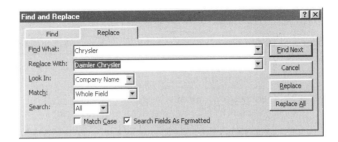

Use the Replace With field to enter text that you want to appear in place of the text in the Find What field. For example, if an employee's name changes, you can find and replace the name easily. If the relationship between the Employees table and the Orders table is set up with referential integrity and cascading updates, the employee name changes wherever it occurs in the Orders table, too.

Verify and replace text strings one at a time by clicking the Find Next and Replace buttons, or replace all instances of the text string by clicking the Replace All button. Be careful using Replace All; Access does what you instruct, so you can inadvertently replace lots of text strings that you shouldn't have.

 TIP You can also use Replace to remove a string. For example, we needed to remove the prefix –SS from the part number field in 500 records in an inventory table. We entered –SS as the Find string, left the Replace With text box blank, enabled Match Case, and set Match to Any Part Of Field before clicking Replace All.

Using Wildcards

You can construct search criteria using *wildcards*, symbols that represent one or more characters. Table 38.1 lists wildcard characters you can use with Find.

TABLE 38.1   WILDCARD SYMBOLS

Wildcard	Usage	Example
*	Can be used at the beginning or the end of a string to match any number of characters.	Par* finds *Parker* and *Parson*. *son finds *Parson* and *Williamson*.
?	Matches any single alphabetic character.	w?ll finds *wall*, *well*, and *will*.
#	Matches any single numeric character.	4#5 finds *405*, *415*, *425*, etc.

Continued ▶

PART

VIII

CREATING AND USING
AN ACCESS DATABASE

TABLE 38.1 (continued) WILDCARD SYMBOLS		
Wildcard	**Usage**	**Example**
[ ]	Matches any single character specified in the brackets.	w[ai]ll finds *wall* and *will*, but not *well*.
-	Identifies any one of a range of characters in ascending order.	[c-h]ill finds *dill*, *fill*, *gill*, and *hill*, but not *kill*, *mill*, etc.
!	Used within brackets to specify any character not in the brackets.	w[!ai]ll finds *well*, but not *wall* or *will*.

Sorting and Filtering Records in Forms

Records in forms are really records stored in tables and viewed through the window of a form. While working with a form, you have essentially the same sorting and filtering options discussed for tables in Chapter 37. There are, however, some sorting and filtering features specific to forms.

When you sort a form and then close it, the sort order is saved with the form automatically. You are not prompted to save changes to the form as you are when you sort in a table. The saved sort order in the form has no effect on the sort order in the underlying table, and changing the sort order in a table doesn't affect the sort order in forms.

Form filters are also saved with and limited to their forms; filters in a form don't affect the underlying table, and filters applied in a table don't affect forms based on the table.

The major difference between filtering a table and filtering a form is the display when you filter by form (refer to Chapter 37). In a table, the Filter By Form window resembles the table's datasheet layout; in a form, the Filter By Form window resembles the form layout.

 WARNING If your users are likely to filter a form and then wonder where all the records went, you may want to consider limiting their access to toolbars and menus in the user interface. Just before you release the database to users, customize the Access toolbar by removing the buttons you don't want users to have (see Appendix A, "Customizing the Office Environment"). Then remove the names of the toolbars from user menus so users can't add or remove buttons. Choose View ➢ Toolbars ➢ Customize. Select the toolbar you want to hide, click Properties on the Toolbars tab, and clear the Allow Showing/Hiding check box. To hide menus from users, choose Tools ➢ Startup and clear the Allow Full Menus, Allow Default Shortcut Menus, and Use Access Special Keys check boxes.

Creating Forms for Multiple Tables

Users rarely get to work with one table at a time. Customers don't call to set up a new account and then call again to place their first order. Forms based on multiple tables are necessary to support the kinds of data entry users require. When you base a form on multiple tables, the result is two forms: one form (a *subform*) nested within another form (the *main form*), or a main form with a button that opens the related form. Use the Form Wizard to create forms that display data from related tables—the *related* part is important, because if you haven't created a relationship between two tables, you can't relate them in a form.

NOTE See "Creating Relationships" in Chapter 37 if you need to verify the relationships between tables in your database.

Multiple Tables, Forms, and Subforms

When you create a form with fields from more than one table, the wizard prompts you to select either a single form or a form and a subform. The choice depends on the use for the form. If you select the Customers and Orders tables in the Northwind database, switching between By Customers (the primary table) and By Orders (the related one) changes the sample in the Form Wizard. Figure 38.6 shows the sample form when By Customers is selected; it's a main form with a subform that shows all the orders a specific customer has placed.

When the form is arranged by the primary table, Customers, the focus is on customers and their orders. The main form includes a datasheet or tabular subform to display the customer's orders: the sunken area of the preview (see Figure 38.6). The subform displays the many order records—a visual representation of the one-to-many relationship between the Customers table and the Orders table. If the main form contains many fields, if there are a lot of records in the subform, or if the data in the related table is used infrequently, choose the Linked Forms option to display the subform as a linked form, as shown in Figure 38.7. The main form contains a button that opens the linked subform.

FIGURE 38.6

*Multiple-table
form arranged
by Customers
(the primary table)*

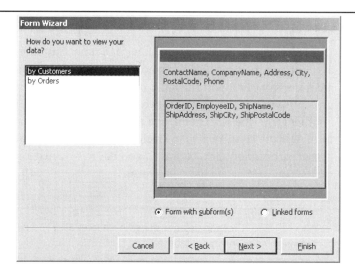

FIGURE 38.7

*To ease crowding in
the main form, create
a linked subform.*

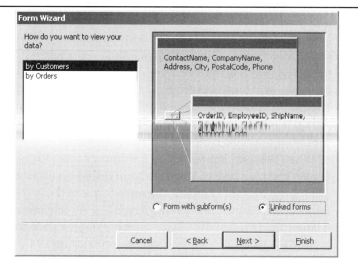

The sample form arranged By Orders is shown in Figure 38.8. When the primary focus of the form is the related table Orders rather than Customers, there is no subform. Each order was placed by one customer, so there is no need for a subform to display multiple customers for a single order.

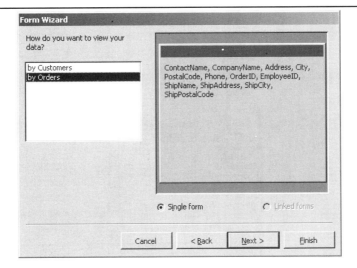

FIGURE 38.8

*The same form
arranged by Orders
(the related table)*

Create forms for a single table with the Form Wizard if you want to omit fields or ensure that the form is labeled with captions rather than field names. When you're creating forms for multiple tables, the Form Wizard is the best tool. While creating the forms, the wizard sets the form properties so that users cannot make changes— such as deleting a linked record—that would violate relationships between the tables.

You can create forms with data from multiple tables in Design view, but it's tedious and time-consuming. If you're interested in efficiency, start every form by using either the Form Wizard or an AutoForm, and then modify the form in Design view. Very few forms (most of them very complex) can be created more quickly when you work solely in Design view.

Creating Forms with the Form Wizard

To create a form with the Form Wizard, follow these steps:

1. Select the Forms tab in the Database window and double-click Create Form By Using Wizard, or choose Form from the menu on the New Object toolbar button and choose Form Wizard in the New Form dialog box. Either way, the Form Wizard opens as shown here.

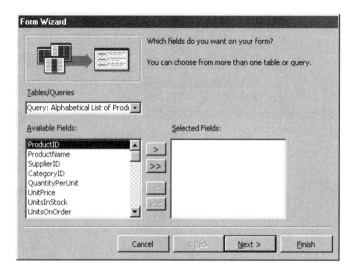

2. In the Form Wizard, select one of the tables you want to use in the Tables/Queries drop-down list.

3. In the Available Fields list, double-click the fields to include, or use the arrow buttons to move fields in order to the Selected Fields list.

4. Select a related table you want to use in the form.

5. Select the fields to include from the related table.

6. Repeat steps 3 and 4 until all fields are selected. Click the Next button.

7. In the next step of the wizard, select how you want to view your data. If the tables have a one-to-many (rather than a one-to-one) relationship, you are asked how you want to view your data—whether the form's primary focus should be the primary or the related table. If you select By [*primary table*], set the Form With Subform(s) or Linked Forms option. Click Next.

NOTE If you choose fields from unrelated tables, the Form Wizard displays an error message. Close the wizard, set the relationships (Tools ➢ Relationships), and start the Form Wizard again.

8. If the form includes a subform, choose the Tabular or Datasheet format. Click Next.

9. Select a style for the main form; Standard is recommended. Click Next.

10. Enter names for the form (using the frm tag) and the subform (using the fsub or sfrm tag). Click Finish to create the form(s).

Modifying Form Design

The forms created with the Form Wizard or AutoForms have limited visual appeal. Fortunately, forms have a Design view, just as tables do, and Access includes many tools for modifying a form's design. To switch to Design view in an open form, click the Design View button on the Database toolbar. To display a form in Design view, select the form in the Database window and click the Design button on the toolbar. The form in Figure 38.9 is shown in Design view.

TIP You spend a lot of time switching between Design view and Form view as you're working in Access. When you change a form's design, it's only logical that you want to see those changes from a user's perspective. Remember, you can use Ctrl+> and Ctrl+< to toggle between Form view and Design view.

PART

VIII

CREATING AND USING
AN ACCESS DATABASE

FIGURE 38.9

A form in Design view

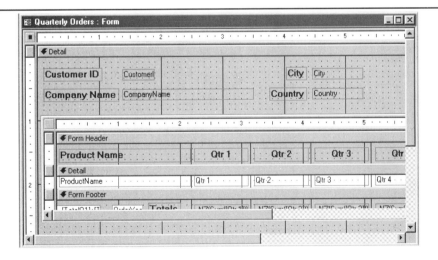

The Design View window includes horizontal and vertical rulers and Form Design and Formatting toolbars. The Toolbox button includes tools to add controls to the form. If the Toolbox doesn't appear when you open a form in Design view, click the Toolbox button on the Form Design toolbar.

In Design view, a form includes several sections and a number of different controls. The sections are:

Form Header Appears at the beginning of the first page of the form and is usually used for titles.

Form Footer Appears at the end of the last page of the form and is used for user tips or other miscellaneous information.

Page Header Is used for printing information at the top of every page in a form.

Page Footer Is used for printing information at the bottom of every page in a form.

Detail Section Displays a record's data.

The Quarterly Orders form, shown previously in Figure 38.9 doesn't have Page Headers and Footers, so those sections don't display by default. If the Form or Page Header and Form Footer bars aren't visible, choose View ➤ Form Header/Footer or View ➤ Page Header/Footer from the menu bar to show them. The Detail section includes the form background and controls, including text boxes that display table data and labels, and the caption or field name from the table. In tabular and datasheet forms, labels appear in the Form Header section, and text boxes appear below the labels in the Detail section. Figure 38.10 shows controls commonly used in Access forms.

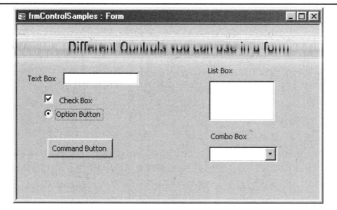

FIGURE 38.10

Common form controls

If you want to rearrange a form, it's easiest to begin by enlarging the form's area. Move the mouse pointer to the bottom of the Detail section, just above the Form Footer. When the pointer changes to an adjustment tool, drag the Footer bar down to increase the height of the Detail area. To increase the Header section, drag the Detail bar down to make the Header area larger. Adjust the form width by dragging the right edge of the form.

 TIP The Design View window includes an extra toolbar and rulers that aren't displayed in Form view, so you can't precisely resize the Form View window with the mouse. To resize the Form View window after you finish working in Design view, switch to Form view, make sure the form window is *not* maximized, and then choose Window ➤ Size To Fit Form from the menu.

Using a Background Picture

When you create a form using the Form Wizard, you can add a background as part of the style selected in the third step of the wizard. When you choose a style other than Standard, you get more than the picture—you get fonts and control properties that don't meet the Windows design standard. Rather than select a nonstandard style, add a background picture in Design view. You can use one of the Access background pictures included in styles or a bitmap picture of your own—perhaps a company logo or a photo.

To add a picture to the background, open the form in Design view. Double-click the *form selector*—the gray box in the upper-left corner of the form window at the intersection of the vertical and horizontal rulers—to open the Form property sheet. In Access 2002, you can also press F4 to open the property sheet. In the property sheet, select the Format tab. Scroll down the list of Format properties and select the Picture property. Click the Build button to open the Insert Picture dialog box. Locate the graphics file you want to use as a background and click OK.

 TIP The pictures used in the Form Wizard styles can be found in the Microsoft Office Styles folder: usually `C:\Program Files\Microsoft Office\Office10\Bitmaps\Styles`. Not there? Use Windows Find, and search for `ACSUMIPT.GIF` (the Sumi background) to locate the correct folder.

Working with Form Controls

To select a control, click it. Handles indicate the control is selected. If you click a control that's already selected, the insertion point appears inside the control so that you can edit text in the control. To reselect the control, click anywhere outside the control and then click the control again.

NOTE Controls that display data, such as text boxes and check boxes, are *bound* (directly tied) to fields in the underlying table; labels, however, are just text on the form and are *unbound*.

To select multiple controls:
- Move the pointer to either ruler bar. The pointer changes to a bold arrow pointing toward the form. Press the mouse button, and a line drops directly through the form. Drag along the ruler to select controls within a vertical or horizontal area. When you release the button, all the controls that the line passed through are selected.
- If the controls you want to select aren't grouped together, you can select one control and hold the Shift key while selecting additional control(s).
- Starting outside any control, drag a rectangle over the controls you wish to select. Hold Shift and click to unselect controls that you don't want to include in the selection.

TIP To specify whether you need to touch or enclose controls to select them, choose Tools ➢ Options to open the Options dialog box. On the Forms/Reports page, choose Par-

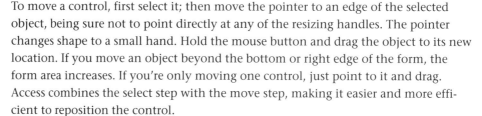

controls completely included in the rectangle.

Delete selected controls by pressing the Delete key on the keyboard.

Moving and Sizing Controls

To move a control, first select it; then move the pointer to an edge of the selected object, being sure not to point directly at any of the resizing handles. The pointer changes shape to a small hand. Hold the mouse button and drag the object to its new location. If you move an object beyond the bottom or right edge of the form, the form area increases. If you're only moving one control, just point to it and drag. Access combines the select step with the move step, making it easier and more efficient to reposition the control.

When you select certain controls—text boxes, check boxes, and option buttons—the corresponding label is also selected.

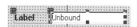

 Point to the edge of the text box (not on a handle) to see the Hand pointer. Move the text box *and* the label by dragging the Hand. To move one control but not the other, point to the move handle on the upper-left corner of the text box or label control. The pointer changes to a finger pointing at the move handle. Drag the control to move it.

 TIP When you click to select a text box, the corresponding label is only partially selected. It *moves* with the text box, but if you change the *format* of the text box, the label format does not change. To format the label, you must click the label to select it.

 Adjust the size of controls as you would any graphic object: by dragging the resizing handles at the corners and sides of the object. Note, however, that changing the size of a text box control does not change the size of its underlying field. To change field size, you must go to the table's Design view and change the field size properties.

TIP For extra precision, select a control and use Shift+arrow keys to resize and Ctrl+arrow keys to move the control.

Adding and Formatting Labels and Controls

You can place and format labels in any section of a form. All labels can be edited and formatted with impunity. Click on a selected label to edit the text in the label.

 WARNING *Don't* change the field name that appears in a text box control. You'll break the binding between the control and its underlying field, and data from the table won't appear in that control. If you're not sure whether a control is a text box or a label, right-click the control and choose Properties. The control type appears in the property sheet title bar.

Adding a Title

The Form Header section is generally used for a form title. Use the Toolbox Label tool to create a title or other text or to add extra information for a user. In the Toolbox, click the Label tool; when you move the pointer back into the design area, it changes to a large letter *A* with crosshairs. Move the pointer into the header area, click where you want to place the label, and type the label text. When you are done entering text, click elsewhere in the form to close the label control. Then you can select the control and use the Formatting toolbar to format the title.

If you make a mistake, you can click the Undo button to reverse your last action. In Access 2002 you have multiple undo capabilities in Design view. That means you can click the button more than once to reverse several actions. Click the drop-down arrow on the Undo button to see the Undo history. Move the mouse down the list to select multiple actions and click to undo them all at once. The Undo history even survives changing views, so you don't have to make sure you're done "undoing" before you switch from Design view to Form view.

Formatting Text

If you know how to format text in Word, Excel, or PowerPoint, you know most of what you need to know to format controls in Access. Select one or more controls and then choose formatting options from the Formatting toolbar, or right-click on the control(s) and select options from the shortcut menu.

Font/Fore Color is the color used for text. Some colors, such as dark blue, make a very attractive form that is easy to read. Other colors, such as yellow, are very hard to read and should be used sparingly, unless you make the background dark and contrasting (which is itself a bad idea.)

The Fill/Back Color is the color for the fill behind the text. The default for labels is transparent, which means the color from the form background appears as the label's background color. The default background color for text boxes is white.

To change the appearance of text, select the controls that contain the text you want to change (to save time, you can select and format several controls at once). Use the Font, Font Size, Weight And Style, Alignment, and Color buttons on the Formatting toolbar to format the selected controls.

Changing Borders

Every Access control has a border. Borders have three properties: color, line width, and special effect.

Although you can't delete the border, you can effectively disable all three properties by choosing Transparent as the border color. Just click the drop-down arrow on the Line/Border Color button and choose Transparent from the top of the color palette. A transparent border has no visible width, color, or effect. This is effective for labels, but text boxes should have borders so that users know where to enter data.

TIP The brief history of PCs is littered with obsolete applications that were functional but made their users feel stupid. Keeping your form design close to the Windows standards makes it easier to use, which helps your users feel reasonably smart. If you're not sure how a control should be formatted, look at any Office dialog box (Print, Save As, Open) for guidance.

You can change the border width using the Line/Border Width button on the Formatting toolbar, selecting widths from a hairline thickness to a 6-point width. Typically, a 1- or 2-point border is appropriate for a text box control, but thicker borders can be used for titles and graphic design.

Border effects differentiate types of controls and draw the user's attention to important controls. The six special effects you can access from the Special Effects button's drop-down list, shown in Figure 38.11, are:

Flat Appropriate for controls, such as labels, that are not used for data entry.

Sunken The best choice for text boxes, for editing or entering data.

Shadowed A good choice for titles.

Raised Another useful choice for data entry or titles, or to draw attention to a part of the screen.

Etched The standard choice for text boxes that cannot be changed.

Chiseled Good for titles. It applies a single inverted line underneath the control.

When you apply the Sunken, Raised, Etched, or Chiseled effects, you turn off any other choices for border color and line width. Only Flat and Shadowed are affected by the border-color and line-width formatting options.

To apply borders and special effects, select the controls you want to change. Then use the Line/Border Color, Line/Border Width, and Special Effects buttons on the Formatting toolbar or the shortcut menu to format the borders for the selected controls.

PART

VIII

CREATING AND USING
AN ACCESS DATABASE

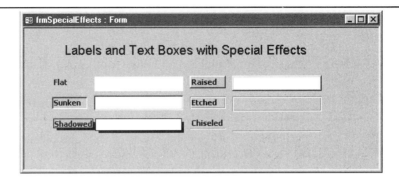

 Changing several controls one by one can be a time-consuming task. You can select and format several controls all at once, or you can use the Format Painter to paint all the formatting—color, borders, special effects, and alignment—from one control onto another. Just follow these steps to do so:

1. Format one control so that it appears as you want it.

2. Select the formatted control.

3. Click the Format Painter.

4. Click an unformatted control. The formatting from the selected control is immediately copied to the second control.

If you're going to apply the selected format to more than one other control, double-click the Format Painter button to lock it on. Click it again to turn it off.

Conditional Formatting

Conditional formatting is displayed when a control's value meets specific criteria that you set. For example, you can conditionally format a Unit Price text box to have bright-red bold text on a yellow background if the Unit Price in the displayed record is more than $100.

To create a conditional format, open the form in Design view. Select the control that you wish to format and choose Format ➣ Conditional Formatting. In the Condition 1 text boxes of the Conditional Formatting dialog box (see Figure 38.12), set a value range in which formatting will apply, and set the formatting with the formatting buttons. The example in Figure 38.12 shows a format for values more than 100; the conditional format is bold text on a shaded background. Click Add if you want to add more conditions to the same control: for example, you may wish to change the color if the value is greater than $50. You can set up to three conditions on a control. Click OK to apply the format; click Delete to remove the conditional format.

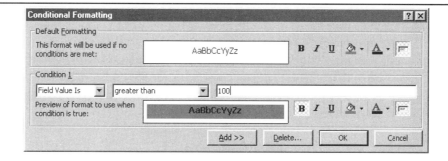

FIGURE 38.12

Create a conditional format to highlight significant values in a form.

In the first condition, you can set a conditional format that is displayed only when the field has *focus:* when the user clicks in or tabs to the field. If there are lots of fields on your form or you're creating forms that will be used by the visually impaired, consider adding this conditional format to all the controls on the form.

 WARNING Conditional formats are applied in the order in which they appear in the Conditional Formatting dialog box. If the value meets the first condition, the format is applied and no other conditions are checked. Therefore, if the first condition bolds values >=100 and the second condition italicizes values >=150, no value will ever be italicized. Reverse the conditions, and the formatting will work as intended.

Dividing Pages and Page Sections

A form that's cluttered or that includes fields representing several different types of information can be hard to use. With Access 2002 you can separate your forms into individual pages or use graphic lines and rectangles to segment the form visually.

 A *page break* is a marker that separates pages in a form that's too long to be displayed on the screen. To insert a page break, click the Page Break button on the Toolbox. When you move the pointer back into the design area, it changes to a crosshair with a piece of paper below it. Click on the form where you want the page break to appear. The Page Break Marker displays on the form, next to the vertical ruler.

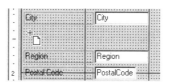

The page break automatically positions itself at the form's left margin. After you add a page break, resize the form so that only one page is visible at a time in Form view (switch to Form view and choose Window ➢ Size To Fit Form).

To move from page to page in a multiple-page form, the user must press the Page Up and Page Down keys (or click in the form's scroll bar).

To delete the page break, switch to Design view; select the Page Break Marker and press the Delete key.

Relative Sizing and Alignment

A form's background has a grid of horizontal and vertical guidelines and points. If the grid points aren't visible, choose View ➢ Grid. When you move a control, it automatically lines up with the grid, both horizontally and vertically. If you try to place the edge of the control between two grid points, Access moves it to align with one grid point or the other. This is a feature called *Snap To Grid*.

 TIP For easier formatting in forms and reports, move the gridlines farther apart. Choose Format on the menu to ensure Snap To Grid is on. Open the property sheet for the entire form (or report). On the Format page, change the Grid X and Grid Y property values to a larger number: 5 or 10.

Sometimes you might want to place controls so they aren't on a grid point—closer together than the grid allows or not as far apart as two grid points require. To do this, you must first turn off Snap To Grid by choosing Format ➢ Snap To Grid. The Snap To Grid feature is not one you need to turn off very often, but working without Snap To Grid is essential for small refinements in your Access forms.

 TIP When you create a form with the Form Wizard or AutoForms, controls are not aligned with the grid. See "Aligning Controls" for hints on lining up controls irrespective of the grid.

Aligning, Sizing, and Spacing Controls

You can manually adjust the size and position of every control on a form. However, Access automates size and positioning features so you can manipulate multiple controls simultaneously for perfect layout results.

Aligning Controls

Begin by selecting two or more controls, and then choose Format ➤ Align or right-click and choose Align from the shortcut menu to open the list of alignment options.

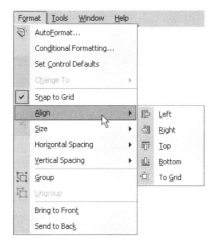

Align ➤ Left aligns the left edges of all selected controls with the leftmost of them. Align ➤ Right works the same way but to the right, as shown in Figure 38.13. Use Align ➤ Top or Align ➤ Bottom to adjust controls on the same horizontal line.

FIGURE 38.13

Select two or more controls and use the Access alignment features.

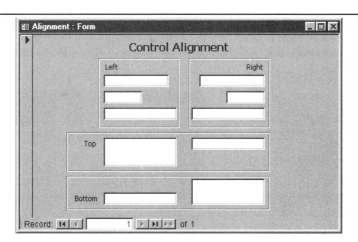

TIP Access can't always align controls that are overlapped, but that doesn't stop it from trying. Separate overlapping controls before attempting to align them.

Sizing Controls

Choosing Format ➤ Size ➤ To Fit or double-clicking any sizing handle instantly resizes labels to fit their text. You can select two or more controls and use the other sizing options to resize all the selected controls to the same size. Tallest and Shortest refer to vertical height, and Widest and Narrowest refer to horizontal width.

Spacing Controls

Spacing allows you to increase or decrease the relative position of selected controls by one grid point either horizontally or vertically. This is valuable if you need to spread out controls or move them closer together for a neater visual layout. You can also use spacing to make sure controls are evenly spaced. Select the controls, and choose Format ➤ Vertical Spacing (or Horizontal Spacing) ➤ Make Equal (or Increase or Decrease).

Rearranging the Tab Order

A form's *tab order*—the sequence of controls you move through when pressing Tab—is assigned when the form is created. After you rearrange controls on a form, the tab order may be out of sequence. Users expect to be able to move through the form sequentially, so an inconsistent tab order almost guarantees data entry errors. To change a form's tab order, choose View ➤ Tab Order, or right-click and choose Tab Order, to open the Tab Order dialog box.

You can set the tab order for each of the three sections on the form, but you'll usually only care about the Detail section. Clicking Auto Order generally rearranges the fields in the correct order, so it always makes sense to try this option first. If the auto order is not correct, you can set the order manually. Click the row selector for a control; then drag the control up or down into position in the tab order.

 TIP You should test how well your forms work each time you make any substantive change. Enter sample data and make sure everything operates as you expect it to.

Formatting Subforms

Making formatting changes to a form that has a subform is in most ways no different than formatting a single form. You can format it just as you would any form, using the Toolbox and the Formatting toolbar. To size a subform, stretch the borders of the subform control in the main form, not in the subform itself. If the subform has a datasheet format, open the main/subform combination in Form view and resize the columns by dragging or double-clicking the column headers.

NEW ▶ When you open a main form that includes a subform, often the subform controls are not accessible. Double-click the subform to open it in its own Design View window or right-click it and choose Subform In New Window.

Adding Controls to Existing Forms

 If you add a field to a table, existing forms won't include the field. Sometimes you change your mind about the fields you omitted when you originally created the form. In both cases, you must add the field to the form in order for users to enter data in the field. To add a field's text box control to the form, click the Field List button on the toolbar to open the Field list. In Access 2002, you can also press F8 to open the Field list from Design view.

You can resize the Field list by dragging its borders as necessary. Or use the scroll bar to view available fields. Select the field you wish to add and press Enter, or drag the desired field from the Field list into the design surface and drop it in place. Proceed with formatting the control as you normally would. Controls created from the Field list are automatically bound to their table fields.

TIP To add a control that enables users to look up a record in the form, don't choose from the Field list. Instead, insert a combo box control from the Toolbox. Make sure the Control Wizards button on the Toolbox is turned on; then click the combo box control and click in your form to launch the Combo Box Wizard.

Formatting Datasheets

A form's Datasheet view looks like its underlying table but only shows the fields you included in the form. Like a Form view, it's just a window into the table where the data is stored. All the formatting changes you can make to a table can also be made to a form's Datasheet view, including row height, column width, hiding, freezing, and conditional formatting.

If the form is already open in Design view (or Form view) and you wish to display it in Datasheet view, just click the drop-down arrow on the View button and choose Datasheet view. All the formatting options can be found on the Format menu.

Changing Properties of Forms and Controls

Every Access object—including controls—has properties. As with field properties and data types, the specific properties for a control depend on the control type. For example, the properties of a text box include its color, font, size, and control source: the table or query and the field that supplies data to the text box. Field properties include size, input masks, and the field type. Form properties include the size of the form, how the form can be viewed, and its record source: the table or query the records come from.

It's not essential to know every available property to work successfully in Access. However, whenever an object doesn't behave as you expect it to, it's a good idea to look for a property that might be affecting its behavior. To view the properties for a control, double-click the control in Design view to open the property sheet, or right-click the control and choose Properties from the shortcut menu.

To open a form's property sheet, double-click the form selector (at the intersection of the vertical and horizontal rulers). A form has four categories of properties (the All tab lists all the properties found on the other four tabs):

Format Properties related to formatting—what the form or control looks like, what buttons and bars are activated, what views are allowed

Data Properties that indicate the record or control source and whether the data can be edited

Event Properties that control events to which you can attach macros and programming code

Other Miscellaneous properties that relate to the object, including, for example, a field's tab order

The property sheet title bar includes the name of the selected object. If you want to look at properties for another control, don't close the property sheet—just click the control to display its property sheet or select from the drop-down list at the top of the property sheet.

 TIP Access 2002 includes voluminous help on each of the control and object properties. With a property sheet open, choose Help ➢ What's This [?] from the menu, and then click the property you'd like information about.

Changing Property Settings on Multiple Fields

Often, you'll want to change the property settings on multiple controls at the same time. If you select more than one control and open the property sheet, only those properties that affect all the selected controls are displayed. For example, if you select a label and a text box, no Data or Event properties are displayed; the text box has Data and Event properties, but the label does not.

 TIP Unless you're feeling very adventurous, you should leave the default settings for properties that you are unfamiliar with.

Hiding Form Features

A number of elements are enabled by default on every form, including scroll bars, record selectors, and navigation buttons. All these elements can be turned off in the form's property sheet. For example, the scroll bars are only needed if parts of the form don't fit on the screen. Record selectors may or may not be necessary. Navigation buttons are generally not needed on a subform. All these features take up valuable screen space and can cause confusion during data entry. You can turn off features you don't need by opening the form's property sheet and changing the item's setting to No on the Format property sheet. These changes, relatively easy to make, can make the form much easier to use.

 MASTERING THE OPPORTUNITIES

Creating a Switchboard and Setting Startup Options

You can make it easier for users to access the forms you create through the use of a switchboard. A switchboard is composed of pages with command buttons that open forms, open reports, close the application, or complete other actions that you select. A database can have only one switchboard. To be efficient, wait to create it until all other forms and reports are done.

To create a switchboard, choose Tools ➢ Database Utilities and select Switchboard Manager. (If Switchboard Manager isn't a choice on the menu, choose Tools ➢ Add-Ins ➢ Add-In Manager and install the Switchboard Manager add-in.) When you are prompted to create a new switchboard, choose Yes. The default switchboard has only one page, which is enough if your users can only take eight or fewer actions. Follow these steps to create items on the main page and to create additional switchboard pages:

1. To add commands to an existing page, click the Edit button to open the Edit Switchboard Page dialog box.

2. Click New to open the Edit Switchboard Item dialog box.

3. Enter the label for the command's button in the text box.

4. Choose a command from the Command drop-down list.

5. If a third text box appears, choose an object (form, report, or macro) for the command.

6. Click OK.

Continued

MASTERING THE OPPORTUNITIES CONTINUED

7. Repeat steps 2 through 6 to add more commands to the page. In the Edit Switchboard Page dialog box, use the Move Up and Move Down buttons to arrange the item list.

8. To add pages to the switchboard, click the New button in the Switchboard Manager dialog box.

9. When you are finished creating pages and items, click Close to close the Switchboard Manager.

The last command on the main page of the switchboard should be Exit Application. If your switchboard contains more than one page, the last command on pages other than the main page should be Go To Switchboard, and the switchboard specified should be the Main Switchboard.

The Switchboard Manager creates a table called Switchboard Items and a form named Switchboard. The form contains Visual Basic code that refers to the form and table, so don't rename either of these objects.

If you need to edit the switchboard, choose Tools ➢ Database Utilities ➢ Switchboard Manager to open the Manager.

To have the switchboard open automatically when a user launches the database, choose Tools ➢ Startup to open the Startup dialog box. In the Display Form/Page control, choose Switchboard. To hide the Database window after the form is displayed, disable the Display Database Window check box. Now in Access 2002 you can even choose an icon for your database. Just click the Build button in the Startup dialog box, and locate and select the icon picture file.

Click OK to set the Startup options. If you need to access the Database window, hold Shift while opening the database to bypass the Startup options.

PART

VIII

CREATING AND USING
AN ACCESS DATABASE

If you've come this far, you'll eventually want to know more about form and control properties and events. Information is close at hand. We recommend the Microsoft Access 2002 Help files. For more information, we suggest *Mastering Access 2002 Premium Edition,* by Alan Simpson and Celeste Robinson (Sybex, 2001).

CHAPTER 39

CREATING REPORTS AND QUERIES

FEATURING

- Creating AutoReports

- Using the Report Wizard

- Previewing and printing reports

- Modifying reports

- Saving a report as a Web page

- Creating a simple query

- Sorting and printing query results

- Creating a parameter query

- Building summary queries

- Using calculations in queries

- Setting crosstab queries

n this chapter, we'll tackle the objects used to get data out of the database: reports and queries. A *report* is the printed output of the data in one or more database tables. Access 2002 gives you the freedom to report data in a variety of ways. You can dump all the fields in a table into a simple report or use only those fields that are needed. Add sorting, grouping, and formatting, and you've got a report to rival those created by much more expensive database-reporting tools. The flexibility to customize reports and to organize the data in useful ways—in other words, to make it accessible—is really what gives Access its name.

When you create forms or reports with fields from more than one table, Access creates a *query* to deliver data to the report or form. The Lookup Wizard, discussed previously in Chapter 37, "Creating the Database Structure," creates queries to retrieve the list to display in the drop-down list. These queries don't appear with the others in the Queries section in the Database window; they're saved as a property of the form, report, or table. You can save these queries separately or create queries from scratch. By modifying a query, you can change the sort order or filter the records displayed. In the second half of this chapter, we'll create and modify queries.

Creating Reports

A report is a static picture of current data. When you save a report, Access saves the controls and information about the report's record source: the table or query needed to present, sort, and filter the data. When you open a report, the data displayed is retrieved from the tables in the database, so the data in a report is as current as the much in the database when the report was opened and printed.

 TIP Reports (except basic AutoReports) created with the Report Wizard include the date and time in the Page Footer. Because a report is always generated "fresh" whenever you open it, the date and time in the Page Footer reflect when you printed the report, not when you created or saved it.

Most reports use either the columnar or tabular format. A *columnar report*, like the report shown in Print Preview in Figure 39.1, shows each field on a separate line in a single column down the page. The fields for one record are printed in full, followed by the fields for the next record. The columnar report is the printed version of a columnar form.

FIGURE 39.1

A columnar report lists each field on a separate line, one record following another.

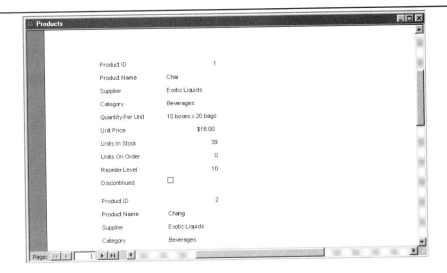

A *tabular report* (shown in Figure 39.2) is like a tabular form; records are oriented horizontally on the page, and may be sorted, grouped, and summarized with totals or averages.

FIGURE 39.2

A tabular report shows records in rows and fields in columns.

Products

Product ID	Product Name	Supplier	Category	Quantity Pe	Unit Price	s In Stock	s On Order
1	Chai	Exotic Liquids	Beverages	10 boxes x 20	$18.00	39	0
2	Chang	Exotic Liquids	Beverages	24 - 12 oz bottl	$19.00	17	40
3	Aniseed Syrup	Exotic Liquids	Condiments	12 - 550 ml bot	$10.00	13	70
4	Chef Anton's Cajun Seaso	New Orleans Cajun	Condiments	48 - 6 oz jars	$22.00	53	0
5	Chef Anton's Gumbo Mix	New Orleans Cajun	Condiments	36 boxes	$21.35	0	0
6	Grandma's Boysenberry S	Grandma Kelly's Ho	Condiments	12 - 8 oz jars	$25.00	120	0
7	Uncle Bob's Organic Dried	Grandma Kelly's Ho	Produce	12 - 1 lb pkgs.	$30.00	15	0
8	Northwoods Cranberry Sau	Grandma Kelly's Ho	Condiments	12 - 12 oz jars	$40.00	6	0
9	Mishi Kobe Niku	Tokyo Traders	Meat/Poultry	18 - 500 g pkg	$97.00	29	0
10	Ikura	Tokyo Traders	Seafood	12 - 200 ml jar	$31.00	31	0
11	Queso Cabrales	Cooperativa de Que	Dairy Products	1 kg pkg.	$21.00	22	30

You can modify any report, but if your ultimate goal is a report that presents all of the information for one record in a column or a rectangular area of the page, start by creating a columnar report. If you want a list of records with the general form of an Excel database, start with a tabular report.

There are three ways to create reports:

- In Design view, where you can design a report completely from scratch

- By choosing one of two AutoReports, which automatically include all the fields in the table or query you select

- With the Report Wizard, which lets you customize a report

In addition, there are two more wizards, each of which creates a specialized report:

- The Chart Wizard, used to visually represent data

- The Label Wizard, used to create mailing and other labels

TIP Labels and stock are available to create name tags, placeholders, business cards, CD labels, and a host of other print documents. If you can track down the label number for a label from one of the 40 or so manufacturers with products supported by Access, you can print them with the Label Wizard.

Creating a report in Access is as simple as creating a form; however, a few additional tricks can help format the report so it looks its best and displays precisely the information you want to see. Sometimes you merely need to show data in some kind of organized manner on individual documents, or a listing of common variables, or other reports bring together independent bits of data and summarize them into useful information that managers can use to make decisions, launch studies, and better understand their organizations.

Generating AutoReports

The simplest reports to produce are AutoReports. As with AutoForms, there are columnar and tabular AutoReports, which provide a good place to start if the data you want is contained in one table or query.

1. On the toolbar, open the New Object button's menu and choose Report from the drop-down list to open the New Report dialog box, shown here.

TIP If you select a table (or a query) from the Database window *before* clicking the New Object button, the table or query name is selected in the New Report dialog box.

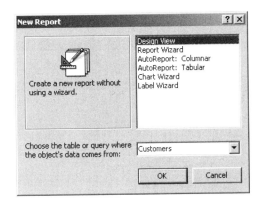

2. In the New Report dialog box, choose AutoReport: Columnar or AutoReport: Tabular. Select the table or query you want to use for the report in the drop-down list.

NOTE If you choose AutoReport from the New Object drop-down list or the Insert menu, Access creates a columnar AutoReport with no date/time in the Page Footer and no layout graphics; select Report to see the New Report dialog box and choose a more complete columnar or tabular AutoReport.

3. Click OK to create the report and open it in Print Preview; a columnar Auto-Report based on the Northwind Categories table is shown in Figure 39.3.

4. To print the report, click the Print button on the toolbar.

When you close the Print Preview window, you are prompted to save the report. The L/R tag for a report is rpt.

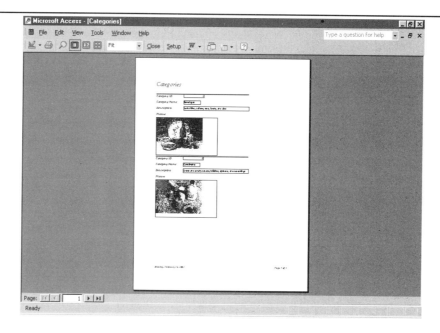

Although AutoReports are fast, they are not incredibly attractive. To create a more professional report, use the Report Wizard.

Using the Report Wizard

The Report Wizard lets you choose the fields you want in the report—including fields from more than one table—and designate how the data should be grouped, sorted, and formatted. When you click Finish, Access creates the report and opens it in Print Preview.

To use the Report Wizard, follow these steps:

1. Select Reports in the Database window and double-click Create Report By Using Wizard.

2. In the first step of the wizard, choose the first table (or query) that includes report fields from the Tables/Queries drop-down list (see Figure 39.4).

3. Use the arrow buttons (right arrow button to select one field or double right arrow button to select all fields, left arrow button to remove a field or double left arrow to remove all fields) or double-click fields in the order in which you want to present them in the report.

4. If you want to include data from another table, select it in the Tables/Queries list. Use the arrow buttons to select the fields you want to include from this table.

FIGURE 39.4

Select a table or query in the Report Wizard.

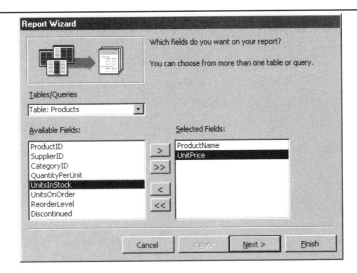

5. When you've finished selecting fields, click Next. If you only selected one field (which will make for a very uninteresting report), skip ahead to step 8.

6. If you selected fields from more than one table, the next step in the wizard asks you to choose the table to use to organize the data (see Figure 39.5). Select one of the tables listed and click Next.

FIGURE 39.5

Organize data by choosing one table as the focus for the report.

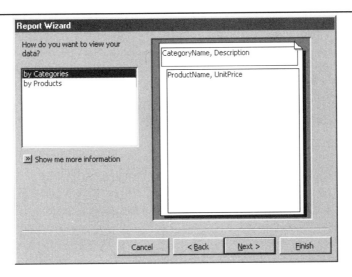

7. In the next step, set the grouping levels for the report. Grouping is megasorting; the field value for the group appears in a header at the beginning of the group. In other words, you use grouping levels to organize the records in your report into clear, logical groups so that, for instance, all products from the same supplier appear together in the report, followed by all products from the next supplier, and so on. Until you become familiar with report results, you may want to use the default choices. Click Next.

8. In the next step, choose sorting options for the report. You can sort by up to four fields (for example, State, City, LastName, FirstName). Specify a sort order by clicking the Ascending/Descending toggle button to the right of the box to switch between ascending (the default) and descending sorts (shown in Figure 39.6).

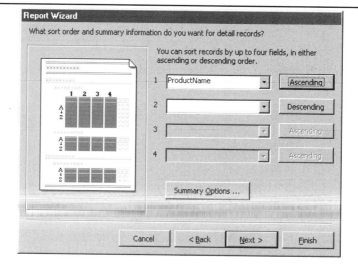

9. If you want to summarize your data by group (for example, with totals or averages), click the Summary Options button (see Figure 39.6), and choose a calculation for each field you want to summarize in the Summary Options dialog box, shown in Figure 39.7. Choose the Summary Only option to hide the table data on the report and present only summary totals. Click Next.

NOTE The Summary Options button is visible only if you have data that can be summarized.

FIGURE 39.7

Set summary options for report fields.

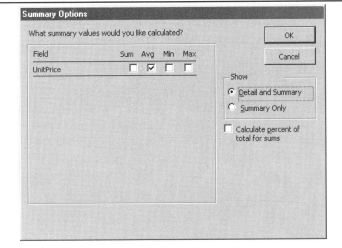

PART

VIII

CREATING AND USING
AN ACCESS DATABASE

10. In the next step, select a layout and an orientation. As you select layouts, the preview changes to reflect your choices. If you enable the Adjust The Field Width check box, report text box controls are truncated so all the fields appear on one page in the selected orientation. If you're going to switch to a smaller font to display complete data, enable the check box. If you intend to rearrange the controls to display all the data, disable this check box. Click Next.

11. In the next step, select a style for the report. Click Next.

12. In the last wizard step, type a title for the report, choose whether you'd like to open the report in Print Preview or Design view, and then click Finish.

Figure 39.8 shows a report based on two tables, Categories and Products. It's grouped by category and sorted within each category by product name.

FIGURE 39.8

A two-table, grouped report created with the Report Wizard

Products by Category

Category	Description	Product Name	Init Price
Beverages	Soft drinks, coffees, teas, beers, and ales		
		Chai	$18.00
		Chang	$19.00
		Chartreuse verte	$18.00
		Côte de Blaye	$263.50
		Guaraná Fantástica	$4.50
		Ipoh Coffee	$46.00
		Lakkalikööri	$18.00
		Laughing Lumberjack Lager	$14.00
		Outback Lager	$15.00
		Rhönbräu Klosterbier	$7.75
		Sasquatch Ale	$14.00
		Steeleye Stout	$18.00
Condiments	Sweet and savory sauces, relishes, spreads, and seasonings		
		Aniseed Syrup	$10.00
		Chef Anton's Cajun Seasoning	$22.00

Printing a Report

Printing a report is simple: open the report in Print Preview and click the Print button on the toolbar. If a report is really long (for example, an invoice report that prints a page for each customer), you may want to print selected pages. Open the report in Print Preview, and use the navigation buttons in the Print Preview window to move to the page you want to print. Note the page number, and choose File ➤ Print. In the Print dialog box, type the page number(s) in the Pages From and To boxes, and click OK.

MASTERING THE OPPORTUNITIES

Saving a Report As a Word Document

To save a report as a Word document (with most of its formatting included), either open the report in Print Preview or select the report name in the Reports section in the Database window. Choose Tools ➤ Office Links ➤ Publish It With MS Word. The report is saved automatically as a rich text format (.rtf) file in your My Documents folder and displayed in Word. However, the file can be opened and edited in most word processing programs.

Modifying a Report in Design View

Most of what you know about Access form design (see Chapter 38, "Creating and Using Forms") can be applied to report design. After you open the report in Design view, maximize the report so you have more room to work. Figure 39.9 shows the Design view of a grouped report named "Products by Category" (previously shown in Print Preview in Figure 39.8). The Report Header includes the title of the report. The Page Footer includes the date the report was printed and page numbers.

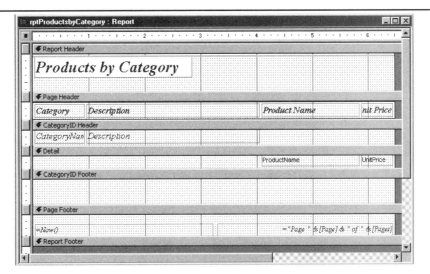

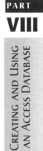

There are seven sections in a report:

Report Header Appears at the top of the report (page 1) and can include the report title and other relevant information. The Northwind Catalog report includes several pages in the Report Header.

Page Header Appears at the top of every printed page of the report.

Group Header Appears at the top of each group; there is a separate Group Header for each grouping level.

Detail Contains data from the tables/queries.

Group Footer Appears at the bottom of the group and can contain summaries (subtotals) for the group data.

Page Footer Appears at the bottom of every page; usually contains the page numbering.

Report Footer Appears on the last page of the report; contains summaries (totals) for all data in the report.

You can incorporate any or all of these sections in a report. Open the View menu to hide or display the Report Header/Footer and the Page Header/Footer. Use the mouse pointer to increase or decrease the size of the sections by dragging section bars up or down.

WARNING Hiding a section isn't like hiding a column or row in Excel. If you hide the page or the Report Headers and Footers, all the controls in the hidden section are deleted.

The Snap To Grid, alignment, and size features all work as they do in forms (see Chapter 38). All the colors, lines, borders, special effects, fonts, and other formatting features you can use with forms are also available in reports (but don't bother with the colors if you're going to print in black and white or grayscale). You can edit any of the report's labels without worrying about affecting the contents of the report, but be careful not to edit the text boxes that contain data fields. If you do, the control is no longer bound to a field, so it won't display data. To be certain that you're editing a label rather than a text box, look at the control's properties (right-click the control and choose Properties to display the control's property sheet).

TIP When you select a control, its name appears in the Object box (just before the font list) on the Formatting toolbar. By default, labels are identified as labels, and bound text boxes are identified by their field names. If you're the only person working on this database and you know you haven't changed the control's name, looking at the Object box is a helpful way to determine which type of control you have selected.

In a report's Design view, there are two preview choices on the View menu: Print Preview and Layout Preview. Print Preview produces the entire report just as it will look when printed, with all the pages.

Layout Preview shows only a few sample records. If you have a database with hundreds of records, it takes time to generate a preview of all the pages. By using a small set of sample data, Layout Preview quickly generates a preview so that you can check design features without a long wait.

Adding Dates and Page Numbers

When you open a report created with the Report Wizard in Design view, the Page Footer contains two unbound text box controls: the current date and the current page number of the total number of pages. This information is important for general efficiency and office organization because it assures you that the report you're reading is current and complete. You can customize both of these controls.

The date control uses the function =Now( ) to retrieve the current date from the operating system when the report is opened or printed. You set the date format in the control's property sheet. Right-click the control and choose Properties. On the Format property sheet, select a Format property: General Date, Long Date, Medium Date, or Short Date.

If you want to add a date to a different part of the report or to a report that lacks a date, choose Insert ➤ Date And Time from the menu to open the Date And Time dialog box.

After you set your preferences and click OK, a text box control with the appropriate code is inserted at the top of the active report section. Drag the control to wherever you want to position it in the report.

If your report is only one page, you might want to delete the page number altogether; select the control and press Delete. If you want to change the page number format, it's easier to delete the control and then reinsert a new page number control with the format you want. Choose Insert ➤ Page Numbers to open the Page Numbers dialog box.

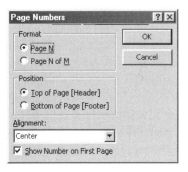

There are two formats: Page N (for example, Page 1) and Page N of M (Page 1 of 2). You can place the page number in the header or the footer and align it with the left, center, or right of the page. For two-sided printing, choose either Inside or Outside alignment. You can also suppress the page number on the first page of a multiple-page report. When you click OK, a page number control appears in the position on the page that you selected in the Page Numbers dialog box.

Changing Sort Order and Grouping Levels

After you've used the wizard to create a report, you can open the report in Design view and change the sort order and grouping levels of the data. *Sorting* organizes items into alphabetical or numerical order, and *grouping* organizes them into categories of similar items. If you group items, you can sort the groups and sort the items within each group. Both grouping and sorting make it much easier for a reader to find and compare specific items in a report.

 Click the Sorting And Grouping button on the Report Design toolbar to open the Sorting And Grouping dialog box.

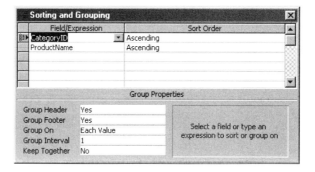

The Sorting And Grouping dialog box is similar to a table Design view. Fields used for sorting and grouping are listed in the rows in the upper portion; select a field to see its Group Properties in the property sheet at the bottom of the dialog box. As illustrated here, the records in the field in the first row, CategoryID, are grouped in this report as indicated by the Sorting And Grouping icon to the left of the Field/Expression column. The Group Header property is set to Yes, indicating that there is a Group Header for the field. The data is then sorted by the field in the second row, ProductName. If you were to click on the ProductName row, you'd see that the Group Header property is set to No, indicating that the report doesn't include a header for product names.

- To rearrange the sorting or grouping order, select a row (click the row selector in front of the row you want) and then click it again to drag it into the desired order.

- To insert a new sort or group level, select the field from the Field/Expression drop-down list.

- To add a header or footer for the group level, set the Group Header or Footer property to Yes.
- To remove a group level, select the row and press the Delete key. Access displays the following warning.

If you click OK, the group level, the group header and footer, and controls in the header or footer are removed from the report. This does not affect the data displayed in the Detail section of the report—except the order of the records—just the summary data for the group.

TIP   If you group by a Date/Time field, you can specify the interval that data should be grouped on in the Group On property: year, quarter, month, week, day, hour, or minute.

Adding and Deleting Report Controls

You can add and delete report controls in the same way that you add or delete form controls.

To add a field to a report, click the Field List button on the Report Design toolbar to open the Field List dialog box, and drag the field name into the appropriate section of the report. You'll probably have to format and resize the label and the text box controls once you drop the field into place. Remember, the Format Painter allows you to quickly format the new control to match others on the report. See Chapter 38 for more information on formatting controls, including use of the Format Painter.

NOTE   A field with a Yes/No data type appears as a check box in the report. You can change it to a toggle button or an option button by choosing Format ➢ Change To.

To delete a field's control from the report, select the control and press Delete.

You can calculate fields in a report by adding a calculated field in the Detail section, but it's easier to add a calculated field to the query underlying the report.

1. To access the query, open the Data tab of the report's property sheet.

2. Click the Build button (the three dots, or ellipsis, at the right end of the field—you must click the field to see it) on the Record Source property to open the query. If the report is based on a table, you are prompted to confirm basing the report on a query. Click Yes.

 NOTE See "Creating Queries" later in this chapter for detailed information on query design and modification.

3. Set up the calculation in the query using the Expression Builder, and then close and save the query.

The calculated field is now available in the report's Field list.

Conditionally Formatting Controls

You can apply conditional formats to text boxes and combo boxes in reports as you do in forms. To recap, conditional formatting allows you to apply special formatting that depends on a field's value. This is a useful tool for drawing a reader's attention to particularly interesting values, such as sales below projections, sales above projections, or inventory numbers for items that need to be reordered.

To create a conditional format, follow these steps:

1. Open the report in Design view.

2. Select the control and choose Format ➤ Conditional Formatting.

3. In the Conditional Formatting dialog box (shown in Figure 39.10), set a value range at which formatting will apply, and set the formatting with the formatting buttons. The example in Figure 39.10 shows a format for values less than 10; the conditional format is shaded.

4. Click Add if you want to add more formatting options to the same control (for example, to add different formatting for values over 50). You can apply up to three conditional formats to a control. Repeat step 3 for each new condition.

Setting a conditional format

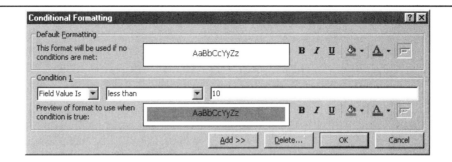

5. Click OK when you're finished.

To remove the conditional format, open the Conditional Formatting dialog box and click Delete. In the Delete Conditional Format dialog box, mark the check boxes for the specific conditional formats you want to delete, and then click OK.

 TIP Conditional formats are applied in the order in which they appear in the Conditional Formatting dialog box. If the value meets the first condition, the format is applied and no other conditions are checked. Therefore, if the first condition bolds values >=100 and the second condition italicizes values >=150, no value will ever be italicized. Reverse the conditions, and the formatting will work as intended.

See "Conditional Formatting" in Chapter 38 for more information.

Saving a Report As a Snapshot

After you create a report, it's easy to show the data to others even if they don't have Access. Save the report as a *snapshot file*: a high-quality picture of each page of the report similar to PDF files created with Adobe Acrobat. Other users can open the file, read the report, and print whichever pages they need. They cannot, however, alter the report.

A snapshot file is read with the Snapshot Viewer, a free program that can be downloaded from the Microsoft Office Developer's Web site or installed from the Office XP CD-ROM. The viewer can be freely distributed, so you can include it with the first snapshot file you send to another user.

PART

VIII

CREATING AND USING
AN ACCESS DATABASE

MASTERING THE OPPORTUNITIES

Using Snapshots on the Web and in E-mail

You can post a snapshot of a report on a Web page by creating a link to the file. Include a link to Microsoft's download page for the Snapshot Viewer to ensure that users can view the file. They only need to download the viewer once, and most Web users are accustomed to downloading add-ins to be able to view files of different types.

You can send report snapshots via e-mail. Your recipients still need the Snapshot Viewer to open and read the snapshot, so include a link to the download page on the Microsoft Web site for your readers' convenience.

Creating a Report Snapshot

To create a snapshot, follow these steps:

1. Select the report in the Database window.

2. Choose File ➢ Export from the menu.

3. In the Export Report dialog box, select Snapshot Format in the Save As Type box.

4. To open the snapshot after it is created, verify that the AutoStart check box is enabled.

5. Select the folder where you want to save the file, enter an appropriate filename, and click Export.

The snapshot is created and displayed in the Snapshot Viewer, shown in Figure 39.11. If the Snapshot Viewer isn't already installed, Access prompts you to install it when you create your first snapshot.

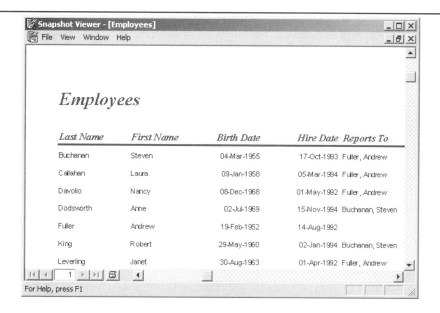

FIGURE 39.11

A report snapshot in the Snapshot Viewer

The snapshot file is saved separately from the database file, in the folder you selected in the Export Report dialog box. You can send it as an attachment in an e-mail message like any other file.

TIP If you want to create an interactive HTML report that's linked to your data and that others can edit or enhance, create a Data Access Page instead of a snapshot. See Chapter 40, "Creating Web Pages with Access," to learn about Data Access Pages.

Creating Queries

One big advantage of a relational database is that data is stored without redundancy in separate tables. There's less data to store, and it's easier to keep data current because there's only one copy of it. But when you want to answer a question such as "How many orders did we get from Massachusetts last year?" you need to join data from related tables to get the answer. Furthermore, you don't want all the data from each related table, just the specific data that answers your question (in this case, the state from a Customers table and numbers of orders from an Orders table).

A *query* displays records and fields from one or more tables based on criteria you specify. Queries are like filters but much more flexible. When you create a query, you can choose which tables to draw data from, which fields you want from the tables, and which sets of records you want from the fields. You can sort a query's resulting set of records any way you want without affecting the sort order in the underlying tables, and you can add calculated fields to perform mathematical operations on the data.

TIP If you use Access to create forms and reports for a SQL Server database, base the forms and reports on queries (not tables), because queries contain only the data you want to display. Your forms and reports are more efficient because SQL Server sends only the data requested for Access to present in the form or report.

Creating Simple Queries

There are different types of Access queries: select queries, parameter queries, crosstab queries, and action queries. Most of the queries used in databases are called *select* queries because they "select" records based on criteria you set; in Access these are commonly referred to as *simple* queries. We'll discuss each query type at length in the following sections of this chapter.

NOTE A query doesn't contain any data itself; instead, it consists of instructions about what data to select and which tables to select the data from. The instructions are in SQL (Structured Query Language). You can see the SQL code for a query by opening the query and then choosing View ➢ SQL View.

Queries, like other database objects, can be created in a variety of ways. You can use one of the query wizards, build your query in Design view, or type SQL statements if you're familiar with SQL and have time to kill. You don't need to create queries for forms or reports; it's easier to use the Form and Report Wizards to retrieve the data you want because the wizard creates the query that the form or report uses. If, however, you need to work with a record set independent of a form or report (for example, if you need to quickly display a list of customers in Oregon and Washington who placed orders worth more than $3,000 last month), a query is faster.

Using the Query Wizard

To create a simple query, select Queries from the Objects list in the Database window. Choose Insert ➤ Query from the Access menu (or open the menu on the New Object toolbar button and select Query); then choose Simple Query Wizard in the New Query dialog box and click OK.

When the Simple Query Wizard (shown in Figure 39.12) starts, choose the first table (or query) that contains the fields you want to include in the query from the Tables/Queries drop-down list. Use the arrow buttons or double-click the fields you want to include in the query. Select any additional tables or queries, and the fields to include. Click Next when you have selected all fields.

PART

VIII

CREATING AND USING AN ACCESS DATABASE

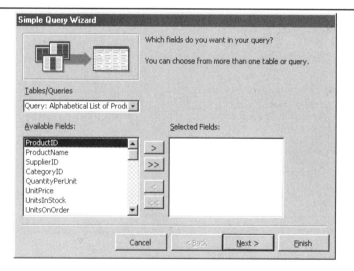

FIGURE 39.12

Select the fields to include in the query in the Simple Query Wizard.

If the fields you selected include a Number or a Currency field, you are asked to choose whether to create a summary or a detail query. To see each record in the query results, choose Detail. To see totals, averages, or other summaries of the data instead of details, choose Summary and set the summation options you want. Click Next.

Give the query a name, and click Finish to run (or "open") the query. Figure 39.13 shows the *result set* produced by a query that selects the ContactName, Country, and Phone fields in the Northwind Customers table.

TIP   The L/R prefix for a simple query is qry.

FIGURE 39.13

A query result set from
the Northwind
Customers table

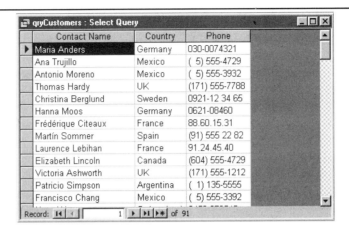

Modifying a Query in Design View

Click the View button on the toolbar to switch the query to Design view (see Figure 39.14). The query window is separated into two panes. In the lower pane (called the *Query By Example grid, QBE grid,* or simply the *grid*) there's one column for each field included in the query. The rows show the field name, the table the field comes from, whether the query is sorted based on the field, whether the field is shown in the query results, and criteria that have been applied to the field to limit the query results.

FIGURE 39.14

Query Design view
includes a table pane
and a QBE grid.

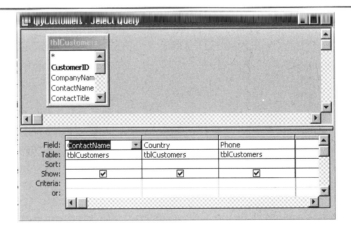

The upper pane (called the *table pane*) shows the tables used in the query and the relationships between the tables.

 TIP To display/hide table names in the grid, choose View ➢ Table Names from the menu.

Changing Criteria

Enter criteria to limit the records displayed in a query so that you display only the records and fields you need to see and nothing else. For example, if you want to see the ContactName, Country, and Phone information only for contacts in Germany, you can use criteria to limit the records to those with the value **Germany** in the Country field.

Criteria are entered in the Criteria row for the appropriate field in the query grid, as shown in Figure 39.15. Don't type the quote marks; Access enters those for you.

FIGURE 39.15

*Entering query criteria
in the grid*

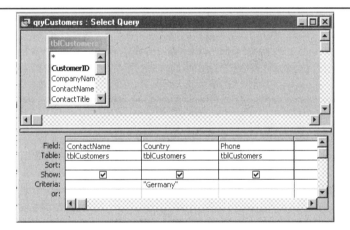

You can enter a specific value (such as **Germany** in the Country field) to show records with that entry; you can also use expressions containing operators to further define the query results. Table 39.1 lists some common comparison operators you can use in queries.

TABLE 39.1   QUERY COMPARISON OPERATORS

Operator	Purpose	Example
AND	Selects records having one characteristic *and* another characteristic in the field.	In the Unit Price field, >20 AND <80 displays records with unit prices between $20 and $80.
OR	Selects records having one characteristic *or* another characteristic in the field.	In the Category field, Seafood OR Meat/Poultry displays Seafood and Meat/Poultry records.
NOT	Selects records that do *not* have the specified characteristic in the field.	In the Category field, NOT Condiments displays all records except those in the Condiments category.
Is Null	Selects records with no entry in the field.	In the ZipCode field, Is Null displays addresses with no zip code entered.
Is Not Null (<> Null)	Selects records that have an entry in the field.	In the PhoneNumber field, Is Not Null displays records with phone numbers entered.
=, <>, >, >=, <, <=	Selects records with a value that's equal to, not equal to, greater than, greater than or equal to, less than, or less than or equal to a specified value.	In the UnitPrice field, > 100 displays items with a unit price more than $100. You can enter an expression either with or without a space following one of these symbols.

Adding and Removing Fields

To add a field to a query, open the query in Design view. In the table pane, double-click the field you want to add to the query. The field is added at the end of the existing fields in the grid, but you can move it to a new position by clicking once on the *column selector* (the gray bar at the top of the column) and then clicking the selector again to drag the column. Double-click the asterisk at the top of the field list to include all fields from the table in the query. The fields are not, however, listed separately in the grid. To include all the fields, listed separately in the grid, double-click the table's title bar in the table pane to select all the fields in the table. Drag the selected fields from the table and drop them in the grid.

TIP To add fields from another table to the query, right-click in the table pane, and then choose Show Table. Select the table you want, and add the fields you want from that table.

To delete a field from a query, click the gray bar at the top of the column to select it and press Delete.

Sometimes you need to include a field in your query—so that you can sort the result set by that field or limit the result set by setting criteria for that field—but don't want to include the field in the result set. In that case, clear the Show check box for the field, which will prevent the field's data from appearing in the result set, and make the changes you want to its Sort and Criteria properties. For example, if you wanted to create a query to show all invoices received within the last week but didn't want to display the actual receipt dates in the result set, you could include the DateReceived field in the query, clear the Show check box for the field, and set its criteria so that only invoices received in the last seven days would appear in the result set.

Understanding Table Joins

If you create a query from related tables, Access displays the relationships as you place the tables in the table pane. If you haven't already defined the relationships between the tables, you can create relationships in the upper pane the same way you do in the Relationships window when defining the database structure (see Chapter 37). However, these relationships are created only for the query—they aren't stored permanently in the database (and thus won't appear automatically in the Relationships window). A relationship between tables, as shown in Figure 39.16, is called a *join*. There are two types of joins: *inner joins* and *outer joins*. Outer joins are further divided into *right outer joins* and *left outer joins*. Double-clicking the join line opens the Join Properties dialog box.

TIP You don't need to worry about remembering the terms "inner" and "outer" join, because the Join Properties dialog box tells you the option to choose to get the results you want.

PART

VIII

CREATING AND USING
AN ACCESS DATABASE

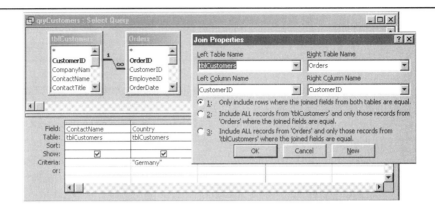

The first join type listed is an *inner join*, also known as an equi-join, which is the default join in queries. In an inner join, the only records displayed in the query result set are those with identical values in the joined fields. In this example, if there are no orders for one of the customers, the customer isn't included in the result set; similarly, an order with no customer is not included in the result set. If you run a query and wonder, "Why are there only 100 customers? I thought we had 240 customers!" blame the inner join.

The second join type (option 2) is a *left outer join*. With a left outer join, all the records in the primary table in the relationship are displayed even if they don't have matching entries in the related table. Customers are included in the result set even if they've never placed an order. This is the join to use to show all the records in a primary table.

A *right outer join* (option 3) includes all the records from the related table (in this example, the Orders table) even if no matching records exist in the primary Customers table. Use a right outer join to show all the records in a related table.

The join line points from the table that will have all records listed to the table that will only have matching records displayed. All three joins use the same tables and relationships, but each returns a different query result set. To remove a join, click the join line and press Delete.

MASTERING TROUBLESHOOTING

Ambiguous Joins

If your query is simple and straightforward, you'll never see the error message "Query contains ambiguous outer joins." But if you create a multiple-table query that's intricate or complex, you may well see this confusing message. Unfortunately, although Access tells you that your query contains ambiguous joins, that's all it tells you. It doesn't tell you what they are or how to fix them.

Ambiguous joins are two or more outer joins that Access can't resolve. If you create a query with two left outer joins to the same table, Access does not know how to process the query. For example, customers place orders and employees take orders. If you design a query with a left outer join between customers and orders *and* a left outer join between employees and orders, Access doesn't know whether to return all employees or all customers. When you see the ambiguous outer join message, it's time to check the joins in your query. Double-click one of the join lines. In the Join Properties dialog box, there are three options.

Join type 1, the inner join, isn't the source of the problem. An inner join returns all records that have entries in *both* the joined fields. If you change all the joins in your query to inner joins, there aren't any outer joins—ambiguous or otherwise—left to create a problem. The result set, however, only includes records with related records in *all* tables in the query.

Join types 2 and 3 tell Access to show all the records in one table—either the left (type 2) or the right (type 3)—and only those records in the other table that have matching entries in the linked field. The join line arrow points from the table from which all records are shown to the table where only records with entries are shown. To resolve ambiguous outer joins, set them up so that all the arrows in the table pane point in the same direction. This allows Access to return, for example, all the records from Table A, all the related records from Table B, and all the records in Table C related to records in Table B. This is simplistic, but it works if it returns the data you require.

If you need to include two outer joins and the result is an ambiguous outer join, you'll need to create two queries. In the first query, include two of the tables with an outer join. Then create a new query that connects this query to the remaining table with an outer join. Separating the request into two queries handles the ambiguity by instructing Access to process first one query, then the other.

PART

VIII

CREATING AND USING
AN ACCESS DATABASE

Sorting a Query

To sort a query so that the records appear in the order you specify, open the query in Design view. Click in the Sort row of the column you want to sort by, and then choose Ascending or Descending from the drop-down list.

You can sort by multiple fields, but the fields need to be in the proper order. Access sorts fields from left to right in the query grid; so if you want to sort customers by last name and then by first name, for example, move the LastName field to the left of the FirstName field in the query grid, and set each to sort Ascending.

 MASTERING THE OPPORTUNITIES

Sorting Drop-Down Lists in Lookup Fields

When you use the Lookup Wizard to create a drop-down list from entries in a table, the wizard creates a query. The query's result set is displayed in the order in which it appears in the table. You can modify the sort order of the query, thereby specifying the sort order for the drop-down list. You can also set criteria to filter the items that are displayed on the drop-down list.

To modify the query behind a lookup field, open the table that includes the field in Design view. Select the field and open the Lookup property tab at the bottom of the table Design View window. Select the Row Source property and click the property's Build button to open and modify the query.

You can also limit the results that the lookup query returns by adding criteria to the grid.

Printing the Results of a Query

When you print a query result set, the results appear in Datasheet view. A query's Datasheet view looks exactly like a table's Datasheet view, and if you need to see the query's result set on paper in a hurry, printing the query is faster than creating and printing a report. To print a query, open the query to display the result set, and click the Print button on the toolbar.

MASTERING THE OPPORTUNITIES

Stealing Queries from Forms and Reports

When you create a form or report based on more than one table, Access creates a query and stores it in the form or report. You can open the form or report and save the query for use outside the form or report by following these steps:

1. Open the form or report in Design view.
2. Open the form or report's property sheet.
3. On the Data tab, select the Record Source property.
4. Click the Build button to open the query.
5. Choose File ➤ Save to save the query. Enter a name when prompted.
6. When you close the query window, you are prompted to update the Record Source property. Choose Yes to base the existing form or report on the query you just saved. Choose No if you don't want to change the form or report's record source.

The saved query appears in the list of queries in the Database window.

PART

VIII

CREATING AND USING
AN ACCESS DATABASE

Creating a Parameter Query

A *parameter query* displays an input box that prompts the user to enter *parameters*, or criteria, for selecting records. Parameter queries are useful when you frequently need to access a subset of a table or tables. For example, if you want to look up the names and phone numbers of customers in a specific state, you can create 50 separate queries, one for each state, or one parameter query that asks you to enter the state abbreviation and displays only the records from that state. It's the same as entering a specific state abbreviation in the Criteria row for the State field in the query grid, but it saves you from having to create a separate query for each state.

To create a parameter query from an existing query, open the query in Design view. In the Criteria cell of the field you want to use as a parameter, enter a question or message (a *prompt*) enclosed in brackets.

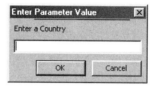

The prompt appears in the Parameters dialog box to ask the user to enter criteria. Every time you run the query, either by opening it or by switching to Datasheet view, you'll see the Parameter dialog box before the query runs.

Enter the parameter and click OK or press Enter.

You can enter more than one prompt. For example, users might want to see records in a particular date range. The following criteria:

`>= [Enter beginning date: mm/dd/yy] AND <= [Enter ending date: mm/dd/yy]`

in the OrderDate field prompts the user twice and uses the parameters to filter the records by OrderDate.

To save the parameter query separately from the simple query you've modified, choose File ➢ Save As and give the parameter query a different name. To change the parameter query back to a select query, delete the prompt from the Criteria cell in the query grid.

Creating a Summary Query

A *summary query* returns summaries or totals rather than detailed records. If the fields you select in the Simple Query Wizard include numeric fields, you can create either a detail or summary query, but you can also turn any select query into a summary query. First, open the query in Design view.

Click the Totals button on the toolbar to display the Totals row of the query grid. All fields in the grid are automatically set to Group By; fields you are not summarizing retain that setting. For fields you want to summarize, click the drop-down arrow in the Totals cell and choose a summary calculation. Table 39.2 lists some of the basic functions used in queries.

TABLE 39.2 QUERY FUNCTIONS

Function	Result	Used with Field Types
Avg	The average of the values in the field.	AutoNumber, Currency, Date/Time, Number
Count	The number of records that hold data in this field. The count includes zeros but not blanks.	All
First	The contents of the field in the first record in the result set.	All
Last	The contents of the field in the last record in the result set.	All
Min	The lowest value in the field.	AutoNumber, Currency, Date/Time, Number, Text
Max	The highest value in the field.	AutoNumber, Currency, Date/Time, Number, Text
StDev	The standard deviation of the values in the field.	AutoNumber, Currency, Date/Time, Number
Sum	The total of the values in the field.	AutoNumber, Currency, Date/Time, Number
Var	The variance of the values in the field.	AutoNumber, Currency, Date/Time, Number

Figure 39.17 shows a summary query based on the Customers table. Data is sorted by the Country field and then grouped by the Count function. The result set illustrated in Figure 39.18 shows the number of customers in each country.

FIGURE 39.17

*A summary query
ready to run*

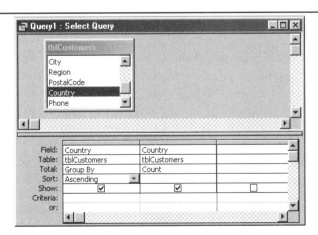

FIGURE 39.18

The summary query's
result set

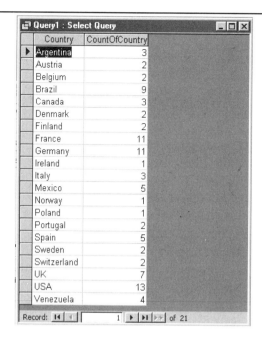

Adding Calculations to Queries

To perform a calculation in a query, you add a new column, called a *calculated field*, to the query. Tables shouldn't include calculated fields based on other fields in the table. ily because you're storing data you can quickly produce when you need it. And because Access isn't Excel, when data changes you need to edit both the original field and the calculated field.

Instead of using calculated fields in tables, add calculated fields to queries to provide up-to-date calculation results. Calculated fields come in various forms. For example, you can multiply one field by another, add two or more fields together, *concatenate* fields (append one to the other), or use constant values (such as a tax rate) in calculations.

Common uses for calculated fields are to calculate Price × Quantity for a subtotal in an Orders query and the sales tax for an order (multiply the calculated subtotal field by the fixed tax rate). You can also use calculated fields with text functions. It's quite common to concatenate (combine), for example, first name and last name to display full names in a single column. See the following sidebar for additional information about concatenating.

Combining and Separating Field Entries

Two frequently performed data manipulation tasks are combining multiple fields into a single field (for example, combining FirstName and LastName fields into a single FullName field), and separating a single field of full names into separate fields for first and last names. Combining (*concatenating*) is a simpler process than separating (*parsing*); combining can be done in a calculated field in a query, and separating is most easily accomplished using Excel 2002 and the Text Import Wizard.

Combining Fields

To combine two fields into one (for example, a FirstName and LastName field into a FullName field), open a query in Design view. Be sure the table with the fields is in the table pane. In the Field cell of a blank column in the QBE grid, type a concatenation expression, such as `FullName:[FirstName]&" "&[LastName]`, and press Enter. In this example, FullName is the new field name, the existing field names are encased in square brackets, and the ampersands (&) join the first name to a space, followed by the last name.

If the table includes a MiddleName or MiddleInitial field that is frequently blank, the formula gets a bit more interesting. The formula `FullName:[FirstName]&" "&[MiddleName]&" "&[LastName]` isn't quite good enough. If there is no middle name, this calculation places two spaces between the first and last name. You need to include the IIF (immediate IF, the Access equivalent of Excel's IF function) function in the formula to handle the spacing based on whether or not the MiddleName field is null: `FullName:[FirstName]&" "&IIF([MiddleName]<>Null,[MiddleName]&" ","")&[LastName]`.

Parsing Text Strings

To separate entries in a field, use Excel to parse the entries and use the Import Wizard (see Chapter 37) to bring the table back into Access. Open Excel and Access in half-screen windows (so you can see them both). Display Tables in the Database window, and then drag the name of the table with the combined entries into the Excel window and drop it in a worksheet to copy the data into the worksheet. Insert a new column on the right side of field you want to parse, and give it a field name in the same row as the other headers. Select all the cells in the field you want to parse, and choose Data ➤ Text To Columns from Excel's menu. In the Convert Text To Columns Wizard, select Delimited, click Next, and then choose Space as the delimiter to separate the names.

Continued

> ### ◀ MASTERING THE OPPORTUNITIES CONTINUED
>
> After you parse the names, save the Excel spreadsheet to a file and bring it back into Access to replace the version that has combined names. Use the Access Import Wizard to import the table (see the section "Importing Data from Spreadsheets and Other Databases" in Chapter 37). Import the table using the existing table name, and click Yes to overwrite the existing table.
>
> This solution assumes that the table doesn't have related records in another table, because when you delete the existing records, you lose links to the related records. If you inherited a poorly designed database and need to parse data without removing it from Access, look in Access Help for information on the Access text functions.

Calculated fields can also calculate with dates. For example, suppose an Employees table includes the year each employee was hired; the Human Resources department would like to quickly calculate the number of years each employee has worked as of the current year. To calculate the years of service, create a query based on the Employees table. In Design view, add a column to the table to contain the calculated field. Click in the Field cell of the column and enter the calculation, or click the Build button on the toolbar to open the Expression Builder.

TIP   Before opening the Expression Builder, save your query to display the current query column names in the Expression Builder.

The Expression Builder gives you more room to build calculation expressions, and it provides the correct spelling of field names (which is critical). Field names in calculations are always encased in square brackets. You can use field names, constant values, operators, and built-in mathematical *functions* in expressions. There are two types of functions: built-in functions included with Access and user-created functions stored in the database modules. To access functions, open the Expression Builder and double-click the Functions folder in the left list box. Click the Built-In Functions folder icon to display the function categories in the center list box and functions in the right list box.

To produce the data the Human Resources department wants, you can use a combination of the Now() function, the Year() function, and a table field. The built-in Access function Now() returns the current Windows date and time, and the function Year() returns the year from a date. By nesting the two functions, you can calculate the current year, `Year(Now())`, and the year hired, `Year([HireDate])`. Then subtract the year hired from the calculated current year: `Year(Now())-Year([HireDate])`. Follow these steps to create the formula using the Expression Builder:

1. Choose the Date/Time category, and double-click Year in the right list box to move it into the expression pane.

2. Select the argument placeholder *<number>* in the expression pane.

3. Double-click the function `Now()` in the right list box to paste it in place of the argument placeholder.

4. Move the insertion point to the end of the expression, and then type a minus symbol or click the minus operator button below the expression pane.

5. Double-click Year in the right list box to move it into the expression pane.

6. Select the argument placeholder for the `Year()` function.

7. In the left list box, click the icon for the query.

8. In the center list box, select `[HireDate]` and double-click `<Value>` in the right list box.

9. Click OK to close the Expression Builder and return to the query.

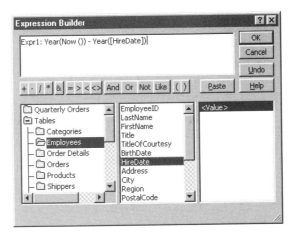

This formula is based on years, so it returns the years of service the employee will have on their anniversary this year. If you need to know the number of years of service as of today's date, use this formula, which subtracts the hire date from today's date, divides the number of days by days in a year, and returns the integer portion of the result: `Int((Now()-[DateHired])/365.25)`.

NOTE For dates stored with two-digit years, Access assumes that dates from 1/1/00 to 12/31/29 fall in the years 2000 through 2029; dates from 1/1/30 to 12/31/99 are assumed to fall in the years 1930 through 1999.

Access names the column Expr1 followed by a colon, but you can select and edit the name in query Design view. (Don't delete the colon.) When you base a form or a report on a query, you choose calculated fields from the list of fields in the Form Wizard, Report Wizard, or Field list as you would table fields.

Formatting and Captioning Calculated Fields

To format calculated field data, right-click on the column selector and choose Properties from the shortcut menu, or select the column you wish to format and choose View ➤ Properties from the menu. Choose a format (and for Number and Currency fields, decimal places) from the list. If you wish, enter a caption for the field.

Creating Crosstab Queries

Crosstab queries summarize information about two or more columns in a table or a query; the Excel equivalent of a crosstab query is a PivotTable Report. To continue our query example, we'll create a crosstab query to show the number of new hires by department each year based on the data in the calculated summary query created in the previous section, shown in Figure 39.19.

FIGURE 39.19

We can base a crosstab query on the results of the qryEmployeeYears query.

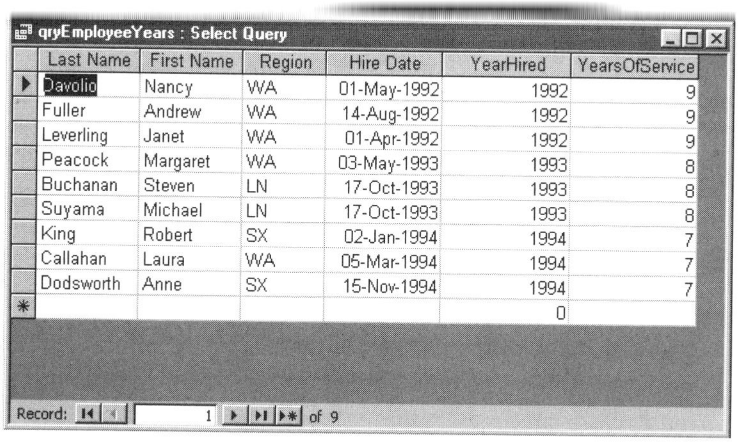

	Last Name	First Name	Region	Hire Date	YearHired	YearsOfService
▶	Davolio	Nancy	WA	01-May-1992	1992	9
	Fuller	Andrew	WA	14-Aug-1992	1992	9
	Leverling	Janet	WA	01-Apr-1992	1992	9
	Peacock	Margaret	WA	03-May-1993	1993	8
	Buchanan	Steven	LN	17-Oct-1993	1993	8
	Suyama	Michael	LN	17-Oct-1993	1993	8
	King	Robert	SX	02-Jan-1994	1994	7
	Callahan	Laura	WA	05-Mar-1994	1994	7
	Dodsworth	Anne	SX	15-Nov-1994	1994	7
*					0	

qryEmployeeYears : Select Query

Record: ◀ ◀ 1 ▶ ▶◀ ▶* of 9

TIP To create a crosstab query that involves more than one table, first use the Simple Query Wizard to create a select query that has all the fields you need, and then base your crosstab query on the select query.

1. To create a crosstab query, display Queries in the Database window and click the New button to open the New Query dialog box. Select Crosstab Query Wizard and click OK.

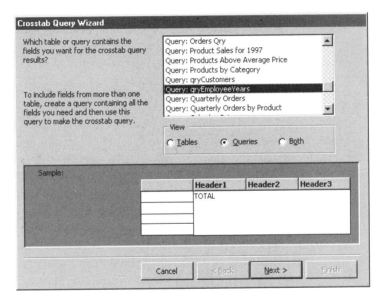

2. In the first step of the wizard, identify the table or query that contains the columns you want to summarize. By default, Access lists tables; if you're basing the new query on an existing query, you must choose Both or Queries. Click Next.

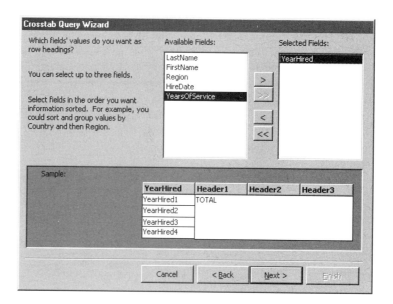

3. In the second step of the wizard, select the fields that contain the information you want to present as rows within the query result set. You can select up to three fields from the table to use as rows. As you select each field, Access adds it to the row headings. (We used the YearHired field for row headings and Region for column headings. We made this choice simply because there are more years than Regions, so placing YearHired on the left side means the completed query is more likely to fit in the width of the computer screen.) When you have selected the row headings, click Next.

4. In the next step, select the single field that you want to use for column headings, and then click Next.

5. The following step has three choices:

- Which field do you want to calculate?
- How do you want to calculate your data?
- Do you want totals for each row?

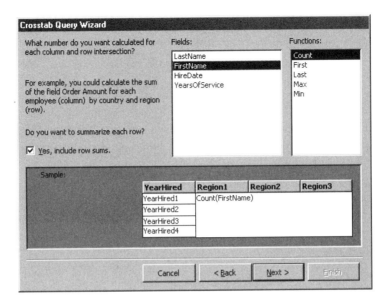

The field you select determines the information that will be summarized in the crosstab query's result set, and the type of field you select determines the summary methods you can choose (see Table 39.1 earlier in this chapter).

6. In the last step of the Crosstab Query Wizard, enter a name for the query. The L/R tag for a crosstab query is qxtb. The results for this example are shown in Figure 39.20.

PART

VIII

CREATING AND USING
AN ACCESS DATABASE

FIGURE 39.20

The crosstab query summarizes the data for each unique row/column combination.

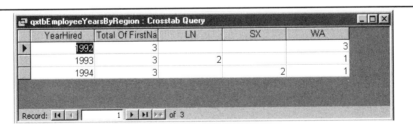

MASTERING THE OPPORTUNITIES

Creating Reports for Crosstab Queries

Crosstab queries are incredibly useful; they summarize data that would require multiple, sophisticated select and summary queries. Reports based on crosstab queries can be problematic, though. When the report is created, the column labels are based on the current values in the field selected as the column field. If the items in the field change, the column labels in the report won't match the column headings in the crosstab query. The solution to this problem is to adjust the Column Headings property of the crosstab query before basing a report on the query so that the query always returns the columns that the report requires, even if the columns contain no data.

Open the crosstab query in Design view. Right-click in the table pane and choose Properties from the shortcut menu, or choose View ➤ Properties from the menu to open the query's property sheet. In the Column Headings property, enter the values from the column field of the crosstab query as a series of strings, enclosed in quotes and separated by commas; for example, "Qtr 1","Qtr 2","Qtr 3","Qtr 4". (Using the query shown in Figure 39.20, you would enter "LN", "SX", "WA"). The strings you enter must exactly match the values that are entered in the table. A query with these column headings will return four columns, one for each quarter in the order specified, even if there is no data for one or more of the quarters.

The column headings also constrain the columns that are included in the result set. If a user mistakenly enters Qtr 5 as a value in the table, Qtr 5 won't be included in the crosstab result set.

Creating Action Queries

Action queries execute specific actions to change or copy large quantities of data. You can use action queries to make a new table out of a query datasheet (a *make-table query*), add a set of records to a table (an *append query*), delete records from a table (a *delete query*), or perform extensive data updates on a table (an *update query*). While you could, for example, use Find and Replace to update a table, action queries are more powerful than menu actions for two reasons: you can include criteria as you would in a select query, and you can run the saved query whenever you need to take the action again.

Creating and Running a Make-Table Query

Sometimes you might need to create a new table from a subset of data in an existing table. For example, suppose you have a large table of historical customer records that you want to keep intact, but you need a separate table of customers who placed orders within the last two years so you can analyze recent purchasing behavior. You can query the historical-data table to select the current customers and then use a make-table query to create a new table from the current-customer query. Here are the steps:

1. First, create a query (including appropriate criteria) that returns the records you want to put in the new table. Open the query in Design view.

2. Click the arrow next to the Query Type button on the toolbar and select Make-Table Query from the drop-down list. The Make Table dialog box appears.

3. In the Table Name text box, enter the name of the table you want to create. Click Current Database to create the new table in the current database, or click Another Database and type the name of a different database you want to put the new table in. Click OK.

4. To preview the records before creating the new table, switch to Datasheet view. Make any changes you need in Design view so that the records and fields you want in the new table are shown in the query.

5. Click Run on the toolbar to create the new table. In the warning message, click Yes. Save the query if you anticipate needing to make a new table with this query again.

Creating and Running an Append Query

If you need to add a group of records from one or more tables to an existing table, run an append query. Here are the steps:

1. First, create a query that returns the records you want to append to another table. The structure—that is, the field names and order—of the records your query returns should match the structure of the table you're appending them to.

2. In query Design view, click the arrow next to the Query Type button on the toolbar, and then click Append Query to display the Append dialog box, shown here.

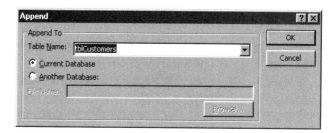

3. In the Table Name drop-down list, select the name of the table you want to append the records to. Click Current Database if the table is in the currently open database, or click Another Database and type the name of a different database where the table is stored. Then click OK.

 NOTE You can also enter a path to a Microsoft FoxPro, Paradox, or dBASE database, or a connection string to a SQL Server database.

4. The Append dialog box closes, and you are returned to the grid that now has an Append To row. Use the query techniques discussed earlier (in the section "Changing Criteria") to select the data you want to append to the table. If the primary key field you're appending has an AutoNumber data type, don't include the field.

5. If the fields you're appending have the same name in both tables, Access automatically fills the matching name in the Append To row that appears in the query's QBE grid. If the fields in the two tables don't have the same name, use the drop-down lists in the Append To row to select the names of the fields in the table you're appending to.

6. To preview the records before you append them, switch to Datasheet view. Make any changes you need in Design view so that the records and fields you want to append are shown in the query.

7. When the records are ready to append, click Run on the toolbar to add the records to the table. In the warning message, click Yes, and then close the query without saving it (unless you anticipate the need to run this append query again; if you do, save it).

Creating and Running a Delete Query

If you want to "clean out" a table (for example, to delete records for discontinued products), create and run a delete query.

 WARNING The results of a delete query are irreversible and can wipe out tremendous amounts of data, so use caution whenever you use a delete query.

You can use a delete query to delete records from a single table in a single action. If you want to delete all related records from multiple tables in a one-to-many relationship, be sure that the table relationships are set up with referential integrity enforced and cascading deletes turned on, so that deleting the records from the "one" table automatically deletes related records in the "many" table. (See the section "Cascading Updates and Deletes" in Chapter 37 to learn more about referential integrity and cascading deletes.)

Follow these steps to create and run a delete query:

1. First, create a query that contains the table of records you want to delete. In query Design view, click the Query Type drop-down arrow on the toolbar, and then choose Delete Query.

2. Use the querying techniques discussed earlier (see "Changing Criteria") to select the records you want to delete.

3. To preview the records before you delete them, switch to Datasheet view. Make any changes you need in Design view so that the records you want to delete are shown in the query.

4. When you're ready to permanently delete the records shown in the query, click the Run button on the toolbar. In the warning message, click Yes.

Creating and Running an Update Query

If you need to make large-scale changes to data in a table, you can run an update query. The advantage of an update query over find-and-replace operations is that you can query for the specific records that need updating before you make the changes so you won't inadvertently change records that shouldn't be changed. An example is a change to the tax rate for a particular city in an Orders table; you don't want to change all the cities' tax rates, just the rates for orders shipped to that specific city.

Follow these steps to create and run an update query:

1. Create a query, selecting the tables or queries that include the records you want to update and the fields you need to set criteria for.

PART

VIII

CREATING AND USING
AN ACCESS DATABASE

2. Open the query in Design view, and click Update Query from the Query Type button drop-down arrow. You won't see a dialog box for update queries. Instead, an Update To row is added to the grid.

3. Use querying techniques to select the records you want to update.

4. In the Update To cell for the fields you want to update, type the expression or value you want to place in the fields.

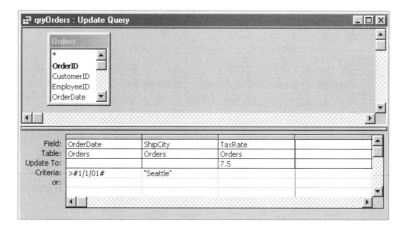

5. To preview the records before you update them, switch to Datasheet view (this list won't show the new values). Make any changes you need in Design view so that the records you want to update are shown in the query.

6. Click Run on the toolbar to complete the updates. In the warning message, click Yes.

MASTERING TROUBLESHOOTING

Compacting and Repairing a Database

Access keeps a history of the forms and reports you create. You can't access the history, but it takes up room in the database. After you've created and modified a number of forms and reports, your database will be large even if it doesn't contain any data. As you add and delete data, it becomes even larger. Access has a utility that can compact the database for you so that it takes up less room, runs faster, and has less chance of

Continued ▐▶

MASTERING THE OPPORTUNITIES CONTINUED

becoming corrupted. A database can become corrupted if Access terminates unexpectedly while you are working in a database. In this case, you will receive a message that the database is corrupted. Don't panic—it can probably be repaired without any dire consequences. To repair a corrupted database or to keep a database in good working condition, follow these steps when the database is open:

1. In a multiuser environment, have all users, except you, close the database.
2. Choose Tools ➤ Database Utilities ➤ Compact And Repair.

Follow these steps if a database is corrupted and you cannot open it, or if you want to make a compacted copy of the database:

1. In a multiuser environment, have all users close the database.
2. Choose Tools ➤ Database Utilities ➤ Compact And Repair.
3. Select the database you want to compact and repair.
4. Click Compact.
5. Select the existing database to overwrite it, or enter a new database name and/or file location.
6. Click Save to compact the database.

You can set Access to compact automatically each time you close the database (as long as no one else has it open). This keeps your database in optimal condition at all times. To do this:

1. On the Tools menu, click Options.
2. Select the General tab.
3. Select the Compact On Close check box.

If you are unable to compact a database, one of several conditions may be the cause:

- Other users may have the database open. To remedy this, ask all other users to close the database.

- You may not have enough space on the drive for both the original and the compacted versions. You may have to choose another drive for the compacted version or delete some unneeded files on the existing drive and try again.

- You don't have adequate permissions to compact the database. You must have both Open/Run and Open Exclusive permissions on the database. To review these permissions, choose Tools ➤ Security ➤ User And Group Permissions.

Continued ▌▶

PART

VIII

CREATING AND USING
AN ACCESS DATABASE

MASTERING TROUBLESHOOTING CONTINUED

- The Access database is set to Read Only or is on a read-only network share. To check the database attributes, choose File ➢ Database Properties and make sure the Read Only check box is not selected. If it is, you must exit the database and change the Read Only attribute in Windows Explorer. If the database is on a read-only network share, you must move the database to a location that has read/write access.

If you are in a networked environment and you are not the database or network administrator, talk to either of these administrators for help in compacting the database.

CHAPTER 40

CREATING WEB PAGES WITH ACCESS

FEATURING

- Creating and using Data Access Pages
- Modifying pages in Design view
- Creating server-generated Web pages
- Creating static Web pages

S ince the earliest versions of Office, each new release has included a significant number of improvements in Web features. Office XP is no exception. In Access 2002, Microsoft's efforts focus on easing programmers' cross-platform data issues with improved XML capabilities. For nonprogrammers, changes to the Data Access Page Designer make it easier than ever to create an engaging Web interface for your database.

Creating Web Pages

You can create three very different kinds of Web pages with Access 2002: dynamic Data Access Pages, server-generated HTML pages, and static Web pages. Each type has advantages and disadvantages. You use different tools to create the different types of pages.

Data Access Pages, created with the Data Access Page Wizard or the Data Access Page Designer, are DHTML (Dynamic HTML) pages that can include Office Web Components. Data Access Pages are interactive. Users can edit and enter database data from a browser, but they must have Office 2000 or Office XP and Internet Explorer (IE) 5 or higher. Therefore, Data Access Pages are suitable for a relatively closed environment, like an intranet, where users need to work interactively with up-to-the-minute data and you know they have the required client-side software.

Server-generated HTML pages let you present live data, but the data cannot be updated from a Web browser. Microsoft Internet Information Server (IIS) is required on the server side to generate the HTML pages; these are not generic "publish anywhere" pages, but they work with a wide variety of browsers. Server-generated HTML pages are useful in a heterogeneous environment like the Internet when you need to deliver current read-only data to a variety of client browsers.

You create static pages when you want users to view—but not change or manipulate—data, and when significant data changes are infrequent. Static pages are purely HTML, so you can publish them on any Web server without being too picky about the Web server or client-side software.

Creating Data Access Pages

Data Access Pages can be posted on a Web site or your company intranet or sent via e-mail to someone off your network. Data Access Pages aren't saved as objects in your database; instead they're saved as separate linked files on your hard drive. They are dynamic Web pages with controls bound directly to the data in your database. Data Access Pages are designed for Internet Explorer 5 or higher; earlier versions of Internet Explorer don't support them.

Just as with other database objects, you can create Data Access Pages in Design view or by using a wizard. Let's start the easy way, with the wizard.

1. Choose Pages in the Objects bar of the Access Database window.

2. On the Pages tab, double-click Create Data Access Page By Using Wizard. The Page Wizard starts, as shown in Figure 40.1. It's very similar to the Report Wizard, and, in fact, your finished Data Access Page resembles an Access report.

3. In the first wizard dialog box (see Figure 40.1), use the Tables/Queries drop-down list to select a table to base your page on, and then select the fields you want to include in the page. If you want to create a page where users can drill down to related records in another table, select the related table in the Tables/Queries drop-down list and select the fields to include from the table. Click Next.

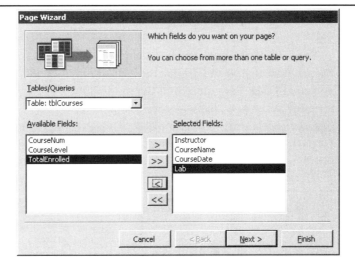

4. In the next step (if you've chosen fields from related tables), group your data as you would in an Access report. See Chapter 39, "Creating Reports and Queries," for additional information about adding grouping levels to a report. Click Next.

5. In the next step in the wizard, set sorting options for the data in the selected records.

6. In the last step of the wizard, name the page. To open the finished page, select the Open The Page option; to open the page in Design view, select Modify The Page's Design. Enable the Apply A Theme check box to select an Office XP theme for your Web page.

7. When you've finished setting options, click Finish to create the Web page.

Access creates a folder named [*page name*]_files and saves Data Access Pages in the same folder as the Access database. Shortcuts to the pages are displayed in the Database window. However, you're not prompted to save until you close the Data Access Page for the first time. If you plan to do extensive work to the page's design, it's a good idea to save it first.

NEW▶ Access 2002 supports relative paths for Data Access Pages. The first time you save a page, you are reminded of this new functionality and prompted about where you should edit the *connection string*, or path to the database.

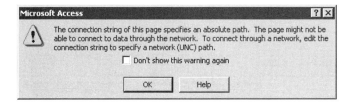

You can edit the connection string just as you would any other property. Open the page in Design view and display the page's properties. (Right-click in the Title area and choose Page Properties from the shortcut menu.) The Connection String property is on the Data tab of the Properties dialog box.

Figure 40.2 shows a rather rough-looking Data Access Page displayed in Access 2002 Form view. Choose File ➢ Web Page Preview to display a Data Access Page in your browser.

An unmodified Data Access Page created with the wizard and displayed in Form view

Course	Introduction to Windows
Level	1
Course Date	10/8/2001
Enrolled	12
Instructor	2
Lab	A14

tblCourses 1 of 8

TIP To delete the page, select the Pages group in the Database window, select the Data Access Page, and click the Delete button. When you delete a page, you are given the choice to delete just the link and keep the page (the unlinked page will be a static snapshot of the data when the page was created) or to delete all the page files.

NEW▶

Figure 40.3 shows a similar Data Access Page in Internet Explorer 5. To create this page, we used the same table (tblCourses) and grouped the data based on CourseType in the Data Access Page Wizard. The result is a *Grouped Data Access Page*. In Access 2002 grouped pages are no longer read-only. Not only do grouped pages offer a slick way to present large quantities of categorized data, users can modify this data too.

 To show (or hide) detail, just click the Expand indicator on the left side of the page. Click again to hide the detail. To see another record for the selected group, just click the Next button on the top toolbar (see Figure 40.3). To display another group, navigate using the second toolbar. You can edit the names that display on these toolbars by changing their properties in Design view.

When a user prints the contents of the browser window, only the data that is displayed is printed. Combine this WYSIWYG printing with the power of grouping with the sorting and filtering toolbar buttons, and you have the tools you need to create a fast and friendly reporting tool for end users.

FIGURE 40.3

Selecting a group in the wizard creates a page with an expandable group.

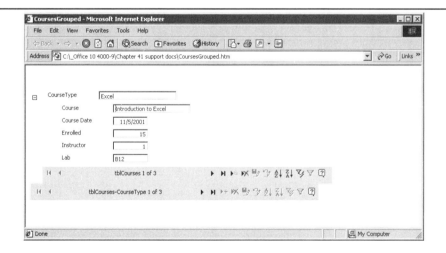

If you've spent considerable time working on a regular form or report, you'll be pleased to know you can move it to the Web in a few quick steps. No need to reinvent the wheel anymore. Just open the form or report in Design view. Then choose File ➤ Save As. In the Save As dialog box, name the page and choose Data Access Page from the As drop-down list.

Using Data Access Pages

Users with a Microsoft Office license can open Data Access Pages in the Internet Explorer browser (version 5 or higher). To test an interactive Data Access Page in its intended environment, open it in IE. The page has a toolbar at the bottom that viewers can use to navigate, sort, or filter the records (see Figure 40.3). Navigating, sorting, and filtering records works here just as it does in Access database forms.

If the Data Access Page was created from a table or an editable query result set, users can edit and enter records in the page as they would in an Access 2002 form. Click the New Record button to display blank fields for entering new data.

If a user makes changes to the data, they must save the changes by clicking the Save button on the Page toolbar; they can undo changes by clicking the Undo button on the toolbar.

WARNING User changes are made directly to the tables in your database, so be careful who has access to editable Data Access Pages.

Working with Pages in Design View

To modify the design of objects on a Data Access Page, open the page in Design view by clicking the Design View button. Figure 40.4 shows the Courses Grouped By Type page from Figure 40.3 in Design view. At the top of the page is a placeholder where you can enter text (Click Here And Type Title Text). The Data Access Page has, at minimum, a header and a navigation section. The lowest-level header is equivalent to the Details section in a form or report. A new header and a navigation section are added for each grouping level, so there are two sets of headers/navigation sections used in Figure 40.4: one for the details (Header: tblCourses) and another for the grouping level (tblCourses-CourseType).

FIGURE 40.4

Open the page in Design view to modify its design.

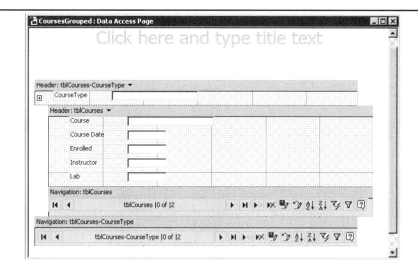

TIP If you don't have FrontPage, you can still design professional Web pages with Access 2002. Open any HTML page in Design view and edit the page even if the page wasn't created in Office. To open a page, select the Pages tab in the Database window and choose Edit An Existing Page.

Adding Fields to the Page

You add fields to the Data Access Page just as you would add a field to a report or form, but you use a beefier version of the Field list that includes fields from every table in the database. Click the Field List button to open the Field List in the task pane, as shown in Figure 40.5. Display fields from different tables by clicking the Expand button in front of the table. Double-click a field to add it to the Data Access Page, or select it and click the Add To Page button.

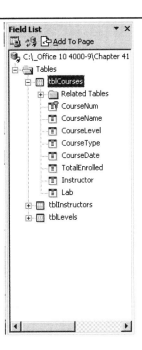

Formatting the Page and Controls

The themes in Access are shared with the other Office 2002 applications. Themes provide an easy way to make sure your Data Access Page has the same look and feel as the Web pages created in Excel, Word, Publisher, or PowerPoint. To change the theme, open the page in Design View and choose Format ➤ Theme from the menu. In the Theme dialog box, preview the different backgrounds, choose other graphical options, and click OK.

NOTE Themes are discussed more fully in Chapter 48, "Simplifying Web Creation," on the companion CD.

Move and resize controls as you would in forms or reports. When you move a control, its label moves with it. Aligning and sizing controls used to be much more tedious here than in a form. All that has changed in Access 2002. Now you can see the actual size of the control while you're sizing. Use the Alignment And Sizing toolbar to align or size controls relative to another control. Alignment, sizing, and property setting work in much the same way as the alignment options in form or report design. The Alignment And Sizing toolbar appears by default.

If you don't see the toolbar, simply right-click any existing toolbar and choose Alignment And Sizing from the shortcut menu, or select View ➤ Toolbars and choose Alignment And Sizing there.

 NOTE You can change Tab Order by opening the property sheet for a control and adjusting its Tab Index property. However, it may be more efficient to open your page in an HTML editor and adjust the Tab Index there.

Changing, Sorting, and Grouping

The sections of the Data Access Page function like an outline. The header for the primary grouping is at the top of the page. If you have two levels of grouping, the secondary grouping header appears next, followed by the third header for the detail. If you have one grouping level (like CourseType in Figure 40.4), you can create a second level by promoting a field from the Courses section.

 Select the field you want to group by; then either click the Promote button on the toolbar or right-click and choose Promote from the shortcut menu. Likewise, when you want to remove a grouping level, select a field in a Group Header, and then either click the Demote button or right-click and choose Demote from the shortcut menu.

 If you prefer a more linear look when you're adjusting grouping levels, click the Data Outline button on the Formatting toolbar to display the outline in its own window, as shown on the following page.

 NEW►

Many of the Data Access Page objects' properties are tied to the grouping levels. To change group properties, open the GroupLevel dialog box, shown in Figure 40.6, by right-clicking the group for which you want to set properties. Choose Group Level Properties from the shortcut menu. Table 40.1 describes the group properties.

> **WARNING** Make sure you right-click the group on the page itself, not in the Data Outline window. If you right-click in the Data Outline window, you can view and set properties on record set only.

FIGURE 40.6

Open the GroupLevel dialog box to set section options.

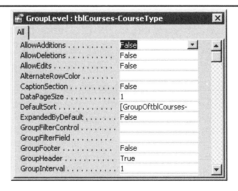

TABLE 40.1   DATA ACCESS PAGE GROUP PROPERTIES

Property	Default	Description
Caption Section	False	Display/hide a section for a title above the Group Header.
Group Header	True	Display/hide the Group Header containing the field control.
Group Footer	False	Display/hide the Group Footer.
Expanded By Default	False	Display/hide records in the level below this level when the page opens.
Data Page Size	Varies	Default is All in lowest-level group, 1 in higher-level groups. Change this setting to All to display all values in a group.
Group Interval	Varies	Number of characters (text fields), date ranges, or numeric ranges used to group data.
Default Sort	N/A	Name of the field you want to sort the grouping level on, or a list of field names separated by commas.
Group Filter Control	N/A	Name of list box or combo box with value used to filter records.
Group Filter Field	N/A	Name of a field in the group's record source that contains the values you want to filter from.

The group properties make it easy to change the Data Access Page layout to make it more useful. Figure 40.7 shows the wizard-created page from Figure 40.3 with just a few additions and changes:

- A title and body text were added in the default locations.
- The controls in the Courses group were rearranged to be listed horizontally. Several labels and one field (Enrolled) were deleted.
- The Label control in the Record Navigation object for the Courses section was edited to display a more "friendly" name.
- The Navigation object for CourseType was deleted.
- In the Courses-Instructor and Courses groups, the Data Page Size property was set to All. In both groups, the Record Navigation Section was turned off automatically, since all records are now displayed.
- Some of the text boxes were bolded.
- The Eclipse theme was applied to the page.

FIGURE 40.7

FIGURE 40.7

A few simple property changes make the page more useful.

CoursesGrouped

Courses By Type

Click the Expand icon (+) to see course details. Click the Collapse icon (-) to hide details for any section.

⊞	CourseType	Excel
⊞	CourseType	Windows
⊟	CourseType	Word

Introduction to Word	10/29/200	Instructor	Steinhoff	Lab	B12
Intermediate Word	10/31/200	Instructor	Steinhoff	Lab	A14
Mail Merge	11/6/2001	Instructor	Nguyen	Lab	B12

Courses

Using the Data Access Page Toolbox

The Data Access Page Toolbox includes a number of controls you're familiar with if you've designed Access forms or reports or if you've created forms using Visual Basic. However, there are other controls specifically for use on Web pages, including the three Office Web Components.

NOTE For information on the Office Web Components, see "Creating Web Pages with Excel" in Chapter 29.

We'll use the improved PivotTable component as an example of how to work with the components in an Access Web page.

PivotTable component   Spreadsheet component

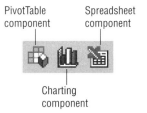

Charting component

To add an Office Web Component to the active Web page, click the component's Toolbox button, and then click on the page to place the component.

NEW▶

No longer must you go through the process of locating the object's control source and selecting its tables and queries to insert fields. Just display the Access Field list and drag fields from the list to the row, column, data, and page areas of the PivotTable component. Access 2002 supports more intuitive drop zones, so it's easy to see where you're dragging fields.

When you've added the fields to the table, spend a moment browsing the object's properties (right-click the pivot table in design view and choose Object Properties from the shortcut menu), which allow you to lock in filters and sort order and to hide or display commands and options when the user opens the page in their browser. Figure 40.8 shows a pivot table illustrating current course enrollments in our Courses By Type page. You can use all three of the Web components to create solid intranet reporting tools; this pivot table, for example, lets any Office 2002 user view total enrollment by course and by instructor without ever opening Access or Excel.

Detailed information about all the intrinsic HTML and COM controls in the Data Access Page Toolbox is beyond the scope of this book, but that shouldn't discourage you from trying those that you haven't used before. Data Access Pages support Visual Basic Script and JavaScript, so they have a lot of flexibility. For more specific information about Data Access Page features, we recommend *Mastering Access 2002 Premium Edition*, by Alan Simpson and Celeste Robinson (Sybex, 2001).

PART
VIII

CREATING AND USING
AN ACCESS DATABASE

FIGURE 40.8

You can add the Office Web Components to any page.

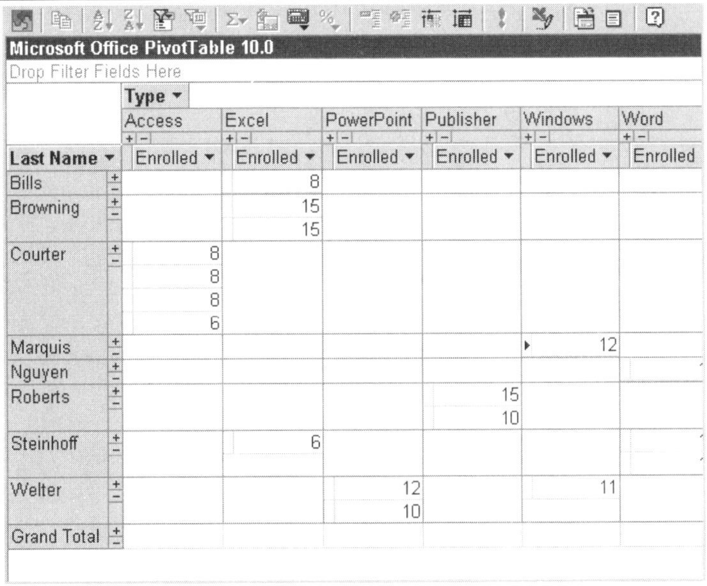

Microsoft Office PivotTable 10.0

Last Name ▼	Access Enrolled ▼	Excel Enrolled ▼	PowerPoint Enrolled ▼	Publisher Enrolled ▼	Windows Enrolled ▼	Word Enrolled
Bills		8				
Browning		15				
		15				
Courter	8					
	8					
	8					
	6					
Marquis					▶ 12	
Nguyen						
Roberts				15		
				10		
Steinhoff		6				
Welter			12		11	
			10			
Grand Total						

Type ▼

Creating Server-Generated HTML Pages

Server-generated HTML pages are the active pages you're used to seeing on the Web exported from forms, tables, or queries. They cannot be updated in a browser, but they are live data. There are two flavors of server-generated pages: ASP and IDC/HTX. ASP (Active Server Pages) is a better format, but the pages require a Web server with Internet Information Server (IIS) version 3 or higher. The IDC/HTX format supported by earlier versions of IIS generates two files: a text file with instructions for connecting to the database and an HTML template for the Web page. With both formats, you have to publish the page on a Web server, which creates the HTML page on demand. Ask your system administrator which version of IIS is installed on your Web server.

 NOTE   When you create a server-generated page, you are asked to specify a data source: an ODBC connection to your database. For more information on creating data sources, see "Retrieving External Data with Microsoft Query" in Chapter 20.

To create a server-generated page, first select the form, table, or query you want to use for the page in the Database window. Then choose File ➤ Export from the menu. In the Save As Type drop-down list, choose either Microsoft IIS 1-2, to create IDC/HTX pages, or Microsoft Active Server Pages. Select a file location, enter a filename, and click Save. If you select Microsoft Active Server Pages, the Output Options dialog box, shown in Figure 40.9, opens so you can enter additional information.

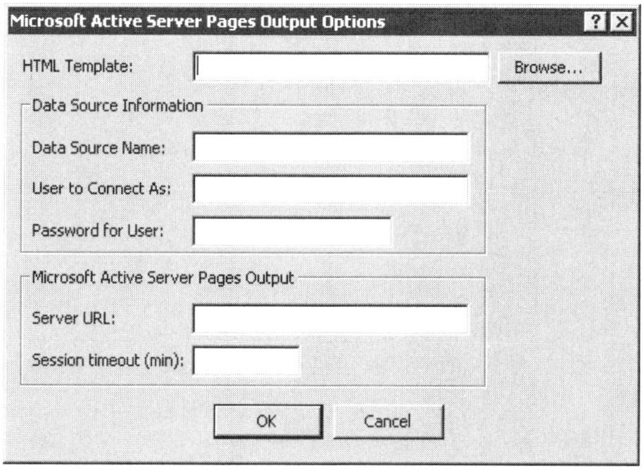

FIGURE 40.9

Enter connection information in the Output Options dialog box.

Microsoft Active Server Pages Output Options

HTML Template: [   ] Browse...

Data Source Information

Data Source Name: [   ]

User to Connect As: [   ]

Password for User: [   ]

Microsoft Active Server Pages Output

Server URL: [   ]

Session timeout (min): [   ]

OK   Cancel

An HTML template is an HMTL file that contains formatting and tags for Access. If you don't select a template, the server applies default formatting. The data source name is the ODBC data source that connects to your database. In the User To Connect As and Password For User text boxes, enter the user name and password for the data source. If you don't enter user names and passwords, the defaults are used (for example, Admin with no password for an Access database). Click OK to create the page.

TIP After you've created a server-generated page, you must publish the page before you can view it, because the server generates the page. Consult your system or Web administrator.

Creating Static HTML Pages

Static HTML pages are snapshots of the data at the time you create the page. There's nothing interactive, dynamic, or even linked here. However, don't overlook their usefulness for data that changes infrequently. Static pages load quickly and are exceptionally egalitarian. If your browser lets you view anything on the Web, it will let you view a static HMTL page. To create a static page, choose the form, table, or query that you want to place on the page from the Database window. Choose File ➤ Export to open the Export As dialog box. Choose HTML Documents as the Save As Type, select a file location, and click Export to create the page. A static HTML page created by exporting the Courses table is shown in Figure 40.10.

PART

VIII

CREATING AND USING
AN ACCESS DATABASE

FIGURE 40.10

Any browser can display static pages like this one.

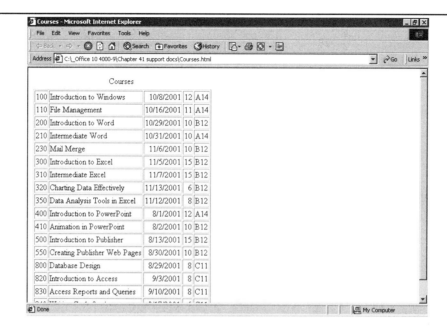

Open the HTML page in Design view to apply a theme or to add a title, a scrolling marquee, or other elements. Remember, you can add Office Web Components if your intended users have IE 5 and Office 2000 or Office XP.

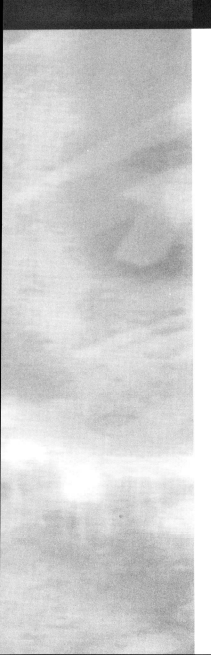

APPENDICES

CUSTOMIZING THE OFFICE ENVIRONMENT

FEATURING

- Working with the Microsoft Office shortcut bar

- Creating Taskbar shortcuts

- Customizing application toolbars

- Customizing shortcut menus

- Setting application options

Microsoft Office XP was designed with a whole host of different users in mind. Some users prefer to use the keyboard as much as possible, while others depend heavily on pointing and clicking. Some users like menus, while others prefer icons. Many users learn one or two ways to complete a task and stop there, while others use a variety of methods depending on the task at hand. In order to make one application suite respond to the needs of so many different work styles, Microsoft has incorporated a variety of ways to customize Office to make it easier for all types of people to become efficient Office users. If you have not taken the time to customize Office to respond to your personal preferences, you are missing out on one of the most important steps to becoming an Office master. In this appendix, we'll show you how to speed up access to applications and tasks with the Office shortcut bar, customize toolbars and menus within applications, and set options that increase your efficiency and maximize your productivity.

Customizing the Office XP Shortcut Bar

When you install Office XP and you choose to install the Office shortcut bar, the shortcut bar is automatically added to the Microsoft Office Tools group on the Windows menu (Start ➤ Programs ➤ Microsoft Office Tools). The shortcut bar is a collection of toolbars designed to provide quick access to commonly used functions: opening documents, creating tasks in Outlook, or launching your browser. The Office shortcut bar behaves the same way as application toolbars do. The default location for the shortcut bar is the right edge of your screen, but, like the Taskbar, it can be dragged to any edge. The shortcut bar illustrated below was placed at the top of the screen, so it's horizontal.

 NOTE The shortcut bar contains more than one toolbar. The toolbar shown here is the Office toolbar, but your shortcut bar may be displaying another toolbar, such as the Favorites toolbar. Click the Office button (the folder icon at the beginning of the toolbar) to display the Office toolbar.

A small Office icon appears in the upper-left corner of the shortcut bar. Click the icon to open the menu shown here:

- Choosing Restore restores the minimized shortcut bar to its prior location. Restore is disabled in the above graphic because the shortcut bar was not minimized when the menu was displayed.
- Minimize minimizes the shortcut bar.
- As with the Windows Taskbar, Auto Hide hides the shortcut bar, giving you more space on the Desktop. When you point to the edge of the screen where the bar is located, it is automatically displayed. If you Auto Hide the Windows Taskbar, you can also Auto Hide the shortcut bar, but you must place it on a different edge of the screen.
- The Customize option lets you change the properties of the shortcut bar, including its color and button settings. In addition, you can add the shortcut bar to the Windows StartUp program group so it will be automatically loaded when you start Windows. These settings are discussed more thoroughly in the next section.
- If you want help with the shortcut bar, choose Help to open the Microsoft Office Shortcut Bar Help dialog box.
- About Microsoft Office displays your Office XP license number and gives you direct access to your computer's system information.
- Exit closes the shortcut bar; when you close the shortcut bar, a dialog box opens, asking whether you wish to display the bar the next time you launch Windows.

The default toolbar displayed in the shortcut bar is the Office toolbar. The shortcut bar can also house additional toolbars with the contents of the Favorites folder, the

APP

A

APPENDICES

Programs menu, Accessories, and your Desktop. To create one of the preconfigured toolbars, right-click the shortcut bar's background to open the shortcut menu:

Choose the toolbar you want, and Office creates it for you. A message box briefly appears, letting you know that the toolbar is being created. To display any other toolbar, click its icon in the shortcut bar.

If you have a lot of program groups (like Microsoft Office or Accessories) on your Programs menu, the Programs toolbar won't be very useful, as you'll have a toolbar linked to lots of program group folders. Clicking a program group button doesn't launch an application; instead, it opens the group folder in a window. Then, you have to select the application you wish to run and close the window. Since the whole idea of using a shortcut bar is to save steps, the Programs choice isn't exactly helpful.

Modifying the Contents and Appearance of the Shortcut Bar

Fortunately, you can customize each of the shortcut bar's toolbars, removing the use-less buttons and adding buttons for the programs and folders you use most frequently. Right-click in the bar's background area or click the Office icon and select Customize from the menu to open the Customize dialog box, shown in Figure A.1. If you mistakenly right-click a button, you'll know it because the shortcut menu for individual buttons doesn't include Customize.

The Customize dialog box has four pages of settings: View, Buttons, Toolbars, and Settings. The View page, shown in Figure A.1, includes options for the colors of individual toolbars on the left side and shortcut bar options on the right side. To change a toolbar's background color, first select the toolbar from the drop-down list. To use the Windows color scheme in your toolbars, enable the Use Standard Toolbar Color check box. To select other colors, click the Change Color button to open the Color dialog box. Select a color, or click the Custom Color button to mix a color using the Color Picker. Select the Use Gradient Fill option if you wish.

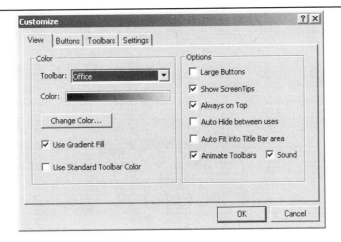

Use the Customize dialog box to change shortcut bar properties.

TIP If the toolbar you want to customize doesn't appear in the list, switch to the Toolbars page and display it.

The options on the right side of the View page apply to the entire shortcut bar:

Large Buttons Makes the buttons easier to see, but the shortcut bar takes up more space on the Desktop.

Show ScreenTips Enabled by default, so when you point to a button, the button's name is displayed.

Always On Top Also on by default, it prevents application windows from encroaching on the shortcut bar.

Auto Hide Between Uses The same as the option available from the shortcut menu.

Auto Fit Into Title Bar Area Places the shortcut bar in the title bar of the active application. At most screen resolutions, this shrinks the buttons, making them hard to see.

Animate Toolbars Sounds much more exciting than it is. When you click (for example) the Programs Toolbar button, the Programs toolbar slides into the shortcut bar.

Sound Enables the switch to another toolbar to be accompanied by a "whoosh" sound.

On the Buttons page (see Figure A.2), you can remove buttons, add files or folders, and rearrange the toolbar buttons. To add a button to the Office toolbar, first select Office from the Toolbar list and then click the check box in front of the application. Use the ↑ and ↓ buttons on the page to move a selected item up (or left when the shortcut bar is displayed horizontally) or down the list. Use the Add Space button to insert a space between the selected button and the next button on the list.

Use the Buttons page of the Customize dialog box to select the programs and folders that will be displayed.

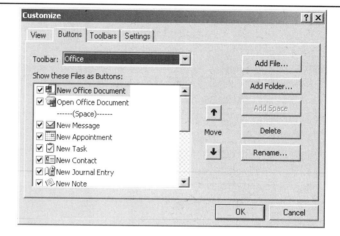

The Add File button lets you add other applications to a toolbar so all your frequently used programs are in one place. Click Add File to open the Add File dialog box, where you must browse to and select the executable file that launches the application you want to add.

> **TIP** You can also click Add File to add shortcuts to other files, such as document templates, that you use frequently. If you keep frequently used templates in the same folder, consider using the Add Folder option to create a shortcut to the folder that holds your templates.

On the Toolbars page (see Figure A.3), you can display, hide, and create toolbars. Use the check boxes to select the toolbars you want to display. To delete a toolbar permanently, click Remove; to change the name of the selected toolbar, click the Rename button. Moving toolbars up or down changes the order of the Toolbar buttons on the shortcut bar.

TIP If you remove one of the toolbars that is included with the shortcut bar, you must run the Office installation program to get it back.

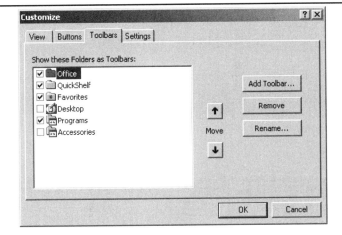

On the Toolbars page, you can add a blank toolbar and populate it with files and folders, or use the contents of a folder to create a new toolbar. (Office uses the second method to create the Desktop and Programs toolbars using the Desktop and Programs folders.) To create a new toolbar, click the Add Toolbar button to open the Add Toolbar dialog box. Enter the name for a blank toolbar, or select the Make Toolbar For This Folder option and click the Browse button to select the folder. A toolbar made from a folder has the folder's name and includes a button for each item in the folder; you can use the Rename button to change the name after it's created.

The Settings page (see Figure A.4) isn't related only to the shortcut bar; it also sets the default location for the templates used by all Office applications. To change the settings for the templates on your local drive, change the User Templates location. The default setting is provided by Office during installation; you should modify it only if you've actually moved the templates to another location. Workgroup templates are generally stored on a network file server. You'll usually have to modify this setting so that Office can locate templates you share with your coworkers.

You can use the Settings page of the Customize dialog box to modify the location for templates.

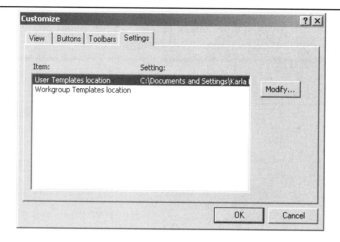

Customizing Application Menus and Toolbars

Office XP is designed to create an environment that supports the way you use each application. When you initially launch an Office application, it displays one row of buttons containing the most frequently used buttons from the Standard and Formatting toolbars. The menus show similarly limited options (see Figure A.5). In order to see all choices under a menu, you must pause a moment or click the Expand button in the bottom of the collapsed menu.

Collapsed menus display only recently used commands.

As you use an application, Office "personalizes" the toolbars and menus by displaying the commands you use. When an entire toolbar or menu is not displayed, the buttons you have used most recently are displayed and others are hidden. For many users, this is enough customization. And for some of us, spontaneously regenerating toolbars are a bit too much customization. If you want to control which menu options and toolbar buttons are visible, you can customize all of the menu bars, toolbars, and most of the Office XP shortcut menus.

Changing Toolbar Options

NEW▶

Microsoft heard users' pleas to make certain toolbar settings available without having to open the Customize dialog box (see below). Now in Office XP, you can click the drop-down arrow at the end of any toolbar and choose Show Buttons On Two Rows.

For additional settings, you must access options for toolbars by right-clicking any Office XP toolbar or menu bar and choosing Customize from the shortcut menu. The Customize dialog box opens. Choose the Options tab to view the options for menus and toolbars (see Figure A.6).

FIGURE A.6

You can change toolbar options in the Customize dialog box.

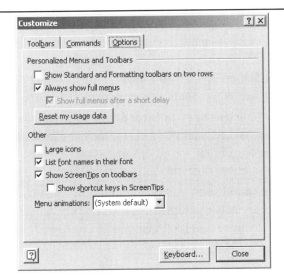

Two options in this dialog box are specific to the application: Show Standard And Formatting Toolbars On Two Rows and Reset My Usage Data. All the other options affect all of Office XP, regardless of which application you set them in. The following list includes all options:

Show Standard And Formatting Toolbars On Two Rows You can turn on the check box to stack the toolbars, which gives more room to display buttons.

Always Show Full Menus With this option turned off, each application shows you a personalized menu (short menu) with the commands you use frequently. Turn this on, and you'll see full menus in all applications.

APP

A

APPENDICES

Show Full Menus After A Short Delay If you like personalized menus, you should probably leave this turned on. If you don't leave it on, then you must actually click the Expand icon at the bottom of a collapsed menu—as opposed to pausing a moment—to see the items you don't select often.

Reset My Usage Data For menus to be personalized, there has to be a mechanism for tracking how often you use different menu options and toolbar buttons. Office tracks and saves your *usage data* when you close each application. This button resets the buttons and the menu commands shown in the personalized menus and toolbars.

Large Icons Intended for users with impaired vision, these are truly large. Just turn them on for a moment, and you'll either love them or rush to return them to their normal size.

List Font Names In Their Fonts This option affects only the Font drop-down list on the Formatting toolbar. It makes it easier to choose a font, but you'll take a slight performance hit, particularly if you have a large number of fonts installed on your computer.

Show ScreenTips On Toolbars Formerly called ToolTips, these are enabled by default; remember that turning them off here turns them off throughout Office.

Show Shortcut Keys In ScreenTips Heads up keyboarders! Here's your opportunity to learn the keyboard shortcuts for toolbar buttons. Enable this setting and you'll see the shortcuts in the screen tips when you point to a button. Look at them enough and you'll have them memorized in no time.

Menu Animations Although interesting initially, these effects (Unfold, Slide, and Random) are not worth the time it takes to animate the menu display.

After you've changed the options, click Close to close the Customize dialog box and apply the options you chose.

 TIP To make toolbars appear and behave as they did in Office 97, you'll need to enable two check boxes: Show Standard And Formatting Toolbars On Two Rows and Always Show Full Menus.

Customizing Toolbars

While the Customize dialog box is open, all displayed toolbars are open for editing. Drag menu items or buttons to new locations to rearrange them, or drop them in the document window to delete them. To add a toolbar button or menu command, click the Commands page of the Customize dialog box. The Commands page from Word is shown in Figure A.7. In the other Office applications, there is no Save In text box at the bottom of the Commands page.

 TIP Now you can customize toolbars in Publisher, just as you can with other Office applications.

FIGURE A.7

Drag commands from the Commands page to a toolbar or menu.

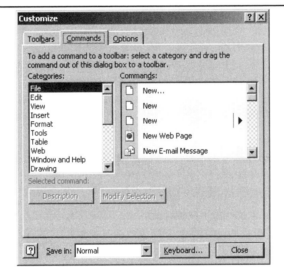

Commands are grouped into categories. Choose a category in the Categories pane, and then locate the command you want to add in the Commands pane. (Click the Description button to see a brief description of the selected command.) Drag the command onto a toolbar or the menu bar. To add a command to an existing menu, point to the menu and place the command in the appropriate place when the menu opens.

 NOTE Choosing the Macros category displays a list of macros that can be added to toolbars. See Chapter 18, "Automating Excel with Macros," for information about creating macros in Office XP.

You can also rearrange, delete, or display toolbar buttons and menu items without opening the Customize dialog box. Simply hold the Alt key while you drag the command.

Each toolbar has its own set of *built-in buttons*. To quickly add or remove built-in buttons on a toolbar, click the More Buttons drop-down arrow and choose Add Or Remove Buttons from the menu. Buttons displayed on the toolbar have a check mark. Click the button name to add or remove the button from the toolbar.

 TIP The default settings for an application's built-in menu and toolbars are retained even after you customize the menu or toolbar. To return a toolbar to its original settings, switch to the Toolbars page of the Customize dialog box, select the toolbar, and then click Reset.

You aren't limited to the built-in toolbars. Creating a new toolbar gives you the opportunity to gather all the toolbar buttons you frequently use in one place. To create an entirely new toolbar, click the New button on the Toolbar page of the Customize dialog box. You are prompted for a new toolbar name, and the application opens the toolbar. Drag buttons onto the toolbar from the Commands list. To copy a button from an existing toolbar, hold down the Ctrl key while dragging the button.

Adding or Modifying Shortcut Keys

Click the Keyboard button in the Customize dialog box to open the Customize Keyboard dialog box shown in Figure A.8. (This option is not available in Outlook.)

Choose the command you wish to add shortcut keys for. A description of the command appears in the Description section of the dialog box. Existing shortcut combinations for the command are displayed in the Current Keys list—in Figure A.8 you can see the three preset combinations for File ➢ Open. If there's already a combination, you may just want to memorize it, or you can add another shortcut combination.

To add a shortcut combination for the selected command, click in the Press New Shortcut Key text box and execute the keystroke combination. If the combination is already assigned to another command, that information appears just below the text box. In Figure A.8, the keystroke combination entered is already used for the Find command on the Edit menu. Click Assign to assign the shortcut to the command, which overwrites the current assignment, or select the information in the Press New Shortcut Key text box and try again. When you have finished creating keyboard shortcuts, close the dialog box.

FIGURE A.8

FIGURE A.8

Change or add shortcut keystrokes in the Customize Keyboard dialog box.

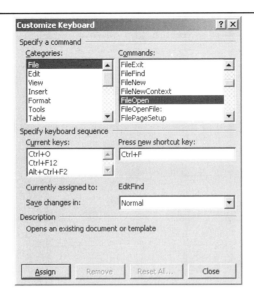

 WARNING Beware of using Alt+key combinations for keyboard shortcuts. Nearly all are used, but the keyboard customization routine doesn't seem to know it. For example, if you enter Alt+F as a shortcut, the Customize Keyboard dialog box tells you that it's currently unassigned although it's the keyboard shortcut used to open the File menu in every Windows program, including the Office XP applications.

Customizing a Shortcut Menu

Starting with Office 2000, users have the ability to customize the shortcut menus. You can't create or delete shortcut menus, but in some applications you can customize them as you would other toolbars. On the Toolbars page of the Customize dialog box in Word, PowerPoint, or Access, enable the Shortcut Menus check box in the Toolbars list. A small toolbar with the three categories of shortcut menus opens.

Click a category to open its list of shortcut menus. Choose the menu you want to customize, as shown in Figure A.9. With the menu open, add commands by dragging them from the Commands page of the Customize dialog box. Delete commands by

APP

A

APPENDICES

dragging them from the menu. You can right-click shortcut menu items and change their options, as you would toolbar item options.

Changing Toolbar Item Options

While the Customize dialog box is open, you can change the properties of toolbar buttons and menu items. Right-click a button to display the shortcut menu of customization options.

Table A.1 summarizes the customization options available on the shortcut menu for individual toolbar items.

TABLE A.1   SEARCH TIPS

Item	Use
Reset	Returns the item to its original image and style.
Delete	Removes the item from the toolbar.
Name	Shows the display name for the command. The ampersand (&) appears before the "hotkey" letter, which is underlined on a menu item.
Copy Button Image	Copies the image so it can be pasted onto another button.
Paste Button Image	Pastes an image from the Clipboard.
Reset Button Image	Restores the default image for the button.
Edit Button Image	Opens the Button Editor. Some button images cannot be edited or changed.
Change Button Image	Displays a palette of button images from which to choose.
Default Style	Displays the command or button in its default style: buttons for toolbars, text for menu items.
Text Only (Always)	Displays text without an image, whether the command is displayed on a toolbar or menu.
Text Only (In Menus)	Displays text without an image on a menu and displays the default image on toolbars.
Image And Text	Displays text and an image.
Begin A Group	Places group dividers on either side of a button or above and below a menu command.
Assign Hyperlink	Creates a hyperlink to open a Web page or document or to insert a picture in the current document.

WARNING   Removing menu commands or changing the image on the Copy button to the image for the Paste button is a swift and reliable way to decrease workplace harmony if you share a computer (and profile) with colleagues.

MASTERING THE OPPORTUNITIES

Creating Document-Specific Toolbars in Word

Creating and displaying toolbars for a specific document used to require Visual Basic code. With Word 2002, you can easily create customized menus, shortcuts, and toolbars for individual documents.

You can save a customized toolbar or set of shortcut keys in the Normal template (NORMAL .DOT), any other active template, or a specific document. The Normal template is loaded each time Word is launched, so customizations saved in Normal become the new default toolbars. When you save in another template, the toolbars and shortcuts are loaded when the template is loaded. If you save changes in the current document, the customized items are displayed only when the document is opened. Use the Save In drop-down list on the Commands page of the Customize dialog box (refer back to Figure A.7) to choose where to save your customized toolbars before clicking OK to close the dialog box. For keyboard shortcuts, use the Save In list in the Customize Keyboard dialog box.

The Assign Hyperlink toolbar option opens up some creative opportunities for presentation of online Word documents. You can create a Supporting Documents toolbar that contains links to other documents and Web pages that your reader might be interested in. Save the customization in the document, and the Supporting Documents toolbar is loaded each time the document is opened.

Setting Application Options

Each Office XP application has other user-customizable option settings. Outlook has the widest range of option settings (although not the most tabs in the Options dialog box) because of the number of modules and the large number of options related to electronic mail. Publisher wins the award for the fewest options.

Options control overall application appearance and behavior. In Excel, for example, option settings determine whether you see sheet tabs, where the cell pointer goes when you press Enter, and how zero values are treated in series charts. In Outlook, Rich Text Format for messages is an option; a mail option determines whether the text of an original message is included in a reply. Word's scroll bars appear or disappear based on an option setting. If an Office program behaves differently than you think it should or remember it did, it's a good idea to check the option settings. To open the Options dialog box in any Office XP application, choose Tools ➤ Options from the menu bar. The Options dialog box for Excel is shown in Figure A.10.

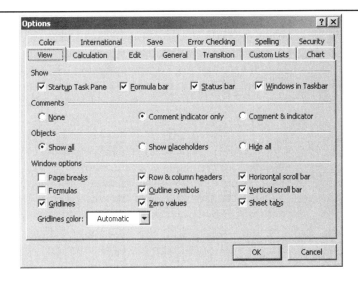

In every application, the settings on the General page include global settings that are required when the application launches, such as the number of recently opened files to display on the File menu and the default file location. The View options display or hide features like scroll bars and the application status bar. Edit options determine how the application should respond to your actions (like selecting and dragging text or cells). Other options differ between applications. Table A.2 lists the types of option settings available in each Office XP application.

TABLE A.2   OFFICE XP OPTIONS

Application	Types of Options
Access	Advanced, Datasheet, Edit/Find, Forms/Reports, General, Keyboard, Tables/Queries, View, Pages, International, Spelling
Excel	Calculation, Chart, Color, Custom Lists, Edit, General, View, Transition, International, Save, Error Checking, Spelling, Security
FrontPage	Configure Editor, General, Reports View, Publish
Outlook	Preferences, Mail Setup, Mail Format, Spelling, Security, Other
PowerPoint	Edit, General, Print, Save, Spelling And Style, View, Security
Publisher	General, Edit, User Assistance, Print, Save
Word	Compatibility, Edit, File Locations, General, Print, Save, Spelling & Grammar, Track Changes, User Information, View, Security

APP

A

APPENDICES

To change options, choose Tools ➤ Options to open the dialog box. If you have a question about a specific option, click the Help button in the title bar of the Options dialog box, then click the option you want to learn about. Office displays a short description of the option. After changing option settings, click OK to close the dialog box and apply the changes.

TROUBLESHOOTING OFFICE XP

Hardly a day goes by when we don't receive at least one question from Office users about something they are having trouble with. Some of the questions result in easy answers: a reference to a page number in the book or a simple "can't be done." Answers to other "How can I" types of questions were included in this edition as Expert Tips, Notes, or Tips.

In this appendix, we've compiled many of the most frequently asked troubleshooting questions and our answers. Questions are arranged by application. Some answers refer to articles in the Microsoft Knowledge Base, an excellent source for troubleshooting tips. The URL for the Knowledge Base is `http://support.microsoft.com`.

All Office XP Applications

Commands Missing or Disabled

These are similar questions, but it's worth knowing the difference among the three.

Question My menus/toolbars don't have the commands and buttons you show in the book. Why not?

Answer In Office XP, the default personalized toolbars (including the menu) replace commands that you seldom use with commands that you use frequently. To find buttons that aren't currently displayed, click the Toolbar Options drop-down arrow at the right end of the toolbar. To see all choices on a menu, just pause for a moment after opening it. The menu uncollapses to display all commands. If you're in a hurry, you can point to the double-down arrows at the bottom of any collapsed menu to uncollapse it immediately. To show all buttons on the Standard and Formatting toolbars, click the Toolbar Options drop-down arrow and choose Show Buttons On Two Rows. To turn off personalized menus, right-click any toolbar and choose Customize. On the Options tab of the Customize dialog box, enable the Always Show Full Menus check box.

Question A specific menu command is grayed out. Why?

Answer Commands, whether on menus or buttons, are disabled (grayed out) when they're unavailable given the status of the application. For example, the Copy and Cut buttons are enabled only when you have something selected, because you can only copy or cut selections. You can't Undo until you've done something, so the Undo button is disabled in a new document until you type some text or take an action.

Question My dialog box doesn't include the buttons that I know were there a month ago. Where did they go?

Answer In the applications other than Outlook, there are only two possibilities: 1) If Office is installed from an Administrative Installation point, your administrator may have changed the available features in the application. 2) The application is broken. Buttons shouldn't disappear from dialog boxes—from toolbars, yes, but not from dialog boxes. Choose Help ➤ Detect And Repair and click Start in the Detect And Repair dialog box to force the application to fix itself. If this does not work, you may need to reinstall the application.

Downloaded Clips Don't Go to the Clip Organizer

Question When I try to download clips from the Microsoft Design Gallery Live, I get the Save As dialog box. I can save the clips as regular files, but shouldn't they go directly to Clip Organizer?

Answer Yes, they should. First, let's make sure you're following the correct procedure to download. When your browser prompts you to Save or Open, you should choose the Open option. This ensures that the clip is downloaded to Clip Organizer. If you save the file to disk, it is downloaded onto your computer as a CIL file rather than an MPF file in Clip Organizer, and it won't be displayed in Clip Organizer. Assuming you're following the correct procedure and the clips are still going astray, there's help on the Clip Gallery Live site that walks you through optimizing your browser so that it recognizes downloaded clips and knows where to put them. Go to http://dgl.microsoft.com/default.asp and click the Help link. Scroll down the Help topics. The link you're looking for is Optimize Your Browser For Downloading Clips On A Windows Computer.

Now, to install all those clips you've already downloaded…. Clip files are saved in CIL format, unless you change that setting during the download. First, find all your CIL files. In Windows 2000, that's Start ➤ Search ➤ For Files Or Folders; then enter ***.cil** in the Search For Files Or Folders Named box. When the search results are displayed, double-click each file to install it in the Downloaded Clips category of Clip Organizer.

Where Are My Sounds?

Question I upgraded from Office 2000 to Office XP and all the sounds I had assigned are gone.

Answer When you upgrade, all Office 2000 files, including sound files, are removed and any system sound assignments that you made are lost. The Office XP sounds are installed the first time that you open an Office XP program. Unfortunately, you'll have to reassign sounds after the upgrade. Choose Sounds And Multimedia in Windows Control Panel to reassign sounds.

No Shortcut Bar

Question I don't have an Office Shortcut bar since installing Office XP. I can see it on the Programs menu, but it doesn't appear when I click it.

Question When I launch the Office XP Shortcut bar, I get the Office 2000 bar instead.

Answer The Office XP Shortcut bar is not included as part of a typical Office XP installation. It's one of the features you get to use only if you set it to Run From My Computer during a custom installation. If you kept previous Office versions when you installed XP, the older version of the Shortcut bar launches when you choose it from the Start menu. If you didn't keep previous versions of Office, there is no Shortcut bar, so nothing appears. Use the Windows Add/Remove feature in Control Panel to install the XP version of the Shortcut bar.

Access 2002

Sorting a Lookup Drop-Down List

Question I'm using a table of employees, tblEmployees, as a drop-down list in another table, tblSuggestions. The primary key in tblEmployees is EmployeeID. How do I sort the drop-down list in tblSuggestions by the employee's name instead of the employee's ID number?

Answer Open tblSuggestions in Design view, then do the following:

1. Select the field that uses the lookup.

2. Click the Lookup property tab.

3. Select the Row Source property. Click the Build button to open the query for the lookup.

4. Sort the query. If you need to add a field or rearrange query fields, note the order of the field that you're storing in the lookup (likely the primary key for tblEmployees, EmployeeID).

5. Close the query. Save changes when prompted to do so.

6. If you added or rearranged fields, make sure the value in the Bound Column property refers to the field being stored in the lookup.

7. Save and close the table.

Lookup Uses Only First Record

Question A table in my database has a lookup for the State field that refers to another table. The lookup displays the list of state names and is supposed to store the two-letter state abbreviation. However, no matter which state I select, the state that gets displayed in the table is Alabama. I've checked the table, and the states and abbreviations are correct.

Answer This usually happens when you've added one or more columns to the query for a Lookup field before the column that contains the unique value you wish to store. Open the table that contains the lookup in Design view. Select the Lookup field. Select the Record Source field, and then click the Build button to open the query that the field is based on. Note which column (first, second, etc.) contains the state abbreviations, then close the query. Choose the Lookup property tab, and make sure the Bound Column property refers to the same column.

Undeleting a Table

Question I accidentally deleted the wrong table from my Access database. Is there any way to undelete it?

Answer If you've already closed or compacted the database or deleted another table, you can't recover the table. If Access is still open, there's hope. Check Microsoft support (http://support.microsoft.com) for article Q209874: "How to Recover a Table Deleted from a Database."

Can't Open Forms

Question I've been working away on my database. When I try to rename a form, an error message appears that says, "The Visual Basic for Applications project in the database is corrupt." When I kill the error message, the form I'm trying to rename disappears. I can't repair the database now, either. What am I supposed to do to get my forms back?

Answer The short answer, unfortunately, is "You can't get your forms back." VBA project corruption is rare, but it's a known problem in Access 2002. You need to export all the tables and queries to a new database, re-create the relationships, and then re-create the forms and reports. While it won't help this time, we suggest that when you're developing a database, you periodically close the database and create a copy. Include the date (and time if you're creating more than one copy a day) in the filename, or number them as you would versions of a document. We usually keep the last two copies of our "backups" so we can revert to the last copy in case of a catastrophe like you've experienced.

Switchboard Doesn't Work After Access 97 Database Is Converted

Question I converted an Access 97 database to Access 2002 and distributed it to other users. Now the switchboard doesn't work for some users. When they click buttons on the switchboard, a message box says the command is not available, or Access closes and creates an error report. Other users report no problems. I can delete and re-create the switchboard in Access 2002 on the "problem" workstations, but isn't there an easier way to fix this?

Answer The button that users are clicking is probably the button that allows them to change the switchboard; some users are clicking it and others are not, which explains why some users aren't reporting problems with the switchboard. We're not sure why you'd want to allow users to change the switchboard, but assuming you do, here's how to fix it without re-creating the switchboard from scratch in Access 2002. The Access Switchboard Manager creates three objects: a table named Switchboard Items, a form named Switchboard, and code behind the form. The form and table convert just fine, but one line of the code behind the form is version-specific. This is a common conversion problem. While objects are converted, the code behind the objects is not. To fix this specific problem in the converted database, open the Switchboard form in Design view. Click the Code button on the Standard toolbar to open the Visual Basic IDE. Choose Edit ➢ Find and search for the command line that includes WZMAIN80 in the current module. In that command line, which begins Application.Run, replace the string WZMAIN80 (used in Access 97) with ACWZMAIN (used in Access 2000 and 2002). Save and close the Visual Basic IDE, then close the form.

Databases Not Consistently Converted

Question We have users in every version of Access since Access 97. I converted an Access 97 database in Access 2002, and I could still open the converted database in Access 2000. Databases that other 2002 users convert open only in Access 2002. What's different?

Answer Access 2002 can create databases in either the Access 2000 or Access 2002 file format. Access 2000 databases can be opened in 2002 or 2000. Access 2002 databases can be opened only in 2002. Check the current Default File Format setting on the Advanced tab of the Options dialog box (Tools ➢ Options).

Excel 2002

Changing the Default File Type

Question I have Excel 2002 on my computer, but the "standard" in my office is another spreadsheet application. How can I change the default setting so all my Excel worksheets are saved in the correct format?

Answer Choose Tools ➢ Options to open the Options dialog box. On the Transition tab, select the appropriate file type from the Save Excel Files As drop-down list.

Gridlines Don't Show

Question Part, but not all, of the cells in one of my worksheets doesn't have gridlines. How do I display them?

Answer When gridlines go missing for only part of a workbook, the gridlines aren't the problem. You've applied a fill (usually white) over the selected cells, and the fill covers the gridlines. Select the range of cells that you can't see gridlines for, open the Fill Color menu (on the Formatting toolbar), and choose No Fill. If all the gridlines are gone, then the Gridlines option is turned off on the View page of the Options dialog box.

Outline Groups Data Incorrectly

Question When I use Excel's Outline feature, the data isn't grouped correctly. When I hide the lowest-level details, some totals are also hidden.

Answer First, make sure that the totals being hidden are formulas, not values. Click a cell with a total and check the formula bar. If it's a number rather than a formula, that's the cause of the problem.

If your worksheet is properly constructed (formulas for summarization, numbers for values), try outlining manually. Turn off AutoOutline and make sure all the data in the worksheet is visible. Select the detail rows or columns (do not select the summary row/column) for a group, then choose Data ➢ Group And Outline ➢ Group to group the detail. Create all the lower-level groups you need, then create the next level by grouping the detail rows/columns and summary rows/columns for that level of detail. See Chapter 19, "Using Excel to Present Information," for more information about outlining.

Empty Cells Behave As If They Have Contents

Question I have an Excel worksheet with a lot of data. When I print the worksheet, I get over a dozen blank pages at the end of the printout. If I click in the database and choose Data ➢ Sort, Excel includes about 150 rows that are empty. I know they're empty because I've selected all the empty rows and columns in the worksheet, then chosen Edit ➢ Clear ➢ All. Still, these empty cells continue to act as if there's something in them. How can I get rid of whatever's there?

Answer You've already done that. Now you need to force Excel to look at the worksheet again and determine what rows and columns are actually occupied. Choose File ➢ Save As and save the file with the same name to force Excel to reset the worksheet ranges.

Pivot Table Doesn't Include Formats

Question When I published my Excel PivotTable using the Office Web Components, the number formatting disappeared. How can I retain it?

Answer You can't. Formatting for text, numbers, alignment, and borders is not included in the published PivotTable.

Cell Selector Jumps All Over the Place

Question When I enter numbers using the numeric keypad, I wind up down in row 23, and no numbers appear in the cell.

Answer Press Num Lock on the keypad.

Chart Doesn't Show Category Axis Labels Correctly

Question I've created a column chart that shows average sales for the last three years. On the category axis, I want to see 1999, 2000, and 2001, but Excel wants to make a bar out of my dates and shows 1, 2, and 3 as category axis labels. I know the data is selected correctly. What gives?

Answer This happens when you use numbers, rather than text, as category labels. Excel assumes the numbers are just another data series and attempts to chart them. But there's an easy fix. At step 2 of the Chart Wizard, click the Series tab. Remove the data series you don't want (Year, in this example). Then click the Collapse button on the Category (X) Axis Labels box. Drag over the dates (or numbers) you want to use to label the category axis. Uncollapse and proceed through the wizard.

FrontPage 2002

Locating Webs Created in FrontPage 98

Question I used FrontPage 98 to create a number of Webs, which I'm having trouble locating in FrontPage 2002. Any hints?

Answer Article Q232684 on the Microsoft site provides a couple of workarounds for locating Webs created in previous versions of FrontPage.

Adding Banner Links from Third Parties

Question I've been accepted into affiliate programs and am setting up some banners to Web sites on my Web. The banners that were e-mailed to me are in HTML code, and the instructions seem to assume I'm using NotePad or some other text editor. How do I include these in FrontPage 2002?

Answer In FrontPage, set up your page, including tables to hold banner images, as you would normally. Position the insertion point where you want to place the banner. Open the e-mail message or the Web site with the banners and copy the HTML string. Switch back to FrontPage and click the HTML tab at the bottom of the page to switch to the HTML code for the page. Paste the HTML string. The banner will not appear in the preview until you've published the page.

Can't Insert a Database

Question When I choose Insert ➤ Database from the menu, the Database command is grayed out. Why can't I insert a database in this page?

Answer Database support comes from your Web server, which must include the FrontPage 2002 server extensions and support ASP (Active Server Pages). Talk to your Web administrator. If your Web is published on a commercial Web server, see if they have a hosting plan that includes ASP support and the FrontPage 2002 extensions. If they do, expect to pay a higher monthly fee.

Outlook 2002

Outlook Runs Floppy Drive

Question I installed Outlook from CD, but it periodically runs my floppy drive. What is it doing?

Answer It's clearly looking for something: a personal folder, sound file, or Office document that you saved on floppy disk that is included in the Journal. Or, the last time you attached a file, you did so from a floppy. You'll find a complete list of things Outlook looks for that could be on a floppy disk in article Q179869 on the Microsoft Web site. One tip worth noting: If you've set Outlook to automatically journal Office documents, don't save Office docs on floppy disks. Save documents on a permanent drive (local or network drive), then use Windows Explorer to copy them to a floppy disk.

Resetting Default Views

Question How can I reset the views in all the Outlook modules to the default views?

Answer Outlook has a number of command switches, including a switch to reset views. This is a one-way street—before you do this, make sure you really want to reset all the views. Then complete these steps:

1. Locate the path to the `Outlook.exe` executable file. The easiest way to do this is to use Windows Find (Start ➢ Find) and find `outlook.exe`. Write down the entire path (for example, `C:\Program Files\Office 2000\Office\Outlook.exe`).

2. Choose Start ➢ Run from the Windows Start menu.

3. In the Run dialog box, enter the entire filename (including the path) for `Outlook.exe` in quotes (for example, `"C:\Program Files\Office 2000\Office\Outlook.exe"`). The quotes are required if spaces are used anywhere in the path. Not sure of the path on your computer? Use Windows Search (Find in Windows 9*x*) to search for `Outlook.exe`.

4. Type a space, then the clean views switch: **/cleanviews**.

5. Click OK.

If, for some bizarre reason, you want to restore the default views each time you start Outlook, add the `/cleanviews` switch to the desktop shortcut you use to start Outlook. For information on other Outlook command-line switches, search Outlook Help for the command.

Arranging Items in Views

Question The Task Pad has disappeared from my calendar. How do I get it back?

Question The Date Navigator is missing from my Outlook Calendar in Day/Week/Month view. How do I turn it back on?

Answer If you display a day, workweek, or week in Day/Week/Month view, the Date Navigator normally appears at the top of the right side of the calendar above the Task Pad. The Task Pad, Date Navigator, and Calendar display share the Information Viewer. If you change the width or height of the display for one, you're taking it away from one or both of the others. For example, you increase the number of months displayed in the Date Navigator by dragging the bottom border of the Date Navigator down over the Task Pad. If you drag it all the way to the bottom of the window, the Task Pad is hidden. To display the Task Pad again, point to the bottom border of the Date Navigator pane; when the pointer changes to an adjustment tool, drag it partway up the window to display the Task Pad. If the Date Navigator is hidden, point to the top border of the Task Pad (just below today's date) and drag down to display the Date Navigator.

DAT E-mail Attachments

Question I own a business that occasionally sends e-mails to about 200 or 300 customers at one time. The last time I sent a mailing to 200 customers, several contacted me and said that there was a DAT file attached! How did this happen, and how do I make sure that it doesn't happen again? I had an attachment to my Web page in the e-mail, but I did not attach anything else.

Answer The problem is not created by Outlook, but rather by the mail service used by the recipients (or, less frequently, your ISP.) We're assuming that every recipient did not receive this DAT file. A DAT file usually is created when the recipient's mail service can't handle formatted mail. We're assuming that you used Outlook Rich Text or HTML to format your e-mail. If that's the case, then some mail services that can only handle plain text dumped the extra format codes (including any Web links) into a DAT file. It really creates no problem—it's just a junk file that can be ignored (you may want to tell recipients that). The only way to avoid this problem is to send the messages to these recipients as plain text. You can change the format of an individual message by opening the message, opening the Format menu, and selecting the format you want to use. You can change the format for all messages on the Mail Format tab of the Options dialog box (Tools ➢ Options).

Mail Sent to Multiple Recipients Not Delivered

Question One of my teams has over 20 members. When I address a message to all of them, about half are returned as undeliverable. If, however, I use the same addresses that I used in the message to send individual messages, everything works fine. The undeliverable addresses aren't the same each time this happens. Any ideas?

Answer There's a known problem with one of the Novell NetWare clients and Outlook that can cause this behavior. For more information, see article Q197320 on the Microsoft site.

Inaccurate Delivery Receipts

Question One of the vendors I send e-mail to is really bad about responding, so I started attaching delivery receipts to his messages. I'm receiving receipts and calling to find out why he hasn't responded, and he says that he never received the message. I know that some e-mail systems don't send delivery receipts at all, so before I really start applying pressure, I want to make sure that delivery receipts that are sent are always accurate.

APP

B

APPENDICES

Answer Don't tighten the thumbscrews yet. Delivery receipts come from your vendor's e-mail server. In most e-mail systems, when the server receives the message and verifies the address, it sends the receipt. However, this doesn't mean that the message was actually sent to the recipient. It could have been held at the server. A few years ago, this happened only when the server was having problems. With the host of new e-mail viruses, however, many system administrators are routinely holding any message with active content (JavaScript, ActiveX components, etc.), messages that have a confirmed virus, or an attachment with a suspect file extension to control viruses in the corporate environment. You may want to ask your vendor to speak with their system administrator to determine if your messages are being held and, if so, why.

PowerPoint 2002

Error Message Appears During PowerPoint Launch

Question When I launch PowerPoint, I always see the same error message about a `ppmusic.ppa` file. If I click OK, I can continue to work in PowerPoint. How do I stop the message from appearing?

Answer This problem occurs only if you upgraded from PowerPoint 97. PowerPoint 2002 is looking for the custom soundtrack add-in that came with PowerPoint 97. You can tell PowerPoint to quit searching for the add-in or, if you used the custom soundtrack add-in in 97 and want to use it in 2002, you can download a PowerPoint 2000 version of the add-in from the Microsoft site. (At the time of this book's publication, there wasn't a 2002 version of the add-in.)

To dump the add-in, choose Tools ➢ Add-ins. In the Add-in dialog box, choose `ppmusic` and click Load. PowerPoint will tell you the add-in is not available and offer to remove it from the list. Click Yes. To download the PowerPoint 2000 version of the add-in, search for `pp2kmus.exe` on the Microsoft Web site.

Error Inserting Movie File

Question I'm trying to insert a movie file and an error message informs me that the file could not be played. What am I doing wrong?

Answer It's nothing you're doing wrong in PowerPoint; you committed this error in your browser when you downloaded and installed another application. Most of the media players you download (RealPlayer, QuickTime, etc.) make changes to your system registry and initialization files, sometimes without your knowledge or consent. The fix is not for the faint of heart, but you'll find it on the Microsoft Web site. Search for article Q212409.

Images Replaced with Red Xs

Question When I open my PowerPoint presentation, there's a red X every place I'd inserted a graphic. How do I get my graphics back?

Answer First, and most important, don't save the presentation. If you save the presentation with red Xs, that's all you'll see in the future. Now, close all other open applications and open the presentation again. If your graphics are there, your presentation was too large for the available memory. Try compressing the pictures in the presentation (File ➢ Save As and choose Compress Pictures from the Tools menu in the Save As dialog box.) If this doesn't work, the problem is either too little memory or an issue with your video driver. If you've recently upgraded your operating system, check with your video card manufacturer for a new driver. And finally, you can also try slowing down the hardware acceleration for the video driver in Windows Control Panel by following these steps:

1. Choose Start ➢ Settings ➢ Control Panel.

2. Double-click the System icon.

3. On the Performance tab, click the Graphics button to open the Advanced Graphic Settings dialog box.

4. Slide the Hardware Acceleration setting toward None from Full.

5. Click OK to close the dialog box.

6. Reboot your computer.

Organization Charts from Previous Version Distorted in PowerPoint 2002

Question I opened a presentation I originally created in PowerPoint 2000. The Organization Chart on Slide 5 doesn't fit on the slide any more. What happened?

Answer This is a known issue with organization charts converted to XP format. The fix requires a bit of registry hacking, so we don't recommend it for beginners. Search the Microsoft Knowledge Base for article Q293213 if you're feeling up to it.

Templates from Previous Versions Missing

Question When I installed Office XP, it wiped out all my existing PowerPoint templates. Can I get them back?

Answer If you've already installed XP, the templates have been deleted—a real shame even if the only templates you had were the standard PowerPoint 2000 templates. The only way to get the 2000 templates back is to reinstall Office 2000. Before installing Office XP, visit the Microsoft Knowledge Base and follow the directions in article Q280558 to create temporary directories for your legacy templates. Install Office XP, then move the templates back to the Office XP Templates folder.

Publisher 2002

Images Don't Print

Question When I print my brochure, the text and lines print but my images don't. I'm printing on an inkjet printer that doesn't have a lot of memory, but I have 128MB on my desktop and I'm closing all other open applications before I print.

Answer Here's a workaround: On the Print tab of the Options dialog box (Tools ➤ Options), enable the Print Line By Line check box. This will slow printing, but still should print the images. You should also check your printer manufacturer's Web site and see if there's a newer driver for your printer.

Inserted Images Very Large

Question When I insert an image, it is often nearly as large as the page, and I have to resize it manually. Is there a setting I can change so images are inserted in normal size?

Answer Not in Publisher, but in Windows. The size of an inserted image is based on your screen resolution compared to the resolution of the screen when the image was saved. If you increase your screen resolution in Windows, images will be smaller when inserted. There's a trade-off, of course: You'll have to work with smaller icons and print. You can also open the images in another application such as Microsoft Photo Editor and resave them using the screen resolution you use in Publisher.

"Continued" Text Doesn't Display

Question I've linked three text boxes in my newsletter so that my article begins at the top of Page 1, continues at the bottom of Page 1, and then finishes on Page 4. When I insert "Continued From" and "Continued On" text, it works only part of the time. I can't get "Continued On" text in the first frame, and I can't get "Continued From" text in the second frame. The rest works just fine.

Answer Sorry, but Publisher displays "Continued On" and "Continued From" text only when the linked frames are on different pages. That explains your mixed results, since only two of the three of the frames are on the same page. You can manually insert text into the first frame that says "Continued Below," but only after you're certain that the text in that frame will not be modified, or your "Continued Below" might appear in the wrong place.

Word 2002

Recovering Corrupt or Damaged Documents

Question How do I recover a corrupt Word document?

Answer Office XP's Document Recovery features—see Chapter 1, "Presenting Office XP: What You Need to Know" for details—decrease the likelihood of developing a corrupt file. However, when it happens, you have a couple of possible solutions. If you can see the file in the Open dialog box, but Word reports that the file is corrupt when you attempt to open it, try Word's text-recovery converter. In Word, choose File ➢ Open. In the Open dialog box, choose Recover Text From Any File in the Files Of Type drop-down list. Select the filename and click Open. If Recover Text From Any File isn't on the list, you'll need to add the file converter from the Office XP CD.

Question What if Word can't recover a corrupt document?

Answer If the file doesn't appear in the Open dialog box and you're willing to try for the text only (without formatting), first close all other applications and all open documents in Word. Choose File ➢ Open. Change the Files Of Type to All Files. Open the folder that contained the file in Windows Explorer or My Computer. Look for a temp file (`.tmp` extension) with a date and time close to the last time the file was successfully opened or saved. Open the file (the file converter may open in Word). The top of the file may contain miscellaneous symbols. Scroll through the document to see if it contains the text you're trying to recover. If it does not, close it without saving and repeat this process with any other likely temp files in the folder.

Animated GIF Won't Play

Question I inserted an animated GIF in a Word document. When I go to Web Page Preview, the GIF isn't animated. Do I need to do something extra to play the GIF?

Answer If you embed a GIF by inserting it as a new object (Insert ➢ Object), the embedded GIF is converted to a regular GIF and it won't play. Use Insert ➢ Picture ➢ ClipArt to insert an animated GIF from the Motion Clips tab of the Media Gallery.

EZP Toolbar Button

Question There's an EZP button on the Standard toolbar. When I click it, the following error message appears: "Word cannot find or run the application." If I delete the button, it reappears. There's no information in Word Help on this button.

Answer The EZP button is installed by EZPhoto, a third-party product used to view photo disks that is not compatible with Word 2002. EZPhoto is an add-in that's loaded when you launch Word, which accounts for its persistence. The fix depends

APP

B

APPENDICES

on your operating system and involves renaming files. For specific information for your operating system, see article Q224727 on the Microsoft site.

Fax Merge in Word 2002

Question I can't merge to faxes in Word 2002. This used to work in Office 2000, but not since I upgraded.

Answer Office always included a fax program that you could use to fax directly from your computer. Office XP does not include any fax software, so you have to have separate fax software that may or may not integrate with Office XP. If it does not, you can go through all the steps of the wizard, but the faxes would have nowhere to go—there is no fax software available to actually send them. If you're looking for fax software, we like Symantec's WinFax Pro. Log on to http://www.symantec.com for more information.

INDEX

Note to the reader: Throughout this index **boldfaced** page numbers indicate primary discussions of a topic. *Italicized* page numbers indicate illustrations.

The Adventure Continues on the CD

 When you've had a chance to explore the main applications in Office XP and are ready for more, slide the accompanying CD into your CD drive and fasten your seat belts. The CD contains full versions of software, shareware, and demos and an electronic book containing 10 bonus chapters and 2 appendices. Look for the CD icon throughout the book for references to material you'll find on the CD. Here's a list of everything you'll find. For a more complete description of each product, click the Readme link on the CD splash screen.

Bonus Chapters and Appendices

"Print and Web Publishing with Microsoft Publisher 2002" (4 chapters), "Collaboration with SharePoint Team Services," "Web Publishing with Microsoft FrontPage 2002" (5 chapters), "Speech Recognition Commands in Office XP," and "Installing Microsoft Office XP."

We've also included an Excel workbook, `WellBilt.xls`, to support your learning in Chapter 17, "Solving Business Problems with the Analysis Tools." This workbook contains the three sample worksheets used in the chapter to illustrate the What If analysis tools.

Free Software

A full version of WebSpice Themes, quality themes and images for use with Office applications.

Shareware. Try some, and then take advantage of the following software:

Microsoft Office–Related Tools Ken Slovack's Outlook Security add-in, Power Utility Pak 2000 for Excel, Outlook Extensions Library (Web link), Teamwork (Web link)

Graphics Tools 160 Textures, 3D Impact Pro, PowerPlug, Presentation Pro, CD Label Creator, Sensiva

General Utilities Adobe Acrobat Reader, WinZip

Web Tools Clickbook, Clipmate, WebWhacker , Grab-a-Site, GrabNet, DropChute, BlackIce Defender (Web link)

Miscellaneous Productivity Tools Macro Express, PlanMagic, Milori Training Tools